THE

CONSTITUTION OF MAN.

BY GEORGE COMBE, ESQ.

ESSAYS ON DECISION OF CHARACTER, &c.

BY JOHN FOSTER, ESQ.

PHILOSOPHY OF SLEEP, AND ANATOMY OF DRUNKENNESS.

BY ROBERT MACNISH, ESQ.

INFLUENCE OF LITERATURE UPON SOCIETY, &c.

BY MADAME DE STAEL.

A TREATISE ON SELF-KNOWLEDGE.

BY JOHN MASON, A. M.

HARTFORD:
PUBLISHED BY SILAS ANDRUS & SON.
1850.

THE

CONSTITUTION OF MAN

CONSIDERED IN

RELATION TO EXTERNAL OBJECTS.

BY

GEORGE COMBE.

Vain is the ridicule with which one sees some persons will divert themselves, upon finding lesser pains considered as instances of divine punishment. There is no possibility of answering or evading the general thing here intended, without denying all final causes.—*Butler's Analogy.*

"ALEXANDRIAN EDITION."

HARTFORD:
PUBLISHED BY SILAS ANDRUS & SON.
1850.

PREFACE

TO THE EDINBURGH EDITION.

This Essay would not have been presented to the public, had I not believed that it contains views of the constitution, condition, and prospects of Man, which deserve attention; but these, I trust, are not ushered forth with any thing approaching to a presumptuous spirit. I lay no claim to originality of conception. My first notion of the natural laws were derived from an unpublished manuscript of Dr Spurzheim, with the perusal of which I was honoured some years ago; and all my inquiries and meditations since have impressed me more and more with a conviction of their importance. The materials employed lie open to all. Taken separately, I would hardly say that a new truth has been presented in the following work. The parts have all been admitted and employed again and again, by writers on morals, from Socrates down to the present day. In this respect, there is nothing new under the sun. The only novelty in this Essay respects the relations which acknowledged truths hold to each other. Physical laws of nature, affecting our physical condition, as well as regulating the whole material system of the universe, are universally acknowledged, and constitute the elements of natural philosophy and chemical science. Physiologists, medical practitioners, and all who take medical aid, admit the existence of *organic laws;* and the science of government, legislation, education, indeed our whole train of conduct through life, proceed upon the admission of laws in morals. Accordingly, the laws of nature have formed an interesting subject of inquiry to philosophers of all ages; but, so far as I am aware, no author has hitherto attempted to point out, in a combined and systematic form, the relations between these laws and the constitution of Man; which must, nevertheless, be done, before our knowledge of them can be beneficially applied. The great object of the following Essay is to exhibit these relations, with a view to the improvement of education, and the regulation of individual conduct.

But, although my purpose is practical, a theory of Mind forms an essential element in the execution of the plan. Without it, no comparison can be instituted between the natural constitution of man and external objects. Phrenology appears to me to be the clearest, most complete, and best supported system of Human Nature, which has hitherto been taught; and I have assumed it as the basis of this Essay. But the practical value of the views now to be unfolded does not depend on Phrenology. This theory of Mind itself is valuable, only in so far as it is *a just exposition* of what previously existed in human nature. We are physical, organic, and moral beings, acting under the sanction of general laws, let the merits of Phrenology be what they may. Individuals will, under the impulse of passion, or by the direction of intellect, hope, fear, wonder, perceive, and act, whether the degree in which they habitually do so, be ascertainable on phrenological principles or not. In so far, therefore, as this Essay treats of the known qualities of Man, it may be instructive even to those who contemn Phrenology as unfounded; while it can prove useful to no one, if it shall depart from the true elements of mental philosophy, by whatever system these may be expounded.

I have endeavoured to avoid all religious controversy. 'The object of Moral Philosophy,' says Mr Stewart, 'is to ascertain the general rules of a wise and virtuous conduct in life, in so far as these rules may be discovered by the unassisted light of nature; that is by an examination of the principles of the human constitution, and of the circumstances in which man is placed.'* By following this method of inquiry, Dr Hutcheson, Dr Adam Smith, Dr Reid, Mr Stewart, and Dr Thomas Brown, have, in succession, produced highly interesting and instructive works on Moral Science; and the present Essay is a humble attempt to pursue the same plan, with the aid of the new lights afforded by phrenology.

* Outlines of Moral Philosophy, p. 1.

Edinburgh, 9th June, 1828

ESSAY

ON

THE CONSTITUTION OF MAN,

AND ITS RELATIONS TO EXTERNAL OBJECTS.

CHAPTER I.

ON NATURAL LAWS.

A STATEMENT of the evidence of a great intelligent First Cause is given in the 'Phrenological Journal,' and in the 'System of Phrenology.' I hold this existence as capable of demonstration. By NATURE, I mean the workmanship of this great Being, such as it is revealed to our minds by our senses and faculties.

In natural science, three subjects of inquiry may be distinguished. 1st. What exists? 2dly. What is the purpose or design of what exists; and, 3dly. Why was what exists designed for such uses as it evidently subserves? For example,—It is a matter of fact that arctic regions and torrid zones exist,—that a certain kind of moss is most abundant in Lapland in mid-winter,—that the rein-deer feeds on it, and enjoys high health and vigor in situations where most other animals would die; farther, it is a matter of fact that camels exist in Africa; that they have broad hoofs, and stomachs fitted to retain water for a length of time, and that they flourish amid arid tracts of sand, where the rein-deer would not live for a day. All this falls under the inquiry, What exists? But in contemplating the foregoing facts, it is impossible not to infer that one object of the Lapland moss is to feed the rein-deer, and one purpose of the deer is to assist man: and that, in like manner, broad feet have been given to the camel to enable it to walk on sand, and a retentive stomach to fit it for arid places in which water is not found except at wide intervals. These are inquiries into the use or purpose of what exists. In like manner, we may inquire, What purpose do sandy deserts and desolate heaths subserve in the economy of nature? In short, an inquiry into the use or purpose of any object that exists, *is merely an examination of its relations to other objects and beings, and of the modes in which it affects them;* and this is quite a legitimate exercise of the human intellect. But, 3dly, we may ask, why were the physical elements of nature created such as they are? Why were summer, autumn, spring, and winter introduced? Why were animals formed of organized matter? These are inquiries why what exists was made such as it is, or into the will of the Deity in creation. Now, man's perceptive faculties are adequate to the first inquiry, and his reflective faculties to the second; but it may well be doubted whether he has powers suited to the third. My investigations are confined to the first and second, and I do not discuss the third.

A *law*, in the common acceptation, denotes a rule of action; its existence indicates an established and constant mode, or process, according to which phenomena take place; and this is the sense in which I shall use it, when treating of physical substances and beings. For example, water and heat are substances; and water presents different appearances, and manifests certain qualities, according to the altitude of its situation, and the degree of heat with which it is combined. When at the level of the sea, and combined with that portion of heat indicated by 32° of Fahrenheit's thermometer, it freezes or becomes solid; when combined with the portion denoted by 212° of that instrument, it rises into vapour or steam. Here water and heat are the substances,—the freezing and rising in vapour are the appearances or phenomena presented by them; and when we say that these take place according to a Law of Nature, we mean only that these modes of action appear, to our intellects, to be established in the very constitution of the water and heat, and in their natural relationship to each other; and that the processes of freezing and rising in vapour are their constant appearances, when combined in these proportions, other conditions being the same.

The ideas chiefly to be kept in view are, 1st. That all substances and beings have received a definite natural constitution; 2dly. That every mode of action, which is said to take place according to a natural law, is inherent in the constitution of the substance, or being, that acts; and, 3dly. That the mode of action described is universal and invariable, wherever and whenever the substances, or beings, are found in the same condition. For example, water, at the level of the sea, freezes and boils, at the same temperature, in China and in France, in Peru and in England; and there is no exception to the regularity with which it exhibits these appearances, when all its conditions are the same: For *cœteris paribus* is a condition which pervades all departments of science, phrenology included. If water be carried to the top of a mountain 20,000 feet high, it boils at a lower temperature than 212°, but this again depends on its relationship to the air, and takes place also according to fixed and invariable principles. The air exerts a great pressure on the water. At the level of the sea the pressure is nearly the same in all quarters of the globe, and in that situation the freezing points and boiling points correspond all over the world; but on the top of a high mountain the pressure is much less, and the vapour not being held down by so great a power of resistance, rises at a lower degree of heat than 212°. But this change of appearances does not indicate a change in the constitution of the water and the heat, but only a variation of the circumstances in which they are placed; and hence it is not correct to say, that water boiling on the tops of high mountains, at a lower temperature than 212°, is an exception to the general law of nature: there never are exceptions to the laws of nature; for the Creator is too wise and too powerful to make imperfect or inconsistent arrangements. The error is in the human mind inferring the law to be, that water boils at 212° in all altitudes; when the real law is only that it boils at that temperature, *at the level of the sea*, in all countries; and that it boils at a lower temperature, the higher it is carried, because there the pressure of the atmosphere is diminished.

Intelligent beings exist, and are capable of modifying their actions. By means of their faculties, the laws impressed by the Creator on physical substances become known to them; and, when perceived, constitute laws to them, by which to regulate their conduct.

For example, it is a physical law, that boiling water destroys the muscular and nervous systems of man. This is the result purely of the constitution of the body, and the relation between it and heat; and man cannot alter or suspend that law. But whenever the human intellect perceives the relation, and the consequences of violating it, the mind is prompted to avoid infringement, in order to shun the torture attached by the Creator to the decomposition of the human body by heat.

Similar views have long been taught by philosophers and divines. Bishop BUTLER, in particular, says: 'An Author of Nature being supposed, it is not so much a deduction of reason as a matter of experience, that we are thus under his government, in the same sense as we are under the government of civil magistrates. Because the annexing pleasure to some actions, and pain to others, in our power to do or forbear, and giving notice of this appointment beforehand to those whom it concerns, *is the proper formal notion of government.* Whether the pleasure or pain which thus follows upon our behaviour, be owing to the Author of Nature's acting upon us every moment which we feel it, or to his having at once contrived and executed his own part in the plan of the world, makes no alteration as to the matter before us. For, if civil magistrates could make the sanctions of their laws take place, without interposing at all, after they had passed them, without a trial, and the formalities of an execution; if they were able to make their laws execute themselves, or every offender to execute them upon himself, we should be just in the same sense under their government then as we are now; but in a much higher degree and more perfect manner. *Vain is the ridicule with which one sees some persons will divert themselves, upon finding* LESSER PAINS CONSIDERED AS INSTANCES OF DIVINE PUNISHMENT. THERE IS NO POSSIBILITY OF ANSWERING OR EVADING *the general thing here intended,* WITHOUT DENYING ALL FINAL CAUSES. For, final causes being admitted, the pleasures and pains now mentioned must be admitted too, as instances of them. And if they are, if GOD annexes delight to some actions, with an apparent design to induce us to act so and so, then he not only dispenses happiness and misery, but also rewards and punishes actions. If, for example, the *pain which we feel upon doing what tends to the destruction of our bodies,* suppose upon too near approaches to fire, or upon wounding ourselves, be *appointed by the Author of Nature to prevent our doing what thus tends to our destruction;* this is ALTOGETHER AS MUCH AN INSTANCE OF HIS PUNISHING OUR ACTIONS, and consequently of our being under his government, as declaring, by a voice from Heaven, that, if we acted so, he would inflict such pain upon us, and inflict it whether it be greater or less.' *

If, then, the reader keep in view that GOD is the creator; that Nature, in the general sense, means the world which he has made; and, in a more limited sense, the particular constitution which he has bestowed on any special object, of which we may be treating, and that a Law of Nature means the established mode in which that constitution acts, and the obligation thereby imposed on intelligent beings to attend to it, he will be in no danger of misunderstanding my meaning.

Every natural object has received a definite constitution, in virtue of which it acts in a particular way. There must, therefore, be as many natural laws, as there are distinct modes of action of substances and beings, viewed by themselves. But substances and beings stand in certain relations to each other, and modify each other's action in an established and definite manner, according to that relationship; altitude, for instance, modifies the effect of heat upon water. There must, therefore, be also as many laws of nature, as there are *relations* between different substances and beings.

It is impossible, in the present state of knowledge, to elucidate all these laws: countless years may elapse before they shall be discovered; but we may investigate some of the most familiar and striking of them. Those that most readily present themselves bear reference to the great classes into which the objects around us may be divided, namely, Physical, Organic, and Intelligent. I shall therefore confine myself to the physical laws, the organic laws, and the laws which characterise intelligent beings.

1st. The Physical Laws embrace all the phenomena of mere matter; a heavy body, for instance, when unsupported, falls to the ground with a certain accelerating force, in proportion to the distance which it falls, and its own density; and this motion is said to take place according to the law of gravitation. An acid applied to a vegetable blue colour, converts it into red, and this is said to take place according to a chemical law.

2dly. Organized substances and beings stand higher in the scale of creation, and have properties peculiar to themselves. They act, and are acted upon, in conformity with their constitution, and are therefore said to be subject to a peculiar set of laws, termed the Organic. The distinguishing characteristic of this class of objects, is, that the individuals of them derive their existence from other organized beings, are nourished by food, and go through a regular process of growth and decay. Vegetables and Animals are the two great subdivisions of it. The organic laws are different from the merely physical. A stone, for example, does not spring from a parent stone; it does not take food from its parent, the earth, or air; it does not increase in vigor for a time, and then decay and suffer dissolution, all which processes characterize vegetables and animals. The organic laws are superior to the merely physical. For example, a living man, or animal, may be placed in an oven, along with the carcass of a dead animal, and remain exposed to a heat, which will completely bake the dead flesh, and yet come out alive, and not seriously injured. The dead flesh is mere physical matter, and its decomposition by the heat instantly commences; but the living animal is able, by its organic qualities, to counteract and resist to a certain extent, that influence. The expression Organic Laws, therefore, indicates that every phenomenon connected with the production, health, growth, decay, and death of vegetables and animals, takes place with undeviating regularity, whenever circumstances are the same. Animals are the chief objects of my present observations.

3dly. Intelligent beings stand still higher in the scale than merely organized matter, and embrace all animals that have distinct consciousness, from the lowest of the inferior creatures up to man. The great divisions of this class are into Intelligent and Animal—and into Intelligent and Moral creatures. The dog, horse, and elephant, for instance, belong to the first class, because they possess some degree of intelligence, and certain animal propensities, but no moral feelings; man belongs to the second, because he possesses all the three These various faculties have received a definite constitution from the Creator, and stand in determinate relationship to external objects: for example, a healthy palate cannot feel wormwood sweet, nor sugar bitter: a healthy eye cannot see a rod partly plunged in water straight, because the water so modifies the rays of light, as to give to the stick the appearance of being crooked; a healthy Benevolence cannot feel gratified with murder, nor a healthy Conscientiousness with fraud. As, therefore, the mental faculties have received a precise constitution, have been placed in fixed and definite relations to external objects, and act regularly, we speak of their acting according to rules or laws, and call these the Moral and Intellectual Laws.

In short, the expression 'laws of nature,' when properly used, signifies the rules of action impressed on

* Butler's Works, Vol. I, p. 44. Similar observations by other authors will be found in the Appendix, No. I.

objects and beings by their natural constitution. Thus, when we say, that by the physical law, a ship sinks when a plank starts from her side, we mean, that, by the constitution of the ship, and the water, and the relation subsisting between them, the ship sinks when the plank starts.

Several important principles strike us very early in attending to the natural laws, viz. 1st. Their independence of each other; 2dly. Obedience to each of them is attended with its own reward, and disobedience with its own punishment; 3dly. They are universal, unbending, and invariable in their operation; 4thly. They are in harmony with the constitution of man.

1. The independence of the natural laws may be illustrated thus;—A ship floats because a part of it being immersed, displaces a weight of water equal to its whole weight, leaving the remaining part above the fluid. A ship, therefore, will float on the surface of the water as long as these physical conditions are observed; no matter although the men in it should infringe other natural laws; as, for example, although they should rob, murder, blaspheme, and commit every species of debauchery; and it will sink whenever the physical conditions are subverted, however strictly the crew and passengers may obey the other laws here adverted to. In like manner, a man who swallows poison, which destroys the stomach or intestines, will die, just because an organic law has been infringed, and because it is independent of others, although the man should have taken the drug by mistake, or been the most pious and charitable individual on earth. Or, thirdly, a man may cheat, lie, steal, tyrannise, and in short break a great variety of the moral laws, and nevertheless be fat and rubicund, if he sedulously observe the organic laws of temperance and exercise, which determine the condition of the body; while, on the other hand, an individual who neglects these, may pine in disease, and be racked with torturing pains, although at the very moment, he may be devoting his mind to the highest duties of humanity.

2. Obedience to each law is attended with its own reward, and disobedience with its own punishment. Thus the mariners who preserve their ship in accordance with the physical laws, reap the reward of sailing in safety; and those who permit its departure from them, are punished by the ship sinking. Those who obey the moral law, enjoy the intense internal delights that spring from active moral faculties; they render themselves, moreover, objects of affection and esteem to moral and intelligent beings, who, in consequence, confer on them many other gratifications. Those who disobey that law, are tormented with insatiable desires, which, from the nature of things, cannot be gratified; they are punished by the perpetual craving of whatever portion of moral sentiment they possess, for higher enjoyments, which are never attained; and they are objects of dislike and malevolence to other beings in the same condition as themselves, who inflict on them the evils dictated by their own provoked propensities. Those who obey the organic laws, reap the reward of health and vigour of body, and buoyancy of mind; those who break them are punished by sickness, feebleness, and languor.

3. The natural laws are universal, invariable, and unbending. When the physical laws are subverted in China or Kamschatka, there is no instance of a ship floating there more than in England; and when they are observed, there is no instance of a vessel sinking in any one of these countries more than in another. There is no example of men, in any country, enjoying the mild and generous internal joys, and the outward esteem and love that attend obedience to the moral law, while they give themselves up to the dominion of brutal propensities. There is no example, in any latitude or longitude, or in any age, of men who entered life with a constitution in perfect harmony with the organic laws, and who continued to obey these laws throughout, being, in consequence of this obedience, visited with pain and disease; and there are no instances of men who were born with constitutions at variance with the organic laws, and who lived in habitual disobedience to them, enjoying that sound health and vigour of body, that are the rewards of obedience.

4. The natural laws are in harmony with the whole constitution of man, the moral and intellectual powers being supreme. For example, if ships had sunk when they were in accordance with the physical law, this would have outraged the perceptions of Causality, and offended Benevolence and Justice; but as they float, the physical is, in this instance, in harmony with the moral and intellectual law. If men who rioted in drunkenness and debauchery, had thereby established health and increased their happiness, this, again, would have been in discord with our intellectual and moral perceptions; but the opposite result is in harmony with them.

It will be subsequently shown, that our moral sentiments desire universal happiness. If the physical and organic laws are constituted in harmony with them, it ought to follow that the natural laws, when obeyed, conduce to the happiness of moral and intelligent beings, who are called on to observe them; and that the evil consequences or punishments resulting from disobedience, are calculated to enforce stricter attention and obedience to the laws, that these beings may escape from the miseries of infringement, and return to the advantages of observance. For example, according to this view, when a ship sinks, in consequence of a plank starting, the punishment ought to impress upon the spectators the absolute necessity of having every plank secure and strong before going to sea again, a condition indispensable to their safety. When sickness and pain follow a debauch, they serve to urge a more scrupulous obedience to the organic laws, that the individual may escape death, which is the inevitable consequence of too great and continued disobedience to these laws, and enjoy health, which is the reward of opposite conduct. When discontent, irritation, hatred, and other mental annoyances, arise out of infringement of the moral law, this punishment is calculated to induce the offender to return to obedience, that he may enjoy the rewards attached to it.

When the transgression of any natural law is excessive, and so great that return to obedience is impossible, one purpose of death, which then ensues, may be to deliver the individual from a continuation of the punishment which could then do him no good. Thus, when, from infringement of a physical law, a ship sinks at sea, and leaves men immersed in water, without the possibility of reaching land, their continued existence in that state would be one of cruel and protracted suffering; and it is advantageous to them to have their mortal life extinguished at once by drowning, thereby withdrawing them from further agony. In like manner, if a man in the vigour of life, so far infringe any organic law as to destroy the function of a vital organ, the heart, for instance, or the lungs, or the brain, it is better for him to have his life cut short, and his pain put an end to, than to have it protracted under all the tortures of an organic existence without lungs, without a heart, or without a brain, if such a state were possible, which, for this wise reason, it is not.

I do not intend to predicate any thing concerning the perfectibility of man by obedience to the laws of nature. The system of sublunary creation, so far as we perceive it, does not appear to be one of optimism; yet benevolent design, in its constitution, is undeniable. Paley says, 'Nothing remains but the first supposition, that God, when he created the human species, wished them happiness, and made for them the provisions which he has made, with that view and for that purpose. The same argument may be proposed in different terms: Contrivance proves design; and the predominant tendency of the contrivance indicates the disposition of the designer. The world *abounds with contrivances;* and ALL THE CONTRIVANCES *which we are acquainted with, are directed to beneficial purposes.*' PALEY's Mor. Phil. Edinb. 1816, p. 51. My object is to discover as many of the contrivances of the Creator, for effecting beneficial purposes, as possible; and to point out in what manner, by accommodating our conduct to these contrivances, we may lessen our misery and increase our happiness.

I do not intend to teach that the natural laws, discernible by unassisted reason, are sufficient for the *salvation* of man without revelation. Human interests regard this world and the next. To enjoy this world, I humbly maintain, that man must discover and obey the natural laws; for example, to ensure health to offspring, the parents must be healthy, and the children after birth must be treated in conformity to the organic laws; to fit them for usefulness in society, they must be instructed in their own constitution,—in that of external objects and beings, and taught to act rationally in reference to these. Revelation does not communicate complete or scientific information concerning the best mode of pursuing even our legitimate temporal interests, probably because faculties have been given to man to discover arts, sciences, and the natural laws, and to adapt his conduct to them. The physical, moral, and intellectual nature of man, is itself open to investigation by our natural faculties; and numerous practical duties resulting from our constitution are discoverable, which are not treated of in detail in the inspired volume; the mode of preserving health, for example; of pursuing with success a temporal calling; of discovering the qualities of men with whom we mean to associate our interests; and many others. My object, I repeat, is to investigate the natural constitution of the human body and mind, their relations to external objects and beings in this world, and the courses of action that, in consequence, appear to be beneficial or hurtful.

Man's spiritual interests belong to the sphere of revelation: and I distinctly declare, that I do not teach, that obedience to the natural laws is sufficient for salvation in a future state. Revelation prescribes certain requisites for salvation, which may be divided into two classes; first, faith or belief; and, secondly, the performance of certain practical duties, not as meritorious of salvation, but as the native result of that faith, and the necessary evidence of its sincerity. The natural laws form no guide as to faith; but so far as I can perceive their dictates and those of revelation coincide in all matters relating to practical duties in temporal affairs.

It may be asked, whether mere *knowledge* of the natural laws is sufficient to insure observance of them? Certainly not. Mere knowledge of music does not enable one to play on an instrument, nor of anatomy to perform skilfully a surgical operation. Practical training, and the aid of every motive that can interest the feelings, are necessary to lead individuals to obey the natural laws. Religion, in particular, may furnish motives highly conducive to this obedience. But, it must never be forgotten, that although mere knowledge is not all-sufficient, it is a primary and indispensable requisite to regular observance; and that it is as impossible, effectually and systematically to obey the natural laws without knowing them, as it is to infringe them with impunity, although from ignorance of their existence. Some persons are of opinion that Christianity alone suffices, not only for man's salvation, which I do not dispute, but for his guidance in all practical virtues, without knowledge of, or obedience to, the laws of nature; but from this notion I respectfully dissent. It appears to me, that one reason why vice and misery, in this world, do not diminish in proportion to preaching, is, because the natural laws are too much overlooked, and very rarely considered as having any relation to practical conduct.

Connected with this subject, it is proper to state, that I do not maintain that the world is arranged on the principle of Benevolence exclusively: my idea is, that it is constituted in harmony with the whole faculties of man; the moral sentiments and intellect holding the supremacy. What is meant by creation being constituted in harmony with the whole faculties of man, is this. Suppose that we should see two men holding a third in a chair, and a fourth drawing a tooth from his head:—While we contemplated this bare act, and knew nothing of the intention with which it was done, and of the consequences that would follow, we would set it down as purely cruel; and say, that, although it might be in harmony with Destructiveness, it could not be so with Benevolence. But, when we were told that the individual in the chair was a patient, the operator a dentist, the two men his assistants, and that the object of all the parties was to deliver the first from violent torture, we would then perceive that Destructiveness had been used as a means to accomplish a benevolent purpose; or, in other words, that it had acted under the supremacy of moral sentiment and intellect, and we would approve of the transaction. If the world were created on the principle of Benevolence exclusively, no doubt the toothach could not exist; but, as pain does exist, Destructiveness has been given to place men in harmony with it, when used for a benevolent end.

To apply this illustration to the works of providence; I humbly suggest it as probable, that if we knew *thoroughly* the design and whole consequences of such institutions of the Creator, as are attended with pain, death, and disease, for example, we should find that Destructiveness was used as a *means*, under the guidance of Benevolence and Justice, to arrive at an end in harmony with the moral sentiments and intellect; in short, that no institution of the Creator has pure evil, or destructiveness alone, for its object. In judging of the divine institutions, the moral sentiments and intellect embrace the results of them to the *race*, while the propensities regard only the individual; and as the former are the higher powers, their dictates are of supreme authority in such questions. Farther, when the operations of these institutions are sufficiently understood, they will be acknowledged to be beneficial for the individual also; although, when partially viewed, this may not at first appear to be the case.

The opposite of this doctrine, viz. that there are institutions of the Creator which have suffering for their exclusive object, is clearly untenable; for this would be ascribing malevolence to the Deity. As, however the existence of pain is undeniable, it is equally impossible to believe that the world is arranged on the principle of Benevolence exclusively; and, with great submission, the view now presented reconciles the existence of Pain with that of Benevolence in a natural way, and the harmony of it with the constitution of the human mind, renders its soundness probable.

CHAPTER II.

OF THE CONSTITUTION OF MAN, AND ITS RELATIONS TO EXTERNAL OBJECTS.

Let us, then, consider the Constitution of Man, and the natural laws to which he is subjected, and endeavour to discover how far the external world is arranged with wisdom and benevolence, in regard to him. Bishop Butler, in the Preface to his Sermons, says, 'It is from considering the relations which the several appetites and passions in the inward frame have to each other, and, above all, the SUPREMACY of reflection or conscience, that we get the idea of the system or constitution of human nature. And from the idea itself, it will as fully appear, that this our nature, *i. e.* constitution, is adapted to virtue as from the idea of a watch it appears, that its nature, *i. e.* constitution or system is adapted to measure time.

'Mankind has various instincts and principles of action as brute creatures have; some leading most directly and immediately to the good of the community, and some most directly to private good.

'Man has several, which brutes have not; particularly reflection or conscience, an approbation of some principles or actions, and disapprobation of others.'

'Brutes obey their instincts or principles of action, according to certain rules; suppose, the constitution of their body, and the objects around them.'

'The generality of mankind also obey their instincts and principles, all of them, those propensities we call good, as well as the bad, according to the same rules, namely, the constitution of their body, and the external circumstances which they are in.'

'Brutes, in acting according to the rules before mentioned, their bodily constitution and circumstances, act suitably to *their whole nature.*

'Mankind also, in acting thus, would act suitably to their whole nature, if no more were to be said of man's nature than what has been now said; if that, as it is a true, were also a complete, adequate account of our nature.

'But that is not a complete account of nature. Somewhat farther must be brought in to give us an adequate notion of it; namely, *that one of those principles of action, conscience, or reflection,* compared with the rest, as they all stand together in the nature of man, *plainly bears upon it marks of authority over all the rest, and claims the absolute direction of them all,* to allow or forbid their gratification;—a disapprobation on reflection being in itself a principle manifestly superior to a mere propension. And the conclusion is, that to allow no more to this superior principle or part of our nature, than to other parts; to let it govern and guide only occasionally, in common with the rest, as its turn happens to come, from the temper and circumstances one happens to be in; *this is not to act conformably to the constitution of man:* neither can any human creature be said to act conformably to his constitution of nature, unless he allows to that superior principle the absolute authority which is due to it.'—*Butler's Works*, vol. ii. *Preface.* The following Essay is founded on the principles here suggested.

SECT. I.—MAN CONSIDERED AS A PHYSICAL BEING.

The human body consists of bones, muscles, nerves bloodvessels, besides organs of nutrition, of respiration, and of thought. These parts are all composed of physical elements, and to a certain extent, are subjected to the physical laws of creation. By the laws of gravitation, the body falls to the ground when unsupported, and is liable to be injured, like any frangible substance; by a chemical law, excessive cold freezes, and excessive heat dissipates, its fluids; and life, in either case is extinguished.

To discover the real effect of the physical laws of nature on human happiness, we would require to understand, 1st. The physical laws themselves, as revealed by mathematics, natural philosophy, natural history, and their subordinate branches; 2dly. The anatomical and physiological constitution of the human body; 3dly. The adaptation of the former to the latter. These expositions are necessary, to ascertain the extent to which it is possible for man to place himself in accordance with the physical laws so as to reap advantage from them, and also to determine how far the sufferings which he endures, fall to be ascribed to their inevitable operation and how far to his ignorance and infringement of them. To treat of these views in detail, would require separate volumes, and I therefore confine myself to a single instance as an illustration of the mode in which the investigation might be conducted.

By the law of gravitation, heavy bodies always tend toward the centre of the earth. Some of the advantages of this law are, that objects remain at rest when properly supported, so that men know where to find them when they are wanted for use; walls, when erected of sufficient thickness and perfectly perpendicular, stand firm and secure, so as to constitute edifices for the accommodation of man. Water descends from the clouds, from the roofs of houses, from streets and fields, and precipitates itself down the channels of rivers, turns mill-wheels in its course, and sets in motion the most stupendous and useful machinery; ships move steadily through the water with part of their hulls immersed, and part rising moderately above it, their masts and sails towering in the air to catch the inconstant breeze; and men are enabled to descend from heights, to penetrate by mines below the surface of the ground, and by diving-bells beneath that of the ocean.

To place man in harmony with this law, the Creator has bestowed on him bones, muscles, and nerves, constructed on the most perfect principles of mechanical science, which enable him to preserve his equilibrium, and to adapt his movements to its influence; also intellectual faculties, calculated to perceive the existence of the law, its modes of operation, the relation between it and himself, the beneficial consequences of observing this relation, and the painful results of infringing it.

Finally, when a person falls over a precipice, and is maimed or killed; when a ship springs aleak and sinks; or when a reservoir pond breaks down its banks and ravages a valley, we ought to trace the evil back to its cause, which will uniformly resolve itself into infringement of a natural law, and then endeavour to discover whether this infringement could or could not have been prevented, by a due exercise of the physical and mental powers bestowed by the Creator on man.

By pursuing this course, we shall arrive at sound conclusions concerning the adaptation of the human mind and body to the physical laws of creation. The subject, as I have said, is too extensive to be here prosecuted in detail, and I am incompetent, besides, to do it justice; but the more minutely any one inquires, the more firm will be his conviction, that in these relations admirable provision is made by the Creator for human happiness, and that the evils which arise from neglect of them, are attributable, to a great extent, to man's not adequately applying his powers to the promotion of his own enjoyment.

SECT. II.—MAN CONSIDERED AS AN ORGANIZED BEING.

Man is an organized being, and subject to the organic laws. An organized being is one which derives its existence from a previously existing organized being, which subsists on food, which grows, attains maturity, decays, and dies. The first law, then, that must be obeyed, to render an organized being perfect in its kind, is that the germ, from which it springs, shall be complete in all its parts, and sound in its whole constitution. If we sow an acorn, in which some vital part has been destroyed altogether, the seedling plant, and the full grown oak, if it ever attain to maturity, will be deficient in the lineaments which were wanting in the embryo root; if we sow an acorn entire in its parts, but only half ripened or damaged, by damp or other causes in its whole texture, the seedling oak will be feeble, and will probably die early. A similar law holds in regard to man. A second organic law is, that the organized being, the moment it is ushered into life, and so long as it continues to live, must be supplied with food, light, air, and other physical aliment requisite for its support, in due quantity, and of the kind best suited to its particular constitution. Obedience to this law is rewarded with a vigorous and healthy development of its powers; and in animals, with a pleasing consciousness of existence and aptitude for the performance of their natural functions; disobedience to it is punished with feebleness, stinted growth, general imperfection, or death. A third organic law, applicable to man, is, that he shall duly exercise his organs, this condition being an indispensable requisite to health. The reward of obedience to this law, is enjoyment in the very act of exercising the functions, pleasing consciousness of existence, and the acquisition of numberless gratifications and advantages, of which labour, or the exercise of our powers, is the procuring means: disobedience is punished with derangement and sluggishness of the functions, with general uneasiness or positive pain, and with the denial of gratification to numerous faculties.

Directing our attention to the constitution of the human body, we perceive that the power of reproduction is bestowed on man, and also intellect, to enable him to discover and obey the conditions necessary for the transmission of a healthy organic frame to his descendants; that digestive organs are given to him for his nutrition, and innumerable vegetable and animal productions are placed around him, in wise relationship to these organs.

Without attempting to expound minutely the organic structure of man, or to trace in detail its adaptation to his external condition, I shall offer some observations in support of the proposition, that the due exercise of the osseous, muscular, and nervous systems, under the guidance of intellect and moral sentiment, and in accordance with the physical laws, contributes to human enjoyment; and, that neglect of this exercise, or an abuse of it, by carrying it to excess, or by conducting it in opposition to the moral, intellectual, or physical laws, is punished with pain.

The earth is endowed with the capability of producing an ample supply for all our wants, provided we expend muscular and nervous energy in its cultivation; while, in most climates, it refuses to produce if we withhold this labour and leave it waste. Farther, the Creator has presented us with timber, metal, wool, and countless materials, which, by means of muscular power, may be converted into clothing, and all the luxuries of life. The fertility of the earth, and the demands of the body for food and clothing, are so benevolently adapted to each other, that with rational restraint on population, a few hour's labour each day from every individual capable of labour, would suffice to furnish all with every commodity that could really add to enjoyment.

In the tropical regions of the globe, for example, where a high atmospheric temperature diminishes the quantum of muscular energy, the fertility and productiveness of the soil are increased in a like proportion, so that less labour suffices. Less labour, also, is required to provide habitations and raiment. In the colder latitudes, muscular energy is greatly increased, and there much higher demands are made upon it. The earth is more sterile, the rude winds require firmer fabrics to resist their violence, and the piercing frosts require a thicker covering to the body.

Farther, the food afforded by the soil in each climate is admirably adapted to the maintenance of the organic constitution in health, and to the supply of the muscular energy requisite for the particular wants of the situation. In the Arctic Regions no farinaceous food ripens; but on putting the question to Dr Richardson, how he, accustomed to the bread and vegetables of the temperate regions, was able to endure the pure animal diet, which formed his only support on his expedition to the shores of the Polar Sea along with Captain Franklin, he replied, that the effects of the extreme dry cold to which they were exposed, living, as they did, constantly in the open air, was to produce a desire for the most stimulating food they could obtain; that bread in such a climate was not only not desired, but comparatively impotent, as an article of diet; that pure animal food, and the fatter the better, was the only sustenance that maintained the tone of the corporeal system, but that when it was abundant (and the quantity required was much greater than in milder latitudes) a delightful vigour and buoyancy of mind and body were enjoyed, that rendered life highly agreeable. Now, in beautiful harmony with these wants of the human frame, these regions abound, during summer, in countless herds of deer, in rabbits, partridges, ducks, in short, in game of every description, and fish; and the flesh of these dried, constitutes delicious food in winter, when the earth is wrapped in one wide-spread covering of snow.

In Scotland, the climate is moist and cold, the greater part of the surface is mountainous, but admirably adapted for raising sheep and cattle, while a certain portion consists of fertile plains, fitted for farinaceous food. If the same law holds in this country, the diet of the people should consist of animal and farinaceous food, the former decidedly predominating. As we proceed to warmer latitudes, we find the soil and temperature of France less congenial to sheep and cattle, but more favourable to corn and wine; and the Frenchman inherits a native elasticity of body and mind, that enables him to flourish in vigour on less of animal food, than would be requisite to preserve the Scottish Highlander in a like gay and alert condition, in the recesses of his mountains. The plains of Hindostan are too hot for the sheep and ox, but produce rice and vegetable spices in prodigious abundance, and the native is healthy, vigorous and active, when supplied with rice and curry, and becomes sick, when obliged to live upon animal diet. He, also, is supplied with less muscular energy from this species of food, and his soil and climate require far less laborious exertion than those of Britain, Germany, or Russia.

So far, then, the external world appears to be wisely and benevolently adapted to the organic system of man, that is, to his nutrition, and to the developement and exercise of his corporeal organs; and the natural law appears to be, that all, if they desire to enjoy the pleasures attending sound and vigorous muscular and nervous systems, must expend in labour the energy which the Creator has infused into these organs. A wide choice is left open to man, as to the *mode* in which he shall exercise his nervous and muscular systems. The labourer, for example, digs the ground, and the squire engages in the chase. The penalty of neglecting this law is debility, bodily and mental, lassitude, imperfect digestion, disturbed sleep, bad health, and, if carried to a certain length, death. The penalty for over-exerting these systems is exhaustion, mental incapacity, the desire of strong artificial stimulants, such as ardent spirits, general insensibility, and grossness of feeling and perception, with disease and shortened life. Society has not recognised this law, and in consequence, the higher orders despise labour, and suffer the first penalty; while the lower orders are oppressed with toil, and undergo the second. The penalties serve to provide motives for obedience to the law, and wherever it is recognised, and the consequences are discovered to be inevitable, men will no longer shun labour as painful and ignominious, but resort to it as a source of pleasure, as well as to avoid the pains inflicted on those who neglect it.

SECT. III.—MAN CONSIDERED AS AN ANIMAL—MORAL—AND INTELLECTUAL BEING.

In the *third* place, man is an animal—moral—and intellectual being. To discover the adaptation of these parts of his nature to his external circumstances, we must first know what are his various animal, moral, and intellectual powers themselves. Phrenology gives us a view of them, drawn from observation; and as I have verified the inductions of that science, so as to satisfy myself that it is the most complete and correct exposition of the Nature of Man which has yet been given, I adopt its classification of facuces as the basis of the subsequent observations. According to Phrenology, then, the Human Faculties are the following:

Order I. FEELINGS.

Genus I. PROPENSITIES—*Common to Man with the Lower Animals.*

1. Amativeness; Produces sexual love.
2. Philoprogenitiveness.—*Uses:* Love of offspring. —*Abuses:* Pampering and spoiling children.
3. Concentrativeness.—*Uses:* It gives the desire for permanence in place, and for permanence of emotions and ideas in the mind.—*Abuses:* Aversion to move abroad; morbid dwelling on internal emotions and ideas, to the neglect of external impressions.
4. Adhesiveness.—*Uses:* Attachment; friendship, and society result from it.—*Abuses:* Clanship for improper objects, attachment to worthless individuals. It is generally large in women.
5. Combativeness.—*Uses:* Courage to meet danger, to overcome difficulties, and to resist attacks.—*Abuses*: Love of contention, and tendency to provoke and assault.
6. Destructiveness.—*Uses:* Desire to destroy noxious objects, and to kill for food. It is very discernible in carnivorous animals.—*Abuses:* Cruelty, desire to torment, tendency to passion, rage, harshness and severity in speech and writing.
7. Constructiveness.—*Uses:* Desire to build and construct works of art.—*Abuses:* Construction of engines to injure or destroy, and fabrication of objects to deceive mankind.
8. Acquisitiveness.—*Uses:* Desire to possess, and tendency to accumulate articles of utility, to provide against want.—*Abuses:* Inordinate desire for property; selfishness; avarice.
9. Secretiveness.—*Uses:* Tendency to restrain within the mind the various emotions and ideas that involuntarily present themselves, until the judgment has approved of giving them utterance; it also aids the artist and the actor in giving expression; and is an ingredient in prudence.—*Abuses:* Cunning, deceit, duplicity, lying, and, joined with Acquisitiveness, theft.

Genus II. SENTIMENTS.

I. *Sentiments common to Man with the Lower Animals.*

10. Self-Esteem.—*Uses:* Self-interest, love of independence, personal dignity.—*Abuses:* Pride, disdain, overweening conceit, excessive selfishness, love of dominion.
11. Love of Approbation.—*Uses:* Desire of the esteem of others, love of praise, desire of fame or glory.—*Abuses:* Vanity, ambition, thirst for praise independent of praiseworthiness.
12. Cautiousness.—*Uses:* It gives origin to the sentiment of fear, the desire to shun danger, to circumspection; and it is an ingredient in prudence. —*Abuses:* Excessive timidity, poltroonery, unfounded apprehensions, despondency, melancholy.
13. Benevolence.—*Uses:* Desire of the happiness of others, universal charity, mildness of disposition, and a lively sympathy with the enjoyment of all animated beings.—*Abuses:* Profusion, injurious indulgence of the appetites and fancies of others, prodigality, facility of temper.

II. *Sentiments proper to Man.*

14. Veneration.—*Uses:* Tendency to worship, adore, venerate, or respect whatever is great and good; gives origin to the religious sentiment.—*Abuses:* Senseless respect for unworthy objects consecrated by time or situation, love of antiquated customs, abject subserviency to persons in authority, superstition.
15. Hope.—*Uses:* Tendency to expect and to look forward to the future with confidence and reliance; it cherishes faith.—*Abuses:* Credulity, absurd expectations of felicity not founded on reason.
16. Ideality.—*Uses:* Love of the beautiful and splendid, the desire of excellence, poetic feeling.—*Abuses:* Extravagance and absurd enthusiasm, preference of the showy and glaring to the solid and useful, a tendency to dwell in the regions of fancy, and to neglect the duties of life.

Wonder.—*Uses:* The desire of novelty, admiration of the new, the unexpected, the grand, and extraordinary.—*Abuses:* Love of the marvellous, astonishment.—*Note.* Veneration, Hope, and Wonder, combined, give the tendency to religion; their abuses produce superstition and belief in false miracles, in prodigies, magic, ghosts, and all supernatural absurdities.

17. Consciousness.—*Uses:* It gives origin to the sentiment of justice, or respect for the rights of others, openness to conviction, the love of truth. *Abuses:* Scrupulous adherence to noxious principles when ignorantly embraced, excessive refinement in the views of duty and obligation, excess in remorse, or self-condemnation.
18. Firmness.—*Uses:* Determination, perseverance, steadiness of purpose.—*Abuses:* Stubbornness, infatuation, tenacity in evil.

Order II. INTELLECTUAL FACULTIES.

Genus I. External Senses.

Feeling or Touch. Taste. Smell. Hearing. Light.	*Uses:* To bring man into communication with external objects, and to enable him to enjoy them. *Abuses:* Excessive indulgence in the pleasures arising from the senses, to the extent of impairing the organs and debilitating the mind.

Genus II. INTELLECTUAL FACULTIES—*which perceive existence.*

19. Individuality—Takes cognizance of existence and simple facts.

Eventuality—Takes cognizance of occurrences and events.

20. Form—Renders man observant of form.
21. Size—Renders man observant of dimensions, and aids perspective.
22. Weight—Communicates the perception of momentum, weight, resistance, and aids equilibrium.
23. Colouring—Gives perception of colours.

Genus III. INTELLECTUAL FACULTIES—*which perceive the relations of external objects.*

24. Locality—Gives the idea of space and relative position.
25. Order—Communicates the love of physical arrangement.
26. Time—Gives rise to the perception of duration.
27. Number—Gives a turn for arithmetic and algebra
28. Tune—The sense of Melody arises from it.
29. Language—Gives a facility in acquiring a knowledge of arbitrary signs to express thoughts—a felicity in the use of them—and a power of inventing them.

Genus IV. REFLECTING FACULTIES—*which compare, judge, and discriminate.*

30. Comparison—Gives the power of discovering analogies and resemblances.
31. Causality—To trace the dependencies of phenomena, and the relation of cause and effect.
32. Wit—Gives the feeling and the ludicrous.
33. Imitation—To copy the manners, gestures, and actions of others, and nature generally.

The first glance at these faculties suffices to show, that they are not all equal in excellence and elevation; that some are common to man with the lower animals; and others peculiar to man. In comparing the human mind, therefore, with its external condition, it becomes an object of primary importance to discover the relative subordination of these different orders of powers. If the Animal Faculties are naturally or necessarily supreme, then external nature, if it be wisely constituted, may be expected to bear direct reference, in its arrangements, to this supremacy. If the Moral and Intellectual Faculties hold the ascendancy, then the constitution of external nature may be expected to be in harmony with them, when predominant. Let us attend to these questions.

SECT. IV.—THE FACULTIES OF MAN COMPARED WITH EACH OTHER; OR THE SUPREMACY OF THE MORAL SENTIMENTS AND INTELLECT.

According to the phrenological theory of human nature, the faculties are divided into Propensities common to man with the lower animals, Sentiments proper to man, and intellect. Every faculty stands in a definite relation to certain external objects;—when it is internally active it desires these objects;—when they are presented to it they excite it to activity, and delight it with agreeable sensations. Human happiness and misery are resolvable into the gratification or denial of gratification of one or more of our active faculties, before described, of the external senses, and the feelings connected with our bodily frame. The faculties, in themselves, are mere instincts; the moral sentiments and intellect are higher instincts than the animal propensities. Every faculty is good in itself, but all are liable to abuse. Their manifestations are right only when directed by *enlightened* intellect and moral sentiment. In maintaining the *supremacy* of the moral sentiments and intellect, I *do not* consider them sufficient to direct conduct by *their mere instinctive suggestions*. To fit them to discharge this important duty, *they must be illuminated by knowledge of science and of moral and of religious duty;* but whenever their dictates, thus enlightened, oppose the solicitations of the propensities, *the latter must yield*, otherwise, *by the constitution of external nature*, evil will inevitably ensue. This is what I mean by nature being constituted in harmony with the supremacy of the moral sentiments and intellect. Let us consider the faculties themselves.

The first three propensities, Amativeness, Philoprogenitiveness, and Adhesiveness, or the group of the domestic affections, desire a conjugal partner, offspring, and friends; the obtaining of these affords them delight,—the removal of them occasions pain. But to render an individual happy, the whole faculties must be gratified harmoniously, or at least the gratification of one or more must not offend any of the others. For example, suppose the group of the domestic affections to be highly interested in an individual, and strongly to desire to form an alliance with him, but that the person so loved is improvident and immoral, and altogether an object which the faculties of Self-esteem, Love of Approbation, Benevolence, Veneration, Conscientiousness, and Intellect, if left dispassionately to survey his qualities, could not approve of; then, if an alliance be formed with him, under the ungovernable impulses of the former faculties, bitter days of repentance must necessarily follow, when these begin to languish, and the latter faculties receive offence from his qualities. If, on the other hand, the domestic affections are guided by intellect to an object pleasing to the latter powers, these themselves will be gratified, they will double the delights afforded by the former faculties, and render the enjoyment permanent.

The great distinction between the animal faculties and the powers proper to man, is, that the object of the former is the preservation of the individual himself, or his family; while the latter have the welfare of others, and our duties to God, as their ends. Even the domestic affections, amiable and respectable as they undoubtedly are when combined with the moral feelings, have self as their object. The love of children, springing from Philoprogenitiveness, when acting alone, is the same in kind as that of the miser for his gold; an intense interest in the object, for the sake of the gratification it affords to his own mind, without regard for the object on its own account. This truth is recognized by Sir Walter Scott. He says, 'Elspat's ardent, *though selfish affection* for her son, *incapable of being qualified by a regard for the true interests of the unfortunate object of her attachment, resembled the instinctive fondness of the animal race for their offspring; and, diving little farther into futurity than one of the inferior creatures, she only felt that to be separated from Hamish, was to die.*'*

In man, this faculty generally acts along with Benevolence, and a disinterested desire of the happiness of the child mingles along with, and elevates the mere instinct of, Philoprogenitiveness; but the sources of these two affections are different, their degrees vary in different persons, and their ends also are dissimilar.

The same observation applies to the affection proceeding from Adhesiveness. When this faculty acts alone, it desires, for its own satisfaction, a friend to love; but, if Benevolence do not act along with it, it cares nothing for the happiness of that friend, except in so far as his welfare may be necessary to its own gratification. The horse feels melancholy when his companion is removed; but the feeling appears to be one of unneasiness at the absence of an object which gratified his Adhesiveness. His companion may have been led to a richer pasture, and introduced to more agreeable society; yet this does not assuage the distress suffered by him at his removal; his tranquillity, in short, is restored only by time causing the activity of Adhesiveness to subside, or by the substitution of another object on which it may exert itself. In human nature, the effect of the faculty, when acting singly, is the same; and this accounts for the fact of the almost total indifference of many persons who were really attached, by Adhesiveness, to each other, when one falls into misfortune, and becomes a disagreeable object to the Self-esteem and Love of Approbation of the other. Suppose two persons, elevated in rank, and possessed of affluence, to have such Adhesiveness, Self-esteem, and Love of Approbation large, with Benevolence and Conscientiousness moderate, it is obvious that, while both are in prosperity, they may really like each other's society, and feel a reciprocal attachment, because there will be mutual sympathy in their Adhesiveness, and the Self-esteem and Love of Approbation of each will be gratified by the rank and circumstances of his friend; but imagine one of them to fall into misfortune, and to cease to be an object gratifying to Self-esteem and Love of Approbation; suppose that he becomes a poor friend instead of a rich and influential one, the harmony between their selfish faculties will be broken, and then Adhesiveness in the one who remains rich will transfer its affection to another individual who may gratify it, and also supply agreeable sensations to Self-esteem and Love of Approbation,—to a genteel friend, in short, who will look well in the eye of the world.

Much of this conduct occurs in society, and the whining complaint is very ancient, that the storms of adversity disperse friends just as the winter winds strip leaves from the forest that gaily adorned it in the sunshine of summer; and many moral sentence are pointed, and episodes finely turned, on the selfishness and corruption of poor human nature. But such friendships were attachments founded on the lower feelings, which, by their constitution, are selfish, and the desertion complained of is the fair and legitimate result of the principles on which both parties acted during the gay hours of prosperity. If we look at the head of Sheridan, we shall perceive large Adhesiveness, Self-esteem, and Love of Approbation, with deficient reflecting organs, and moderate Conscientiousness. He

* Chronicles of the Canongate, vol. i. p. 281.

has large Individuality, Comparison, Secretiveness, and Imitation, which gave him talents for observation and display. When these earned him a brilliant reputation, he was surrounded by friends, and he himself probably felt attachment in return. But his deficient morality prevented him from loving his friends with a true, disinterested, and honest regard; he abused their kindness, and, as he sunk into poverty and wretchedness, and ceased to be an honour to them, or to excite their Love of Approbation, they almost all deserted him. But the whole connexion was founded on selfish principles; Sheridan honoured them, and they flattered Sheridan; and the abandonment was the natural consequence of the cessation of gratification to their selfish feelings. I shall by-and-by point out the sources of a loftier and a purer friendship, and its effects.

To proceed with the propensities: Combativeness and Destructiveness, also are in their nature purely selfish. If aggression is committed against us, Combativeness draws the sword and repels the attack; Destructiveness inflicts vengeance for the offence; both feelings are obviously the very opposite of benevolent. I do not say, that, in themselves, they are despicable or sinful; on the contrary, they are necessary, and, when legitimately employed, highly useful; but still self is the object of their supreme regard.

The next organ is Acquisitiveness, and self is eminently its object. It desires blindly to possess, is pleased with accumulating, and suffers great uneasiness in being deprived of its objects. It is highly useful, like all the other faculties, for even Benevolence cannot give away until Acquisitiveness has acquired. There are friendships, particularly among mercantile men, founded on Adhesiveness and Acquisitiveness, just as in fashionable life they are founded on Adhesiveness and Love of Approbation. Two individuals fall into a course of dealing, by which each reaps profit by transactions with the other: this leads to intimacy, and Adhesiveness probably mingles its influence, and produces a feeling of actual attachment. The moment, however, that the Acquisitiveness of the one suffers the least inroad from that of the other, and their interests clash, they are apt, if no higher principle unite them, to become bitter enemies. It is probable that, while these fashionable and commercial friendships last, the parties may profess great recriprocal esteem and regard, and that, when a rupture takes place, the one who is depressed, or disobliged, may recall these expressions and charge them as hypocritical; but they really were not so: each probably felt from Adhesiveness and gratified Love of Approbation something which he coloured over, and perhaps believed to be disinterested friendship; but if each would honestly probe his own conscience, he would be obliged to acknowledge that the whole basis of the connexion was selfish; and hence, that the result is just what every man ought to expect, who places his reliance for happiness chiefly on the lower propensities.

Secretiveness is also selfish in its nature; for it suppresses feelings that might injure us with other individuals, and desires to find out secrets that may enable its possessor to guard self against hostile plots or designs. In itself it does not desire, in any respect, the benefit of others.

Self-esteem is, in its very essence and name, selfish; it is the love of ourselves, and the esteem of ourselves *par excellence.*

Love of Approbation, although many think otherwise, is also in itself a purely selfish feeling. Its real desire is applause to ourselves, to be esteemed ourselves, and if it prompt us to do services, or to say agreeable things to others, it is not from love of them, but purely for the sake of obtaining self-gratification.

Suppose, for example, we are acquainted with a person who has committed an error in some public duty, who has done or said something that the public disapprove of, and which we see to be really wrong, Benevolence and Conscientiousness would prompt us to lay before our friend the very head and front of his offending, and conjure him to forsake his error, and publicly make amends:—Love of Approbation, on the other hand, would either render us averse to speak to him on the subject, lest he should be offended, or prompt us to extenuate his fault, and represent it as either positively no error at all, or as extremely trivial. If we analyze the motive which prompts to this course, we shall find that it is not love of our friend, or consideration for his welfare, but fear lest, by our presenting to him disagreeable truths, he should feel offended at us, and deprive us of the gratification afforded to our Love of Approbation by his good opinion: in short, the motive is purely selfish.

Another illustration occurs. A manufacturer in a country town, having acquired a considerable fortune by trade, applied part of it in building a princely mansion, which he furnished in the richest and most expensive style of fashion. He asked his customers, near and distant, to visit him when calling on business, and led them into a dining-room or drawing-room that absolutely dazzled them with its magnificence. This excited their wonder and curiosity, which was precisely the effect he desired; he then led them over his whole apartments, and displayed before them his grandeur and taste. In doing so, he imagined that he was conferring a high pleasure on them, and filling their minds with an intense admiration of his greatness; but the real effect was very different. The motive of his conduct was not love of them, or regard for their happiness or welfare; it was not Benevolence to others that prompted him to build the palace; it was not Veneration, nor was it Conscientiousness. The fabric sprung from Self-esteem and Love of Approbation combined, no doubt, with considerable Intellect and Ideality. In leading his humble brethren in trade through the princely halls, over the costly carpets, and amidst the gilding, burnishing, and rich array, that every where met their eyes,he exulted in the consciousness of his own importance, and asked for their admiration, not as an expression of respect for any real benefits conferred upon them, but as the much relished food of his own selfish vanity.

Let us attend, in the next place, to the effect of this display on those to whom it was addressed. To gain their esteem or affection, it was necessary to manifest towards them real Benevolence, real regard, and impartial justice; in short, to cause another individual to love us, we must make him the object of the moral sentiments, which have his good and happiness for their end. Here, however, these were not the inspiring motives of the conduct, and the want of them would be instinctively felt. The customers, who possessed the least shrewdness, would ascribe the whole exhibition to the vanity of the owner, and they would either pity or hate him; if their own moral sentiments predominated, they would pity; if their Self-esteem and Love of Approbation were paramount, these would be offended at his assumed superiority, and would rouse Destructiveness to hate him. It would only be the silliest and the vainest who would be at all gratified; and their satisfaction would arise from the feeling, that they could now return to their own circle, and boast how great a friend they had, and in how grand a style they had been entertained,—this display being a direct gratification of their own Self-esteem and Love of Approbation, by their identifying themselves with him. Even this pleasure could be reaped only where the admirer was so humble in rank as to entertain no idea of rivalship, and so limited in intellect and sentiments as not to perceive the worthlessness of the qualities by which he was captivated.

In like manner, when persons, even of more sense than the manufacturer here alluded to, give entertainments to their friends, they sometimes fail in their object from the same cause. They wish to show off themselves as their leading motive, much more than to confer real happiness upon their acquaintances; and, by the irreversible law of human nature, this must fail in exciting good-will and pleasure in the minds of those to whom it is addressed, because it disagreeably affects their Self-esteem and Love of Approbation. In short, to be really successful in gratifying our friends, we must keep our own selfish faculties in due subordination, and pour out copious streams of real kindness from the higher sentiments, animated and elevated by intellect; and all who have experienced the heart-felt joy and satisfaction attending an entertainment conducted on this principle, will never quarrel with the homeliness of the fare, or feel uneasy about the absence of fashion in the service.

Cautiousness is the next faculty, and is a sentiment instituted to protect self from danger, and has clearly a regard to individual safety as its primary object.

This terminates the list of the feelings common to man with the lower animals,* and which, as we have seen, have self preservation as their leading objects. They are given for the protection and advantage of our animal nature, and, when duly regulated, are highly useful, and also respectable, viewed with reference to that end; but they are sources of innumerable evils when allowed to usurp the ascendancy over the moral faculties, and to become the leading springs of our social intercourse.

I proceed to notice the moral sentiments which constitute the proper human faculties, and to point out their objects and relations.

Benevolence has no reference to self. It desires purely and disinterestedly the happiness of its objects; it loves for the sake of the person beloved; if he be well, and the sunbeams of prosperity shine warmly around him, it exults and delights in his felicity. It desires a diffusion of joy, and renders the feet swift and the arm strong in the cause of charity and love.

Veneration also has no reference to self. It looks up with a pure and elevated emotion to the being to whom it is directed, whether God or our fellow-men, and delights in the contemplation of their venerable and admirable qualities. It desires to find out excellence, and to dwell and feed upon it, and renders self lowly, humble, and submissive.

Hope spreads its gay wing in the boundless regions of futurity. It desires good, and expects it to come; 'it incites us to aim at a good which we can live without;' its influence is soft, soothing, and happy; but self is not its direct or particular object.

Ideality delights in perfection from the pure pleasure of contemplating it. So far as it is concerned, the picture, the statue, the landscape, or the mansion, on which it abides with intensest rapture, will be as pleasing, although the property of another, as if all its own. It is a spring that is touched by the beautiful wherever it exists; and hence its means of enjoyment are as unbounded as the universe is extensive.

Wonder seeks the new and the striking, and is delighted with change; but there is no desire of appropriation to self in its longings.

Conscientiousness stands in the midway between self and other individuals. It is a regulator of our animal feelings, and points out the limit which they must not pass. It desires to do to another as we would have another to do to us, and thus is a guardian of the welfare of our fellow men, while it sanctions and supports our personal feelings within the bounds of a due moderation. It is a noble feeling; and the mere consciousness of its being bestowed upon us, ought to bring home to our minds an intense conviction that the Author of the universe is at once wise and just.

Intellect is universal in its application. It may become the handmaid of any of the faculties; it may devise a plan to murder or to bless, to steal or to bestow, to rear up or to destroy; but, as its proper use is to observe the different objects of creation, to mark their relations, and direct the propensities and sentiments to their proper and legitimate enjoyments, it has a boundless sphere of activity, and, when properly exercised and applied, is a source of high and inexhaustible delight.

Keeping in view the great difference now pointed out between the animal and properly human faculties, the reader will perceive that three consequences follow from the constitution of these powers: *First,* All the faculties, when in excess, are insatiable, and, from the constitution of the world, never can be satisfied. They indeed may be soon satisfied on any particular occasion. Food will soon fill the stomach; indulgence will speedily assuage Amativeness; success in a speculation will render Acquisitiveness quiescent for the moment: a triumph will satisfy for the time Self-esteem and Love of Approbation; a long concert will fatigue Tune; and too long a discourse afflict Casuality. But after repose they will all *renew their solicitations.* They must all therefore be regulated; and, in particular, the lower propensities, from having self as their primary objects, and being blind to consequences, do not set limits to their own indulgence; and hence lead to misery to the individual, and injury to society, when allowed to exceed the limits prescribed by the superior sentiments and intellect.

As this circumstance attending the propensities is of great practical importance, I shall make a few observations in elucidation of it. The births and lives of children depend upon circumstances, over which unenlightened men have but a limited control; and hence an individual, whose supreme happiness springs from the gratification of Philoprogenitiveness will, by the mere predominance of that propensity, be led to neglect or infringe the natural laws, on which the lives and welfare of children depend, and which can be observed only by active moral and intellectual faculties. Hence he will be in constant danger of anguish and disappointment, by the removal of his children, or by their undutiful conduct and immoral behaviour. Besides, Philoprogenitiveness, acting along with Self-esteem and Love of Approbation, would, in each parent, desire that *his* children should possess the highest rank, the greatest wealth, and be distinguished for the most splendid talents. Now the highest, the greatest, the most splendid of any qualities, necessarily imply the existence of inferior degrees, and are not attainable except by one. The animal faculties, therefore, must be restrained in their desires, and directed to their objects by the human faculties, by the sentiments of Conscientiousness, Benevolence, Veneration, and Intellect, otherwise they will inevitably lead to disappointment. In like manner, Acquisitiveness desires wealth, and, as nature affords only a certain number of quarters of grain annually, a certain portion of cattle, of fruit, of flax, and other articles, from which food, clothing, and wealth, are manufactured; and as this quantity, divided equally among all the members of a state, would afford but a moderate portion to each, it is self-evident that, if all desire to acquire and possess a large amount, ninety-nine out of the hundred must be disappointed. This disappointment, from the very constitution of nature, is inevitable to the greater number; and when individuals form schemes of aggrandisement, originating from desires communicated by the animal faculties alone, they would do well to keep this law of nature in view. When we look around, we see how few make rich; how few succeed in accomplishing all their lofty anticipations for the

* Benevolence is stated in the works on Phrenology as common to man with the lower animals; but in them it appears to produce rather passive meekness and good nature, than actual desire for each other's happiness. In the human race this last is its proper function; and, viewed in this light, I here treat of it as exclusively a human faculty.

advancement of their children; how few attain the summit of ambition, compared with the multitudes who fall short. Love of Approbation and Self-esteem when unregulated, desire the highest station of ambition; but, as these faculties exist in all men, and only one can be greatest, they will prompt one man to defeat the gratification of another. All this arises, not from error and imperfection in the institution of the Creator but from blindness in men to their own nature, to the nature of external objects, and to the relations established between these: in short, blindness to the principles of the divine administration of the world.

Secondly. The animal propensities being inferior in their nature to the human faculties, their gratifications when not approved of by the latter, leave a painful feeling of discontent and dissatisfaction in the mind, occasioned by the secret disclamation of their excessive action by the higher feelings. Suppose, for example a young person to set out in life, with the idea that the great object of existence is to acquire wealth, to rear and provide for a family, and to attain honor and distinction among men; all these desires spring from the propensities alone. Imagine him to rise early and sit up late, to put forth all the energies of a powerful mind in buying, selling, and making rich, and that he is successful; it is obvious, that, in prompting to this course of action, Benevolence, Veneration, and Conscientiousness, had no share; and that, in pursuing it, they have not received direct and intended gratification; they would have anxiously and wearily watched the animal faculties, longing for the hour when they were to say Enough; their whole occupation, in the mean time, being to restrain them from such gross extravagances as would have defeated their own ends. In the domestic circle, again, a spouse and children would gratify Philoprogenitiveness and Adhesiveness, and their advancement would please Self-esteem and Love of Approbation; but here also the moral sentiments would act the part of mere spectators and sentinels to impose restraints; they would receive no direct enjoyment, and would not be recognised as the fountain of the conduct. In the pursuit of honor, suppose an office of dignity and power, or high rank in society, the mainsprings of exertion would still be Self-esteem and Love of Approbation, and the moral sentiments would be compelled to wait in tiresome vacuity, without having their energies called directly into play, so as to give them full scope in their legitimate sphere.

Suppose, then, this individual to have reached the evening of life, and to look back on the pleasures and pains of his past existence, he must feel that there has been vanity and vexation of spirit,—the want of a satisfying portion; and for this sufficient reason, that the highest of his faculties have been all along scarcely employed. In estimating, also, the real affection and esteem of mankind which he has gained, he will find it to be small or great in exact proportion to the degree in which he has manifested, in his habitual conduct, the lower or the higher faculties. If society has seen him selfish in his pursuit of wealth, selfish in his domestic affections, selfish in his ambition; although he may have gratified all these feelings without positive encroachment on the rights of others, they will still look coldly on him, they will feel no glow of affection towards him. no elevated respect, no sincere admiration; he will see and feel this, and complain bitterly that all is vanity and vexation of spirit. But the fault has been his own; love, esteem, and sincere respect, arise, by the Creator's laws, not from contemplating the manifestations of plodding, selfish faculties, but only from the display of Benevolence, Veneration, and Justice, as the motives and end of our conduct; and the individual supposed has reaped the natural and legitimate produce of the soil which he cultivated, and eaten the fruit which he has reared.

Thirdly. The higher feelings, when directed by enlightened intellect, have a boundless scope for gratification; their least indulgence is delightful, and their highest activity is bliss; they cause no repentance, leave no void, but render life a scene at once of peaceful tranquillity and sustained felicity; and, what is of much importance, conduct proceeding from their dictates carries in its train the highest gratification to the animal propensities themselves, of which the latter are susceptible. At the same time, it must be observed, that the sentiments err, and lead also to evil, when not regulated by enlightened intellect; that intellect in its turn must give due weight to the existence and desires of both the propensities and sentiments, as elements in the human constitution, before it can arrive at sound conclusions regarding conduct; and that rational actions and true happiness flow from the gratification of all the faculties *in harmony* with each other; the sentiments and intellect bearing the directing sway.

This proposition may be shortly illustrated. Imagine an individual to commence life, with the thorough conviction that the higher sentiments are the superior powers, and that they ought to be the sources of his actions, the first effect would be to cause him to look habitually outward on other men and on his Creator, instead of looking inward on himself as the object of his highest and chief regard. Benevolence would shed on his mind the conviction, that there are other human beings as dear to the Creator as he, as much entitled to enjoyment as he, and that his duty is to seek no gratification to himself which is to injure them; but, on the contrary, to act so as to confer on them, by his daily exertions, all the services in his power. Veneration would give a strong feeling of reliance on the power and wisdom of God, that such conduct would conduce to the highest gratification of all his faculties; it would add also an habitual respect for his fellow men, as beings deserving his regard, and whose reasonable wishes he was bound to yield a willing and sincere obedience. Lastly, Conscientiousness would prompt him to apply the scales of rigid justice to his animal desires, and to curb and restrain each so as to prevent the slightest infraction on what is due to his fellow men.

Let us trace, then, the operation of these principles in ordinary life. Suppose a friendship formed by such an individual; his first and fundamental principle is Benevolence, which inspires with a sincere, pure, and disinterested regard for his friend; he desires his welfare for his friend's sake; next Veneration reinforces this love by the secret and grateful acknowledgment, which it makes to Heaven for the joys conferred upon the mind by this pure emotion, and also by the habitual deference which it inspires towards our friend himself, rendering us ready to yield where compliance is becoming, and curbing our selfish feelings when these would intrude by interested or arrogant pretensions on his enjoyment; and thirdly, Conscientiousness, ever on the watch proclaims the duty of making no unjust demands on the Benevolence of our friend, but of limiting our whole intercourse with him on an interchange of kindness, good offices, and reciprocal affection. Intellect, acting along with these principles, would point out, as an indispensable requisite to such an attachment, that the friend himself should be so far under the influence of the sentiments, as to be able, in some degree, to meet them; for, if he were immoral, selfish, vainly ambitious, or, in short, under the habitual influence of the propensities, the sentiments could not love and respect him; they might pity him as unfortunate, but love him they could not, because this is impossible by the very laws of their constitution.

Let us now attend to the degree in which such a friendship would gratify the lower propensities. In the first place, how would Adhesiveness exult and rejoice in such an attachment! It would be overpowered with delight, because, if the intellect were convinced that the friend habitually acknowledged the supremacy of the higher sentiments, Adhesiveness might pour forth all its ardour, and cling to its object with the closest bonds of affection. The friend would not encroach on us for evil, because his Benevolence and Justice would oppose this ; he would not lay aside restraint, and break through the bounds of affection by undue familiarity, because Veneration would forbid this ; he would not injure us in our name, person, or reputation, because Conscientiousness, Veneration, and Benevolence, all combined, would prevent such conduct. Here then Adhesiveness, freed from the fear of evil, from the fear of deceit, from the fear of dishonour, because a friend who should habitually act thus, could not possibly fall into dishonour, would be at liberty to take its deepest draught of affectionate attachment ; it would receive a gratification which it is impossible it could attain, while acting in combination with the purely selfish faculties. What delight, too, would such a friendship afford to Self-esteem and Love of Approbation ! There would be an internal approval of ourselves, that would legitimately gratify Self-esteem : because it would arise from a survey of pure motives, and just and benevolent actions. Love of Approbation also, would be gratified in the highest degree ; for every act of affection, every expression of esteem, from such a friend, would be so purified by Benevolence, Veneration, and Conscientiousness, that it would form the legitimate food on which Love of Approbation might feast and be satisfied ; it would fear no hollowness beneath, no tattling in absence, no secret smoothing over for the sake of mere effect, no envyings, and no jealousies. In short, friendship founded on the higher sentiments, as the ruling motives, would delight the mind with gladness and sunshine, and gratify all the faculties, animal, moral, and intellectual, *in harmony* with each other.

By this illustration, the reader will understand more clearly what I mean by the harmony of the faculties. The fashionable and commercial friendships of which I spoke, gratified the propensities of Adhesiveness, Love of Approbation, Self-esteem, and Acquisitiveness, but left out, as fundamental principles, all the higher sentiments :—there was, therefore, a want of harmony in these instances, an absence of full satisfaction, an uncertainty and changeableness, which gave rise to only a mixed and imperfect enjoyment while the friendship lasted, and to a feeling of painful disappointment, and of vanity and vexation, when a rupture occurred. The error, in such cases, consists in founding attachment on the lower faculties, seeing they, by themselves, are not calculated to form a stable basis of affection, instead of building it on them and the higher sentiments, which afford a foundation for real, lasting, and satisfactory friendship. In complaining of the vanity and vexation of attachments springing from the lower faculties exclusively, we are like men who should try to build a pyramid on its smaller end, and then, lament the hardness of their fate, and speak of the unkindness of Providence, when it fell. A similar analysis of all other pleasures founded on the animal propensities chiefly, would give similar results. In short, happiness must be viewed by men as connected inseparably with the exercise of the three great classes of faculties, the moral sentiments and intellect exercising the directing and controlling sway, before it can be permanently attained.

SECT. V.—THE FACULTIES OF MAN COMPARED WITH EXTERNAL OBJECTS.

Having considered man as a *physical* being, and briefly adverted to the adaptation of his constitution to the physical laws of creation ; having viewed him as an organised being, and traced the relations of his organic structure to his external circumstances ; having taken a rapid survey of his *faculties*, as an animal, moral, and intellectual being,—with their uses and the forms of their abuse—and having contrasted these faculties with each other, and discovered the supremacy of the moral sentiments and intellect, I proceed to compare his faculties with *external objects*, in order to discover what provision has been made for their gratification.

1. Amativeness is a feeling obviously necessary to the continuance of the species ; and one which, properly regulated, is not offensive to reason ;—opposite sexes exist to provide for its gratification.*
2. Philoprogenitiveness is given, and offspring exist.
3. Concentrativeness is conferred,—and the other faculties are its objects.
4. Adhesiveness is given,—and country and friends exist.
5. Combativeness is bestowed,—and physical and moral obstacles exist, requiring courage to meet and subdue them.
6. Destructiveness is given,—and man is constituted with a carnivorous stomach, and animals to be killed and eaten exist. Besides, the whole combinations of creation are in a state of decay and renovation. In the animal kingdom almost every species of creatures is the prey of some other ; and the faculty of Destructiveness places the human mind in harmony with this order of creation. Destruction makes way for renovation, and the act of renovation furnishes occasion for the activity of our powers ; and activity is pleasure. That destruction is a natural institution is unquestionable. Not only has nature taught the spider to construct a web for the purpose of ensnaring flies, that it may devour them, and constituted beasts of prey with carnivorous teeth, but she has formed even plants, such as the Drosera, to catch and kill flies, and use them for food. Destructiveness serves also to give weight to indignation, a most important defensive as well as vindicatory purpose. It is a check upon undue encroachment, and tends to constrain mankind to pay regard to the rights and feelings of each other. When properly regulated. it is an able assistant to justice.
7. Constructiveness is given,—and materials for constructing artificial habitations, raiment, ships, and various other fabrics that add to the enjoyment of life, have been provided to give it scope.
8. Acquisitiveness is bestowed,—and property exists capable of being collected, preserved, and applied to use.
9. Secretiveness is given,—and our faculties possess internal activity requiring to be restrained, until fit occasions and legitimate objects present themselves for their gratification ; which restraint is rendered not only possible but agreeable, by the propensity in question. While we suppress and confine one feeling within the limits of our own consciousness, we exercise and gratify another in the very act of doing so.
10. Self-Esteem is given,—and we have an individual existence and individual interests, as its objects.
11. Love of Approbation is bestowed,—and we are surrounded by our fellow men, whose good opinion is the object of its desire.
12. Cautiousness is given, and it is admirably adapted to the nature of the external world. The human body is combustible, is liable to be destroyed by violence, to suffer injury from extreme wet and winds, &c ; and it is necessary for us to be habitually watchful to avoid these sources of calamity. Accordingly, Cautiousness is bestowed on us as an ever watchful sentinel, constantly whispering, 'Take care.' There is ample scope for the legitimate and pleasureable exercise of all our faculties, without running into these evils, provided we know enough, and are watchful enough ; and, therefore,

* The nature and sphere of activity of the phrenological faculties is explained at length in the 'System of Phrenology,' to which I beg to refer. Here I can only indicate general ideas.

Cautiousness is not overwhelmed with inevitable terrors. It serves merely as a warder to excite us to beware of sudden and unexpected danger; it keeps the other faculties at their post, by furnishing a stimulous to them to observe and trace consequences, that safety may be insured; and, when these other faculties do their duty in proper form, the impulses of Cautiousness are not painful, but the reverse: they communicate a feeling of internal security and satisfaction, expressed by the motto *Semper paratus;* and hence this faculty appears equally benevolent in its design, as the others which we have contemplated.

Here, then, we perceive a beautiful provision made for supporting the activity of, and affording legitimate gratification to, the lower propensities. These powers are conferred on us clearly to support our animal nature, and to place us in harmony with the external objects of creation. So far from their being injurious or base in themselves, they possess the dignity of utility, and the estimable quality of being sources of high enjoyment, when legitimately indulged. The phrenologist, therefore, would never seek to extirpate, nor to weaken them too much. He desires only to see their excesses controlled, and their exercise directed in accordance with the great institutions and designs of the Creator.

The next class of faculties is that of the moral sentiments proper to man. These are the following:

Benevolence is given,—and sentient and entelligent beings are created, whose happiness we are able to increase, thereby affording it its scope and delight. It is an error to imagine, that creatures in misery are the only objects of benevolence, and that it has no function but the excitement of pity. It is a wide-spreading fountain of generous feeling, desiring for its gratification not only the removal of pain, but the maintenance and augmentation of positive enjoyment; and the happier it can render its objects, the more complete are its satisfaction and delight. Its exercise, like that of all the other faculties, is a source of great pleasure to the individual himself; and nothing can be conceived more admirably adapted for affording it scope, than the system of creation exhibited on earth. From the nature of the human faculties, each individual, without injuring himself, has it in his power to confer prodigious benefits, or, in other words, to pour forth the most copious streams of benevolence on others, by legitimately gratifying their Adhesiveness, Constructiveness, Acquisitiveness, Love of Approbation, Self-Esteem, Cautiousness, Veneration, Hope, Ideality, Conscientiousness, and their Knowing and Reflecting Faculties.

Veneration.—The legitimate object of this faculty is the Divine Being; and I assume here, that Phrenology enables us to demonstrate the existence of God. The very essay in which I am now engaged, is an attempt at an exposition of some of his attributes, as manifested in this world. If we shall find contrivance, wisdom, and benevolence in his works, unchangeableness, and no shadow of turning in his laws; perfect harmony in each department of creation, and shall discover that the evils which afflict us are much less the direct objects of his arrangements than the consequences of ignorant neglect of institutions calculated for our enjoyment,—then we shall acknowledge in the Divine Being an object whom we may love with our whole soul, reverence with the deepest emotions of veneration, and on whom Hope and Conscientiousness may repose with a perfect and unhesitating reliance. The exercise of this sentiment is in itself a great positive enjoyment, when the object is in harmony with all our other faculties. Further, its activity disposes us to yield obedience to the Creator's laws, the object of which is our own happiness; and hence its exercise is in the highest degree provided for. Revelation unfolds the character and intentions of God where reason cannot penetrate, but its doctrines do not fall within the limits prescribed to this Essay.

Hope is given,—and our understanding, by discovering the laws of nature, is enabled to penetrate into the future. This sentiment, then, is gratified by the absolute reliance which Causality warrants us to place on the stability and wisdom of the Divine arrangements; its legitimate exercise, in reference to this life, is to give us a vivifying faith, that while we suffer evil, we are undergoing a chastisement for having neglected the institutions of the Creator, the object of which punishment is to force us back into the right path. Revelation presents to Hope the certainty of a life to come; and directs all our faculties in points of Faith.

Ideality is bestowed,—and not only is external nature invested with the most exquisite loveliness, but a capacity for moral and intellectual refinement is given to us, by which we may rise in the scale of excellence, and at every step of our progress reap direct enjoyment from this sentiment. Its constant desire is for 'something more excellent still:' in its own immediate impulses it is delightful, and external nature and our own faculties respond to its call.

Wonder prompts to admiration, and desires something new. When we contemplate man endowed with intellect to discover a Deity and to comprehend his works, we cannot doubt of Wonder being provided with objects for its intensest exercise; and when we view him placed in a world where all old things are constantly passing away, and a system of renovation is incessantly proceeding, we see at once how vast a provision is made for the gratification of his desire of novelty, and how admirably it is calculated to impel his other faculties to activity.

Conscientiousness exists,—and it is necessary to prove that all the divine institutions are founded in justice, to afford it full satisfaction. This is a point which many regard as involved in much obscurity: I shall endeavour in this Essay to lift the veil, for to me justice appears to flow through every divine institution.

One difficulty in regard to Conscientiousness, long appeared inexplicable; it was, how to reconcile with Benevolence the institution by which this faculty visits us with remorse, *after* offences are actually committed, instead of arresting our hands by an irresistible veto before them, so as to save us from from the perpetration altogether. The problem is solved by the principle, 'That happiness consists in the activity of our faculties, and that the arrangement of punishment after the offence is far more conducive to activity than the opposite. For example, if we desired to enjoy the highest gratification of Locality, Form, Colouring, Ideality, and Wonder, in exploring a new country, replete with the most exquisite beauties of scenery, and most captivating natural productions, and if we found among these, precipices that gratified Ideality in the highest degree, but which endangered life when we advanced so near as to fall over them, and neglected the law of gravitation, whether would it be most bountiful for Providence to send an invisible attendant with us, who, whenever we were about to approach the brink, should interpose a barrier, and fairly cut short our advance, without requiring us to bestow one thought upon the subject, and without our knowing when to expect it and when not,—or to leave all open, but to confer on us, as he has done, eyes fitted to see the precipice, faculties to comprehend the law of gravitation, Cautiousness to make us fear the infringement of it, and then to leave us to enjoy the scene in perfect safety if we used these powers, but to fall over and suffer pain by bruises and death if we neglected to exercise them? It is obvious that the latter arrangement would give far more scope to our various powers; and if active faculties are the sources of pleasure, as will be shown in the next section, then it would contribute more to our enjoyment than the other. Now, Conscientiousness punishing after the fact, is analogous in the moral world, to this arrangement in the physical. If Intellect, Benevolence, Veneration, and Conscientiousness, do their parts, they will give distinct intimations of disapprobation before commission of the offence, just as Cautiousness will give intimations of danger at sight of the cliff; but if these are disregarded, and we fall over the moral precipice, remorse follows as the punishment, just as pain is the chastisement for tumbling over the physical brink. The object of both institutions is, to permit and encourage the most vigorous and unrestrained exercise of our faculties, in accordance with the physical, moral, and intellectual laws of nature, and to punish us only when we transgress these limits.

FIRMNESS is bestowed,—and the other faculties of the mind are its objects. It supports and maintains their activity, and gives determination to our purposes.

The next Class of Faculties is the Intellectual.

The provisions in external nature for the gratification of the *Senses* of Hearing, Seeing, Smelling, Taste, and Touch or Feeling, are so obvious that it is unnecessary to enlarge upon them.

INDIVIDUALITY and EVENTUALITY, or the powers of observing things that exist, and occurrences, are given, and 'all the truths which Natural Philosophy teaches, depend upon *matter of fact*, and that is learned by observation and experiment, and never could be discovered by reasoning at all.' Here, then, is ample scope for the exercise of these powers.

FORM, SIZE, WEIGHT, LOCALITY, ORDER, NUMBER, } are bestowed, { and the sciences of Geometry, Arithmetic, Algebra, Geography, Chemistry, Botany, Mineralogy, Zoology, Anatomy, and various others, exist, as the fields of their exercise. The first three sciences are almost the entire products of these faculties; the others result chiefly from them, when applied on external objects.

COLOURING, TIME, TUNE, } are given, { and these, aided by Constructiveness, Form, Locality, Ideality, and other faculties, find scope in Painting, Sculpture, Poetry, and the other fine arts.

LANGUAGE is given,—and our faculties inspire us with lively emotions and ideas, which we desire to communicate by its means to other indviduals.

COMPARISON, CAUSALITY, WIT, } exist, { and these faculties, aided by Individuality, Form, Size, Weight, and others already enumerated, find ample gratification in Natural Philosophy, in Moral, Political and Intellectual Science, and their different branches.

IMITATION is bestowed,—and every where man is surrounded by beings and objects whose actions and appearances it may benefit him to copy.

SECT. VI.—ON THE SOURCES OF HUMAN HAPPINESS, AND THE CONDITIONS REQUISITE FOR MAINTAINING IT.

Having now given a rapid sketch of the Constitution of Man, and its relations to external objects, we are prepared to inquire into the sources of his happiness, and the conditions requisite for maintaining it.

The *first* and most obvious circumstance which attracts attention, is, that all enjoyment must necessarily arise from *activity* of the various systems of which the human constitution is composed. The bones, muscles, nerves, digestive and respiratory organs, furnish pleasing sensations, directly or indirectly, when exercised in conformity with their nature; and the external senses, and internal faculties, when excited, supply the whole remaining perceptions and emotions, which, when combined, constitute life and rational existence. If these were habitually buried in sleep, or constitutionally in active, life, to all purposes of enjoyment, might as well be extinct; for existence would be reduced to mere vegetation, without Consciousness.

If, then, Wisdom and Benevolence have been employed in constituting Man, we may expect the arrangements of creation, in regard to him, to be calculated *as a leading object to excite* his various powers, corporeal and mental, *to activity*. This, accordingly, appears to me to be the case; and the fact may be illustrated by a few examples. A certain portion of nervous and muscular energy is infused by nature into the human body every twenty-four hours, and it is delightful to expend this vigour. To provide for its expenditure, the stomach has been constituted so as to require regularly returning supplies of food, which can be obtained only by nervous and muscular exertion; the body has been created destitute of covering, yet standing in need of protection from the elements of Heaven; but this can be easily provided by moderate expenditure of corporeal strength. It is delightful to repair exhausted nervous and muscular energy by wholesome aliment; and the digestive organs have been so constituted, as to perform their functions by successive stages, and to afford us frequent opportunities of enjoying the pleasure of eating. In these arrangements, the design of supporting the various systems of the body in activity, for the enjoyment of the individual, is abundantly obvious. A late writer justly remarks, that 'a person of feeble texture and indolent habits has the bone smooth, thin, and light; but nature, solicitous for our safety, in a manner which we could not anticipate, combines with the powerful muscular frame a dense and perfect texture of bone, where every spine and tubercle is completely developed.' 'As the structure of the parts is originally perfected by the action of the vessels, the function or operation of the part is made the stimulus to those vessels. The cuticle on the hand wears away like a glove; but the pressure stimulates the living surface to force successive layers of skin under that which is wearing, or, as anatomists call it, desquamating; by which they mean, that the cuticle does not change at once, but comes off in squamæ or scales.

Directing our attention to the Mind, we discover that Individuality, and the other Perceptive Faculties, desire, as *their* means of enjoyment, to know existence, and to become acquainted with the qualities of external objects; while the Reflecting Faculties desire to know their dependences and relations. 'There is something,' says an eloquent writer, 'positively agreeable to all men, to all, at least, whose nature is not most grovelling and base, in gaining knowledge for its own sake. When you see any thing for the first time, you at once derive some gratification from the sight being new; your attention is awakened, you desire to know more about it. If it is a piece of workmanship, as an instrument, a machine of any kind, you wish to know how it is made; how it works; and what use it is of. If it is an animal, you desire to know where it comes from; how it lives; what are its dispositions, and, generally, its nature and habits. This desire is felt, too, without at all considering that the machine or the animal may ever be of the least use to yourself practically; for, in all probability, you may never see them again. But you feel a curiosity to learn all about them, *because they are new and unknown to you.* You, accordingly make inquiries; you *feel a gratification* in getting answers to your questions, that is, *in receiving information,* and in knowing more,—in being better informed than you were before. If you ever happen again to see the same instrument or animal you find it agreeable to recollect having seen it before and to think that you know something about it. If you see another instrument or animal, in some respects like, but differing in other particulars, you find it pleasing to *compare them together,* and to note in what they agree, and in what they differ. Now, all this kind of gratification is of a pure and disinterested nature, and has no reference to any of the common purposes of life; yet it is a pleasure—an enjoyment. You are nothing the richer for it; you do not gratify your palate, or any other bodily appetite; and yet it is so pleasing that you would give something out of your pocket to obtain it, and would forego some bodily enjoyment for its sake. The pleasure derived from science is exactly of the like nature, or rather it is the very same.'* This is a correct and forcible exposition of the pleasures attending the active exercise of our intellectual faculties.

Supposing the human faculties to have received their present constitution, two arrangements may be fancied as instituted for the gratification of these powers. 1st. Infusing into them at birth *intuitive knowledge* of every object which they are fitted ever to comprehend; or, 2dly. Constituting them only as *capacities* for gaining knowledge by exercise and application, and surrounding them with objects bearing such relations towards them, that when observed and attended to, they shall afford them high gratification; and, when unobserved and neglected, they shall occasion them uneasiness and pain; and the question occurs, Which mode would be most conducive to enjoyment? The general opinion will be in favor of the first; but the second appears to me to be preferable. If the first meal we had eaten had for ever prevented the recurrence of hunger, it is obvious that all the pleasures of satisfying a healthy appetite would have been then at an end; so that this apparent bounty would have greatly abridged our enjoyment. In like manner, if, our faculties being constituted as at present, intuitive knowledge had been communicated to us, so that, when an hour old, we should have been thoroughly acquainted with every object, quality, and relation that we could ever comprehend, all provision for the sustained activity of many of our faculties would have been done away with. When wealth is acquired, the miser's pleasure in it is diminished. He grasps after *more* with increasing avidity. He is supposed irrational in doing so; but he obeys the instinct of his nature. What he possesses no longer satisfies Acquisitiveness; it is like food in the stomach, which gave pleasure in eating, and would give pain were it withdrawn, but which, when there, is attended with little positive sensation. The Miser's pleasure arises from the *active state* of Acquisitiveness, and only the pursuit and obtaining of *new treasure* can *maintain this state.* The same law is exemplified in the case of Love of Approbation. The gratification which it affords depends upon its *active state,* and hence the necessity for *new incense* and *higher mounting* in the scale of ambition, is constantly experienced by its victims. Napoleon, in exile, said, 'Let us live upon the past:' but he found this impossible; his predominating desires originated in Ambition and Self-esteem; and the past did not stimulate these powers, or maintain them in constant activity. In like manner, no musician, artist, poet, or philosopher, would reckon himself happy, however extensive his attainments, if informed, Now you must stop, and live upon the past; and the reason is still the same. New ideas, and new emotions, best excite and maintain in activity the faculties of the mind, and activity is essential to enjoyment. If these views be correct, the consequences of imbuing the mind with intuitive knowledge, would not have been unquestionably beneficial. The limits of our acquirements would have been reached; our first step would have been our last; every object would have become old and familiar; Hope would have had no object of expectation; Cautiousness no object of fear; Wonder no gratification in novelty; monotony, insipidity, and mental satiety, would apparently have been the lot of man.

* Objects, Advantages, and Pleasures of Science, page 1.

According to the view now advanced, creation, in its present form, is more wisely and benevolently adapted to our constitution than if intuitive instruction had been showered on the mind at birth. By the actual arrangement, numerous noble faculties are bestowed; their objects are presented to them; these objects are naturally endowed with qualities fitted to benefit and delight us, when their uses and proper applications are discovered, and to injure and punish us for our ignorance, when their properties are misunderstood or misapplied; but we are left to find out all these qualities and relations by the exercise of the faculties themselves. In this manner, provision is made for ceaseless activity of the mental powers, and this constitutes the greatest delight. Wheat, for instance, is produced by the earth, and admirably adapted to the nutrition of the body; but it may be rendered more grateful to the organ of taste, more salubrious to the stomach, and more stimulating to the nervous and muscular systems, by being stripped of its external skin, ground into flour, and baked by fire into bread. Now, the Creator obviously pre-arranged all these relations, when he endowed wheat with its properties, and the human body with its qualities and functions. In withholding congenial and intuitive knowledge of these qualities and mutual relations, but in bestowing faculties of Individuality, Form, Colouring, Weight, Constructiveness, &c, fitted to find them out; in rendering the exercise of these faculties agreeable; and in leaving man, in this condition, to proceed for himself,—he appears to me to have conferred on him the highest boon. The earth produces also hemlock and foxglove; and, by the organic law, those substances, if taken in certain moderate quantities, remove diseases; if in excess, they occasion death: but, again, man's observing faculties are fitted, when applied under the guidance of Cautiousness and Reflection, to make this discovery; and he is left to make it in this way, or suffer the consequences of neglect.

Farther, water, when elevated in temperature, becomes steam; and steam expands with prodigious power; this power, confined by muscular energy, exerted on metal, and directed by intellect, is capable of being converted into the steam-engine, the most efficient, yet humble servant of man. All this was clearly pre-arranged by the Creator; and man's faculties were adapted to it; but still we see him left to observe and discover the qualities and relations of water for himself. This duty, however, must be acknowledged as benevolently imposed, the moment we discover that the Creator has made the very exercise of the faculties pleasurable, and arranged external qualities and relations so beneficially, that, when known, they carry a double reward in adding by their positive influence to human gratification.

The Knowing Faculties, as we have seen, observe the mere external qualities of bodies, and their simpler relations. The Reflecting Faculties observe relations also; but of a higher order. The former, for example, discover that the soil is clay or gravel; that it is tough or friable; that it is wet, and that excess of water impedes vegetation; that in one season the crop is large, and in the next deficient. The reflecting faculties take cognizance of the *causes* of these phenomena. They discover the *means* by which wet soil may be rendered dry; clay may be pulverized; light soil may be invigorated; and all of them made more productive; also the relationship of particular soils to particular kinds of grain. The inhabitants of a country who exert their knowing faculties in observing the qualities of their soil, their reflecting faculties in discovering its capabilities and relations to water, lime, manures, and the various species of grain, and who put forth their muscular and nervous energies in accordance with the dictates of these powers, receive a rich reward in a climate improved in salubrity, in an abundant supply of food, besides much positive enjoyment attending the exercise of the powers themselves. Those communities, on the other hand, who neglect to use their mental faculties and muscular and nervous energies, are punished by ague, fever, rheumatism, and a variety of painful affections, arising from damp air; are stinted in food; and, in wet seasons, are brought to the very brink of starvation by total failure of their crops. This punishment is a benevolent admonition from the Creator, that they are neglecting a great duty, and omitting to enjoy a great pleasure; and it will cease as soon as they have fairly redeemed the blessings lost by their negligence, and obeyed the laws of their being.

The winds and waves appear, at first sight, to present insurmountable obstacles to man leaving the island or continent on which he happens to be born, and to his holding intercourse with his fellows in distant climes: But, by observing the relations of water to timber, he is able to construct a ship; by observing the influence of the wind on a physical body placed in a fluid medium, he discovers the use of sails; and, finally, by the application of his faculties, he has found out the expansive quality of steam, and traced its relations until he has produced a machine that enables him almost to set the roaring tempest at defiance, and to sail straight to the stormy north, although its loudest and its fiercest blasts oppose. In these instances, we perceive external nature admirably adapted to support the mental faculties in habitual activity, and to reward us for the exercise of them.

It is objected to this argument, that it involves an inconsistency. Ignorance, it is said, of the natural laws, is necessary to happiness, in order that the faculties may obtain exercise in discovering them;—nevertheless, happiness is impossible till these laws shall have been discovered and obeyed. Here, then, it is said, ignorance is represented as at once *essential* to, and *incompatible* with enjoyment. The same objection, however, applies to the case of the bee. Gathering honey is necessary to its enjoyment; yet it cannot subsist and be happy till it has gathered honey, and therefore that act is both essential to, and incompatible with its gratification. The fallacy lies in losing sight of the natural constitution both of the bee and of man. While the bee possesses instinctive tendencies to roam about the fields and flowery meadows, and to exert its energies in labour, it is obviously beneficial to it to be furnished with motives and opportunities for doing so; and so it is with man to obtain scope for his bodily and mental powers. Now, gathering knowledge is to the mind of man what gathering honey is to the bee. Apparently with the view of effectually prompting the bee to seek this pleasure, honey is made essential to its subsistence. In like manner, and probably with a similar design, knowledge is made indispensable to human enjoyment. Communicating intuitive knowledge of the natural laws to man, *while his present constitution continues*, would be the exact parallel of gorging the bee with honey in midsummer, when its energies are at their height. When the bee has completed its store, winter benumbs its powers, which resume their vigour only when its stock is exhausted, and spring returns to afford them scope. No torpor resembling that of winter seals up the faculties of the human race; but their ceaseless activity is amply provided for. *First*, The laws of nature, compared with the mind of any individual, are of boundless extent, so that every one may learn something new to the end of the longest life. *Secondly*, By the actual constitution of man, he must make use of his acquirements habitually, otherwise he will lose them. *Thirdly*, Every individual of the race is born in utter ignorance, and starts from zero in the scale of knowledge, so that he has the laws to learn for himself.

These circumstances remove the apparent inconsistency. If man had possessed intuitive knowledge of all nature, he could have had no scope for exercising his faculties in *acquiring* knowledge, in *preserving* it, or in *communicating* it. The infant would have been as wise as the most revered sage, and forgetfulness would have been necessarily excluded.

Those who object to these views, imagine that after the human race has acquired knowledge of all the natural laws, if such a result be possible, they *will be in the same condition as if they had been created with intuitive knowledge;* but this does not follow. Although the *race* should acquire the knowledge supposed, it is not an inevitable consequence that *each individual* will necessarily enjoy it all; which, however, would follow from intuition. The entire soil of Britain belongs to the landed proprietors as a class; but each does not possess it *all;* and hence every one has scope for adding to his territories; with this advantage, however, in favour of knowledge, that the acquisitions of one do not impoverish another. Farther, although the race should have learned all the natural laws, their children would not intuitively inherit their ideas, and hence the activity of every one, as he appears on the stage, would be provided for; whereas, by intuition, every child would be as wise as his grandfather, and parental protection, filial piety, and all the delights that spring from difference in knowledge between youth and age, would be excluded. 3*d*, *Using* of acquirements, is, by the actual state of man, essential to the preservation as well as the enjoyment of them. By intuition all knowledge would be habitually present to the mind without effort or consideration. On the whole, therefore, it appears that man's nature being what it is, the arrangement by which he is endowed with powers to acquire knowledge, but left to find it out for himself, is both wise and benevolent.

It has been asked, 'But is there no pleasure in science but that of discovery? Is there none in using the knowledge we have attained? Is there no pleasure in playing at chess after we know the moves? In answer, I observe, that if we know beforehand all the moves that our antagonist intends to make and all our own, which must be the case if we know *everything* by intuition, we shall have no pleasure. The pleasure really consists in discovering the intentions of our antagonist, and in calculating the effects of our own play; a certain degree of ignorance of both of which is indispensable to gratification. In like manner, it is agreeable first to discover the natural laws, and then to study 'the moves' that we ought to make, in consequence of knowing them. So much, then, for the *sources* of human happiness.

In the *second* place, To reap enjoyment in the *greatest quantity*, and to maintain it *most permanently*, the faculties must be gratified *harmoniously:* In other words, if, among the various powers, the *supremacy* belongs to the moral sentiments, then the aim of our habitual conduct must be the attainment of objects suited to gratify them. For example, in pursuing wealth or fame as the leading object of existence, full gratification is not afforded to Benevolence, Veneration, and Conscientiousness, and, consequently, complete satisfaction cannot be enjoyed ; whereas, by seeking knowledge, and dedicating life to the welfare of mankind, and obedience to God, in our several vocations, these faculties will be gratified, and wealth, fame, health, and other advantages, will flow in their train, so that the whole mind will rejoice, and its delights will remain permanent as long as the conduct continues to be in accordance with the supremacy of the moral powers and the laws of external creation.

Thirdly, To place human happiness on a secure basis, the laws of external creation themselves must accord with the dictates of the moral sentiments, and intellect must be fitted to discover the nature and relations of both, and to direct the conduct in coincidence with them.

Much has been written about the extent of human ignorance ; but we should discriminate between absolute incapacity to know, and mere want of information arising from not having used this capacity to its full extent. In regard to the first, or our capacity to know, it appears probable that, in this world, we shall never know the essence, beginning, or end of things ; because these are points which we have no faculties calculated to reach : But the same Creator who made the external world constituted our faculties, and if we have sufficient data for inferring that His intention is, that we shall enjoy existence here while preparing for the ulterior ends of our being ; and if it be true that we can be happy here only by becoming acquainted with the qualities and modes of action of our own minds and bodies, with the qualities and modes of action of external objects, and with the relations established between them ; in short, by becoming thoroughly conversant with those natural laws, which, when observed, are pre-arranged to contribute to our enjoyment, and which, when violated, visit us with suffering, we may safely conclude that our mental capacities are wisely adapted to the attainment of these objects, whenever we shall do our own duty in bringing them to their highest condition of perfection, and in applying them in the best manner.

If we advert for a moment to what we already know, we shall see that this conclusion is supported by high probabilities. Before the mariner's compass and astronomy were discovered, nothing would seem more utterly beyond the reach of the human faculties than traversing the enormous Atlantic or Pacific Oceans ; but the moment these discoveries were made, how simple did this feat appear, and how completely within the scope of human ability ! But it became so, not by any addition to man's mental capacities, nor by any change in the physical world ; but by the easy process of applying Individuality, and the other knowing faculties, to observe, Causality to reflect, and Constructiveness to build ; in short, to perform their natural functions. Who that, forty years ago, regarded the small-pox as a scourge, devastating Europe, Asia, Africa, and America, would not have despaired of the human faculties ever discovering an antidote against it? and yet we have lived to see this end accomplished by a simple exercise of Individuality and Reflection, in observing the effects of, and applying vaccine innoculation. Nothing appears more completely beyond the reach of the human intellect, than the cause of volcanoes and earthquakes ; and yet some approach towards its discovery has recently been made.*

Sir Isaac Newton observed, that all bodies which refracted the rays of light were combustible, except one, the diamond, which he found to possess this quality, but which he was not able, by any powers he possessed, to burn. He did not conclude, however, from this, that the diamond was an exception to the uniformity of nature. He inferred, that, as the same Creator made the refracting bodies which he was able to consume, and the diamond, and proceeded by uniform laws, the diamond would, in all probability, be found to be combustible, and that the reason of its resisting his power, was ignorance on his part of the proper way to produce its conflagration. A century afterwards, chemists made the diamond blaze with as much vivacity as Sir Isaac Newton had done a wax candle. Let us proceed, then, on an analogous principle. If the intention of our Creator was, that we should enjoy existence while in this world, then He knew what was necessary to enable us to do so; and He will not be found to have failed in conferring on us powers fitted to accomplish His design, provided we do our duty in developing and applying them. The great motive to exertion is the conviction, that increased knowledge will furnish us with increased means of doing good,—with new proofs of benevolence and wisdom in the Great Architect of the Universe.

The human race may be regarded as only in the beginning of its existence. The art of printing is an invention comparatively but of yesterday, and no imagination can yet conceive the effects which it is destined to produce. Phrenology was wanting to give it full efficacy, especially in *moral science,* in which little progress has been made for centuries. Now that this desideratum is supplied, may we not hope that the march of improvement will proceed in a rapidly accelerating ratio?

SECT. VII.—APPLICATION OF THE NATURAL LAWS TO THE PRACTICAL ARRANGEMENTS OF LIFE.

If a system of living and occupation were to be framed for human beings, founded on the exposition of their nature, which I have now given, it would be something like this.

1st. So many hours a day would require to be dedicated by every individual in health, to the exercise of his nervous and muscular systems, in labour calculated to give scope to these functions. The reward of obeying this requisite of his nature would be health, and a joyous animal existence ; the punishment of neglect is disease, low spirits, and death.

2dly. So many hours a day should be spent in the sedulous employment of the knowing and reflecting faculties ; in studying the qualities of external objects, and their relations ; also the nature of all animated beings, and their relations ; not with the view of accumulating mere abstract and barren knowledge, but of enjoying the positive pleasure of mental activity, and of turning every discovery to account, as a means of increasing happiness, or alleviating misery. The leading object should always be to find out the relationship of every object to our own nature, organic, animal, moral, and intellectual, and to keep that relationship habitually in mind, so as to render our acquirements directly gratifying to our various faculties. The reward of this conduct would be an incalculably great increase of pleasure, in the very act of acquiring knowledge of the real properties of external objects, together with a great accession of power in reaping ulterior advantages, and in avoiding disagreeable affections.

3dly. So many hours a day ought to be devoted to the cultivation and gratification of our moral sentiments ; that is to say, in exercising these in harmony with intellect, and especially in acquiring the habit of admiring, loving, and yielding obedience to the Creator and his institutions. This last object is of vast importance. Intellect is barren of practical fruit, however rich it may be in knowledge, until it is fired and prompted to act by moral sentiment. In my view, knowledge by itself is comparatively worthless and impotent compared with what it becomes when vivified by elevated emotions. It is not enough that Intellect is informed ; the moral faculties must simultaneously co-operate ;

* Vide Cordier, in Edin. New Phil. Journ. No. VIII, p. 273.

yielding obedience to the precepts which the intellect recognises to be true. One way of cultivating the sentiments would be for men to meet and act together, on the fixed principles which I am now endeavouring to unfold, and to exercise on each other in mutual instruction, and in united adoration of the great and glorious Creator, the several faculties of Benevolence, Veneration, Hope, Ideality, Wonder, and Justice. The reward of acting in this manner would be a communication of direct and intense pleasure to each other: for I refer to every individual who has ever had the good fortune to pass a day or an hour with a really benevolent, pious, honest, and intellectual man, whose soul swelled with adoration of his Creator, whose intellect was replenished with knowledge of his works, and whose whole mind was instinct with sympathy for human happiness, whether such a day did not afford him the most pure, elevated, and lasting gratification he ever enjoyed. Such an exercise, besides, would invigorate the whole moral and intellectual powers, and fit them to discover and obey the divine institutions.

Phrenology is highly conducive to this enjoyment of our moral and intellectual nature. No faculty is bad, but, on the contrary each, when properly gratified, is a fountain of pleasure; in short, man possesses no feeling, of the legitimate exercise of which an elightened and ingenuous mind need be ashamed. A party of thorough practical phrenologists, therefore, meets in the perfect knowledge of each other's qualities; they respect these as the gifts of the Creator, and their great object is to derive the utmost pleasure from their legitimate use, and to avoid every approximation to abuse of them. The distinctions of country and temperament are broken down by unity of principle; the chilling restraints of Cautiousness, Self-esteem, Secretiveness, and Love of Approbation, which stand as barriers of eternal ice between human beings in the ordinary intercourse of society, are gently removed; the directing sway is committed to Benevolence, Veneration, Conscientiousness, and Intellect; and then the higher principles of the mind operate with a delightful vivacity unknown to persons unacquainted with the qualities of human nature.

Intellect also ought to be regularly exercised in arts, science, philosophy, and observation.

I have said nothing of dedicating hours to the direct gratification of the animal powers; not that they should not be exercised, but that full scope for their activity will be included in the employments already mentioned. In muscular exercises, Combativeness, Destructiveness, Constructiveness, Acquisitiveness, Self-esteem, and Love of Approbation, may all be gratified. In contending with and surmounting physical and moral difficulties, Combativeness and Destructiveness obtain vent; in working at a mechanical employment, requiring the exertion of strength, these two faculties, and also Constructiveness and Acquisitiveness, will be exercised; in emulation who shall accomplish most good, Self-esteem and Love of Approbation will obtain scope. In the exercise of the moral faculties, several of these, and others of the animal propensities, are employed; Amativeness, Philoprogenitiveness, and Adhesiveness, for example, acting under the guidance of Benevolence, Veneration, Conscientiousness, Ideality and Intellect receive direct enjoyment in the domestic circle. From proper direction also, and from the superior delicacy and refinement imparted to them by the higher powers, they do not infringe the moral law, and leave no sting or repentance in the mind.

Finally a certain portion of time would require to be dedicated to taking of food and sleep.

All systems hitherto practised have been deficient in providing for one or more of these branches of enjoyment. In the community at Orbiston, formed on Mr. Owen's principles, music, dancing, and theatrical entertainments were provided; but the people soon tired of these. They had not corresponding moral and intellectual instruction. The novelty excited them, but there was nothing substantial behind. In common society, very little either of rational instruction or amusement is provided. The neglect of innocent amusement is a great error.

If there be truth in these views, they will afford answers to two important questions, that have puzzled philosophers in regard to the progress of human improvement. The first is, Why should man have existed so long, and made so small an advance in the road to happiness?* If I am right in the fundamental proposition, that activity in the faculties is synonymous with enjoyment of existence,—it follows that it would have been less wise and benevolent towards man, constituted as he is, to have communicated to him intuitively perfect knowledge, thereby leaving his mental powers with diminished motives to activity, than to bestow on him faculties endowed with high susceptibility of action, and to surround him with scenes, objects, circumstances, and relations, calculated to maintain them in ceaseless excitement; although this latter arrangement necessarily subjects him to suffering while ignorant, and renders his first ascent in the scale of improvement difficult and slow. It is interesting to observe, that, according to this view, although the first pair of the human race had been created with powerful and well balanced faculties, but of the same nature as at present; if they were not also intuitively inspired with knowledge of the whole creation, and its relations, their first movements as *individuals* would have been *retrograde:* that is, as *individuals*, they would, through pure want of information, have infringed many natural laws, and suffered evil; while, as *parts of the race*, they would have been decidedly *advancing:* for every pang they suffered would have led them to a new step in knowledge, and prompted them to advance towards a much higher condition than that which they at first occupied. According to the hypothesis now presented, not only is man really benfited by the arrangement which leaves him to discover the natural laws for himself, although, during the period of his ignorance, he suffers much evil from unacquaintance with them; but *his progress* towards knowledge and happiness must from the very extent of his experience, *be actually greater* than can at present be conceived. Its extent will become more obvious, and his experience itself more valuable, after he has obtained a view of the real theory of his constitution. He will find that past miseries have at least exhausted countless errors, and he will know how to avoid thousands of paths that lead to pain; in short, he will then discover that errors in conduct resemble errors in philosophy, in this, that they give additional importance and practicability to truth, by the demonstration which they afford of the evils attending departures from its dictates. The grand sources of human suffering at present arise from bodily disease and mental distress, and, in the next chapter these will be traced to infringement, through ignorance or otherwise, of physical, organic, moral, or intellectual laws, which, when expounded, appear in themselves calculated to promote the happiness of the race. It may be supposed that, according to this view, as knowledge accumulates, enjoyment will decrease; but ample provision is made against this event, by withholding intuition from each generation as it appears on the stage; each successive age must acquire knowledge for itself; and, provided ideas are new, and suited to the faculties, the pleasure of acquiring them from instructors, is only second to that of discovering them for ourselves; and, probably countless ages may elapse before *all* the facts and relations of nature shall have been explored, and the possibility of discovery exhausted. If the universe be infinite, knowledge can never be complete.

* In offering a solution of this problem, I do not inquire why man has received his present constitution.

The second question is, Has man really advanced in happiness, in proportion to his increase in knowledge? We are apt to entertain erroneous notions of the pleasures enjoyed by past ages. Fabulists have represented them as peaceful, innocent and gay; but if we look narrowly at the condition of the savage and barbarian of the present day, and recollect that these are the states of all individuals previous to the acquisition of knowledge, we shall not much or long regret the pretended diminution of enjoyment by civilization. Phrenology renders the superiority of the latter condition certain, by showing it to be a law of nature, that, until the intellect is extensively informed, and the moral sentiments assiduously exercised, the animal propensities bear the predominant sway; and that wherever they are supreme, misery is an inevitable concomitant. Indeed, the answer to the objection that happiness has not increased with knowledge, appears to me to be found in the fact, that until phrenology was discovered, the nature of man was not scientifically known; and in consequence, that not one of his institutions, civil or domestic, was correctly founded on the principle of the supremacy of the moral sentiments, or in accordance with the other laws of his constitution. Owing to the same cause, also, much of his knowledge has necessarily remained partial, and inapplicable to use; but after this science shall have been appreciated and applied, clouds of darkness, accumulated through long ages that are past, may be expected to roll away, as if touched by the rays of the meridian sun, and with them many of the miseries that attend total ignorance or imperfect information.*

CHAPTER III.

TO WHAT EXTENT ARE THE MISERIES OF MANKIND REFERABLE TO INFRINGEMENTS OF THE LAWS OF NATURE?

In the present chapter, I propose to inquire into some of the evils that have afflicted the human race; also whether they have proceeded from abuses of institutions benevolent and wise in themselves, and calculated, when observed, to promote the happiness of man, or from a defective or vicious constitution of nature, which he can neither remedy nor improve.

SECT. I.—CALAMITIES ARISING FROM INFRINGEMENTS OF THE PHYSICAL LAWS.

The proper way of viewing the Creator's institutions, is to look, first, to their uses, and to the advantages that flow from observance of them; and, secondly, to their abuses, and the evils consequent thereon.

In Chapter II, some of the benefits conferred on man, by the law of gravitation, are enumerated; and I may here advert to the evils originating from that law, when human conduct is in opposition to it. For example, men are liable to fall from horses, carriages, stairs, precipices, roofs, chimneys, ladders, masts, or slip in the street, &c. by which accidents life is frequently altogether extinguished, or rendered miserable from lameness and pain; and the question arises, Is human nature provided with any means of protection against these evils, at all equal to their frequency and extent?

The lower animals are equally subject to this law; and the Creator has bestowed on them external senses, nerves, muscles, bones, an instinctive sense of equilibrium, the sense of danger, or cautiousness, and other faculties, to place them in accordance with it. These appear to afford sufficient protection to animals placed in all ordinary circumstances; for we very rarely discover any of them, in their natural condition, killed or mutilated by accidents referable to gravitation. Where their mode of life exposes them to extraordinary danger from this law, they are provided with additional securities. The monkey, which climbs trees, enjoys great muscular energy in its legs, claws, and tail, far surpassing, in proportion to its gravitating tendency, or its bulk and weight, what is bestowed on the legs and arms of man; so that, by means of them, it springs from branch to branch, in nearly complete security against the law in question. The goat, which browses on the brinks of precipices, has received a hoof and legs, that give precision and stability to its steps. Birds, which are destined to sleep on branches of trees, are provided with a muscle passing over the joints of each leg, and stretching down to the foot, which, being pressed by their weight, produces a proportionate contraction of their claws, so as to make them cling the faster, the greater their liability to fall. The fly, which walks and sleeps on perpendicular walls, and the ceilings of rooms, has a hollow in its foot, from which it expels the air, and the pressure of the atmosphere on the outside of the foot holds it fast to the object on which the inside is placed. The sea-horse, which is destined to climb up the sides of ice-hills, is provided with a similar apparatus. The camel, whose native region is the sandy deserts of the torrid zone, has broad-spreading hoofs to support it on the loose soil. Fishes are furnished with air bladders, by dilating and contracting of which they can accommodate themselves with perfect precision to the law of gravitation.

In these instances, the lower animals, under the sole guidance of their instincts, appear to be placed admirably in harmony with gravitation, and guaranteed against its infringement. Is man, then, less an object of love with the Creator? Is he alone left exposed to the evils that spring inevitably from its neglect? His means of protection are different, but when understood and applied, they will probably be found not less complete. Man, as well as the lower animals, has received bones, muscles, nerves, an instinct of equilibrium,* and organs of Cautiousness; but not in equal perfection, in proportion to his figure, size, and weight, with those bestowed on them:—The difference, however, is far more than compensated by other organs, particularly those of Constructiveness and Reflection, in which he greatly surpasses them. Keeping in view that the external world, in regard to man, is arranged on the principle of supremacy in moral sentiments and intellect, we shall probably find, that the calamities suffered by him from the law of gravitation, are referable to predominance of the animal propensities, or to neglect of proper exercise of his intellectual powers. For example, when coaches break down, ships sink, men fall from ladders, &c, how generally may the cause be traced to decay in the vehicle, the vessel, or ladder, which a predominating Acquisitiveness alone prevented from being repaired; or when men fall from houses, scaffolds, or slip on the streets, &c, how frequently should we find their muscular, nervous, and mental energies, impaired by preceding debaucheries; in other words, by predominance of the animal faculties, which, for the time, diminished their natural means of accommodating themselves to the law from which they suffer. Or, again, the slater, in using a ladder, assists himself by Constructiveness and Reflection; but, in walking along the ridge of a house, or standing on a chimney, he takes no aid from these faculties; he trusts to the mere instinctive power of equilibrium, in which he is inferior to the lower animals, and, in so doing, clearly violates the law of his nature, that requires him to use reflection, where instinct is deficient. Causality and Constructiveness could invent means by which, if he slipped from a roof or chimney, his fall might be arrested. A small chain, for instance, attached by one

* Readers who are strangers to phrenology, and the evidence on which it rests, may regard the observations in the text as extravagant and enthusiastic; but I respectfully remind them, that, while they judge in comparative ignorance it has been my endeavour to subject it to the severest scrutiny. Having found its proofs irrefragable; and being convinced of its importance, I solicit their indulgence in speaking of it as it appears to my own mind.

* Vide Essay on Weight, Phren. Journ. vol. ii. p. 412.

end to a girdle round his body, and the other end fastened by a hook and eye to the roof, might leave him at liberty to move about, and break his fall, in case he slipped. How frequently, too, do these accidents happen, after disturbance of the faculties and corporeal functions by intoxication?

The objection will probably occur, that in the gross condition in which the mental powers exist, the great body of mankind are incapable of exerting habitually that degree of moral and intellectual energy, which is indispensable to observance of the natural laws; and that, therefore, they are, in point of fact, less fortunate than the lower animals. I admit, that, at present, this representation is to a considerable extent just: but nowhere do I perceive the human powers exercised and instructed, in a degree at all approaching to their limits. Let any person recollect of how much greater capacity for enjoyment and security from danger he has been conscious, at a particular time, when his whole mind was filled with, and excited by, some mighty interest, not only allied to, but founded in, morality and intellect, than in that languid condition which accompanies the absence of elevated and ennobling motives, and he may form some idea of what man is capable of reaching when his powers shall have been cultivated to the extent of their capacity. At the present moment, no class of society is systematically instructed in the constitution of their own minds and bodies, in the relations of these to external objects, in the nature of these objects, in the natural supremacy of the moral sentiments, in the principle that activity in the faculties is the only source of pleasure, and that the higher the powers, the more intense the delight; and, if such views be to the mind, what light is to the eyes, air to the lungs, and food to the stomach, there is no wonder that a mass of inert *mentality*, if I may use such a word, should everywhere exist around us, and that countless evils should spring from its continuance in this condition. If active moral and intellectual faculties are the natural fountains of enjoyment, and the external world is created with reference to this state; it is as obvious that misery must result from animal supremacy and intellectual torpidity, as that flame, which is constituted to burn only when supplied with oxygen, must inevitably become extinct, when exposed to carbonic acid gas. Finally, if the arrangement by which man is left to discover and obey the laws of his own nature, and of the physical world, be more conducive to activity, than intuitive knowledge, the calamities now contemplated appear to be instituted to force him to his duty; and his duty, when understood, will constitute his delight.

While, therefore, we lament the fate of individual victims to the law of gravitation, we cannot condemn that law itself. If it were suspended, to save men from the effects of negligence, not only would the proud creations of human skill totter to their base, and the human body rise from the earth, and hang midway in the air, but our highest enjoyments would be terminated, and our faculties become positively useless, by being deprived of their field of exertion. Causality, for instance, teaches that similar causes will always, *cœteris paribus*, produce similar effects; and, if the physical laws were suspended or varied, to accommodate man's negligence or folly, it is obvious that this faculty would be without an object, and that no definite course of action could be entered upon with confidence in the result. If, then, this view of the constitution of nature were kept steadily in view, the occurrence of one accident of this kind would suggest to Reflection means to prevent others.

Similar illustrations and commentaries might be given, in regard to the other physical laws to which man is subject; but the object of the present Essay being merely to evolve principles, I confine myself to gravitation, as the most obvious and best understood.

I do not mean to say, that, by the mere exercise of intellect, man may absolutely guarantee himself against all accidents; but only that the more ignorant and careless he is, the more he will suffer, and the more intelligent and vigilant, the less; and that I can perceive no limits to this rule. The law of most civilized countries recognizes this principle, and subjects owners of ships, coaches, and other vehicles, in damages arising from gross infringements of the physical laws. It is unquestionable that the enforcement of this liability has increased security in travelling in no trifling degree.

SECT. II.—ON THE EVILS THAT BEFALL MANKIND, FROM INFRINGEMENT OF THE ORGANIC LAWS.

An organised being, I have said, is one which derives its existence from a previously existing organised being, which subsists on food, grows, attains maturity, decays and dies. Whatever the ultimate object of the Creator in constituting organised beings, may be, it will scarcely be denied, that part of his design is, that they should enjoy their existence here; and, if so, every particular part of their systems will be found conducive in its intention to this end. The first law, then, that must be obeyed, to render an organised being perfect in its kind, is, that the germ from which it springs shall be complete in all its parts, and sound in its whole constitution; the second is, that the moment it is ushered into life, and as long as it continues to live, it shall be supplied with food, light air, and every physical aliment necessary for its support: and the third law is, that it shall duly exercise its functions. When all these laws are obeyed, the being should enjoy pleasure from its organised frame, if its Creator is benevolent; and its constitution should be so adapted to its circumstances, as to admit of obedience to them, if its Creator is wise and powerful. Is there, then, no such phenomenon on earth, as a human being existing in full possession of organic vigour, from birth till advanced age when the organised system is fairly worn out? Numberless examples of this kind have occurred, and they show no demonstration, that the corporeal frame of man is so constituted, as to admit the *possibility* of his enjoying organic health and vigour, during the whole period of a long life. In the life of Captain COOK it is mentioned, that 'one circumstance peculiarly worthy of notice is, the perfect and uninterrupted health of the inhabitants of New Zealand. In all the visits made to their towns, where old and young, men and women, crowded about our voyagers, they never observed a single person who appeared to have any bodily complaint; nor among the numbers that were seen naked, was once perceived the slightest eruption upon the skin, or least mark which indicated that such an eruption had formerly existed. Another proof of the health of these people is the facility with which the wounds they at any time receive are healed. In the man who had been shot with the musket ball through the fleshy part of his arm, the wound seemed to be so well digested, and in so fair a way of being perfectly healed, that if Mr COOK had not known that no application had been made to it, he declared that he should certainly have inquired, with a very interested curiosity, after the vulnerary herbs and surgical art of the country. An additional evidence of human nature's being untainted with disease in New Zealand, is the great number of old men with whom it abounds. Many of them, by the loss of their hair and teeth, appeared to be very ancient, and yet none of them were decrepit. Although they were not equal to the young in muscular strength, they did not come in the least behind them with regard to cheerfulness and vivacity. Water, as far as our navigators could discover, is the universal and only liquor of the New Zealanders. It is greatly to be wished that their happiness in this respect may never be destroyed by such a connexion with the European nations, as shall introduce that fondness for spirituous liquors which hath been so fatal to the Indians of North America.'—*Kippis' Life of Captain Cook.* Dublin, 1788, p. 100.

Now, as a natural law never admits of an exception; for example, as no man ever sees without eyes, or digests without a stomach, we are entitled to say, that the best condition in which an organized being has ever been found, is fairly within the capabilities of the race. A human being, vigorous and healthy from the cradle to the grave, could no more exist, unless the natural constitution of his organs permitted it, of design, than vision could exist without eyes. Health and vigour cannot result from infringement of the organic laws; for then pain and disease would be the objects of these laws, and beneficence, wisdom, and power, could never be ascribed to the Creator, who had established them. Let us hold, then, that the organised system of man, in itself—admits of the possibility of health, vigour, and organic enjoyment, during the full period of life; and proceed to inquire into the causes why these advantages are not universal.

One organic law, is, that the germ of the infant being must be complete in all its parts, and perfectly sound in its condition, as an indispensable requisite to its vigorous development, and full enjoyment of existence. If the corn that is sown is weak, wasted, and damaged, the plants that spring from it will be feeble, and liable to speedy decay. The same law holds in the animal kingdom; and I would ask, has it hitherto been observed by man? It is notorious that it has not. Indeed, its existence has been either altogether unknown, or in a very high degree disregarded by human beings. The feeble, the sickly, the exhausted with age, and the incompletely developed, through extreme youth, marry, and, without the least compunction regarding the organization which they shall transmit to their offspring, send into the world miserable beings, the very rudiments of whose existence are tainted with disease. If we trace such conduct to its source, we shall find it to originate either in animal propensity, intellectual ignorance, or more frequently in both. The inspiring motives are generally merely sensual appetite, avarice, or ambition, operating in the absence of all just conceptions of the impending evils. The punishment of this offence is debility and pain, transmitted to the children, and reflected back in anxiety and sorrow on the parents. Still the great point to be kept in view, is, that these miseries are not legitimate consequences of *observance* of the organic laws, but the direct chastisement of their *infringement.* These laws are unbending, and admit of no exception; they must be fulfilled, or the penalties of disobedience will follow. On this subject profound ignorance reigns in society. From such observations as I have been able to make, I am convinced that the union of certain temperaments and combinations of mental organs in the parents, are highly conducive to health, talent, and morality in the offspring, and *vice versa*, and that these conditions may be discovered and taught with far greater certainty, facility, and advantage, than is generally imagined. It will be time enough to conclude that men are naturally incapable of obedience to the organic laws, after their intellects have been instructed, their moral sentiments trained to the observance of the Creator's natural institutions, as at once their duty, their interest, and a grand source of their happiness; and they have continued to rebel.

A second organic law regards nutriment, which must be supplied of a suitable kind, and in due quantity. This law requires also free air, light, cleanliness, and attention to every physical arrangement by which the functions of the body may be favored or impaired. Have mankind, then, obeyed or neglected this institution? I need scarcely answer the question. To be able to obey institutions, we must first know them. Before we can know the organic constitution of our body, we must study that constitution, and the study of the human constitution is anatomy and physiology. Before we can be acquainted with its relations to external objects, we must learn the existence and qualities of these objects, (unfolded by chemistry, natural history, and natural philosophy), and compare them with the constitution of the body. When we have fulfilled these conditions, we shall be better able to discover the laws which the Creator has instituted in regard to our organic system. It will be said, however, that such studies are impracticable to the great bulk of mankind, and, besides, do not appear much to benefit those who pursue them. They are impracticable only while mankind prefer founding their public and private institutions on the basis of the propensities, instead of that of the sentiments. I have mentioned, that exercise of the nervous and muscular systems is required of *all* the race by the Creator's fiat, that if all, who are capable, would obey this law, a moderate extent of exertion, agreeable and salubrious in itself, would suffice to supply our wants, and to surround us with every beneficial luxury; and that a large portion of unemployed time would remain. The Creator has bestowed on us Knowing Faculties, fitted to explore the facts of these sciences, Reflecting Faculties to trace their relations, and Moral Sentiments calculated to feel interest in such investigations, and to lead us to reverence and obey the laws which they unfold; and, finally he has made this occupation, when entered upon with a view of tracing His power and wisdom in the subjects of our studies, and of obeying His institutions, the most delightful and invigorating of all vocations. In place, then, of such a course of education being impracticable, every arrangement of the Creator appears to be prepared in direct anticipation of its actual accomplishment.

The second objection, that those who study these sciences are not more healthy and happy, as organized beings, than those who neglect them, admits also of an easy answer. Parts of these sciences are taught to a few individuals, whose, main design in studying them is to apply them as means of acquiring wealth and fame; but they have nowhere been taught as connected parts of a great system of natural arrangements, fraught with the highest influences on human enjoyment; and in no instance have the intellect and sentiments been systematically directed to the natural laws, as the grand fountains of happiness and misery to the race, and trained to observe and obey them as the Creator's institutions.

A third organic law, is, that all our functions shall be duly exercised; and is this law observed by mankind? Many persons are able, from experience, to attest the severity of the punishment that follows from neglecting to exercise the nervous and muscular systems, in the lassitude, indigestion, irritability, debility, and general uneasiness that attend a sedentary and inactive life. But the penalties that attach to neglect of exercising the *brain* are much less known, and therefore I shall notice them more at length. How often have we heard the question asked, What is the use of education? The answer might be illustrated by explaining to the inquirer the nature and objects of the various organs of the body, such as the limbs, lungs, eyes, and then asking him if he could perceive any advantage to a being so constituted, in obtaining access to earth, air, and light. He would, at once, declare, that they were obviously of the very highest utility to him, for they were the only conceivable objects, by means of which these organs could obtain scope for action, which action we suppose him to know to be pleasure. To those, then, who know the constitution of the intellectual and moral powers of man, I need only say, that the objects introduced to the mind by education, bear the same relation to them that the physical elements of nature bear to the nerves and muscles; they afford them scope for action, and yield them delight. The meaning which is commonly attached to the word *use* in such cases, is how much *money*, *influence*, or *consideration*, will education bring; these being the only objects of strong desire with which uncultivated minds are acquainted; and they do not perceive in what way education can greatly gratify such propensities. But the moment the mind is opened to the perception of its constitution and to the natural laws, the great advantage of moral and intellectual cultivation, as a means of exercising the faculties, and of directing the conduct in obedience to these laws, becomes apparent.

But there is an additional benefit arising from healthy activity of brain, which is little known. The brain is the fountain of nervous energy to the whole body, and different modifications of that energy appear to take place, according to the mode in which the faculties and organs are affected. For example, when misfortune and disgrace impend over us, the organs of Cautiousness, Self-esteem, Love of Approbation, &c. are painfully excited; and then they transmit an impaired or a positively noxious nervous influence to the heart, stomach, intestines, and thence to the rest of the body; the pulse becomes feeble and irregular, digestion is deranged, and the whole corporeal frame wastes. When, on the other hand, the cerebral organs are agreeably affected, a benign and vivifying nervous influence pervades the frame, and all the functions of the body are performed with more pleasure and completeness. Now, it is a law, that the quantum of nervous energy increases with the number of cerebral organs roused to activity. In the retreat of the French from Moscow, for example, when no enemy was near, the soldiers became depressed in courage, and enfeebled in body, they nearly sunk to the earth through exhaustion and cold; but no sooner did the fire of the Russian guns sound in their ears, or the gleam of their bayonets flash in their eyes, than new life seemed to pervade them. They wielded powerfully the arms, which a few moments before, they could scarcely carry or trail on the ground. No sooner, however, was the enemy repulsed, than their feebleness returned. The theory of this is, that the approach of the combat called into activity a variety of additional faculties; these sent new energy through every nerve, and while their vivacity was maintained by the external stimulus, they rendered the soldiers strong beyond their merely physical condition. Many persons have probably experienced the operation of the same principle. When sitting feeble and listless by the fire, we have heard of an accident having occurred to some beloved friend, who required our instantaneous aid, or an unexpected visiter has arrived, in whom our affections were bound up, in an instant our lassitude was gone, and we moved with an alertness and animation that seemed surprising to ourselves. The cause was the same; these events roused Adhesiveness, Benevolence, Love of Approbation, Intellect, and a variety of faculties, which were previously dormant, and their influence invigorated the limbs. Dr Sparmann, in his Voyage to the Cape, mentions, that 'there was now again a great scarcity of meat in the wagon; for which reason my Hottentots began to grumble, and reminded me that we ought not to waste so much of our time in looking after insects and plants, but give a better look out after the game. At the same time, they pointed to a neighbouring dale overrun with wood, at the upper edge of which, at the distance of about a mile and a quarter from the spot where we then were, they had seen several buffaloes. Accordingly, we went thither; but though our fatigue was lessened by our Hottentots carrying our guns for us up a hill, yet we were quite out of breath, and overcome by the sun, before we got up to it. Yet, what even now appears to me a matter of wonder is, *that as soon as we got a glimpse of the game, all this languor left us in an instant.* In fact, we each of us strove to fire before the other, so that we seemed entirely to have lost sight of all prudence and caution.' 'In the mean time, our temerity, which chiefly proceeded from hurry and ignorance, was considered by the Hottentots as a proof of spirit and intrepidity hardly to be equalled.

It is part of the same law that the more agreeable the mental stimulus, the more benign is the nervous influence transmitted to the body.

If we imagine a man or woman, who has received from nature a large and tolerably active brain, but who has not enjoyed the advantages of a scientific or extensive education, so as to feel an interest in moral and intellectual pursuits for their own sake, and who, from possessing wealth sufficient to remove the necessity for labor, is engaged in no profession, we shall find a perfect victim to infringement of the natural laws. The individual ignorant of these laws, will, in all probability, neglect nervous and muscular exercises, and suffer the miseries arising from impeded circulation and impaired digestion; in entire want of every object on which the energy of his brain might be expended, its stimulating influence on the body will be withheld, and the effects of muscular inactivity tenfold aggravated; all the functions will, in consequence, become enfeebled; lassitude, uneasiness, anxiety, and a thousand evils, will arise, and life, in short, will become a mere endurance of punishment for infringement of institutions, calculated, in themselves to promote happiness and afford delight, when known and obeyed. This fate frequently overtakes uneducated females, whose early days have been occupied with business, or the cares of a family, but which occupations have ceased before old age had diminished corporeal vigour; it overtakes men also, who, uneducated, retire from active business in the prime of life. In some instances, these evils accumulate to such a degree that the brain itself gives way, its functions become deranged, and insanity is the result.

It is worthy of remark, that the more elevated the objects of our study, the higher in the scale are the mental organs which are exercised, and the higher the organs the more pure and intense is the pleasure; and hence, a vivacious and regularly supported excitement of the moral sentiments and intellect, is, by the organic law, highly favourable to health and corporeal vigour. In the fact of a living animal being able to retain life in an oven that will bake dead flesh, we see an illustration of the organic law rising above the purely physical: and, in the circumstance of the moral and intellectual organs transmitting the most favorable nervous influence to the whole bodily system, we have an example of the moral and intellectual law rising higher than the mere organic.

No person after having his intellect and sentiments imbued with a perception of, and belief in, the natural laws, as now explained, can possibly desire idleness, as a source of pleasure; nor can he possibly regard muscular exertion and mental activity, when not carried to excess, as any thing else than enjoyments kindly vouchsafed to him by the benevolence of the Creator. The notion that moderate labour and mental exertion are evils, can originate only from ignorance, or from viewing the effects of over-exhaustion as the result of the natural law, and not as the punishment for infringement of it.

If, then, we sedulously inquire, in each particular instance, into the *cause* of the sickness, pain, premature death, and general derangement of the corporeal frame of man, which we see around us, and endeavour to discover whether it has originated in obedience to the physical and organic laws, or sprung from an infringement of them, we shall be able to form some estimate how far bodily suffering is justly attributable to imperfections of nature, and how far to our own ignorance and neglect of divine institutions.

The foregoing principles being of much practical importance, may, with propriety, be elucidated by a few cases of actual occurrence. Two or three centuries ago, various cities in Europe were depopulated by the plague, and, in particular, London was visited by an awful mortality from this cause, in the reign of Charles the Second. The people of that age attributed this scourge to the inscrutable decrees of Providence, and some to the magnitude of the nation's moral iniquities. According to the views now presented, it must have arisen from infringement of the *organic laws*, and been intended to enforce stricter obedience to them in future. According to this view, there was nothing inscrutable in its causes or objects, which, when clearly analysed, appear to have had no direct reference to the moral condition of the people: I say *direct* reference to the moral condition of the people, because it would be easy to show, that the physical, organic, and all the other natural laws, are connected indirectly, and constituted in harmony, with the moral law: and that infringement of the one often leads to disobedience to another, and brings a double punishment on the offender. But, in the mean time, I observe that the facts recorded in history exactly correspond with the theory now propounded. The streets of London were excessively narrow, the habits of the people dirty, and no adequate provision was made for removing the filth unavoidably produced by a dense population. The great fire in that city, which happened soon after the pestilence, afforded an opportunity of remedying in some degree, the narrowness of the streets; and habits of increasing cleanliness abated the filth; these changes brought the people into a closer obedience to the organic laws, and no plague has since returned. Again, till very lately, thousands of children died yearly of the small-pox, but, in our day, vaccine inoculation saves ninety-nine out of a hundred, who, under the old system, would have died. The theory of its operation is not known, but we may rest assured, that it places the system more in accordance with the organic laws, than in the cases where death ensued. A gentleman, who died about ten years ago at an advanced period of life, told me, that, six miles west from Edinburgh, the country was so unhealthy in his youth, that every spring the farmers and their servants were seized with fever and ague, and required regularly to undergo bleeding, and a course of medicine, to prevent attacks, or restore them from their effects. At the time, these visitations were believed to be sent by Providence, and to be inherent in the constitution of things; after, however, said my informant, an improved system of agriculture and draining was established, and vast pools of stagnant water formerly left between the ridges of the field were removed, dunghills carried to a distance from the houses, and the houses themselves made more spacious and commodious, every symptom of ague and marsh-fever disappeared from the district, and it became highly salubrious. In other words, as soon as the gross infringement of the organic laws was abated by a more active exertion of the muscular and intellectual powers of man, the punishment ceased. In like manner, how many calamities occurred in coal-pits, in consequence of infringement of a physical law, viz. by introducing lighted candles and lamps into places filled with hydrogen gas, that had emanated from seams of coal, and which exploded, scorched, and suffocated the men and animals within its reach, until Sir Humphrey Davy discovered that the Creator had established such a relation betwixt flame, wire-gauze, and hydrogen gas, that by surrounding the flame with gauze, its power of exploding hydrogen was counteracted. By the simple application of a covering of wire-gauze, put over and around the flame, it is prevented from igniting gas beyond it, and colliers are now able to carry, with safety, lighted lamps into places highly impregnated with inflammable air. I have been informed, that the accidents from explosion, which still occasionally occur in coal mines, arise from neglecting to keep the lamps in perfect condition.

It is needless to multiply examples in support of the proposition, that the organized system of man, in itself, admits of a healthy existence from infancy to old age, provided its germ has been healthy, and its subsequent condition has been uniformly in harmony with the physical and organic laws; but it has been objected, that although the human faculties may perhaps be adequate to discover these laws, and to record them in books, yet they are totally incapable of retaining them in the memory, and of formally applying them in every act of life. If, it is said, we could not move a step without calculating and adjusting the body to the law of gravitation, and could never eat a meal without a formal rehearsal of the organic laws, life would become oppressed by the pedantry of knowledge, and rendered miserable by petty observances and trivial details. The answer to this is, that all our faculties are adapted by the Creator to the external world, and act *instinctively* when their objects are placed in the proper light before them. For example, in walking on a foot-path in the country during day, we are not conscious, in adjusting our steps to the inequalities of the surface, of being overburdened by mental calculation. In fact, we perform this adjustment with so little trouble, that we are not aware of having made *any particular* mental or muscular effort. But, on returning at night, when we cannot see, we stumble, and discover, for the first time, how important a duty our faculties had been performing during day, without our having adverted to their labours. Now, the simple medium of light is sufficient to bring clearly before our eyes the inequalities of ground; but to make the mind equally familiar with the nature of the countless objects, and their relations, which abound in external nature, an intellectual light is necessary, which can be struck out only by exercising and applying the knowing and reflecting faculties; but the moment that light is obtained, and the qualities and relationships in question are perceived by its means, the faculties, so long as the light lasts, *will act instinctively* in adapting our conduct to the nature of the objects, just as in accommodating our movements to the unequal surface of the ground. It is no more necessary for us to go through a course of physical, botanical, and chemical reasoning, before we are able to abstain from eating hemlock, after its properties are known, than it is to go through a course of mathematical demonstration, before lifting the one foot higher than the other, in ascending a stair. At present, physical and political science, morals and religion, are not taught as parts of one connected system; nor are the relations between them and the constitution of man pointed out to the world. In consequence, theoretical knowledge and practice are often widely separated. Some of the advantages of the scientific education now recommended would be the following:

In the 1st place, the physical and organic laws, when truly discovered, appear to the mind as institutions of the Creator, wise and salutary in themselves, unbending in their operation, and universal in their application. They interest our intellectual faculties, and strongly impress our sentiments. The necessity of obeying them, comes upon us with all the authority of a mandate of God. While we confine ourselves to a mere recommendation to beware of damp, to observe temperance, or to take exercise, without explaining the *principle*, the injunction carries only the weight due to *the authority of the individual* who gives it, and is addressed to only two or three faculties, Veneration and Cautiousness, for instance, or Self-love in him who receives it. But if we are made acquainted with the elements of the physical world, and with those of our organised system,—with the uses of the different parts of the latter, and the conditions necessary to their healthy action,—with the causes of their derangement, and the pains consequent thereon: and if the obligation to attend to these conditions be enforced on our moral sentiments and intellect; then the motives to observe the physical and organic laws, as well as *the power of doing so*, will be prodigiously increased. Before we can dance well, we must not only *know the motions*, but our muscles must be trained *to execute them*. In like manner, to enable us to act on precepts, we must not only comprehend their meaning but our intellects and sentiments must be disciplined into actual performance. Now, the very act of acquiring connected scientific information concerning the natural world, its qualities, and their relations, is to the intellect and sentiments what practical dancing is to the muscles, it *invigorates them;* and, as obedience to the natural laws must spring from them, exercise renders it more easy and delightful.

2. It is only by being taught the *principle* on which consequences depend, that we see the *invariableness* of the results of the physical and organic laws; acquire confidence in, and respect for the laws themselves; and fairly endeavour to accommodate our conduct to their operation. Dr Johnson defines 'principle' to be 'fundamental truth; original postulate; first position from which others are deduced;' and in these senses I use the word. The human faculties are instinctively active, and desire gratification; but Intellect itself must have fixed data, on which to reason, otherwise it is itself a mere impulse. The man in whom Constructiveness and Weight are powerful, will naturally betake himself to constructing machinery; but, if he be ignorant of the principles of mechanical science, he will not direct his efforts to as important ends, and attain them as successfully, as if his intellect were stored with these. Principles are deduced from the *laws* of nature. A man may make music by the instinctive impulses of Time and Tune; but there are immutable laws of harmony; and, if ignorant of these, he will not perform so invariably, correctly, and in good taste, as if he knew them. In every art and science, there are principles referable solely to the constitution of nature, but these admit of countless applications. A musician may produce gay, grave, solemn, or ludicrous tunes, all good of their kind, by following the laws of harmony; but he will never produce one good piece by violating them. While the inhabitants west of Edinburgh allowed the stagnant pools to deface their fields, some seasons would be more healthy than others; and, while the cause of the disease was unsuspected, this would confirm them in the notion that health and sickness were dispensed by an overruling Providence, on inscrutable principles, which they could not comprehend; but the moment the cause was known, it would be found that the most healthy seasons were those that were cold and dry, and the most sickly those that were warm and moist; and they would then perceive, that the superior salubrity of one year, and unwholesomeness of another, were clearly referable to *one principle*, and would be both more strongly prompted, and rendered morally and intellectually more capable of applying the remedy. If some intelligent friend had merely told them to drain their fields, and remove their dung-hills, they would not probably have done it; but whenever their intellects were enlightened, and their sentiments roused, to appreciate the advantages of adopting, and disadvantages of neglecting, the improvement, it became easy.

The truth of these views may be still farther illustrated by examples. A young gentleman of Glasgow, whom I knew, went out, as a merchant to North America. Business required him to sail from New York to St Domingo. The weather was hot, and he, being very sick, found the confinement below deck, in bed, as he said, intolerable; that is, this confinement was, for the moment, more painful than the course which he adopted, of laying himself down at full length on the deck, in the open air. He was warned by his fellow passengers, and the officers of the ship, that he would inevitably induce fever by this proceeding: but he was utterly ignorant of the physical and organic laws; his intellect had been trained to regard only wealth and present pleasure as objects of real importance; t could perceive no necessary connexion between exposure to the mild and grateful sea breeze of a warm climate and fever, and he obstinately refused to quit his position. The consequence was, that he was rapidly taken ill, and lived just one day after arriving at St Domingo. Knowledge of chemistry and physiology would have enabled him, in an instant, to understand that the sea air, in warm climates, holds a prodigious quantity of water in solution, and that damp and heat, operating together on the human organs, tend to derange their healthy action, and ultimately to destroy them entirely: and if his sentiments had been deeply imbued with a feeling of the indispensable duty of yielding obedience to the institutions of the Creator, he would have actually enjoyed, not only a *greater desire*, but a *greater power* of supporting the temporary inconvenience of the heated cabin, and might, by possibility, have escaped death.

Captain Murray, R. N. mentioned to Dr A. Combe, that, in his opinion, most of the bad effects of the climate of the West Indies might be avoided by care and attention to clothing; and so satisfied was he on this point, that he had petitioned to be sent there in preference to the North American station, and had no reason to regret the change. The measures which he adopted, and their effects, are detailed in the following interesting and instructive letter:

'*Assynt, April* 22, 1827

'MY DEAR SIR,

'I should have written to you before this, had I not been anxious to refer to some memorandums, which I could not do before my return home from Coul. I attribute the great good health enjoyed by the crew of his Majesty's ship Valorous, when on the West India station, during the period I had the honour of commanding her, to the following causes. 1st, To the keeping the ship perfectly *dry* and *clean;* 2dly, To habituating the men to the wearing of flannel *next* the *skin;* 3dly, To the precaution I adopted, of giving each man a proportion of his allowance of cocoa *before* he left the ship in the *morning*, either for the purpose of watering, or any other duty he might be sent upon; and, 4thly, To the cheerfulness of the crew.

'The Valorous sailed from Plymouth on the 24th December, 1823, having just returned from the coast of Labrador and Newfoundland, where she had been stationed two years, the crew, including officers, amounting to 150 men. I had ordered the purser to draw two pairs of flannel drawers, and two shirts extra for each man, as soon as I knew that our destination was the West Indies; and, on our sailing, I issued two of each to every man and boy in the ship, making the officers of each division responsible for the men of their respective divisions wearing these flannels during the day and night; and, at the regular morning nine o'clock musters, I inspected the crew personally; for you can hardly conceive the difficulty I have had in *forcing* some of the men to use flannel at first; although I never yet knew one who did not, from choice, adhere to it, when once fairly adopted. The only precaution after this, was to *see* that, in bad weather, the watch, when relieved, did not turn in in their wet clothes, which the young hands were apt to do, if not looked after; and their flannels were shifted every Sunday.

'Whenever fresh beef and vegetables could be procured at the contract price, they were always issued in preference to salt provision. Lime juice was issued whenever the men had been fourteen days on ship's provisions; and the crew took their meals on the main deck, except in very bad weather.

'The quarter and main decks were scrubbed with

sand and water, and wet holy stones, every morning at daylight. The lower deck, cock-pit, and store-rooms were scrubbed every day after breakfast, with dry holy stones and hot sand, until quite *white*, the sand being carefully swept up, and thrown overboard. The pump-well was also swabbed out dry, and then scrubbed with holy stones and hot sand; and here, as well as in every part of the ship which was liable to damp, Brodiestoves were constantly used, until every appearance of humidity vanished. The lower deck and cock-pit were washed once every week in dry weather; but Brodie-stoves were constantly kept burning in them, until they were quite dry again.

'The hammocks were piped up, and in the nettings, from 7 A. M. until dusk, when the men of each watch took down their hammocks alternately, by which means, only one-half of the hammocks being down at a time, the tween decks were not so crowded, and the watch relieved was sure of turning into a dry bed on going below. The bedding was aired every week, once at least. The men were not permitted to go on shore in the heat of the sun, or where there was a probability of their getting *spirituous liquors;* but all hands were indulged with a run on shore, when out of reach of such temptation.

'I was employed on the coast of Caraccas, the West India Islands, and Gulf of Mexico; and, in course of service, I visited Trinidad, Margarita, Cocha, Cumana, Nueva Barcelona, Laguira, Porto Cabello, and Maracaibo, on the coast of Caraccas; all the West India Islands, from Tobago to Cuba, both inclusive; as also, Caraçao and Aruba, and several of those places repeatedly; also to Vera Cruz and Tampico, in the Gulf of Mexico, which you will admit must have given a trial to the constitutions of my men, after two years amongst the icebergs of the Labrador, without an intervening summer between that icy coast and the coast of Caraccas; yet I arrived in England on June 24th, without having buried a single man or officer belonging to the ship, or indeed having a single man on the sick list; from which I am satisfied that a *dry* ship will always be a healthy one in any climate. When in command of the Recruit, of 18 guns, in the year 1809, I was sent to Vera Cruz, where I found the ——— 46, the ——— 42, the ——— 18, and ——— gun-brig; we were joined by the ——— 36, and the ——— 18. During the period we remained at anchor (from 8 to 10 weeks,) the three frigates, lost from 30 to 50 men each, the brigs 16 to 18, the ——— most of her crew, with two different commanders; yet the Recruit, although moored in the middle of the squadron, and constant intercourse held with the other ships, did not lose a man, and had none sick. Now, as some of these ships had been as long in the West Indies as the Recruit, we cannot attribute her singularly healthy state to *seasoning*, nor can I to superior cleanliness, because even the breeches of the carronades, and all the pins, were polished bright in both ——— and ———, which was not the case with the Recruit. Perhaps her healthy state may be attributed to cheerfulness in the men; to my never allowing them to go on shore in the morning, on an empty stomach; to the use of dry sand and holy-stone for the ship; to never working them in the sun; perhaps to accident. Were I asked my opinion, I would say that I firmly believe that cheerfulness contributes more to keep a ship's company healthy, than any precaution that can be adopted; and that, with this attainment, combined with the precautions I have mentioned, I should sail for the West Indies, with as little anxiety as I would for any other station. My Valorous fellows were as cheerful a set as I ever saw collected together.'

Suppose that two gentlemen were to ascend one of the Scottish mountains, in a hot summer day, and to arrive at the top, bathed in perspiration, and exhausted with fatigue. That one of them knew intimately the physical and organic laws, and that, all hot and wearied as he was, he should button up his coat closer about his body, wrap a handkerchief about his neck, and continue walking, at a quick pace, round the summit, in the full blaze of the sun. That the other, ignorant of these laws, should eagerly run to the base of a projecting cliff; stretch himself at full length on the turf, under its refreshing shade; open his vest to the grateful breeze; and, in short, give himself up entirely to the present luxuries of coolness and repose;—the former, by warding off the rapid chill of the cool mountain air, would descend with health unimpaired; while the latter would carry with him, to a certainty, the seeds of rheumatism, consumption, or fever, from permitting perspiration to be instantaneously checked, and the surface of the body to be cooled with an injurious rapidity. I have put these cases hypothetically, because, although I have seen and experienced the benefits of the former method, I have not directly observed the opposite. No season, however, passes in the Highlands, in which some tragedy of the latter description does not occur; and, from the minutest information that I have been able to obtain, the causes have been such as are here described.

I shall conclude these examples by a case which is illustrative of the points under consideration, and which I have had too good an opportunity of observing in all its stages.

An individual in whom it was my duty as well as pleasure, to be greatly interested, had resolved on carrying Mr Owen's views into practical effect, and got an establishment set agoing on his principles, at Orbiston, in Lanarkshire. The labour and anxiety which he underwent at the commencement of the undertaking, gradually impaired an excellent constitution; and, without perceiving the change, he, by way of setting an example of industry, took to digging with the spade, and actually worked for fourteen days at this occupation, although previously unaccustomed to labour. This produced hæmoptysis. Being unable now for bodily exertion, he gave up his whole time to directing and instructing the people, about 250 in number, and for two or three weeks *spoke the whole day*, the effusion from his lungs continuing. Nature rapidly sunk under this irrational treatment; and at last he came to Edinburgh for medical advice. When the structure and uses of his lungs were explained to him, and when it was pointed out that his treatment of them had been equally injudicious as if he had thrown lime or dust into his eyes, after inflammation, he was struck with the extent and consequences of his own ignorance, and exclaimed, How greatly he would have been benefitted if one month of the five years which he had been forced to spend in a vain attempt at acquiring a mastery over the Latin tongue, had been dedicated to conveying to him information concerning the structure of his body, and the causes which preserve and impair its functions. He had departed too widely from the organic laws to admit of an easy return; he was seized with inflammation of the lungs, and with great difficulty got through that attack; but it impaired his constitution so grievously, that he died, after a lingering illness of eleven months. He acknowledged, however, even in his severest pain, that he suffered under a just law. The lungs, he saw, were of the first-rate importance to life, and their proper treatment was provided for by this tremendous punishment, inflicted for neglecting the conditions requisite to their health. Had he given them rest, and returned to obedience to the organic law, at the first intimation of departure from it, the door stood wide open and ready to receive him; but, in utter ignorance, he persevered for weeks in direct opposition to these conditions, till the fearful result ensued.

This last case affords a striking illustration of the independence of the different institutions of the Creator, and of the necessity of obeying *all* of them, as the only condition of safety and enjoyment. The individual here alluded to, was deeply engaged in a most benevolent and disinterested experiment for promoting the welfare of his fellow creatures; and superficial observers would say that this was just an example of the inscrutable decrees of Providence, which visited him with sickness, and ultimately with death, in the very midst of his most virtuous exertions. But the institutions of the Creator are wiser than the imaginations of such men. The first principle on which existence on earth, and all its advantages depend, is obedience to the physical and organic laws. The benevolent Owenite neglected these, in his zeal to obey the moral law; and, if it were possible to dispense with the one, by obeying the other, the whole theatre of man's existence would speedily become deranged, and involved in inexplicable disorder.

Having traced bodily sufferings, in the case of individuals, to neglect of, or opposition to, the organic laws, by their progenitors or by themselves, I next advert to another set of calamities, that may be called social miseries, and which obviously spring from the same causes; but of which latter fact complete evidence was not possessed until Phrenology was discovered. And, first, in regard to evils of a domestic nature:—One fertile source of unhappiness arises from persons uniting in marriage whose tempers, talents, and dispositions do not harmonize. If it be true that natural talents and dispositions are connected by the Creator with particular configurations of brain, then it is obviously one of His institutions that, in forming a compact for life, these should be attended to.* If we imagine an individual endowed with the splendid cerebral development of RAPHAEL, under a mere animal impulse, uniting himself for life with a female, possessing a brain like that of MARY MACINNES,† which by no possibility, could sympathise with his, this proceeding would be as direct an obstacle to happiness, as if a man were to surround himself with ice to remove sensations of cold. Until Phrenology was discovered, no natural index to mental qualities, that could be practically relied on, was possessed, and each individual was left to his own sagacity in directing his conduct; but the natural law never bended one iota to accommodate itself to that state of ignorance. The Creator having bestowed on mankind faculties fitted to discover Phrenology, having constituted them so that their greatest enjoyment should consist in activity, framed his institutions in such a way as to confer happiness when they were discovered, and observed, and to carry punishment when unknown and infringed, as an arrangement at once benevolent and wise for the race. If it be the fact, that natural talents and dispositions are indicated by cerebral development; and if an individual, after this truth reaches his mind, shall form a connexion fitted to occasion him sorrow, it is obvious that he must do so from one of two causes, either from contempt of the effects of development of brain, and a secret belief that he may evade its consequences, which is just contempt of an organic law, and disbelief in its consequences; or, secondly, from the predominance of avarice, or some animal or other feeling precluding his yielding obedience to what he sees to be an institution of the Creator. In either case, he must abide the consequences; and although these may be grievous, they cannot be complained of as unjust. In the play of the Gamester, Mrs Beverly is represented as a most excellent wife, acting habitually under the guidance of the moral sentiments and intellect; but she is married to a being who, while he adores her, reduces her to beggary and misery. His sister utters an exclamation to this effect:—Why did just Heaven unite such an angel to so heartless a thing! The parallel of this case occurs too often in real life; only it is not 'just Heaven' that makes such matches, but ignorant and thoughtless human beings, who imagine themselves absolved from all obligation to study and obey the natural laws of Heaven, as announced in the general arrangement of the universe. Phrenology will put it in the power of mankind to mitigate these evils, when they choose to adopt its dictates as a practical rule of conduct.

The justice and benevolence of rendering the individuals themselves unhappy who neglect this great institution of the Creator, become more striking when in the next place, we consider the effects, by the organic law, of such conduct on the children of these ill-assorted unions.

Physiologists, in general, are agreed, that a vigorous and healthy constitution of body in the parents, communicates existence, in the most perfect state, to the offspring,* and many observers of mankind, as well as medical authors, have remarked, also the transmission, by hereditary descent, of mental talents and dispositions.

Dr KING, in speaking of the fatality which attended the House of Stewart, says, 'If I were to ascribe their calamities to another cause (than an evil fate,) or endeavour to account for them by any natural means, I should think they were chiefly owing to a certain *obstinacy of temper*, which appears to have *been hereditary and inherent* in all the Stuarts, except Charles II.'

It is well known that the caste of the Brahmins is the highest in point of intelligence as well as rank of all the castes in Hindostan; and it is mentioned by the missionaries as an ascertained fact, that *their* children are naturally more acute, intelligent, and docile, than the children of the inferior castes, age and other circumstances being equal.

Dr GREGORY, in treating of the temperaments in his *Conspectus Medicinæ Theoreticæ*, says, 'Hujusmodi varietates non corporis modo, verum et animi quoque, plerumque congenitæ, nonnun quam hæreditariæ, observantur. Hoc modo parentes sæpe in proles reviviscunt; certe parentibus liberi similes sunt, non vultum modo et corporis formam, sed animi indolem, et virtutes, et vitia. Imperiosa gens Claudia diu Romæ floruit, impigra, ferox, superba; eadem illachrymabilem Tiberium, tristissimum tyrennum, produxit; tandem in immanem Caligulam, et Claudium, et Agrippinam, ipsumque demum Neronem, post sexcentos annos, desitura.'†—Cap. i. sect. 16.

Phrenology reveals the principle on which these phenomona take place. Mental talents and dispositions are determined by the size and constitution of the brain. The brain is a portion of our organised system, and as such is subject to the organic laws, by one of which its qualities are transmitted by hereditary descent. This law, however faint or obscure it may appear in individual cases, becomes absolutely undeniable in nations. When we place the collection of Hindoo, Charib, Negro, New Holland, North American, and European skulls, possessed by the Phrenological Society, in juxtaposition, we perceive a national form and combination of organs in each actually obtruding itself upon our notice, and corresponding with the mental characters of the respective tribes; the cerebral development of one tribe is seen to differ as widely from that of another, as the European mind does from that of the New Hollander. Here, then, each Hindoo, Chinese, New Hollander, Negro, and Charib, obviously inherits from his parents a certain general type of head; and so does each European. If, then, the general forms and proportions are thus so palpably transmitted, can we

* See Appendix, Note 2.

† Cases of these heads are sold in the shops, and will be found in many Phrenological Collections.

* Very young hens lay small eggs; but a breeder of fowls will never set these to be hatched, because the animals produced be feeble and imperfectly developed. They select the largest and freshest eggs, and endeavour to rear the healthiest stock possible.

† Parents frequently live again in their offspring. It is quite certain that children resemble their parents, not only in countenance and the form of their body, but also in their mental dispositions, in their virtues and vices, &c.

doubt that the individual varieties follow the same rule, modified slightly by causes peculiar to the parents of the individual? The differences of national *character* are equally conspicuous as those of national *brains*, and it is surprising how permanently both endure. It is observed by an author in the *Edinburgh Review*, that 'the Vicentine district is, as every one knows, and has been for ages, an intergral part of the Venetian dominions, professing the same religion, and governed by the same laws, as the other continental provinces of Venice; yet the English character is not more different from the French, than that of the Vicentine from the Paduan; while the contrast between the Vicentine and his other neighbours, the Veronese, is hardly less remarkable.'—No. lxxxiv. p. 459.

If, then, form, size, and constitution of brain, are transmitted from parents to children, if these determine natural mental talents and dispositions, which in their turn exercise the greatest influence over the happiness of individuals through the whole of life, it becomes extremely important to discover according to what laws this transmission takes place. Three principles present themselves to our consideration, at the first aspect of the question. Either, in the first place, the constitution and qualities of brain, which the parents themselves inherit at birth, are transmitted absolutely, so that the children, sex following sex, are exact copies, without variation or modification, of the one parent or the other; or, secondly, the natural and inherent qualities of the father and mother combine, and are transmitted in a modified form to the offspring; or, thirdly, the qualities of the children are determined jointly by the constitution of the stock, and by the faculties which predominate in power and activity in the parents, at the particular time when the organic existence of each child commences.

Experience shows that the *first* cannot be the law; for, as often mentioned, a real law of nature admits of no exceptions, and it is well established, that the minds of children are *not exact* copies, without variation or modification, of those of the parents, sex following sex. Neither can the second be the law, because it is equally certain that the minds of children, although *sometimes, are not always*, in talents and disposition, perfect modifications of those of the father and mother. If this law prevailed, no child would be a copy of the father, none a copy of the mother, nor of any collateral relation, but each would be invariably a compound of the two parents, and all the children would be exactly alike, sex only excepted. Experience shows, that this cannot be the law. What then, does experience say to the *third* idea, that the mental character of each child is determined by the particular qualities of the stock, combined with those which predominate in the parents, when its existence commenced.

I have already adverted to the influence of the stock, and shall now illustrate that of the condition of the parents, when existence is communicated.

A strong illustration, in the case of the lower animals, appeared in the Edinburgh Review, No. lxxxiv. p. 457.

'Every one conversant with beasts,' says the reviewer, 'knows, that not only their natural, but that many of their acquired qualities, are transmitted by the parents to their offspring. Perhaps the most curious example of the latter fact may be found in the pointer.

'This animal is endowed with the natural instinct of winding game, and stealing upon his prey, which he surprises, having first made a short pause, in order to launch himself upon it with more security of success. This sort of *semicolon* in his proceedings, man converts into a *full stop*, and teaches him to be as much pleased at seeing the bird or beast drop by the shooter's gun, as at taking it himself. The staunchest dog of this kind, and of the original pointer, is of Spanish origin, and our own, is derived from this race, crossed with that of the foxhound, or other breed of dog, for the sake of improving his speed. This mixed and factitious race, of course, naturally partakes less of the true pointer character; that is to say, is less disposed to stop, or at least he makes a shorter stop at game. The *factitious pointer is, however, disciplined, in this country, into staunchness; and, what is most singular*, THIS QUALITY IS, IN A GREAT DEGREE INHERITED BY HIS PUPPY, who, may be seen earnestly standing at swallows or pigeons in a farm-yard. For intuition, though it leads the offspring to exercise his parents' faculties, does not instruct him how to direct them. The preference of his master afterwards guides him in his selection, and teaches him what game is better worth pursuit. On the other hand, the pointer of pure Spanish race, unless he happen to be well broke himself, which in the south of Europe seldom happens, produces a race which are all but unteachable, according to our notions of a pointer's business. They will make a stop at their game, as natural instinct prompts them, but seem incapable of being drilled into the habits of the animal, which education has formed in this country, and has rendered as I have said, in some degree, capable of transmitting his acquirements to his descendants.

'Acquired habits are hereditary in other animals besides dogs. English sheep, probably from the greater richness of our pastures, feed very much together; while Scotch sheep are obliged to extend and scatter themselves over their hills, for the better discovery of food. Yet the English sheep, on being transferred to Scotland, *keep their old habit of feeding in a mass*, though so little adapted to their new country; so do their descendants; and the English sheep is not thoroughly naturalized into the necessities of his place *till the third generation*. The same thing may be observed as to the nature of his food, that is observed in his mode of seeking it. When turnips were introduced from England into Scotland, *it was only the third generation* which heartily adopted this diet, the first having been starved into an acquiescence in it.'

In these instances, long continued impressions on the parents appear to have at last effected change of disposition in the offspring.

'We have seen,' says an author whom I have already quoted, 'how wonderfully the *bee* works—according to rules discovered by man thousands of years after the insect had followed them with perfect accuracy. The same little animal seems to be acquainted with principles of which we are still ignorant. We can, by crossing, vary the forms of cattle with astonishing nicety; but we have no means of altering the nature of an animal, once born, by means of treatment and feeding. This power, however, is undeniably possessed by the bees. When the queen-bee is lost, by death or otherwise, they choose a grub from among those who are born for workers; they make three cells into one, and placing the grub there, they build a tube round it; they afterwards build another cell, of a pyramidal form, into which the grub grows: they feed it with peculiar food, and tend it with extreme care. It becomes, when transformed from the worm to the fly, not a worker, but a queen-bee.'—*Objects, Advantages, and Pleasures of Science*, p. 33. It is difficult to conceive that man will ever possess such a power as this last.

Man, however, as an organized being, is subject to laws similar to those which govern the organization of the lower animals. Dr Pritchard, in his Researches into the Physical History of Mankind, has brought forward a variety of interesting facts and opinions on this subject of transmission of hereditary qualities in the human race. He says, 'Children resemble, in feature and constitution, both parents, but, I think, more generally the father. In the breeding of horses and oxen, great importance is attached, by experienced propagators, to the male. In sheep, it is commonly observed that black rams beget black lambs. In the human species, also, the complexion chiefly follows that of the father; and I believe it to be a general fact, that the offspring of a *black father* and white mother is *much darker* than the progeny of a *white father* and a black mother.'—Vol. ii, p. 551. These facts appear to me to be referable to both causes. The stock must have had some influence, but the mother, in all these cases, is not impressed by her own colour, because she does not look on herself; while the *father's* complexion must strikingly attract her attention, and may, in this way, give the darker tinge to the offspring.*

Dr Pritchard states the result of his investigations to be, First, That the organization of the offspring is always modelled according to the type of the *original structure* of the parent; and Secondly, 'That changes, produced by external causes in the appearance or constitution of the individual are temporary; and, in general, acquired characters are transient; they terminate with the individual, and have no influence on the progeny.'—Vol. ii, p. 536. He supports the first of these propositions by a variety of facts occurring 'in the porcupine family,' 'in the hereditary nature of complexion,' and, 'in the growth of supernumerary fingers or toes, and corresponding deficiencies.' 'Maupertuis has mentioned this phenomenon; he assures us, that there were two families in Germany, who have been distinguished for several generations by six fingers on each hand, and the same number of toes on each foot,' &c. He admits, at the same time, that the *second* proposition is of more difficult proof, and that an opinion contrary to it 'has been maintained by some writers, and a variety of singular facts have been related in support of it.' But many of these relations, as he justly observes, are obviously fables.

In regard to the foregoing propositions, I would observe, that a manifest distinction exists between transmission of monstrosities, or mutilations, which constitute additions to, or abstractions from, the natural lineaments of the body, and transmission of a mere tendency in particular organs to a greater or less development of their natural functions. This last appears to me to be influenced by the state of the parents, at the time when existence is communicated to the offspring. On this point Dr Pritchard says, 'The opinion which formerly prevailed, and which has been entertained by some modern writers, among whom is Dr Darwin, that at the period when organization commences in the ovum, that is, at or soon after the time of conception, the structure of the fœtus is capable of undergoing modification from impressions on the mind or senses of the parent, does not appear altogether so improbable. It is contradicted, at least, by no fact, in physiology. It is an opinion of very ancient prevalence, and may be traced to so remote a period, that its rise cannot be attributed to the speculations of philosophers, and it is difficult to account for the origin of such a persuasion, unless we ascribe it to facts which happened to be observed,' p. 556.

A striking and undeniable proof of the effect on the character and dispositions of children, produced by the form of brain transmitted to them by hereditary descent, is to be found in the progeny of marriages between Europeans, whose brains possess a favourable development of the moral and intellectual organs, and Hindoos, and native Americans, whose brains are inferior. All authors agree, and report the circumstance as singularly striking, that the children of such unions are decidedly superior in mental qualities to the native, while they are still inferior to the European parent. Captain Franklin says, that the half-bred American Indians 'are upon the whole a good looking people; and, where the experiments have been made, have shown much expertness in learning, and willingness to be taught, they have, however, been sadly neglected,' p. 86. He adds, 'It has been remarked, I do not know with what truth, that half breeds show more personal courage than the pure breeds.' Captain Basil Hall, and other writers on South America, mention that the offspring of native American and Spanish parents, constitute the most active, vigorous, and powerful portion of the inhabitants of these countries; and many of them rose to high commands during the revolutionary war. So much is this the case in Hindostan, that several writers have already pointed to the mixed race there, as obviously destined to become the future sovereigns of India. These individuals inherit from the native parent a certain adaptation to the climate, and from the European parent a higher development of brain, the two combined constituting their superiority.

* Black hens lay dark-coloured eggs.

Another example of the same law occurs in Persia. In that country, it is said that the custom has existed for ages among the nobles, of purchasing beautiful female Circassian captives, and forming alliances with them as wives. It is ascertained that the Circassian form of brain stands comparatively high in the development of the moral and intellectual organs.* And it is mentioned by some travellers, that the race of nobles in Persia is the most gifted in natural qualities, bodily and mental, of any class of that people; a fact diametrically opposite to that which takes place in Spain, and other European countries, where the nobles intermarry constantly with each other, and set the organic laws altogether at defiance.

The degeneracy and even idiocy of some of the noble and royal families of Spain and Portugal, from marrying nieces, and other near relations, is well known; and defective brains, in all these cases are observed.

The father of NAPOLEON BONAPARTE, says Sir WALTER SCOTT, 'is stated to have possessed a very handsome person, a talent for eloquence, and a vivacity of intellect which he transmitted to his son.' 'It was in the middle of civil discord, fights, and skirmishes, that CHARLES BONAPARTE married LÆTITIA RAMOLINI, one of the most beautiful young women of the island, and possessed of a great deal of firmness of character. She partook of the dangers of her husband during the years of civil war, and is said to have accompanied him on horseback on some military expeditions or perhaps hasty flights, shortly before her being delivered of the future Emperor.'—*Life of* NAPOLEON BONAPARTE, vol. iii, p. 6.

The murder of DAVID RIZZIO was perpetrated by armed nobles, with many circumstances of violence and terror, in the presence of Mary, Queen of Scotland, shortly before the birth of her son, afterwards James the First of England. The constitutional liability of this monarch to emotions of fear, is recorded as a characteristic of his mind; and it has even been mentioned that he started involuntarily at the sight of a drawn sword. Queen Mary was not deficient in courage, and the Stuarts, both before and after James the First, were distinguished for this quality; so that he was a marked exception to the dispositions of his family. Napoleon and James form striking contrasts; and it may be remarked that the mind of Napoleon's mother appears to have risen to the danger to which she was exposed, and braved it; while the circumstances in which Queen Mary was placed, were calculated to inspire her with fear alone.

Farther evidence of the same law may still be mentioned. Esquirol, the celebrated French medical writer, in adverting to the causes of madness, mentions that many children whose existence dated from periods when the horrors of the French Revolution were at their height, turned out subsequently to be weak, nerv-

* In Mr W. Allan's picture of the Circassian Captives, the form of the head is said to be a copy from nature, taken by that artist, when he visited the country. It is engraved by Mr James Stewart with great beauty and fidelity, and may be consulted as an example of the superiority of Circassian development of the brain.

ous, and irritable in mind, extremely susceptible of impressions, and liable, by the least extraordinary excitement, to be thrown into absolute insanity. Again, in a case which fell under my observation, the father of a family was sick, had a partial recovery, but relapsed, declined, and in two months died. Seven months after his death, a son was born, of the full age; and the origin of whose existence was referable to the period of the partial recovery. At that time, and during the subsequent two months, the faculties of the mother were in the highest state of excitement, in ministering to her husband, to whom she was greatly attached; and, after his death, the same excitement continued to operate, for she was then loaded with the charge of a numerous family, but not depressed; for her circumstances were comfortable. The child is now more than ten years old; and, while his constitution is the most delicate, his development of the mental organs, and the natural activity of these, is decidedly the greatest of the family. Another illustration of the same law is found in the fact, that, when two parties marry very young, the eldest of their children generally inherits a less favorable development of the moral and intellectual organs, than those produced in more mature age,—which is in exact correspondence with the doctrine, that the animal faculties in men, in general, are most vigorous in early life, and will then be most readily transmitted to offspring. Indeed, it appears difficult to account for the wide varieties in the form of the brain in children of the same family, unless on the principle, that the organs which predominate in activity and vigor in the parents, at the time when existence is communicated, determine the tendency of corresponding organs to develop themselves largely in the children. If this is really the law of nature, as there is great reason for believing, then parents, in whom combativeness and destructiveness are in habitual activity, will transmit these organs, in a state of high development and excitement, to their children; and those in whom the moral and intellectual organs exist in supreme vigour, will transmit these in greatest perfection.

This view is in harmony with the fact that children generally, although not universally, resemble the parents in their mental qualities; because the largest organs being naturally the most active, the general and habitual state of the parents will be strongly marked by those which predominate in size in their own brains; and on the principle of predominance in activity and energy causing the transmission of similar qualities to the offspring, the children will, in this way, very generally resemble the parents. But they will not always do so; because, even Mary Macinnes, in whom the moral and intellectual organs were extremely deficient, might have been exposed to external influences which, for the time being, might have excited them to unwonted vivacity; and, according to the rule, as now explained, a child, dating its existence from that period, might have inherited a higher organization of brain than her own. Or, a person with a very excellent moral development, might, by some particular occurrence, have his animal propensities roused to unwonted vigour, and his moral sentiments thrown, for the time, into the shade; and any offspring connected with that condition, would prove inferior to himself in the development of the moral organs, and greatly surpass him in the size of those of the propensities.

I do not present these views as ascertained phrenological science, but as inferences strongly supported by facts, and consistent with known phenomena. If we suppose them to be true, they will greatly strengthen the motives for preserving the *habitual* supremacy of the moral sentiments and intellect, when, by doing so, improved moral and intellectual capacities may be conferred on offspring. If it be true that this lower world, so far as man is concerned, is framed to harmonize with the supremacy of the higher faculties of the mind, what a noble prospect would this law open up of the possibility of man ultimately becoming capable of placing himself more fully in accordance with the Divine institutions, than he has hitherto been able to accomplish; and, in consequence, of reaping numberless enjoyments that appear destined for him by his Creator, and avoiding thousands of miseries that now render his life a series of calamities. The views here expounded also harmonize with the second principle of this Essay, namely, That, as activity in the faculties is the fountain of enjoyment, the whole constitution of nature is designedly framed to call on them for ceaseless exertion. What scope for observation, reflection, the exercise of moral sentiments, and regulating of animal impulse, does not this picture of nature present!

I cordially agree, however, with Dr Pritchard, that this subject is still involved in very great obscurity. 'We know not,' says he, 'by what means any of the facts we remark are effected; and the utmost we can hope to attain, is, by tracing the connexion of circumstances, to learn from what combinations of them we may expect to witness particular results,'—Vol. ii, p. 542. But much of the darkness may be traced to the past ignorance of mankind concerning the functions of the brain. If we consider that it has all along been the most important organ of our system; that, from its office, mental impressions must almost necessarily have exercised a powerful influence over the development of its parts, and that the relative size of these determines the predominance of particular talents and dispositions; but, nevertheless, that all past observations have been conducted without the knowledge of these principles; it will not appear marvellous that merely confusion and contradiction have existed in the results drawn. At the present moment, accordingly, almost all that phrenologists can pretend to accomplish, is, to point out the mighty void; to offer an exposition of its causes; and to state such inferences as their own very limited observations have hitherto enabled them to deduce. Far from pretending to be in possession of certain and complete knowledge on this subject, I am inclined to think, that, although every conjecture now hazarded were true, several centuries of observation will probably be required to render the principles completely practical. At present we have almost no information concerning the effects, on the children, of different temperaments, of different combinations in the cerebral organs, of differences of age, &c. in the parents.

It is astonishing, however, to what extent mere pecuniary interests excite men to investigate and observe the Natural Laws, and how small an influence moral and rational considerations exert in leading them to do so. Before a common insurance company will undertake the risk of paying £100, on the death of an individual, they require the following questions to be answered by credible and intelligent witnesses:

'1. How long have you known Mr A B?

'2. Has he had the gout?

'3. Has he had a spitting of blood, asthma, consumption, or other pulmonary complaint?

'4 Do you consider him at all predisposed to any of these complaints?

'5. Has he been afflicted with fits, or mental derangement?

'6. Do you think his constitution perfectly good, in the common acceptation of the term?

'7. Are his habits in every respect strictly regular and temperate?

'8. Is he at present in good health?

'9. Is there any thing in his form, habits of living, or business, which you are of opinion may shorten his life?

'10. What complaints are his family most subject to?

'11. Are you aware of any reason why an insurance might not with safety be effected on his life?'

A man and woman about to marry, have in the general case, the health and happiness of five or more human beings depending on their attention to consideration, essentially the same as the foregoing, and yet how much less scrupulous are they than the mere speculators in money.

There is no moral difficulty in admitting and admiring the wisdom and benevolence of the institution, by which good qualities are transmitted from parents to children; but it is frequently held as unjust to the latter, that they should inherit parental deficiencies, and so be made to suffer for sins which they did not commit. In solving this difficulty, I must again refer to the supremacy of the moral sentiments, as the theory of the constitution of the world. The animal propensities are all selfish, and regard only the immediate and apparent interest of the individual; while the higher sentiments delight in that which communicates the greatest quantity of enjoyment to the greatest number. Now, let us suppose the law of hereditary descent to be abrogated altogether, that is to say, that each individual of the race at birth were endowed with fixed natural qualities, without the slightest reference to what his parents had been, or done;—this form of constitution would obviously cut off every possibility of improvement *in the race*. Every phrenologyist knows, that the New Hollanders, Charibs, and other savage tribes, are distinguished by great deficiencies in the moral and intellectual organs.* If, however, it be true, that considerable development of intellectual organs is indispensable to the comprehension of science, and the practice of virtue, it would, on the present supposition, be impossible to raise the New Hollanders, as a people, one step higher in capacity for intelligence and virtue than they now are. We might cultivate each generation up to the limit of its powers, but there the improvement, and a low one it would be, would stop; for the next generation, being produced with brains equally deficient in the moral and intellectual regions, no principle of increasing amelioration would exist. The same remarks are applicable to every tribe of mankind. If we assume modern Europeans as the standard, then, if the law of hereditary descent were abrogated, every deficiency that at this moment is attributable to imperfect or disproportionate development of brain, would be irremediable, and continue as long as the race existed. Each generation might be cultivated till the summit level of its capacities was attained, but there each succeeding generation would remain. When we contrast with this prospect the very opposite effects flowing from the law of hereditary transmission of qualities in an increasing ratio, the whole advantages are at once perceived to be on the side of the latter constitution. According to this rule, the children of the individuals who have obeyed the organic, the moral, and the intellectual laws, would start from the highest level of their parents, not only in acquired knowledge, but in consequence of that very obedience, they would inherit an enlarged development of the moral and intellectual organs, and thereby enjoy an increasing capability of discovering and obeying the Creator's institutions. This improvement, will, no doubt, have its limits; but it may probably extend to that point at which man will be capable of placing himself in harmony with the natural laws. The effort necessary to *maintain* himself there, will still provide for the activity of his faculties.

2dly, We may suppose the law of hereditary descent to be limited to the transmission of good, and abrogated as to the transmission of bad qualities; and it may be thought that this arrangement would be more benevolent and just. There are objections to this view, however, which do not occur at once to the mind. We see as matter of fact, that a vicious and debased parent is actually defective in the moral and intellectual organs. Now, if his children should take up exactly the same development as himself, this would be transmission of imperfections, which is the very point objected to; or, if he were to take up a development fixed by nature, and not at all referable to that of the parent; this would render the whole race stationary in their first condition, without the possibility of improvement in their capacities, which also we have seen would be an evil greatly to be deprecated.

3dly. The bad development might be supposed to transmit, by hereditary descent, a good development; but this would set at naught the supremacy of justice and benevolence; it would render the consequences of contempt for, and violation of the divine laws, and of obedience to them, in this particular, precisely alike. The debauchee, the cheat, the murderer, and the robber, would according to this view, be able to look upon the prospects of their prosperity, with the same confidence in their welfare and happiness, as the pious and intelligent Christian, who had sought to know God and to obey his institutions during his whole life. Certainly no individual, in whom the higher sentiments prevail, will for a moment regard this imagined change as any improvement on the Creator's arrangements. What a host of motives to moral and religious conduct would at once be withdrawn, were such a spectacle of divine government exhibited to the mind. In proportion as the brain is improved, the aptitude of man for discovering and obeying the natural laws will be increased. For example, it appears to me that the native American savages, and native New Hollanders, cannot, with their present brains, adopt European civilization. The reader will find in the Phrenological Collections specimens of their skulls, and, on comparing them with those of Europeans, he will observe that in the former, the organs of reflecting intellect, Ideality, Conscientiousness, and Benevolence, are greatly inferior in size to the same organs in the latter. If, by obeying the organic laws, the moral and intellectual organs of these savages could be considerably enlarged, they would *desire* civilization, and would adopt it when offered. If this view be well founded, all means used for their cultivation, which are not calculated at the same time to improve their cerebral organization, will be limited in their effects by the narrow capacities attending their present development. In youth, all the organs of the body are more susceptible of modification than in advanced age; and hence the effects of education on the young may arise from the greater susceptibility of the brain to impressions at that period than later.

4thly. It may be supposed that human happiness would have been more completely secured, by endowing all individuals at birth with that degree of development of the moral and intellectual organs, which would have best fitted them for discovering and obeying the Creator's institutions, and by preventing all aberrations from this standard; just as the lower animals appear to have received instincts and capacities, adjusted with the most perfect wisdom to their conditions. Two remarks occur on this supposition. First; We are not competent at present to judge correctly how far the development actually bestowed on the human race, is, or is not, wisely adapted to their circumstances; for there may, by possibility, be departments in the great system of human society, exactly suited to all existing forms of brain, not imperfect through disease, if our knowledge were sufficient to discover them. The want of a natural index to the mental dispositions and capacities of individuals, and of a philosophical theory of the constitution of society, has hitherto precluded the possibility of arriving at sound conclusions on this question. It appears to me probable, that while there may be great room for improvement in the talents and dispositions of vast numbers of individuals, the imperfections of the race in general may not be so great, as

* This fact is demonstrated by specimens in most Phrenological Collections.

we, in our present state of ignorance of the aptitudes of particular persons for particular situations, are prone to infer. But, secondly, on the principle that activity in the faculties is the fountain of enjoyment, it may be considered whether additional motives to the exercise of the moral and intellectual powers, and consequently, greater happiness, are not conferred by leaving men, within certain limits, to regulate the talents and tendencies of their descendants, than by endowing each individual with the best qualities, independently of the conduct of his parents.

On the whole, therefore, there seems reason for concluding, that the actual institution, by which both good and bad qualities* are transmitted, is fraught with higher advantages to the race, than the abrogation of the law of transmission altogether; or than the supposed change of it, by which bad men would transmit good qualities to their children. The actual law, when viewed by the moral sentiments and intellect, both in its principles and consequences, appears beneficial and expedient. When an individual sufferer, therefore, complains of its operation, he regards it through the animal faculties alone; his self-love is annoyed and he carries his thought no farther. He never stretches his mind forward to the consequences to mankind at large, if the law which grieves him were reversed. The animal faculties regard nothing beyond their own immediate and apparent interest, and they do not even discern it correctly; for no arrangement that is beneficial for the race can be injurious to individuals, if its operations in regard to them were distinctly traced. The abrogation of the rule, therefore, under which they complain, would, we may be certain, bring ten thousand times greater evils, even upon themselves, than its continuance.

On the other hand, an individual sufferer under a hereditary pain, in whom the moral and intellectual faculties predominate, who should see the principle and consequences of the institution of hereditary descent, as now explained, would not murmur at them as unjust; he would bow with submission, to an institution, which he perceived to be fraught with blessings to the race, when it was known and observed, and the very practice of this reverential acquiescence would be so delightful, that it would diminish, in a great degree, the severity of the evil. Besides, he would see the door of mercy standing widely open, and inviting his return; he would perceive that every step which he made in his own person towards exact obedience to the Creator's institutions, would remove by so much the organic penalty transmitted through his parents' transgressions, and that his posterity would reap the full benefits of his more dutiful observance.

It may be objected to the law of hereditary transmission of organic qualities, that the children of a blind and lame father have sound eyes and limbs: But, in the 1st place, these defects are generally the result of accident or disease, occurring either during pregnancy, or posterior to birth, and seldom or never the operation of nature; and, consequently, the original physical principles remaining entire in the constitution, the bodily imperfections are not transmitted to the progeny. 2dly. Where the defects are congenite or constitutional, it frequently happens that they are transmitted through successive generations. This is exemplified in deafness, in blindness, and even in the possession of supernumerary fingers or toes. The reason why such peculiarities are not transmitted to all the progeny, appears to be simply that, in general, only one parent is defective. If the father, for instance, be blind or deaf, the mother is generally free from that imperfection, and her influence naturally extends to, and modifies the result in, the progeny.

If the law of hereditary transmission of mental qualities be, as now explained, dependent on the organs in highest excitement in the parents, it will account for the varieties, along with the general resemblance, that occur in children of the same marriage. It will account also for the circumstance of genius being sometimes transmitted and sometimes not. Unless *both* parents possess the developments and temperament of genius, the law would not certainly transmit these qualities to the children; and even although both did possess these endowments, they would be transmitted only on condition of the parents obeying the organic laws, one of which forbids that excessive exertion of the mental and corporeal functions, which exhausts and debilitates the system; an error almost universally committed by persons endowed with high original talent, under the present condition of ignorance of the natural laws, and erroneous fashions and institutions of society. The supposed law would be disproved by cases of weak, imbecile, and vicious children, being born to parents whose own constitution and habits had been in the highest accordance with the organic, moral, and intellectual laws; but no such cases have hitherto come under my observation.

Farther; after birth, it is quite certain that the organs most active in the parents have a decided tendency to cause and increase in the size of corresponding organs in the children, by habitually exciting and exercising them, which favors their growth. According to this law, habitual severity, chiding, and imperious conduct, proceeding from over-active Self-esteem and Destructiveness in the parents, rouse these faculties in the children, produce hatred and resistance, and increase the activity of the same organs, while those of the moral sentiments and intellect are left in a state of apathy.

Rules, however, are best taught by examples; and I shall, therefore, proceed to mention some facts that have fallen under my own notice, or been communicated to me from authentic sources, illustrative of the practical consequences of infringing the law of hereditary descent.

A man, aged about fifty, possessed a brain, in which the animal, moral and knowing intellectual organs were all strong, but the reflecting weak. He was pious, but destitute of education; he married an unhealthy young woman, deficient in moral development, but of considerable force of character; and several children were born. The father and mother were far from being happy; and when the children attained to eighteen or twenty years of age, they were adepts in every species of immorality and profligacy; they picked their father's pockets, stole his goods, and got them sold back to him, by accomplices, for money, which was spent in betting and cock fighting, drinking, and low debauchery. The father was heavily grieved; but knowing only two resources, he beat the children severely as long as he was able, and prayed for them; his own words were, that 'if *after that*, it pleased the Lord to make vessels of wrath of them, the Lord's will must just be done.' I mention this last observation, not in jest, but in great seriousness. It was impossible not to pity the unhappy father; yet, who that sees the institutions of the Creator to be in themselves wise, but in this instance to have been directly violated, will not acknowledge that the bitter pangs of the poor old man were the consequences of his own ignorance; and that it was an erroneous view of the divine administration, which led him to overlook his own mistakes, and to attribute to the Almighty the purpose of making vessels of wrath of his children, as the only explanation which he could give of their wicked dispositions. Who that sees the cause of his misery must not lament that his piety should

* In using the popular expressions 'good qualities, and 'bad qualities,' I do not mean to insinuate, that any of the tendencies bestowed on man are essentially bad in themselves. Destructiveness and Acquisitiveness, for example, are, when properly directed, unquestionably good; but they become the sources of evil, when their organs are too large, in proportion to those of the moral sentiments and intellect. By bad qualities, therefore, I always mean either disease, or unfavorable proportions among the different organs.

not have been enlightened by philosophy, and directed to obedience, in the first instance, to the organic institutions of the Creator, as one of the prescribed conditions, without observance of which he had no title to expect a blessing upon his offspring.

In another instance, a man, in whom the animal organs, particularly those of Combativeness and Destructiveness, were very large, but with a pretty fair moral and intellectual development, married, against her inclination, a young woman, fashionable and showily educated, but with a very decided deficiency and Conscientiousness. They soon became unhappy and even blows were said to have passed between them, although they belonged to the middle rank of life. The mother, in this case, employed the children to deceive and plunder the father, and, latterly, spent the produce in drink. The sons inherited the deficient morality of the mother, and the ill temper, of the father. The family fireside became a theatre of war, and, before the sons attained majority, the father was glad to get them removed from his house, as the only means by which he could feel even his life in safety from their violence ; for they had by that time retaliated the blows with which he had visited them in their younger years ; and he stated that he actually considered his life to be in danger from his own offspring.

In another family, the mother possesses an excellent development of the moral and intellectual organs, while, in the father, the animal organs predominate in great excess. She has been the unhappy victim of ceaseless misfortune, originating from the misconduct of her husband. Some of the children have inherited the father's brain, and some the mother's ; and of the sons whose heads resembled the father's, several have died through mere debauchery and profligacy under thirty years of age ; whereas, those who resemble the mother are alive and little contaminated, even amidst all the disadvantages of evil example.

On the other hand, I am not acquainted with a single instance in which the moral and intellectual organs predominated in size, in both father and mother, and whose external circumstances also permitted their general activity, in which the *whole* children did not partake of a moral and intellectual character, differing slightly in degrees of excellence one from another, but all presenting the decided predominance of the human over the animal faculties.

There are well-known examples of the children of religious and moral fathers exhibiting dispositions of a very inferior description ; but in all of these instances that I have been able to observe, there has been a large development of the animal organs in the one parent, which was just controlled, but not much more, by the moral and intellectual powers ; and in the other parent, the *moral* organs did not appear to be in large proportion. The unfortunate child inherited the large animal development of the one, with the defective moral development of the other ; and, in this way, was inferior to both. The way to satisfy one's self on this point, is to examine the heads of the parents. In all such cases, a large base of the brain, which is the region of the animal propensities, will very probably be found in one or other of them.

Another organic law of the animal kingdom deserves attention ; viz. that by which marriages betwixt blood relations tend decidedly to the deterioration of the physical and mental qualities of the offspring. In Spain kings marry their nieces, and, in this country, first and second cousins marry without scruple ; although every philosophical physiologist will declare that this is in direct opposition to the institutions of nature. This law holds also in the vegetable kingdom. 'A provision, of a very simple kind, is, in some cases, made to prevent the male and female blossoms of the same plant from breeding together, this being found to hurt the breed of vegetables, just as breeding in and in does the breed of animals. It is contrived, that the dust shall be shed by the male blossom before the female is ready to be affected by it, so that the impregnation must be performed by the dust of some other plant, and in this way the breed be crossed.'—*Objects &c, of Science*, p. 33.

On the same principle, it is found highly advantageous in agriculture not to sow grain of the same stock in constant succession on the same soil. In individual instances, if the soil and plants are both possessed of great vigour and the highest qualities, the same kind of grain may be reaped in succession twice or thrice, with less perceptible deterioration than where these elements of reproduction are feeble and imperfect ; and the same thing appears in the animal kingdom. If the first individuals connected in near relationship, who unite in marriage, are uncommonly robust, and possess very favorably developed brains, their offspring may not be *so much* deteriorated below the common standard of the country as to attract particular attention, and the law of nature is, in this instance, supposed not to hold ; but it does hold, for to a law of nature there never is an exception. The offspring are uniformly inferior to what they *would have been*, if the parents had united with strangers in blood of *equal vigour and cerebral development*. Whenever there is any remarkable deficiency in parents who are related in blood, these appear in the most marked and aggravated forms in the offspring. This fact is so well known, and so easily ascertained, that I forbear to enlarge upon it. So much for miseries arising from neglect of the organic laws in forming the *domestic compact*.

I proceed to advert to those evils which arise from overlooking the operation of the same laws in ordinary relations of society.

How many little annoyances arise from the misconduct of servants and dependants in various departments of life ; how many losses, and sometimes ruin, arise from dishonesty and knavery in confidential clerks, partners, and agents. A mercantile house of great reputation, in London, was ruined and became bankrupt, by a clerk having embezzled a prodigious extent of funds, and absconded to America ; another company in Edinburgh, was talked of about a year ago, which had sustained a great loss by a similar piece of dishonesty ; a company in Paisley was ruined by one of the partners having collected the funds, and eloped with them to the United States ; and lately, several bankers, and other persons, suffered severely in Edinburgh, by the conduct of an individual, some time connected with the public press. If it be true, then, that the mental qualities and dispositions of individuals are indicated and influenced by the development of their brains, and that their actual conduct is the result of this development, operated upon by their external circumstances, including in this latter every moral and intellectual influence coming from without, is it not obvious, that one and all of the evils here enumerated flowed from infringement of the natural institutions, that is to say, from having placed human beings decidedly deficient in moral or intellectual qualities in situations where these were required in a higher degree than they possessed them ?

If any man were to go to sea in a paper boat, which the very fluidity of the element would dissolve, no one would be surprised at his being drowned : and, in like manner, if the Creator has constituted the brain so as to exert a great influence on the mental dispositions, and if, nevertheless, men are pleased to treat this fact with neglect and contempt, and to place individuals, naturally deficient in the moral organs, in situations where a great degree of these sentiments is required, they have no cause to be surprised if they suffer the penalties of their own misconduct, in being plundered and defrauded.

Although I can state, from experience, that it is possible, by the aid of Phrenology, to select individuals whose moral and intellectual qualities may be relied on; yet the extremely limited extent of our practical knowledge in this respect falls to be confessed. To be able to judge accurately what combination of natural talents and dispositions in an individual will best fit him for any given employment, we require to have seen a variety of combinations tried in that particular department, and to have noted their effects. It is impossible, at least for me, to anticipate with unerring certainty, what these effects will be: but I have ever found nature constant and after once discovering, by experience, an assortment of qualities suited to a particular duty, I have found no subsequent exception to the rule. Cases in which the predominance of particular regions of the brain as the moral and intellectual, is very decided, present fewest difficulties; although, even in them, the very deficiency of animal organs may sometimes incapacitate an individual for important stations; but where the three classes of organs, the animal, moral, and intellectual, are nearly *in æquilibrio*, the most opposite results may ensue by external circumstances exciting the one or the other to decided predominance in activity.

Having now adverted to calamities by external violence,—to bad health,—unhappiness in the domestic circle, arising from ill-advised unions, and viciously disposed children,—to the evils of placing individuals, as servants, clerks, partners, public instructers, &c, in situations to which they are not suited, by their natural qualities, and traced all of them to infringements or neglect of the physical or organic laws, I proceed to advert to the last, and what is reckoned the greatest of all calamities, DEATH, and which itself is obviously a part of the organic law. Baron Cuvier, after stating that the world we inhabit was at first fluid, and that highly crystalline rocks were deposited before animal or vegetable life began, has demonstrated, that then came the lowest orders of zoophytes and of vegetables, —next fishes and reptiles,—and trees in vast forests, giving origin to our present beds of coal, then quadrupeds and birds, and shells and plants, *resembling* those of the present era, but all of which, as species, have utterly perished from the earth; next came alluvial rocks, containing bones of mammoths, &c, and last of all came man. (Cuvier's Preface to his Ossemens Fossiles, and papers by Dr Fleming in Chalmer's Journal.) This shows that destruction of vegetable and animal life were institutions of nature before man became an inhabitant of the globe. It is beyond the compass of philosophy to explain *why* the world was so constituted. I therefore make no inquiry *why* death was instituted, and refer, of course, only to the dissolution of organized bodies, and not at all to the state of the soul or mind after its separation from the body. These belong to Revelation.

Let us view the dissolution of the body abstractedly from personal considerations, as a mere natural arrangement. Death, then, appears to be a result of the constitution of all organized beings; for the very definition of the genus, is, that the individuals grow, attain maturity, decay, and die. The human imagination cannot conceive how the former part of this series of movements could exist without the latter, as long as space is necessary to corporeal existence. If all the vegetable and animal productions of nature, from creation downwards, had grown, attained maturity, and there remained, this world would not have been capable of containing one thousandth part of them; so that, on this earth, decaying and dying appear indispensably necessary to admit of reproduction and growth. Viewed abstractedly, then, organized beings live as long as health and vigour continue; but they are subjected to a process of decay, which impairs gradually all their functions, and at last terminates in their dissolution. Now, in the vegetable world, the effect of this law, is, to surround us with young forests, in place of the monotony of everlasting stately full grown woods, standing forth in awful endless majesty, without variation in leaf or bough;—with the vernal bloom of the meadows changing gracefully into the vigour of summer, and the maturity of autumn;—with the rose, first simply and delicately budding, next fresh and lovely in its blow and then rich and luxuriant in its perfect condition. In short, when we advert to the law of death, as instituted in the vegetable organized kingdom, and as related to our own faculties of Ideality, Wonder, &c, which desire and delight in the very changes which death introduces, we without hesitation exclaim, that all is wisely, admirably, and wonderfully made. Turning again, to the animal kingdom, the same fundamental principle prevails. Death removes the old, the worn out, and decaying, and, in their place, the organic law introduces the young, the gay, and the vigorous, to tread the stage with increased agility and delight.

This transfer of existence may readily be granted to be beneficial to the young; but, at first sight, it appears the opposite of benevolent to the old. To have lived at all, is felt as giving a right to continue to live; and the question arises, how can the institution of death, as the result of the organic laws, be reconciled with Benevolence and Justice?

In treating of the supremacy of the sentiments, I pointed out, that the grand distinction between them and the propensities, consist in this, that the former are disinterested, generous, and fond of the general food, and the latter altogether selfish in their desires. It is obvious, that death, as an institution of the Creator, must affect these two classes of faculties in the most different manner. The propensities, being confined in their gratification to self, and having no reference to the welfare of any other creature, a being endowed only with them and reflecting intellect, and enabled, by the latter, to discover death and its consequences, would regard it as the most appalling of visitations, and would see in it only utter extinction of all enjoyment. The lower animals, then, whose whole being is composed of the inferior propensities, and several *knowing* faculties, would see death, if they could at all anticipate it, only in this light. So tremendously fearful would it appear to them, as the extinguisher of every pleasure which they had ever felt or could conceive, that we may safely predicate, that the bare prospect of it would render their lives wretched, and that nothing could compensate the agonies of terror, with which an habitual consciousness of it would inspire them. But, by depriving them of *reflecting* organs, the Creator has kindly and effectually preserved them from the influence of this evil. He has thereby rendered them completely blind to its existence. There is not the least reason to believe, that any one of the lower animals, while in health and vigour, has the slightest conception that it is a mortal creature, any more than a tree has that it will die. In consequence, it lives in as full enjoyment of the present, as if it were assured of every agreeable sensation being eternal. Death always takes the individual by surprise, whether it comes in the form of violence, suppressing life in youth, or of slow decay by age; therefore, it really operates in their case as a transference of existence from one being to another, without consciousnesss of the loss in the one which dies. Let us, however, trace the operations of death, in regard to the lower animals, a little more in detail.

It will not be disputed, that the world is calculated to contain and support only a definite number of living creatures, that the lower animals have received from nature powers of reproduction far beyond what is necessary to supply the waste of life by natural decay, and that they do not possess intellect sufficient to restrain their numbers within the limits of their means of subsistence. Here, therefore, is an institution in which destruction of life, to a great extent, is necessarily implied. Philosophy cannot tell why death was instituted at first, but, according to the views maintained in this Essay, we should expect to find it connected with, and regulated by, benevolence and justice; that is to say, that it should not be inflicted for the sole purpose of extinguishing the life of individuals, to their damage, without any other result; but that the general system under which it takes place should be, on the whole, favourable to the enjoyment of the race; and this accordingly is the fact. Violent death, and the devouring of one animal by another, are not purely benevolent because pure benevolence would never inflict pain; but they are instances of destruction guided by benevolence; that is, wherever death proceeds under the institutions of nature, it is accompanied with enjoyment or beneficial consequences to one set of animals or another. Herbivorous animals are exceedingly prolific, yet the supply of vegetable food is limited. Hence, after multiplying for a few years, extensive starvation, the most painful and lingering of all deaths, and the most detrimental to the race, would inevitably ensue; but carnivorous animals have been instituted who kill and eat them; and by this means not only do carnivorous animals reap the pleasures of life, but the numbers of the herbivorous are restrained within such limits, that the individuals among them enjoy existence while they live. The destroyers, again, are limited in their turn: The moment they become too numerous, and carry their devastations too far their food fails them, and, in their conflicts for the supplies that remain, they extinguish each other, or die of starvation. Nature seems averse from inflicting death extensively by starvation, probably because it impairs the constitution long before it extinguishes life, and has the tendency to produce degeneracy in the race. It may be remarked, also, speculatively, that herbivorous animals must have existed in considerable numbers before the carnivorous began to exercise their functions; for many of the former must die, that one of the latter may live; if a single sheep and a single tiger had been placed together at first, the tiger would have eaten up the sheep at a few meals, and died itself of starvation, in a brief space afterwards. In natural decay, the organs are worn out by mere age, and the animal sinks into gradual insensibility, unconscious that dissolution awaits it. Further, the wolf, the tiger, the lion, and other beasts of prey, instituted by the Creator as instruments of violent death, are provided, in addition to Destructiveness, with large organs of Cautiousness and Secretiveness, that prompt them to steal upon their victims with the unexpected suddenness of a mandate of annihilation, and they are impelled also to inflict death in the most instantaneous and least painful method; the tiger and lion spring from their covert with the rapidity of the thunderbolt, and one blow of their tremendous paws, inflicted at the junction of the head with the neck, produces instantaneous death. The eagle is taught to strike its sharp beak into the spine of the birds which it devours, and their agony endures scarcely for an instant. It has been objected, that the cat plays with the unhappy mouse, and prolongs its tortures; but the cat that does so, is the pampered and well fed inhabitant of a kitchen; the cat of nature is too eager to devour, to indulge in such luxurious gratifications of Destructiveness and Secretiveness. It kills in a moment, and eats. Here, then, is actually a regularly organized process for withdrawing individuals of the lower animals from existence, almost by a fiat of destruction, and thereby making way for a succession of other occupants.

Man is not so merciful towards the lower creatures: but he might be so. Suppose the sheep in the hands of man, were to be guillotined, and not maltreated before its execution, the creature would never know that it had ceased to live. And, by the law which I have already explained, man does not with impunity add one unnecessary pang to the death of the lower animals. In the brutal butcher who inflicts torments on calves, sheep, and cattle, while driving them to the slaughter, and who puts them to death in the way supposed to be the most conducive to the gratification of his Acquisitiveness, such as bleeding them to death, by successive stages, prolonged for days, to whiten their flesh,—the animal faculties of Destructiveness, Acquisitiveness, Self-esteem, &c. predominate so decidedly in activity, over the moral and intellectual powers, that he is necessarily excluded from all the enjoyments attendant on the supremacy of the human faculties; he besides, goes into society under the influence of the same base combination, and suffers at every hand animal retaliation, so that he does not escape with impunity for his outrages against the moral law. Here, then, we can perceive nothing malevolent in the institution of death, in so far as regards the lower animals. A pang certainly does attend it; but while Destructiveness must be recognized in the pain, Benevolence is equally perceptible in its effects.

I mentioned formerly, that the organic law rises above the physical, and the moral and intellectual law above the organic; and the present occasion affords an additional illustration of this fact. Under the physical law, no remedial process is instituted to arrest, or restore, against the consequences of infringement. If a mirror falls, and is smashed, by the physical law it remains ever after in fragments; if a ship sinks, it lies still at the bottom of the ocean, chained down by the law of gravitation. Under the organic law, on the other hand, a distinct remedial process is established. If a tree is blown over, every root that remains in the ground will double its exertions to preserve life; if a branch is lopped off, new branches will shoot out in its place; if a leg in an animal is broken, the bone will reunite; if a muscle is severed, it will grow together; if an artery is obliterated, the neighbouring arteries will enlarge their dimensions, and perform its functions. The Creator, however, not to encourage animals to abuse this benevolent institution, has established pain as an attendant on infringement of the organic law, and made them suffer for the violation of it, even while he restores them. It is under this law that death has received its organic pangs. Instant death is not attended with pain of any perceptible duration; and it is only when a lingering death occurs in youth and middle age, that the suffering is severe; dissolution, however, does not occur at these periods *as a direct and intentional result of the organic laws*, but as the consequence of infringement of them under the fair and legitimate operation of these laws, the individual whose constitution was at first sound, and whose life has been in accordance with their dictates, lives till old age fairly wears out his organized frame, and then the pang of expiration is little perceptible.* The pains of premature death, then, are the punishments of infringement of the organic law, and the object of that chastisement probably is to impress upon us the necessity of obeying them that we may live, and to prevent our abusing the remedial process inherent to a great extent in our constitution.

Let us now view death as an institution appointed to man. If it be true, that the organic constitution of man, when sound in its elements, and preserved in ac-

* The following table is copied from an interesting article by Mr William Fraser, on the History and Constitution of Benefit or Friendly Societies, published in the Edinburgh New Philosophical Journal for October, 1827, and is deduced from Returns by Friendly Societies in Scotland for various years, from 1750 to 1821. It shows how much sickness is dependant on age.

Average Sickness for each Individual.

Age.	Weeks and Decimals.	Weeks.	Days.	Hours.	Proportion of sick members
Under 20	0.3797	0	2	16	1 in 136.95
20–30	0.5916	0	4	3	1 " 87.89
30–40	0.6865	0	4	19	1 " 75.74
40–50	1.0273	1	0	4	1 " 50.61
50–60	1.8806	1	6	3	1 " 27.65
60–70	5.6337	5	4	10	1 " 9.23
Above 70	16.5417	16	3	19	1 " 3.14

cordance with the organic laws, is fairly calculated to endure in health from infancy to old age, and that death when it occurs during the early or middle periods of life, is the consequence of departures from the physical and organic laws, it follows, that, even in premature death, a benevolent principle is discernible. Although the remedial process restores animals from moderate injuries, yet the very nature of the organic law must place a limit to it. If life had been preserved, and health restored, after the brain had been blown to atoms, by a bomb shell, as effectually as a leg that is broken, and a finger that is cut are healed, this would have been an actual abrogation of the organic law; and all the curbs which that law imposes on the lower propensities, and all the incitements which the observance of it affords to the higher sentiments, and intellect, would have been lost. The limit, then, is this; that any departure from the law against which restoration is permitted, shall be moderate in extent, and shall not involve, to a great degree, any organ essential to life, such as the brain, the lungs, the stomach, or intestines. The very maintenance of the law, with all its advantages, requires that restoration from grievous derangement of these organs should not be permitted. When we reflect on the hereditary transmission of qualities to children, we clearly perceive benevolence to the race in the institution, which cuts short the life of an individual in whose person essential organs are so deeply diseased by departures from the organic law, as to be beyond the limits of the remedial process; for the extension of the punishment of his errors over an innumerable posterity is thereby prevented. In premature death, then, we see two objects accomplished; first; the individual sufferer is withdrawn from agonies which could serve no beneficial end to himself; he has transgressed the limits of recovery, and prolonged life would be protracted misery; secondly; the race is guaranteed from the future transmissions of his disease by hereditary descent.

The disciple of Mr Owen, formerly alluded to, who had grievously transgressed the organic law, and suffered a punishment of equal intensity, observed, when in the midst of his agony,—'Philosophers have urged the institution of death, as an argument against divine goodness, but not one of them could experience, for five minutes, the pain which I now endure, without looking upon it as a most merciful arrangement. I have departed from the natural institutions, and suffer the punishment; but, in death, I see only the Creator's benevolent hand, stretched out to terminate my agonies, when they cease to serve any beneficial end.' On this principle, the death of a feeble and sickly child is an act of mercy to it. It withdraws a being, in whose person the organic laws have been violated, from useless suffering; cutting short, thereby, also, the transmission of its imperfections to posterity. If, then, the organic institutions which inflict pain and disease as punishments for transgressing them, are founded in benevolence and wisdom; and, if death, in the early and middle periods of life, is an arrangement for withdrawing the transgressor from farther suffering, after return to obedience is impossible, and protecting the race from the consequences of his errors, it also is in itself wise and benevolent.

This, then, leaves us only death in old age as a natural and unavoidable institution of the Creator. It will not be denied, that, if old persons, when their powers of enjoyment are fairly exhausted, and their cup of pleasure full, could be removed from this world, as we have supposed the lower animals to be, in an instant, and without pain or consciousness, to make way for a fresh and vigorous offspring, about to run the career which the old have terminated, there would be no lack of benevolence and justice in the arrangement. At present, while we live in habitual ignorance and neglect of the organic institutions, death probably comes upon us with more pain and agony, even in advanced life, than might be its legitimate accompaniment, if we placed ourselves in accordance with these; so that we are not now in a condition to ascertain the natural quantum of pain necessarily attendant on death. Judging from analogy, we may conclude, that the close of a long life, founded at first, and afterwards spent, in accordance with the Creator's laws, would not be accompanied with great organic suffering, but that an insensible decay would steal upon the senses. Be this, however, as it may, I observe, in the next place, that as the Creator has bestowed on man animal faculties that fear death, and reason that carries home to him the conviction that he must die, it is an interesting inquiry, Whether he has provided any *natural* means of relief, from the consequences of this combination of terrors? He has bestowed moral sentiments on man, and arranged the whole of his existence on the principles of their supremacy; and these, when duly cultivated and enlightened, are calculated to withdraw from him the terrors of death, in the same manner as unconsciousness of its existence saves the lower animals from its horrors.

In regard to the lower animals killed by violence, if reason sees, on the one hand, a momentary pang in parting with life, it perceives the continued existence and enjoyment of beasts of prey, as an advantage attending it on the other, so that every animal that is devoured ministers to the continued life of another. The process is still one of a transfer of existence.

In regard to man, again, the moral sentiments and intellect perceive,

1st. That Amativeness, Philoprogenitiveness, and Adhesiveness, are provided with direct objects of gratification, in consequence of the institution of death. If the same individuals had lived here for ever, there would have been no field for the enjoyment that flows from the domestic union, and the rearing of offspring. The very institution of these propensities prove, that producing and rearing young, form part of the design of creation; and the successive production of young appears necessarily to imply removal of the old.

2dly. All the other faculties would have been limited in their gratifications. Conceive, for a moment, how much exercise is afforded to our intellectual and moral powers, in acquiring knowledge, communicating it to the young, and in providing for their enjoyments; also, what a delightful exercise of the higher sentiments is implied in the intercourse between the aged and the young; all which pleasures would have been unknown, if there had been no young in existence, which there could not have been, without a succession of individuals.

3dly. Constituted as man is, the succession of individual withdraws beings whose physical and mental constitutions have run their course, and become impaired in sensibility, and substitutes, in their place, fresh and vigorous minds and bodies, far better adapted for the enjoyment of creation.

4thly. If I am right in the position, that the organic laws transmit, in an increasing ratio, the qualities most active in the parents to their offspring, the law of succession provides for a far higher degree of improvement in the race than could ever have been reached by the permanency of a single generation.

Let us inquire, then, how the moral sentiments are affected by death in old age, as a natural institution.

Benevolence, glowing with a disinterested desire for the diffusion and boundless increase of enjoyment, utters no complaint against death in old age, as a transference of existence from a being impaired in its capacity for usefulness and pleasure, to one fresh and vigorous in all its powers, and fitted to carry forward, to a higher point of improvement, every beneficial measure previously begun. Conscientiousness, if thoroughly enlightened, perceives no infringement of justice in a guest, satiated with enjoyment, being called on to retire from the banquet, to permit a stranger with a keener and more youthful appetite to partake; and Veneration, when instructed by intellect that this is the institution of the Creator, and made acquainted with its objects, bows in humble acquiescence to the law. Now, if these powers have acquired, in any individual, that complete supremacy which they are clearly intended to hold, he will be placed by them as much above the terror of death, as a natural institution, as the lower animals are, by being ignorant of its existence. And unless the case were so, man would, by the very knowledge of death, be rendered, during his whole life, more miserable than they.

In these observations, I have said nothing of the prospects of a future existence as a palliative of the evils of dissolution, because I was bound to regard death, in the first instance, as the result of the organic law, and to treat of it as such. But no one who considers that the prospects of a life to come, are directly addressed to Veneration, Hope, Benevolence, and Intellect, can fail to perceive that this consolation also is clearly founded on the principle, that supremacy in the sentiments is intended by the Creator to protect man from its terrors.

The true view of death, then, as a natural institution, is, that it is an essential part of the very system of organization; that birth, growing, and arriving at maturity, as completely imply decay and death in old age, as morning and noon imply evening and night, as spring and summer imply harvest, or as the source of a river implies a termination of it. Besides, organized beings are constituted by the Creator to be the food of other organized beings, so that some must die that others may live. Man, for instance, cannot live on stones, or earth, or water, which are not organized, but on vegetable and animal substances; so that death is as much, and as essentially, an inherent part of organization as life itself. If vegetables, animals, and men, had been destined for a duration like that of the mountains,—instead of creating a primitive pair of each, and endowing these with extensive powers of reproduction, so as to usher into existence young beings to grow up to maturity by insensible degrees, we may presume, from analogy, that the Creator would have furnished the world with its definite compliment of living beings, perfect at first in all their parts and functions, and that these would have remained, like hills, without diminution, and without increase.

To prevent, then, all chance of being misapprehended, I repeat, that I do not at all allude to the state of the soul or mind, after death, but merely to the dissolution of organized bodies; that, according to the soundest views which I am able to obtain of the natural law, pain and death in youth and middle age, in the human species, are consequences of departure from the Creator's laws; while death in old age, by insensible decay, is an essential and apparently indispensable part of the system of organized existence; that this arrangement admits of the succession of individuals, substituting the young and vigorous for the feeble and decayed; that it is directly the means by which organized beings live, and indirectly the means by which Amativeness, Philoprogenitiveness, and a variety of other faculties obtain gratification; that it admits of the race ascending to a great extent in the scale of improvement, both in their organic and mental qualities; that the moral sentiments, when supreme in activity, and enlightened by intellect, so as to perceive its design and consequences, are calculated to place man in harmony with it; while religion addresses its consolation to the same faculties, and completes what reason leaves undone.

If the views now unfolded be correct, death, in old age, will never be abolished, as long as man continues an organized being; but pain and premature death will constantly decrease, in the exact ratio of his obedience to the physical and organic laws. It is interesting to observe, that there is already some evidence of this process being actually in progress. About seventy years ago, tables of the average duration of life, in England, were compiled for the use of the Life Insurance Companies; and from them it appears, that the average of life was then twenty-eight years; that is, 1,000 persons being born, and the years which each of them lived being added together, and divided by 1,000, gave twenty-eight to each. By recent tables, it appears that the average is now thirty-two years to each; that is to say, by superior morality, cleanliness, knowledge, and general obedience to the Creator's institutions, fewer individuals now perish in infancy, youth, and middle age, than did seventy years ago. Some persons have said, that the difference arises from errors in compiling the old tables, and that the superior habits of the people are not the cause. It is probable, however, that there may be a portion of truth in both views. There may be some errors in the old tables, but it is quite natural that increasing knowledge and stricter obedience to the organic laws, should diminish the number of premature deaths. If this idea be correct, the average duration of life should go on increasing; and our successors, two centuries hence, may probably attain to an average of forty years, and then ascribe to errors in our tables our low average of thirty-two.*

SECT. III.—CALAMITIES ARISING FROM INFRINGEMENT OF THE MORAL LAW.

We come now to consider the Moral Law, which is proclaimed by the higher sentiments and intellect acting harmoniously, and holding the animal propensities in subjection. In surveying the moral and religious codes of different nations, and the moral and religious opinions of different philosophers, every reflecting mind must have been struck with their diversity. Phrenology, by demonstrating the differences of combination in their faculties, enables us to account for these varieties of sentiment. The code of morality framed by a legislator, in whom Destructiveness, Secretiveness, Acquisitiveness, and Self-esteem were large, and Conscientiousness, Benevolence, and Veneration small, would be very different from one instituted by another lawgiver, in whom this combination was reversed. In like manner, a system of religion, founded by an individual, in whom Destructiveness, Wonder, and Cautiousness were very large and Veneration, Benevolence, and Conscientiousness deficient, would present views of the Supreme Being widely dissimilar to those which would be promulgated by a person in whom the last three faculties and intellect decidedly predominated. Phrenology shows, that the particular code of morality and religion, *which is most completely in harmony with the whole faculties of the individual*, will necessarily appear to him to be the best, *while he refers only to the dictates of his individual mind, as the standard of right and wrong*. But if we are able to show, that the *whole scheme of external creation is arranged in harmony with certain principles, in preference to others*, so that enjoyment flows upon the individual from without, when his conduct is in conformity with them, and that evil overtakes him when he departs from them, we shall then obviously prove, that the former is the morality and religion established by the Creator; andthat individual men who support different codes, must necessarily be deluded by imperfections in their own minds. That constitution of mind, also, may be pronounced to be the best, which harmonizes most completely with the morality and religion established by the Creator's arrangements. In this view, *morality becomes a science*, and departures from its dic-

* While the above paragraph was in the press, an interesting article on the 'Diminished Mortality in England,' appeared in the Scotsman newspaper, of 16th April, 1828. It coincides with the views of the text; and, as it proceeds on scientific data, it is printed in the Appendix, No. III.

tates may be demonstrated as practical follies, injurious to the real interest and happiness of the individual, just as errors in logic are capable of refutation to the understanding. Before we can be in a condition to perceive this, it is obvious that we must know, first, The nature of man, physical, animal, moral and intellectual; secondly, The relations of the different parts of that nature to each other; and, Thirdly, the relationship of the whole to God and external objects. The present Essay is an attempt, (a very feeble and imperfect one indeed,) to arrive, by the aid of phrenology, at a demonstration of morality as a science. The interests dealt with in the investigation are so elevating, and the effort itself so delightful, that the attempt carries its own reward, however unsuccessful in its results.

Assuming, then, that, among the faculties of the mind, the higher sentiments and intellect hold the natural supremacy, I shall endeavour to show, that obedience to the dictates of these powers is rewarded with pleasing emotions in the mental faculties themselves, and with the most beneficial external consequences; whereas disobedience is followed by deprivation of these emotions, by painful feelings within the mind, and great external evil.

First. Obedience is attended by pleasing emotions in the faculties. It is scarcely necessary to dwell on the circumstance, that every propensity, sentiment, and intellectual faculty, when gratified in harmony with all the rest, is a fountain of pleasure. How many exquisite thrills of joy arise from Philoprogenitiveness, Adhesiveness, Acquisitiveness, Constructiveness, Love of Approbation, and Self-esteem, when gratified in accordance with the moral sentiments; who that has ever poured forth the aspirations of Hope, Ideality, Wonder, and Veneration, directed to an object in whom Intellect and Conscientiousness also rejoiced, has not experienced the deep delight of such an exercise? Or, who is a stranger to the grateful pleasures attending an active Benevolence? Turning to the intellect, again, what pleasures are afforded by the scenery of nature, by painting, poetry, and music, to those who possess the combination of faculties related to these studies? And how rich a feast does not philosophy yield to those who possess high reflecting organs, combined with Concentrativeness and Conscientiousness? The reader is requested, therefore, to keep steadily in view, that these exquisite rewards are attached by the Creator to the active exercise of our faculties, in accordance with the moral law; and that one punishment, clear, obvious, and undeniable, inflicted on those who neglect or infringe the law, is *deprivation* of these pleasures. This is a consideration very little attended to; because mankind, in general, live in such habitual neglect of the moral law, that they have, to a very partial extent, experienced its rewards, and do not know the enjoyment they are deprived of by its infringement. Before its full measure can be judged of, the mind must be instructed in its own constitution, in that of external objects, and in the relationship established between it and them, and between it and the Creator. Until a tolerably distinct perception of these truths is obtained, the faculties cannot enjoy repose, nor act in full vigour or harmony: while, for example, our forefathers regarded the marsh fevers, to which they were subjected, from deficient draining of their fields, and the outrages on person and property, attendant on the wars waged by the English against the Scots, or by one feudal lord against another, even on their own soil, not as punishments for particular infringements of the organic and moral laws, to be removed by obedience to these laws, but as inscrutable dispensations of God's providence, which it behooved them meekly to endure, but not to avert,—so long as such notions were entertained, the full enjoyment which the moral and intellectual faculties were fairly calculated by the Creator to afford, could not be experienced. Benevolence would pine in dissatisfaction; Veneration would flag in its devotions, and Conscientiousness would suggest endless surmises of disorder and injustice in a scheme of creation, under which such evils occurred, and were left without a remedy; the full tide of moral, religious, and intellectual enjoyment could not possibly flow, until views, more in accordance with the constitution and desires of the moral faculties were obtained. The same evil afflicts mankind still to a prodigious extent. How is it possible for the Hindoo, Mussulman, Chinese, or the native American, while they continue to worship deities, whose qualities outrage Benevolence, Veneration, and Conscientiousness,—and remain in profound ignorance of almost all the Creator's natural institutions, in consequence of infringing which they suffer punishment without ceasing, to form even a conception of the gratifications which the moral and intellectual nature of man is calculated to enjoy, when exercised in harmony with the Creator's real character and institutions? This operation of the moral is not the less real, because many do not recognise it. Sight is not a less excellent gift to those who see, because some men born blind have no conception of the extent of pleasure and advantage from which the want of it cuts them off.

The qualities manifested by the Creator may be inferred from the works of creation; but it is obvious, that, to arrive at the soundest views, we would require to know his institutions thoroughly. To a grossly ignorant people, who suffer hardly from transgression of his laws, the Deity will appear infinitely more severe and mysterious than to an enlightened nation who know them, avoid the penalties of infringement, and trace the principles of his government through many parts of his works. The character of the Divine Being, under the natural system, will thus go on rising in exact proportion as his works shall be understood. The low and miserable conceptions of God formed by the vulgar Greeks and Romans, were the reflections of their own ignorance of natural, moral, and political science. The discovery and improvement of phrenology must necessarily have a great effect on natural religion. Before phrenology was known, the moral and intellectual constitution of man was unascertained;—in consequence, the relations of external nature towards it could not be competently judged of; and, while these were involved in obscurity, many of the ways of Providence must have appeared mysterious and severe, which in themselves are quite the reverse. Again, as bodily suffering and mental perplexity would bear a proportion to this ignorance, the character of God would appear to the natural eye in that condition, much more unfavorable than it will do after these clouds of darkness shall have passed away.

Some persons, in their great concernment about a future life, are liable to overlook the practical direction of the mind in the present. When we consider the nature and objects of the mental faculties, we perceive that a great number of them have the most obvious and undeniable reference to this life; for example, Amativeness, Philoprogenitiveness, Combativeness, Destructiveness, Acquisitiveness, Secretiveness, Cautiousness, Self-esteem, and Love of Approbation, with Size, Form, Colour, Weight, Tune, Wit, and probably other faculties, stand in such evident relationship to this particular world, with its moral and physical arrangements, that if they were not capable of legitimate application here, it would be difficult to assign a reason for their being bestowed on us. We possess also Benevolence, Veneration, Hope, Ideality, Wonder, Conscientiousness, and Reflecting Intellect, all of which appear to be particularly adapted to a higher sphere. But the important consideration is, that here on earth these two sets of faculties are combined; and on the same principle that led Sir Isaac Newton to infer the combustibility of the diamond, I am disposed to expect that the external world, when its constitution and relations shall be sufficiently understood, will be found to be in harmony with all our faculties, and of course that the character of the Deity, as unfolded by the works of creation, will more and more gratify our moral and intellectual powers, in proportion as knowledge advances. The structure of the eye is admirably adapted to the laws of light; that of the ear to the laws of sound; that of the muscles to the laws of gravitation; and it would be strange if our mental constitution was not as wisely adapted to the general order of the external world.

This principle, then, is universal, and admits of no exception, That inactivity and want of power, in every faculty, is attended with deprivation of the pleasures attendant on its vivacious exercise. He who is so deficient in Tune that he cannot distinguish melody, is cut off from a vast source of gratification enjoyed by him who possesses that organ vigorous and highly cultivated; and the same principle holds in the case of every other organ and faculty. Criminals and profligates of every description, therefore, from the very constitution of human nature, are excluded from great enjoyments attending virtue; and this is the first natural punishment to which they are inevitably liable. Persons also, who are ignorant of the constitutions of their own minds, and the relations between external objects, not only suffer many direct evils on this account; but, through, the consequent inactivity of their faculties, are besides, deprived of many exalted enjoyments. The works of creation, and the character of the Deity, are the legitimate objects of our highest powers; and hence he who is blind to their qualities loses nearly the whole benefit of his moral and intellectual existence. If there is any one to whom these gratifications are unknown, or appear trivial, he must either, to a very considerable degree, be still under the dominion of the animal propensities, or his views of the Creator's character and institutions, must not be in harmony with the natural dictates of the moral sentiments and intellect.

But in the second place, as the world is arranged on the principle of the supremacy of the moral sentiments and intellect, observance of the moral law is attended with external advantages, and infringement of it with positive evil consequences; and, from this constitution, arises the second natural punishment of misconduct.

Let us trace the advantages of obedience.—In the domestic circle; if we preserve habitually Benevolence, Conscientiousness, Veneration, and Intellect supreme, it is quite undeniable, that we shall raise the moral and intellectual faculties of children, servants, and assistants, to love us, and to yield us willing service, obedience, and aid. Our commands will then be reasonable, mild, and easily executed, and the commerce will be that of love. With our equals, again, in society, what would we not give for a friend in whom we were perfectly convinced of the supremacy of the sentiments: what love, confidence, and delight, would we not repose in him? To a merchant, physician, lawyer, magistrate, or an individual in any public employment, how invaluable would be the habitual supremacy of the sentiments? The Creator has given different talents to different individuals, and limited our powers, so that we execute any work best by confining our attention to one department of labour,—an arrangement which amounts to a direct institution of separate trades and professions. Under the natural laws, then, the manufacturer may pursue his calling with the entire approbation of all the moral sentiments, for he is dedicating his talents to supply the wants of his fellow men; and how much more successful will he not be, if his every wish is accompanied by the desire to act benevolently and honestly towards those who are to consume and pay for the products of his labour? He cannot gratify his Acquisitiveness half so successfully by any other method. The same remark applies to the merchant, the lawyer, and physician. The lawyer and physician, whose whole spirits breathe a disinterested desire to consult, as a paramount object, the best interests of their clients and patients, not only obtain the direct reward of gratifying their own moral faculties, which is no slight enjoyment, but they reap a positive gratification to their Self-esteem and Love of Approbation, in a high and well-founded reputation, and to their Acquisitiveness, in increasing emolument, not grudgingly paid, but willingly offered, from minds that feel the worth of the services bestowed.

There are three conditions required by the moral and intellectual law, which must all be observed to ensure its rewards; 1st. The department of industry selected must be really useful to human beings: Benevolence demands this; 2dly. The quantum of labor bestowed must bear a just proportion to the natural demand for the commodity produced: Intellect requires this; and, 3dly. In our social connexions, we must imperatively attend to the organic law, that different individuals possess different developments of the brain, and in consequence different natural talents and dispositions, and we must rely on each only to the extent warranted by his natural endowment.

If, then, an individual has received, at birth, a sound organic constitution, and favourably developed brain, and if he live in accordance with the physical, the organic, the moral, and intellectual laws, it appears to me that, in the constitution of the world, he has received an assurance from the Creator, of provision for his animal wants, and a high enjoyment in the legitimate exercise of his various mental powers.

I have already observed, that, before we can obey the Creator's institutions, we must know them, and that the science which teaches the physical laws, is natural philosophy; that the organic laws belong to the department of anatomy and physiology; and I now add, that it is the business of the political economist to unfold the kinds of industry that are really necessary to the welfare of mankind, and the degrees of labour that will meet with a just reward. The leading object of political economy, as a science, is to increase enjoyment, by directing the application of industry. To attain this end however, it is obviously necessary that the nature of man,—the constitution of the physical world,—and the relations between these, should be known. Hitherto, the knowledge of the first of these elementary parts has been very deficient, and, in consequence, the whole superstructure has been weak and unproductive, in comparison of what it may become, when founded on a more perfect basis. Political economists have never dreamt, that the world is arranged on the principle of supremacy of the moral sentiments and intellect; and, consequently, that, to render man happy, *his leading pursuits must be such as will exercise and gratify these powers*, and that his life will necessarily be miserable, if devoted entirely to the production of wealth. They have proceeded on the notion, that the accumulation of wealth is the *summum bonum*; but all history teaches, that national happiness does not increase in proportion to national riches; and until they shall perceive and teach, that intelligence and morality are the foundation of all lasting prosperity, they will never interest the great body of mankind, nor give a valuable direction to their efforts.

If the views contained in the present Essay be sound, it will become a leading object with future masters in that science, to demonstrate the necessity of civilized man limiting his physical, and increasing his moral and intellectual occupations, as the only means of saving himself from ceaseless punishment under the natural laws.

The idea of men, in general, being taught natural philosophy, anatomy, and physiology, political economy, and the other sciences that expound the natural laws, has been sneered at, as utterly absurd and ridiculous.

But I would ask, in what occupations are human beings so urgently engaged, that they *have no leisure* to bestow on the study of the Creator's laws? A course of natural philosophy would occupy sixty or seventy hours in the delivery; a course of anatomy and physiology the same; and a course of phrenology can be delivered pretty fully in forty hours! These, twice or thrice repeated, would serve to initiate the student so that he could afterwards advance in the same paths, by the aid of observation and books. Is life, then, so brief, and are our hours so urgently occupied by higher and more important duties, that we cannot afford those pittances of time to learn the laws that regulate our existence! No. The only difficulty is in obtaining the *desire* for the knowledge; in seeing the necessity and advantage of it, and then time will not be wanting. No idea can be more preposterous, than that of human beings having no time to study and obey the natural institutions. These laws punish so severely, when neglected, that they cause the offender to lose tenfold more time in undergoing his chastisement, than would be requisite to obey them. A gentleman extensively engaged in business, whose nervous and digestive systems had been impaired by neglect of the organic laws, was desired to walk in the open air at least one hour a-day; to repose from all exertion, bodily and mental, for one full hour after breakfast, and another full hour after dinner, because the brain cannot expend its energy in thinking and in aiding digestion at the same time; and to practise moderation in diet; which last he regularly observed; but he laughed at the very idea of his having three hours a-day to spare for attention to his health. The reply was, that the organic laws admit of no exception, and that he must either obey them, or take the consequences; but that the time lost by the punishment would be double or treble that requisite for obedience; and, accordingly, the fact was so. Instead of his attending an appointment, it is quite usual for him to send a note, perhaps, at two in the afternoon, in these terms:—'I was so distressed with headache last night, that I never closed my eyes, and to-day I am still incapable of being out of bed.' On other occasions, he is out of bed, but apologizes for incapacity to attend to business, on account of an intolerable pain in the region of the stomach. In short, if the hours lost in these painful sufferings were added together, and distributed over the days when he is able for duty, he would find them far outnumber those which would suffice for obedience to the organic laws, and with this difference in the results; by neglect he loses both his hours and his enjoyment; whereas, by obedience, he would be rewarded by aptitude for business, and a pleasing consciousness of existence.

We shall understand the operation of the moral and intellectual laws, however, more completely, by attending to the evils which arise from neglect of them.

As to Individuals. At present, the almost universal persuasion of civilized man, is, that happiness consists in the possession of wealth, power, and external splendor; objects related to the animal faculties and intellect much more than to the moral sentiments. In consequence, each individual sets out in the pursuit of these as the chief business of his life; and, in the ardour of the chase, he recognizes no limitations on the means which he may employ, except those imposed by the municipal law. He does not perceive or acknowledge the existence of natural laws, determining not only the sources of his happiness, but the steps by which it may be attained. From this moral and intellectual blindness, merchants and manufacturers, in numberless instances, hasten to be rich beyond the course of nature; that is to say, they engage in enterprises far exceeding the extent of their capital, or capacity; they place their property in the hands of debtors, whose natural talents and morality are so low, that they ought never to have been trusted with a shilling; they send their goods to sea without insuring them, or leave them uninsured in their own warehouses; they ask pecuniary accommodation from other merchants to enable them to carry on their undue speculations, and become security for them in return, and both fall in consequence of blindly following Acquisitiveness to extremities; or they live in splendor and extravagance, far beyond the extent of the natural return of their capital and talents. In every one of these instances, the calamity is obviously the consequence of infringement of the moral and intellectual law. The lawyer, medical practitioner, or probationer in the church, who is disappointed in his reward, will be found erroneously to have placed himself in a profession, for which his natural talents and dispositions did not fit him, or to have pursued his vocation under the guidance chiefly of the lower propensities, preferring selfishness to honorable regard for the interests of his employers. Want of success in these professions, appears to me to be owing, in a high degree, to three causes; first, The brain being too small, or constitutionally lymphatic, so that the mind does not act with sufficient energy to make an impression; secondly, some particular organs indispensably requisite to success, being very deficient, as Language, or Causality, in a lawyer, the first rendering him incapable of ready utterance, and the second destitute of that intuitive sagacity, which sees at a glance the bearing of the facts and principles founded on by his adversary, so as to estimate the just inferences that follow, and to point them out. A lawyer, who is weak in this power, appears to his client like a pilot who does not know the shoals and the rocks. His deficiency is perceived whenever difficulty presents itself, and he is pronounced unsafe to take charge of great interests; he is then passed by, and suffers the responsibility of an erroneous choice of profession; or, thirdly, Predominance of the animal and selfish faculties. The client and the patient discriminate instinctively between the cold, pithless, but pretending manner of Acquisitiveness and Love of Approbation, and the unpretending, genuine warmth of Benevolence, Veneration, and Conscientiousness; and they discover very speedily that the intellect inspired by the latter sees more clearly, and manages more successfully, their interests, than when animated only by the former; the victim of selfishness either never rises, or sinks, wondering why his merits are neglected.

In all these instances, the failure of the merchant, and the bad success of the lawyer, &c. are the consequences of having infringed the natural laws; so that the evil they suffer is the punishment for having failed in a great duty, not only to society, but to themselves.

The greatest difficulties, however, present themselves, in tracing the operation of the moral and intellectual laws, in the wide field of social life. An individual may be made to comprehend how, if he commits an error, he should suffer a particular punishment; but when calamity overtakes whole classes of the community, each person absolves himself from all share of the blame, and regards himself as simply the victim of general but inscrutable visitation. Let us, then, examine briefly the Social Law.

In regarding the human faculties, we perceive that numberless gratifications spring from the social state. The muscles of a single individual could not rear the habitations, build the ships, forge the anchors, construct the machinery, or, in short, produce the countless enjoyments that every where surround us, in consequence of men being constituted, so as instinctively to combine their powers and skill, to obtain a common end. Here, then, are prodigious advantages resulting directly from the social law; but, in the next place, social intercourse is the means of affording direct gratification to a variety of our mental faculties. If we live in solitude, the propensities of Amativeness, Philoprogenitiveness, Adhesiveness, Love of Approbation, the sentiments of Benevolence, Veneration, Conscientiousness, Wonder, Language, and the reflecting faculties, would be deprived, some of them absolutely, and others of them nearly, of all opportunities of gratification. The social law, then, is the source of the highest delights of our nature, and its institution indicates the greatest benevolence and wisdom towards us, in the Creator.

Still, however, this law does not suspend or subvert the laws instituted for man as an individual. If we imagine an individual to go to sea for his own gratification in a ship, the natural laws require that his intellectual faculties shall be instructed in navigation, also in the nature of the coasts and seas which he traverses; that he shall know and avoid the shoals, currents, and eddies; that he shall trim his canvass in proportion to the gale; and that his animal faculties shall be so much under subjection to his moral sentiments, that he shall not abandon himself to drunkenness, sloth, or any animal indulgence, when the natural laws, require him to be watchful at his duty. If he obey the natural laws, he will be safe as an individual; and if he disobey them he will be drowned.* Now, if a crew, and passengers desire to avail themselves of the social law, that is, to combine their powers and activity under one leader or chief, by doing which they may sail in a large ship, have ample stores of provisions, divide their labour, enjoy each other's society, &c.; and if at the same time they fulfil the moral and intellectual laws, by placing, in the situation of captain, an individual fully qualified for that duty, they will enjoy the reward in sailing safely, and in comfort; if they disregard these laws, and place an individual in charge of the ship, whose intellectual faculties are weak, whose animal propensities are strong, whose moral sentiments are in abeyance, and who, in consequence, habitually neglects the natural laws, then they will suffer the penalty in being wrecked.

I know it will be objected that the crew and passengers do not appoint the captain; but, in every case, except impressment in the British navy, they may go in, or stay out, of a particular ship, as they discover the captain to possess the natural qualities or not. This, at present, I am aware, ninety-nine individuals out of the hundred never inquire into; but so do ninety-nine out of the hundred neglect many of the other natural laws, and suffer the penalty, because their moral and intellectual faculties have never yet been instructed in their existence and effects, or trained to observe and obey them. But they have the power from nature of obeying them, if properly taught and trained; and, besides, I give this merely as an illustration of the mode of operation of the social law.

Another example may be given. By employing servants, the labours of life are rendered less burdensome to the master; but he must employ individuals who know the moral law, and who possess the desire to act under it; otherwise, as a punishment for neglecting this requisite, he may be robbed, cheated, or murdered in bed. Phrenology presents the means of observing this law, in a degree quite unattainable without it, by the facility which it affords of discovering the natural talents and dispositions of individuals.

By entering into copartnerships, merchants, and other persons in business, may extend their employment, and gain advantages beyond those they could reap, if labouring as individuals. But, by the natural law, each must take care that his partner knows, and is inclined to obey, the moral and intellectual law, as the only condition on which the Creator will permit him *securely* to reap the *advantages* of the social compact. If a partner in China is deficient in intellect and moral sentiments, another in London may be utterly ruined. It is said that this is the innocent suffering for or along with the guilty; but it is not so. It is an example of a person seeking to obtain the *advantages* of the social law, without conceiving himself bound to obey the conditions required by it; the first of which is, that those individuals, of whose services he avails himself, shall observe the moral and intellectual laws.

Let us now advert to the calamities which overtake whole classes of men, or COMMUNITIES, under the social law, trace their origin, and see how far they are attributable to infringement of the Creator's laws.

If I am right in representing the whole faculties of man as intended by the Creator to be gratified, and the moral sentiments and intellect, as the higher and directing powers, with which all natural institutions are in harmony; it follows, that if large communities of men, in their systematic conduct, habitually seek the gratification of the inferior propensities, and allow either no part, or too small and inadequate a part, of their time to the regular employment of the higher powers, they will act in direct opposition to the natural institutions; and will, of course, suffer the punishment in sorrow and dissapointment. Now, to confine ourselves to our own country, it is certain that, until within these few years, the labouring population of Britain were not taught that it was any part of their duty, as rational creatures, to restrain their propensities, so as not to multiply their numbers beyond the demand for their labours, and the supply of food for their offspring; and up to the present hour this most obvious and important doctrine is not admitted by one in a thousand, and not acted upon as a practical principle by one in ten thousand of those whose happiness or misery depends on observance of it. The doctrine of Malthus, that 'population cannot go on perpetually increasing, without pressing on the limits of the means of subsistence, and that a check of some kind or other must, sooner or latter, be opposed to it,' just amounts to this,—that the means of subsistence are not susceptible of such rapid and unlimited increase as population, and in consequence that the Amative propensity must be restrained by reason, otherwise it will be checked by misery. This principle is in accordance with the views of human nature maintained in this Essay, and applies to all the faculties; thus Philoprogenitiveness, when indulged in opposition to reason, leads to spoiling children, which is followed directly by misery both to them and their parents. Acquisitiveness, when uncontrolled by reason, leads to avarice or theft, and these again carry suffering in their train.

But so far from attending to such views, the lives of the inhabitants of Britain generally are devoted to the acquisition of wealth, of power and distinction, or of animal pleasure; in other words, the great object of the labouring classes, is to live and gratify the inferior propensities; of the mercantile and manufacturing population, to gratify Acquisitiveness and Self-esteem; of the more intelligent class of gentlemen, to gratify Self-esteem and Love of Approbation, in political, literary or philosophical eminence; and of another portion, to gratify Love of Approbation, by supremacy in fashion; and these gratifications are sought by means not in accordance with the dictates of the higher sentiments, but by the joint aid of the intellect and propensities. If the supremacy of moral sentiment and intellect be the natural law, then, as often observed, every circumstance connected with human life must be in harmony with it; that is to say, first, After rational restraint on population, and with the proper use of machinery, such moderate labour as will leave ample time for the systematic exercise of the higher powers, will suffice to provide for human wants: and, secondly, If this exercise be neglected, and the time which ought to be dedicated to it be employed in labour to gratify the propensities, direct evil will ensue; and this accordingly appears to me to be exactly the result.

* I waive at present the question of storms, which he could not foresee, as these fall under the head of ignorance of natural laws, which may be subsequently discovered

By means of machinery, and the aids derived from science, the ground can be cultivated, and every imaginable necessary and luxury produced in ample abundance, by a moderate expenditure of labour by any population not in itself superabundant. If men were to stop whenever they had reached this point, and dedicate the residue of each day to moral and intellectual pursuits, the consequence would be, ready and steady because not overstocked, markets. Labour, pursued till it provided abundance, but not redundant superfluity, would meet with a certain and just reward: and would yield also, a vast increase of happiness; for no joy equals that which springs from the moral sentiments and intellect excited by the contemplation, pursuit, and observance, of the Creator's institutions. Farther, morality would be improved; for men being happy, would cease to be vicious; and, lastly, There would be improvement in the organic, moral, and intellectual capabilities of the race; for the active moral and intellectual organs in the parents would increase the volume of these in their offspring; so that each generation would start not only with greater stores of acquired knowledge than their predecessors possessed, but with higher natural capabilities of turning these to account.

Before merchants and manufacturers can be expected to act in this manner, a great change must be effected in their sentiments and perceptions; but so was a striking revolution effected in their ideas and practices of the tenantry west of Edinburgh, when they removed the stagnant pools between each ridge of land, and banished ague from their district. If any reader will compare the state of Scotland during the thirteenth, fourteenth, and fifteenth centuries, correctly and spiritedly represented in Sir Walter Scott's Tales of a Grandfather, with its present condition, in regard to knowledge, morality, religion, and the comparative ascendency of the rational over the animal part of our nature, he will perceive so great an improvement in later times, that the commencement of the millennium itself, in five or six hundred years hence, would scarce be a greater advance beyond the present, than the present is over the past. If the laws of the Creator be really what are here represented, and if they were once taught as elementary truths to every class of the community, and the sentiment of Veneration called in to enforce obedience to them, a set of new motives and principles would be brought into play, calculated to accelerate the change; especially if it were seen, what, in the next place, I proceed to show, that the consequences of neglecting these laws are the most serious visitations of suffering that can well be imagined. The labouring population of Britain is taxed with exertion for ten, twelve, and some even fourteen hours a day, exhausting their muscular and nervous energy, so as utterly to incapacitate them, and leaving, besides, no leisure; for moral and intellectual pursuits. The consequence of this is, that all markets are overstocked with produce; prices first fall ruinously low; the operatives are then thrown idle, and left in destitution of the necessaries of life, until the surplus produce of their formerly excessive labours, and perhaps something more, are consumed; after this takes place, prices rise too high in consequence of the supply falling rather below the demand; the labourers resume their toil, on their former system of excessive exertion; they again overstock the market, and again are thrown idle, and suffer dreadful misery.

In 1825-6-7 we witnessed this operation of the natural laws: large bodies of starving and unemployed labourers were then supported on charity. How many hours did they not stand idle, and how much of excessive toil would not these hours have relieved, if distributed over the periods when they were overworked? The results of that excessive exertion were seen in the form of untenanted houses, of shapeless piles of goods decaying in warehouses, in short, in every form in which misapplied industry could go to ruin. These observations are strikingly illustrated by the following official report, copied from the public newspapers:

'State of the Unemployed Operatives, resident in Edinburgh, who are supplied with work by a Committee, constituted for that purpose, according to a list made up on Wednesday, the 14th March, 1827.

'The number of unemployed operatives who have been remitted by the Committee for work, up to the 14th of March, are	1481
'And the number of cases they have rejected, after having been particularly investigated, for being bad characters, giving in false statements, or being only a short time out of work, &c. &c. are	446
Making together,	1927

'Besides those, several hundred have been rejected by the Committee, as, from the applicants's *own* statements, they were not considered as cases entitled to receive relief, and were not, therefore, remitted for investigation.

'The wages allowed is 5s. per week, with a peck of meal to those who have families. Some youths are only allowed 3s. of wages.

'The particular occupations of those sent to work are as follows:—242 masons, 634 labourers, 66 joiners, 19 plasterers, 76 sawyers, 19 slaters, 45 smiths, 40 painters, 36 tailors, 55 shoe makers, 20 gardeners, 229 various trades. Total 1481.'

Edinburgh is not a manufacturing city, and if so much misery existed in it in proportion to its population, what must have been the condition of Glasgow, Manchester, and other manufacturing towns?*

Here, then, the Creator's laws show themselves paramount, even when men set themselves systematically to infringe them. He intended the human race, under the moral law, not to pursue Acquisitiveness excessively, but to labour only a certain and a moderate portion of their lives; and although they do their utmost to defeat this intention, they cannot succeed; they are constrained to remain idle as many days and hours, while their surplus produce is consuming, as would have served for the due exercise of their moral and intellectual faculties and the preservation of their health, if they had dedicated them regularly to these ends from day to day, as time passed over their heads. But their punishment proceeds: the extreme exhaustion of nervous and muscular energy, with the absence of all moral and intellectual excitement, create the excessive craving for the stimulus of ardent spirits which distinguishes the labouring population of the present age; this calls into predominant activity the organs of the Animal Propensities, these descend to the children by the law already explained; increased crime, and a deteriorating population, are the results: and a moral and intellectual incapacity for arresting the evils, becomes greater with the lapse of every generation.

According to the principles of the present Essay, what are called by commercial men 'times of prosperity,' are seasons of the greatest infringement of the natural laws, and precursors of great calamities. Times are not reckoned prosperous, unless *all* the industrious population is employed during *the whole day*, hours of eating and sleeping only excepted, in the production of *wealth*. This is a dedication of their whole lives to the service of the propensities, and must necessarily terminate in punishment, if the world is constituted on the principle of supremacy of the higher powers.

This truth has already been illustrated more than once in the history of commerce. The following is a resent example.

By the combination laws, workmen were punishable for uniting to obtain a rise of wages, when an extraordinary demand occurred for their labour. These laws being obviously unjust, were at length repealed. In summer and autumn 1825, however, commercial men conceived themselves to have reached the highest point of prosperity, and the demand for labour was unlimited. The operatives availed themselves of the opportunity to better their condition formed extensive combinations; and because their demands were not complied with,

*In the Appendix, No. IV, several interesting documents are given, in further elucidation of these principles.

struck work, and continued idle for months in succession. The master manufacturers clamoured against the new law, and complained that the country would be ruined, if combinations were not again declared illegal, and suppressed by force. According to the principles of this Essay, the just law must from the first have been *the most beneficial for all parties* affected by it; and the result amply confirmed this idea. Subsequent events proved that the extraordinary demand for labourers in 1825 was entirely factitious, fostered, by an overwhelming issue of bank paper, much of which ultimately turned out to be worthless; in short, that, during the combinations, the master manufacturers were engaged in an extensive system of speculative over-production, and that the combinations of the workmen presented a *natural check* to this erroneous proceeding. The ruin that overtook the masters in 1826 arose from their having accumulated, under the influence of unbridled Acquisitiveness, vast stores of commodities which were not required by society; and to have compelled labourers, by force, to manufacture more at their bidding, would obviously have been to aggravate the evil. It is a well known fact, accordingly, that those masters whose operatives most resolutely refused to work, and who, on this account clamoured loudest against the law, were the greatest gainers in the end. Their stock of goods were sold out at high prices during the speculative period; and when the revulsion came, instead of being ruined by the fall of property, they were prepared, with their capitals at command, to avail themselves of the depreciation, to make new and highly profitable investments. Here again, therefore, we perceive the law of justice vindicating itself and benefiting by its operation even those individuals who blindly denounced it as injurious to their interests. A practical faith in the doctrine that the world is arranged by the Creator, in harmony with the moral sentiments and intellect, would be of unspeakable advantage both to rulers and subjects; for they would then be able to pursue with greater confidence the course dictated by moral rectitude, convinced that the result would prove beneficial, even although, when they took the first step, they could not distinctly perceive by what means.

In the whole system of education and treatment of the labouring population, the laws of the Creator such as I have now endeavoured to expound them, are neglected, and their moral and intellectual cultivation is scarcely known. The Schools of Art, and 'the Library of Useful Knowledge,' are laudable attempts at a better order of things; and I hail with joy their increase; but they too much exclude the science of human nature, and in consequence, will long remain comparatively barren. From indications which already appear, however, I think it probable that the labouring classes will ere long recognise Phrenology, and the natural laws, as deeply interesting to themselves; and whenever their minds shall be opened to rational views of their own constitution as men, and their condition as members of society, I venture to predict that they will devote themselves to improvement, with a zeal and earnestness that in a few generations will change the aspect of their class.

The consequences of the present system of departing from the moral law, on the middle orders of the community, are in accordance with its effects on the lower. Uncertain gains, continual fluctuations in fortune, absence of all reliance on moral and intellectual principles in their pursuits, a gambling spirit, an insatiable appetite for wealth, alternately extravagant joys of excessive prosperity and bitter miseries of disappointed ambition, render the whole lives of merchants vanity and vexation of spirit. Nothing is more essential to human happiness than fixed principles of action, on which we can rely for our present safety and future welfare; and the Creator's laws when seen and followed, afford this support and delight to our faculties in the highest degree. It is one, not of the least, of the punishments that overtake the middling classes for neglect of these laws, that they do not, as a permanent condition of mind, feel secure and internally at peace with themselves. When the excitement of business has subsided, vacuity and craving are felt within. These proceed from the moral and intellectual faculties calling aloud for exercise; but, through ignorance of their own nature, fashionable amusements, or intoxicating liquors, are resorted to, and, with these, a vain attempt is made to fill up the void of life. I know that this class ardently desires a change that would remove the miseries described, and will zealously co-operate in the diffusing of knowledge, by which means alone it can be introduced.

The responsibility which overtakes the higher classes is equally obvious. If they do not engage in some active pursuits, so as to give scope to their energies, they suffer the evils of ennui, morbid irritability, and excessive relaxation of the functions of mind and body, which carry in their train more suffering than is entailed even on the operatives by excessive labour. If they pursue ambition in the senate or in the field, or in literature or philosophy, their real success is in exact proportion to the approach which they make to observance of the supremacy of the sentiments and intellect. Franklin, Washington, and Bolivar, may be contrasted with Sheridan, and Bonaparte, as illustrations. Sheridan and Napoleon did not, systematically, pursue objects sanctioned by the higher sentiments and intellect as the end of their exertions; and no person, who is a judge of human emotions, can read their lives, and consider what must have passed within their minds, without coming to the conclusion, that, even in their most brilliant moments of external prosperity, the canker was gnawing within, and that there was no moral relish of the present or reliance on the future; but a mingled tumult of inferior propensities and intellect, carrying with it an habitual feeling of unsatisfied desires.

Let us now consider the effect of the moral law on NATIONAL prosperity.

If the Creator has constituted the world in harmony with the dictates of the higher sentiments, the highest prosperity of each particular nation should be thoroughly compatible with that of every other; that is to say, England, by sedulously cultivating her own soil, pursuing her own courses of industry, founding her internal institutions and her external relations on the principles of Benevolence, Veneration, and Justice, which imply abstinence from wars of aggression, from conquest, and from all selfish designs of commercial monopoly, would be in the highest condition of prosperity and enjoyment that nature would admit of; and every step that she deviated from these principles, would carry an inevitable punishment along with it. The same statement might be made relative to France and every other nation. According to this principle, also, the Creator should have conferred on each nation some peculiar advantages of soil, climate, situation, or genius, which would enable it to carry on amicable intercourse with its fellow states, in a beneficial exchange of the products peculiar to each; so that the higher one rose in morality, intelligence, and riches, it ought to become so much the more estimable and valuable as a neighbour to all the surrounding states. This is so obviously the real constitution of nature, that proof of it is superfluous.

England, however, as a nation, has set this law at absolute defiance. She has led the way in taking the propensities as her guides, in founding her laws and institutions on them, and in following them out in her practical conduct. England invented restrictions on trade, and carried them to the greatest height; she conquered colonies, and ruled them in the full spirit of selfishness; she encouraged lotteries, and fostered the slave trade, carried paper money and the most avaricious spirit of manufacturing and speculating in commerce to their highest pitch; defended corruption in Parliament, distributed churches and seats on the bench of justice, on principles purely selfish; all in direct opposition to the supremacy of the moral law. If the world had been created in harmony with predominance of the animal faculties, England should have been a most felicitous nation; but as the reverse is the case, we should expect a severe national responsibility to flow from these departures from the divine institutions; and grievous accordingly has been, and, I fear, will be, the punishment.

The principle which regulates national responsibility is, that the precise combination of faculties which leads to the national transgression, carries in its train the punishment. Nations are under the moral and intellectual law, as well as individuals. A carter who half starves his horse, and unmercifully beats it, to supply, by the stimulous of pain, the vigour that nature intended to flow from abundance of food, may be supposed to practise this barbarity with impunity in this world, if he evade the eye of Mr Martin, and that of the police; but this is not the case. The hand of Providence reaches him by a direct punishment: He fails in his object, for blows cannot supply the vigour which, by the constitution of the horse, flows only from sufficiency of wholesome food. In his conduct he manifests an excessive Combativeness and Destructiveness, with deficient Benevolence, Veneration, Justice, and Intellect, and he cannot reverse this character, by merely averting his eyes and his hand from the horse. He carries these dispositions into the bosom of his family, and into the company of his associates, and a variety of evil consequences ensue. The delights that spring from active moral sentiments and intellectual powers are necessarily unknown to him; and the difference between these pleasures, and the sensations attendant on his moral and intellectual condition, are as great as between the external splendour of a king and the naked poverty of a beggar. It is true that he has never felt the enjoyment, and does not know the extent of his loss; but still the difference exists; *we* see it, and know that, as a direct consequence of this state of mind, he is excluded from a very great and exalted pleasure. Farther; his active animal faculties rouse the Combativeness, Destructiveness, Self-esteem, Secretiveness, and Cautiousness, of his wife, children, and associates, against him, and they inflict on him animal punishment. He, no doubt, goes on to eat, drink, blaspheme, and abuse his horse, day after day, apparently as if Providence approved of his conduct; but he neither feels, nor can any one who attends to his condition believe him to feel, *happy;* he is uneasy, discontented, and disliked,—all which sensations are his punishment, and it is fairly owing to his own grossness and ignorance that he does not connect it with his offence. Let us apply these remarks to nations. England, for instance, under the impulses of an excessively strong Acquisitiveness, Self-esteem, and Destructiveness, for a long time protected the slave trade. Now, according to the law which I am explaining, during the periods of greatest sin in this respect, the same combination of faculties ought to be found working most vigorously in her other institutions, and producing punishment for that offence. There ought to be found in these periods a general spirit of domineering and rapacity in her public men, rendering them little mindful of the welfare of the people; injustice and harshness in her taxations and public laws; and a spirit of aggression and hostility towards other nations, provoking retaliation of her insults. And, accordingly, I have been informed, as a matter of fact, that, while these measures of injustice were publicly patronised by the government, its servants vied with each other in injustice towards it, and that its subjects dedicated their talents and enterprise towards corrupting its officers, and cheating it of its due. Every trader who was liable to excise or custom duties, evaded the one-half of them, and felt no disgrace in doing so. A gentleman, who was subject to the excise laws fifty years ago, described to me the condition of his trade at that time. The excise officers, he said, regarded it as an understood matter, that at least one-half of the goods manufactured were to be smuggled without being charged with duty; but then, said he, 'they made us pay a moral and pecuniary penalty that was at once galling and debasing. We required to ask them to our table at all meals, and place them at the head of it in our holiday parties; when they fell into debt, we were obliged to help them out of it; when they moved from one house to another, our servants and carts were in requisition to perform this office; and, by way of keeping up discipline upon us, and also to make a show of duty, they chose every now and then to step in and detect us in a fraud, and get us fined; if we submitted quietly, they told us that they would make us amends, by winking at another fraud; and generally did so; but if our indignation rendered passive obedience impossible, and we spoke our mind of their character and conduct, they enforced the law on *us*, while they relaxed it on our neighbours; and these being rivals in trade, undersold us in the market, carried away our customers, and ruined our business. Nor did the bondage end here. We could not smuggle without the aid of our servants; and as they could, on occasion of any offence given to themselves, carry information to the head quarters of excise, we were slaves to them also, and were obliged tamely to submit to a degree of drunkenness and insolence, that appears to me now perfectly intolerable. Farther; this evasion and oppression did us no good; for all the trade were alike, and we just sold our goods so much cheaper the more duty we evaded; so that our individual success did not depend upon superior skill and superior morality, in making an excellent article at a moderate price, but upon superior capacity for fraud, meanness, sycophancy, and every possible baseness. Our lives were any thing but enviable. Conscience, although greatly blunted by practices that were universal, and viewed as inevitable, still whispered that they were wrong; our sentiments of self-respect very frequently revolted at the insults to which we were exposed, and there was a constant feeling of insecurity from the great extent to which we were dependent upon wretches whom we internally despised. When the government took a higher tone, and more principle and greater strictness in the collection of the duties were enforced, we thought ourselves ruined; but the reverse has been the case. The duties, no doubt, are now excessively burdensome from their amount; but that is their least evil. If it was possible to collect them from every trader with perfect equality, our independence would be complete, and our competition would be confined to superiority in morality and skill. Matters are much nearer this point now than they were fifty years ago; but still they would admit of considerable improvement.' The same individual mentioned, that, in his youth, now seventy years ago, the civil liberty of the people of Scotland was held by a weak tenure. He knew instances of soldiers being sent in times of war, to the farm-houses, to carry off, by force, young men for the army; and as this was against the law, they were accused of some imaginary offence, such as a trespass, or an assault, which was proved by false witnesses, and the magistrate, perfectly aware of the farce, and its object, threatened the victim with transportation to the colonies, as a felon, if he would not enlist; which he, of course, unprotected and overwhelmed by power and injustice, was compelled to consent to.

If the same minute representation were given of other departments of private life, during the time of the greatest immoralities on the part of the government, we would find that this paltering with conscience and character in the national proceedings, tended to keep down the morality of the people, and fostered in them a rapacious and gambling spirit, to which many of the evils that have since overtaken us have owed their orgin.

But we may take a more extensive view of the subject of national responsibility.

In the American war England desired to gratify her Acquisitiveness and Self-esteem, in opposition to Benevolence and Justice, at the expense of the transatlantic colonies. This roused the animal resentment of the latter, and the lower faculties of the two nations came into collision; that is to say, they made war on each other; England to support a dominion in direct hostility to the principles which regulate the moral government of the world, in the expectation of becoming rich and powerful by success in that enterprise; the Americans, to assert the supremacy of the higher sentiments, and to become free and independent. According to the principles which I am now unfolding, the greatest misfortune that could have befallen England would have been success, and the greatest advantage, failure in her attempt; and the result is now acknowledged to be in exact accordance with these views. If England had subdued the colonies in the American war, every one must see to what an extent her Self-esteem, Acquisitiveness and Destructiveness would have been let loose upon them; this, in the first place, would have roused their animal faculties, and led them to give her all the annoyance in their power, and the fleets and armies requisite to repress this spirit would have far counterbalanced, in expense, all the profits she could have wrung out of the colonists, by extortion and oppression. In the second place, the very exercise of these animal faculties by herself, in opposition to the moral sentiments, would have rendered her government at home an exact parallel of that of the carter in his own family. The same malevolent principles would have overflowed on her own subjects, the government would have felt uneasy, the people rebellious, discontented, and unhappy, and the moral law would have been amply vindicated by the suffering which would have every where abounded. The consequences of her failure have been exactly the reverse. America has sprung up into a great and moral nation, and actually contributes ten times more to the wealth of Britain, standing as she now does, in her natural relation to this country, than she ever could have done, as a discontented and oppressed colony. This advantage is reaped without any loss, anxiety, or expense; it flows from the divine institutions, and both nations profit by and rejoice under it. The moral and intellectual rivalry of America, instead of prolonging the predominance of the propensities in Britain, tends strongly to excite the moral sentiments in her people and government; and every day that we live, we are reaping the benefits of this improvement in wiser institutions, deliverance from endless abuses, and a higher and purer spirit pervading every department of the executive administration of the country. Britain, however, did not escape the penalty of her attempt at the infringement of the moral laws. The pages of her history, during the American war, are dark with suffering and gloom, and at this day we groan under the debt and difficulties then partly incurred.

If the world be constituted on the principles of the supremacy of the moral sentiments and intellect, the method of one nation seeking riches and power, by conquering, devastating, or obstructing the prosperity of other states, must be *essentially futile.* Being in opposition to the moral constitution of creation, it must occasion misery while in progress, and can lead to no result except the impoverishment and mortification of the people who pursue it. The national debt of Britain has been contracted chiefly in wars, originating in commercial jealousy and thirst of conquest; in short, under the suggestions of Combativeness, Destructiveness, Acquisitiveness, and Self-esteem. Did not our ancestors, therefore, impede their own prosperity and happiness, by engaging in these contests? and have any consequences of them reached us, except the burden of paying nearly thirty millions of taxes annually; as the price of the gratification of their propensities? Would a statesman, who believed in the doctrine of this Essay, have recommended these wars *as essential to national prosperity*? If the twentieth part of the sums had been spent in objects recognised by the moral sentiments, for example, in instituting seminaries of education, penitentiaries, making roads, canals, public granaries, &c. &c. how different would have been the present condition of the country!

After the American followed the French revolutionary war. Opinions are at present more divided upon this subject; but my view of it, offered with the greatest deference, is the following. When the French Revolution broke out, the domestic institutions of England were, to a considerable extent, founded and administered on principles in opposition to the supremacy of the sentiments. A clamour was raised by the nation for reform of abuses. If my leading principle is sound, every departure from the moral law in nations, as well as in individuals, carries its punishment with it from the first hour of its commencement, till its final cessation; and if Britain's institutions were then, to any extent corrupt and defective, she could not too speedily have abandoned them, and adopted purer and loftier arrangements. Her government, however, clung to the suggestions of the propensities, and resisted every innovation. To divert the national mind from causing a revolution at home, they embarked in a war abroad; and, for a period of twenty-three years, let loose the propensities on France with headlong fury, and a fearful perseverance. France, no doubt, threatened the different nations of Europe with the most violent interference with their governments; a menace wholly unjustifiable, and that called for resistance. But the rulers of that country were preparing their own destruction, in exact proportion to their departures from the moral law; and a statesman, who knew and had confidence in the constitution of the world, as now explained, could have listened to the storm in complete composure, prepared to repel actual aggression, and left the exploding of French infatuation to the Ruler of the Universe, in unhesitating reliance on the efficacy of his laws. But England preferred a war of aggression. If this conduct was in accordance with the sentiments, we should now, like America, be reaping the reward of our obedience to the moral law, and plenty and rejoicing should flow down our streets like a stream. But mark the contrast. This island exhibits the spectacle of millions of men, toiled to the extremity of human endurance, for a pittance scarcely sufficient to sustain life; weavers labouring for fourteen or sixteen hours a day for eight pence, and frequently unable to procure work, even on these terms; other artisans exhausted almost to death by laborious drudgery, who, if better recompensed, seek compensation and enjoyment in the grossest sensual debauchery, drunkenness, and gluttony; master-traders and manufacturers anxiously labouring for wealth, now gay in the fond hope that all their expectations will be realised, then sunk in deep despair by the breath of ruin having passed over them; landholders and tenants now reaping unmeasured returns from their properties, then pining in penury, amidst an overflow of every species of produce; the government cramped by an overwhelming debt and the prevalence of ignorance and selfishness on every side, so that it is impossible for it to follow with a bold step the most obvious dictates of reason and justice, owing to the countless prejudices and imaginary interests which every where obstruct the path of improvement. This resembles much more punishment for transgression, than reward for obedience to the divine institutions.

If every man in Britain will turn his attention inward, and reckon the pangs of disappointment which he has felt at the subversion of his own most darling schemes, by unexpected turns of public events, or the deep inroads on his happiness which such calamities, overtaking his dearest relations and friends, have occasioned to him; the numberless little enjoyments in domestic life, which he is forced to deny himself, by the taxation with which they are loaded; the obstructions to the fair exercise of his industry and talents presented by stamps, licenses, excise laws, custom-house duties *et hoc genus omne;* he will discover the extent of responsibility attached by the Creator to national transgressions. From my own observation, I would say, that the miseries inflicted upon individuals and families, by fiscal prosecutions, founded on excise laws, stamp laws, post-office laws, &c. all originating in the necessity of providing for the national debt, are equal to those arising from some of the most extensive natural calamities. It is true, that few persons are prosecuted without having offended; but the evil consists in presenting men with enormous temptations to infringe mere financial regulations not always in accordance with natural morality, and then inflicting ruinous penalties for transgression. Men have hitherto expected the punishment of their offences in the thunderbolt, or the yawning earthquake; and believed, that because the sea did not swallow them up, or the mountain fall upon them and crush them to atoms, Heaven was taking no cognizance of their sins; while, in point of fact, an omnipotent, an all-just, and an all-wise God, had arranged before they erred, an ample retribution in the very consequences of their transgressions. It is by looking to the *principles* in the mind, from which transgressions flow, and attending to their whole operations and results, that we discover the real theory of the divine government. When men shall be instructed in the laws of creation, they will discriminate more accurately than heretofore between natural and factitious evils, and become less tolerant of the latter.

The Spaniards, under the influence of Acquisitiveness, Self-esteem, Love of Approbation, and a blind Veneration, conquered South America, inflicted upon its wretched inhabitants the most atrocious cruelties, and continued to weigh, for three hundred years, like a moral incubus, upon that quarter of the globe. The responsibility now shows itself. By the laws of the Creator, nations require to obey the moral law to be happy; that is, to cultivate the arts of peace, to be industrious, upright, intelligent, pious, and humane. The reward of such conduct is individual happiness, and national greatness and glory. There shall then be none to make them afraid. The Spaniards disobeyed all these laws in the conquest of America, they looked to rapine and foreign gold, and not to industry, for wealth; this fostered avarice and pride in the government, baseness in the nobles, indolence, ignorance, and mental depravity in the people; led them to imagine happiness to consist, not in the exercise of the moral and intellectual powers, but in the gratification of all the inferior feelings to the outrage of the higher. Intellectual cultivation was utterly neglected, the sentiments ran astray into the regions of bigotry and superstition, and the propensities acquired a fearful ascendency. These causes made them the prey of internal discord and foreign invaders; and Spain, at this moment, suffers an awful responsibility.*

In surveying ths present aspect of Europe, we perceive astonishing improvements achieved in physical science. How much is implied in the mere names of the steam-engine, power-looms, rail-roads, steam-boats, canals, and gas-lights; and yet of how much misery are several of these inventions at present the direct sources, in consequence of being almost exclusively dedicated to the gratification of the propensities. The leading purpose to which the steam-engine in almost all its forms of application is devoted, is the accumulation of wealth, or the gratification of Acquisitiveness and Self-esteem; and few have proposed, by its means, to lessen the hours of toil to the lower orders of society, so as to afford them opportunity and leisure for the cultivation of their moral and intellectual faculties, and thereby to enable them to render a more perfect obedience to the Creator's institutions. Physical has far outstripped moral science; and, it appears to me, that, unless the light of Phrenology open the eyes of mankind to the real constitution of the world, and at length induce them to modify their conduct, in harmony with the laws of the Creator, their future physical discoveries will tend only to deepen their wretchedness. Intellect, acting as the ministering servant of the propensities, will lead them only farther astray. The science of man's whole nature, animal, moral, and intellectual, was never more required to guide him than at present, when he seems to wield a giant's power, but in the application of it to display the ignorant selfishness, wilfulness, and absurdity of an overgrown child. History has not yielded, and cannot yield, half her fruits, until mankind shall be possessed of a true theory of their own nature.

SECT. IV.—MORAL ADVANTAGES OF PUNISHMENT.

After the intellect and moral sentiments have been brought to recognize the principles of the Divine administration, so much wisdom, benevolence, and justice, are discernible in the natural laws, that our whole nature is meliorated in undergoing the punishments annexed to them. Punishment endured by one individual also serves to warn others against transgression. These facts afford another proof that a grand object of the arrangement of creation is the improvement of the moral and intellectual nature of man. So strikingly conspicuous, indeed, is the meliorating influence of suffering, that many persons have supposed this to be the primary object for which it is sent; a notion which, with great deference, appears to me to be unfounded in principle, and dangerous in practice. If evils and misfortunes are mere mercies of Providence, it follows that

* Cowper recognises these principles of divine government as to nations, and has embodied them in the following powerful verses:

The hand that slew till it could slay no more,
Was glued to the sword-hilt with Indian gore,
Their prince, as justly seated on his throne
As vain imperial Philip on his own,
Tricked out of all his royalty by art,
That stript him bare, and broke his honest heart,
Died by the sentence of a shaven priest,
For scorning what they taught him to detest.
How dark the veil, that intercepts the blaze
Of Heaven's mysterious purposes and ways;
God stood not, though he seemed to stand aloof,
And at this hour the conqueror feels the proof:
The wreath he won drew down an instant curse,
The fretting plague is in the public purse,
The cankered spoil corrodes the pining state,
Starved by that indolence their minds create.

Oh! could their ancient Incas rise again,
How would they take up Israel's taunting strain!
Art thou too fallen, Iberia? Do we see
The robber and the murd'rer weak as we?
Thou that hast wasted Earth, and dared despise
Alike the wrath and mercy of the skies,
Thy pomp is in the grave, thy glory laid
Low in the pits thine avarice has made.
We come with joy from our eternal rest,
To see th' oppressor in his turn oppressed.
Art thou the god, the thunder of whose hand
Rolled over all our desolated land,
Shook principalities and kingdoms down,
And made the mountains tremble at his frown?
The sword shall light upon his boasted powers,
And waste them, as the sword has wasted ours.
'Tis thus Omnipotence his law fulfils,
And Vengeance executes what Justice wills.

Cowper's Poems.—Charity p. 156

a headache consequent on a debauch, is not intended to prevent a repetition of drunkenness, so much as to prepare the debauchee for 'the invisible world;' and that shipwreck in a crazy vessel is not designed to render the merchant more cautious, but to lead him to heaven.

It is however undeniable, that in innumerable instances pain and sorrow are the direct consequences of our own misconduct; at the same time it is obviously benevolent in the Deity to render it beneficial directly as a warning against future transgression, and indirectly as a means of purifying the mind; nevertheless, if we shall imagine that in some instances it is dispensed as a direct punishment for particular transgressions, and in others, only on account of sin in general, and with the view of meliorating the spirit of the sufferer, we shall ascribe inconsistency to the Creator, and expose ourselves to the danger of attributing our own afflictions to his favour, and those of others, to his wrath; thus fostering in our minds self-conceit and uncharitableness. Individuals who entertain the belief that bad health, worldly ruin, and sinister accidents, befalling them, are not punishments for infringement of the laws of nature, but particular manifestations of the love of the Creator toward themselves, make slight inquiry into the natural causes of their miseries, and bestow few efforts to remove them. In consequence, the chastisements endured by them, neither correct their own conduct, nor deter others from committing similar transgressions. Some religious sects, who espouse these notions, literally act upon them, and refuse to inoculate with the cow-pox to escape contagion, or take other means of avoiding natural calamities. Regarding these as dispensations of Providence, sent to prepare them for a future world, they conceive that the more of them the better. Farther; these ideas, besides being repugnant to the common sense of mankind, are at variance with the principle that the world is arranged so as to favour virtue and discountenance vice; because favouring virtue means obviously that the favoured virtuous will positively enjoy more happiness, and, negatively, suffer fewer misfortunes than the vicious. The view, then, now advocated, appears less exceptionable, viz. that punishment serves a double purpose, directly to warn us against transgression; and indirectly, when rightly apprehended, to subdue our lower propensities, and purify and vivify our moral and intellectual powers.

Bishop Butler coincides in this interpretation of natural calamities. 'Now,' says he, 'in the present state, all which we enjoy, *and* A GREAT PART OF WHAT WE SUFFER, *is put in our power.** For *pleasure and pain are the consequences of our actions;* and we are endued by the Author of our nature with capacities of foreseeing these consequences.' 'I know not that we have any one kind or degree of enjoyment, but by the means of our own actions. And, *by prudence and care*, we may, for the most part, pass our days in tolerable ease and quiet; or, on the contrary, we may, *by rashness, ungoverned passion, wilfulness*, or *even by negligence*, make ourselves *as miserable as ever we please*. And many do please to make themselves extremely miserable; *i. e.* they do what they knew beforehand will render them so. They follow those ways, the fruit of which they knew, by instruction, example, experience, will be disgrace, and poverty, and sickness, and untimely death. This every one observes to be the general course of things, though it is to be allowed, we cannot find by experience, that *all* our sufferings are owing to our own follies.'—*Analogy*, p. 40. In accordance with this last remark, I have treated of *hereditary* diseases; and evils resulting from convulsions of physical nature may be added to the same class.

It has been objected that physical punishments, such as the breaking of an arm by a fall, are often so disproportionally severe, that the Creator must have had some other and more important object in view in appointing them, than to serve as mere motives to physical observance; and that that object must be to influence the mind of the sufferer, and to draw his attention to concerns of higher import.

In answer, I remark, that the human body is liable to destruction by severe injuries; and that the degree of suffering, in general, bears a just proportion to the danger connected with the transgression. Thus, a slight surfeit is attended only with headache or general uneasiness, because it does not endanger life: a fall on any muscular part of the body is followed either with no pain, or only a slight indisposition, for the reason that it is not seriously injurious to life; but when a leg or arm is broken, the pain is intensely severe, because the bones of these limbs stand high in the scale of utility to man. The human body is so framed that it may fall nine times, and suffer little damage, but the tenth time a limb may be broken, which will entail a painful chastisement. By this arrangement the mind is kept alive to danger to such an extent, as to ensure general safety, while at the same time it is not overwhelmed with terror by punishments too severe and too frequently repeated. In particular states of the body, a slight wound may be followed by inflammation and death; but these are not the results simply of the wound, but the consequences of a previous derangement of health, occasioned by departures from the organic laws.

On the whole, therefore, no adequate reason appears for regarding the consequences of physical accidents in any other light than as direct punishments for infringement of the natural laws, and indirectly as a means of accomplishing moral and religious improvement.

* These words are printed in Italics in the original.

CHAPTER IV.

ON THE COMBINED OPERATION OF THE NATURAL LAWS.

Having now unfolded several of the natural laws, and their effects, and having also attempted to show that each is inflexible and independent in itself, and requires absolute obedience, so that a man who shall neglect the physical law will suffer the physical punishment, although he may be very attentive to the moral law; that one who infringes the organic law will suffer organic punishment, although he may obey the physical law; and that a person who violates the moral law will suffer the moral punishment, although he should observe the other two; I proceed to show the mutual relationship between these laws, and to adduce some instances of their joint operation.

The great fires in Edinburgh, in November, 1824, when the Parliament Square and a part of the High Street, were consumed, will serve as one example. That calamity may be viewed in the following light:—The Creator constituted the countries of England and Scotland, and the English and Scottish nations, with such qualities and relationships, that the individuals of both kingdoms would be most happy in acting towards each other, and pursuing their separate vocations, under the supremacy of the moral sentiments. We have lived to see this practised, and to reap the rewards of it. But the ancestors of the two nations did not believe in this constitution of the world, and they preferred acting on the principles of the propensities; that is to say, they waged furious wars, and committed wasting devastations, on each other's properties and lives. This was clearly a violent infringement of the moral law; and it is obvious from history that the two nations were equally ferocious, and delighted reciprocally in each other's calamities. One effect of it was to render personal safety an object of paramount importance. The hill on which the Old Town of Edinburgh is built, was naturally surrounded by marshes, and presented a perpendicular front, to the west, capable of being crowned with a castle. It was appropriated with avidity, and the metropolis of Scotland founded there, obviously and undeniably under the inspiration purely of the animal faculties. It was fenced round, and ramparts built to exclude the fierce warriors who then inhabited the south of the Tweed; and also to protect the inhabitants from the feudal banditti who infested their own soil. The space within the walls, however, was limited and narrow; the attractions to the spot were numerous, and to make the most of it, our ancestors erected the enormous masses of high, confused, and crowded buildings which now compose the High Street of this city, and the wynds or alleys, on its two sides. These abodes, moreover, were constructed, to a great extent, of timber, for not only the joists and floors, but the partitions between the rooms, were of massive wood. Our ancestors did all this in the perfect knowledge of the physical law, that wood ignited by fire is not only consumed itself, but envelopes in inevitable destruction every combustible object within its influence. Farther; their successors, even when the necessity had ceased, persevered in the original error, and in the perfect knowledge that every year added to the age of such fabrics, increased, their liability to burn, they allowed them to be occupied not only as shops filled with paper, spirits, and other highly combustible materials, but introduced gas-lights, and let off the upper floors for brothels, introducing thereby into the heart of this magazine of conflagration, the most reckless and immoral of mankind. The consummation was the tremendous fires of November, 1824, the one originating in a whiskey-cellar, and the other in a garret brothel, which consumed the whole Parliament Square and a part of the High Street, destroying property to the extent of many thousands of pounds, and spreading misery and ruin over a considerable portion of the population of Edinburgh. Wonder, consternation, and awe were forcibly excited at the vastness of this calamity; and in the sermons that were preached, and the dissertations that were written upon it, much was said of the inscrutable ways of Providence, that sent such visitations upon the people, enveloping the innocent and the guilty in one common sentence of destruction.

According to the exposition of the ways of Providence which I have ventured to give, there was nothing wonderful, nothing vengeful, nothing arbitrary, in the whole occurrence. The surprising thing was, that it did not take place generations before. The necessity for these fabrics originated in gross violation of the moral law; they were constructed in high contempt of the physical law; and, latterly, the moral law was set at defiance, by placing in them inhabitants abandoned to the worst habits of recklessness and intoxication. The Creator had bestowed on men faculties to perceive all this, and to avoid it, whenever they chose to exert them; and the destruction that ensued was the punishment of following the propensities, in preference to the dictates of intellect and morality. The object of the destruction, as a natural event, was to lead men to avoid repetition of the offences: but the principles of the divine government are not yet comprehended; Acquisitiveness whispers that more money may be made of houses consisting of five or six floors, under one roof, than of only two; and erections, the very counterparts of the former, are now rearing their heads on the spot where the others stood, and, sooner or later, they also will be overtaken by the natural laws, which never slumber or sleep.

The true method of arriving at a sound view of calamities of every kind, is to direct our attention, in the first instance, to the law of nature, from the operation of which they have originated; then to find out the uses and advantages of that law, when observed; and to discover whether the evils under consideration have arisen from violation of it. In the present instance, we ought never to lose sight of the fact, that the houses in question stood erect, and the furniture in safety, by the very same law of gravitation which made them topple to the foundation when it was infringed; that mankind enjoy all the benefits which result from the combustibility of timber as fuel, by the very same law which renders it a devouring element, when unduly ignited; that, by the same moral law, which, when infringed, leads to the necessity of ramparts, fortifications, crowded lanes, and extravagantly high houses, we enjoy, now that we observe it better, that security of property and life which distinguishes modern Scotland from ancient Caledonia.

This instance affords a striking illustration of the manner in which the physical and organic laws are constituted in harmony with, and in subserviency to, the moral law. We see clearly that the leading cause of the construction of such erections as the houses of the Old Town of Edinburgh (with the deprivation of free air, and liability to combustion that attend them,) arose from the excessive predominance of Combativeness, Destructiveness, Self-esteem and Acquisitiveness, in our ancestors; and although the ancient personages who erected these monuments of animal supremacy, had no conception that, in doing so, they were laying the foundations of a severe punishment on themselves and their posterity; yet, when we compare the comforts and advantages that would have accompanied dwellings constructed under the inspiration of Benevolence, Ideality, and enlightened Intellect, with the contaminating, debasing, and dangerous effects of their workmanship, we perceive most clearly that they actually were the instruments of chastising their own transgressions, and of transmitting that chastisement to their posterity, so long as the animal supremacy shall be prolonged. Another example may be given.

Men, by uniting under one leader, may, in virtue of the social law, acquire prodigious advantages to themselves, which singly they could not obtain; and I stated, that the condition under which the benefits of that law were permitted, was, that the leader should know and obey the natural laws that were conducive to success; if he neglected these, then the same principle which gave the social body the benefit of his observing them, involved them in the punishment of his infringement; and that this was just, because, under the natural law, the leader must necessarily be chosen by the social body, and they were responsible for not attending to his natural qualities. Some illustrations of the consequences of neglect of this law may be stated, in which the mixed operation of the physical and moral laws will appear.

During the French war, a squadron of English men-of-war was sent to the Baltic with military stores, and, in returning home up Channel, they were beset, for two or three days, by a thick fog. It was about the middle of December, and no correct information was possessed of their exact situation. Some of the commanders proposed lying-to all night, and proceeding only during day, to avoid running ashore unawares. The commodore was exceedingly attached to his wife and family, and stated his determination to pass Christmas with them in England, if possible, and ordered the ships to sail straight on their voyage. The very same night they all struck on a sand-bank off the coast of Holland; two ships of the line were dashed to pieces, and every soul on board perished. The third ship drew less water, was forced over the bank by the waves, was stranded on the beach, the crew saved, but led to a captivity of many years' duration. Now, these vessels were destroyed under the physical law; but this calamity owed its origin to the predominance of the animal over the moral and intellectual faculties in the commodore. The gratification which he sought to obtain was individual and selfish; and, if his Benevolence, Veneration, Conscientiousness, and Intellect, had been as alert and carried as forcibly home to his mind the operation of the physical laws, and the welfare of the men under his charge ; nay, if these faculties had been sufficiently alive to see the danger to which he exposed his own life, and the happiness of his own wife and children, —he never could have followed the precipitate course which consigned himself, and so many brave men, to a watery grave, within a few hours after his resolution was formed.

Very lately the Ogle Castle East Indiamen was offered a pilot coming up Channel, but the captain refused assistance, professing his own skill to be sufficient. In a few hours the ship ran aground on a sand-bank, and every human being perished in the waves. This also arose from the physical law, but the unfavourable operation of it sprung from Self-esteem, pretending to knowedge which the intellect did not possess ; and, as it is only by the latter that obedience can be yielded to the physical laws, the destruction of the ship was indirectly the consequence of infringement of the moral and intellectual laws.

An old sailor, whom I lately met on the Queensferry passage, told me, that he had been nearly fifty years at sea, and once was in a fifty gun ship in the West Indies. The captain, he said, was a 'fine man ;' he knew the climate, and foresaw a hurricane coming, by its natural signs ; and, on one occasion, in particular, he struck the topmasts, lowered the yards, lashed the guns, made each man supply himself with food for thirty-six hours, and scarcely was this done when the hurricane came ; the ship lay for four hours on her beam-ends in the water ; but all was prepared ; the men were kept in vigour during the storm, and fit for every exertion ; the ship at last righted, suffered little damage, and proceeded on her voyage. The fleet which she convoyed was dispersed, and a great number of the ships foundered. Here we see the supremacy of the moral and intellectual faculties, and discover to what a surprising extent they present a guarantee, even against the fury of the physical elements in their highest state of agitation.

One of the most instructive illustrations of the connexion between the different natural laws is presented in Captain Lyon's brief narrative of an unsuccessful attempt to reach Repulse Bay, in his Majesty's ship Griper, in the year 1824.

Captain Lyon mentions, that he sailed in the Griper on 13th June, 1824, in company with his Majesty's surveying vessel Snap, as a store-tender. The Griper was 180 tons burden, and 'drew 16 feet 1 inch abaft, and 15 feet 10 inches forward.'—p. 2. On the 26th, he 'was sorry to observe that the Griper, from her great depth and sharpness forward, pitched very deeply.'—p. 3. She sailed so ill, that 'in a stiff breeze and with studding-sails set, he was unable to get above four knots an hour out of her, and she was twice whirled round in an eddy in the Pentland Frith, from which she could not escape.'—p. 6. On the 3d July, 'being now fairly at sea, I caused the Snap to take us in tow, which I had declined doing as we passed up the east coast of England, although our little companion had much difficulty in keeping under sufficiently low sail for us, and by noon we had passed the Stack Back.' 'The Snap was of the greatest assistance, the Griper frequently towing at the rate of five knots, in cases where she would not have gone three.'—p. 10. 'On the forenoon of the 16th, the Snap came and took us in tow ; but at noon on the 17th, strong breezes and a heavy swell obliged us again to cast off. We scudded while able, but our depth on the water caused us to ship so many heavy seas, that I most reluctantly brought to under storm stay-sails. This was rendered exceeding mortifying, by observing that our companion was perfectly dry, and not affected by the sea.' p. 13. 'When our stores were all on board, we found our narrow decks completely crowded by them. The gang-ways, forecastle, and abaft the mizen-mast, were filled with casks hawsers, whale-lines, and stream-cables, while on our straitened lower decks we were obliged to place casks and other stores, in every part but that allotted to the ship's company's mess-tables ; and even my cabin had a quantity of things stowed away in it.'—p. 21. 'It may be proper to mention, that the *Fury* and *Hecla*, which were enabled to stow *three* years' provisions, were each exactly *double* the size of the Griper, and the Griper carried two years' and a half's provisions,—pp 22, 23.

Arrived in the Polar Seas, they were visited by a storm, of which Captain Lyon gives the following description : We soon, however, came to fifteen fathoms, and I kept right away, but had then only ten ; when, being unable to see far around us, and observing, from the whiteness of the water, that we were on a bank, I rounded to at 7 A. M., and tried to bring up with the starboard anchor, and seventy fathoms chain, but the stiff breeze and heavy sea caused this to part in half an hour, and we again made sail to the north-eastward : but finding that we came suddenly to seven fathoms and that the ship could not possibly work out again, as she would not face the sea, or keep steerage-way on her, I most reluctantly brought her up with three bowers and a stream in succession, yet not before we had shoaled to five and a half. This was between 8 and 9 A. M., the ship pitching bows under, and a tremendous sea running. At noon, the starboard-bower anchor parted, but the others held.

'As there was every reason to fear the falling of the tide, which we knew to be from twelve to fifteen feet on this coast, and in that case the total destruction of the ship, I caused the long-boat to be hoisted out, and with the four smaller ones to be stored to a certain extent, with arms and provisions. The officers drew lots for their respective boats, and the ship's company were stationed to them. The long-boat having been filled full of stores, which could not be put below, it became requisite to throw them overboard, *as there was no room for them on our very small and crowded decks, over which heavy seas were constantly sweeping*. In making these preparations for taking to the boats, it was evident to all, that the long-boat was the only one that had the slightest chance of living under the lee of the ship, should she be wrecked, but every officer and man drew his lot with the greatest composure, though two of our boats would have swamped the instant they were lowered. Yet, such was the noble feeling of those around me, that it was evident, that, had I ordered the boats in question to be manned, their crews would have entered them without a murmur. In the afternoon, on the weather clearing a little, we discovered a low beach all around astern of us, on which the surf was running to an awful height, and it appeared evident that no human powers could save us. At 3 P. M. the tide had fallen to twenty-two feet, (*only six feet more than we drew,*) *and the ship, having been lifted by a tremendous sea, struck with great violence the length of her keel.* This we naturally conceived was the forerunner of her total wreck, and we stood in readiness to take the boats, and endeavour to hang under her lee. She continued to strike with sufficient force to have burst any less fortified vessel, at intervals of a few minutes, whenever an unusual heavy sea passed us. And, as the water was so shallow, these might almost be called breakers rather than waves, for each in passing burst with great force over our gangways, and as every sea 'topped,' our decks were continually, and frequently deeply, flooded. All hands took a little refreshment, for some had scarcely been below for twenty four hours, and I had not been in bed for three nights. Although few, or none of us, had any idea that we should survive the gale, we did not think that our comforts should be entirely neglected, and an order was therefore given to the men to put on their best and warmest clothing, to enable them to support life as long as possible. Every man, therefore, brought his bag on deck, and dressed himself ; and in the fine athletic forms which stood before me, I did not see one muscle quiver, nor the slightest sign of alarm. The officers each secured some useful instrument about them, for the purposes of observation, although it was acknowledged by all that not the slightest hope remained. And now that every thing in our power had been done, I called all hands aft, and to a merciful God offered prayers for our preservation. I thanked every one for their excellent conduct, and cautioned them, as we should, in all probability, soon appear before our Maker, to enter his presence as men resigned to their fate. We then all sat down in groups, and, sheltered from the wash of the sea, by whatever we could find, many of us endeavoured to obtain a little sleep. Never, perhaps, was witnessed a finer scene than on the deck of my little ship, when all the hope of life had left us. Noble as the character of the British sailor is always allowed to be in cases of danger; yet I did not believe it to be possible, that, amongst forty-one persons, not one repining word should have been uttered. The officers sat about, wherever they could find a shelter from the sea, and the men lay down conversing with each other with the most perfect calmness. Each was at peace with his neighbour and all the world, and I am firmly persuaded that the resignation which was then shown to the will of the Almighty, was the means of obtaining his mercy. At about 6 P. M., the rudder, which had already received some very heavy blows, rose, and broke up the after-lockers, and this was the last severe shock that the ship received. We found by the well that she made no water, and by dark she struck no more. God was merciful to us, and the tide, almost miraculously fell no lower. At dark heavy rain fell, but was borne in patience, for it beat down the gale, and brought with it a light air from the northward. At 9 P. M., the water had deepened to five fathoms. The ship kept off the ground all night, and our exhausted crew obtained some broken rest.'—p. 76.

In humble gratitude for his deliverance, he called the place 'The Bay of God's mercy,' and 'offered up thanks and praises to God, for the mercy he had shown to us.'

On 12th September, they had another gale of wind, with cutting showers of sleet, and a heavy sea. '*At such a time as this*,' says Captain Lyon '*we had fresh cause to deplore the extreme dullness of the Griper's sailing; for though almost any other vessel would have worked off this lea-shore, we made little or no progress on a wind, but remained actually pitching, forecastle under, with scarcely steerage-way*, to preserve which I was ultimately obliged to keep her nearly two points off the wind.'—p. 98.

Another storm overtook them, which is described as follows;—'Never shall I forget the dreariness of this most anxious night. Our ship pitched at such a rate that it was not possible to stand, even below; while on deck we were unable to move, without holding by ropes, which were stretched from side to side. The drift snow flew in such sharp heavy flakes, that we could not look to windward, and it froze on deck to above a foot in depth. The sea made incessant breaches quite fore and aft the ship, and the temporary warmth it gave while it washed over us, was most painfully checked, by its almost immediately freezing on our clothes. To these discomforts were added, the horrible uncertainty as to whether the cables would hold until daylight, and the conviction also, that if they failed us, we should be instantly dashed to pieces; the wind blowing directly to the quarter in which we knew the shore must lie. Again, should they continue to hold us, we feared, by the ship's complaining so much forward, that the bitts would be torn up, or that she would settle down at her anchors, overpowered by some of the tremendous seas which burst over her. At dawn on the 13th, thirty minutes after four A. M., we found that the best bower cable had parted; and, as the gale now blew with terrific violence from the north, there was little reason to expect that the other anchors would hold long; or, if they did, *we pitched so deeply, and lifted so great a body of water each time that it was feared the windlass and forecastle would be torn up, or she must go down at her anchors;* although the ports were knocked out, and a considerable portion of the bulwark cut away, she could scarcely discharge one sea before shipping another, and the decks were frequently flooded to an alarming depth.

'At six A. M., all farther doubts on this particular account were at an end; for, having received two overwhelming seas, both the other cables went at the same moment, and we were left helpless, without anchors, or any means of saving ourselves, should the shore, as we had every reason to expect, be close astern. And here, again, I had the happiness of witnessing the same tranquillity as was shown on the 1st of September. There was no outcry that cables were gone; but my friend Mr. Manico, with Mr. Carr the gunner, came aft as soon as they recovered their legs, and, in the lowest whisper, informed me that the cables had all parted. The ship, in trending to the wind, lay quite down on her broadside, and as it then became evident that nothing held her, and that she was quite helpless, each man instinctively took his station; while the seamen at the leads, having secured themselves as well as was in their power, repeated their soundings, on which our preservation depended, with as much composure as if we had been entering a friendly port. Here, again, that Almighty power, which had before so mercifully preserved us, granted us his protection.'—p. 100.

Nothing can be more interesting and moving than this narrative; it displays a great predominance of the moral sentiments and intellect,but sadly unenlightened as to the natural laws. I quoted, in Captain Lyon's own words, his description of the Griper, loaded to such excess that she drew sixteen feet water; that she was incapable of sailing; that she was whirled round in an eddy in the Pentland Frith; that seas broke over her that did not wet the deck of the little Snap, not half her size. Captain Lyon knew all this; and also the roughness of the climate to which he was steering; and, with these outrages of the physical law staring him in the face, he proceeded on his voyage, without addressing, so far as we perceive, one remonstrance to the Lords of the Admiralty on the subject of this infringement of every principle of common prudence. My opinion is, that Captain Lyon was not blind to the errors committed in his equipment, or to their probable consequences; but that his powerful sentiment of Veneration, combined with Cautiousness and Love of Approbation, (misdirected in this instance), deprived him of courage to complain to the Admiralty, through fear of giving offence: or that, if he did complain, they have prevented him from stating the facts in his narrative. To the tempestuous north he sailed; and his greatest dangers were clearly referable to the very infringements of the physical laws which he describes. When the tide ebbed, his ship reached to within six feet of the bottom, and, in the hollow of every wave, struck with great violence: but she was loaded at least four feet too deeply, by his own account; so that, if he had done his own duty, she would have had four feet of additional water, or ten feet in all, between her and the bottom, even in the hollow of the wave,—a matter of the very last importance, in such a critical condition. Indeed, with four feet more water, she would not have struck. Besides, if less loaded, she would have struck less violently. Again, when pressed upon a lea-shore, her incapability of sailing was a most obvious cause of danger; in short, if Providence is to be regarded as the cause of these calamities, there is no impropriety which man can commit, which may not, on the same principles, be charged against the Creator.

But the moral law again shines forth in delightful splendour, in the conduct of Captain Lyon and his crew, when in the most forlorn condition. Piety, resignation, and manly resolution, then animated them to the noblest efforts. On the principle, that the power of accommodating the conduct to the natural laws, depends on the activity of the sentiments and intellect, and that the more numerous the faculties that are excited, the greater is the energy communicated to the whole system, I would say, that, while Captain Lyon's sufferings were, in a great degree, brought on by his infringements of the physical laws, his escape was, in a great measure, promoted by his obedience to the moral law; and that Providence, in the whole occurrences, proceeded on the broad and general principle, which sends advantage uniformly as the reward of obedience, and evil as the punishment of infringement, of every particular law of creation.

That storms and tempests have been instituted for some benevolent end, may, perhaps, be acknowledged, when their causes and effects are fully known, which at present is not the case. But, even amidst all our ignorance of these, it is surprising how small a portion of evil they would occasion, if men obeyed the laws which are actually ascertained. How many ships perish from being sent to sea in an old worn out condition, and ill equipped, through mere Acquisitiveness; and how many more, from captains and crews being chosen who are greatly deficient in knowledge, intelligence, and morality, in consequence of which they infringe the physical laws. We ought to look to all these matters, before complaining of storms as natural institutions.

The last example of the mixed operation of the natural laws which I shall notice, is that which followed from the mercantle distresses of 1825-6. I have traced the origin of that visitation to excessive activity of Acquisitiveness, and a general ascendancy of the animal and selfish faculties over the moral and intellectual powers. The punishments of these offences were manifold. The excesses infringed the moral law, and the chastisement for this was deprivation of the tranquil, steady enjoyment that flows only from the sentiments, with severe suffering in the ruin of fortune and blasting of hope. These disappointments produced mental anguish and depression; which occasioned unhealthy action in the brain. The action of the brain being disturbed, a morbid nervous influence was transmitted to the whole corporeal system; bodily disease was superadded to mental sorrow, and, in some instances, the unhappy sufferers committed suicide to escape from these aggravated evils. Under the organic law, the children produced in this period of mental depression, bodily distress, and organic derangement, will inherit weak bodies, with feeble and irritable minds, a hereditary chastisement of their father's transgressions.

In the instances now given, we discover the various laws acting in perfect harmony, and in subordination to the moral and intellectual. If our ancestors had not forsaken the supremacy of the moral sentiments, such fabrics at the houses in the Old Town of Edinburgh never would have been built; and if the modern proprietors had returned to that law, and kept profligate and drunken inhabitants out of them, the conflagration might still have been avoided. In the case of the ships, we saw that wherever intellect and sentiment had been relaxed, and animal motives permitted to assume the supremacy, evil had speedily followed; and that where the higher powers were called forth, safety had been obtained. And, finally, in the case of the merchants and manufacturers, we traced their calamities directly to placing Acquisitiveness and Ambition above Intellect and sentiment.

Formidable and appaling, then as these punishments are, yet, when we attend to the laws under which they occur, and perceive that the object and legitimate operation of every one of them, when observed, is to produce happiness to man; and that the punishments have the sole object in view of forcing him back to this enjoyment, we cannot, under the supremacy of the sentiments and intellect, fail to bow in humility before them, as at once wise, just, and beneficent.

CONCLUSION.

The question has frequently been asked, What is the practical use of Phrenology, even supposing it to be true? A few observations will enable us to answer this inquiry; and, at the same time to present a brief summary of the doctrine of the preceding Essay.

Prior to the age of Galileo, the earth and sun presented to the eye phenomena exactly similar to those which they now exhibit; but their motions appeared in a very different light to the understanding.

Before the age of Newton, the revolutions of the planets were known as matter of fact; but the understanding was ignorant of the principle of their motions.

Previous to the dawn of modern chemistry, many of the qualities of physical substances were ascertained by observation, but their ultimate principles and relations were not understood.

Knowledge may be rendered beneficial in two ways, either by rendering the substance discovered directly subservient to human enjoyment; or, where this is impossible, by modifying human conduct in harmony with its qualities. While knowledge of any department of nature remains imperfect and empirical, the unknown qualities of the objects belonging to it, may render our efforts either to apply or to accord with those which are known, altogether abortive. Hence it is only after ultimate principles have been discovered, their relations ascertained, and this knowledge has been systematised, that science can attain its full character of utility. The merits of Galileo and Newton consist in having rendered this service to astronomy.

Before the appearance of Drs Gall and Spurzheim. mankind were practically acquainted with the feelings and intellectual operations of their own minds; and anatomists, knew the appearances of the brain. But the science of Mind was very much in the same state as that of the heavenly bodies prior to Galileo and Newton. This remark is borne out by the following considerations;

First. No unanimity prevailed among philosophers concerning the elementary feelings and intellectual powers of man. Individuals, deficient in Conscientiousness, for instance denied that the sentiment of justice was a primitive mental quality of mind. Others, deficient in Veneration, asserted that man was not naturally prone to worship, and ascribed religion to the invention of priests.

Secondly. The extent to which the primitive faculties differ in relative strength, was matter of dispute, or of vague conjecture; and there was no agreement whether many actual attainments were the gifts of nature, or the results of mere cultivation.

Thirdly. Different modes of the same feeling were often mistaken for different feelings; and modes of action of all the intellectual faculties were mistaken for faculties themselves.

Fourthly. The brain, confessedly the most important organ of the body, and that with which the nerves of the senses, of motion, and of feeling directly communicate, had no ascertained functions. Mankind were ignorant of its uses, and of its influence on the mental faculties. They indeed still dispute that its different parts are the organs of different mental powers, and that the vigour of manifestation bears a proportion, *cæteris paribus*, to the size of the organ.

If, in physics, imperfect and empirical knowledge renders the unknown qualities of bodies liable to frustrate the efforts of man to apply or to accommodate his conduct to their known qualities; and if only a complete and systematic exhibition of ultimate principles, and their relations, can confer on science its full character of utility,—the same doctrine applies with equal or greater force to the philosophy of man. For example,

Politics embrace forms of government, and the relations between different states. All government is designed to combine the efforts of individuals, and to regulate their conduct when united. To arrive at the best means of accomplishing this end, systematic knowledge of the nature of man seems highly important. A despotism, for example, may restrain some abuses of the lower propensities, but it assuredly impedes the exercise of reflection, and others of the highest and noblest powers. A form of government can be suited to the nature of man only when it is calculated to permit the legitimate use and to restrain the abuses, of all his mental feelings and capacities; and how can such a government be devised, while these principles, with their spheres of action, and external relations, are imperfectly ascertained. Again; all relations between different states must also be in accordance with the nature of man, to prove permanently beneficial; and the question recurs, How are these to be framed while that nature is matter of conjecture? Napoleon disbelieved in a sentiment of justice as an innate quality of mind; and, in his relations with other states, relied on fear and interest as the grand motives of conduct: but that sentiment existed; and combined with other faculties which he outraged, prompted Europe to hurl him from his throne. If Napoleon had comprehended the principles of human nature, and their relations, as forcibly and clearly as the principles of mathematics, in which he excelled, his understanding would have greatly modified his conduct, and Europe would have escaped prodigious calamities.

Legislation, civil and criminal, is intended to regulate and direct the human faculties in their efforts at gratification; and, to be useful, laws must accord with the constitution of these faculties. But how can salutary laws be enacted, while the subject to be governed, or human nature, is not accurately understood? The inconsistency and intricacy of the laws even in enlightened nations, have afforded themes for the satirist in every age; and how could the case be otherwise? Legislators provided rules for directing the qualities of human nature, which they conceived themselves to know; but either error in their conceptions, or the effects of other qualities unknown or unattended to, defeated their intentions. The law, for example, punishing heresy with burning, was addressed by our ancestors to Cautiousness, Self-love, and other inferior feelings; but Intellect, Veneration, Conscientiousness, and Firmness, were omitted in their estimate of human principles of action; and these set their law at defiance.

There are many laws still in the statute book, equally at variance with the nature of man.

Education is intended to enlighten the intellect and moral sentiments, and train them to vigour. But how can this be successfully accomplished, when the faculties and sentiments themselves, the laws to which they are subjected, and their relations to external objects, are unascertained. Accordingly, the theories and practices observed in education are innumerable and contradictory, which could not happen if men knew the constitution of the object which they were training.

Morals and Religion, also, cannot assume a systematic and demonstrable character, until the elementary qualities of mind, and their relations shall be ascertained.

It is presumable that the Deity, in creating the moral powers and the external world, really adapted the one to the other; so that individuals and nations, in pursuing morality, must, in every instance, be promoting their best interests, and, in departing from it, must be sacrificing them to passion or to illusory notions of advantage. But, until the nature of man, and the relationship between it and the external world, shall be scientifically ascertained, and systematically expounded, it will be impossible to support morality by the powerful demonstration of interest, as here supposed, coinciding with it. The tendency in most men to view expediency as not always coincident with justice affords a striking proof of the limited knowledge of the constitution of man and the external world still prevalent in society.

The diversities of doctrine in religion also obviously owe their origin to ignorance of the primitive faculties and their relations. The faculties differ in relative strength in different individuals, and each person is most alive to objects and views connected with the powers predominant in himself. Hence, in reading the Scriptures, one is convinced that they establish Calvinism; another, possessing a different combination of faculties, discovers in them Lutheranism; and a third is satisfied that Socinianism is the only true interpretation. These individuals have, in general, no distinct conception that the views which strike them most forcibly, appear in a different light to minds differently constituted. A correct interpretation of revelation must harmonize with the dictates of the moral sentiments and intellect holding the animal propensities in subordination. It may legitimately go beyond what they, unaided, could reach; but it cannot contradict them because this would be setting the revelation of the bible in opposition to the inherent dictates of the faculties constituted by the Creator, which cannot be admitted; as the Deity is too powerful and wise to be inconsistent. But mankind will never be induced to bow to such interpretations, while each takes his individual mind as a standard of human nature in general, and conceives that his own impressions are synonymous with absolute truth. The establishment of the nature of man, therefore on a scientific basis, and in a systematic form, must aid the cause both of morality and religion.

The professions, pursuits, amusements, and hours of exertion of individnals, ought also to bear reference to their physical and mental constitution; but hitherto no guiding principle has been possessed to regulate practice in these important particulars,—another evidence that the science of man has been unknown.

But we require only to attend to the scenes daily presenting themselves in society, to obtain irresistible demonstration of the consequences resulting from the want of a true theory of human nature, and its relations. Every preceptor in schools, every professor in colleges, every author, editor, and pamphleteer, every member of Parliament, counsellor, and judge, has a set of notions of his own, which in his mind hold the place of a system of the philosophy of man; and although he may not have methodised his ideas, or even acknowledged them to himself as a theory, yet they constitute a standard to him by which he practically judges of all questions in morals, politics, and religion; he advocates whatever views coincide with them, and condemns all that differ from them, with an unhesitating dogmatism as the most pertinacious theorist on earth. Each also despises the notions of his fellows, in so far as they differ from his own. In short, the human faculties too generally operate simply as instincts, exhibiting all the confliction and uncertainty of mere feeling, unenlighted by perception of their own nature and objects. Hence public measures in general, whether relating to education, religion, trade, manufactures, the poor, criminal law, or to any other of the dearest interests of society, instead of being treated as branches of one general system of economy, and adjusted each on scientific principles in harmony with all the rest, are supported or opposed on narrow and empirical grounds, and often call forth displays of ignorance, prejudice, selfishness, intolerance, and bigotry, that greatly obstruct the progress of improvement. Indeed, unanimity, even among sensible and virtuous men, will be impossible, so long as no standard of mental philosophy is admitted to guide individual feelings and perceptions. But the state of things now described could not exist if education embraced a true system of human nature and its relations.

If, then, phrenology be true, it will, when matured, supply the deficiencies now pointed out.

But, here, another question naturally presents itself, How are the views now expounded, supposing them to contain some portion of truth, to be rendered practical? In answer I remark, that the institutions and manners of society indicate the state of mind of the influential classes at the time when they prevail. The trial and burning of old women as witches, point out clearly the predominance of Destructiveness and Wonder over Intellect and Benevolence in those who were guilty of such cruel absurdities. The practices of wager of battle, and ordeal by fire and water, indicate Combativeness, Destructiveness, and Veneration, to have been in great activity in those who permitted them, combined with much intellectual ignorance of the natural constitution of the world. In like manner, the enormous sums willingly expended in war, and the small sums grudgingly paid for public improvements ; the intense energy displayed in the pursuit of wealth ; and the general apathy evinced in the search after knowledge and virtue unequivocally proclaim activity of Combativeness Destructiveness, Acquisitiveness, Self-esteem and Love of Approbation ; with comparatively moderate vivacity of Benevolence and Intellect in the present generation. Before, therefore, the practices of mankind can be altered, the state of their minds must be changed. No practical error can be greater than that of establishing institutions greatly in advance of the mental condition of the people. The rational method is first to instruct the intellect, then to interest the sentiments, and, last of all, to form arrangements in harmony with, and resting on, these as their basis.

The views developed in the preceding chapters, if founded in nature, may be expected to lead, ultimately, to considerable changes in many of the customs and pursuits of society ; but to accomplish this effect, the principles themselves must first be ascertained to be true ; then they must be sedulously taught ; and when the public mind has been thoroughly prepared, then only ought important practical alterations to be proposed. It appears to me that a long series of years will be necessary to bring even civilized nations into a condition systematically to obey the natural laws.

The preceding chapters may be regarded, in one sense, as an introduction to an Essay on Education. If the views unfolded in them be in general sound, it will follow that education has scarcely yet commenced. If the Creator has bestowed on the body, on the mind, and on external nature, determinate constitutions, and arranged these so as to act on each other, and to produce happiness or misery to man, according to certain definite principles, and if this action goes on invariably, inflexibly, and irresistibly, whether men attend to it or not, it is obvious that the very basis of useful knowledge must consist in an acquaintance with these natural arrangements ; and that education will be valuable in the exact degree in which it communicates such information, and trains the faculties to act upon it. Reading, writing, and accounts, which make up the instruction enjoyed by the lower orders, are merely *means of acquiring knowledge*, but do not *constitute* it. Greek, Latin, and mathematics, which are added in the education of the middle classes, are still only *means* of obtaining information ; so that, with the exception of a few who pursue physical science, society dedicates very little attention to the study of the natural laws. In following out the views now discussed, therefore, each individual, according as he becomes acquainted with the natural laws, ought to obey them, and to communicate his experience of their operations to others ; avoiding at the same time all attempts at subverting, by violence, established institutions, or outraging public sentiment by intemperate discussions. The doctrine now unfolded, if true, authorises us to predicate that the most successful method of meliorating the condition of mankind, will be that which appeals most directly to their moral sentiments and intellect ; and, I may add from experience and observation, that, in proportion as any individual becomes acquainted with the real constitution of the human mind, will his conviction of the efficacy of this method increase.

The next step ought to be to teach those laws to the young.* Their minds, not being pre-occupied by prejudices, will recognise them as congenial to their constitution ; the first generation that has embraced them from infancy will proceed to modify the institutions of society into accordance with their dictates ; and in the course of ages they may at length be acknowledged as practically useful. All *true* theories have ultimately been adopted and influenced practice ; and I see no reason to fear that the present will prove an exception. The failure of all previous systems is the natural consequence of their being unfounded ; if this one shall resemble them, it will deserve, and assuredly will meet with, a similar fate. A perception of the importance of the natural laws will lead to their observance, and this will be attended with an improved development of brain, thereby increasing the desire and capacity for obedience.

Finally. If it be true that the Natural Laws must be obeyed as a preliminary condition to happiness in this world, and if virtue and happiness be inseparably allied, the religious instructors of mankind may probably discover in the general and prevalent ignorance of these laws, one reason of the limited success which has hitherto attended their own efforts at improving the condition of mankind ; and they may perhaps perceive it to be not inconsistent with their sacred office, to instruct men in the natural institutions of the Creator, in addition to his revealed will, and to recommend obedience to both. They exercise so vast an influence over the best members of society, that their countenance may hasten, or their opposition retard, by a century, the practical adoption of the natural laws, as guides of human conduct.

* Some observations on education will be found in the Phrenological Journal, vol. iv, p. 407.

APPENDIX.

NOTE I.

NATURAL LAWS.—Text, p. 3.

In the text it is mentioned, that many philosophers have treated of the Laws of Nature. The following are examples:

Mr Stewart says, 'To examine the economy of nature in the phenomena of the lower animals, and to compare their instincts with the physical circumstances of their external situation, forms one of the finest speculations of Natural History; and yet it is a speculation to which the attention of the natural historian has seldom been directed. Not only Buffon, but Ray and Derham have passed it over slightly; nor, indeed, do I know of any one who has made it the object of a particular consideration but Lord Kames, in a short Appendix to one of his Sketches.—*Elements of the Philosophy of the Human Mind*, vol. iii, p. 368.

Mr Stewart also uses the following words:—' Numberless examples show that nature has done no more for man than was necessary for his preservation, leaving him to make many acquisitions for himself, which she has imparted immediately to the brutes.

'My own idea is, as I have said on a different occasion, that both *instinct* and *experience* are here concerned, and that the share which belongs to each in producing the result, can be ascertained by an appeal to facts alone.'—Vol. iii, ch. 338.

Montesquieu introduces his Spirit of Laws by the following observations:—' Laws, in their most general signification, are the necessary relations derived from the nature of things. In this sense, all beings have their laws; the Deity has his laws; the material world its laws; the intelligences superior to man have their laws; the beasts their laws; man his laws.

'Those who assert that *a blind fatality produced the various effects we behold in this world*, are guilty of a very great absurdity: for can any thing be more absurd than to pretend that a blind fatality could be productive of intelligent beings?

'There is, then, a primitive reason; and laws are the relations which subsist between it and different beings, and the relations of these beings among themselves.

'God is related to the universe as creator and preserver; *the laws by which he has created all things are those by which he preserves them. He acts according to these rules*, because he knows them: he knows them because he has made them; and he made them because they are relative to his wisdom and power, &c.

'*Man, as a physical being, is, like other bodies, governed by invariable laws.*'—Spirit of Laws, b. i, c. i.

Justice Blackstone observes, that 'Law, in its most general and comprehensive sense, signifies a rule of action; and *is applied indiscriminately to all kinds of action, whether animate or inanimate, rational or irrational.* Thus we say, the laws of motion, of gravitation, of optics, or mechanics, as well as the laws of nature and of nations. Thus, when the Supreme Being formed the universe, and created matter out of nothing, he impressed certain *principles* upon that matter, from which it can never depart, and without which it would cease to be. When he put that matter into motion, he established *certain laws of motion*, to which all moveable bodies must conform.'—'If we farther advance from mere inactive matter to *vegetable and animal life*, WE SHALL FIND THEM STILL GOVERNED BY LAWS; more numerous, indeed, but *equally fixed and invariable*. The whole progress of plants, from the seed to the root, and from thence to the seed again;—the method of animal nutrition, digestion, secretion, and all other branches of vital economy;—are *not left to chance*, or the will of the creature itself, but are performed in a wondrous involuntary manner, and *guided by unerring rules laid down by the great Creator*. This, then, is the general signification of a law, a rule of action dictated by some superior being; and in those creatures that have neither power to think, nor the will, such laws must be invariably obeyed, so long as the creature itself subsists; for its existence depends on that obedience.—*Blackstone's Commentaries on the Laws of England*, vol. i, sect. 2.

'The word *law*,' says Mr Erskine, 'is frequently made use of, both by *divines and philosophers*, in a large acceptation, to express *the settled method of God's providence*, by which he preserves the order of the MATERIAL WORLD *in such a manner, that nothing in it may deviate from that uniform course which he has appointed for it.* And as brute matter is merely passive, without the least degree of choice upon its part, *these laws are* INVIOLABLY OBSERVED *in the material creation, every part of which continues to act, immutably, according to the rules that were from the beginning prescribed to it by infinite wisdom.* Thus philosophers have given the appellation of *law* to that motion which incessantly pervades and agitates the universe, and is ever changing the form and substance of things, dissolving some, and raising others, as from their ashes, to fill up the void: Yet so, that amidst all the fluctuations by which particular things are affected, the universe is still preserved without diminution. Thus also they speak of the *laws* of fluids, of gravitation, &c. and *the word is used, in this sense, in several passages of the sacred writings;* in the book of Job, and in Proverbs viii, 29, where God is said to have given *his law* to the seas that they should not pass his commandment.'—*Erskine's Institutes of the Law of Scotland*, book i, tit. i, sect. 1.

Discussions about the Laws of Nature, rather than inquiries into them, were common in France, during the Revolution, and having become associated in imagination, with the crimes and horrors of that period, they continue to be regarded by some individuals, as inconsistent with religion and morality. A coincidence between the views maintained in the preceding Essay, and a passage in Volney, has been pointed out to me as an objection to the whole doctrine. Volney's words are the following:—'It is a law of nature, that water flows from an upper to a lower situation; that it seeks its level; that it is heavier than air; that all bodies tend towards the earth; that flame rises towards the sky; that it destroys the organization of vegetables and animals; that air is essential to the life of certain animals; that, in certain cases, water suffocates and kills them; that certain juices of plants, and certain minerals, attack their organs, and destroy their life;—and the same of a variety of facts.

'Now, since these facts, and many similar ones, are constant, regular, and immutable, they become so many real and positive commands, to which man is bound to conform, under the express penalty of punishment attached to their infraction, or well-being connected with their observance. So that if a man were to pretend to see clearly in the dark, or is regardless of the progress of the seasons, or the action of the elements; if he pretends to exist under water, without drowning; to handle fire without burning himself; to deprive himself of air without suffocating; or to drink poison without destroying himself; he receives for each infraction of the law of nature, a corporal punishment proportioned to his transgression. If, on the contrary, he observes these laws, and founds his practice on the precise and regular relation which they bear to him, he preserves his existence, and renders it as happy as it is capable of being rendered; and since all these laws, considered in relation to the human species, have in view only one common end, that of their preservation and their happiness; whence it has been agreed to assemble together the different ideas, and express them by a single word, and call them collectively by the name of the "*Law of Nature.*"—VOLNEY'S *Law of Nature*, 3d edit. pp. 21, 24.

I feel no embarrassment by this coincidence; but remark, first, That various authors, quoted in the text and in this note, advocated the importance of the laws of nature, long before the French Revolution was heard of; secondly, That the existence of the laws of nature is as obvious to the understanding, as the existence of the external world, and of the human mind and body themselves to the senses; thirdly, That these laws, being inherent in creation, must have proceeded from the Deity; fourthly, That if the Deity is powerful, just, and benevolent, they must harmonize with the constitution of man; and, lastly, That if the laws of nature have been instituted by the Deity, and been framed in wise, benevolent, and just relationship to the human constitution, they must at all times form the highest and most important subjects of human investigation, and remain altogether unaffected by the errors, follies, and crimes of those who endeavour to expound them; just as religion continues holy, venerable, and uncontaminated, notwithstanding the hypocrisy, wickedness, and inconsistency of individuals professing themselves her interpreters and friends.

That the views of the natural laws themselves, advocated in this Essay, are diametrically opposite to the practical conduct of the French revolutionary ruffians, requires no demonstration. My fundamental principle is, that man can enjoy happiness on earth only by placing his habitual conduct under the supremacy of the moral sentiments, and intellect, and that this is the *law of his nature*. No doctrine can be more opposed than this to fraud, robbery, blasphemy, and murder.

It may be urged, that all past speculations about the laws of nature have proved more imposing than useful; and that while the laws themselves afford materials for elevated declamation on the part of philosophers, they form no secure guides even to the learned, and much less to the illiterate, in practical conduct. In answer, I would respectfully repeat what has frequently been urged in the text, that, before we can discover the laws of nature, applicable to man, we must know, first, The constitution of man himself; secondly, The constitution of external nature; and, thirdly, We must compare the two. But, previous to the discovery of Phrenology, the mental constitution of man was a matter of vague conjecture, and endless debate; and the connexion between his mental powers and his organized system, was involved in the deepest obscurity. The brain, the most important organ of the body, had no ascertained functions. Before the introduction of this science, therefore, men were rather impressed with the unspeakable importance of a knowledge of the laws of nature, than acquainted with the laws themselves; and even the knowedge of the external world actually possessed, could not, in many instances, be rendered available, on account of its relationship to the qualities of man being unascertained, and unascertainable, so long as these qualities themselves were unknown.

NOTE II.

ORGANIC LAWS.—Text, p. 21.

It is a very common error, not only among philosophers, but among practical men, to imagine that the *feelings* of the mind are communicated to it through the medium of the *intellect;* and, in particular, that if no indelicate objects reach the eyes, or expressions penetrate the ears, perfect purity will necessarily reign within the soul; and, carrying this mistake into practice, they are prone to object to all discussion of the subjects treated of under the 'Organic Laws,' in works designed for general use. But their principle of reasoning is fallacious, and the practical result has been highly detrimental to society. The *feelings* have existence and activity distinct from the *intellect;* they spur it on to obtain their own gratification; and it may become either their slave or guide, according as it is enlightened concerning their constitution and objects, and the laws of nature to which they are subjected. The most profound philosophers have inculcated this doctrine; and, by phrenological observation, it is demonstrably established. The organs of the feelings are distinct from those of the intellectual faculties; they are larger; and, as each faculty, *cæteris paribus*, acts with a power proportionate to the size of its organ, the feelings are obviously the active or impelling powers. The cerebellum, or organ of Amativeness, is the largest of the whole mental organs; and, being endowed with natural activity, it fills the mind spontaneously with emotions and suggestions which may be directed, controlled, and resisted, in outward manifestation, by intellect and moral sentiment, but which cannot be prevented from arising, nor eradicated after they exist. The whole question, therefore, resolves itself into this, Whether it is most beneficial to enlighten and direct that feeling, or (under the influence of an error in philosophy, and false delicacy founded on it,) to permit it to riot in all the fierceness of a blind animal instinct, withdrawn from the eye of reason, but not thereby deprived of its vehemence and importunity. The former course appears to me to be the only one consistent with reason and morality; and I have adopted it in reliance on the good sense of my readers, that they will at once discriminate between practical instruction concerning this feeling, addressed to the intellect, and lascivious representations addressed to the mere propensity itself; with the latter of which the enemies of all improvement may attempt to confound my observations. Every function of the mind and body is instituted by the Creator; all may be abused; and it is impossible regularly to avoid abuse of them, except by being instructed in their nature, objects, and relations. This instruction ought to be addressed exclusively to the intellect; and, when it is so, it is science of the most beneficial description. The propriety, nay necessity, of acting on this principle, becomes more and more apparent, when it is considered that the discussions of the text suggest only intellectual ideas to individuals in whom the feeling in question is naturally weak, and that such minds perceive no indelicacy in knowledge which is calculated to be useful; while, on the other hand, persons in whom the feeling is naturally strong, are precisely those who stand in need of direction, and to whom, of all others, instruction is the most necessary.

Fortified by these observations, I venture to record some additional facts communicated by persons on whose accuracy reliance may be placed.

A gentleman, who has paid much attention to the rearing of horses, informed me, that the male race-horse, when excited, but not exhausted, by running, has been found by experience, to be in the most favourable condition for transmitting swiftness and vivacity to his offspring. Another gentleman stated, that he was himself present when the pale gray colour of a male horse was objected to; that the groom thereupon presented before the eyes of the male another female from the stable, of a very particular, but pleasing, variety of colours, asserting, that the latter would determine the complexion of the offspring; and that in point of fact it did so. The experiment was tried in the case of a second female, and the result was so completely the same, that the two young horses, in point of colour, could scarcely be distinguished, although their spots were extremely uncommon. The account of Laban and the peeled rods laid before the cattle to produce spotted calves, is an example of the same kind.

Portal mentions the hereditary descent of blindness and deafness. His words are: 'Morgagni has seen three sisters dumb "*d'origine*.' Other authors also cite examples, and I have seen like cases myself.' In a note, he adds, 'I have seen three children out of four of the same family blind from birth by amaurosis, or *gutta serena*.'—*Portal, Memoires sur Plusieurs Maladies*, tome iii, p. 193. Paris, 1808.

In the Quarterly Journal of Agriculture, No. I, there are several valuable articles illustrative of the Organic Laws in the inferior animals. I select the following examples:

'Every one knows that the hen of any bird will lay eggs although no male be permitted to come near her; and that those eggs are only wanting in the vital principle which the impregnation of the male conveys to them. Here, then, we see the female able to make an egg, with yolk and white, shell and every part, just as it ought to be, so that we might, at the first glance, suppose that here, at all events, the female has the greatest influence. But see the change which the male produces. Put a Bantam cock to a large sized hen and she will instantly lay a small egg; the chick will be short, in the leg, have feathers to the foot, and put on the appearance of the cock; so that it is a frequent complaint where Bantams are kept, that they make the hens lay small eggs, and spoil the breed. Reverse the case; put a large dung-hill cock to Bantam hens, and instantly they will lay larger eggs, and the chicks will be good-sized birds, and the Bantam will have nearly disappeared. Here, then, are a number of facts known to every one, or at least open to be known by every one, clearly proving the influence of the male in some animals; and as I hold it to be an axiom that nature never acts by contraries, never outrages the law clearly fixed in one species, by adopting the opposite course in another,—therefore, as in the case of an equilateral triangle on the length of one side being given we can with certainty demonstrate that of the remaining; so, having found these laws to exist in one race of animals, we are entitled to assume that every species is subjected to the self-same rules,—the whole bearing, in fact, the same relation to each other as the radii of a circle.'

'*A Method of obtaining a greater number of One Sex, at the option of the Proprietor, in the Breeding of Live Stock.*—Extracted from the Quarterly Journal of Agriculture, No. I, p. 63.

'In the Annales de l'Agriculture Française, vols. 37, and 38, some very interesting experiments are recorded, which have lately been made in France, on the Breeding of Live Stock. M. Charles Girou de Buzareingues proposed, at a meeting of the Agricultural Society of Séverac, on the 3d of July, 1826, to divide a flock of sheep into two equal parts, so that a greater number of males or females, at the choice of the proprietor, should be produced from each of them. Two of the members of the Society offered their flocks to become the subjects of his experiments, and the results have now been communicated, which are in accordance with the author's expectations.

'The first experiment was conducted in the following manner: He recommended very young rams to be put to the flock of ewes, from which the proprietor wished the greater number of females in their offspring; and, also, that during the season when the rams were with the ewes, they should have more abundant pasture than the other; while, to the flock from which the proprietor wished to obtain male lambs chiefly, he recommended him to put strong and vigorous rams four or five years old. The following tabular view contains the result of this experiment.

FLOCK FOR FEMALE LAMBS.

Age of the Mothers.	Sex of the Lambs. Males.	Females.
Two years,	14	26
Three years,	16	29
Four years,	5	21
Total,	35	76
Five years and older,	18	8
Total,	53	84

N. B. There were three twin births in this flock. Two rams served it, one fifteen months, the other nearly two years old.

FLOCK FOR MALE LAMBS.

Age of the Mothers.	Sex of the Lambs. Males.	Females.
Two years,	7	3
Three years,	16	14
Four years,	33	14
Total,	55	31
Five years and older,	25	24
Total,	80	55

N. B. There were no twin births in this flock. Two strong rams, one four, the other five years old, served it.

'The second experiment is thus related by the author:

'During the summer of 1826, M. Cournuéjouls kept, upon a very dry pasture, belonging to the village of Bez, a flock of 106 ewes, of which 84 belonged to himself, and 22 to his shepherds. Towards the end of October, he divided his flock into two sections, of 42 heads each, the one composed of the strongest ewes, from four to five years old; the other of the weakest beasts under four or above five years old. The first was destined to produce a greater number of females than the second. After it was marked with pitch in my presence, it was taken to much better pasture behind Panouse, where it was delivered to four male lambs, about six months old, and of good promise. The second remained upon the pasture of Bez, and was served by two strong rams, more than three years old.

'The ewes belonging to the shepherds, which I shall consider as forming a third section, and which are in general stronger and better fed than those of the master, because their owners are not always particular in preventing them from trespassing on the cultivated lands, which are not enclosed, were mixed with those of the second flock. The result was that the

	Males.	Females.
First section gave,	15	25
The second,	26	14
The third,	10	12
In the First section there were Two Twin Births,	0	4
In the Second and Third there were also Two,	3	1

'Besides these very decisive experiments, M. Girou relates some others, made with horses and cattle, in which his success in producing a greater number of one sex rather than another also appears. The general law, as far as we are able to detect it, seems to be, that, when animals are in good condition, plentifully supplied with food, and kept from breeding as fast as they might do, they are most likely to produce females. Or, in other words, when a race of animals is in circumstances favourable for its increase, nature produces the greatest number of that sex which in animals that do not pair, is most efficient for increasing the numbers of the race: But, if they are in a bad climate, or on stinted pasture, or, if they have already given birth to a numerous offspring, then nature, setting limits to the increase of the race, produces more males than females. Yet, perhaps, it may be premature to attempt to deduce any law from experiments which have not yet been sufficiently extended. M. Girou is disposed to ascribe much of the effect to the age of the ram, independent of the condition of the ewe.'

Note III.

DEATH.—Text, p. 35.

The decreasing Mortality of England is strikingly supported by the following extract from the Scotsman of 16th April 1828. It is well known that this paper is edited by Mr Charles Maclaren, a gentlemen whose extensive information, and scrupulous regard to accuracy and truth, stamp the highest value on his statements of facts: and whose profound and comprehensive intellect warrants a well-grounded reliance on his philosophical conclusions.

'Diminished Mortality in England. The diminution of the annual mortality in England amidst an alleged increase of crime, misery, and pauperism, is an extraordinary and startling fact, which merits a more careful investigation than it has received. We have not time to go deeply into the subject: but we shall offer a remark or two on the question, how the apparent annual mortality is affected by the introduction of the cow-pox, and the stationary or progressive state of the population. In 1780, according to Mr Rickman, the annual deaths were 1 in 40, or *one-fortieth* part of the population died every year; in 1821, the proportion was 1 in 58. It follows, that, out of any given number of persons, 1000 or 10,000 scarcely more than two deaths take place now for three that took place in 1780, or the mortality has diminished 45 per cent. The parochial registers of burials in England, from which this statement is derived, are known to be incorrect, but as they continue to be kept without alteration in the same way, the errors for one year, are justly conceived to balance those of another, and they thus afford *comparative* results upon which considerable reliance may be placed.

A community is made up of persons of many various ages among whom the law of mortality is very different. Thus, according to the Swedish tables, the deaths among children from the moment of birth up to 10 years of age, are 1 in 22 per annum; from 10 to 20, the deaths are only 1 in 185. Among the old again, mortality is of course great. From 70 to 80, the deaths are 1 in 9; from 80 to 90, they are 1 in 4. Now a community like that of New York or Ohio, where marriages are made early and the births are numerous, necessarily contains a large proportion of young persons, among whom the proportional mortality is low, and a small proportion of the old who die off rapidly. A community in which the births are numerous, is like a regiment receiving a vast number of a young and healthy recruits and in which, of course, as a whole, the annual deaths will be few compared with those in another regiment chiefly filled with veterans, though among the persons at any particular age, such as 20, 40, or 50, the mortality will be as great in the one regiment as the other. It may thus happen, that the annual mortality among 1000 persons in Ohio may be considerably less than in France, while the *Expectation of Life*, or the chance which an individual has to reach to a certain age, may be no greater in the former country than in the latter; and hence we see that a diminution in the rate of mortality is not a certain proof of an increase in the value of life, or an improvement in the condition of the people.

But the effect produced by an increased number of births is less than might be imagined, owing to the very great mortality among infants in the first year of their age. Not having time for the calculations necessary to get at the precise result, which are pretty complex, we avail ourselves of some statements given by Mr. Milne in his work on Annuities. Taking the Swedish tables as a basis, and supposing the law of mortality to remain the same for each period of life, he has compared the proportional number of deaths in a population which is stationary, and in one which increases 15 per cent. in 20 years. The result is, that when the mortality in the stationary society is *one* in 36. 13, that in the progressive society is one in 37. 33, a difference equal to 3 1-3 per cent. Now, the population of England and Wales increased 34.3 per cent. in the 20 years ending in 1821, but in the interval from 1811 to 1821. the rate was equivalent to 39 1-4 per cent, upon 20 years; and the apparent diminution of mortality arising from this circumstance must of course have been about 8 1-2 per cent. We are assuming, however, that the population was absolutely stationary at 180, which was not the case. According to Mr Milnes (p. 437,) the average annual increase in the five years ending 1784, was 1 in 155; in the ten years ending 1821, according to the census, it was 1 in 60. Deducting, then, the proportional part corresponding to the former, which is 3 1-4 there remains 5 1-4. If Mr Milne's tables, therefore, are correct, *we may infer that the progressive state of the population causes a diminution of* 5 1-4 *per cent. in the annual mortality*—a diminution which is only *apparent*, because it arises entirely from the great proportion of births, and is not accompanied with any real increase in the value of human life.

'A much greater change—not apparent but real—was produced by the introduction of the vaccination in 1798. It was computed, that, in 1795, when the population of the British Isles was 15, 000,000, the deaths produced by the small-pox amounted to 36,000, or nearly 11 per cent. of the whole animal mortality. (See article *Vaccination* in the Supplement to Encylopedia Brittanica, p. 713.) Now, since not more than one case in 330 terminates fatally under the cow-pox system, either directly by the primary infection, or from the other disease supervening: the whole of the young persons destroyed by the small-pox might be considered as saved were vaccination universal, and always properly performed. This is not precisely the case, but one or one and a-half per cent. will cover the deficiencies; and we may therefore conclude, that *vaccination has diminished the annual mortality fully nine per cent.* After we had arrived at this conclusion by the process described, we found it confirmed by the authority of Mr Milne, who estimates in a note to one of his tables, that the mortality of 1 in 40, would be diminished to 1 in 43—5, by exterminating the small-pox. Now, this is almost precisely 9 per cent.

'We stated, that the diminution of the annual mortality between 1780 and 1821 was 45 per cent., according to Mr Rickman. If we deduct this from 9 per cent. for the effect of vaccination, and 5 per cent. as only apparent, resulting from the increasing proportion of births—31 per cent. remains, *which, we apprehend, can only be accounted for by an improvement in the habits, morals, and physical condition of the people.* Independently, then, of the two causes alluded to, the value of human life since 1780, has increased in a ratio which would diminish the annual mortality from 1 in 40 to 1 in 52 1-2,—a fact which is indisputably of great importance, and worth volumes of declamation in illustrating the true situation of the labouring classes. We have founded our conclusion on data derived entirely from English returns ; but there is no doubt that it applies equally to Scotland. It is consoling to find, from this very unexceptionable species of evidence, that though there is much privation and suffering in the country, the situation of the people has been, on the whole, progressively improving during the last forty years. But how much greater would the advance have been, had they been less taxed, and better treated ? and how much room is there still for future melioration, by spreading instruction, amending our laws, lessening the temptations to crime, and improving the means of correction and reform ? In the mean time it ought to be some encouragement to philanthropy to learn that it has not to struggle against invincible obstacles, and that even when the prospect was least cheering to the eye, its efforts were silently benefitting society.'

It has been mentioned to me, that the late Dr Monro, in his anatomical lectures, stated, that, as far as he could observe, the human body as a machine, was perfect,—that it bore within itself no marks by which we could possibly predicate its decay,—that it was apparently calculated to go on for ever,—and that we learned only by experience that it would not do so ; and some persons have conceived this to be an authority against the doctrine maintained in Chap. III, Sect. 2, that death is apparently inherent in organization. In answer, I beg to observe, that if we were to look at the sun only for one moment of time, say at noon, no circumstance, in its appearance would indicate that it had ever risen, or that it would ever set ; but, if we had traced its progress from the horizon to the meridian, and down again till the long shadows of evening prevailed, we should have ample grounds for inferring, that, if the same causes that had produced these changes continued to operate, it would undoubtedly at length disappear. In the same way, if we were to confine our observations on the human body to a mere point of time, it is certain that, from the appearances of that moment, we could not infer that it had grown up, by gradual increase, or that it would decay ; but this is the case only, because our faculties are not fitted to penetrate into the essential nature and dependences of things. Any man, who had seen the body decrease in old age, could, without hesitation, predicate, that, if the same causes which had produced that effect went on operating, dissolution would at last inevitably occur ; and if his Causality were well developed, he would not hesitate to say that a *cause* of the decrease and dissolution must exist, although he could not tell by examining the body what it was. By analysing alcohol, no person could predicate, independently of experience, that it would produce intoxication ; and nevertheless, there must be a cause in the constitution of the alcohol, in that of the body, and in the relationship between them, why it produces this effect. The notion, therefore, of Dr Monro, does not prove that death is not an essential law of organization, but only that the human faculties are not able, by dissection, to discover that the cause of it is inherent in the bodily constitution itself. It does not follow however, that this inference may not be legitimately drawn from phenomena collected from the whole period of corporeal existence.

Note IV.

INFRINGEMENT OF THE MORAL LAWS.—Text, p. 44.

The deterioration of the operative classes of Britain which I attribute to excessive labour, joined with great alternations of high and low wages, and occasionally with absolute idleness and want, is illustrated by the following extracts :—

'UNEMPLOYED WEAVERS IN LANARKSHIRE. On Saturday last, a meeting of weavers' delegates from the various districts in this neighbourhood, was held in the usual place. The object of the meeting was to receive from the several districts an account of the number of weavers out of employment, which statement it was intended to lay before the Lord Provost and Magistrates. The following are the returns given in :—Anderston contains 708 looms, of which 386 are idle. Baillieston-toll contains 150 looms, of these 98 are empty. The district of North Bridgeton contains, in whole, between 400 and 500 looms. The returns are only from about one half of this district, which contains 150 empty looms. For the centre and south districts of Bridgeton, the accounts are incomplete. In the former 180 and in the latter 60 empty looms were taken up. In Charleston there are 132 idle. In Cowcaddens, of 300 looms, 120 are idle. In Clyde,Bell, and Tobago Streets,of about 500 looms, there are 74 idle ; and 100 working webs which cannot average 7d. a-day. In Drygate, there are 105 idle ; In Drygate-toll 73 ; in Duke Street 18. In Gorbals,containing 365 looms, there are 223 idle. In Havannah, out of 130 looms, there are 48 idle. In the district of Keppoch-hill, of 70 weavers, there are 20 idle. The district of King Street is divided into ten wards ; returns are only given in from four, which contain 70 empty looms. In Pollockshaws, containing about 800 looms,there are 216 idle. In Rutherglen there are 167 idle. In Springbank, of 141 weavers, there are 58 unemployed ; and in Strathbungo, containing 104 looms, there are 28 idle, 25 of whom are married men. Parkhead, Camlachie, and some other extensive districts, have not yet given in their returns. The delegates, before separating, appointed a general meeting to be held in the Green this day, to decide upon an address to the Magistrates, requesting them to endeavour to procure employment for the idle hands.'—*Glasgow Chronicle, Tuesday, March,* 1826.

'SHEEP TRADE. The late commercial crisis, like a death-blow, has paralysed the whole activity of the country, and left scarcely a single branch of its trade and industry unscathed. It was at first fondly hoped that the storm would pass without such remote districts as our own having much reason to complain of its visitation ; but nothing, as the present instance proves, is more certain than that the distresses of the commercial, must also in all cases be more or less felt by the agricultural classes of the community. The demand for wool has now so far ceased as to operate most injuriously upon the price of sheep, which cannot presently be sold but at a very considerable loss to the farmer. In the latter part, or "back season," as it is called, of 1824, black-faced ewes—their example applies equally to the other kinds—were bought in for wintering at from 8s. to 12s. a head ; and in the spring of 1825, immediately before lambing-time, these were disposed of in the English markets at so great a profit, that every farmer who could at all enter into the speculation, bought up at the end of the ensuing harvest, as much of that description of stock as his quantity of keep would reasonably permit. The number of sheep over those of the preceding year, which were bought up for this purpose, may be judged of from the fact, that the highest inlay price of 1824 was the lowest of

1825—the rate for the latter year being, for black-faced ewes, from 12s to 18. But the present crisis came, —the manufacturers of England were obliged to retrench at meals in the article of mutton,—the demand on the part of the butchers consequently ceased; and now those sheep which were purchased at so extravagant a rate, are necessarily sold, upon an average, at a loss of 2s. a-head upon the inlay price, without at all estimating the expense of keep. We know one extensive moorland farmer, who calculates upon losing two hundred pounds in the present year from this cause alone, besides a vast loss which he must also sustain in consequence of the reduced price of wool. This cessation of demand in England was unfortunately not fully ascertained until several droves of lambing ewes had been despatched to that quarter; and the embarrassment of those who are placed in this predicament is the more afflicting, as their knowledge has been acquired too late to allow of their availing themselves of the House of Muir, and other northern markets.'—*Dumfries Courier, March*, 1826.

'*Details upon the Subject of Weavers' Wages, from the last Report of emigration extracted from the Scotsman Newspaper, of* 10*th November*, 1827.

'Joseph Foster a weaver, and one of the deputies of an emigration society in Glasgow, states that the labour is all paid by the piece; the hours of working are various, sometimes eighteen or nineteen out of twenty-four, and even all night once or twice a-week; and that the wages made by such labour, after deducting the necessary expenses, will not amount to more than from 4s. 6d. to 7s. per week, some kinds of work, paying better than others. When he commenced working as a weaver, from 1800 to 1805, the same amount of labour that now yields 4s. 6d. to 5s. would have yielded 20s. There are about 11,000 hand-looms going in Glasgow and its suburbs, some of which are worked by boys and girls, and he estimates the average net earnings of each hand-weaver at 5s 6d. The principle subsistence of the weavers is oatmeal and potatoes, with occasionally some salt herring.

'Major Thomas Moodie, who had made careful inquiries into the state of the poor at Manchester, states, that the calico and other light plain work at Bolton and Blackburn, yields the weaver from 4s. to 5s. per week, by fourteen hours of daily labour. In the power-loom work, one man attends two looms, and earns from 7s. 6d. to 14s. per week, according to the fineness of the work. He understood that during the last ten years, weavers' wages had fallen on an average about 15s. per week.

'Mr Thomas Hunton, manufacturer, Carlisle, states, that there are in Carlisle and its neighbourhood about 5500 families, or from 18,000 to 20,000 persons dependent on weaving. They are all hand-weavers, and are now in a very depressed state, in consequence of the increase of power-loom and factory weaving* in Manchester and elsewhere. Taking fifteen of his men, he finds that five of them, who are employed on the best work, had earned 5s. 6d. per week for the preceding month deducting the necessary expenses of loom-rent, candles, tackling, &c.; the next five, who are upon work of the second quality, earned 3s. 11d.; and the third five earned 3s. 7 1-2per week. They work from fourteen to sixteen hours a-day, and live chiefly on potatoes, butter-milk, and herrings.

'Mr W. H. Hyett, Secretary to the Charity Committee in London, gives a detailed statement, to show, that in the Hundred of Blackburn, comprising a population of 150,000 persons, 90,000 were out of employment in 1826! In April last, when he gave his evidence before the Committee, these persons had generally found work again, but at very low wages. They were labouring from twelve to fourteen hours a-day, and gaining from 4s. to 5s. 6d. per week.'

'Poor Rates, 28*th March*, 1828.—A document of great importance, though of a description by no means cheering, has been presented to the House of Commons,—the annual Abstract of the Returns of the Poor Rates levied and expended, with comparisons, showing their increase or diminution. The accounts show the expenditure of the year ending 25th March, 1827, compared with the previous year. The total sum levied in all the counties of England and Wales, in the last year, was £7,489,694; the sum expended for the relief of the poor, £6,179,877. The increase in that year throughout the whole of England and Wales, is nine per cent; nine per cent. in one year on the whole sum expended. It is true that this is in part to be accounted for by the temporary distress of the manufacturing districts. (In Lancaster, the increase was forty-seven, in the West Riding of York, thirty-one per cent;) but we are sorry to find, that in only three counties of England was there any the most trifling diminution. In Berks two, Hampshire five, Suffolk four per cent. The poor rates in England, therefore, amount to nearly double the whole landed rental of Scotland.'

'*Extract from the Lord-Advocate's Speech in the House of Commons*, 11*th March*, 1828, *on the additional Circuit Court of Glasgow.*

'The Lord-Advocate, in rising to move for leave to bring in a bill to "authorize an additional Court of Justiciary to be held at Glasgow, and to facilitate criminal trial in Scotland," said he did not anticipate any opposition to the motion. A great deal had been said of the progress of crime in this country, but he was sorry to say crime in Scotland had kept pace with that increase. A return had been made of the number of criminal commitments in each year, so far back as the year 1805. In that year the number of criminal commitments for all Scotland amounted only to 85. In 1809 it had risen to between 200 and 300; in 1819—20, it had increased to 400; and by the last return, it appeared, that, in 1827, 661 persons had been committed for trial. He was inclined to think, that the great increase of crime, particularly in the west of Scotland, was attributable, in no small degree, to the number of Irish who daily and weekly arrived there. He did not mean to say that the Irish themselves were in the habit of committing more crime than their neighbours; but he was of opinion, that their numbers tended to reduce the price of labour, and that an increase of crime was the consequence. Another cause was the great disregard manifested by parents for the moral education of their children. Formerly the people of Scotland were remarkable for the paternal care which they took of their offspring. That had ceased in many instances to be the case. Not only were parents found who did not pay attention to the welfare of their children, but who were actually parties to their criminal pursuits, and participated in the fruits of their unlawful proceedings. When crime was thus on the increase, it was necessary to take measures for its speedy punishment. The great city of Glasgow, which contained 150,000 inhabitants, and to which his proposed measure was meant chiefly to apply, stood greatly in need of some additional jurisdiction. This would appear evident, when it was considered that the court which met there for the trial of capital offences, had also to act in the districts of Renfrew, Lanark, and Dunbarton. In 1812, the whole number of criminals tried in Glasgow was only 31; in 1820, it was 83; in 1823, it was 85; and in 1827, 211. —The learned lord concluded by moving for leave to bring in a bill to authorize an additional circuit court of justiciary to be held at Glasgow. and to facilitate criminal trial in Scotland.'

* In what is called factory weaving, an improved species of hand-loom is employed, in which the dressing and preparation of the web is effected by machinery, and the weaver merely sits and drives the shuttle.

THE END.

CONTENTS OF THE CONSTITUTION OF MAN.

CHAPTER I.

CHAPTER II.

CHAPTER III.

CHAPTER IV.

APPENDIX.

ESSAYS

IN A

SERIES OF LETTERS,

ON THE FOLLOWING SUBJECTS:

ON A MAN'S WRITING MEMOIRS OF HIMSELF.

ON DECISION OF CHARACTER.

ON THE APPLICATION OF THE EPITHET ROMANTIC.

ON SOME OF THE CAUSES

BY WHICH EVANGELICAL RELIGION HAS BEEN

RENDERED LESS ACCEPTABLE TO PERSONS

OF CULTIVATED TASTE.

BY JOHN FOSTER,

AUTHOR OF 'GLORY OF THE AGE,' &c.

HARTFORD:

PUBLISHED BY SILAS ANDRUS & SON.

1850.

AUTHOR'S PREFACE.

Perhaps it will be thought that pieces written so much in the manner of set compositions as the following, should not have been denominated Letters; it may, therefore, be proper to say, that they are so called because they were actually addressed to a friend. They were written, however, with the intention to print them, if, when they were finished, the writer could persuade himself that they deserved it; and the character of authors is too well known for any one to be surprised that he *could* persuade himself of this.

When he began these letters, his intention was to confine himself within such limits, that essays on twelve or fifteen subjects might have been comprised in a volume. But he soon found that an interesting subject could not be so fully unfolded as he wished, in such a narrow space. It appeared to him that many things which would be excluded, as much belonged to the purpose of the essay as those which would be introduced.

It will not seem a very natural manner of commencing a course of letters to a friend to enter formally on a subject, in the first sentence. In excuse for this abruptness it may be mentioned, that an introductory letter went before that which appears first in the series; but as it was written in the presumption that a considerable variety of subjects would be treated in the compass of a moderate number of letters, it is omitted, as being less adapted to precede what is executed in a manner so different from the design.

When writing which has occupied a considerable length, and has been interrupted by considerable intervals, of time, which is also on very different subjects, and was, perhaps, meditated under the influence of different circumstances, is at last all read over in one short space, this immediate succession and close comparison make the writer sensible of some things of which he was not aware in the slow separate stages of his progress. On thus bringing the following essays under one review, the writer perceives some reason to apprehend that the spirit of the third may appear so different from that of the second as to give an impression of something like inconsistency. The second may seem to represent that a man may effect almost every thing; the third, that he can effect scarcely any thing. The writer, however, persuades himself that the one does not assert the efficacy of human resolution and effort under the same conditions under which the other asserts their inefficacy; and that, therefore, there is no real contrariety between the principles of the two essays. From the evidence of history and familiar experience we know that under certain conditions, and within certain limits, (very contracted ones indeed,) an enlightened and resolute human spirit has great power, this greatness being relative, of course, to the measures of things within a small sphere; while it is equally obvious that this enlightened and resolute spirit, disregarding these conditions, and attempting to extend its agency over a much wider sphere, shall find its power baffled and annihilated, till it draws back again within the contracted boundary. Now the great power of the human mind within the narrow limit may be distinctly illustrated at one time, and its impotence beyond that limit, at another; but the assemblage of sentiments and exemplifications most adapted to illustrate, and without any very material exaggeration, that power alone, will form apparently so strong a contrast with the assemblage of thoughts and facts proper for illustrating that imbecility alone, that on a superficial view the two representations may appear contradictory. And the author appeals to the experience of such thinking men as are accustomed to commit their thoughts to writing, whether they have not sometimes, on comparing the pages in which they had endeavoured to place one truth in the strongest light, with those in which they have endeavoured a strong but yet not extravagant exhibition of another, felt a momentary difficulty to reconcile them, even while satisfied of the substantial justness of both. The whole doctrine on any extensive moral subject necessarily includes two views which may be considered as its extremes; and if these are strongly stated quite apart from their relations to each other, both the representations may be perfectly true, and yet may require, in order to the readers perceiving their consistency, a recollection of many intermediate ideas.

In the fourth essay, it was not intended to take a comprehensive or systematic view of the causes contributing to prevent the candid attention and the cordial admission due to evangelical religion, but simply to select a very few which had particularly attracted the author's observation. One or two more would have been specified and slightly illustrated, if that the essay had not been already too long.

ESSAY I.

ON A MAN'S WRITING MEMOIRS OF HIMSELF

LETTER I.

Affectionate Interest with which we revert to our past Life—It deserves a brief Record for our own use—Very few things to be noted of the Multitude that have occurred—Direction and Use of such a Review as would be required for writing a Memoir—Importance of our past Life considered as the Beginning of an endless Duration of Existence—General Deficiency of Self-Observation—Oblivion of the greatest number of our past Feelings—Occasional Glimpses of vivid Recollection—Associations with Things and Places—The different and unknown Associations of different Persons with the same Places.

MY DEAR FRIEND,

EVERY one knows with what interest it is natural to retrace the course of our own lives. The past states and periods of a man's being are retained in a connexion with the present by that principle of self-love, which is unwilling to relinquish its hold on what has once been his. Though he cannot but be sensible of how little consequence his life can have been in the creation, compared with many other trains of events, yet he has felt it more important to himself than all other trains together; and you will very rarely find him tired of narrating again the little history, or at least the favorite parts of the little history, of himself.

To turn this partiality to some account, I recollect having proposed to two or three of my friends that they should write, each principally however for his own use, memoirs of their own lives, endeavouring not so much to enumerate the mere facts and events of life, as to discriminate the successive states of the mind, and the progress of character. It is in this progress that we acknowledge the chief importance of life to consist: but even as supplying a constant series of interests to the passions, and separately from every consideration of moral and intellectual discipline, we have all accounted our life an inestimable possession, which it deserved incessant cares and labours to retain, and which continues in most cases to be still held with anxious attachment. What has been the object of so much partiality, and has been delighted and painted by so many emotions, might claim, even if the highest interest were out of the question, that a short memorial should be retained by him who has possessed it, has seen it all to this moment depart, and can never recal it.

To write memoirs of many years, as twenty, thirty, or forty, seems, at the first glance, a ponderous task. To reap the products of so many acres of earth indeed might, to one person, be an undertaking of mighty toil. But the materials of any value that all past life can supply to a recording pen, would be reduced by a discerning selection to a very small and modest amount. Would as much as one page of moderate size be deemed by any man's self-importance to be due, on an average, to each of the days that he has lived? No man would judge more than one in ten thousand of all his thoughts, sayings, and actions, worthy to be mentioned, if memory were capable of recalling them. Necessarily a very large portion of what has occupied the successive years of life was of a kind to be utterly useless for a history of it; because it was merely for the accommodation of the time. Perhaps in the space of forty years, millions of sentences are proper to be uttered, and many thousands of affairs requisite to be transacted, or of journeys to be performed, which it would be ridiculous to record. They are a kind of material for the common expenditure and waste of the day. And yet it is often by a detail of this subordinate economy of life, that the works of fiction, the narratives of age, the journals of travellers, and even grave biographical accounts, are made so unreasonably long. As well might a chronicle of the coats that a man has worn, with the colour and date of each, be called his life, for any important uses of relating its history. As well might a man, of whom I inquire the dimensions, the internal divisions, and the use, of some remarkable building, begin to tell me how much wood was employed in the scaffolding, where the mortar was prepared, or how often it rained while the work was proceeding.

But, in a deliberate review of all that we can remember of past life, it will be possible to select a certain proportion which may with the most propriety be deemed the history of the man. What I am recommending is, to follow the order of time, and reduce your recollections, from the earliest period to the present, into as simple a statement and explanation as you can, of your feelings, opinions, and habits, and of the principal circumstances through each stage that have influenced them, till they have become at last what they now are.

Whatever tendencies nature may justly be deemed to have imparted in the first instance, you would probably find the greater part of the moral constitution of your being composed of the contributions of many years and events, consolidated by degrees into what we call character; and by investigating the progress of the accumulation, you would be assisted to judge more clearly how far the materials are valuable, the mixture congruous, and the whole conformation worthy to remain unaltered. With respect to any friend that greatly interests us, we have always a curiosity to obtain an accurate account of the past train of his life and feelings; and though there may be several reasons for such a wish, it partly springs from a consciousness how much this retrospective knowledge would assist to decide or confirm our estimate of that friend; but our estimate of ourselves is of more serious consequence.

The elapsed periods of life acquire importance too from the prospect of its continuance. The smallest thing becomes respectable, when regarded as the commencement of what has advanced, or is advancing, into magnificence. The first rude settlement of Romulus would have been an insignificant circumstance, and might justly have sunk into oblivion, if Rome had not at length commanded the world. The little rill, near the source of one of the great American rivers, is an interesting object to the traveller, who is apprised, as he steps across it, or walks a few miles along its bank, that this is the stream which runs so far, and which gradually swells into so immense a flood. So, while I anticipate the endless progress of life, and wonder through what unknown scenes it is to take its course, its past years lose that character of vanity which would seem to belong to a train of fleeting perishing moments, and I see them assuming the dignity of a commencing eternity. In them I have *begun* to be that conscious existence which I *am* to be through infinite duration: and I feel a strange emotion of curiosity about this little life, in which I am setting out on such a progress; I cannot be content without an accurate sketch of the windings thus far of a stream which is to bear me on forever. I try to imagine how it will be to recollect, at a far distant point of my era, what I was when here; and wish, if it were possible, to retain, as I advance, the whole course of my existence within the scope of clear reflection; to fix in my mind so strong an idea of what I have been in this original period of my time, that I shall possess this idea in ages too remote for calculation.

The review becomes still more important, when I learn the influence which this first part of the progress will have on the happiness or misery of the next.

One of the greatest difficulties in the way of executing the proposed task will have been caused by the extreme deficiency of that self-observation, which, to any extent, is no common employment either of youth or any later age. Men realize their existence in the surrounding objects that act upon them, and from the *interests* of self, rather than in that very *self*, that interior being that is thus acted upon. So that this being itself, with its thoughts and feelings, as distinct from the objects of those thoughts and feelings, but rarely occupies its own deep and patient attention. Men carry their minds as they carry their watches, content to be ignorant of the mechanism of their movements, and satisfied with attending to the little exterior circle of things, to which the passions, like indexes, are pointing. It is surprising to see how little self-knowledge a person not watchfully observant of himself may have gained, in the whole course of an active, or even an inquisitive life. He may have lived almost an age, and traversed a continent, minutely examining its curiosities, and interpreting the half-obliterated characters on its monuments, unconscious the while of a process operating on his own mind, to impress or to erase characteristics of much more importance to him than all the figured brass or marble that Europe contains. After having explored many a cavern or dark ruinous avenue, he may have left undetected a darker recess in his character. He may have conversed with many people, in different languages, on numberless subjects; but, having neglected those conversations with himself by which his whole moral being should have been kept continually disclosed to his view, he is better qualified perhaps to describe the intrigues of a foreign court, or the progress of a foreign trade; to represent the manners of the Italians, or the Turks; to narrate the proceedings of the Jesuits, or the adventures of the Gypsies; than to write the history of his own mind.

If we had practised habitual self-observation, we could not have failed to make important discoveries. There have been thousands of feelings, each of which, if strongly seized upon, and made the subject of reflection, would have shown us what our character was, and what it was likely to become. There have been numerous incidents, which operated on us as tests, and so fully brought out our prevalent quality, that another person, who should have been discriminately observing us, would instantly have formed a decided estimate. But unfortunately the mind is generally too much occupied by the feeling or the incident itself, to have the slightest care or consciousness that any thing *could* be learnt, or *is* disclosed. In very early youth it is almost inevitable for it to be thus lost to itself even amidst its own feelings, and the external objects of attention; but it seems a contemptible thing, and certainly is a criminal and dangerous thing, for a man in mature life to allow himself this thoughtless escape from self-examination.

We have not only neglected to observe what our feelings indicated, but have also in a very great degree ceased to remember what they were. We may justly wonder how our minds could pass away successively from so many scenes and moments which seemed to us important, each in its time, and retain so light an impression, that we have now nothing to tell about what once excited our utmost emotion. As to my own mind, I perceive that it is becoming uncertain of the exact nature of many feelings of considerable interest, even of comparatively recent date; of course, the remembrance of what was felt in early life is exceedingly faint. I have just been observing several children of eight or ten years old, in all the active vivacity which enjoys the plentitude of the moment without 'looking before or after;' and while observing, I attempted, but without success, to recollect what I was at that age. I can indeed remember the principal events of the period, and the actions and projects to which my feelings impelled me; but the feelings themselves, in their own pure juvenility, cannot be revived, so as to be described and placed in comparison with those of maturity. What is become of all those vernal fancies which had so much power to touch the heart? What a number of sentiments have lived and revelled in the soul that are now irrevocably gone! They died, like the singing birds of that time, which now sing no more.

The life that we then had, now seems almost as if it could not have been our own. When we go back to it in thought, and endeavour to recal the interests which animate it, they will not come. We are like a man returning, after the absence of many years, to visit the embowered cottage where he passed the morning of his life, and finding only a relic of its ruins.

But many of the propensities which still continue, probably originated then: and our not being able to explore them up to those remote sources renders a *complete* investigation of our moral and intellectual characters forever impossible. How little, in those years, we were aware, when we met with the incident, or heard the conversation, or saw the spectacle or felt the emotion, which were the first causes of some of the chief permanent tendencies of future life, how much and how vainly we might, long afterward, wish to ascertain the origin of those tendencies. But if we cannot absolutely reach their origin, it will however be interesting to trace them back through all the circumstances which have increased their strength.

In some occasional states of the mind, we can look back much more clearly, and to a much greater distance, than at other times. I would advise to seize those short intervals of illumination which sometimes occur without our knowing the cause, and in which the genuine aspect of some remote event, or long-forgotten image, is recovered with extreme distinctness by vivid spontaneous glimpses of thought such as no effort could have commanded; as the sombre features and minute objects of a distant ridge of hills become strikingly visible in the strong gleams of light which transiently fall on them. An instance of this kind occurred to me but a few hours since, while reading what had no perceptible connexion with a circumstance of my early youth, which probably I have not recollected for many years, and which had no unusual interest at the time that it happened. That circumstance came suddenly to my mind with a clearness of representation which I was not able to retain for the length of an hour, and which I could not by the strongest effort at this instant renew. I seemed almost to *see* the walls and windows of a particular room, with four or five persons in it, who were so perfectly restored to my imagination, that I could recognise not only the features, but even the momentary expressions of their countenances, and then tones of their voices.

According to different states of the mind too, retrospect appears longer or shorter. It may happen that some memorable circumstance of very early life shall be so powerfully recalled, as to contract the wide intervening space, by banishing from the view, a little while, all the series of intermediate remembrances; but when this one object of memory retires again to its remoteness and indifference, and all the others resume their proper places and distances, the retrospect appears long.

Places and things which have an association with any of the events or feelings of past life, will greatly assist the recollection of them. A man of strong associations finds memoirs of himself already written on the places where he has conversed with happiness or misery. If an old man wished to animate for a moment the languid and faded ideas which he retains of his youth, he might walk with his crutch across the green, where he once played with companions who are now probably laid to repose in another spot not far off. An aged saint may meet again some of the affecting ideas of his early piety, in the place where he first thought it happy to pray. A walk in a meadow, the sight of a bank of flowers, perhaps even of some one flower, a landscape with the tints of autumn, the descent into a valley, the brow of a mountain, the house where a friend has been met, or has resided, or has died, have often produced a much more lively recollection of our past feelings, and of the objects and events which caused them, than the most perfect description could have done; and we have lingered a considerable time for the pensive luxury of thus resuming the departed state.

But there are many to whom local associations present images which they fervently wish they could forget; images which haunt the places where crimes had been perpetrated, and which seemed to approach and glare on the criminal as he hastily passes by, especially if in the evening or in the night. No local associations are so impressive as those of guilt. It may here be observed, that as each one has his own separate remembrances, giving to some places an aspect and a significance which he alone can perceive, there must be an unknown number of pleasing, or mournful, or dreadful associations, spread over the scenes inhabited or visited by men. *We* pass without any awakened consciousness by the bridge, or the wood, or the house, where there is something to excite the most painful or frightful ideas in the next man that shall come that way, or possibly the companion that walks along with us. How much there is in a thousand spots of the earth, that is invisible and silent to all but the conscious individual!

I hear a voice you cannot hear;
I see a hand you cannot see.

LETTER II.

All past Life an Education—Discipline and influence from—direct Instruction—Companionship—Books—Scenes of Nature—and the State of Society.

We may regard our past life as a continued though irregular course of education; and the discipline has consisted of instruction, companionship, reading, and the diversified influence of the world. The young mind eagerly came forward to meet the operation of some or all of these modes of discipline, though without the possibility of a thought concerning the important process under which it was beginning to pass. In some certain degree we have been influenced by each of these parts of the great system of education; it will be worth while to inquire how far, and in what manner.

Few persons can look back to the early period when they were most directly the subjects of instruction, without a regret for themselves, (which may be extended to the human race,) that the result of instruction, excepting that which leads to evil, bears so small a proportion to its compass and repetition. Yet *some* good consequences will follow the diligent inculcation of truth and precept on the youthful mind; and our consciousness of possessing certain advantages derived from it will be a partial consolation in the review that will comprise so many proofs of its comparative inefficacy. You can recollect perhaps, the instructions to which you feel yourself permanently the most indebted, and some of those which produced the greatest effect at the time, those which surprised, delighted, or mortified you. You can remember the facility or difficulty of understanding, the facility or difficulty of believing, and the practical inferences which you drew from principles, on the strength of your own reason, and sometimes in variance with those made by your instructers You can remember what views of truth and duty were most frequently and cogently presented, what passions were appealed to, what arguments were employed, and which had the greatest influence. Perhaps your present idea of the most convincing and persuasive mode of instruction, may be derived from your early experience of the manner of those persons with whose opinions you felt it the most easy and delightful to harmonize, who gave you the most agreeable consciousness of your faculties expanding to the light, like morning flowers, and who, assuming the least of dictation, exerted the greatest degree of power. You can recollect the submissiveness with which your mind yielded to instructions as from an oracle, or the hardihood with which you dared to examine and oppose them. You can remember how far they became, as to your own conduct, an internal authority of reason and conscience, when you were not under the inspection of those who inculcated them; and what classes of persons or things around you they induced you to dislike or approve. And you can perhaps imperfectly trace the manner and the particulars in which they sometimes aided, or sometimes counteracted, those other influences which have a far stronger efficacy on the character than instruction can boast.

Most persons, I presume, can recollect some few sentiments or conversations which made so deep an impression, perhaps in some instances they can scarcely tell why, that they have been thousands of times recalled, while all the rest have been forgotten; or they can advert to some striking incident, coming in aid of instruction, or being of itself a forcible instruction, which they seem even now to see as clearly as when it happened, and of which they will retain a perfect idea to the end of life. The most remarkable circumstances of this kind deserve to be recorded in the supposed memoirs. In some instances, to recollect the instructions of a former period, will be to recollect too the excellence, the affection, and the death, of the persons who gave them. Amidst the sadness of such a remembrance, it will be a consolation that they are not entirely lost to us. Wise monitions, when they return on us with this melancholy charm, have more pathetic cogency than when they were first uttered by the voice of a living friend. It will be an interesting occupation of the pensive hour, to recount the advantages which we have received from the beings who have left the world, and to reinforce our virtues from the dust of those who first taught them.

In our review, we shall find that the companions of our childhood, and of each succeeding period, have had a great influence on our characters. A creature so conformable as man, and at the same time so capable of being moulded into partial dissimilarity by social antipathies, cannot have conversed with his fellow beings thousands of hours, walked with them thousands of miles, undertaken with them numberless enterprises, smaller and greater, and had every passion, by turns, awakened in their company, without being immensely affected by all this association. A large share, indeed, of the social interest may have been of so common a kind, and with persons of so common an order, that the effect on the character has been too little peculiar to be strikingly perceptible during the progress. We were not sensible of it, till we came to some of those circumstances and changes in life, which make us aware of the state of our minds by the manner in which new objects are acceptable or repulsive to them. On removing into a new circle of society, for instance, we could perceive, by the number of things in which we found ourselves uncongenial with the new acquaintance, the modification which our sentiments had received in the preceding social intercourse. But in some instances we have been sensible, in a very short time, of a powerful force operating on our opinions, tastes and habits, and throwing them into a new order. This effect is inevitable, if a young susceptible mind happens to become familiarly acquainted with a person in whom a strongly individual cast of character is sustained and dignified by uncommon mental resources; and it may he found that, generally, the greatest measure of effect has been produced by the influence of a very small number of persons; often of one only, whose extended and interesting mind had more power to surround and assimilate a young, ingenuous being, then the collective influence of a multitude of the persons, whose characters were moulded in the manufactory of custom, and sent forth like images of clay of kindred shape and varnish from a pottery. I am supposing, all along, that the person who writes memoirs of himself, is conscious of something more peculiar than a mere dull resemblance of that ordinary form of character for which it would seem hardly worth while to have been a man. As to the crowd of those who are faithfully stamped, like bank notes, with the same marks, with the difference only of being worth more guineas or fewer, they are mere particles of a glass, mere pieces and bits of the great vulgar or the small; *they* need not write their history, it may be found in the newspaper chronicle, or the gossip's or the sexton's narrative.

It is obvious, in what I have suggested respecting the research through past life, that all the persons who are recalled to the mind, as having had an influence on us, must stand before it in judgment. It is impossible to examine our moral and intellectual growth without forming an estimate, as we proceed, of those who retarded, advanced, or perverted it. Our dearest relatives and friends cannot be exempted. There will be to some instances the necessity of blaming where we wish to give entire praise; though perhaps some worthy motives and generous feelings may, at the same time, be discovered in the conduct where they had hardly been perceived or allowed before. But, at any rate, it is important that in no instance the judgment be duped into delusive estimates, amidst the examination, and so as to deprave the principles of the examination, by which we mean to bring ourselves to rigorous justice. For if any indulgent partiality, or mistaken idea of that duty which requires a kind and candid feeling to accompany the clearest discernment of defects, may be permitted to beguile our judgment out of the decisions of jutsice in favour of others, self-love, a still more indulgent and partial feeling, will not fail to practise the same beguilement in favour of ourselves. But indeed it would seem impossible, besides being absurd, to apply one set of principles to judge of ourselves, and another to judge of those with whom we have associated.

Every person of tolerable education has been considerably influenced by the books he has read; and remembers with a kind of gratitude several of those that made the earliest and the strongest impression. It is pleasing at a more advanced period to look again into the early favourites; though the mature person may wonder how some of them had once power to absorb his passions, make him retire into a lonely wood in order to read unmolested, repel the approaches of sleep, or infect it, when it came, with visions. A capital part of the proposed task would be to recollect the books that have been read with the greatest interest, the periods when they were read, the succession of them, the partiality which any of them inspired to a particular mode of life, to a study, to a system, of opinions or to a class of human characters; to note the counteraction of later ones (where we have been sensible of it) to the effect produced by the former; and then to endeavour to estimate the whole and ultimate influence.

Considering the multitude of facts, sentiments, and characters, which have been contemplated by a person who has read much, the effect, one should think, must have been very great. Still, however, it is probable that a very small number of books will have the pre-eminence in our mental history. Perhaps your memory will promptly recur to six or ten that have contributed more to your present habits of feeling and thought than all the rest together. And here it may be observed, that when a few books of the same kind have pleased us emphatically, they too often form an almost exclusive taste, which is carried through all future reading, and is pleased only with books of that kind.

It might be supposed that the scenes of nature, an amazing assemblage of phenomena if their effect were not lost through familiarity, would have a powerful influence on all opening minds, and transfuse into the internal economy of ideas and sentiment something of a character and a colour correspondent to the beauty, vicissitude, and grandeur, which continually press on the senses. On minds of genius they often have this effect; and Beattie's Minstrel may be as just as it is a captivating description of the feelings of such a spirit. But on the greatest number this influence operates feebly; you will not see the process in children, nor the result in mature persons. The charms of nature are objects only of sight and hearing, not of sensibility and imagination. And even the sight and hearing do not receive impressions sufficiently distinct or forcible for clear recollection; it is not, therefore, strange that these impressions seldom go so much deeper than the senses as to awaken pensiveness or enthusiasm, and fill the mind with an interior permanent scenery of beautiful images at its own command. This defect of fancy and sensibility is unfortunate amidst a creation infinitely rich with grand and beautiful objects, which imparting something more than images to a mind adapted and habituated to converse with nature, inspire an exquisite sentiment that seems like the emanation of a spirit residing in them. It is unfortunate, I have thought within these few minutes, while looking out on one of the most enchanting nights of the most interesting season of the year, and hearing the voices of a company of persons, to whom I can perceive that this soft and solemn shade over the earth, the calm sky, the beautiful stripes of clouds, the stars, and the waning moon just risen, are things not in the least more interesting than the walls, ceilings, and candle-light of a room. I feel no vanity in this instance; for probably a thousand aspects of night, not less striking than this, have appeared before my eyes and departed, not only without awakening emotion, but almost without attracting notice.

If minds in general are not made to be strongly affected by the phenomena of the earth and heavens, they are however all subject to be powerfully influenced by the appearances and character of the *human* world. I suppose a child in Switzerland, growing up to a man, would have acquired incomparably more of the cast of his mind from the events, manners, and actions of the next village, though its inhabitants were but his occasional companions, than from all the mountain scenes, the cataracts, and every circumstance of beauty or sublimity in nature around him. We are all true to our species, and very soon feel its importance to us, (though benevolence be not the basis of the interest,) far beyond the importance of any thing we see besides. You may have observed how instantly even children will turn their attention away from any of the more ample aspects of nature, however rare or striking, if human objects present themselves to view in any active manner. This 'leaning to our kind' brings each individual not only under the influence attending direct companionship with a few, but under the operation of numberless influences, from all the moral diversities of which he is a spectator in the living world,—a complicated, though often insensible tyranny, of which every fashion, folly, and vice, may exercise its part.

Some persons would be able, in the review of life, to recollect very strong and influential impressions made, in almost the first years of it, by some of the facts which they witnessed in surrounding society. But whether the operation on us of the plastic power of the community began with impressions of extraordinary force or not, it has been prolonged through the whole course of our acquaintance with mankind. It is no little effect for the living world to have had on us, that very many of our present *opinions* are owing to what we have seen and experienced in it. That thinking which has involuntarily been kept in exercise upon it, however remiss and desultory, could not fail to result in a number of settled notions, which may be said to be shaped upon its facts and practices. We could not be in sight of it, and in intercourse with it, without the formation of opinions adjusted to what we found in it; and thus far it has been the creator of our mental economy. But its operation has not stopped here. It will not confine itself to occupying the understanding, and yield to be a mere subject for judgments to be formed upon; but all the while that its judge is directing upon it the exercise of his opinion, it is re-actively throwing on him various moral influences and infections.

LETTER III.

Very powerful Impressions sometimes from particular Facts, tending to form discriminated Characters—Yet very few strongly discriminated and individual Characters found—Most Persons belong to general classes of Character—Immense Number and Diversity of Impressions, of indefinitely various tendency, which the moral Being has undergone in the course of Life—Might be expected that such a Confusion of Influences would not permit the Formation of any settled Character—That such a Character is, nevertheless, acquired and maintained, is owing to some one leading Determination, given by whatever means, to the Mind, generally in early Life—Common self-deceptive Belief that we have maintained moral Rectitude and the Exercise of sound Reason under the Impressions that have been forming our Characters.

A person, capable of being deeply interested, and who is accustomed to reflect on his feelings, will have observed in himself this subjection to the influences of what has been presented to him in society; and will acknowledge that in one or a few instances they have seemed, at the time, of sufficient force to go far toward new-moulding the whole habit of the mind. Recollect your own experience. After witnessing some remarkable transaction, or some new and strange department of life and manners, or some striking disclosure of character, or after listening to some extraordinary conversation, or impressive recital of facts, you have been conscious that what you have heard or seen has given your mind some one strong determination, of a nature resulting from the quality of that which has made the impression. Though the dispositions already existing must no doubt have been prepared to receive the operation of this new cause in one certain manner, (since every one would not have been affected in the same manner,) yet the feelings have been thrown into an order so different, that you seemed to have acquired a new moral being. The difference has been not merely in their temporary energy, but also in their direction. In the state thus suddenly formed, some of the dispositions of which you had been conscious before, seemed to be lost, while others, that previously had little strength, were grown into an imperious prevalence; or even a new one appeared to have been originated.* While this state continues, a man is another character; and if the moral tendency thus excited or created could be prolonged through the sequel of his life, the difference might be such, that it would be by means only of his person that he would be recognized for the same, while an observer who should not know the cause, would be perplexed and surprised at the change. Now this permanence of the new moral direction might be effected, if the impression which causes it were so intensely powerful as to haunt him ever after; or if he were subjected to a long succession of impressions of the same tendency, without any opposite or strongly different ones intervening to break the process.

You have witnessed perhaps a scene of injustice and oppression, and have retired with an indignation which has tempted you to imprecate vengeance. Now supposing that the hateful image of this scene were to be revived in your mind for a long time, as often as any iniquitous circumstance in society presents itself to your notice, and that you had an entire persuasion that your feeling was the pure indignation of virtue: or, supposing that you were repeatedly to witness similar instances, without emotion becoming languid by familiarity with them, the consequence might be that you would acquire the spirit of Draco or Minos.

It is easy to imagine the impression of a few atrocious facts on a mind of ardent passions converting a humane horror of cruelty into the vindictive fanaticism of Montbar the Buccaneer;† and I have known instances of a similar effect, in a fainter degree. A person of gentler sensibility, by accidentally witnessing a scene of distress of which none of the circumstances caused disgust toward the sufferers, or indignation against others as the cause of the sorrow, having once tasted the pleasure of soothing woes which perhaps death alone can remove, might be led to seek other instances of distress, acquire both an aptitude and a partiality for the friendly office, and become a pensive philanthropist. The extreme disgust, excited by some extravagance of ostentatious wealth, or some excess of dissipated frivolity, and awaked again at every succeeding and inferior instance of the same kind, with a much stronger aversion than would have been excited in these inferior instances, if the disgusted feeling did not run into the vestiges of the first indelible impression, may produce a cynic or a miser, a recluse or a philosopher. Numberless other illustrations might be brought to show how much the characters of human beings, entering on life, with such unwarned carelessness of heart, are at the mercy of the incalculable influences which may strike them from any point of the surrounding world.

It is true that, notwithstanding so many influences are acting on men, and some of them apparently of a kind and of a force to produce in their subjects a striking peculiarity, comparatively few characters determinately marked from all around them are found to arise. In looking on a large company of persons whose dispositions and pursuits are substantially alike, we cannot doubt that several of them have met with circumstances, of which the natural tendency must have been to give them a determination of mind extremely dissimilar to the character of those whom they now so much resem-

* So great an effect, however, as this last, is perhaps rarely experienced from even the most powerful causes, except in early life.

† See Abbe Raynal's History of the Indies

ble. And why does the influence of such circumstances fail to produce such a result? Partly, because the influences that are of a more peculiar and specific operation are overborne and lost in that wide general influence which accumulates and conforms each individual to the crowd; and partly, because even were there no such general influence to steal away the impressions of a more peculiar tendency, few minds are of so fixed and faithful a consistence as to retain, in continued efficacy, impressions of a kind which the common course of life is not adapted to reinforce, nor prevailing example to confirm. The mind of the greater proportion of human beings, if attempted to be wrought into any boldly specific form, proves like a half-fluid substance, in which angles, or circles, or any other figures, may be cut, but which recovers, while you are looking, its former state, and closes them up; or like a quantity of dust, which may be raised into momentary reluctant shapes, but which is relapsing even amidst the operation toward its undefined mass.

But if characters marked with strong individual peculiarity are somewhat rare, such as bear some considerably prominent generic distinction are very numerous; the decidedly avaricious for instance, the devoted slaves of fashion, and the eager aspirers to power, in however confined a sphere, the little Alexanders of a mole-hill, quite as ambitious, in their way, as the great Alexander of a world. It is observable here, how much more obviously the unworthy distinctions of human character are presented to the thoughts than those of contrary quality. And it is a melancholy illustration of the final basis of character, that is, human nature itself, that both the distinctions which designate a bad class, and those which constitute a bad individual peculiarity, are attained with far the greatest frequency and facility. While, however, I have the most entire conviction of this mighty inclination to evil, which is the grand cause of all the diversified forms of evil, and while, at the same time, I cannot divest myself of the vulgar belief of a great native difference between different men, in the original modification of those principles which are to be unfolded by the progress of time into intellectual powers and moral dispositions; I yet cannot but perceive that the *immediate* causes of the greater portion of the prominent *actual* character of human beings are to be found in those moral elements through which they pass. And if one might be pardoned for putting in words, so fanciful an idea as that of its being possible for a man to live back again to his infancy, through all the scenes of his life, and to give back from his mind and character, at each time and circumstance, as he re-passed it, exactly that which he took from it, when he was there before, it would be most curious to see the fragments and *exuviæ* of the moral man lying here and there along the retrograde path, and to find what he was in the beginning of this train of modifications and acquisitions. Nor can it be doubted that any man, though his original tendencies (which possibly have been brought under a series of events calculated to favour their development) were ever so defined, might, by being led through a different train, opposite to those native tendencies, have been now an extremely different man from what he is, even the measure of his intellectual cultivation being the same.

Here a person even of your age, might pause, and look back with great interest on the world of circumstances through which life has been drawn. Consider what thousands of situations, appearances, incidents, persons, you have been present to, each in its moment. The review will present to you something like a chaos, with all the moral, and all other elements, confounded together; and you may reflect till you begin almost to wonder how an individual retains even the same essence through all the diversities vicissitudes, and counteractions of influence, that operate on it during its progress through the confusion. But though the essence is the same, and might defy an universe to extinguish, absorb, or change it; its modification, its condition, and habits, will show where it has been and what it has undergone. You may descry on it the marks and colours of many of the things by which, in passing, it has been touched or arrested.

Consider the number of meetings with acquaintance, friends, or strangers; the number of conversations you have held or heard; the number of exhibitions of good or evil, virtue or vice; the number of occasions on which you have been disgusted or pleased, moved to admiration or to abhorrence; the number of times that you have contemplated the town, the rural cottage, or verdant fields; the number of volumes that you have read; the times that you have looked over the present state of the world, or gone by means of history into past ages; the number of comparisons of yourself with other persons, alive or dead, and comparisons of them with one another; the number of solitary musings, of solemn contemplations of night, of the successive subjects of thought, and of animated sentiments that have been kindled and extinguished. Add all the hours and causes of sorrow that you have known. Through this lengthened, and, if the number could be told, stupendous multiplicity of things, you have advanced while all their heterogeneous myriads have darted influence upon you, each one of them have some definable tendency. A traveller round the globe would not meet a greater variety of seasons, prospects, and winds, than you might have recorded of the circumstances affecting the progress of your character, in your moral journey. You could not wish to have drawn to yourself the agency of a vaster diversity of causes; you could not wish, on the supposition that you had gained advantage from all these, to wear the spoils of a greater number of regions. The formation of the character from so many materials reminds one of that mighty appropriating attraction, which, on the hypotheses that the resurrection should re-assemble the same particles which composed the body before, must draw them from dust, and trees, and animals, from ocean, and winds.

It would scarcely be expected that a being which should be conducted through such anarchy of discipline, in which the endless crowd of influential powers seem waiting each to take away what the last had given, should be permitted to acquire, or to retain, any settled form of qualities at all. The more probable result would be, either several qualities disagreeing with one another, or a blank neutrality. And in fact, a great number of nearly such neutralities are found every where; persons, who, unless their sharing of the general properties of human nature, a little modified by the insignificant distinction of some large class, can be called character, have no character. It is therefore somewhat strange, if you, and if other individuals have come forth with moral features of a strongly marked and consistently combined cast, from the infinity of miscellaneous impressions. If the process has been so complex, how comes the result to be so simple? How has it happened that the *collective* effect of these numerous and jarring operations on your mind, is that which only a *few* of these operations would have seemed adapted to produce, and quite different from that which many others of them would naturally have produced, and do actually produce, in many other persons? Here you will perceive that some one capital determination must long since have been by some means established in your mind, and that, during your progress, this grand determination has kept you susceptible of the effect of some influences, and fortified against many others. Now, what was the prevailing determination, whence did it come, how did it acquire its power? Was it an original tendency and insuppressible impulse of your nature? or the result of your earliest impressions; or of some one class of impressions repeated oftener than any other; or of one single impression of extreme force? What was it, and whence did it come? This is the great secret in the history of character; for, it is scarcely necessary to observe, that as soon as the mind is under the power of a predominant tendency, the difficulty of growing into the maturity of that form of character, which this tendency promotes or creates, is substantially over. Because, when a determining principle is become predominant, it not only produces a partial insensibility to all impressions, that would counteract it, but also continually augments its own ascendancy, by means of a faculty or fatality of finding out every thing, and attracting and meeting every impression, that is adapted to coalesce with it and strengthen it; like the instinct of animals, which instantly selects from the greatest variety of substances those which are fit for their nutriment. Let a man have some leading and decided propensity, and it will be surprising to see how many more things he will find, and how many more events will happen, than any one could have imagined, of a nature to reinforce it. And sometimes even circumstances which seemed of an entirely counteractive order, are strangely seduced by this predominant principle into an operation that confirms it; just in the same manner as polemics most self-complacently avow their opinions to be more firmly established by all that the opponent has objected.

It would be easy to enlarge without end on the influences of the surrounding world in forming the character of each individual; and no one would deny that to a considerable extent such a representation is true. But yet a man may be unwilling to allow that he has been quite so servilely passive as he would probably find that he has been, if it were possible for him to make a complete examination. He may be disposed to think that his reason has been an independent power, has kept a strict watch, and passed a right judgment on his moral progress, has met the circumstances of the external world on terms of examination and authority, and has *permitted* only such impressions to be received, or at least only such consequences to follow from them, as is wisely approved. But I would tell him, that he has been a very extraordinary man, if the greater part of his time has not been spent entirely without a thought of reflecting what impressions were made on him, and what was their tendency; and even without a consciousness that the effect of any impressions was of importance to his moral habits. He may be assured that he has been subjected to many gentle gradual processes, and has met many critical occasions, on which, and on the consequences of which to himself, he exercised no attention or opinion. And again, it is unfortunately true, that even should attention be awake, and opinions be formed, the faculty which forms them is very servile to the other parts of the human constitution. If it could be extrinsic to the man, a kind of domestic Pythia, or an attendant genius, like the demon of Socrates it might then be a dignified regulator of the influences which are acting on his character to decide what should not affect him, what should affect him, and in what manner; though even then, its disapproving dictates would often be inefficacious against the powerful impressions which create an impulse in the mind, and the repetition of them which confirms that impulse into a habit. But the case is, that this faculty, though mocked with imperial names, being condemned to dwell in the mind in the company of far more active powers than itself, and earlierex ercised, becomes humbly obsequious to them. The passions easily beguile this majestic reason, or judgment, into neglect, or bribe it into acquiescence, or repress it into silence, while *they* receive the impressions, and while *they* acquire from those impressions that determinate direction which will constitute the character. If, after thus much is done during the weakness, or without the notice, or without the leave, or under the connivance or corruption of the judgment, it be called upon to perform its part in estimating the quality and actual effect of the modifying influences, it has to perform this judicial work with just that degree of rectitude which it can have acquired and maintained under the operation of those very influences. In acting the judge, it is itself in subjection to the effect of those impressions of which its office was to have previously decided whether they should not be strenuously repelled. Thus its opinions will unconsciously be perverted; like the answers of the ancient oracles, dictated for the imaginary god by beings of a very terrestrial sort, though the sly intervention could not be percived. It is quite a vulgar observation, how pleased a man may be with the formation of his own character, though *you* laugh at the gravity of his persuasion, that his tastes, preferences, and qualities have on the whole grown up under the sacred and faithful guardianship of judgment, while in fact his judgment has accepted every bribe that has been offered to betray him.

LETTER IV.

Most of the Influences under which the Characters of Men are forming, unfavourable to Wisdom, Virtue, and Happiness—Proof of this, if a Number of Persons, suppose a Hundred, were to give a clear Account of the Circumstances that have most affected the state of their Minds—a few Examples—a Misanthropist—a lazy prejudiced Thinker—a man fancying himself a Genius—a Projector—an Antiquarian in Excess—a petty Tyrant.

You will agree with me, that in a comprehensive view of the influences which have formed, and are forming, the characters of men, we shall find, religion excepted, but little cause to felicitate our species. Make the supposition that any assortment of persons, of sufficient number to comprise the most remarkable distinctions of character, should write memoirs of themselves so clear and perfect as to explain, to your discernment at least, if not to their own consciousness, the entire process by which their minds have attained their present state, recounting all the most impressive circumstances. If they were to read these memoirs to you in succession, and if your benevolence could so long be maintained in full exercise, and your rules for estimating lost nothing of their determinate principle in their application to such a confusion of subjects, you would often, during the disclosure, regret to observe how many things may be the causes of irretrievable mischief. Why is the path of life, you would say, so haunted as if with evil spirits of every diversity of noxious agency, some of which may patiently accompany, or others of which may suddenly cross, the unfortunate wanderer? And you would regret to observe into how many forms of intellectual and moral perversion the human mind readily yields itself to be modified.

As *one* of the number concluded the account of himself, your observation would be, I perceive, with compassion, the process under which you have become a misanthropist. If your juvenile ingenuous ardour had not been chilled on your entrance into society, where your most favourite sentiments were not at all comprehended by some, and by others deemed wise and proper enough, perhaps for the people of the millennium; if you had not felt the mortification of relatives being uncongenial, of persons whom you were anxious to render happy being indifferent to your kindness, or of apparent friendships proving treacherous or transitory; if you had not met with such striking instances of hopeless stupidity in the vulgar, or of vain self-importance in the learned, or of the coarse or supercilious arrogance of the persons whose manners were always regulated by the consideration of the number of guineas by which they were better than you; if your mortifications had not given you a keen faculty of perceiving the all pervading selfishness of mankind, while, in addition, you had perhaps a peculiar opportunity to observe the apparatus of systematic villany, by which combinations of men are able to arm their selfishness to oppress or ravage the world, you might even now perhaps have been the persuasive instructer of beings, concerning whom you are wondering why they should have been made in the form of rationals; you might have conciliated to yourself and to goodness where you repel and are repelled; you might have been the apostle and pattern of benevolence, instead of the grim solitaire. Yet not that the world should bear all the blame. Frail and changeable in virtue, you *might* perhaps have been good under a series of auspicious circumstances; but the glory had been to be victoriously good against malignant ones. Moses lost none of his generous concern for a people, on whom *you* would have invoked the waters of Noah or the fires of Sodom to return; and that Greater than Moses, who endured from men such a matchless excess of injustice, while for their sake alone he sojourned and suffered on earth, was not alienated to live a misanthropist, nor to die one.

A *second* sketch might exhibit external circumstances not producing any effect more serious than an intellectual stagnation. When it was concluded, your recollection might be,—If I did not know that mental freedom is a dangerous thing in situations where the possessor would feel it a singular attainment; and if I did not prefer even the quiescence of unexamining belief, when tolerably right in the most material points, to the indifference or scepticism which feels no assurance or no importance in any belief, or to the weak presumption that darts into the newest and most daring opinions as *therefore* true—I should deplore that your life was destined to preserve its sedate course so entirely unanimated by the intellectual novelties of the age, the agitations of ever-moving opinion; and under the habitual and exclusive influence of one individual, worthy perhaps, and in certain degree sensible, but of unenlarged views, whom you have been taught and accustomed to regard as the comprehensive repository of all the truth requisite for you to know, and from whom you have derived, as some of your chief acquisitions, an assurance of the labour of inquiry being needless and a superstitious horror of innovation, without even knowing what points are threatened by it.

At the end of *another's* disclosure, you would say, How unfortunate, that you could not believe there might be respectable and valuable men, that were not born to be wits or poets. And how unfortunate were those first evenings that you were privileged to listen to a company of men who could *say* more fine things in an hour than their biographers will be able, without a little panegyric fiction, to record them to have *done* in the whole space of life. It was then you discovered that *you* too were of the progeny of Apollo, and that you had been iniquitously transferred at your nativity into the hands of ignorant foster-parents, who had endeavored to degrade and confine you to the sphere of regular employments and sober satisfactions. But, you would 'tower up to the region of your sire.' You saw what wonderful things might be found to be said on all subjects; you found it not so very difficult yourself to say *different* things from other people; and every thing that was not *common* dulness, was therefore pointed, every thing that was not sense by any *vulgar* rule, was therefore sublime. You adopted a certain vastitude of phrase, mistaking extravagance of expression for greatness of thought. You set yourself to dogmatize on books, and the abilities of men, but especially on their prejudices; and perhaps to demolish, with the air of an exploit, some of the trite observations and maxims current in society. You awakened and surprised your imagination, by imposing on it a strange new tax of colours and metaphors; a tax reluctantly and uncouthly paid, but perhaps in some one instance so luckily, as to gain the applause of these gifted (if they were not merely eccentric) men. This was to you the proof and recognition of fraternity; and it has since been the chief question that has interested you with each acquaintance and in each company, whether they too could perceive what you were so happy to have discovered, yet so anxious that the acknowledgment of others should confirm; your own persuasion, however, became as pertinacious as ivy climbing a wall. It was almost of course to attend to necessary pursuits with reluctant irregularity, though suffering by the consequences of neglecting them, and to feel indignant that *genius* should be reproached for the disregard of these ordinary duties to which it ought never to have been subjected.

During a *projector's* story of life and misfortunes, you might regret that he should ever have heard of Harrison's time-piece, the perpetual motion, or the Greek-fire.

After an *antiquarian's* history, you might be allowed to congratulate yourself on not having fallen under the spell which confines a human soul to inhabit, like a spider in one of the corners, a dusty room, consecrated with religious solemnity to old coins, rusty knives, illuminated mass books, swords and spurs of forgotten kings, and slippers of their queens; with perhaps a Roman helmet, the acquisition of which was the first cause of the collection and of the passion, elevated imperially over the relics of kings and queens and the whole museum, as the eagle once waved over the kingdoms and the world. And you might be inclined to say, I wish that helmet had been a pan for charcoal, or had been put on the head of one of the quiet equestrian warriors in the Tower, or had aided the hauntings and rattlings of the ghost of Sir Godfrey in the baron's castle where he was murdered, or had been worn by Don Quixote instead of the barber's bason, or had been the cauldron of Macbeth's witches, been in any other shape, place, or use, rather than dug up an antiquity, in a luckless hour, in a bank near your garden.

I compassionate you,—would, in a *very* benevolent hour, be again your language to the wealthy unfeeling *tyrant of a family and a neighbourhood*, who seeks, in the overawed timidity and unretaliated injuries of the unfortunate beings within his power,—the gratification that should have been sought in their happiness. Unless you had brought into the world some extraordinary refractoriness to the influence of evil, the process that you have undergone could not easily fail of being efficacious. If your parents idolized their own importance in their son so much, that they never opposed your inclinations themselves, nor permitted it to be done by any subject to their authority; if the humble companion, sometimes summoned to the honour of amusing you, bore your caprices and insolence with the meekness without which he had lost his enviable privilege; if you could despoil the garden of some harmless, dependent neighbour of the carefully reared flowers, and torment his little dog or cat, without his daring to punish you or to appeal to your infatuated parents; if aged men addressed you in a submissive tone, and with the appellation of 'Sir,' and their aged wives uttered their wonder at your condescension, and pushed their grandchildren away from around the fire for your sake, if you happened, though with the strut of pertness, and your hat on your head, to enter one of their cottages, perhaps to express your contempt of the homely dwelling, furniture, and fare; if, in maturer life, you associated with vile persons, who would forego the contest of equality, to be your allies in trampling on inferiors; and if, both then and since, you have been suffered to deem your wealth the compendium or equivalent of every ability, and every good quality—it would indeed be immensely strange if you had not become, in due time, the miscreant, who may thank the power of the laws in civilized society, that he is not assaulted with clubs and stones; to whom one could cordially wish the opportunity and the consequences of attempting his tyranny among some such people as those *submissive* sons of nature in the forests of North America; and whose dependents and domestic relatives may be almost forgiven when they shall one day rejoice at his funeral.

LETTER V.

An Atheist—Slight Sketch of the Process by which a Man in the humbler Order of Abilities and Attainments may become one.

I will imagine only one case more, on which you would emphatically express your compassion, though for one of the most daring beings in the creation, a *contemner of God*, who explodes his laws by denying his existence.

If you were so unacquainted with mankind, that this character might be announced to you as a rare or singular phenomenon, your conjectures, till you saw and heard the man, at the nature and the extent of the discipline through which he must have advanced, would be led toward something extraordinary. And you might think that the term of that discipline must have been very long; since a quick train of impressions, a short series of mental gradations, within the little space of a few months and years, would not seem enough to have matured such an awful heroism. Surely the creature that thus lifts his voice, and defies all invisible power within the possibilities of infinity, challenging whatever unknown being may hear him, and may appropriate that title of Almighty which is pronounced in scorn, to evince his existence, if he will, by his vengeance, was not as yesterday a little child that would tremble and cry at the approach of a diminutive reptile.

But indeed it is heroism no longer, if he *knows* that there is no God. The wonder then turns on the great process, by which a man could grow to the immense intelligence that can know that there is no God. What ages and what lights are requisite for THIS attainment! This intelligence involves the very attributes of Divinity, while a God is denied. For unless this man is omnipresent, unless he is at this moment in every place in the universe, he cannot know but there may be in some place manifestations of a Deity, by which even *he* would be overpowered. If he does not know absolutely every agent in the universe, the one that he does not know may be God. If he is not himself the chief agent in the universe, and does not know what is so, that which is so may be God. If he is not in absolute possession of all the propositions that constitute universal truth, the one which he wants may be, that there is a God. If he cannot with certainty assign the cause of all that he perceives to exist, that cause may be a God. If he does not know every thing that has been done in the immeasurable ages that are past, some things may have been done by a God. Thus, unless he knows all things, that is, precludes another Deity by being one himself, he cannot know that the Being whose existence he rejects, does not exist. But he must *know* that he does not exist, else he deserves equal contempt and compassion for the temerity with which he firmly avows his rejection and acts accordingly. And yet a man of ordinary age and intelligence may present himself to you with the avowal of being thus distinguished from the crowd; and if he would describe the manner in which he has attained this eminence, you would feel a melancholy interest in contemplating that process of which the result is so portentous.

If you did not know that there are more than a few such examples, you would say, in viewing this result, I *should* hope this is the consequence of some malignant intervention so occasional that ages may pass away before it return among men; some peculiar conjunction of disastrous influences must have lighted on your selected soul; you have been struck by that energy of evil which acted upon the spirits of Pharaoh and Epiphanes. But give your own description of what you have met with in a world which has been deemed to present in every part the indications of a Deity. Tell of the mysterious voices which have spoken to you from the deeps of the creation, falsifying the expressions marked on its face. Tell of the new ideas, which, like meteors passing over the solitary wanderer, gave you the first glimpses of truth while benighted in the common belief of the Divine existence. Describe the whole train of causes that have operated to create and consolidate that state of mind, which you carry forward to the great experiment of futurity under a different kind of hazard from all other classes of men.

It would be found, however, that those circumstances, by which even a man who had been presented from his infancy with the ideas of religion, could be elated into a contempt of its great object, were far from being extraordinary. They might have been met by any man, whose mind had been cultivated and exercised enough to feel interested about holding any systems of opinions at all, whose pride had been gratified in the consciousness of having the liberty of selecting and changing opinions, and whose habitual assent to the principles of religion, had neither the firmness resulting from decisive arguments, nor the warmth of pious affection.* Such a person had only, in the first place, to come into intimate acquaintance with a man, who had the art of alluding to a sacred subject in a manner which, without appearing like intentional contempt, divested it of its solemnity; and who had possessed himself of a few acute observations or plausible maxims, not explicitly hostile to revealed religion, but which, when opportunely brought into view in connexion with some points of it, tended to throw a slight degree of doubt on their truth and authority. Especially if either or both of these men had any decided moral tendencies and pursuits of a kind which Christianity condemned, the friend of intellectual and moral freedom was assiduous to insinuate, that, according to the principles of reason and nature at least, it would be difficult to prove the wisdom or the necessity of some of those dictates of religion, which must, however, be admitted, be revered, because divine. Let the mind have once acquired a feeling, as if the sacred system might in some points be invalidated, and the involuntary inference would be rapidly extended to other parts, and to the whole. Nor

* It will be obvious that I am describing the progress of one of the humbler order of aliens from all religion, and not that by which the great philosophic leaders have ascended the dreary eminence, where they look with so much complacency up to a vacant heaven, and down to the gulf of annihilation. Their progress undoubtedly is much more systematic and deliberate, and accompanied often by a laborious speculation, which though in ever so perverted a train, the mind is easily persuaded to identify, because it *is* laborious, with the search after truth and the love of it. While however it is in a persevering train of thought, and not by the hasty movements of a more vulgar mind, that they pursue their deviation from some of the principles of religion into a final abandonment of it all, they are very greatly mistaken, if they assure themselves that the moral causes which contribute to guide and animate their progress are all of a sublime order; and if they could be fully revealed to their own view, they might perhaps be severely mortified to find what vulgar motives, while they were despising vulgar men, have ruled their intellectual career. Pride, which idolizes self, which revolts at every thing that comes in the form of dictates, and exults to find that there is a possibility of controverting whether any dictates come from a greater than mortal source; repugnance as well to the severe and sublime morality of the laws reputed of divine appointment, as to the feeling of accountableness to an all-powerful Authority, that will not leave moral laws to be enforced solely by their own sanctions; contempt of inferior men; the attraction of a few brilliant examples; the fashion of a class; the ambition of showing what ability can do, and what boldness can dare—if such things as these, after all, have excited and directed the efforts of a philosophic spirit, the unbelieving philosopher must be content to acknowledge plenty of companions and rivals among little men, who are quite as capable of being actuated by these elevated principles as himself.

was it long probably before this new instructer plainly avowed his own entire emancipation from a popular prejudice, to which he was kindly sorry to find a *sensible* young man still in captivity. But he had no doubt that the deductions of enlightened reason would successfully appeal to every liberal mind. And accordingly, after perhaps a few months of frequent intercourse, with the addition of two or three books, and the ready aid of all the recollected vices of pretended Christians and pretended Christian churches, the whole venerable magnificence of Revelation was annihilated. Its illuminations respecting the Divinity, its miracles, its Messiah, its authority of moral legislation, its regions of immortality and retribution, the sublime virtues and devotion of its prophets, apostles, and martyrs, together with the reasonings of so many accomplished advocates, and the credibility of history itself, were vanished all away; while the convert, exulting in his disenchantment, felt a strange pleasure to behold nothing but a dreary train of impostures and credulity stretching over those past ages which lately were gilded with so divine a vision, and the thickest Egyptian shades fallen on that total vast futurity which the spirit of inspiration had partially and very solemnly illuminated.

Nothing tempts the mind so powerfully on, as to have successfully begun to demolish what has been deemed to be most sacred. The soldiers of Cæsar probably had never felt themselves so brave, as after they had cut down the Massilian grove; nor the Philistines, as when the ark of the God of Israel was among their spoils: the mind is proud of its triumphs in proportion to the reputed greatness of what it has overcome. And many examples would seem to indicate, that the first proud triumphs over religious faith involve some fatality of advancing, however formidable the mass of arguments which may obstruct the progress, to farther victories. But perhaps the intellectual difficulty of the progress might be less than a zealous believer would be apt to imagine. As the ideas which give the greatest distinctness to our conception of a Divine Being are imparted by revelation, and rest on its authority, the rejection of that revelation would in a great measure banish those ideas, and destroy that distinctness. We have but to advert to pure heathenism, to perceive what a faint conception of this Being could be formed by the strongest intellect in the absence of revelation; and after the *rejection* of it, the mind would naturally be carried very far back toward that darkness, so that some of the attributes of the Deity would immediately become, as they were with the heathens, subjects of doubtful conjecture and hopeless speculation. But from this state of thought it is perhaps no vast transition to that, in which his being also shall begin to appear a subject of doubt; since the reality of a being is with difficulty apprehended, in proportion as its attributes are undefinable. And when the mind is brought into doubt, we know it easily advances to disbelief, if to the smallest plausibility of arguments be added any powerful moral cause for wishing such a conclusion. In the present case there *might* be a very powerful cause, besides that pride of victory which I have just noticed. The progress in guilt, which generally follows a rejection of revelation, makes it still more and more desirable that no object should remain to be feared. It was not strange, therefore, if this man read with avidity, or even strange if he read with something which his wishes completed into conviction, a few of the writers, who have attempted the last achievement of presumptuous man. After inspecting these pages a while, he raised his eyes, and the Great Spirit was gone. Mighty transformation of all things! The luminaries of heaven no longer shone with his splendour; the adorned earth no longer looked fair with his beauty; the darkness of night had ceased to be rendered solemn by his majesty; life and thought were not an effect of his all-pervading energy; it was not his providence that supported an infinite charge of dependent beings; his empire of justice no longer spread over the universe; nor had even that universe sprung from his all-creating power. Yet when you saw the intellectual course brought to this signal conclusion, though aware of the force of each preceding and predisposing circumstance, you might nevertheless be somewhat struck with the suddenness of the final decision, and might be curious to know what kind of argument and eloquence could so quickly finish the work. You would examine those pages with the expectation probably of something more powerful than subtlety attenuated into inanity, and in that invisible and impalpable state, mistaken by the reader, and willingly admitted by the perverted writer, for profundity of reasoning; than attempts to destroy the certainty, or preclude the application, of some of those great familiar principles which must be taken as the basis of human reasoning, or it can have no basis; than suppositions which attribute the order of the universe to such causes as it would be felt ridiculous to pronounce adequate to produce the most trifling piece of mechanism; than mystical jargon which, under the name of *nature*, alternately exalts almost into the properties of a god, and reduces far below those of a man, some imaginary and undefineable agent or agency, which performs the most amazing works without power, and displays the most amazing wisdom without intelligence; than a zealous preference of that part of every great dilemma which merely confounds and sinks the mind, to that which elevates while it overwhelms; it than a constant endeavour to degrade as far as possible every thing that is sublime in our speculations and feelings, or than monstrous parallels between religion and mythology. You would be still more unprepared to expect on so solemn a subject the occasional wit, or affectation of wit, which would seem rather prematurely expressive of exultation that the grand Foe is retiring.

A feeling of complete certainty would hardly be thus rapidly attained; but a slight degree of remaining doubt, and consequent apprehension, would not prevent this disciple of darkness from accepting the invitation to pledge himself to the cause in some associated band, where profaneness and vice would consolidate impious opinions without the aid of augmented conviction; and where the fraternity, having been elated by the spirit of social daring to say, What is the Almighty that *we* should serve him? the individuals might acquire each a firmer boldness to exclaim, Who is the Lord that *I* should obey his voice? Thus easy it is, my friend, for a man to meet that train of influences which may seduce him to live an infidel, though it may betray him to die a terrified believer; that train of which the infatuation, while it promises him the impunity of non-existence, and degrades him to desire it, impels him to fill the measure of his iniquity, till the divine wrath come upon him to the uttermost.

LETTER VI.

The Influence of Religion counteracted by almost all other Influences—Pensive Reflections on the imperfect Manifestation of the Supreme Being—on the inefficacy of the Belief of such a Being—on the Strangeness of that Inefficacy—and on the Debasement and Infelicity consequent on it—Happiness of a devout Man.

In recounting so many influences that operate on man, it is grievous to observe that the incomparably noblest of all, religion, is counteracted with a fatal success by a perpetual conspiracy of almost all the rest, aided by the intrinsic predisposition of our nature, which yields itself without such consenting facility to every impression tending to estrange it still farther from God.

It is a cause for wonder and sorrow, to see millions of rational creatures growing into their permanent habits, under the conforming efficacy of every thing which they ought to resist, and receiving no part of those habits from impressions of the Supreme Object. They are content that a narrow scene of a diminutive world, with its atoms and evils, should usurp and deprave and finish their education for immortality, while the Infinite Spirit is here, whose transforming companionship would exalt them into his sons, and, in defiance of a thousand malignant forces attempting to stamp on them an opposite image, lead them into eternity in his likeness. Oh why is it so possible that this greatest inhabitant of every place where men are living, should be the last whose society they seek, or of whose being constantly near them they feel the importance? Why is it possible to be surrounded with the intelligent Reality, which exists wherever we are, with attributes that are infinite, and not feel, respecting all other things which may be attempting to press on our minds and affect their character, as if they retained with difficulty their shadows of existence, and were continually on the point of vanishing into nothing? Why is this stupendous Intelligence so retired and silent, while present, over all the scenes of the earth, and in all the scenes of the earth, and in all the paths and abodes of men? Why does he keep his glory invisible behind the shades and visions of the material world? Why does not this latent glory sometimes beam forth with such a manifestation as could never be forgotten, nor ever be remembered without an emotion of religious fear? And why, in contempt of all that he *has* displayed to excite either fear or love, is it still possible for a rational creature so to live, that it must finally come to an interview with him in a character completed by the full assemblage of those acquisitions, which have separately been disapproved by him through every stage of the accumulation? Why is it possible for feeble creatures to maintain their little dependent beings fortified and invincible in sin, amidst the presence of divine purity? Why does not the thought of such a Being strike through the mind with such intense antipathy to evil, as to blast with death every active principle that is beginning to pervert it, and render gradual additions of depravity, growing into the solidity of habit, as impossible as for perishable materials to be raised into structures amidst the fires of the last day? How is it possible to forget the solicitude, which should accompany the consciousness that such a Being is continually darting upon us the beams of observant thought, (if we may apply such a term to Omniscience;) that we are exposed to the piercing inspection, compared to which the concentrated attention of all the beings in the universe besides, would be but as the powerless gaze of an infant? Why is faith, that faculty of spiritual apprehension, so absent, or so incomparably more slow and reluctant to receive a just perception of the grandest of its objects, than the senses are adapted to receive the impressions of theirs? While there is a Spirit pervading the universe with an infinite energy of being, why have the few particles of dust which encloses *our* spirits the power to intercept all sensible communication with it, and to place them as in a vacuity, where the sacred Essence had been precluded or extinguished?

The reverential submission, with which you ought to contemplate the mystery of omnipotent benevolence forbearing to exert the agency, which could assume an instantaneous ascendency in every mind over the causes of depravation and ruin, will not avert your compassion from the unhappy persons who are practically 'without God in the world.' And if, by some vast enlargement of thought, you could comprehend the whole measure and depth of disaster contained in this exclusion, (an exclusion under which, to the view of a serious mind, the resources and magnificence of the creation would sink into a mass of dust and ashes, and all the causes of joy and hope into disgust and despair,) you would feel a distressing emotion at each recital of a life in which religion had no share; and you would be tempted to wish that some spirit from the other world, possessed of eloquence that might threaten to alarm the slumbers of the dead, would throw himself in the way of this one mortal, and this one more, to protest, in sentences of lightning and thunder, against the infatuation that can at once acknowledge there is a God, and be content to forego every connexion with him, but that of danger. You would wish they should rather be assailed by the 'terror of the Lord,' than retain the satisfaction of carelessness till the day of his mercy be past.

But you will not need such enlargement of comprehension, in order to compassionate the situation of persons who, with reason sound to think, and hearts not strangers to feeling, have advanced far into life, perhaps near to its close, without having felt the influence of religion. If there is such a Being as we mean by the term God, the ordinary intelligence of a serious mind will be quite enough to see that it must be a melancholy thing to pass through life, and quit it, just as if there were not. And sometimes it will appear as strange as it is melancholy: especially to a person who has been pious from his youth. He would be inclined to say, to a person who has nearly finished an irreligious life, What would have been justly thought of you, if you could have been the greatest part of your time in the society of the wisest and best man on earth, (were it possible to have ascertained that individual,) and have acquired no degree of conformity; much more, if you could all the while, have acquired progressively the meanness, prejudices, follies, and vices, of the lowest society, with which you might have been exposed at intervals to mingle? You might have been asked how *this* was possible. But then through what defect or infatuation of mind have you been able, during so many years spent in the presence of a God, to continue even to this hour as clear of all marks and traces of any divine influences having operated on you, as if the Deity were but a poetical fiction, or an idol in some temple of Asia?—Evidently, as the immediate cause, through want of thought concerning him.

And why did you not think of him? Did a most solemn thought of him never *once* penetrate your soul, while admitting the proposition that there is such a Being? If it never did, what is reason, what is mind, what is man? If it did once, how could its effects stop there? How could a deep thought, on so singular and momentous a subject, fail to impose on the mind a permanent necessity of frequently re-calling it; as some awful or magnificent spectacle will haunt you with a long recurrence of its image, even if the spectacle itself were seen no more?

Why did you not think of him? How could you estimate so meanly your mind with all its capacities, as to feel no regret that an endless series of trifles should seize, and occupy as their right, all your thoughts, and deny them both the liberty and the ambition of going on to the greatest Object? How, while called to the contemplations which absorb the spirits of Heaven, could you be so patient of the task of counting the flies of a summer's day?

Why did you not think of Him? You knew yourself to be in the hands of some Being from whose power you could not be withdrawn; was it not an equal defect of curiosity and prudence to indulge a careless confidence that sought no acquaintance with his nature and his dispositions, nor ever anxiously inquired what conduct should be observed toward him, and what expectations might be entertained from him? You would have been alarmed to have felt yourself in the power of a mysterious stranger, of your own feeble species; but let the stranger be omnipotent, and you cared no more.

Why did you not think of Him? One would deem that the thought of him must, to a serious mind, come second to almost every thought. The thought of virtue would suggest the thought of both a lawgiver and a rewarder; the thought of crime, of an avenger; the thought of sorrow, of a consoler; the thought of an inscrutable mystery, of an intelligence that understands it; the thought of that ever-moving activity which prevails in the system of the universe, of a supreme agent; the thought of the human family, of a great father; the thought of all being not necessary and self-existent, of a creator; the thought of life, of a preserver; and the thought of death, of an uncontrollable disposer. By what dexterity, therefore, of irreligious caution, did you avoid precisely every track where the idea of him would have met you, or elude that idea if it came? And what must sound reason pronounce of a mind which, in the train of millions of thoughts, has wandered to all things under the sun, to all the permanent objects or vanishing appearances in the creation, but never fixed its thought on the Supreme Reality; never approached, like Moses, 'to see this great sight?'

If it were a thing which we might be allowed to imagine, that the Divine Being were to manifest himself in some striking manner to the senses, as by some resplendent appearance at the midnight hour, or by rekindling on an elevated mountain the long extinguished fires of Sinai, and uttering voices from those fires; would he not compel from you an attention which you now refuse? Yes, you will say, he would then seize the mind with irresistible force, and religion would become its most absolute sentiment; but he only presents himself to faith. Well, and is it a worthy reason for disregarding him, that you *only believe* him to be present and infinitely glorious? Is it the office of faith to veil or annihilate its object? Cannot you reflect, that the grandest representation of a spiritual and divine Being to the senses would bear not only no proportion to his glory, but no relation to his nature; and could be adapted only to an inferior dispensation of religion, and to a people who, with the exception of a most extremely small number of men, had been totally untaught to carry their thoughts beyond the objects of sense? Are you not aware, that such a representation would considerably tend to restrict you in your contemplation to a defined image, and therefore a most inadequate and subordiate idea of the divine Being? While the idea admitted by faith, though less immediately striking, is capable of an illimitable expansion, by the addition of all that progressive thought can accumulate, under the continual certainty that all is still infinitely short of the reality?

On the review of a character thus grown, in the exclusion of the religious influences, to the mature and perhaps ultimate state, the sentiment of pious benevolence would be, I regard you as an object of great compassion: unless there can be no felicity in friendship with the Almighty, unless there be no glory in being assimilated to his excellence, unless there be no eternal rewards for his devoted servants, unless there be no danger in meeting him, at length, after a life estranged equally from his love and his fear. I deplore, at every period and crisis in the review of your life, that religion was not there. If religion had been there, your youthful animation would neither have been dissipated in the frivolity which, in the morning of the short day of life, fairly and formally sets aside all serious business for *that* day, nor would have sprung forward into the emulation of vice, or the bravery of profaneness. If religion had been there, that one despicable companion, and that other malignant one, would not have seduced you into their society, or would not have retained you to share their degradation. And if religion had accompanied the subsequent progress of your life, it would have elevated you to rank, at this hour, with those saints who will soon be added to 'the spirits of the just.' Instead of which, what are you now, and what are your expectations from that world, where piety alone can hope to find such a sequel of life, as will inspire exultation in the retrospect of this introductory period, in which the mind began to converse with the God of eternity?

On the other hand, it would be interesting to record, or to hear, the history of a character which has received its form, and reached its maturity, under the strongest operations of religion. We do not know that there is a more beneficent or a more direct mode of the divine agency in any part of the creation than that which 'apprehends' a man, as apostolic language expresses it, amidst the unthinking crowd, and leads him into serious reflection, into elevated devotion, into progressive virtue, and finally into a nobler life after death. When he has long been commanded by this influence, he will be happy to look back to its first operations, whether they were mingled in early life almost insensibly with his feelings, or came on him with mighty force at some particular time, and in connexion with some assignable and memorable circumstance, which was apparently the instrumental cause. He will trace all the progress of this his better life, with grateful acknowledgment to the sacred power which has advanced him to a decisiveness of religious habit that seems to stamp eternity on his character. In the greater majority of things, habit is a greater plague than ever afflicted Egypt; in religious character, it is a grand felicity. The devout man exults in the indications of his being fixed and irretrievable. He feels this confirmed habit as the grasp of the hand of God, which will never let him go. From this advanced state he looks with firmness and joy on futurity, and says, I carry the eternal mark upon me that I belong to God; I am free of the universe; and I am ready to go to any world to which he shall please to transmit me, certain that every where, in height or depth, he will acknowledge me for ever.

LETTER VII.

Self-knowledge being supposed the principal Object in writing the Memoir, the train of exterior Fortunes and Actions will claim but a subordinate Notice in it—If it were intended for the amusement of the Public, the Writer would do well to fill it rather with Incident and Action—Yet the mere mental History of some Men would be interesting to reflecting Readers—of a Man, for example, of a speculative Disposition, who has passed through many Changes of Opinion—Influences that warp Opinion—Effects of Time and Experience on the Notions and Feelings cherished in Early Life—Feelings of a sensible old Man on viewing a Picture of his own Mind drawn by himself when he was young—Failure of excellent Designs; Disappointment of sanguine Hopes—Degree of Explicitness required in the Record—Conscience—Impudence and canting false Pretences of many Writers of "Confessions"—Rosseau.

The preceding letters have attempted to exhibit only general views of the influences by which a reflective man may perceive the moral condition of his mind to have been determined.

In descending into more particular illustrations, there would have been no end of enumerating the local circumstances, the relationships of life, the professions and employments, and the accidental events, which may have affected the character. A person who feels any interest in reviewing what has formed thus far his education for futurity, may carry his own examination into the most distinct particularity.—A few miscellaneous observations will conclude the essay.

You will have observed that I have said comparatively little of that which forms the exterior, and in general account the main substance, of the history of a man's life—the train of his fortunes and actions. If an adventurer or a soldier writes memoirs of himself for the information or amusement of the public, he may do well to keep his narrative alive by a constant crowded course of facts; for the greater part of his readers will excuse him the trouble of investigating, and he might occasionally feel it a convenience to be excused from disclosing, if he had investigated, the history and merits of his internal principles. Nor can this ingenuousness be any part of his duty, any more than it is that of a fiddler at a ball, so long as he tells all that probably he professes to tell, that is, where he has been, what he has witnessed, and the more reputable portion of what he has done. Let him go on with his lively anecdotes, or his legends of the marvellous, or his gazettes of marches, stratagems and skirmishes, and there is no obligation for him to turn either penitent or philosopher on our hands. But I am supposing a man to retrace himself through his past life, in order to acquire a deep self-knowledge, and to record the investigation for his own instruction. Through such a retrospective examination, the exterior life will hold but the second place in attention, as being the imperfect offspring of that internal state, which it is the primary and more difficult object to review. From an effectual inquisition into this inner man, the investigator may proceed outward, to the course of his actions; of which he will thus have become qualified to form a much juster estimate, than he could by any exercise of judgment upon them regarded merely as exterior facts. No doubt that sometimes also, in a contrary process, the judgment will be directed upon the dispositions and principles within by a consideration of the actions without, which will serve as a partial explication of the interior character. Still it is that interior character, whether displayed in actions or not, which forms the leading object of inquiry. The chief circumstances of his practical life will, however, require to be noted, both for the purpose of so much illustration as they will afford of the state of his mind, and because they mark the points, and distinguish the stages of his progress.

Though in memoirs intended for publication, a large share of incident and action would generally be necessary, yet there are some men whose mental history alone might be very interesting to reflective readers; as, for instance, that of a thinking man, remarkable for a number of complete changes of his speculative system. From observing the usual tenacity of views once deliberately adopted in mature life, we regard as a curious phenomenom the man whose mind has been a kind of caravansera of opinions, entertained awhile, and then sent on pilgrimage; a man who has admired and dismissed systems with the same facility with which John Buncle found, adored, married, and interred, his succession of wives, each one being, for the time, not only better than all that went before, but the best in the creation. You admire the versatile aptitude of a mind, sliding into successive forms of belief in this intellectual metempsychosis by which it animates so many new bodies of doctrines in their turn. And as none of those dying pangs which hurt you in a tale of India, attend the desertion of each of these speculative forms which the soul has awhile inhabited, you are extremely amused by the number of transitions, and eagerly ask what is to be the next; for you never deem the present state of such a man's views to be for permanence, unless perhaps when he has terminated his course of believing every thing, in ultimately believing nothing. Even then, unless he is very old, or feels more pride in being a sceptic, the conqueror of all systems, than he ever felt in being the champion of one, even then, it is very possible he may spring up again, like a vapour of fire from a bog, and glimmer through new mazes, or retrace his course through half of those which he trod before. You will observe, that no respect attaches to this Proteus of opinion, after his changes have been multiplied; as no party expect him to remain with them, nor deem him much of an acquisition if he should. One, or perhaps two, considerable changes, will be regarded as signs of a liberal inquirer, and therefore the party to which his first or his second intellectual conversion may assign him, will receive him gladly. But he will be deemed to have abdicated the dignity of reason, when it is found that he can adopt no principles but to betray them; and it will be perhaps justly suspected that there is something extremely infirm in the structure of that mind, whatever vigor may mark some of its operiations, to which a series of very different, and sometimes contrasted theories, can appear in succession demonstratively true, and which imitates sincerely the perverseness which Petruchio only affected, declaring that which was yesterday, to a certainty, the sun, to be to-day, as certainly, the moon.

It would be curious to observe in a man who should make such an exhibition of the course of his mind, the sly deceit of self-love. While he despises the system which he has rejected, he does not deem it to imply so great a want of sense in *him* once to have embraced it, as in the rest, who were then or are now its disciples and advocates. No, in *him* it was no debility of reason, it was at the utmost but a merge of it; and probably he is prepared to explain to you that such peculiar circumstances, as might warp even a very strong and liberal mind, attended his consideration of the subject, and misled him to admit the belief of what others prove themselves fools by believing.

Another thing apparent in a record of changed opinions would be what I have noticed before, that there is scarcely any such thing in the world as simple conviction. It would be amusing to observe how reason had, in one instance, been overruled into acquiescence by the admiration of a celebrated name, or in another, into opposition by the envy of it; how most opportunely reason discovered the truth just at the time that interests could be essentially served by avowing it; how easily the impartial examiner could be induced to adopt some part of another man's opinions, after that other had zealously approved some favourite, especially if unpopular, part of his; as the Pharisees almost became partial even to Christ, at the moment that he defended one of their doctrines against the Sadducees. It would be curious to see how a respectful estimate of a man's character and talents might be changed, in consequence of some personal inattention experienced from him, into depreciating invective against him or his intellectual performances, and yet the railer, though actuated solely by petty revenge, account himself, all the while, the model of equity and sound judgment. It might be seen how the patronage of power could elevate miserable prejudices into revered wisdom, while poor old Experience was mocked with thanks for her instruction: and how the vicinity or society of the rich, and, as they are termed, great, could perhaps transmute a soul that seemed to be of the stern consistence of the early Roman republic, into the gentlest wax on which Corruption could wish to imprint the venerable creed, 'The right divine of kings to govern wrong,' with the pious and loyal inference of the flagrant iniquity of expelling Tarquin. I am supposing the *observer* to perceive all these accommodating dexterities of reason; for it were probably absurd to expect that any mind should itself be able, in its review, to detect all its own obliquities, after having been so long beguiled, like the mariners in a story which I remember to have read, who followed the direction of their compass, infallibly right as they could have no doubt, till they arrived at an enemy's port, where they were seized and made slaves. It happened that the wicked captain, in order to betray the ship, had concealed a large loadstone at a little distance on one side of the needle.

On the notions and expectations of one stage of life, I suppose all reflecting men look back with a kind of contempt, though it may be often with a mingling wish that some of its enthusiasm of feeling could be recovered,—I mean the period between childhood and maturity. They will allow that their reason was *then* feeble, and they are prompted to exclaim, What fools we have been—while they recollect how sincerely they entertained and advanced the most ridiculous speculations on the interests of life, and the questions of truth; how regretfully astonished they were to find the mature sense of some of those around them so completely wrong; yet in other instances what veneration they felt for authorities for which they have since lost all their respect; what a fantastic importance they attached to some most trivial things;* what complaints against their fate were uttered on account of disappointments which they have since recollected with gaiety or self-congratulation; what happiness of Elysium they expected from sources which would soon have failed to impart even common satisfaction; and how certain they were that the feelings and opinions then predominant would continue through life.

If a reflective aged man were to find at the bottom of an old chest, where it had lain forgotten fifty years, a record which he had written of himself when he was young, simply and vividly describing his whole heart and pursuits, reciting verbatim many recent passages of the language sincerely uttered to his favourite companions; would he not read it with more wonder than almost any other writing could at his age inspire? His consciousness would be strangely confused in the attempt to verify his identity with such a being. He would feel the young man, thus introduced to him, separated by so wide a distance of character as to render all congenial communion impossible. At every sentence he might repeat, Foolish youth! I have no sympathy with your feelings, I can hold no converse with your understanding. Thus you see that in the course of a long life a man may be several moral persons, so various from one another, that if you could find a real individual that should nearly exemplify the character in one of these stages, and another that should exemplify it in the next, and so on to the last, and then bring these several persons together into one society, which would thus be a representation of the successive states of one man, they would feel themselves a most heterogeneous party, would oppose and probably despise one another, and soon separate, not caring if they were never to meet again. The dissimilarity in mind between the two extremes, the youth of seventeen and the sage of seventy, might perhaps be little less than that in countenance; and as the one of these contrasts might be contemplated by an old man, if he had a true portrait for which he sat in the bloom of life, and should hold it beside a mirror in which he looks at his present countenance, the other would be powerfully felt if he had such a genuine and detailed memoir as I have supposed.† Might it not be worth while for a self-observant person in early life, to preserve for the inspection of the old man, if he should live so long, such a mental likeness of the young one? If it be not drawn near the time, it can never be drawn with sufficient accuracy.

If this sketch of life were not written till a very mature or an advanced period of it, a somewhat interesting point would be, to distinguish the periods during which the mind made its greatest progress in the enlargement of its faculties, and the time when they appeared to have reached and acknowledged their insuperable limits. And if there have been vernal seasons, if I may so express it, of goodness also, periods separated off from the latter course of life by some point of time, subsequent to which the Christian virtues have had a less generous growth, this is a circumstance still more worthy to be strongly marked. No doubt it will be with a reluctant hand that a man marks either of these circumstances; for he could not reflect without regret, that many children may have grown into maturity and great talent, and many unformed or defective characters into established excellence, since the period when he ceased to become abler or better. Pope, for instance, at the age of fifty, would have been incomparably more mortified than, as Johnson says, his readers are, at the fact, if he had perceived it, that he could not then write materially better than he had written at the age of twenty. And the consciousness of having passed many years without any moral and religious progress, ought to be not merely the regret for an infelicity, but the remorse of guilt; since, though natural causes must somewhere have circumscribed and fixed the extent of the intellectual power, an incessant advancement in the nobler distinctions has still continued to be possible, and will be possible, till the evening of rational life. The instruction resulting from a clear estimate of what has been effected or not in this capital concern, is the chief advantage to be derived from recording the stages of life, comparing one part with another, and bringing the whole into a comparison with the standard of perfection, and the illustrious human examples which have approached that standard the nearest. In forming this estimate, we shall keep in view the vast series of advantages and monitions, which has run parallel to the train of years; and it will be inevitable to recollect, sometimes with mortification bordering on anguish, the sanguine calculations of improvement of the best kind, which at various periods the mind was delighted to make for other given future periods, should life be protracted till then, and promised itself most *certainly* to realize by the time of their arrival. The mortification will be still more grievous, if there was at those past seasons something more hopeful than mere confident presumptions, if there were actual favourable omens, which partly justified while they raised, in ourselves and others anticipations that have mournfully failed. My dear friend it is very melancholy that EVIL must be so palpable, so hatefully conspicuous, to an enlightened conscience in every retrospect of a human life.

If the supposed memoirs are to be carried forward as life advances, each period being recorded as soon as it has elapsed, they should not be composed by small daily or weekly accumulations, (though this practice may on another ground have its value,) but at certain considerable intervals, as at the end of each year, or any other measure of time that is ample enough for some definable alteration to have taken place in the character or attainments.

It is needless to say that the *style* should be as simple as possible—unless indeed the writer accounts the theme worthy of being bedecked with brilliants and flowers. If he idolizes his own image so much as to think it deserves to be enshrined in a frame of gold, why let him enshrine it.

Should it be asked what degree of explicitness ought to prevail through this review, in reference to those particulars on which conscience has fixed the deepest mark of condemnation; I answer, that if a man writes it exclusively for his own use, he ought to signify both the nature of the delinquency and the measure of it, so far at least as to secure to his mind a most defined recollection of the facts, and of the verdict pronounced by conscience before its emotions were quelled by time. Such honest distinctness is necessary, because this will be the most useful part of his record for reflection to dwell upon; because this is the part which self-love is most willing to diminish and memory to dismiss; because he may be certain that mere general terms or allusions of censure will but little aid the cultivation of his humility; and because this license of saying so

* I recollect a youth of some acquirements, who earnestly wished the time might one day arrive, when his name should be adorned with the addition of D. D. which he deemed one of the sublimest of human distinctions.

† Since a character, and a set of opinions, once formed, not unfrequently continue substantially through life, perhaps the moral and intellectual difference between the stages, is not quite as great as the physical. Some people have in fact but three or four stages in the whole of life.

much about himself in the character of a biographer may become only a temptation to the indulgence of vanity, and a protection from the shame of it, unless he can maintain the feeling in earnest that it is really at a confessional, and a severe one, that he is giving his account.

But perhaps he wishes to hold this record open to an intimate relative or friend; perhaps even thinks it might supply some interest and some lessons to his children. And what then? Why then it is perhaps too probable that though he could readily confess some of his faults, there may have been certain states of his mind, and certain circumstances in his conduct, which he cannot easily persuade himself to present to such inspection. Such a difficulty of being quite ingenuous is in every instance a cause for deep regret. Should not a man tremble to feel himself involved in a difficulty of confiding to an equal and a mortal, what has been all observed by the Supreme Witness and Judge? And the consideration of the large proportion of men constituting such instances, throws a melancholy hue over the general human character. It has several times in writing this essay occurred to me what strangers men may be to one another, whether as to the influences which have determined their characters, or as to the less obvious parts of their conduct. What strangers too we may be, with persons who have any power and caution of concealment, to the principles which are at this moment prevailing in the heart. Each mind has an interior apartment of its own, into which none but himself and the Divinity can enter. In this retired place, the passions mingle and fluctuate in unknown agitations. Here all the fantastic and all the tragic shapes of imagination have a haunt, where they can neither be invaded nor descried. Here the surrounding human beings, while quite unconscious of it, are made the subjects of deliberate thought, and many of the designs respecting them revolved in silence. Here projects, convictions, vows, are confusedly scattered, and the records of past life are laid. Here in solitary state, sits Conscience, surrounded by her own thunders, which sometimes sleep, and sometimes roar, while the world does not know. The secrets of this apartment, could they have been even but very partially brought forth, might have been fatal to that eulogy and splendour with which many a piece of biography has been exhibited by a partial and ignorant friend. If, in a man's own account of himself, written on the supposition of being seen by any other person, the substance of the secrets of this apartment is brought forth, he throws open the last asylum of his character, where it is well if there be nothing found that will distress and irritate his most intimate friend, who may thus become the ally of his conscience to condemn, without the leniency which even conscience acquires from self-love. And if it is not brought forth, where is the integrity or value of the history; and what ingenuous man could bear to give a delusive assurance of his being, or having been, so much more worthy of applause or affection than conscience all the while pronounces? It is obvious then that a man whose sentiments and designs, or the undisclosed parts of whose conduct, have been stained with deep delinquency, must keep his record most sacred to himself; unless he feels such an unsupportable longing to relieve his heart by confiding its painful consciousness, that he can be content to hold the regard of his friend on the strength of his penitence and recovered virtue. As to the rest, whose memory of the past is sullied by shades if not by stains, they must either in the same manner retain this delineation for solitary use, or limit themselves in writing it, to a deliberate and strong expression of the *measure* of conscious culpabilities, and their effect in the general character, with a certain reserve and indefiniteness of explanation that shall equally avoid particularity and mystery; or else, they must consent to meet their friends, who are likewise human and have had their deviations, on terms of mutual ingenuous acknowledgment. In this confidential communication, each will learn to behold the other's transgressions fully as much in that light in which they certainly are infelicities to be commiserated, as in that in which they are also faults or vices to be condemned; while both will earnestly endeavour to improve by their remembered errors. The apostle seems to encourage such a confidence, where he says, 'Confess your faults one to another, and pray one for another.'

But I shall find myself in danger of becoming ridiculous amidst these scruples about an entire ingenuousness to a confidential friend or two, while I glance into the literary world, and observe the number of historians of their own lives, who magnanimously throw the complete cargo, both of their vanities and their vices, before the whole public. Men who can gaily laugh at themselves for ever having even pretended to goodness; men who can tell of having sought consolation for the sorrows of bereaved tenderness, in the recesses of debauchery; men whose language betrays that they deem a spirited course of profligate adventures a much nobler thing than the stupidity of vulgar virtues, and who seem to claim the sentiments with which we regard an unfortunate hero, for the disasters into which these adventurers led them; venal partisans, whose talents would hardly have been bought, if their venom had not made up the deficiency; profane travelling coxcombs; players, and the makers of immoral plays—all these can narrate the course of a contaminated life with the most ingenuous effrontery. Even courtezans, grieved at the excess of modesty with which the age is afflicted, have endeavored to diminish the evil, by presenting themselves before the public, in their narratives, in a manner very analogous to that in which the Lady Godiva is said to have consented, from a most generous inducement, to pass through the city of Coventry. They can gravely relate, perhaps, with intermingled paragraphs and verses of plaintive sensibility, (a kind of weeds in which sentiment without principle apes and mocks mourning virtue,) the whole nauseous detail of their transitions from proprietor to proprietor. They can tell of the precautions for meeting some 'illustrious personage,' accomplished in depravity even in his early youth, with the proper adjustment of time and circumstances to save him the scandal of such a meeting; the hour when they crossed the river in a boat; the arrangements about money; the kindness of the personage at one time, his contemptuous neglect at another; and every thing else that can turn the compassion with which we deplore their first misfortunes and errors, into detestation of the effrontery which can even take to itself a merit in proclaiming the commencement, sequel, and all, to the wide world.

With regard to all the classes of self-describers who thus think the publication of their vices necessary to crown their fame, one should wish there were some public special mark and brand of emphatical reprobation, to reward this tribute to public morals. Men that court the pillory for the pleasure of it, ought to receive the honour of it too, in all those contumelious salutations which suit the merits of vice grown proud of its impudence. Those that 'glory in their shame' should like other distinguished personages, 'pay a tax for being eminent.' Yet I own the public itself is to be consulted in this case; for if the public welcomes such productions, it shows there are readers who feel themselves akin to the writers, and it would be hard to deprive congenial souls of the luxury of their appropriate sympathies. If such is the taste, it proves that a considerable portion of the public deserves just that kind of respect for its virtue, which is very significantly implied in this confidence of its favour.

One is indignant at the cant pretence and title of Confessions, sometimes adopted by these narrators of their own disgrace; as if it were to be believed that penitence and humility would ever excite men to call thousands to witness an unnecessary disclosure of what oppresses them with grief and shame. If they would be mortified that only a few readers should think it worth their while to see them thus performing the work of self-degradation, like the fetid heroes of the Dunciad in a ditch, is it because they would gladly incur the contempt and disgust of multitudes in order to serve the cause of virtue? No, this title of Confessions is only a nominal deference to morality, necessary indeed to be paid, because mankind never forget to insist, that the *name* of virtue shall be devoutly respected, even while vice obtains from them that practical favour on which these writers place their reliance for toleration or applause.

This slight homage being duly rendered and occasionally repeated, they trust in the character of the community that they shall not meet this kind of condemnation, and they have no desire for the kind of pity which would strictly belong to criminals; nor is it any part of their penitence, to wish that society may become better by the odious repellency of their example. They are glad the age continues such, that even *they* may have claims to be praised; and honour of some kind, and from some quarter, is the object to which they aspire, and the consequence which they promise themselves. Let them once be convinced, that they make such exhibitions under the absolute condition of subjecting themselves irredeemably to opprobrium, as in Miletus the persons infected with a rage for destroying themselves were by a solemn decree assured of being exposed, after the perpetration of the deed, in naked ignominy—and these literary suicides will be heard of no more.

Rousseau has given a memorable example of this voluntary humiliation. And he has honestly assigned the degree of contrition which accompanied the self-inflicted penance, in the declaration, that this document, with all its dishonours, shall be presented in his justification before the Eternal Judge. If we could, in any case, pardon the kind of ingenuousness which he has displayed, it would certainly be in the disclosure of a mind so wonderfully singular as his.* We are almost willing to have such a being preserved, to all the unsightly minutæ and anomalies of its form, to be placed, as an unique, in the moral museum of the world.

Rousseau's impious reference to the Divine Judge, leads me to suggest, as I conclude, the consideration, that the history of each man's life, though it should not be written by himself or by any mortal hand, is thus far unerringly recorded, will one day be finished in truth, and one other day yet to come will be brought to a final estimate. A mind accustomed to grave reflections is sometimes led involuntarily into a curiosity of awful conjecture, which asks, What are those very words which I should read this night, if, as to Belshazzar, a hand of prophetic shade were sent to write before me the identical sentences in which that final estimate will be declared?—

* There is indeed one case in which this kind of honesty would be so singularly useful to mankind, that it would deserve almost to be canonized into a virtue. If statesmen, including ministers, popular leaders, ambassadors, &c. would publish before they go in the triumph of virtue to the 'last audit,' or leave to be published after they are gone, each frank exposition of motives, cabals, and manœuvres, it would give dignity to that blind adoration of power and rank in which mankind have always superstitiously lived, by supplying just reasons for that adoration. It would also give a new aspect to history; and perhaps might tend to a happy exorcism of that evil spirit which has never allowed nations to remain at peace.

ESSAY II.

ON DECISION OF CHARACTER.

LETTER I.

Examples of the Distress and Humiliation incident to an irresolute Mind—Such a Mind cannot be said to belong to itself—Manner in which a Man of decisive Spirit deliberates and passes into Action—Cæsar—Such a Spirit prevents the Fretting away, in harassing Alterations of Will of the animated Feelings required for sustaining the Vigour of Action—Averts impertinent Interference—Acquires, if free from Harshness of Manner, an undisputed and beneficial Ascendancy over Associates—Its last Resource inflexible Pertinacity—Instance in a Man on a Jury.

MY DEAR FRIEND,

We have several times talked of this bold quality, and acknowledged its great importance. Without it, a human being, with powers at best but feeble, and surrounded by innumerable things tending to perplex, to divert, or to oppress, their operations, is indeed a pitiable atom the sport of diverse and casual impulses. It is a poor and disgraceful thing, not to be able to reply, with some degree of certainty, to the simple questions, What will you be? What will you do?

A little acquaintance with mankind will supply numberless illustrations of the importance of this character. You will often see a person anxiously hesitating a long time between different, or opposite determinations, though impatient of the pain of such a state, and ashamed of its debility. A faint impulse of preference alternates toward the one, and toward the other; and the mind, while thus held in a trembling balance, is vexed that it cannot get some new thought, or feeling, or motive, that it has not more sense, more resolution, more of any thing that would save it from envying even the decisive instinct of brutes. It wishes that any circumstance might happen, or any person might appear, that could deliver it from the miserable suspense.

In many instances, when a determination *is* adopted it is frustrated by this indecision. A man, for example, resolves to make a journey to-morrow, which he is not under an absolute necessity to make, but the inducements appear, this evening, so strong, that he does not think it possible he can hesitate in the morning. In the morning, however, these inducements have unaccountably lost much of their force. Like the sun that is rising at the same time, they appear dim through a mist; and the sky lowers, or he fancies that it lowers; recollections of toils and fatigues ill repaid in past expeditions rise and pass into anticipations; and he lingers, uncertain, till an advanced hour determines the question for him, by the certainty that it is now too late to go.

Perhaps a man has conclusive reasons for wishing to remove to another place of residence. But when he is going to take the first actual step towards executing his purpose, he is met by a new train of ideas, presenting the possible, and magnifying the unquestionable, disadvantages and uncertainties of a new situation; awakening the natural reluctance to quit a place to which habit has accommodated his feelings, and which has grown *warm* to him, if I may so express it, by his having been in it so long; giving new strength to his affection for the friends whom he must leave, and so detaining him still lingering, long after his serious judgment may have dictated to him to be gone.

A man may think of some desirable alteration in his plan of life; perhaps in the arrangements of his family, or in the mode of his intercourse with society.—Would it be a good thing? He thinks it would be a good thing. It certainly would be a very good thing. He wishes it were done. He will attempt it *almost* immediately. The following day, he doubts whether it would be quite prudent. Many things are to be considered. May there not be in the change some evils of which he is not aware? Is this a proper time? What will the people say?—And thus, though he does not formally renounce his purpose, he shrinks out of it, with a wish that he could be fully satisfied of the propriety of renouncing it. Perhaps he wishes that the thought had never occurred to him, since it has diminished his self-complacency, without promoting his virtue. But the next day, his conviction of the wisdom and advantage of such a reform comes again with great force. Then, Is it so practicable as I was at first willing to imagine? Why not? Other men have done much greater things; a resolute mind is omnipotent; difficulty is a stimulus and a triumph to a strong spirit; 'the joys of conquest are the joys of man.' What need I care about people's opinion? It shall be done. He makes the first attempt. But some unexpected obstacle presents itself; he feels the awkwardness of attempting an unacustomed manner of acting; the questions or the ridicule of his friends disconcert him; his ardour abates and expires. He again begins to question, whether it be wise, whether it be necessary, whether it be possible; and at last, surrenders his purpose, to be perhaps resumed when the same feelings return, and to be in the same manner again relinquished.

While animated by some magnanimous sentiments which he has heard or read, or while musing on some great example, a man may conceive the design, and partly sketch the plan, of a generous enterprise; and his imagination revels in the felicity that would follow, to others and to himself, from its accomplishment. The splendid representation always centres in himself as the hero that is to realize it.

Yet a certain consciousness in his mind doubtfully asks, Is this any thing more than a dream; or am I really destined to achieve such an enterprise? Destined!—and why are not this conviction of its excellence, this conscious duty of performing the noblest things that are possible, and this passionate ardour, enough to secure that I shall effect it? He feels indignant at that failing part of his nature which puts him so far below his own conceptions, and below the examples which he is admiring; and this feeling assists him to resolve, that he will undertake this enterprise, that he certainly will, though the Alps or the Ocean lie between him and the object. Again his ardour slackens; distrustful of himself, he wishes to know how the design would appear to other minds; and when he speaks of it to his associates, one of them wonders, another laughs, and another frowns. His pride attempts, while with them, a manful defence; but his mind is gradually descending toward their level, he becomes ashamed to entertain a visionary project, which therefore, like a rejected friend, desists from intruding on him or following him, and he subsides, at last, into what he labours to believe, a man too rational for the schemes of ill-calculating enthusiasm. And it were strange if the effort to make out this favourable estimate of himself did not succeed, while it is so much more pleasant to attribute one's defect of enterprise to wisdom, which on maturer thought disapproves of it, than to imbecility which shrinks from it.

A person of undecisive character wonders how all the embarassments in the world happened to meet exactly in *his* way, to place him just in that one situation for which he is peculiarly unadapted, and in which he is also willing to think no other man could have acted with such facility or confidence. Incapable of setting up a firm purpose on the basis of things as they are, he is often employed in vain speculations on some different supposable state of things, which would have saved him from all this perplexity and irresolution. He thinks what a determined course he could have pursued, *if* his talents, his health, his age, had been different; if he had been acquainted with some one person sooner; if his friends were, in this or the other point, different from what they are; or if fortune had showered her favours on him. And he gives himself as much license to complain, as if all these advantages had been among the rights of his nativity, but refused, by a malignant or capricious fate, to his life. Thus he is occupied—instead of catching with a vigilant eye, and seizing with a strong hand, all the possibilities of his actual situation.

A man without decision can never be said to belong to himself; since, if he dared to assert that he did, the puny force of some cause, about as powerful, you would have supposed, as a spider, may make a capture of the hapless boaster the very next moment, and triumphantly exhibit the futility of the determinations by which he was to have proved the independence of his understanding and his will. He belongs to whatever can seize him; and innumerable things do actually verify their claim on him, and arrest him as he tries to go along; as twigs and chips, floating near the edge of a river, are intercepted by every weed, and whirled in every little eddy. Having concluded on a design, he may pledge himself to accomplish it,—*if* the hundred diversities of feeling which may come within the week, will let him. As his character precludes all foresight of his conduct, he may sit and wonder what form and direction his views and actions are destined to take to-morrow; as a farmer has often to acknowledge the next day's proceedings are at the disposal of its winds and clouds.

This man's opinions and determinations always depend very much on other human beings; and what chance for consistency and stability, while the persons with whom he may converse, or transact, are so various? This very evening, he may talk with a man whose sentiments will melt away the present form and outline of his purposes, however firm and defined he may have fancied them to be. A succession of persons whose faculties were stronger than his own, might, in spite of his irresolute reaction, take him and dispose of him as they pleased. An infirm character practically confesses itself made for subjection, and the man so constituted passes, like a slave, from owner to owner. Sometimes indeed it happens, that a person of this sort falls into the train, and under the permanent ascendancy of some one stronger character, which thus becomes through life the oracle and guide, and gives the inferior a steady will and plan. This, when the leading character is virtuous, is a fortunate relief to the feeling, and an advantageous point gained to the utility, of the subordinate appended mind.

It is inevitable that the regulation of every man's plan must greatly depend on the course of events which come in an order not to be foreseen or prevented. But in accommodating the plans of conduct to the train of events, the difference between two men may be no less than that, in the one instance, the man is subservient to the events, and in the other, the events are made subservient to the man. Some men seem to have been taken along by a succession of events, and, as it were, handed forward in quiet passiveness from one to another; without any determined principle in their own characters, by which they could constrain those events to serve a design formed antecedently to them, or apparently in defiance of them. The events seized them as a neutral material, not they the events. Others, advancing through life, with an internal invincible determination of mind, have seemed to make the train of circumstances, whatever they were, conduce as much to their chief design as if they had taken place on purpose. It is wonderful how even the apparent casualties of life seem to bow to a spirit that will not bow to them, and yield to assist a design, after having in vain attempted to frustrate it. You may have seen such examples, though they are comparatively not numerous. You may have seen a man of this strong character in a state of indecision concerning some affair, in which it was requisite for him to determine, because it was requisite for him to act. But, in this case, his manner would assure you that he would not remain long undecided; you would wonder if you found him still at a loss the next day. If he explained his thoughts, you would perceive that their clear process, evidently at each effort approaching nearer to the result, must certainly reach it ere long. The deliberation of such a mind is a very different thing from the fluctuation of the other. To *know how* to obtain a determination, is one of the first symptoms of a rationally decisive character.

When the decision was formed, and the purpose fixed, you would feel an entire assurance that something would absolutely be done. It is characterestic of such a mind, to think for effect; and the pleasure of escaping from temporary doubt gives an additional impulse to the force with which it is carried into action. Such a man will not re-examine his conclusions with endless repetition, and he will not be delayed long by consulting other persons, after he has ceased to consult himself. He cannot bear to sit still among unexecuted decisions and unattempted projects. We wait to hear of his achievements, and are confident we shall not wait long. The possibility of the means may not be obvious to us, but we know that every thing will be attempted, and that such a mind is like a river, which, in whatever manner it is obstructed, will make its way somewhere. It must have cost Cæsar many anxious hours of deliberation, before he decided to pass the Rubicon; but it is probable he suffered but few to elapse after his decision, before he did pass it. And any one of his friends, who should have been apprised of this determination, and understood his character, would have smiled contemptuously to hear it insinuated that though Cæsar had resolved, Cæsar would not dare; or that though he might cross the Rubicon, whose opposite bank presented to him no hostile legions, he might come to other rivers, which he would not cross; or that either rivers, or any other obstacle, would deter him from prosecuting the determination from this ominous commencement to its very last consequence.

One signal advantage possessed by a mind of this character is, that its passions are not wasted. The whole measure of passion of which any mind, with important transactions before it, is capable, is not more than enough to supply interest and energy to its practical exertions; and therefore as little as possible of this sacred fire should be extended in a way that does not augment the force of action. But nothing can less contribute to vigour of action, than protracted anxious fluctuation, intermixed with resolutions decided and revoked, while yet nothing causes a greater expense of feeling. The heart is fretted and exhausted by being subjected to an alternation of contrary excitements, with the ultimate mortifying consciousness of their contributing to no end. The long-wavering deliberation, whether to perform some bold action of difficult virtue, has often cost more to feeling than the action itself, or a series of such actions, would have cost; with the great disadvantage too of being relieved by none of that invigoration, which, to the man in action, would have sprung from the spirit of the action itself, and have renovated the ardour which it was expending. A person of decisive character, by consuming as little passion as possible in dubious musings and abortive resolutions, can secure its utmost value and use, by throwing it all into effective operation.

Another advantage of this character, is, that it exempts from a great deal of interference and persecution, to which an irresolute man is subjected. Weakness, in every form, tempts arrogance; and a man may be allowed to wish for a kind of character with which stupidity and impertinence may not make so free. When a firm decisive spirit is recognised, it is curious to see how the space clears around a man, and leaves him room and freedom. This disposition to interrogate, dictate, or banter, preserves a respectful and politic distance, judging it not unwise to keep the peace with a person of so much energy. A conviction that he understands and that he wills with extraordinary force, silences the conceit that intended to perplex or instruct him, and intimidates the malice that was disposed to attack him. There is a feeling, as in respect to Fate, that the decrees of so inflexible a spirit *must* be right, or that, at least, they *will* be accomplished.

But not only will he secure the freedom of acting for himself, he will obtain also by degrees the coincidence of those in whose company he is to transact the business of life. If the manners of such a man are free from arrogance, and he can qualify his firmness with a moderate degree of insinuation; and if his measures have partly lost the appearance of being the dictates of his will, under the wider and softer sanctions of some experience that they are reasonable; both competition and fear will be laid to sleep, and his will may acquire an unresisted ascendency over many who will be pleased to fall into the mechanism of a system, which they find makes them more successful and happy than they could have been amidst the anxiety of adjusting plans and expedients of their own, and the consequences of often adjusting them ill. I have known several parents, both fathers and mothers, whose management of their families has answered this description; and has displayed a striking example of the facile complacency with which a number of persons, of different ages and dispositions, will yield to the decisions of a firm mind, acting on an equitable and enlightened system.

The last resource of this character, is, hard inflexible pertinacity, on which it may be allowed to rest its strength, after finding it can be effectual in none of its milder forms. I remember admiring an instance of this kind, in a firm, sagacious and very estimable old man, whom I well knew, and who is now dead. Being on a jury, in a trial of life and death, he was completely satisfied of the innocence of the prisoner; the other eleven were of the opposite opinion. But he was resolved the man should not be condemned; and as the first effort for preventing it, very properly made application to the *minds* of his associates, spending several hours in labouring to convince them. But he found he made no impression, while he was exhausting the strength which was to be reserved for another mode of operation. He then calmly told them, it should now be a trial who could endure confinement and famine the longest, and they might be quite assured he would sooner die than release them at the expense of the prisoner's life. In this situation they spent about twenty-four hours; when at length all acceded to his verdict of acquittal.

It is not necessary to amplify on the indispensable importance of this quality, in order to the accomplishment of any thing eminently good. We instantly see, that every path to signal excellence is so obstructed and beset, that none but a spirit so qualified can pass. But it is time to examine what are the elements which compose the character.

LETTER III.

Brief Inquiry into the Constituents of this commanding Quality—Corporeal Constitution—Possibility, nevertheless, of a firm Mind in a feeble Body—Confidence in a Man's own Judgment—This is an uncommon Distinction—Picture of a Man who wants it—This Confidence distinguished from Obstinacy—Partly founded on Experience—Takes a high Tone of Independence in devising Schemes—Distressing Dilemmas.

Perhaps the best mode would be to bring into our thoughts in succession, the most remarkable examples of this character that we have known in real life, or that we have read of in history or even in fiction, and attentively to observe, in their conversations, manners, and actions, what principles appear to produce, or to constitute, this commanding distinction. You will easily pursue this investigation yourself. I lately made a partial attempt, and shall offer you a number of suggestions.

As a previous observation, it is beyond all doubt that very much depends on the constitution of the body. It would be for physiologists to explain, if it were explicable, the *manner* in which corporeal organization affects the mind; I only assume it as a fact, that there is in the material construction of some persons, much more than of others, some quality which augments, if it does not create, both the stability of their resolution, and the energy of their active tendencies. There is something that, like the ligatures which one class of the Olympic combatants bound on their hands and wrists, braces round, if I may so describe it, and compresses the powers of the mind, giving them a steady, forcible spring and re-action, which they would presently lose if they could be transferred into a constitution of soft, yielding, treacherous debility. The action of strong character seems to demand something firm in its corporeal basis, as massive engines require, for their weight and for their working, to be fixed on a solid foundation. Accordingly I believe it would be found, that a majority of the persons most remarkable for decisive character, have possessed great constitutional firmness. I do not mean an exemption from disease and pain, nor any certain measure of mechanical strength, but a tone of vigour, the opposite to lassitude, and adapted to great exertion and endurance. This is clearly evinced in respect to many of them, by the prodigious labours and deprivations which they have borne in prosecuting their designs. The physical nature has seemed a proud ally of the moral one, and with a hardness that would never shrink, has sustained the energy that could never remit.

A view of the disparities between the different races of animals inferior to man, will show the effect of organization on disposition. Compare, for instance, a lion with the common beasts of our fields, many of them composed of a larger bulk of animated substance. What a vast superiority of courage, impetuous movement, and determined action; and we attribute this difference to some great dissimilarity of modification in the composition of the animated material. Now it is probable that a difference somewhat analogous subsists between some human bodies and others, and that this is no small part of the cause of the striking inequalities in respect to decisive character. A very decisive man has probably more of the physical quality of a *lion* in his composition than other men.

It is observable that women in general have less inflexibility of character than men; and though many moral influences contribute to this difference, the principal cause may probably be something less firm in the corporeal texture. Now that physical quality, whatever it is, from the existence of a smaller measure of which in the constitution of the frame, women have less firmness than men, may be possessed by one man more than by men in general, in a greater degree of difference than that by which men in general exceed women.

If there have been found some resolute spirits powerfully asserting themselves in feeble vehicles, it is so much the better; since this would authorize a hope, that if all the other grand requisites can be combined, they may form a strong character, in spite of the counteraction of an unadapted constitution. And on the other hand, no constitutional hardness will form the true character, without those grand principles; though it may produce that false and contemptible kind of decision which we term *obstinacy;* a stubbornness of temper, which can assign no reasons but mere will, for a constancy which acts in the nature of dead weight rather than of strength; resembling less the re-action of a powerful spring, than the gravitation of a big stone.

The first prominent mental characteristic of the person whom I describe, is, a complete confidence in his own judgment. It will perhaps be said, that this is not so uncommon a qualification. I however think it is uncommon. It is indeed obvious enough, that almost all men have a flattering estimate of their own understanding, and that so long as this understanding has no harder task than to form opinions which are not to be tried in action, they have a most self-complacent assurance of being right. This assurance extends to the judgments which they pass on the proceedings of others. But let them be brought into the necessity of adopting actual measures in an untried proceeding, where, unassisted by any previous example or practice, they are reduced to depend on the resources of pure judgment alone, and you will see, in many cases, this confidence of opinion vanish away. The mind seems all at once placed in a misty vacuity, where it reaches round on all sides, but can find nothing to take hold of. Or if not lost in vacuity, it is overwhelmed by confusion; and feels as if its faculties were annihilated as soon as it begins to think of schemes and calculations among the possibilities, chances, and hazards, which overspread a wide, untrodden field; and this conscious imbecility becomes severe distress, when it is believed that consequences, of serious or unknown good or evil, are depending on the decisions which are to be formed amidst so much uncertainty. The thought painfully recurs at each step and turn, I may be right, but it is more probable I am wrong. It is like the case of a rustic walking in London, who, having no certain direction through the vast confusion of streets to the place where he wishes to be, advances, and hesitates, and turns, and inquires, and becomes, at each corner, still more inextricably perplexed.* A man in this situ-

* 'Why does not the man call a hackney-coach?' a gay reader, I am aware, will say of a person so bemazed in a great town. So he might, certainly; and the gay reader and I have only to deplore that there is no parallel convenience for the assistance of perplexed understandings.

ation feels he shall be very unfortunate if he cannot accomplish more than he can understand. Is not this frequently, when brought to the practical test, the state of a mind not much disposed, in general, to undervalue its own judgment?

In cases where judgment is not so completely bewildered, you will yet perceive a great practical distrust of it. A man has perhaps advanced a considerable way toward a decision, but then lingers at a small distance from it, till necessity, with a stronger hand than conviction, impels him upon it. He cannot see the whole length of the question, and suspects the part beyond his sight to be the most important, because it *is* beyond. He fears that certain possible consequences, if they should follow, would cause him to reproach himself for his present determination. He wonders how this or the other person would have acted in the same circumstances; eagerly catches at any thing like a respectable precedent; and looks anxiously round to know what each person thinks on the subject; while the various and opposite opinions to which he listens, perhaps only serve to confound his perception of the track of thought by which he had hoped to reach his conclusion. Even when that conclusion is obtained, there are not many minds that might not be brought a few degrees back into dubious hesitation, by a man of respected understanding saying, in a confident tone, Your plan is injudicious; your selection is unfortunate; the event will disappoint you.

It cannot be supposed that I am maintaining such an absurdity as that a man's complete reliance on his own judgment is necessarily a proof of that judgment being correct and strong. Intense stupidity may be in this point the rival of clear-sighted wisdom. I had once some knowledge of a person, whom no mortal, not even Cromwell, could have excelled in the article of confidence in his judgment, and consequent inflexibility of conduct; while at the same time his successive schemes were ill-judged to a degree that made his disappointments ridiculous rather than pitiable. He was not an example of that simple obstinacy which I have mentioned before; for he considered his measures, and did not want for reasons which satisfied himself beyond a doubt of their being most judicious. This confidence of opinion may be possessed by a person in whom it will be contemptible or mischievous; but its proper place is in a very different character, and without it there can be no dignified actors in human affairs.

If, after observing how foolish this confidence appears as a feature in a weak character, it be inquired what it is in a justly decisive person's manner of thinking, which authorizes him in this firm assurance that his view of the concerns before him is comprehensive and accurate; he may, in answer, justify his confidence upon such grounds as these: that he is conscious that objects are presented to his mind with an exceedingly distinct and perspicuous aspect, not like the shapes of moon-light, or like Ossian's ghosts, dim forms of uncircumscribed shade; that he sees the different parts of the subject in an arranged order, not in dispersed fragments; that in each deliberation the main object keeps its clear pre-eminence, and he perceives the bearings which the subordinate and conducive ones have on it; that perhaps several dissimilar trains of thought lead him to the same conclusion; and that he finds his judgment does not vary according to the moods of his feelings.

It may be presumed that a high degree of this character is not attained without a considerable measure of that kind of certainty, with respect to the relations of things, which can be acquired only from experience and observation; though an extreme vigilance in the exercise of observation, and a strong and strongly exerted power of generalizing on experience, may have made a comparatively short time enough to supply a large share of the wisdom derivable from these sources; so that a man may be rich in the benefits of experience, and therefore may have all the decision of judgment legitimately founded on that accomplishment, long before he is old. This experimental knowledge he will be able to apply in a direct and immediate manner, and without refining it into general principles, to some situations of affairs, so as to anticipate the consequences of certain actions in those situations as confidently and rationally as the kind of fruit to be produced by a given kind of tree. Thus far the facts of his experience will serve him as precedents. At the next step, he will be able to apply this knowledge, now converted into general principles, to a multitude of cases bearing but a partial resemblance to any thing he has actually witnessed. And then, in looking forward to the possible occurrence of altogether new combinations of circumstances, he can trust to the resources which he is persuaded his intellect will open to him, or is humbly confident, if he is a devout man, that the Supreme Intelligence will not suffer to be wanting to him, when the occasion arrives. In proportion as his views include, at all events, more certainties than those of other men, he is less fearful of contingencies. And if, in the course of executing his design, unexpected disastrous events should befal, but which are not owing to any thing wrong in the plan and principles of that design, but to foreign causes; it will be characteristic of a strong mind to attribute these events discriminately to their own causes, and not to the *plan*, which, therefore, instead of being disliked and relinquished, will be still as much approved as before, and the man will proceed calmly to the sequel of it without any change of arrangement;—unless indeed these sinister events should be such as to alter the whole state of things to which the plan was correctly adapted, and so to create a necessity on this account for an entirely new one to be formed.

Without absolutely despising the understandings of other men, he will perceive their dimensions compared with his own, which will preserve its independence through every communication and encounter. It is however a part of this very independence, that he will hold himself at liberty to alter his opinion, if the information which may be communicated to him, shall give sufficient reason. And as no one is so sensible of the importance of a complete acquaintance with a subject as the man who is always endeavouring to think conclusively, he will listen with the utmost attention to the *information*, which may be received sometimes from persons for whose *judgment* he has no great respect. The information which they may afford to him is not at all the less valuable for the circumstance, that his practical inferences from it may be quite different from theirs. Counsel will in general have only so much weight with him as it supplies knowledge which may assist his judgment; he will yield nothing to it as authority; but he may hear it with more candor and good temper, from being conscious of this independence of his judgment, than the man who is afraid lest the first person that begins to persuade him, should confound his determination. He feels it entirely a work of his own to deliberate and to resolve, amidst all the advice which may be attempting to control him. If, with an assurance of his intellect being of the highest order, he also holds a commanding station, he will feel it gratuitous to consult with any one, excepting merely to receive statements of facts. This appears to be exemplified in the man, who has lately shown the nations of Europe how large a portion of the world may, when Heaven permits, be at the mercy of the solitary workings of an individual mind.

The strongest trial of this determined style of judgment is in those cases of urgency where something must immediately be done, and where the consequences of deciding right or wrong are of great importance; as in the office of a medical man in treating a patient whose situation, while it renders some hazardous means indispensable, also renders it extremly doubtful which ought to be selected. A still stronger illustration is the case of a general, who is compelled, in the very instant, to make dispositions on which the event of a battle, the lives of thousands of his men, or perhaps almost the fate of a nation, may depend. He may even be reduced to an alternative which appears equally dreadful on both sides. Such a dilemma is described in Denon's account of one of the sanguinary conflicts between the French and Mamelukes, as having for a while held General Desaix, though a very decisive commander, in a state of anguish.

LETTER III.

Energy of Feeling as necessary as Confidence of Opinion—Conduct that results from their Combination—Effect and Value of a Ruling Passion—Great Decision of Character invests even wicked Beings with something which we are tempted to admire—Satan—Zanga—A Spanish Assassin—Remarkable Example of this Quality in a Man who was a Prodigal and became poor, but turned Miser and became rich—Howard—Whitefield—Christian Missionaries.

This indispensable basis, confidence of opinion, is however not enough to constitute the character in question. For many persons, who have been conscious and proud of a much stronger grasp of thought than ordinary men, and have held the most decided opinions on important things to be done, have yet exhibited, in the listlessness or inconstancy of their actions, a contrast and a disgrace to the operations of their understandings. For want of some cogent feeling impelling them to carry every internal decision into action, they have been still left where they were; and a dignified judgment has been seen in the hapless plight of having no effective forces to execute its decrees.

It is evident then, (and I perceive I have partly anticipated this article in the first letter,) that another essential principle of the character is, a total incapability of surrendering to indifference or delay the serious determinations of the mind. A strenuous *will* must accompany the conclusions of thought, and constantly incite the utmost efforts for their practical accomplishment. The intellect must be invested, if I may so describe it, with a glowing atmosphere of passion, under the influence of which, the cold dictates of reason take fire, and spring into active powers.

Revert once more in your thoughts to the persons most remarkably distinguished by this decision. You will perceive, that instead of allowing themselves to sit down delighted after the labour of successful thinking, as if they had completed some great thing, they regard this labour but as a circumstance of preparation, and the conclusions resulting from it as of no more value, till applied to the greater labour which is to follow, than the entombed lamps of the Rosicrucians. They are not disposed to be content in a region of mere ideas, while they ought to be advancing into the field of corresponding realities; they retire to that region sometimes, as ambitious adventurers anciently went to Delphi, to consult, but not to reside. You will therefore find them almost uniformly in determined pursuit of some object, on which they fix a keen and steady look, and which they never lose sight of, while they follow it through the confused multitude of other things.

A person actuated by such a spirit, seems by his manner to say, 'Do you think that I would not disdain to adopt a purpose which I would not devote my utmost force to effect; or that having thus devoted my exertions, I will intermit or withdraw them, through indolence, debility, or caprice; or that I will surrender my object to any interference except the uncontrollable dispensations of Providence? No, I am linked to my determination with iron bands; it clings to me with the tenacity of my fate, of the accomplishment of which, the frustration of my purpose may indeed be doomed as a part, but is doomed so only through calamity or death.

This display of systematic energy seems to indicate a constitution of mind in which the passions are commensurate with the intellectual part, and at the same time hold an inseparable correspondence with it, like the faithful sympathy of the tides with the phases of the moon. There is such an equality and connexion, that subjects of the decisions of judgment become proportionally and of course the objects of passion. When the judgment decides with a very strong preference, that same strength of preference, actuating also the passions, devotes them with energy to the object, so long as it is thus approved; and this will produce such a conduct as I have described. When therefore a firm, self-confiding, and unaltering judgment fails to make a decisive character, it is evident either that the passions in that mind are too languid to be capable of a strong and unremitting excitement, which defect makes an indolent or irresolute man; or that they perversely sometimes coincide with judgment and sometimes clash with it, which makes an inconsistent or versatile man.

There is no man so irresolute as not to act with determination in many single cases, where the motive is powerful and simple, and where there is no need of plan and perseverance; but this gives no claim to the term *character*, which expresses the habitual tenour of a man's active being. The character may be displayed in the successive unconnected undertakings, which are each of limited extent, and end with the attainment of their particular objects. But it is seen to the greatest advantage in those grand schemes of action, which have no necessary point of conclusion, which continue on through successive years, and extend even to that dark period when the agent himself is withdrawn from human sight.

I have repeatedly remarked to you in conversation, the effect of what has been called a Ruling Passion. When its object is noble, and an enlightened understanding directs its movements, it appears to me a great felicity; but whether its object be noble or not it infallibly creates, where it exists in great force, that active, ardent constancy, which I describe as a capital feature of the decisive character. The Subject of such a commanding passion wonders, if indeed he were at leisure to wonder, at the persons who pretend to attach importance to an object which they make none but the most languid efforts to secure. The utmost powers of the man are constrained into the service of the favourite Cause by this passion, which sweeps away, as it advances, all the trivial objections and little opposing motives, and seems almost to open a way through impossibilities. The spirit comes on him in the morning as soon as he recovers his consciousness, and commands and impels him through the day, with a power from which he could not emancipate himself if he would. When the force of habit is added, the determination becomes invincible, and seems to assume rank with the great laws of nature, making it nearly as certain that such a man will persist in his course as that in the morning the sun will rise.

A persisting, untameable efficacy of soul gives a seductive and pernicious dignity even to a character and a course which every moral principle forbids us to approve. Often in the narrations of history and fiction, an agent of the most dreadful designs compels a sentiment of deep respect for the unconquerable mind displayed in their execution. While we shudder at his activity, we say with regret, mingled with an admiration which borders on partiality, What a noble being this would have been, if goodness had been his destiny! The partiality is evinced in the very selection of terms, by which we show that we are tempted to refer his atrocity rather to his destiny than to his choice. I wonder whether an emotion like this, has not been experienced by each reader of Paradise Lost, relative to the Leader of the infernal spirits; a proof, if such were the fact, that a very serious error has been committed by the greatest poet. In some of the high examples of ambition, we almost revere the force of mind which impelled them forward through the longest series of action, superior to doubt and fluctuation, and disdainful of ease, of pleasures, of opposition, and of danger. We bow to the ambitious spirit which reached the true sublime in the reply of Pompey to his friends, who dissuaded him from hazarding his life on a tempestuous sea in order to be at Rome on an important occasion; 'It is necessary for me to go; it is not necessary for me to live.'

Revenge has produced wonderful examples of this unremitting constancy to a purpose. Zanga is a well supported illustration. And you may have read a real instance of a Spaniard, who, being injured by another inhabitant of the same town, resolved to destroy him: the other was apprised of this, and removed with the utmost secrecy, as he thought, to another town at a considerable distance, where however he had not been more than a day or two, before he found that his enemy was arrived there. He removed in the same manner to several parts of the kingdom, remote from each other; but in every place quickly perceived that his deadly pursuer was near him. At last he went to South America, where he had enjoyed his security but a very short time, before his unrelenting enemy came up with him, and accomplished his purpose.

You may recollect the mention, in one of our conversations, of a young man who wasted, in two or three years, a large patrimony in profligate revels with a number of worthless associates who called themselves his friends, and who, when his last means were exhausted, treated him of course with neglect or contempt. Reduced to absolute want, he one day went out of the house with an intention to put an end to his life; but wandering a while almost unconsciously, he came to the brow of an eminence which overlooked what were lately his estates. Here he sat down, and remained fixed in thought a number of hours, at the end of which he sprang from the ground with a vehement, exulting emotion. He had formed his resolution, which was, that all these estates should be his again; he had formed his plan too, which he instantly began to execute. He walked hastily forward, determined to seize the very first opportunity, of however humble a kind, to gain any money, though it were ever so despicable a trifle, and resolved absolutely not to spend, if he could help it, a farthing of whatever he might obtain. The first thing that drew his attention was a heap of coals shot out of carts on the pavement before a house. He offered himself to shovel or wheel them into the place where they were to be laid, and was employed. He received a few pence for the labour; and then, in pursuance of the saving part of his plan, requested some small gratuity of meat and drink, which was given him. He then looked out for the next thing that might chance to offer; and went, with indefatigable industry, through a succession of servile employments in different places, of longer and shorter duration, still scrupulously avoiding, as far as possible, the expense of a penny. He promptly seized *every* opportunity which could advance his design without regarding the meanness of occupation or appearance. By this method he had gained after a considerable time, money enough to purchase in order to sell again, a few cattle, of which he had taken pains to understand the value. He speedily but cautiously turned his first gains into second advantages; retained without a single deviation his extreme parsimony; and thus advanced by degrees into larger transactions and incipient wealth. I did not hear, or have forgotten, the continued course of his life; but the final result was, that he more than recovered his lost possessions, and died an inveterate miser, worth 60,000*l*. I have always recollected this as a signal instance, though in an unfortunate and ignoble direction, of decisive character, and of the extraordinary *effect* which, according to general laws, belongs to the strongest form of such a character.

But not less decision has been displayed by men of virtue. In this distinction no man ever exceeded, for instance, or ever will exceed, the late illustrious Howard.

The energy of his determination was so great, that if, instead of being habitual, it had been shown only for a short time on particular occasions, it would have appeared a vehement impetuosity; but by being unintermitted, it had an equability of manner which scarcely appeared to exceed the tone of a calm constancy, it was so totally the reverse of any thing like turbulence or agitation. It was the calmness of an intensity kept uniform by the nature of the human mind forbidding it to be more, and by the character of the individual forbidding it to be less. The habitual passion of his mind was a measure of feeling almost equal to the temporary extremes and paroxysms of common minds: as a great river, in its customary state, is equal to a small or moderate one when swollen to a torrent.

The moment of finishing his plans in deliberation, and commencing them in action, was the same. I wonder what must have been the amount of that bribe, in emolument or pleasure that would have detained him a week inactive after their final adjustment. The law which carries water down a declivity, was not more unconquerable and invariable than the determination of his feelings toward the main object The importance of this object held his faculties in a state of excitement which was too rigid to be affected by lighter interests, and on which therefore the beauties of nature and of art had no power. He had no leisure feeling which he could spare to be diverted among the innumerable varieties of the extensive scene which he traversed; all his subordinate feelings lost their separate existence and operation, by falling into the grand one. There have not been wanting trivial minds, to mark this as a fault in his character. But the mere men of taste ought to be silent respecting such a man as Howard; he is above their sphere of judgment. The invisible spirits, who fulfil their commission of philanthrophy among mortals, do not care about pictures, statues, and sumptuous buildings; and no more did he, when the time in which he must have inspected and admired them, would have been taken from the work to which he had consecrated his life. The curiosity which he might feel, was reduced to wait till the hour should arrive, when its gratification should be presented by conscience, which kept a scrupulous charge of all his time, as the most sacred duty of that hour. If he was still at every hour, when it came, fated to feel the attractions of the fine arts but the second claim, they might be sure of their revenge; for no other man will ever visit Rome under such a despotic consciousness of duty, as to refuse himself time for surveying the magnificence of its ruins. Such a sin against taste is very far beyond the reach of common saintship to commit. It implied an inconceivable severity of conviction, that he had *one thing to do*, and that he who would do some great thing in this short life, must apply himself to the work with such a concentration of his forces, as, to idle spectators who live only to amuse themselves, looks like insanity.

His attention was so strongly and tenaciously fixed on his object, that even at the greatest distance, as the Egyptian pyramids to travellers, it appeared to him with a luminous distinctness as if it had been nigh, and beguiled the toilsome length of labour and enterprise by which he was to reach it. It was so conspicuous before him, that not a step deviated from the direction, and every movement and every day was an approximation. As his method referred every thing he did and thought to the end, and as his exertion did not relax for a moment, he made the trial, so seldom made, what is the utmost effect which may be granted to the last possible efforts of a human agent: and therefore what he did not accomplish, he might conclude to be placed beyond the sphere of mortal activity, and calmly leave to the immediate disposal of Providence.

Unless the eternal happiness of mankind be an insignificant concern, and the passion to promote it an inglorious distinction, I may cite George Whitefield as a noble instance of this attribute of the decisive character, this intense necessity of action. The great Cause which was so languid a thing in the hands of many of its advocates, assumed in his administrations an unmitigable urgency.

Many of the Christian missionaries among the heathens, such as Brainerd, Elliot, and Schwartz, have displayed memorable examples of this dedication of their whole being to their office, this abjuration of all the quiescent feelings.

This would be the proper place for introducing (if I did not hesitate to introduce in any connexion with mere human instances) the example of Him who said, 'I must be about my Father's business. My meat and drink is to do the will of Him that sent me, and to finish his work. I have a baptism to be baptized with, and how am I straitened till it be accomplished.'

LETTER IV.

Courage a chief Constituent of the Character—Effect of this in encountering Censure and Ridicule—Almagro, Pizarro, and De Luques—Defiance of Danger—Luther—Daniel—Another indispensable Requisite to Decision is the full Agreement of all the Powers of the Mind—Lady Macbeth—Richard III—Cromwell—A Father who had the opportunity of saving one of two Sons from Death.

After the illustrations on the last article, it will seem but a very slight transition when I proceed to specify Courage, as an essential part of the decisive character. An intelligent man, adventurous only in thought, may sketch the most excellent scheme, and after duly admiring it, and himself as its author, may be reduced to say, What a noble spirit that would be which should dare to realize this! A noble spirit! Is it I? And his heart may answer in the negative, while he glances a mortified thought of inquiry round to recollect persons who would venture what he dares not, and almost hopes not to find them. Or if by extreme effort he has brought himself to a resolution of braving the difficulty, he is compelled to execrate the timid lingerings that still keep him back from the trial. A man endowed with the complete character, might say, with a sober consciousness as remote from the spirit of bravado as it is from timidity, Thus, and thus, is my conviction and my determination; now for the phantoms of fear; let me look them in the face; they will find I am not made of trembling materials: 'I dare do all that may become a man.' I shall firmly confront every thing that threatens me in the prosecuting of my purpose, and I am prepared to meet the consequences of it when it is accomplished. I should despise a being, though it were myself, whose agency could be held enslaved by the gloomy shapes of imagination, by the haunting recollections of a dream, by the whistling or the howling of winds, by the shriek of owls, by the shades of midnight, or by the threats and frowns of man. I should be indignant to feel that, in the commencement of an adventure, I could think of nothing but the deep pit by the side of the way where I must walk, into which I may slide, the mad animal which it is not impossible that I may meet, or the assassin who may lurk in a thicket of yonder wood. And I disdain to compromise the interests that rouse me to action, for the privilege of a disgraceful security.

As the conduct of a decisive man is always individual, and often singular, he may expect some serious trials of courage. For one thing, he may be encountered by the strongest disapprobation of many of his connexions, and the censure of the greater part of the society where he is known. In this case, it is not a man of common spirit that can show himself just as at other times, and meet their anger in the same undisturbed manner as he would meet some ordinary inclemency of the weather; that can without harshness or violence, continue to effect every moment some part of his design, coolly replying to each ungracious look and indignant voice, I am sorry to oppose you: I am not unfriendly to you, while thus persisting in what excites your displeasure; it would please me to have your approbation and concurreuce, and I think I should have them if you would seriously consider my reasons; but meanwhile, I am superior to opinion, I am not to be intimidated by reproaches, nor would your favour and applause be any reward for the sacrifice of my object. As you can do without my approbation, I can certainly do without yours; it is enough that I can approve myself, it is enough that I can appeal to the last authority in the creation. Amuse yourselves, as you may, by continuing to censure or to rail; *I* must continue to act.

The attack of contempt and ridicule is perhaps a still greater trial of couaage. It is felt by all to be an admirable thing, when it can in no degree be ascribed to the hardness of either stupidity or confirmed depravity, to sustain for a considerable time, or in numerous instances, the looks of scorn, or an unrestrained shower of taunts and jeers, with a perfect composure, which shall immediately after, or even at the time, proceed on the business that provokes all this ridicule. This invincibility of temper will often make even the scoffers themselves tired of the sport; they begin to feel that against such a man it is a poor sort of hostility to laugh. There is nothing that people are more mortified to spend in vain than their scorn. Till, however, a man becomes a veteran, he must reckon on sometimes meeting this trial; and I instantly know—if I hear him anxiously reply, to an important suggestion of any measure to be adopted, But will they not laugh at me?—I know that he is not the person whom this essay attempts to describe. A man of the right kind would say, They will smile, they will laugh, will they? Much good may it do them. I have something else to do than to trouble myself about their mirth. I do not care if the whole neighbourhood were to laugh in a chorus. I should indeed be sorry to see or hear such a number of fools, but pleased enough to find that they did not consider me as one of their stamp. The good to result from my project will not be less, because vain and shallow minds that cannot understand it, are diverted at it and at me. What should I think of my pursuits, if every trivial, thoughtless being could comprehend or would applaud them; and of myself, if my courage needed levity and ignorance for their allies, or could shrink at their sneers?

I remember, that on reading the account of the project of conquering Peru, formed by Almagro, Pizarro, and De Luques, while abhorring the principle and the design of the men, I could not help admiring the hardihood of mind, which made them regardless of scorn. These three individuals, before they had obtained any associates, or arms, or soldiers, or a complete knowledge of the power of the kingdom they were to conquer, celebrated a solemn mass in one of the great churches, as a pledge and a commencement of the enterprise, amidst the astonishment and contempt expressed by a multitude of people for what was deemed a monstrous project. They however proceeded through the service, and afterwards to their respective departments of preparation, with an apparently entire insensibility to all this triumphant scorn; and thus gave the first proof of possessing that invincible firmness with which they afterwards prosecuted their design, till they attained a success, the destructive process and many of the results of which humanity will for ever deplore.

Milton's Abdiel is a noble illustration of the courage that defies scorn.

But in some of the situations where decision of character is to be evinced, a man will be threatened by evils of a darker aspect than disapprobation or contempt. He may apprehend serious sufferings; and very often, to dare as far as conscience or a great cause required, has been to dare to die. In almost all plans of great enterprise, a man must systematically dismiss, at the entrance, every wish to stipulate for safety with his destiny. He voluntarily treads within the precincts of danger; and though it is possible that he may escape, he ought to be prepared with the fortitude of a self-devoted victim. This is the inevitable condition on which heroes, travellers or missionaries among savage nations, and reformers on a grand scale, must commence their career. Either they must allay their fire of enterprise, or they must hold themselves in readiness to be exploded by it from the world.

The last decisive energy of a rational courage, which confides in the Supreme Power, is very sublime. It makes a man, who intrepidly dares every thing that can oppose or attack him within the whole sphere of mortality; who would retain his purpose unshaken amidst the ruins of the world; who will still press toward his object while death is impending over him.

It was in the true elevation of this character that Luther, when cited to appear at the Diet of Worms, under a very questionable assurance of safety from high authority, said to his friends, who conjured him not to go, and justly brought the example of John Huss, who, in a similar situation, and with the same pledge of protection, had notwithstanding been burnt alive, 'I am called in the name of God to go, and I would go, though I were certain to meet as many devils in Worms as there are tiles on the houses.'

A reader of the Bible will not forget Daniel, braving in calm devotion the decree which virtually consigned him to the den of lions; or Shadrach, Meshach and Abed-nego, saying to the tyrant, 'We are not careful to answer thee in this matter,' when the furnace was in sight.

The combination of these several essential principles constitutes that state of mind which is the grand requisite to decision of character, and perhaps its most striking distinction, that is, the full agreement of the mind with itself, the co-operation of all its powers and all its dispositions.

What an unfortunate task it would be for a charioteer, who had harnessed a set of horses however strong, if he could not make them draw together; if, while one of them would go forward, another was restive, another struggled backward, another started aside. If even one of the four were unmanageably perverse, while the three were obedient, an aged beggar with his crutch might leave Phæton behind. So in a human being, unless the chief forces act consentaneously, there can be no inflexible vigour, either of will or of execution. *One* dissentient principle in the mind not only deducts so much from the strength and mass of its agency, but counteracts and embarrasses all the rest. If the judgment holds in low estimation that which yet the passions incline a man to pursue, his pursuit will be irregular and inconstant, though it may have occasional fits of animation, when those passions happen to be highly stimulated. If there is an opposition between judgment and habit, though the man will probably continue to act mainly under the direction of habit in spite of his opinions, yet sometimes the intrusion of those opinions will have for the moment an effect like that of Prospero's wand on the limbs of Ferdinand; and to be alternately impelled by habit, and checked by opinion, will be a state of vexatious debility. If two principal passions are opposite to each other, they will utterly distract any mind, whatever might be the force of its faculties when acting without embarrassment. The one passion may be somewhat stronger than the other, and therefore just prevail barely enough to give a feeble impulse to the conduct of the man; but no powerful impulse can be given, till the disparity of these two rivals becomes greater, in consequence of the gradual weight of habit, or the reinforcement supplied by some new impressions, being added to the preponderating passion. The disparity must be no less than an absolute predominance of the one and subjection of the other, before the prevailing passion will have at liberty from the intestine conflict any large measure of its force to throw activity into the system of conduct. If, for instance, a man feels at once the love of fame which is to be gained only by arduous exertions, and an equal degree of the love of pleasure which precludes those exertions; if he is eager to show off in splendour, and yet anxious to save money; if he has the curiosity of adventure, and yet that solicitude for his safety, which forbids him to climb a precipice, descend into a cavern, or explore a dangerous wild; if he has the stern will of a tyrant, and yet the relentings of a man; if he has the ambition which would subdue his fellow-mortals, counteracted by the humanity which would not hurt them; we can easily anticipate the irresolute, contradictory tenour of his actions. Especially if conscience, that great troubler of the human breast, loudly declares against a man's wishes or projects, it will be a fatal enemy to decision, till it either reclaim the delinquent passions, or be debauched or murdered by them.

Lady Macbeth may be cited as a harmonious character, though the epithet seems strangely applied. She had capacity, ambition, and courage; and she willed the death of the king. Macbeth had still more capacity, ambition, and courage; and he also willed the murder of the king. But he had, besides, humanity, generosity, conscience, and some measure of what forms the *power* of conscience, the fear of a Superior Being. Consequently, when the dreadful moment approached, he felt an insupportable conflict between these opposite principles, and when it was arrived, his utmost courage began to fail. The worst part of his nature fell prostrate under the power of the better; the angel of goodness arrested the demon that grasped the dagger; and would have taken that dagger away, if the pure demoniac firmness of his wife, who had none of these counteracting principles, had not shamed and hardened him to the deed.

The poet's delineation of Richard III, gives a dreadful specimen of this indivisibility of mental impulse. After his determination was fixed, his whole mind with the compactest fidelity supported him in prosecuting it Securely privileged from all interference of doubt that could linger, or humanity that could soften, or timidity that could shrink, he advanced with a grim, concentrated constancy through scene after scene of atrocity, still fulfilling his vow to 'cut his way through with a bloody axe.' He did not waver while he pursued his object, nor relent when he seized it.

Cromwell, (whom I mention as a parallel, not to Richard's depravity, but to his inflexible vigour) lost his mental consistency in the latter end of a career distinguished by as much decision as the world ever saw. It appears that the wish to be a king, at last arose in a mind which had execrated royalty, and battled it from the land. As far as he really had any republican principles and partialities, this new desire must have been a very uncomplacent associate for them, and must have produced a schism in the breast where all the strong forces of thought and passion had acted till then in concord. The new form of ambition became just predominant enough to carry him, by slow degrees, through the embarrassment and the shame of this incongruity, into an irresolute determination to assume the crown; so irresolute, that he was reduced again to a mortifying indecision by the remonstrances of some of his friends, which he could have slighted, and by an apprehension of the public disapprobation, which he could have braved, if some of the principles of his own mind had not shrunk or revolted from the design. When at last the motives for relinquishing this design prevailed, it was by so small a degree of predominance, that his reluctant refusal of the offered crown was the voice only of half his soul.

Not only two distinct counteracting passions, but one passion interested for two objects, both equally desirable, but of which the man must be sacrificed, may annihilate in that instance the possibility of determined conduct. I recollect reading in an old divine, a story from an older historian, applicable to this remark. A father went to the agents of a tyrant, to endeavour to redeem his two sons, military men, who with some other captives of war were condemned to die. He offered, as a ransom, to surrender his own life and a large sum of money. The tyrant's agents who had them in charge, informed him that this equivalent would be accepted for one of his sons, and for one only, because they should be accountable for the execution of two persons; he might therefore choose which he would redeem. Anxious to save even one of them thus at the expense of his own life, he yet was unable to decide which would die, by choosing the other to live, and remained in the agony of this dilemma so long that they were both irreversibly ordered for execution.

LETTER V.

Formidable Power of Mischief which this high Quality gives to bad Men—Care required to prevent its rendering good Men unconciliating and overbearing—Independence and over-ruling Manner in Cosultation—Lord Chatham—Decision of Character not incompatible with Sensibility and mild Manners—But probably the Majority of the most eminent Examples of it deficient in the kinder Affections—King of Prussia—Situations in which it may be an absolute Duty to act in Opposition to the Promotings of those Affections.

It were absurd to suppose that any human being can attain a state of mind capable of acting in all instances invariably with the full power of determination; but it is obvious that many have possessed a habitual and very commanding measure of it; and I think the preceding remarks have taken account of its chief characteristics and constituent principles. A number of additional observations remain.

The slightest view of human affairs shows what fatal and ample mischief may be caused by men of this character, when misled or wicked. You have but to recollect the conquerors, despots, bigots, unjust conspirators, and single villains of every class, who have blasted society by the relentless vigour which could act consistently and heroically wrong. Till therefore the virtue of mankind be greater, there is reason to be pleased that so few of them are endowed with extraordinary decision.

When this character is dignified by wisdom and principle, great care is yet required in the possessors of it to prevent it from becoming unamiable. As it involves much practical assertion of superiority over other human beings, the manner ought to be as mild and conciliating as possible; else pride will feel provoked, affection hurt, and weakness oppressed. But this manner is not the one which will be most natural to such a man; rather it will be that of sternness, reserve, and incompliance. He will have the appearance of keeping himself always at a distance from social equality; and his friends will feel as if their friendsihp were continually sliding into subserviency; while his intimate connexions will think he does not attach the due importance either to their opinions or to their regard. His manner, when they differ from him, or complain, will be in danger of giving the impression of careless inattention, and sometimes of disdain.

When he can accomplish a design in his own person alone, he may separate himself to the work with the cold self-inclosed individuality on which no one has any hold, which seems to recognize no kindred being in the world, which takes little account of good wishes and kind concern, any more than it cares for opposition; which seeks neither aid nor sympathy, and which seems to say, I do not want any of you, and I am glad that I do not; leave me alone to succeed or die. This has a very repellent effect on the friends who wished to feel themselves of some importance, in some way or other, to a person whom they are constrained to respect. When assistance is indispensable to his undertakings, his mode of signifying it will seem rather to command the co-operation, than to invite it.

In consultation, his manner will indicate that when he is equally with the rest in possession of the circumstances of the case, he does not at all expect to hear any opinions that shall correct his own; but is satisfied that either his present conception of the subject is the just one, or that his own mind must originate that which shall be so. This striking difference will be apparent between him and his associates, that *their* manner of receiving *his* opinions is that of agreement or dissent; *his* manner of receiving *theirs* is that of sanction or rejection. He has the tone of authoritatively deciding on what they say, but never of submitting to decision of what himself says. Their coincidence with his views does not give him a firmer assurance of his being right, nor their dissent any other impression than that of their incapacity to judge. If his feeling took the distinct form of a reflection, it would be, Mine is the business of comprehending and devising, and I am here to rule this company, and not to consult them; I want their docility and not their arguments; I am come, not to seek their co-operation in thinking, but to determine their concurrence in executing what is already thought for them. Of course, many suggestions and reasons which appear important to those from whom they come, will be disposed of by him with a transient attention, or a light facility, that will seem very disrespectful to persons who possibly hesitate to admit that he is a demi-god, and that they are but idiots. Lord Chatham, in going out of the House of Commons, just as one of the speakers against him concluded his speech by emphatically urging what he perhaps rightly thought the unanswerable question, '*Where* can we find means to support such a war?' turned round a moment, and gaily replied, 'Gentle Shepherd, tell me where.'

Even the assenting convictions, and practical compliances, yielded by degrees to this decisive man, may be somewhat undervalued; as they will appear to him no more than simply coming, and that perhaps very slowly, to a right apprehension; whereas himself understood and decided justly from the first, and has been right all this while.

He will be in danger of extending but little tolerance to the prejudices, hesitation, and timidity, of those with whom he has to act. He will say to himself, I wish there were any thing like manhood among the beings called men; and that they could have the sense and spirit not to let themselves be hampered by so many silly notions and childish fears. Why cannot they either determine with some promptitude, or let me, that can, do it for them? Am I to wait till debility become strong, and folly wise? If full scope be allowed to these tendencies, they will make even a man of eleva ed virtue a tyrant, who, in the consciousness of the right intention, and the assurance of the wise contrivance, of his designs, will hold himself justified in being regardless of every thing but the accomplishment of them.

He will forget all respect for the feelings and liberties of beings who are to be regarded as but a subordinate machinery, to be actuated, or to be thrown aside when not actuated, by the spring of his commanding spirit.

I have before asserted that this strong character may be exhibited with a mildenss of manner, and that, generally, it will thus best secure its efficacy. But this mildness must often be at the cost of great effort; and how much considerate policy or benevolent forbearance it will require, for a man to exert his utmost vigour in the very task, as it will appear to him at the time, of cramping that vigour! Lycurgus appears to have been a high example of mild patience in the firm prosecution of designs which were to be effected among a perverse multitude.

It is probable that the men most distinguished for decision, have not, in general, possessed a large share of tenderness; and it is easy to imagine that the laws of our nature will with great difficulty allow the combination of the refined sensibilities with a hardy, never-shrinking, never-yielding constancy. Is it not almost of the essence of this constancy to be free from even the *perception* of such impressions as cause a mind, weak through susceptibility, to relax or waver; just as the skin of the elephant, or the armour of the rhinoceros, would be but indistinctly sensible to the application of a force by which a small animal, with a skin of thin and delicate texture, would be pierced or lacerated to death? No doubt, this firmness consists partly in overcoming feelings, but it may consist partly too in not having them. To be tremblingly alive to gentle impressions, and yet to be able to preserve, when the prosecution of a design requires it, an immoveable heart, amidst the most imperious causes of subduing emotion, is perhaps not an impossible constitution of mind, but it must be the rarest endowment of humanity.

If you take a view of the first rank of decisive men, you will observe that their faculties have been too much bent to arduous effort, their souls have been kept in too military an attitude, they have been begirt with too much iron, for the melting movements of the heart. Their whole being appears too much arrogated and occupied by the spirit of severe design, compelling them to work systematically toward some defined end, to be sufficiently at ease for the indolent complacency, the soft lassitude, of gentle affections, which love to surrender themselves to the present felicities, forgetful of all 'enterprises of great pith and moment.' The man seems rigorously intent still on his own affairs, as he walks, or regales, or mingles with domestic society; and appears to despise all the feelings that will not take rank with the grave labours and decisions of intellect, or coalesce with the unremitting passion which is his spring of action: he values not feelings which he cannot employ either as weapons or as engines. He loves to be actuated by a passion so strong as to compel into exercise the utmost force of his being, and fix him in a tone, compared with which, the gentle affections, if he had felt them, would be accounted tameness, and their exciting causes, insipidity.

Yet we cannot willingly allow that tenderness is totally incompatible with the most impregnable inflexibility; nor can we help believing that such men as Timoleon, Alfred, and Gustavus Adolphus, must have been very fascinating domestic associates, whenever the urgency of their affairs would allow them to withdraw from the interests of statesmen and warriors, to indulge the affections of men: most fascinating, for, with a relative or friend who had any right perceptions, all the value of their stronger character would be recognized in the gentler one; the man whom nothing could subdue, would exalt the quality of the tenderness which softened him to recline.

But it were much easier to enumerate a long train of ancient and modern names of men, who have had the decision without the softness. Perhaps indeed they have yielded sometimes to some species of love, as a mode of amusing their passions for an interval, till greater engagements have summoned them into their proper element; when they have shown how little the sentiment ever belonged to the heart, by the ease with which they could relinquish the temporary favourite. In other cases, where there have not been the selfish inducements, which this passion supplies, to the exhibition of something like softness, and where they have been left to the pure sympathies of humanity alone, no rock on the face of the earth could be harder.

The celebrated King of Prussia occurs to me, as a capital instance of the decisive character; and there occurs to me, at the same time, one of the anecdotes of his life.* Intending to make, in the night, an important movement in his camp, which was in sight of the enemy, he gave orders that by eight o'clock all the lights in the camp should be put out, on pain of death. The moment that the time was past, he walked out himself to see whether all were dark. He found a light in the tent of a Captain Zietern, which he entered just as the officer was folding up a letter. Zietern knew him, and instantly fell on his knees to entreat his mercy. The king asked to whom he had been writing; he said it was a letter to his wife, which he had retained the candle these few minutes beyond the time in order to finish. The king coolly ordered him to rise, and write one line more, which he should dictate. This line was to inform his wife, without any explanation, that by such an hour the next day, he should be a dead man. The letter was then sealed, and despatched as it had been intended; and, the next day, the Captain was executed. I say nothing of the justice of the punishment itself; but this cool barbarity to the affection both of the officer and his wife, was enough to brand the character indelibly. It proved how little the decisive hero and pretended philosopher was susceptible of such an affection, or capable of sympathizing with its pains.

At the same time, it is proper to observe, that the case may easily occur, in which a man *must* be resolute to act in a manner which may make him appear to want the finer feelings. He must do what he knows will cause pain to persons who will feel it severely. He may be obliged to resist affectionate wishes, expostulations, entreaties, and tears. Take this same instance. If the wife of Zietern had come to supplicate for him, not only the remission of the punishment of death, but an exemption from any other severe punishment, which was perhaps justly due to the violation of such an order, on so important an occasion, it had then probably been the duty and the virtue of the commander to deny the most interesting suppliant, and to resist the most pathetic appeals which could have been made to his feelings.

LETTER VI.

Circumstances tending to consolidate this Character—Opposition—Desertion—Marius—Satin—Charles de Moor—Success has the same Tendency—Cæsar—Habit of Associating with Inferiors—Voluntary means of forming or confirming this Character—The Acquisition of perfect Knowledge in the Department in which we are to act—The Cultivation of a connected and Conclusive Manner of reasoning—The resolute commencement of Action in a Manner to commit ourselves irretrievably—Ledyard—The choice of a dignified Order of Concerns—The Approbation of Conscience—Yet melancholy to consider how many of the most distinguished Possessors of the Quality have been wicked.

VARIOUS assignable circumstances may contribute much to confirm the character in question. I shall just notice two or three.

* The authenticity of this anecdote, which I read in some trifling fugitive publication many years since, has been questioned.

And first *opposition*. The passions which inspirit men to resistance, and sustain them in it, such as anger, indignation, and resentment, are evidently far stronger than those which have reference to friendly objects; and if any of these strong passions are frequently excited by opposition, they infuse a certain quality into the general temperament of the mind which remains after the immediate excitement is past. They continually strengthen the principle of re-action; they put the mind in the habitual array of defence and self-assertion, and often give it the aspect and the posture of a gladiator, when there appears no confronting combatant. When these passions are felt by the man whom I describe, it is probable that each excitement is followed by a greater increase of this principle of re-action than in other men, because this result is so congenial with his naturally resolute disposition. Let him be opposed then, through the whole course of an extended design, or in the general tenour of his actions; and this constant opposition would render him the service of an ally by corroborating his inflexibility. An irresolute mind indeed might be quelled and subjugated by a formidable kind of opposition; but the strong wind which blows out a taper, augments a powerful fire, if there is fuel enough to an indefinite intensity.

I believe you will find in fact that many of the individuals most eminently decisive in conduct, have made their way through opposition and contest; in which they have acquired both a prompt acuteness of faculty, and an inflexibility of temper, which even strong minds could never have attained in the tame security of facile, friendly coincidence. Very often, however, it is granted the firmness matured by such discipline is accompanied, in a man of virtue, with a Catonic severity, and in a mere man of the world, with an unhumanized, repulsive hardness.

Desertion is another cause which may conduce to consolidate this character. A kind, mutually reclining dependence, is certainly the happiest state of human beings; but this necessarily prevents the development of some great individual powers which would be forced into action by a state of desertion. I lately happened to notice, with some surprise, an ivy, which being prevented from attaching itself to the rock beyond a certain point, had shot off into a bold, elastic stem, with an air of as much independence as any branch of oak in the vicinity. So a human being, thrown, whether by cruelty, justice, or accident, from all social support and kindness, if he has any vigour of spirit, and is not in the bodily debility of either childhood or age, will instantly begin to act for himself with a resolution which will appear like a new faculty. And the most absolute inflexibility is likely to characterize the resolution of an individual who is obliged to deliberate without consultation, and execute without assistance. He will disdain to concede to beings that have rejected him, or to forego a single particle of his designs or advantages, for the sake of the opinions or the will of all the world. Himself, his pursuits, and his interests, are emphatically his own. 'The world is not his friend, nor the world's law,' and therefore he becomes regardless of every thing but its power, of which his policy carefully takes the measure, in order to ascertain his own means of action and impunity, as set against the world's means of annoyance, prevention, and retaliation.

If this person has but little humanity or principle, he will become a misanthrope, or perhaps a villain, that will resemble a solitary wild beast of the night, which makes prey of every thing it can overpower, and cares for nothing but fire. If he is capable of grand conception and enterprise, he may, like Spartacus, make a daring attempt against the whole social order of the state where he has been oppressed. If he has great humanity and principle, he may become one of the noblest of mankind, and display a generous virtue to which society had no claim, and which it is not worthy to reward, if it should at last become inclined. No, he will say, give your rewards to another; as it has been no part of my object to gain them, they are not necessary to my satisfaction. I have done good, without expecting your gratitude, and without caring for your approbation. If conscience and my Creator had not been more auspicious than you, none of these virtues would ever have opened to the day. When I ought to have been an object of your compassion, I might have perished; now, when you find I can serve your interests, you will affect to acknowledge me and reward me; I will not accept your rewards.—In either case, virtuous or wicked, the man who has been compelled to do without assistance, will spurn interference.

Common life would supply illustrations of the effect of desertion. Some of the most resolute men have become such, partly from being left friendless in early life. The case has also sometimes happened, that a wife and mother, remarkable perhaps for gentleness and acquiescence before, has been compelled, after the death of her husband on whom she depended, and when she has met with nothing but neglect or unkindness from relatives and those who had been deemed friends, to adopt a plan of her own, and has executed it with a resolution which has astonished even herself.

One regrets that the signal examples, real or fictitious, that most readily present themselves, are still of the depraved order. I fancy myself to see Marius sitting on the ruins of Carthage, where no arch or column that remained unshaken amidst the desolation, could present a stronger image of a firmness beyond the power of calamitous events to subdue. The rigid constancy which had before distinguished his character, would be aggravated by his finding himself thus an outcast from all human society; and he would proudly shake off every sentiment that had ever for an instant checked his designs by reminding him of social obligations. The lonely individual was placed in the alternative of becoming the victim or the antagonist of the power of the empire. While, with a spirit capable of confronting that power, he resolved, amidst those ruins, on a great experiment, he would enjoy a kind of sullen luxury in surveying the dreary situation, and recollecting the circumstances of his expulsion; since they would seem to him to sanction an unlimited vengeance; to present what had been his country as the pure legitimate prize for desperate achievement; and to give him a proud consequence in being reduced to maintain singly a quarrel against the bulk of mankind. He would exult that his desolate condition gave him a proof of his possessing a mind which no misfortunes could repress or intimidate, and that it kindled an animosity intense enough to force that mind from firm endurance into impetuous action. He would feel as if he became stronger for enterprise, in proportion as he became more inexorable; and the sentiment with which he quitted his solitude would be, Rome expelled her patriot, let her receive her evil genius.

The decision of Satan, in Paradise Lost, is represented as consolidated by his reflections on his hopeless banishment from heaven, which oppress him with sadness for a moment, but he soon resumes his invincible spirit, and utters the impious but subl me sentiment,

> 'What matter where, if I be still the same.'

You remember how this effect of desertion is represented in Charles de Moor. His father's supposed cruel rejection consigned him irretrievably to the career of atrocious enterprise, in which, notwithstanding the most

Possibly enough it might be one of the many but half true stories which could not fail to go abroad concerning a man who made, in his day, so great a figure. But as it does not at all misrepresent the general character of his mind, since there are many incontrovertible facts proving against him as a great degree of deliberate cruelty as this anecdote would charge on him, the want of means to prove this one fact does not seem to impose any necessity for omitting the illustration.

interesting emotions of humanity and tenderness, he persisted with heroic determination till he considered his destiny as accomplished.

Success tends considerably to reinforce this character. It is true that a man possessing it in a high degree will not lose it by occasional failure; for if the failure was caused by something entirely beyond the reach of all human knowledge and ability, he will remember that fortitude is the virtue required in meeting unfavourable events which in no sense depended on him; if by something which *might* have been known and prevented, he will feel that even the experience of failure completes his competence, by admonishing his prudence, and enlarging his understanding. But as all schemes and measures of action have reference to some end, and if wise, are correctly adapted to attain that end, continual failure would show something essentially wrong in a man's system, and either destroy his confidence, or prove it to be mere absurdity or obstinacy. On the contrary, when a man has ascertained by experiment the justness of his calculations and the extent of his powers, when he has measured his force with various persons, when he has braved and conquered difficulty, and partly seized the prize, he will advance with increasing assurance to the trials which still await him.

In some men whose lives have been spent in constant perils, continued success has produced a confidence beyond its rational effect, by inspiring a persuasion that the common laws of human affairs were, in their case, superseded by the decrees of a peculiar destiny, securing them from almost the possibility of disaster; and this superstitious feeling, though it has displaced the unconquerable resolution from its rational basis, has yet often produced the most wonderful effects. This persuasion dictated Cæsar's expression to the mariner who was terrified at the storm and billows, 'What art thou afraid of? Thy vessel carries Cæsar.' This idea had some influence among the intrepid men in the time of the English Commonwealth.

The wilfulness of an obstinate person is sometimes fortified by some single instance of remarkable success in his undertakings, which is promptly recalled in every case where his decisions are questioned or opposed, as a proof that he must in this instance too be right; especially if that one success happened contrary to your predictions.

I shall only add, and without illustration, that the habit of associating with *inferiors*, among whom a man can always, and therefore does always, take the lead, is very conducive to a subordinate kind of decision of character. You may see this exemplified any day in an ignorant country 'squire among his vassals; especially if he wears the superadded majesty of Justice of the Peace.

In viewing the characters and actions of the men who have possessed the supreme degree of the quality which I have attempted to describe, one cannot but wish it were possible to know how much of this astonishing superiority was created by the circumstances in which they were placed; but it seems inevitable to believe that there was some vast difference from ordinary men in the very structure of the mind. In observing lately a man who appeared too vacant almost to think of a purpose, too indifferent to resolve upon it, and too sluggish to execute it if he had resolved, I was distinctly struck with the idea of the difference between him and Marius, of whom I happened to have been thinking; and I felt it utterly beyond my power to believe that any circumstances on earth, though ever so perfectly combined and adapted, would have produced in this man, if placed under their fullest influence from his childhood, any resemblance (beyond perhaps a diminutive kind of revenge and cruelty) of the formidable Roman.

It is needless to discuss whether a person who is practically evinced, at the age of maturity, to want the stamina of this character, can, by any process, acquire it. Indeed such a person cannot have sufficient force of *will* to make the complete experiment. If there is the unconquerable *will* that would persist to seize all possible means, and apply them in order to attain such an end, it would prove the existence already of a high degree of the character sought; and if there is not this *will*, how then is the supposed attainment possible?

Yet though it is improbable that a very irresolute man can ever become a habitually decisive one, it should be observed, that since there are many *degrees* of determined character, and since the essential principles of it, partially existing in those degrees, cannot be supposed subject to an absolute and ultimate limitation, like the dimension of the bodily stature, it might be possible to apply a discipline which should advance a man from the first degree to the second, and from that to the third, and how much farther—it will be well worth his trying, after he shall have made this first progress. I have but a very imperfect conception of the discipline; but will suggest a hint or two.

And in the first place, the indispensable necessity of a clear and comprehensive knowledge of the concerns before us, seems too obvious for remark; and yet no man has been sufficiently sensible of it, till he has been placed in circumstances which forced him to act before he had time, or after he had made ineffectual efforts, to obtain the needful information. The pain of having brought things to an unfortunate issue, is hardly greater than that of proceeding in the conscious ignorance which continually threatens such an issue. While thus proceeding without plan or guide, because he positively cannot be permitted to remain in inaction, a man looks round for information as eagerly as a benighted wanderer would for the light of a human dwelling. He perhaps labours to recal what he thinks he once heard or read in relation to a similar situation, without dreaming at the time he heard or read it, that such instruction could ever be of importance to him; and is distressed to find that he cannot accurately recollect it. He would give a considerable sum, if some particular book could be brought to him at the instant; or a certain document which he believes to be in existence; or the detail of a process, the terms of a prescription, or the model of an implement. He thinks how many people know, without its being of any present use to them, exactly what could be of such important service to him, if he could know it. In some cases, a line, a sentence, a monosyllable of affirming or denying, or a momentary sight of an object, would be inexpressibly valuable and welcome. And he resolves that if he can once happily escape from the present difficulty, he will apply himself day and night to obtain knowledge, rather than be so involved and harassed again. It might even be of service to have been occasionally forced to act under the disadvantage of conscious ignorance, if the affair was not very important, nor the consequence very injurious, as an effectual lesson on the necessity of knowledge in order to decision either of plan or execution. It is indeed an extreme case that will compel a considerate man to act without knowledge; yet he may often be necessitated to proceed to action, when he is sensible his information does not extend to the whole of the concern in which he is going to commit himself. And in this case, he will feel no little uneasiness, while transacting that part of it in which his knowledge is competent, when he looks forward to the point where that knowledge terminates; unless he is conscious of a very prompt faculty of catching information at the moment that he wants it for use; as Indians set out on a long journey with but a small stock of provision because they are certain that their bows or guns will procure it by the way. It is one of the nicest points of wisdom to decide how much less than complete knowledge in any question of practical interest, will warrant a man to venture on an undertaking, in the presumption that the deficiency will be supplied in time to prevent either perplexity or disaster.

A thousand familiar instances show the effect of perfect knowledge on determination. An artizan may be said to be decisive as to the mode of working a piece of iron or wood, because he is certain of the proper process and the effect. A man perfectly acquainted with the intricate paths of a district, takes the right one without a moment's hesitation; while a stranger who has only some very vague information, is lost in perplexity. It is easy to imagine what a number of circumstances may occur in the course of a life or even of a year, in which a man cannot thus readily determine, and thus, confidently proceed, without an extent and an exactness of knowledge which few persons have application enough to acquire.

In connexion with the necessity of knowledge, I would suggest the importance of cultivating, with the utmost industry, a conclusive manner of reasoning. In the first place, let the general course of thinking *be* reasoning; for it should be remembered that this name does not belong to a series of thoughts and fancies which follow one another without deduction or dependence, and which can therefore no more bring a subject to a proper issue, than a number of separate links will answer the mechanical purpose of a chain. The conclusion which terminates such a series, does not deserve the name of *result*, since it has little more than a casual connexion with what went before; the conclusion might as well have taken place in an earlier point of the train, or have been deferred till that train had been extended much farther. Instead of having been busily employed in this kind of thinking, for perhaps many hours, a man might as well have been sleeping all the time; since the single thought which is now to determine his conduct, might have happened to be the first thought that occurred to him on awaking. It only *happens* to occur to him now; it does not follow from what he has been thinking all these hours; at least he cannot prove that some other thought might not just as properly have come in its place, at the end of this long series. It is easy to see how feeble that determination is likely to be, which is formed on so narrow a ground as the last accidental idea that comes into the mind, or on so loose a ground as this crude uncombined assemblage of ideas. Indeed it is difficult to form a determination at all on such slight ground. A man delays, and waits for some more satisfactory thought to occur to him; and perhaps he has not waited long, before an idea arises in his mind of a quite contrary tendency to the last. As this additional idea is not, more than that which preceded it, the result of any process of reasoning, nor brings with it any arguments, it is likely to give place soon to another, and still another; and they are all in succession of equal authority, that is, of none. If at last an idea occurs to him which seems of considerable authority, he may here make a stand, and adopt his resolution, with firmness, as he thinks, and commence the execution. But still, as he cannot *verify* the authority of the principle which has determined him, his resolution is likely to prove treacherous and evanescent in any serious trial. A principle so little defended and established by sound reasoning, is not terra firma for a man to trust himself upon: it is only as a slight incrustation on a yielding element; it is like the sand on the surface of the lake Serbonis, which broke away under the unfortunate army which had begun to advance on it, mistaking it for solid ground.—These remarks may seem to refer only to a *single instance* of deliberation; but they are equally applicable to all the deliberations and undertakings of a man's life; the same closely connected manner of thinking, which is so necessary to give firmness of determination and of conduct in a particular instance, will, if habitual, greatly contribute to form a decisive character.

Not only should thinking be thus reduced by a rigid discipline, to a train, in which all the parts at once depend upon and support one another, but also this train should be followed on to a full conclusion. It should be held as an absolute law, that the question must be disposed of before it is let alone. The mind may carry on this accurate process to some length, and then stop through indolence, or divert through levity; but it can never possess that rational confidence in its opinions which is requisite to the character in question, till it is conscious of acquiring them from trains of reasoning which are followed on to their result. The habit of thinking thus completely is indispensable to the character in general; and in any particular instance, it is found that short pieces of trains of reasoning, though correct as far as they go, are inadequate to qualify a man for the immediate concern. They are besides of little value for the assistance of future thinking; because from being left thus incomplete, they are but slightly retained by the mind, and soon sink away; in the same manner as walls left unfinished speedily moulder.

After these remarks, I should take occasion to observe, that a vigorous exercise of thought may sometimes for a while seem to increase the difficulty of decision, by discovering a great number of unthought-of reasons for a measure and against it, so that even a discriminating mind may, during a short space, find itself in the state of the magnetic needle under the equator. But no case in the world can really have this perfect equality of opposite reasons; nor will it long appear to have it, in the estimate of a clear and strongly exerted intellect, which after some time will ascertain, though the difference is small, which side of the question has twenty, and which has but nineteen.

Another thing that would powerfully assist toward complete decision, both in the particular instance, and in the general spirit of the character, is for a man to place himself in a situation like that in which Cæsar placed his soldiers, when he burnt the ships which brought them to land. If his judgment is *really* decided, let him commit himself irretrievably by doing something which shall compel him to do more, which shall necessitate him to do all. If a man resolves as a general intention to be a philanthropist, I would say to him, Form some actual plan of philanthropy, and begin the execution of it to-morrow, (perhaps I should say *to-day*,) so explicitly, that you cannot relinquish it without becoming despicable even in your own estimation. If a man would be a hero, let him, if it is possible to find a good cause in arms, go instantly to the camp. If a man would be a traveller through distant countries, let him actually prepare to set off. Let him not still dwell, in imagination, on mountains, rivers, and temples; but give directions about his remittances, his clothes, or the carriage, or the vessel, in which he is to go. Ledyard surprised the official person who asked him how soon he could be ready to set off for the interior of Africa, by replying promptly and firmly, 'To-morrow.'

Again, it is highly conducive to a manly firmness, that the interests in which it is exerted, should be of a dignified order, so as to give the passions an ample scope, and a noble object. The degradation that should devote these passions to mean and trivial pursuits, would, in general, I should think, likewise debilitate their energy, and therefore preclude strength of character.

And finally, if I would repeat that one should think a man's own conscientious approbation of his conduct must be of vast importance to his decision in the outset, and his persevering constancy, I must at the same time acknowledge that it is astonishing to observe how many of the eminent examples have been very wicked men. These must certainly be deemed also examples of the original want, or the depravation, or the destruction, of the moral sense.

I am sorry, and I attribute it to defect of memory, that a greater proportion of the illustrations introduced in this essay, are not as conspicuous for goodness as for power. It is melancholy to contemplate beings, whom our imagination represents as capable, (when they possessed great external means in addition to the force of their minds,) of the grandest utility, capable of vindicating each good cause which has languished in a world adverse to all goodness, and capable of intimidating the collective vices of a nation or an age—becoming themselves the very centres and volcanoes of those vices; and it is melancholy to follow them in serious thought, from this region, of which not all the powers and difficulties and inhabitants together, could have subdued their adamantine resolution, to the Supreme Tribunal where that resolution must tremble and melt away.

ESSAY III.

ON THE APPLICATION OF THE EPITHET ROMANTIC.

LETTER I.

Great convenience of having a number of Words that will answer the Purposes of Ridicule or Reprobation without having any precise Meaning—Puritan—Methodist—Jacobin—The word Romantic of the greatest Service to Persons, who, wanting to show their Scorn, have not wherewithal in the way of Sense or Wit—Whenever this Epithet is applied, let the exact meaning be demanded—Does it attribute, to what it is applied to, the kind of Absurdity prevalent in the works called Romances?—That absurdity was from the predominance, in various Modes, of Imagination over Judgment—Mental Character of the early Romance Writers—Opposite Character of Cervantes—Delightful, delusive, and mischievous Operation of a predominant Imagination—Yet desirable, for several Reasons, that the Imagination should have this Ascendancy in early Life.

MY DEAR FRIEND,

A thoughtful judge of sentiments, books, and men, will often find reason to regret that the language of censure is so easy and so undefined. It costs no labour, and needs no intellect, to pronounce the words, foolish, stupid, dull, odious, absurd, ridiculous. The weakest or most uncultivated mind may therefore gratify its vanity, laziness, and malice, all at once, by a prompt application of vague, condemnatory words, where a wise and liberal man would not feel himself warranted to pronounce without the most deliberate consideration, and where such consideration might perhaps terminate in applause. Thus the most excellent performances, whether in the department of thinking, or of action, might be consigned to contempt, if there were no better judges, on the authority of those who could not even understand them. A man who wishes some decency and sense to prevail in the circulation of opinions, will do well, when he hears these decisions of ignorant arrogance, to call for a precise explication of the manner in which the terms apply to the subject.

There is a competent number of words for this use of cheap censure; but though a man deems himself to be giving no mean proof of sagacity in this confident readiness to condemn, even with this impotence of language, he may however, have a certain consciousness that there is, in some other minds, a keen dexterity which would find expressions to bite harder than the words, dull, stupid, and ridiculous, which he is repeating many times to compensate for the incapacity of hitting off the right thing at once. These vague epithets describe nothing, discriminate nothing; they express no species, are as applicable to ten thousand things as to this one, and he has before employed them on a numberless diversity of subjects. But he can perceive that censure or contempt has the smartest effect, when its expressions have an appropriate peculiarity, which adapts them more precisely to the present subject than to another; and he is therefore not quite satisfied with the expressions which say 'about it and about it,' but do not say the thing itself; which rather show his mischievous will than prove his mischievous power. He wants words and phrases which would make the edge of his clumsy meaning fall just where it ought. Yes, he wants words; for his meaning is sharp, he knows, if only the words would come.

Discriminative censure must be conveyed, either in a sentence which expresses some marked and acute turn of thought, instead of simply applying an epithet, or in an epithet so specifically appropriate, that the single word is sufficient to fix the condemnation by the mere precision with which it describes. But as the censurer perhaps cannot succeed in either of these ways, he is willing to seek some other resource. And he may often find it in cant terms, which have a more spiteful force, and seem to have more particularity of meaning, than plain, common words, without needing any shrewdness for their application. Each of these is supposed to denominate some one class or character of scorned or reprobated things, but leaves it so imperfectly defined, that dull malice may venture to assign to the class any thing which it would desire to throw under the odium of the denomination. Such words serve for a mode of collective execution, somewhat like the vessels which, in a season of outrage in a neighbouring country, received a promiscuous crowd of reputed criminals, of unexamined and dubious similarity, and were then sunk in the flood. You cannot wonder that such compendious words of decision, which can give quick vent to crude impatient censure, emit plenty of antipathy in a few syllables, and save the condemner the difficulty of telling exactly what he wants to mean, should have had an extensive circulation.

Puritan was, doubtless, welcomed as a term most luckily invented or recalled when it began to be applied in contempt to a class of men, of whom the world was not worthy. Its peculiarity gave it almost such an advantage as that of a proper name among the lumber of common words by which they were described and reviled; while yet it meant any thing, every thing, which the vain world disliked in the devout and conscientious character. To the more sluggish it saved, and to the more loquacious it relieved, the labour of endlessly repeating, 'demure rogues,' 'sanctimonious pretenders,' 'formal hypocrites.'

This term has long since lost its point, and is almost forgotten; but some word of a similar cast was indispensably necessary to the vulgar of both kinds. The vain and malignant spirit which had descried the elevated piety of the Puritans, sought about (as Milton describes the wicked one in Paradise) for some convenient form in which it might again come forth to hiss at zealous Christianity; and in another lucky moment fell on the term *Methodist.* If there is no *sense* in the word, as now applied, there seems however to be a great deal of aptitude and execution. It has the advantage of being comprehensive as a general denomination, and yet opprobrious as a special badge, for every thing that ignorance and folly may mistake for fanaticism, or that malice may wilfully assign to it. Whenever a grave formalist feels it his duty to sneer at those operations of religion on the passions, which he never felt, he has only to call them *methodistical;* and notwithstanding that the word is both so trite and so vague, he feels as if he had uttered a good pungent thing. There is satiric smartness in the word, though there be none in the man. In default of keen faculty in the mind, it is delightful thus to find something that will do as well, ready bottled up in odd terms. It is not less convenient to a profligate, or a coxcomb, whose propriety of character is to be supported by laughing indiscriminately at religion in every form; the one, to evince that his courage is not sapped by conscience, the other, to make the best advantage of his instinct of catching at impiety as a substitute for sense. The word *Methodism* so readily sets aside all religion as superstitious folly, that they pronounce it with an air as if no more needed to be said. Such terms have a pleasant facility of throwing away the matter in question to scorn, without any trouble of making a definite, intelligible charge of extravagance or delusion, and attempting to prove it.

In politics, *Jacobinism* has, of late years, been the brand by which all sentiments alluding to the principles of liberty, in a way that could be taken to censure the measures of the ascendant party in the State, have been consigned to execration. What a quantity of noisy zeal would have been quashed in dead silence, if it had been possible to enforce the substitution of statements and definitions for this unmeaning, vulgar, but most efficacious term of reproach. What a number of persons have vented the superabundance of their loyalty, or their rancour, by means of this and two or three similar words, who, if by some sudden lapse of memory they had lost these two or three words, and a few names of persons, would have looked round with an idiotic vacancy, totally at a loss what was the *subject* of their anger or their approbation. One may here catch a glimpse of the policy of men of a superior class, in employing these terms as much as the vulgar, in order to keep them in active currency. If a rude populace, whose understandings they despise, and do not wish to improve, could not be excited and kept up to loyal animosity, but by means of a clear comprehension of what they were to oppose, and why, a political party would have but feeble hold on popular zeal, and might vociferate, and intrigue, and fret itself to nothing. But if a single word can be made the symbol of all that is absurd and execrable, so that the very sound of it shall irritate the passions of this ignorant and scorned multitude, as dogs have been taught to bark at the name of a neighbouring tyrant, it is a commodious thing for managing these passions to serve the interests of those who despise, while they flatter, their duped auxiliaries. The popular passions are the imps and demons of the political conjurer, and he can raise them, as other conjurers affect to do theirs, by terms of gibberish.

The epithet *romantic* has obviously no similarity to these words in its coinage, but it is considerably like them in the mode and effect of its application. For having partly quitted the rank of plain epithets, it has become a convenient exploding word, of more special, deriding significance than the other words of its order, such as wild, extravagant, visionary. It is a standard expression of contemptuous despatch, which you have often heard pronounced with a very self-complacent air, that said, 'How much wiser I am than some people,' by the indolent and animate on what they deemed impracticable, by the apes of prudence on what they accounted foolishly adventurous, and by the slaves of custom on what startled them as singular. The class of absurdities which it denominates, is left so undefined, that all the views and sentiments which a narrow, cold mind could not like or understand in an ample and fervid one, might be referred hither; and yet the word *seems* to discriminate their character so conclusively as to put them out of argument. With this cast of significance, and vacancy of sense, it is allowed to depreciate without being accountable; it has the license of a parrot, to call names without being taxed with insolence. And when any sentiments are decisively stigmatized with this denomination, it would require considerable courage to rescue and defend them; since the imputation which the epithet fixes on them will pass upon the advocate; and he may expect to be himself enrolled among the heroes of whom Don Quixotte is the time immemorial commander-in-chief. At least he may be assigned to that class which occupies a dubious frontier space between the rational and the insane.

If, however, the suggestions and sketches which I had endeavoured to exhibit as interesting and practicable, were attempted to be turned into vanity and 'thin air' by the enunciation of this epithet, I would say, Pray now what do you mean by *romantic?* Have you, as you pronounce it, any precise conception in your mind, which you can give in some other words, and then distinctly fix the charge? Or is this a word, which, because it is often used in some such way as you now use it, may be left to tell its own meaning better than the speaker knows how to explain it? Or perhaps you mean, that the ideas which I am expressing associate in your mind with the fantastic images of Romance; and that you cannot help thinking of enchanted castles, encounters with giants, solemn exorcisms, fortunate surprises, knights and wizards, dragons and griffins. You cannot exactly distinguish what the absurdity in my notion *is*, but you fancy what it is *like*. You therefore condemn it, not by giving a definition, but by applying an epithet which assigns it to a class of things already condemned; for evidently the epithet should signify a resemblance to what we have condemned in the works of romance. Well then, take advantage of this resemblance, to bring your censure into a discriminative form. Explain with precision the chief points in which the absurdity of the works of romance has consisted, and then show how the same distinctions characterize my notions or schemes. I will then renounce at once all my visionary follies, and be henceforward at least a very sober, if I cannot be a very rational man.

The great, general characteristic of those works has been the ascendancy of imagination over judgment. And the description is correct as applied to the books, even supposing the makers of them to have been ever so well endowed with intellect. If they choose. for their amusement, to lay a sound judgment a while to rest, to stimulate their imagination to the wildest extravagances, and to write them as they went on, the book might be nearly the same thing as if produced by a mind in which sound judgment had no place; it would display imagination *actually* ascendant by the writer's voluntary indulgence, though, not *necessarily* so by the constitution of his mind. It was a different case, if a writer kept his judgment active, amidst these extravagances, for the very purpose of managing and directing them to some particular end, of satire or sober truth. But, however, the romances of the ages of chivalry and the preceding times, were composed under neither of these intellectual conditions. They were not the productions either of men who, possessing a strong judgment, chose formally to forego its exercise, in order to riot a while in scenes of extravagant fancy, only keeping that judgment so far awake as to retain a continual consciousness in what degree they *were* extravagant; or of men designing to give effect to truth or malice under the disguise of a fantastic exhibition. It is evident that the authors were under the real and permanent ascendancy of imagination; and though they must have perceived that the operations of this faculty went to an excess in some of its wildest flights, yet it might reach a very great degree of extravagance without their being conscious of any excess at all. They could drive on their career through monstrous absurdities of description and narration, without being sensible of inconsistency and improbability, and with an air as if they really reckoned on being believed. And the general state of intellect of the age in which they lived seems to have been well fitted to allow them the utmost license. This irrationality of the romancers, and the age, provoked the powerful mind of Cervantes to expose it, by means of a parallel and still more extravagant representation of the prevalence of imagination over reason, drawn in a ludicrous form, by which he rendered the folly palpable even to the sense of that age. From that time the delirium abated; the works which inspirited its ravings having been blown away almost beyond the reach of bibliomaniac curiosity; and the fabrication of such is become a lost branch of manufacture.

Yet romance was in some form to be retained, as indispensable to the craving of the human mind for something more vivid, more elated, and more wonderful, than the plain realities of life; as a kind of mental balloon, for mounting into the air from the ground of ordinary experience. To afford this extrarational kind of luxury, it was requisite the fictions should still partake, in a *limited degree*, of the quality of the earlier romance. The writers were not to be the *dupes* of wild fancy; they were not to feign marvels in such a manner as if they knew no better; they were not wholly to lose sight of the actual system of things, but to keep within *some* measures of relation and proportion to it; and yet they were required to disregard the strict laws of verisimilitude in shaping their inventions, and to extend them with an indulgence and daring of fancy very considerably beyond the bounds of probability. Without this, their fictions would have lost what was regarded as the essential quality of romance.

If, therefore, the epithet Romantic, as now employed for description and censure of character, sentiments, and schemes, is to be understood as expressive of the quality which is characteristic of that class of fictions, it imputes, in substance, a great, excess of imagination in proportion to judgment; and it imputes, in particulars, such errors as naturally result from that excess.—It may be worth while to look for some of the practical exemplifications of this unfortunate disproportion between the two faculties.

It should first be noted, that a defective judgment is, not necessarily accompanied by a romantic disposition, since the imagination may be as inert as the judgment is weak: and this double and equal deficiency produces mere dulness. But it is obvious that a weak judgment may be accompanied with a great force of that faculty which can so powerfully assert itself even in childhood, in dreams, and in the state of insanity.

Again, there may be an intellect not *positively* feeble (supposing it estimated separately from the other power) yet practically reduced to debility by a disproportionate imagination, which continually invades its sphere, and takes every thing out of its hands. And then the case is made worse by the unfortunate circumstance, that the exercise of the faculty which should be repressed, is incomparably more easy and delightful, than of that which should be promoted. Indeed the term *exercise* is hardly applicable to the activity of a faculty which can be active without effort, which is so far from needing to be stimulated to its works of magic, that it often scorns the most serious injunctions to forbear. It is not exercise, but indulgence; and even minds possessing much of the power of understanding, may be disposed to undergo but little of the labour of it, when amidst the ease of the deepest indolence they can revel in the activity of a more animating employment. Imagination may be indulged till it usurp an entire ascendency over the mind, and then every subject presented to that mind will excite imagination, instead of understanding, to work; imagination will throw its colours where the intellectual faculty ought to draw its lines; imagination will accumulate metaphors where reason ought to deduce arguments; images will take the place of thoughts, and scenes of disquisitions. The whole mind may become at length something like a hemisphere of cloud-scenery, filled with an ever-moving train of changing, melting forms, of every colour, mingled with rainbows, meteors, and an occasional gleam of pure sun-light, all vanishing away, the mental, like this natural imagery, when its hour is up, without leaving any thing behind but the wish to recover the vision. And yet, the while, this series of visions may be mistaken for operations of thought, and each cloudy image be admitted in the place of a proposition or a reason; or it may even be mistaken for something sublimer than thinking. The influence of this habit of dwelling on the beautiful, fallacious forms of imagination, will accompany the mind into the most serious speculations, or rather musings, on the real world, and what is to be done in it, and expected; as the image, which the eye acquires from looking at any dazzling object, still appears before it wherever it turns. The vulgar materials that constitute the actual economy of the world, will rise up to its sight in fictitious forms, which it cannot disenchant into plain reality, nor will even suspect to be deceptive. It cannot go about with sober, rational inspection, and ascertain the nature and value of all things around it. Indeed such a mind is not disposed to examine, with any careful minuteness, the real condition of things. It is content with ignorance, because environed with something more delicious than such knowledge, in the Paradise which imagination creates. In that Paradise it walks delighted, till some imperious circumstance of real life call it thence, and gladly escapes thither again when the avocation is past. There, every thing is beautiful and noble as could be desired to form the residence of an angel. If a tenth part of the felicities that have been enjoyed, the great actions that have been performed, the beneficent institutions that have been established, and the beautiful objects that have been seen in that happy region, could have been imported into this terrestrial place—what a delightful thing, my dear friend, it would have been to awake each morning to see such a world once more.

It is not strange that a faculty, of which the exercise is so easy and bewitching, and the scope infinite, should obtain a predominance over judgment, especially in young persons, and in those who have been brought up, like Rasselas and his companions, in a state of seclusion from the sight and experience of the world. Indeed a considerable vigour of imagination, though it be at the expense of a frequent predominance over juvenile understanding, seems even necessary, in early life, to cause a generous expansion of the passions by giving the most lively aspect to the objects which must attract them, in order to draw forth the activity of our being. It may also contribute to prepare the mind for the exercise of that faith which converses with things unseen, but converses with them through the medium of those ideal forms in which imagination presents them, and in which only a strong imagination can present them impressively.* And I should deem it the indication of a character not destined to excel in the liberal, the energetic, or the devout qualities, if I observed in the youthful age a close confinement of thought to bare truth and minute accuracy, with an entire aversion to the splendours, amplifications, and excursions of fancy. This opinion is warranted by instances of persons so distinguished in youth, who have become subsequently very sensible indeed, but dry, cold, precise, devoted to detail, and incapable of being carried away one moment by any inspiration of the beautiful or the sublime. They seem to have only the bare intellectual stamina of the human mind, without the addition of what is to give it life and sentiment. They give one an impression similar to that made by the leafless trees which you remember our observing in winter, admirable for the distinct exhibition of their branches and minute ramifications so clearly defined on the sky, but destitute of all the green, soft luxury of foliage which is requisite to make a perfect tree. And even the affections existing in such minds seem to have a bleak abode, somewhat like those bare, deserted nests which you have often seen in such trees.

If, indeed, the signs of this exclusive understanding indicated also such an extraordinary vigour of the faculty, as to promise a very great mathematician or metaphysician, one would perhaps be content to forego some of the properties which form a complete mind, for the sake of this pre-eminence of one of its endowments; even though the person were to be so defective in sentiment and fancy, that, as the story goes of an eminent mathematician, he could read through a most animated and splendid epic poem, and on being asked what he thought of it, gravely reply, 'What does it prove?' But the want of imagination is never an evidence, and perhaps but rarely a concomitant, of superior understanding.

Imagination may be allowed the ascendency in early youth; the case should be reversed in mature life; and if it is not, a man may consider his mind either as not the most happily constructed, or as unwisely disciplined. The latter indeed is probably true in every such instance.

LETTER II.

One of the Modes of this ascendancy justly called Romantic is, the unfounded Persuasion of something peculiar and extraordinary in a Person's Destiny—This vain Expectation may be relative to great Talent and Achievement, or to great Felicity—Things ardently anticipated which not only cannot be attained but would be unadapted to the Nature and Condition of Man if they could—A Person that hoped to out-do rather than imitate Gregory Lopez, the Hermit—Absurd Expectations of Parents—Utopian Anticipations of Philosophers—Practical Absurdity of the Age of Chivalry—The extravagant and Exclusive Passion for what is Grand.

THE ascendancy of imagination operates in various modes; I will endeavour to distinguish those which may justly be called romantic.

The extravagance of imagination in romance has very much consisted in the display of a destiny and course of life totally unlike the common condition of mankind. And you may have observed in living individuals, that one of the effects sometimes produced by the predominance of this faculty is, a persuasion in a person's own mind that he is born to some peculiar and extraordinary destiny, while yet there are no extraordinary indications in the person or his circumstances. There was something rational in the early pre-sentiment which some distinguished men have entertained of their future career. When a celebrated general of the present times exclaimed, after performing the common military exercise in a company of juvenile volunteers, 'I shall be a commander-in-chief,'* a sagacious observer of the signs of talents yet but partially developed, might have thought it indeed a rather sanguine, but probably not a quite absurd, anticipation. An elder and intelligent associate of Milton's youth might without much difficulty have believed himself listening to an oracle, when so powerful a genius avowed to him, that he regarded himself as destined to produce a work which should distinguish the nation and the age. The opening of uncommon faculties may be sometimes attended with these anticipations, and may be allowed to express them, perhaps, even, as a stimulus, encouraged to indulge them. But in most instances these magnificent presumptions form, in the observer's eye, a ludicrous contrast with the situation and powers of the person that entertains them. And, in the event, how few such anticipations have proved themselves to have been the genuine promptings of an extraordinary mind.

The visionary presumption of a peculiar destiny is entertained in more forms than that which implies a confidence of possessing uncommon talent. It is often the flattering self-assurance simply of a life of singular felicity. The captive of fancy fondly imagines his prospect of life as a delicious vale, from each side of which every stream of pleasure is to flow down to his feet; and while it cannot but be seen that innumerable evils do harass other human beings, some mighty spell is to protect him against them all. He takes no deliberate account of what is inevitable in the lot of humanity, of the sober probabilities of his own situation, or of those principles in the constitution of his mind which are perhaps unfavourable to happiness.

If this excessive imagination is composed with tendencies to affection, it makes a person *sentimentally* romantic. With a great, and what might, in a better endowed mind, be a just contempt of the ordinary rate of attachments, both in friendship and love, he indulges a most assured confidence that his peculiar lot is to realize all the wonders of generous, virtuous, noble, unalienable friendship, and of enraptured, uninterrupted, and unextinguishable love, that fiction ever talked in her dreams; while perhaps a shrewd, indifferent observer can see nothing in the nativity or character of the man, or in the qualities of the human creatures that he adores, or in the principles on which his devotion is founded, to promise an elevation or permanence of felicity beyond the destiny of common mortals.

If a passion for variety and novelty accompanies this extravagant imagination, it will exclude from its bold sketches of future life every thing like confined regularity, and common, plodding occupations. It will suggest that *I* was born for an adventurer, whose story will one day amaze the world. Perhaps I am to be an universal traveller; and there is not on the globe a grand city, or ruin, or volcano, or cataract, but I must

* The Divine Being is the only one of these objects which a Christian would wish it possible to contemplate without the aid of imagination; and every reflective man has felt how difficult it is to apprehend even this object without the intervention of an image. In thinking of the transactions and personages of history, the final events of time foretold by prophecy, the state of good men in another world, the superior ranks of intelligent agents, &c, he has often had occasion to wish his imagination much more vivid.

* Related of Moreau

see it. Debility of constitution, deficiency of means, innumerable perils, unknown languages, oppressive toils and the shortness of life, are very possibly all left out of the account.

If there is in the disposition a love of what is called glory, and an almost religious admiration of those capacious and intrepid spirits, one of which has often decided in one perilous day the destiny of armies and of empires, a predominant imagination may be led to revel amidst the splendors of military exploit, and to flatter the man that he too is to be a hero, a great general.

When a mind under this influence recurs to precedents as a foundation and a warrant of its expectations. they are never the usual, but always the extraordinary examples, that are contemplated. An observer of the ordinary instances of friendship is perhaps heard to assert, that the sentiment is sufficiently languid in general to admit of an entire self-interest, of absence without pain, and of final indifference. Well, so let it be; Damon and Pythias were friends of a different sort, and our friendship is to be like theirs. Or if the subject of musing and hope is the union in which love commonly results, it may be true and obvious enough that the generality of instances would not seem to tell of more than a mediocrity of happiness in this relation; but a visionary person does not live within the same world with these examples. The few instances which have been recorded of tender and never-dying enthusiasm, together with the numerous ones which romance and poetry have created, form the class to which he belongs, and from whose enchanting history, excepting their misfortunes, he reasons to his own future experience. So too the man, whose fancy anticipates political or martial achievement, allows his thoughts, to revert continually to those names which a rare conjunction of talents and circumstances has elevated into fame; forgetting that many thousands of men of great ability have died in at least comparative obscurity, for want of situations in which to display themselves; and never suspecting that himself perhaps has not abilities competent to any thing great, if some extraordinary event were now just to place him in the most opportune concurrence of circumstances. That there has been one very signal man to a million, more avails to the presumption that he shall be a signal man, than there having been a million to one signal man, infers a probability of his remaining one of the multitude.

You will generally observe, that persons thus self-appointed, in either sex, to be exceptions to the usual lot of humanity, endeavour at a kind of consistency of character, by a great aversion to the common modes of action and language, and an habitual affectation of something extraordinary. They will perhaps disdain regular hours, usual dresses, and common forms of transacting business; this you are to regard as the impulse of a spirit whose high vocation requires it to renounce all signs of relation to vulgar minds.

The epithet romantic then may be justly applied to those presumptions, (if entertained after the childish or very youthful age,) of a peculiarly happy or important destiny in life, which are not clearly founded on certain palpable distinctions of character or situation, or which greatly exceed the sober prognostics afforded by those distinctions. It should be observed here that *wishes* merely do not constitute a character romantic. A person may sometimes let his mind wander into vain wishes for all the fine and strange things on earth, and yet be far too sober to expect any of them. In this case however he will often check and reproach himself for the folly of entertaining the wish.

The absurdity of such anticipations consists simply in the improbability of their being realized, and not in their objects being uncongenial with the human mind; but another effect of the predominance of imagination may be a disposition to form schemes or indulge expectations essentially incongruous with the nature of man. Perhaps however you will say, What is that nature? Is it not a mere passive thing, variable almost to infinity, according to climate, to institutious, and to the different ages of time? Even taking it in a civilized state, what relation is there between such a form of human nature as that displayed at Sparta, and, for instance, the modern society denominated Quakers, or the Moravion Fraternity; And how can we ascertain what is congenial with it or not, unless itself were first ascertained? Allow me to say, that I speak of human nature in its most general principles, only, as social self-interested, inclined to the wrong, slow to improve, passing through several states of capacity and feeling in the successive periods of life, and the few other such permanent distinctions. Any of these distinctions may vanish from the sight of a visionary mind, while forming, for itself or for others, such schemes as could have sprung only from an imagination become wayward through its excess of power. I remember, for example, a person, very young I confess, who was so enchanted with the stories of Gregory Lopez, and one or two more pious hermits, as almost to form the resolution to betake himself to some wilderness and live as Gregory did. At any time, the very word *hermit* was enough to transport him, like the witch's broomstick, to the solitary hut, which was delightfully surrounded by shady, solemn groves, mossy rocks, crystal streams, and gardens of radishes. While this fancy lasted, he forgot the most obvious of all facts, that man is not made for habitual solitude, nor can endure it without misery, except when transformed into a superstitious ascetic, nor probably even then.*

Contrary to human nature, is the proper description of those theories of education, and those flatteries of parental hope, which presume that young people in general may be matured to eminent wisdom, and adorned with the universality of noble attainments, by the period at which in fact, the intellectual faculty is but beginning to operate with any thing like clearness and force. Because some individuals, remarkable exceptions to the natural character of youth, have in their very childhood advanced beyond the youthful giddiness, and debility of reason, and have displayed, at the age of perhaps twenty, a wonderful assemblage of all the strong and all the graceful endowments, it therefore only needs a proper system of education to make other young people (at least those of *my* family, the parent thinks,) be no longer what nature has always made youth to be. Let this be adopted, and we shall see multitudes at that age possessing the judgment of sages, or the diversified acquirements and graces of all-accomplished gentlemen and ladies. And what, pray, are the beings which are to become, by the discipline of eight or ten years, such finished examples of various excellence? Not, surely, these boys here, that love nothing so much as tops, marbles, and petty mischief—and those girls, that have yet attained but few ideas beyond the dressing of dolls? Yes, even these!

The same charge of being unadapted to man, seems applicable to the speculations of those philosophers and philanthropists, who have eloquently displayed the happiness, and asserted the practicability, of an equality of property and modes of life throughout society. Those who really anticipated or projected the practical trial of the system, must have forgotten on what planet those apartments were built, or those arbours were growing, in which they were contemplating such visions. For in these visions they beheld the ambition of one part of the inhabitants, the craft or audacity of another, the avarice of another, the stupidity or indo-

* Lopez indeed was often visited by pious persons who sought his instructions; this was a great modification of the loneliness, and of the trial involved in enduring it: but my hermit was fond of the idea of an uninhabited island, or of a wilderness so deep that these good people would not have been able to come at him, without a more formidable pilgrimage than was ever yet made for the sake of obtaining instruction.

lence of another, and the selfishness of almost all, as mere adventitious faults, superinduced on the character of the species, and instantly flying off at the approach of better institutions, which shall prove, to the confusion of all the calumniators of human nature, that nothing is so congenial to it as industry, moderation, and disinterestedness. It is at the same time but just to acknowledge, that many of them have admitted the necessity of such a grand transformation as to make man another being previously to the adoption of the system. This is all very well: when the proper race of *men* shall come from Utopia, the system and polity may very properly come along with them; or these sketches of it, prepared for them by us may be carefully preserved here, in volumes more precious than those of the Sibyls, against their arrival. Till then, the sober observers of the human character will read these beautiful theories as romances, adapted to excite sarcastic ridicule in their splenetic hours, when they are disgusted with human nature, and to produce deep melancholy in their benevolent ones, when they commiserate it.

It hardly needs to be said, that the character of the age of chivalry may be cited as an illustration of the same kind. One of its most prominent distinctions was, an immense incongruity with the simplest principles of human nature. For instance, in the concern of love: a generous young man became attached to an interesting young woman—interesting as he believed, from having once seen her; for probably he never heard her speak. His heart would naturally prompt him to seek access to the object whose society, it told him, would make him happy; and if in a great measure debarred from that society, he would surrender himself to the melting mood of the passion, in the musings of pensive retirement. But this was not the way. He must abandon for successive years her society and vicinity, and every soft indulgence of feeling, and rush boldly into all sorts of hardships and perils, deeming no misfortune so great as not to find constant occasions of hazarding his life among the roughest foes, or if he could find or fancy them, the strangest monsters; and all this, not as the allievation of despair, but as the courtship of hope. And when he was at length betrayed to flatter himself that such a probation, through every kind of patience and danger, might entitle him to throw his trophies and himself at her imperial feet, it was very possible she might be affronted that he had presumed to be still alive. It is unnecessary to refer to the other parts of the institution of chivalry, the whole system of which would seem more adapted to any race of beings exhibited in the Arabian Nights, or to any still wilder creation of fancy, than to a community of creatures appointed to live by cultivating the soil, anxious to avoid pain and trouble, seeking the reciprocation of affection on the easiest terms, and nearest to happiness in regular pursuits, and quiet, domestic life.

One cannot help reflecting here, how amazingly accommodating this human nature has been to all institutions but wise and good ones; insomuch that an order of life and manners, formed in the wildest deviation from all plain sense and native instinct, could be practically adopted, to some extent, by those who had rank and courage enough, and adored and envied by the rest of mankind. Still, the genuine tendencies of nature have survived the strange but transient modifications of time, and remain the same after the age of chivalry is gone far toward that oblivion, to which you will not fail to wish that many other institutions might speedily follow it. Forgive the prolixity of these illustrations, intended to show, that schemes and speculations respecting the interests either of an individual or of society, which are inconsistent with the natural constitution of man, may, except where it should be reasonable to expect some supernatural invention, be denominated romantic.

The tendency to this species of romance, may be caused, or very greatly promoted, by an exclusive taste for what is *grand*, a disease to which some few minds are subject. They have no pleasure in contemplating the system of things as the Creator has ordered it, a combination of great and little, in which the great is much more dependent on the little than the little on the great. They cut out the grand objects, to dispose them into a world of their own. All the images in their intellectual scene must be colossal and mountainous. They are constantly seeking what is animated into heroics, what is expanded into immensity, what is elevated above the stars. But for great empires, great battles, great enterprises, great convulsions, great geniusses, great temples, great rivers, there would be nothing worth naming in this part of the creation.* All that belongs to connexion, gradation, harmony, regularity, and utility, is thrown out of sight behind these forms of vastness. The influence of this exclusive taste will reach into the system of projects and expectations. The man will wish to summon the world to throw aside its tame, accustomed pursuits, and adopt at once more magnificent views and objects, and will be indignant at mankind that they cannot or will not be sublime. Impatient of little means and slow processes, he will wish for violent transitions and entirely new institutions. He will perhaps determine to set men the example of performing something great, in some ill-judged, sanguine project in which he will fail; and, after being ridiculed by society, both for the scheme and its catastrophe, may probably abandon all the activities of life, and become a misanthrope the rest of his days.

LETTER III.

The Epithet applicable to Hopes and Projects inconsistent with the known Relations between Ends and Means—Reckoning on happy Casualties—Musing on Instances of good Luck—Novels go more than half the Length of the older Romance in promoting this pernicious Tendency of the Mind—Specimen of what they do in this way.—Fancy magnifies the smallest Means into an apparent Competence to the greatest Ends—This delusive Calculation apt to be admitted in Schemes of Benevolence—Projects for civilizing Savage Nations—Extravagant Expectations of the Efficacy of direct Instruction, in the Lessons of Education, and in Preaching—Reformers apt to overrate the Power of Means—The Fancy about the Omnipotence of Truth—Our Expectations ought to be limited by what we actually see and know of human Nature—Estimate of that Nature—Prevalence of Passion and Appetite against Conviction.

One of the most obvious distinctions of the works of romance is, an utter violation of all the relations between ends and means. Sometimes such ends are proposed as seem quite dissevered from means, inasmuch as there are scarcely any supposable means on earth to accomplish them: but no matter; if we cannot ride we must swim, if we cannot swim we must fly: the object is effected by a mere poetical omnipotence that wills it. And very often practicable objects are attained by means the most fantastic, improbable, or inadequate; so that there is scarcely any resemblance between the method in which they are accomplished by the dexterity of fiction, and that in which the same things must be attempted in the actual economy of the world. Now, when you see this absurdity of imagination prevailing in the calculations of real life, you may justly apply the epithet, romantic.

Indeed a strong and habitually indulged imagination may be so absorbed in the end, if it is not a concern of

* Just as, to employ a humble comparison, a votary of fashion, after visiting a crowded public place which happened at that time not to be graced by the presence of many people of consequence, tells you, with an affected tone, 'There was not a creature there.'

absolute, immediate urgency, as for a while quite to forget the process of attainment. It has incantations to dissolve the rigid laws of time and distance, and place a man in something so like the presence of his object, that he seems half to possess it ; and it is hard, while occupying the verge of Paradise, to be flung far back in order to find or make a path to it, with the slow and toilsome steps of reality. In the luxury of promising himself that what he wishes will by some means take place at some time, he forgets that he is advancing no nearer to it—except on the wise and patient calculation that he must, by the simple movement of growing older, be coming somewhat nearer to every event that is yet to happen to him. He is like a traveller, who, amidst his indolent musings in some soft bower, where he has sat down to be shaded a little while from the rays of noon, falls asleep, and dreams he is in the midst of all the endearments of home, insensible that there are many hills and dales for him yet to traverse. But the traveller will awake ; so too will the man of fancy, and if he has the smallest capacity of just reflection, he will regret to have wasted in reveries the time which ought to have been devoted to practical exertions.

But even though reminded of the necessity of intervening means, the man of imagination will often be tempted to violate their relation with ends, by permitting himself to dwell on those happy *casualties*, which the prolific sorcery of his mind will promptly figure to him as the very things, if they would but occur, to accomplish his wishes at one, without the toil of a sober process. If they would occur—and things as strange *might* happen : he reads in the newspapers that an estate of ten thousand per annum was lately adjudged to a man who was working on the road. He has even heard of people dreaming that in such a place something valuable was concealed ; and that, on searching or digging that place, they found an old earthen pot, full of gold and silver pieces of the times of good King Charles the Martyr. Mr. B. was travelling by the mail-coach, in which he met with a most interesting young lady, whom he had never seen before ; they were mutually delighted, and were married in a few weeks. Mr C., a man of great merit in obscurity, was walking across a field when Lord D., in chase of a fox, leaped over the hedge, and fell off his horse into a ditch. Mr C., with the utmost alacrity and kind solicitude, helped his lordship out of the ditch, and recovered for him his escaped horse. The consequence was inevitable ; his lordship, superior to the pride of being mortified to have been seen in a condition so unlucky for giving the impression of nobility, commenced a friendship with Mr C. and introduced him into honourable society and the road to fortune. A very ancient maiden lady of a large fortune happening to be embarrassed in a crowd, a young clergyman offered her his arm, and politely attended her home ; his attention so captivated her, that she bequeathed to him, soon after, her whole estate, though she had many poor relations.

That class of fictitious works called *novels*, though much more like real life than the romances which preceded them, (and which are recently, with some alterations, partly come into vogue again,) is yet full of these lucky incidents and adventures, which are introduced as the chief means toward the ultimate success. A young man without fortune, for instance, is precluded from making his addresses to a young female in a superior situation, whom he believes not indifferent to him, until he can approach her with such worldly advantages as it might not be imprudent or degrading for her to accept. Now how is this to be accomplished ? —Why, I suppose, by the exertion of his talents in some fair and practicable department ; and perhaps the lady, besides, will generously abdicate for his sake some of the trappings and luxuries of rank. You really suppose this is the plan ? I am sorry you have so much less genius than a novel-writer. This young man has an uncle, who has been absent a long time, nobody knew where, except the young man's lucky stars. During his absence, the old uncle has gained a large fortune, with which he returns to his native land, at a time most opportune for every one, but a highwayman, who, attacking him in a road through a wood, is frightened away by the young hero, who happens to come there at the instant, to rescue and recognize his uncle, and to be in return recognized and made the heir to as many thousands as the lady or her family could wish.—Now what is the intended impression of all this on the reader's mind ? Is he to think it very *likely* that *he* too has some old uncle, or acquaintance at least, returning with a shipload of wealth from the East Indies ; and very *desirable* that the highwayman should make one such attempt more ; and very *certain* that in that case he shall be there in the nick of time to catch all that fortune sends ? One's indignation is excited at the immoral tendency of such lessons to young readers, who are thus taught to regard all sober, regular plans for compassing an object with disgust or despondency, and to muse on improbabilities till they become foolish enough to expect them, and to be melancholy when they find they may expect them in vain. It is unpardonable that these pretended instructers by example should thus explode the calculations and exertions of manly resolution, destroy the connexion between ends and means, and make the rewards of virtue so depend on chance, that if the reader does not either regard the whole fable with contempt, or promise himself he shall receive the favours of fortune in some similar way, he must close the book with the conviction that he may hang or drown himself as soon as he pleases ; that is to say, unless he has learnt from some other source a better morality and religion than these books will ever teach him.

Another deception in respect to means, is the facility with which fancy passes along the train of them, and reckons to their ultimate effect at a glance, without resting at the successive stages, and considering the labours and hazards of the protracted process from each point to the next. If a given number of years are allowed requisite for the accomplishment of an object, the romantic mind vaults from one last day of December to another, and seizes at once the whole product of all the intermediate days, without condescending to recollect that the sun never shone yet on three hundred and sixty-five days at once, and that they must be slowly told and laboured one by one. If a favourite plan is to be accomplished by means of a certain large amount of property, which is to be produced from what is at present a very small one, the calculations of a sanguine mind can change shillings into guineas, and guineas into hundreds of pounds, incomparably faster than, in the actual experiment, these lazy shillings can be compelled to improve themselves into guineas, and the guineas into hundreds of pounds. You remember the noble calculation of Alnaschar on his basket of earthen ware, which was so soon to obtain him the Sultan's daughter.

Where imagination is not delusive enough to embody future casualties as effective means, it may yet represent very inadequate ones as competent. In a well-balanced mind, no conception will grow into a favourite purpose, unaccompanied by a process of the understanding, deciding its practicability by an estimate of the means ; in a mind under the influence of fancy, this is a subordinate after-task. By the time that this comes to be considered, the projector is too much enamoured of an end that is deemed to be great, to abandon it because the means are suspected to be little. But then they must cease to *appear* little ; for there must be an apparent proportion between the means and the end. Well, trust the whole concern to this plastic faculty, and presently every insignificant particle of means, and every petty contrivance for their management, will swell into magnitude; pigmies and Lilliputians with their tiny arrows will soon grow up into giants wielding spears; and the diffident consciousness which was at first somewhat afraid to measure the plan against the object, will give place to a generous scorn of the timidity of doubting. The mind will most ingeniously place the apparatus between its eye and the object at a distance, and be delighted to find that the one looks as large as the other.

The consideration of the deluded calculations on the effect of insufficient means, would lead to a wide variety of particulars; I will only touch slightly on a few. Various projects of a *benevolent* order would come under this charge. Did you ever listen to the discussion of plans for the civilization of barbarous nations without the intervention of conquest? I have, with interest and with despair.* That very many millions of the species should form only a brutal adjunct to civilized and enlightened man, is a melancholy thing, notwithstanding the whimsical attempts of some ingenious men to represent the state of wandering savages as preferable to every other condition of life; a state for which, no doubt, they would have been sincerely glad to abandon their fame and proud refinements. But where are the means to reclaim these wretched beings into the civilized family of man? A few examples indeed are found in history, of barbarous tribes being formed into well-ordered and considerably enlightened states by one man, who began the attempt without any power but that of persuasion, and perhaps delusion. There are perhaps other instances, of the success obtained by a small combination of men employing the same means; as in the great undertaking of the Jesuits in South America. But have not these wonderful facts been far too few to be made a standard for the speculations of sober men? And have they not also come to us with too little explanation to illustrate any general principles? To me it appears extremely difficult to comprehend how the means recorded by historians to have been employed by some of the unarmed civilizers, could have produced so great an effect. In observing the half-civilized condition of a large part of the population of these more improved countries, and in reading what travellers describe of the state and dispositions of the various orders of savages, it would seem a presumption unwarranted by any thing we ever saw of the powers of the human mind to suppose that any man, or any ten men now on earth, if landed and left on a savage coast, would be able to transform a multitude of stupid or ferocious tribes into a community of mild intelligence and regular industry. We are therefore led to believe that the few unaccountable instances conspicuous in the history of the world, of the success of one or a few men in this work, must have been the result of such a combination of favourable circumstances, co-operating with their genius and perseverance, as no other man can hope to experience. Such events seem like Joshua's arresting the sun and moon, things that have been done, but can be done no more. Pray, which of you, I should say, could expect to imitate with success, or indeed would think it right if he could, the deception of Manco Capac, and awe a wild multitude into order by a commission from the sun? What would be your first expedient in the attempt to substitute that regularity and constraint which they hate, for that lawless liberty which they love? How could you reduce them to be conscious, or incite them to be proud, of those wants, for being subject to which they would regard you as their inferiors; wants of which, unless they could comprehend the refinement, they must necessarily despise the debility? By what magic are you to render visible and palpable any part of the world of science or of abstraction, to beings who have hardly words to denominate even their sensations? And by what concentrated force of all kinds of magic together, that Egypt or Chaldea ever pretended, are you to introduce humanity and refinement among such creatures as the Northern Indians, described by Mr. Hearne? If an animated young philanthropist still zealously maintained that it might be done, I should be amused to think how that warm imagination would be quelled, if he were obliged to make the practical trial. It is easy for him to be romantic while enlivened by the intercourse of cultivated society, while reading of the contrivances and the patience of ancient legislators, or while infected with the enthusiasm of poetry. He feels as if he could be the moral conqueror of a continent. He becomes a Hercules amidst imaginary labours; he traverses untired, while in his room, wide tracts of the wilderness; he surrounds himself with savage men, without either trembling or revolting at their aspects or fierce exclamations; he makes eloquent speeches to them, though he knows not a word of their language, which language indeed, if he did know it, would perhaps be found totally incapable of eloquence; they listen with the deepest attention, are convinced of the necessity of adopting new habits of life, and speedily soften into humanity, and brighten into wisdom. But he would become sober enough, if compelled to travel a thousand miles through the desert, or over the snow, with some of these subjects of his lectures and legislation; to accompany them in a hunting excursion; to choose in a stormy night between exposure in the open air and the smoke and grossness of their cabins; to observe the intellectual faculties narrowed almost to a point, limited to a scanty number of the meanest class of ideas; to find by repeated experiments that *his* kind of ideas could neither reach their understanding nor excite their curiosity; to see the ravenous appetite of wolves succeeded for a season by a stupidity insensible even to the few interests which kindle the utmost ardour of a savage; to witness loathsome habits occasionally diversified by abominable ceremonies; or to be for once the spectator of some of the circumstances which accompany the wars of savages.

But there are many more familiar illustrations of the extravagant estimate of means. One is, the expectation of far too much from mere direct instruction. This is indeed so general, that it will hardly be termed romantic, except in the most excessive instances. Observe it, however, a moment in the concern of education. Nothing seems more evident than the influence of external circumstances, distinct from the regular discipline of the parent or tutor, in forming the character of youth. And nothing seems more evident than that direct instruction, though an useful ally to the influence of these circumstances when they are auspicious, is a feeble counteractor if they are malignant. And yet this mere instruction is enough in the account of thousands of parents, to lead the youth to wisdom and happiness; even that very youth whom the united influence of almost all things else which he is exposed to see, and hear, and participate, is drawing with the unrelaxing grasp of a fiend to destruction.

A too sanguine opinion of the efficacy of instruction, has sometimes been entertained by those who teach from the pulpit. Till the dispensations of a better age shall be opened on the world, the measure of effect which may reasonably be expected from preaching, is to be determined by a view of the visible effects which are actually produced on congregations from week to week; and this view is far from flattering. One might appeal to preachers in general—What striking improvements are apparent in your societies? When you inculcate charity on the Sunday do the misers in your congregations liberally open their chests and purses to the distressed on Monday? Might I not ask as well, whether the rock and trees really *did* move at the voice of Orpheus? After you have unveiled even the scenes of

* I here place out of view that religion by which Omnipotence will at length transform the world.

eternity to the gay and frivolous, do you find in more than some rare instances a dignified seriousness take place of their follies? What is the effect, on the elegant, splendid professors of Christianity, of your inculcation of that solemn interdiction of their habits, 'Be not conformed to this world?' Yet, notwithstanding this melancholy state of facts, some preachers, from the persuasion of a mysterious apostolic sacredness in the office, or from a vain estimate of their personal talents, or from mistaking the applause with which the preacher has been flattered, for the proof of a salutary effect on the minds of the hearers, and some from a much worthier cause, the affecting influence of sacred truth on their own minds, have been inclined to anticipate immense effects from their public ministrations. Melancthon was a romantic youth when he began to preach. He expected that all must be inevitably and immediately persuaded, when they should hear what he had to tell them. But he soon discovered as he said, that old Adam was too hard for young Melancthon. In addition to the grand fact of the depravity of the human heart, there are so many causes operating injuriously through the week on the characters of those who form a congregation, that a thoughtful man often feels a melancholy emotion amidst his religious addresses, from the reflection that he is making a feeble effort against a powerful evil, a single effort against a combination of evils, a temporary and transient effort against evils of continual operation, and a purely intellectual effort against evils, many of which act on the senses. When the preacher considers the effect naturally resulting from the sight of so many bad examples, the communications of so many injurious acquaintances, and hearing and talking of what would be, if written, so many volumes of vanity and nonsense, the predominance of fashionable dissipation in one class, and of vulgarity in another; he must indeed imagine himself endowed with the power a super-human eloquence, if the instructions, expressed in an hour or two on the Sabbath, and soon forgotten, as he might know, by most of his hearers, are to leave something in the mind, which shall be through the week the efficacious repellant to the contact and contamination of all these forces of mischief. But how soon he would cease to imagine such a power in his exhortations, if the greater number of his hearers could sincerely and accurately tell him, toward the end of the week, in what degree these admonitions had affected and governed them, in opposition to their corrupt tendencies and their temptations. What would be, in the five or six days, the number of the moments and the instances in which these instructions would be proved to have been effectual, compared with the whole number of moments and circumstances to which they were justly applicable? How often, while hearing such a week's detail of the lives of a considerable proportion of the congregation, a man would have occasion to say, By whose instructions were these persons influenced *then*, in that neglect of devout exercises, that excess of levity, that waste of time, that avowed contempt of religion, that language of profaneness and imprecation, those contrivances of selfishness, those paroxysms of passion, that study of sensuality, or that general and obdurate depravity?

But the preacher whom I deem too sanguine, may tell me, that it is not by means of any force which *he* can throw into his religious instructions, that he expects them to be efficacious: but that he believes a *divine* energy will accompany what is undoubtedly a message from heaven. I am pleased with the piety, and the sound judgment, (as I esteem it,) with which he expects the conversion of careless or hardened men from nothing *less* than the operation of a power strictly divine. But I would remind him, that the probability, at any given season, that such a power will intervene, must be in proportion to the frequency or infrequency with which its intervention is actually manifested in the general course of experience. In other words, it is in proportion to the number of happy transformations of character which we see taking place under the efficacy of religious truth.

Reformers in general are very apt to overrate the power of the means by which their theories are to be realized. They are forever introducing the story of Archimedes, who was to have moved the world if he could have found any second place on which to plant his engines; and imagination discloses to moral and political projectors a cloud-built and truly extramundane position which they deem to be exactly such a convenience in their department as the mathematician, whose converse with demonstrations had saved *part* of his reason from being run away with by his fancy, confessed to be a desideratum in his. This terra firma is called the Omnipotence of Truth.

It is presumed, that truth must at length, by the force of indefatigable inquiry, become generally victorious, and that all vice, being the result of a mistaken judgment of the nature or the means of happiness, must therefore accompany the exit of error. Of course, it is presumed of the present times also, or of those immediately approaching, that in every society and every mind where truth is clearly admitted, the reforms which it dictates must substantially follow. I have the most confident faith that the empire of truth, advancing under a far mightier agency than a mere philosophic inquiry, is appointed to irradiate the latter ages of a dark and troubled world; and, on the strength of prophetic intimations, I anticipate its coming sooner, by at least a thousand centuries, than a disciple of that philosophy which rejects revelation, as the first proud step towards the improvment of the world, is warranted, by a view of the past and present state of mankind, to predict. The assurance from the same authority is the foundation for believing, that when that sacred empire shall overspread the world, the virtue of character will correspond to the illuminations of understanding. But in the present state of the moral system, our expectations of the effect of truth on the far greater number of the persons who shall admit its convictions, have no right to exceed the rules of probability which are taught by facts. It would be gratifying no doubt to believe, that the several powers in the human constitution are so combined, that to gain the judgment would be to secure the whole man. And if all history, and all memory of our observation and experience, could be merged in Lethe, it might be believed, perhaps a few hours. How could an attentive observer believe it longer? Is it not obvious that very many persons, with a most absolute conviction, by their own ingenuous avowal, that one certain course of action is virtue and happiness, and another, vice and misery, do yet habitually choose the latter? It is not improbable that several millions of human beings are at this very hour thus acting in violation of the laws of goodness, while those laws are clearly admitted, not only as impositions of moral authority, but as the vital principles of their own true self-interest.* And did not even the best men confess a fierce discord between the tendencies of their nature, and the dictates of that truth which

* The criminal himself has the clearest consciousness that he violates the dictates of his judgment. How trifling is the subtilty which affects to show that he does not violate them, by alleging, that every act of choice must be preceded by a determination of the judgment, and that therefore in choosing an evil, a man does at the time judge it to be on some account preferable, though he may know it to be wrong. It is not to be denied that the choice does imply such a conclusion of the judgment. But this conclusion is made according to a narrow and subordinate scale of estimating good and evil, while the mind is conscious that, judging according to a larger scale, the opposite conclusion is true. It judges a thing better for immediate pleasure, which it knows to be worse for ultimate advantage. The criminal, therefore, may be correctly said to act according to his judgment, in choosing it for present pleasure. But since it is the great office of the judgment to decide what is wisest and best on the whole, the man may truly be said to act against his judgment, who acts in opposition to the conclusion which it forms on this greater scale.

they revere? They say with St Paul, 'That which I do, I allow not; for what I would, that I do not; but what I hate, that I do; to will is present with me, but how to perform that which is good, I find not; the good that I would, that I do not, and the evil which I would not, that I do.' Every serious self-observer recollects instances,in which a temptation, exactly addressed to his passions or his habits, has prevailed in spite of the sternest interdict of his judgment, pronounced at the very crisis. Perhaps the most lawful sanctions by which the judgment can ever enforce its authority, were distinctly brought to his view at the same moment with its convictions. In the subsequent hour he had to reflect, that the ideas of God, of a future account, of a world of retribution, could not prevent him from violating his conscience. That he did not dwell deliberately on these ideas, is nothing against my argument. It is in the nature of the passions not to permit the mind to fix strongly and durably on those considerations which oppose and condemn them. But what greater power than this, is requisite for their fatal triumph? If the passions *can* thus prevent the mind from strongly fixing on the most awful considerations when distinctly presented, they can destroy the efficacy of that truth which presents them. Truth can do no more than discriminate the good from the evil before us, and declare the consequences of our choice. When this is inefficacious, its power has failed. And no fact can be more evident than that its power often thus fails. I should compassionate the self-complacency of the man who was not conscious he had to deplore many violations of his own clearest convictions. And in trying the efficacy of truth on others, it would be found, in numberless instances, that to have informed and convinced a man, may be but little toward emancipating him from the habits which he sincerely acknowledges to be wrong. There is then no such inviolable connexion as some men have supposed between the admission of truth, and consequent action. And therefore, however great is the value of truth, the expectations that presume its omnipotence, without extraordinary intervention are, romantic delusion.

You will observe that in this case of trying the efficacy of the truth on others, I have supposed the great previous difficulty of presenting it to the understanding so luminously as to impress irresistible conviction, to be already overcome; though the experimental reformer will find this introductory work such an arduous undertaking, that he will be often tempted to abandon it as a hopeless one.

LETTER IV.

Christianity the grand appointed Means of reforming the World—But though the Religion itself be a Communication from Heaven, the Administration of it by human Agents is to be considered as a merely human Means, excepting so far as a special Divine Energy is made to accompany it—Its comparatively small success proves in what an extremely limited measure that Energy accompanies it—Impotence of Man to do what it leaves undone—Irrational to expect from its progressive Administration a measure of success indefinitely surpassing the present State of its Operations, till we see some Signs of a great Change in the Divine Government of the World—Folly of Projects to reform mankind which disclaim religion—Nothing in human Nature to meet and give effect to the Schemes and Expedients of the Moral Revolutionist—Wretched State of that Nature—Sample of the absurd Estimates of its condition by the irreligious Members of Society.

As far as the gloomy estimate of means and of plans for the amendment of mankind may appear to involve the human administration of the religion of Christ, I am anxious not to seem to fail in justice to that religion by which I entirely believe, and rejoice to believe, that every improvement of a sublime order yet awaiting our race must be affected. And I trust I do not fail, since I keep in my mind a most clear distinction between Christianity itself as a divine thing, and the administration of it by a system of merely human powers and means. These means are indeed of divine appointment, and to a certain extent are accompanied by a special divine agency. But how far this agency accompanies them is seen in the measure of their success. Where *that* stands arrested, the fact itself is the proof that the superior operation does not go farther with these means. There it stops, and leaves them to accomplish, if they can, what remains. And oh, what remains? If the general transformation of mankind into such persons as could be justly deemed true disciples of Christ, were regarded as the object of his religion, how mysteriously small a part of that object has this divine agency ever yet been exerted to accomplish! And then, the awful and immense remainder evinces the inexpressible imbecility of the means, when left to be applied as a mere human administration. I need not illustrate its incompetency by citing the vast majority, the numerous millions of Christendom, nor the millions of even our own country, on whom this religion has no direct influence. I need not observe how many of these have heard or read the evangelic declaration ten thousand times, nor with what perfect insensibility vast numbers can receive its most luminous ideas, and most cogent enforcements, which are but like arrows meeting the shield of Ajax. Probably each religious teacher can recollect, besides his general experience, very particular instances, in which he has set himself to exert the utmost force of his mind, in reasoning, illustration, and serious appeal, to impress some one important idea, on some one class of persons to whom it was most specifically applicable; and has perceived the plainest indications, both at the instant and immediately after, that it was an attempt of the same kind as that of demolishing a tower by attacking it with pebbles. Nor do I need to observe how generally, if a momentary impression is made, it is forgotten the following hour.

A man convinced of the truth and supreme excellence of Chrstianity, yet entertaining a more flattering notion of the reason and moral dispositions of man than the judgment which that religion passes upon them, may be very reluctant to admit that there is such a fatal disproportion between the apparatus, if I may call it so, of the Christian means as left to be applied by mere human energy, and the object which is to be attempted with them. But how is he to avoid it? Will he, in this one excepted instance, reject the method of inference from facts? He cannot look upon the world of facts and contradict the representation in the preceding paragraph, unless his fancy is so illusive as to interpose a vision, an absolute dream, between his eyes and the obvious reality. He cannot affirm that there are *not* an immense number of persons, even educated persons, receiving the Christian declarations with indifference, or rejecting them with contempt mingled with their carelessness. The right means are applied, and with all the force that human effort can give them, but with a suspension, in these instances, of the divine agency,—and this is the effect! While the fact stands out so palpably to view, I am doomed to listen with wonder, when some of the professed believers and advocates of the gospel avowing high anticipations of its progressive efficacy, chiefly or solely by means of the intrinsic force which it carries as a rational address to rational creatures. I cannot help inquiring what length of time is to be allowed for the experiment, which is to prove the adequacy of the means independently of an extraordinary intervention. Nor can it be impertinent to ask what is, thus far, the state of the experiment and the success, among those who reject the idea of such a divine agency, as a tenet of fanaticism. Might it not be prudent, to moderate the expressions of contempt for the persuasion which excites an importunity for extraordinary influence from the Almighty, till the success without it shall be greater? The utmost arrogance of this contempt will venture no comparison between the respective success, in the conversion of vain and wicked men, of the Christian means as administered by those who implore and rely upon this special agency of Heaven, and by those who deny any such operation on the mind; deny it in sense and substance, whatever accommodating phrases they may sometimes employ. Indeed, has there been any success at all, of that high order, to vindicate the calculations of this latter class from the imputaton of all that should be meant by the word Romantic?

But, when I introduced the mention of reformers and their projects, I was not intending any reference to delusive presumptions of the operations of Christianity, but to those speculations and schemes for the amendment of mankind which anticipate their effect independently of its assistance; some of them perhaps silently coinciding with several of its principles, while others expressly disclaim them. Unless these schemes bring with them, like spirits from Heaven, an intrinsic competence to the great operation, without being met or aided by any considerable degree of favourable disposition in the nature of the Subject, it is probable that they will disappoint their fond projectors. There is no avoiding the ungracious perception, in viewing the general character of the race, that, after some allowance for what is called natural affection, and for compassionate sympathy, (an excellent principle, but extremely limited and often capricious in its operation,) the main strength of human feeling consists in the love of sensual gratification, of distinction, of power, and of money. And by what suicidal inconsistency are these principles to lend their force to accomplish the schemes of pure reason and virtue, which, they will not fail to perceive, are plotting against them?* And if *they* have far too perfect an instinct to be trepanned into such an employment of their force, and yet are the preponderating agents in the human heart, what *other* active principles of it can the renovator of human character call to his effectual aid, against the evils which are accumulated and defended by what is at once the baser and the stronger part? Whatever principles of a better kind there may be in the nature, they can hold but a feeble and inert existence under the predominance of the worse, and could make but a faint insurrection in favour of the invading virtue, the very worst of them may indeed seem to become its allies when it happens, as it occasionally will, that the course of action which reforming virtue forces, falls in the same line in which these meaner principles can promote their interests. Then, and so far, an unsound coincidence may take place, and the external effect of those principles may be clad in specious appearances of virtue; but the moment that the reforming projector summons their co-operation to a service in which they must desert their own object and their corrupt character, they will desert *him*. As long as he is condemned to depend, for the efficacy of his schemes, on the aid of so much pure propensity as he shall find in the corrupted subject, he will be nearly in the case of a man attempting to climb a tree by laying hold, first on this side, and then on that, of some rotten twig, which still breaks off in his hand, and lets him fall among the nettles.

Look again to the state of facts. Collective man *is* human nature; and the conduct of this assemblage, under the diversified experiments continually made on it, expresses its true character, and indicates what may be expected from it. Now then, to what principle in human nature, as thus illustrated by trial, could you with confidence appeal in favour of any of the great objects which a benevolent man desires to see accomplished? If there were in it any one grand principle of goodness which an earnest call, and a great occasion, would raise into action, to assert or redeem the character of the species, one should think it would be what we call, incorrectly enough, Humanity. Consider then, in this nation for instance, which extols its own generous virtues to the sky, what lively and rational appeals have been made to the whole community, respecting the slave trade,* the condition of the poor, and the hateful mass of cruelty inflicted on brute animals, not to glance toward the horrid sacrifices in that temple of Moloch named honourable war which has been kept open more than half the past century;—appeals substantially in vain: And why in vain? If humanity *were* a powerful principle in the nature of the community, they would not, in contempt of knowledge, expostulation, and spectacles of misery, persist in the most enormous violations of it. Why in vain? but plainly because there is not enough of the virtue of humanity, not even in what is deemed a highly cultivated state of the human nature, to answer to the pathetic call. Or if this be not the cause, let the idolaters of human divinity call, like the worshippers of Baal, in a louder voice. Their success will too probably be the same; they will obtain no extraordinary exertion of power, though they cry from morning till the setting sun. And meanwhile the observer, who foresees their disappointment, would think himself warranted, but for the melancholy feeling that the nature in question is his own, to mock their expectations,—You know that a multitude of exemplifications might be added. And the thought of so many great and interesting objects, relating to the human economy, as a sober appreciation of means seems to place beyond the reach of the moral revolutionist,† will often, if he has genuine benevolence, make him sad. He will repeat to himself, 'How easy it is to conceive these inestimable improvements, and how nobly they would exalt my species; but how to work them into the actual condition of man!—Are there somewhere in possibility,' he will ask, 'intellectual and moral engines mighty enough to perform the great process? Where in darkness is the sacred repository in which they lie? What Marraton‡ shall explore the unknown way to it? The man who would not be glad, in exchange for the discovery of this treasury of powers, to shut up for ever the mines of Potosi, would deserve to be immured as the last victim of those deadly caverns.'

But each speculative visionary thinks the discovery is made? and while surveying his own great magazine of expedients, consisting of Fortunatus's cap, the philosopher's stone, Aladdin's lamp, and other equally efficient articles, he is confident that the work may speedily be done. These powerful instruments of melioration perhaps lose their individual names under the

* I am here reminded of the Spanish story of a village where the devil, having made the people excessively wicked, was punished by being compelled to assume the appearance and habit of a friar, and to preach so eloquently, in spite of his internal repugnance and rage, that the inhabitants were completely reformed.

* Happily this topic of accusation is in a measure now set aside: but it would have remained as immoveable as the continent of Africa, if the Legislature had not been forced into a conviction that, on the whole, the slave trade was not advantageous in point of pecuniary interest. At least the guilt would so have remained upon the nation acting in its capacity of a state.—This note is added subsequently to the first edition.—It may be subjoined, in qualification of the reproach relative to the next article,—the condition of the poor—that during a later period, there has been a great increase of the attention and exertion directed to that condition; which has, nevertheless, become worse.

† It is obvious that I am not supposing this moral revolutionist to be armed with any power but that of persuasion. If he were a monarch, and possessed virtue and talents equal to his power, the case would be materially different. Even then, he would accomplish but little compared with what he could imagine, and would desire; yet, to all human appearance, he might be the instrument of wonderfully changing the condition of society within his empire. If the soul of Alfred could return to the earth!

‡ Spectator, No 56.

general denomination of Philosophy, a term that would be venerable, if it could be saved from the misfortune of being hackneyed into cant, and from the impiety of substituting its expedients in the place of divine power. But it is of little consequence what denomination the projectors assume to themselves or their schemes: it is by their fruits that we shall know them. Their work is before them; the scene of moral disorder presents to them the plagues which they are to stop, the mountain which they are to remove, the torrent which they are to divert, the desert which they are to clothe in verdure and bloom. Let them make their experiment, and add each his page to the gloomy records in which experience contemns the folly of imagination.*

All the speculations and schemes of the sanguine projectors of all ages, have left the world still a prey to infinite legions of vices and miseries, an immortal band, which has trampled in scorn on the monuments and the dust of the self-idolizing men who dreamed, each in his day, that they were born to chase these evils out of the earth. If these vain demigods of an hour, who trusted to change the world, and who perhaps wished to change it only to make it a temple to their fame, could be awaked from the unmarked graves into which they sunk, to look a little while round on the world for some traces of the success of their projects, would they not be eager to retire again into the chambers of death, to hide the shame of their remembered presumption? The wars and tyranny, the rancour, cruelty, and revenge, together with all the other unnumbered vices and crimes with which the earth is still infested, are enough, if the whole mass could be brought within the bounds of any one even the most extensive empire, to constitute its whole population literally infernals, all but their being incarnate, and that indeed they would soon, through mutual destruction, cease to be. Hitherto the fatal cause of these evils, the corruption of the human heart, has sported with the weakness, or seduced the strength, of all human contrivances to subdue them. Nor do I perceive any signs as yet that we are commencing a better era, in which the means that have failed before, or the expedients of a new and more fortunate invention, shall become irresistible, like the sword of Michael in our hands. The nature of man still 'casts ominous conjecture on the whole success.' While *that* is corrupt, it will pervert even the very schemes and operations by which the world should be improved, though their first principles were pure as heaven; and revolutions, great discoveries, augmented science, and new forms of polity, will become in *effect* what may be denominated the sublime mechanics of depravity.

* In reading lately some part of a tolerably well-written book published a few years since, I came to the following passage, which, though in connexion indeed with the subject of elections, expresses the author's general opinion of the state of society, and of the means of exalting it to wisdom and virtue. 'The bulk of the community begin to examine, to feel, to understand, their rights and duties. They only require the fostering care of the Philosopher to ripen them into complete rationality, and furnish them with the requisites of political and moral action.' Here I paused to indulge my wonder. The fostering care of the Philosopher! Why then is not the Philosopher about his business? Why does he not go and indoctrinate a company of peasants in the intervals of a ploughing or a harvest day, when he will find them far more eager for his instructions than for drink? Why does he not introduce himself among a circle of farmers, who cannot fail, as he enters, to be very judiciously discussing, with the aid of their punch and their pipes, the most refined questions respecting their rights and duties, and wanting but exactly his aid, instead of more punch and tobacco, to possess themselves completely of the requisites of political and moral action? The population of a manufactory, is another most promising seminary, where all the moral and intellectual endowments are so nearly 'ripe,' that he will seem less to have the task of cultivating than the pleasure of reaping. Even among the company in the ale-house, though the Philosopher might at first be sorry, and might wonder, to perceive a slight merge of the moral part of the man in the sensitive, and to find in so vociferous a mood that inquiring reason which, he had supposed, would be waiting for him with the silent, anxious docility of a pupil of Pythagoras, yet he would find a most powerful predisposition to truth and virtue, and there would be every thing to hope from the accuracy of his logic, the comprehensiveness of his views, and the beauty of his moral sentiments. But perhaps it will be explained, that the Philosopher does not mean to visit all these people in person; but that having first secured the source of influence, having taken entire possession of princes, nobility, gentry, and clergy, which he expects to do in a very short time, he will manage them like an electrical machine, to operate on the bulk of the community. Either way the achievement will be great and admirable; the latter event seems to have been predicted in that sibylline sentence, 'When the sky falls, we shall catch larks.'

LETTER V.

Melancholy Reflections—No Consolation amidst the mysterious Economy but in an Assurance that an infinitely good Being presides, and will at length open out a new moral World—Yet many moral Projectors are solicitous to keep their Schemes for the Amendment of the World clear of any reference to the Almighty—Even good Men are guilty of placing too much Dependence on subordinate Powers and Agents—The Representations in this Essay not intended to depreciate to nothing the Worth and Use of the whole Stock of Means, but to reduce them, and the Effects to be expected from them, to a sober Estimate—A humble Thing to be a Man—Inculcation of devout Submission, and Diligence, and Prayer—Sublime Quality, and indefinite Efficacy, of this last, as a Means—Conclusion; briefly marking out a few general Characters of Sentiment and Action to which, though very uncommon, the Epithet Romantic is unjustly applied.

This view of moral and philosophical projects, added to that of the limited exertion of energy which the Almighty has made to attend, as yet, the dispensation of the gospel, and accompanied with the consideration of the impotence of human efforts to make that dispensation efficacious where his will does not, forms a melancholy and awful account. In the hours of pensive thought, the serious observer, unless he can fully resign the condition of man to the infinite wisdom and goodness of his Creator, will feel an emotion of horror, as if standing on the verge of a hideous gulf, into which almost all the possibilities, and speculations, and efforts, and hopes, relating to the best improvements of mankind, are brought down in a long abortive series by the torrent of ages, to be lost in final despair.

To an atheist of enlarged sensibility, if that were a possible character, how gloomy, beyond all power of description, must be the long review, and the undefinable prospect, of this triumph of evil, unaccompanied, as it must appear to his thoughts, by any sublime, intelligent process, converting, in some manner unknown to mortals, this evil into good, either during the course, or in the result. A devout theist, when he becomes sad amidst his contemplations, recovers a solemn and submissive tranquillity, by reverting to his assurance of such a wise and omnipotent conduct. As a believer in revelation, he is consoled by the confidence both that this train of evils will be converted into good in the effect, and that the evil itself in this world will at a future period almost cease. He is persuaded that the Great Spirit, who presides over this mysterious scene, has yet an energy of operation in reserve to be unfolded on the earth, such as its inhabitants have never, except in a few momentary glimpses, beheld, and that when his kingdom comes, those powers will be manifested, to command the chaos of turbulent and malignant elements into a new moral world.

And is it not strange, my dear friend, to observe how carefully some philosophers, who deplore the condition of the world, and profess to expect its melioration, keep their speculations clear of every idea of Divine Interposition? No builders of houses or cities were ever more attentive to guard against the access of inundation or fire. If *He* should but touch their prospective theories of improvement, they would renounce them, as defiled, and fit only for vulgar fanaticism. Their system of providence would be profaned by the intrusion of the Almighty. Man is to effect an apotheosis for himself, by the hopeful process of exhausting his corruptions. And should it take all but an endless series of ages, vices, and woes, to reach this glorious attainment, patience may sustain itself the while by the thought that when it is realized, it will be burdened with no duty of religious gratitude. No time is too long to wait, no cost too deep to incur, for the triumph of proving that we have no need of that one attribute of a Divinity, which creates the grand interest in acknowledging such a Being, the benevolence that would make us happy. But even if this triumph should be found unattainable, the independence of spirit which has laboured for it, must not at last sink into piety. This afflicted world, 'this poor terrestrial citadel of man,' is to lock its gates, and keep its miseries, rather than admit the degradation of receiving help from God.

I wish it were not true, that even men who firmly believe in the general doctrine of the divine government of the world, are often betrayed into the impiety of attaching an excessive importance to human agency in its events. How easily a creature of their own species is transformed by a sympathetic pride into a god before them! If what they deem the cause of truth and justice, advances with a splendid front of distinguished names of legislators, or patriots, or military heroes, it must then and must therefore triumph; nothing can withstand such talents, accompanied by the zeal of so many faithful adherents. If these shining insects of fame are crushed, or sink into the despicable reptiles of corruption, alas, then, for the cause of truth and justice! All this while, there is no solemn reference to the 'Blessed and only Potentate.' If, however, the foundations of their religious faith have not been shaken, and they possess any docility to the lessons of time, they will after a while be taught to withdraw their dependence and confidence from all subordinate agents, and habitually regard the Supreme Being as the only power in the creation.

Perhaps it is not improbable, that the grand moral improvements of a future age may be accomplished in a manner that shall leave nothing to man but humility and grateful adoration. His pride so obstinately ascribes to himself whatever good is effected on the globe, that perhaps the Deity will evince his own interposition, by events as evidently independent of human power as the rising of the sun. It may be that some of them may take place in a manner but little connected even with human operation. Or if the activity of men shall be employed as the means of producing all of them, there will probably be as palpable a disproportion between the instruments and the events, as there was between the rod of Moses and the stupendous phenomena which followed its being stretched forth. No Israelite was foolish enough to ascribe to the rod the power that divided the sea; nor will the witnesses of the moral wonders to come attribute them to man.

I hope these extended observations will not appear like an attempt to exhibit the whole stock of means, as destitute of all value, and the industrious application of them as a labour without reward. It is not to depreciate a thing, if, in the attempt to ascertain its real magnitude, it is proved to be little. It is no injustice to mechanical powers, to say that slender machines will not move rocks and massive timbers; nor to chemical ones, to assert that though an earthquake may fling a promontory from its basis, the explosion of an ounce of gunpowder will not.—Between moral powers also, and the objects to which they are applied, there are eternal laws of proportion; and it would seem a most obvious principle of good sense, that an estimate moderately correct of the force of each of our means according to these laws, as far as they can be ascertained, should precede every application of them. Such an estimate has no place in a mind under the ascendency of imagination, which, therefore, by extravagantly magnifying its means, inflates its projects with hopes which may justly be called Romantic. The best corrective of such irrational expectation is an appeal to experience. There is an immense record of experiments, which will tell the power of almost all the engines, as worked by human hands, in the whole moral magazine. And if a man expects any one of them to produce a greater effect than ever before, it must be because the talents of him who repeats the trial, transcend those of all former experimenters, or else because the season is more auspicious.

The estimate of the power of means, obtained by the appeal to experience, is indeed most humiliating: but what then? It is a humble thing to be a man. The feebleness of means is, in fact, the feebleness of him that employs them; for the most inconsiderable means, when wielded by celestial powers, can produce the most stupendous effects. Till, then, the time shall arrive for us to assume a nobler rank of existence, we must be content to work on the present level of our nature, and effect that little which we can effect; unless it be greater magnanimity and piety to resolve that because our powers are limited to do only little things, they shall therefore, as if in revenge for such an economy, do nothing. Our means will do something; that something is what they were meant to effect in our hands, and not that something else which we all wish they would effect, and a visionary man presumes they will.

This disproportion between the powers and means which mortals are confined to wield, and the great objects which all good men would desire to accomplish, is a part of the appointments of Him who determined all the relations in the universe; and He will see to the consequences. For the present, he seems to say to his servants, 'Forbear to inquire why so small a part of those objects to which I have summoned your activity, is placed within the reach of your powers. Your feeble ability for action is not accompanied by such a capacity of understanding, as would be requisite to comprehend why that ability was made no greater. Even if it had been made incomparably greater, would there not still have been objects before it too vast for its operation? Must not the highest of created beings still have something in view, which they feel they can but partially accomplish till their powers are enlarged? Must there not be an end of improvement in my creation, if the powers of my creatures had become perfectly equal to the magnitude of their designs? How mean must be the spirit of that being that would not make an effort now, toward the accomplishment of something higher than he will be able to accomplish till hereafter. Because mightier labourers would have been requisite to effect all that you wish, will you therefore murmur that I have honoured you, the inferior ones, with the appointment of making a noble exertion? If there is but little power in *your* hands, is it not because I retain the power in *mine*? Are you afraid lest that power should fail to do all things right, only because *you* are so little made its instruments? Be grateful that *all* the work is not to be done without you, and that a God employs you in that in which he also is employed. But remember, that while the employment is yours, the success is altogether his; and that your diligence therefore, and not the effect which it produces, will be the test of yuor characters. Good men have been employed in all ages under the same economy of inadequate means, and what appeared to them inconsiderable success. Go to your labours: every sincere effort will infallibly be one step more in your own progress to a perfect state; and as to the Cause, when *I* see it necessary for a God to interpose in his own manner, I will come.'

I should deem a train of observations of the melancholy hue which shades some of the latter pages of this essay, useless, or perhaps even noxious, were I not convinced that a serious exhibition of the feebleness of human agency in relation to all great objects, might aggravate the impression, often so faint, of the absolute supremacy of God, of the total dependence of all mortal effort on him, and of the necessity of devoutly regarding his intervention at every moment. It might promote that last attainment of a zealously good man, the resignation to be as diminutive an agent as God pleases, and as unsuccessful a one. I am assured also that, in a pious mind, the humiliating estimate of means and human power, and the consequent sinking down of all lofty expectations founded on them, will leave one single means, and that far the best of all, to be held not only of undiminished but of more eminent value than ever was ascribed to it before. The noblest of all human means must be that which obtains the exertion of divine power. The means which, introducing no foreign agency, are applied directly and immediately to their objects, seem to bear such a defined proportion to those objects, as to assign and limit the probable effect. This strict proportion exists no longer, and therefore the possible effects become too great for calculation, when *that* expedient is solemnly employed, which is appointed as the means of engaging the divine energy to act on the object. If the only means by which Jehoshaphat sought to overcome his superior enemy, had been his troops, horses, and arms, the proportion between these means and the end would have been nearly assignable, and the probable result of the conflict a matter of ordinary calculation. But when he said, 'Neither know we what to do, but our eyes are up unto thee,' he moved (I speak it reverently) a new and infinite force to invade the host of Moab and Ammon; and the consequence displayed, in their camp, the difference between an irreligious leader, who could fight only with arms and on the level of the plain, and a pious one, who could thus assault from Heaven. It may not, I own, be perfectly correct, to cite, in illustration of the efficacy of prayer, the most wonderful ancient examples. Nor is it needful, since the experience of devout and eminently rational men, in latter times, has supplied a great number of striking instances of important advantages so connected with prayer, that they deemed them the evident result of it. This experience, taken in confirmation of the assurances of the Bible, warrants ample expectations of the efficacy of an earnest and habitual devotion;* provided still, as I need not remind you, that this means be employed as the grand auxiliary of the other means, and not alone, till all the rest are exhausted or impracticable. And I am convinced that every man, who, amidst his serious projects, is apprised of his dependence on God, as completely as that dependence is a fact, will be impelled to pray, and anxious to induce his serious friends to pray, almost every hour. He will as little, without it, promise himself any noble success, as a mariner would expect to reach a distant coast by having his sails spread in a stagnation of the air.—I have intimated my fear that it is visionary to expect an unusual success in the human administration of religion, unless there are unusual omens; now a most emphatical spirit of prayer would be such an omen; and the individual who should solemnly determine to try its last possible efficacy, might probably find himself becoming a much more prevailing agent in his little sphere. And if the whole, or the greater number, of the disciples of Christianity, were, with an earnest, unalterable resolution of each, to combine that heaven should not withhold one single influence which the very utmost effort of conspiring and persevering supplication would obtain, it would be the sign that a revolution of the world was at hand.

My dear friend, it is quite time to dismiss this whole subject; though it will probably appear to you that I have not entirely lost and forgotten the very purpose for which I took it up, which certainly was to examine the correctness of some not unusual applications of the epithet Romantic. It seemed necessary first to describe the characteristics of that extravagance which ought to be given up to the charge with some exemplifications. The attempt to do this, has led me into a length of detail far beyond all expectation. The intention was, next, to display and to vindicate, in an extended illustration, several schemes of life, and models of character; but I will not carry the subject any farther. I shall only just specify, in concluding, two or three of those points of character, on which the censure of being romantic has improperly fallen.

One is, a disposition to take high examples for imitation. I have condemned that extravagance, which presumes on the same career of action and success that has been the destiny of some individuals, so extraordinary as to be the most conspicuous phenomena of history. But this is a very different thing from the disposition to contemplate with emotion the class of men who have been illustrious for their excellence and their wisdom, to observe with deep attention the principles that animated them and the process of their attainments, and to keep them in view, as the standard of character. A man, may without a presumptious estimate of his talents, or the expectation of passing through any course of unexampled events, indulge the ambition to resemble and follow, in the essential determination of their characters, those sublime spirits who are now removed to the kingdom where they 'shine as the stars for ever and ever.'

A striking departure from the order of custom in that rank to which a man belongs, by devoting the privileges of that rank to a mode of excellence which the people who compose it never dreamed to be a duty, will by them be denominated Romantic. They will wonder why a man that ought to be just like themselves should affect quite a different style of life, should attempt unusual plans of doing good, should distaste the society of his class, and should put himself under some extraordinary discipline of virtue, though every point of his system may be the dictate of reason and conscience.

The irreligious will apply this epithet to the determination to make, and the zeal to inculcate, great exertions and sacrifices for a purely moral ideal reward. Some gross and palpable prize is requisite to excite their energies; and therefore self-denial repaid by conscience, beneficence, without fame, and the delight of resembling the Divinity, appear very visionary felicities.

The epithet will often be applied to a man who feels it an imperious duty, to realize, as far as possible, and as soon as possible, every thing which in theory he approves and applauds. You will often hear a circle of perhaps respectable persons agreeing entirely that this one is an excellent principle of action, and that other an amiable quality, and a third a sublime excellence, who would be amazed at your fanaticism if you were to adjure them thus: 'My friends, from this moment you are bound, from this moment we are all bound, on peril of the displeasure of God, to realize in ourselves, to the last possible extent, all that we have thus applauded.' Through some fatal defect of conscience, there is a very general feeling, regarding the high order of moral and religious attainments, that though it is a glorious and happy exaltation to possess them, yet it is perfectly safe to stop contented where we are. One is confounded to hear irritable persons applauding a character of self-command; persons who trifle away their days admiring the instances of a strenuous improvement of time; rich persons praising examples of extraordinary beneficence which they know far surpass themselves, though without larger means; and all expressing their deep respect for the men who have been most eminent for devotional habits;—and yet apparently with no consciousness that they are themselves placed in a solemn

* Here I shall not be misunderstood to believe the multitude of stories which have been told by deluded fancy, or detestable imposture.

election of henceforth striving in earnest to exemplify this very same pitch of character, or of being condemned in the day of Judgment.

Finally, in the application of this epithet, but little allowance is generally made for the very great difference between a man's entertaining high designs and hopes for himself alone, and his entertaining them relative to other persons. It may be very romantic for a man to promise himself to effect such designs upon others as it may be very reasonable to meditate for himself. If he feels the powerful, habitual impulse of conviction, prompting him to the highest attainments of wisdom and excellence, he may perhaps justly hope to approach them himself, though it would be most extravagant to extend the same hope to all the persons to whom he may try to impart the impulse. I specify the attainments of *wisdom* and *excellence*, because, to the distinction between the designs and hopes which a man might entertain for himself, and those which he might have respecting others, it is necessary to add a farther distinction as to the nature of those which he might entertain only for himself. His extraordinary plans and expectations for himself might be of such a nature as to depend on other persons for their accomplishment, and might therefore be as extravagant as if other persons alone had been their object. Or, on the contrary they may be of a kind which shall not need the co-operation of other persons, and may be realized independently of their will. The design of acquiring immense riches, or becoming the commander of an army, or the legislator of a nation, must in its progress be dependent on other beings besides the individual, in too many thousand points for a considerate man to presume that he shall be fortunate in them all. But the schemes of eminent personal attainments, not being dependent in any of these ways, are romantic only when there is some fatal intellectual or moral defect in the mind itself which has adopted them.

ESSAY IV.

ON SOME OF THE CAUSES BY WHICH EVANGELICAL RELIGION HAS BEEN RENDERED UNACCEPTABLE TO PERSONS OF CULTIVATED TASTE.

LETTER I.

Nature of the Displacency with which some of the most peculiar Features of Christianity are regarded by many cultivated Men who do not deny or doubt the Divine Authority of the Religion—Brief Notice of the Term Evangelical.

MY DEAR FRIEND,

While this life is passing so fast away, it is striking to observe the various forms of character in which men choose to spend this introductory season of their being, and to enter on its future greater stage. If some one of these forms is more eligible than all the rest for entering on that greater stage, a thoughtful man will surely wish for that to be his own; and to ascertain which it is, is the most important of all his inquiries. We, my friend, are persuaded that the inquiry, if serious, will soon terminate, and that the Christian character will be selected as the only one, in which it is wise to await the call into eternity. Indeed the assurance of our external existence itself rests but on that authority which dictates also the right introduction to it.

The Christian character is simply a conformity to the whole religion of Christ. But this implies a cordial admission of that whole religion; and it meets, on the contrary, in many minds not denying it to be a communication from God, a disposition to shrink from some of its peculiar distinctions, or to modify them. I am not now to learn that the substantial cause of this is that repugnance in human nature to what is purely divine, which revelation affirms, and all history proves, and which perhaps some of the humiliating points of the Christian system are more adapted to provoke, than any thing else that ever came from Heaven. Nor do I need to be told how much this chief cause has aided and aggravated the power of those subordinate ones, which may have conspired to prevent the success of evangelical religion among one class of persons; I mean persons of a refined taste, and whose feelings concerning what is great and excellent have been disciplined to accord to a literary or a philosophical standard. But even had there been less of this natural aversion in such minds, or had there been none, some of the causes which have acted on them, would, nevertheless, have tended, necessarily, as far they had any operation at all, to lessen the attraction of pure Christianity.—I wish to illustrate several of these causes, after briefly describing the anti-christian feelings in which I have observed their effect.

It is true that many persons of taste have, without any precise disbelief of the Christian truth, so little concern about religion in any form, that the unthinking dislike which they may occasionally feel to the evangelical principles hardly deserves to be described. These are to be assigned, whatever may be their faculties or improvements, to the numerous triflers, on whom we can pronounce only the general condemnation of irreligion, their feelings not being sufficiently marked for a more discriminative censure. But the aversion to the evangelical system is of a more defined character, as it exists in a mind too serious for the follies of the world and the neglect of all religion, and in which the very aversion becomes, at times, the subject of painful and apprehensive reflection, from a consciousness that it is an unhappy symptom, if that view of the subjects by which it is excited, has really the sanction of divine revelation. If a person of such a mind disclosed himself to you, he would describe how the elevated sentiment, inspired by the contemplation of other sublime subjects, is confounded, and sinks mortified into the heart, when this new subject is presented to his view. It seems to require almost a total change of his mental habits to admit this as the most interesting subject of all, while yet he dares not reject the authority which supports its claims. The dignity of religion, as a general and refined speculation, he may have long acknowledged ; but it appears to him as if it lost part of that dignity, in taking the specific form of the evangelical system ; just as if an ethereal being were reduced to combine his radiance and subtlety with an earthly nature. He is aware that religion in the abstract, or, in other words, the principles which constitute the obligatory relation of all intelligent creatures to the Supreme Being, must receive a special modification, by means of the addition of some other principles, in order to become a peculiar religious economy for a particular race of those creatures, especially for a little and a guilty race. And the Christian revelation assigns the principles by which this religion in the abstract, the religion of the universe, is thus modified into the peculiar form required for the nature and condition of man. But when he contemplates some of these principles, which do indeed place our nature and condition in a very humbling point of view, he can with difficulty avoid regretting that our relations with the Divinity should be fixed according to *such* an economy. The gospel appears to him like the image in Nebuchadnezzar's dream, refulgent indeed with a head of gold ; the sublime truths which are independent of every peculiar dispensation are luminously exhibited ; but the doctrines which are added as descriptive of the peculiar circumstances of the Christian economy, appear less splendid, and as if descending towards the qualities of iron and clay. In admitting this portion of the system as a part of the truth, his feelings amount to the wish that a different theory *had been true*. It is therefore with a degree of shrinking reluctance that he sometimes adverts to the ideas peculiar to the gospel. He would willingly lose this specific scheme of doctrines in a more general theory of religion, instead of resigning every wider speculation for this scheme, in which God has comprised, and distinguished by a very peculiar character, all the religion which he wills to be known, or to be useful, to our world. He would gladly evade the conviction that the gospel is so far from being merely one of the modes, or merely even the best of the modes, of religion, that it is, as to us, the comprehensive and exclusive mode ; insomuch that he who has not a religion concordant with the New Testament, is without a religion. He suffers himself to pass the year in a dissatisfied uncertainty, and a criminal neglect of deciding whether his cold reception of the specific views of Christianity will render unavailing his regard for those more general truths respecting the Deity, moral rectitude, and a future state, which are necessarily at the basis of the system. He is afraid to examine and determine the question, whether it will be safe to rest in a scheme composed of the general principles of wisdom and virtue, selected from the Christian oracles and the speculations of philosophy, harmonized by reason, and embellished by taste. If it were safe, he would much rather be the dignified professor of such a philosophic refinement of Christianity, than yield himself to be completely humbled into a submissive disciple of Jesus Christ. This refined system would be clear of the unwelcome peculiarities of Christian doctrine, and it would also allow some different ideas of the nature of moral excellence. He would not be so explicitly condemned for indulging a disposition, to admire and imitate some of those models of character, which, however opposite to pure Christian excellence, the world has always idolized.

I wish I could display in the most forcible manner, the considerations which show how far such a state of mind is wrong. But my object is, to remark on a few of the causes which may have contributed to it.

I do not, for a moment, place among these causes that continual dishonour which the religion of Christ has suffered through the corrupted institutions, and the depraved character of individuals or communities of what is called the Christian world. Such a man as I have supposed, understands what its tendency and dictates really are, so far at least that, in contemplating the bigotry, persecution, hypocrisy, and worldly ambition, which have stained, and continue to stain, the Christian history, his mind instantly dissevers by a decisive glance of thought, all these evils, and the pretended Christians who are accountable for them, from the religion which is as distinct from them as the Spirit that pervades all things is pure from matter and from sin. In his view, these odious things and these wicked men that have arrogated and defiled the Christian name, sink out of sight through a chasm, like Korah, Dathan, and Abiram, and leave the camp and the cause holy, though they leave the numbers small. It needs so very moderate a share of discernment, in a Protestant country at least, where a well-known volume exhibits the religion itself, genuine and entire as it came from heaven, to perceive the utter disconnexion and antipathy between it and all these abominations, that to take them as congenial and inseparable, betrays, in every instance, a detestable want of principle, or a pitiable want of sense. The defect of cordiality toward the religion of Christ, in the persons that I am accusing does not arise from this debility or this injustice. They would not be less equitable to Christianity than they would to some estimable man, whom they would not esteem the less because villains that hated him, knew, however, so well the excellence of his name and character, as gladly to employ them to aid their schemes, or to shelter their crimes.—But, indeed, these remarks are not strictly to the purpose ; since the prejudice which a weak or corrupt mind receives from such a view of the Christian history, operates, as we see by facts, not discriminatively against particular characteristics of Christianity, but against the whole system, and leads toward a denial of its divine origin. On the contrary, the class of persons now in question fully admit its divine authority, but feel a deep dislike to some of its most peculiar distinctions. These peculiarities they may wish, as I have said, to refine away ; but in moments of impartial seriousness, are constrained to admit the conviction, or something very near the conviction, of their being inseparable from the sacred economy. This however fails to subdue or conciliate the heart ; and the dislike to some of the parts has often an influence on the affections in regard to the whole. That portion of the system which they think they *could* admire, is admitted with the coldness of a mere speculative assent, from the intruding recollection of its being combined with something else which they cannot admire. Those distinctions from which they recoil, are chiefly comprised in that view of Christianity which, among a large proportion of the professors of it, is denominated, in a somewhat specific sense, Evangelical ; and therefore I have adopted this denomination in the title of this letter. Christianity, taken in this view, contains—a humiliating estimate of the moral condition of man, as a being radically corrupt—the doctrine of redemption from that condition by the merit and sufferings of Christ—the doctrine of a divine influence being necessary to transform the character of the human mind, in order to prepare it for a higher station in the universe—and a grand moral peculiarity by which it insists on humility, penitence, and a separation from the spirit and habits of the world.—I do not see any necessity for a more formal and amplified description of that mode of understanding

Christianity which has assumed the distinctive epithet Evangelical; and which is not, to say the least, more discriminatively designated among the scoffing part of the wits, critics and theologians of the day, by the terms Fanatical, Calvinistical, Methodistical.

I may here notice that, though the greater share of the injurious influences on which I may remark operates more pointedly against the peculiar *doctrines* of Christianity, yet some of them are fatally hostile to that *moral spirit* which is so essentially inherent that the religion must partly retain it, even when reduced as far as it can be toward the condition of a mere philosophical theory. And I would observe, finally, that though I have specified the more refined and intellectual class of minds, as indisposed to the religion of Christ by the causes to which I refer, and though I keep them chiefly in view, yet the influence of some of these causes extends to many persons of subordinate mental rank.

LETTER II.

One of the Causes of the Displacency is, that Christianity, being the Religion of a great Number of Persons of weak and uncultivated Minds, presents its Doctrines to the view of Men of Taste associated with the Characteristics of those Minds; and though some Parts of the Religion instantaneously redeem themselves from that Association by their philosophic Dignity, other Parts may require a considerable Effort to detatch them from it—This easily done if the Men of taste were powerfully pre-occupied and affected by the Religion—Reflections of one of them in this Case—But the Men of Taste now in question are not in this Case—Several Specific Causes of injurious Impression from this Association of Evangelical Doctrines and Sentiments with the intellectual Littleness of the Persons entertaining them—Their Deficiency and Dislike of all strictly intellectual Exercise on Religion—Their reducing the whole of Religion to one or two favourite Notions, and continually dwelling on them—The perfect Indifference of some of them to general Knowledge, even when not destitute of Means of acquiring it; and the consequent voluntary and contented Poverty of the irreligious Ideas and Language—Their Admiration of Things in a literary Sense utterly bad—Their Complacency in their Deficiencies—Their injudicious Habits and Ceremonies—their unfortunate Metaphors and Similes—Suggestion to religious Teachers that they should not run to its last possible Extent the Parallel between the Pleasures of Piety and those of Eating and Drinking—Mischief of such Practices—Effect of the ungracious Collision between uncultivated Seniors and a young Person of Literary and Philosophic Taste—Expostulation with this intellectual young Person, on the Folly and Guilt of suffering his Mind to take the Impression of Evangelical Religion from any Thing which he knows to be inferior to that Religion itself, as exhibited by the New Testament, and by the most elevated of its Disciples.

In the view of an intelligent and honest mind the religion of Christ stands as clear of all connexion with the corruption of men, and churches, and ages, as when it was first revealed. It retains its purity like Moses in Egypt, or Daniel in Babylon, or the Saviour of the world himself, while he mingled with scribes and pharisees, or publicans and sinners. But though it thus instantly and totally separates itself from all appearance of relation to the vices of bad men, a degree of effort may be required in order to display it, or to view it, in an equally perfect separation from the weakness of good ones. It is in *reality* no more *identified* with the one than with the other; its essential sublimity is as incapable of being reduced to littleness, as its purity is of uniting with vice. But it may have a vital connexion with a weak mind, while it necessarily disowns a wicked one; and the qualities of that mind with which it confessedly unites itself, will much more seem to adhere to it, than of that with which all its principles plainly in antipathy. It will be more natural to take those persons who are acknowledged the real subjects of its influence as illustrations as its nature, than those on whom it is the heaviest reproach that they pretend to be its friends. The perception of its nature and dignity must be very vivid, in the man who can observe it in its state of intimate combination with the thoughts, affections, and language of its disciples, without losing sight for one moment of its essential qualities and lustre. No possible associations indeed can diminish the grandeur of some parts of the Christian system. The doctrine of immortality, for instance, cannot be reduced to take even a transient appearance of littleness, by the meanest or most uncouth words and images that shall ever be employed to represent it. But there are some other points of the system which have not the same obvious philosophic sublimity. And these principles are capable of acquiring, from the mental defects of their believers, such associations as will give a character very different from our common ideas of sublimity to so much as they constitute of the evangelical economy. One of the causes, therefore, which I meant to notice, as having excited in persons of taste a sentiment unfavourable to the reception of evangelical religion, is that this is the religion of many weak and uncultivated minds.

The schools of philosophy have been composed of men of superior faculties and extensive accomplishments, who could sustain, by eloquence and capacious thought, the dignity of the favourite themes; so that the proud distinctions of the disciples and advocates appeared as the attributes of the doctrines. The adepts could attract refined and aspiring spirits, by proclaiming that the temple of *their* goddess was not profaned by being a rendezvous for vulgar men. On the contrary, it is the beneficent distinction of the gospel, that notwithstanding it is of a magnitude to interest and to surpass angelic investigation, (and therefore assuredly to pour contempt on the pride of human intelligence that rejects it for its *meanness*,) it is yet most expressly sent to the class which philosophers have always despised. And a good man feels it a cause of grateful joy, that a communication has come from heaven, adapted to effect the happiness of multitudes, in spite of natural debility or neglected education. He is grateful to him who has 'hidden these things from the wise and prudent, and revealed them to babes,' while he observes that confined capacities do not preclude the entrance, and the permanent residence, of that sacred combination of truth and power, which finds no place in the minds of many philosophers, and wits, and statesmen. But it is not to be denied that the natural con sequence follows. Contracted and obscure in its abode, the inhabitant will appear, as the sun through a misty sky, with but little of its magnificence, to a man who can be content to receive his impression of the intellectual character of the religion from the mode of its manifestation from the minds of its disciples; and in doing so, can indolently and perversely allow himself to regard the weakest mode of its displaying itself, as its truest image. In taking such a dwelling, the religion seems to imitate what was prophesied of its author, that, when he should be seen, there would be no beauty that he should be desired. This humiliation is inevitable; for unless miracles are wrought, to impart to the less intellectual disciples an enlarged power of thinking, the evangelic truth must accommodate itself to the dimensions and unrefined habitudes of their minds. And perhaps the exhibitions of it will come forth with more of the character of those minds, than of its own celestial distinctions: insomuch that if there were no declaration of the sacred system, but in the forms of conception and language in which they declare it, even a candid man might hesitate to admit it as the most glorious gift of Heaven. Happily, he finds its quality declared by other oracles; but while from them he receives it in his own character, he is tempted to wish he could detach it from all the associations which he feels it has acquired from the humbler exhibition. And he does not greatly wonder that other men of the same intellectual habits, and with a less candid and profound solicitude to receive with simplicity every thing that really comes from God, should have admitted an injurious impression from these associations.

They would not make this impression on a man already devoted to the reign of Jesus Christ. No passion that has become predominant is ever cooled by any thing which can be associated with its object, while that object itself continues unaltered. The passion is even willing to verify its power, and the merit of that which interests it, by sometimes letting the unpleasing associations surround and touch the object for an instant, and then chasing them away; and it welcomes with augmented attachment that object coming forth from them unstained; as happy spirits at the last day will receive with joy their bodies recovered from the dust in a state of purity that will leave every thing belonging to the dust behind. A zealous Christian exults to feel in contempt of how many counteracting circumstances he can still love his religion; and that this counteraction, by exciting his understanding to make a more defined estimate of its excellence, has but made him love it the more. It has now pre-occupied even those avenues of taste and imagination, by which alone the ungracious effect of associations could have been admitted. The thing itself is close to his mind, and therefore the causes which would have misrepresented it, by coming between, have lost their power. As he hears the sentiments of sincere Christianity from the weak and illiterate, he says to himself—All this is indeed little, but I am happy to feel that the subject itself is great, and that this humble display of it cannot make it appear to me, different from what I absolutely know it to be; any more than a clouded atmosphere can diminish my impression of the grandeur of the heavens, after I have so often beheld the pure azure, and the host of stars. I am glad that it has in this man all the consolatory and all the purifying efficacy, which I wish that my more elevated views of it may not fail to have in me. This is the chief end for which a divine communication can have been granted to the world. If this religion, instead of being designed to make its disciples pure and happy amidst their littleness, had required to receive lustre from their mental dignity, it would have been sent to none of us. At least, not to me; for though I would be grateful for an order of ideas somewhat superior to those of my uncultivated fellow Christian, I am conscious that the noblest forms of thought in which I apprehend, or could represent, the subject, do but contract its amplitude, do but depress its sublimity. Those superior spirits who are said to rejoice over the first proof of the efficacy of divine truth, have rejoiced over its introduction, even in so humble a form, into the mind of this man, and probably see in fact but little difference, in point of speculative greatness, between his manner of viewing and illustrating it and mine. If Jesus Christ could be on earth as before, he would receive this disciple, and benignantly approve, for its operation on the heart, that faith in his doctrines, which men of taste might be tempted to despise for its want of intellectual refinement And since all his true disciples are destined to attain greatness at length, the time is coming, when each pious though now contracted mind will do justice to this high subject. Meanwhile, such as this subject will appear to the intelligence of immortals, and such as it will be expressed in their eloquence, such it really is now; and I should deplore the perversity of my mind, if I felt more disposed to take the character of the religion from that style of its exhibition in which it appears humiliated, than from that in which I am assured it will be sublime. If while we are all advancing to meet the revelations of eternity, I have a more vivid and comprehensive idea than these less privileged Christians, of the glory of our religion, as displayed in the New Testament, and if I can much more delightfully participate the sentiments which devout genius has uttered in the contemplation of it, I am therefore called upon to excel them as much in devotedness to this religion, as I have a more luminous view of its excellence.

Let the spirit of the evangelical system once gain the ascendency, and it may thus defy the impressions tending to associate disagreeable ideas with its principles; as the angels in the house of Lot forced away the unworthy assailants. But it requires a most extraordinary energy of conviction to obtain a cordial reception for these principles, if such impressions have pre-occupied the mind. And that they should thus have pre-occupied the man of taste, is not wonderful, if you consider how early, how often, and by what diversities of the same general cause, they may have been made on him. As the gospel comprises an ample assemblage of intellectual views, and as the greater number of Christians are inevitably disqualified to do justice to them, even in any degree, by the same causes which disqualify them to do justice to other intellectual subjects, it is not improbable, that the greater number of expressions which he has heard in his whole life, have been utterly below the subject. Obviously this is a very serious circumstance; for if he had heard as much spoken on any other intellectual subject, as, for instance, poetry, or astronomy, for which perhaps he has a passion, and if a similar proportion of what he had heard had been as much below the subject, he would probably have acquired but little partiality for either of those studies. And it is a very melancholy disposition against the human heart, that the gospel needs fewer unfavourable associations to become repulsive in it, than any other important subject.

The injurious impressions have perhaps struck his mind in many ways. For instance, he has met with some zealous Christians, who not only were very slightly acquainted with the evidences of the truth, and the illustrations of the reasonableness, of their religion, but who actually felt no interest in the inquiry. Perhaps more than one individual attempted to deter him from pursuing it, by suggesting that inquiry either implies doubt, which was pronounced a criminal state of mind, or will probably lead to it, as a judgment on the profane curiosity which, on such a subject, was not satisfied with implicitly believing. It was thought that an attempt to examine the foundation would be likely to end in a wish to demolish the structure.

He may sometimes have heard the discourse of sincere Christians, whose religion involved no intellectual exercise, and, strictly speaking, no *subject* of intellect. Separately from their feelings, it had no definition, no topics, no distinct succession of views. And if he or some other person attempted to talk on some part of the religion *itself*, as a thing definable and important, independently of the feelings of any individual, and as consisting in a vast congeries of ideas, relating to the divine government of the world, to the general nature of the economy disclosed by the Messiah, to the distinct doctrines in the theory of that economy, to moral principles, and to the greatness of the future prospects of man,—they seemed to have no concern in *that* religion, and impatiently interrupted the subject with the observation—That is not experience.

Others he has heard continually recurring to two or three points of opinion, selected perhaps in conformity to a system, or perhaps in consequence of some casual direction of the individual's thoughts, and asserted to be the life and essence of Christianity. These opinions he has heard zealously though not argumentatively defended, even when they were not attacked or questioned. If they *were* called in question, it was an evidence not less of depraved principle than of perverted judgment. All other religious truths were represented as deriving their authority and importance purely from these, and indeed as deriving so little authority and importance, that it was almost needless ever to advert to them. The neglect of constantly repeating and enforcing these opinions was said to be the chief cause of the melancholy failure attending the efforts to promote Christianity in the world, and of the decay of particular religious societies. Though he could not perceive how these points were essential to Christianity, even admitting them to be true, they were made the sole and decisive standard for distinguishing between a genuine and a false profession of it. And perhaps they were abruptly applied in eager haste to any sentiment which *he* happened to express concerning religion, as a test of its quality, and a proof of its corruptness.

In some instances, he may have observed some one idea or doctrine, though not especially sanctioned by any system, to have so monopolized the mind, that every conversation, from whatever point of the compass it started, was certain to find its way to the favourite topic, while he was sometimes fretted, sometimes amused, and never much improved, by observing its progress to the appointed place. If his situation and connexions rendered it unavoidable for him often to hear this unfortunate manner of discoursing on religion, his mind probably fell into a fault very similar to that of his well-meaning acquaintance. As this worthy man could never speak on the subject without soon bringing the whole of it down to one particular point, so the more refined and intellectual listener became unable to think on the subject without adverting immediately to the narrow illustration of it exhibited by this one man. In consequence of this connexion of ideas, he perhaps felt disinclined to think on the subject at all; or, if he was disposed or constrained to think of it, he was so averse to let his views of Christianity thus converge to the littleness of a point, that he laboured to expand them, till they lost all specifically evangelical distinctions in the wildness of generality and abstraction.

Again—the majority of Christians are precluded, by their condition in life, from any acquirement of general knowledge. It would be unpardonable in this more cultivated man, not to make the allowance for the natural effect of this circumstance on the extent of their religious ideas. But he has met with numbers, who had no inconsiderable means, both as to money, judging by their unnecessary expenses, and as to leisure, judging by the quantity of time consumed in useless chat, or in needless sleep, to furnish their minds with various information, but who were quite on a level, in this respect, with those of the humblest rank. They never even suspected that knowledge could have any connexion with religion; or that they could not be as clearly and amply in possession of the great subject as a man whose faculties had been exercised, and whose extended acquaintance with things would supply an endless series of ideas illustrative of religion. He has perhaps even heard them make a kind of merit of their indifference to knowledge, as if it were the proof or the result of a higher value for religion. If a hint of wonder was insinuated at their reading so little, and within so very confined a scope, it would be replied, that they thought it enough to read the Bible; as if it were possible for a person whose mind fixes with inquisitive attention on what is before him, even to read through the Bible without thousands of such questions being started in his thoughts as can be answered only from sources of information extraneous to the Bible. But he perceived that this reading the Bible was no work of inquisitive thought; and indeed he has commonly found that those who have no wish for any thing like a general improvement in knowledge, have no disposition for the real business of thinking even in religion, and that their discourse on that subject is the exposure of intellectual poverty. He has seen them live on for a number of years content with the same confined views, the same meagre list of topics, and the same uncouth religious language. In so inconsiderable a space of time, the diligent investigation of truth would have given much more clearness to their faculties, and much more precision to the articles of their belief. They might have ramified the few leading articles, into a rich diversity of subordinate principles and important inferences. They might have learned to place the Christian truth in all those combinations with the other parts of our knowledge, by which it is enabled to present new and striking aspects, and to multiply its arguments to the understanding, and its appeals to the heart. They might have rendered nature, history, and the present views of the moral world, tributary to the illustration and the effect of their religion. But they neglected, and even despised, all these means of enlarging their ideas of a subject which they professed to hold of infinite importance. Yet, perhaps, if this man of more intellectual habits showed but little interest in conversing with them on that subject, or seemed designedly to avoid it, this was considered as pure aversion to religion; and what had been uninteresting to him as a doctrine, then became revolting as reproof.*

He may not unfrequently have heard worthy but illiterate persons expressing their utmost admiration of saying, passages in books, or public discourses, which he could not help perceiving to be hardly sense, or to be the dictates of conceit, or to be common-place inflated to fustian. While, on the other hand, if he has introduced a favourite passage, or an admired book, they have perhaps shown no perception of its beauty, or expressed a doubt of its tendency, from its not being in canonical diction. Or, perhaps they have directly avowed that they could not understand it, in a manner that very plainly implied that *therefore* it was of no value. Possibly when he has expressed his high admiration of some of the views of the gospel, such, for instance, as struck the mind of Rousseau, he has been mortified to find that some sublime distinctions of the religion of Christ are lost to many of his disciples, from being of too abstract a kind for the apprehension of any but improved and reflective men.

If he had generally found in those professed Christians whose intellectual powers and attainments were small, a candid humility, instructing them, while expressing their animated gratitude for what acquaintance with religion they had been able to attain, and for the immortal hopes springing from it, to feel that they had but a confined view of the subject which is of immense variety and magnitude, he would have been too much pleased by this amiable feeling, to be much repelled by the defective character of their conceptions and expressions. But often, on the contrary, he has observed such a complacent sense of sufficiency in the little sphere, as if it self-evidently comprised every thing which it is possible, or which it is of consequence, for any mind to see in the Christian religion. They were like persons who should doubt the information that an infinitely greater number of stars can be seen through a telescope than they ever beheld, and who should have no curiosity to try.

Many Christians may have appeared to him to attach an extremely disproportionate importance to the precise *modes* of religious observances, not only in the hour of controversy respecting them, when they are always extravagantly magnified, but in the habitual course of their religious references. These modes may be either such as are adhered to by whole communities of Christians, perhaps as their respective marks of distinction from one another; of any smaller ceremonial peculiarities, devised and pleaded for by particular individuals or families.

The religious habit of some Christians may have disgusted him excessively. Every thing which could even distantly remind him of grimace, would inevitably do this; as, for instance, a solemn lifting up of the eyes,

* I own that what I said of Jesus Christ's gladly receiving one of the humbler intellectual order for his disciple, will but ill apply to some of the characters that I describe.

artificial impulse of the breath, grotesque and regulated gestures and postures in religious exercises, an affected faltering of the voice, and, I might add, abrupt religious exclamations in common discourse, though they were even benedictions to the Almighty, which he has often heard so ill-timed as to have an irreverent and almost a ludicrous effect. In a mind such as I am supposing, the happiest improvement in point of veneration for genuine religion will produce no tolerance still for such habits. Nor will the dislike to them be lessened by ever so perfect a conviction of the sincere piety of any of the persons who have fallen into them.

In the conversation of illiterate Christians he has perhaps frequently heard the most unfortunate metaphors and similes, employed to explain or enforce evangelical sentiments ; and probably, if he twenty times recollected one of those sentiments, or if he heard a similar one from some other quarter, the repulsive figure was sure to recur to his imagination. If he has heard so many of these, that each Christian topic has acquired its appropriate images, you can easily conceive what a lively perception of the importance of the subject itself must be requisite to overcome the disgust and banish the associations. The feeling accompanying these topics, as connected with these ideas, will be somewhat like that which spoils the pleasure of reading a noble poet, Virgil, for instance, when each admired passage recalls the images into which it has been degraded in that kind of imitation denominated *travesty*. It may be added, that the reluctance to think of the subject because it is connected with these ideas, strengthens that connexion. For often the earnest wish not to dwell on the disagreeable images, produces a mischievous reaction by which they press in more forcibly. The tenacity with which ideas adhere to the mind, is in proportion to the degree of interest, whether pleasing or unpleasing, which accompanies them ; and an idea cannot well be accompanied by a stronger kind of interest than the earnest wish to escape from it. If we could cease to dislike it, it would soon cease to haunt us. It may also be observed, that the infrequency of thinking upon the evangelical subjects, will confirm the injurious associations. The same mental law operates in regard to subjects as to persons. If any unfortunate incident, or any circumstance of expression or conduct, displeased us in our first meeting with a person, it will be strongly recalled each subsequent time that we see him, if we meet him but seldom ; on the contrary, if our intercourse with a person becomes frequent or habitual, such a first unpleasing circumstance, and many following ones may be forgotten. This observation might be of some use to a man that really wishes to dissolve in his mind the connexion between evangelical subjects and such disagreeable ideas ; as he will perceive that one of the most effectual means would be, to make those subjects familiar by often thinking on them.

While remarking on the effect of unpleasing images employed to illustrate Christian principles, I cannot help wishing that religious teachers were aware of the propriety of not amplifying the less dignified class of those metaphors which it may be proper enough sometimes to introduce, and which perhaps are employed, in a short and transient way in the Bible. I shall notice only that common one in which the benefits and pleasures of religion are represented under the image of food. I do not recollect that, in the New Testament at least, this metaphor is ever drawn to a great length. But from the facility of the process, it is not strange that it has been amplified both in books and discourses into the most extended descriptions ; and the dining-room has been exhausted of images, and the language ransacked for substantives and adjectives, to stimulate the spiritual palate. The metaphor is combined with so many terms in our language, that it will sometimes unavoidably occur ; and when employed in the simplest and shortest form, it may, by transiently suggesting the analogy, assist the thought without lessening the subject. But it is degrading to spiritual ideas to be extensively and systematically transmuted, I might say *cooked*, into sensual ones. The analogy between meaner things and dignified ones should never be pursued farther than one or two points of necessary illustration ; for if it is traced to every circumstance in which a resemblance can be found or fancied, the meaner thing no longer serves the humble and useful purpose of merely illustrating some qualities of the great one, but becomes formally its representative and equal. By their being made to touch at all points, the meaner is constituted a scale to measure and to limit the magnitude of the superior, and thus the importance of the one shrinks to the insignificence of the other. It will take some time for a man to recover any great degree of solemnity in thinking on the delights or the supports of religion, after he has seen them reduced into all the forms of eating and drinking. In such detailed analogies it often happens, that the most fanciful, or that the coarsest points of the resemblance, remain longest in the thoughts. When the mind has been taught to descend to a low manner of considering divine truth, it will easily descend to the lowest. There is no such violent tendency to abstraction and sublimity in the minds of the generality of readers and hearers, as to render it necessary to take any great pains for the purpose of retaining their ideas in some small degree of alliance with matter.

The preceding pages are a short description of some of the prominent circumstances of repellency, which are connected with evangelical religion by means of its uncultivated and injudicious professors ; and more might have been added. After such a description, it would be unjust not to observe that some Christians, of a subordinate intellectual order, are distinguished by such an unassuming simplicity, by so much refinement of conscience, and by a piety so fervent and even exalted, that it would imply a very perverted state of mind in a cultivated man, if these examples did not operate, notwithstanding the confined scope of their ideas, to attract him toward the faith which renders them so happy and excellent, rather than to repel him from it. But I am *supposing* his mind to be in a perverted state, and am far from the impiety of defending him. This supposition, however, being made, I feel no surprise, on surveying the majority of the persons composing evangelical communities, that this man has acquired an accumulation of prejudices against some of the distinguishing features of the gospel. Permitting himself to feel as if the circumstances which thus diminish or distort an order of Christian sentiments, were inseparable from it, he is inclined to regret that there should be any divine sanctions against his framing for himself, on the foundation of those principles in Christianity which he cannot but admire, but with a qualifying intermixture of foreign elements, a more liberalized scheme of religion.

It was especially unfortunate if, in the advanced stage of this man's perhaps highly cultivated youth, while he was exulting in the conscious enlargement of intellect, and the quickening and vivid perceptiveness of taste, but was still to be regarded as in a degree the subject of *education*, it was his lot to have the principles of religion exhibited and inculcated in a repulsive language and cast of thought by the seniors of his family or acquaintance. In that case, the unavoidable frequency of intercouse must have rendered the counteractive operation of the unpleasing circumstances, associated with Christian truth, almost incessant. And it would naturally become continually stronger. For each repetition of that which offended his refined intellectual habits, would incite him to value and cherish them the more, and to cultivate them according to a standard still more foreign from all congeniality with his instructers. These habits he began and continued to acquire from books of elegant sentiment or philosophical research, which he read in disregard of the advice, perhaps, to read scarcely any but works specifically religious. To such studies he has again and again returned with an animated rebound from systematic common-places, whether delivered in private or in public instruction ; and has felt the full contrast between the force, lustre, and mental richness, accompanying the moral speculations or poetical visions of genius, and the manner in which the truths of the gospel had been conveyed. He was not serious and honest enough to make, when in retirement, any deliberate trial of abstracting these truths from the shape in which they were thus unhappily set forth, in order to see what they would appear in a better. He could easily have transferred them into this better form ; or, at least, if he could not, he had but a very small portion of that mental 'superiority' of which he was congratulating himself that his disgusts were an evidence. But his sense of the duty of doing this was perhaps less cogent, from his perceiving that the evangelical doctrines were inculcated by his relatives with no less deficiency of the means of proving them true, than of rendering them interesting ; and he could easily discern that his instructers had received the articles of their faith implicitly from a class of teachers, or a religious community, without even a subsequent exercise of reasoning to confirm what they had thus adopted. They believed these articles through the habit of hearing them, and maintained them by the habit of believing them. The recoil of his feelings, therefore, did not alarm his conscience with the conviction of its being absolutely the truth of God, that, under this uninviting form, he was reluctant to embrace. Unaided by such a conviction already existing in him, and unarmed with a force of argument sufficient to impress it, the seriousness, perhaps sometimes harsh seriousness, of his friends, incessantly asserting his mind to be in a fatal condition, till he should think and feel exactly as they did, was little likely to conciliate his repugnance. When sometimes their admonitions took the mild or pathetic tone, his respect for their piety, and his gratitude for their affectionate solicitude, had perhaps a momentary effect to make him earnestly wish he could abdicate every intellectual refinement, and adopt in pious simplicity all their feelings and ideas. But as the contracted views, the rude figures, and the mixture of systematic and illiterate language, recurred, his mind would again revolt, and compel him to say, They cannot, will not, be my mode of religion.

Now, one wishes there had been some enlightened friend to say to such a man, Why will you not understand that there is no necessity for this to be the *mode* of your religion ? By what want of acuteness do you fail to distinguish between the mode, (a mere extrinsic and casual mode,) and the substance ? In the world of nature you see the same simple elements wrought into the plainest and most beautiful, into the most diminutive and the most majestic forms. So the same simple principles of Christian truth may constitute the basis of a very inferior, or a very noble, order of ideas. The principles themselves have an invariable quality ; but they were not imparted to man to be fixed in the mind as so many bare scientific propositions, each confined to one single mode of conception, without any collateral ideas, and to be always expressed in one unalterable form of words. They are placed there in order to spread out, if I might so express it, into a great multitude and diversity of ideas and feelings. These ideas and feelings, forming round the pure, simple principles, will correspond, and will make those principles seem to correspond, to the meaner or more dignified intellectual rank of the mind. Why will you not perceive that the subject which takes so humble a style in its less intellectual believers, unfolds greater proportions through a gradation of larger and still larger faculties, and with facility occupies the whole capacity of the amplest, in the same manner as the ocean fills a gulf as easily as a creek ? Through this series it retains an identity of its essential principles, and appears progressively a nobler thing only by gaining a position for more nobly displaying itself. Why will you not follow it through this gradation, till it reach the point where it is presented in a greatness of character, to correspond with the improved state of your mind ? Never fear lest the gospel should prove not sublime enough for the elevation of your thoughts. If you could attain an intellectual eminence from which you would look with pity on the rank which you at present hold, you would still find the dignity of this subject occupying your level, and rising above it. Do you doubt this ? What then do you think of such spirits, for instance, as those of Milton and Pascal ? And by how many degrees of the intellectual scale shall yours surpass them, to authorize your feeling that to be little which they felt to be great ? They were often conscious of the magnificence of Christian truth filling, distending, and exceeding, their faculties, and sometimes wished for greater powers to do it justice. In their noblest contemplations, they did not feel their minds elevating the subject, but the subject elevating their minds. Now, consider that their views of the gospel were, in essence, the same with those of its meanest sincere disciples ; and that therefore many sentiments which, by their unhappy form have disgusted you so much, bore a faithful though humble analogy to the ideas of these sublime Christians. Why then, while hearing such sentiments, have you not learnt the habit of darting upward, by means of this analogy, to the noblest style of the subject, instead of abandoning the subject itself in the recoil from the unfortunate mode of presenting it ? Have you not cause to fear that your dislike goes deeper than the mode of its appearance ? For, else, would you not anxiously seek, and rejoice to meet the divine subject in that lustre of array, that transfiguration of aspect, by which its grandeur is thus redeemed ?

I would make a solemn appeal to the understanding and the conscience of such a man. I would say to him, Is it among the excellences of a mind of taste, that it loses, when the religion of Christ is concerned, all the value of its discrimination ? Do you not absolutely know that the littleness which you see investing that religion is adventitious ? Are you not certain that in hearing the discourse of such men, if they were now to be found, as those that I have named, the evangelical truths would appear to you most sublime, and that they cannot be less noble in fact than they would appear as displayed from those minds ? But even suppose that *they* also failed, and that all modern Christians, without exception, had conspired to give an unimpressive aspect to the subject of their profession, do you never read the New Testament ? If you do, is it in that state of susceptible seriousness, without which you will have no just perception of its character ; without which you are but like an ignorant clown who, happening to look at the heavens, perceives nothing more awful in that wilderness of suns than in the row of lamps along the streets ? If you do read that book in the better state of feeling, I have no comprehension of the mechanism of your mind, if the first perception would not be that of a simple venerable dignity, and if the second would not be that of a certain abstract, undefinable magnificence ; a perception of something which, behind this simplicity, expands into a greatness beyond the compass of your mind ; an impression like that with which a thoughtful man would have looked on the countenance of Newton, after he had published his discoveries, feeling a kind of mystical absorption in the attempt to comprehend the magnitude of the soul residing within that form. When in this state of serious susceptibility, have you not also perceived, in the character and the manner of the first apostles of this truth, while they were declaring it, an expression of dignity, altogether different from that of other distinguished men, and much more refined and heavenly? If you examined the cause, you perceived that the dignity arose partly from their being employed as living oracles of this truth, and still more from their whole characters being pervaded by its spirit. And have you not been sometimes conscious, for a moment, that if it possessed your soul in the same manner as it did theirs, it would make you one of the most elevated of mortals? You would then display a combination of sanctity, devotion, disinterestedness, superiority to external things, energy, and exulting hope, in comparison of which the ambition of a conqueror, or the pride of a self-admiring philosopher, would be a very vulgar kind of dignity. You acknowledge these representations to be just; you allow that the kind of sublimity which you have sometimes perceived in the New Testament, that the qualities of the apostolic spirit, and that the intellectual and moral greatness of some modern Christians, express the genuine character of the evangelical religion, and therefore evince its dignity. But then, is it not most disingenuous in you to allow the meanness which you know to be but associated and separable, to be admitted by your own mind as an excuse for its alienation from what is acknowledged to be the very contrary of meanness? Ought you not to turn on yourself, with indignation at that want of rectitude which resigns you to the effect of these associations, or with contempt of the debility which tries in vain to break them? Is it for *you* to be offended at the mental weakness of Christians? you, whose intellectual vigour, and whose sense of justice, but leave you to sink helpless in the fastidiousness of sickly taste, and to lament that so many inferior spirits have been consoled and saved by this divine faith as to make it impossible for you to embrace it, even though your own salvation depend on it? At the very same time perhaps this weakness takes the form of pride. Let that pride speak out; it would be curious to hear it say, that your mental refinement perhaps *might* have permitted you to take your ground on that eminence of the Christian faith where Milton and Pascal stood, *if* so many humbler beings did not disgrace it, by occupying the declivity and the vale.

But, after all, what need of referring to illustrious names, as if the claims of that which you acknowledge to be from heaven should be made to depend on the number of those who have received it gracefully; or, as if a rational being could calmly wait for his taste to be conciliated, before he would embrace a system by which his immortal interest is to be secured? Is the difference, as declared by the Supreme Authority, between the consequences of cordially receiving or not receiving the evangelical system so small, that a solemn contemplation of it would not overwhelm you with wonder and mortification that so subordinate a counteraction could so long have made you unjust to yourself? And if you avoid this contemplation, will therefore the difference, and the ultimate loss, prove the less serious because you would not exercise thought enough to anticipate it? If the consequence should prove to be inexpressibly disastrous, will a perversity of refinement appear a worthy cause for which to have incurred it? You deserve to be disgusted with a divine communication, and to lose its inestimable benefits, if you can thus let every thing have a greater influence on your feelings concerning it than its truth and importance, and if its accidental and separable associations with littleness, can counteract its essential inseparable ones with the Governor and Redeemer of the world, with happiness, and with eternity. With what compassion you might be justly regarded by an illiterate but zealous Christian, whose interest in the truths of the New Testament at once constitutes the best felicity here, and carries him rapidly toward the kingdom of his Father; while you are standing aloof, and perhaps thinking, that if he and all such as he were dead, you might, after a while, acquire the spirit which should impel you also toward heaven. But why do you not feel your individual concern in this great subject as absolutely as if all men were dead, and you heard alone in the earth the voice of God; or, as if you saw, like the solitary exile of Patmos, an awful appearance of Jesus Christ, and the visions of hereafter? What is it to you that many Christians have given an aspect of littleness to the gospel, or that a few have displayed it in majesty?

LETTER III.

Another Cause the Peculiarity of Language adopted in religious Discourse and Writing—Classical Standard of Language—The theological Deviation from it barbarous—Surprise and Perplexity of a sensible heathen Foreigner, who, having learnt our Language according to its best Standard alone, should be introduced to hear a public evangelical Discourse—Distinctive Characters of this Theological Dialect—Reasons against employing it—Competence of our Language to express all religious Ideas without the aid of this uncouth Peculiarity—Advantages that would attend the Use of the Language of mere general Intelligence, with the addition of an extremely small Number of Words that may be considered as necessary technical Terms in Theology.

Another cause which I think has tended to render evangelical religion less acceptable to persons of taste, is the *peculiarity of language* adopted in the discourses and books of its teachers, as well as in the religious correspondence and conversation of Christians. I do not refer to any past age, when an excessive quaintness deformed the style of composition, both on religion and all other subjects: my assertion is respecting the diction at present in use.

The works collectively of the best writers in the language have created and substantially fixed a standard of general phraseology. If any department is exempted from the authority of this standard, it is the low one of humour and buffoonery, in which the writer may coin and fashion phrases according to his whim. But in the language of higher, and of what may be called middle subjects, that authority is the law. It does indeed allow indefinite varieties of what is called style, since twenty pure and able writers might be cited, who have had each a different style; but yet there is a certain general character of expression which they have mainly concurred to establish. This compound result of all their modes of writing is become sanctioned as the classical manner of employing the language, as the form in which it constitutes the most pure general vehicle of thought. And, though it is difficult to define this standard, yet a well-read person of taste instantly feels when it is transgressed or deserted, and pronounces that no classical writer has employed that phrase or would have combined those words in such a manner.

Now the deviations from this standard must be, first, by mean or vulgar diction, which is below it; or, secondly, by a barbarous diction, which is *out* of it, or foreign to it; or, thirdly, by a diction which, though foreign to it, is yet not to be termed barbarous, because it is elevated entirely above the authority of the standard, by a super-human force or majesty of thought, or a super-human communication of truth.

I might make some charge against the language of divines under the first of these distinctions; but my present attention is to what seems to me to come under the second character of difference from the standard, that of being barbarous. The phrases peculiar to any trade, profession, or fraternity, are barbarous, if they were not low: they are commonly both. The language of law is felt by every one to be barbarous in the extreme, not only by the huge lumber of its technical terms, but by its very structure, in such parts of it as do not consist of technical terms. The language of science is barbarous, as far as it differs arbitrarily, and in more than the use of those terms which are indispensable to the science, from the pure general model. And I am afraid that, on the same principle, the accustomed diction of evangelical religion also must be pronounced barbarous. For I suppose it will be instantly allowed, that the mode of expression of the greater number of evangelical divines,* and of those taught by them, is widely different from the standard of general language, not only by the necessary adoption of some peculiar terms, but by a continued and systematic cast of phraseology; insomuch that in reading or hearing five or six sentences of an evangelical discourse, you ascertain the school by the mere turn of expression, independently of any attention to the quality of the ideas. If, in order to try what those ideas would appear in an altered form of words, you attempted to reduce a paragraph to the language employed by intellectual men in speaking or writing well on general subjects, you would find it must be absolutely a version. There is no room and no need to collect phrases and quotations; but you know how easily it could be done; and the specimens would give the idea of an attempt to create, out of the general mass of the language, a dialect which should be intrinsically spiritual; and so excessively appropriated to Christian doctrine as to be totally unserviceable for any other subject, and to become ludicrous when applied to it.† And this being extracted, like the Sabbath from the common course of time, the general range of diction is abandoned, with all its powers, diversities, and elegance, to secular subjects and the use of the profane. It is a kind of popery of language, vilifying every thing not marked with the signs of the holy church, and forbidding any one to minister to religion except in consecrated speech.

Supposing that a heathen foreigner had acquired a full acquaintance with our language in its most classical construction, yet without learning any thing about the gospel, (which it is true enough he might do,) and that he then happened to read or hear an evangelical discourse—he would be exceedingly surprised at the strange cast of phraseology. He would probably be more arrested and occupied by the singularity of the diction than by that of the ideas; whereas the general course of the diction should appear but the same as that to which he had been accustomed. It should be such that he would not even think of *it*, but only of the new subject and peculiar ideas which it should present to his view; unless there could be some advantage in the necessity of looking at these ideas through the mist and confusion of the double medium, created by the superinduction of an uncouth dialect on a plain language. —Or, if he were *not* a stranger to the subject, but had acquired its leading principles from some author or speaker, who employed (with the addition of a very small number of peculiar terms) the same style in which any other serious subject would have been illustrated, he would still be not less surprised. 'Is it possible,' he would say, as soon as he could apprehend what he was attending to, 'that these are the very same views which lately presented themselves with such lucid simplicity to my understanding? Or, is there something more, of which I am not aware, conveyed and concealed under these strange devices of phrase? Is this another stage of the religion, the school of the adepts, in which I am not yet initated? And does religion then, every where, as well as in *my* country, affect to show and guard its importance by relinquishing the simple language of intelligence, and assuming an obscure dialect of its own? Or, is this the diction of an individual only, and of one who really intends but to convey the same ideas that I have elsewhere received in so much more clear and direct a vehicle of words? But then, in what remote corner, placed beyond the authority of criticism and the circulation of literature, where a noble language stagnates into barbarism, did this man study his religion and acquire his phrases? Or, by what inconceivable perversion of taste and of labour has he framed, for the sentiments of his religion, a mode of expression so uncongenial with the eloquence of his country, and so adapted to dissociate them from all connexion with that eloquence?'

My dear friend, if I were not conscious of a solemn and cordial veneration for evangelical religion itself, I should be more afraid to trust myself in making these observations on the usual manner of expressing its ideas. If I am candid, I am willing to be corrected. Perhaps my description of this manner exaggerates; but that there is a great and systematical difference between it and the true classical diction, is most palpably obvious, and I cannot help regarding it as an unfortunate circumstance. It gives the gospel too much the air of a professional thing, which must have its peculiar cast of phrases, for the mutual recognition of its proficients, in the same manner as other professions, arts, and mysteries, have theirs. This is officiously placing the singularity of littleness to draw attention to the singularity of greatness, which in the very act it misrepresents and obscures. It is giving an uncouthness of mein to a beauty which should attract all hearts. It is teaching a provincial dialect to the rising instructer of a world. It is imposing the guise of a cramped, formal ecclesiastic on what is destined for an universal monarch.

Would it not be an improvement in the administration of religion, by discourse and writing, if Christian truth were conveyed in that neutral vehicle of expression which is adapted indifferently to common serious subjects? But it may be made a question, whether it *can* be perfectly conveyed in such language. This point, therefore, requires a little consideration. The diction on which I have animadverted may be distinguished into three parts.

The first a peculiar mode of using various common words. And this peculiarity consists partly in expressing ideas by such single words as do not simply and directly belong to them, instead of other single words which do simply and directly belong to them, and in general language are used to express them;* and partly in using such combinations of words as make uncouth phrases. Now, is this necessary? The answer to the question is immediately obvious as to the former part of the description; there can be no need to use one common word in an affected manner to convey an idea which there is another common word at hand to express in the simplest and most usual manner. And

* When I say evangelical divines, I concur with the opinion of those, who deem a considerable, and, in an intellectual and literary view, a highly respectable class of the writers who have professedly taught Christianity, to be not strictly evangelical. They might rather be denominated moral and philosophical divines, treating very ably on the generalities of religion, and on the Christian morals, but not placing the economy of redemption exactly in that light in which the New Testament appears to me to place it. Some of these have avoided the kind of dialect on which I am animadverting, not only by means of a diction more classical and dignified in the general principles of its structure, but also by avoiding the ideas with which the phrases of his dialect are commonly associated. I may, however, here observe, that it is by no means altogether confined to the specifically evangelical department of writing and discourse, though it there prevails the most, and with the greatest number of phrases. It extends in some degree, into the majority of writing on religion in general, and may therefore be called the theological, almost as properly as the evangelical dialect.

† This is so true, that it is no uncommon expedient with the would-be wits, to introduce some of the spiritual phrases, in speaking of any thing which they wish to render ludicrous; and they are generally so far successful as to be rewarded by the laugh or the smile of the circle, who probably may never have had the privilege of hearing wit, and have not the sense or conscience to care about religion.

* As, for instance, walk and conversation, instead of conduct, actions, or deportment; flesh, instead of, sometimes body, some times natural inclination;

then as to phrases, consisting of an uncouth combination of words which are common, and have no degree of technicality,—are they necessary? They are not absolutely necessary, unless each of these combinations conveys a thought of so exquisitely singular a signification, that no other conjunction of terms could have expressed it; a thought which was never suggested by one mind to another till these three or four words happened to fall out of the general order of the language into the cluster of a peculiar phrase; a thought which cannot be expressed in the language of another country that has not a correspondent idiom; and which will vanish from the world if ever this phrase shall be forgotten. But these combinations of words have no such pretensions. They will seldom appear to express a meaning which it required such a fortunate or such a dexterous expedient to bring and to retain within the scope of our ideas. Very often their sense is of so general and common a kind, that you could easily have expressed it in five or ten different forms of words. Some of these phrases would seem to have been originally the mere produce of affectation; and some to have been invented to give an appearance of particular significance to ideas which were so plain and common, that they seemed to have no force as exhibited in the ordinary cast of diction. In religion, as in other departments, artificial turns of expression have often been resorted to, in order to relieve the obvious plainness of the thought. In whatever manner, however, the language was first perverted into these artificial modes, it would be easy to try whether they are become such special and privileged vehicles of thought that no other forms of words can express what is supposed to be their sense. And it would be found that these phrases, as it is within our familiar experience that all phrases, consisting of only common words, and having no relation to art or science, can be exchanged for several different combinations of words, without materially altering the thought or lengthening the expression. I conclude, then, that what I have described as the first part of the theological dialect, the peculiar mode of using common words, is not absolutely necessary as a vehicle of Christian truths.

The second part of the diction consists, not in a peculiar mode of using common words, but in a class of words peculiar in themselves, as being seldom used except by divines, but of which the meaning can with perfect ease be expressed, without definition or circumlocution, by other single terms which are in general use. For example, edification, tribulation, blessedness, godliness, righteousness, carnality, lusts, (a term peculiar and theological only in the plural,) could be exchanged for parallel terms too obvious to need mentioning. It is true, indeed, that there are very few terms, if any, perfectly synonymous. But when there are several words of very similar though not exactly the same signification, and none of them belong to an art or science, the one which is selected is far more frequently used in that *general* meaning by which it is merely equivalent to the others, than in that precise shade of meaning by which it is distinguished from them. The words instruction, improvement, for instance, may not express exactly the sense of edification; but the word edification is probably not often used by a writer or speaker with any recollection of that peculiarity of its meaning by which it differs from the meaning of improvement or instruction. This is still more true of some other words, as, for example, tribulation and affliction. Whatever small difference of import these words may have from their etymology, it is probable that no man *ever* wrote tribulation rather than affliction *on account* of that difference. If, in addition to these two, the word distress has occurred to the mind, the selection of any one from the three has perhaps always been determined by habit, or accident, rather than by any perception of a distinct signification. The same remark will, in a great measure, apply to the words blessed, happy, righteous, virtuous, carnal, sensual, and a multitude of others. So that though there are few words in strict truth synonymous, yet there are very many which are so in *effect*, even by the allowance and sanction of the most rigid laws to which the best writers have conformed their composition. Perhaps this is a defect in human thinking, of which the ideal perfection may be, that every conception should be so exquisitely discriminative and precise, that no two words, which have the most refined shade of difference in their meaning, should be equally and indifferently eligible to express that conception. But what writer or speaker will ever even aspire to such perfection?—not to say, that if he did, he would soon find the vocabulary of the most copious language deficient of single, direct terms to mark all the sensible modifications of his ideas. If a divine felt that he had such extreme discrimination of thought, that he meant something clearly different by the words, carnal, godly, edifying, and so of many others, from what he could express by the words, sensual, pious, religious, instructive, he would certainly do right to adhere to the more peculiar words; but if he does not, he may perhaps improve the vehicle, without hurting the material, of his religious communications, by adopting the general and classical mode of expression.

The third distinction of the theological dialect consists in words almost peculiar to the language of divines, and for which equivalent terms *cannot* be found, except in the form of definition or circumlocution. Sanctification, grace, covenant, salvation, and a few more, may be assigned to this class. These may be called, in a qualified sense, the technical terms of evangelical religion. Now, separately from any religious considerations, it is plainly necessary, in a literary view, that all those terms that express a modification of thought which there are no other words competent to express, without great circumlocution, should be retained. They are requisite to the perfection of the language. And then, in considering those terms as connected with the Christian truth, I am ready to admit, that it will be of advantage to that truth, for some of those peculiar modes of thought of which it partly consists, to be permanently denominated by certain peculiar words which shall stand as its technical terms. But here several thoughts suggest themselves.

First, The definitions of some of these Christian terms are not absolutely unquestionable. The words have assumed the specific formality of technical terms, without having completely the quality and value of such terms. A certain laxity in their sense render them of far less use, in their department, than the terms of science, especially of mathematical science, are in theirs. Technical terms have been the lights of science, but, in many instances, the shades of religion. It is most unfortunate, when, in disquisitions or instructions, the grand leading words on which the force of all the rest depends, have not a precise and indisputable signification. The effect is similar to that which takes place in the ranks of an army, when an officer has a doubtful opinion, or gives indistinct orders. What I would infer from these observations, is, that a Christian writer or speaker will occasionally do well, instead of using the peculiar term, to express at length in other words, at the expense of much circumlocution, that idea which he would have wished to convey if he had used that peculiar term. I do not mean that he should do this so often as to render the term obsolete. It might be useful sometimes, especially in verbal instruction, both to introduce the term, and to give such a sentence as I have described. Such an expletive repetition of the idea will more than compensate for the tediousness by the clearness.*

* It is needless to observe that this would be a superfluous labour, with respect to the most simple of the peculiar words; such for instance, as salvation.

Secondly, If the definitions of the Christian peculiar terms were even as precise and fixed as those of scientific denominations, yet the nature of the subject is such as to permit an indolent mind to pronounce or to hear these terms without recollecting those definitions. In delivering or writing, and in hearing or reading, a mathematical lecture, both the teacher and the pupil are compelled to form in their minds the exact idea which each technical term has been defined to signify; else the whole train of words is mere sound and inanity. But in religion, a man has a feeling of having some general ideas connected with all the words as he hears them, though he perhaps never studies, or does not retain, the definition of one. I shall have occasion to repeat this remark, and therefore do not enlarge here. The inference is the same as under the former observation; it is, that the technical terms of Christianity will contribute little to precision of thought, unless the ideas which they signify are often expressed at length in other words, either in explanation of those terms when introduced, or in substitution for them when omitted.

Thirdly, It is not in the power of single theological terms, however precise their definitions may at any time have been, to secure to their respective ideas an unalterable stability. Unless the ideas themselves, by being often expressed in common words, preserve the signification of the terms, the terms will not preserve the accuracy of the ideas. This is true no doubt of the technical terms of science; but it is true in a much more striking manner of the peculiar words in theology. If the technical terms of science, at least of the strictest kind of science, were to cease to mean what they had been defined to mean, they would cease to mean any thing, and the change would be only from knowledge to ignorance. But, in the Christian theology, the change might be from truth to error; since the peculiar words might cease to mean what they were once defined to mean, by being employed in a different sense. It may not be difficult to conjecture in what sense conversion and regeneration, two more of the peculiar words, were used by the reformers, and the men who may be called the fathers of the established church of this country; but what sense have they subsequently borne in the writings of many of its divines? The peculiar words may remain, when the ideas, which they were intended to perpetuate, are gone. Thus, instead of being the signs of those ideas, they become their monuments, and monuments profaned into abodes for the living enemies of the departed. It must indeed be acknowledged, that in many cases innovations of doctrine have been introduced partly by ceasing to employ the words which designated the doctrines which it was wished to render obsolete; but, it is probable, they may have been still more frequently and successfully introduced under the advantage of retaining the terms while the principles were gradually subverted. And therefore I shall be pardoned for repeating this once more, that since the peculiar words can be kept in one invariable signification only by keeping that signification clearly in sight by means of something separate from these words themselves, it would be wise in Christian authors and speakers sometimes to express the ideas in common words, either in expletive and explanatory connexion with the peculiar terms, or occasionally, instead of them. I would still be understood to approve most entirely of the habitual use of a few of this class of terms; while the above observations may tend to deduct very much from the usual estimate of their value and importance.

These pages have attempted to show, in what particulars the language adopted by a great proportion of Christian divines might be modified, and yet remain faithful to the principles of Christian doctrine.—Such common words as have acquired an affected cast in theological use, might give place to the other common words which express the ideas in a plain and unaffected manner; and the phrases formed of common words uncouthly combined, may be dismissed. Many peculiar and antique words might be exchanged for other single words, of equivalent signification, and in general use. And the small number of peculiar terms acknowledged and established as of permanent use and necessity, might, even separately from the consideration of modifying the diction, be often, with advantage to the explicit declaration and clear comprehension o Christian truth, made to give place to a fuller expression, in a number of common words, of those ideas ot which these peculiar terms are the single signs.

Now, such an alteration would bring the language of divines nearly to the classical standard. If evangelical sentiments could be faithfully presented in an order of words of which so small a part should belong exclusively to those sentiments, they could be presented in what should be substantially the diction of Addison or Pope. And, if even Shaftesbury, Bolingbroke, and Hume, could have become Christians by some mighty and sudden efficacy of conviction, and had determined to write thenceforth in the spirit of the Apostles, they would have found, if these observations are correct, no radical change necessary in the structure of their language. An enlightened believer in Christianity might have been sorry, if, in such a case, he had seen any of them superstitiously labouring to acquire all the phrases of a school, instead of applying at once to its new and its noblest use a diction fitted for the vehicle of universal thought. Are not *they* yet sufficient masters of language, it might have been asked with surprise, to express all their thoughts with the utmost precision? As their language had been found sufficiently specific to injure the gospel, it would have been strange if it had been too general to serve it. The required alteration would probably have been little more than to introduce familiarly the obvious denominations of the Christian topics and objects, such as, redemption, heaven, Mediator, Christ, Redeemer, with the others of a similar kind, and a very few of those almost technical words which I have admitted to be indispensable. The habitual use of such denominations would have left the general order of their composition the same. And it would have been striking to observe by how comparatively small a difference of terms a diction which had appeared most perfectly pagan, could be christianized, when the writer had turned to Christian subjects, and felt the Christian spirit. On the whole, then, I conclude that, with the exception which I have distinctly made, the evangelical principles may be clearly exhibited in what may be called a neutral diction. And if they may, I can imagine some reasons to justify the wish that it had been more generally employed.

It will be permitted me to repeat, as one of these reasons, the consideration of the impression made by the style which I have described on those persons of cultivated taste whom this essay has chiefly in view. I am aware that they are greatly inclined to make an idol of their taste; and I am aware also that no species of irreligion can be much worse than to sacrifice to this idol any thing which essentially belongs to Christianity. If any part of evangelical religion, separately from all injurious associations, were of a nature to displease a finished taste, the duty would evidently be to repress its claims and murmurs. We should dread the presumption which would require of the Deity, that his spiritual economy should be, both in fact and in a manner obvious to our view, subjected or correspondent in all parts to those laws of order and beauty, which we have learnt partly from the relations of the material world, and partly from the arbitrary institutions and habits of society. But, at the same time, it is a most unwise policy for religion, that the sacrifice of taste, which ought, if required, to be submissively made to any part of either its essence or its form as really displayed from heaven.

should be exacted to any thing unnecessarily and ungracefully superinduced by man.

As another reason, I would observe, that the disciples of the religion of Christ would wish it to mingle more extensively and familiarly with social converse, and all the serious objects of human attention. But then it should have every facility, that would not compromise its genuine character, for doing so. And a peculiar phraseology is the direct contrary of such facility, as it gives to what is already by its own nature eminently distinguished from common subjects, an *artificial* strangeness, which makes it difficult for discourse to slide into it, and revert to it, and from it, without a formal and ungraceful transition. The subject is placed in a condition like that of an entire foreigner in company, who is debarred from taking any share in the conversation, till some one interrupts it by turning it directly to him, and beginning to talk with him in the foreign language. You have sometimes observed, when a person has introduced religious topics, in the course of perhaps a tolerably rational conversation on other interesting subjects, that, owing to the cast of expression, fully as much as to the difference of the subject, it was done by an entire change of the whole tenour and bearings of the discourse, and with as formal an announcement as the bell ringing to church. Had his religious diction been more of a piece with the common train of sensible language, he might probably have introduced the subject sooner, and certainly with a much better effect.

A third consideration, is, that evangelical sentiments would be less subject to the imputation of fanaticism, if their language were less contrasted with that of other classes of sentiments. Here it is unnecessary to say, that no pusillanimity were more contemptible than that which, to escape this imputation, would surrender the smallest vital particle of the religion of Christ. We are to keep in solemn recollection his declaration, 'Whosoever shall be ashamed of me and my words, of him also shall the Son of Man be ashamed.' Any model of terms, which could not be superseded without precluding some idea peculiar to the gospel from the possibility of being easily and most faithfully expressed, it would be for his disciples to retain, in spite of all the ridicule of the most antichristian age. But I am, at every step, supposing that every part of the evangelical system can be most perfectly exhibited in a diction but little peculiar; and, that being admitted, would it not be better to avert the imputation, as far as this difference of language could avert it? Better, I do not mean, in the way of protective convenience to any cowardly feeling of the man who is liable to be called a fanatic for maintaining the evangelical principles; he ought, on the ground both of Christian fidelity and of manly independence, to be superior to caring about the charge; but better, as to the light in which these principles might appear to the persons who meet them with this prejudice. You may have observed that in attributing fanaticism, they often fix on the phrases, at least as much as on the absolute substance, of evangelical doctrines. Now would it not be better to show them what these doctrines are, as divested of these phrases, and exhibited clearly in that vehicle in which other important truths are presented; and thus, at least, to obviate and disappoint their propensity to seize on a mode of exhibition so convertible to the ludicrous, in defence against any claim to seriousness respecting the substantial matter? If sometimes their grave attention, their corrected apprehension, their partial approbation, might be gained, it were a still more desirable effect. And we can recollect instances in which a certain degree of this good effect has resulted. Persons who had received unfavourable impressions of some of the peculiar ideas of the gospel, from having heard them advanced almost exclusively in the modes of phrase on which I have remarked, have acknowledged their prejudices to be diminished, after these ideas had been presented, in the simple, general language of intellect. We cannot, indeed, so far forget the lessons of experience, and the inspired declarations concerning the disposition of the human mind, as to expect that any improvement in the mode of exhibiting Christian truth will render it irresistible. But it were to be wished that every thing should be done to bring reluctant minds into doubt, at least, whether, if they cannot be evangelical, it be because they are too sensible and refined.

As a farther consideration in favour of adopting a more general language, it may be observed, that hypocrisy would then find a much greater difficulty, as far as speech is concerned, in supporting its imposture. The usual language of hypocrisy, at least of vulgar hypocrisy, is cant; and religious cant is often an affected use of the phrases which have been heard employed as appropriate to evangelical truth; with which phrases the hypocrite has connected no distinct ideas, so that he would be confounded if a sensible examiner were to require an accurate explanation of them; while yet nothing is more easy to be sung or said. Now, were this diction, for the greater part, to vanish from Christian society, leaving the truth in its mere essence behind,—and were, consequently, the pretender reduced to assume the guise of religion on the wide and laborious plan of acquiring an understanding of its leading principles, so as to be able to assign them discriminately in language of his own,—the part of a hypocrite would be much less easily acted, and less frequently attempted. Religion would therefore be seldomer dishonoured by the mockery of a false semblance.

Again—if this alteration of language were introduced, some of the sincere disciples of evangelical religion would much more distinctly feel the necessity of a positive intellectual hold on the principles of their profession. A systematic recurring formality of words tends to prevent a perfect understanding of the subject, by furnishing for complex ideas a set of ready-framed signs, (like stereotype in printing,) which a man learns to employ without really having the combinations of thought of which those ideas consist. Some of the simple ideas which belong to the combination may be totally absent from his mind—the others may be most faintly apprehended: there is no precise construction therefore of the thought; and thus the sign which he employs, stands in fact for nothing. If, on hearing one of these phrases, you were to turn to the speaker, and say, Now, what *is* that idea? What do you plainly mean by that expression?—you would often find with how indistinct a conception, with how littte attention to the very idea itself, the mind had been contented. And this contentment you would often observe to be, not a humble acquiescence in a consciously defective apprehension of some principle of which a man feels and confesses the difficulty of attaining more than a partial conception, but the satisfied assurance that he fully understands what he is expressing. On another subject, where there were no settled forms of words to beguile him into the feeling as if he thought and understood when in fact he did not, and where words must have been selected to define his own apprehension of the thought, his embarrassment how to express himself would have made him conscious of the indistinctness of his conception, and have compelled an intellectual effort. But it is against all justice, that Christian truth should be believed and professed with a less concern for precision, and at the expense of less mental exercise, than any other subject would require. And of how little consequence it would seem to be, in *this* mode of believing, whether a man entertains one system of principles, or the opposite.

But if such arguments could not be alleged, it would still seem far from desirable, without evident necessity, to clothe evangelical sentiment in a diction varying in more than a few indispensable terms from the general standard, for the simple reason, that it must be barbarous; unless, as I have observed, it be raised quite above the authority of this standard, and of the criticism and the taste which appeal to it by the majesty of inspiration which we have no more to expect, or by the mighty intellectual action of a genius almost transcending human nature. I do not know whether it is absolutely impossible that there should arise a man whose manner of thinking shall be so incomparably original and sublime, as to authorize him to throw the language into a new order, all his own; but it is questionable whether there ever appeared such a writer, in any language which had been cultivated to its maturity. Even Milton, who might, if ever mortal might, be warranted to sport with all established authorities, and to seize at will every unsanctioned mode of expression into which uncontrollable genius could stray, is, notwithstanding, for having presumed in a certain degree to create for himself a peculiar diction, censured by Johnson as having written in a 'Babylonish dialect.' And Johnson's own mighty force of mind has not saved his own peculiar structure of language from being condemned by all men of taste. The magic of Burke's eloquence is not enough to preclude a perception of its being much less perfect than it might have been, had the same marvellous affluence of thought been expressed in a language of less arbitrary, capricious, and mannerish construction. No more have the most distinguished evangelical divines, who have adhered to the spiritual dialect, impressed on it either a dignity to overawe literary taste, or a grace to conciliate it. Nor does it, with me, derive any sanction from being not the language of an individual only, but of a numerous and pious class; nor from its long established use; nor yet from the preeminence of its subject, since I think that subject suffers in its dignity of appearance by being presented in this vehicle.

LETTER IV.

Answer to the Plea, in behalf of the Dialect in Question, that it is formed from the Language of the Bible—Description of the Manner in which it is formed—This Way of employing biblical Language very different from simple Quotation—Grace and Utility with which brief Forms of Words, whether Sentences or single Phrases, may be introduced from the Bible, if they are brought in as pure Pieces and Particles of the Sacred Composition, set in our own Composition as something distinct from it and foreign to it—But the biblical Phraseology in the Theological Dialect, instead of thus appearing in distinct bright Points and Gems, is modified and mixed up throughout the whole Consistence of the Diction, so as at once to lose its own venerable Character, and to give a pervading Uncouthness without Dignity to the whole Composition—Let the Scripture Language be quoted often, but not degraded into a barbarous compound Phraseology—Even if it were advisable to construct the Language of Theological Instruction in some kind of Resemblance to that of the Bible, it would not follow that it should be constructed in Imitation of the Phraseology of an antique Version—License to very old Theologians to retain in a great Degree this peculiar Dialect—Young ones recommended to learn to employ in Religion the Language in which cultivated Men talk and write on general Subjects—The vast Mass of Writing in a comprehensive literary Sense bad, on the Subjects of Evangelical Theology, one great Cause of the Distaste felt by Men of intellectual Refinement—Several Kinds of this bad Writing specified—Wish for another Caliph Omar.

In defence of the diction which I have been describing, it will be said, that it has grown out of the language of the Bible. To a great extent this is evidently true. Many phrases, indeed, which casually occurred in the writings of divines, and many which were laboriously invented by those who wished to give to divinity a complete, systematic arrangement, and therefore wanted denominations or titles for the multitude of articles in the artificial distribution, have been naturalized into the theological dialect. But a large proportion of its phrases consists partly in such combinations of words as were taken originally from the Bible, and still more in such as have been made in an intentional resemblance of the characteristic language of that book.

Before I make any farther remarks, I do not know whether it may be necessary, in order to prevent misapprehension, to advert to the high advantage and propriety of often introducing sentences from the Bible,—not only in theological, but in all grave, moral composition. Passages of the inspired writings must necessarily be cited, in some instances, in proof of the truth of opinions, and may be most happily cited, in many others, to give a venerable and impressive air to serious sentiments which would be admitted without a formal reference to authority. Both complete sentences, and striking, short expressions, consisting perhaps sometimes of only two or three words, may be thus introduced with an effect at once useful and ornamental, while they appear pure and unmodified amidst the composition, as simple particles of scripture, quite distinct from the diction of the writer who inserts them. When thus appearing in their own genuine quality, as lines or parts of lines taken from a venerable book which is written in a manner very different from our common mode of language, they continue to be of a piece with that book. They are read as expressions, foreign to the surrounding composition, and, without an effort, referred to the work from which they are brought; in the same manner as passages, or striking, short expressions, adopted from some respected and well-known classic in our language. Whatever dignity characterizes the great work itself, is possessed also by these detached pieces in the various places where they are inserted. And if they are judiciously inserted, they impart their dignity to the sentiments which they are employed to enforce. This employment of the sacred expressions may be very frequent, as the Bible contains such an immense variety of ideas, applicable to all manner of interesting subjects. And from its being so familiarly known, its sentences or shorter expressions may be introduced without the formality of noticing, either by words or any other mark, from what volume they are drawn. These observations are more than enough to obviate any imputations of wanting a due sense of the dignity and force which may be imparted by a judicious introduction of the language of the Bible.

It is a different mode of using biblical language, that constitutes so considerable a part of the dialect which I have ventured to disapprove. When insertions are made from the Bible in the manner here described as effective and ornamental, the composition comprises two kinds of diction, each bearing its own separate character; the one being the diction which belongs to the author, the other that of the sacred book whence the citations are drawn. We pass along the course of his language with the ordinary feeling of being spoken to in a common, general phraseology; and when we meet with the insertions of direct scripture expression, they are recognized in their own peculiar character, as something foreign to the author's diction, and with the sense that we are reading just so much of the Bible itself. This distinct recognition of the two separate characters of language prevents any impression of an uncouth, heterogeneous consistence. But in the theological dialect, that part of the phraseology which has a biblical cast, is neither the one of these two kinds of language nor the other, but an inseparable mixture of both. For the expressions resembling those of scripture are blended and moulded into the very substance of the diction. I say *resembling;* for though some of them are precisely phrases from the Bible, yet most of them are phrases a little modified from the form in which they occur in the sacred book, by changing or adding a word, by giving an artificial turn to the beginning or the end, or by compounding two phrases into one. There are also, as I have already observed, many forms of expression cast in imitation of the biblical, by taking some one word almost peculiar to the Bible, and connecting it with one, or with several, of the common words, in a very peculiar construction separately from which it is seldom introduced. In this manner the scriptural expressions, instead of appearing as shining points on a darker ground, as gems advantageously set in an inferior substance, are reduced to become a constituent part of the dialect, in which they lose their genuine quality and their lustre. They are not brought, in each single instance, directly from the scriptures by the distinct selection of the person who uses them, but merely recur to him in the common usage of the diction, and generally without a recollection of their sacred origin. They are habitually employed by the school of divines, and therefore are now, in no degree, of the nature of quotations introduced for their special appositeness in particular instances, as the expressions of a venerable human author would be repeated.

This is the kind of biblical phraseology which I could wish to see less employed,—unless it is either more venerable or more lucid than that which I have recommended. We may be allowed to doubt how far such a cast of language can be venerable, after considering, that it gives not the smallest assurance of striking or elevated thought, since in fact a great quantity of most inferior writing has appeared in this kind of diction; that it is not *now* actually learnt from familiarity with the scriptures; that the incessant repetition of its phrases in every kind of religious exercise and performance wears out any solemnity it might ever have had; and that it is the very usual concomitant of a too systematic and cramped manner of thinking. It may be considered also, that phrases of whatever quality or high origin, if they do not stand separate in the composition, but are made essentially of a piece with the dialect, take, in point of dignity, the quality of that dialect, so that if the whole of it is not dignified, the particular part is not: if the whole character of the peculiar language of divines is not adapted to excite veneration, that proportion of it which has been formed out of the scripture phraseology is not adapted to excite it. And again, let it be considered, that in almost all cases, an attempt to imitate the peculiarity of form in which a venerable object is presented, instead of being content to aim at a coincidence of general qualities, not only fails to excite veneration, but excites the contrary sentiment; especially when all things in the form of the venerable model are homogeneous, while the imitation exhibits some features of resemblance incongruously combined with what is mainly and unavoidably of a different cast. A grand, ancient edifice, of whatever order, or if it were of a construction peculiar to itself, would be an impressive object; but a modern little one raised in its neighbourhood, in a style of building substantially of the most vulgar kind, but with a number of antique windows and angles in imitation of the grand structure, would be a grotesque and ridiculous one.

Scriptural phrases, then, can no longer make a solemn impression, when modified and vulgarized into the texture of a language which, taken altogether, is the reverse of every thing that can either attract or command. Such idioms may indeed remind one of prophets and apostles, but it is a recollection which prompts to say, Who are these men that, instead of seriously introducing at intervals the direct words of those revered dictators of truth, seem to be mocking the sacred language by a barbarous, imitative diction of their own? They may affect the forms of a divine solemnity, but there is no fire from heaven. They may show something like a burning bush, but it is without an angel.

As to perspicuity, it will not be made a question whether that is one of the recommendations of this corrupt modification of the biblical phraseology. Without our leave, the mode of expression habitually associated with the general exercise of our intelligence, conveys ideas to us the most easily and the most clearly. And not unfrequently even in citing the pure expressions of scripture, especially in doctrinal subjects, a religious instructer will find it indispensable to add a sentence, in order to expose the sense in a more obvious manner.

If it should be feared that the use of a language in which the biblical phrases are not in this manner blended, might have a tendency to make the reader or hearer forget the Bible, or recollect it only as an antiquated book, it may surely be assumed, that devout men, in illustrating religious subjects, will too often introduce the pure, unmodified expressions of that book to admit any danger of its being forgotten. And though these should occur much seldomer in the course of their sentences than the half-scriptural phrases are repeated in that diction on which I have remarked, they would probably remind us of the Bible in a more advantageous manner, than a dialect which has lost the dignity of a sacred language without acquiring the grace of a classical one. I am sensible in how many points the illustration would not apply; but it would partly answer my purpose to observe, that if it were wished to promote the study of some venerated human author, suppose Hooker, the way would not be to attempt incorporating a great number of his turns of expression into the essential structure of our own diction, which would generally have a most uncouth effect, but to make respectful references, and often to insert in our composition sentences, and parts of sentences, distinctly *as his*.

Let the oracles of inspiration be cited continually, both as authority and illustration, in a manner that shall make the mind instantly refer each expression that is introduced to the venerable book from which they are taken; but let *our* part of religious language be simply ours, and let those oracles retain their characteristic form of expression unimitated, unparodied, to the end of time.*

* In the above remarks, I have not made any distinction between the sacred books in their own language, and as translated. It might not however be improper to notice, that though there is a great peculiarity of manner in the original scriptures, yet a certain small proportion of the phraseology which appears in the translated scriptures, does not belong to the essential structure of the original composition, but is to be ascribed to the state of the language at the time when the translation was made. A translation, therefore, made now, and conformed to the present mature state of the language, in the same degree in which the earlier translation was conformed to the state of the language at that time, would make an alteration in some parts of that phraseology which the theological dialect has attempted to incorporate and imitate. If therefore it were the duty of divines to take the biblical mode of expression for their model, it would still be quite a work of supererogation to take this model in a wider degree of difference from the ordinary language of serious thoughts than as it would appear in such a later version. This would be a homage, not to the real diction of the sacred scriptures, but to the earlier cast of our own language. At the same time it must be admitted, both that the change of expression, which a later version might, on merely philological principles, be justified by the progress and present standard of our language for making, would not be great; and that every sentiment of prudence and devotional taste forbids to make quite so much alteration as those principles might warrant. All who have long venerated the scriptures in their somewhat antique version, would protest against their being laboriously modernized into every nice conformity with the present standard of the language, and against any other than a very literal translation. If it could be supposed that our language had not yet attained a fixed state, but that it would progressively change for ages to come, it would be desirable that the translation of the Bible should always continue, except in what might essentially affect the sense, a century behind, for the sake of that venerable air which a degree of antiquity confers on the form of that which is in its substance so eminently sacred. But I cannot allow that the same law is to be extended to the language of divines. They have no right to assume the same ground and the same distinctions as the Bible; they ought not to affect to keep it company. There is no solemn dignity in their writings, which can claim to be invested with a venerable peculiarity. Imitate the Bible or not, their composition is merely of the ordinary human quality, and subject to the same rules as that of their contemporaries who write on other subjects. And if they remain behind the advanced state of the classical diction, those contemporaries will not allow them

An advocate for the theological diction, who should not maintain its necessity or utility on the ground that a considerable proportion of it has grown out of the language of scripture, may think it has become necessary in consequence of so many people having been so long accustomed to it. I cannot but be aware that many respectable teachers of Christianity, both in speaking and writing, are so habituated to put their ideas in this cast of phraseology, that it would cost them a very great effort to make any material change. Nor could they acquire, if the change were attempted, a happy command of a more general language, without being intimately conversant with good writers on general subjects, and observant of their manner of composition. Unless, therefore, this study has been cultivated, or is intended to be cultivated, it will, perhaps, be better to adhere to the accustomed mode of expression with all disadvantages. Younger theological students, however, are supposed to be introduced to those authors who have displayed the utmost extent and powers of language in its freest form; and it may not be amiss for them to be told that evangelical ideas would incur no necessary corruption or profanation by being conveyed in so liberal and lucid a diction. With regard also to a considerable proportion of Christian readers and hearers, I am sensible that a reformed language would be excessively strange to them. But may I not allege, without any affectation of paradox, that its being so strange to them would be a proof of the necessity of adopting it, at least in part, and by degrees? For the manner in which some of them would receive this altered dialect, would prove that the customary phraseology had scarcely given them any clear ideas. It would be found, as I have observed before, that the peculiar phrases had been, not so much the vehicles of ideas, as the substitutes for them. These hearers and readers have been accustomed to chime to the sound without apprehending the sense; insomuch that if they hear the very ideas which these phrases signify, or did signify, expressed ever so simply in other language, they do not recognise them; and are instantly on the alert with the epithets, sound, orthodox, and all the watch-words of ecclesiastical suspicion. For such Christians, the diction is the convenient asylum of ignorance, indolence, and prejudice.

But I have enlarged far beyond my intention, which was only to represent, with a short illustration, that this peculiarity is unfavourable to a cordial reception of evangelical doctrines in minds of cultivated taste. This I know to be a fact from many observations in real life, especially among intellectual young persons, not altogether averse to serious subjects, nor inclined to listen to the cavils against the divine authority of Christianity itself.

After dismissing the consideration of the peculiar diction of divines, I meant to have taken a somewhat more general view of the accumulation of bad writing, under which the evangelical theology has been buried; and which has contributed to render its principles less welcome to persons of accomplished mental habits. A large proportion of that writing may be called bad, on more accounts than merely the theological peculiarity of dialect. But it is an invidious topic, and I shall make only a few observations

Evidences of an intellect superior in some degree to the common level, with a literary execution disciplined to great correctness, and partaking somewhat of elegance, are requisite on the lowest terms of acceptance for good writing, with cultivated readers; excepting indeed that one requisite alone in a pre-eminent degree, superlatively strong sense, will command attention and even admiration, in the absence of all the graces, and notwithstanding much incorrectness in the workmanship of the composition. Below this pitch of single or of combined quality, a book cannot, as a literary performance, please, though its subject be the most interesting on earth; and for acceptableness, therefore, the subject is unfortunate in coming to those persons in that book. A disgusting cup will spoil the finest element which can be conveyed in it, though that were the nectar of immortality.

Now, in this view, I suppose it will be acknowledged that the evangelical cause has not, on the whole, been happy in its prodigious list of authors. A number of them have displayed a high order of excellence; but one regrets as to a much greater number, that they did not revere the dignity of their religion too much to beset and suffocate it with their superfluous offerings. To you I do not need to expatiate on the character of the collective Christian library. It will have been obvious to you that a great many books form the perfect vulgar of pious authorship; an assemblage of the most subordinate materials that can be called thought, in language too grovelling to be called style. Some of these writers seem to have concluded that the greatness of the *subject* was to do every thing, and that they had but to pronounce, like David, the name of 'the Lord of Hosts,' to give pebbles the force of darts and spears. Others appear to have really wanted the perception of any great difference, in point of excellence, between the meaner and the nobler modes of writing. If they had read alternately Barrow's pages and their own, they probably would have been hardly sensible of the superiority of his. A number of them, citing, in a perverted sense, the language of St. Paul, 'not with excellency of speech,' 'not with enticing words of man's wisdom,' 'not in the words which man's wisdom teacheth,' expressly disclaim every thing that belongs to fine writing, not exactly as what they could not have exhibited or attained, but as what they judge incompatible with the simplicity of evangelical truth and intentions. In the books of each of these classes you are mortified to see how low religious thought and expression *can* sink; and you almost wonder how it was possible for the noblest ideas that are known to the sublimest intelligences, the ideas of God, of providence, of redemption, of eternity, to come into a serious human mind without imparting some small occasional degree of dignity to the train of thought. The indulgent feelings, which you entertain for the intellectual and literary deficiency of humble Christians in their religious communications in private, are with difficulty extended to those who make for their thoughts this demand on public attention; it was necessary for them to be Christians, but what made it their duty to become authors? Many of the books are indeed successively ceasing, with the progress of time, to be read or known; but the new supply continually brought forth is so numerous, that a person who turns his attention to religious reading is certain to meet a variety of them. Now only suppose a man who has been conversant and enchanted with the works of eloquence, refined taste, or strong reasoning, to meet a number of these books in the outset of his more serious inquiries; in what light would the religion of Christ appear to him, if he did not find some happier delineations of it?

There is another large class of Christian books, which bear the marks of learning, correctness, and a disciplined understanding; and by a general propriety leave but little to be censured; but which display no invention, no prominence of thought, nor living vigour of expression: all is flat and dry as a plain of sand. It is perhaps the thousandth iteration of commonplaces, the listless attention to which is hardly an action of the mind: you seem to understand it all, and mechanically assent while you are thinking of something else. Though the author has a rich, immeasurable field of possible varieties of reflection and illustration around him, he seems doomed to tread over again the narrow space of ground long since trodden to

to excuse themselves by pretending to identify themselves with the Bible.

dust, and in all his movements appears clothed in sheets of lead.

There is a smaller class that might be called mock-eloquent writers. These saw the effect of brilliant expression in those works of eloquence and poetry where it was dictated and animated by energy of thought, and very reasonably wished that Christian sentiments might assume a language as impressive as any subject had ever employed to fascinate or command. But unfortunately, they forgot that eloquence resides essentially in the thought, and that no words can make that eloquent, which will not be so in the plainest that could fully express the sense. Or, probably, they were quite confident of the excellence of their thoughts. Perhaps they concluded them to be vigorous and sublime from the very circumstance that they refused to be expressed in plain language. The writers would be but little inclined to suspect of poverty or feebleness the thoughts which seemed so naturally to be assuming, in their minds and on their page, such a magnificent style. A gaudy verbosity is always eloquence in the opinion of him that writes it ; but what is the effect on the reader? Real eloquence strikes on your mind with irresistible force, and leaves you not the possibility of asking or thinking whether it *be* eloquence ; but the sounding sentences of these writers leave you cool enough to examine with doubtful curiosity a language that seems threatening to move or astonish you, without actually doing it. It is something like the case of a false alarm of thunder ; where a sober man, that is not apt to startle at sounds, looks out to see whether it be not the rumbling of a cart. Very much at your ease, you contrast the pomp of the expression with the quality of the thoughts ; and then read on for amusement, or cease to read from disgust. In a serious hour, indeed, the feeling of being amused, is prevented by the regret, that it should be possible for an ill-judged style of writing to bring the most important subjects in danger of something worse than failing to interest. The unpleasing effect which it has on your own mind will lead to apprehend its having a very injurious one on many others.

A principal device in the fabrication of this style, is, to multiply epithets, dry epithets, laid on the outside, and into which none of the vitality of the sentiment is found to circulate. You may take a great number of the words out of each page, and find that the sense is neither more nor less for your having cleared the composition of these epithets of chalk of various colours, with which the tame thoughts had submitted to be dappled and made fine.

Under the denomination of mock-eloquence may also be placed the mode of writing which endeavours to excite the passions, not by presenting striking ideas of the object of passion, but by the appearance of an emphatical enunciation of the writer's own feelings concerning it. You are not made to perceive how the thing itself has the most interesting claims on your heart ; but you are required to be affected in mere sympathy with the author, who attempts your feelings by frequent exclamations, and perhaps by an incessant application to his fellow-mortals, or to their Redeemer, of all the appellations and epithets of passion, and sometimes of a kind of passion not appropriate to the object. To this last great Object, especially, such forms of expression are occasionally applied, as must revolt a man who feels that he cannot meet the same being at once on terms of adoration and of caressing equality.

It would be going beyond my purpose, to carry my remarks from the literary merits, to the moral and theological characteristics, of Christian books ; else a very strange account could be given of the injuries which the gospel has suffered from its friends. You might often meet with a systematic writer, in whose hands the whole wealth, and variety, and magnificence of revelation, shrink into a meagre list of doctrinal points, and who will let no verse in the Bible say a syllable till it has placed itself under one of them. You may meet with a Christian polemic, who seems to value the arguments for evangelical truth as an assassin values his dagger, and for the same reason ; with a descanter on the invisible world, who makes you think of a popish cathedral, and from the vulgarity of whose illuminations you are excessively glad to escape into the solemn twilight of faith ; or with a grim zealot for a theory of the divine attributes, which seems to delight in representing the Deity as a dreadful king of furies, whose dominion is overshaded with vengeance, whose music is the cries of victims, and whose glory requires to be illustrated by the ruin of his creation.

It is quite unnecessary to say, that the list of excellent Christian writers would be very considerable. But as to the vast mass of books that would, by the consenting adjudgment of all men of liberal cultivation, remain after this deduction, one cannot help deploring the effect which they must have had on unknown thousands of readers. It would seem beyond all question that books which, though even asserting the essential truths of Christianity, yet utterly preclude the full impression of its character ; which exhibit its claims on admiration and affection with insipid feebleness of sentiment ; or which cramp its simple majesty into an artificial form at once distorted and mean ; must be seriously prejudicial to the influence of this sacred subject, though it be admitted that many of them have sometimes imparted a measure of instruction and a measure of consolation. This they might do, and yet convey very contracted and inadequate ideas of the subject at the same time.* There are a great many of them into which an intelligent Christian cannot look without rejoicing that *they* were not the books from which he received his impressions of the glory of his religion. There are many which nothing would induce him, even though he do not materially differ from them in the leading articles of his belief, to put into the hands of an inquiring young person ; which he would be sorry and ashamed to see on the table of an infidel ; and some of which he regrets to think may still contribute to keep down the standard of religious taste, if I may so express it, among the public instructers of mankind. On the whole, it would appear, that a profound veneration for Christianity would induce the wish, that, after a judicious selection of books had been made, the Christians also had their Caliph Omar, and their General Amrou.

LETTER V.

A grand Cause of the displacency encountered by Evangelical Religion among Men of Taste is, that the great School in which that Taste is formed, that of Polite Literature, taken in the widest Sense of the Phrase, is hostile to that Religion—Modern Literature intended principally to be animadverted on—Brief Notice of the ancient—Heathen Theology, Metaphysics, and Morality—Harmlessness of the two former ; Deceptiveness of the last—But the chief Influence is from so much of the History as may be called Biography, and from the Poetry—Homer—Manner in which the Interest he excites is hostile to the Spirit of the Christian Religion—Virgil.

The causes which I have thus far considered, are associated immediately with the *object*, and, by misre-

* It is true enough that on every other subject, on which a multitude of books have been written, there must have been many which in a literary sense were bad. But I cannot help thinking that the number coming under this description, bear a larger proportion to the excellent ones in the religious department than in any other. One chief cause of this has been, the mistake by which many good men professionally employed in religion, have deemed their respectable mental competence to the office of public speaking, the proof of an equal competence to a work, which is subjected to much severer literary and intellectual laws.

presenting it, render it less acceptable to refined taste; but there are other causes, which operate by perverting the very principles of this taste itself, so as to make it dislike the religion of Christ, even though presented in its own full and genuine character, cleared of all these associations. I shall remark chiefly on one of these causes.

I fear it is incontrovertible, that far the greatest part of what is termed Polite Literature, by familiarity with which taste is refined, and the moral sentiments are in a great measure formed, is hostile to the religion of Christ; partly, by introducing insensibly a certain order of opinions unconsonant, or at least not identical, with the principles of that religion; and still more, by training the feelings to a habit alien from its spirit. And in this assertion, I do not refer to writers palpably irreligious, who have laboured and intended to seduce the passions into vice, or the judgment into the rejection of divine truth; but to the general assemblage of those elegant and ingenious authors who are read and admired by the Christian world, held essential to a liberal education and to the progressive accomplishment of the mind in subsequent life, and studied often without an apprehension, or even a thought, of their injuring the views and temper of spirits advancing, with the New Testament for their chief instructer and guide, into another world.

It is *modern* literature that I have more particularly in view; at the same time, it is obvious that the writings of heathen antiquity have continued to operate till now with their own proper influence, that is, a correctly heathenish influence, in the very sight and presence of Christianity, on the minds of many who have admitted the truth of that religion. This is just as if an eloquent pagan priest had been allowed constantly to accompany our Lord in his ministry, and had divided with him the attention and interest of his disciples, counteracting, of course, as far as his efforts were successful, the doctrine and spirit of the Teacher from heaven.*

The few observations which the subject may require to be made on ancient literature, will be directed chiefly to one part of it. For it will be allowed, that the purely speculative part of that literature has in a great measure ceased to interfere with the intellectual discipline of modern times. It obtains too little attention, and too little deference, to contribute much toward fixing the mind in those habits of thought and feeling which prevent the cordial admission of the doctrines and spirit of the gospel. Several learned and fanatical devotees to antiquity and paganism, have indeed made some effort to recall the long departed veneration for the dreams and subtleties of ancient philosophy. But they might, with perhaps a better prospect for success, recommend the building of temples or a pantheon, and the revival of all the institutions of idolatrous worship. The greater number of intelligent, and even learned men, would feel but little regret in consigning (if it could be consigned,) the much larger proportion of that philosophy to oblivion; except they may be supposed to love it as heathenism more than they admire it as wisdom; or unless their pride would wish to retain it as a contrast to their own more rational theories.

The ancient speculations on religion include, indeed some very noble ideas relating to a Supreme Being; but these ideas do not produce, in an intelligent man, any degree of partiality for that immense system, or rather chaos, of fantastic folly by which they are environed. He separates them from that chaos as something not strictly belonging to heathenism, nor forming a part of it. He considers most of them as the traditionary remains of divine communications to man in the earliest ages. A few of them were, perhaps, the utmost efforts of human intellect, at some happy moments excelling itself. But whether they are referred to the one origin or the other, they stand so conspicuously above the general assemblage of the pagan speculations on the subject of the Deity, that they throw a solemn contempt on those speculations. They throw contempt on the greatest part of the theological doctrine of even the very philosophers that expressed them. They rather seem to direct our contemplation and affection toward a religion divinely revealed, than to obtain any degree of favour for those notions of a God, which sprung and indefinitely multiplied from a melancholy combination of ignorance and depraved imagination. As to the apparent analogy between some of the notions of pagan religion, and one or two of the most, specific articles of Christianity, those notions are presented in such fantastic, and varying, and often monstrous, shapes, that the analogy is not close and constant enough to pervert our conception, or to preclude our admission of the defined propositions of the evangelic faith.

The next part of the pure speculations of the ancients, is, their metaphysics. And whatever may be the effect of metaphysical study in general, or of the particular systems of modern philosophers, with regard to the cordial and simple admission of Christian doctrines, the ancient metaphysics may certainly be pronounced harmless, from holding so little connexion with modern opinions. Later philosophers, by means of a far better method of inquiry, have opened quite a new order of metaphysical views; and persons with but a very small share of the acuteness and ingenuity of those ancient framers of ideal systems, can now wonder at their being so fantastic. The only attraction of abstract speculations is in their truth; and therefore when the persuasion of their truth is gone, all their influence is extinct. That which could please the imagination or interest the affections, might in a considerable degree continue to please and interest them, though convicted of fallacy. But that which is too subtle to please the imagination, loses all its power when it is rejected by the judgment. And this is the predicament to which time has reduced the metaphysics of the old philosophers. The captivation of their systems seems almost as far withdrawn from us as the songs of their Syrens, or the enchantments of Medea.

The didatic morality of the heathen philosophers comes much nearer to our interests, and has probably continued to have a considerable influence on the sentiments of cultivated men. After being detained a great while among the phantoms and the monsters of mythology, or following through the mazes of ancient metaphysics that truth which occasionally appears for a moment, but still for ever retires before the pursuer, the student of antiquity is delighted to meet with a sage who comes to him in a character of *reality*, with the warm, living eloquence of a doctrine which speaks to him in direct instruction concerning duty and happiness. And since it is necessarily the substantial object of this instruction to enforce goodness, he feels but little cause to guard against any perversion of his principles. He entirely forgets that goodness has been defined and enforced by another authority; and that though

*It is, however, no part of my object in these letters to remark on the influence, in modern times, of the fabulous deities that infested the ancient works of genius. That influence is at the present time, I should think, extremely small, from the fables being so stale: all readers are sufficiently tired of Jupiter, Apollo, Minerva, and the rest. So long, however, as they could be of the smallest service, they were piously retained by the Christian poets of this and other countries, who are now under the necessity of seeking out for some other mythology, the northern or the eastern, to support the languishing spirit of poetry. Even the ugly pieces of wood, worshipped in the South Sea islands, will probably at last receive names that may more commodiously hitch into verse, and be invoked to adorn and sanctify the belles lettres of the next century. The poet has no reason to fear that the supply of gods may fail; it is, at the same time, a pity, one thinks, that a creature so immense should have been placed in a world so small as this, where all nature, all history, all morals, all true religion, and the whole resources of innocent fiction, are too little to furnish materials enough for the wants and labours of his genius.

its main substance, as matter of practice, must be much the same in the dictates of that authority, and in the writings of Epictetus, or Cicero, or Antoninus, yet there is a material difference in some parts of the detail, and a most important one in the principles that constitute the basis. While he is admiring the beauty of virtue as displayed by one accomplished moralist, and its lofty independent spirit as exhibited by another, he is not inclined to suspect that any thing in their sentiments, or his animated participation of them, can be wrong.

But the part of ancient literature which has had incomparably the greatest influence on the character of cultivated minds, is that which has turned, if I may so express it, moral sentiments into real beings and interesting companions, by displaying the life and actions of eminent individuals. A few of the personages of fiction are also to be included. The captivating spirit of Greece and Rome resides in the works of the biographers; in so much of the history as might properly be called biography, from its fixing the whole attention and interest on a few signal names; and in the works of the principal poets.

No one, I suppose, will deny, that both the characters and the sentiments, which are the favourites of the poet and the historian, become the favourites also of the admiring reader; for this would be to deny the excellence of the poetry and eloquence. It is the high test and proof of genius that a writer can render his subject interesting to his readers, not merely in a general way, but in the *very same manner* in which it interests himself. If the great works of antiquity had not this power, they would long since have ceased to charm. We could not long tolerate what revolted, while it was designed to please, our moral feelings. But if their characters and sentiments really do thus fascinate the heart, how far will this influence be coincident with the spirit and with the design of Christianity?*

Among the poets, I shall notice only the two or three pre-eminent ones of the Epic class. Homer, you know, is the favourite of the whole civilized world; and it is many centuries since there needed one additional word of homage to the amazing genius displayed in the Iliad. The object of inquiry is, what kind of predisposition will be formed toward Christianity in a young and animated spirit, that learns to glow with enthusiasm at the scenes created by Homer, and to indulge an ardent wish, which that enthusiasm will probably awaken, for the possibility of emulating some of the principal characters. Let this susceptible youth, after having mingled and burned in imagination among heroes, whose valour and anger flame like Vesuvius, who wade in blood, trample on dying foes, and hurl defiance against earth and heaven; let him be led into the company of Jesus Christ and his disciples, as displayed by the evangelists, with whose narrative, I will suppose, he is but slightly acquainted before. What must he, what can he, do with his feelings in this transition? He will find himself flung as far as 'from the centre of the utmost pole;' and one of these two opposite exhibitions of character will inevitably excite his aversion. Which of them is that likely to be, if he is become thoroughly possessed with the Homeric passions?

Or if, on the other hand, you will suppose a person have first become profoundly interested by the New Testament, and to have acquired the spirit of the Saviour of the world, while studying the evangelical history; with what sentiments will *he* come forth from conversing with heavenly mildness, weeping benevolence, sacred purity, and the eloquence of divine wisdom, to enter into a scene of such actions and characters, and to hear such maxims of merit and glory, as those of Homer? He would be still more confounded by the transition, had it been possible for him to have entirely escaped that depravation of feeling which can think of crimes and miseries with but little emotion, and which we have all acquired from viewing the whole history of the world composed of scarcely any thing else. He would find the mightiest strain of poetry employed to represent ferocious courage as the greatest of virtues, and those who do not possess it as worthy of their fate, to be trodden in the dust. He will be taught, at least it will not be the fault of the poet if he is not taught, to forgive a heroic spirit for finding the sweetest luxury in insulting dying pangs, and imagining the tears and despair of distant relatives. He will be incessantly called upon to worship revenge, the real divinity of the Iliad, in comparison of which the Thunderer of Olympus is but a despicable pretender to power. He will be taught that the most glorious and enviable life is that, to which the greatest number of other lives are made a sacrifice; and that it is noble in a hero to prefer even a short life attended by this felicity, to a long one which should permit a longer life also to others. The dire Achilles, a being whom, if he really existed, it had deserved a conspiracy of the tribes then called nations to chain or to suffocate, is rendered interesting even amidst the horrors of revenge and destruction, by the intensity of his affection for his friend, by the melancholy with which he appears in the funeral scene of that friend, by one momentary instance of compassion, and by his solemn references to his own approaching death. A reader, who has even passed beyond the juvenile ardour of life, feels himself interested, in a manner that excites at intervals his own surprise, in the fate of this stern destroyer; and he wonders, and he wishes to doubt, whether the moral that he is learning be, after all, exactly no other than that the grandest employment of a great spirit is the destruction of human creatures, so long as revenge, ambition, or even caprice, may choose to regard them under an artificial distinction, and call them *enemies*. But this, my dear friend, is the real and effective moral of the Iliad, after all that critics have so gravely written about lessons of union, or any other subordinate moral instructions, which they discover or imagine in the work. Who but critics ever thought or cared about these instructions? Whatever is the chief and grand impression made by the whole work on the ardent minds which are most susceptible of the influence of poetry, *that* is the real moral; and Alexander, and, by reflection from him, Charles XII. correctly received the genuine inspiration.

If it be said that such works stand on the same ground, except as to the reality or accuracy of the facts, with an eloquent history, which simply *exhibits* the actions and characters, I deny the assertion. The actions and characters are presented in a *manner* which prevents their just impression, and empowers them to make an opposite one. A transforming magic of genius displays a number of atrocious savages in a hideous slaughter-house of men, as demigods in a temple of glory. No doubt an eloquent history might be so written as to give the same aspect to such men, and such operations; but that history would deserve to be committed to the flames. A history that should present a perfect display of human miseries and slaughter, would incite no one, that had not attained the last possibility of depravation, to imitate the principal actors. It would give the same feeling as the sight of a field of dead and dying men after a battle is over; a sight at which the soul would shudder, and earnestly wish that this might be the last time the sun should behold such a spectacle: but the tendency of the Homeric poetry, and of a great part of epic poetry in general, is to insinuate the glory of repeating such a tragedy. I therefore ask again, how it would be possible for a man, whose mind was first

* It may be noticed here, that a great part of what could be said on heathen literature as opposed to the religion of Christ, must necessarily refer to the peculiar moral spirit of that religion. It would border on the ridiculous to represent the martial enthusiasm of ancient historians and poets as counteracting the peculiar doctrines of the gospel, meaning by the term those dictates of truth that do not directly involve moral precepts.

completely assimilated to the spirit of Jesus Christ, to read such a work without a most vivid antipathy to what he perceived to be the moral spirit of the poet? And if it were not too strange a supposition, that the most characteristic parts of the Iliad had been read in the presence and hearing of our Lord, and by a person animated by a fervid sympathy with the work—do you not instantly imagine Him expressing the most emphatical condemnation? Would not the reader have been made to know, that in the spirit of that book he could never become a disciple and a friend of the Messiah? But then, if he believed this declaration, and were serious enough to care about being the disciple and friend of the Messiah, would he not have deemed himself extremely unfortunate to have been seduced, through the pleasures of taste and imagination, into habits of feeling which rendered it impossible, till they could be destroyed, for him to receive the only true religion, and the only Redeemer of the world? To show *how* impossible it would be, I wish I may be pardoned for making another strange and indeed a most monstrous supposition, namely, that Achilles, Diomede, Ulysses, and Ajax, had been real persons, living in the time of our Lord, and had become his disciples and yet (excepting the mere exchange of the notions of mythology for Christian opinions,) had retained entire the state of mind with which their poet has exhibited them. It is instantly perceived that Satan, Beelzebub, and Moloch, might as consistently have been retained in heaven. But here the question comes to a point: if these great examples of glorious character, pretending to coalesce with the transcendant Sovereign of virtues, would have been probably the most enormous incongruity existing, or that ever had existed, in the whole universe, what harmony can there be between a man who has acquired a considerable degree of congeniality with the spirit of these heroes, and that paramount Teacher and Pattern of excellence? And who will assure me that the enthusiast for heroic poetry does *not* acquire a degree of this congeniality? But unless I can be so assured, I necessarily persist in asserting the noxiousness of such poetry.

Yet the work of Homer is, notwithstanding, the book which Christian poets have translated, which Christian divines have edited and commented on with pride, at which Christian ladies have been delighted to see their sons kindle into rapture, and which forms an essential part of the course of a liberal education, over all those countries on which the gospel shines. And who can tell how much that passion for war which, from the universality of its prevalence, might seem inseparable from the nature of man, may, in the civilized world, have been reinforced by the enthusiastic admiration with which young men have read Homer, and similar poets, whose genius transforms what is, and ought always to appear, purely horrid, into an aspect of grandeur?

Should it be asked, And what ought to be the practical consequence of such observations? I may surely answer that I cannot justly be required to assign that consequence. I cannot be required to do more than exhibit in a simple light an important point of truth. *If* such works do really impart their own genuine spirit to the mind of an admiring reader, in proportion to the degree in which he admires, and *if* this spirit is totally hostile to that of Christianity, and *if* Christianity ought really and in good faith to be the supreme regent of all moral feeling, then it is evident that the Iliad, and all the books which combine the same tendency with great poetical excellence, are among the most mischievous things on earth. There is but little satisfaction, certainly, in illustrating the operation of evils without proposing any adequate method of contending with them. But, in the present case, I really do not see what a serious observer of the character of mankind can offer. To wish that the works of Homer, and some other great authors of antiquity, should cease to be read, is just as vain as to wish they had never been written. As to the far greater number of readers, it were equally in vain to wish that pure Christian sentiments might be sufficiently recollected, and loved, to accompany the study, and constantly prevent the injurious impression of the works of pagan genius. The few maxims of Christianity to which the student may have assented without thought and for which he has but little veneration, will but feebly oppose the influence; the spirit of Homer will vanquish as irresistibly as his Achilles vanquished. It is also most perfectly true, that so long as pride, ambition, and vindictiveness hold so mighty a prevalence in the character and in the nature of our species, they would still amply display themselves, though the stimulus of heroic poetry were withdrawn by the annihilation of all those works which have invested the worst passions, and the worst actions with a glare of grandeur. With or without classical ideas, men and nations will continue to commit offences against one another, and to avenge them; to assume an arrogant precedence, and account it noble spirit; to celebrate their deeds of destruction and call them glory; to idolize the men who possess, and can infuse, the greatest share of an infernal fire; to set at nought all principles of virtue and religion in favour of a thoughtless, vicious mortal who consigns himself in the same achievement to fame and perdition; to vaunt in triumphal entries, or funeral pomps, or strings of scalps, how far human skill and valour can excel the powers of famine and pestilence: men and nations will continue thus to act, till some new dispensation of Heaven shall establish the reign of Christianity. In that better season, perhaps the great works of ancient genius will be read with such a state of mind as can receive the intellectual improvement derivable from them, and at the same time as little coincide or be infected with their moral spirit, as in the present age we venerate their mythological vanities.

In the mean time, one cannot believe that any man who seriously reflects how absolutely the religion of Christ claims a conformity of his whole nature, will without regret feel himself animated, even for a moment, with a class of sentiments of which the habitual prevalence would be the total preclusion of Christianity. And it seems to show how little this religion is really understood, or even considered, in any of the countries denominated Christian, that so many who profess to adopt it never once thought of guarding their own minds, and those of their children, against the eloquent seductions of a spirit which is mortally opposite. Probably they would be more intelligent and vigilant, if any other interest than that of the professed religion were endangered. But a thing which injures them only in *that* concern, is sure to meet with all possible indulgence.

With respect to religious parents and preceptors, whose children and pupils are to receive that liberal education which must inevitably include the study of these great works, it will be for them to accompany the youthful readers throughout, with an effort to show them, in the most pointed manner, the inconsistency of many of the sentiments, both with moral rectitude in general, and with the special dictates of Christianity. And in order to give the requisite force to these dictates, it will be an important duty to illustrate to them the amiable tendency, and to prove the awful authority, of this dispensation of religion. This careful effort will often but very partially prevent the mischief; but it seems to be all that can be done.

Virgil's work is a kind of lunar reflection of the ardent effulgence of Homer; surrounded, if I may extend the figure, with as beautiful a halo of elegance and tenderness as perhaps the world ever saw. So much more refined an order of sentiment might have rendered the heroic character far more attractive to a mind that can melt as well as burn, if there had actually been a hero in the poem. But none of the personages intended for heroes excite the reader's enthusiasm enough to assimilate the tone of his feelings. No fiction or history of human characters and actions will ever powerfully transfuse its spirit, without some one or some very few individuals of signal peculiarity or greatness, to concentrate and embody the whole energy of the work. There would be no danger, therefore, of any one's becoming an idolater of the god of war through the inspiration of the Æneid, even if a larger proportion of it had been devoted to martial enterprise. Perhaps the chief counteraction to Christian sentiments which I should apprehend to an opening, susceptible mind, would be a depravation of its ideas concerning the other world, from the picturesque scenery which Virgil has opened to his hero in the regions of the dead, and the solemn and interesting images with which he has shaded the avenue to them. Perhaps, also, the affecting sentiments which precede the death of Dido might tend to lessen, especially in a pensive mind, the horror of that impiety which would throw back with violence the possession of life into the hands of Him who gave it.

LETTER VI

Lucan—Influence of the moral Sublimity of his Heroes—Plutarch—The Historians—Antichristian Effect of admiring the moral Greatness of the eminent Heathens—Points of essential Difference between Excellence according to Christian Principles, and the most elevated Excellence of the Heathens—An unqualified Complacency in the latter produces an alienation of Affection and Admiration from the former.

When I add the name of Lucan, I must confess that notwithstanding the offence to taste from a style too ostentatious and inflated, none of the ancient authors would have so much power to seduce my feelings, in respect to moral greatness, into a temper not coincident with Christianity. His leading characters are widely different from those of Homer, and of a greatly superior order. The mighty genius of Homer appeared and departed in a rude age of the human mind, a stranger to the intellectual enlargement which would have enabled him to combine in his heroes the dignity of thought, instead of mere physical force, with the energy of passion. For want of this, they are great heroes without being great *men.* They appear to you only as tremendous fighting and destroying animals; a kind of human Mammoths. The rude efforts of personal conflict are all they can understand and admire, and in their warfare their minds never reach to any of the sublimer results even of war; their chief and final object seems to be the mere savage glory of fighting, and the annihilation of their enemies. When the heroes of Lucan, both the depraved and the nobler class, are employed in war, it seems but a small part of what they can do, and what they intend; they have always something farther and greater in view than to evince their valour, or to riot in the vengeance of victory. Even the ambition of Pompey and Cæsar seems almost to become a grand passion, when compared to the contracted as well as detestable aim of Homer's chiefs; while this passion too is confined to narrow and vulgar designs, in comparison with the views which actuated Cato and Brutus.—The contempt of death, which in the heroes of the Iliad often seems like an incapacity or an oblivion of thought, is in Lucan's favourite characters the result, or at least the associate, of profound reflection; and this strongly contrasts their courage with that of Homer's warriors, which is, (according indeed to his own frequent similes,) the daring of wild beasts. Lucan sublimates martial into moral grandeur. Even if you could deduct from his great men all that which forms the specific martial display of the hero, you would find their greatness little diminished; they would be commanding and interesting men still. The better class of them, amidst war itself, hate and deplore the spirit and ferocious exploits of war. They are indignant at the vices of mankind for compelling *their virtue* into a career in which such sanguinary glories can be acquired. And while they deem it their duty to exert their courage in a just cause, they regard camps and battles as vulgar things, from which their thoughts often turn away into a train of solemn contemplations in which they approach sometimes the empyreal region of sublimity. You have a more absolute impression of grandeur from a speech of Cato, than from all the mighty exploits that epic poetry ever blazoned. The eloquence of Lucan's moral heroes does not consist in images of triumphs and conquests, but in reflections on virtue, suffering, destiny and death; and the sentiments expressed in his own name have often a melancholy tinge which renders them irresistibly interesting. He might seem to have felt a presage, while musing on the last of the Romans, that their poet was soon to follow them. The reader becomes devoted both to the poet and to these illustrious men; but, under the influence of this attachment, he adopts all their sentiments, and exults in the sympathy; forgetting, or unwilling to reflect, whether this state of feeling is concordant with the religion of Christ, and with the spirit of the apostles and martyrs. The most seducing of Lucan's sentiments, to a mind enamoured of pensive sublimity, are those concerning death. I remember the very principle which I would wish to inculcate, that is, the necessity that a believer of the gospel should preserve the Christian tenour of feeling predominant in his mind, and clear of incongruous mixture, having struck me with great force amidst the enthusiasm with which I read many times over the memorable account of Vulteius, the speech by which he inspired his gallant band with a passion for death, and the reflections on death with which the poet closes the episode. I said to myself, with a sensation of conscience, 'What are these sentiments with which I am burning? Are these the just ideas of death? Are they such as were taught by the Divine Author of our religion? Is this the spirit with which St Paul approached his last hour? And I felt a painful collision between this reflection and the passion inspired by the poet. I perceived with the clearest certainty that the kind of interest which I felt was no less than a real adoption, for the time, of the very same sentiments by which he was animated.

The epic poetry has been selected for the more pointed application of my remarks, from the conviction that it has had a much greater influence on the moral sentiments of succeeding ages than all the other poetry of antiquity, by means of its impressive display of individual great characters. And it will be admitted that the moral spirit of the epic poets, taken together, is as little in opposition to the Christian theory of moral sentiments as that of the collective poetry of other kinds. The just and elevated sentiments to be found in the Greek tragedies, tend to lead to the same habits of thought as the best of the pagan didactic moralists. And these sentiments infuse themselves more intimately into our minds when thus coming warm in the course of passion and action, and speaking to us with the emphasis imparted by affecting and dreadful events; but still are not so forcibly impressed as by the insulated magnificence of such striking and sublime individual characters as those of epic poetry. The mind of the reader does not retain for months and years an animated recollection of some personage whose name incessantly recalls the sentiments which he uttered, or which his conduct made us feel. Still, however, the moral spirit of the Greek tragedies acts with a considerable force on a susceptible mind; and if there should be but half as great a difference between the quality of the instructions which they will insinuate, and the principles of evangelical morality, as there was between the religious knowledge and moral spirit of the men themselves who wrote and contended for their own fame in Greece, and the divine illumination and noble character of those apostles that opened a commission from heaven to transform the world, the student may have some cause to be careful lest his Athenian morality should disincline him to the doctrines of a better school.

I shall not dwell long on the biography and history, since it will be allowed that their influence is very nearly coincident with that of the epic poetry. The work of Plutarch, the chief of the biographers, (a work so necessary, it would seem, to the consolations of a Christian, that I have read of some author who did not profess to disbelieve the New Testament, declaring that if he were to be cast on a desert island, and could have one book, and but one, it should be this,) the work of Plutarch delineates a greatness partly of the same character as that celebrated by Homer, and partly of the more dignified and intellectual kind which is so commanding in the great men of Lucan, several of whom, indeed, are the subjects also of the biographer. Various distinctions might, no doubt, be remarked in the impression made by great characters as illustrated in poetry, and as exposed in the plainness of historical record: but I am persuaded that the habits of feeling which will grow from admiring the one or the other, will be substantially the same as to a cordial reception of the religion of Christ.

A number of the men exhibited by the biographers and historians, rose so eminently above the general character of the human race, that their names have become inseparably associated with our ideas of moral greatness. A thoughtful student of antiquity enters this majestic company with an impression of mystical awfulness, resembling that of Ezekiel in his vision. In this select and revered assembly we include only those who were distinguished by elevated virtue, as well as powerful talents and memorable actions. Undoubtedly the magnificent powers and energy without moral excellence, so often displayed on the field of ancient history, compel a kind of prostration of the soul in the presence of men, whose surpassing achievements seem to silence for a while, and but for a while, the sense of justice which must execrate their ambition and their crimes; but where greatness of mind seems but secondary to greatness of virtue, as in the examples of Phocion, Epaminondas, Aristides, Timoleon, Dion, and a considerable number more, the heart applauds itself for feeling an irresistible captivation. This number indeed is small, compared with the whole galaxy of renowned names; but it is large enough to fill the mind, and to give as venerable an impression of pagan greatness, as if none of its examples had been the heroes whose fierce brilliance lightens through the blackness of their depravity; or the legislators, orators, and philosophers, whose wisdom was degraded by hypocrisy, venality, or vanity.

A most impressive part of the inflnence of ancient character on modern feelings, is derived from the accounts of two or three of the greatest philosophers, whose virtue, protesting and solitary in the times in which they lived, whose intense devotedness to the pursuit of wisdom, and whose occasional sublime glimpses of thought, darting beyond the sphere of error in which they were enclosed and benighted, present them to the mind with something like the venerableness of the prophets of God. Among the exhibitions of this kind, it is unnecessary to say that Xenophon's Memoir of Socrates stands unrivalled and above comparison.

Sanguine spirits without number have probably been influenced in modern times by the ancient history of mere heroes; but persons of a reflective disposition have been incomparably more affected by the contemplation of those men, whose combination of mental power with illustrious virtue constitutes the supreme glory of heathen antiquity. And why do I deem the admiration of this noble display of moral excellence pernicious to these reflective minds, in relation to the religion of Christ? For the simplest possible reason; because the principles of that excellence are not identical with the principles of this religion; as I believe every serious and self-observant man, who has been attentive to them both, will have verified in his own experience. He has felt the animation which pervaded his soul, in musing on the virtues, the sentiments, and the great actions of these dignified men, suddenly expiring, when he has attempted to prolong or transfer it to the virtues, sentiments, and actions of the apostles of Jesus Christ. Sometimes he has, with mixed wonder and indignation, remonstrated with his own feelings, and has said, I know there is the highest excellence in the religion of the Messiah, and in the characters of his most magnanimous followers; and surely it is *excellence* also that attracts me to those other illustrious men; why then cannot I take a full delightful interest in them both? But it is in vain; he finds this amphibious devotion impossible. And he will always find it so; for, antecedently to experience, it would be obvious that the order of sentiments which was the life and soul of the one form of excellence, is extremely distinct from that which is the animating spirit of the other. If the whole system of a Christian's sentiments is required to be adjusted to the economy of redemption, they must be widely different from those of the men, however wise or virtuous who never thought or heard of the Saviour of the world; else where is the peculiarity or importance of this new dispensation, which does, however, both avow and manifest a most signal peculiarity, and with which Heaven has connected the signs and declarations of its being of infinite importance? If, again, a Christian's grand object and solicitude is to please God, this must constitute his moral excellence, (even though the *facts* were the same,) of a very different nature from that of the men who had not in firm faith any god that they cared to please, and whose highest glory it might possibly become, that they boldly differed from their deities; as Lucan undoubtedly intended it as the most emphatical applause of Cato, that he was the inflexible patron and hero of the cause which was the aversion of the gods.* If humility is required to be a chief characteristic in a Christian's mind, he is here again placed in a state of contrariety to that love of glory which accompanied, and was applauded as a virtue while it accompanied, almost all the moral greatness of the heathens. If a Christian lives for eternity, and advances towards death with the certain expectation of judgment, and of a new and awful world, how different must be the essential quality of his serious sentiments, as partly created, and totally pervaded, by this mighty anticipation, from the order of feeling of the virtuous heathens, who had no positive or sublime expectations beyond death! The interior essences, if I may so speak, of the two kinds of excellence, sustained or produced by these two systems of thought, are so different, that they will hardly be more convertible or compatible in the same mind than even excellence and turpitude. Now it appears to me that the enthusiasm, with which a mind of deep and thoughtful sensibility dwells on the history of sages, virtuous legislators, and the noblest class of heroes, of heathen antiquity, will be found to beguile that mind into an order of sentiments congenial with theirs, and therefore thus seriously different from the spirit and principles of Christianity.† It is not exactly that the judg-

* Victrix causa Diis placuit, sed victa Catoni.

† If it should be said that, in admiring pagan excellence, the mind takes the mere facts of that excellence, separately from the principles, and as far as they are identical with the facts of Christian excellence, and then, connecting Christian principles with them, converts the whole into a Christian character before it cordially admires, I appeal to experience while I assert that this is not true. If it were, the mind would be able to turn with full complacency from an affectionate admiration of an illustri

ment admits distinct pagan propositions, but the heart insensibly acquires an unison with many of the sentiments which *imply* those propositions, and are wrong, unless those propositions are right. It forgets that a different state of feeling, corresponding to a greatly different scheme of propositions, is appointed by the Sovereign Judge of all things as (with relation to *us*) an indispensable preparation for entering the eternal paradise;* and that now, no moral distinctions, however splendid, are excellence in his sight, if not conformed to this standard. It slides into a persuasion that, under *any* economy, to be exactly like one of those heathen examples would be a competent qualification for any world to which good spirits are to be assigned. The devoted admirer contemplates them as the most enviable specimens of his nature, and almost wishes he could have been one of them; without reflecting that this would have been under the condition probably, among many other circumstances, of adoring Jupiter, Bacchus or Æsculapius, and of despising even the deities that he adored; and under the condition of being a stranger to the son of God, and to all that he has disclosed and accomplished for the felicity of our race. It would even throw an ungracious chill on his ardour, if an evangelical monitor should whisper, 'Recollect Jesus Christ,' and express his regret that these illustrious men could not have been privileged to be elevated into Christians. If precisely the word 'elevated' were used, the admonished person might have a feeling, at the instant, as if it were not the *right* word. But this state of mind is no less than a serious hostility to the gospel, which these feelings are practically pronouncing to be at least unnecessary; and therefore that noblest part of ancient literature which tends to produce it, is inexpressibly injurious. It had been happy for many cultivated and aspiring minds, if the men whose characters form the moral magnificence of the classical history, had been such atrocious villains, that their names could not have been recollected without execration. Nothing can be more disastrous than to be led astray by eminent virtue and intelligence, which can give a sense of grandeur, or of an alliance with grandeur, in the deviation.

It will require a very affecting impression of the Christian truth, a very strongly marked idea of the Christian character, and a habit of thinking with sympathetic admiration of the most elevated class of Christians, to preserve entire the evangelical spirit among the examples of what might pardonably have been deemed the most exalted style of man, if a revelation had not been received from heaven. Some views of this excellence it were in vain for a Christian to forbid himself to admire; but he must learn to admire under a serious restriction, else every emotion is a desertion of his cause. He must learn to assign these men in thought to another sphere, and to regard them as beings under a different economy with which our relations are dissolved; as marvellous specimens of a certain imperfect kind of moral greatness, formed on a model foreign to true religion, which model is crumbled to dust and given to the winds. At the same time, he may well deplore, while viewing some of these men, that, if so much excellence could be formed on such a model, the sacred system on which his own character professes to be formed should not have raised him almost to heaven. So much for the effect of the most interesting part of ancient literature.

In the next letter I shall make some observations, in reference to the same object on modern polite literature. Many of these must unavoidably be very analogous to those already made; since the greatest number of the modern fine writers acquired much of the character of their minds from those of the ancient world. Probably, indeed, the ancients have exerted a much more extensive influence in modern times by means of the modern writers to whom they have communicated their moral spirit, than immediately by their own works.

ous heathen, to admire, in the very same train of feeling, and with still warmer emotion, the excellence of St Paul; which is not the fact.

* I hope none of these observations will be understood to insinuate the impossibility of the future happiness of virtuous heathens. But a disquisition on the subject would here be out of place.

LETTER VII.

When a Communication, declaring the true Theory of both Religion and Morals, was admitted as coming from Heaven, it was reasonable to expect that, from the Time of this Revelation to the End of the World, all by whom it was so admitted would be religiously careful to maintain, in whatever they taught on Subjects within its cognizance, a systematic and punctillious Conformity to its Principles—Absurdity, Impiety, and pernicious Effect, of disregarding this sovereign Claim to Conformity—The greatest Number of our fine Writers have incurred this Guilt, and done this Mischief—They are Antichristian, in the first Place, by Omission; they exclude from their moral sentiments the modifying interference of the Christian Principles—Extended Illusftration of this Fact, and o the Consequences.

To a man who had long observed the influences which tyrannize over human passions and opinions, it would not, perhaps, have appeared strange, that when the Grand Renovator came on earth, and during the succeeding ages, a number of the men whose superior talents were to carry on the course of literature, and guide the progress of the human mind, should reject his religion. These I have placed out of the question, as it is not my object to show the injuries which Christianity has received from its avowed enemies. But it might have been expected, that all the intelligent men, from that hour to the end of time, who should really *admit* this religion, would perceive the sovereignty, and universality of its claims, and feel that every thing unconsonant with it ought instantly to vanish from the whole system of approved sentiments and the whole school of literature, and to keep as clearly aloof as the Israelites from the boundaries that guarded Mount Sinai. It might have been presumed, that all principles which the new dispensation rendered obsolete, or declared or implied to be wrong, should no more be regarded as belonging to the system of principles to be henceforward received and taught, than dead bodies in their graves belong to the race of living men. To retain or recall them would, therefore, be as offensive to the judgment, as to take up these bodies and place them in the paths of men, would be offensive to the senses; and as absurd as the practice of the ancient Egyptians, who carried their embalmed ancestors to their festivals. It might have been supposed, that whatever Christianity had actually substituted, abolished, or supplied, would therefore be *practically* regarded by these believers of it as substituted, abolished or supplied; and that they would, in all their writings, be at least as careful of their fidelity in this great article, as a man who adopts the Newtonian philosophy would be certain to exclude from his scientific discourse all ideas that seriously implied the Ptolemaic or Tychonic system to be true. Necessarily, a number of these literary believers would write on subjects so completely foreign to what comes within the cognizance of Christianity, that a pure neutrality, which should avoid all interference with it, would be all that could be claimed from them in its behalf; though, at the same time, one should feel some degree of regret, to see a man of enlarged mind exhausting his ability and his life on these foreign subjects, without devoting some short interval to the service of that which he believes to be of far surpassing moment.*

* I could not help feeling a degree of this regret in reading lately the memoirs of the admirable and estimable Sir William

But the great number who choose to write on subjects that come within the relations of the Christian system, as on the various views of morals, the distinctions and judgments of human character, and the theory of happiness, with almost unavoidable references sometimes to our connexion with Deity, to death, and to a future state, ought to have written every page under the recollection, that these subjects are not left free for careless or arbitrary sentiment, since the time that 'God has spoken to us by his Son;' and that the noblest composition would be only so much eloquent impiety, if discordant with the dictates of the New Testament. Had this been a habitual recollection amidst the studies of the fine writers of the Christian world, an ingenuous mind might have read alternately their works and those of the evangelists and apostles, without being confounded by a perception of antipathy between the inspirations of genius and the inspirations of heaven.

I confine my view chiefly to the elegant literature of our own country. And it may be presumed, independently of any actual comparison, that this (the literature of directly vicious and infidel tendency being put out of view on both sides,) is much less exceptionable than the belles lettres of the other parts of modern Europe; for this plain reason, that the extended prevalence of the happy light of the Reformation, through almost the whole period that has produced our works of genius and taste, must necessarily, by presenting the religion of Christ in an aspect more true to its genuine dignity, have compelled from the intellectual men who could not reject its truth, a respect which the same class of men in popish countries would be but little inclined to feel; or which would generally be, if they did feel it, but the homage of superstition, which injured the sacred cause another way.

I do not assign any class of writers formally theological to the polite literature of a country, not even the distinguished sermon-writers of France; as it is probable that works of direct theology have formed but a small part of that school of thinking and taste, in which the generality of cultivated men have acquired the moral conformation of their minds. That school is composed of poets, moral philosophers, historians, essayists, and you may add the writers of fiction. If the great majority of these authors have injured, and still injure their pupils in the most important of all their interests, it is a very serious consideration, both in respect to the accountableness of the authors, and the final effect on their pupils. I maintain that they are guilty of this injury.

On so wide a field, my dear friend, it would be in vain to attempt making particular references and selections to verify all these remarks. I must appeal for their truth to your own acquaintance with our popular fine writers.

In the first place, and as a general observation, the alleged injury has been done, to a great extent, by Omission, or rather it should be called Exclusion. And here I do not refer so much to that unworthy care, which seems prevalent through the works of our ingenious authors, to avoid *formally* treating on any topics of a precisely evangelical kind, as the absence of that Christian tinge and modification, (indicated partly by the occasional expression of Christian recollections, and partly by a solicitous, though it were a tacit, conformity to every principle of the Christian theory,) which should be diffused universally through the sentiments that regard man as a moral being. Consider how small a portion of the serious subjects of thought can be detached from all connexion with the religion of Christ, without narrowing the scope to which he meant it to extend, and repelling its intervention where he intended it to intervene. The book which unfolds it, has exaggerated its comprehensiveness, and the first distinguished Christian had a delusive view of it, if it does not actually claim to mingle its principles with the whole system of moral ideas, so as to impart to them a specific character: in the same manner as the element of fire, interfused through the various forms and combinations of other elements, produces throughout them, even when latent, a certain important modification, which they would instantly lose, and therefore lose their perfect condition, by its exclusion.

And this claim to extensive interference, made, as a matter of authority, for the Christian principles, appears to be supported by their *nature*. For they are not of a nature which necessarily restricts them to a peculiar department, like the principles which constitute some of the sciences. We should at once perceive the absurdity of a man who should be attempting to adjust all his ideas on general subjects according to the principles of geometry, and who should maintain (if any man could do so preposterous a thing,) that geometrical laws ought to enter into the essence of our reasoning on politics and morals. This I own is taking an illustration in the extreme; since geometrical and moral truth are not only very different, but of a nature essentially distinct. Let any other class of principles foreign to moral subjects be selected, in order to its being shown how absurd is the effect of an attempt to stretch them beyond their proper sphere, and force them into some connexion with ideas with which they have no relation. Let it be shown how such principles can in no degree modify the subject to which they are attempted to be applied, nor mingle with the reasons concerning it, but refuse to touch it, like magnetism applied to brass. I would then show that, on the contrary, the Christian principles have something in their nature which has a relation with something in the nature of almost all serious subjects. Their being extended to those subjects, therefore, is not an arbitrary and forced application of them; it is merely permitting their cognizance and interfusion in whatever is essentially of a common nature with them. It must be evident in a moment that the most general doctrines of Christianity, such as those of a future judgment, and immortality, if believed to be true, have a direct relation with every thing that can be comprehended within the widest range of moral speculation and sentiment. It will also be found that the more particular doctrines, such as those of the moral depravity of our nature, an atonement made by the sacrifice of Christ, the interference of a special divine influence in renewing the human mind, and educating it for a future state, together with all the inferences, conditions, and motives resulting from them, cannot be admitted and religiously regarded, without combining themselves, in numberless instances, with a man's ideas on moral subjects. I mean, that it is in their very *nature* thus to interfere and find out a relation with these ideas, even if there were no divine requirement that they should. That writer must, therefore, have retired beyond the limits of an immense field of important and most interesting speculations, must indeed have retired beyond the limits of *all* the speculation most important to man, who can say that nothing in the religion of Christ bears, in any manner, or any part of his subject any more than if he were a philosopher of Satan.

Jones. Some of his researches in Asia have incidentally served, in a very important manner, the cause of religion; but did he think the last possible direct service had been rendered to Christianity, that his accomplished mind was left at leisure for hymns to the Hindoo gods? Was not this even a violation of the neutrality, and an offence, not only against the gospel, but against theism itself? I know what may be said about personification, license of poetry, and so on; but should not a worshipper of God hold himself under a solemn obligation to abjure all tolerance of even poetical figures that can seriously seem, in any way whatever, to recognise the pagan divinities, or abominations, as the prophets of Jehovah would have called them? What would Elijah have said to such an employment of talents in his time? It would have availed little to have told him that these divinities were only personifications (with their appropriate representative idols) of objects in nature, of elements, or of abstractions. He would have sternly replied, And was not Baal, whose prophets I destroyed, the same?

And, in thus habitually interfering and combining with moral sentiments and speculations, the Christian principles will greatly modify them. The evangelical ideas will stand in connexion with the moral ones, not simply as *additional* ideas in the train of thinking, but as ideas which impart or dictate a particular character to the rest. A writer whose mind is so possessed with the Christian principles that they thus continually suggest themselves in connexion with his serious speculations, will unavoidably present a moral subject in a somewhat different aspect, even if he make no express references to the gospel, from that in which it would be presented by another writer, whose habits of thought were clear of evangelical recollections. And in every train of thinking in which the serious recognition of those principles would produce this modification, it ought to be produced ; so that the very last idea within the compass of speculation which would have a different cast as a ray of the gospel falls, or does not fall, upon it, should be faithfully exhibited in that light. The Christian principles cannot be true, without determining what shall be true in the mode of representing all those subjects with which they hold a connexion. Obviously, as far as the gospel *can* go, and does by its relations with things thus claim to go, with a modifying power, it cannot be a matter of indifference whether it *do* go or not ; for nothing on which its application would have this effect, would be equally right as so modified and as not so modified. That which is made precisely correct by this qualified condition, must, therefore, separately from it, be incorrect. He who has sent a revelation to declare the theory of sacred truth, and to order the relations of all moral sentiment with that truth, cannot give his sanction at once to this final constitution, and to that which disowns it. He, therefore, disowns that which disowns the religion of Christ. And what he disowns he condemns ; thus placing all moral sentiments in the same predicament, with regard to the Christian economy, in which Jesus Christ placed his contemporaries, 'He that is not with me is against me.' The order of ideas thus dissentient from the Christian system, presumes the existence, or attempts the creation, of some other economy.

Now, in casting a recollective glance over our elegant literature, the far greater part, as far as I am acquainted with it, appears to me to fall under this condemnation. After a comparatively small number of names and books are excepted, what are called the British Classics, with the addition of very many works of great literary merit that have not quite attained that rank, present an immense vacancy of christianized sentiment. The authors do not exhibit the signs of having ever deeply studied Christianity, or of retaining any discriminative and serious impression of it. Whatever has strongly occupied a man's attention, affected his feelings, and filled his mind with ideas, will even unintentionally show itself in the train and cast of discourse : these writers do not in this manner betray that their faculties have been occupied and interested by the special views unfolded in the evangelic dispensation. Of their being solemnly conversant with these views, you discover no notices analogous, for instance, to those which appear in the writing or discourse of a man, who has lately passed some time amidst the wonders of Rome or Egypt, and who shows you, by almost unconscious allusions and images occurring in his language even on other subjects, how profoundly he has been interested in comtemplating triumphal arches, temples, pyramids, and tombs. Their minds are not naturalized, if I may so speak, to the images and scenery of the kingdom of Christ, or to that kind of light which the gospel throws on all objects. They are somewhat like the inhabitants of those towns within the vast salt mines of Poland, who, beholding every object in their region by the light of lamps and candles only, have in their conversation no expressions describing things in such aspects as never appear but under the lights of heaven. You might observe, the next time that you open one of these works, how far you may read, without meeting with an idea of such a nature, or so expressed, as could not have been, unless Jesus Christ had come into the world ;* even though the subject be one of those which he came to illuminate, and to enforce on the mind by new and most cogent arguments. And where so little of the light and rectifying influence of these communications has been admitted into the habits of thought, there will be very few cordially reverential and animated references to the great Instructer himself. These will perhaps not oftener occur than a traveller in some parts of Africa, or Arabia, comes to a spot of green vegetation in the desert. You might have read a considerable number of volumes, without becoming apprised that there is such a dispensation in existence, or that such a sublime minister of it had ever appeared among men. And you might have diligently read, for several years, and through several hundred volumes, without at all discovering its nature or importance, or that the writers, when alluding to it, admitted any peculiar and essential importance to belong to it. You would only have conjectured it to be a scheme of opinions and discipline which had appeared in its day, as many others had appeared, and left us, as the rest have left us, to follow our speculations very much in our own way, taking from them, indifferently, any notions that we may approve.

You would have supposed that these writers had heard of one Jesus Christ, as they had heard of one Confucius, as a teacher whose instructions are admitted to contain many excellent things, and to whose system a liberal mind will occasionally advert, well pleased to see China, Greece, and Judea, as well as England, producing their philosophers, of various degrees and modes of illumination, for the honour of their respective countries and periods, and for the concurrent promotion of human intelligence. All the information which they would have supplied to your understanding, and all the conjectures to which they would have prompted your inquisitiveness, would have left you, if not instructed from other sources, to meet the real religion itself, when at length disclosed to you, as a thing of which you had but slight recognition, except by its name as a wonderful novelty. How little you would have expected, from their literary and ethical glimpses, to find the case to be, that the system, so insignificantly and carelessly acknowledged in the course of their fine sentiments, is the actual and sole economy by the provisions of which their happiness can be secured, by the laws of which they will be judged, which has declared the relations of man with his Creator, and specified the exclusive ground of acceptance ; which is therefore of infinite consequence to you, and to them, and to all their readers, as fixing the entire theory of the condition and destinies of man on the final principles to which all theories and sentiments are solemnly required to be 'brought into obedience.'

Now, if the writers who have thus preserved the whole world of interesting ideas which they have unfolded free from any evangelical intermixture, are really the chief instructers of persons of taste, and form, from early life, their habits of feeling and thought, it is easy to see that they must produce a state of mind very uncongenial with the gospel. Views habitually presented to the mind, during its most susceptible periods, and through the main course of its improvements, in every varied light of sublimity and beauty, with every fascination of that taste, ingenuity, and eloquence, which it has learnt still more to admire each year as its faculties have expanded, will have become the settled order of its ideas. And it will feel the same complacency in this

* Except, perhaps, in respect to humanity and benevolence, on which subject his instructions have improved the sentiments even of infidels, in spite of the rejection of their divine authority

intellectual order, that as inhabitants of the material world, we do in the great arrangement of nature, in the green, blooming earth, and the magnificent hemisphere of heaven.

LETTER VIII.

More Specific forms of their contrariety to the Principles of Revelation—Their Good Man is not a Christian—Contrasted with St Paul—Their Theory of Happiness essentially different from the Evangelical—Short Statement of both—In moralizing on Life, they do not habitually consider, and they prevent their Readers from considering, the present State as introductory to another—Their Consolations for Distress, Old Age, and Death, widely different on the whole, from those which constitute so much of the Value of the Gospel — The Grandeur and Heroism in Death, which they have represented with irresistible Eloquence, emphatically and perniciously opposite to the Christian Doctrine and examples of Sublimity and Happiness in Death—Examples from Tragedy.

It will be proper to specify, somewhat more distinctly, several of the particulars in which I consider the generality of our fine writers as disowning or contradicting the evangelical dispensation, and, therefore beguiling their readers into a complacency in an order of sentiments that is unconsonant with it.

And one thing extremely obvious to remark, is, that the *good man*, the man of virtue, who is of necessity constantly presented to view in the volumes of these writers, *is not a Christian*. His character could have been formed, thongh the Christian revelation had never been opened on the earth, or though all the copies of the New Testament had perished ages since ; and it might have appeared admirable, but not peculiar. It has no such complexion and aspect as would have appeared foreign and unacountable in the absence of the Christian truth, and have excited wonder what it should bear relation to, and on what model, in what school, such a confirmation of principles and feelings could have taken its consistence. Let it only be said that this man of virtue had conversed whole years with the instructions of Socrates, Plato, Cicero, and perhaps Antoninus, and all would be explained ; nothing would lead to ask, 'But if so, with whom has he conversed *since*, to lose so completely the appropriate character of his school, under the broad impression of some other mightier iufluence ?'

The good man of our polite literature never talks with affectionate devotion of Christ, as the great High Priest of his profession, as the exalted Friend, whose injunctions are the laws of his virtues, whose work and sacrifice are the basis of his hopes, whose doctrines guide and awe his reasonings, and whose example is the pattern which he is earnestly aspiring to resemble. The last intellectual and moral disignation in the world by which it would occur to you to describe him, would be those by which the apostles so much exulted to be recognized, a disciple, and a servant, of Jesus Christ ; nor would he (I am supposing this character to become a real person,) be at all gratified by being so described. You do not hear him avowing that he deems the habitual remembrance of Christ essential to the nature of that excellence which he is cultivating. He rather seems, with the utmost coolness of choice, adopting virtue as according with the dignity of a rational agent, than to be in the least degree impelled to it by any relations with the Saviour of the world.

On the supposition of a person realizing this character having fallen into the company of St Paul, you can easily imagine the total want of congeniality. Though both avowedly devoted to truth, to virtue, and perhaps to religion, the difference in the cast of their sentiments would have been as great as that between the physical constitution and habitudes of a native of the country at the equator, and those of one from the arctic regions. Would not that law of the apostle's feelings by which there was a contitual intervention of ideas concerning one object, in all subjects, places, and times, have appeared to this man of virtue and wisdom, inconceivably mystical ? In what manner would he have listened to the emphatical expressions respecting the love of Christ constraining us, living not to ourselves, but to him that died for us and rose again, counting all things but loss for the knowledge of Christ, being ardent to win Christ and be found in him, and trusting that Christ should be magnified in our body, whether, by life or by death ? Perhaps St Paul's energy, and the appearance of its being accompanied by a vigorous intellect, might have awed him into silence. But amidst that silence, he, must, in order to defend his self-complacency, have decided that the apostle's mind had fallen, notwithstanding its strength, under the dominion of an irrational association ; for he would have been conscious that no such ideas had ever kindled his affections, and that no such affections had ever animated his actions ; and yet *he* was indubitably a good man. according to a generally approved standard, and could, in another style, be as eloquent for goodness as St Paul himself. He would therefore have concluded, either that it was not necessary to be a Christian, or that this order of feelings was not necessary to that character. But if the apostle's sagacity had detected the cause of this reserve, and the nature of his associate's reflections, he would most certainly have declared to him with great solemnity that both these things were necessary —or that he had been deceived by inspiration ; and he would have parted from this self-complacent man with admonition and compassion. Now, would St Paul have been wrong ? But if he would have been right, what becomes of those authors, whose works, whether from neglect or design, tend to satisfy their readers of the perfection of a form of character which he would have pronounced essentially defective ?

Again—moral writings are instructions on the subject of happiness. Now the doctrine of this subject is declared in the evangelical testimony : it had been strange indeed if it had not, when the happiness of man was expressly the object of the communication. And what, according to this communication, are the essential requisites to that condition of the mind without which no man ought to be called happy ; without which ignorance or insensibility alone can be content, and folly alone can be cheerful ? A simple reader of the Christian scriptures will reply that they are—a change of heart, called conversion, the assurance of the pardon of sin through Jesus Christ, a habit of devotion approaching so near to intercourse with the Supreme Object of devotion that revelation has called it 'communion with God,' a process of improvement called sanctification, a confidence in the divine Providence that all things shall work together for good, and a conscious preparation for another life, including a firm hope of eternal felicity. And what else can he reply ? What else can you reply ? Did the lamp of heaven ever shine more clearly since Omnipotence lighted it, than these ideas display themselves through the New Testament ? *Is* this then absolutely the true, and the only true, account of happiness ? It is not that which our accomplished writers in general have chosen to sanction. Your recollection will tell you that they have most certainly presumed to avow, or to insinuate, a doctrine of happiness which implies much of the Christian doctrine to be a needless intruder on our speculations, or an imposition on our belief ; and I wonder that this serious fact should so little have alarmed the Christian students of elegant literature. The wide difference between the dictates of the two authorities is too evident to be overlooked ; for the writers in question have very rarely, amidst an immense assemblage of sentiments concerning happiness, made any reference to what the New Testament so explicitly declares to be its constituent and vital principles. How many times you might read the sun or the moon to its repose, before you would find an assertion or a recognition, for instance of a change of the mind being requisite to happiness, in any terms commensurate with the significance which this article seems to bear in all the varied propositions and notices of it in the New Testament. Some of these writers appear hardly to have admitted or to have recollected even the maxim, that happiness must essentially consist in something so fixed in the mind itself as to be substantially independent of worldly condition; for their most animated representations of it are merely descriptions of fortunate combinations of external circumstances, and of the feelings immediately caused by them, which will expire the moment that these combinations are broken up. The greater number, however, have fully admitted so plain a truth, and have given their illustrations of the doctrine of happiness accordingly. And what appears in these illustrations of the brightest image of happiness? It is, probably, that of a man feeling an elevated complacency in his own excellence, a proud consciousness of rectitude; possessing extended views, cleared from the mists of ignorance, prejudice, and superstition; unfolding the generosity of his nature in the exercise of beneficence; without feeling, however, any grateful incitement from remembrance of the transcendent generosity of the Son of Man; maintaining, in respect to the events and bustle of the surrounding scene, a dignified indifference, which can let the world go its own way, undisturbed by its disordered course; and living in a cool resignation to fate, without any strong expressions of a specific hope, or even solicitude, with regard to the termination of life and to all futurity. Now, notwithstanding a partial coincidence of this description with the Christian theory of happiness,* it is evident that on the whole the two modes are so different that the same man cannot realize them both. The consequence is clear; the natural effect of incompetent and fallacious schemes, prepossessing the mind by every grace of genius, will be an aversion to the Christian scheme; which will be seen to place happiness in elements and relations much less flattering to what will be called a noble pride; to make it consist in something of which it were a vain presumption for the man to fancy that *himself* can be the sovereign creator.

It is, again, a prominent characteristic of the Christian Revelation, that, having declared this life to be but the introduction to another, it systematically preserves the recollection of this great truth through every representation of every subject; so that the reader is not allowed to contemplate any of the interests of life in a view which detaches them from the grand object and conditions of life itself. An apostle could not address his friends on the most common concerns, for the length of a page, without the final references. He is like a person whose eye, while he is conversing with you about an object, or a succession of objects, immediately near, should glance every moment toward some great spectacle appearing on the distant horizon. He seems to talk to his friends in somewhat of that manner of expression with which you can imagine that Elijah spoke, if he remarked to his companion any circumstance in the journey from Bethel to Jericho, and from Jericho to the Jordan; a manner betraying the sublime anticipation which was pressing on his thoughts. The correct consequence of conversing with our Lord and his apostles would be, that the thought of immortality should become almost as habitually present and familiarized to the mind as the countenance of a domestic friend; that it should be the grand test of the value of all pursuits, friendships, and speculations; and that it should mingle a certain nobleness with every thing which it permitted to occupy our time. Now how far will the discipline of modern polite literature coincide?

I should be pleased to hear a student of that literature seriously profess that he is often and impressively reminded of futurity; and to have it shown that ideas relating to this great subject are presented in sufficient number, and in a proper manner, to produce an affect which should form a respectable proportion of the *whole* effect produce by these authors on susceptible minds. But there is no ground for expecting this satisfaction. It is true that the idea of immortality is so exceedingly grand, that many writers of genius who have felt but little genuine interest in religion, have been laid by their perception of what is sublime to introduce an illusion which is one of the most powerful means of elevating the imagination. And the energy of their language has been worthy of the subject. In these instances, however, it is not always found that the idea is presented exactly in that light which both shows its individual grandeur, and indicates the extent of its necessary connexion with other ideas; it appears somewhat like a majestic ower, which a traveller in some countries may find standing in a solitary scene, no longer surrounded by that great assemblage of buildings, that ample city, of which it was raised to be the centre, the strength, and the ornament. Immortality had been had recourse to in one page of an ingenious work as a single topic of sublimity, in the same manner as a stupendous natural phenomenon, or a brilliant achievment, has been described in another. The author's object might rather seem to have been to supply an occasional gratification to taste, than to reduce the mind and all its feelings under the perpetual dominion of a grand practical principle.

It is true also, that a graver class of fine writers, who have expressed considerable respect for religion and for Christianity, and who, though not writing systematically on morals, have inculcated high moral principles, have made references to a future state as the hope and sanction of virtue. But these references are made less frequently than the connexion between our present conduct and a future life would seem to claim. And the manner in which they are made sometimes indicates either a deficiency of interest in the great subject, or a pusillanimous anxiety not to offend those readers who would think it too directly religious. It is sometimes adverted to as if rather from a conviction, that if there is a future state, moral speculation must be defective, even to a degree of absurdity, without some allusions to it, than from feeling a profound delight in the contemplation of it. When the idea of another life is introduced to aggravate the force of moral principles, and the authority of conscience, it is done at times in a manner which appears like a somewhat *reluctant* acknowledgment of the deficiency of all inferior sanctions. The consideration is suggested in a transient glimpse, after the writer has eloquently expatiated on every circumstance by which the present life can supply motives to goodness. In some instances, a watchful reader will also perceive what appears too much like care to divest the idea, when it *must* be introduced, of all direct references to that sacred person who first completely opened the prospect of immortality, or to some of those other doctrines which he taught in immediate connexion with this great truth. There seems reason to suspect the writer of having been pleased that, though it is indeed to the gospel alone that we owe the assurance of immortality, yet it was a subject so much in the conjectures and speculation of the heathen sages, that he may mention it without therefore so expressly recognizing the gospel as in the case of introducing some truth of which not only the evidence, but even the first explicit conception, was communicated by that dispensation.

* No one can be so absurd as to represent the notions which pervade the works of polite literature as totally and at all points, opposite to the principles of Christianity; what I am asserting, is, that in some important points they are substantially and essentially different, and that in others they disown the Christian modification.

Taking this defective kind of acknowledgment of a future state, together with that entire oblivion of the subject which prevails through an ample portion of elegant literature, I think there is no hazard in saying, that a reader who is satisfied without any other instructions, will learn almost every other lesson sooner than the necessity of habitually living for eternity. Many of these writers seem to take as much care to guard against the inroad of ideas from this solemn quarter, as the inhabitants of Holland do against the irruption of the sea; and their writings do really form a kind of moral dyke against the invasion from the other world. They do not instruct a man to act, to enjoy, and to suffer, as a being that may by to-morrow have finally abandoned this orb: every thing is done to beguile the feeling of his being 'a stranger and a pilgrim on the earth.' The relation which our nature bears to the circumstances of the present state, and which individuals bear to one another, is mainly the ground on which their considerations of duty proceed and conclude. And their schemes of happiness, though formed for beings at once immortal and departing, include little which avowedly relates to that world to which they are removing, nor reach beyond the period at which they will properly but begin to live. They endeavour to raise the groves of an earthly paradise, to shade from sight that vista which opens to the distance of eternity.

Another article in which the anti-Christian tendency of a great part of our productions of taste and genius is apparent, is, the kind of consolation administered to distress, old age, and death. Things of a mournful kind make so large a portion of the lot of humanity, that it is impossible for writers who take human life and feelings for their subject, to avoid (nor indeed have they endeavoured to avoid) contemplating man in those conditions in which he needs every benignant aid to save him from despair. And here, if any where, we may justly require an absolute coincidence of all moral instructions with the religion of Christ: since consolation is eminently its distinction and its design; since a being in distress has peculiarly a right not to be trifled with by the application of unadapted expedients; and since insufficient consolations are but to mock it, and deceptive ones are but to betray. It should then be clearly ascertained by the moralist, and never forgotten, what are the consolations provided by this religion, and under what condition they are offered.

Christianity offers even to the irreligious, who relent amidst their sufferings, the alleviation springing from inestimable promises made to penitence: any other system, which should attempt to console them, simply as suffering, and without any reference to the moral and religious state of their minds, would be mischievous, if it were not inefficacious. What are the principal sources of consolation to the pious, is immediately apparent. The victim of sorrow is assured that God exercises his paternal wisdom and kindness in afflicting his children; that this necessary discipline is to refine and exalt them by making them 'partakers of his holiness;' that he mercifully regards their weakness and pains, and will not let them suffer beyond what they shall be able to bear; that their great Leader has suffered for them more than they can suffer, and compassionately sympathizes still; that this short life was not meant so much to give them joy, as to prepare them for it; and that patient constancy shall receive a resplendent crown. An aged Christian is soothed by the assurance that his almighty friend will not despise the enfeebled exertions, nor desert the oppressed and fainting weakness, of the last stage of his servant's life. When advancing into the shade of death itself, he is animated by the faith that the great sacrifice has taken the malignity of death away; and that the divine presence will attend the dark steps of this last and lonely enterprise, and show the dying traveller and combatant with evil that even this melancholy gloom is the very confine of paradise, the immediate access to the region of eternal life.

Now, in the greater number of the works to which I am referring, what are the modes of consolation which sensibility, reason, and eloquence, have most generally exerted themselves to apply to the mournful circumstances of life, and to its close? You will readily recollect such as these: a man is suffering—well, it is the common destiny, every one suffers sometimes, and some much more than he; it is well it is no worse. If he is unhappy now, he *has* been happy, and he could not expect to be always so. It were ridiculous to complain that his nature was constituted capable of suffering, or placed in a world where it is exposed to the causes of it. If it were not capable of pain, it would not of pleasure. Would he be willing to lose his being, to escape these ills? Or would he consent, if such a thing were possible, to be any person else? The sympathy of each kind relative and friend will not be wanting. His condition may probably change for the better; there is hope in every situation; and meanwhile, it is an opportunity for displaying manly fortitude. A strong mind can proudly triumph over the oppression of pain, the vexations of disappointment, and the tyranny of fortune. If the cause of distress is some irreparable deprivation, it will be softened by the lenient hand of time.*

The lingering months of an aged man are soothed almost, it is pretended, into cheerfulness by the respectful attention of his neighbours; by the worldly prosperity and dutiful regard of the family that he has brought up; by the innocent gayety and amusing frolics of their children; and by the consideration of his fair character in society. If he is a man of thought, he has the added advantage of some philosophical considerations; the cares and passions of his former life are calmed into a wise tranquillity; he thinks he has had a competent share of life; it is as proper and necessary for mankind to have their 'exits,' as their 'entrances;' and his business will now be to make a 'well-graced' retreat from the stage, like a man that has properly acted his part, and may retire with applause.

As to the means of sustaining the spirit in death, the general voice of these authors asserts the grand and only all-sufficient one to be the recollection of a well-spent life. To this chief source of consolation you will find various additional suggestions; as for instance, that death is in fact a far less tremendous thing than that dire form of it by which imagination and superstition are haunted; that the sufferings of death are less than men often endure in the course of life; that it is only like one of those transformations with which the world of nature abounds; and that it is easy to conceive, and reasonable to expect, a more commodious vehicle and habitation. It would seem almost unavoidable to glance a momentary thought toward what revelation has signified to us of 'the house not made with hands,' of the 'better country, that is, the heavenly.' But yet the greater number of the writers of taste advert to the subject with apparent reluctance, except it can be done, on the one hand, in the manner of pure philosophical conjecture, or on the other, under the form of images, bearing some analogy to the visions of classical poetry.†

* Can it be necessary to notice here again, that every system of moral sentiments must inevitably contain some principles which the gospel does not disapprove? Various particulars in this assemblage of consolations are compatible, in a subordinate place, with the dictates of Christianity. But the enumeration, altogether, and exclusively of the grand Christian principles, forms a scheme of consolation quite different from that of the religion of Christ.

† I am infinitely far from disliking philosophical speculation, or even daring flights of fancy, on this high subject. On the contrary, it appears to me strange that any one should solemnly entertain the belief of a life to come, without its exciting both the intellectual faculty and the imagination to their highest exercise. What I mean to censure in the mode of referring to another life, is, the care to avoid any direct resemblance or re

The arguments for resignation to death are not so much drawn from future scenes, as from a consideration of the evils of the present life, the necessity of submitting to a general and irreversible law, the dignity of submitting with that calmness which conscious virtue is entitled to feel, and the improbability (as these writers sometimes intimate) that any very formidable evils are to be apprehended after death, except by a few of the very worst of the human race. Those arguments are in general rather aimed to quiet fear than to animate hope. The pleaders of them seem more concerned to convey the dying man in peace and silence out of the world, than to conduct him to the celestial felicity. Let us but see him embarked on his unknown voyage in fair weather, and we are not accountable for what he may meet, or where he may be carried, when he is gone out of sight. They seldom present a lively view of the distant happiness, especially in any of those images in which the Christian revelation has intimated its nature. In which of these books, and by which of the real or fictitious characters whose last hours and thoughts they sometimes display, will you find, in terms or in spirit, the apostolic sentiments adopted, 'To depart and be with Christ is far better,' 'Willing rather to be absent from the body, and present with the Lord?' The very existence of that sacred testimony which has given the only genuine consolations in death, and the only just conceptions of the realities beyond it, seems to be scarcely recollected; while the ingenious moralists are searching the exhausted common-places of the stoic philosophy, or citing the dubious maxims of a religion moulded according to the corrupt wishes of mankind, or even recollecting the lively sayings of the few whose wit has expired only in the same moment with life, to fortify the pensive spirit for his last removal. 'Is it not because there is not a God in Israel, that ye have sent to inquire of Baalzebub the God of Ekron?'

Another order of sentiments concerning death, of a character too bold to be called consolations, has been represented as animating one class of human beings. In remarking on Lucan, I noticed that desire of death which has appeared in the expressions of great minds, sometimes while merely indulging solemn reflections when no danger or calamity immediately threatened, but often in the conscious approach towards a fatal catastrophe. Many writers of later times have exerted their whole strength, and have even excelled themselves, in representing the high sentiments in which this desire has displayed itself; genius has found its very gold mine in this field. If this grandeur of sentiment had awakened piety while it exalts the passions, some of the poets would have ranked among our greatest benefactors. Powerful genius, aiding to inspire a Christian triumph in the prospect of death, might be revered as a prophet, might be almost loved as a benignant angel. No man's emotions perhaps have approached nearer to enthusiasm than mine, in reading the thoughts which are made to be expressed by sages and reflective heroes in this prospect. I have always felt these passages as the last and mightiest of the enchantments of poetry, capable of inspiring for a little while a contempt of all ordinary interests, of the world which we inhabit, and of life itself. While the enthusiast is elated with such an emotion, nothing may appear so desirable as some noble occasion of dying; such an occasion as that supplied by the legal injustice which awarded the hemlock to Socrates, or by the destiny which at Philippi involved Brutus in the ruin of a great design for the liberty of the world.* Poetry has delighted to display personages of this high order, in the same fatal predicament; and the situation of such men has appeared inexpressibly enviable, by means of those sublime sentiments by which they illuminated the gloom of death. The reader has loved to surround himself in imagination with that gloom, for the sake of irradiating it with that sublimity. All other greatness has been for a while eclipsed by the greatness of thought displayed by these contemplative and magnanimous spirits, though untaught by religion, when advancing to meet their fate. But the Christian faith recalls the mind from this enchantment to recollect that the Christian spirit in dying can be the only right and noble one, and to consider whether these examples be not exceedingly different. Have not the most enlightened and devout Christians, whether they have languished in their chambers, or passed through the fire of martyrdom, manifested their elevation of mind in another strain of eloquence? The examples of greatness in death, which poetry has exhibited, generally want all those sentiments respecting the pardon of sin, and a Mediator through whom it is obtained, and often the explicit idea of meeting the Judge, with which a Christian contemplates his approaching end. Their expressions of intrepidity and exultation have no analogy with the language of an incomparable saint and hero, 'Oh death, where is thy sting? O grave, where is thy victory? Thanks be to God, who giveth us the victory through our Lord Jesus Christ.' The kind of self-authorized confidence of taking possession of some other state of being, as monarchs would talk of a distant part of their empire which they were going to enter; the proud apostrophes to the immortals, to prepare for the great and rival spirit that is coming; their manner of consigning to its fate a good but falling cause, which will sink when they are gone, there not being virtue enough in earth or heaven to support or vindicate it; their welcoming death as a kind of glad revenge against a hated world and a despicable race,—are not the humility nor the benevolence with which a Christian dies. If a Christian will partly unite with these high spirits in being weary of a world of dust and trifles, in defying the pains of death; in panting for an unbounded liberty, it will be at the same time with a most solemn commitment of himself to the divine mercy, which *they* forget, or were never instructed, to implore. And as to the vision of the other world, you will observe a great difference between the language of sublime poetry and that of revelation, in respect to the nature of the sentiments and triumphs of that world, and still more, perhaps, in respect to the associates with whom the departing spirit expects soon to mingle. The dying magnanimity of poetry anticipates high converse with the souls of heroes, and patriots, and perhaps philosophers; a Christian feels himself going, (I may accommodate the passage,) to 'an innumerable company of angels, to the general assembly and church of the first born, to God the Judge of all, to the spirits of just men made perfect, and to Jesus the Mediator of the new covenant.'

In defence of those who have thus rendered death attractive by other means than the evangelical views, it may be said, that many of the personages whom their scenes exhibit in the contemplation of death, or in the approach to it, were necessarily, from the age or country in which they lived or are feigned to have lived, unacquainted with Christianity; and that therefore it would have been absurd to represent them as animated by Christian sentiments. Certainly. But I then ask, on what principle men of genius will justify themselves for *choosing*, with a view to the instruction of the heart, as they profess, examples, of which they cannot preserve the consistency, without making them pernicious? Where is the conscience of that man, who is

cognition of the ideas which the New Testament has given to guide, in some small, very small degree, our conjectures.

* Poetry will not easily exceed many of the expressions which mere history has recorded. I should little admire the capability of feeling, or greatly admire the Christian temper, of the man who could without emotion read, for instance, the short observations of Brutus to his friend, (in contemplation even of a self-inflicted death,) on the eve of the battle which extinguished all hope of freedom: 'We shall either be victorious, or remove beyond the power of those that are so. We shall deliver our country by victory, or ourselves by death.'

most anxious that every sentiment expressed by the historical or fictitious personage, in the fatal season, should be harmonious with every principle of the character,—but feels not the smallest concern about the consistency of selecting or creating the character itself, with his conviction of the absolute authority of the religion of Christ ? In glancing forward, he knows that his favourite is to die, and that he cannot die as a Christian : yet he is to die with the most elevated moral dignity. Would it not, therefore, be a dictate of conscience to warn his readers, that he hopes to display the exit with a commanding sublimity of which the natural effect will be, to make them no more wish to die as Christians ? But how would he feel while seriously writing such a warning ? Might it not be said to him, And are *you* then willing to die otherwise than as a Christian ? If you are, you virtually pronounce Christianity to be a feeble, and, to be consistent, should avow the rejection. If you are not, how can you endeavour to seduce your readers into an enthusiastic admiration of such a kind of death as you wish that you may not die ? How can you endeavour to inspire those sentiments, which would excite your apprehension and compassion for the state of your reader's mind, if you heard him utter them in his last hours ? Is it *necessary* to the pathos and sublimity of poetry, to introduce characters which cannot be justly represented without falsifying our view of the most serious of all moral subjects ? If this *be* necessary, it would be better that poetry with all its charms were exploded, than that the revelation of God should not attain its end, and fix its own ideas of death, clearly and alone, in the minds of beings whose manner of preparing for it is of infinite consequence. But this is far from being the dilemma ; since innumerable examples could be found, or rationally imagined, of Christian greatness in death. Is not then this preference of examples inimical to Christianity, and is not the sympathetic animation which so easily expresses their appropriate feelings, and informs them with their utmost energy, a worse kind of infidelity, as it is far more mischievous, than that of the cold dealer in cavils and quibbles against the gospel ? What is the Christian belief of that poet worth, who would not, on reflection, feel self-reproach for the affecting scene, which has, for a while, made each of his readers rather wish to die with Socrates, or with Cato, than with St John ? What would have been thought of the pupil of an apostle, who after hearing his master describe the spirit of a Christian's departure from the world, in language which he believed to be of conclusive authority, and which asserted or clearly implied that this alone was greatness in death, should have taken the first occasion to expatiate with enthusiasm on the closing scene of a philosopher, or on the exit of a stern hero, that, acknowledging in the visible world no object for either confidence or fear, departed with the aspect of a being who was going to summon his gods to judgment for the misfortunes of his life ? And how will these careless men of genius give their account to the Judge of the world, for having virtually taught many aspiring minds that, notwithstanding his first coming was to conquer for man the king of terrors, there needs no recollection of him, in order to look toward death with noble defiance or sublime desire ?

Some of their dying personages are so consciously uninformed of the realities of the invisible state, that the majestic sentiments which they disclose on the verge of life, can only throw a slight glimmering on unfathomable darkness ; but some anticipate the other world, as I have already observed, in very defined images. I recollect one of them, after some just reflections on the vanity and wretchedness of life, thus expressing his complacency in view of the great deliverer :

'Death joins us to the great majority ;
'Tis to be born to Platos and to Cæsars ;
'Tis to be great forever.
'Tis pleasure, 'tis ambition then, to die.'

Another, an illustrious female, in a tragedy which I lately read, welcomes death with the following sentiments :

—'Oh 'tis wondrous well !
Ye gods of death that rule the Stygian gloom !
Ye who have greatly died, I come ! I come !
The hand of Rome can never touch me more ;
Hail ! perfect freedom, hail !'

'My free spirit should ere now have join'd
That great assembly, those devoted shades,
Who scorned to live till liberty was lost ;
But, ere their country fell, abhorr'd the light.'

'Shift not thy colour at the sound of death ;
It is to me perfection, glory, triumph.
Nay, fondly would I choose it, though persuaded
It were a long, dark night without a morning ;
To bondage far prefer it, since it is
Deliverance from a world where Romans rule.'

—'Then let us spread
A bold, exalted wing, and the last voice we hear,
Be that of wonder and applause.'

'And is the sacred moment then so near ?
The moment when yon sun, those heavens, this earth,
Hateful to me, polluted by the Romans,
And all the busy, slavish race of men,
Shall sink at once, and straight another state
Rise on a sudden round ?
Oh to be there !'*

You will recollect to have read many that are equally improper to engage a Christian's full sympathy, and therefore improper for a poet, admitting Christianity, to have written in order to engage that sympathy. It is a pernicious circumstance in passages of this strain, that some of the general sentiments of anticipation and high emotion which might be expressed by a dying Christian, are combined so intimately with other ideas and a predominant state of feeling contradictory to Chritianity, as to tempt the mind by the approbation of the one into a tolerance of the other.

Sometimes even very bad men are made to display such dignity in death, as at once to excite a sympathy with their false sentiments, and to lessen the horror of their crimes. I recollect the interest with which I read, many years since, in Dr Young's Busiris, the proud, magnanimous speech at the end of which the tyrant dies : the following are some of the lines :

'I thank these wounds, these raging pains, which promise
An interview with equals soon elsewhere.
Great Jove, I come !'

Even the detestable Zanga, though conscious that 'to receive him hell blows all her fires,' appears, (if I recollect right,) with a fine elevation in the prospect of death, by means, partly indeed of the sentiments of returning justice, but chiefly of heroic courage. To create an occasion of thus compelling us to do homage to the dying magnanimity of wicked men, is an insult to the religion which condemns such magnanimity as madness. It is no justification to say, that such instances have been known, and therefore such representations but imitate reality ; for if the laws of criticism do not enjoin, in works of genius, a careful adaptation of all examples and sentiments to the purest moral purpose, as a far higher duty than the study of resemblance to the actual world, the laws of piety most certainly do. Let the men who have so much literary conscience about this verisimilitude, content themselves with the office of mere historians, and then they may relate without guilt, if the relation be simple and unvarnished, all the facts and speeches of depraved greatness within

* This is not, perhaps, one of the best specimens ; it is the last that has come under my notice. I am certain of having read many, but have not, just now, the means of finding them again.

the memory of the world. But when they choose the higher office of inventing and combining, they are accountable for all the consequences. They create a new person, and in sending him into society, they can choose whether his example shall tend to improve or to pervert the minds that will be compelled to admire him.

It is an immense transition from such instances as those which I have been remarking upon, to Rousseau's celebrated description of the death of his Eloisa, which would have been much more properly noticed in an earlier page. It is long since I read that scene, one of the most striking specimens probably of original conception and interesting sentiment that ever appeared; but though the representation is so extended as to include every thing which the author thought needful to make it perfect, there is no explicit reference to the peculiarly evangelical causes of complacency in death. Yet the representation is so admirable, that the serious reader is tempted to suspect even his own mind of fanaticism, while he is expressing to his friends the wish that they, and that himself, may be animated, in the last day of life, by a class of ideas which this eloquent writer would have been ashamed to introduce.

LETTER IX.

The Estimate of the depraved moral Condition of Human Nature is quite different in Revelation and Polite Literature—Consequently, the Redemption by Jesus Christ which appears with such momentous Importance in the one, is, in comparison, a Trifle in the other—Our fine Writers employ and justify antichristian Motives to Action; especially the Love of Fame—The Morality of this Passion argued—The earnest Repression of it shown to be a Duty—Some of the lighter Order of our popular Writers have aided the Counteraction of Literature to Evangelical Religion by careless or malignant Ridicule of Things associated with it—Brief Notice of the several Classes of fine Writers, as lying under the Charge of contributing to alienate Men of Taste from the Doctrines and moral Spirit of the New Testament—Moral Philosophers—Historians Essayists—Addison—Johnson—The Poets—Exception in favour of Milton, &c.—Pope—Antichristian Quality of his Essay on Man—Novels—Melancholy Reflection on the Review—Conclusion.

Does it not appear to you, my dear friend, that an approving reader of the generality of our ingenious authors will entertain an opinion of the moral condition of our species very different from the divine declarations? The governor of all intelligent creatures has spoken of this nation or family of them, as exceedingly remote from conformity to that standard of perfection which alone can ever be his rule of judgment. And this is pronounced not only of vicious individuals, who are readily given up to condemnation by those who form the most partial or the proudest estimate of human nature, but of the constitutional quality of that nature itself. The moral part of the constitution of man is represented as placing him immensely below that rank of dignity and happiness to which, by his intellectual powers, and his privilege of being immortal, he would otherwise have seemed adapted to belong. The descriptions of the human condition are such as if the nature had, by a dreadful convulsion, been separated off at each side from a pure and happy system of the creation, and had fallen down an immeasurable depth, into depravation and misery. In this state man is represented as loving, and, therefore, practically choosing, the evils which subject him to the condemnation of God; and it is affirmed that no expedient, but that very extraordinary one which Christianity has revealed, can change this condition, and avert this condemnation with its formidable consequences.

Every attempt to explain the wisdom and the precise ultimate intention of the Supreme Being in constituting a nature subject in so fatal a degree to moral evil, will fail. But even if a new revelation were given to turn this inquiry into noon-day, it would make no difference in the actual state of things. An extension of knowledge could not reverse the fact, that the human nature has displayed through every age the most aggravated proofs of being in a deplorable and hateful condition, whatever were the reasons for giving a moral agent a constitution which it was foreseen would soon be found in this condition. Perhaps, if there were a mind expanded to a comprehension so far beyond all other created intelligences, that it could see at once the whole order of the universe, and look into distant ages, it might understand in what manner the melancholy fact could operate to the perfection of the vast system; and according to what principles, and in reference to what ends, all that has taken place within the empire of the eternal monarch is right. But in this contemplation of the whole, it would also take account of the separate condition of each part; it would perceive that this human world, whatever are its relations to the universe, has its own distinct economy of interests, and stands in its own relation and accountableness to the righteous governor; and that, regarded in this exclusive view, it is an awful spectacle. Now, to this exclusive sphere of our condition and interests revelation confines our attention; and pours contempt, though not more than experience pours, on all attempts to reason on those grand, unknown principles, according to which the Almighty disposes the universe; all our estimates, therefore, of the state and relations of man must take the subject on this insulated ground. Considering man in this view, the sacred oracles have represented him as a more melancholy object than Nineveh or Babylon in ruins; and an infinite aggregate of obvious facts confirms the doctrine. This doctrine, then, is absolute authority in our speculations on human nature. But to this authority the writers in question seem to pay, and to teach their readers to pay, but little respect. And unless those readers are preoccupied by the grave convictions of religious truth, rendered still more grave by painful reflection on themselves, and by observation on mankind; or unless they are capable of enjoying a malicious or misanthropic pleasure, like Mandeville and Swift, in detecting and exposing the degradation of our nature, it is not wonderful that they should be prompt to entertain the sentiments which insinuate a much more flattering estimate. Our elegant and amusing moralists no doubt copiously describe and censure the follies and vices of mankind; but many of these, they maintain, are accidental to the human character, rather than a disclosure of intrinsic qualities. Others do indeed spring radically from the nature; but they are only the wild weeds of a virtuous soil. Man is still a very dignified and noble being, with strong dispositions to all excellence, holding a proud eminence in the ranks of existence, and, (if such a Being is adverted to,) high in the favour of his Creator. The measure of virtue in the world vastly exceeds that of depravity; we should not indulge a fanatical rigour in our judgments of mankind; nor be always reverting to an ideal perfection; nor accustom ourselves to contemplate the Almighty always in the dark majesty of justice. None of their speculations seem to acknowledge the gloomy fact which the New Testament so often asserts or implies, that all men are, 'by nature children of wrath.'

It is quite of course that among sentiments of this order, the idea of the redemption by Jesus Christ, (if any allusion to it should occur,) can appear with but an equivocal meaning, and with none of that transcendent importance with which his own revelation has displayed it. While man is not considered as lost, the mind cannot do justice to the expedient, or to, 'the only name under heaven,' by which he can be redeemed. Accordingly the gift of Jesus Christ does not appear to be habitually recollected as the most illustrious instance of the beneficence of God that has ever come to hnman knowledge, and as the single fact which, more than all others, has relieved the awfulness of the mystery in which our world is enveloped. No thankful joy seems to beam forth at the thought of so mighty an interposition, and of him who was the agent of it. When it is difficult to avoid making some allusion to him, he is acknowledged rather in any of his subordinate characters, than as absolutely a Redeemer; or if the term Redeemer, or, our Saviour, is introduced, it is with an awkward formality, which betrays that its meaning is but little relished, or but little understood. Jesus Christ is regarded rather as having added to our moral advantages, than as having conferred that without which all the rest were in vain; rather as having made the passage to a happy futurity somewhat more commodious, than as having formed the passage itself over what was else an impassable gulf. Thus that comprehensive sum of blessings, called in the New Testament salvation, or redemption, is shrunk into a comparatively inconsiderable favour, which a less glorious messenger might have brought, which a less magnificent language than that dictated by inspiration might have described and which a less costly sacrifice might have secured.

It is consistent with this delusive idea of human nature, and these faint impressions of the gospel, that these writers commonly represent eternal felicity as the pure reward of merit. I believe you will find this, as far as any illusions are made to the subject, the prevailing opinion through the school of polite literature. You will perceive it to be the real opinion of many writers who do sometimes advert, in some phrase employed by way of respectful ceremony to *our national creed*, to the work or sacrifice of Christ.

I might remark on the antichristian motives to action which are more than tolerated among these authors: I will only notice one, the love of glory; that is, the desire of being distinguished, admired, and praised.

No one will deny that to wish for the favourable opinion of the human beings around us, is, to a certain extent, and under certain conditions, consistent with the Christian laws. In the first place a material portion of human happiness depends on the attachment of relatives and friends, and it is right for a man to wish for the happiness resulting from such attachment. But the degree in which he will obtain attachment, will depend very much on the higher or the lower estimate which these persons entertain of his qualities and abilities. In order, therefore, to possess a great degree of their affection, it is right for him to wish, while he endeavours to deserve, that their estimate might be high.

In the next place it is almost too plain to need an observation, that if it were possible for a man to desire the respect and admiration of mankind *purely* as a mean of giving a greater efficacy to his efforts for their welfare, and for the promotion of the cause of heaven, while he would be equally gratified that any other man, in whose hands this mean would have exactly the same effect, should obtain the admiration instead of himself, this would be something more than innocent; it would indicate a most noble state of mind. But where is the example?

In the third place, as the Creator has fixed this desire in the essential constitution of our nature, he intended its gratification, in some restricted degree, to be a direct and immediate cause of pleasure. The good opinion of mankind, expressed in praise, pleases us by the same necessary and inexplicable laws according to which mutual affection pleases us, or according to which we are gratified by music, or the beauties and gales of spring. To a certain extent, therefore, it is innocent to admit the gratification of this desire, simply for the sake of this pleasure.

But to what extent? It is very apparent that this desire has, if I may so express it, an immense voracity. It has within itself no natural principle of limitation, since it is incapable of being gratified to satiety. The applause of a continent has not satisfied some men, nor would that of the whole globe. To what extent, I repeat, may the desire be indulged? Evidently not beyond that point where it begins to introduce its acessories, disdainful comparison, or envy, or competition or ungenerous wishes. But I appeal to each man who has deeply reflected on himself, or observed those around him, whether, this desire, under even a considerably limited degree of indulgenee, does not introduce these accessories; and whether, in order to exclude them from his own mind, he has not often felt it necessary to adopt a severity of restriction approaching near an endeavour to suppress the very desire itself. In wishing to prohibit an *excess* of its indulgence, he has perceived that even a very small degree has amounted, or most powerfully tended, to that excess—with that exception perhaps, of that modification of the desire which has had reference to engaging the affection of relations or a few friends. The measure, therefore, of this desire, which may be permitted consistently with perfect innocence, will be found to be exceedingly small.

Again, the desire cannot be cherished without becoming a motive of action exactly in the degree in which it is cherished. Now if the supreme, though not only motive of action in a pious mind, must be the wish to please God, it is evident that the passion which supplies another motive, ought not to be allowed in a degree that will empower this motive involved in it to contest, in the mind, the supremacy of the pious motive. But here I again appeal to the reflective man of conscience, whether he has not felt that a very small degree of indulgence of the desire of human applause is enough, not only to render the motive involved in it strong enough to maintain a rivalry with what should be the supreme motive, but absolutely to prevail over it. In each pursuit or performance in which he has excelled, or endeavoured to excel, has he not felt with grief and indignation that his thoughts much more promptly turned to the consideration of human praise, than of divine approbation? And when he has been able in some measure to repress this passion, has he not found that a very slight stimulus was competent to restore its impious ascendency? Now what is the inference from these observations? What can it be but absolutely this, that though the desire of human applause is in some certain small degree innocent, yet that since it so mightily tends to an excess destructive of the very essence of piety, it ought, (excepting in the cases where human estimation is sought purely as a means toward some valuable end,) to be opposed and repressed in a manner NOT MUCH LESS general and unconditional than if it were purely evil; and that all those things and books which tend, on the contrary, to animate it with new force, are most pernicious? And such an inference is concordant with the spirit of the New Testament which, though not requiring the absolute extinction of the desire of human applause, yet alludes to most of its operations with censure, exhibits probably no approved instance of its indulgence, and abounds with the most emphatically cogent representations, both of its pernicious influence when it predominates in the mind and of its powerful tendency to acquire this predominance. Insomuch that a serious reader of this book feels that the degree to which the most indulgent Christian casuistry can tolerate this desire, is a degree *which it will be certain to reach and to exceed in his mind in spite of the most systematical opposition.* He will perceive that the question is not so much how far he may encourage it, as by what means he may repress it; and that in the effort to repress it, there is no possibility of going to an excess. The most resolute and persevering exertion will still leave so much of this passion as Christianity will pronounce a fault or a vice. He will be anxious to assemble, in aid of the discipline by which he endeavours to repress the feeling, all the arguments of reason, all striking examples, and all the interdictions of the Bible.

Now I think I cannot be mistaken in asserting, that much the greater number of our fine writers have done the direct contrary of what I have thus represented a devout reader of the New Testament as feeling necessary to be done. Which of their advocates will venture to deny, that they really have encouraged the love of applause, of fame, of glory, or whatever else it may be called, in a degree which, if the preceding argument is just, places them in the most pointed hostility with the Christian religion? Their good sense has, indeed, often, without adverting to the religious considerations, admitted the conviction, and compelled the acknowledgment, of the inanity of this glory. Almost all our ingenious writers have, in one place or another, expressed a contempt of the 'fool to fame.' They perceived the truth, but as the truth did not make them free, they were willing after all to dignify a passion to which they felt themselves irretrievable slaves. And they have laboured to do it by celebrating, with every splendid epithet, the men who were impelled by this passion through the career in which they were the idols of mankind and their own; by describing glory as the best incentive to noble actions, and their worthiest reward; by placing the temple of virtue (proud station of the goddess) in the situation to be a mere introduction to that of Fame; by lamenting that so few, and their unfortunate selves not of the number, can 'climb the steep where that proud temple shines afar:' and by intimating a charge of meanness of spirit against those, who have no generous ardour to distinguish themselves from the crowd by deeds calculated and designed to command admiration. If sometimes the ungracious recollection strikes them, and seems likely to strike their readers, that this admiration is infinitely capricious and perverse, since men have gained it without claims, and lost it without demerit, and since all kinds of fools have offered the incense to all kinds of villains, they escape from the disgust and from the benefit of this recollection by saying, that it is *honourable* fame that noble spirits seek; for they despise the ignorant multitude, and seek applause by none but worthy actions, and from none but worthy judges. Almost every one of these writers sometimes mentions the approbation of the Supreme Being, as that to which wise and good men will beyond all things aspire; but such an occasional acknowledgment feebly counteracts the effect of many glowing sentiments and descriptions of a contrary tendency. I must read once more, and with a habit of mind adapted to receive impressions in a very different manner, the assemblage of our elegant classics, before I can be convinced that the above representation is unjust; and if it is correct, there can be no question whether they have instructed their readers to tolerate, and even to cherish, anti-christian motives of action.

I will only remark on one particular more, namely, that the lighter order of these writers, and some even of the graver, have increased the unacceptableness of Christian doctrines to men of taste, by their manner of ridiculing the cant and extravagance by which hypocrisy, enthusiasm, or the peculiarities of a sect or a period, may have disgraced them. Sometimes, indeed, they have selected and burlesqued modes of expression which were *not* cant, and which ignorance and impiety alone would have dared to ridicule. And often, in exposing to contempt the follies of language or manners, by which a Christian of good taste deplores that the profession of the gospel should ever have been deformed, they take not the smallest care to preserve a clear separation between what taste and sense have a right to explode, and what piety commands to reverence. By this criminal carelessness, (unless, indeed, it were *design*,) they have fixed disagreeable and irreverent associations on the evangelical truth itself, for which many persons, afterwards become more seriously convinced of that truth, have had cause to wish those pages or volumes had gone into the fire, instead of coming into their hands. Many others, who have not become thus seriously affected, retain the impression and cherish the disgust. Gay writers ought to know that this is dangerous ground.

I am sorry that this extended censure on works of genius and taste could not be prosecuted with a more marked application, and with more discriminate references than the continual repetition of the expressions, 'elegant literature,' and 'these writers.' It might be a service of some value to the evangelical cause, if a work were written containing a faithful and serious estimate, individually, of the most popular writers of the last century and a half, in respect to the important subject of these comments; with formal citations from some of their works, and a candid statement of the general tendency of others. In an essay like this it is impossible to make an enumeration of names, or pass a judgment, except in a very slight, occasional manner, on any particular author. Even the several *classes* of authors, which I mentioned some time back, as coming under the accusation, shall detain you but a short time.

The moral philosophers for the most part seem anxious to avoid every thing that might subject them to the appellation of Christian divines. They regard their department as a science complete in itself; and they investigate the foundation of morality, define its laws, and affix its sanctions, in a manner generally so distinct from Christianity, that the reader would almost conclude that religion to be *another* science complete in itself.* An *entire* separation, indeed, it is hardly possible to preserve; since Christianity has decided some moral questions on which reason was dubious or silent; and since that final retribution which the New Testament has so luminously foreshown, is evidently the greatest of sanctions. To make *no* reference, while inculcating moral principles, to a judgment to come, after it has been declared, on what has been confessed to be divine authority, would look like systematic irreligion. But still it is striking to observe how small a portion of the ideas, which distinguish the New Testament from other books, many moral philosophers have thought indispensable to a theory in which they professed to include the sum of the duty and interests of man. A serious reader is constrained to feel that either there is too much in *that* book, or too little in theirs. He will perceive that, in the inspired book, the moral principles are intimately interwoven with all those doctrines which could not have been known without that revelation. He will find, also, in this superior book, a vast number of ideas avowedly designed to interest the *affections* in favour of all moral principles and virtues. These ideas are taken from a consideration of the divine mercy, the compassion of the Redeemer, and other topics to which moral philosophers have very rarely alluded. And though the same definition would apply to any given virtue as illustrated in the inspired and in the philosophical page, yet the manner in which it bears on the conscience and on the heart is materially different. The difference becomes momentous, if it should be found that the sacred authority pronounces the virtues of a good man not to be the cause of his acceptance with God, and that the philosophic moralists disclaim any other. On the whole, it must be concluded that there cannot but be something very defective in the theory of morality which makes so slight an acknowledgment of the religion of Christ, and takes so little of its peculiar character. The philosophers place the religion in the relation of a diminutive satellite to the world of moral

* When it happens, sometimes, that a moral topic hardly can be disposed of without some recognition of its involving, or being intimately connected with, a theological doctrine it is curious to notice with what an air of indifference somewhat partaking of contempt, one of these writers will observe, that that view of the matter is the business of the divines, with whose department he does not pretend to interfere.

and eternal interests; useful, as throwing a few rays on that side of it on which the solar light of human wisdom could not directly shine; but that it can impart a vital warmth, or that it claims the ascendant power and honours, some of them seem not to have a suspicion.

Without doubt, innumerable reasonings and conclusions may be advanced on moral subjects which shall be *true* on a foundation of their own, equally in the presence of the evangelical system and in its absence. Without any reference to that system, or if it had never been appointed or revealed, it had been easy to illustrate, the utility of virtue, the elevation which it confers on a rational being, its conformity with the orders of the universe, and many other views of the subject. It would also have been easy to pass from virtue in the abstract into an illustration and enforcement of the several distinct virtues as arranged in a practical system. And if it should be asked, Why may not some writers employ their speculations on those parts and views of moral truth which are independent of the gospel, leaving it to other men to Christianize the whole by the addition of the evangelical relations, motives and conditions? I readily answer, That this may sometimes very properly be done. An author may render valuable service by explaining, for instance, the utility of virtue in general, or of any particular virtue, or by a clear illustration of any other circumstance of the moral system. In doing this, he would expressly take a marked ground, and aim at a specific object. He would not let it be imagined for a moment that this particular view of the subject of morals involved all the relations of that subject with the interests of man, and with God. It would be fully understood that a multitude of other considerations were indispensable to a complete moral theory. But the charge against the moral philosophers is meant to be applied to those who have professed to consider morals under a comprehensive view, including all the relations in which they are connected with duty and happiness; and who, in this comprehensive view, seem quite to have forgotten the implication of moral with evangelical truth, since they neither include the evangelical ideas in their speculations, nor appear sensible of a defect.

When I mention our Historians, it will instantly occur to you, that the very foremost names in this department imply every thing that is deadly to the Christian religion itself, as a divine communication, and therefore lie under condemnation of a different kind. But as to the generality of those who have not been regarded as enemies to the Christian cause, have they not forgotten what was due from its friends? The historian intends his work to have the effect of a series of moral estimates of the persons whose actions he records; now, if he believes that a Judge of the world will come at length, and pronounce on the very characters that his work adjudges, it is one of the simplest dictates of good sense, that all the awards of the historian should be faithfully coincident with the judgments which may be expected from that supreme authority on the last day. Those distinctions of character, which the historian applauds as virtues, or censures as vices, should be exactly the same qualities, which the language already heard from that judge certifies us that he will applaud or condemn. It is worse than foolish to erect a literary court of morals and human character, of which the maxims, the language, the decisions, and the judges, will be equally the objects of contempt before him whose intelligence will instantly distinguish and place in light the right and the wrong of all time. What a wretched abasement will overwhelm on that day some of the pompous historians, who were called by others, and deemed by themselves, the high authoritative censors of an age, and whose verdict was to fix on each name immortal honour or infamy, if they shall find many of the questions and the decisions of that tribunal proceed on principles which they would have been ashamed to apply, or never took the trouble to understand. How they will be confounded, if some of the men whom they had extolled, are consigned to ignominy, and some that they had despised, are applauded by the voice at which the earth will tremble and be silent. But such a sad humiliation will, I think, be apprehended for many of the historians, by every serious Christian reader who shall take the hint of this subject along with him through their works. He will not seldom feel that the writers seem uninformed, while they remark and decide on actions and characters, that a final lawgiver has come from heaven, or that he will come, or on what account he will come, yet once more. Their very diction often abjures the plain Christian denominations of good and evil; nor do I need to enumerate the specious and fallacious terms which they have employed in their place. How, then, can a mind which learns to think in *their* manner, learn, at the same time, to think in *his* from whose opinion it will, however, be found no light matter to have dissented, when they shall be declared for the last time in this world?

The various interesting sets of short Essays, especially the Spectator and Rambler, must have had, during a season at least, a very considerable influence on the moral taste of the public; and probably they have a considerable influence still. The very ample scope of the Spectator gave a fair opportunity for a serious writer to introduce, excepting pure science, a little of every subject connected with the condition and happiness of men. How did it happen that the stupendous circumstance of the redemption by the Messiah, of which the importance is commensurate with the whole interests of man, with the value of his immortal spirit, with the government of his Creator in this world, and with the happiness of eternity, should not have been a few times, in the long course of that work, fully and solemnly exhibited? Why should not a few of the most peculiar of the doctrines comprehended in the subject have been clothed with the fascinating elegance of Addison, from whose pen many persons would have received an occasional evangelical lesson with incomparably more candour than from any professed divine? A pious and benevolent man, such as the avowed advocate of Christianity ought to be, should not have been contented that so many thousands of minds as his writings were adapted to instruct and to charm should have been left, for any thing that he very explicitly attempted to the contrary in his most popular works, to end a life which he had contributed to refine, acquainted but slightly with the grand security of happiness after death. Or, if it was not his duty to introduce in a formal manner any of the most specifically evangelical subjects, it might at least have been expected, that some of the many serious essays contained in the Spectator should have had more of a Chirstian tinge, more references to the sentiments of the gospel, intermingled with the speculations concerning the Deity, and the gravest moral subjects. There might easily have been more assimilation of what may, as it now stands, be called a *literary* religion, to the spirit of the New Testament. From him also, as a kind of dictator among the majority of the elegant writers of the age, it might have been expected that he would have set himself, with the same decision and noble indignation which his Cato had shown against the betrayers of Roman liberty and laws, to denounce that ridicule which has wounded religion by a careless or by a crafty manner of holding up its abuses to scorn: but of this the Spectator itself is not free from examples.

Addison wrote a book expressly in defence of the religion of Christ; but to be the dignified advocate of a cause, and to be its humble disciple, may be very different things. An advocate has a feeling of making himself important—he seems to *confer* something on the cause; but as a disciple, he must feel littleness, humanity, and submission. Self-admiration might find more to gratify it in becoming the *patron* of a beggar, than the *servant* of the greatest potentate. Addison was, moreover, very unfortunate, for any thing like justice to the gospel, in the class of persons with whom he associated, and whom he was anxious to please. One can imagine with what a perfect storm of ridicule he would have been greeted, on entering one of his celebrated coffee-houses of wits, on the day after he should have published in the Spectator, a paper, for instance, on the necessity of being devoted to the service of Jesus Christ. The friendship of the world ought to be a 'pearl of great price,' for its cost is very serious.

The powerful and lofty mind of Johnson was much more capable of scorning the ridicule, and defying the opposition, of wits and worldlings. And yet it is too probable that his social life was eminently unfavourable to a deep and simple consideration of Christian sentiment; and that the very ascendency by which he intimidated and silenced impiety, contributed to the injury. He associated with men of whom many were very learned, some were extremely able, but of whom comparatively few made any decided profession of piety; and, perhaps, a considerable number were such as would in other society have shown a strong propensity to irreligion. This, however, seldom dared to appear undisguisedly in Johnson's presence; and it is impossible not to revere the strength and noble severity that made it so cautious. But this repression of irreligion had the effect of rendering many men acceptable associates, with whom his judgment, his conscience, and all his moral feelings, would have forbidden much friendly intercourse, if those men had habitually assumed the freedom of fully disclosing themselves. Decorum in respect to religion being preserved, he could take a most lively interest in the company of men who drew forth the utmost force and stores of his mind, in conversations on literature, moral philosophy, and general intelligence, and who could enrich every subject of social argument by their learning, their genius, or their knowledge of mankind. But if there was at the same time a repressed impiety latent in their minds, it was impossible that it should not infuse into the sentiments which they communicated, a certain quality uncongenial with Christianity, though every thing avowedly opposed to it were in his company avoided. Now, through the complacency which he felt in such intellectual intercourse, this quality would, in some degree, steal into his own ideas and feeling. For it is not in the power of the strongest and most vigilant mind, amidst the animated interchange of eloquence, to avoid some degree of assimilation to even the least approved sentiments of men whose intellectual wealth or energy gives so much pleasure, and commands so much respect. Thus the very predominance by which he could repress the direct irreligion of statesmen, scholars, wits, and accomplished men of the world, might, by retaining him their intimate or frequent associate, subject him to meet the influence of that irreligion acting in a manner too indirect and refined to excite his hostility or his caution.

But, indeed, if his caution was excited, there might still be a possibility of self-deception in the case. He would feel it, and justly feel it, so great an achievement to constrain such men as I have described, to adopt, at least by acquiescence, when with him, a better style of moral sentiment, cleared of all obvious irreligion, that he might be too much disposed to be satisfied himself with such an order of sentiments. It would be difficult for him to admit that what was actually a victory over impiety, could be itself less than Christianity. It is hard for a man to suspect himself deficient in that very thing in which he not only excels other men, but mends them. Nothing can well be more unfortunate for Christian attainments, than to be habitually in society where a man will feel as if he displayed a saintly eminence of character by obtaining a decent silence or partial assent on subjects, on which it has been the delight of wise and devout men to expatiate.

If there be any truth in the representations which compose so large a part of this essay, Johnson's continual immersion, if I may so express it, in the studies of polite literature, must have subjected him to no small measure of an influence, which it requires a more intimate and habitual familiarity with the Christian principles than perhaps we are warranted to believe he maintained, to prevent being injurious to a man's views and feelings concerning religion.

It must, however, be admitted that this illustrious author, who, though here mentioned only in the class of essayists, is to be ranked among the greatest of moral philosophers, is less at variance with the principles which appear to be displayed in the New Testament, than almost any other distinguished writer of either of these classes. But few of his speculations, comparatively, tend to beguile the reader and admirer into that spirit which, on turning to the instructions of Jesus Christ and his apostles, would feel estrangement or disgust; and he has more explicit and solemn references to the grand purpose of human life, to a future judgment, and to eternity, than almost any other of our elegant moralists has had the piety or the courage to make. There is so much that most powerfully coincides and co-operates with Christian truth, that the disciple of Christianity the more regrets to meet occasionally a sentiment, respecting perhaps the review of life, the consolations in death, the effect of repentance, or the terms of acceptance with God, which he cannot reconcile with the evangelical theory, nor with those principles of Christian faith in which Johnson avowed his belief. In such a writer he cannot but deem such deviations a matter of grave culpability.

Omission is his other capital fault. Though he did introduce in his serious speculations, as I have observed, more distinct allusions to religious ideas than most other moralists, yet he did not introduce them so often as may be claimed from a writer who frequently carries seriousness to the utmost pitch of solemnity. There scarcely ever was an author, not formally theological, in whose works a large proportion of explicit Christian sentiment was more requisite for a consistent entireness of character, than in the moral writings of Johnson. No writer ever more completely exposed and blasted the folly and vanity of the greatest number of human pursuits. The visage of Medusa could not have darted a more fatal glance against the tribe of gay triflers, the competitors of ambition, the proud possessors of wealth, or the men who consume their life in useless speculations. His severe and just condemnation strikes indeed at almost all classes, and all the most favourite employments of mankind. But it was so much the more peculiarly his duty to insist, still more fully than he did, on that one model of character, that one grand employment of life, which is enjoined by heaven, and which will stand the test of the most rigid moral speculation, and of the final account. No author has more impressively displayed the misery of human life: he laid himself under so much the stronger obligation to unfold most explicitly the only effectual consolations, the true scheme of felicity as far as it is attainable on earth, and the delightful prospect of that better region which has so often inspired exultation in the most melancholy situations. No writer has better illustrated the rapidity of time, and the shortness of life; he ought so much the more fully to have dwelt on the views of that eternity at which his readers are reminded that they will so quickly arrive. No writer will easily make more poignant reflections on the pains of guilt: was it not indispensable that he should oftener have directed the mind suffering this deepest distress to that great sacrifice once offered for sin? No writer represents with more accurate and mortifying truth the failure of human resolutions, and the feebleness of human efforts, in the contest against corrupt inclination, depraved habit, and temptation: why did not this melancholy contemplation and experience prompt a very frequent recollection, and a most emphatical expression of the importance, of that divine assistance, without which the Bible has fully warned us that our labours will fail?

In applying the censure to the poets, it is very gratifying to meet with so much to applaud in the most elevated of all their tribe. Milton's genius might harmoniously have mingled with the angels that announced the Messiah to be come, or that on the spot and at the moment of his departure predicted his coming again; might have shamed to silence the muses of paganism; or softened the pains of a Christian martyr. Part of the poetical works of Young, those of Cowper, Watts, and a few others, have animated a very great number of minds with sentiments, which they did not feel it necessary to repress or extinguish in order to listen with complacency to the language of Christ and his apostles. But as to the great majority of the poets, it would be most curious to try what kind of religious system, and what view of the economy of man, would be formed by the assemblage of all the sentiments belonging or alluding to the subject throughout their works; if such an experiment were worth the trouble, and there were any person sufficiently in the state of the ingenuous Huron to perform it justly. But it would be exceedingly amusing to observe the process and the fantastic result; it would, in the next place, be very sad to consider, that these fallacies have been insinuated by the charms of poetry into countless thousands of minds, with a beguilement that has, first, diverted them from a serious attention to the gospel, then formed them to a habitual dislike of it, and finally operated to betray some of them to the doom which, beyond the grave, awaits the neglect of Jesus Christ.

You have probably seen Pope cited as a Christian poet, by some pious authors, whose anxiety to impress reluctant genius into an appearance of favouring Christianity, has credulously seized on any occasional verse which seemed an echo of the sacred doctrines. No reader can admire more than I, the discriminate thought, the finished execution, and the galaxy of poetical felicities, by which Pope's writings are distinguished. But I cannot refuse to perceive, that almost every allusion in his lighter works to the names, the facts, and the topics, that peculiarly belong to the religion of Christ, is in a style and spirit of profane banter; and that, in most of his graver ones, where he meant to be dignified, he took the utmost care to divest his thoughts of all the mean vulgarity of Christian associations. 'Off! ye profane!' might seem to have been his address to all evangelical ideas, when he began his Essay on Man; and they were obedient, and fled; for if you detach the detail and illustrations, so as to lay bare the outline and general principles of the work, it will stand confest an elaborate attempt to redeem the whole theory of the condition and interests of men, both in life and death, from all the explanations imposed on it by an unphilosophical revelation from heaven. And in the happy riddance of this despised though celestial light, it exhibits a sort of moon-light vision, of thin, impalpable abstractions, at which a speculatist may gaze, with a dubious wonder whether they are realities or phantoms; but which a practical man will in vain try to seize and turn to account, and which an evangelical man will disdain to accept in substitution for those applicable and affecting forms of truth with which his religion has made him conversant. But what deference to Christianity was to be expected, when such a man as Bolingbroke was the genius whose imparted splendours was to illuminate, and the demigod* whose approbation was to crown, the labours which were to conjoin these two venerable names, according to the wish of the poet, in everlasting fame?

* He is so named somewhere in Pope's works.

If it be said for some parts of these dim speculations, that though Christianity comes forward as the practical dispensation of truth, yet there must be, in remote abstraction behind it, some grand, ultimate, elementary truths, of which this dispensation does not inform us, or which it reduces from their pure recondite into a more palpable and popular form; I answer, And what did the poet, or 'the master of the poet and the song,' know about these truths, and how did they come by their information?

A serious observer must acknowledge with regret, that such a class of productions as novels, in which folly tries to please in a greater number of shapes than the poet enumerates in the Paradise of Fools, is capable of producing a very considerable effect on the moral taste of the community. A large proportion of them, however, consist too much of pure folly to have any more specific counteraction to Christian principles than that of mere folly in general; excepting, indeed, that the most flimsy of them will occasionally contribute their mite of mischief, by alluding to a Christian profession in a manner that identifies it with the cant by which hypocrites have aped it, or the extravagance with which fanatics have distorted it. But a great and direct force of counteracting influence proceeds from those which eloquently display characters of eminent vigour and virtue, when that virtue is founded on no basis consolidated by religion; but on a mixture of refined pride with generous feeling, or expressly on those philosophical principles which are too often accompanied, in these works, by an avowed or strongly intimated contempt of every idea of any religion, especially the Christian. If the case is mended in those into which an awkward religion has found its way, it is rather because the characters excite less interest, than because that which they *do* excite is favourable to religion. No reader is likely to be impressed with the dignity of being a Christian by seeing, in one of these works, an attempt to combine that character with the fine gentleman by means of a most ludicrous apparatus of amusements and sacraments, churches and theatres, morning-prayers and evening-balls. Nor will it perhaps be of any great service to the Christian cause, that some others of them profess to exemplify and defend, against the cavils and scorn of infidels, a religion of which it does not appear that the writers would have discovered the merits, had it not been established by law. One may doubt whether any one will be more than amused by the venerable priest, who is introduced probably among wicked lords and giddy girls, to maintain the sancity of terms, and attempt the illustration of doctrines, which these well-meaning writers do not perceive that the worthy gentleman's college, diocesan and library, have but very imperfectly enabled him to understand. If the reader even wished to be more than amused, it is easy to imagine how much he would be likely to be instructed and affected, by such an illustration or fence of the Christian religion, as the writer of a fashionable novel would deem a graceful expedient for filling up his plot.

One cannot close such a review of our fine writers without melancholy reflections. That cause which will raise all its zealous friends to a sublime eminence on the last and most solemn day the world has to behold, and will make them great forever, presented its claims full in sight of each of these authors in his time. The very lowest of those claims could not be less than a conscientious solicitude to beware of every thing that could in any point injure the sacred cause. This claim has been slighted by so many as have lent attraction to an order of moral sentiments greatly discordant with its principles. And so many are gone into eternity under the charge of having employed their genius, as the magicians their enchantments against Moses, to counteract the Saviour of the world.

Under what restrictions, then, ought the study of polite literature to be conducted? I cannot but have foreseen that this question must return at the end of these observations; and I can only answer as I have answered before. Polite literature will necessarily continue to be the grand school of intellectual and moral cultivation. The evils, therefore, which it may contain, will as certainly affect in some degree the minds of the successive students, as the hurtful influence of the climate, or of the seasons, will affect their bodies. To be thus affected, is a part of the destiny under which they are born, in a civilized country. It is indispensable to acquire the advantage; it is inevitable to incur the evil. The means of counteraction will amount, it is to be feared, to no more than palliatives. Nor can these be proposed in any specific method. All that I can do is, to urge on the reader of taste the very serious duty of continually recalling his mind, and if he is a parent or preceptor, of cogently representing to his pupils, the real character of the religion of the New Testament, and the reasons which command an inviolable adherence to it.

ESSAY V.

ON POPULAR IGNORANCE.

MY PEOPLE ARE DESTROYED FOR LACK OF KNOWLEDGE.—*Hosea.*

CHAPTER I.

HISTORICAL REVIEW OF THE GENERAL CONDITION OF MANKIND, IN AN INTELLECTUAL RESPECT, AT DIFFERENT PERIODS.

SECTION I.

Indifference of the Human Mind to representations of Misery.

It may excite in us some sense of wonder, and perhaps of self-reproach, to reflect with what a stillness and indifference of the mind we can read and repeat sentences asserting facts which are awful calamities; especially if we perceive that this repose of feeling remains undisturbed when the calamities so pronounced have all the aggravation of being of a moral and spiritual nature. And this indifference is not an extraordinary thing, the mere transient effect of occasional heaviness and languor. The self-inspector must often be compelled to acknowledge it as an indication of the moral habit of his mind, that ideas of misery and destruction, though expressed in the plainest, strongest language, seem to come with but a faint glimmer on his apprehension, and die away without being able to awake one emotion of that sensibility which so many comparatively trifling causes can bring into exercise.

Will the hearers of the sentence just now repeated from the sacred book, give a moment's attention to the manner in which it impresses them? Would you find it difficult to say what idea, or whether any thing that can properly be denominated an idea at all, has been formed by the sound of words bearing so melancholy a significance? And would you be constrained to own that they excite no interest which would not instantly give place to that of the smallest of your own concerns, suggested in the course of your thoughts, or to the tendency to wander loose among casual fancies, or to feelings of the ludicrous, if any little unlucky or whimsical incident were to happen? It is at least too probable that this is true of the majority of any numerous assemblage, even though concerns of the gravest interest be ostensibly the object of their meeting. And perhaps even many of even the most serious will confess, they are mortified to find what strong repeated painful exertion it requires, to fix the mind so effectually as to move its affections to any depth, though the subjects appealing to them be unspeakably mournful.

That the 'people are destroyed,' is perceived to have the sound of a lamentable declaration. But the import which it languidly conveys to the mind, sinks into insignificance as received into a state of feeling which, if reducible to distinct thought would be expressed to this effect;—that the people's destruction, in whatever sense of the word, is, doubtless, a deplorable thing, but quite a customary and ordinary matter, the prevailing fact, indeed, in the general state of this world; that, in truth, they seemed to be made but to be destroyed, for that they have always been, in a variety of ways, the subjects of destruction; that, subjected in common with all living corporeal beings on earth to the doom of death, and to a fearful diversity of causes tending to inflict it, they have also appeared, through their long sad history, consigned to a spiritual and moral destruction, if that term be applicable to a condition the reverse of wisdom, goodness, and happiness; that, in short, such a sentence as that taken from the prophet, is too merely an expression of what has been always and over the whole world self-evident, to exite any particular attention or emotion.

Thus the destruction, in every sense of the word, of human creatures, is so constantly obvious, as mingled and spread throughout the whole system of things in which we are placed, that the mind has been insensibly wrought to that guarded state which we acquire in defence of our own ease, against any grievance which is habitually present to us. The instinctive policy, with respect to this prevailing destruction, has been—not to feel. And the art of maintaining this exemption, by all the requisite devices, avoidances, and fallacies, has become almost mechanical. When fully matured, it appears like a wonderful adventitious power, added to the natural faculties of the mind,—a power of *not seeing*, (though with eyes open, and perfectly endowed with sight,) what is obviously and glaringly presented to view on all sides. There is, indeed, a dim general recognition that such things are; the hearing of a bold denial of their existence might provoke the mind in re-action to go out in intent observation to take account of them; and their reality and dreadful excess would then be asserted in emphatic terms of contradiction to that denial, their impression continuing in force as long as required for maintaining that contradiction; but, in the ordinary state of feeling, the mind preserves a comfortable dulness of perception towards the melancholy vision, and sees it as if it saw it not.

This habitual and fortified insensibility may, indeed, be sometimes broken in upon with violence, by the sudden occurrence of some particular instance of human destruction, in either import of the word, some example of peculiar aggravation, or happening under extraordinary and striking circumstances, or very near us in place or interest. An emotion is excited of pity, or terror, or horror; so strong, that if the person has been habitually thoughtless, and has no wish to be otherwise, he fears he shall never be able to recover his state of careless ease; or, if of a more serious disposition, thinks it impossible he can ever cease to feel an awful and salutary effect. This more serious person perhaps also thinks it must be inevitable that henceforward his feelings will be more alive to the miseries of mankind. But how mighty is the power of habit against any single impressions made in contravention to it! Both the thoughtless and the more reflective man may probably find, that a comparatively short lapse of time suffices to relieve them from any thing more than slight momentary reminiscences of what had struck them with such painful force, and to restore, in regard to the general view of the acknowledged misery of the human race, nearly the accustomed tranquillity. The course of feeling bears some resemblance to a listless stream of water, which, after having been provoked into turbulence and ebullition, by a massive substance flung into it, or by its precipitation at a rapid, relapses, in the progress of a few fathoms and a few moments, into its former sluggishness of current.

But is it well that this should be the state of feeling, while a fatal process is going on under which the people are destroyed? Is there not cause to suspect some unsound principles in a tranquillity to which it makes no material difference whether the multitude be destroyed or saved? which would hardly, perhaps, have been excited to an act of deprecation at the view of what Ornan beheld, and which might have permitted the privileged patriarch to sink in a soft slumber at the moment when the ark was felt to move from its ground. Is it possible to conceive that beings put in one place, so near together, so much alike, and under such a complication of connexions and dependences, can yet really be so insulated, as that some of them may, without any thing wrong in feeling, behold, with unmoved composure, innumerable companies of the rest in such a condition, that it had been better for them not to have existed?

To such a condition a vast multitude have been consigned by the 'lack of knowledge.' And we have to appeal to whatever there is of benevolence and conscience in those who deem themselves happy instances of exemption from this deplorable consignment and who ascribe their state of inestimable privilege to knowledge, it being a consequence which has resulted, under the blessing of heaven, from information, from truth, having been communicated to their minds. Amidst the benefit and delight of what they thus possess in consequence of knowing, they might make, sometimes, the trial of how far they can go toward conceiving what their condition would be under a negation of that possession by a negation of its cause. It may, indeed, be alleged that the mind has not the power to place itself in any effectual imagination of the predicament of suffering, or having suffered, an annihilation of its knowledge; that it cannot follow out a supposed process of putting out one bright fixed truth within it, and another, in order to conceive the state it would be in if they were extinguished. It is true that such a voluntary artificial eclipse of the light of the soul is not practicable: all that is possible in this way, is an imperfect recollection, as a matter of experience, of the ignorance which actually preceded one part, and another, of the knowledge, in the progress of its attainment: the recollection will be very imperfect in those persons, especially who were well instructed in their childhood. But though you cannot perform in imagination a series of acts of *unlearning*, realizing to yourselves, through out the retrogradation, what you would be, intellectually, at each successive extinction of a portion of knowledge, you *can* go backward along this train in the way of supposing the negation of the valuable *benefits* which have arisen to you from knowledge. Distinguishing the respective advantage accruing to you at each stage, and from each particular part, of your knowledge progressively acquired, you can so make the supposition of that advantage not having become yours, as to conceive, in some measure, in what state you would have been in the absence of it. And, while going through this process, you may consider that you are making out a representation of the condition of innumerable beings of your race.

It may be presumed of many in a numerous grave assemblage of persons, that if their attention were directed to take an account of the benefit they have received through the medium of knowledge, they might in sober truth, and the spirit of gratitude, say they do not well know where to begin the long enumeration, nor how to bring into one estimate so ample a diversity of valuable things. It might be something like being asked to specify, in brief terms, what a highly improved portion of the ground, in a tract rude and sterile if left to itself, has received from cultivation. No little time would be required to consider and recount what it has received. The fancy is carried back through a gradation of states and appearances, in which the now fertile spots, and picture-like scenes, and commodious passes, may or must have existed in the advance from the original rudeness. The estimate of what has ultimately been effected, rises at each stage in this retrospect of the progress, in which so many valuable changes and additions still required to be followed by something more, to complete the scheme of improvement. In thus tracing backward the condition of a now fair and productive place of human dwelling and subsistence, it may easily be recollected, what a vast number of the earth's inhabitants there are whose places of dwelling are in all those states of worse cultivation and commodiousness, and what multitudes leading a miserable and precarious life amidst the inhospitableness of the waste howling wilderness. Each presented circumstance of fertility or shelter, salubrity or beauty, may be named as what is wanting to a much greater number of the occupants of the world, then enjoy such an advantage.

If, in like manner, a person richly possessed of the benefits imparted by means of knowledge, finds, in attempting to estimate the amount of good thus acquired, that the kind and modes of it, in their variety, combinations, and gradations from less to greater, rise so fast on his view, that his computing faculty loses itself among them, he may be reminded that this account of his wealth is, in truth, that of many other men's poverty. A comparison for compassion may be made at the view of one important advantage after another, ascertained to have been from this source and observed through their progress of enlargement, while he thinks what it would be to suffer a depravation of all this good, or a reduction to its smallest measure, and then realizes to himself the melancholy fact, that parallel to such a state is that of the multitude in every direction. —But truly what a state that must be, if men still but very partially enlightened, and feeling themselves in all respects imperfect, and also exposed to sorrows and doomed to death, can, nevertheless, look down upon it with compassion, in consequence of what knowledge has done for them! To what a depth this implies that their fellow mortals are sunk by the 'lack of knowledge.'

We may say to persons so favoured,—If knowledge has been made the cause that you are beyond all comparison better qualified to make the short sojourn on this earth to the greatest advantage, think what a fatal thing that must be which condemns so many, whose lot is contemporary, and in vicinity with yours, to pass through the most precious possibilities of good unprofited, and at last to look back on life as a lost adventure. If through knowledge you have been introduced into a new and superior world of ideas and realities, and your intellectual being there brought into exercise among the highest interests, and into communication with the noblest objects, think of that state of the soul to which this better economy has no existence. If knowledge rendered efficacious has become, in your minds, the light and joy of the Christian faith and hope, look at the state of those whose minds have never been cultivated to an ability to entertain the evangelical truths even as mere intellectual notions. In a word, what a state and what a calamity you deem the abandonment of human spirits to ignorance to be, when you would not for the wealth, literally, of an empire or a world, consent, were it possible, to descend into it from that to which you have been advanced by means of knowledge.

But in this state have the multitude been from the time of the prophet, whose words we have cited, down to this hour. Our design is to offer, without much formality of method, a series of observations descriptive of the wretchedness, especially in a moral point of view, naturally and inseparably attending on prevailing ignorance in the people; though it might perhaps be contended that the emphatic sentence of this ancient denunciator referred rather to the punishment inflicted by divine judicial appointment on the guilt involved in that ignorance, and on the crimes resulting from it. Exact distinctions, however, as to the mode in which the fatal consequence was connected with the cause, would be in little account with him who was deploring so sad a calamity.

SECTION II.

Disastrous Consequences of Ignorance in the Ancient Israelites.

The prophets had their exalted privilige of dwelling amidst the illuminations of heaven, effectually countervailed by the daily spectacle of the grossest manifestations and mischiefs of ignorance, among the very people for whose instruction they were under the prophetic vocation. One of the most striking of the characteristics by which their writings so forcibly seize the imagination, is that strange fluctuating visionary light and gloom, caused by the continual intermingling and contrast of the emanations from the spirit of infinite wisdom, with the disclosures from the dark debased souls of the people. We are tempted to pronounce that nation not only the most perverse, but the most unintelligent and stupid of all human tribes. The revealed law of god in the midst of them; the prophets and other organs and modes of oracular communication; religious ordinances and emblems; facts, made and expressly intended to embody truths, in long and various series; the whole system of their superhuman government constituted as a school—all these were ineffectual to create so much just thought in their minds, as to save them from the vainest and the vilest fancies, delusions, and superstitions.

But, indeed, this very circumstance, that knowledge shown on them from him that knows all things, may, in part, account for a stupidity that appears so peculiar and marvellous. The nature of man is in such a moral condition, that any thing is the less acceptible for coming directly from God; it being quite consistent, that the state of mind which is declared to be 'enmity against him,' should have a dislike to his coming so near, as to impart his communications, as it were, by his immediate act, and bearing on them the fresh and sacred impression of his hand. The supplies for man's temporal being are conveyed to him through an extended medium, through a long process of nature and art, which seems to place the great first cause at a commodious distance; and those gifts are, on that account, more welcome, on the whole, than if they were sent like the manna. The manna itself would not, probably, have been so soon loathed, had it been produced in what we call the regular course of nature. And with respect to the intellectual communications which were given to constitute the light of knowledge in their souls, there can, on the same principle, be no doubt that they would more willingly have opened their minds to receive them, and exercised their faculties upon them, if they could have appeared as something originating in human wisdom, or at least as something which had been long surrendered by the divine revealer, to maintain itself in the world on much the same terms as the doctrines worked out from mere human speculation. But truth declared to them, and inculcated on them, through a continual immediate manifestation of the sovereign intelligence, had a glow of divinity (if we may so express it) that was unspeakably offensive to their minds, which therefore receded with instinctive avoidance. They were averse to look toward that which they could not see without seeing God; and thus they were hardened in ignorance, through a re-action of human depravity against the too luminous approach of the divine presence to give them wisdom.

But, in whatever degree the case might be thus, as to the cause, the fact is evident, that the Jewish people were not more remarkable for this state of privilege, than for the little benefit, in point of mental light, which they acquired under a dispensation specially and miraculously constituted and administered for their instruction. The sacred history of which they are the subject, exhibits every mode in which the intelligent faculties may resist, evade, or pervert the truth; every way in which the decided preference for darkness may avail to defy what might have been presumed to be irresistible irradiations; every condition of ignorance which makes it be also guilt; and every form of practical mischief in which the natural tendency of ignorance is shown. A great part of what the devout teachers of that people had to address to them, wherever they appeared among them, was in reproach of their ignorance, and in order, if possible, to dispel it. We may, in some degree, conceive the grievous manner in which it was continually encountering them. If we should imagine one of these well instructed and benevolent teachers going into a promiscuous company of the people, in a house, or open place in a village, and asking them, with a view at once to see into their minds and inform them, say ten plain questions, relative to matters somewhat above the ordinary secular concerns of life, but essential for them to understand, it is but making the case similar to what might happen in much later and nearer states of society, if we suppose him not to obtain from the whole company rational answers to more than three, or two, or even one, of those questions, notwithstanding that every one of them might be designedly so framed as to admit of an easy reply from the most prominent of the dictates of the 'law and the prophets,' and the right application of the most memorable of the facts in the national history. In his earlier experiments he might be very reluctant to admit the fact, that so many of his countrymen, in one spot, could have been so faithfully maintaining the ascendency of darkness in their spirits, while surrounded by divine manifestations of truth. He might be willing to suspect he had not been happy in the form of words in which his queries had been conveyed. But it may be believed that all his changes and adaptations of expression, to elicit from the contents of his auditors' understandings something fairly answering to his questions, might but complete the proof that the thing sought was not there. And while he might be looking from one to another, with regret not unmingled with indignation at an ignorance at once so unhappy and so criminal, they probably might little care, excepting some very slight feeling of mortified pride, that they were thus proved to be nearly pagans in knowledge within the immediate hearing of the oracles of God.

Or we may represent to ourselves this benevolent promoter of improvement endeavouring to instruct such a company, not in the way of interrogation, but in the ordinary manner of discourse, and that he *assumed* the existence in their minds of those principles, those points of knowledge, which would have suggested the proper replies to the questions on the former supposition to have been put to them. You can well conceive what reception the reasonings, advices, or reproofs, proceeding on such an assumption, would find among the hearers, according to their respective temperaments. Some would be content with knowing nothing at all about the matter, which, they would perhaps say, might be, for aught they knew, something very wise; and, according to their greater or less degree of patience and sense of decorum, would wait in quiet and perhaps sleepy dulness for the end of the irksome lecture, or escape from it by slyly stealing off, or by an open and ostentatiously noisy manner of going away. To others it would all seem ridiculous absurdity, and they would readily laugh aloud if any one would begin. A few possessed of some natural shrewdness, would set themselves to catch at something in the way of cavil, with awkward aim, but good will. While perhaps one or two, of better disposition, imperfectly descrying at moments something true and important in what was said, and convinced of the friendly intention of the speaker, might feel a transient regret for what they would with honest shame call the stupidity of their own minds, accompanied with some resentment against those to whose neglect it was greatly attributable. The teacher must have been a man very little exercised in observing looks and manner, as indications, if he did not after a while perceive that he had no effective hold on the mental faculties of the living figures before him. And if he could have heard their talk about him and his discourse, at their evening rendezvous, he might have been compelled to pronounce himself nearly as foolish as any of them, for having so thoughtlessly assumed men's being in possession of principles which they might have learnt by serious attention during a few days, and which they were not fit to live one day without. At the same time, he would have been moved to utter the most bitter reproaches against the gross incompetence and wicked neglect in the system and office of public instruction, of which the intellectual condition of such a company of persons could not but be taken as an evidence and consequence. And in fact there is no class more conspicuous in reprobation in the solemn invectives of the prophets, than those whose special duty it was to instruct the Jewish people.

Now if such were the state of their intelligence, what would the consequences naturally be? How would this friend of truth and the people *expect* to find their piety, their morals, and their happiness, affected by such destitution of knowledge? Do men gather grapes of thorns, or figs of thistles? We are supposing them to be in ignorance of four parts out of five, or even a still greater proportion, of what the supreme wisdom was maintaining an extraordinary dispensation to declare to them. Why to declare, but because each particular in this manifestation, was adapted to set and preserve something right which other means were not competent to rectify? Consider then the case of minds to which one, and a second, and a third, and the much greater number, of the indispensable points of information thus given in divine testimony, were wanting; of which minds, therefore, the estimates, volitions, passions, the principles of action, and the actions too, were abandoned to take, as it were, their chance for good or evil. But, if we may continue to use such a term, *had* they any chance for good in such an abandonment? From what known principal in the human nature was good to be fallen upon through an impulse that made the rational discrimination of it needless? It were truly an exceedingly probable thing that by a kind of beneficent instinct, without any determination given by knowledge, good would be found and chosen by that nature which can so often resist knowledge, conscience, and the divine authority combined to constrain it to such a choice! And besides, the absence of knowledge is likely to be something more and worse than simple ignorance. Even that mere negation would be sure to have its mischiefs. But the vacancy of truth would probably be found replenished with positive error There might not, indeed, be thought enough, of any kind, for the formation of opinions or prejudices distinctly and definitely the opposites to the truths that were wanting; but such false notions as there were in the mind, however crude, and however deficient in number for constituting a full system of error, would be found sufficient to spread their influence to all the points left unoccupied by truth. It is frightful to see what a space, in an ignorant mind, one false notion can fill, so as to be virtually the reverse of a great number of distinct truths that are wanting there, as effectually the reverse, for practical influence, as if, instead of one, this false notion were a number of distinct errors, formally standing in place of so many truths. And thus the supposed visitor for instruction would find that the ignorance of the people was not only the want of direction to good, and of defence against evil, but a positive active power of mischief.

And also, he would be made to perceive that, while the absence of right apprehensions was practically equivalent to wrong ones, that small portion of knowledge which an ignorant people might really possess could be of very little avail. For one thing, from its being most confined in its compass, and scanty in its particulars, there would be a vast number of things and occasions by which it would not, (as bearing no direct relation to them,) be called into exercise, and in which, therefore, the bad activities generated from ignorance would be left to have their unrestrained play. For another thing, a few notions conformable to truth cannot, in understandings left mainly in ignorance, and so given up, as we have seen, to error, maintain the clearness and power of truth for application even to the very things to which those notions are applicable. A mind holding but a little of truth will, commonly, hold that little with both a feeble apprehension, and a great liability to have it perverted to subserve the errors that occupy that same mind. The conjunction of truths is of the utmost importance for preserving the genuine tendency, and securing the efficacy, of each. It is an unhappy 'lack of knowledge' when there is not enough to preserve, to what there is of it, the honest beneficial quality of knowledge. How many of the follies, excesses, and crimes, in the course of the world, have taken their pretended warrant from some fragment of truth, dissevered from the connexion of truths indispensable to its right operation, and in that detached state easily perverted into coalescence with the most noxious principles, which concealed and gave effect to their malignity by the advantage of this combination.

There was no want of exemplifications of all we have said of ignorance, in the conduct of that ancient people at present in our view. Doubtless an awful share of the iniquities which, by their necessary tendency and by the divine vindictive appointment, brought plagues and destruction upon them, were committed in violation of what they knew. But that also it was in part from the non-admission into their minds, of the information which pressed almost in a palpable form on their very senses, that they were betrayed into crimes and consequent miseries, is evident equally from the language of the prophets, and from the surprise which they sometimes seem to have felt on finding themselves involved in retributive suffering. How could such things as these, (they have seemed to say of their conduct, with sincere unknowing amazement,) bring on us such inflictions? It seemed as if they had never so much as dreamed of such a consequence; and their monitors had to represent to them, that it had been through their own stupid inattention to divine dictates and warnings, if they did not know that such proceedings would have such a termination.

How one portion of knowledge admitted, with the exclusion of other truths equally indispensable to be known, may not only be quite unavailing, but be perverted to coincide with destructive error, is dreadfully illustrated in the final catastrophe of that favoured guilty nation. They were in possession of the one important point of knowledge, that a Messiah was to come. They held this assurance not slightly, but with strong conviction, and as a matter of the greatest interest. But then, that this knowledge might have its appropriate and happy effect, it was indispensable for them to know also the character of this Messiah, and the real nature of his great design. This they did not, because they would not, learn, and were absolutely ignorant of. Literally the whole people, with an exception awfully diminutive, had failed, or rather refused, to admit, as to that part of the subject, the inspired declarations. Now comes the fatal consequence of knowing only one thing of several that require to be inseparable in knowledge. They formed to themselves a false idea of the Messiah, according to their own vain and worldly imaginations. They extended the full assurance which they justly entertained of his coming, to this false notion of what he was to be and to accomplish when he should come. From this it was natural and inevitable that when the true Messiah should come they would not recognize him, and that their hostility would be excited against a person who, while evidently the reverse of all their favourite and confident ideas of that glorious character, demanded to be acknowledged as realizing the declarations of heaven concerning it. And thus they were placed in an incomparably worse situation for receiving him when he did appear, than if they had had no knowledge at all that a Messiah was to come. For on that supposition they might have received him as a most striking moral phenomenon, with curiosity, and wonder, and as little prejudice as it is possible in any case for depravity and ignorance to feel toward sanctity and wisdom. But this delusive pre-occupation of their minds formed a direct grand cause for their rejecting Jesus Christ. And how fearful was the final consequence of *this* 'lack of knowledge!' How truly, in all senses, the people were destroyed! The violent extermination at length of multitudes of them from the earth, was but as the omen and commenement of a deeper perdition. And the terrible memorial is a perpetual admonition what a curse it is *not to know*. For he by the rejection of whom these despisers devoted themselves to perish, while he looked on their great city, and wept at the doom which he beheld impending, said, *If* thou hadst *known*, even thou in this thy day———.

SECTION III.

Miseries resulting from the Ignorance of Pagans.

So much for that selected people:—we need not dwell long on the state of the whole world beside, as exemplifying the perniciousness of the want of knowledge.

The ignorance which pervaded the heathen nations, was fully equal to the utmost result that could have been calculated from all the causes contributing to thicken the mental darkness. The feeble traditional glimmering of the truth that had been originally received by divine communication, had long since become nearly extinct, having as it were gone out in the act of lighting up certain fantastic inventions of doctrine, of which the element was exhaled from the corruptions of the human soul. In other words, the grand principles of truth, imparted by the creator to the early inhabitants of the earth, had gradually lost their clearness and purity, and at length passed out of existence in yielding somewhat of their semblance and authority, through some slight deceptive analogy, to the vanities of fancy and notion which sprang from the inventive depravity of man. And thus, if we except so much instruction as we may deem to have been conveyed by the extraordinary and sometimes dreadful interpositions of the governor of the world, (and it was in but an extremely limited degree that these had actually the effect of illumination,) the human tribes were surrendered to their own understanding for all that they were to know and think. Melancholy predicament! The understanding, the intellect, the reason, (whatever name or distinction we designate it by,) which had not sufficed even for seeing the necessity of preserving the true light from heaven, was to be competent to give light in its absence. Under the disadvantage of this loss,—after the setting of the sun—it was to exercise itself on an unlimited diversity of important things, inquiring, comparing, and deciding. All those things, if examined far, extended into mystery. All genuine thinking was a hard repellent labour. The senses were feeble organs for the action of intellect on exterior existence. Casual impressions had a mighty force of perversion. The appetites and passions would infallibly, for the most part, occupy and actuate the whole man. When his imagination was put in activity, it would not be at all more favourable to the attainment of truth. His interest, according to the gross apprehension of it, would in numberless instances require, and therefore would gain, false judgments for justification of the manner of pursuing it. And all this while, there was no grand standard and test to which the notions of things could be brought. If there were some spirits of larger and purer thought, that went out in the honest search of truth, they must have felt an oppression of utter hopelessness in looking round on a world of doubtful things, on no one of which they could obtain the dictate of a supreme intelligence. There was no sovereign demonstrator in communication with the earth, to tell wretched man what to think in any of a thousand questions which arose to confound him. There were, instead, impostors, magicians, vain theorists, prompted by ambition and superior native ability to abuse the credulity of their fellow mortals, which they did with such success as to become their oracles, their dictators, or even their gods. The multitude most naturally surrendered themselves to all such delusions. If it was, perhaps, possible that their feeble and degraded reason, in the absence of divine light, and but little disciplined by education, might by earnest exertion have attained to judge better, that exertion was precluded by indolence, by the immediate wants and unavoidable employments of life, by love of amusement, by subjection, even of the mind, to superiors and national institutions, and by the tendency of human individuals to fall, if we may so express it, in dead conformity and addition to the lump.

The result of all these causes, the sum of all these effects, was that unnumbered millions of living beings, whose value was in their intelligent and moral nature, were, as to that nature, in a condition analogous to what their physical existence would have been under a total and permanent eclipse of the sun. It was perpetual night in their souls, with all the phenomena incident to night. The physical economy around them presented its open and brightened aspect; there was a true light coming on them every morning in material beams from the sky; they saw one order of things aright,—that which they were soon to leave, look back upon as a dream when one awaketh. But there was subsisting present with them, unapprehended except in faint and delusive glimpses, another order of things involving their greatest interests, with no luminary to make that apparent to them, after the race had willingly forgotten the primary instructions from their creator.

The dreadful consequences of this 'lack of knowledge,' as appearing in the religion and morals of the nations, and through these affecting their welfare, equalled and even surpassed all that might in theory have been presaged from the cause.

This ignorance could not annihilate the *principle* of religion in the spirit of man, but in removing the awful repression of the idea of one exclusive sovereign divinity it left that spirit to form its religion in its own manner. And as the creating gods might be the most appropriate way of celebrating the deliverance from the most imposing idea of one supreme being, depraved and insane invention took this with ardor. The mind threw a fictitious divinty into its own phantasms, and into the objects in the visible world. It is amazing to observe how, when one solemn principle was taken away, the promiscuous numberless crowd of almost all shapes of fancy and of matter became, as it were, instinct with ambition, and mounted into gods. They were alternately the toys and the tyrants of their miserable creator. They appalled him often, and often he could make sport with them. For overawing him by their supposed power they made him a compensation by descending to a fellowship with his follies and vices. But indeed this was a condition of their creation; they *must* own their mortal progenitor by sharing his depravity, even amidst the lordly domination over him and the universe. We may safely affirm, that the mighty artificer of deifications, the corrupt soul of man, never once, in its almost infinite diversification of device in their production, struck out a form of absolute goodness. No, if there were a million of deities, there should not be one that should be authorized by perfect rectitude in itself to punish *him;* not one by which it should be possible for him to be rebuked without having a right to recriminate.

Such a pernicious creation of active delusions it was that took the place of religion in the absence of knowledge. And to this intellectual obscuration, and this legion of pestilent fallacies, swarming like the locusts from the smoke of the bottomless pit in the vision of St John, the fatal effect on morals and happiness corresponded. Indeed the mischief done there perhaps even exceeded the proportion of the ignorance and the false theology; according to the general rule, that any thing wrong in the mind will be the *most* wrong where it comes the nearest to its ultimate practical effect.

The people of those nations, (and the same description is applicable to modern heathens,) did not know the essential nature of perfect moral goodness, or virtue. How should they know it? A depraved mind would not find in itself any native conception to give the bright form of it. There were no living examples of it. The men who held the pre-eminence in the community were generally, in the most important points, its reverse. It was for the *divine* nature, manifesting itself and contemplated, to have presented the archetype of the idea of perfect rectitude, whence might have been derived the modified examplar for human virtue. And so *would* the idea of perfect moral excellence have come to dwell and shine in the understanding, if it had been the true divinity that men beheld in their contemplations of a superior existence. But when the gods of their heaven were little better than their own evil qualities, exalted to the sky to be thence reflected back upon them invested with Olympian charms and splendors, their ideas of deity would evidently cooperate with all that made it impossible for them to conceive a perfect model for human excellence. See the mighty labour of human depravity to confirm its dominion! It would translate itself to heaven, and usurp divinity, in order to come down thence with a sanction for man to be wicked,—in order by a falsification of the qualities of the supreme nature, to preclude his forming the true idea of what would be perfect rectitude in his own.

A system which could thus associate all the modes of moral turpitude with the most lofty and illustrious forms of existence, would go far toward vitiating essentially the entire theory of moral good and evil. And if, in spite of all its power of subversion, any moral principles still maintained their ground in the convictions of the understanding, and there asserted their claim with a voice which nothing could silence, such a system would nevertheless greatly contribute to defraud them of practical efficacy.

But, how small was the number of pure moral principles, (if indeed any,) that among the people of the heathen nations *did* maintain themselves in the convictions of the understanding. The darkness to which the privation of the divine light had abandoned them, gave free action to all the perversities of thought and desire that went to the abrogation, in speculative acknowledgment, in judgment, of almost all the essential principles and specific rules of the true morality. And of this melancholy privilege, the naturally rebelling temper of the mind against those principles and rules availed itself in every possible way, operating to this effect, of erasing from the understanding the just notions and traces of morality, partly by the direct means of the influence of the passions and appetites, and partly, as we have just described, by the corrupt agency more circuitously brought to bare on the same object through a falsification of religion.

And so mighty was the success of this anti-moral operation, that iniquities without number took the name and repute of virtues. It is quite tremendous to consider how large a proportion of all the vices and crimes of which mankind were ever guilty, have actually constituted, in one nation and age, and another, a part of the approved moral and religious system. It is questionable if we could select from the worst forms of depravity any one which has not been at least admitted among the authorized customs, if not even appointed among the institutes of the religion, of some tribe of the human race. And when thus sanctioned, these depravities might without restraint diffuse an infection of their quality through every thing in the social economy in which they were contained. This was as natural an effect as that which would follow from the admission, among a close assemblage of persons, of an individual who was sickening of the plague. Wherever, therefore, in the imperfect notices afforded us of ancient nations, we find any one virulent iniquity holding an authorized place in custom or religion, we may confidently make a very large inference, even where the record is silent.

Every thing that, under the advantage of this destitution of knowledge, operated to the destruction of the true morality, both in theory and practice, must have had a fatal reinforcement of its power in that part of this ignorance which respected hereafter. The doctrine of a future existence and retribution did not, in any rational and salutary form, interfere in the adjustment of the system of life. What there was of such a notion in the minds of the pagans, was too fantastic in its conception, or too slightly held in faith, either to become itself, as from its own nature and authority, a definer and prescriber of genuine virtues, (by the rule of inference—if this is so, then such and such ought to be the conduct of the expectants,) or to give efficacy to what might have been yet retained of natural reason to discern between good and evil. Imagine, if you can, the withdrawment of this doctrine from the minds of those whose present faith is the whole of revealed truth. Suppose the grand idea wholly obliterated, or faded to a shadowy and dubious trace of what it had been, or transmuted into a poetic dream of classic or barbarian mythology, and how many moral principles would be found to have vanished with it. How many things which it had imposed would have ceased to be duties, or would continue such only on the strength, and in the proportion, of some very minor consideration which might remain to enforce them, perhaps in an altered and deteriorated form. If some things retained the undeniable quality of duty, by virtue of a close relation to the matter of benefit or mischief, of the most obvious and tangible kind, the sense of obligation would be destitute of all solemnity, from the abolition of all its relations to deity, eternity, an invisible world, and a judgment to come. It would therefore have none of that emphasis of impression which can sometimes dismay and quell the opposing passions, as by a mysterious visitation from an unseen power. It would be deprived of that which forms the chief force of conscience. And it would have no strength to uphold in the higher quality of *principle*, that which would be constantly degenerating into mere policy, and rationally justifying itself in doing so.

The withdrawment, we say, of the grand truth in question, from a man's faith, would necessarily break up the moral government over his conscience. How evident then is it, that among the people of the heathen lands, under a disastrous ignorance of this and all the sublime truths that are fit to rule an immortal being during his sojourn on earth, no man could feel any peremptory obligation to be universally virtuous, or adequate motives to excite the endeavour to approach that high attainment, even were there not a perfect inability to form the true conception of it. How evident too it is, that the general mass would be horribly depraved. We may indeed, at times, notwithstanding the dreadfulness of the results easily foreseen as inevitable from such causes, be somewhat surprised at reading of some transcendent enormities; but we feel no wonder at the substance of the exhibition of such a state of those nations as the sacred scriptures affirm, in descriptions to which the other records of antiquity add their testimony and their ample illustrations. Let the spectacle be looked on in thought, of vast national multitudes, filled, agitated, and impelled, by the restless forces of passions and appetites. Say what measure and what kinds of restraint there should be on such crowds, so actuated, to keep them from rushing into evil. Take off, as far as you dare, any given restraint, to see what will follow. Take off or withhold from these beings, possessed and inflamed as you see them to be,—remove from them all the coercion that could be applied in the form of just ideas of the righteous almighty governor; a luminous exposition of what it is for moral agents to be good, and what to be evil, with the vast importance of the difference, and the prospect of a judgment, retribution, and eternal existence. All this being removed from resting on and grasping the spirits of the innumerable assemblage, imagine them yielded up for their passions and appetites to have the dominion, excepting so far as it shall be opposed and limited by something else than those solemn counteractions, something remaining or supplied when they are annihilated. And *what* will, for this use, so remain or be supplied? What a lamentable scene ensues, if all that will be left or be found to maintain the opposition and repression is, from within, so much innate blind preference for goodness as even such a state of things cannot destroy, and from without, that measure of resistance which all men make to one another's bad inclinations, in self-defence.

It is true, indeed, that this last does prevent an infinity of actual mischief. There is involved in the very constitution of things a principle by which a coarse self-interest prevents, under providence, more practical evil, beyond comparison more, than all other causes together. The man inclined to perpetrate an iniquity, of the nature of a wrong to his fellow-mortals, is apprized that he shall provoke a reaction, to resist or punish him; that he shall incur as great an evil as that he is disposed to do, or greater; that either summary revenge will strike him, or a process instituted in organized society will vindictively reach his property, liberty, or life. This defensive array, of all men against all men, restrains to stop within the mind an immensity of wickedness which is there burning to come out into action. But for this, Noah's flood had been rendered needless. But for this, our planet might have been accomplishing its circles round the sun for thousands of years past without a human inhabitant. By virtue of this great law in the constitution of things, it was possible for the race to subsist, notwithstanding all that ignorance of the divine being, of heavenly truth, and of uncorrupt morality, in which we are contemplating the heathen nations as benighted. But while it thus prevented utter destruction, it had no corrective operation on the depravity of the heart. It was not through a judgment of things being essentially evil that they were forborne; it was not by means of conscience that depraved propensity was kept under restraint. It was but by a hold on the meaner principles of his nature, that the offender in will was arrested in prevention of the deed. Thus the immense multitudes were virtually as bad as they would actually have been if they had dared for fear of one another. But besides, how very partial was the effect of this restraint, even in the exterior operation to which it was confined. Men *did* dare, in contempt of this preventive defensive array, to commit a stupendous amount of crimes against one another, to say nothing of their moral self-destruction, or of that view of their depravity in which it is to be considered as against God. While there was no force of beneficent truth to invade the dreadful cavern of iniquity in the mind, and there to combat and conquer it, there would be sure to be often no want of audacity to send it forth into action at all hazards.

Something might be said, no doubt, in behalf of what might be supposed to be done for the pagan nations by legislation, considered, not in its character of director of the coercive and retributive force in the community, but strictly in the capacity of a moral preceptor. But besides that legislators who themselves, in common with the people of their nations, looked on human existence and duty through a worse than twilight medium, who had no divine oracles to speak wisdom to them, and were, some of them, reduced to begin their operations with the lie that pretended they had,—besides that such legislators would inevitably be, in many of their principles and enactments, at variance with eternal rectitude,—besides this fatal defect, legislation bore upon it too plainly that character of self-interest, of mutual self-defence and menace, to which we have adverted, to be an efficacious teacher of morals, in any deeper sense than the prevention of a certain measure of external crime. Every one knew well that the pure approbation and love of goodness were not the source of law, but that it was an arrangement originating and deriving all its force from self-love, a contrivance by which each man was glad to make the collective strength of society his guarantee against his neighbour's presumed wish and interest to do him wrong. While happy that his neighbour was under this restraint, he was often vexed to be under it also himself; but on the whole deemed this security worth the cost of suffering this interdict on his own inclinations, perhaps as judging it probable that his neighbour's were still much worse than his own. We repeat, that a preceptive system thus estimated would but ill instruct the judgment in the pure principles of virtue, and could not come with the weight of authority and sanctity on the conscience. We may here observe, by the way, how evident was the necessity, that the rules and sanctions of morality, to come in simplicity and power on the human mind, should primarily emanate from a being exalted above all implication and competition of interests with man.

Thus we see, that in the darkened economy of the heathens there was nothing to be applied, with a grand corrective restraining operation, directly and internally, to the mighty depraved energy of the passions and appetites. That was left in awful predominance in the innumerable multitude. And to the account of what this energy of feeling tending to evil would accomplish, let there be added all that could result from the cooperation of intellect. Only reflect for a moment on the extent of human genius, in its powers of invention, combination, diversification, and then think of all this faculty, in an immense number of minds, through many ages, and in every imaginable variety of situation, impelled to its utmost exertion in the service of sin, as it would of course, and was in fact. Reflect how many ideas, available to the purpose, would spring up casually, or be suggested by circumstances, or be attained by the earnest study of beings goaded in pursuit of change and novelty. The simple modes of iniquity were put under an active ministry of art, to combine, innovate, and augment. And consequently all conceivable,—literally all conceivable forms of immorality were brought to imagination, most of them into experiment, and the greater number into prevailing practice, in those nations: insomuch that the sated monarch would have imposed nearly as difficult a task on ingenuity in calling for the invention of a new vice, as of a new pleasure. They would perhaps have been identical demands when he was the person to be pleased.

If such depravity did not, as viewed in itself and alone, appear equivalent to the gravest import of the terms, 'the people are destroyed,' the attendant misery instantly rushes on our sight to complete their verification. There may not be wanting a class of vain sneering mortals who receive no impression of any serious truth in the maxim that wicked nations must be miserable ones, and will say, 'the state of the ancient heathens as referred to in exemplification, is a matter of most trivial interest to us, just fit to give some show and exaggeration to a common-place. They might be wretched enough; and perhaps also the matter has been extravagantly magnified for the service of a favourite theme, or to afford indulgence to rhetorical excess. At any rate, it is not now worth while to go so far back to trouble ourselves about it. The ancient heathens had their day and their destiny, and it is of very little importance to us what they were or suffered.' And whose compass of thought, we would ask, is evinced, whose apprehension of the higher and permanent relations of things, whose aptitude to derive admonition and wisdom from the past, whose contemplation of the divine government as one system from the beginning to the end,—if nothing can powerfully strike the mind but a thing of the present moment? There were doubtless some reckless souls that could sport in great self-complacency in view of the ruins of Jerusalem, sometime after the Roman legions had left it and its myriads of dead inhabitants to silence, and would have made light of a reference to it as an example of the consequences of the wickedness of a people; but would not exactly these have been the most likely to provoke the next avenging visitation, and to perish in it? The ancient triflers with the wretchedness and destruction of their race, who thought it but an impertinent moralizing that attempted to recall such funereal spectacles for admonition, assuredly found themselves at last to be fools. And *we* are convicted of exceeding stupidity, if the dreadful exhibition of the general misery of a world is felt, (when to be looked back upon through some intervening ages) too insignificant a thing to illustrate to us the very truth, to enforce on us the very instruction, which it so prominently and peculiarly offers,—we might almost say fulminates, so glaring is the fact that a condition emphatically unhappy, manifested, in those nations of old, the natural tendency of ignorance of the most important truths.

It is true that the mental darkness which we are representing as so greatly the cause of their wickedness and unhappiness, had the effect, in a measure, of protecting them from some kinds of suffering. They had not illumination enough, to have conscience enough, for inflicting the severest pains of remorse, and of 'the fearful looking for of fiery indignation.' But that they were wretched was practically acknowledged in the very quality of what they ardently and universally sought as the highest felicities of existence. Those delights were violent and tumultuous, in all possible ways and degrees estranged from reflection, and adverse to it. The whole souls of great and small, in the most barbarous and in the more polished state, were passionately set upon revelry, upon expedients for inflaming the indulgences of licentiousness to extravagance, madness, and monstrous enormity; upon concourses of multitudes for pomps, celebrations, shows, games, combats; on the riots of exultation and revenge after victories. The ruder nations had, in their way, however pitiable in their attempts at magnificence, their grand festive, triumphal, and demoniac confluxes and revellings. To these joys of tumult, the people of the savage and the more cultivated nations sacrificed every thing belonging to the peaceful economy of life, with a desparate frantic fury. And all this was the confession that there was little felicity in the heart or in the home. Nor could all this be itself happiness: even if the vain elation could be called so while it lasted, it was brief in each instance, and it subsided in an aggravated dreariness of the soul.

The fact of their being unhappy had a still more gloomy attestation in the mutual enmity which seems to have been of the very essence of life, so fatal a principle that it could not be spared an hour. No, they could not live without this luxury drawn from the fountains of death! What is the most conspicuous material of ancient history, what is it that glares out the most hideously from that darkness and oblivion into which the old world has in so great a degree retired, but the incessant furies of miserable mortals against their fellow-mortals, 'hateful and hating one another?' We cannot look that way but we see the whole field covered with inflicters and sufferers, not seldom interchanging those characters. If that field widens to our view, it is still to the utmost line to which the shade clears away, a scene of cruelty, oppression, and slavery; of the strong trampling on the weak, and the weak often attempting to bite at the feet of the strong; of rancorous animosities and murderous competitions of persons raised above the mass of the community; of treacheries and massacres; and of war, between hordes, and cities, and nations, and empires, war *never*, in spirit, intermitted, and suspended sometimes in act only to acquire renewed force for destruction, or to find another assemblage of hated creatures to cut in pieces. Powerful as 'the spirit of the first-born Cain' has continued, down to our own age, and in the most improved division of mankind, there was nevertheless, in the ancient pagan race, (as there is in some portions of the modern,) a more complete uncontrolled actuation of the all-killing, all-devouring fury, a more absolute possession of Moloch.

Now it is *as misery* that we are exhibiting all this depravity. To be thus *was suffering*. The corruption and the torment are inseparable in description, and they were so in reality. And both together were a natural result of being ignorant of God and all the most important truth. A comprehensive estimate of the condition of those tribes, on a larger scale, would, we need not observe, include some minor things of less gloomy character, but not availing to change the general aspect of the picture. How emphatically then, as of the Jewish tribes when they rejected the divine illuminations, and found the consequence, it may be pronounced of the heathen nations that surrounded them, 'the people were destroyed for lack of knowledge.'

We might have been allowed to comprehend in the account of their miserable condition *all* the kinds of infelicity inseparable from their ignorance. We should then have recounted such topics as these : the unhappiness of being without an assurance of an all-comprehending and merciful providence, and of wanting therefore the best support in sorrow and calamity ; the uncontrolable impatience, or the deep melancholy, with which the more thoughtful persons must have seen departing from life, with no anticipation approaching to a defined hope of ever meeting them in a life elsewhere, the relatives or associates who were dear to them in exception to prevailing selfishness and hostility ; and the gloomy and perhaps sometimes alarmed sentiment, with which they must have thought of their own continual approach towards death. But, as the sentence we adopted, to introduce these observations, evidently implies the people's *iniquity* while pronouncing that they are destroyed, we have wished to give the prominence, in the representation, to the misery which they suffered by necessary result, or rather in the very fact, of their being wicked, and wicked in natural consequences of being estranged from the knowledge of the true religion and the divinely authorized morality.

We shall not, we trust, incur the imputation of such an absurdity as to imagine, that had that knowledge prevailed among them, to the extent of being present in all their minds, there could then have been scarcely any thing of this wickedness and misery : these evils have a deeper source than even ignorance. But it would be no less an absurdity to deny, that something of the highest importance toward the desired practical end is accomplished, if it is made sure that the dictates and impulses of a corrupt will shall be encountered, like Balaam by the angel, by a clear manifestation of their bad and ruinous tendency, by a convinced judgment, a protesting conscience, and the aspect of the almighty judge,—instead of their being under the tolerance of a judgment not instructed to condemn them, or, (as ignorance is sure to quicken into error,) perverted to reinforce them by its sanction.

Having thus shown, at greater length than was first intended, how the ancient state of mankind both Jews and Gentiles, verified the expression of the prophet, we shall glance rapidly over the long subsequent periods, and come down to our own times. In doing so, however, we need not take farther account of Jews or heathens. Nor shall we do more than just name the Mahomedan imposture, though that is, perhaps, the most signal instance in the world and all time, of a malignant delusion maintained directly and immediately by ignorance, by a solemn determination and even a fanatic zeal not to receive one new idea. This execrable delusion is so strong and absolute in ignorance, is so identified with it, and so systematically repels at all points the approach of knowledge, that it is difficult to conceive a mode of its extermination that shall not involve some fearful destruction, in the most literal sense, of the people. And such a catastrophe it is probable the great body of them, in this temper of mind prevailing among them at the hour, would choose to incur by preference, we do not say to a serious patient consideration of the true religion, but even to the admission among them of a system merely favouring knowledge in general, an order of measures which should urge upon the adults, and peremptorily enforce for the children, a discipline of intellectual improvement. There would be little national hesitation of choice, (at least in the central regions of the dominion of this hateful imposture,) between the introduction of any general system of expedients for driving them from their stupefaction into something like thinking and learning, and a general plague, to rage as long as any remained for victims.

SECTION IV.

Awful Abominations directly flowing from the Ignorance and Errors of Popery.

But let us now look a moment at the intellectual state of the people denominated Christian, during the long course of ages preceeding the Reformation. The acquisition made by earth from heaven, of Christianity, might have seemed to bring with it an inevitable necessity of an immense difference speedily and for permanence taking place, in regard to the competence of men's knowledge to prevent their destruction. It was as if, in the physical system, some one production, far more salutary to life than all the other things furnished from the elements, had been reserved by the creator to spring up in a later age, after many generations of men had been languishing through life, and prematurely dying, from the deficient virtue of their sustenance and remedies. The image of the inestimable plant had been shown to the prophets in their visions, but the reality was now given ; its fruit had 'the seed in itself,' and it was for all people to cultivate it. But, while by the greater part of mankind it was not accounted worth admission to a place on their blasted desolated soil, the manner in which its virtue was frustrated among those who pretended to regard it, as it was, the best gift of the divine beneficence, is recorded in eternal reproach of the Christian nations.

As the hostility of heathenism, in the direct endeavours to extirpate the Christian religion, became evidently hopeless, in the realms within the Roman empire, there was a grand change of the policy of evil : and all manner of reprobate things, heathenism itself among them, rushed as by general conspiracy, into treacherous conjunction with Christianity, retaining their own quality under the sanction of its name, and by a rapid process reducing it to surrender almost every thing distinctive of it but that dishonoured name. There were indeed in existence the sacred oracles, and these could not be essentially falsified. But there was no lack of expedients and pretexts for keeping them in a great measure secreted, and a kind of reverence might be pretended in doing so. In the progress of version from their original languages, they could be stopped short in a language but little less unintelligible to the bulk of the people, in order that this 'profane vulgar' might never hear the very words of God, but only such report as it should please certain men, at their discretion, to give of what he had said. But even though the people had understood the language, in the usage of social converse, there was a grand security against them in keeping them so destitute of the knowledge of letters that the bible, if such a rare thing ever did happen to fall into any of their hands, would be no more to them than a scroll of hieroglyphics. When to this was added, the great cost of a copy of so large a book before the invention of printing, it remained perhaps just worth while, (and it would be a matter of very little difficulty or daring,) to make it, in the matured state of the system, an offence, and a sacrilegious invasion of sacerdotal privilege, to look into a bible. If it might seem hard thus to constitute a new sin, in addition to the long list already denounced by the divine law, amends were made by indulgently rescinding some article in that list, and qualifying the rules of obligation with respect to them all.

In this retirement and latency of the sacred authorities from all communication with men's minds, the Christian world was left in possession of merely the names of the solemn realities of religion. These names, thus vacated, were available to all evil. They were as unfilled vessels of the sanctuary, into which crafty and wicked men might clandestinely introduce the most malignant preparations. And such men did improve their opportunity to the utmost. How prolific was the invention of the falsehoods and absurdities of notion, and of the vanities and corruptions of practice, which it was managed to make these names designate and sanction; while it was also managed, with no less sedulity and success, that the inventors and propagators should be held in submissive reverence by the community, as the oracular depositaries of truth. That community had not knowledge enough of any other kind, to create a resisting and defensive power against this imposition in the concern of religion. A sound exercise of reason on other subjects, a moderate degree of instruction in literature and science rightly so called, might have given some competence to question, to examine, to call for evidence, and to detect some of the fallacies imposed for Christian faith. But the general mind was on all sides pressed and borne down to its fate. All re-action was subdued; and the people were reduced to exist in one huge, unintelligent, monotonous, substance, united by the interfusion of a vile superstition, which just kept it enough mentally alive for all the uses of cheats and tyrants,—a proper subject for the dominion of 'our Lord God the Pope,' as he was sometimes denominated, and might be denominated with perfect impunity, as to any excitement of revolting or indignation, in millions of beings, bearing the form of men, and the name of Christians.

Such *was*,—it is easy to conceive what *should* have been,—the condition of existence of this vast mass, which was thus assimilated and reduced into a material fit for all the bad uses, to which priestcraft could wish to put the souls and bodies of its slaves. The mighty aggregate of Christendom *should* have consisted of so many beings having each, in some degree, the independent beneficial use of his *mind;* all of them trained to the object of being made sensible of their responsibility to their creator, for the exercise of their reason on the matters of belief and choice; all of them capacitated for improvement by being furnished with the rudiments and instrumental means of knowledge; and all having within their easy reach, in their own language, the scriptures of divine truth.

Can any doubt arise, whether there were in the Christian states resources competent, if so applied, to secure to all the people an elementary instruction, and the possession of the bible? Alas! all nations, sufficiently raised above perfect barbarism to exist as states, have in all ages consumed, in some way or other else than they should, an infinitely greater amount of resources than would have sufficed, after comfortable physical subsistence was provided for, to afford a moderate share of instruction to all the people. And in those popish ages, that expenditure alone which went to ecclesiastical use, would have been far more than adequate to this beneficent purpose. Think of the boundless cost for supporting the magnificence and satiating the rapacity of the hierarchy, from its triple-crowned head, down through all the orders, consecrated under that head to maintain the delusion and share the spoil. Recollect the immense system of policy, for jurisdiction and intrigue, every agent of which was a consumer. Recollect the pomps and pageants, for which the general resources were to be taxed; while the general industry was injured by the interruption of useful employment, and the diversion of the people to such dissipation as their condition qualified them to indulge in. Think also of the incalculable cost of ecclesiastical structures, the temples of idolatry, as in truth they may be adjudged to have been. One of the most striking situations for a religious and reflective Protestant is, that of passing some solitary hour under the lofty vault, among the superb arches and columns, of any of the most splendid of these edifices remaining at this day in our own country. If he has sensibility and taste, the magnificence, the graceful union of so many diverse inventions of art, the whole mighty creation of genius that so many centuries since quitted the world without leaving even a name, will come with magical impression on his mind, while it is contemplatively darkening into the awe of antiquity. But he will be recalled,—the sculptures, the inscriptions, the sanctuaries enclosed off for the special benefit, after death, of persons who had very different concerns during life from that of the care of their salvation, and various other insignia of the original character of the place, will help to recall him,—to the thought, that these proud piles were in fact raised to celebrate the conquest, and prolong the dominion, of the power of darkness over the souls of the people. They were as triumphal arches, erected in memorial of the extermination of that truth which was given to be the life of men.

As he looks round, and looks upward, on the prodigy of design, and skill, and perseverance, and tributary wealth, he may image to himself the multitudes that, during successive ages, frequented this fane in the assured belief, that the idle ceremonies and impious superstitions, which they there performed or witnessed, were a service acceptable to heaven, and to be repaid in blessings to the offerers. He may say to himself, Here, on this very floor, under that elevated and decorated vault, in a 'dim religious light' like this, but with the darkness of the shadow of death in their souls, they prostrated themselves to their saints, or their 'queen of heaven;' nay, to painted images and toys of wood or wax, to some ounce or two of bread and wine, to fragments of old bones, and rags of clothing. Hither they came, when conscience, in looking either back or forward, dismayed them, to purchase remission with money or atoning penances, or to acquire the privilege of sinning in a certain manner, or for a certain time, with impunity; and they went out at yonder door in the perfect confidence that the priest had secured, in the one case the suspension, in the other the satisfaction, of the divine law. Here they solemnly believed, as they were taught, that, by donatives to the church, they delivered the souls of their departed sinful relatives from their state of punishment; and they went out at that door resolved to bequeath some portion of their possessions, to operate in the same manner for themselves another day, in case of need. Here they were convened to listen in reverence to some representative emissary from the man of sin, with new dictates of blasphemy or iniquity to be promulgated in the name of the almighty; or to witness the trickery of some detestable farce, devised to cheat or fright them out of whatever remainder the former impositions might have left to them of sense, conscience, or property. Here, in fine, there was never presented to their understanding, from their childhood to their death, a comprehensive honest declaration of the laws of duty, and the pure doctrines of salvation. To think! that they should have mistaken for the house of God, and the very gate of heaven, a place where the power of darkness had so short a way to come from his appropriate dominions, and his agents and purchased slaves so short a way to go thither. If we could imagine a momentary visit from him who once entered a fabric of sacred denomination with a scourge, because it was made the resort of a common traffic, with what aspect and voice, with what infliction but the 'rebuke with flames of fire,' would he have entered this mart of iniquity, assuming the name of his sanctuary, where the traffic was in delusions, crimes, and the souls of men? It was even as if, to use the prophet's language, the very 'stone cried out of the wall, and the beam out of the timber answered it,' in denunciation; for a portion of the means of building, in the case of some of these edifices, was obtained as the price of dispensations and pardons.

In such a hideous light would the earlier history of one of these mighty structures, pretendedly consecrated to Christianity, be presented to the reflecting protestant; and then would recur the idea of its cost, as relative to what that expenditure might really have done for Christianity and the people. It absorbed in the construction, sums sufficient to have supplied even manuscript bibles, costly as they were, to all the families of a province; and in the revenues appropriated to its ministration of superstition, enough to have provided men to teach all those families to read those bibles.

In all this, and in the whole constitution of the grand apostacy, involving innumerable forms of mischief and abomination to which our object does not require any allusion, how sad a spectacle is held forth of the people destroyed for lack of knowledge. If, as one of their plagues, an inferior one in itself, they were plundered, as we have seen, of their worldly goods, it was that the spoil might subserve to a still greater wrong. What was lost to the accommodation of the body, was to be made to contribute to the depravation of the soul. It supplied means for multiplying the powers of the grand ecclesiastical machinery, and confirming the intellectual despotism of the absolute authorities in religion. Those authorities enforced on the people, on pain of final perdition, and acquiescence in principles and ordinances which, in effect, precluded their direct access to the almighty, and the saviour of the world, interposing between them and the divine majesty a very extensive, complicated, and heathenish mediation, which in a great measure substituted itself for the real and exclusive mediation of Christ, obscured by its vast creation of intercepting vanities, the glory of the eternal being, and thus almost extinguished the true worship. But how calamitous was such a condition!—to be thus intercepted from direct intercourse with the supreme spirit, and to have the solemn and elevating sentiment of devotion flung downward, on objects and phantoms which even the most superstitious could not pay homage to, without some indistinct sense of degradation.

It was, again a disastrous thing to be under a directory of practical life framed for the convenience of a corrupt system, a rule which enjoined many things wrong, allowed a dispensation from every thing that was right, and abrogated the essential principle and groundwork of true morality. Still again, it was an unhappy thing, that the consolations in sorrow and the view of death should either be too feeble to animate, or should animate only by deluding. And it was the consummation of evil in the state of the people of those dark ages, it was, emphatically, to be 'destroyed,' that the grand doctrines of redemption should have been essentially vitiated or formally supplanted, so that multitudes of the people were betrayed to rest their final hopes on a ground unauthorized by the judge of the world. In this most important matter, the spiritual authorities were subjects themselves of the fatal delusion in which they held the community; and well they deserved to be so, in judicial retribution of their wickedness in imposing on the people, deliberately and on system, innumerable things which they knew to be false.

We have often mused, and felt a gloom and dreariness spreading over the mind while we have mused, on descriptions of the aspect of a country after a pestilence has left it in desolation, or of a region where the people are perishing by famine. It has seemed a mournful thing to behold, in contemplation, the multitude of lifeless forms, occupying in silence the same abodes in which they had lived, or scattered upon the gardens, fields, and roads; and then to see the countenances of the beings yet languishing in life, looking despair, and impressed with the signs of approaching death. We have even sometimes had the vivid and horrid picture offered to our imagination, of a number of human creatures shut up by their fellow-mortals in some strong hold, under an entire privation of sustenance; and presenting each day their imploring, or infuriated, or grimly sullen, or more calmly woeful countenances, at the iron and impregnable grates; each succeeding day more haggard, more perfect in the image of despair; and after a while appearing each day one fewer, till at last all are gone. Now shall we feel it as a *relief* to turn in thought from the inhabitants of a country, or from those of such ar accursed prison-house, thus pining away, to behold the different spectacle of numerous national tribes, or any small selection of persons on whose *minds* are displayed the full effects of knowledge denied; who are under the process of whatever destruction it is, that spirits can suffer from the want of the vital aliment to the intelligent nature, especially from a 'famine of the words of the Lord.'

To bring the two to a close comparison, suppose the case, that some of the persons thus doomed to perish in the tower were in possession of the genuine light and consolations of Christianity, perhaps even had actually been adjudged to this fate, (no extravagant supposition,) for zealously and persistingly endeavouring the restoration of the purity of that religion to the deluded community. Let it be supposed that numbers of that community, having conspired to obtain this adjugment, frequented the precincts of the fortress to see their victims gradually perishing. It would be perfectly in the spirit of the popish superstition, that they should believe themselves to have done God service, and be accordingly pleased at the sight of the more and more deathlike aspect of the emaciated countenances. The while, they might be in the enjoyment of 'fulness of bread.' We can imagine them making convivial appointments within sight of the prison grates, and going from the spectacle to meet at the banquet. Or they might delay the festivity, in order to have the additional luxury of knowing that the tragedy was consummated; as Bishop Gardiner would not dine till the martyrs were burnt. Look at these two contemporary situations, that of the persons with truth and immortal hope in their minds, enduring this slow and painful reduction of their bodies to dissolution, and that of those who, while their bodies fared sumptuously, were thus miserably perishing in soul, through ignorance wrought into error and intense depravity: and say which was the more calamitous predicament.

If we have no hesitation in pronouncing, let us consider whether we have ever been grateful enough to God for the dashing in pieces so long since, in this land, of a system which maintains, to this hour, much of its stability over the greater part of Christendom. If we regret that certain fragments of it are still held in veneration here, and that so tedious a length of ages should be required, to work out a complete mental rescue from what usurped the faculties of our ancestors, let us at the same time look at the various states of Europe, small and great, where this superstition continues to hold the minds of the people in its odious grasp, and verify to ourselves what we have to be thankful for, by thinking how *our* minds could subsist on their mummeries, masses, absolutions, legends, relics, mediation of saints, and corruptions, even to complete reversal, of the evangelical doctrines.

It was, however, but very slowly that the people of our land realized the benefits of the Reformation, glorious as that event was, regarded as to its progressive and its ultimate consequences. Indeed, the thickness of the preceding darkness was strikingly manifested by the deep shade which still continued stretched over the nation, in spite of the newly risen luminary, the beams of which lost much of their fire in pervading it to reach the popular mind, and came with the faintness of an obscured and tedious dawn.

Long there lingered enough of night for the evil spirit

of popery to walk abroad in great power. How deplorably deficient and partial must have been the utmost effect to be obtained by a change of formularies, and of a portion of the hierarchy, with some curtailment of the ceremonial, when that effect was to be wrought upon profound ignorance fortified by being in the form of an inveterate superstition! and when the innovation in doctrine had no accompanying prodigies to strike the senses, in default of finding a qualified recipient in the reason, of beings who had never been trained to deal intellectually with any thing in all existence, nor could be ever the wiser for the volume of inspiration itself, had it been, in their native language, in every house, instead of being hardly in one house in five hundred.

It was doubtless a good thing at any rate, and a most important alteration, that a man should cease and refuse to worship relics and wafers, to rest his confidence on penance and priestly absolution, and to regard the virgin and saints as in effect the supreme regency of heaven; a very good thing even though he *could* not read, nor apprehend the precise meaning and force of terms in the very argument on the strength of which he made his transition. Yes, this was a valuable thing gained; but not even thus much *was* gained, but in an exceedingly limited measure, during a long period of time. The superstition, long after being supplanted, as a national institution, by the reformed order of things, maintained a dominion but little diminished over a large proportion of the people, though reduced to consult, in its formal observances, the policy of saving appearances. As far as to this policy, it was an excellent and persuasive argument that the state had decreed, and would resolutely enforce, a change in religion, that is to say till it should be the sovereign pleasure of a succeeding monarch, readily seconded by a majority of the ecclesiastical authorities, just to turn the whole matter round from north to south. But the argument would find its main strength expended upon this policy; its efficacy of persuasion would go no farther; for what force could it carry inward to act upon the fixed tenets of the mind, to destroy there the effect of the earliest and ten thousand subsequent impressions, of inveterate habit, and of ancient authority? Was it to enforce itself in the form of saying, that the government, in church and state, was wiser than the people, and therefore the best judge in every matter? This, as a general proposition, was what the people most firmly believed; it has always been their prevailing faith. But then, was the benefit of that conviction to go exclusively to the government of just that particular time,—a government which, by its innovations and demolitions, was exhibiting a contemptuous dissent from all past government remembered in the land? Were the people not to hesitate a moment to take this innovating government's word for it that all their forefathers, up through an unknown length of ages, had been fools and dupes in reverencing, in their time the wisdom and authority of *their* governors? The most unthinking and submissive would feel that this was too much; especially after they had seen proof that the government so demanding, might, on the substitution of just one individual for another at its head, revoke its own last year's decrees and ordinances, and punish those who should contumaciously continue to be ruled by them. You summon us, they might have said to their government, at your arbitrary dictate to renounce, as what you are pleased to call idolatries and abominations, the faith and rites held sacred by twenty generations of our ancestors and yours. We are to do this on peril of your highest displeasure, and that of God, whom you so easily assume as your authority or ally; now who will insure us that, within a few months, there may not be a vindictive inquisition made who among us has been the most obsequiously prompt to offer wicked insult to the holy catholic apostolic church?

Thus baffled must the force of the state authority have been on the minds of the multitude. Nor would this deficiency of influence be supplied by the authority of the class held next to the government in the right to claim deference, since the people well knew, in their respective neighbourhoods, that many of the persons of consequence throughout the country had never in reality renounced the ancient religion. And while deficient in these means of enforcement, the reformed religion was naturally so much the less attractive, to vast numbers, for appearing shorn, in a material degree, of the pomp which is always the delight of the ignorant, and for having no privileges to offer in the way of commutation and indulgence in matters of conscience. When such were the recommendations which it had *not*, and when that which it *had*, was, that it appealed to the understanding *that it was true*, no wonder the unintelligent multitude were very slow to yield their assent and submission. Great numbers of them were faithful to the infatuation in which they had been brought up, and did not become proselytes. But even as to those who did, while it was a happy deliverance, as we have said, to escape on almost any terms from the utter grossness of popery, still they would carry into their better faith, (it is of the uneducated people that we speak,) much of the unhappy effect of that previous debasement of their mental existence. A man cannot be completely ignorant and stupified as to truth in general, and have a luminous apprehension of one of its particulars. There would not be in men's minds a similitude to what we image to ourselves of Goshen in the preternatural night of Egypt, a space defined out in full brightness with a precise limit amidst the general thick darkness. The rejection and substitution of religious ideas, in the perfectly illiterate converts from popery, would not appear with a magnitude of change and contrast proportioned to the difference between a compost of lying vanities and vile practical principles, and a religion which had originally come on earth in the light and sanctity of the third heaven. There had been inflicted for life and to be prolonged for generations downward, among the common people, the doom of entertaining genuine Christianity itself, restored by the reformation, with an excessively inadequate apprehension of its attributes,—as in the primitive ages a good man might have entertained a heaven-commissioned visitant as a respectable human sojourner, unaware that it was an angel. Happy for both the worthy ancient, and the honest though rude and ignorant adopter of the reformed religion, when that which they entertained repaid them according to its own quality of an angel, and not in proportion to their inadequate reception. This consideration of how much good was, we may believe, conferred by the restored true religion on many honest disciples, (notwithstanding that, from the profound ignorance in which barbarism and superstition had sunk and kept them, they were utterly incapable of forming more than a meagre and degraded conception of it,) affords more of a relief than any other thing presented in the dreary spectacle of the period in which popery was slowly retiring, with a protracted effort to maintain its dominion at every step of its retreat.

SECTION V.

Intellectual Condition of the Mass of Population in England since the reign of Elizabeth.

Of a very different kind, however, are the circumstances most readily exhibiting themselves to view in alleviation of the gloom with which we might contemplate that period of our history; or rather they would beguile us out of the perception of its being a gloomy scene at all. For we all look back with pleasure to that age of our nation when Elizabeth reigned. How can we refuse to indulge a delightful sympathy with the energy of those times, and an elation at beholding the splendid unparalleled allotment to her reign and service, of statesmen, heroes, and literary geniuses, but for whom 'that bright occidental star' would have left no such brilliant track of fame behind her? But, all this while, what was the intellectual state of the people, properly so denominated, and what should we deem it ought to have been in order to be in due proportion to the magnificence of these their representive chiefs? There is evidence that it was, what the infernal blight and blast of popery might be expected to have left it, generally and most wretchedly degraded. What it was, is shown by the facts, that it was found impossible, even under the inspiring auspices of the literate Elizabeth, with her constellation of geniuses, orators, scholars, to supply the churches generally with officiating persons capable of going with decency through the task of the public service, made ready, as every part of it was, to their hands; and that to be able to read, was the very marked distinction of here and there an individual. It requires little effort but that of going low enough, to complete the general account in conformity to such facts.

And here we cannot help remarking what a deception we suffer to pass on us from history. It celebrates some period in a nation's career as pre-eminently illustrious, for magnanimity, lofty enterprise, literature, and original genius. There was perhaps a learned and vigorous monarch, and there were Cecils and Walsinghams, and Shakspeares and Spensers, and Sidneys and Raleighs, with many other powerful thinkers and actors to render it the proudest age of our national glory. And we thoughtlessly admit on our imagination this splendid exhibition, as representing, in some indistinct manner, the collective state of the people in that age! The etheral summits of a tract of the moral world are conspicuous and fair in the lustre of heaven, and we take no thought of the immensely greater proportion of it which is sunk in gloom and covered with fogs. The general mass of the population, whose physical vigour, indeed, and courage, and fidelity to the interests of the country, were of such admirable avail to the purposes, and under the direction, of the mighty spirits that wielded their rough agency,—this great mass was sunk in such mental barbarism, as to be placed at about the same distance from their illustrious intellectual chiefs, as the hordes of Scythia from the most elevated minds of Athens. It was nothing to this great debased multitude spread over the country, existing in the coarsest habits, destitute, in the proportion of ten thousand to one, of cultivation, and still to a considerable extent enslaved by the popish superstition,—it was nothing directly, to them, as to drawing forth their minds into free exercise and acquirement, that there were, within the circuit of the island, a profound scholarship, a most disciplined and vigorous reason, a masculine eloquence, and genius breathing enchantment. Both the actual possessors of these noble things, and the portion of society forming, around them, the sphere immediately pervaded by the delight and instruction imparted by them, might as well, for any thing they diffused of this luxury and benefit among the general multitude, have been a Brahminical cast, dissociated by an imagined essential distinction of nature. This prostrate multitude grovelled through life as through dark subterraneous passages, to their graves. Yet *they* were the *nation; they* formed the great aggregate which under that name and image of consociation, has been historically mocked with an implied community in the application of the superb epithets, which a small proportion of the men of that age claimed by a striking *exception* to the condition of the mass. History too much consults our love of effect and pomp, to let us see in a close and distinct manner any thing

'On the low level of the inglorious throng;'

and our attention is borne away to the intellectual splendor exhibited among the most favoured aspirants of the seats of learning, or in councils, in courts camps, and heroic and romantic enterprises, and in some immortal works of genius. And thus we are as if gazing with delight at a prodigious public bonfire, while in all the cottages round, the people are shivering for want of fuel.

Our history becomes very bright again with the intellectual and literary riches of a much later period, often denominated a golden age,—that which was illustrated by the talents of Addison, Pope, Swift, and their numerous secondaries in fame, and which was amply furnished, too, with its philosophers, statesmen, and heroes. And what had been effected by the lapse of four or five ages, according to the average term of human life, since the earlier grand display of mind, to advance the mental condition of the general population toward a point, at which it would be prepared for ready and intelligent communication with this next tribe of highly endowed spirits? By this time, the class of persons who sought knowledge on a wider scale than what sufficed for the ordinary affairs of life, who took an interest in literature, and constituted the *Authors' Public*, extended somewhat beyond the people of condition, the persons formally receiving a high education, and those whose professions involved some necessity, and might create some taste for reading. But still they *were* a *class*, and that with a limitation marked and palpable, to a degree very difficult for us now to conceive. They were in contact, indeed, on the one side, with the great thinkers, moralists, poets, and wits, but not with the great mass of the people on the other. They received the emanations of the powerful assemblage of talent and knowledge, but did not serve as conductors to convey them down indefinitely into the community. While these distinguished minds, and this class instructed and animated by them, formed the superior part of the great national body, that body, the collective national being, was intellectually in a condition too much resembling what we have sometimes heard of a human frame in which, (through an injury in the spinal marrow,) some of the most important functions of vitality have terminated at some precise limit downward, and the inferior extremities have been devoid of sensation and the power of action.

It is on record, that works admirably adapted to find readers, and to make them, had but an extremely confined and slowly widening circulation, according to *our* standard of the popular success of the productions of distinguished genius. It is even apparent in allusions to the people in these works themselves, that 'the lower sort,' 'the vulgar herd,' 'the canaille,' 'the mob,' 'the many-headed beast,' 'the million,' (and even these designations often meant something short of the lowest class of all,) were no more thought of in any relation to a state of cultivated intelligence than Turks or Tartars. The writers are habitually seen, in the very mode of addressing their readers, recognizing them as a kind of select community; and any references to the main bulk of society are unaffectedly in a manner implying, that it is just merely recollected as a herd of beings existing on quite other terms, and for other purposes, than we fine writers, and you, our admiring readers. Indeed it is apparent in our literature of that age, (a feature siill more prominent in that of France, at that and down to a much later period,) that the main national population were held by the mental lords in the most genuine sovereign contempt, as creatures to which souls were given just to render their bodies mechanically serviceable.

Wrong as such a feeling was, there is no doubt that the actual state of the people was perfectly adapted to excite it, in men whose large and richly cultivated minds did not contain philanthrophy or Christianity enough to regret the popular debasement as a calamity. For while they were indulging their pride in the elevation, and their taste in all the luxuries and varieties, within the range of that ampler higher existence enjoyed by such men, and could even infuse a refinement and a grace into the very turpitude of the elegant part of society, the great liviug crowd of the nation would appear to them as—a good stout race of animals, indeed, and well fitted for their appointed use, supposing it an use which left mind out of the account, but—as a contemptable and offensive mass of barbarism, if to be viewed in any reference to what man is in his higher style were revelling in an unlimited opulence of ideas, the majority of the inhabitants of the island were reduced to subsist on the most beggarly pittance on which mind be barely kept alive. Probably they had still fewer ideas than the people of the former age which we have been describing. For many of those with which popery had occupied the faith and fancy of those earlier people, had now vanished from the popular mind, without being replaced in equal number by better ideas, or by ideas of any kind. And then their vices had the whole grossness of vice, and their favourite amusements were at best rude and boisterous, and a large proportion of them detestably savage and cruel. So that when we look at the shining wits, poets, and philosopbers, of that age, they appear like gaudy flowers growing in a putrid marsh.

And to a much later period the same dreadful ignorance, with all its appropriate consequences, formed the intellectual and moral condition of the inhabitants of England. Of England! which had through many centuries made so great a figure in Christendom; which has been so splendid in arms, liberty, legislation, science, and all manner of literature; which has boasted its universities of early establishment and proudest fame, of munificently endowed and possessed of stupendous accumulations of literary treasure; and which has had, through the charity of individuals, such a multitude of minor institutions for education, that it was thought it could be afforded to let many of them fall into desuetude, as to *that* purpose. Of England! so long after the reformation, and all the while under the superintendence and tuiton of an ecclesiastical establishment extending both its instruction and jurisdiction over every part of the realm, conjunct and armed with the power of the state, supported by an immense revenue, and furnished with mental qualifications from the most venerable institutions for instruction perhaps in the world. Thus favoured had England been, thus was she favoured at the period under our reviw, (the former part of the last century,) with the facilities, the provisions, the great intellectual apparatus, to be wielded in whatsoever modes she might devise, and with whatever strength of hand she chose to apply, for promoting her several millions of rational, accountable, immortal beings, somewhat beyond a state of mere physical existence. When therefore, notwithstanding all this, an awful proportion of them were under the continual process of destruction for want of knowledge, what a tremendous responsibility was insensibly borne by whatever portion of the community it was that stood, either by formal vocation, or by the general obligation inseparable from ability, in the relation of guardianship to the rest.

But here some voice of patriotic scepticism may be heard to say, Surely this is a wantonness of reproach. Is it possible that that could be so flagrant and mighty an evil, which the combined power, wealth, intelligence, and religion of England so long tranquilly suffered to be prevalent in the state of the people? England has been a nation breathing another spirit than to tolerate long any gross moral deformity, which her utmost energy could remove or modify.

Alas! this would be a thoughtless and rash encomium. There is no saying *what* a civilized and Christian nation; (so called,) may not tolerate. Recollect the slave trade, which, with the magnitude of a national concern, continued its infernal course of abominations while one generation after another of Englishmen passed away; and the united illumination, conscience, and power, of the country, maintained as faithful a peace with it, as if the divine anger had been apprehended against whatever should attempt its molestation. The being sensible of the true characters of good and evil in the world around us, is a thing strangely subject to the effect of habit, not only in the uncultivated bulk of the community, but also in the more select and responsible persons. The highly instructed and intelligent men, through a series of generations, shall have directly within their view an enormous nuisance and iniquity, and yet shall very rarely think of it, and never be made restless by its annoyance; and so its odiousness shall never be decidedly apprehended till some individual or two, as by the acquisition of a new moral sense, receive a sudden intuition of its nature, a disclosure of its most interior essence and malignity,—the essence and malignity of that very thing which has been offering its quality to view, without the least reserve, and in the most flagrant signs, to millions of observers.

Thus it has been with respect to the barbarous ignorance under which nine-tenths, at the least, of the population of our country, have been, during a number of ages subsequent to the Reformation, surrendered to every thing low, vicious, and wretched. This state of things was manifest in its whole breadth of debasement and national dishonour, to statesmen, to dignified and subordinate ecclesiastics, to magistrates, to the philosophic contemplators of actual human nature, and to all those whose rank and opulence brought them hourly proofs what influence they could exert on the people below them. And still it appeared all very right, at least substantially so, that the multitudes, constituting the grand living agency through the realm, should remain in such a condition that, when they died, the country should lose nothing but so much living body, and the quantum of vice which had probably helped to keep it in action. It is a most ungracious thing that we should have to add, that a large proportion of these classes not only were slow to admit the reformed doctrine which began at length to pronounce all this to be wrong, but systematically decried the speculations, and plans, which philanthropy was growing earnest to bring to some practical bearing on the object of giving the people, at last, the use and value of their souls as well as their hands. The philanthropists wondered, perhaps, rather inconsiderately, at this phenomenon; and it gave them, as by force, more insight into human nature. This unwelcome manner of having the insight sharpened does not tend to make its subsequent exercise very indulgent. But nevertheless, they are willing to forego any shrewd investigation into the causes of the later silence or acquiescence of some of these opposers, and of the motives instigating others of them to the adoption, though in a frowning and repellent mood, of measures tending in their general effect to the same end. Were they even compelled to entertain an unfavourable judgment or suspicion of those motives, they would recollect an example, not altogether foreign to the nature of their business, and quite in point to their duty, that of the great Apostle's magnanimous conception of the right policy and calculation for the zealous promoter of a good cause. He exulted to seize, and to bring into his capacious reckoning, the very proceedings promoted by a rival or hostile disposition toward himself, when they were such that they *must*, however intended, conduce to his great object. Some preached Christ of envy, and strife, and contention, supposing to add afflictions to his bonds; but, says he, What then? notwithstanding every way, whether in pretence or truth, Christ is preached—*the thing itself is done*,—and I therein rejoice, yea, and will rejoice. This is the high style and the great scale of ambition and policy, which will not let a good cause lose the advantage of any thing that may have unwittingly pronounced its name, though without the genuine spirit to serve it; and which assumes as something gained for it, all things that in their leading effect advance it, notwithstanding any offensive subordinate aim of their action. He who is to this degree devoted to the cause, may triumphantly say to those who are doing what necessarily advances it, but on a principle unamicable to him,—I am far more pleased by what you are in point of fact contributing, whatever be the temper, to the great object which I am intent upon, than it is possible for you to aggrieve me by letting me perceive that you would not be sorry for the frustration of *my* schemes and exertions for its service.

We revert but for one moment to the review of past times. We aid that long after the brilliant show of talent, and the creation of literary supplies for the national use, in the early part of the last century, the deplorable mental condition of the people remained in no very great degree altered. To look on that bright and sumptuous display, regarded as in connexion with the subsequent state of the popular cultivation, is like going out from some magnificent apartment, with its lustres music, refections, and assemblage of elegant personages, into the gloom and fog and cold of a winter night, beset too by shivering beggars.

Take a few hours, indulgence in the literary luxuries of Addison and Pope, and then turn to some authentic plain representation of the attainments and habits of the mass of the people, at the time when Whitefield and Wesley commenced their invasion of the barbarous community. But the benevolent reader, (or let him be a patriotically proud one,) is quite reluctant to recognize his country, his celebrated Christian nation, the most enlightened in the world, in a populace for the far greater part as perfectly estranged from the page of knowledge as if printing, or even letters, had never been invented ; the younger part finding their supreme delight in rough frolic and savage sports, the old sinking down into impenetrable stupefaction with the decline of the vital principle.

If he would please himself with the courage, and a certain natural rudimental good sense, which are acknowledged to have characterized the people, he has to observe these beset and befooled by a multitude of the most contemptible superstitions, — contemptible not only for their stupid absurdity, but also as having in general nothing of that pensive, lofty, and poetical character, which superstition itself is capable of assuming, and did assume in the northernmost part of the island.

As to religion, there is no hazard in saying, that several millions of them had no farther notion of it than that it was an occasional, or in the opinion of perhaps one in twenty, a regular attendance at church, hardly taking into the account that they were to be taught any thing there. And what *were* they taught ! The state of their notions would be, so to speak, brought out, it would be made apparent what they were taught or not taught, when so strong and general asensation was produced by the irruption among them of the two reformers just named, proclaiming, as they both did, notwithstanding their considerable difference, the grand principles which the venerable reformers, so called by eminence, had made the very essence of the national creed. And, bearing with them this quality of a test, which would prove, by the manner of their reception, the nature of popular Christianity, how were these men received ? Why, on account of their doctrine, fully as much as of the zeal with which they promulgated it, they were generally received with as complete an impression of novelty and outlandishness, as any of our voyagers and travellers of discovery have been by the barbarous tribes who had never before seen civilized man, or as the Spaniards on their arrival in Mexico or Peru. They might, as the voyagers have done, experience every local difference of moral temperament, from that which hailed them with acclamations, to that which went off in a volley of mud and brickbats ; but through all these varieties of greetings, there was a strong sense of something novel and passing strange in what they proclaimed as religion. 'Thou bringest certain strange things to our ears,' was an expression not uttered more fully in the meaning of the words by any hearer of an apostle, preaching in a heathen city. And to many of the auditors, it was a matter of nearly as much difficulty as it would to an inquisitive heathen, and required as new a posture of the mind, to obtain a clear view of the evangelical doctrines, though they were the very same which had been held forth by the fathers and martyrs of the English church.

We have alluded to the violence, which sometimes encountered the endeavour to restore these doctrines to the knowledge and faith of the people. And if any one should have thought that, in the descriptions we have been giving, too frequent and willing use has been made of the epithet 'barbarous,' and similar words, as if we could have a perverse pleasure in degrading our nation, we should request him to select for himself the appropriate terms for estimating that state of the people, in point of sense and decency, to say nothing of religion, which could admit of such a thing as the following becoming a fact, in their history ; namely that, in a vast number of instances and places, where some person, unexceptionable in character as far as known, and sometimes well known to be of undeniable worth, has attempted to address a number of the inhabitants, under a roof or under the sky, on what it imported them beyond all things in the world to know and consider, a multitude has rushed together shouting and howling, raving and cursing, and accompanying, in many of the instances, their ferocious cries and yells with loathsome or dangerous missiles ; dragging or driving the preacher from his humble stand, forcing him, and the few that wished to encourage and hear him, to flee for their lives sometimes not without serious injury before they could escape. And these savage tumults have, in many cases, been well understood to be instigated or abetted by persons, whose advantage of superior condition in life, or even express vocation to instruct the people better, has been infamously lent in defence of the perpetrators against shame, or remorse, or legal punishment, for the outrage.

There would be no hazard, we believe, in affirming, that since Wesley and Whitefield began the conflict with the heathenism of the country, there have been in it hundreds of occurrences answering in substance to this description. From any one, therefore, who should be inclined to accuse us of harsh language, we may well repeat the demand in what terms, *he* would think he gave the true character of a mental and moral condition, manifested in such explosions of obstreperous savage violence as the Christian missionaries among eastern idolaters never have the slightest cause to apprehend. These occurrences were so far from uncommon half a century back, that they might fairly be taken as symptoms of a habitual state. Yet the good and zealous men whose lot it was to be, in various places, thus set upou by a furious rabble of many hundreds, the foremost of them active in direct violence, and the rest venting their ferocious delight in a hideous blending of ribaldry and execration. of joking and cursing, were taxed with a canting hypocrisy, or a fanatical madness, for speaking of the prevailing ignorance and barbarism in terms equivalent to our sentence from the prophet, 'The people are destroyed for lack of knowledge,' and deploring that the existing institutions were utterly inefficient for any revolution in this empire of darkness. But those, whom direct danger could not deter from renewing and indefinitely repeating such attempts at all hazards, were little likely to be appalled by these contumelies of speech. They might have laughed at the persons so abusing them, and said, 'Now really you are inconsiderately wasting your labour. Don't you know, that on the score of this same business we have sustained the battery of stones, bricks, and the contents of the ditch? And is it possible you should think, that we can much care for the force of mere words, gibes, and sneers, after that? Albeit the opprobrious phrases *have* all the coarse violence of a proud rich proprietor, or the more highly inspirited tone of invective learnt in a college, they are quite another kind of thing to be the mark for, than such assailments as have come from the brawny arms of some of your peasants.' It is gratifying to see thus exemplified, in the endurance of evil for a good cause, the effect of that provision in our nature for economizing the expense of feeling through which the encountering of the greater reduces the less to insignificance.

That our descriptive observations do not exaggerate the popular ignorance, with its natural concommitants, as prevailing at the middle, and down far beyond the middle, of the last century, many of the elderly and middle-aged persons among us can readily confirm from what they remember of the testimony of their immediate ancestors, some of them perhaps not very long removed from the world. It will easily be recollected what pictures they gave, of the moral scene spread over the country when they were young. They could convey lively images of the situations in which the vulgar notions and manners had their free display, by representing the assemblages, and the cast of communication, at fairs, revels, and other rendezvous of amusement, or in the field of rural employment, or on the village green, or in front of the mechanic's shop. They could recount various anecdotes characteristic of the times; and repeat short dialogues, or single sayings, which expressed the very essence of what was to the population of the township or province, instead of law and prophets, or sages or apostles. They could describe how free from all sense of shame whole families would seem to be, from grandsires down to the third rude reckless generation, for not being able to read; and how well content, when there was some one individual in the neighbourhood who could read an advertisement, or ballad, or last dying speech of a malefactor, for the benefit of the rest. They could describe the awful desolation of the land, with respect to any enlightening and impressive religious instruction in the places of worship, and what wretched and delusive notions of religion such of them as cared to pay any attention at all to its public observances, were permitted and authorized, by their appointed spiritual guides, to carry with them to their last hour; at which hour, some ceremonial form was to be a passport to heaven. A little bread and wine, under an ecclesiastical designation, and with the recital of some sentences regarded much in the nature of an incantation,—and all was safe! The sinner expiring believed so, and the sinners surviving were allowed to form their plan of life on a calculation of the same final resource.*

Thus the past age has left, as imparted through immediate tradition, an image of its character in the minds of the generation now themselves growing old. Here and there, indeed, there lingers, long after the departure of the great company to which he belonged, an ancient who retains in some degree this image immediately from the reality, as having become of an age to look at the world, and take a share in its activities, about the middle of the last century. It might be an employment of considerable though rather melancholy interest, for a person visiting many parts of the land, to put in requisition, in each place, for a day or two, the most faithful of the memories of the most narrative of the oldest people, for the materials from which to form an estimate of the mental and moral state of the main body of the inhabitants, of town or country, in the period of which they themselves saw the latter part, and retain also many recollections of what their progenitors testified of the former. With the removal of these persons the image of that age, in its most vivid delineation on the mind, will become extinct. It will soon, therefore, be no otherwise to be acquired than from written memorials.

But if we could have it placed before the mental eye in all the luminousness of a supernatural manifestation, are we sure we should not have the mortification of perceiving that the change, from that condition of popular attainments and habits to the present, has been but in a humiliating proportion to the ostensible amount of the advantages, which we are apt to be elated in recounting as the boast and happiness of a later age? If we had *not* this mortifying impression, if on the contrary, the people of the present times, thus brought into comparison, appeared so much less ignorant and debased as a moderate efficacy of their greater advantages would have rendered them, then, it is certain, we should behold those former people presented in a still darker character than we have been depicting. For what must that moral condition have been, if it was worse than the present by any thing near the difference of a tolerably fair improvement of the additional means latterly afforded? If it has taken so much to make the present generation *but* what it is, what must they have been to whom as means, and in whom as effect, all this was wanting?

The means wanting to the former generations, and that have sprung into existence for the latter, may be briefly named. There has been a vast extension of the system of preaching, by the classes of Christians that arose under the influence of the happy innovation of Whitefield and Wesley, but especially by the followers of the latter; a connexion of Christians which, (while, many of us differ materially from their theological tenets and while we may attribute to them some certain modicum too much of ambition in capacity of a religious body, combined with a good deal too much tendency to servility to power in capacity of citizens, also a small portion more than is *defensively* necessary of the Ishmaelitish quality, as toward other sects of dissenters, and some exemplification of the difficulty of perfectly combining temperance and zeal in religious feelings,) we must acknowledge to be doing incalculable good in the nation, more good probably than any other religious denomination. We may add, the progressive formation of a serious zealous evangelical ministry in the established church, and the rapid extension of the dissenting worship and teaching.

* The form of an address to an auditory, retained thus far and still farther on in the original composition of these observations, (conformably to the purpose for which they had first been meditated and used,) it is so expressly marked in the paragraph which here immediately follows, that it cannot well be modified to fall without awkwardness into the course of the composition in its present more general character. In a note it may be read or passed by. It stands thus:

'Some of you can hardly fail to be, at this moment, recollecting descriptions which you may have heard given by persons of the preceding generation, of the condition, as they could remember it, of the people of some districts in the neighbourhood of this city, (Bristol.) In those accounts they described some of the persons and leagues of persons, of local notoriety, whose daring and address gave them the precedence in an uncivilized community; related incidental rencounters and conversations with individuals of the inhabitants; and detailed the circumstances of some formidable affray, or some mischievous or fatal violence committed against strangers passing through the country. And perhaps it was told in what manner religion itself and its teachers were received by them, when it was begun to be introduced, in a form absolutely new to them, by those its worthy champions who could set at nought abuse and danger when an attempt was to be made to rescue men's souls. Such of you as have the clearest remembrance of these recitals by contemporaries and observers of the facts, will acknowledge that no general terms can aggravate or equal the wildness and gloominess of the scene, in which an ignorance, nearly as profound as any thing we can well imagine in the centre of Africa, had its legitimate effect, in the cherishing, letting loose, and justifying of all the active propensities to evil, and that with a remarkable local advantage of system and compact. The depraved spirit of the population, acting with such a collectiveness of force, might be said to constitute a great moral steam-engine of iniquity,—if a fancied analogy between the then state of the mind in the district, and the now conspicuous mechanical appearances on it, may warrant such a metaphor.'

These being things of directly *religious* operation, it perhaps might seem for a moment questionable whether they are more than very partially to the purpose, in an enumeration of the agencies for banishing the *ignorance* of the community. But we hardly need to say, that true religion, besides that it *is* knowledge, of the most important order, in whatever degree it occupies the understanding, is a marvellous improver of the *sense* of uneducated persons, by creating in them a habit of serious thought, which has in many instances been seen to have the effect of making them appear to have acquired, in the space of a very few years, double the measure of intellectual faculty they had ever shown before.

And then there have been the diversified causes and expedients, contributing to the increase of knowledge among the people in a mode less specifically directed to the religious effect. There was the grand novelty of Sunday schools, which conferred immense benefit themselves, and encouraged instead of superceding the formation of other schools. There was a large production and circulation of tracts, which showed how well entertainment might be made, by the proper hands, to subserve moral and religious instruction without lessening its seriousness, and which will remain a monument of the talent, knowledge, and benevolence, of that distinguished benefactor of her country and age, Mrs. H. More, perhaps even pre-eminent above her many excellent works in a higher strain. Later issues of tracts, in different forms of composition, to the amount almost of an inundation, have solicited millions of thoughtless beings to begin to think. The enormous flight of periodical miscellancies, and of newspapers, must be taken as both the indication and the cause that hundreds of thousands of persons were giving some attention to the matters of general information, where their grandfathers were, during the intervals of time allowed by their employments, prating, brawling, sleeping, or drinking, the hours away.

When we come down to a comparatively recent time, we see the bible 'going up on the breadth of the land;' schools, of a construction, devised as in rivalry of the multiplied forces in the finest mechanical inventions, in a hopeful progress toward general adoption; and an extensive practice, by the instrumentality of missionary and other benevolent institutions, of rendering familiar to common knowledge a great number of such interesting and important facts, in the state of other countries and our own, as would formerly have been far beyond the sphere of ordinary information.

The statement would be signally deficient, if we omitted to observe, that the prodigious commotion in the political world, during a third part of a century, has been a grand cause, in whatever proportion it may be judged that the attendant evil has balanced against the good, of any observable rising of the popular mind from its former stagnation. In all time there has not been a combination of events with principles that has, within so short a period, stirred to the very bottom the mind of so vast a portion of the race. The mighty spirit of the commotion has not only agitated men's passions and tempers, but through these, and with all the force of these, has reached their opinions.

But reverting to the account of minor and more specific instrumentality, in our own country, we may add, that for a good many years past, there has been a most prolific inventiveness in making almost every sort of information offer itself in brief, familiar, and attractive forms, adapted to youth or to adult ignorance; so that knowledge, which was formerly a thing to be searched and dug for, 'as for hid treasures,' has seemed at last beginning to effloresce through the surface of the ground on all sides of us. And, now, when we have put all these things together, we may well pause to indulge again our wonder what *could* have been the mental situation of the inferior orders, the great majority of our nation, antecedently to the creation of this modern comprehensive economy of so many influences and means, for awakening them to something of an intelligent existence.

CHAPTER II.

VARIOUS ILLUSTRATIONS OF THE EVILS ATTENDANT ON AN UNEDUCATED STATE OF A PEOPLE.

SECTION I.

Degradation of the lower class shown by contrast with something better within that class itself.

The gloomy review of the past, however, may here be terminated. And how happy were it, if here also terminated the prevalence of that which makes it so gloomy, if all these later multiplied means for forming a more enlightened race, were seen to have had so much success, that, with respect to the people of our country, the prophet's expression, which led us into the train of description, might here be dismissed as a mere sentence of history. But we are compelled to see how slow is the progress of mankind toward thus rendering obsolete any of the darker lines of the sacred book. So completely, so desperately, had the whole popular body and being been pervaded by the stupifying power of the long reign of ignorance,—with such heavy reluctance, at the best, does the human mind open its eyes to admit light,—and so incommensurate as yet, even on the supposition of its having much less of this reluctance, has been in quantity the whole new supply of means for a happy change,—that we have still before us a most melancholy spectacle.

Even that proportion of beneficial effect which actually has resulted from this new creation and co-operation of means, but serves to bring out to view, in more ungracious manifestation, the ignorance and debasement, still obviously constituting the character of immensely the greater part of the population of our land; as a dreary waste is made to look still more dreary by the little inroads of cultivation and beauty in its hollows, and the faint advances of an unwonted green upon its borders. The degradation of the lower class is the most forcibly illustrated, as seen in contrast with something better within that class itself. It is not with the great literati and philosophers, that men would ever think of comparing the untutored rustics, and labourers in handicraft. The two classes were as antipodes of the moral world, and could not be kept in sight both at once. They were regarded as having their respective places in the system, as formed for quite different modes of moral subsistence, as hardly required on the one side, or permitted on the other, to recognize in each other a common nature; as being, in short, under an allotment which rendered it idle to speculate on any expedients for their approximation, or to regret, that no slight humble participation could be afforded to the one class, of that in the fulness of which the other deems itself to verify the nobleness of the rational nature. But now, when such a humble participation *has* been afforded, a description of people has been formed, contiguous to the multitude, or rather intermingled with them; and it is between this improved portion and the general crowd, that the grievous contrast arises. It certainly were ridiculous enough to fix on a labouring man and his family, and affect to deplore that he is doomed not to behold the depths and heights of science, not to expatiate over the wide field of history, not to luxuriate among the delights, refinements, and infinite diversities of literature; and that his family are not growing up in a training to every high accomplishment, after the pattern of some neighbouring family, favoured by fortune, and perhaps unusual ability combined with the highest cultivation in those at their head. But it is a quite different thing to take this man and his family, unable perhaps, both himself and they, even to read, and therefore sunk in all the debasement of ignorance,—and compare them with another man and family in the same sphere of life, but who have received the utmost improvement within the reach of that situation, and learnt to set the proper value on the advantage; who often employ the leisure hour in reading, (sometimes socially and with intermingled converse,) such instructive and innocently entertaining things as they can procure, are detached from constant and chosen society with the absolute vulgar, have acquired much of the decorums of life, can take some intelligent interest in the great events of the world, and are prevented, by what they read and hear, from forgetting that there is another world. It is, we repeat, after thus seeing what may, and in particular instances does exist, in a humble condition, that we are compelled to regard as an absolutely horrible spectacle the still prevailing state of our national population.

The brief display which we would attempt, in several of the most prominent particulars, of the evils of an uneducated state of the people, is not to be regarded as peculiarly and exclusively a representation of the popular condition in this country, as if meant precisely as a portrait. But a general description of what is naturally inseparable from prevailing ignorance in the national multitude will necessarily be, in substance, a picture of our people; and it is chiefly from what is too conspicuous among them, and our specific illustrations will be taken.

The subject is to the last degree unattractive. It is totally unsusceptible of that something partaking of magnificence in the display, which so readily, though mischievously, throws itself over some of the forms in which depravity and misery make a prey of mankind. Nor does it afford any thing of that wild and picturesque character, in which some of the fantastic shapes of pagan superstition array themselves to our view. The representation, too, while it displays degradation and wretchedness in one whole class, reflects ungraciously, at least by implication, on other classes who may be supposed to look at the spectacle. And also, the whole matter of the exhibition must have the disadvantage, as to arresting attention, of being mere obvious facts plain to the view of whoever looks around him. But indeed, ought it not to be so much the better, when we are pleading for a certain mode of benevolent exertion, that every one can see, and that no one can deny, the sad reality of all that forms the object and imposes the duty, of that exertion?

Look, then, at the neglected ignorant class in their childhood and youth. One of the most obvious circumstances is, that there is not formed in their minds any thing of the nature of an estimate of the life before them. The human being should, as early as possible, have fixed within him a notion of what he is in existence for, of what the life before him is for. It ought to be among the chief of the things which he early becomes aware of, that the course of activity he is beginning should have a leading principle of direction, some predominant aim, a general and comprehensive purpose, paramount to the divers particular objects he may pursue. It should be as much in his settled apprehension as the necessity of his having an employment in order to live, that there is something it imports him to be, which he will not become, merely by passing from one day into another, by eating, growing taller and stronger, seizing what share he can of noisy sport, and performing appointed portions of work; and that *not* to be, that which it is so imports him to be, will of necessity be to be worthless and miserable.

We are not entertaining the extravagant fancy of the possibility, except in some rare instances of premature thoughtfulness, of turning inward into deep habitual reflection, the spirit that naturally goes outward, in these vivacious, active, careless beings, when we assert that it *is* possible to teach many of them with a degree of success, in very juvenile years, to apprehend and admit such a principle. We have many times seen this exemplified in fact. We have found some of them appearing apprized that *life is for something as a whole*; and that, to answer that general purpose, a mere succession of interests and activities, each engaged in for his own sake, will not suffice. They could comprehend, that the multiplicity of interests and activities in detail, instead of being allowed, without plan or pervading principle, to constitute and be that general purpose, were to be things selected and regulated in reference and amenableness to it. By the comprehensive and presiding object, we do not rigorously and exclusively mean the religious concern, (though that is the most essential thing in it,) but the combination of all those interests and attainments, for the sake of which it is worth while to have the activities of life disposed into a system, instead of being left to casualty. The scheme will bear toward ultimate felicity; but will also take large account of what is to be attempted and hoped for in this life.

Now, we no more expect to find any such idea of a presiding purpose of life, than we do the profoundest philosophical reflection, in the minds of the uneducated children and youth. They think nothing at all about their existence and life in any moral reference whatever. They know no good that is to have been endowed with a rational rather than a brute nature, excepting that thus they have the privilege of tormenting brutes with impunity. They think nothing about what they shall become, and very little about what shall become of them. There is nothing that tells them of the relations, for good and evil, of present things with future and remote ones. The whole energy of their moral and intellectual nature goes out as in brute instinct on present objects, to make the most they can of them for the moment, taking the chance for whatever may be next. They are left totally devoid even of the thought, that what they are doing is the beginning of a life; their whole faculty is engrossed in the doing of it; and whether it signify any thing to the next ensuing stage of life, or to the last, is as foreign to any calculation of theirs, as the idea of reading their destiny in the stars. Not only, therefore, is there an entire preclusion from their minds of the faintest hint of a monition, that they should live for the grand final object pointed to by religion, but also, for the most part, of all consideration of the attainment of a reputable condition and character in life. The creature of so many faculties, and entering on an endless career, is seen in the predicament of snatching, as its utmost reach of purpose, at the low amusements and vices of each passing day; and cursing its privations and tasks, and often also the sharers of those privations, and the exactors of those tasks.

When these are grown up into the mass of mature population, what will it be, as far as their quality shall go toward constituting the quality of the whole? Alas! it will be, to that extent, just a continuation of the ignorance, debasement, and misery, so conspicuous in the bulk of the people now. And to *what* extent? Calculate that from the unquestionable fact, that hundreds of thousands of the human beings in our land, between the ages, say, of eight and sixteen, are at this hour thus abandoned to go forward into life at random, as to the use they shall make of it,—(if, indeed, it can be said to be at random, when there is strong tendency and temptation to evil, and no discipline to good.) Looking at this proportion, does any one think there will be, on the whole, wisdom and virtue enough in the community to render this black infusion imperceptible or innoxious?

But are we accounting it absolutely inevitable that the sequel must be in full proportion to this present fact,—*must* be every thing that this fact threatens, and *can* lead to,—as we should behold persons carried down in a mighty torrent, where all interposition is impossible, or as the Turks look at the progress of a conflagration or a plague ? It is in order to 'frustrate the tokens' of such melancholy divination, to arrest something of what a destructive power is in the act of carrying away, to make the evil spirit find, in the next stages of his march, that, all his enlisted host have not followed him, and to quell somewhat of the triumph of his boast, 'my name is Legion, for we are many ;'—it is for this that the friends of improvement, and of mankind, are called upon for efforts beyond those which are requisite for maintaining, in its present extent of operation, the system of expedients, for instructing, before it be too late, the yet youthful tribe.

SECTION II.

Uncultivated minds abandoned to seek their pleasures in sensual gratification.

Another obvious circumstance in the state of the untaught class is, that they are abandoned, in a direct unqualified manner, to seek their chief good in sensual gratification. The very narrow scope to which their condition limits them in the pursuit of this, will not prevent its being to them the most desirable thing in existence, since for any other mode of happiness their scope is narrower *still*. By the very constitution of the human nature, the mind seems half to belong to the senses, it is so shut within them, affected by them, dependent on them, and impotent but through their medium. And while, by this necessary hold which they have on what would call itself a spiritual being, they absolutely will engross to themselves, as of clear right, a large share of its interest and exercise they will strive to possess themselves of the other half too. And they will have it, if it has not been carefully otherwise claimed and pre-occupied. And when the senses have thus usurped the whole mind for their service, how will you get any of it back ? Try, if you will, whether this is a thing so easy to be done. Present to the minds, so engrossed with the desires of the senses, that their main action is but in these desires and the consideration how to fulfil them,—offer to their view nobler objects, which are appropriate to the spiritual being, and observe whether that being promptly shows a sensibility to the worthier objects, as congenial to its nature, and, obsequious to the new attraction, disengages itself from what has wholly absorbed it.

Nor would we require that the experiment be made by presenting something of a precisely religious nature, to which there is an innate aversion for religion's own sake separately from its being an intellectual thing,—an aversion even though the mental faculties *be* cultivated. It may be made with something that ought to have power to please the mind as simply a being of intelligence, imagination, and sentiment, a pleasure which may not be altogether foreign, in some of its modes, to the senses themselves ; as when, for instance, it is to be imparted by something fine or grand in the natural world, or in the works of art. Let this refined solicitation be addressed to the grossly uncultivated, in competition with some low indulgence, with the means for example, of gluttony and inebriation. See how the subjects of your experiment, (intellectual and moral natures, though they are,) answer to these respective offered gratifications. Observe how these more dignified attractives encounter and overpower the meaner, and reclaim the usurped debased spirit. Or rather, observe whether they can avail, for more than an instant, so much as to divide its attention. But indeed you can foresee the result so well, that you may spare the labor. Still less could you deem it to be of the nature of an experiment, (which implies uncertainty,) to make the attempt with ideal forms of nobleness or beauty, with intellectual, poetical, or moral captivations.

Yet this addiction to sensuality, beyond all competition of worthier modes and means of interest, does not altogether refuse to admit of some division and diversion of the vulgar feelings, in favour of some things of a more mental character, provided they be vice. A man so neglected in his youth that he can hardly spell the names of Alexander, Cæsar, or Bonaparte, may feel the strong incitement of ambition. This, instead of raising him, may only propel him forward, so to speak, on the level of his debased condition and society, and it is a favourable supposition that makes him 'the best wrestler on the green,' or a manful pugilist ; for it is probable his grand delight may be, to indulge himself in an oppressive insolent arrogance toward such as are unable to maintain a strife with him on terms of fair rivalry, making his will the law to all whom he can force or frighten into submission.

SECTION III.

The devotion to sensuality and coarse pleasures a ready introduction to habits of cruelty.

The devotement to coarse sensuality admits, again, of occasional competition and suspension in behalf of the pleasures of cruelty ; a flagrant characteristic, generally, of uncultivated degraded human creatures, both where the whole community consists of such, as in barbarous and savage tribes, and where they form a large portion of it, as in this country. It is hardly worth while to put in words, the acknowledgment of the obvious and odious fact, that a considerable share of mental attainment is sometimes inefficient to extinguish this infernal principle of human nature, by which it is gratifying to witness and inflict suffering, even separately from any prompting of revenge. All of us have seen examples of this inefficiency. But why do we regard them as peculiarly hateful, and brand them with the most intense reprobation, but *because* it is judged the fair and natural tendency of mental cultivation to repress that principle, insomuch that a surpassing virulence of depravity is evinced by the failure of that discipline to produce this effect ? But then, think of that discipline being almost wholly withheld, so that the ordinary, and the extraordinary, degrees of this execrable propensity may go into action in their unmitigated malignity.

And such a consequence of the absence of that discipline, is manifest in the lower portion of our self-extolled community ; notwithstanding a diminution, which the progress of education and religion has effected, in certain of the once most favourite and customary practices of cruelty. These very practices, nevertheless, still keep their ground in some of the more heathenish parts of the country ; and if it were possible, that the more improved notions and taste of the more respectable classes could admit of any countenance being given to their revival, in the more civilized parts, it would be found that even there too large a portion of the people is, to this hour, left in a disposition which would welcome the return of savage exhibitions. It may be, that some of the most atrocious forms and degrees of cruelty would hardly please the greater number of them ; for there have been instances in which an English populace has shown indignation at extreme and *unaccustomed* perpetrations of this kind, even to the extent of cruelly revenging them. Perhaps not many would be delighted with such scenes as those which, in the *Place de Greve*, used to be a gratification to a multitude of all ranks of the Parisians. But how many odious facts, characteristic of our people, have come under every one's observation.

Who has not seen numerous instances of the delight with which advantage is taken of weakness or simplicity, to practise upon them some sly mischief, or inflict some open mortification; and of the unrepressed glee with which many spectators can witness or abet the malice? And if, in such a case, an indignant observer has hazarded a remark or expostulation to any of them, the full stare, and the quickly succeeding laugh and retort of brutal scorn, has thrown open to his revolting sight the state of the recess within, where the moral sentiments are; and shown how much the preceptions and notions had been indebted to the cares of the instructor. Could he help thinking what was deserved somewhere, by individuals or by the local community collectively, for suffering a being to grow up to quite or nearly the complete dimensions and features of manhood, with so vile a thing in it in substitution for what a soul should be? We need not remark, what every one has noticed, how much the vulgar are amused by seeing vexatious or injurious incidents, (if only not quite disastrous or tragical ones,) befalling persons against whom they can have no resentment; how ferocious often their temper and means of revenge when they *have* causes of resentment; or how intensely delighted, in company, it is true, with many that are called their betters, in beholding several of their fellow-mortals, whether in anger or athletic competition, covering each other with bruises, deformity and blood.

Our institutions, however, protect, in some considerable degree, man against man, as being framed in a knowledge of what would else become of the community. But observe a moment what are the dispositions of the vulgar as indulged, and with little preventive interference of those institutions, on the inferior animals. To a large proportion of the class it is, in their youth at least, one of the most vivid exhilaration to witness the terrors and anguish of living beings. If there is heard at a distance a howl that strikes you as almost infernal, one of your first conjectures in explanation would be, that a company of rationals may be witnessing the writhings, agonies and cries, of some animal struggling for escape or for life, while it is suffering the infliction, perhaps, of stones and kicks, or the application of the more directly fatal instruments of violence. If you hear in the clamour a sudden burst of fiercer exultation, you will surmise that just then the deadly blow or stab has been given. There is hardly an animal on the whole face of the country, of size enough, and enough within reach, to be a sufficient object of attention, that would not be persecuted to death if no consideration of ownership interposed. The children of the uncultivated families are allowed, without a check, to exercise and improve the hateful disposition, on flies, young birds, and other feeble and harmless creatures; and they are actually encouraged to do it on what, under the denomination of vermin, are represented in the formal character of enemies, almost in such a sense as if a moral responsibility attached to them, and they were therefore not only to be destroyed as a nuisance, but deserving to be punished as offenders.

The destruction of sympathy, with the consequent carelessness of inflicting pain, combined inseparably, as this will probably always be, with the *love* of inflicting it, must be confirmed by the horrid spectacle of slaughter all over the land; a spectacle sought for gratification by the children and youth of the lower order; and in many places so publicly exhibited that they cannot well avoid seeing it, and its savage preliminary circumstances, sometimes directly wanton aggravations, perhaps in diabolic revenge of a struggle to resist or escape. Horrid, we call it because it is the infliction, on millions of sentient and innocent creatures every year, in what calls itself a humane and Christian nation, of anguish perfectly unnecessary to the purpose. And it is a flagrant dishonour to such a country, and to the class that virtually, by rank, and formally, by official power, have presided over its economy, one generation after another, that so hideous a fact should never, as far as we can remember to have heard, have moved even a thought of authoritative interference. An inconceivable daily amount of suffering, inflicted on unknown thousands of creatures, dying in slow anguish, when their death might be without pain as being instantaneous, is accounted no deformity in the social system, no incongruity with the national profession of a religion of which the essence is charity and mercy, nothing to sully the polish, or offend the refinement, of what will be seriously asserted to be, in its higher portions, a pre-eminently civilized and humanized community. Precious and well protected polish and refinement, and humanity, and Christian civilization! to which it is a matter of easy indifference to know, that in the neighbourhood of their abode, in whatever part of the whole country it may be, those tortures of butchery are, unnecessarily, inflicted, which could not be actually witnessed by persons in whom the pretension to these fine qualities is any thing better than affectation, without intolerable sensations of horror.

They are known to be inflicted, and yet this is a trifle not worth an effort toward innovation on inveterate custom, on the part of the influential classes; who may be far more worthily intent on changing the fashion of a dress, or possibly some new refinement in the cookery of the dead bodies of the victims. It is a matter far below legislative attention; while the powers of definition are exhausted under the stupendous accumulation of regulations and interdictions for the good order of society. So hardened may the moral sense of a community be by universal and continual custom, that we are perfectly aware these very remarks will provoke the ridicule of many; and provoke it not at all the less that not one man of them can deny, or affect to deny, that the manner of the practice referred to steels and depraves, to a dreadful degree, a vast number of the human beings immediately employed in it, and, as a spectacle, powerfully contributes to confirm, in a much greater number, exactly that which it is, by eminence, the object of moral tuition to counteract—men's disposition to make light of all suffering but their own.

Now this one thing, exactly this one disposition, is the grand principle of moral depravity on earth,—this not caring for what is endured by other beings that are made liable to suffer. Estrangement from the supreme goodness, indeed, is the primary *cause;* but this very thing, this not caring for the sufferings of other beings, is the substantial practical essence of the iniquity which forms the curse and blast of this wretched world. And yet, we repeat it, a civilized and Christian nation feels not the slightest self-displacency, for its allowing a certain unhappy but necessary part in the economy of the world to be executed, (by preference to a harmless method,) in a manner which probably does more to corroborate in the vulgar class this essential principle of depravity, than all the expedients of amelioration yet applied are doing to expel it.

Were it not vain and absurd to muse on supposable new principles in the constitution of the moral system, there is one that we might have been tempted to wish for, namely, that of all suffering *unnecessarily* and wilfully inflicted by man on any class of sentient existence, a bitter intimation and participation might be conveyed to him through a mysterious law of nature, enforcing an avenging sympathy in severe proportion to that suffering, on all the men, be where they might, who were really accountable for its being inflicted.

After children and youth are trained to behold with something worse than hardened indifference, with a feeling of stimulant amusement, the sufferings of creatures dying for the service of man, it is no wonder if they are barbarous in their treatment of those that serve him by their life. And in fact nothing is more obvious as a prevailing, if we may not say general abomination, than the cruel habits of the lower class toward the labouring animals placed within their power. Of whatever quality and condition those animals may be, they have experienced enough of human nature; but generally its diabolic disposition is the most fully exercised on those that have been already the greatest sufferers. Meeting, wherever we go, with some of these starved, abused, exhausted figures, we shall not unfrequently meet with also another figure accompanying them,—that of a ruffian, young or old, who with a visage of rage, and accents of hell, in wrecking his utmost malevolence on a wretched victim for being slow in performing, or quite failing to perform, what the excess of loading, and perhaps the feebleness of old age, have rendered difficult or absolutely impracticable; or for shrinking from effort, to be made by a pressure on bleeding sores, or for loosing the right direction through blindness, and that occasioned by hardship or savage violence. Many of the exacters of animal labour really seem to resent it as a kind of presumption and insult to the slave, that it should be any thing else than a machine, that the living being should betray under its toils that it suffers, that it is pained, weary, or reluctant. And if, by outrageous abuse, it should be excited to some manifestation of resentment, that is a crime for which the sufferer would be likely to incur such a fury and repetition of blows and lacerations, as to die on the spot, but for an interfering admonition of interest against destroying so much property, and losing so much service. When that service has utterly exhausted, often before the term of old age, the strength of those wretched animals, there awaits many of them a last short stage of still more remorseless cruelty, that in which it is become a doubtful thing whether the utmost efforts to which the emaciated disease sinking frame can be forced by violence, are worth the trouble of that violence, the delays and accidents, and the expense of the scanty supply of subsistence. As they must at all events very soon perish, it has ceased to be of any material consequence, on the score of interest, how grossly they may be abused; and their tormentors seem delighted with this release from all restraint on their dispositions. Those dispositions, as indulged in some instances, when the miserable creatures are formally consigned to be destroyed, cannot be much exceeded by any thing we can attribute to fiends. Some horrible exemplifications were adduced, not as single casual circumstances, but as usual practices, by a patriotic senator some years since, in endeavouring to obtain a legislative enactment in mitigation of the sufferings of the brute tribes. The design vanished to nothing in the house of commons, under the effect of argument and ridicule from a person distinguished for intellectual cultivation; whose resistance was not only against that specific measure, but avowedly against the principle itself on which *any* measure of the same tendency could ever be founded.*

If some advocate for things as they are in the lower classes, should be inclined to interpose here with a remark, that after *such* a reference, we have little right to ascribe to those classes, as if it were peculiarly one of their characteristics, the insensibility to the sufferings of the brute creation, and to number it formally among the results of the 'lack of knowledge,' we can only reply, that however those of higher order may explode any attempt to make the most efficient authority of the nation bear repressively upon the evil, and however it may in other ways be abetted by them, it is, at any rate, in those inferior classes chiefly that the actual perpetrators of it are found. It is not a little to say in favour of cultivation, that it generally renders those who have the benefit of it incapable of practising, *themselves*, those cruelties which they are, indeed, far too little sensible how much they may be virtually countenancing, by some things which they do, and some things which they omit or refuse to do.

* Lord Erskine's memorable Bill, triumphantly scouted by the late Mr. Windham.

SECTION IV

Uneducated persons have vague, limited, unsteady, and often perverted notions of right and wrong.

If we did not trust to be indulged in an exemption, in a course of observations on such a subject, from any rigorous enforcement of the laws of order, we ought to have put nearer the beginning of these illustrations, from notorious fact, of the state of an uneducated people, that obvious characteristic—a rude, limited, unsteady, and often perverted, sense of right and wrong in general.

It is curious to look into a large volume of religious casuistry, for instance Bishop Taylor's *Ductor Dubitantium*, and reflect what a conscience disciplined in the highest degree might be, and then observe what this regulator of the soul actually is where there has been any dicipline of reason at all; and where there is no deep religious sentiment to rectify the perceptions, in the absence of an accurate intellectual discrimination of things. This sentiment being wanting, dispositions and conduct will not be taken account of according to the distinction between holiness and sin; and in the absence of instructed understanding, they connot be brought to the test of the distinguishing law between propriety and turpitude; nor estimated upon any moral and comprehensive notion of utility. The evidence of all this is thick and close around us; so that every serious observer has been struck and almost shocked to observe, in what a very small degree conscience is a *necessary* attribute of the human creature; and how nearly a non-entity the whole system of moral principles may be, as to any recognition of it by an unadapted spirit. While that system is of a substance veritable and eternal, and stands forth in its exceeding breadth, marked with the strongest characters and prominence, it comes before these persons with hardly a shadow's virtue and reality, except in a few things of the grossest bulk, if we may so express it; their conscience having little sense of its vocation as respecting the evil of any thing done, or questioned whether to be done, in matters short of very palpable and flagrant iniquity. It is therefore probable, they have considerably protracted exemptions from any interference of conscience at all; it is certain that they experience no such pertinacious attendance of it, as to feel habitually a monitory intimation, that without great thought and care they will inevitably do something wrong. But what may we judge and presage of the moral fortunes of a sojourner, of naturally corrupt propensity, in this bad world, who is not haunted, even to a degree of alarm, by this monitory sense, through every day of his life?

As he moves hither and thither on the scene, he has his perception of what is existing and passing on it; there are continually meeting his senses numberless moving and stationary objects; and among the latter there are many forms of limitation and interdiction; there are high walls, and gates, and fences, and bricks of torrents and precipices; in short, an order of things on all sides signifying to him, with more or less of menace,—Thus far and no farther. And he is in a general way obsequious to this arrangement. We do not ordinarily expect to see him carelessly violating the most decided of the artificial lines of warning-off, nor daring across those dreadful ones of nature. But the while, as he is nearly destitute of that faculty of the soul which would perceive, (analogously to the effect of coming in contact with something charged with that element which causes the lightning,) the awful interceptive lines of that other arrangement which he is in the midst of as a subject of the laws of God, we see with what insensibility he can transgress those prohibitory significations of the almighty will, which are to devout men as lines streaming with an infinitely more formidable than material fire. And if we look toward his future course of life, the natural sequel foreseen is, that those lines of divine interdiction which he has not conscience to perceive as meant to deter him, he will seem, nevertheless, to have, through his corruptions, a strong recognition of, but in another quality—as temptations to attract him.

But to leave these terms of generality, and advert to a few particulars of illustration:—Recollect how commonly persons of the class described are found utterly violating truth, not in hard emergencies only, but as a habitual practice, and apparently without the slightest reluctance or compunction, their moral sense perfectly at rest under the accumulation of a thousand deliberate falsehoods. It is seen that by far the greatest proportion of them think it no harm to take little unjust advantages in their dealings, by deceptive management; and very many would take the greatest but for fear of temporal consequences; would do it, that is to say, without inquietude of conscience, in the proper sense. It is uniformly the testimony of experience, from persons who have had the most to transact with them and to employ them, that the indispensable rule of proceeding is to assume generally their want of principle, and leave it to time and prolonged trial to establish rather slowly, the individual exceptions. Those unknowing admirers of human nature, or of English character, who are disposed to exclaim against this as an illiberal rule, may be recommended to act on what they will therefore deem a liberal one—at their cost.

In any species of wrong which has the salvo of custom in its favour, the most palpable iniquity of the practice shall not force any moral debate upon it on the mind. From recent accounts it appears, that the entire coast of our island is not even yet clear of those people called *wreckers*, who regarded it as all fair and right to appropriate whatever they could seize, of the lading of vessels cast ashore, including, often, what they could tear from the personal possession of the unfortunate beings who might just be escaping from the most dreadful peril. The cruelty we have so largely attributed to our English vulgar, never recoils on them in a compulsion to detest themselves. The habitual indulgence of the irascible, vexatious, and malicious tempers, to the plague or terror of all within reach, scarcely ever becomes a subject of judicial estimate, as a character viewed in the abstract, with then a reflection of that estimate on the man's own self to whom the character belongs. He reflects but just enough to say to himself that it is all right and deserved, and unavoidable too, for that he is unpardonably crossed and provoked; nor will he be driven from this self-approval, though it be evident to every one else that the provocations are comparatively slight. The inconvenience and vexation incident to low libertinism, will make the offenders fret at themselves indeed for having been such fools, but it is in general with an extremely trifling degree of the sense of guilt. Suggestions of reprehension, in even the discreetest terms, and from persons confessedly the best authorized to apply them, would most commonly be answered by a grinning defying carelessness, or abusive retort; instead of any betrayed signs of even an internal acknowledgement of deserving reproof. And while thus the censure of a fellow-mortal finds nothing in their minds to meet it, in the way of owning its justice, this stupid self-complacency is undisturbed also on the side toward heaven. A mere philosopher, that should make little account of religion, beyond its adaptedness to be applied to enforce and aggravate the sense of obliga ion with respect to rules of conduct, and would not, pr ›vided it may have this effect, care much about its t uth or falsehood, might be disposed to assert, that the gnorant and debased part of the population, of this Christian and protestant country, are but so much the worse for the riddance of some parts of the superstitions of former ages. There were admitted even in those times, he might say, *some* right injunctions of morality, considered as an external practical concern. These might be, and actually were, infixed in the popular mind as matter of conscience, by the great array of things pretendedly divine and demi-divine which surrounded, and pressed closely and powerfully on, the mind of the multitude. Whereas now, when this great array is vanished, there is nothing, absolutely nothing, to enforce moral principles and rules on the ignorant portion of the people with the mighty authority of divine sanction; since they have not, in their exemption from the superstitions of their ancestors come under any solemn and commanding effect of the true idea of the divine majesty. And it is undeniable that this is the state of conscience among them. The vague faint notion, as they conceive it, of a being who is said to be the creator, governor, lawgiver, and judge, and who is somewhere in the sky, has not, to many of them, the smallest force of intimidation from evil, at least when they are in health and day-light. One of the large sting-armed insects of the air does not alarm them less. A certain transitory fearfulness, that sometimes comes upon them, points more to the devil, and perhaps sometimes the ghosts of the dead, than to the almighty. It may be, indeed, that this feeling is in its ultimate principle, if it were ever followed up so far, an acknowledgment of justice and power in God, reaching to wicked men through these hostile beings as a kind of instrumentality; but beyond these proximate objects of apprehension the idea of invisible spiritual power is inexpressibly vacant and feeble.

Even what notion they do conceive of the greatness of God tends little to restrain the dispositions to sin, or to impress the sense of guilt after it is committed. He is too great, they readily say, to mind the little matters that such creatures as we may do amiss; they can do *him* no harm. The idea, too, of his bounty, is so coarsely formed as to be a protection against all conscious reproach of ingratitude toward him: he has made us to need all this that it is said he does for us; and it costs him nothing, it is no labour, and he is not the less rich; and besides, we have toil, and want, and plague enough, notwithstanding any thing that he gives.

It is probable this unhappiness of their condition, oftener than any other cause, brings God into their thoughts, and that as a being against whom they have a quarrel on account of it. And this strongly assists the reaction against whatever would enforce the sense of guilt on the conscience. When he has done so little for us, (something like this is the sentiment,) he cannot think it any such great matter if we *do* sometimes come a little short of his commands. There is no doubt that their recollections of him as a being to murmur against for their allotment, are more frequent, more dwelt upon, and with more of an excited feeling, than their recollections of him as a being whom they ought to have loved and served, but have offended against. The very idea of such offence, as one of the things which constitute wickedness, is so slightly conceived, (because he is invisible, and because he is secure against all injury,) that if the thoughts of one of these persons *should*, by some rare occasion, be thrown into the direction of unwillingly seeing his own faults, it is probable his impiety would appear the most inconsiderable thing in the account, that he would easily forgive himself the negation of all acts and feelings of devotion toward the supreme being, and the countless multiplication of insults to him by profane language.

To conclude this part of the melancholy description, it may be observed of the class in question, that they have but very little notion of guilt, or possible guilt, in any thing but external practice. That busy interior existence, which is the moral person, genuine and complete; the thoughts, imaginations, volitions; the motives, projects, deliberations, devices; the indulgence of the ideas of what they cannot or dare not practically realize,—all this, we have reason to believe, passes nearly exempted from jurisdiction, even of that feeble and undecisive kind which *may* occasionally attempt a little interference with their actions. They do indeed take such notice of the quality of these things within, as to be aware that some of them are not to be disclosed in their communications; which prudential caution has of course little to do with conscience, when the things so withheld are internally cherished in perfect disregard of the omniscient observer, and with hardly the faintest monition that the essence of the guilt is the same, with only a difference in degree, in intending or deliberately desiring an evil, and, in acting it.

It is not natural obtuseness of mental faculty that we are attributing all this while, to the uneducated class of our people, in thus exposing the deplorable defectiveness of their discernment between right and wrong. If it were, there might arise somewhat of the consolation afforded in contemplating some of the very lowest of the savage tribes of mankind, by the idea that such outcasts of the rational nature must stand very nearly divested of accountableness, through absolute natural want of mind. But in the barbarians of our country we shall often observe a very competent, and now and then an abundant share of native sense. We may see it evinced in respect to the very questions of morality, in cases where they are quite compelled, as will occasionally happen, to feel themselves brought within the cognizance of some plain principle of distinction between right and wrong. In such cases we have witnessed a sharpness and activity of intellect which have excited almost our admiration. What contrivance of deception, and artful evasion. What dexterity of quibble, and captious objection, and petty sophistry. What vigilant observance how the plea in justification takes effect, and address in changing it if they perceive it is not the right one. What quickness to avail themselves of any mistake, or apparent concession in the examiner or reprover. What readiness of resource for reply or subterfuge. What copious rhetoric in exaggeration of the cause which tempted to do wrong, or the great good hoped to be effected by the little deviation from the right—a good surely enough to excuse so trifling an impropriety. What facility of placing between themselves and the censure, the recollected example of some good man who has been 'overtaken in a fault.'

Here *is* mind, after all, we have been prompted to exclaim; mind educating itself to evil, in default of that discipline which should have educated it to good. How much of the wisdom of evil, (if we may be allowed the expression,) there is faculty enough in the neglected corrupt popular mass of this nation to attain, by the exercise into which the individual's mind is carried by its own bad impulse, with the advantage too of a most extensive co-operation. And how freely the advantage has always been conceeded to each of these self-improvers in depraved sense, that he should have as great a number as he could desire of associates and co-operators; that no attempt should be made, in a strenuous manner, on a large scale, to diminish the immense tribe! Multitudes beyond calculation, have been, through every period, abandoned to this destructive process of self-education, and to assist one another in it. Where then has been that character of parental guardianship, which seems to be ascribed when poets, orators, and patriots, are inspired with tropes, and talk of England and her children? This imperial matron of their rhetoric seems to have little cared how much she might be disgraced in the larger portion of her progeny, or how little cause they might have to all eternity to remember her with gratitude. She has had far other concern about them, and employment for them, than that of their being taught the value of their spiritual nature, and carefully trained to be enlightened, good, and happy. Laws against crime, it is true, she has enacted for them in great plenty. She has also maintained public sabbath observances to remind them of religion, of which observances the reading of a book of sports was, at one period, long after her adoption of the reformation in religion, an indispensable part. But she might plainly see what all this did *not* accomplish. It was a glaring fact before her eyes, that a vast number of her children were brought up in a mental rudeness akin to that of Muscovite boors. She had most ample resources indeed for supplying the remedy; but, provided that the productions of the soil and the workshop were duly forthcoming, she thought it of no consequence, it should seem, that the operative hands belonged to degraded minds. And then, too, as at all times, her lofty ambition destined a good proportion of them to the consumption of martial service, she perhaps judged that the less they were trained to think, the more fit they might be to be actuated mechanically, as an instrument of blind impetuous force. Or perhaps she thought it would be rather an inconsistency, to be making much of the inner existence of a thing which was to be so unceremoniously cut or dashed to pieces. And besides, a certain measure of instruction to think, especially if consisting, in a considerable part, of the inculcation of religion, might have done something to disturb that Mahomedan notion, which she was by no means desirous to expel from her fleets and armies, that death for 'king and country' clears off all accounts for sin.

SECTION V.

General effects of the want of knowledge in a community, and the facility with which a vacant mind receives wrong impressions.

Let us direct our attention a little while to the effects of the privation of knowledge, as they may be seen displayed in the several parts of the economy of life, in the uneducated portion of the community. Observe those people in their daily occupations. None of us need to be told that of the prodigious diversity of manual employments, some consist of, or include, operations of such minuteness or complexity, and so much demanding nicety, arrangement, or combination, as to necessitate the constant and almost entire attention of the mind; nor that nearly all of them must require its full attention at times, at particular stages, changes, and adjustments, of the work. We give this its full weight, in prevention of any extravagant notion of how much it is possible to think of other things during the working time. It is however to be recollected, that persons of a class superior to the numerous one we have in view, take the chief share in the departments of operation which require the most of mental effort,—those which demand extreme precision, or inventive contrivance, or taste, or scientific skill. We may also take into the account of the allotment of employments to the uncultivated multitude, how much facility is acquired by habit, how much use there is of instrumental mechanism, (the grand exempter from the responsibility, that would lie on the mind,) and how merely general and very slight an attention is exacted, in the ordinary course of some of the occupations. These things being considered, we may venture perhaps to assume, on an average of those employments, that the persons engaged in them might be, as much at least as one third part of the time, without detriment to the manual performance, giving the thoughts to other things with attention enough for interest and improvement. This is particularly true of the plainer parts of the labours of agriculture.

But as the case at present is, what does become,

during such portion of the time, of the ethereal essence which inhabits the corporeal labourer, this spirit created for thought, knowledge, and immortality? Can we without regret know, that in very many of the persons in the situations supposed, it suffers a dull absorption, subsides into the mere physical nature, is sunk and sleeping in the animal warmth and functions, and lulled and rocked, as it were, in its lethargy, by the bodily movements in the works which it is not necessary for it to keep habitually awake to direct? In being, at the same time, under a *general* responsibility for their right execution, it has a kind of license and protection for this somnolency. The employment *is something to be minded,* though but now and then requiring a full attention, and therefore it seems an exemption from the claim to mind any thing else: as a person retained for some service which requires but occasionallly an active exercise, will excuse the indolence which declines taking in hand, as he very properly might, any other business in the intervals, under the pretext that he has his appointment; and so, when not under the immediate calls of that appointment, he will go to sleep, even in the full light of day, with an easy conscience.

Let not any such folly be imputed to us here, as that we are fancying the labouring class, in this age and country, to be placed under a moderate demand of their thoughts, for their immediate necessities. Many of them experience, amidst their employment, a severe arrest of those thoughts which the employment itself would leave free. The lot of that classs seems to be placed in a melancholy disproportion, between what *must* be given to the cares and toils for mere subsistence, and what *can,* at most, be given to the interests of the noble part of their nature. It is a strange and sad spectacle, to behold so many myriads of spiritual beings under the doom, of consuming the greatest share of their energy and time in just supporting so many bodies in the struggle to live; a struggle, not in the general sense merely, that the body must, by the laws of our nature, compel to the concern of its life and well-being a great deal of the mind's attention and activity; nor in the general sense merely of that sentence, 'in the sweat of thy brow thou shalt eat thy bread;' but in the more special sense, that through the adventitious effect of some dreadful disorder of the social economy in this part of the world, at this time, the utmost that the exertions of the body and mind together can do, but barely suffices, in some instances, does not suffice, for the mere protraction of life,—comfortable life being altogether out of the question. The course of the administration of the civilized states, and the recent dire combustion into which they have almost unanimously rushed, as in emulation which of them should with the least reserve, and with the most desperate rapidity annihilate the resources which should have been for the subsistence and competence of their people, have resulted in such destitution and misery as were never suffered in this country before, except as immediately inflicted by the local visitation of some awful calamity. The state very many of our people, at this hour, is nearly what might be conceived as the consequence of a failure of the accustomed produce of the earth. Not a few might give the image of families driven out into a desert, from abodes destroyed in the ravage of war.

We were wishing to introduce a suggestion how the labouring people's thoughts might be partly employed, during their daily task, and consistently with industry and good workmanship. Alas! what a state of things is exhibited where the very name of industry, the virtue universally honoured, the topic of so many human and divine inculcations, cannot be spoken without offering a bitter insult; where the heavy toil, denounced on man for his transgression, in the same sentence as death, is in vain implored as the greatest possible privilege; or thought of in despair as a blessing too great to be attainable; and when the reply of the artizan, to an unwitting admonition, that even amidst his work, he might have some freedom for useful thinking may be, 'Thinking! I have no work to confine my thinking; I may, for that, employ it all on other subjects; but those subjects are, whether I please or not, the plenty and luxury in which many creatures of the same kind as myself are rioting, and the starvation which and my family are suffering.'

We hope in Providence, more than in any wisdom shown by men, that this melancholy state of things will be alleviated, otherwise than by the extinction of a considerable portion of suffering humanity. We trust to see the time, when a Christian monitor shall no longer be silenced by the apprehension of such a reply, when he would suggest to the humble class that they should strive against being reduced to mere machines amidst their manual employments; that it is miserable to have the whole mental existence shrunk and shrivelled as it were to the breadth of the material they are working upon; that the noble interior agent, which lends itself to maintain the external activity, and direct the operations required of the bodily powers for the body's welfare, has eminently a right and claim to have employments on its own account, during such parts of those operations as do not of necessity monopolize its attention. It has a right to take its privilege, by a rule analogous to what would be applicable, in the case of a man of great general intelligence or science having the charge of directing a common workman, in a business of no considerable novelty or difficulty, and who would interfere when really acquired; but would not give up all other thought and employment to be a constant mere looker-on, during operations of so ordinary a nature that he could not really fix his attention on them.

But how is the mind of the labourer or artizan to be delivered from the blank and stupified state, during the parts of his employment that do not necessarily engross his thoughts? How, but by its having within some store of subjects for thought; in a word, by the possession of knowledge? How can it be sensibly alive and active, when it is placed fully and decidedly out of communication with all things that are friendly to intellectual life, all things that apply a beneficent stimulus to the faculties, all things, of this world or another, that are the most inviting or commanding to thought and emotion? We can imagine this ill-fated spirit, thus detached from all vital connexion, secluded from the whole universe, and enclosed as by a wall of incarceration,—we can imagine it sometimes moved with an indistinct longing for its appropriate interests; and going round and round by this dark dead wall, to seek for any spot where there might be a chance of escape, or any crevice where a living element for the soul transpires; and then, as feeling it all in vain, relapsing into inertion and slumber. Some ignorant minds have instinctive impulses of this kind; though many, it is possible, are so deeply stupified as to be habitually much at ease. But let them have received, in their youth and progressively afterwards, a considerable measure of interesting information, respecting, for instance, the many striking objects on the globe they inhabit, the memorable events of past ages, the origin and uses of remarkable works within their view, remaining from ancient times; the causes of effects and phenomena familiar to their observation as now unintelligible facts; the prospects of man, from the relation he stands in to time and eternity, and God, explained by the great principles and facts of religion, and that religion, declared by a direct revelation from heaven. Let there be fixed in their minds so many ideas of these kinds, as might be imparted by a comparatively humble education, (one quite compatible with the destination to a life of ordinary employment,) and even involuntarily the thoughts would often recur to these subjects, in those moments and hours when the manual occupation can, and actually will, be prosecuted with but little of exclusive attention. Slight incidents, casual expressions, would sometimes suggest these subjects ; by association they would suggest one another. The mere reaction of a somewhat cultivated spirit against invading dulness, might recal some of the more amusing and elating ones ; and they would fall like a gleam of sunshine on the imagination. An emotion of conscience, a self-reflection, an occuring question of duty a monitory sensation of defective health, would sometimes point to the serious and solemn ones. The mind might thus go a great way, to recreate or profit itself, and, on coming back again, find all safe in the process of the field or the loom. The man would thus come from these processes with more than the bare earnings to set against the fatigue. There would thus be scattered some appearances to entertain, and some sources and productions to refresh, over what were else a dead and barren flat of existence.

There is no romancing in all this ; we have known instances of its verification to a very pleasing and exemplary extent. We have heard persons of the class in question tell of the exhilarating imaginations, or solemn reflections, which, through the reminiscences of what they had read in youth or more advanced years, had visited their minds ; and put them as it were in communication for a while with diversified, remote, and elevated objects, while in their humble employments under the open sky or the domestic roof. And is not this, (if it be true, after all, that the intellectual immortal nature is by emphasis the man,) is not this vastly better than that this mind should lie nearly as dormant, during the labourer's hours of business, as his attendant of the canine species shall be sometimes seen to do in the corner of the field where he is at work?

But perhaps it will be said, that the minds of the uncultivated order are not generally in this state of utter inanity during their common employments ; but are often awake and busy enough in recollections, fancies, projects, and the tempers appropriate ; and that they abundantly show this when they stop sometimes in their work to talk ; or talk as they are proceeding in it. So much the stronger, we answer, the argument for supplying them with knowledge ; for it were better their mental being *were* sunk in lethargy, than busy among the imaged transactions, the wishes, and the schemings, which will be the most likely to occupy the faculties of persons abandoned to ignorance, vulgarity, and therefore probably to vice.

We may add to the representation, the manner in which they spend the part of their time not required to be devoted to the regular, nor to the occasional, exercise of their industry. It is too true that many of them may plead as they do, that excepting Sunday, the utmost suspension of toil allowed them is little more than what, being caused by weariness, is absolutely needed for complete repose. This is particularly the case of the females, especially those who have the chief cares of the family. Nevertheless, it is within our constant observation that a considerable proportion of the men, a large one of the younger men, do in fact, include, for substance, their manual employments within such limits of time, as often to leave several hours in the day to be spent nearly as they please. And in what manner, for the most part, is this precious time expended by those of no mental cultivation? It is very true, again, that in many departments of labour, a diligent exertion during even this limited space of the day, occasions such a degree of lassitude and heaviness as to render it almost inevitable, especially in certain seasons of the year, to surrender some moments of the spare time, beyond what is necessary for taking the supports of life, to a kind of listless subsidence of all the powers, corporeal and mental. But after all these allowances fully conceded, a great proportion of the class under contemplation have in some days several hours, and in the whole six days of the week, on an average of the year, many hours, to be given, as they choose, to useful purposes or to waste; and again we ask, where the mind has been left waste how *is* that time mostly expended?

If the persons are of a phlegmatic temperament, we shall often see them just simply annihilating those portions of time. They will for an hour, or for hours together, if not disturbed by some cause from without, sit on a bench, or lie down on a bank of hillock, or lean on a wall, or fill the fire-side chair, yielded up to utter vacancy and torpor, not asleep perhaps, but more exempt from mental excitement than if they were ; since the dreams, that would probably visit their slumbers, would most certainly be a more lively train of ideas than any they have awake. Of a piece with this, is the habit, among many of this order of people, of giving formally to sleep as much as one-third part, sometimes considerably more, of the twenty-four hours. Certainly there is a mounful number of cases in which infirmity, care, fatigue, and the comfortlessness and penury of the humble dwelling, effectually plead for a large allowance of this balm of oblivion. But very many surrender themselves to this excess from destitution of any thing to keep their minds awake, especially in the evenings of the winter. What a contrast is here suggested to the imagination of those who have read Dr. Henderson's, and other recent descriptions, of the habits of the people of Iceland!

These, however, are their most harmless modes of wasting the time. For while we might think of the many hours merged by them in apathy and needless sleep, with a wish that those hours could be recovered to the account of their existence, we might well think with a wish that the hours could be struck out of it which they may sometimes give, instead, to conversation ; in parties where ignorance, coarse vulgarity, and profaneness, are to support the dialogue on topics the most to their taste ; always including, as the most welcome to that taste, the depravities and scandals of the neighbourhood ; while all the reproach and ridicule, expended with the warmest good will on those depravities, have uniformly the strange result, of making the censors the less disinclined themselves to practise them, and only a little better instructed how to do it with impunity. In many instances there is the additional mischief, that these assemblings for corrupt communication find their resort at the public house, where intemperance and ribaldry may season each other, if the pecuniary means can be afforded, even at the cost of distress at home. But short of this depravity, the worthlessness of the communications of a number of grossly ignorant beings is easy to be imagined, besides that most of us have been made judges of their quality by numberless occasions of unavoidably hearing samples of them.

In the finer seasons of the year, much of these leisure spaces of time can be expended out of doors; and we have still only to refer each one to his own observation of the account to which they are turned, in the lives of beings whose lot allows but so contracted a portion of time to be, at the best, applied directly to the highest purposes of life. Here the hater of all such schemes of improvement, as would threaten to turn the lower order into what that hater may probably call Methodists, in other words, into rational creatures and Christians, comes in with a ready cant of humanity and commiseration. And why, he says, with an affected indignation of philanthropy, why should not the poor creatures enjoy a little fresh air and cheerful sunshine, and have a chance for keeping their health, confined as many of them are, for the greatest part of their time, in narrow squalid rooms, unwholesome shops, or one kind or other of disagreeable places and employments? Very true, we answer ; and why should they not be collected in groups by the road side, in readiness for any thing that, in passing, may furnish occasions for gross jocularity, practising some impertinence, or uttering some jeering scurrility, at the expense of persons going by; shouting with laughter at the effect of the sport, and inspiriting it all with infernal imprecations? Or why should they not form a little conventicle for cursing, blaspheming, and blackguard obstreperousness in the street, about the entrance of one of the haunts of intoxication; where they are perfectly safe from that far worse mischief of a gloomy fanaticism, with which they might have been smitten if seduced to frequent the meeting-house twenty paces off? Or why should not the children, growing into the stage called youth, be turned loose through the lanes, roads, and fields, to form a brawling impudent rabble, trained by their association to every low vice, and ambitiously emulating, in voice, visage, and manners, the drabs and ruffians of maturer growth? Or why should not the young men and women collect in clusters, or range about or beyond the neighbourhood in bands, for revel, frolic, and all kinds of coarse mirth, to come back late at night to quarrel with their wretched elders, who perhaps envy them their capacity for such wild gaities and strollings, while rating them for their disorderly habits? We say, where can be the harm of all this? What reasonable and benevolent man would think of making any objection to it? Reasonable and benevolent,—for these are qualities expressly boasted by the opposers of an improved education of the people, while in such opposition they virtually avow their approbation of all that we have here described.

We have allowed most fully the plea of how little time, *comparatively*, could be afforded by the lower classes from their indispensable employments to the concern of mental improvement; and also that of the fatigue consequent on them, and causing a temporary incapacity of effort in any other way. But here we see that, nevertheless, time, strength, and wakefulness, and spring and spirit for exertion, *are* found for a vast deal of busy diversion.

This is the manner in which the spare time of the week-days goes to waste, and worse; but the Sunday is welcomed as giving scope for the same things on a larger scale. It is very striking to consider, that several millions, we may safely assert, of our English people, come to what should be years of discretion, are almost completely exempt from any manner of conscience respecting this seventh part of time, not merely as to any required consecration of it to religion, but as to its being under any claim or of any worth at all, otherwise than for amusement. It is actually regarded by them as a section of time far less under obligation than any other. They take it as so absolutely at their free disposal, by a right so exlusively vested in their taste and will, that a demand made even in behalf of their own most important interests is contemptuously repelled as an interference. If the idea occurs at all of claims which they have heard that God should make on the hours, it is dismissed with the thought that it really cannot signify to him how creatures condemned by his appointment to toil all the rest of the week, may wish to spend this one day, on which the secular taskmaster manumits them, and he, the spiritual one, might surely do as much. An immense number pay no attention whatever to any sort of religious worship; and multitudes of those that do afford an hour to such an observance, do it either as a mode of amusement, or by way of taking a license of exemption from any farther accountableness as to the manner in which they may like to spend the day. It is the natural consequence of all this, that there is more folly, if not more crime, committed on this than on all the other six days together.

Thus man, at least *ignorant* man, is unfit to be trusted with any thing under heaven; since a remarkable appointment for raising the general tenor of moral existence, has, with these persons, the effect of sinking it. Those favoured portions of their time, interposed a regular and frequent intervals, with a mark of the divine benediction upon them, might, without any approach toward the punctilious and burdensome austerity in the manner of improving them which some good men in former times enjoined, be the means of diffusing a degree of light and dignity over the whole series of their days; whereas an unhappily large number of those of our people who are now arrived near the close of that long series, have to look back on the Sundays as having been made, in a peculiar manner, the dishonour and bane of their life. One of the most melancholy views in which a human being can be presented to us, is when we behold a man of perhaps seventy years sunk in the gross stupidity of an almost total ignorance of all the most momentous subjects, and reflect that more than three thousand Sundays have passed over him, of which every hour successively *has been his time*, since he came to an age of some natural capacity for mental exercise. Perhaps some compassionate friend may have been pleading in his behalf—Alas! what opportunity, what time, has the poor mortal ever had? His lot has been to labour hard through the week, throughout almost his whole life. Yes, we answer, but he has had three thousand Sundays; what would not even the most moderate improvement of so immense a quantity of time have done for him? But the ill-fated man, (perhaps rejoins the commiserating pleader,) had no advantages of education, had nothing in any sense deserving that name. There, we reply, you strike the mark. Sundays are of no practical value, nor bibles, nor the enlarged knowledge of the age, nor heaven nor earth, to beings brought up in estrangement from all right discipline of their minds. And therefore we are pleading for the schemes and institutions which will not *let* human beings be thus brought up.

In so pleading, we can happily appeal to a conspicuous fact in evidence that the intellectual and religious culture, in the introductory stages of life, tends to secure that the persons so trained shall be, after they are grown up, much more sensible than the uncultivated, of the value of means and opportunities, and more disposed to avail themselves of them. Look at the numbers now attending, and with a deportment not unsuitable, public worship and instruction, as compared with what the proportion is remembered or recorded to have been half a century since, or any time previous to the great exertions of benevolence, to save the children of the inferior classes from preserving the likeness of the minds of their forefathers.

It can be testified also, by persons whose observation has been the longest in the habit of following children and youth from the instruction of the school institutions into mature life, that in a gratifying number of instances, they have been seen permanently retaining too much love of improvement, and too much of the habit of an useful employment of their minds, to sink, in their ordinary daily occupations, into that wretched inanity we were representing; or to consume the free intervals of time in the listlessness, or worthless gabble, or vain sports, of which their neighbours furnished plenty of example and temptation.

SECTION VI.

Gross ignorance produces a degraded state of domestic society.

These representations have partly included, what we may yet specify distinctly as one of the unhappy effects of gross ignorance—*a degraded state of domestic society.*

That form of community is seen to have a peculiar tendency to fall below the level of complacent and dignified association, and strongly requires the intervention of every preventive and corrective cause. Human beings cannot be together without having constantly, though it may be somewhat indistinctly, a certain sense of claiming from one another something meant and suited to please. This is fully recognized when strangers fall into company for a few hours. The members of the domestic society have each this same feeling that the others should please them; but their passing so very large a portion of their time together is adverse to their *giving* what they thus mutually claim. To be through so long a time maintaining a study and effort to please one another, would be too long and costly a suspension of their individual wills, tastes, and humors; for to please each one himself, rather than others, is the predominant principle of human feeling after all. Hence the absence, in domestic society, of the attentiveness, the tone of civility, the habits of little concessions and accommodations, voluntary and supernumerary, which are observable in the temporary intercourse of acquaintance, and, as we have said, of strangers. Where the claim is perpetual, each one seems prompted by a natural impulse to a manner of deportment which has the ungraciousness of asserting his freedom.

And then consider, in so close a kind of community, what near and intimate witnesses they are of all one another's faults, weaknesses, tempers, perversities; of whatever is offensive in manner, or unseemly in habit; of all the irksome, humiliating, or even ludicrous, circumstances and situations. And also, in this close association, the bad moods, the strifes, and resentments, are pressed into immediate lasting corrosive contact with whatever should be the most vital to social happiness. If there be, into the account, the wants, anxieties, and vexations of severe poverty, they will generally aggravate all that is destructive to domestic complacency and decorum.

Now add gross ignorance to all this, and see what the picture will be. How many families we have seen where the parents were only the older and stronger animals than their children, whom they could teach nothing but the methods and tasks of labour. They naturally could not be the mere companions, for alternate play and quarrel, of their children, and were disqualified by mental rudeness to be their respected guardians. There were about them these young and rising forms, containing the inextinguishable principle which was capable of entering on an endless progression of wisdom, goodness, and happiness; needing numberless suggestions, explanations, admonitions, and brief reasonings, and a training to follow the thoughts of written instruction. But nothing of all this from the parental mind. Their case was as hopeless for receiving this benefit, as the condition, for physical nutriment, of infants attempting to draw it, (we have heard of so affecting and mournful a fact,) from the breast of a dead parent. These unhappy heads of families possessed no resources for engaging and occupying, for at once amusing and instructing, the younger minds; no descriptions of the most wonderful objects, or narratives of the memorable events, to set, for superior attraction, against the idle stories of the neighbourhood; no assemblage of admirable examples, from the sacred or other records of human character, to give a beautiful real form to virtue and religion, and promote an aversion to base companionship.

Requirement and prohibition must be a part of the family economy, perpetually in operation of course; and in such examples we have seen the family government exercised, or attempted to be exercised, in the roughest barest shape of will and menace, with no aptitude or means of imparting to injunction and censure a convincing and persuasive quality. Not that the seniors should allow their government to be placed on such a ground, that, in every thing they enforce or forbid, they may be liable to have their reasons demanded by the children. Far from it; but at the same time, it should not be obvious to the natural shrewdness of the children that their domestic authorities really *have* no reasons better than an obstinate or capricious will, so that they should plainly perceive there is no reason for their submission but the necessity imposed by their dependence. But this must often be the unfurtunate case in such families.

Now imagine a week, month, or year, of the intercourse in such a domestic society, the course of talk, the mutual manners, and the progess of mind and character; where there is a sense of drudgery approaching to that of slavery, in the unrelenting necessity of labour; where there is none of the interest of imparting knowledge or receiving it, or of reciprocating knowledge that has been imparted and received; where there is not an acre, if we might express it so, of intellectual space around them, clear of the thick universal fog of ignorance; where, especially, the luminaries of the spiritual heaven, the attributes of the almighty, the grand phenomenon of redeeming meditation, the solemn realities of a future state and another world, are totally obscured in that shade; where the conscience and the discriminations of duty are dull and indistinct, from the youngest to the oldest; where there is no genuine respect felt or shown on the one side, nor affection unmixed with vulgar petulence and harshness, expressed perhaps in wicked imprecations, on the other; where a mutual coarseness of manners and language has the effect, without their being aware of it as a cause of debasing their worth in one another's esteem, all round; and where, notwithstanding all, they absolutely must pass a great deal of time together, to converse, and to display their dispositions toward one another, and exemplify what the primary relations of life are reduced to when divested of all that is to give them dignity endearment, and conduciveness to the highest advantage of existence.

Home has but little to please the young members of such a family, and a great deal to make them eager to escape out of the house; which is also a welcome riddance to the elder persons, when it is not in neglect or refusal to perform the allotments of labour. So little is the feeling of a peaceful cordiality created among them by their seeing one another all within the habitation, that, not unfrequently, the passer-by may learn the fact of their collective number being there, from the sound of a low strife of mingled voices, some of them betraying youth replying in anger and contempt to maturity or age. It is wretched to see how early this liberty is boldly taken. As the children perceive nothing in the *minds* of their parents that should awe them into deference, the most important difference left between them is that of physical strength. The children, if of hardy disposition, to which they are perhaps trained in battles with their juvenile rivas, soon show a certain degree of daring against this superior strength. And as the difference lessens, and by the time it has nearly ceased, what is so natural as that they should assume equality, in manners and in following their own will; But equality assumed where there should be subordination, inevitably involves contempt toward the party against whose claim it is asserted.

The relative condition of such parents as they sink in old age, is most deplorable. And all that has preceded leads, by a natural course, to that consequence which we have sometimes beheld, with feelings emphatically gloomy,—the almost perfect indifference with which the descendants, and a few other near relatives, of a poor old man of this class, would consign him to the grave. A human being was gone out of the world, a being whom they had been near all their lives, some of them sustained in their childhood by his labours, and yet not one heart, at any one moment, felt the sentiment—I have lost.——They never could regard him with respect, and their miserable education had not taught them humanity enough to regard him in his declining days as an object of pity. Some decency of attention was perhaps shown him, or perhaps not, in his last hours. His being become a dead, instead of a living man was a burden taken off; and the insensibility and levity, somewhat disturbed and repressed at the sight of his expiring struggle, and of his being lowered into the grave, recovered, by the day after his interment, if not on the very same evening, their accustomed tone, never more to be interrupted by the effect of any thought of him. It is a very melancholy spectacle to see an ignorant thoughtless father, surrounded by his untaught children, at the sight of whom our thought thus silently accosts him, The event which will take you finally from among them, perhaps after forty or fifty years of intercourse with them. will leave no more impression on their affections, than the cutting down of a decayed old tree in the neighbourhood of your habitation.

There are instances of rare occurrence, in which the dark and thoughtless spirit of the head of such a family is, late in life, far too late for their welfare, roused by an influence from heaven into earnest thoughtfulness and conscience. When the sun thus breaks out in radiance toward the close of his gloomy day, and when, in the energy of this new life, he puts forth the best efforts of his untaught soul to acquire a little divine knowledge, to be a lamp to him in entering ere long the shades of death, with what bitter regrets he looks back to the period when a number of human beings now scattered from him, and here and there pursuing their course in careless ignorance, were growing up under his roof, within his charge but in utter estrangement from all discipline of wisdom. And most gladly would he lay down his life to make the impression, on the now harder state of their minds, which instruction might have been rendered efficacious to make upon them in that early season.

Another thing is to be added, to this representation of the evils attendant on an uncultivated state of the people, namely—that this mental rudeness puts them decidedly out of communication with the superior and cultivated classes. It does so to a degree most pernicious to their own and the general welfare. It is of great consequence to a nation, that whatever there is in it of dignity and refinement, of liberalized feeling and deportment, and of intelligence, should have its effect downward, through all the gradations of the social condition, even to the lowest. It is easy to conceive such an effect, so pervading them all, that there should be perceptible, in every class, a modification betraying a beneficent influence of those the most eminent and enlightened. But in order to this, the subordinate ranks must be in a certain degree in communication, on favourable and amicable terms, with the higher. We have known individual instances of such a friendly approximation, and of the benefit of it. Each reader may probably recollect an example, in the case of some man in humble station, but who has had, (for his condition,) an excellent education; having been well instructed and exercised in his youth in the elements of useful knowledge; having had good principles diligently inculcated upon him; having subsequently instructed himself, to the best of his very confined means and opportunity, through a habit of reading; and exhibiting in his manners all the decorums of a respectable human being. It has been seen, that such a man, has not found, in his superiors in station and attainment, any disposition to shun him; and has not felt in himself or his situation any reason why he should seek to shun them. He would occasionally fall into conversation with the wealthy and accomplished proprietor, or the professional man of learning, in the neighbourhood. He maintained toward them a modest deference, but yet with an honest freedom of avowing his opinion, and making his observations on the matters brought in question. His intelligent manner of attending to what they said, his perfect understanding of the language naturally employed by cultivated sense, the considerateness and pertinence of his replies, and the chastened independence, just amounting to the absence of servility and awkward timidity, greatly pleased those persons of superior rank, and induced various friendly and useful attentions, on their part, to him and his family. He and his family thus experienced a direct benefit of superior sense, civility, and good principle, in a humble condition; and were put under a new responsibility to preserve a character for those distinctions. Now think of the incalculable advantage to society, if any thing approaching to this were the general state of social relation, between the lower and the higher orders.

On the contrary, there is no medium of complacent communication between the classes of higher condition and endowment, and an ignorant coarse populace. Except on occasion of giving orders or magisterial rebukes, the gentleman will never think of accosting the clowns in his vicinity. They, on their part, are desirous to avoid him; excepting when any of them may have a purpose to gain, by arresting his attention with an ungainly cringe; or when some of those, that have no kind of dependence on him, are disposed to cross his way with a look and strut of rudeness, to show how little they care for him. The servility, and the impudence, almost equally repress, in him, all friendly disposition toward a voluntary intercourse with the class. There is thus as complete a dissociation between the two orders, as mutual dislike, added to every imaginable dissimilarity, can create. And this broad, ungracious separation, intercepts all modifying influence, that might otherwise have passed, from the intelligence and refinement of the one, upon the barbarism of the other.

But there is, in human nature, a pertinacious disposition to work disadvantages, in one way or other, into privileges. The people, in being thus consigned to a low and alien ground, in relation to the cultivated part of society, are put in possession, as it were, of a territory of their own; where they can give their disposition freer play, and act out their characters in their own manner; under none of the necessity or policy which, had they occupied a ground where they must have been in communication with persons of superior order, they would have felt of partially conforming to the tastes and manners of those superiors. They thu enjoy a great emancipation; a degrading and pernicious one indeed, but one of which they are certain to make the full license. In all things and situations, it is one of the first objects with human beings, to verify experimentally the presumed extent of their liberty and privilege. In this dissociation, the people are rid of the many salutary restraints and incitements, which they would have been made to feel, if on terms of friendly recognition with the respectable part of the community; they have neither honour nor disgrace, from that quarter, to take into their account; and this contributes to extinguish all sense and care of respectability of character,—a sense and care which will never be maintained by any regard to one another's estimates, which they are far enough from holding in reverence: in truth there is a kind of tacit mutual understanding among them, that, for the benefit of them all, they are systematically to set aside all high notions and nice responsibilities of character and conduct.

And what is the natural consequence of their being thus abandoned to themselves, free from all the influence they would have been under in a state of friendly contiguity, if we may so express it, to the cultivated orders? Times may have been, when the great mass, thus detached, combined such a quietude with their ignorance, that they had none but submissive feelings in relation to their superiors, whose property, almost, they were inured to consider themselves: when it never occurred to them to make a question, why there should be so vast a difference of condition between beings of the same race, when there were never unfolded to their view, the portentious possibilities included in the fact of the immense superiority of numbers, and therefore of the physical force, of the lower order as put in comparison with the higher. But the times of this perfect, unquestioning, unmurmuring, succumbency, under the actual allotment, have passed away; except in such regions as the Russian empire, where they have yet long to continue. In the other principal states of Europe, and especially in our own, the grossest ignorance of the people has no where prevented them from acquiring a sense of their strength and importance; with a certain ill conceived, but stimulant notion, of some change which they think ought to take place in their condition. How, indeed, should it have been possible, for any considerable proportion of them to remain unaware of this strength and importance, while the whole civilized world was shaken with a practical and tremendous controversy, between the two grand opposed orders of society, concerning their respective rights; or that they should not have taken a strong, and, from the rudeness of their mental condition, a fierce interest, in the principle and progress of the strife? And how should they have failed to hear, that during this commotion, innumerable persons from the lowest class, signalizing themselves by talent and daring, had taken, by main strength, the advantageous ground formerly deemed in a great measure the peculiar right, as if by a law of nature of those who held their claim in virtue of their nativity?

The effect of all this is gone deep into the minds, of great numbers who are not excited, in consequence, to any worthy exertion for raising themselves, individually, from their degraded condition, by the earnest improvement and application of their faculties and means. The feeling of many of them seems to be, that they must and will sullenly abide by the ill-starred fate of their class, till some great comprehensive alteration, in their favour, shall absolve them from that bond of hostile sentiment, in which they make common cause against the superior orders; and shall create a state of things in which it shall be worth while for the individual to make an effort to raise himself. We can at best, (they seem to say,) but barely maintain, with the utmost difficulty, a miserable life; and you talk to us of cultivation, of discipline, of moral respectability, of efforts to come out from our degraded rank! No, we shall even stay where we are, till it is seen how the question is settled between the people of our sort, and those who will have it that they are of a far worthier kind. There may then, perhaps, be some chance for such as we; and if not, the less we are disturbed about improvement, knowledge, and all those things, the better, while we are bearing the heavy load a few years, to die like those before us.

We said they are banded in a hostile sentiment. It is true, that among such a degraded populace there is very little kindness, or care for one another's interests. They all know too well what they all are not, to be much attached to one another. But it is infinitely easier, for any set of human beings, to maintain a community of feeling in hostility to something else, than in benevolence toward one another; for here no sacrifice is required of any one's self-interest. And it is certain, that the subordinate portions of society, in this and several other nations, have come to regard the occupants of the tracts of fertility and sunshine, the possessors of opulence, splendor, and luxury, with a deep settled systematic aversion,—to use the most moderate term; with a disposition to contemplate in any other light than that of a calamity, an extensive downfall of the favorites of fortune, when a brooding imagination figures such a thing as possible; and with but very slight hints, from conscience, of the iniquity of the most tumultuary accomplishment of such a catastrophe. In a word, so far from considering their own welfare as identified with the stability of the existing social order, they consider it as something that would spring from the ruin of that order. They have lost all that veneration by habit, partaking somewhat perhaps of the nature of a superstition, which had been protracted downward, though progressively attenuated with the lapse of time, from the feudal ages into the last century. They have quite lost, too, in this disastrous age, that sense of competence, and possible well-being, which might have harmonized their feelings with a social economy under which they have enjoyed such a state. Whatever the actual economy may have of wisdom in its institutions, and of splendor, and fulness of all good things, in some parts of its apportionment, they feel that what is allotted to most of *them*, in its arrangements, is pressing hardship, galling unremitting poverty. And while thus thrown loose from the former ties to the social order, their minds have not been seized upon to be put under the substitutional ones which sound instruction alone could impose. Wise instruction might have made them capable of understanding, how a considerable proportion of the evil may have been inevitable from uncontrollable causes; of admitting in their consciences that national calamities are visitations of divine judgment, of which they were to reflect whether they had not deserved a heavy share; and of comprehending that, at all events, rancour, violence, and disorder, cannot be the way to alleviate any of the evils, but to aggravate them all. But, we repeat it, there are millions in this land, and if we include the neighboring island politically united to it, many millions, who have received no instruction adequate, in the smallest degree, to counteract the natural effect of the distresses of their condition, or to create a new principle of adherence to the established order, in place of those which time and the innovation of opinions have worn out.

Thus alienated, and thus not reclaimed, there is a large proportion of human strength and feeling not in vital combination with the social system, but aloof from it, looking at it with 'gloomy and malign regard,' in a state progressive toward a fitness to be impelled against it with a dreadful shock, under the actuating energy of whatever daring powerful spirits might arise, intent on its demolition, and favoured by opportune conjunctures of circumstances. There have not been wanting examples to show, with what fearful effect this hostility may come into action, in the crisis of the fate of a nation's ancient system; where this alienated portion of its own people, rushing in, have revenged upon it the neglect of their tuition; that neglect which had abandoned them to so utter a 'lack of knowledge,' that they really understood no better than to expect their own solid advantage in general havoc and disorder. But how bereft of sense the *state* too must be, that would thus *let* a multitude of its people grow up in a condition of mind to believe that the sovereign expedient for their welfare is to be found in spoliation and destruction! It might easily have comprehended, what it was reasonable to expect from the matured dispositions and strength, of such of its children as it abandoned to be nursed by the wolf.

While this principle of ruin was working on, by a steady and natural process, this supposed infatuated state was, it is extremely possible, directing its chief care to maintain the splendor of a court, or to extort the means for prosecuting some object of vain and wicked ambition, some project of conquest and military glory.

SECTION VII.

Answer to a very common, but futile objection. Advantages of a general diffusion of knowledge, in connexion with religion, illustrated.

But there may be persons ready to ask here, whether it be so certain that giving the people of the lower or der more knowledge, and sharpening their faculties, will really tend to the preservation of good order. Would not such improvement elate them, to a most extravagant estimate of their own worth and importance; and therefore result in insufferable arrogance, both in the individuals and the class? Would they not, on the strength of it, be continually assuming to sit in judgment on the proceedings and claims of their betters, even in the most lofty stations; and demanding their own pretended rights, with a troublesome and probably turbulent pertinacity? Would they not, since their improvement cannot from their condition in life, be large and deep, be in just such a half-taught state, as would make them exactly fit to be wrought upon by all sorts of crafty schemers, fierce declaimers, empirics, and innovators? Is it not, in short, too probable that, since an increase of mental power is available to bad uses as well as good, the results would greatly preponderate on the side of evil?

They would do well to put the objection in direct terms, and say, Understanding is to be men's guide to right conduct, and therefore the less understanding they have, the more safe are we against their going wrong. But not to dwell on the absurdity of denying, that the more mental light people have, the better qualified, in that proportion, must they be to discern their duty, nor on the tendency of an argument, if such questions contain one, which goes to depreciate the desire of truth, and all that has been venerated as wisdom, and all literature, and divine revelation, and our rational nature itself,—not to insist on this absurdity, we can most confidently answer from matter of fact. It is proved by fact, that giving the people more knowledge and more sense, does not tend to disorder and insubordination; does not excite them to impatience and extravagant claims; does not spoil them for the ordinary business of life, imposed by duty and necessity; does not make them the dupes of knaves; nor prompt them to seek the benefit of the improvement of their faculties in turning knaves themselves. Employers can testify, from all sides, that there is a striking general difference between those bred up in ignorance and rude vulgarity, and those who have been trained through the well ordered schools for the humble classes; a difference exceedingly in favour of the latter, who are found not only more apt at understanding and executing, but more decorous, more respectful, more attentive to orders, more ready to see and acknowledge the propriety of good regulations, and more disposed to a practical acquiescence in them; far less inclined to ebriety and low company; and more to be depended on in point of honesty. In almost any part of the country, where the experiment has been zealously prosecuted for a moderate number of years, a long resident observer can discern a modification in the character of the neighbourhood; a mitigation of the former brutality of manners; a less frequency of brawls and quarrels, and less tendency to draw together into rude riotous assemblages. There is especially a marked difference on the Sabbath, on which multitudes attend public worship, whose forefathers used to be found in those very assemblages on that day; and who would themselves, in all probability, have followed the same course, but for the tuition which has led them into a better. In many instances, the children have carried from the schools inestimable benefits home to their unhappy families; winning even their depraved thoughtless parents into consideration and concern about their most important interests,—a precious repayment of all the long toils and cares endured to support them through the period of childhood, and an example of that rare class of phenomena, in which a superlative beauty arises from the inversion of the general order of nature.

Even the frightful statements of the increase, in recent years, of active juvenile depravity, especially in the metropolis, include a gratifying testimony in favour of education. The advocates of schools have had the triumph of its being shown, that it was not from *these* seminaries that such delinquents were to go out, to evince that the improvement of intelligence may be but the greater ability for fraud and mischief. No, it was uniformly found to have been in very different places of resort, that these wretches had been almost from their infancy, accomplished for crime; and that their training had not taken or needed any assistance from an exercise on literary rudiments, from bibles, catechisms, or religious and moral poetry, or from an attendance on public worship. Indeed, as if it were through an intervention of Providence to confound the cavillers, the children and youth of the schools were found to have been more generally preserved from defection to the league of premature reprobates, than a moral calculator, with the quality of human nature kept in his sight, would have ventured to anticipate, upon a moderate estimate of the influence of instruction.

Experience equally falsifies the notion that knowledge, imparted to the lower orders, beyond what is necessary to the handling of their tools, tends to factious turbulence; to a re-action, (in pursuance of certain wild principles and theories,) against law and regular government in society. The maintainers of which notion should also affirm, that the people of Scotland have long been about the most disaffected tumultuary, revolutionary rabble in Europe; and that the Cornish miners, at this day so worthily distinguished at once by exercised intellect and religion, are incessantly on the point of insurrection, against their employers or the state. And we shall be just as ready to believe them if they also assert, that, in those popular irregularities which have too often disturbed, in particular places, the peace of our country, the clamorous bands or crowds, collected for purposes of intimidation or demolition, have consisted chiefly of the more cultivated part of the poorer inhabitants;—yes, or that this class furnished one in a hundred of the numbers forming such lawless bands; even though many of these more instructed of the people might be suffering, with their families, the utmost extremity of want, the direct pressure of that hunger which, as well as oppression, may 'make a wise man mad.' Many of these, in their desolate abodes, with tears of parents and children mingled together, have been committing themselves to their father in heaven, at the time that the ruder part of the population have been carrying alarm, and sometimes mischief, through the district, and so confirming the faith, we may suppose, of sundry magnates of the neighbourhood, who had vehemently asserted, a few years before, the pernicious tendency of educating the people.

It would be less than what is due to suffering humanity, to leave this topic without observing, that if a numerous portion of the community should be sinking under severe, protracted, unmitigated distress, distress on which there appears to them no dawn of hope from ordinary causes, it is not to be held a disparagement to the value of education, if some of those who have enjoyed a measure of that advantage, in common with a greater number who have not, should become feverishly agitated with imaginations of great sudden changes in the social system; and be led to entertain suggestions of irregular violent expedients for the removal of insupportable evils. It must, in all reason, be acknowledged the last lesson, which education could be expected to teach with practical effect, that one part of the community should be willing to resign themselves, as far as they can see, to destruction, that the others may live in sufficiency and tranquillity. Such heroic devotement might not be difficult in the sublime elation of Thermopylæ; but it is a very different matter in a melancholy cottage, and in the midst of famishing children.

After thus referring to matter of fact, for contradiction of the notion, that the mental cultivation of the lower classes might render them less subject to the rules of good order, we have to observe, in farther reply, that we are not heard insisting on the advantages of increased knowledge, and mental invigoration, among the people, *unconnected with the inculcation of religion.* Nor is this essential point forgotten or neglected in the actual system of procedure, in the institutions of which we are the advocates. Undoubtedly, their conductors and zealous friends account knowledge valuable absolutely, as being the apprehension of things as they are; a prevention of delusion; and so far a fitness for right volitions. But they consider religion, (besides being itself the primary and infinitely the most important part of knowledge,) as a principal indispensable for securing the full benefit of all the rest. It is desired and endeavoured, that the understandings of these opening minds may be taken possession of, by just and solemn ideas of their relation to the eternal almighty being; that they may be taught to apprehend it as an awful reality, that they are perpetually under his inspection; and as a certainty, that they must at length appear before him in judgment, and find, in another life, the consequences of what they are in spirit and conduct here It is impressed upon them, that his will is the supreme law; that his declarations are the most momentous truth known on earth; and his favour and condemnation the greatest good and evil. And it is wished, and endeavoured, to be by the light of this divine wisdom that they are disciplined in other parts of knowledge; so that nothing they learn may be detached from all sensible relation to it, or have a tendency contrary to it. Thus it is sought to be secured, that, as the pupil's mind grows stronger, and multiplies its resources, and he therefore has necessarily more power and means for what is wrong, there may be luminously presented to him, as if celestial eyes visibly beamed upon him, the most solemn ideas that can enforce what is right.

Such is the discipline mediated for preparing the subordinate classes to pursue their individual welfare, and act their part as members of the community. They are to be trained in early life to diligent employment of their faculties, tending to strengthen them, regulate them, and give their possessors the power of effectually using them. They are to be exercised to form clear correct notions, instead of crude vague delusive ones. The subjects of these ideas will be, a very considerable number of the most important facts and principles; which are to be presented to their understandings with a patient repetition of efforts to fix them there as knowledge that cannot be forgotten. By this measure of substantial acquirement and by the habit formed in so acquiring, they will be qualified for making farther attainment in future time, if they are disposed to improve their opportunities. During this progress, and in connexion with many of its exercises, their duty is to be enforced on them, in the various, forms in which they will have to make a choice, between right and wrong in their conduct toward society. There will be inculcated justice, prudence, inoffensiveness, estrangement from the counsels and leagues of vain and bad men; love of peace, hatred of all disorder and violence, and a respect for institutions designed and necessary to prevent these evils. All this will be taught directly from the holy scriptures, from which authority will also be inculcated, all the while, the principles of religion. And religion, while its grand reference is to the state of the soul towards God, and to eternal interests, yet takes every principle and rule of morals under the full sanction of its authority; making the primary obligation and responsibility be towards God, of every thing that is a duty with respect to men. So that, with the subjects of this education, the sense of *propriety* shall be *conscience*, the consideration of how they ought to be regulated, in their conduct as a part of the community, shall be the recollection that their master in heaven dictates the laws of that conduct, and will judicially hold them amenable for every part of it.

And, as far as any judgment can be formed of means as adapted to ends, is not this endeavour to fix religious principles in ascendency, the way to bring up citizens fit to preserve the great social compact? Or perhaps far less interference of the divine sanctions, would do quite as well, for securing peace and good order among the mulitude, provided they be but kept in profound ignorance,—the religious principles being rendered unnecessary to them, just in the proportion of their want of other knowledge. This is, at least virtually, said by the disapprover of the designs for educating the people. For, it were most idle for these persons to pretend, that they would have the people, in some way or other, put in the state of understanding the principal truths, and acknowledging the sanctions, of religion, *as a special and separate attainment*, while remaining destitute of mental cultivation in the general sense. If those who would so pretend, were to see the actual phenomenon; if it were to come before them as a real fact,—(an extremely ignorant man entertaining a lively and influential sense of religion,)—would they not greatly marvel? Would they not be nonplussed in trying to understand such a thing? What if there were whispered to them, just then, some of the phrases at which they had often sneered; for example *divine grace*; which the man himself might very possibly be guilty of naming? *We* shall not deny the possibility of such a phenomenon *from such a cause.* But here we are speaking of the course required in human proceeding, by practical rational methods, toward the attainment of an object attainable through discipline. And how, it may well be demanded, is this supposed education to be conducted, which shall preserve the people's general ignorance inviolate, and yet inculcate religion with the due efficacy for making them virtuous citizens? How introduce the subject into minds unformed to admit any thing but the impressions of sense; never made to affix a meaning to the very terms to be employed; never opened to a capacity of comprehending any one idea approaching to greatness or remoteness; and infinitely repugnant to *begin* so unwonted and uncouth an exercise with the topic of religion, of all subjects in the world? No, assuredly, the good order of a populace, left in stupid ignorance, cannot be preserved by the effect of so slight an infusion of religion, as these pretended good friends of theirs would instil into their mental grossness. It must be done by something far stronger; and if it actually *is* done already, in nearly the required degree, with no more of religion than this, it is done by other means; and therefore much hypocritical canting about the necessity of religion in the lower orders, to the safety of the state, might be spared to such persons as we have heard uttering it together with more than a doubt of the prudence of qualifying these same lower orders even to read the bible.

But all this while, we are forgetting to inquire how much is to be understood as included in that good order, that deference and subordination, which it has been apprehended that the possession of more mind and knowledge, by the people, might disturb or destroy. May not the notion of it, as entertained by some persons, be conceived somewhat according to the model of an earlier age, or of some eastern dominion? Is it required, that the sentiment of obsequiousness should be, in the people, like the instinct by which a lower order of animals as in awe of a higher, by which the common tribe of beasts would shrink at the sight of lions? Or is the deference expected to be of an absolute, unconditional kind, as to something claiming it by simple divine right, as the prophets or judges of Israel did? Are the people to be prevented from considering their relation to the community, any farther than the labours it is their assigned part to perform in it, and the respect they are to pay to the higher orders of it? Are they to entertain no questions, respecting the right adjustment of their condition, in the arrangements of the great social body? Are they forbidden ever to admit a single doubt, of its being quite a matter of course, that every thing that ought to be is done, and in such manner as it ought to be, for the interests of their class; or, therefore, to pretend to any such right as that of representing, complaining, and remonstrating?

A subordination founded in such principles, and required to such a degree, it is true enough that the communication of knowledge is not the way to perpetuate. For the first use, which men infallibly make, of an enlargement of their faculties and ideas, will be to take a larger view of their interests; and they may happen, as soon as they do so, to think they discover that it was quite time; and the longer they do so, to retain still less and less of implicit faith, and those interests will be done justice too without their own vigilance and intervention. An educated people must be very slow indeed in their learning, if they do not soon grow out of all belief in the *necessary* wisdom, and rectitude, of any class of human creatures whatever. They will see how unreasonable it were to expect, that any class will fail in fidelity to the great natural principle, of making its own advantage the first object; and therefore they will not be apt to listen, with the gravity which in other times and regions may have been shown in listening, to injunctions of gratitude for the willingness, evinced by the higher orders, to take on them the trouble of watching and guarding the people's welfare, by keeping them and all their interests in a proper course.

But neither will it *necessarily* be in the spirit of hostility, in the worst sense of the word, that a more instructed people will thus show a diminished credulity of reverence, toward the predominant ranks in the social economy; and will keep in habitual exercise upon them a somewhat suspicious observation, and a judicial estimate; with an honest freedom in sometimes avowing disapprobation, and strongly asserting any right which is believed to be endangered. This will only be expressing that, since all classes naturally consult, by preference, their own interests, it is plainly unfit, that one portion of the community should be trusted with an unlimited discretion, in ordering what affects the welfare of the others; and that, in all prudence, the people must withhold an entire affiance, and unconditional unexamining acquiescence; till some such thing as a commission of angels shall come to harmonise, and then administer, interests which are placed so unappeasably at strife:—for as to what is so often asserted of those interests being in reality the same, it is evidently impossible for either party, even while believing so, to concede to the other the exclusive adjustment of the practical mode of identification.

But only let the utmost that is possible be done, to train the people, from their early years, to a sound use of their reason, under a discipline for imparting a valuable portion of knowledge, and assiduously inculcating the principles of social duty and of religion; and then something may be said, to good purpose, to their understanding and conscience, while they are maintaining the inevitable competition of claims with their superiors. They will then be capable of seeing put in a fair balance, many things which headlong ignorance would have taken all one way. They will be able to appreciate many explanations, alleged causes of delay, statements of difficulty between opposing reasons; which would be thrown away on an ignorant populace. And it would be an inducement to their making a real exertion of the understanding, that they thus found themselves so formally put upon their responsibility for its exercise,—that they were summoned to a rational discussion, instead of being addressed in the style of Pharaoh to the Israelites. The strife of interests would thus come to be carried on with less fierceness and malice, in the spirit and manner, on the part of the people. And the ground itself of the contention, the substance of the matters in contest, would be gradually diminished—by the concessions of the higher classes to the claims of the lower: for there is no affecting to dissemble, that a great mental and moral improvement of the people would necessitate, though there were not a single movement of rude force in the case, important concessions to them, on the part of the superior orders. A people advanced to such a state, would make its moral power felt in a thousand ways, and every moment. This general augmentation of mind and virtue would send forth, against all arrangements, and inveterate usages, of the nature of invidious repression and exclusion, an energy, which could no more be resisted than the power of the sun, when he advances in the spring to annihilate the relics and vestiges of the winter. This plastic influence would modify the institutions of the national community, to a state adapted to secure all the popular interests; and to convey the genuine, collective opinion, to bear directly on the counsel and transaction of national concerns. That opinion would have a weight which could not be set at defiance, and an unperverted fidelity of manifestation, which would leave no possibility of affecting to take an opposite one as the genuine.

That such consequences would inevitably follow a highly improved general state of the people, must be freely acknowledged to those, who cannot consent to their receiving the utmost practicable cultivation. And is it *because* this would follow, that these disapprovers would deprecate such a cultivation? Then let them say, what it is that *they* are hoping for from an opposite system. *What* is it, that they are seriously promising themselves, from the auspicious influence of all the ignorance, that can henceforward be retained among the population of this part of the world? They see, that in this country, and other of the great states of Europe, there is gone forth, among the great mass of the people, a spirit of revolt from the sense of obligation toward institutions simply as existing or as ancient; a spirit that re-acts, with deep and settled antipathy, against some of the arrangements and claims, of the order into which the national community has been disposed by institutions and the course of events; a spirit which regards some of the appointments, and requirements, of that order, as little better than adaptations of the system to the will, and gratification, of the more fortunate portion of the species. We need not repeat, with what dreadful commotion the pervasion of this spirit has wrought, both in its own proper action and explosive force, and as excited to preternatural energy in the conflict with the arrayed power of the old order of things. And is it extinguished? Is it subdued? Is it in the slightest degree reduced?—reduced we mean, as a principle fixed in the decided form of an opinion, and actuating, with the strength and sanction of this its possession of the judgment, the wishes and strongest passions; and often kindling, in the more restless and sanguine spirits, imaginations of supposeable changes, and of the expedients for accomplishing them.

Is it, we repeat, repressed? There may be persons who cannot believe it possible, 'good easy men,' that it can have lived in spite of a world of war and legislation aimed at its destruction, to come forth, with unabated vigour, at the opportune junctures in the future progress of events; like some great serpent, meeting and glaring upon the sight again, with his appalling glance and uninjured length of volume, after a storm of missiles has sent him to his retreat, and been poured in there with destructive intention after him. But these must be the dullest, or most spell-bound in their faculties, of all prognosticators. Repressed!—what is it that is manifesting itself in the most remarkable events in the old, and what has been named the new world, at this very hour? And what are the measures of several of the great state authorities of Europe, and the apparent agitation, and as it were fitful changes of feeling between rashness and dismay, in the adoption of those measures in some of the states, but a confession, that after all, this spirit is growing stronger? Every year renders it but more evident, that the principle in action is something far different from a superficial transient irritation; that it has gone the whole depth of the mind; has possessed itself of the very judgment and conscience, of an innumerable legion, extending, continually, to a still greater number. No doubt is permitted to remain, whether the real current of the popular feeling has made a portentous change in its direction, to return to its ancient course, when the stream of some great branch of the Mississippi shall resume the channel, which it has abandoned by making for itself a new one into the Mexican Gulf. For when once the great mass of the lower and larger division of the community, shall have become filled with an absolute, and almost unanimous conviction, that they, the grand physical agency of that community; that they, the operators, the producers, the preparers, of almost all it most essentially wants; that they, the part, therefore, of the social assemblage so obviously the most essential to its existence, and on which all the rest must depend;—that they are placed in a condition, in the great social arrangement, which does not do justice to this their importance, which does not adequately reward these their services;—we say, when this shall have become the feeling and the conviction, to the very centre of the mind, in the millions of Europe, we would put it as a question to the judgment of a sober man, how this state of feeling is to be reversed or neutralized, while those circumstanaes of the economy which have caused it are remaining. But then we put it to his judgment at the next step, what the consequence must ultimately be. Will he pretend not to foresee, that the power of so vast a combination of wills and agents, must sooner or later, in one manner or another, affect a great modification in the arrangements of the social system? What plan, then, is he supposing adopted to prevent it? Are the higher and more privileged portions of the national communities to have, henceforward, just this one grand object of their existence, this chief employment for all their knowledge, means, and power, namely to keep down the lower orders of their fellow-citizens, by mere stress of coercion and punishment? Are they resolved, and prepared, for a rancorous interminable hostility in prosecution of such a benign purpose; with, of course, a continual exhaustion upon it of the means, which might be applied to diminish that wretchedness of the people, which has been, and must continue to be, the grand corroborator of the principles that have passed like an earthquake under the foundations of the old social systems? But supposing this *should* be the course pursued, how long can it be effectual? That must be a very firm structure, must be of gigantic mass or most excellent basis and conformation, against which the ocean shall unremittingly wear and foam in vain. And it does not appear what there can be of such impregnable consistenc in any particular construction of the social order which is, by the supposition to be resolved to be maintained in sovereign immutability, in permanent frustration of the persevering, ever-growing, aim and impulse of the great majority, pressing on to achieve important innovations in their favour; innovations in those systems of institution and usage, under which they will never cease to think they have had far less happiness heretofore than they ought to have had. We cannot see how this impulse can be so repelled or diverted that it shall not prevail at length, to the effect of either bearing down, or wearing away a portion of the order of things which the ascendent classes in every part of Europe would have fondly wished to maintain in perpetuity, without one particle of surrender.

But though they cannot preserve its entireness, the manner in which it shall yield to alteration is in a great measure at their command. And here is the important consideration. If a movement has really begun in the general popular mind of the nations, and if the principle of it is growing and insuppressible, so that it must in one manner or another ultimately prevail, what will the state be of any national community where it shall be an unenlightened, half barbarous, people that so prevails?—a people no better informed, perhaps, than to believe that all the hardship and distress endured by themselves and their forefathers were wrongs, which they suffered from the higher orders; than to ascribe to bad government, and the rapacity and selfishness of the rich, the very evils caused by inclement seasons; and than to assume it as beyond question, that the whole accumulation of their resentments, brought out into action at last, is but justice demanding and effecting a retribution.

In such an event, what would not the superior orders be glad to give and forego, in compromise with principles, tempers, and demands, which they will know they should never have had to encounter, to the end of time, if, instead of spending their vast advantages on merely their own state and indulgence, they had applied them in a mode of operation and influence tending to improve, in every way, the situation and character of the people? It is true, that such a wild triumph of overpowering violence would necessarily be short. A blind turbulent monster of popular power never can for a long time maintain the domination of a political community. It would rage and riot itself out of breath and strength, succumb under some strong coercion of its own creating, and lie subject and stupified, till its spirit should be recovered and incensed for new commotion. But this impossibility of a very prolonged reign of confusion, would be little consolation for the classes, against whose privileged condition the first tremendous eruption should have driven. It would not much cheer a man who should see his abode carried away, and his fields and plantations devastated, to tell him that what had inflicted this ruin was but a transient mountain torrent. A short prevalence of the overturning force would have sufficed, for the subversion of the proudest longest established state of privilege; and most improbable would it be, that those who lost it in the tumult, would find the new authority, which would arise as that tumult subsided, either able or disposed to restore it. They might perhaps, (on a favorable supposition,) survive in personal safety, but in humiliated fortunes, to ruminate on their manner of occupying their former elevated situation, and of employing its ample means of power, a due portion of which applied to promote the universal education of the community, with an accompanying liberal yet very gradual concession of privileges to the people, would have prevented the catastrophe.

Let us urge then, that a zealous endeavor to render it absolutely impossible that, in any change whatever, the destinies of a nation should fall under the power of an ignorant infuriated multitude, may take place of the presumption that there *is* no great change to be ever effected by the progressive and conscious importance of the people; a presumption than which nothing can appear more like infatuation; when we look at the recent scenes and present temperament of the moral world. Educate the people; train them to sound sense; civilize them; promote the reformation of their morals; inculcate the principles of religion, simply and solemnly *as* religion, as a thing directly of divine dictation, and not as if half of its authority were in virtue of human institutions; let the higher orders generally make it perfectly evident to the multitude that they are desirous to improve them, raise them, and promote their happiness; and then *whatever* the demands of the people as a body, thus improving in understanding and the sense of justice, shall come to be, and *whatever* modification their preponderance may ultimately enforce on the great social arrangements, it will be infallibly certain that there never *can* be a love of disorder, an insolent anarchy, a prevailing spirit of revenge and devastation. Such a conduct of the ascendent classes would, in this nation at least, secure that as long as the world lasts, there never would be any formidable commotion, or violent sudden changes. All those modifications of the national economy which an improving people would aspire and would deserve to obtain, would be gradually accomplished, in a manner by which no party would be injured, and all would be the happier.

CHAPTER III.

THE FATAL INAPTITUDE WHICH IGNORANCE CREATES, OR CONSTITUTES, FOR RECEIVING RELIGIOUS INSTRUCTION.

SECTION I.

Uneducated minds destitute of any religious notions, and fortified against all approach of truth.

We do not know whether any of these observations will be accounted foreign to the purpose, of illustrating the effects of popular ignorance. However that may be, we shall pursue the course of illustration toward its conclusion, by describing somewhat more fully here than in the former stages, the manner in which the want of mental improvement affects the people in regard to the most important concern of all, religion. It is true, that this has been already very expressly adverted to, and perhaps more than once; but the topic seems to merit a considerable amplification; and will better excuse, than any other, the fault of a too evident repetition. What we would especially remark upon is, the wretched inaptitude which ignorance creates or constitutes for receiving religious instruction. But first a few sentences relative to what there actually is of religious notion in the minds of the uneducated,—to show whether, as far as that great subject is concerned, education may be spared.

Some notion of such a thing, something different in their consciousness from the absolute negation of the idea, something that faintly responds to the terms in which a person conversing with them would express the idea, in the way of questioning them on the subject, may be presumed to exist in the minds of all who are advanced a considerable way into youth, or come to mature age, in a country where all have the monitory spectacle of edifices for religious use, on spots appointed also for the interment of the dead. If this sort of measured caution in the assumption should seem bordering on the ridiculous, we would recommend those who would smile at it to make some little experiments. It would not be difficult to insinuate themselves, on road or field, into the company of some of the innumerable rustics who have grown up destitute of every thing worth calling education; or of the equally ill-fated beings in the alleys, precincts, and lower employments of towns. They might manage to avoid an abruptness and judicial formality, which would prevent the readiness to be communicative, while they contrived to question, in effect rather than express form, some of these persons respecting God, Jesus Christ, the human soul, the invisible world. And we can assure them they would in many instances receive such answers as would amaze them. The exposure made to them in these answers would break up, as by a sudden shock, their easy complacent assurance, (were it possible they had been so unknowing as to cherish such a feeling,) that almost all the people must, by some means or other, have been brought to be tolerably apprised of a few first principles of religion; that this *could* not have failed to be the case in a community acknowledging, in its collective capacity, a considerable responsibility that its members should not be left totally destitute of the most essential of all things to their well-being. This agreeable assurance would vanish, like a dream interrupted, at the spectacle thus presented, of persons nearly, very nearly, as devoid of those first principles, after living eighteen, thirty, forty, or twice forty years, under the superintendence of that community, as if they had been the aboriginal rovers of the American forests, or natives of unvisited coral-built spots in the ocean.

If these examiners were to prosecute the investigation widely, and their reflections grew more pensive with their discoveries, they might become sensible of a very altered estimate of this our Christian tract of the earth. From appearing to them so peculiarly auspicious, as if almost by some virtue of its climate, to the cultivation and enlargement of religious understanding in the people, it might come to appear to them as favourable to the developement of *all things rather than that.* Plants and trees, the diversity of animal forms and powers, the human frame, the features enlarging or enlarged to manhood in the persons looked upon while making the answers to the exposed examiner, with their passions also, and prevailing dispositions—see how all things can unfold themselves in our territory, and grow and enlarge to their completeness, excepting the ideas of the human soul relating to the almighty, and to the grand purpose of its existence!

The supposed answers would, in many instances, betray, that any thought of God at all was of very rare occurrence, as never having become strongly associated with any thing beheld in the whole creation. We should think it probable, as we have said before, that with many, while in health, weeks often pass away without the idea being once so presented as to hold the mind, so to speak, looking at it for one moment of time. If they could be set to any such task as that of retracing, at the end of the day or week, what has come into their minds, and what their thoughts have dwelt upon, it would no more be recalled that this idea had encountered them, than that a splendid meteor had passed through the air before them. Yet during such a space of time, their thoughts, such as they are, shall have run through incalculable thousands of changes; and even the divine name itself may have been pronounced by them a multitude of times, in jocularity or imprecation. This is a state very near absolute atheism.

But the idea of God which has, by some means, found its way into their minds to abide thereso nearly in silence and oblivion,—what is it, when some direct call does really evoke it? It is generally a gross approximation of the conception of the infinite being to the likeness of man. If what they have heard of his being a spirit, has indeed some little effect in prevention of the total debasement of the idea, it prevents it rather by confusion than by magnificence. It may somewhat restrain and baffle the tendency of the imagination to a direct degrading definition; but it does so by turning the idea as into a wide attenuated cloud. And ever and anon, this cloudy diffusion is again drawing in, and shaping, toward an image, enormous perhaps, and spectral, and portentous across the firmament, but in some strong analogy to the human mode of personality.

The divine attribute which it apprehended by them with most of an impression of reality, is a certain vastness of power. But through the grossness of their intellectual atmosphere, this appears to them rather in the character of something prodigiously huge, than sublimely glorious. As considered in his quality of moral judicial governor, God is regarded by some of them as more disposed, than there is any reasonable cause, to be displeased with what is done in this world. But the far greater number have no prevailing sentiment that he takes any very vigilant account or concern.* And even those who entertain the more ungracious apprehension, have it not in sufficient force to make them, once in whole months, deliberately think it worth while to care what he may disapprove.

The notions that should answer to the doctrine of a providence, are a confusion of some crude idea of a divine superintendence, with stronger fancies and impressions of luck and chance; and these still farther, and most uncouthly, confounded by the admixture of the ancient heathen notion of fate, reduced from its philosophy to its dregs. In many instances, however, this obtains such a predominance, as to lesson the confusion, and withal to preclude, in a great measure, the sense of accountableness. In neither of these states of intellectual desolation is there any serious admisson, at least during the enjoyment of health, of the duty or advantage of prayer.

The supposed examiner may endeavour to elicit the notions concerning the redeemer of the world. They would be found, in numerous instances, amounting literally to no more than, that Jesus Christ was a worthy kind of man, (the word has actually been 'gentleman,' in more than one instance that we have heard told from unquestionable authority,) who once, somewhere, (these national Christians had never in their lives thought of inquiring when or where,) did a great deal of good, and was very ill used by bad people. The people now, they think, bad as they may be, would not do so in the like case. Some of these persons may have casually been at church; and are just aware that his name often recurs in its services; they never considered why; but they have a vague impression of its repetition having some kind of virtue, perhaps rather in the nature of a spell. The names of the four evangelists are by some held literally and technically available for such an use.

A few steps withdrawn from this thickest of the mental fog, there are many, who are not entirely uninformed of something having been usually affirmed, by religious teachers, of Jesus Christ's being more than a man, and of his having done something of great importance toward preventing our being punished for our sins. This combination of a majestic superiority to the human nature, with the fact of his being yet confessedly human, just passes their minds like a shape formed of a shadow, as one of the unaccountable things that may be as it is said, for what they know, but which they need not trouble themselves to think about. As to the great things said to be done by him, to save men from being punished, they see indeed no necessity for such an expedient, but if it is so, very right, and so much the better; for between that circumstance in our favour, and God's being too good, after all that is said of his holiness and wrath, to be severe on such poor creatures as men, we must have a good chance of coming off safely at last. But multitudes of the miserably poor, however wicked, have a settled assurance of this coming off well at last, independently of any thing effected for men by the mediator: they shall not be exempted, they believe, from any future suffering in consideration of their having suffered so mnch here. There is nothing, in the scanty creedof great numbers, more firmly held than this.

It is true, they believe that the most atrociously wicked must go to a state of punishment after death. They consider murderers, especially as under this doom. But the offences which they deem to deserve it, form but a short catalogue. It is indeed enlarged sometimes, in the case of the individual, by the addition of an offence which he would not have accounted so heinous, but that it has happened to be committed against *him*. We can recollect the exultation of sincere faith, seen mingling with the anger of an offended man, while *predicting*, as well as imprecating, this retribution of some injury he had suffered; a real injury, indeed, in some degree; yet of a kind which he would have held in small account, had he only seen it done to another person As to the nature of that future punishment, the ideas of these neglected minds, go scarcely at all beyond the images of corporeal anguish, conveyed by the well known metaphors.

It is most striking to observe how wholly negative are their conceptions of the future happiness, which it should seem they expect to obtain, as the necessary alternative of the evil they so easily assure themselves of escaping. The ordinary images employed in religious discourse to represent it, (if they should ever have heard enough of such discourse to be acquainted with those images,) are very little congenial to their notions of pleasure; and no more would the abstracted and elevated ideas be so, if they had intellect and thought enough to reach so far. Here the reflection again returns, what an inexpressible poverty of mind there is, when the people have no longer a mythology, and yet have not obtained in its place any knowledge of the true religion. The martial vagrants of Scandinavia glowed with the vivid anticpations of Valhalla; the savages of the western continent had their animating visions of the 'land of souls;' the modern Christian barbarians of England, who also expect to live after death, do not know what they mean by their phrase of 'going to heaven.'

Most of this class of persons think very little in any way whatever of the invisible spiritual economy. And many of them wish to think, if possible, still less. For they are liable to be occasionally affected with dark hints and hauntings of an unseen world. But it is very remarkable, how little these may contribute to enforce the salutary impressions of religion. A man, who is, for instance, subject to the terror of apparitions, shall not therefore be in the smallest degree the less profane, except just at the time that this terror is upon him. A number of persons, of whom not one durst have walked, alone, at midnight, round a lonely church, encompassed with graves, and among them perhaps the recent one a notoriously, wicked man, will nevertheless, on a fine Sunday morning, form a row of rude idlers, standing in the road to this very church, to vent their jokes on the persons going thither to attend the offices of religion, and on those offices themselves.

Such, as regarding religion, is the state out of which it is desired to redeem a multitude of the people of this land. Or rather we should say, it is sought to save a multitude from being consigned to it. For consider, in the next place, (what we wished especially to point at, in this last and most important article in the enumeration of the evils of ignorance,) consider what a fatal inaptitnde for receiving the truths of religion, is created by the neglect of training minds to the exercise of their faculties, and the acquirement of elementary information.

How inevitably it must be so, from the nature of the case!—There is a sublime economy of invisible realities. There is the supreme existence, an infinite and eternal spirit. There are spiritual existences, that have kindled into brightness and power, from nothing, at his creating will. There is an universal government, omnipotent, all-wise, righteous, of that supreme being, over the creation. There is the immense tribe of human spirits, in a most peculiar and tremendous predicament, held under eternal obligation of conformity to a law which emanates from the holiness of its sovereign

* Some have no very distinct impression the one way or the other. Not very long since, a friend of the writer, in one of the midland counties, fell into talk, on a Sunday, with a man who had been in some very plain violation of the consecrated character of the day. He seriously animadverted on this, adding, Don't you think God will be displeased at and punish such conduct? or words to that effect. The man, after a moments consideration, answered, with unaffected cool simplicity, exactly thus: 'That's according as how he takes it.'

author, but perverted to a state of disconformity to it, and opposition to him. Next, there is a marvellous anomaly of moral government, the constitution of a new state of relation between the supreme governor and this alienated race, through a mediator, who makes an atonement for humau iniquity, and stands representative before almighty justice, for those who gratefully accord to the mysterious appointment, and consign themselves to his charge. There are the several doctrines declaratory of this new constitution through all its parts. There is the view of religion in its operative character, the combination of its doctrines and precepts with a divine agency on the mind, transforming and disciplining it. And all this while, there is the invisible world, to which the spirits of men proceed at death, in possession of a conscious existence to be retained for ever; and there is the certain prospect of a final judgment and a retribution.

Look at this solemn ideal scene, so distinct, and stretching to such remoteness, from the field of ordinary things; consisting of elements of which it is for intellect alone to apprehend the reality; of objects with which intellect alone can hold converse. Look at this scene; and then consider, what manner of beings you are calling upon to enter into it by contemplation. Beings who have never learned to think at all. Beings who have hardly ever once, in their whole lives, made a real effort, to direct and concentrate the action of their faculties on any thing abstracted from the objects palpable to the senses; whose entire attention has been engrossed, from their infancy, with the common business, the low amusements and gratifications, the idle talk, the local occurrences, which formed the whole compass of the occupation, and practically acknowledged interests, of their progenitors. Beings who have never been made, in the least, familiar with even the matters of fact, those especially of the scripture history, which stand in the most obvious relation to religion, and have given a substantial form, as it were, to some of its truths. Beings who will thus combine, as we have said before, the utmost aversion to any attempt at a purely intellectual exercise, with whatever dislike it is in our nature to feel toward this class of subjects. What kind of ideas should you imagine to be raised in their minds, by all the words you might employ, to place within their intellectual vision some portion of this spiritual order of things,—even should you be able, which you often would not, to engage any effort of attention to the subject? And yet we have heard men, who had been disciplined in the most splendid institutions for mental cultivation in the world, pertinaciously maintain, that the common people need not be taught so much as to be able tu read the bible, in order to their attaining a competent knowledge of religion; for that they may learn as much of it by an attendance at church, as it can be of any use for them to know.

Do such men ever make an immediate, personal experiment, on this happy facility with which mature ignorance learns religion? We may appeal to those pious and benevolent persons who have made the most numerous trials, for testimony to the inaptitude of uneducated people to receive that kind of instruction. You have visited, perhaps, some numerous family, or Sunday assemblage of several related families; to which you had access without awkward intrusion, in consequence of the acquaintance arising from near neighbourhood, or of little services you had rendered, or of the circumstance of any of their younger children coming to your charity schools. You were soon made sensible what a desert you were in, as to all religious thought, by indications unequivocal to your perception, though, it may be, not reducible, in a few words, to exact description. And those indications were perhaps almost equally apparent in the young persons, those advanced to the middle of life, and those who were evidently destined not long to remain in it, the patriarch, perhaps, and the eldest matron, of the kindred company. You attempted by degrees, with all managements of art, as if you had been seeking to gain a favour for yourselves, to train into the talk some topic bearing toward religion; and which could be followed up to a more explicit reference to that great subject, without the abruptness which causes instant silence and recoil. We will suppose, that the gloom of such a moral scene was not augmented to you, by the mortification of observing impatience of this suspension of their usual and favourite tenor of discourse, betrayed in marks of suppressed irritation, or rather by the withdrawing of one, and another, from the company. But it was quite enough to render the moments and feelings some of the most disconsolate you had ever experienced, to have thus immediately before you a number of rational beings as in a dark prison house, and to feel the impotence of your friendly efforts to bring them out. Their darkness of ignorance infused into your spirit the darkness of melancholy, when you perceived that the fittest words you could think of, in every change and combination in which you could dispose them, failed to impart, to their understanding, the most elementary and essential ideas of the most momentous subject.

You thought again, perhaps, and again, Surely *this* mode of expression, or *this*, as it is in words familiar to them, will define the meaning to their apprehension. But you were forced to perceive that the common words and phraseology of the language, those which make the substance of ordinary discourse on ordinary subjects, had not, for the understandings of these persons, an indifferent and general applicableness. It seemed as if the perfectly neutral and general portion of the language had become in its meaning special and exclusive for their own sort of topics. Their narrow associations had rendered it incapable of conveying sense to them on matters foreign to their habits. When used on a subject to which they were quite unaccustomed, it became like a stream which, though one and the same current, flows clear on the one side, and muddy (as we sometimes see for a space) on the other,—and to them it was clear only at their own edge. And if even the plain popular language turned dark on their understandings when employed in explanation of religion, it is easy to imagine what had been the success of any thing approaching to a more technical expression of the subject, though it went no farther than such terms as are used in the bible.

You continued, however, the effort, for a while. As desirous to show you due civility, some of the persons, perhaps the oldest, would give assent to what you said, with some sign of acknowledgement ol the importance of the concern. In expressing this assent, they would say something which they took to be equivalent to what you had said. And when it was an intelligible idea that they uttered, it would probably show the grossest possible misconception of the first principles of religion; something clumsily analogous to its worst perversions by popery, or approaching to very paganism. You tried, perhaps, with repeated modifications of your expression, and attempts at illustration, to loosen the false notion, and to place the true one in such a near obviousness to the apprehension, that at least the difference should be seen, and (perhaps you hoped) a little movement excited to think farther of the subject, and make a serious question of it. But all in vain. The hoary unhappy subject of your too late instruction, either would still take it that it came all to the same thing; or, if compelled to perceive that you were trying to make him *unthink* his poor old notions, and learn something new and contrary, would probably retreat, in a little while, into a half sullen half despondent silence, after observing, that he was too old, 'the worse was the luck,' to be able to learn about such things, which he never had, like you, the 'scholarship' and the time for.

In several of the party you perceive the signs of almost a total blank. They seemed but to be waiting for any trifling incident to take their attention, and keep their minds alive. Some one with a little more of listening curiosity, but without caring about the subject, might have to observe, that it seemed to him the same kind of thing that the Methodist parson, (the term most likely to be used,) was lately saying in such a one's funeral sermon. It is too possible that one or two of the visages of the company, of the younger people especially, might wear, during a good part of the time, somewhat of a derisive smile, meaning, 'What odd kind of stuff all this is;' as if they could not help thinking it most ludicrously strange, that any one should be talking of God, of the Saviour of mankind, of the facts of the bible, the welfare of the soul, the shortness and value of life, and a future account, when he might be talking of the neighbouring fair, past or expected, or the local quarrels, or the last laughable incident or adventure of the hamlet. It is particularly observable, that grossly ignorant persons are very apt to take a ludicrous impression from high aud solemn subjects; at least when introduced in any other time or way than in the ceremonial of public religious service; when brought forward as a personal concern, demanding consideration every where, and which may be urged by individual on individual. You have commonly enough observed this provoke the grin of stupidity and folly. And if you asked yourselves, (for it were in vain to ask *them*,) why it produced this so perverse effect, you had only to consider that, to minds abandoned through ignorance to be totally engrossed and besotted by the immediate objects of sense, the grave assumption, and emphatic enforcement, of the transcendent importance of a wholly unseen and spiritual economy, has much the appearance and effect of a great lie attempted to be passed upon them. You might indeed recollect also, that the most that some of them may have learnt about religion, is, that it, and those who profess it, *may* be laughed at, for that they are so by multitudes, not of their own vulgar order only, but including many of the wealthy, the genteel, the magisterial, and the dignified in point of rank.

Individuals of the most ignorant class may stroll into a place of worship, bearing their character so conspicuously in their appearance and manner as to draw the particular notice of the preacher, while addressing the congregation. It may be, that having taken their stare round the place, they go out, just, perhaps, when he is in the midst of a marked, prominent, and even picturesque illustration, possibly from some of the striking facts or characters of the scripture narrations, which had not made the slightest ingress on their thoughts or imagination. Or they are pleased to stay through the service; during which his eye is frequently led to where several of them may be seated together. Without an appearance of addressing them personally, he shall be excited to direct a special effort toward what he surmises to be the state of their minds. He may in this effort acquire an additional force, emphasis, and pointedness of delivery; but especially his utmost mental force shall be brought into action to strike upon their faculties, with vivid rousing ideas, plainly and briefly expressed. And he fancies, perhaps, that he has at least arrested their attention; that what is going from his mind is in some manner or other taking a place in theirs; when some inexpressibly trivial occurring circumstances shows him, that the hold he has on them is not of the strenghth of a spider's web. Those thoughts, those intellects, those souls, are instantly and wholly gone—from a representation of one of the awful visitations of divine judgment in the ancient world—a description of sublime angelic agency, as in some recorded fact in the bible—an illustration of the discourse, miracles, or expiatory sorrows of the redeemer of the world—a strong appeal to conscience on past sin—a statement, in form, perhaps, of example, of an important duty in given circumstances—a cogent enforcement of some specific point as of most essential moment in respect to eternal safety;—from the attempted grasp, or supposed seizure, of any such subject, these rational spirits started away, with infinite facility, to the movements occasioned by the falling of a hat from a peg.

By the time that any semblance of attention returns the preacher's address may have taken the form of pointed interrogation, with very defined supposed facts; or even real ones, to give the question and its principle as it were a tangible substance. Well; just at the moment when his questions converged to a point, which was to have been a dart of conviction striking the understanding, and compelling the common sense and conscience of the auditors to answer for themselves,—at that moment, he perceives two or three of the persons he had particularly in view begin in active whispering, prolonged with the accompaniment of the appropriate vulgar smiles. They may possibly relapse at length, through sheer dullness, into tolerable decorum; and the instructor, not quite losing sight of them, tries yet again to impel some serious ideas through the obtuseness of their mental being. But he can clearly perceive, after the animal spirits have thus been a little quieted by the necessity of sitting still awhile, the signs of a perfectly stupid vacancy, which is hardly sensible that any thing is actually saying, and probably makes, in the case of some of the individuals, what is mentally but a slight transition to yawning and sleep.

Utter ignorance is a most effectual fortification to a vicious state of the mind. Prejudice may perhaps be removed; unbelief may be reasoned with; even demoniacs have been capable of bearing witness to the truth; but the stupidity of confirmed ignorance, not only defeats the ultimate efficacy of the means for making men wiser and better, but stands in preliminary defiance to the very act of their application. It reminds us of an account, in one of the relations of the French Egyptian campaigns, of the attempt to reduce a garrison posted in a bulky fort of mud. Had the defences been of timber, the besiegers might have burnt them; had they been of stone, even blocks of granite, they might have shaken and ultimately breached them by the incessant battery of their cannon; or they might have undermined and blown them up. But the huge mound of mud received the iron missiles without effect; they just struck in and were dead; so that the mighty engines of attack and demolition were utterly baffled.

The most melancholy of the exemplifications of the effect of ignorance, as constituting an incapacity for receiving religious instruction, have been presented to those, who have visited persons thus devoid of knowledge in sickness and the approach to death. Supposing them to manifest alarm and solicitude, it is deplorable to see how powerless their understandings are, for any distinct conception of what, or why, it is that they fear, or regret, or desire. The objects of their apprehension come round them as vague forms of darkness, instead of distinctly exhibiting dangers and foes, which they might steadily contemplate, and think how to escape or encounter. And how little does the benevolent instructor find it possible for him to do, when he applies his mind to the painful task of reducing this gloomy confused vision to the plain truth of their unhappy situation, set in order before their eyes.

He deems it necessary to speak of the most elementary principles—the perfect holiness, and justice of God—the corresponding holiness, and the all-comprehending extent, of his law, appointed to his creatures—the absolute duty of conformity to it in every act, word, and thought—the necessary condemnation consequent on failure—the dreadful evil, therefore of sin, both in its principle and consequences. God—perfect holiness—justice—law—universal conformity—sin—

condemnation! Alas! the hapless auditor has no such sense of the force of terms, and no such analogical ideas, as to furnish the medium for conveying these representations to his understanding. He never had, at any time; and now there may be in his mind all the additional confusion and incapacity of fixed attention, arising from pain, debility, and sleeplessness. All this therefore passes before him with a tenebrious glimmer, and is gone; like lightening faintly penetrating to a man behind a thick black curtain.

The instructor attempts a personal application, endeavouring to give the disturbed conscience a rational direction, and a distinct cognizance. But he finds, as he might expect to find, that a conscience without knowledge has never taken but a very small portion of the man's habits of life under its jurisdiction; and that it seems a most hopeless thing to attempt to send it back reinforced, to reclaim and conquer, through all the past, the whole extent of its rightful but never assumed dominion. As conscience has not necessarily received, by its present alarm, the benefit of a larger exercise of the understanding, it is absolutely incapable of admitting the monitor's estimate of the measure of guilt involved in omission, and in an irreligious state of the mind, as a dreadful addition to the account of criminal action. The person is totally and honestly unable to conceive of substantial guilt in any thing of which he can ask, what injury it has done to any body, This single point—whether positive harm has been done to any one,—comprehends the whole essence and sum of the conscious accountableness of very ignorant people. As to a duty absolute in the nature of things, of a duty as owing to themselves, or a duty as imposed by the almighty,—*that their minds should be in a certain prescribed state*,—there does really require a perfectly new manner of the action of intellect to enable them to descry its existence. Material wrong, *very* material wrong, to their fellow mortals, they are sensible they should not do; it is very little farther than so, that a sense of being amenable even to God is distinctly admitted; beyond that, they are absolved from jurisdiction; they are their own property, without an obligation even to themselves, as to the manner in which the possession may be held and ordered. The effect of their having thus habitually made nothing of the state of the mind, now meets the supposed instructor. He presses on this side of the province of conscience, on account of its vast importance; and partly, too, because he would avoid, except in a case of notoriously bad character, the invidiousness of seeming directly to reproach the sick man's outward conduct. But to give in an hour the understanding which it requires the discipline of many years to render competent! How vain the attempt! The man's sense of guilt fixes almost exclusively on something that has been improper in the practical courses. He professes to acknowledge the evil of this; and perhaps with a certain stress of expression, intended, by an apparent respondence to the serious emphasis which the monitor is laying on another part of the accountableness and guilt, to take him off from thus endeavouring, as it appears to the ignorant sufferer, to make him more of a sinner than there is any reason. By continuing to insist on the subject, the instructor may find himself in danger of being regarded as having taken upon him the unkind office of accuser in his own name, and of his own will and authority.

In the inculcation of the necessity of repentance, he will perceive the indistinctness of apprehension, respecting the difference between that kind of forced recoil from sin which is caused by dread of impending consequences, and the antipathy to its essential nature. And even if this distinction, which admits of very easy forms of exemplification, should thus be rendered in a degree perceptible in itself, the man cannot make the application. The instructor observes, as one of the most striking results of a want of disciplined mental exercise, an utter inability for self-inspection. There is before his eyes, looking at him, but a stranger to himself, a man on whose mind no other minds, except one, can shed a life of self-manifestation, to save him from the most fatal mistakes.

If the monitor would turn, (rather from an impulse to leave the gloom of the scene, than from any thing he sees even faintly approaching toward a right apprehension of the austerer truths of religion,) if he would turn his efforts, to the effect of directing on this dark spirit the benign rays of the Christian redemption, what is he to do for terms,—yes, for very terms? Mediator, sacrifice, atonement, satisfaction; faith, reliance; even the expression believing in Christ; merit of the death of Christ, acquittal, acceptance, justification:—he knows, or will soon learn, that he might as well talk in the language of the occult sciences. And he is forced down to such expedients of grovelling paraphrase, and humiliating analogy, that he becomes sensible his method of endeavoring to make a divine subject intelligible, is to divest it of all its radiance, and reduce it, in order that it may not confound, to the rank of things which have not majesty enough to impress with awe. And after this has been done, to the utmost of his ability, and to the unavoidable weariness of his suffering auditor, he is distressed to think of the proportion between any such slight ideas as this man's mind now possesses of the economy of redemption, and the stupendous magnitude of the interest in which he stands dependent on it. Some crude sentiment, as, that he 'hopes Jesus Christ will stand his friend;' that it was very good of the Saviour to think of us; that he wishes he knew what to do to get his help; that Jesus Christ has done him good in other things, and he hopes he will now again at the last;*—such expressions will afford little to alleviate the gloomy feelings, with which the serious visitor descends from the chamber in which, perhaps, a few days after, he hears that the man he conversed with is a dead body.

But such benevolent visitors have to tell of still more melancholy exemplifications of the effects of ignorance in the close of life. They have seen the neglect of early cultivation, and the subsequent estrangement from all knowledge and thinking, except about business and folly, result in such a stupefaction of mind, that irreligious and immoral persons, approaching death, and fully aware that they were, and by no means in a state of physical lethargy, were absolutely incapable of being alarmed at the near approach of death. They did not deny, nor in the infidel sense disbelieve, what was said to them of the awfulness of that event, and its consequences; but they had actually never thought enough of death to have any solemn associations with the idea. And their faculties were become so rigid, so stiffened, as it were, they could not now acquire them; no, not while the portentious spectre was unveiling his visage to them, in near and still nearer approach; not when the element of another world was beginning to penetrate to their souls, through the rents of their mortal tabernacle. It appeared that literally their thoughts *could not* go out from what they had been through life immersed in, to contemplate, (with any realizing feeling,) a grand change of being, expected so soon to take place. They could not go to the fearful brink to look off. It was a stupor of the soul not to be awaked but by the actual plunge into the realities of eternity. In such a case, there probably appeared the instinctive repugnance to death. But the feeling was, If it must be so, there is no help for it; and as to what may come after, we must take our chance. In this temper and manner, we recollect a sick man, of this untaught class,

* Such an expression as this would hardly have occurred but from recollection of fact, in the instance of an aged farmer, (the owner of the farm,) in his last illness. In the way of reassuring his somewhat doubtful hope that Christ would not fail him when now had recourse to, at his extreme need, he said, (to the writer,) 'Jesus Christ has sent me a deal of good crops.'

answering the inquiry how he felt himself, 'Getting worse; I suppose I shall make a die of it.' And his pious neighbours, earnestly exhorting him to solemn concern and preparation, could not make him sensible there was occasion for any extraordinary disturbance of mind. And yet this man was not inferior to those around him in sense for the common business of life.

After a tedious length of suffering, and when death is plainly inevitable, it is not very uncommon for the persons under this infatuation to express a wish for its arrival, simply as a deliverance from what they are enduring, without troubling themselves with a thought of what may follow. 'I hope it will please God soon to release me,' was the expression, to his religious medical attendant, of such an ignorant and insensible mortal, within an hour of his death, which was evidently and directly brought on by his vices. And he uttered it without a word, or the smallest indicated emotion, of penitence or solicitude; though he had passed his life in a neighbourhood abounding with the public means of religious instruction and warning.

When earnest, persisting, and seriously menacing admonitions, of pious visitors or friends, almost literally compel such unhappy persons to some precise recognition of the subject, their answers will often be faithfully representative, and a consistent completion, of their course through mental darkness, from childhood to the mortal hour. We recollect the instance of a wicked old man, who, within that very hour, replied to the urgent admonitions, by which a religious neighbour felt it a painful duty to make a last effort to alarm him, 'What, do you believe that God can think of damning me because I may have been as bad as other folk? I am sure he will do no such thing: he is far too good for that.'

We cannot close this detailed illustration of so gloomy a subject, without again adverting to a rare, it is true, but most admirable phenomenon, for which the observers may, if they choose, go round the whole circle of their philosophy, and begin again, to find any adequate cause, other than the most immediate agency of the almighty spirit. Here and there an instance occurs to the delight of the Christian philanthropist, of a person brought up in utter ignorance and barbarian rudeness, and so continuing till late, sometimes very late in life; and then, at last, after the long petrifying, effect of time and habit, suddenly seized upon by a mysterious power, and taken, with an alarming and irresistible force, out of the dark hold in which the spirit has lain imprisoned and torpid, into the sphere of thought and feeling.

This we notice, not so much to show how far a divine influence surpasses all other applications, to the human mind, as for the purpose of again remarking, how wonderfully this great moral change may effect the obtuse intellectual faculties; which it appears, in the most signal of these instances, almost to create anew. It is exceedingly striking to observe how the contracted rigid soul seems to soften, and grow warm, and expand, and quiver with life. With the new energy infused, it painfully struggles to work itself, into freedom, from the wretched contortion in which it has so long been fixed, as by the impressed spell of some infernal magic. It has been seen filled with a painful and indignant emotion at its own ignorance; actuated with a restless earnestness to be informed; acquiring an unwonted applicableness of its faculties to thought; attaining a perception, combined of intelligence and moral sensibility, to which numerous things are becoming discernible and affecting, that they were as non-existent before. It is not in the very utmost strength of their import that we employ such terms of description; but we have known instances in which the change, the intellectual change, has been so conspicuous, within a brief space of time, that even an infidel observer must have forfeited all claim to be esteemed a man of sense, if he would not acknowledge,—This that you call divine grace, whatever it may really be, is the strangest awakener of faculties after all. And to a devout man, it is a spectacle of most enchanting beauty thus to see the immortal plant, which has been under a malignant blast while sixty or seventy years have passed over it, coming out at length in the bloom of life.

We cannot hesitate to draw the inference, that if religion is so auspicious to the intellectual faculties, the cultivation and exercise of those faculties must be of great advantage to religion.

SECTION II.

Mischievous operation of ignorance in disposing the mind to receive every species of absurdity as religious truth.

Perhaps we should not finally dismiss the subject of the effect of ignorance, as creating an incapacity of receiving religious instruction, without just noticing its mischievous operation on many who are disposed to attend to such instruction, in fitting their minds to receive, as religious truth, all manner of absurdities.

We have expressly said, (what indeed did not need to be said,) that such a noble exemplification as above described, is very rare. If we come down to a very considerably lower degree, we shall find the examples numerous, among the uneducated subjects of genuine religion, of persons remarkably improved in the power and exercise of their reason; and we may assume that *some* share of this improvement reaches to all who are really under this most beneficent influence in the creation.* But still it must be acknowledged of too many, who are in a measure, we may candidly believe, under the genuine efficacy of religion, that they have attained, under its influence, but so diminutive a proportion of the improvement of intellect, that they can be well pleased with a great deal of absurdity of religious notions and language. While, however, we confess and regret that it is so, we should not overlook the obvious causes and excuses for it; partly in the constitution of the mind, partly in extraneous circumstances. Many whose attention is in honest earnestness drawn to religion, are naturally endowed with so scanty a portion of the thinking power, strictly so denominated, that it would have required high cultivation to raise them to the level of very moderate understanding. There are some who appear to have a natural invincible tendency to an uncouth fantastic mode of forming their notions. It is in the nature of others, that whatever cultivation they might have received, it would still have been by their passions, rather than, by any due proportion by their reason, that an important concern would have taken and retained hold of them. In the case of too many, there may have been associated with the causes of their first effectual religious impressions, with the instructions and instructors, perhaps, that first drew them into the full interest of the subject, circumstances unfortunately tending to prevent a sound rational discipline, of the understanding which was coming into exercise on that subject.

Now suppose all these worthy persons, with these circumstances against them, to be also under the one great sad calamity of an utterly neglected education; and is it any wonder they can receive with approbation, a great deal of what is a heavy disgrace to the name of

* Really under this influence, we repeat, pointedly; for we justly put all others out of the account. It is nothing, as against our asserted principle or fact, that great numbers who may contribute to swell a public bustle about religion, who may run together at the call of whim imposture, or insanity, assuming that name; who may acquire, instead of any other folly, a turn for talking, disputing, or ranting, about that subject; it is nothing, in short, that any, who are not in real conscientious seriousness, the disciples of religion, can be shown to be no better for it, in point of improved understanding.

religious doctrine and ministration? Where is the wonder, that crudeness of conception should not disappoint and offend minds that have not, ten times since they came into the world, been compelled to form two ideas with precision, and then combine them with strictness, beyond the narrow scope of their ordinary pursuits? Where is the wonder, if many such persons take noise and fustian, for something zealous and something lofty; if they mistake a wheedling cant for affectionate solicitude; if they defer to pompous egotism and dogmatical assertion, from the obvious interest, which those who cannot inquire much for themselves, have to believe their teacher is an oracle; if they are delighted with whimsical conceits as strokes of discovery and surprise, and yet at the same time are pleased with common-place, and endless repetition, as an exemption from mental effort; and if they are gratified by vulgarity of diction and illustration, as bringing religion to the level where they are at home? Nay, if an artful pretender, or half lunatic visionary, or some poor set of dupes of their own inflated self-importance, should give out, that they are come into the world for the manifestation, at last, of true Christianity, which the divine revelation has failed, till their advent, to explain to any of the numberless devout and sagacious examiners of it, what is there in the minds of the most ignorant class of the persons desirous to secure the benefits of religion, that can be relied on to certify them, that they shall not forego the greatest blessing ever offered to them by setting at nought these pretensions?

It is grievous to think there should be a large snd almost perpetual stream of words, conveying crudities, extravagances, arrogant dictates of ignorance, pompous nothings, vulgarities, catches of idle fantasy, and impertinences of the speaker's vanity, as religious instruction, to assemblages of ignorant people. But then, how to turn this current away, to waste itself, as it deserves, in the swamps of the solitary desert? The thing to be wished is, that it were possible to put some strong coercion on the *minds*, (we deprecate all other restraint,) of the teachers, a compulsion to feel the necessity of information, sense, disciplined thinking, the correct use of words, and the avoidance at once of soporific formality and wild excess. There are signs of amendment, certainly; but while the passion of human beings for notoriety lasts, (which will be yet a considerable time,) there will not fail to be men, in any number required, ready to exhibit in religion, in any manner in which the people are willing to be pleased with them. The effectual method will be, to take the matter in the inverted order, and endeavour to secure that those who assemble to be taught, shall already have learnt so much *by other means*, as to impose upon their teachers the necessity of wisdom. But by what other means, except the discipline of the best education possible to be given to them, and the subsequent voluntary self improvement to which it may be hoped that such an education would often lead?

We cannot dismiss this topic, of the unhappy effect of extreme ignorance on persons religiously disposed, in rendering them both liable and inclined to receive their ideas of the highest subject in a disorderly, perverted, and debased form, mixed largely with other men's folly and their own, without again remarking a pleasing testimony to the connexion between genuine religion and intelligence. It arises from the fact, apparent to any discriminating observer, that, as a general the most truly pious of the illiterate disciples of religion, those who have the most of its devotional feeling, do certainly manifest more of the operation of judgment in their religion than is evinced by those of less solemn and devout sentiment. The former will unquestionably be found, when on a level as to the measure of natural faculty and the want of previous cultivation, to show more discernment, to be less captivated by noise and extravagance, and more intent on really understanding *what it is* that they profess to believe and love.

Thus we have endeavoured, we are afraid with too much prolixity and repetition, to describe the evils attendant on a neglected state of the minds of the people. The representation is far enough from comprehending all those even of magnitude and prominence; but it displays that portion of them which is the most serious and calamitous, as being the effect which the people's ignorance has on their moral and religious interests. And we think no one who has attentively surveyed the state and character of the lower orders of the community, in this country, will impute exaggeration to the picture. It is rather to be feared that the reality is of much darker shade; and that a more strikingly gloomy exhibition might be formed, by such a process as the following:—That a certain number, twenty, or less or more, of the most observant of the religious philanthropic persons, who have had most intercourse with the classes in question, for the purposes of instruction, charitable aid, or perhaps of furnishing employment, should relate the most characteristic circumstances and anecdotes within their own experience, illustrative of this mental and moral condition; and that these should be arranged, without any comment, under the respective heads of the preceding sketch, or of a more comprehensive enumeration. Let each of them repeat, in so many words, the most notable things he had heard uttered as expressing notions of deity, or any part of religion; or respecting the ground and extent of duty and accountableness; or the termination of life, and a future retribution. Let the recital include both the expressions of individual conception, and those of the most prevailing maxims and common-places; and let them be the sayings of persons in health, and of those languishing and dying. Then let there be produced a numerous assortment of characteristic samples of practical conduct; conduct not alone proceeding, in a general way, from corrupt disposition; but bearing the special marks of the cast and direction given to that disposition by extreme ignorance. The assemblage of things thus recounted, when the actual circumstances were also added of the wretchedness corresponding and inseparable, would constitute such an exhibition of fact, as any description of those evils in general terms would incur the charge of rhetorical excess in attempting to rival. We can well imagine, that some of these persons of large experience may have accompanied us through the foregoing series of illustrations with a feeling, that they could have displayed the subject with a more impressive prominence.

SECTION III.

The preceding remarks exemplified by the condition of England.

And now again the grievous reflection comes upon us, that all this is the description of a large portion of the people of our own nation. Of this nation, the theme of so many lofty strains of panegyric. Of this nation, stretching forth its powers in ambitious enterprise, with infinite pride and cost, to all parts of the globe;—just as if a family were seen eagerly intent on making some new appropriation, or going out to maintain some new competition or feud with its neighbours, or mixing perhaps in the strife of athletic games, or drunken frays, at the very time that several of its members are lying dead in the house. So that the fame of the nation resounded, and its power made itself felt, in every clime, it was not worth a consideration that a vast proportion of its people were systematically consigned, through ignorance and its inseparable irreligion and depravities, to wretchedness and even final perdition. It is matter for never-ending amazement, that during one generation after another, the presiding wisdom in this chief of Christian and Protestant states, should have thrown out the living strength of that state, into almost every mode of agency under heaven, rather than that of promoting the state itself to the condition of a happy community of cultivated beings. What stupendous infatuation, what disastrous ascendency of the power of darkness, that this energy should have been sent forth to pervade all parts of the world in quest of objects, to inspirit and accomplish innumerable projects, political and military, and to lavish itself, even to exhaustion and fainting at its vital source, on every alien interest; while here, at home, a great portion of the social body was in a moral and intellectual sense dying and putrefying over the land. And it was thus perishing for want of the vivifying principle of knowledge, which one fifth part of this mighty amount of exertion would have been sufficient to diffuse into every corner and cottage of the island. Within its circuit, a countless multitude were seen passing away their mortal existence little better, in any view, than mere sentient shapes of matter, and by their depravity inexpressibly worse; and yet this hideous fact had not the weight of the very 'dust of the balance,' in the deliberation, whether a grand exertion of the national vigour and resource could have any object so worthy, (with God for the judge, the while,) as some scheme of foreign aggrandizement, some interference in remote quarrels, an avengement, by anticipation, of wrongs pretended to be foreseen, or the obstinate prosecution of some fatal career, begun in the very levity of pride, or from the casual ascendency of some perverse and irritated individual or party.

The national *honour*, perhaps, would be alleged in a certain matter of punctilio, for the necessity of undertakings of incalculable consumption, by men who could see no national *disgrace* in the circumstance, that several millions of the persons composing the nation could not read the ten commandments. Or the national *safety* has been pleaded, to a similar purpose, in terms of patriotic emphasis, upon some very slight symptoms of danger; and the pleaders would have suspected alienation of mind in any adviser suggesting,—'Do you, instead, apply your best efforts, and the nation's means, to raise the barbarous population from their ignorance aud debasement, and you really may venture some little trust in divine providence for the nation's safety meanwhile.'

If a serious and religious man, looking back through one or two centuries, were enabled to take, with an adequate comprehension of intellect, the sum and value of so much of the astonishing course of the national exertions of this country, as the supreme judge has put to the criminal account of pride and and ambition; and if he could then place in contrast to the transactions on which that mighty amount has been expended, a sober estimate of what so much exerted vigour *might* have accomplished, for the intellectual and moral exaltation of the people, it could not be without an emotion of horror that he would say, Who is to be accountable who *has been* accountable, for this difference? He would no longer wonder at any plagues and judgments, which may have been inflicted on such a state. And he would solemnly adjure all those, especially, who profess in a peculiar manner to feel the power of the Christian religion, to beware how they implicate themselves, by avowed or even implied approbation, in what must be a matter of fearful account before the highest tribunal. For *some or other* persons, such a course *must* have been a matter of account. Such a moral agency could not throw off its responsibility into the air, to be dissipated and lost, like the black smoke of forges or volcanoes. This one grand thing, (the improvement of the people,) left undone, while a thousand arduous things have been done or strenuously endeavoured, cannot be less than an awful charge *somewhere*. And where?—but on all who have voluntarily co-operated and concurred in systems and schemes, which could deliberately put *such* a thing last? Last! nay, not even that; for they have till recently, as we have seen, thrown it almost wholly out of consideration. A long succession of men are gone to this audit. Let the rest beware.

We were supposing a thoughtful man to draw out to his view a parallel and contrast exhibiting, on the one side, the series of objects on which, during several ages, an enormous exertion of the national energy has been directed; and on the other those improvements of the people which might have been effected by so much of that exertion as he deems to have been wasted. In this process, he might often be inclined to single out particular parts and points in the disapproved series, to be put in special contrast over against the possibilities on the opposite line. For example; there perhaps occurs to his view some island, of inconsiderable extent, the haunt of pestilence, rendered productive solely by means involving the most flagrant iniquity; an iniquity which it avenges by opening a premature grave for many of his countrymen, and being a most powerful moral corrupter of others. Such a blasted spot, nevertheless, may have been one of the most material objects of a widely destructive war, which has in effect sunk incalculable treasure in the sea, and in the sands, ditches and fields of plague-infested shores; with a dreadful sacrifice too of blood, life, and all the best moral feelings and habits. Its possession, perhaps, was the prize and triumph of all the grand exertion; the equivalent for all the cost, misery, and crime.

Or there may occur to him the name of some fortress, in a less remote region, where the Christian nations seem to have vied with one another which of them should deposit the greatest number of victims, securely kept in the charge of death, to rise and testify for them, at the last day, how much they have been governed by the peaceful spirit of their professed religion. He reads that his countrymen, conjoined with others, have battled round this fortress, wasting the vicinity, but richly manuring the soil with blood. They have co-operated in hurling upon the abodes of thousands of inhabitants within its walls, a thunder and lightning incomparably more destructive than that of nature; and have put fire and earthquake under the fortifications; shouting, 'to make the welkin ring,' at sight of the consequent ruin and chasm, which have opened an entrance for hostile rage. They have taken the place,—and then they have surrendered it. The next year perhaps they have taken it again; to be again at last given up, upon compulsion or in the acknowledgment of right, to the very same party to which it had belonged previously to all this horrible commotion. The operations in this local and very narrow portion of the grand affray of monarchies, he may calculate to have cost his country, as much as the amount earned by the toils of the whole life of all the inhabitants of one of its considerable towns; if he can set aside from his view, long enough for such a mere pecuniary reckoning, the more portentous part of the account,—the carnage, the crimes, and the devastation committed on the foreign tract, the place of abode of people who had little interest in the contest, and no power to prevent it. And why all this? He may not be able to divest himself of the principles that should rule the judgment of a moralist and a Christian, in order to think like a statesman, and therefore may find no better reason than that, when despots would quarrel, Britain must take the occasion to prove itself a great power, by bearing a high hand amidst their rivalries; though this should be at the expense of having this scene at home chequered between children learning little more than how to curse, and old persons dying without knowing how to put words together to pray.

The question may have been, in one part of the world or another, which of two wicked individuals of the same family, competitors for sovereign authority, should be actually invested with it, they being equal in the qualifications and dispositions to make the worst use of it. And the decision of such a question was worthy, that England should expend what remained of her depressed strength from previous exertions of it in some equally meritorious cause.

Or the supposed reviewer of our history may find, somewhere in his retrospect, that a certain brook or swamp in a wilderness, or stripe of waste, or settlement of boundaries in respect to some insignificant traffic, was difficult of adjustment between jealous, irritated, and mutually incursive neighbours; and therefore national honour and interest equally required that war should be lighted up, sea and land, through several quarters of the globe. Or a dissension may have arisen upon the matter of some petty tax on an article of commerce; an absolute will had been rashly signified on the subject; pride had committed itself, and was peremptory for persisting; and the resolution was to be prosecuted through a wide tempest of destruction protracted perhaps many years; and only terminating in the loss, as to the leading power concerned, of infinitely more than this 'least fatal arbitrement' had been determined on as the means of maintaining;—besides the absolutely fathomless amount of every kind of cost in this progress to final frustation. But there would be no end of recounting facts of this order.

Now the comparative estimator has to set against a large array of things of this character, the forms of imagined good, which might, during the ages of this retrospect, have been realized by an incomparably less exhausting series of exertion, an exertion, indeed, continually renovating its own resources. Imagined good, we said;—alas! the evil stands in long and awful display on the ground of history; the hypothetical good presents itself as but a dream; with this difference, that there is resting on the conscience of beings somewhere still existing, an eternal accountableness for its not having been a reality.

For such an *island*, as we have supposed our comparer to read of, he can, in imagination, look on a space of proportional extent in any part of his native country, taking a district as a detached section of a general national picture. And he can figure to himself the result, resplendent upon this tract, of so much energy there beneficently expended as that island had cost: an energy, we mean, *equivalent in measure*; while in the infinitely different *mode* of an exertion, by all appropriate means, to improve the reason, manner, and morals of the people. What a prevalence of intelligence, what a delightful civility of deportment, what repression and almost disappearance of the most gross obtrusive forms of vice, what domestic decorum, attentive education of the children, gravity and understanding in attendance on public offices of religion, sense and good order in assemblages for the assertion and exercise of civil and political rights!

We were supposing his attention fixed awhile on the recorded operations against a strongly fortified place, in a region marked through every part with the traces and memorials of the often renewed conflicts of the Christian states. And we suppose him to make a collective mixed estimate of all kinds of human ability put forth around and against that particular devoted place, as a detached portion of the whole enormous quantity of exertion, expended by his country in all that region, in the campaigns of a war, or of a century's wars. He may then again endeavour, by a rule of equivalence, to conceive the same amount of exertion in quite another way; to imagine human forces equal in *quantity* to all that putting forth of strength, physical, mental, and financial, for annoyance and destruction, expended, instead, in the operation of effecting the utmost improvement which they *could* effect, in the mental cultivation and the morals of the inhabitants of one large town in his own country.

In figuring to himself the channels and instrumentality, through which this great stream of energy might pass into this operation, he will soon have many specific means presented to his view: Schools, of the most perfect appointment, in every section and corner of the town; a system of friendly, but cogent and peremptory dealing, with all the people of inferior condition, relatively to the necessity of their practical accordance to the plans of education;* an exceedingly copious supply, for individual possession, of the best books of elementary knowledge, accompanied, as we need not say, by the sacred volume; a number of assortments of useful and pleasing books for circulation, established under strict order, and with appointments of honorary and other rewards to those who gave evidence of having made the best use of them; a number of places of resort where various branches of the most generally useful and attainable knowledge and arts should be explained and applied, by every expedient of familiar, practical, and entertaining illustration, admitting a degree of co-operation by those who attended to see and hear; and an abundance of commodious places for religious instruction on the sabbath, where there should be intelligent and zealous men to impart it. Our speculator has a good right to suppose a high degree of these qualifications in his public teachers of religion, when he is to imagine something parallel in this department to the skill and ardor displayed in the supposed military operations. He may add to such an apparatus, a police, (if we may employ that rather ungracious term,) faithful and vigilant against every cognizable form of neglect and immorality. And besides all this, there will be a great variety of undefined and optional activity of benevolent, and intelligent men of local influence.

Under so auspicious a combination of discipline, he will not indeed fancy, in his transient vision, that he beholds Athens revived; but he will in sober consistency, we think, with what is known of the relation of cause and effect, imagine a place surpassing any actual town or city now on earth. And let it be distinctly kept in view, that to produce the effect exhibited in this ideal spectacle, he is just supposing to have been expended, on the population of the town, a measure of exertion and means equal, (as far as agencies in so different a form and direction can be brought to a rule of comparative estimate,) to what has been expended by his country in investing, battering, undermining, burning, taking, and perhaps retaking, one particular foreign town, in one or several campaigns.

If he should perchance be sarcastically questioned, how can he allow himself in so strange a conceit as that of supposing such a quantity of moral forces concentrated to act in one exclusive spot, while the rest of the country remained under the old course of things; or in such an absurdity as that of fancying that any *any* quantity of those forces could effectually raise one local section of the people eminently aloft, while continuing surrounded and unavoidably in constant intercourse with the general mass, remaining still sunk in degradation—he has to reply that he is fancying no such thing. For while he is thus converting, in imagination, the military exertions against one foreign town, into intellectual and moral operations on one town at home, why may he not, in similar imagination, make a whole country correspond to a whole country? He may conceive the grand incalculable amount of exertion made by his country in marshal operations over all that wide foreign territory of which he has selected a particular spot, to have been, on the contrary, expended in the

* It is here most confidently presumed, that any man who looks, in a right state of his senses, at the manner in which the children are still brought up, in many parts of the land, will hear with unlimited contempt any hypocritical protest against so much interference with the discretion, the liberty of parents; the discretion, the liberty, forsooth, of bringing up their children a nuisance on the face of the earth!

supposed beneficent process on the great scale of this whole nation. Then would the supposed popular improvement in the one particular town, so far from being a strange insulated phenomenon, absurd to be conceived as existing in exception and total contrast to the general state of the people, be but a portion and specimen of that state.

He may proceed along the series of such confronted representations as far as bitter mortification will let him. But he will soon be sick of this process of comparison. And how sick will he thenceforward be, to perpetual loathing, of the vain raptures with which an immoral and antichristian patriotism can review a long history of what it will call national glory, acquired by national energy ambitiously consuming itself in a continual succession and unlimited extent of extraneous operations, of that kind which has been the grand curse of the human race ever since the time of Cain; while the one thing needful of national welfare, the very *summum bonum* of a state, has been regarded with contemptuous indifference.

These observations are not made on any assumption, that England could in all cases have kept clear of implications of foreign interests and remote and sanguinary contests. But they are made on the assumption of what is admitted and deplored by every thoughtful religious man, whose understanding and moral sense are not wretchedly prostrated in homage to a prevailing system, and chained down by a superstition that dare not question the wisdom and probity of high national authorities and counsels. What is so admitted and deplored by the true and Christian patriots is, that this nation has gone to an awfully criminal extent beyond the line of necessity; and it has been extremely prompt to find occasions for appearing again, and still again, in array for the old work of waste and death; and that, taking into the account the high advantage enjoyed by its preponderating classes for forming a religious judgment, it has shown during several generations and down into our own age, an astonishing insensibility to the dictates of Christianity and the warning of accountableness to the sovereign judges.

These observations assume, too, with perfect confidence, that there CANNOT be, in the world, any such thing as a nation habitually absolved from the duty of raising its people from brutish ignorance, in consideration of a necessity and duty of expending its vigour and means in foreign enterprise. The concern of redeeming the people from a besotted condition of their reason and conscience, is a duty at all events and to an entire certainty; is a duty imperative and absolute; and any pretended necessity for such a direction of the national exertion as would be incompatible with a paramount attention to this, must be an imposition too gross to furnish an excuse for being imposed on.

SECTION IV.

Indications of a better age approaching—with remarks on some visionary projects, for meliorating the condition of mankind.

Such as we have described has been, for ages, the degraded state of the multitude. And such has been the indifference manifested in regard to it by the superior, the refined, the ascendant portion of the community; who, generally speaking, could see these sharers with them of the dishonoured human nature, in endless numbers around them, in the city and the field, without its ever flashing on conscience that on them was lying a solemn accountableness, destined to press one day with all its weight, for what excluded these beings from the sphere of rational existence. It never occurred to many of them as a question of the smallest moment, in what manner the mind might live in all these bodies, if only it were there in competence to make them efficient as machines and implements. Contented to be gazed at, to be envied, or to be regarded as too high even for envy, and to have the rough business of the world performed by these inhalers of the vital air, they perhaps thought, if they reflected at all on the subject, that the best and most privileged state of such beings was to be in the least possible degree morally responsible; and that therefore it would but be doing them an injury to enlarge their knowledge. And might not the thought be suggested at some moment, (see how many things may be envied in their turns?) how happy *they* should be, if with the vast superiority of their advantages they could be just as little accountable? And yet even at such moments they were little thinking how much it *was* for which they would, in consequence of those advantages, be summoned to answer; little anticipating they should ever be arraigned on a charge, to which they would vainly wish to be permitted to plead, 'Were we our brothers' keepers?' If an office designated by those terms, had been named to them as forming a part of their duty, their thoughts might have beaten about in various conjectures and protracted perplexity, before it had come explicitly to their apprehension, that the objects of that office were in a peculiar manner the understandings, principles, and consciences, of the vulgar mass We repeat that we speak generally, and not universally.

But we think a great revolution is evidently beginning; a far more important one, by its higher principle and more expansive and beneficent consequences, than the ordinary events of that name. What have commonly been the matter and circumstances of revolutions? The last deciding blow in a deadly competition of equally selfish parties; actions and re-actions of ambition and revenge; the fiat of a predominating potentate or conqueror; a burst of blind fury, suddenly sweeping away an old despotism, but overwhelming, too, all attempts to substitute a better institution; plots, massacres, battles, dethronements, restorations: all ordinary things. How little of the sublime of moral agency has there been, with one or two partial exceptions, in these mighty commotions; how little wisdom or virtue, or reference to the supreme patron of national interests; how little nobleness, or even distinctness of purpose, or consolidated advantage of success! But here is a revolution with different phenomena. It displays its quality and project in activities, of continually enlarging scope and power, for the universal diffusion of the divine revelation; in enterprises to attempt an opening of the doors of all the immense prison-houses of human spirits in every region; in schemes, (advancing with a more quick and widening impulse into effect than good designs were wont to do in former times,) for rendering education and the possession of valuable knowledge universal; in multiplying exertions, in all official and unofficial forms, for making it impossible to mankind to avoid hearing the voice of religion; and all this taking advantage of the new and powerful movement in the general mind; as earnest bold adventurers have sometimes availed themselves of a formidable torrent to be conveyed whither the stream in its accustomed state would never have carried them; or as we have heard of heroic assailants seizing the moment of an awful tempest of thunder and lightning, to break through the enemy's lines. These are the insignia by which it may well express disdain to take its rank with ordinary revolutions.

Do these appear but a feeble array, to be recounted as the signs and forces of a great revolution, to the mere political projectors and calculators, whose object is to ameliorate the state and character of the people? And what, alas! can *you* do, we might ask them, by expedients relying on any different class of forces from these? As a preliminary point, how are you to *obtain*, (if your theory of an improved state of the people require that there be obtained in the *first instance*,) any materially altered political arrangements in their favour? In what manner can you promise yourselves to bring into effect a theory, that should presume a hasty concession of privileges to the people by the superior orders of the community, while those orders have to allege in justification of refusal, that the people are so ignorant, and so exceedingly corrupt, as to be totally unfit for the possession of any such privileges, even supposing them, abstractedly speaking, their right?

But suppose the leading classes did *not* refuse any one thing you would ask, for reducing your theory to practise, or to experiment. Suppose the people instated in the fulness of what you would call the privileges rightfully appropriate to their situation in the community; placed on just such a ground in the great political arrangement as you would wish to claim and vindicate for them, in order to raise them, as you think, to respectability and happiness. Suppose them placed there at this moment; and what then? How,—through what mode of the salutary effect of this change,—are the felicitous consequences to follow? You know, yes, you absolutely know, that a vast majority of the multitude are, at this hour, as wretchedly ignorant, and as dreadfully corrupt, as any of those esteemed their enemies have represented them. Hardly any language on this subject can exceed the odious truth. Nor can any thing on earth be more contemptible than that strain of talking which affects a confidence in their sound judgment, their steady principles, there well ordered dispositions, and so forth; and which in addressing them, adopts phrases of encomium and difference, and makes a kind of boasting in their name, as if in them where to be found the main substance of what there is of sterling worth in the land. It is but an incipient and exceedingly partial appearance of transformation that the most sanguine of us can, as yet, profess to perceive, as the result of all the new and augmented moral forces in recent times brought into operation; so inveterate, so obdurate, so profound in evil, is that popular condition attempted to be corrected. The great mass is still most deplorably corrupt. And yet you really can, notwithstanding, place it, in imagination, under some *merely* political auspicious adjustment which shall act upon it with a more immediate and powerful efficacy of correction, than any alterative influence of higher education and inculcated religion. But how? Through the medium of what principles? Think in what terms you shall name these merely political vitalites, so mighty for a moral regeneration. Would you, perhaps, talk of—the dignified sense of independence; the generous, the liberalizing, the ennobling sentiments of freedom; the self-respect, and conscious responsibility of men in the full exercise of their rights; the manly disdain of what is base; and the innate sense and love of what is worthy and honourable, which would spontaneously develope itself on the removal of certain ungenial circumstances in the political constitution of society, which have had the effect of winter on the moral nature of its inferior portions? It would be difficult to believe you were not aware that all this, in such a manner of putting it forth, in fragrant nonsense.

But perhaps you will say, that your scheme of means for the desired renovation of the state and character of the people, is *not* exclusively political. Your chief power, you own, your Hercules in the operations for placing them on a happier ground, is indeed to be a highly improved form of the political framing together of the national community because in the attainment of this there would be an end of many bad impressions now strongly and habitually affecting the people and the commencement of as many beneficent influences, to come upon them with a direct immediate action, and an action not merely affecting a proportion of them as individuals, but falling on them generally as one great body. This, you think, would be such a mighty and comprehensive advantage, that it must stand primary in a rational scheme for the grand object. Bnt then, you will say, for subordinate and subsidiary means, to follow in detail, under this chief improver of the people, you do not fail to set a high value on plans of education, and efforts for diffusing the knowledge of religion; that in reality you are never imagining the possibility of the full accomplishment of the object without the assistance of these means: they are always *included* in your speculation, though accounted in it as secondary and instrumental, under the paramount importance of what you must still insist on placing first. Do you say so? Then confess that those persons are right at all events, who are zealous to bring into operation immediately the expedients thus admitted by yourselves to be indispensible somewhere in the process; who will do it as *so much gained at any rate*, in dispute of the reluctance of the economy around them to dispose itself into an order, under which the benificent design might have a greater power and more rapid efficacy. Whatever order of things you would conceive as the most propitious to the improvement of the people, what would that improvement itself consist in, for its most valuable part, but exactly that which is endeavoured to be imparted *now* by the men who will not wait for the fortunate aspects and conjunctions of your political astrology? We should say, which *is* imparted by them; for they find that in some measure their scheme for infusing that best improvement *can* be brought in contact with the mind of the humbler order, in its juvenile portion; and that already, as from the garment of the redeemer, a sanative virtue goes out of it. And shall they despise this measure of utility, just because they have reason to wish it were a thousand times as much? They acknowledge with regret the exceedingly limited reach and force of their operations, as compared with the immensity of the assemblage of intellectual and moral existence requiring to be operated upon; but who, nevertheless, are the truer friends of the people,—they, who find an intrinsic value in such means as there are, in the absence of whatever means there are not, and actively exert themselves that the people may be the better *so far;* or you, who rate all means as but cyphers, unless a certain favourite one be at their head; and seem almost content that, till it *shall* be there, the people should remain jnst as they are for mere evidence that no scheme but yours can do them good?

But some of those persons who, whenever they think of great plans of utility to a nation, inevitably think also of that which directs the nation's organized strength, and of the forms of institution, and of the prevailing spirit, according to which that strength is made to act, have to plead, that it is not on specfic circumstances wrong in the political arrangement, that they are resting so much of the emphasis of their regrets or wishes; that it is not from this or that particular formal correction of institutions, that they are imagining, in melancholy musings, how much good might flow to pour life and vigour into the process for reforming and exalting the people. They say, that whatever they might perhaps, on examination, deem wrong in political mechanism, their ungracious feeling toward states, and those who have presided in the management of them, is of this more general and solemn purport,—that those national systems and administrators have never, in the plenitude of immense power, actually wrought to this grand effect, of saving the people from a dreadful mental degradatlon. It is on this enormous practical failure that they dwell, with such deep displacency, rather than on precise defects in the construction of states, theoretically considered. And then they say, that the contemplation of this fact has the effect of reducing almost to folly, in their view, the little schemes and efforts of individuals directed toward such an object.

Now we earnestly wish it might be granted by the

almighty, that the political institutions of the nations might speedily take a form, and come under an administration, that *would* apply the energy of the state to so sublime a purpose; and we always consider the question whether they do this, or the degree in which they do it, as the grand test of their merits. But then, we must suggest it to the persons thus on the point of turning the awful omissions of states into a license for individuals to do nothing, to consider what, after all, has been the criminal neglect of which nations in their character of states have been guilty, but the neglect of which the individuals composing them have been guilty. And are individuals *now* absolved from all such responsibility; and the more so, that the conviction of the importance of the object is come upon them with such a new and mighty force? When they say, reproachfully, that the nation in its collective capacity, as a body politic, neglects a most important duty, does this amount to the very same thing as saying that *they* perform their share? In actually not performing it, by what principle do they transfer the blame on the state? Would they, in effect, prostitute the language of religion, and say, In thee we live, move, and have a being? Or, in imitation of what the pagans of the East are rid of all sense of guilt by believing of their gods, namely, that the gods so pervade or rather essentially *constitute* their faculties and wills, that whatever they do or refuse to do, it is not they, but literally the gods that do it, or refuse,—in imitation of this will these persons account themselves but as particles of matter, actuated and necessitated in all things by a sovereign mythological something denominated the State?

It is not so that they feel with respect to those other interests and projects, which they are really in earnest to promote, though those concerns may lie in no greater proportion than the one in question does within the scope of their individual ability. The incubus has then vanished; and they find themselves in possession of a free agency, and a degree of power which they are by no means disposed to underrate. What is there then that should reduce them, as individnal agents, to such utter and willing insignificance in the present affair? Besides, they may form themselves, in indefinite number, into combination. And is there no power in any collective form in which they can be associated, save just that one in which the aggregation is constituted under the political shape and authority denominated a state? Or does the matter come at last to this, that they grow alarmed in conscience at the high-toned censure they have been stimulated and betrayed to pronounce on the state, for neglect of its greatest duty; that they relapse into the obsequiousness of hesitating, whether to attempt to do good of a kind which that high agent has left undone; that they must wait for the sanction of its great example; that till the 'shout of kings is among them' it were better not to march against the vandalism and the paganism which are, the while, quite at their ease, destroying the people?

But if this had always been the way in which private individuals, single or associated, had accounted of themselves and their possible exertions, in regard to great general improvements, but very few would ever have been accomplished. For the case has commonly been, that the schemes of such improvements have originated with persons not invested with political power; have been urged on by the accession and co-operation of such individuals; and at length slowly and reluctantly acceded to by the holders of the dominion over the community, the last to admit what may long have appeared to the majority of thinking men, no less than demonstrative evidence of the propriety and advantage of the reformation.

In all probability, the improvement of mankind is destined, under divine providence, to advance just in proportion as good men feel the responsibility for it resting on themselves, *as individuals*, and are actuated by a bold sentiment of independenee, (humble, at the same time, in reference to the necessity of a celestial agency,) in the prosecution of it. Each person who is standing still to look, with grief or indignation, at the evils which are overrunning the world, would do well to recollect what he may have read of some gallant partizan, who, perceiving where a prompt movement, with the force at his own command, would make an impression infallibly tending to the success of the warfare, could not endure to lose the time till some great sultan should find it convenient to come in slow march, and the pomp of state, to take on him the general direction of the compaign.

But happpily, such admonitions are becoming every day of more limited application; and we return with pleasure to the animating idea of that great revolution of which we were noting the introductory signs. It is a revolution in the manner of estimating the souls of the people, and consequently in the judgment of what should be done for their welfare. Through many ages, that immense multitude had been but obscurely presented to view in the character of rational improvable creatures. They were recognized but as one large mass, of equivocal moral substance, but faintly distinguishable into iudividuals; a breadth of insignificant sameness, undiscernible in marked features and aspects of mental character; existing, and to be left to exist, in their own manner; and that manner hardly worth concern or inquiry. Little consideration could there be of how much spiritual immortal essence might be going to waste, while this multitude was reduced to this kind of collective nothingness on the field of contemplation. But now it is as if a mist were rising and dispersing from that field, and leaving this mighty assemblage of spiritual beings exhihited to view in such a light from heaven as they were never beheld in before, except by the eyes of Apostles, and of a small number that in every age have resembled them.

It is true, this manifestation forms so melancholy a vision, that if we had only to behold it *as a spectacle*, we might well desire that the misty obscurity might descend upon it again, to shroud it from sight; while we should be left to indulge and elate our imaginations by dwelling on the pomps and splendours of the terrestrial scene,—the mighty empires, the heroes, the victories, the triumphs; the refinements and enjoyments of the most highly cultivated of the race; the brilliant performances of genius, and the astonishing reach of science. So the tempter would have beguiled our Lord into a complacent contemplation of the kingdoms and glories of the world. But he was come to look on a different aspect of it! Nor could he be withdrawn from the gloomy view of its degradation and misery. And a good reason why. For the sole object for which he had appeared in the only world where temptation could even in form approach him, was to begin in operation, and finish in virtue, a design for changing that state of degradation and misery. In the prosecution of such a design, and in the spirit of that divine benevolence in which it sprung, he could endure to fix on the melancholy and odious character of the scene, the contemplation which was vainly attempted to be diverted to any other of its aspects. What indeed, could sublunary pomps and glories be to him in any case; but emphatically what, when his object was to redeem the people from darkness and destruction?

Those who, actuated by a spirit in some remote resemblance to his, have entered deeply into the state of the people, such as it is found in our own nation, have often been appalled at the spectacle disclosed to them. They have been astonished to think what *can* have been the direction, while successive ages have passed away, of so many thousands of acute and vigilant mental eyes, that so dreadful a sight should scarcely have been descried. They have been aware in describing it as they actually saw it, they would be regarded by some as gloomy fanatics, tinctured with insanity by the influence of some austere creed ; and that others, of kinder nature, but whose sensibility has more of self-indulging refinement than tendency to active benevolence, wonld almost wish that so revolting an exhibition had never been made, though the fact be actually so. There may have been moments, when even they themselves have experienced a temporary recoil of their benevolent zeal, under the impression at once of the immensity of the evil and its grievously offensive quality. At times, the rudeness of the subjects, and perhaps the ungracious reception and thankless requital, of their philanthropic labours, aggravating the general feeling of the miserableness, (so to express it,) of seeing so much misery, have lent sednction to the temptations to ease and self-indulgence. Why should *they*, just they of all men, condemn themselves to dwell so much in the most dreary climate of the moral world, when they could perhaps have taken their almost constant abode in a little elysium of elegant knowledge, taste, and refined society ? Then was the time to revert to the example of him 'who, though he was rich, for our sakes became poor.'

Or, again, their thoughts may not unfrequently be turned on that view of things, which we have described as so habitual, and of such withering effect, with men who speculate on benevolence with but little of its spirit. They may have dwelt too long on the consideration, of how much the higher and more amply furnished powers leave such generous designs to proceed as they can, in the mere strength of private individual exertion. And they may have yielded to gloomy and repressive feelings after the fervour of indignant ones : for indignation, unless animated by a very sanctified principle, is very apt, when it cools, to become despondency. It is as if, (they have said,) armies and giants would stand aloof, to amuse themselves, while we are to be committed and abandoned in the ceaseless toil of a conflict, which these armies and giants have no business even to exist as such but for tbe very purpose of waging. We are, if we will,—and if we will we may let it alone—to try to effect in diminutive pieces, and detached local efforts, a little share of that, to which the greatest human force on earth might be applied to operate on system, and to the widest compass. —So they have said, perhaps, and been tempted to leave their object to its destiny.

But really it is now too late for this resentful and desponding abandonment. They cannot now retire in the tragical dignity of despair. It must be a matter more forlorn that would admit of their saying, as in parody or travesty of Cato, 'Witness heaven and earth, we have done our duty, but the stars and fate are against us ; and here it becomes us to terminate a strife, which would degenerate into the ridiculous if prosecuted against impossibilities. On the contrary, the zeal which could begin so onerous a work, and prosecute it thus far, could not now remit without betraying its past ardor to the condemnation and ridicule due to a fantastic caprice. Is it for the projectors of a noble edifice for public utility, to abandon the undertaking when it has risen from its foundation to be seen above the ground ; or is just come to be level with the surface of the waters, in defiance of which it has been commenced, and the violence of which it was designed to control, or the unfordable depths and streams of which it was to bear people over ? Let the promoters of education and Christian knowledge among the inferior classes, reflect what has already been accomplished ; regarding it, we once again repeat, as quite the incipient stage. It is most truly as yet the day of small things ; but let them recount the individuals whom, nevertheless, they have seen rescued from what had all the the signs of a destination to the lowest debasement, and utter ruin ; some of whom are returning animated thanks, and will do so in the hour of death, for what these, their best human friends, have been the means of imparting to them. Let them recollect of how many families they have seen the domestic condition pleasingly, and in some instances eminently and delightfully amended. And let them reflect how they have trampled down prejudices, greatly silenced a heathenish clamour, and provoked the imitative and rival efforts of many who, but for them, would have been most cordially willing for all such schemes to lie in abeyance to the end of time. Let them think of all this, and then go on and try, (we speak reverently,) what God and they can do, whether the authorities that govern the nations will or will not lend their powers vigorously in aid ; whether, when the the infinite importance of the concern is represented to them, they will hear, or whether they will forbear.

But let them never fear but the time will come, when the rulers and the ascendent classes in states will comprehend it to be their best policy to promote all possible improvement of the people. It will be given to them to understand, that the highest glory of those at the head of great communities, must consist in the eminence attained by those communities generally, in whatever it is that constitutes the most valuable and honorable superiority of one man or class over others. They will one day have learnt to esteem it a far nobler form of power to *lead* an immense combination of intelligent minds, than to command and coerce a great aggregation of brute force. They will come to feel, that it is better for them to have a people who can understand and rationally approve their purposes and measures, than one bent in stupid submission,—or rather one fermenting in ignorant disaffection, continually believing them to be wrong, and without sense enough to appreciate the arguments to prove them right. And a time will come, when it will not be left to the philanthropic speculatists alone, to make the comparative estimate between what has been effected by the enormously expensive apparatus of coercive and penal administration,—the prisons, prosecutions, transportations, and a vast military police,—and what *might* have been effected by one half of that expenditure devoted to popular reformation, to be accomplished by means of schools, and every practicable variety of methods for effecting, that men's understanding and conscience shall stand confronting them in the way, like the angel with the sword, when they are inclined or tempted to go wrong. All this will come to pass in due time. But meanwhile, let the promoters of a good cause act on the consideration, that no time is *theirs*, but the present.

SECTION V.

Moderate computations to be made for the effects of knowledge communicated: advantages actually gained : improvement in benevolent institutions : general considerations.

We have not come so near the end of our observations, without having been many times reminded, that there will be persons ready to impute sanguine extravagance to our expectations of the results, to follow from such means and exertions for improving the popular education as are already in progress ; we mean especially the schools which benevolence is multiplying over the land, the kind and measure of subsequent reading for which it is hoped not a few of their pupils will have acquired a taste, and the habit established of attendance on public Christian instruction. And what *is* it, then, how much is it, we ask, that the advocates of the system, profess to anticipate ? Are they heard maintaining that the communication of knowledge, or true notions of things, to youthful minds, will infallibly ensure their virtue and happiness? They are not quite so new to the world, to experimental labours in the business of tuition, or to self-observation. They have constantly within their view a mournful illustration of the quality of human nature, in the circumstance, of the great difference of assurance with which the effects may be predicted of ignorance on the one hand, and knowledge on the other. There is very nearly an absolute certainty of success in the method for making clowns, sots, vagabonds and ruffians. You may safely leave it to themselves to carry on the process for becoming complete. Let human creatures grow up without discipline, destitute therefore of salutary information, sound judgment, or any conscience but what will shape itself to whatever they like, and serve in the manner of some vile friar pander in the old plays,—and no one thinks of taking any credit for foresight in saying they will be a noxious burden on the earth; except indeed in those tracts of it where they seem to have their fair business, in being matched against the wolves and bears of the wildernes. When they infest what should be a civilized and Christianized part of the world, the philanthropist is sometimes put in doubt whether to repress, or indulge, the sentiment which tempts him to complacency in the operations of an epidemic which is thinning their members.

The consequences of ignorance are certain, unless almost a miracle interpose; but unhappily those of knowledge are of diffident and very restricted calculation. It is the testimony of all ages that men may see and even approve the better, and yet follow the worse. It is the hapless predicament of our nature, that the noblest of its powers, the understanding, has but imperfectly and precariously that commanding hold on the others, which is essential to the good order of the soul; as in a machine where the secondary wheels should be liable to be thrown by a slight movement out of the catch and grapple of the master one. Nay, worse than so, these moral powers, when detached from the control of the understanding, may have a powerful action of their own, from the impulse of another principle: indeed it is this impulse that causes the detachment from that control. It is really frightful to look at the evidence, from facts, that these active powers *may* grow strong in the depravity which will set the judgment at defiance, during the very time that the judgment is training, and not without success, to an ability to dictate to them what is right. We cannot pay any serious attention to the fancy of those, who will have it that when the passions and will go wrong, it *must* be because the understanding has not a just apprehension. This gross assumption, in what is purely a question of fact, is in flat contradiction to an infinity of evidence, of men deliberately and distinctly avowing their conviction of the evil quality, and fatal consequences, of courses which they are soon afterwards seen pursuing, and without the smallest pretence of a change of opinion; of men still avowing the same conviction, and sometimes in strong terms of self-reproach, in the checks and pauses of their career; and of men in the near prospect of death and judgment expressing, in bitter regret, the acknowledgment that they had persisted in acting wrong while they knew better. And this assumption so wilfully made against such evidence, is to be maintained for no better reason, that appears, than that human nature cannot, must not, shall not, be so absurd and depraved as to be capable of such madness. As if human nature were taking the smallest trouble to assume before them any equivocal appearance to cozen them into a favourable opinion; as if it suspended its determined propensities in complaisance to their denying that it has them. It has, and keeps, and shows its character, without the leave of those who would resolve its moral turpitude into error in its understanding. But for understanding—it should be time to take care of their own, when they find themselves asserting, in other words, that there is actually as much virtue in the world as there is knowledge of its principles. We should rather have surmised that, deplorably deficient as that knowledge is, the reduction of it all to practice would make a glorious change in England and Europe.

The persons, therefore, whose zeal is combined with knowledge in the prosecution of plans for the extension of education, proceed on a calculation of an effect more limited, in apparent proportion to the means, and less positively, (even in that more limited measure,) to be reckoned on in a given single instance, than they would have been justified in anticipating in many other departments of operation. They would, for example, predict with more confidence the results of an undertaking to cultivate any tract of waste land, or to reclaim a bog, or to render mechanical forces and contrivance available in a difficult untried mode of application, or, in many cases, the successful results of the application of the healing art to diseased body. They still remember what moral nature they are calculating on, and calculating *for good.* And in their more gloomy moments they perhaps fall into a comparison of *their* calculation on it for good, with that which an enemy of mankind might please himself in making on it for evil; both of them having respect to the same particular human beings, and both keeping in view this fact of the very imperfect command of the judgment over the active powers of the mind. In some such moments they would be glad of an exchange between their respective degrees of probability. That is to say, let a man, if such there be, who could be pleased with the depravity and misery of the race, a sagacious judge, too, of their moral constitution, and a veteran observer of their conduct,—let him look over a hundred children in one of the benevolent schools, and indulge himself in prognosticating, on the strength of the fact to which we have adverted, the proportion, in numbers and degree, in which these children will, in subsequent life, exemplify the *failure* of what is done for their wisdom and welfare,—there may be times, we say, when the friends of these institutions would be glad to transfer the portion in which, and the probability with which, he so prognosticates evil from the nature of the beings, to their own hopes of the good to be effected by discipline. In other words, there are times when they would say, 'evil be thou my good,' in the sense of wishing that the respective proportions of power, with which the agencies of good and evil are affecting the subjects in question, could be exchanged between them.

But we shall know where to stop in the course of observations of this darkening colour; and we shall take off the point of the derider's taunt, just forthcoming, that we are here unsaying, in effect, all that we have been so laboriously urging about the value and absolute necessity of knowledge to the people. It was proper to show, that the prosecutors of these designs are not suffering themselves to be beguiled out of a perception of what there is in the nature of their subjects of a tendency to frustate them, and of certain power to reduce their efficacy to a very partial measure of the effect desired. It was to be shown that they are not unknowing enthusiasts; but then, in keeping clear of the vain extravagancies of hope, they are not to surrender their confidence that something great and important can be done: it should be possible for a man to be sober, short of being dead. They are not to gravitate down into a state of feeling as if the understanding had been proved to have *no* sway upon the moral powers; as if, therefore, any presumption upon the relation between means and ends must in this great department of action be illusory. It might not, indeed, be amiss for them to be *told* that the case is so, by those who would desire, from whatever motive, to repress their efforts and defeat their designs; as so downright a blow at their favourite object would but serve to provoke them, to a determined exercise of thought to ascertain more definitely what there really is for them to form their schemes and calculations upon, and therefore to verify to themselves the reasons they have for persisting, in confidence that the labour will not be lost. And the instant they apply themselves, in this severe sobriety, to the estimates, they have the fact conspicuous before them, that there is at any rate such an efficacy in cultivation, that it is quite certain a well cultivated people *cannot* remain on the same degraded moral level as a neglected ignorant one,—or any where near it. None of those even that value such designs the least, ever pretend to foresee, after they shall have taken effect, an undiminished prevalence of rudeness and brutality of manners, of delight in spectacles and amusements of cruelty, of noisy revelry, of sottish intemperance, or of disregard of character. It is not pretended to be foreseen that the poorer classes will then continue to display so much of that heedless and almost desperate improvidence, respecting their temporal means and prospects, which has aggravated the calamities of the present times. It is not predicted that an universal school discipline will bring up several millions to the neglect, and many of them in the impudent contempt, of attendance on the ministrations of religion. The result will at all hazards, by every one's acknowledgment, be *the contrary of all this*.

But more specifically:—The promoters of the plans of popular education see a most important advantage gained in the very outset, and as perhaps the smallest matter in the account of emolument, in the obvious fact, that in their schools a very large portion of time is employed well, that otherwise would infallibly be employed ill. Let any one introduce himself into one of these places of assemblage, where there has been time to mature the arrangements into the most efficient system. He should not enter as an important personage, in patronizing and judicial state, to demand the respectful looks of the whole tribe from their attention to their printed rudiments and their slates; but glide in as a quiet observer, just to survey at his leisure the character and operations of the scene. Undoubtedly he will descry here and there the signs of inattention, weariness, or vacancy, not to say of perverseness. Even these individuals, however, are out of the way of practical harm; and at the same time he will see a multitude of youthful spirits acknowledging the duty of directing their best attention to something altogether foreign to their wild amusements; of making a protracted effort in one mode or another of the strange business of *thinking*. He will perceive in many the unequivocal indications of a real grave and earnest effort made to acquire, with the aid of visible signs and implements, a command of what is invisible and immaterial. They are thus treading in the precincts of an intellectual economy; the economy of thought and truth, in which they are to live for ever; and never, to eternity, will they have to regret *this* period and part of their employments. He will be delighted to think how many disciplined actions of the mind, how many just ideas, distinctly admitted, that were strangers at the beginning of the day's exercise, (and among these ideas some to remind them of God and their highest interest,) —there will have been by the time the busy and well ordered company breaks up in the evening, and leaves silence within these walls. He will not indeed grow romantic in hope; he knows too much of the nature to which these beings belong; knows therefore that the desired results of this discipline will but partially follow; but still rejoices to think that partial result, which will most certainly follow, will be worth incomparably more than all it will have cost.

Now let him, when he has contemplated this scene, consider how the greatest part of this numerous company *would* have been employed during the same hours, (whether of the sabbath or other days,) but for such a provision of means for their instruction. And, for the contrast, he has only to leave the school, and walk a mile round the neighbourhood, in which it will be very wonderful, (we may say this of most parts of England,) if he shall not, in a populous district and on a fine day, meet with a great number of wretched disgusting imps, straggling or in knots, in the activity of mischief and nuisance, or at least the full cry of vile and profane language; with here and there, as a lord among them, an elder larger one growing fast into an insolent blackguard. He may make the comparison, quite sure that such as they are, and so employed, would many now under the salutary discipline of yonder school have been, but for its institution. But the two classes, so beheld in contrast,—might they not seem to belong to two different nations? Do they not seem growing into two extremely different orders of character? Do they not even seem preparing for different worlds in the final distribution?

The friends of these designs for a general and highly improved education, may proceed farther in this course of verifying to themselves the grounds of their assurance of happy results. A number of ideas decidedly the most important that were ever formed in human thought, or imparted from the supreme mind, will be so taught in these institutions, that it is absolutely certain they will be fixed irrevocably and for ever in the minds of many of the pupils. It will be as impossible to erase these ideas from their memories as to extinguish the stars. And in the case of many, perhaps the majority, of these youthful beings, advancing into the temptations of life, these grand ideas, thus fixed deep in their souls, will distinctly present themselves to judgment and conscience an incalculable number of times. What a number, if the sum of all these reminiscences of these ideas, in all the minds now assembled in a numerous school, could be conjectured! But if one in a hundred of these recollections, if one in a thousand, shall have the efficacy that it ought to have, who can compute the amount of the good resulting from the tuition which shall have so enforced and fixed these ideas that they shall infallibly be thus recollected? And it is altogether out of reason to hope that the desired efficacy will, as often as once in a thousand times, attend the luminous rising again of a solemn idea to the view of the mind? Is still less than *this* to be hoped for our unhappy nature, and that too while a beneficent God has the superintendence of it?

The institutions themselves will gradually improve in both the manner and the compass of their discipline. They will acquire a more vigorous mechanism, (if we may so name it,) and a more decidedly intellectual character. In this latter respect, it is but comparatively of late years that schools for the inferior classes have ventured any thing beyond the humblest pretensions. Mental cultivation—intellectual and moral discipline—almost the word education itself—were terms of denomination which they were reverently cautious of taking in vain. They would have been regarded as of too ambitious an import, as seeming to betray somewhat of the impertinence of a *disposition*, (for the idea of the *practicability* of any such invasion would have been scorned,) to encroach on a ground exclusively appropriate to the superior orders. Schools for the poor were to be as little as possible scholastic. They were to have every possible assimilation to the workshop, excepting perhaps in one particular,—that of working hard: for the scholars were literally to throw time away rather than be occupied with any thing beyond the merest rudiments. Their advocates and petitioners for aid were to avow and plead how little it was that they pretended or presumed to teach. The argument in their behalf was either to begin or end with saying, that they *only* taught reading and writing; or if it could not be denied that there was to be some meddling with the first rules of arithmetic,—we may safely appeal to some of these pleaders whether they did not, twenty or thirty years since, bring out this addition with the management and hesitation of a confession and apology. It is a prominent characteristic of that happy revolution we have spoken of as in commencement, that this aristocratic notion of education is breaking up. The theory of the subject is loosening into enlargement; and no longer presumes, or will not much longer presume, to impose a niggardly restriction on the extent of what shall be sought to be accomplished in schools for the inferiors of the community.

As these institutions go on, augmenting in number and improving in organization, their pupils will bring their quality and efficacy to the proof, as they grow to maturity, and go forth to act their part in society. And there can be no doubt, that while too many of them may probably be mournful examples of the evil genius of the corrupt nature, and the infection of a bad world, prevailing against the better influences of instruction, and may descend toward the old wretched condition of the people, a very considerable proportion will take and permanently maintain a far higher ground. They will have become imbued with an element, which will have put them in strong repulsion to that coarse vulgar that will be sure to continue in existence, in this country, long enough to be a trial of the moral taste of this better cultivated race. It will be seen that they cannot associate with it by choice, and in the spirit of companionship. And while *they* are thus withheld on their part, from approximating, it may be hoped that the repelling principle will be converted into attraction in the case of a certain less ill affected portion of that vulgar. Its entire numbers cannot remain careless, contemptuous, or merely and malignantly envious, at sight of the advantages obtained, through the sole medium of personal improvement, by those who had otherwise been exactly on the same level as themselves. The effect on pride, in some, and on better propensities, it may be hoped, in others, will be to excite them to make their way upward to a community which, they will clearly see, could commit no greater folly than to come downward to them. And we will presume a friendly disposition in most of those who shall have been raised to this higher ground, to meet such aspirers and help them to ascend.

And while they will thus draw upward the less immovable and hopless part of the mass below them, they will themselves on the other hand be placed, by the respectability of their understanding and manners, within the influence of the higher cultivation of the classes above them; a great advantage, as we have taken occasion to notice in a former stage of these observations. —We must not, however, attribute high cultivation, as quite a thing of course in the classes above them, meaning by this designation the superiority in property and what is called condition in life. For in truth, too many of these more privileged persons may be observed to betray a disgraceful deficiency of what is indispensible in the mind in order to dignify their station. But here another important advantage is suggested as likely to accrue from the better education of the common people, namely, that their rising attainments would compel not a few of their superiors to betake themselves to mental improvement, in order to keep their desired distance. Would it not be a most excellent thing that they should find themselves thus incommodiously pressed upon by a new and strange circumstance in the creation, and forced to preserve that ascendency for which wealth and station would formerly suffice, at the coast, now, of a good deal more reading, thinking, and general self-discipline? Would it be a worthy sacrifice, that to spare some substantial agriculturists, idle gentlemen, and sporting or promenading ecclesiastics, such an afflictive necessity, the actual tillers of the ground, and the workers in manufacture and mechanics, should continue to be kept in stupid ignorance?

It is very possible this may excite a smile, as the threatening of a necessity or a danger of these privileged persons, which it is thought they may be comfortably assured is very remote. This danger,—that a good many of them, or rather of those who are coming in the course of nature to succeed them in the same rank, will find that its relative consequence cannot be sustained but at a very considerably higher pitch of mental qualification,—is threatened upon no stronger presages than the following:—Allow us first to take it for granted, that no very long course of years will have passed before the case comes to be, that a large proportion of the children of the lower classes are trained through a laborious discipline, during a series of years, in such schools as every thing possible is done to render efficient. Then, if we include in one computation all the time they will have spent in real mental exercise and acquirement there, and all those pieces and intervals of time which we may reasonably hope that many of them will employ to the same purpose in the subsequent years, a good proportion of them will have employed, by the time they reach middle age, many thousands of hours more than people in their condition have heretofore done, in a way the most directly tending to the improvement of their minds. And how must we be estimating the natural capacities of these inferior classes, or the perceptions of the higher, not to foresee as a consequence, that these latter will find their relative situation greatly altered, with respect to the measure of knowledge and mental power requisite as one most essential constituent of their superiority, in order to command the unfeigned deference of their inferiors?

Our strenuous promoters of the schemes for cultivating the minds of all the people, are not afraid of professing to foresee, that when schools, of that completely disciplinarian organization which they will gradually attain, shall have become general, and shall be vigourously seconded by all those auxiliary expedients for popular instruction which are also in progress, a very pleasing modification will become apparent in the character, the moral colour, if we might so express it, of the people's ordinary employment. The young persons so instructed, being appointed, for the most part, to the same occupations to which they would have been destined had they grown up in utter ignorance and vulgarity, are expected to give striking evidence that the meanness, the debasement almost, which had characterized many of those occupations, in the view of the more refined classes, was in truth the debasement of the men rather than of the callings; which, it is anticipated, will change to an appearance of much more respectability, as associated with the sense, decorum, and self-respect of the performers, than they had borne when blended and polluted with all the low habits, manners, and language, of ignorance and vulgar grossness. And then for the degree of excellence in the performance—who will be the persons most likely to excel, in the many branches of workmanship and business which admit of being better done in proportion to the degree of intelligence directed upon them? And again, who will be most in requisition for those offices of management and superintendence, where something must be confided to judgment and discretion, and where the value is felt, (often grievously felt from the want,) of some power of combination and foresight?

Such as these are among the subordinate benefits reasonably, we might say infallibly, calculated upon. Our philanthropists are confident in foreseeing also, that very many of these better disciplined young persons will be valuable co-operators against that ignorance from which themselves have been so happily saved; will exert an influence, by their example and the steady avowal of their opinions, against the vice and folly in their vicinity; and will be useful advisers of their neighbours in their perplexities, and sometimes moderators in their discords. It is predicted, with a confidence so much resting on general grounds of probability, as hardly to need the instances already afforded in various parts of the country to confirm it, that here and there one of the well instructed humbler class will become an able and useful public teacher of the most important truth. It is, in short, anticipated with delightful assurance, that great numbers of those who will go forth from under the friendly guardianship which is now preparing to take the charge of their youthful minds, will be examples, through life and at its conclusion, of the power and felicity of religion.

Here we can suppose it not improbable that some one may, in pointed terms, put the question—Do you then, at last, mean to affirm that you can, by the course of discipline spoken of, absolutely secure that effectual operation and ascendency of religion in the mind, which shall place it in the right condition toward God, and in a state of fitness for passing, without fear or danger, into the scenes of its future endless existence?

Certainly we should think, there might have been many expressions and sentiments in the preceding train of observations, of a nature to preclude any such question; but let it be asked, since there can be no difficulty to reply. We do *not* affirm that any form of discipline, the wisest and best in the power of the wisest and best men to apply, is competent of itself thus to subject the mind to the power of religion. On the contrary, we believe that grand effect can be accomplished only by a special influence of the divine being, operating by the means of such a discipline, or, if he pleases, without. But next we have to say, that it is perfectly certain, notwithstanding, that the application of these human means will, in a multitude of instances, be efficacious to that sublime effect.

This certainty arises from a few very plain general considerations. The first is, that the whole system of means appointed by the almighty to be employed as a human process for presenting religion solemnly in view before men's minds, and enforcing it upon them, is an appointment *expressly intended* for working that great effect which secures their endless felicity, though to what extent in point of number, is altogether unknown to the subordinate agents. With some awful exceptions of obdurate malignant infidelity, (as in the case of the Jews in the time of our Lord,) in which it was plainly signified that the manifestation and enforcement of divine truth would not, and should not have this blessed effect—with these exceptions, the whole order of expedients in this great course of operation is most formally represented, by him that has commanded their employment, as to be employed in a confident expectation of attaining, in a proportion to be determined by himself, the great end to which these expedients are avowedly directed. The appointment is most evidently not one of mere exercise for the faculties and submissive obedience of those who are summoned to be active in its execution.

Accordingly, there are in the divine revelation very many explicit and animating assurances, that their exertion shall certainly be in a measure successful, in the highest sense of the word. And if these assurances are made in favour of the exertions for inculcating religion, generally, that is on men of all conditions and ages, they may be assumed with a still stronger confidence in favour of those for impressing it on young minds, before they can be pre-occupied and hardened by the depravities of the world. But besides, there are some of these expressions of promised success given in special favour of this one part of the application of the great general process; affording rays of hope which have in ten thousand instances animated the diligence of pious parents, and the other benevolent instructors of children.

There is also palpable and striking matter of fact, to confirm the certainty, that an education in which religious instruction shall be mingled in the mental discipline, will be rendered, in many instances, efficacious to the formation of a religious character. This obvious fact is, that a much greater proportion of the persons so educated do actually become the subjects of religion, than of a similar number of those brought up in ignorance and profligacy. Take collectively any number of families in which such an education prevails, and the same number in which it does not, and follow the young persons respectively into subsequent life. But any one who hears the suggestion, feels there is no need to wait the lapse of time and follow their actual course. As instructed by what he has already seen in society, he can go forward with them prophetically, with an absolute certainty that a much greater proportion of the one tribe, than of the other, will become persons not only of moral respectability, but of decided religion. Here then is practical evidence, that while discipline must disclaim any absolute power to produce this effect, there is, nevertheless, such a constitution of things that it infallibly will, as an instrumental cause, in many instances produce it.

The state of the matter, then, is very simple. The supreme cause of men's being 'made wise to salvation,' in appointing a system of means, to be put by human activity in operation toward this effect, has connected certainly and inseparably with that system, some portion of the accomplishment of this sovereign good which would not take place in the absence of such application of means:—only he has placed this certainty in the system of operation *as taken generally and comprehensively;* leaving, as to human foresight, an *uncertainty* with respect to the particular instances in which the desired success shall be attained. His subordinate agents are to proceed on this positive assurance that the success *shall be somewhere,* though they cannot know that it will be in this one case, or in the other. 'In the morning sow thy seed, and in the evening withhold not thy hand; for thou knowest not whether shall prosper, this, or that.' If they rate the value of their agency so high, as to hold it incompatible with their dignity that any part of their labours should be performed under the condition of possibly being unsuccessful, they may be assured that such is not exactly the estimate in which they stand in the judgment of him to whom they look for the acceptance of their services, and for the reward.

But it may be added, that the great majority of those who are intent on the schemes for enlightening and reforming mankind, are entertaining a confident hope of the approach of a period when the success will be far greater in proportion to the measure of exertion, in every department of the system of instrumentality for that grand object. We cherish this confidence, not on the strength of any pretension to be able to resolve prophetic emblems and numbers into precise dates and events of the present and approaching times. We rest it on a much more general mode of combining the very extraordinary indications of the period we live in, with the substantial purport of the divine predictions. There unquestionably gleams forth, through the plainer lines and through the mystical imagery of prophecy, the vision of a better age, in which the application of the truths of religion to men's minds will be irresistible. And what should more naturally be interpreted as one of the dawning signs of its approach, than a sudden wide movement at once to clear their intellects and bring the heavenly light to shine close upon them; accompanied by a prodigious breaking up in the old system of the world, which hardly recognized in the inferior millions the very existence of souls to need such an illumination?

The labourers in the institutions for instructing the young descendants of those millions, may often regret to perceive how little the process is as yet informed with the energy which is thus to pervade the world. But let them regard as one great undivided economy and train of operation, these initiatory efforts and all that is to follow, till that time 'when all shall know the Lord;' and take by anticipation, as in fraternity with the happier future labourers, their just share of that ultimate triumph. Those active spirits, in the happier stages, will look back with this sentiment of kindred and complacency to those who sustained the earlier toils of the good cause, and did not suffer their zeal to languish under the comparative smallness of their success.

SECTION VI.

Concluding remarks.

We shall conclude with a few sentence in the way of reply to another question, which we can surmise there may be persons ready to ask, after this long iteration of the assertion of the necessity of knowledge to the common people. The question would be to this effect: What do you, all this while mean to assign as the *measure* of knowledge proper for the people to be put in possession of?—for you do not specify the kinds, nor limit the extent: you talk in vague general terms of mental improvement; you leave the whole matter indefinite and for all that appears, the people are never to know when they know enough.

We answer, that we *do* leave the extent undefined, and should request to be informed where, and why, the line of circumscription and exclusion should be drawn.

We could wish, in the first place, to be certified, whether it is to be considered as yet at all a settled point, in what the value and importance of the human nature does really consist. It is indeed quite an uniformly assumed thing in the language of both divines and philosophers, that the worth, the dignity, the importance, of man, are in his rational immortal nature; and that therefore the best condition of *that* is his true felicity and glory, and the object chiefly to be aimed at in all that is done by him, and for him, on earth. But whether this should be regarded as any thing more than the elated faith of ascetics, or a fine dogma of academic speculation? For we often see, and it is very striking to see, how principles which pass for infallible truth within the province of thinking and doctrine, and are directly applicable, with most emphatic importance, to great practical interests may be disowned and repelled, as perfectly foreign, intrusive, and visionary, when they come demanding to have their appropriate place and power in the actual state of things. But is it really admitted, as the great practical principle, that the mind the intelligent imperishable existence, is the supremely valuable thing in man? Is it then admitted, inevitably, that the discipline, the correction, the improvement, the maturation, of this spiritual being, to the highest attainable degree, is the great object to be desired by men, for themselves, and one another. That is to say, that knowledge, cultivation, salutary exercise, wisdom, all that can conduce to the perfection of the mind, form the state in which it is due to man's nature that he should be endeavoured to be placed. But then, this is due to his nature by an absolutely *general* law. He cannot be so circumstanced in the order of society that this shall *not* be due to it. No situation in which the arrangements of the world, or say of Providence, may place him, can constitute him a specific kind of creature, to which is no longer fit and necessary that which is necessary to the well-being of man considered generally, as a spiritual immortal nature. The essential law of this nature cannot be abrogated by men's being placed in humble and narrow circumstances, in which a very large portion of their time and exertions are required for mere subsistence. This accident of a confined situation is no more a reason why their minds should not require the best possible cultivation than would be the circumstance that the body in which a man's mind is lodged, happens to be of smaller dimensions than those of other mind.

That under the disadvantages of this humble situation they *cannot* acquire all the mental improvement, desirable for the perfection of their intelligent nature,—that the situation renders it impracticable,—is quite another matter. So far as this inhibition is real and absolute, it must be submitted to as one of the infelicities of their lot. What we are insisting on is, that by the law of their nature there is to them the same general necessity as to any other human beings, of that which is essential to the well-being of the mind; and that therefore they should be advanced in this improvement *as far as they can.* A greater degree of this advancement will conduce more to their welfare than a less.

This might be confirmed by easy and obvious illustration. A poor man, cultivated in a small degree, has acquired a few just ideas of an important subject, which lies out of the scope of his daily employments for subsistence. Be that subject what it may, if those ideas are of any use to him, by what principle would one idea more, or two, or twenty, be of *no* use to him? Of no use, when all the thinking world knows, that every additional clear idea of a subject is valuable by a ratio of progress much greater than that of the mere numerical increase, and that by a large addition of ideas a man trebles the value of those with which he began. He has read a small meagre tract on the subject, or perhaps only an article in a magazine, or an essay in the literary column of a provincial newspaper. Where would be the harm, on supposition he can fairly afford the time, in consequence of husbanding it for this very purpose, of his reading a well written concise book, which would give him a clear comprehensive view of the subject?

But perhaps another branch of the tree of knowledge bends its fruit temptingly to his hand. And if he should indulge, and gain a tolerably clear notion of one more interesting subject, (still punctually regardful of the duties of his ordinary vocation,) where, we say again, is the harm? Converse with him; observe his conduct; compare him with a wretched clown in a neighbouring dwelling; and say that he is the worse for having thus much of the provision for a mental subsistence. But if thus much has contributed greatly to his advantage, why should he be interdicted still farther attainments? Are you alarmed for him, if he will needs go the length of acquiring some knowledge of geography, the solar system, and the history of his own country and of the ancient world?* Let him proceed; supply him gratuitously with some of the best books on these subjects; and if you shall converse with him again, after another year or two of his progress, and compare him once more with the ignorant, stunted, cankered beings in his vicinity, you will see whether there be any thing essentially at variance, between his narrow circumstances in life and his mental enlargement.

You are willing, perhaps, that he *should* acquire some knowledge of ancient times, and can trust him with Goldsmith's histories of Greece and Rome; But if he should then by some means find his way into such a work as that of Rollin, or betray that he covets an acquaintance with those of Gillies, or even Mitford,—it is all over with him for being an useful member of society

* These denominations of knowledge, so strange as they will to some persons appear, in such a connexion, we have ventured to write from observing, that they stand in the schemes of elementary instruction in the missionary schools for the children of the natives of Bengal. But of course we are to acknowledge, that the vigorous high-toned spirits of those Asiatic idolaters, are adapted to receive a much superior style of cultivation to any of which the feeble progeny of England can be supposed to be capable.

in his humble situation. You would consent to his reading a slender abridgment of voyages and travels; but what *is* to become of him if nothing less will content him than the whole length story of Captain Cook? He will direct, it is to be hoped, some of his best attention to the supreme subject of religion. And you would quite approve of his reading some useful tracts, some manuals of piety, some commentary on a catechism, some volume of serious plain discourses; but he is absolutely undone if his ambition should rise at length to Stillingfleet, or Howe, or Jeremy Taylor. And yet all this while we can believe that he acquits himself with exemplary regularity and industry in his allotted labours; and that even in this very capacity he is preferred by the men of business to the illiterate tools in his neighbourhood; nay, most likely preferred, in the more technical sense of the word, to the honourable, but often sufficiently vexatious office, of directing and superintending the operations of those tools.

And where, now, is the evil he is incurring, or causing, during this progress of violating, step after step, the circumscription by which the aristocratic compasses were again and again, with reluctant extension to successive greater distances, defining the scope of the knowledge proper for a man of his condition? It is a bad thing, is it, that he has a great variety of ideas to relieve the tædium incident to the sameness of his course of life; that, with many things which had else been bare unmeaning facts and objects, he has many interesting associations, like woodbines and roses wreathing round the stumps of trees; that the world is a translated and intelligible volume before his eyes; that he has a power of applying himself to *think* of what becomes at any time necessary for him to understand. Is it a judgment upon him for his temerity, that he has so much to impart to his children as they are growing up, and that if some of them are already come to maturity, they know not where to find a man to respect more than their father? Or if he takes a part in the converse and devotional exercises of religious society, is no one there the better for the clearness and plenitude of his thoughts and the propriety of his expression? But there would be no end of the preposterous suppositions fairly attachable to the notion, that the mental improvement of the common people has some proper limit of arbitrary prescription, on the ground simply of their *being* the common people, and quite distinct from the restriction which their circumstances may invincibly impose on their ability.

Taken in this latter view, we acknowledge that their condition would be a subject for most melancholy contemplation, if we did not hope for better times. The benevolent reflector when sometimes led to survey in thought the endless myriads of beings with minds within the circuit of a country like this, will have a momentary vision of them as they would be if all improved to the highest mental condition to which it is *naturally possible* for them to be exalted; a magnificent spectacle but it instantly fades and vanishes. And the sense is so powerfully upon him of the unchangeable economy of the world, which even if the fairest fondest visions of the millennium itself were realized, would still render such a thing *actually* impossible, that he hardly regrets the bright scene was but a beautiful cloud, and melts away. His imagination then descends to view this immense tribe of rational beings in another, and comparatively moderate state of the improvement of their faculties, a state not one third part so lofty as that in which he had beheld all the individuals improved to the highest degree of which each is naturally capable; and he thinks, that the condition of man's abode on earth *might* admit of their being raised to *this* elevation. But he soon sees, that till a mighty change shall take place in the system according to which the nations are managing their affairs, this too is impossible; and with regret he sees even this inferior ideal spectacle pass away, to rest on an age in distant prospect. At last he takes his imaginary stand on what he feels to be a very low level of the supposed improvement of the general popular mind; and he says, Thus much, at the least, should be a possibility allowed by the circumstances of the people under *any* tolerable order of the disposition of national interests;—and then he turns to look down upon an actual condition in which care, and toil, and distress, render it utterly impossible for a great proportion of the people to reach, or even approach, this his last and lowest conception of what the state of their minds ought to be.

In spite of all the optimists, it is a grievous reflection, after the race has had so many thousands of years on earth to improve its condition, that all the experience, the philosophy, the science, the art, the power acquired by mind over matter—that all the contributions of all departed and all present spirits and bodies, yes, and all religion too, should have come but to this;—to this, that in what is esteemed the most favoured and improved nation of all terrestrial space and time, a vast proportion of the people are absolutely found in a condition which confines them, with all the rigor of necessity, to the veriest childhood of intelligent existence, without its innocence.

But at the very same time, and while compassion is rising at such a view, there comes in on the other hand, the reflection, that even in the actual state of things, there are a considerable number of the people who *might* acquire a valuable share of improvement which they do not. Great numbers of them grown up, waste by choice, and multitudes of children waste through utter neglect, a large quantity of precious time, which their narrow circumstances still leave free from the iron dominion of necessity. And they will waste it, it is certain that they will, till education shall have become general, and much more vigorous in discipline. If through a miracle there were to come down on this country, with a sudden delightful affluence of temporal amelioration, resembling the vernal transformation from the dreariness of winter, an universal prosperity so that all should be placed in ease and plenty, it would require another miracle to prevent this benignity of heaven from turning to a dreadful mischief. What would the great tribe of the uneducated people do with the half of their time, which we may suppose that such a state would give to their voluntary disposal? Every one can answer infalliby, that the far greater number of them would consume it in idleness, vanity, or abomination. Educate them, then, educate them;—or, in all circumstances and events, calamitous or prosperous, they are still a race made in vain!

In quitting the subject, we wish to express, in strong terms, the applause and felicitations due to those excellent individuals, found here and there, who in very humble circumstances, and perhaps with very little advantage of education in their youth, have been excited to a strenuous continued exertion for the improvement of their minds, by which they have made, (the unfavourable situation considered,) admirable attainments, which are now passing with inestimable worth into the instruction of their families, and a variety of usefulness within their sphere. They have nobly struggled with their threatened destiny, and have overcome it. When they think, with regret, how confined, after all, is their portion of knowledge, as compared with the rich possessions of those, who have had from their infancy all facilities and the amplest time for its acquirement, let them be consoled by reflecting, that the value of mental progress is not to be measured solely by the quantity of knowledge possessed, but partly, and indeed still more, by the corrective invigorating effect produced on the mental powers by the resolute exertions made in attaining it. And therefore, since, under their great disadvantages, it has required a much greater degree of this resolute exertion in them to force their way victoriously out of ignorance, than it has required in those who have had every thing in their favour, to make a long free career over the field of knowledge, they may be assured they have obtained a greater benefit in *proportion* to the measure of what they have attained to know. This persistence of a determined will to do what has been so difficult to be done, has infused a peculiar energy into the exercise of their powers; a valuable point of compensation, to be set against the circumstance, that they have not equally with the ampler possessors of knowledge, the advantage of illustrating and perfecting one principle of it by the accession of many others Let them persevere in this worthy self-discipline, appropriate to the introduction of an endless mental life. Let them go on from strength to strength;—but solemnly taking care, that all their improvements may tend to such a result, that at length the rigor of their lot and the confinement of mortality itself bursting at once from around them, may give them to those intellectual revelations, that everlasting sun-light of the soul, in which the truly wise will expand all their faculties in a happier economy.

END OF THE ESSAYS.

CONTENTS OF FOSTER'S ESSAYS.

THE

PHILOSOPHY

OF

SLEEP.

BY

ROBERT MACNISH,

AUTHOR OF "THE ANATOMY OF DRUNKENNESS," AND MEMBER OF THE FACULTY OF PHYSICIANS AND SURGEONS OF GLASGOW.

HARTFORD:
PUBLISHED BY SILAS ANDRUS & SON.
1850.

PREFACE TO THE SECOND EDITION

The present edition of THE PHILOSOPHY OF SLEEP is so different from its predecessor, that it may almost be regarded as a new treatise. The work has been, in a great measure, re-written, the arrangement altered, and a great accession made to the number of facts and cases: the latter, many of which are now published for the first time, will, I hope, add much to its value. Some of them have occurred in my own practice; and for others, I am indebted to the kindness of several ingenious friends. Notwithstanding every care, the work is far from being what it ought to be, and what I could have wished; but, imperfect as it is, it may, perhaps, stimulate some other inquirer to investigate the subject more deeply, and thus give rise to an abler disquisition. So far as I know, this is the only treatise in which an attempt is made to give a complete account of Sleep. The subject is not an easy one; and, in the present state of our knowledge, moderate success is probably all that can be looked for.

In the first edition Dr Gall's theory, that the brain is composed of a plurality of organs, each organ being the seat of a particular mental faculty, was had recourse to for the purpose of explaining the different phenomena of Sleep; in the present edition, this doctrine is more prominently brought forward. The great objection to the prevailing metaphysical systems is, that none of their positions can be proved; and that scarcely two writers, agree upon any particular point. The disciples of Gall, on the one hand, assume that his system, having ascertainable facts to illustrate it, is at all times susceptible of demonstration—that nothing is taken for granted; and that the inquirer has only to make an appeal to nature to ascertain its fallacy or its truth. The science is entirely one of observation: by that it must stand or fall, and by that alone ought it to be tested. The phrenological system appears to me the only one capable of affording a rational and easy explanation of all the phenomena of mind. It is impossible to account for dreaming, idiocy, spectral illusions, monomania, and partial genius in any other way. For these reasons, and for the much stronger one, that having studied the science for several years with a mind rather hostile than otherwise to its doctrines, and found that nature invariably vindicated their truth, I could come to no other conclusion than that of adopting them as a matter of belief, and employing them for the explanation of phenomena which they alone seem calculated to elucidate satisfactorily. The system of Gall is gaining ground rapidly among scientific men, both in Europe and America. Some of the ablest physiologists in both quarters of the globe have admitted its accordance with nature; and, at this moment, it boasts a greater number of proselytes than at any previous period of its career. The prejudices still existing against it, result from ignorance of its real character. As people get better acquainted with the science, and the formidable evidence by which it is supported, they will think differently.

Many persons who deny the possibility of estimating individual character, with any thing like accuracy, by the shape of the head, admit the great phrenological principle that the brain is composed of a plurality of organs. To them, as well as to those who go a step farther, the doctrine laid down in the present work will appear satisfactory. An admission that the brain is the material apparatus by which the mind manifests itself, and that each mental faculty is displayed through the medium of a particular part of the brain, is all that is demanded in considering the philosophy of the science. These points are only to be ascertained by an appeal to nature. No man can wisely reject phrenology without making such an appeal.

THE

PHILOSOPHY OF SLEEP.

CHAP. I.

INTRODUCTION.

Sleep is the intermediate state between wakefulness and death: wakefulness being regarded as the active state of all the animal and intellectual functions, and death as that of their total suspension.

Sleep exists in two states; in the complete and the incomplete. The former is characterized by a torpor of the various organs which compose the brain, and by that of the external senses and voluntary motion. Incomplete sleep, or dreaming, is the active state of one or more of the cerebral organs while the remainder are in repose: the senses and the volition being either suspended or in action according to the circumstances of the case. Complete sleep is a temporary metaphysical death, though not an organic one—the heart and lungs performing their offices with their accustomed regularity under the control of the involuntary muscles.

Sleep is variously modified, as we shall fully explain hereafter, by health and disease. The sleep of health is full of tranquillity. In such a state we remain for hours at a time in unbroken repose, nature banqueting on its sweets, renewing its lost energies, and laying in a fresh store for the succeeding day. This accomplished, slumber vanishes like a vapour before the rising sun; languor has been succeeded by strength; and all the faculties, mental and corporeal, are recruited. In this delightful state, man assimilates most with that in which Adam sprang from his Creator's hands, fresh, buoyant, and vigourous; rejoicing as a racer to run his course, with all his appetencies of enjoyment on edge, and all his feelings and faculties prepared for exertion.

Reverse the picture, and we have the sleep of disease. It is short, feverish, and unrefreshing, disturbed by frightful or melancholy dreams. The pulse is agitated, and, from nervous excitation, there are frequent startings and twitchings of the muscles. Nightmare presses like an incarnation of misery upon the frame—imagination, distempered by its connexion with physical disorder, ranging along the gloomy confines of terror, holding communication with hell and the grave, and throwing a discolouring shade over human life.

Night is the time for sleep; and assuredly the hush of darkness as naturally courts to repose as meridian splendour flashes on us the necessity of our being up at our labour. In fact, there exists a strange, but certain sympathy between the periods of day and night, and the performance of particular functions during these periods. That this is not the mere effect of custom, might be readily demonstrated. All nature awakes with the rising sun. The birds begin to sing; the bees to fly about with murmurous delight. The flowers which shut under the embrace of darkness, unfold themselves to the light. The cattle arise to crop the dewy herbage; and 'man goeth forth to his labour until the evening.' At close of day, the reverse of all this activity and motion is observed. The songs of the woodland choir, one after another, become hushed, till at length twilight is left to silence, with her own star and her falling dews. Action is succeeded by listlessness, energy by languor, the desire of exertion by the inclination for repose. Sleep, which shuns the light, embraces darkness, and they lie down together under the sceptre of midnight.

From the position of man in society, toil or employment of some kind or other is an almost necessary concomitant of his nature—being essential to healthy sleep, and consequently to the renovation of our bodily organs and mental faculties. But as no general rule can be laid down as to the quality and quantity of labour best adapted to particular temperaments, so neither can it be positively said how many hours of sleep are necessary for the animal frame. When the body is in a state of increase, as in the advance from infancy to boyhood, so much sleep is required, that the greater portion of existence may be fairly stated to be absorbed in this way. It is not mere repose from action that is capable of recruiting the wasted powers, or restoring the nervous energy. Along with this is required that oblivion of feeling and imagination which is essential to, and which in a great measure constitutes, sleep. But if in mature years the body is adding to its bulk by the accumulation of adipose matter, a greater tendency to somnolency occurs than when the powers of the absorbents and exhalents are so balanced as to prevent such accession of bulk. It is during the complete equipoise of these animal functions that health is enjoyed in greatest perfection; for such a state presupposes exercise, temperance, and the tone of the stomach quite equal to the process of digestion.

Sleep and stupor have been frequently treated of by physiological writers as if the two states were synonymous. This is not the case. In both there is insensibility; but it is easy to awake the person from sleep, and difficult, if not impossible, to arouse him from stupor. The former is a necessary law of the animal economy; the latter is the result of diseased action.

Birth and death are the Alpha and Omega of existence; and life, to use the language of Shakspeare, 'is rounded by a sleep.'

When we contemplate the human frame in a state of vigour, an impression is made on the mind that it is calculated to last forever. One set of organs is laying down particles and another taking them up, with such exquisite nicety, that for the continual momentary waste there is continual momentary repair; and this is capable of going on with the strictest equality for a half a century.

What is life? Those bodies are called living in which an appropriation of foreign matter is going on; death is where this process is at an end. When we find blood in motion, the process of appropriation is going on. The circulation is the surest sign of life. Muscles retain irritability for an hour or two after circulation ceases, but irritability is not life. Death is owing to the absence of this process of appropriation.

Bichat has divided life into two varieties, the *organic* and the *animal*. The first is common to both vegetables and animals, the last is peculiar to animals alone. Organic life applies to the functions which nourish and sustain the object—animal life to those which make it a sentient being; which give it thought, feeling, and motion, and bring it into communication with the surrounding world. The processes of assimilation and excretion exist both in animals and vegetables: the other vital processes are restricted solely to animals. The digestive organs, the kidneys, the heart, and the lungs, are the apparatus which carry into effect the organic life of animals. Those which manifest animal life are the brain, the organs of the senses, and the voluntary powers. Sleep is the suspension of animal life; and during its continuance the creature is under the influence of organic life alone.

Notwithstanding the renovating influence of sleep, which apparently brings up the lost vigour of the frame to a particular standard, there is a power in animal life which leads it almost imperceptibly on from infancy to second childhood, or that of old age. This power, sleep, however, healthy, is incapable of counteracting. The skin wrinkles, and everywhere shows marks of the ploughshare of Saturn; the adipose structure dissolves; the bones become brittle; the teeth decay or drop out; the eye loses its exquisite sensibility to sight; the ear to sound; and the hair is bleached to whiteness. These are accompanied with a general decay of the intellectual faculties; there is a loss of memory, and less sensibility to emotion; the iris hues of fancy subside to twilight; and the sphere of thought and action is narrowed. The principle of decay is implanted in our nature, and cannot be counteracted. Few people, however, die of mere decay, for death is generally accelerated by disease. From sleep we awake to exertion—from death not at all, at least on this side of time. Methuselah in ancient, and Thomas Parr in modern times, ate well, digested well, and slept well; but at length they each died. Death is omnivorous. The worm which crawls on the highway and the monarch on his couch of state, are alike subjected to the same stern and inexorable law; they alike become the victims of the universal tyrant.

CHAPTER II.

SLEEP IN GENERAL.

Every animal passes some portion of its time in sleep. This is a rule to which there is no exception; although the kind of slumber and the degree of profoundness in which it exists in the different classes are extremely various. Some physiologists lay it down as a general rule, that the larger the brain of an animal the greater is the necessity for a considerable proportion of sleep. This, however, I suspect is not borne out by facts. Man, for instance, and some birds, such as the sparrow, have the largest brains in proportion to their size, and yet it is probable that they do not sleep so much as some other animals with much smaller brains. The serpent tribe, unless when stimulated by hunger, (in which case they will remain awake for days at a time waiting for their prey,) sleep much more than men or birds, and yet their brain are proportionally greatly inferior in size: the boa, after dining on a stag or goat, will continue in profound sleep for several days. Fishes,* indeed, whose brains are small, require little sleep; but the same remark applies to birds,† which have large brains, and whose slumber is neither profound nor of long continuance. The assertion, therefore, that the quantum of sleep has any reference to the size of the brain may be safely looked upon as unfounded. That it has reference to the quality of the brain is more likely, for we find that carnivorous animals sleep more than such as are herbivorous; and it is probable that the texture, as well as form, of the brains of these two classes is materially different. This remark, with regard to the causes of the various proportions of sleep required by the carnivorous and herbivorous tribes, I throw out not as as a matter of certainty, but merely as surmise which seems to have considerable foundation in truth.

In proportion as man exceeds all other animals in the excellency of his physical organization, and an intellectual capability, we shall find that in him the various phenomena of sleep are exhibited in greater regularity and perfection. Sleep seems more indispensably requisite to man than to any other creature, if there can be supposed to exist any difference where its indispensability is universal, and where every animal must, in some degree or other, partake of it; but, as regards, man, it is certain that he sustains any violation of the law ordaining regular periods of repose with less indifference than the lower grades of creation—that a certain proportion of sleep is more essential to his existence than theirs—that he has less power of enduring protracted wakefulness, or continuing in protracted sleep—and that he is more refreshed by repose and more exhausted by the want of it than they. The sleep of man, therefore, becomes a subject of deeper interest and curiosity than that of any other animal, both on account of the more diversified manner in which it displays itself, and the superior opportunity which exists of ascertaining the various phenomena which in the inferior animals can only be conjectured or darkly guessed at.

Sleep, being a natural process, takes place in general without any very apparent cause. It becomes, as it were, a habit, into which we insensibly fall at stated periods, as we fall into other natural or acquired habits. But it differs from the latter in this, that it cannot in any case be entirely dispensed with, although by custom we may bring ourselves to do with a much smaller portion than we are usually in the practice of indulging in. In this respect it bears a strong analogy to the appetite for food or drink. It has a natural tendency to recur every twenty-four hours, and the periods of its accession coincide with the return of night.

But though sleep becomes a habit into which we would naturally drop without any obvious, or very easily discovered cause, still we can often trace the origin of our slumbers; and we are all acquainted with many circumstances which either produce or heighten them. I shall mention a few of these causes.

Heat has a strong tendency to produce sleep. We often witness this in the summer season; sometimes in the open air, but more frequently at home, and above all in a crowded meeting. In the latter case the soporific tendency is greatly increased by the impurity of the air. A vitiated atmosphere is strongly narcotic, and when combined with heat and monotony, is apt to induce slumber, not less remarkable for the rapidity of its accession than its overpowering character. In such a situation, the mind in a few minutes ceases to act, and sinks into a state of overpowering oblivion. The slumber, however, not being a natural one, and seldom occurring at the usual period, is generally short: it rarely exceeds an hour; and when the person awakes from it, so far from being refreshed, he is unusually dull, thirsty, and feverish, and finds more than com

* As a proof that fishes sleep, Aristotle, who seems to have paid more attention to their habits than any modern author, states, that while in this condition they remain motionless, with the exception of a gentle movement of the tail—that they may then be readily taken by the hand, and that, if suddenly touched, they instantly start. The tunny, he adds, are surprised and surrounded by nets while asleep, which is known by their showing the white of their eyes.

† The sleep of some birds is amazingly light. Such is the case with the goose which is disturbed by the slightest noise, and more useful than any watch-dog for giving warning of danger. It was the cackling of the sacred geese that saved the capitol of Rome from the soldiers of Brennus, when the watch-dogs failed to discover the approach of an enemy.

mon difficulty in getting his mental powers into their usual state of activity.

A heated church and a dull sermon are almost sure to provoke sleep. There are few men whose powers are equal to the task of opposing the joint operation of two such potent influences. They act on the spirit like narcotics, and the person seems as if involved in a cloud of anconite or belladonna. The heat of the church might be resisted, but the sermon is irresistable. Its monotony falls in leaden accents upon the ear, and soon subdues the most powerful attention. Variety, whether of sight or sound, prevents sleep, while monotony of all kinds is apt to induce it. The murmuring of a river, the sound of a Eolian harp, the echo of a distant cascade, the ticking of a clock, the hum of bees under a burning sun, and the pealing of a remote bell, all exercise the same influence. So conscious was Boerhaave of the power of monotony, that in order to procure sleep for a patient, he directed water to be placed in such a situation as to drop continually on a brass pan. When there is no excitement, sleep is sure to follow. We are all kept awake by some mental or bodily stimulus, and when that is removed our wakefulness is at an end. Want of stimulus, especially in a heated atmosphere, produces powerful effects; but where sufficient stimulus exists, we overcome the effects of the heat, and keep awake in spite of it. Thus, in a crowded church, where a dull, inanimate preacher would throw the congregation into a deep slumber, such a man as Massilon, or Chalmers, would keep them in a state of keen excitement. He would arrest their attention, and counteract whatever tendency to sleep would otherwise have existed. In like manner, a prosing, monotonous, long-winded acquaintance is apt to make us doze, while another of a lively, energetic conversation keeps us brisk and awake. It will generally be found that the reasoning faculties are those which are soonest prostrated by slumber, and the imaginative the least so. A person would more readily fall asleep if listening to a profound piece of argumentation, than to a humorous or fanciful story; and probably more have slumbered over the pages of Bacon and Locke, than over those of Shakspeare and Milton.

Cold produces sleep as well as heat, but to do so a very low temperature is necessary, particularly with regard to the human race; for, when cold is not excessive, it prevents, instead of occasioning slumber: in illustration of which, I may mention the case of several unfortunate women, who lived thirty-four days in a small room overwhelmed with the snow, and who scarcely slept during the whole of that period. In very northern and southern latitudes, persons often lose their lives by lying down in a state of drowsiness, occasioned by intense cold. The winter sleep, or hybernation of animals, arises from cold; but as this species of slumber is of a very peculiar description; I have discussed it separately in another part of the work.

The finished gratification of all ardent desires has the effect of inducing slumber; hence, after any keen excitement, the mind becomes exhausted, and speedily relapses into this state. Attention to a single sensation has the same effect. This has been exemplified in the case of all kinds of monotony, where there is a want of variety to stimulate the ideas, and keep them on the alert. 'If the mind,' says Cullen, 'is attached to a single sensation, it is brought very nearly to the state of the total absence of impression;' or, in other words, to the state most closely bordering upon sleep. Remove those stimuli which keep it employed, and sleep ensues at any time.

Any thing which mechanically determines the blood to the brain, acts in a similar manner, such as whirling round for a great length of time, ascending a lofty mountain, or swinging to and fro. The first and last of these actions give rise to much giddiness, followed by intense slumber, and at last by death, if they be continued very long. By lying flat upon a millstone while performing its evolutions, sleep is soon produced and death, without pain, would be the result, if the experiment were greatly protracted. Apoplexy, which consists of a turgid state of the cerebral vessels, produces perhaps the most complete sleep that is known, in so far that, while it continues it is utterly impossible to waken the individual: no stimulus, however powerful, has any influence in arousing his dormant faculties. When the circulating mass in the brain is diminished beyond a certain extent, it has the same effect on the opposite state; whence excessive loss of blood excites sleep.

Opium, hyoscyamus, aconite, belladonna, and the whole tribe of narcotics, induce sleep, partly by a specific power which they exert on the nerves of the stomach, and partly by inducing an apoplectic state of the brain. The former effect is occasioned by a moderate—the latter by an over dose.

A heavy meal, especially if the stomach is at the same time weak, is apt to induce sleep. In ordinary circumstances, the nervous energy or sensorial power of this viscus is sufficient to carry on its functions; but when an excess of food is thrown upon it, it is then unable to furnish, from its own resources, the powers requisite for digestion. In such a case it draws upon the whole body—upon the chest, the limbs, &c., from whence it is supplied with the sensorial power of which it is deficient; and is thus enabled to perform that which by its own unassisted means it never could have accomplished. But mark the consequences of such accommodation! Those parts, by communicating vigor to the stomach, become themselves debilitated in a corresponding ratio, and get into a state analogous to that from which they had extricated this viscus. The extremities become cold, the respiration heavy and stertorous, and the brain torpid. In consequence of the torpor of the brain, sleep ensues. It had parted with that portion of sensorial energy which kept it awake, and by supplying another organ is itself thrown into the state of sleep. It is a curious fact, that the feeling of sleep is most strong while the food remains on the stomach, shortly after the accession of the digestive process, and before that operation which converts the nourishment into chyle has taken place.

When, therefore, the sensorial power is sufficiently exhausted, we naturally fall asleep. As this exhaustion, however, is a gradual process, so is that of slumber. Previous to its accession, a feeling of universal lassitude prevails, and exhibits itself in yawning,* peevishness, heaviness, and weakness of the eyes; indifference to surrounding objects, and all the characteristics of fatigue. If the person be seated, his head nods and droops; the muscles become relaxed; and, when circumstances admit of it, the limbs are thrown into the recumbent position, or that most favorable for complete inaction. The senses then become unconscious of impressions, and, one after the other, part with sensation; the sight first, then taste, smell, hearing, and touch, all in regular order. The brain does not all at once glide into repose: its different organs being successively thrown into this state; one dropping asleep, then another, then a third, till the whole are locked up in the fetters of slumber. This gradual process of intellectual obliteration is a sort of confused dream—a mild delirium which always precedes sleep. The ideas have no resting-place, but float about in the con-

* We yawn before falling asleep and when we wake; yawning, therefore, precedes and follows sleep It seems an effort of nature to restore the just equilibrium between the flexor and extensor muscles. The former have a natural predominancy in the system; and on their being fatigued, we, by an effort of the will, or rather by a species of instinct, put the latter into action for the purpose of redressing the balance, and poising the respective muscular powers. We do the same thing on awaking, or even on getting up from a recumbent posture—the flexors in such circumstances having prevailed over the extensors, which were in a great measure inert.

fused tabernacle of the mind, giving rise to images of the most perplexing description. In this state they continue for some time, until, as sleep becomes more profound, the brain is left to thorough repose, and they disappear altogether.

Sleep produces other important changes in the system. The rapidity of the circulation is diminished, and, as a natural consequence, that of respiration: the force of neither function, however, is impaired; but, on the contrary, rather increased. Vascular action is diminished in the brain and organs of volition, while digestion and absorption shall proceed with increased energy. The truth of most of these propositions it is not difficult to establish.

The diminished quickness of the circulation is shown in the pulse, which is slower and fuller than in the waking state; that of respiration in the more deliberate breathing which accompanies sleep. Diminished action of the brain is evident from the abolition of its functions, as well as direct evidence. A case is related by Blumenbach, of a person who had been trepanned, and whose brain was observed to sink when he was asleep, and swell out when he was awake. As for the lessened vascular action in the voluntary powers, this is rendered obvious by the lower temperature on the surface which takes place during the slumbering state. Moreover, in low typhus, cynanche maligna, and other affections attended with a putrid diathesis, the petechiæ usually appear during sleep when the general circulation is least vigorous, while the paroxysms of reaction or delirium take place, for the most part, in the morning when it is in greater strength and activity.

In some individuals the stronger and more laborious respiration of sleep is made manifest by that stertorous sound commonly denominated snoring. Stout apoplectic people—those who snuff much or sleep with their mouths open, are most given to this habit. It seems to arise principally from the force with which the air is drawn into the lungs in sleep. The respiratory muscles being less easily excited during this state do not act so readily, and the air is consequently admitted into the chest with some degree of effort. This, combined with the relaxed state of the fauces, gives rise to the stertorous noise. Snuffing, by obstructing the nasal passages and thus rendering breathing more difficult, has the same effect; consequently snuffers are very often great snorers. The less rapidly the blood is propelled through the lungs, the slower is the respiration, and the louder the stertor becomes. Apoplexy, by impairing the sensibility of the respiratory organs, and thus reducing the frequency of breathing, produces snoring to a great extent; and all cerebral congestions have, to a greater or less degree, the same effect.

That sleep increases absorption is shown in the disappearance or diminution of many swellings, especially œdema of the extremities, which often disappears in the night and recurs in the daytime, even when the patient keeps his bed, a proof that its disappearance does not not always depend on the position of the body: that it increases digestion, and, as a natural consequence, nutrition, is rendered probable by many circumstances: hence it is the period in which the regeneration of the body chiefly takes place. Were there even no augmentation given to the assimilative function, as is maintained by Broussais and some other physiologists, it is clear that the body would be more thoroughly nourished than when awake, for all those actions which exhaust it in the latter condition are quiescent, and it remains in a state of rest, silently accumulating power, without expending any.

Sleep lessens all the secretions, with one exception—that of the skin. The urinary, salivary, and bronchial discharges, the secretions from the nose, eyes, and ears, are all formed less copiously than in the waking state. The same rule holds with regard to other secretions—hence diarrhœa, menorrhagia, &c., are checked during the intervals of slumber.

From the diminished vascular action going on upon the surface, we would be apt to expect a decrease of perspiration, but the reverse is the case. Sleep relaxes the cutaneous vessels, and they secrete more copiously than in the waking state. According to Sanctorius, a person sleeping some hours undisturbed, will perspire insensibly twice as much as one awake. This tendency of sleep to produce perspiration is strikingly exhibited in diseases of debility; whence the nocturnal sweats so prevailing and so destructive in all cachectic affections. Sanctorius farther states, that the insensible perspiration is not only more abundant, but less acrimonious during sleep than in the waking state; that, if diminished during the day, the succeeding sleep is disturbed and broken, and that the diminution in consequence of too short a sleep, disposes to fever, unless the equilibrium is established, on the following day, by a more copious perspiration.

Sleep produces peculiar effects upon the organs of vision. *A priori*, we might expect that, during this state, the pupil would be largely dilated in consequence of the light being shut out. On opening the eyelids cautiously it is seen to be contracted; it then quivers with an irregular motion, as if disposed to dilate, but at length ceases to move, and remains in a contracted state till the person awakes. This fact I have often verified by inspecting the eyes of children. Sleep also communicates to these organs a great accession of sensibility, so much so, that they are extremely dazzled by a clear light. This, it is true, happens on coming out of a dark into a light room, or opening our eyes upon the sunshine even when we are awake, but the effect is much stronger when we have previously been in deep slumber.

Sleep may be natural or diseased—the former arising from such causes as exhaust the sensorial power, such as fatigue, pain, or protracted anxiety of mind; the latter from cerebral congestion, such as apoplexy or plethora. The great distinction between these varieties is, that the one can be broken by moderate stimuli, while the other requires either excessive stimuli, or the removal of the particular cause which gave rise to it.

During complete sleep no sensation whatever is experienced by the individual: he neither feels pain, hunger, thirst, nor the ordinary desires of nature. He may be awakened to a sense of such feelings, but during perfect repose he has no consciousness whatever of their existence—if they can indeed be said to exist where they are not felt. For the same reason, we may touch him without his feeling it; neither is he sensible to sounds, to light, or to odours. When, however, the slumber is not very profound, he may hear music or conversation, and have a sense of pain, hunger, and thirst; and, although not awakened by such circumstances, may recollect them afterwards. These impressions, caught by the senses, often give rise to the most extraordinary mental combinations, and form the groundwork of the most elaborate dreams.

I am of opinion that we rarely pass the whole of any one night in a state of perfect slumber. My reason for this supposition is, that we very seldom remain during the whole of that period in the position in which we fall asleep. This change of posture must have been occasioned by some emotion, however obscure, affecting the mind, and through it the organs of volition, whereas in complete sleep we experience no emotion whatever.

The position usually assumed in sleep has been mentioned; but sleep may ensue in any posture of the body; persons fall asleep on horseback, and continue riding in this state for a long time without been awakened. Horses sometimes sleep for hours in the standing posture; and the circumstance of somnambulism shows that the same thing may occur in the human race.

Some animals, such as the hare, sleep with their eyes open; and I have known similar instances in the human subject. But the organ is dead to the ordinary stimulus of light, and sees no more than if completely shut.

Animals which prey by night, such as the cat, hyena, &c., pass the greater part of their time in sleep; while those that do not, continue longer awake than asleep. The latter slumber part of the night and continue awake so long as the sun continues above the horizon. The propensity of the former to sleep in the day time seems to proceed from the structure of their eyes; as they see much better in darkness than in light, and consequently pass in slumber that period in which their vision is of least avail to them. It is a very curious fact, however, that these animals, when kept in captivity, reverse the order of their nature, and remain awake by day while they sleep by night. This fact has been ascertained in the menagerie at Paris. In such cases I apprehend that some corresponding change must take place in the structure of the eyes, assimilating them to those animals which naturally sleep by night.

M. Castel observes,* that the greater part of animals sleep longer in winter than in summer. It is precisely on account of perspiration that in the first of these seasons sleep is more necessary than in the second. In winter, the want of perspiration during the day is furnished in sleep; in summer, the diurnal sweat supplies that of the night, and renders much sleep less necessary. In other words, during summer the perspiration is so much excited by atmospheric temperature, that a shorter time is sufficient to give issue to the fluids which have to be expelled by this means. For the same reason, the inhabitants of very cold climates sleep more than those who live in the warmer latitudes.

The profoundness of sleep differs greatly in different individuals. The repose of some is extremely deep; that of others quite the reverse. One will scarcely obey the roar of cannon; another will start at the chirping of a cricket or the faintest dazzling of the moonbeams. Heavy-minded, phlegmatic people generally belong to the former class; the irritable, the nervous, and the hypochondriac to the latter, although we shall at times find the cases reversed with regard to the nature of sleep enjoyed by these different temperaments. Man is almost the only animal in whom much variety is to be found in this respect. The lower grades are distinguished by a certain character, so far as their slumber is concerned, and this character runs through the whole race; thus, all hares, cats, &c., are light sleepers; all bears, turtles, badgers, &c., are the reverse. In man, the varieties are infinite. Much of this depends upon the age and temperament of the individual, and much upon custom.

The profoundness of sleep differs also during the same night. For the first four or five hours, the slumber is much heavier than towards morning. The cause of such difference is obvious; for we go to bed exhausted by previous fatigue, and consequently enjoy sound repose, but, in the course of a few hours, the necessity for this gradually abates, and the slumber naturally becomes lighter.

That sleep from which we are easily roused is the healthiest: very profound slumber partakes of the nature of apoplexy.

On being suddenly awakened from a profound sleep our ideas are exceedingly confused; and it is sometime before we can be made to comprehend what is said to us. For some moments, we neither see, nor hear, nor think without our usual distinctness, and are, in fact, in a state of temporary reverie.

When there is a necessity for our getting up at a certain hour, the anxiety of mind thus produced not only prevents the sleep from being very profound, but retards its accession; and even after it does take place, we very seldom oversleep ourselves, and are almost sure to be awake at, or before, the stipulated time.

Shortly after falling asleep, we often awake with a sudden start, having the mind filled with painful impressions; although we often find it impossible to say to what subject they refer. Some persons do this regularly every night, and there can be no doubt that it proceeds from the mind being tortured by some distressing vision; which, however, has faded away without leaving behind it any feeling, save one of undefinable melancholy. There are some persons who are sure to be aroused in this startling and painful manner if they happen to fall asleep in the position in which they at first lay down, who nevertheless escape if they turn themselves once or twice before falling into repose. This fact we must take as we find it: any explanation as to its proximate cause seems quite impracticable.

Disease exercises a powerful influence upon sleep. All affections attended with acute pain prevent it, in consequence of the undue accumulation which they occasion of sensorial power. This is especially the case where there is much *active* determination of blood to the head, as in phrenetic affections, and fevers in general.

Sleep is always much disturbed in hydrothorax; and almost every disease affects it, more or less; some preventing it altogether, some limiting the natural proportion, some inducing fearful dreams, and all acting with a power proportioned to the direct or indirect influence which they exercise upon the sensorium.

From the increased irratibility of the frame and relaxed state of the cutaneous vessels during sleep, the system at that time is peculiarly apt to be acted upon by all impressions, especially of cold; and those who fall asleep exposed to a current of air are far more apt to feel the consequences thereof than if they were broad awake. By a law of nature the sensibility of the system is increased by any suspension of the mental or voluntary powers, for the same reason that it is diminished, while these powers resume their action. In drunkenness, for instance, where the mind is vehemently excited, we are far less susceptible of cold than in a state of sobriety.

Sleep is much modified by habit. Thus, an old artillery-man often enjoys tranquil repose, while the cannon are thundering around him; an engineer has been known to fall asleep within a boiler, while his fellows were beating it on the outside with their ponderous hammers; and the repose of a miller is nowise incommoded by the noise of his mill. Sound ceases to be a stimulus to such men, and what would have proved an inexpressible annoyance to others, is by them altogether unheeded. It is common for carriers to sleep on horseback, and coachman on their coaches. During the battle of the Nile, some boys were so exhausted, that they fell asleep on the deck amid the deafening thunder of that dreadful engagement. Nay, silence itself may become a stimulus, while sound ceases to be so. Thus, a miller being very ill, his mill was stopped that he might not be disturbed by its noise; but this so far from inducing sleep, prevented it altogether; and it did not take place till the mill was set a-going again. For the same reason, the manager of some vast iron-work who, slept close to them amid the incessant din of hammers forges, and blast furnaces, would awake if there was any cessation of the noise during the night. To carry the illustration still farther, it has been noticed, that a person who falls asleep near a church, the bell of which is ringing, may hear the sound during the whole of his slumber, and be nevertheless aroused by its sudden cessation. Here the sleep must have been imperfect, otherwise he would have been insensible to the sound: the noise of the bell was no stimulus; it was its ces-

* 'Journal Complémentaire.'

sation which, by breaking the monotony, became so, and caused the sleeper to awake.

The effects of habit may be illustrated in various ways. 'If a person, for instance, is accustomed to go to rest exactly at nine o'clock in the evening, and to rise again at six in the morning, though the time of going to sleep be occasionally protracted till twelve, he will yet awake at his usual hour of six; or, if his sleep be continued by darkness, quietude or other causes, till the day be farther advanced, the desire for sleep will return in the evening at nine.'

Persons who are much in the habit of having their repose broken, seldom sleep either long or profoundly, however much they may be left undisturbed. This is shown in the cases of soldiers and seamen, nurses, mothers, and keepers.

Seamen and soldiers on duty can, from habit, sleep when they will, and wake when they will. The Emperor Napoleon was a striking instance of this fact. Captain Barclay, when performing his extraordinary feat in walking a mile an hour for a thousand successive hours, obtained at last such a mastery over himself, that he fell asleep the instant he lay down. Some persons cannot sleep from home, or on a different bed from their usual one: some cannot sleep on a hard, others on a soft bed. A low pillow prevents sleep in some, a high one in others. The faculty of remaining asleep for a great length of time, is possessed by some individuals. Such was the case with Quin, the celebrated player, who could slumber for twenty-four hours successively—with Elizabeth Orvin, who spent three-fourths of her life in sleep—with Elizabeth Perkins, who slept for a week or a fortnight at a time—with Mary Lyall, who did the same for six successive weeks—and with many others, more or less remarkable. In Bowyer's life of Beattie, a curious anecdote is related of Dr Reid, viz., that he could take as much food and immediately afterwards as much sleep as were sufficient for two days.

A phenomenon of an opposite character is also sometimes observed, for there are individuals who can subsist upon a surprisingly small portion of sleep. The celebrated General Elliot was an instance of this kind: he never slept more than four hours out of the twenty-four. In all other respects he was strikingly abstinent; his food consisting wholly of bread, water, and vegetables. In a letter communicated to Sir John Sinclair, by John Gordon, Esq. of Swiney, Caithness, mention is made of a person named James Mackay, of Skerray, who died in Strathnaver in the year 1797, aged ninety-one: he only slept, on an average, four hours in the twenty-four, and was a remarkably robust and healthy man. Frederick the Great, of Prussia, and the illustrious surgeon, John Hunter, only slept five hours in the same period; and the sleep of the active-minded is always much less than that of the listless and indolent. The celebrated French General Pichegru, informed Sir Gilbert Blane, that, during a whole year's campaigns, he had not above one hour's sleep in the twenty-four. I know a lady who never sleeps above half an hour at a time, and the whole period of whose sleep does not exceed three or four hours in the twenty-four; and yet she is in the enjoyment of excellent health. Gooch gives an instance of a man who slept only for fifteen minutes out of the twenty-four hours, and even this was only a kind of dozing, and not a perfect sleep: notwithstanding which, he enjoyed good health, and reached his seventy-third year. I strongly suspect there must be some mistake in this case, for it is not conceivable that human nature could subsist upon such a limited portion of repose. Instances have been related of persons who *never slept*; but these must be regarded as purely fabulous.

The period of life modifies sleep materially. When a man is about his grand climateric, or a few years beyond it, he slumbers less than at any former period of life; but very young children always sleep away the most of their time. At this early period, the nerves being extremely sensitive and unaccustomed to impressions, become easily fatigued. As the children get older, the brain besides becoming habituated to impressions, acquires an accession of sensorial power, which tends to keep it longer awake. For the first two or three years, children sleep more than once in the twenty-four hours. The state of the fœtus has been denominated, by some writers, a continued sleep, but the propriety of this definition may be doubted; for the mind having never yet manifested itself, and the voluntary organs never having been exercised, can hardly be said to exist in slumber, a condition which supposes a previous waking state of the functions. Middle-aged persons who lead an active life, seldom sleep above eight or nine hours in the twenty-four, however much longer they may lie in bed; while a rich, lazy, and gormandizing citizen will sleep twelve or thirteen hours at a time.

Sleep is greatly modified in old people. They usually slumber little, and not at all profoundly. Sometimes, however, when they get into a state of dotage, in consequence of extreme old age, the phenomena of childhood once more appear, and they pass the greater part of their time in sleep. The repose of the aged is most apt to take place immediately after taking food, while they often solicit it in vain at that period at which, during the former years of their lives, they had been accustomed to enjoy it. The celebrated de Moivre slept twenty hours out of the twenty-four, and Thomas Parr latterly slept away by far the greater part of his existence.

Those who eat heartily, and have strong digestive powers, usually sleep much. The great portion of sleep required by infants is owing, in part, to the prodigious activity of their digestive powers. The majority of animals sleep after eating, and man has a strong tendency to do the same thing, especially when oppressed with heat. In the summer season, a strong inclination is often felt, to sleep after dinner, when the weather is very warm.

A heavy meal, which produces no uneasy feeling while the person, will often do so if he fall asleep. According to Dr. Darwin, this proceeds from the sensorial actions being increased, when the volition is suspended. The digestion from this circumstance goes on with increased rapidity. 'Heat is produced in the system faster than it is expended; and, operating on the sensitive actions, carries them beyond the limitations of pleasure, producing, as is common in such cases, increased frequency of pulse.' In this case, incomplete sleep is supposed, for, when the slumber is perfect, no sensation whatever, either painful or the reverse, can be experienced.

In recovering from long protracted illness, accompanied with great want of rest, we generally sleep much—far more, indeed, than during the most perfect health. This seems to be a provision of nature for restoring the vigour which had been lost during disease, and bringing back the body to its former state. So completely does this appear to be the case, that as soon as a thorough restoration to health takes place, the portion of sleep diminishes till it is brought to the standard at which it originally stood before the accession of illness.

After continuing a certain time asleep, we awake, stretch ourselves, open our eyes, rub them, and yawn several times. At the moment of awaking, there is some confusion of ideas, but this immediately wears away. The mental faculties from being in utter torpor, begin to act one after the other;* the senses do the

* 'In the gradual progress from intense sleep, when there can be no dream, to the moment of perfect vigilance, see what occurs. The first cerebral organ that awakes enters into the train of thinking connected with its faculty: some kind of *dream* is the result; as organ after organ awakes, the dream becomes more vivid; and as the number of active organs increases, so

same. At last, the mind, the senses, and the locomotion being completely restored, what are our sensations? Instead of the listlessness, lassitude, and general fatigue experienced on lying down, we feel vigorous and refreshed. The body is stronger, the thoughts clearer and more composed; we think coolly, clearly, rationally, and can often comprehend with ease what baffled us on the previous night.

One or two other points remain to be noticed. On awaking, the eyes are painfully affected by the light, but this shortly wears away, and we then feel them stronger than when we went to bed. The muscular power, also, for a few seconds, is affected. We totter when we get up; and if we lay hold of any thing, the hand lacks its wonted strength. This, however, as the current of nervous energy is restored throughout the muscles, immediately disappears; and we straightway possess redoubled vigour. On examining the urine, we find that it is higher in its colour than when we lay down. The saliva is more viscid, the phlegm harder and tougher, the eyes glutinous, and the nostrils dry. If we betake ourselves to the scale, we find that our weight has diminished in consequence of the nocturnal perspirations; while, by subjecting our stature to measurement, we shall see that we are taller by nearly an inch than on the preceding night. This fact was correctly ascertained in a great variety of instances, by Mr. Wasse, Rector of Aynho in Northumberland; and is sufficiently accounted for by the intervertebral cartilages recovering their elasticity, in consequence of the bodily weight being taken off them during the recumbent posture of sleep.

Such are the leading phenomena of sleep. With regard to the purposes which it serves in the economy, these are too obvious to require much detail. Its main object is to restore the strength expended during wakefulness; to recruit the body by promoting nutrition and giving rest to the muscles; and to renovate the mind by the repose which it affords the brain. Action is necessarily followed by exhaustion; sleep by checking the one restrains the other, and keeps the animal machine in due vigour. Mr Carmichael supposes sleep to be the period when assimilation goes on in the brain. In this respect, I believe that the brain is not differently situated from the rest of the body. There, as elsewhere, the assimilative process proceeds both in the slumbering and in the waking state; but that it is only at work in the brain during sleep analogy forbids us to admit. So long as circulation continues, a deposition of matter is going on; and circulation, we all know, is at work in the brain as in other organs, whether we be asleep or awake. According to Richerand, one of the great purposes, served by sleep, is to diminish the activity of the circulation, which a state of wakefulness has the invariable effect of increasing. 'The exciting causes' he observes, 'to which our organs are subject during the day, tend progressively to increase their action. The throbbings of the heart, for instance, are more frequent at night than in the morning; and this action, gradually, accelerated, would soon be carried to such a degree of activity as to be inconsistent with life, if its velocity were not moderated at intervals by the recurrence of sleep.'

To detail the beneficent purposes served by sleep in the cure of diseases, as well as in health, would be a work of supererogation. They are felt and recognised by mankind as so indispensable to strength, to happiness, and to life itself, that he who dispenses with that portion of repose required by the wants of nature, is in reality curtailing the duration of its own existence.

does the complication of dreams; and if all the internal organs are awake, the man is still asleep until his awakening senses bring him into direct communication with the world.'

Carmichael's Memoir of Spurzheim, p. 92.

CHAPTER III.

DREAMING.

In perfect sleep, as we have elsewhere stated, there is a quiescence of all the organs which compose the brain; but when, in consequence of some inward excitement, one organ or more continues awake, while the remainder are in repose, a state of incomplete sleep is the result, and we have the phenonmena of dreaming. If, for instance, any irritation, such as pain, fever, drunkenness, or a heavy meal, should throw the perceptive organs into a state of action while the reflecting ones continue asleep, we have a consciousness of objects, colors, or sounds being presented to us, just as if the former organs were actually stimulated by having such impressions communicated to them by the external senses;* while in consequence of the repose of the reflecting organs, we are unable to rectify the illusions, and conceive that the scenes passing before us, or the sounds that we hear, have a real existence. This want of mutual co-operation between the different organs of the brain accounts for the disjointed nature, the absurdities, and incoherencies of dreams.

Many other doctrines have been started by philosophers, but I am not aware of any which can lay claim even to plausibility; some, indeed, are so chimerical, and so totally unsupported by evidence, that it is difficult to conceive how they ever entered into the imaginations of their founders. Baxter, for instance, in his 'Treatise on the Immortality of the Soul,' endeavours to show that dreams are produced by the agency of some spiritual beings, who either amuse, or employ themselves seriously, in engaging mankind in all those imaginary transaction with which they are employed in dreaming. The theory of Democritus and Lucretius is equally whimsical. They accounted for dreams by supposing that spectres, and simulacra of corporeal things constantly emitted from them, and floating up and down in the air, come and assault the soul in sleep. The most prevailing doctrine is that of the Cartesians, who supposed that the mind was continually active in sleep; in other words, that during this state we were always dreaming. Hazlitt, in his 'Round Table,' has taken the same view of the subject, and alleges, that if a person is awakened at any given time and asked what he has been dreaming about, he will at once be recalled to a train of associations with which his mind has been busied previously. Unfortunately for this theory it is not sustained by facts; experiments made on purpose having shown that, though in some few instances, the individual had such a consciousness of dreaming as is described, yet in the great majority he had no consciousness of any thing of the kind. The doctrine, therefore, so far as direct evidence is concerned must fall to the ground; and yet, unsupported as it is either by proof or analogy, this is the fashionable hypothesis of the schools, and the one most in vogue among our best metaphysical writers.

There is a strong analogy between dreaming and insanity. Dr. Abercrombie defines the difference between the two states to be, that in the latter the erroneous impression, being permanent, affects the conduct; whereas in dreaming, no influence on the conduct is produced, because the vision is dissipated on awaking. This definition is nearly, but not wholly correct; for in somnambulism and sleep-talking, the conduct is influenced by the prevailing dream. Dr. Rush has, with great shrewdness, remarked, that a dream may be considered as a transient paroxysm of delirium, and delirium as a permanent dream.

Man is not the only animal subject to dreaming. We have every reason to believe that many of the lower

* This internal stimulation of particular organs without the concurrence of outward impressions by the senses, is more fully stated under the head of Spectral Illusions.

animals do the same. Horses neigh and rear, and dogs bark and growl in their sleep. Probably, at such times, the remembrance of the chase or the combat was passing through the minds of these creatures; and they also not unfrequently manifest signs of fear, joy, playfulness, and almost every other passion.* Ruminating animals, such as the sheep and cow, dream less; but even they are sometimes so affected, especially at the period of rearing their young. The parrot is said to dream, and I should suppose some other birds do the same. Indeed the more intellectual the animal is, the more likely it is to be subject to dreaming. Whether fishes dream it is impossible to conjecture: nor can it be guessed, with any thing like certainty, at what point in the scale of animal intellect, the capability of dreaming ceases, although it is very certain there is such a point. I apprehend that dreaming is a much more general law than is commonly supposed, and that many animals dream which are never suspected of doing so.

Some men are said never to dream, and others only when their health is disordered: Dr. Beattie mentions a case of the latter description. For many years before his death, Dr. Reid had no consciousness of ever having dreamed; and Mr. Locke takes notice of a person who never did so till his twenty-sixth year, when he began to dream in consequence of having had a fever. It is not impossible, however, but that, in these cases, the individuals may have had dreams from the same age as other people, and under the same circumstances, although probably they were of so vague a nature, as to have soon faded away from the memory.

Dreams occur more frequently in the morning than in the early part of the night; a proof that the sleep is much more profound in the latter period than in the former. Towards morning, the faculties, being refreshed by sleep, are more disposed to enter into activity; and this explains why, as we approach the hours of waking, our dreams are more fresh and vivid. Owing to the comparatively active state of the faculties, morning dreams are more rational—whence the old adage, that such dreams are true.

Children dream almost from their birth; and if we may judge from what, on many occasions, they endure during sleep, we must suppose that the visions which haunt their young minds are often of a very frightful kind. Children, from many causes, are more apt to have dreams of terror than adults. In the first place, they are peculiarly subject to various diseases, such as teething, convulsions, and bowel complaints, those fertile sources of mental terror in sleep; and, in the second place, their minds are exceedingly susceptible of dread in all forms, and prone to be acted on by it, whatever shape it assume. Many of the dreams experienced at this early period, leave au indelible impression upon the mind. They are remembered in after-years with feelings of pain; and, blending with the more delighful reminiscences of childhood, demonstrate that this era, which we are apt to consider one varied scene of sunshine and happiness, had, as well as future life, its shadows of melancholy, and was not untinged with hues of sorrow and care. The sleep of infancy, therefore, is far from being that ideal state of felicity which is commonly supposed. It is haunted with its own terrors, even more than that of adults; and, if many of the visions which people it are equally delightful, there can be little doubt that it is also tortured by dreams of a more painful character than often fall to the share of after-life.

In health, when the mind is at ease, we seldom dream; and when we do so our visions are generally of a pleasing character. In disease, especially of the brain, liver, and stomach, dreams are both common and of a very distressing kind.

Some writers imagine, that as we grow older, our dreams become less absurd and inconsistent, but this is extremely doubtful. Probably, as we advance in life, we are less troubled with these phenomena than at the period of youth, when imagination is full of activity, and the mind peculiarly liable to impressions of every kind; but when they do take place, we shall find them equally preposterous, unphilosophical, and crude, with those which haunted our early years. Old people dream more, however, than the middle-aged, owing doubtless to the more broken and disturbed nature of their repose.

I believe that dreams are uniformly the resuscitation or re-embodiment of thoughts which have formerly, in some shape or other, occupied the mind. They are old ideas revived either in an entire state, or heterogeneously mingled together. I doubt if it be possible for a person to have, in a dream, any idea whose elements did not, in some form, strike him at a previous period. If these break loose from their connecting chain, and become jumbled together incoherently, as is often the case, they give rise to absurd combinations; but the elements still subsist, and only manifest themselves in a new and unconnected shape. As this is an important point, and one which has never been properly insisted upon, I shall illustrate it by an example. I lately dreamed that I walked upon the banks of the great canal in the neighbourhood of Glasgow. On the side opposite to that on which I was, and within a few feet of the water, stood the splendid portico of the Royal Exchange. A gentleman, whom I knew, was standing upon one of the steps, and we spoke to each other. I then lifted a large stone, and poised it in my hand, when he said that he was certain I could not throw it to a certain spot which he pointed out. I made the attempt, and fell short of the mark. At this moment, a well known friend came up, whom I knew to excel at *putting* the stone; but, strange to say, he had lost both his legs, and walked upon wooden substitutes. This struck me as exceedingly curious; for my impression was that he had only lost one leg, and had but a single wooden one. At my desire he took up the stone, and, without difficulty, threw it beyond the point indicated by the gentleman upon the opposite side of the canal. The absurdity of this dream is extremely glaring; and yet, on strictly analyzing it, I find it to be wholly composed of ideas which passed through my mind on the previous day, assuming a new and ridiculous arrangement. I can compare it to nothing but to cross readings in the newspapers, or to that well known amusement which consists in putting a number of sentences, each written on a separate piece of paper, into a hat, shaking the whole, then taking them out one by one as they come, and seeing what kind of medley the heterogeneous compound will make, when thus fortuitously put together. For instance, I had, on the above day, taken a walk to the canal, along with a friend. On returning from it, I pointed out to him a spot where a new road was forming, and where, a few days before, one of the workmen had been overwhelmed by a quantity of rubbish falling upon him, which fairly chopped off one of his legs, and so much damaged the other that it was feared amputation would be necessary. Near this very spot there is a park, in which, about a month previously, I practised throwing the stone. On passing the Exchange on my way home, I expressed regret at the lowness of its situation, and remarked what a fine effect the portico would have were it placed upon more elevated ground. Such were the previous circum stances, and let us see how they bear upon the dream. In the first place, the canal appeared before me. 2. Its situation is an elevated one. 3. The portico of the exchange, occurring to my mind as being placed too low, became associated with the elevation of the canal,

* 'The stag-hounds, weary with the chase,
Lay stretched upon the rushy floor,
And urged in dreams the forest race
From Teviot-stone to Eskdale moor.'
Lay of the last Minstrel.

and I placed it close by on a similar altitude. 4. The gentleman I had been walking with, was the same whom, in the dream, I saw standing upon the steps of the portico. 5. Having related to him the story of the man who lost one limb, and had a chance of losing another, this idea brings before me a friend with a brace of wooden legs, who, moreover, appears in connexion with putting the stone, as I know him to excel at that exercise. There is only one other element in the dream which the preceding events will not account for, and that is, the surprise at the individual referred to having more than one wooden leg. But why should he have even one, seeing that in reality he is limbed like other people? This also, I can account for. Some years ago he slightly injured his knee while leaping a ditch, and I remember of jocularly advising him to get it cut off. I am particular in illustrating this point with regard to dreams, for I hold, that if it were possible to analyze them all, they would invariably be found to stand in the same relation to the waking state as the above specimen. The more diversified and incongruous the character of a dream, and the more remote from the period of its occurrence the circumstances which suggest it, the more difficult does its analysis become; and, in point of fact, this process may be impossible, so totally are the elements of the dream often dissevered from their original source, and so ludicrously huddled together. This subject shall be more fully demonstrated in speaking of the remote causes of dreams.

Dreams generally arise without any assignable cause, but sometimes we can very readily discover their origin. Whatever has much interested us during the day, is apt to resolve itself into a dream; and this will generally be pleasurable, or the reverse, according to the nature of the exciting cause. If, for instance, our reading or conversation be of horrible subjects, such as spectres, murders, or conflagrations, they will appear before us magnified and heightened in our dreams. Or if we have been previously sailing upon a rough sea, we are apt to suppose ourselves undergoing the perils of shipwreck. Pleasurable sensations during the day are also apt to assume a still more pleasurable aspect in dreams. In like manner, if we have a longing for any thing, we are apt to suppose that we possess it. Even objects altogether unattainable are placed within our reach: we achieve impossibilities, and triumph with ease over the invincible laws of nature.

A disordered state of the stomach and liver will often produce dreams. Persons of bad digestion, especially hypochondriacs, are harassed with visions of the most frightful nature. This fact was well known to the celebrated Mrs Radcliffe, who, for the purpose of filling her sleep with those phantoms of horror which she has so forcibly embodied in the 'Mysteries of Udolpho,' and 'Romance of the Forest,' is said to have supped upon the most indigestible substances; while Dryden and Fuseli, with the opposite view of obtaining splendid dreams, are reported to have eaten raw flesh. Diseases of the chest, where the breathing is impeded, also give rise to horrible visions, and constitute the frequent causes of that most frightful modification of dreaming—nightmare.

The usual intoxicating agents have all the power of exciting dreams. The most exquisite visions, as well as the most frightful, are perhaps those occasioned by narcotics. These differences depend on the dose and the particular state of the system at the time of taking it. Dreams also may arise from the deprivation of customary stimuli, such as spirits, or supper before going to bed. More frequently, however, they originate from indulging in such excitations.

A change of bed will sometimes induce dreams; and, generally speaking, they are more apt to occur in a strange bed than in the one to which we are accustomed.

Dreams often arise from the impressions made upon the senses during sleep. Dr Beattie speaks of a man on whom any kind of dream could be induced, by his friends gently speaking in his presence upon the particular subject which they wished him to dream about. I have often tried this experiment upon persons asleep, and more than once with a like result. I apprehend, that when this takes place, the slumber must have been very imperfect. With regard to the possibility of dreams being produced by bodily impressions, Dr Gregory relates that having occasion to apply a bottle of hot water to his feet when he went to bed, he dreamed that he was making a journey to the top of Mount Etna, and that he found the heat of the ground almost insufferable. Another person having a blister applied to his head, imagined that he was scalped by a party of Indians; while a friend of mine happening to sleep in damp sheets, dreamed that he was dragged through a stream. A paroxysm of gout during sleep, has given rise to the persons supposing himself under the power of the Inquisition, and undergoing the torments of the rack. The bladder is sometimes emptied during sleep, from the dreaming idea being directed (in consequence of the unpleasant fullness of the viscus) to this particular want of nature. These results are not uniform, but such is the path in which particular bodily states are apt to lead the imagination; and dreams, occurring in these states, will more frequently possess a character analogous to them than to any other modified, of course, by the strength of the individual cause, and fertility of the fancy.

Some curious experiments in regard to this point, were made by M. Giron de Buzareingues, which seems to establish the practicability of a person determining at will the nature of his dreams. By leaving his knees uncovered, he dreamed that he travelled during night in in a diligence: travellers, he observes, being aware that in a coach it is the knees that get cold during the night. On another occasion, having left the posterior part of his head uncovered, he dreamed that he was present at a religious ceremony performed in the open air. It was the custom of the country in which he lived to have the head constantly covered, except on particular occasions, such as the above. On awaking, he felt the back of his neck cold, as he had often experienced dnring the real scenes, the representation of which had been conjured up by his fancy. Having repeated this experiment at the end of several days, to assure himself that the result was not the effect of chance, the second vision turned out precisely the same as the first. Even without making experiments, we have frequent evidence of similar facts; thus, if the clothes chance to fall off us, we are liable to suppose that we are parading the streets in a state of nakedness, and feel all the shame and inconvenience which such a condition would in reality produce. We see crowds of people following after us and mocking our nudity; and we wander from place to place, seeking a refuge under this ideal misfortune. Fancy, in truth, heightens every circumstance, and inspires us with greater vexation than we would feel if actually labouring under such an annoyance. The streets in which we wander are depicted with the force of reality; we see their windings, their avenues, their dwelling-places, with intense truth. Even the inhabitants who follow us are exposed to view in all their various dresses and endless diversities of countenance. Sometimes we behold our intimate friends gazing upon us with indifference, or torturing with annoying impertinence. Sometimes we see multitudes whom we never beheld before; and each individual is exposed so vividly, that we could describe or even paint his aspect.

In like manner, if we lie awry, or if our feet slip over the side of the bed, we often imagine ourselves standing upon the brink of a fearful precipice, or falling from its beetling summit into the abyss beneath.* If the

* Dr Currie, in allusion to the visions of the hypochondriac observes, that if he dream of falling into the sea, he awakes just as

rain or hail patter against our windows, we have often the idea of a hundred cataracts pouring from the rocks; if the wind howl without, we are suddenly wrapt up in a thunderstorm, with all its terrible associations; if the head happen to slip under the pillow, a huge rock is hanging over us, and ready to crush us beneath its ponderous bulk. Should the heat of the body chance to be increased by febrile irritation or the temperature of the room, we may suppose ourselves basking under the fiery sun of Africa; or if, from any circumstance, we labour under a chill, we may then be careering and foundering among the icebergs of the pole, while the morse and the famished bear are prowling around us, and claiming us for their prey. Dr Beattie informs us, that once, after riding thirty miles in a high wind, he passed the night in visions terrible beyond description. The extent, in short, to which the mind is capable of being carried in such cases, is almost incredible. Stupendous events arise from the most insignificant causes —so completely does sleep magnify and distort every thing placed within its influence. The province of dreams is one of intense exaggeration—exaggeration beyond even the wildest conceptions of Oriental romance.

A smoky chamber, for instance, has given rise to the idea of a city in flames. The conflagrations of Rome and Moscow may then pass in terrific splendor before the dreamer's fancy. He may see Nero standing afar off, surrounded by his lictors and guards, gazing upon the imperial city wrapt in flames; or the sanguinary fight of Borodino, followed by the burning of the ancient capital of Russia, may be presented before him with all the intenseness of reality. Under these circumstances, his whole being may undergo a change. He is no longer a denizen of his native country, but of that land to which his visions have transported him. All the events of his own existence fade away; and he becomes a native of Rome or Russia, gazing upon the appalling spectacle.

On the other hand, the mind may be filled with imagery equally exaggerated, but of a more pleasing character. The sound of a flute in the neighborhood may invoke a thousand beautiful and delightful associations. The air is, perhaps, filled with the tones of harps, and all other varieties of music—nay, the performers themselves are visible; and while the cause of this strange scene is one trivial instrument, we may be regaled with a rich and melodious concert. For the same reason a flower being applied to the nostrils may, by affecting the sense of the smell, excite powerfully the imagination, and give the dreamer the idea of walking in a garden.

There is one fact connected with dreams which is highly remarkable. When we are suddenly awaked from a profound slumber by a loud knock at, or by the rapid opening of the door, a train of actions which it would take hours, or days, or even weeks to accomplish, sometimes passes through the mind. Time, in fact, seems to be in a great measure annihilated. An extensive period is reduced, as it were, to a single point, or rather a single point is made to embrace an extensive period. In one instant, we pass through many adventures, see many strange sights, and hear many strange sounds. If we are awaked by a loud knock, we have perhaps the idea of a tumult passing before us, and know all the characters engaged in it—their aspects, and even their very names. If the door open violently, the flood-gates of a canal may appear to be expanding, and we may see the individuals employed in the process, and hear their conversation, which may seem an hour in length. If a light be brought into the room, the notion of the house being in flames perhaps invades us, and we are witnesses to the whole conflagration from its commencement till it be finally extinguished. The thoughts which arise in such situations are endless, and assume an infinite variety of aspects. The whole, indeed, constitutes one of the strangest phenomena of the human mind, and calls to recollection the story of the Eastern monarch, who, on dipping his head into the magician's water pail, fancied he had travelled for years in various nations, although he was only immersed for a single instant. This curious psychological fact, though occurring under somewhat different circumstances, has not escaped the notice of Mr De Quincey, better known as the 'English Opium-Eater.' 'The sense of space, says he, 'and, in the end, the *sense of time* were both powerfully affected. Buildings, landscapes, &c., were exhibited in proportions so vast as the bodily eye is not fitted to receive. Space swelled, and was amplified to an extent of unutterable infinity. This, however, did not disturb me so much as the expansion of time. I sometimes seemed to have lived for seventy or a hundred years in one night; nay, sometimes had feelings representative of a millennium passed in that time, or however, of a duration beyond the limits of any human experience.' It is more easy to state the fact of this apparent expansion of time in dreams than to give any theory which will satisfactorily account for it. I believe that, whenever it occurs, the dream has abounded in events and circumstances which, had they occurred in reality, would have required a long period for their accomplishment. For instance, I lately dreamed that I made a voyage to India—remained some days in Calcutta—then took ship for Egypt, where I visited the cataracts of the Nile, and the pyramids: and, to crown the whole, had the honor of an interview with Mehemit Ali, Cleopatra, and the Sultan Saladin. All this was the work of a single night, probably of a single hour, or even a few minutes; and yet it appeared to occupy many months.

I must also mention another circumstance of a somewhat similar kind, which though it occur in the waking condition, is produced by the peculiar effect of previous sleep upon the mind. Thus, when we awake in a melancholy mood, the result probably of some distressing dream, the remembrance of all our former actions, especially those of an evil character, often rushes upon us as from a dark and troubled sea.* They do not appear individually, one by one, but come linked together in a close phalanx, as if to take the conscience by storm, and crush it beneath their imposing front. The whole span of our existence, from childhood downwards, sends them on; oblivion opens its gulphs snd impels them forwards; and the mind is robed in a cloud of wretchedness, without one ray of hope to brighten up its gloom. In common circumstances, we possess no such power of grouping so instantaneously the most distant and proximate events of life; the spell of memory is invoked to call them successively from the past; and they glide before us like shadows, more or less distinct according to their remoteness, or the force of their impress upon the mind. But in the case of which I speak, they start abruptly forth from the bosom of time, and overwhelm the spirit with a crowd of most sad and appalling reminiscences. In the crucible of our distorted imagination, every thing is exaggerated and invested with a blacker gloom than belongs to it; we see, at one glance, down the whole vista of time; and each event of our life is written there in gloomy and distressing characters. Hence the mental depression occurring under these circumstances, and even the remorse which falls, like bitter and unrefreshing dews, upon the heart.

We have seldom any idea of past events in dreams; if such are called forth, they generally seem to be pre-

the waters close over him, and is sensible of the precise gurgling sound which those experience who actually sink under water. In falling from heights, during dreams, we always awake before reaching the ground.

* Something similar occurs in drowning. Persons recovered from this state have mentioned that, in the course of a single minute, almost every event of their life has been brought to their recollection.

sent and in the process of actual occurrence. We may dream of Alexander the Great, but it is as of a person who is co-existent with ourselves.

Dreams being produced by the active state of such organs as are dissociated from, or have not sympathised in, the general slumber, partake of the character of those whose powers are in greatest vigour, or farthest removed from the somnolent state. A person's natural character, therefore, or his pursuits in life, by strengthening one faculty, make it less susceptible, than such as are weaker, of being overcome, by complete sleep ; or, if it be overcome, it awakes more rapidly from its dormant state, and exhibits its proper characteristics in dreams. Thus, the miser dreams of wealth, the lover of his mistress, the musician of melody, the philosopher of science, the merchant of trade, and the debtor of duns and bailiffs. In like manner, a choleric man is often passionate in his sleep ; a vicious man's mind is filled with wicked actions ; a virtuous man's with deeds of benevolence ; a humorist's with ludicrous ideas. Pugnacious people often fight on such occasions, and do themselves serious injury by striking against the posts of the bed ; while persons addicted to lying, frequently dream of exercising their favourite vocation.

For such reasons persons who have a strong passion for music often dream of singing and composing melodies ; and the ideas of some of our finest pieces are said to have been communicated to the musician in his sleep. Tartini, a celebrated violin player, is said to have composed his famous *Devil's Sonata* from the inspiration of a dream, in which the Devil appeared to him and challenged him to a trial of skill upon his own fiddle. A mathematician, in like manner, is often engaged in the solution of problems, and has his brain full of Newton, Euler, Euclid, and Laplace ; while a poet is occupied in writing verses, or in deliberating upon the strains of such bards as are most familiar to his spirit ; it was thus in a dream that Mr Coleridge composed his splendid fragment of Kubla Khan.* To speak phrenologically : if the organ of *size* be large, then material images more than sounds or abstractions possess the mind, and every thing may be magnified to unnatural dimensions ; if *color* be fully developed, whatever is presented to the mental eye is brilliant and gaudy, and the person has probably the idea of rich paintings, shining flowers, or varied landscapes : should *locality* predominate, he is carried away to distant lands, and beholds more extraordinary sights than Cook, Ross, or Franklin ever described. An excess of *cautiousness* will inspire him with terror ; an excess of *self-esteem* cause him to be placed in dignified situations ; while *imitation* may render him a mimic or a player ; *language*, a wrangler or philologist ; *secretiveness*, a deceiver ; *acquisitiveness*, a thief. Occasionally, indeed, the reverse is the case, and those trains of thoughts in which we mostly indulge are seldom or never the subjects of our dreams. Some authors even assert that when the mind has been strongly impressed with any peculiar ideas, such are less likely to occur in dreams than their opposites ; but this is taking the exception for the general rule, and is directly at variance with both experience and analogy. In fact, whatever propensities or talents are strongest in the mind of the individual, will, in most cases, manifest themselves with greatest readiness and force in dreams ; and where a faculty is very weak it will scarcely manifest itself at all. Thus, one person who has large *tune* and small *casuality* will indulge in music, but seldom in ascertaining the nature of cause and effect ; while another, with a contrary disposition of organs, may attempt to reason upon abstract truths, while music will rarely intrude into the temple of his thoughts. It is but fair to state, however, that the compositions, the reasonings, and the poems which we concoct in sleep, though occasionally superior to those of our waking hours,* are generally of a very absurd description ; and, how admirable soever they have appeared, their futility is abundantly evident when we awake. To use the words of Dr Parr, 'In dreams we seem to reason, to argue, to compose ; and in all these circumstances, during sleep, we are highly gratified, and think that we excel. If, however, we remember our dreams, our reasonings we find to be weak, our arguments we find to be inconclusive, and our compositions trifling and absurd.' The truth of these remarks is undeniable ; but the very circumstance of a man's dreams turning habitually upon a particular subject—however ridiculously he may meditate thereupon—is a strong presumption that that subject is the one which most frequently engrosses his faculties in the waking state ; in a word, that the power most energetic in the latter condition is that also most active in dreams.

Dreams are sometimes useful in affording prognostics of the probable termination of several diseases. Violent and impetuous dreams occurring in fevers generally indicate approaching delirium ; those of a gloomy, terrific nature give strong grounds to apprehend danger ; while dreams of a pleasant cast may be looked upon as harbingers of approaching recovery. The visions, indeed, which occur in a state of fever are highly distressing ; the mind is vehemently hurried on from one train of ideas to another, and participates in the painful activity of the system. Those generated by hypochondria or indigestion are equally afflicting, but more confined to one unpleasant idea—the intellect being overpowered, as it were, under the pressure of a ponderous load, from which it experiences an utter incapacity to relieve itself. The febrile dream has a fiery, volatile, fugitive character : the other partakes of the nature of nightmare, in which the faculties seem frozen to torpor, by the presence of a loathsome and indolent fiend.

Other diseases and feelings besides fever give a character to dreams. The dropsical subject often has the idea of fountains, and rivers, and seas, in his sleep ; jaundice tinges the objects beheld with its own yellow and sickly hue ; hunger induces dreams of eating agreeable food ; an attack of inflammation disposes us to see all things of the colour of blood ; excessive thirst presents us with visions of dried up streams, burning sand-plains, and immitigable heat ; a bad taste in the mouth, with every thing bitter and nauseous in the vegetable world.

* The following is the account he himself gives of the circumstance :—'In the summer of the year 1797, the author, then in ill-health, had retired to a lonely farm-house between Porlock and Linton, on the Exmoor confines of Somerset and Devonshire. In consequence of a slight indisposition, an anodyne had been prescribed, from the effects of which he fell asleep in his chair at the moment that he was reading the following sentence, or words of the same substance, in 'Purchas's Pilgrimage :—'Here the Khan Kubla commanded a palace to be built, and a stately garden thereunto. And thus ten miles of fertile ground were enclosed with a wall.' The author continued for about three hours in a profound sleep, at least of the external senses, during which time he had the most vivid confidence, that he could have composed not less than from two to three hundred lines; if that indeed can be called composition in which all the images rose up before him as *things*, with a parallel production of the correspondent expressions, without any sensation or consciousness of effort. On awaking, he appeared to himself to have a distinct recollection of the whole : and taking his pen, ink, and paper instantly and eagerly wrote down the lines that are here preserved At this moment he was unfortunately called out by a person on business from Porlock, and detained by him above an hour ; and on his return to his room, found, to his no small surprise and mortification, that though he still retained some vague and dim recollection of the general purport of the vision ; yet, with the exception of some eight or ten scattered lines and images, all the rest had passed away like the images on the surface of a stream into which a stone had been cast, but alas ! without the after restoration of the latter.'

* Such was the case with Cabanis, who often, during dreams, saw clearly into the bearings of political events which had baffled him when awake ; and with Condorcet, who, when, engaged in some deep and complicated calculations, was frequently obliged to leave them in an unfinished state, and retire to rest, when the results to which they led were at once unfolded in his dreams.

If, from any cause, we chance to be relieved from the physical suffering occasioning such dreams, the dreams themselves also wear away, or are succeeded by others of a more pleasing description. Thus, if perspiration succeed to feverish heat, the person who, during the continuance of the latter, fancied himself on the brink of a volcano, or broiled beneath an African sun, is transported to some refreshing stream, and enjoys precisely the pleasure which such a transition would produce did it actually take place.

Some authors imagine that we never dream of objects which we have not seen; but the absurdity of this notion is so glaring as to carry its own refutation along with it. I have a thousand times dreamed of such objects.

When a person has a strong desire to see any place or object which he has never seen before, he is apt to dream about it; while, as soon as his desire is gratified, he often ceases so to dream. I remember of hearing a great deal of the beauty of Rouen Cathedral, and in one form or other it was constantly presented before my imagination in dreams; but having at last seen the cathedral I never again dreamed about it. This is not the invariable result of a gratified wish; but it happens so often that it may be considered a general rule.

Sometimes we awake from dreams in a pleasing, at other times in a melancholy mood, without being able to recollect them. They leave a pleasurable or disagreeable impression upon the mind, according doubtless to their nature; and yet we cannot properly remember what we were dreaming about. Sometimes, though baffled at the time, we can recall them afterwards, but this seldom happens.

It often happens that the dreamer, under the influence of a frightful vision, leaps from his bed and calls aloud in a paroxysm of terror. This is very frequently the case with children and persons of weak nerves; but it may happen even with the strongest minded. There is something peculiarly horrible and paralyzing in the terror of sleep. It lays the energies of the soul prostrate before it, crushes them to the earth as beneath the weight of an enormous vampyre, and equalizes for a time the courage of the hero and the child. No firmness of mind can at all times withstand the influence of these deadly terrors. The person awakes panic-struck from some hideous vision; and even after reason returns and convinces him of the unreal nature of his apprehensions, the panic for some time continues, his heart throbs violently, he is covered with cold perspiration, and hides his head beneath the bed-clothes, afraid to look around him, lest some dreadful object of alarm should start up before his affrighted vision. Courage and philosophy are frequently opposed in vain to these appalling terrors. The latter dreads what it disbelieves; and spectral forms, sepulchral voices, and all the other horrid superstitions of sleep arise to vindicate their power over that mind, which, under the fancied protection of reason and science, conceived itself shielded from all such attacks, but which, in the hour of trial, often sinks beneath their influence as completely as the ignorant and unreflecting mind, who never employed a thought as to the real nature of these fantastic and illusive sources of terror. The alarm of a frightful dream is sometimes so overpowering, that persons under the impression thus generated, of being pursued by some imminent danger, have actually leaped out of the window to the great danger and even loss of their lives. In the 9th volume of the 'Philosophical Transactions of the Royal Society of London,' a curious case is given by Archdeacon Squire, of a person who, after having been dumb for years, recovered the use of his speech by means of a dream of this description: 'One day, in the year 1741, he got very much in liquor, so much so, that on his return at home at night to the Devizes, he fell from his horse three or four times, and was at last taken up by a neighbour, and put to bed in a house on the road. He soon fell asleep; when, dreaming that he was falling into a furnace of boiling wort, it put him into so great an agony of fright, that, struggling with all his might to call out for help, he actually did call out aloud, and recovered the use of his tongue that moment, as effectually as ever he had it in his life, without the least hoarseness or alteration in the old sound of his voice.'

There have been instances where the terror of a frightful dream has been so great as even to produce insanity. Many years ago, a woman in the West Highlands, in consequence of a dream of this kind, after being newly brought to bed, became deranged, and soon after made her escape to the mountains, where for seven years, she herded with the deer, and became so fleet that the shepherds and others, by whom she was occasionally seen, could never arrest her. At the end of this term, a very severe storm brought her and her associates to the valley, when she was surrounded, caught, and conveyed to her husband, by whom she was cordially received and treated with the utmost kindness. In the course of three months, she regained her reason, and had afterwards several children. When caught, her body is said to have been covered with hair, thus giving a color to the story of Orson and other wild men of the wood.

Instances have not been wanting where, under the panic of a frightful vision, persons have actually committed murder. They awake from such a dream—they see some person standing in the room, whom they mistake for an assassin, or dreadful apparition; driven to desperation by terror, they seize the first weapon that occurs, and inflict a fatal wound upon the object of their alarm. Hoffbauer, in his Treatise on Legal Medicine, relates a case of this kind. Although he does not state that the circumstances which occasioned the panic was a previous dream of terror, I do not doubt that such, in reality, must have been the case. 'A report,' says he, 'of the murder committed by Bernard Schidmaizig was made by the Criminal College of Silesia. Schidmaizig awoke suddenly at midnight: at the moment of awaking, he beheld a frightful phantom (at least his imagination so depicted it) standing near him, (in consequence of the heat of the weather he slept in an open coach-house.) Fear, and the obscurity of the night, prevented him from recognizing any thing distinctly, and the object which struck his vision appeared to him an actual spectre. In a tremulous tone, he twice called out, *who goes there?*—he received no answer, and imagined that the apparition was approaching him. Frightened out of his judgment, he sprung from his bed, seized a hatchet which he generally kept close by him, and with this weapon assaulted the imaginary spectre. To see the apparition, to call out *who goes there?* and to seize the hatchet where the work of a moment: he had not an instant for reflection, and with one blow the phantom was felled to the ground. Schidmaizig uttered a deep groan. This, and the noise occasioned by the fall of the phantom, completely restored him to his senses; and all at once the idea flashed across his mind that he must have struck down his wife, who slept in the same coach-house. Falling instantly upon his knees, he raised the head of the wounded person, saw the wound which he had made, and the blood that flowed from it; and in a voice full of anguish exclaimed *Susannah, Susannah, come to yourself!* He then called his eldest daughter, aged eight years, ordered her to see if her mother was recovering, and to inform her grandmother that he had killed her. In fact, it was his unhappy wife who received the blow, and she died the next day.'*

* This case is highly important in a legal point of view; and to punish a man for acting similarly in such a state would be as unjust as to inflict punishment for deeds committed under the influence of insanity or somnambulism. 'This man,' as Hoffbauer properly remarks, 'did not enjoy the free use of his senses: he knew not what he saw: he believed that he was repulsing an unlooked for attack. He soon recognised the place where he usually slept; it was natural that he should seize the hatchet

The passion of horror is more frequently felt in dreams than at any other period. Horror is intense dread, produced by some unknown or superlatively disgusting object. The visions of sleep, therefore, being frequently undefined, and of the most revolting description, are apt to produce this emotion, as they are to occasion simple fear. Under its influence, we may suppose that fiends are lowering upon us; that dismal voices, as from the bottomless pit, or from the tomb, are floating around us; that we are haunted by apparitions; or that serpents, scorpions and demons are our bed-fellows. Such sensations are strongly akin to those of nightmare; but between this complaint and a mere dream of terror, there is a considerable difference. In incubus, the individual feels as if his powers of volition were totally paralyzed; and as if he were altogether unable to move a limb in his own behalf, or utter a cry expressive of his agony. When these feelings exist, we may consider the case to be one of nightmare: when they do not, and when notwithstanding his terror, he seems to himself to possess unrestrained muscular motion, to run with ease, breathe freely, and enjoy the full capability of exertion, it must be regarded as a simple dream.

Dr Elliotson has remarked, with great acuteness, that dreams, in which the perceptive faculties alone are concerned, are more incohereut, and subject to more rapid transitions than those in which one or more of the organs of the feelings are also in a state of activity. 'Thus, in our dreams, we may walk on the brink of a precipice, or see ourselves doomed to immediate destruction by the weapon of a foe, or the fury of a tempestuous sea, and yet feel not the slightest emotion of fear, though, during the perfect activity of the brain, we may be naturally disposed to the strong manifestation of this feeling; again we may see the most extraordinary object or event without surprise, perform the most ruthless crime without compunction, and see what, in our waking hours, would cause us unmitigated grief, without the smallest feeling of sorrow.'

Persons are to be found, who, when they speak much during sleep, are unable to remember their dreams on awaking, yet recollect them perfectly if they do not speak. This fact is not very easily accounted for. Probably when we are silent, the mind is more directed upon the subject of the dream, and not so likely to be distracted from it. There is perhaps another explanation. When we dream of speaking, or actually speak, the necessity of using language infers the exercise of some degree of reason; and, thus the incongruities of the dream being diminished, its nature becomes less striking, and consequently less likely to be remembered. Though we often dream of performing impossibilities, we seldom imagine that we are relating them to others.

When we dream of visible objects, the sensibility of the eyes is diminished in a most remarkable manner; and on opening them, they are much less dazzled by the light than if we awoke from a slumber altogether unvisited by such dreams. A fact equally curious is noticed by Dr. Darwin, in his 'Zoonomia,'—'If we sleep in the day time, and endeavor to see some object in dreams, the light is exceedingly painful to our eyes; and, after repeated struggles, we lament in our sleep that we cannot see it. In this case, I apprehend, the eyelid is in some measure opened by the vehemence of our sensations; and the iris being dilated, shows as great, or greater sensibility than in our waking hours.'

There are some persons to whom the objects of their dreams are always represented in a soft, mellow lustre, similar to twilight. They never seem to behold any thing in the broad glare of sunshine; and, in general, the atmosphere of our vision is less brilliant than that through which we are accustomed to see things while awake.

since he had taken the precaution to place it beside him; but the idea of his wife and the possibility of killing her were the last things that occurred to him.'

The most vivid dreams are certainly those which have reference to sight. With regard to hearing, they are less distinctly impressed upon the mind, and still more feebly as regards smell, or taste. Indeed, some authors are of opinion that we never dream of sounds, unless when a sound takes place to provoke a dream: and the same with regard to smell and taste; but this doctrine is against analogy, and unsupported by proof. There are, beyond doubt, certain parts of the brain which take cognizance of taste, odors, and sounds, for the same reason that there are others which recognise forms, dimensions, and colors. As the organs of the three latter sensations are capable of inward excitement, without any communication, by means of the senses, with the external world, it is no more than analogical to infer that, with the three former, the same thing may take place. In fever, although the individual is ever so well protected against the excitement of external sounds, the internal organ is often violently stimulated, and he is harassed with tumultuous noises. For such reasons, it is evident that there may be in dreams a consciousness of sounds, of tastes, and of odors, where such have no real existence from without.

Dreams are sometimes exceedingly obscure, and float like faint clouds over the spirit. We can then resolve them into nothing like shape or consistence, but have an idea of our minds being filled with dim, impalpable imagery, which is so feebly impressed upon the tablet of memory, that we are unable to embody it in language, or communicate its likeness to others.

At other times, the objects of sleep are stamped with almost supernatural energy. The dead, or the absent, whose appearance to our waking faculties had become faint and obscure, are depicted with intense truth and reality; and even their voices, which had become like the echo of a forgotten song, are recalled from the depths of oblivion, and speak to us as in former times. Dreams therefore, have the power of brightening up the dim regions of the past, and presenting them with a force which the mere effects of unassisted remembrance could never have accomplished our waking hours.

This property of reviving past images, is one of the most remarkable possessed by sleep. It even goes the length, in some cases, of recalling circumstances which had been entirely forgotten, and presenting them to the mind with more than the force of their original impression. This I conceive to depend upon a particular part of the brain—that, for instance, which refers to the memory of the event—being preternaturally excited; hence forgotten tongues are sometimes brought back to the memory in dreams, owing doubtless to some peculiar excitement of the organ of *Language*. The dreamer sometimes converses in a language of which he has no knowledge whatever when he awakes, but with which he must at one period have been acquainted. Phenomena of a similar kind occasionally occur in madness, delirium, or intoxication, all of which states have an analogy to dreaming. It is not uncommon, for instance, to witness in the insane an unexpected and astonishing resusciation of knowledge—an intimacy with events and languages of which they were entirely ignorant in the sound state of their minds. In like manner, in the delirium attendant upon fevers, people sometimes speak in a tongue* they know nothing of in

* A girl was seized with a dangerous fever, and, in the delirious paroxysm accompanying it, was observed to speak in a strange language which, for some time, no one could understand. At last it was ascertained to be Welsh—a tongue she was wholly ignorant of at the time she was taken ill, and of which she could not speak a single syllable after her recovery. For some time the circumstance was unaccountable, till, on inquiry, it was found she was a native of Wales, and had been familiar with the language of that country in her childhood, but had wholly forgotten it afterwards. During the delirium of fever, the obliterated impressions of infancy were brought to her mind, and continued to operate there so long as she remained under the mental excitation occasioned by the disease, but no longer,

health; and in drunkenness events are brought to the memory which desert it in a state of sobriety.* Analogous peculiarties occur in dreams. Forgotten facts are restored to the mind. Sometimes those adhere to it and are remembered when we awake: at other times—as can be proved in cases of sleep-talking—they vanish with the dream which called them into existence, and are recollected no more.

I believe that the dreams of the aged, like their memory, relate chiefly to the events of early life, and less to those of more recent occurrence. My friend, Dr Cumin, has mentioned to me the case of one of his patients, a middle-aged man, whose visions assumed this character in consequence of severe mental anxiety. Owing to misfortunes in trade, his mind had been greatly depressed: he lost his appetite, became restless, nervous, and dejected; such sleep as he had was filled with incessant dreams, which at first were entirely of events connected with the earliest period of his life, so far as he recollected it, and never by any chance of late events. In proportion as he recovered from this state, the dreams changed their character, and referred to circumstances farther on in life; and so regular was the progression, that, with the march of his recovery, so was the onward march of his dreams. During the worst period of his illness, he dreamed of occurrences which happened in boyhood: no sooner was convalescence established than his visions had reference to manhood; and on complete recovery they were of those recent circumstances which had thrown him into bad health. In this curious case, one lateral half of the head was much warmer than the other. This was so remarkable as to attract the notice of the barber who shaved it.

One of the most remarkable phenomena of dreams is the absence of surprise. This, indeed, is not invariable, as every one must occasionally have felt the sensation of surprise, and been not a little puzzled in his visions to account for the phenomena which present themselves; but, as a general rule, its absence is so exceedingly common, that, when surprise does occur, it is looked upon as an event out of the common order, and remarked accordingly. Scarcely any event, however incredible, impossible, or absurd, gives rise to this sensation. We see circumstance at utter variance with the laws of nature, and yet their discordancy, impracticability, and oddness, seldom strike us as at all out of the usual course of things. This is one of the strongest proofs that can be alleged in support of the dormant condition of the reflecting faculties. Had these powers been awake, and in full activity, they would have pointed out the erroneous nature of the impressions conjured into existence by fancy: and shown us truly that the visions passing before us were merely the chimeras of excited imagination—the airy phantoms of imperfect sleep.

In visions of the dead, we have a striking instance of the absence of surprise. We almost never wonder at beholding individuals whom we yet know, in our dreams, to have even been buried for years. We see them among us, and hear them talk, and associate with them on the footing of fond companionship. Still the circumstance seldom strikes us with wonder, nor do we attempt to account for it. They still seem alive as when they were on earth, only all their qualities, whether good or bad, are exaggerated by sleep. If we hated them while in life, our animosity is now exaggerated to a double degree. If we loved them, our affection becomes more passionate and intense than ever. Under these circumstances, many scenes of most exquisite pleasure often take place. The slumberer supposes himself enjoying the communionship of those who were dearer to him than life, and has far more intense delight than he could have experienced, had these individuals been in reality alive, and at his side.

'I hear thy voice in dreams
  Upon me softly call,
Like echo of the mountain streams
  In sportive waterfall:
I see thy form, as when
  Thou wert a living thing,
And blossomed in the eyes of men
  Like any flower of spring.'

Nor is the passion of love, when experienced in dreams, less vivid than any other emotion, or the sensation to which it gives rise less pleasurable. I do not here allude to the passion in its physical sense, but to that more moral and intellectual feeling, the result of deep sensibility and attachment. Men who never loved before, have conceived a deep affection to some particular woman in their dreams, which, continuing to operate upon them after they awoke, has actually terminated in a sincere and lasting fondness for the object of their visionary love. Men, again, who actually are in love, dream more frequently of this subject than of any thing else—fancying themselves in the society of their mistresses, and enjoying a happiness more exquisite than is compatible with the waking state—a happiness, in short, little removed from celestial. Such feelings are not confined to men; they pervade the female breast with equal intensity; and the young maiden, stretched upon the couch of sleep, may have her spirit filled with the image of her lover, while her whole being swims in the ecstacies of impassioned, yet virtuous attachment. At other times, this pure passion may, in both sexes, be blended with one of a grosser character; which also may acquire an increase of pleasurable sensation: to such an extent is every circumstance, whether of delight or suffering, exaggerated by sleep.

For the same reason that the lover dreams of love, does the newly married woman dream of children They, especially if she have a natural fondness for them—if she herself be pregnant, or possess an ardent longing for offspring—are often the subject of her sleeping thoughts; and she conceives herself to be encircled by them, and experiencing intense pleasure in their innocent society. Men who are very fond of children often experience the same sensations; and both men and women who are naturally indifferent in this respect, seldom dream about them, and never with any feelings of peculiar delight.

During the actual process of any particular dream, we are never conscious that we are really dreaming: but it sometimes happens that a second dream takes place, during which we have a consciousness, or a suspicion, that the events which took place in the first dream were merely visionary, and not real. People, for instance, sometimes fancy in sleep, that they have acquired wealth: this may be called the first dream; and during its progress they never for a moment doubt the reality of their impressions; but a second one supervenes upon this, and they then begin to wonder whether their riches be real or imaginary—in other words, they try to ascertain whether they had been previously dreaming or not. But even in the second dream we are unconscious of dreaming. We still seem to ourselves to be broad awake—a proof that in dreams we are never aware of being asleep. This unconsciousness of being asleep during the dreaming state, is referable to the quiescent condition of the reasoning powers. The mind is wholly subject to the sceptre of other faculties; and whatever emotions or images they invoke seem to be real, for want of a controlling power to point out their true character.

for so soon as the state of mind which recalled these impressions was removed, they also disappeared, as she was as ignorant of Welsh as before she was taken ill.

* Mr Combe mentions the case of an Irish porter to a warehouse, who, in one of his drunken fits, left a parcel at the wrong house, and when sober could not recollect what he had done with it; but the next time he got drunk, he recollected where he had left it, and went and recovered it.

'You stood before me like a thought,
A dream remembered in a dream.'

Those troubled with deafness do not hear distinctly such sounds as they conceive to be uttered during sleep. Dr. Darwin speaks of a gentleman who, for thirty years, had entirely lost his hearing, and who in his dreams never seemed to converse with any person except by the fingers or in writing: he never had the impression of hearing them speak. In like manner, a blind man seldom dreams of visible objects, and never if he has been blind from his birth. Dr Blacklock, indeed, who became blind in early infancy, may seem an exception to this rule. While asleep, he was conscious of a sense which he did not possess in the waking state, and which bears some analogy to sight. He imagined that he was united to objects by a sort of distant contact, which was effected by threads or strings passing from their bodies to his own.

The illusion of dreams is much more complete than that of the most exquisite plays. We pass, in a second of time, from one country to another; and persons who lived in the most different ages of the world are brought together in strange and incongruous confusion. It is not uncommon to see, at the same moment, Robert the Bruce, Julius Cæsar, and Marlborough in close conversation. Nothing, in short, however monstrous, incredible, or impossible, seems absurd Equally striking examples of illusion occur when the person awakes from a dream, and imagines that he hears voices or beholds persons in the room beside him. In the first cases we are convinced, on awaking, of the deceptive nature of our visions, from the utter impossibility of their occurrence; they are at variance with natural laws; and a single effort of reason is sufficient to point out their absolute futility. But when the circumstances which seem to take place are not in themselves conceived impossible, however unlikely they may be, it is often a matter of the utmost difficulty for us to be convinced of their real character. On awaking, we are seldom aware that, when they took place, we laboured under a dream. Such is their deceptive nature, and such the vividness with which they appear to strike our senses, that we imagine them real; and accordingly often start up in a paroxysm of terror, having the idea that our chamber is invaded by thieves, that strange voices are calling upon us, or that we are haunted by the dead. When there is no way of confuting these impressions, they often remain ineradicably fixed in the mind, and are regarded as actual events, instead of the mere chimeras of sleep. This is particularly the case with the weak-minded and superstitious, whose feelings are always stronger than their judgments; hence the thousand stories of ghosts and warnings with which the imaginations of those persons are haunted—hence the frequent occurrence of nocturnal screaming and terror in children, whose reflecting faculties are naturally too weak to correct the impressions of dreams, and point out their true nature—hence the painful illusions occurring even to persons of strong intellect, when they are debilitated by watchfulness, long-continued mental suffering, or protracted disease. These impressions often arise without any apparent cause: at other times, the most trivial circumstances will produce them. A voice, for instance, in a neighbouring street, may seem to proceed from our own apartment, and may assume a character of the most appalling description; while the tread of footsteps, or the knocking of a hammer over-head, may resolve itself into a frightful figure stalking before us.

'I know,' says Mr Waller, 'a gentleman who is living at this moment a needless slave to terror, which arises from a circumstance which admits easily of explanation. He was lying in his bed with his wife, and, as he supposed, quite awake, when he felt distinctly the impression of some person's hand upon his right shoulder, which created such a degree of alarm that he dared not to move himself in bed, and indeed could not, if he had possessed the courage. It was some time before he had it in his power to awake his wife, and communicate to her the subject of his terror. The shoulder which had felt the impression of the hand, continued to feel benumbed and uncomfortable for some time. It had been uncovered, and most probably, the *cold* to which it was exposed was the cause of the phenomenon.'*

An attack of dreaming illusion, not, however, accompanied with any unpleasant feeling, occurred to myself lately. I had fallen accidentally asleep upon an armchair, and was suddenly awaked by hearing, as I supposed, two of my brothers talking and laughing at the door of the room, which stood wide open. The impressions were so forcible, that I could not believe them fallacious, yet I ascertained that they were so entirely; for my brothers had gone to the country an hour before, and did not return for a couple of hours afterwards.

There are few dreams involving many circumstances, which are, from beginning to end, perfectly philosophical and harmonious: there is usually some absurd violation of the laws of consistency, a want of congruity, a deficiency in the due relation of cause and effect, and a string of conclusions altogether unwarranted by the premises. Mr Hood, in his 'Whims and Oddities,' gives a curious illustration of the above facts. 'It occurred,' says he, 'when I was on the eve of marriage, a season when, if lovers sleep sparingly, they dream profusely. A very brief slumber sufficed to carry me, in the night coach, to Bogner, It had been concerted between Honoria and myself that we should pass the honeymoon at some such place upon the coast. The purpose of my solitary journey was to procure an appropriate dwelling, and which, we had agreed upon, should be a little pleasant house, with an indispensable look-out upon the sea. I chose one accordingly, a pretty villa, with bow windows, and a prospect delightfully marine. The ocean murmur sounded incessantly from the beach. A decent elderly body, in decayed sables, undertook on her part to promote the comfort of the occupants by every suitable attention, and, as she assured me, at a very reasonable rate. So far the nocturnal faculty had served me truly: a day dream could not have proceeded more orderly: but alas! just here, when the dwelling was selected, the sea-view was secured, the rent agreed upon, when every thing was plausible, consistent, and rational, the incoherent fancy crept in, and confounded all—by marrying me to the old woman of the house!'

There are no limits to the extravagancies of those visions sometimes called into birth by the vivid exercise of the imagination. Contrasted with them, the wildest fictions of Rabelais, Ariosto, or Dante, sink into absolute probabilities. I remember of dreaming on one occasion that I possessed ubiquty, twenty resemblances of myself appearing in as many different places, in the same room; and each being so thoroughly possessed by my own mind, that I could not ascertain which of them was myself, and which my double, &c. On this occasion, fancy so far travelled into the regions of absurdity, that I conceived myself riding upon my own back—one of the resemblances being mounted upon another, and both animated with the soul appertaining to myself. in such a manner that I knew not whether I was the *carrier* or the *carried.* At another time, I dreamed that I was converted into a mighty pillar of stone, which reared its head in the midst of a desert, where it stood for ages, till generation after generation melted away before it. Even in this state, though unconscious for possessing any organs of sense, or being else than a mass of lifeless stone, I saw every object around—the mountains growing bald with age—the forest trees drooping in decay; and I heard whatever

* Waller's 'Treatise on the Incubus or Nightmare.'

sounds nature is in the custom of producing such as the thunder-peal breaking over my naked head, the winds howling past me, or the ceaseless murmur of streams. At last I also waxed old, and began to crumble into dust, while the moss and ivy accumulated upon me, and stamped me with the aspect of hoar antiquity. The first of these visions may have arisen from reading Hoffman's 'Devil's Elixir,' where there is an account of a man who supposed he had a double, or, in other words, was both himself and not himself; and the second had perhaps its origin in the Heathen Mythology, a subject to which I am extremely partial, and which abounds in stories of metamorphosis.

Such dreams as occur in a state of drunkenness are remarkable for their extravagance. Exaggeration beyond limits is a very general attendant upon them; and they are usually of a more airy and fugitive character than those proceeding from almost any other source. The person seems as if he possessed unusual lightness, and could mount into the air, or float upon the clouds, while every object around him reels and staggers with emotion. But of all dreams, there are none which, for unlimited wildness, equal those produced by narcotics. An eminent artist, under the influence of opium, fancied the ghastly figures in Holbein's 'Dance of Death' to become vivified—each grim skeleton being endowed with life and motion, and dancing and grinning with an aspect with hideous reality. The 'English Opium Eater,' in his 'Confessions,' has given a great variety of eloquent and appalling descriptions of the effects produced by this drug upon the imagination during sleep. Listen to one of them:—

'Southern Asia is, and has been for thousands of years, the part of the earth most swarming with human life; the great *officina gentium*. Man is a weed in those regions. The vast empires, also, into which the enormous population of Asia has always been cast, give a farther sublimity to the feelings associated with all Oriental names or images. In China, over and above what it has in common with the rest of Southern Asia, I am terrified by the modes of life, by the manners, and the barrier of utter abhorrence and want of sympathy placed between us by feelings deeper than I can analyze. I could sooner live with lunatics or brute animals. All this, and much more than I can say, or have time to say the reader must enter into before he can comprehend the unimaginable horror which these dreams of Oriental imagery and mythological tortures impressed upon me. Under the connecting feeling of tropical heat and vertical sunlights, I brought together all creatures, birds, beasts, reptiles, all trees and plants, usages and appearances, that are found in all tropical regions, and assembled them together in China or Indostan. From kindred feelings I soon brought Egypt and all her gods under the same law. I was stared at, hooted at, grinned at, chattered at, by monkeys, by paroquets, and cockatoos. I ran into pagodas: and was fixed for centuries at the summit, or in the secret rooms; I was the idol; I was the priest; I was worshipped; I was sacrificed. I fled from the wrath of Brama through all the forests of Asia: Vishnu hated me: Seeva laid in wait for me. I came suddenly upon Isis and Osiris: I had done a deed, they said, which the ibis and the crocodile trembled at. I was buried for a thousand years, in stone coffins, with mummies and sphinxs, in narrow chambers, at the heart of eternal pyramids. I was kissed, with cancerous kisses, by crocodiles, and laid confounded with all unutterable slimy things, amongst reeds and Nilotic mud.'

Again; 'Hitherto the human face had mixed often in my dreams, but not so despotically, nor with any special power of tormenting. But now that which I have called the tyranny of the human face began to unfold itself. Perhaps some part of my London life might be answerable for this. Be that as it may, now it was that upon the rocking waters of the ocean, the human face began to appear; the sea appeared paved with innumerable faces, upturned to the heavens: faces imploring, wrathful, despairing, surged upwards by thousands, by myriads, by generations, by centuries:—my agitation was infinite—my mind tossed and surged with the ocean.'

I have already spoken of the analogy subsisting between dreaming and insanity, and shall now mention a circumstance which occurs in both states, and points out a very marked similitude of mental condition. The same thing also occasionally, or rather frequently, takes place in drunkenness, which is, to all intents and purposes, a temporary paroxysm of madness. It often happens, for instance, that such objects or persons as we have seen before and are familiar with, become utterly changed in dreams, and bear not the slightest resemblance to their *real* aspect. It might be thought that such a circumstanee would so completely annihilate their identity as to prevent us from believing them to be what, by us, they are conceived; but such is not the case. We never doubt that the particular object or person presented to our eyes appears in its true character. In illustration of this fact, I may mention, that I lately visited the magnificent palace of Versailles in a dream, but that deserted abode of kings stood not before me as when I have gazed upon it broad awake; it was not only magnified beyond even its stupendous dimensions, and its countless splendors immeasurably increased, but the very aspect itself of the mighty pile was changed; and instead of stretching its huge Corinthian front along the entire breadth of an elaborate and richly fantastic garden, adorned to profusion with alcoves, fountains, waterfalls, statues, and terraces, it stood alone in a boundless wilderness—an immense architectural creation of the Gothic ages, with a hundred spires and ten thousand minarets sprouting up, and piercing with their pointed pinnacles the sky. The whole was as different as possible from the reality, but this never once occurred to my mind; and, while gazing upon the visionary fabric, I never doubted for an instant that it then appeared as it had ever done, and was in no degree different from what I had often previously beheld.

Another dream I shall relate in illustration of this point. It was related to me by a young lady, and, independent of its illustrative value, is well worthy of being preserved as a specimen of fine imagination. 'I dreamed,' said she, 'that I stood alone upon the brink of a dreadful precipice, at the bottom of which rolled a great river. While gazing awe-struck upon the gulph below, some one from behind laid a hand upon my shoulder, and, on looking back, I saw a tall, venerable figure with a long, flowing, silvery beard, and clothed in white garments, whom I at once knew to be the Saviour of the world. "Do you see," he inquired, "the great river that washes the foundation of the rock upon which you now stand? I shall dry it up, so that not a drop of its waters shall remain, and all the fishes that are in it shall perish." He then waved his hand, and the river was instantly dried up; and I saw the fishes gasping and writhing in the channel, where they all straightway died. "Now," said he, "the river is dried up and the fishes are dead; but to give you a farther testimony of my power, I shall bring back the flood, and every creature that was wont to inhabit it shall live again." And he waved his hand a second time, and the river was instantly restored, its dry bed filled with volumes of water, and all the dead fishes brought back unto life. On looking round to express to him my astonishment at those extraordinary miracles, and to fall down and worship him, he was gone; and I stood by myself upon the precipice, gazing with astonishment at the river which rolled a thousand feet beneath me.' In this fine vision, the difference between the aspect of Christ as he appeared in it, and as he is represented in the sacred writings, as well as in paintings, did not suggest itself to the mind of the dreamer. He came in the guise of an aged man, which is diametrically opposite to our habitual impressions of his aspect. If it be asked what produces such differences between the reality and the representation, I apprehend we must refer it to some sudden second dream or flash of thought breaking in upon the first, and confusing its character. For instance, I have a dream of an immense Gothic pile, when something about Versailles, somehow, occurs to my mind, and this I immediately associate with the object before me. The lady has the idea of an old man in her dream, and the thought of Christ happening to come across her at the instant, she identifies it involuntarily with the object of her vision. There is yet another explanation of the latter. The old man has the power of working a great miracle; so had Christ, and she is thus led to confound the two together. She, it is true, imagines she knows the old man at once to be the Saviour, without any previous intimation of his miraculous gifts; but, this, very possibly, may be a mistake; and the knowledge which she only acquires after witnessing his power, she may, by the confusion attendant on dreams, suppose to have occurred to her in the first instance. These facts, combined with the dormant state of the reflecting faculties, which do not rectify the erroneous impressions, render the explanation of such dreams sufficiently easy, however puzzling, and unaccountable at first sight.

In some cases, the illusion is not merely confined to sleep, but extends itself to the waking state. To illustrate this I may state the following circumstance: Some years ago, my impressions concerning the aspect and localities of Inverness, were strangely confused by a dream which I had of that town, taking so strong a hold upon my fancy as to be mistaken for a reality. I had been there before, and was perfectly familiar with the appearance of the town, but this was presented in so different a light, and with so much force by the dream, that I, at last, became unable to say which of the two aspects was the real one. Indeed, the visionary panorama exhibited to my mind, took the strongest hold upon it; and I rather felt inclined to believe that this was the veritable appearance of the town, and that the one which I had actually beheld, was merely the illusion of the dream. This uncertainty continued for several years, till, being again in that quarter, I satisfied myself on the real state of the case. On this occasion, the dream must have occurred to my mind some time after it had happened, and taken such a firm hold upon it as to dethrone the reality, and taken its place. I remember distinctly of fancying that the little woody hill of Tomnachurich was in the centre of the town, although it stands at some distance from it; that the principle steeple was on the opposite side of the street to that on which it stands; and that the great mountain of Ben-Wevis, many miles off, was in the immediate neighborhood.

The power of imagination is perhaps never so vividly displayed, as in those dreams which haunt the guilty mind. When any crime of an infamous character has been perpetrated, and when the person is not so utterly hardened as to be insensible of his iniquity, the wide storehouse of retributive vengeance is opened up, and its appalling horrors poured upon him. In vain does he endeavor to expel the dreadful remembrance of his deeds, and bury them in forgetfulness; from the abyss of slumber they start forth, as the vampyres start from their sepulchres, and hover around him like the furies that pursued the footsteps of Orestes; while the voice of conscience stuns his ears with murmurs of judgment and eternity. Such is the punishment reserved for the guilty in sleep. During the busy stir of active existence, they may contrive to evade the memory of their wickedness—to silence the whispers of the 'still small voice' within them, and cheat themselves with a semblance of happiness; but when their heads are laid upon the pillow, the flimsy veil which hung between them and crime, melts away like an illusive vapor, and displays the latter in naked and horrid deformity. Then, in the silence of night, the 'still small voice' is heard like an echo from the tomb; then, a crowd of doleful remembrances rush in upon the criminal, no longer to be debarred from visiting the depths of his spirit; and when dreams succeed to such broken and miserable repose, it is only to aggravate his previous horrors, and present them in a character of still more overwhelming dread.*

"Though thy slumber may be deep,
Yet thy spirit shall not sleep;
There are shades which will not vanish,
There are thoughts thou canst not banish;
By a power to thee unknown,
Thou canst never be alone;
Thou art wrapt as with a shroud,
Thou art gathered in a cloud;
And forever shalt thou dwell
In the spirit of this spell."

Such are the principal phenomena of dreams; and from them it will naturally be deduced, that dreaming may occur under a great variety of circumstances; that it may result from the actual state of the body or mind, previous to falling asleep; or exist as a train of emotions which can be referred to no apparent external cause. The forms it assumes are also as various as the causes giving rise to it, and much more striking in their nature. In dreams, imagination unfolds, most gorgeously, the ample stores of its richly decorated empire; and in proportion to the splendor of that faculty in any individual, are the visions which pass before him in sleep. But even the most dull and passionless, while under the dreaming influence, frequently enjoy a temporary inspiration: their torpid faculties are aroused from the benumbing spell which hung over them in the waking state, and lighted up with the Promethean fire of genius and romance; the prose of their frigid spirits is converted into magnificent poetry; the atmosphere around them peopled with new and unheard-of imagery; and they walk in a region to which the proudest flights of their limited energies could never otherwise have attained.

I shall conclude this chapter with a few words on the management of dreams.

When dreams are of a pleasing character, no one cares any thing about their removal: it is only when they get distressing and threaten to injure the health of the individual, by frequent recurrence, that this becomes an important object. When dreams assume the character of nightmare, they must be managed according to the methods laid down for the cure of that affection. In all cases, the condition of the digestive organs must be attended to, as any disordered state of these parts is

* 'No fiction of romance presents so awful a picture of the ideal tyrant as that of Caligula by Suetonius. His palace—radiant with purple and gold, but murder every where lurking beneath flowers; his smiles and echoing laughter. masking (yet hardly meant to mask) his foul treachery of heart; his hideous and tumultuous dreams; his baffled sleep, and his sleepless nights, compose the picture of an Æschylus. What a master's sketch lies in those few lines:—'Incitabatur insomnio maxime; neque enim plus tribus horis nocturnis quiescebat; ac ne his placida quiete, at pavida miris rerum imaginibus; ut qui inter ceteras pelagi quondam speciem colloquentem secum videre visus sit. Ideoque magna parte noctis, vigiliæ cubandique tædio, nunc toro residens, nunc per longissimas porticus vagus, invocare identidem atque expectare lucem consueverat;'—*i. e.* But above all, he was tormented with nervous irritation, by sleeplessness; for he enjoyed not more than three hours of nocturnal repose: nor even these in pure, untroubled rest, but agitated by phantasmata of portentous augury; as, for example, upon one occasion he fancied he saw the sea, under some definite impersonation, conversing with himself. Hence it was, and from this incapacity of sleeping, and from weariness of lying awake, that he had fallen into habits of ranging all the night long through the palace, sometimes throwing himself on a couch, sometimes wandering along the vast corrodors—watching for the earliest dawn, and anxiously invoking its approach.'—*Blackwood's Magazine*, vol. xxxiii. p. 59.

apt to induce visions of a very painful character. For this purpose, mild laxatives may become useful ; and if the person is subject to heartburn, he should use a little magnesia, chalk, or carbonate of soda, occasionally. Attention, also, must be paid to the diet ; and as suppers, with some people, have a tendency to generate dreams of all kinds, these meals should, in such cases, be carefully avoided. At the same time, great care should be taken not to brood over any subject upon lying down, but to dispel, as soon as possible, all intrusive ideas, especially if they are of a painful nature. If there is any unpleasant circumstances, such as hardness, irregularity, &c., connected with the bed, which tends to affect sleep, and thus induce dreams, it must be removed. Late reading, the use of tea or coffee shortly before going to rest, or any thing which may stimulate the brain, ought likewise to be avoided.

If dreaming seems to arise from any fulness of the system, blooding and low diet will sometimes effect a cure. Mr Stewart, the celebrated pedestrian traveller, states that he never dreamed when he lived exclusively upon vegetable food. This, however, may not hold true with every one. 'When dreams arise from a diminution of customary stimuli, a light supper, a draught of porter, a glass of wine, or a dose of opium, generally prevent them. Habitual noises, when suspended should be restored.'*

In speaking of dreams representative of danger, I may mention that there are instances of persons, who, having determined to remember that the perils seen in them are fallacious, have actually succeeded in doing so, while asleep ; and have thus escaped the terrors which those imaginary dangers could otherwise have produced. Haller relates a case of this kind ; and Mr Dugald Stewart mentions that the plan was successfully adopted by Dr Reid to get rid of the distress of those fearful visions by which he was frequently annoyed. Whenever, in a dream, the Doctor supposed himself on the brink of a precipice, or any other dangerous situation, it was his custom to throw himself over, and thus destroy the illusion. Dr Beattie also relates, that at one time he found himself in a dangerous situation upon the parapet of a bridge. Reflecting that he was not subject to pranks of this nature, he began to fancy that it might be a dream, and determined to pitch himself over, with the conviction that this would restore him to his senses, which accordingly took place.† I could never manage to carry this system into effect in an ordinary dream of terror, but I have sometimes succeeded in doing so during an attack of nightmare ; and have thus very materially mitigated the alarm produced by that distressing sensation. This intellectual operation may also be successfuly employed to dispel the lowness of spirits under which we often awake from unpleasant visions by teaching us that the depression we experience is merely the result of some unnatural excitement in the brain. Indeed, all kinds of melancholy, not based upon some obvious foundation, might be mitigated or dispelled altogether, could we only oppose our feelings with the weapons of reason, and see things as they really are, and not as they only seem to be.

CHAPTER IV.

PROPHETIC POWER OF DREAMS.

Dreams have been looked upon by some, as the occasional means of giving us an insight into futurity, This opinion is so singularly unphilosophical, that I would not have noticed it, were it not advocated even by persons of good sense and education. In ancient times, it was so common as to obtain universal belief ; and the greatest men placed as implicit faith in it as in any fact of which their own senses afforded them cognizance. That it is wholly erroneous, however, cannot be doubted ; and any person who examines the nature of the human mind, and the manner in which it operates in dreams, must be convinced, that under no circumstances, except those of a miracle. in which the ordinary laws of nature are triumphed over, can such an event ever take place. The sacred writings testifiy that miracles were common in former times ; but I believe no man of sane mind will contend that they ever occur in the present state of the world. In judging of things as now constituted, we must discard supernatural influence altogether, and estimate events according to the general laws which the great ruler of nature has appointed for the guidance of the universe. If, in the present day, it were possible to conceive a suspension of these laws, it must, as in former ages, be in reference to some great event, and to serve some mighty purpose connected with the general interests of the human race ; but if faith is to be placed in modern miracles, we must suppose that God suspended the above laws for the most trivial and useless of purposes —as, for instance, to intimate to a man that his grandmother will die on a particular day, that a favourite mare has broke her neck, that he has received a present of a brace of game, or that a certain friend will step in and take pot-luck with him on the morrow.

At the same time, there can be no doubt that many circumstances occurring in our dreams have been actually verified ; but this must be regarded as altogether the effect of chance ; and for one dream which turns out to be true, at least a thousand are false. In fact, it is only when they are of the former description, that we take any notice of them ; the latter are looked upon as mere idle vagaries, and speedily forgotten. If a man, for instance, dreams that he has gained a law-suit in which he is engaged, and if this circumstance actually takes place, there is nothing at all extraordinary in the coincidence : his mind was full of the subject, and, in sleep, naturally resolved itself into that train of ideas in which it was most deeply interested. Or if we have a friend engaged in war, our fears for his safety will lead us to dream of death or captivity, and we may see him pent up in a hostile prison-house, or lying dead upon the battle plain. And should these melancholy catastrophies ensue we call our vision to memory ; and, in the excited state of mind into which we are thrown, are apt to consider it as a prophetic warning, indicative of disaster. The following is a very good illustration of this particular point.

Miss M——, a young lady, a native of Ross-shire, was deeply in love with an officer who accompanied Sir John Moore in the peninsular war. The constant danger to which he was exposed, had an evident effect upon her spirits. She became pale and melancholy in perpetually brooding over his fortunes ; and, in spite of all that reason could do, felt a certain conviction, that when she last parted with her lover, she had parted with him for ever. In vain was every scheme tried to dispel from her mind the awful idea ; in vain were all the sights which opulence could command, unfolded before her eyes. In the midst of pomp and gaiety, when music and laughter echoed around her, she walked as a pensive phantom, over whose head some dreadful and mysterious influence hung. She was brought by her affectionate parents to Edinburgh, and introduced into all the gaiety of that metropolis, but nothing could restore her, or banish from her mind the insupportable load which oppressed it. The song and the dance were tried in vain : they only aggravated her distress

* Rush's Medical Iuquiries.

† These facts do not controvert what is elsewhere stated of a person never being aware, during the actual process of a dream, that he was dreaming. While the above dreams were in progress, the individuals never doubted that they were dreaming : the doubt, and the actions consequent upon it, were after-operations.

and made the bitterness of despair more poignant. In a surprisingly short period, her graceful form declined into all the appalling characteristics of a fatal illness; and she seemed rapidly hastening to the grave, when a dream confirmed the horrors she had long anticipated, and gave the finishing stroke to her sorrows. One night, after falling asleep, she imagined she saw her lover, pale, bloody, and wounded in the breast, enter her apartment. He drew aside the curtains of the bed, and with a look of the utmost mildness, informed her that he had been slain in battle, desiring her, at the same time, to comfort herself, and not take his death too seriously to heart. It is needless to say what influence this vision had upon a mind so replete with woe. It withered it entirely, and the unfortunate girl died a few days thereafter, but not without desiring her parents to note down the day of the month on which it happened, and see if it would be confirmed, as she confidently declared it would. Her anticipation was correct, for accounts were shortly after received that the young man was slain at the battle of Corunna, which was fought on the very day, on the night of which his mistress had beheld the vision.

This relation, which may be confidently relied upon, is one of the most striking examples of identity between the dream and the real circumstances with which I am acquainted, but it must be looked upon as merely accidental. The lady's mind was deeply interested in the fate of her lover, and full of that event which she most deeply dreaded—his death. The time of this occurrence, as coinciding with her dream, is certainly curious; but still there is nothing in it which can justify us in referring it to any other origin than chance. The following events, which occurred to myself, in August 1821, are almost equally remarkable, and are imputable to the same fortuitous cause.

I was then in Caithness, when I dreamed that a near relation of my own, residing three hundred miles off, had suddenly died: and immediately thereafter awoke in a state of inconceivable terror, similar to that produced by a paroxysm of nightmare. The same day, happening to be writing home, I mentioned the circumstance in a half-jesting, half-earnest way. To tell the truth, I was afraid to be serious, lest I should be laughed at for putting any faith in dreams. However, in the interval between writing and receiving an answer, I remained in a state of most unpleasant suspense. I felt a presentiment that something dreadful had happened, or would happen; and although I could not help blaming myself for a childish weakness in so feeling, I was unable to get rid of the painful idea which had taken such rooted possession of my mind. Three days after sending away the letter, what was my astonishment when I received one written the day subsequent to mine, and stating that the relative of whom I had dreamed, had been struck with a fatal shock of palsy the day before—*viz.* the very day on the morning of which I had beheld the appearance in my dream! My friends received my letter two days after sending their own away, and were naturally astonished at the circumstance. I may state that my relation was in perfect health before the fatal event took place. It came upon him like a thunderbolt, at a period when no one could have the slightest anticipation of danger.

The following case will interest the reader, both on its own account, and from the remarkable coincidence between the dream and the succeeding calamity; but, like all other instances of the kind, this also must be referred to chance.

'Being in company the other day, when the conversation turned upon dreams, I related one, which as it happened to my own father, I can answer for the perfect truth of it. About the year 1731, my father, Mr D. of K——, in the County of Cumberland, came to Edinburgh to attend the classes, having the advantage of an uncle in the regiment then in the Castle, and remained under the protection of his uncle and aunt, Major and Mrs Griffiths, during the winter. When spring arrived, Mr D. and three or four young gentlemen from England, (his intimates,) made parties to visit all the neighboring places about Edinburgh, Roslin, Arthur's Seat, Craig-Millar, &c., &c. Coming home one evening from some of those places, Mr D. said, 'We have made a party to go a-fishing to Inch-Keith tomorrow, if the morning is fine, and have bespoke our boat; we shall be off at six;' no objection being made, they separated for the night.

'Mrs Griffiths, had not been long asleep, till she screamed out in the most violent agitated manner, 'The boat is sinking; save, oh, save them!' The Major awaked her, and said, 'Were you uneasy about the fishing party?' 'Oh no,' said she, 'I had not once thought of it.' She then composed herself, and soon fell asleep again; in about an hour, she cried out in a dreadful fright, 'I see the boat is going down.' The Major again awoke her, and she said, 'It has been owing to the other dream I had; for I feel no uneasiness about it.' After some conversation, they both fell sound asleep, but no rest could be obtained for her; in the most extreme agony, she again screamed, 'They are gone; the boat is sunk!' When the Major awakened her, she said, 'Now I cannot rest; Mr D. must not go, for I feel, should he go, I would be miserable till his return; the thoughts of it would almost kill me.'

'She instantly arose, threw on her wrapping-gown, went to his bedside, for his room was next their own, and with great difficulty she got his promise to remain at home. 'But what am I to say to my young friends whom I was to meet at Leith at six o'clock?' 'With great truth you may say your aunt is ill, for I am so at present; consider, you are an only son, under our protection, and should any thing happen to you, it would be my death.' Mr D. immediately wrote a note to his friends, saying he was prevented from joining them, and sent his servant with it to Leith. The morning came in most beautifully, and continued so till three o'clock, when a violent storm arose, and in an instant the boat, and all that were in it, went to the bottom, and were never heard of, nor was any part of it ever seen.'*

Equally singular is the following case, from the 'Memoirs of Lady Fanshawe.'

'My mother being sick to death of a fever, three months after I was born, which was the occasion she gave me suck no longer, her friends and servants thought to all outward appearnce she was dead, and so lay almost two days and a night; but Dr Winston coming to comfort my father, went into my mother's room, and looking earnestly on her face, said, 'She was so handsome, and now looks so lovely, I cannot think she is dead;' and suddenly took a lancet out of his pocket, and with it cut the sole of her foot, which bled. Upon this, he immediately caused her to be laid upon the bed again, and to be rubbed, and such means, as she came to life, and opening her eyes, saw two of her kinswomen stand by her, my Lady Knollys and my Lady Russell, both with great wide sleeves, as the fashion then was, and said, 'Did not you promise me fifteen years, and are you come again' which they not understanding, persuaded her to keep her spirits quiet in that great weakness wherein she then was; but some hours after, she desired my father and Dr Howlsworth might be left alone with her, to whom she said, 'I will acquaint you, that during the time of my trance I was in great quiet, but in a place I could neither distinguish nor describe; but the sense of leaving my girl, who is dearer to me than all my children, remained a trouble upon my spirits. Suddenly I saw two by me, clothed in long white garments, and methought I fell down upon my face upon the dust; and they asked

* 'Blackwood's Edinburgh Magazine,' vol. xix. p. 73.

why I was so troubled in so great happiness. I replied, O let me have the same grant given to Hezekiah, that I may live fifteen years to see my daughter a woman: to which they answered, It is done: and then, at that instant, I awoke out of my trance!' and Dr Howlsworth did there affirm, that that day she died made just fifteen years from that time.'

A sufficiently striking instance of such coincidence occurs in the case of Dr Donne, the metaphysical poet; but I believe that, in this case, it was a spectral illusion rather than a common dream. Two days after he had arrived in Paris, he was left alone in a room where he had been dining with Sir Robert Drury and a few companions. 'Sir Robert returned about an hour afterwards. He found his friend in a state of ecstacy, and so altered in his countenance, that he could not look upon him without amazement. The Doctor was not able for some time to answer the question, *what had befallen him?*—but a long and perplexed pause, at last said, 'I have seen a dreadful vision since I saw you; I have seen my dear wife pass twice by me through this room, with her hair hanging about her shoulders, and a dead child in her arms. This I have seen since I saw you.' To which Sir Robert answered, 'Sure, Sir, you have slept since I went out; and this is the result of some melancholy dream, which I desire you to forget, for you are now awake.' Donne replied, 'I cannot be more sure that I now live, than that I have not slept since I saw you; and am as sure that at her second appearing she stopped, looked me in in the face and vanished.''* It is certainly very curious that Mrs Donne, who was then in England, was at this time sick in bed, and had been delivered of a dead child, on the same day, and about the same hour, that the vision occurred. There were distressing circumstances in the marriage of Dr Donne which account for his mind being strongly impressed with the image of his wife, to whom he was exceedingly attached; but these do not render the coincidence above related less remarkable.

I do not doubt that the apparition of Julius Cæsar, which appeared to Brutus, and declared it would meet him at Philippi, was either a dream or a spectral illusion—probably the latter. Brutus, in all likelihood, had some idea that the battle which was to decide his fate would be fought at Philippi: probably it was a good military position, which he had fixed upon as a fit place to make a final stand; and he had done enough to Cæsar to account for his own mind being painfully and constantly engrossed with the image of the assasinated Dictator. Hence the verification of this supposed warning—hence the easy explanation of a supposed supernatural event.

At Newark-upon-Trent, a curious custom, founded upon the preservation of Alderman Clay and his family by a dream, has prevailed since the days of Cromwell. On the 11th March, every year, penny loaves are given away to any one who chooses to appear at the town hall and apply for them, in commemoration of the alderman's deliverance, during the siege of Newark by the parliamentary forces. This gentleman, by will, dated 11th December, 1694, gave to the mayor and aldermen one hundred pounds, the interest of which was to be given to the vicar yearly, on condition of his preaching an annual sermon. Another hundred pounds were also appropriated for the behoof of the poor, in the way above mentioned. The origin of this bequest is singular. During the bombardment of Newark by Oliver Cromwell's forces, the alderman dreamed three nights successively that his house had taken fire, which produced such a vivid impression upon his mind, that he and his family left it; and in a few days the circumstances of his vision actually took place, by the house being burned down by the besiegers.

Dr Abercrombie relates the case of a gentleman in Edinburgh, who was affected with an aneurism of the popliteal artery, for which he was under the care of two eminent surgeons. About two days before the time appointed for the operation, his wife dreamed that a change had taken place in the disease, in consequence of which an operation would not be required. 'On examining the tumor in the morning, the gentleman was astonished to find that the pulsation had entirely ceased; and, in short, this turned out to be a spontaneous cure. To persons not professional, it may be right to mention that the cure of popliteal aneurism, without an operation, is a very uncommon occurrence, not happening, perhaps, in one out of numerous instances, and never to be looked upon as probable in any individual case. It is likely, however, that the lady had heard of the possibility of such a termination, and that her anxiety had very naturally embodied this into a dream: the fulfilment of it, at the very time when the event took place, is certainly a very remarkable coincidence.'*

Persons are said to have had the period of their own death pointed out to them in dreams. I have often heard the case of the late Mr M. of D—— related in support of this statement. It is certainly worth telling, not on account of any supernatural character belonging to it, but simply from the extraordinary coincidence between the dream and the subsequent event. This gentleman dreamed one night that he was out riding, when he stopped at an inn on the road side for refreshment, where he saw several people whom he had known some years before, but who were all dead. He was received kindly by them, and desired to sit down and drink, which he accordingly did. On quitting this strange company, they exacted a promise from him that he would visit them that day six weeks. This he promised faithfully to do; and, bidding them farewell, he rode homewards. Such was the substance of his dream, which he related in a jocular way to his friends, but thought no more about it, for he was a person above all kind of superstition. The event, however, was certainly curious enough, as well as melancholy; for on that very day six weeks on which he had engaged to meet his friends at the inn, he was killed in attempting to spring his horse over a five-barred gate. The famous case of Lord Lyttleton† is also cited as an example of a similar kind, but with less show of reason, for this case is now very generally supposed to be an imposition; and so will almost every other of the same kind, if narrowly investigated. At the same time, I do not mean to doubt that such an event, foretold in a dream, may occasionally come to pass; but I would refer the whole to fortuitous coincidence. Men dream, every now and then, that they will die on a certain day, yet how seldom do we see those predictions fulfiled by the result! In very delicate people, indeed, such a visionary communication, by acting fatally upon the mind, might be the means of occasioning its own fulfilment. In such cases, it has been customary for the friends of the individual to put back the clock an hour or two, so as to let the fatal period pass by without his being aware of it; and as soon as it was fairly passed, to inform him of the circumstance, and laugh him out of his apprehension.

There is another way in which the apparent fulfilment of a dream may be brought about. A good illustration in point is given by Mr Combe. The subject of it was one Scott, executed in 1823, at Jedburg, for murder. 'It is stated in his life, that some years be-

* Hibbert's Philosophy of Apparitions, p. 354.

* Abercrombie's Inquiries concerning the Intellectual Powers, p. 282, 1st edit.

† 'Of late it has been said and published, that the unfortunate nobleman had previously determined to take poison, and of course had it in his own power to ascertain the execution of the prediction. It was, no doubt, singular that a man, who meditated his exit from the world, should have chosen to play such a trick upon his friends. But it is still more credible that a whimsical man should do so wild a thing, than that a messenger should be sent from the dead, to tell a libertine at what precise hour he should expire.'—*Scott's Letters on Demonology*, p. 361

fore the fatal event, he had dreamed that he had committed a murder, and was greatly impressed, with the idea. He frequently spoke of it, and recurred to it as something ominous, till at last it was realized. The organ of *Destructiveness* was large in the head, and so active that he was an enthusiast in poaching, and prone to outrage and violence in his habitual conduct. This activity of the organ might take place during sleep, and then it would inspire his mind with destructive feelings, and the dream of murder would be the consequence. From the great natural strength of the propensity, he probably may have felt, when awake, an inward tendency to this crime; and, joining this and the dream together, we can easily account for the strong impression left by the latter on the mind.' *

One method in which death may appear to be foretold is, by the accession of frightful visions immediately before the fatal illnesses. This, however, goes for nothing in the way of argument, for it was the state of the system shortly before the attack of disease which induced such dreams. According to Silamachus, the epidemic fever which prevailed at Rome was ushered in by attacks of nightmare; and Sylvius Deleboe, who describes the epidemic which raged at Leyden in 1669, states, that previous to each paroxysm of the fever, the patient fell asleep, and suffered a severe attack of nightmare. The vulgar belief, therefore, that unpleasant dreams are ominous of death, is not destitute of foundation; but the cause why they should be so is perfectly natural. It is the incipient disease which produces the dreams, and the fatal event which often follows, is a natural consequence of that disease.

It is undoubtedly owing to the faculty possessed by sleep, of renewing long-forgotten ideas, that persons have had important facts communicated to them in dreams. There have been instances, for example, where valuable documents, sums of money, &c, have been concealed, and where either the person who secreted them or he who had the place of their concealment communicated to him, may have forgotten every thing therewith connected. He may then torture his mind in vain, during the walking state, to recollect the event; and it may be brought to his remembrance, at once, in a dream. In such cases, an apparition is generally the medium through which the seemingly mysterious knowledge is communicated. The imagination conjures up some phantom that discloses the secret; which circumstance, proceeding, in reality, from a simple operation of the mind, is straightway converted into something supernatural, and invested with all the attributes of wonder and awe. When such spectral forms appear, and communicate some fact which turns out to be founded on truth, the person is not always aware that the whole occurred in a dream, but often fancies that he was broad awake when the apparition appeared to him and communicated the particular intelligence. When we hear, therefore, of hidden treasures, wills, &c, being disclosed in such a manner, we are not always to scout the report as false. The spectre divulging the intelligence was certainly the mere chimera of the dreamer's brain, but the facts revealed, apparently by this phantom, may, from the above circumstance, be substantially true. The following curious case is strikingly in point, and is given by Sir Walter Scott in his notes to the new edition of 'The Antiquary'

'Mr R——d of Bowland, a gentleman of landed property in the Vale of Gala, was prosecuted for a very considerable sum, the accumulated arrears of tiend, (or tithe,) for which he was said to be indebted to a noble family, the titulars (lay impropriators of the tithes.) Mr R——d was strongly impressed with the belief that his father had, by a form of process peculiar to the law of Scotland, purchased these lands from the titular, and, therefore, that the present prosecution was groundless. But after an industrious search among his father's papers, an investigation of the public records, and a careful inquiry among all persons who had transacted law business for his father, no evidence could be recovered to support his defence. The period was now near at hand when he conceived the loss of his lawsuit to be inevitable, and he had formed the determination to ride to Edinburgh next day, and make the best bargain he could in the way of compromise. He went to bed with this resolution, and, with all the circumstances of the case floating upon his mind, had a dream to the following purpose. His father, who had been many years dead, appeared to him, he thought, and asked him why he was disturbed in his mind. In dreams, men are not surprised at such apparitions. Mr R——d thought that he informed his father of the cause of his distress, adding, that the payment of a considerable sum of money was the more unpleasant to him, because he had a strong consciousness that it was not due, though he was unable to recover any evidence in support of his belief. 'You are right, my son,' replied the paternal shade; 'I did acquire right to these tiends, for payment of which you are now prosecuted. The papers relating to the transaction are now in the hands of Mr ——, a writer, (or attorney,) who is now retired from professional business, and resides at Inveresk, near Edinburgh. He was a person whom I employed on that occasion for a particular reason, but who never on any other occasion transacted business on my account. It is very possible,' pursued the vision, 'that Mr —— may have forgotten a matter which is now of a very old date; but you may call it to his recollection by this token, that when I came to pay his account, there was difficulty in getting change for a Portugal piece of gold, and we were forced to drink out the balance at a tavern.'

'Mr R——d awoke in the morning with all the words of the vision imprinted on his mind, and thought it worth while to walk across the country to Inveresk, instead of going straight to Edinburgh. When he came there, he waited on the gentleman mentioned in the dream, a very old man. Without saying anything of the vision, he inquired whether he remembered having conducted such a matter for his diseased father. The old gentleman could not at first bring the circumstance to his recollection, but on mention of the Portugal piece of gold, the whole returned upon his memory; he made an immediate search for the papers, and recovered them—so that Mr R——d carried to Edinburgh the documents necessary to gain the cause which he was on the verge of losing.

'The author has often heard this story told by persons who had the best access to know the facts, who were not likely themselves to be deceived, and were certainly incapable of deception. He cannot, therefore, refuse to give it credit, however extraordinary the circumstances may appear. The circumstantial character of the information given in the dream, takes it out of the general class of impressions of the kind, which are occasioned by the fortuitous coincidence of actual events with our sleeping thoughts. On the other hand, few will suppose that the laws of nature were suspended, and a special communication from the dead to the living permitted, for the purpose of saving Mr. R——d a certain number of hundred pounds. The author's theory is, that the dream was only the recapitulation of information which Mr R——d had really received from his father while in life, but which at first he merely recalled as a general impression that the claim was settled. It is not uncommon for persons to recover, during sleep, the thread of ideas which they have lost during their waking hours. It may be added, that this remarkable circumstance was attended with bad consequences to Mr R——d; whose health and spirits were afterwards impaired, by the attention which he thought himself obliged to pay to the visions of the

* Combe's System of Phrenology, p. 511, 3d edit.

night.' This result is a melancholy proof of the effect sometimes produced by ignorance of the natural laws. Had Mr R——d been acquainted with the nature of the brain, and of the manner in which it is affected in sleep, the circumstance above related would have given him no annoyance. He would have traced the whole chain of events to their true source; but, being ignorant of this, he became the victim of superstition, and his life was rendered miserable.

CHAPTER V.

NIGHTMARE.

Nightmare may be defined a painful dream, accompanied with difficult respiratory action, and a torpor in the powers of volition. The reflecting organs are generally more or less awake; and, in this respect, nightmare differs from simple dreaming, where they are mostly quiescent.

This affection, the Ephialtes of the Greeks, and Incubus of the Romans, is one of the most distressing to which human nature is subject. Imagination cannot conceive the horrors it frequently gives rise to, or language describe them in adequate terms. They are a thousand times more frightful than the visions conjured up by necromancy or *diablere;* and far transcend every thing in history or romance, from the fable of the writhing and asp-encircled Laocoon to Dante's appalling picture of Ugolino and his famished offspring, or the hidden tortures of the Spanish inquisition. The whole mind, during the paroxysm, is wrought up to a pitch of unutterable despair: a spell is laid upon the faculties, which freezes them into inaction; and the wretched victim feels as if pent alive in his coffin, or overpowered by resistless and immitigable pressure.

The modifications which nightmare assumes are infinite; but one passion is almost never absent—that of utter and incomprehensible dread. Sometimes the sufferer is buried beneath overwhelming rocks, which crush him on all sides, but still leave him with a miserable consciousness of his situation. Sometimes he is involved in the coils of a horrid, slimy monster, whose eyes have the phosphorescent glare of the sepulchre, and whose breath is poisonous as the marsh of Lerna. Every thing horrible, disgusting, or terriffic in the physical or moral world, is brought before him in fearful array; he is hissed at by serpents, tortured by demons, stunned by the hollow voices and cold touch of apparitions. A mighty stone is laid upon his breast, and crushes him to the ground in helpless agony; mad bulls and tigers pursue his palsied footsteps: the unearthly shrieks and gibberish of hags, witches, and fiends float around him. In whatever situation he may be placed, he feels superlatively wretched; he is Ixion working for ages at his wheel: he is Sisyphus rolling his eternal stone: he is stretched upon the iron bed of Procrustes: he is prostrated by inevitable destiny beneath the approaching wheels of the car of Juggernaut. At one moment, he may have the consciousness of a malignant demon being at his side: then to shun the sight of so appalling an object, he will close his eyes, but still the fearful being makes its presence known; for its icy breath is felt diffusing itself over his visage, and he knows that he is face to face with a fiend. Then, if he look up, he beholds horrid eyes glaring upon him, and an aspect of hell grinning at him with even more than hellish malice. Or, he may have the idea of a monstrous hag squatted upon his breast—mute, motionless, and malignant; an incarnation of the evil spirit—whose intolerable weight crushes the breath out of his body, and whose fixed, deadly, incessant stare petrifies him with horror and makes his very existence insufferable.

In every instance, there is a sense of oppression and helplessness; and the extent to which these are carried, varies according to the violence of the paroxysm. The individual never feels himself a free agent; on the contrary he is spell-bound by some enchantment, and remains an unresisting victim for malice to work its will upon. He can neither breathe, nor walk, nor run, with his wonted facility. If pursued by an imminent danger, he can hardly drag one limb after another; if engaged in combat, his blows are utterly ineffective; if involved in the fangs of any animal, or in the grasp of an enemy, extrication is impossible. He struggles, he pants, he toils, but it is all in vain: his muscles are rebels to the will, and refuse to obey its calls. In no case is there a sense of complete freedom: the benumbing stupor never departs from him; and his whole being is locked up in one mighty spasm. Sometimes he is forcing himself through an aperture too small for the reception of his body, and is there arrested and tortured by the pangs of suffocation produced by the pressure to which he is exposed; or he loses his way in a narrow labyrinth, and gets involved in its contracted and inextricable mazes; or he is entombed alive in a sepulchre, beside the mouldering dead. There is, in most cases, an intense reality in all that he sees, or hears, or feels. The aspects of the hideous phantoms which harass his imagination are bold and defined; the sounds which greet his ear appalling distinct; and when any dimness or confusion of imagery does prevail, it is of the most fearful kind, leaving nothing but dreary and miserable impressions behind it.

Much of the horror experienced in nightmare will depend upon the natural activity of the imagination, upon the condition of the body, and upon the state of mental exertion before going to sleep. If, for instance, we have been engaged in the perusal of such works as 'The Monk,' 'The Mysteries of Udolpho,' or 'Satan's Invisible World Discovered;' and if an attack of nightmare should supervene, it will be aggravated into sevenfold horror by the spectral phantoms with which our minds have been thereby fillled. We will enter into all the fearful mysteries of these writings, which, instead of being mitigated by slumber, acquire an intensity which they never could have possessed in the waking state. The apparitions of murdered victims, like the form of Banquo, which wrung the guilty conscience of Macbeth, will stalk before us; we are surrounded by sheeted ghosts, which glare upon us with their cold sepulchral eyes; our habitation is among the vaults of ancient cathedrals, or among the dungeons of ruined monasteries, and our companions are the dead.

At other times, an association of ludicrous images passes through the mind: every thing becomes incongruous, ridiculous, and absurd. But even in the midst of such preposterous fancies, the passion of mirth is never for one moment excited: the same blank despair, the same freezing *inertia*, the same stifling tortures, still harass us; and so far from being amused by the laughable drama enacted before us, we behold it with sensations of undefined horror and disgust.

In general, during an attack, the person has the consciousness of an utter inability to express his horror by cries. He feels that his voice is half choked by impending suffocation, and that any exertion of it, farther than a deep sigh or groan, is impossible. Sometimes, however, he conceives that he is bellowing with prodigious energy, and wonders that the household are not alarmed by his noise. But this is an illusion: those outcries which he fancies himself uttering, are merely obscure moans, forced with difficulty and pain from the stifled penetralia of his bosom.

Nightmare takes place under various circumstances. Sometimes, from a state of perfect sleep, we glide into it, and feel ourselves unconsciously overtaken by its attendant horrors: at other times, we experience it stealing upon us like a thief, at a period when we are all but awake, and aware of its approach. We have then our senses about us, only, perhaps a little deadened and confused by incipient slumber ; and we feel the gradual advance of the fiend, without arousing ourselves, and scaring him away, althongh we appear to possess the full ability of doing so. Some persons, immediately previous to an attack, have sensations of vertigo and ringing in the ears.

At one time, nightmare melts into unbroken sleep or pleasing dreams ; and when we awake in the morning with merely the remembrance of having had one of its attacks ; at another, it arouses us by its violence, and we start out of it with a convulsive shudder. At the moment of throwing off the fit, we seem to turn round upon the side with a mighty effort, as if from beneath the pressure of a superincumbent weight ; and, the more thoroughly to awake ourselves, we generally kick violently, beat the breast, rise up in bed, and cry out once or twice. As soon as we are able to exercise the voice or voluntary muscles with freedom, the paroxysm is at an end ; but for some time after, we experience extreme terror, and often cold shivering, while the heart throbs violently, and the respiration is hurried. These two latter circumstances are doubted by Dr Darwin, but I am convinced of their existence, both from what I have experienced in my own person, and from what I have been told by others ; indeed, analogy would irresistibly lead us to conclude that they must exist ; and whoever carefully investigates the subject, will find that they do almost universally.

An opinion prevails, that during incubus the person is always upon his back ; and the circumstances of his usually feeling as if in that posture, together with the relief which he experiences on turning round upon his side, are certainly strong presumptions in favour of its accuracy. The sensations, however, which occur, in this state, are fallacious in the highest degree. We have seldom any evidence either that he was on his back, or that he turned round at all. The fact, that he supposed himself in the above position during the fit, and the other fact, that, on recovering from it, he was lying on his side, may have produced the illusion ; and, where he never moved a single muscle, he may conceive that he turned round after a prodigious effort. I have had an attack of this disorder while sitting in an arm-chair, or with my head leaning against a table. In fact, these are the most likely positions to bring it on, the lungs being then more completely compressed than in almost any other posture. I have also had it most distinctly while lying on the side, and I know many cases of a similar description in others. Although, therefore, nightmare may take place more frequently upon the back than upon the side, the opinion that it occurs only in the former of these postures, is altogether incorrect ; and where we are much addicted to its attacks, no posture whatever will protect us.

Persons not particulary subject to incubus, feel no inconvenience, save temporary terror or fatigue, from any occasional attack which they may have ; but those with whom it is habitual, are apt to experience a certain degree of giddiness, ringing in the ears, tension of the forehead, flashing of light before the eyes, and other symptoms of cerebral congestion. A bad taste in the mouth, and more or less fulness about the pit of the stomach, are sometimes experienced after an attack.

The illusions which occur, are perhaps the most extraordinary phenomena of nightmare ; and so strongly are they often impressed upon the mind, that, even on awaking, we find it impossible not to believe them real. We may, for example, be sensible of knockings at the door of our apartment, hear familiar voices calling upon us, and see individuals passing through the chamber. In many cases, no arguments, no efforts of the understanding will convince us that these are merely the chimeras of sleep. We regard them as events of actual occurrence, and will not be persuaded to the contrary. With some, such a belief has gone down to the grave : and others have maintained it strenuously for years, till a recurrence of the illusions under circumstances which rendered their real existence impossible, has shown them that the whole was a dream. Many a good ghost story has had its source in the illusions of nightmare.

The following case related by Mr Waller gives a good idea of the strength of such illusive feelings.

'In the month of February, 1814, I was living in the same house with a young gentlemen, the son of a peer of the United Kingdom, who was at that time under my care, in a very alarming state of health ; and who had been, for several days, in a state of violent delirium. The close attention which his case required from me, together with a degree of personal attachment to him, had rendered me extremely anxious about him ; and as my usual hours of sleep suffered a great degree of interruption from the attendance given to him, I was from that cause alone, rendered more than usually liable to the attacks of nightmare, which consequently intruded itself every night upon my slumbers. The young gentleman in question, from the violence of his delirium, was with great diffiiculty kept in bed ; and had one or twice eluded the vigilance of his attendants, and jumped out of bed, an accident of which I was every moment dreading a repetition. I awoke from one sleep one morning about four o'clock—at least it apppeared to me that I awoke—and heard distinctly the voice of this young gentleman, who seemed to be coming hastily up the stairs leading to my apartment, calling me by name in the manner he was accustomed to do in his delirium ; and, immediately after, I saw him standing by my bedside, holding the curtains open, expressing all that wildness in his looks which accompanies a violent delirium At the same moment, I heard the voices of his two attendants coming up the stairs in search of him, who likewise came into the room and took him away. During all this scene I was attempting to speak, but could not articulate ; I thought, however, that I succeeded in attempting to get out of bed, and assisting his atendants in removing him out of the room ; after which, I returned to bed, and instantly fell asleep. When I waited upon my patient in the morning, I was not a little surprised to find that he was asleep ; and was uttterly confounded on being told that he had been so all night ; and as this was the first sleep he had enjoyed for three or four days, the attendants were very minute in detailing the whole particulars of it. Athough this account appeared inconsistent with what I conceived I had seen, and with what I concluded they knew as well as myself, I did not, for some time, perceive the error into which I had been led, till I observed that some of my questions and remarks were not intelligible ; then I began to suspect the true source of the error, which I should never have discovered had not experience rendered these hallucinations familiar to me. But the whole of this transaction had so much consistency and probability in it, that I might, under different circumstances, have remained forever ignorant of having been imposed upon in this instance, by my senses.'*

During nightmare, the deepness of the slumber varies much at different times. Sometimes we are in a state closely approximating upon perfect sleep ; at other times we are almost completely awake ; and it will be remarked, that the more awake we are, the greater is the violence of the paroxysm. I have experienced the affection stealing upon me while in perfect possession of my faculties, and have undergone the greatest tortures, being haunted by spectres, hags, and every sort of phantom—having, at the same time, a full conscious-

* Waller's Treatise.

ness that I was labouring under incubus, and that all the terrifying objects around me were the creations of my own brain. This shows that the judgment is often only very partially affected, and proves also that nightmare is not merely a disagreeable dream, but a painful bodily affection. Were it nothing more than the former, we could rarely possess a knowledge of our condition; for, in simple visions, the reflecting organs are almost uniformly quiescent, and we scarcely ever, for a moment, doubt the reality of our impressions. In nightmare, this is often, perhaps generally, the case; but we frequently meet with instances, in which, during the worst periods of the fit, consciousness remains almost unimpaired.

There are great differences in the duration of the paroxysm, and also in the facility with which it is broken. I know not of any method by which the period to which it extends can be estimated, for the sufferer has no data to go by, and time, as in all modifications of dreaming, is subjected to the most capricious laws—an actual minute often appearing to embrace a whole hour. Of this point, therefore, we must be contented to remain in ignorance; but it may be conceived that the attack will be as various in its duration, as in the characters which it assumes—in one case being ten times as long as in another. With regard to the breaking of the fit, the differences are equally great. At one time, the slightest agitation of the body, the opening of the chamber door, or calling softly to the sufferer, will arouse him; at another, he requires to be shaken violently, and called upon long and loudly, before he is released.

Some people are much more prone to incubus than others. Those whose digestion is healthy, whose minds are at ease, and who go supperless to bed, will seldom be troubled with it. Those, again, who keep late hours, study hard, eat heavy suppers, and are subject to bile, acid, or hypochondria, are almost sure to be more or less its victims. There are particular kinds of food, which pretty constantly lead to the same result, such as cheese, cucumbers, almonds, and whatever is hard to be digested. Hildesheim, in his 'De Affectibus Capitis,' justly remarks, that 'he who wishes to know what nightmare is, let him eat chestnuts before going to sleep, and drink feculent wine after them.'

Certain diseases, also, are apt to induce it, such as asthma, hydrothorax, agina pectoris, and other varieties of dyspnœa. Men are more subject to it than women, probably from their stomachs being more frequently disordered by intemperance, and their minds more closely occupied. Sailors, owing to the hard and indigestible nature of their food, are very frequently its victims; and it is a general remark that it oftener occurs at sea than on shore. It seems probable that much of the superstitious belief of these men, in apparitions, proceeds from the phantoms which nightmare calls into existence. Unmarried women are more annoyed by it than those who are married; and the latter, when pregnant, have it oftener than at other times. Persons who were extremely subject to the complaint in their youth, sometimes get rid of it when they reach the age of puberty, owing, probably, to some change in the constitution which occurs at this period.

There have been different opinions with regard to the proximate cause of incubus, and authors have generally looked upon it as involved in considerable obscurity. An impeded circulation of blood in the pulmonary arteries, compression of the diaphragm by a full stomach, and torpor of the intercostal muscles, are all mentioned as contributing wholly, or partially, to the event. I am of opinion that either of these states may cause nightmare, but that, in most cases, they are all combined. Any thing, in fact, which impedes respiration, may give rise to the disorder, whether it be asthma, hydrothorax, distended stomach, muscular torpor, or external compression. The causes, then, are various, but it will be found that, whatever they may be, their ultimate operation is upon the lungs.

We have already seen that, in ordinary sleep, particular states of the body are apt to induce visions: it is, therefore easily conceivable that a sense of suffocation, such as occurs in nightmare, may give birth to all the horrid phantoms seen in that distemper. The physical sufferings in such a case, exalts the imagination to its utmost pitch: fills it with spectres and chimeras; and plants an immovable weight or malignant fiend upon the bosom to crush us into agony. Let us see how such physical sufferings is brought about.

Any disordered state of the stomach may produce it. This organ may be so distended with food or wind as to press upon the diaphragm, lessen the dimensions of the chest, obstruct the movements of the heart, and thereby impede respiration. Circumstances like these alone are sufficient to produce nightmare; and the cause from the first is purely mechanical.

Secondly. The state of the stomach may call forth incubus by means circuitous or indirect. In this case the viscus is unequal to the task imposed upon it of digesting the food, either from an unusual quantity being thrown upon it, from the food being of an indigestible nature, or from actual weakness. Here the sensorial power latent in this organ, is insufficient to carry it through with its operations, and it is obliged to draw upon the rest of the body—upon the brain, the respiratory muscles, &c, for the supply of which it is deficient. The muscles of respiration, in giving their portion, reduce themselves to a state of temporary debility, and do not retain a sufficient share to execute their own actions with due vigour. The pectorels, the intercostals, and the diaphragm became thus paralyzed; and, the chest not being sufficiently dilated for perfect breathing, a feeling of suffocation inevitably insues. In like manner, the muscles of volition, rendered inert by the subtraction of their quota of sensorial power, are unable to exercise their functions, and remain, during the paroxysm, in a state of immovable torpor. This unequal distribution of nervous energy continues till, by producing some excessive uneasiness, it stimulates the will to a violent effort, and breaks the fit; and so soon as this takes place, the balance becomes redressed, and the sensorial equilibrium restored.

Physical suffering of that kind which impedes breathing, may also be occasioned by many other causes—by pneuomonia, by empyema, by aneurism of the aorta, by laryngitis by croup, by external pressure; and, accordingly, either of these may give rise to nightmare. If we chance to lie down with a pillow or heavy cloak upon the breast, or to sleep with the body bent forward, and the head supported upon a table, as already mentioned, we may be seized with it; and, in truth, whatever, either directly or indirectly, acts upon the respiratory muscles, and impedes their operation, is pretty sure to bring it on. Even a weak or disordered stomach, in which there is no food, by attracting to itself a portion of their sensorial power to aid its own inadequacies, may induce it. The disorder, therefore, takes place under various circumstances—either by direct pressure upon the lungs, as in distended stomach, or hydrothorax; or by partial torpor of the stomach or muscles of respiration, owing to a deficiency of nervous energy. These physical impediments coexisting with, or giving rise to a distempered state of the brain, sufficiently account for the horrors of nightmare.

Why are hard students, deep thinkers, and hypochondriacs unusually subject to incubus? The cause is obvious. Such individuals have often a bad digestion: their stomachs are subject to acidity, and other functional derangements, and therefore, peculiarly apt to generate the complaint. The sedentary life, and habits of intellectual or melancholy reflection in which they indulge, have a tendency not merely to disturb the digestive apparatus, but to act upon the whole cerebral system: hence, they are far more liable to dreams of every kind than other people, in so far as their minds are more intently employed; and when, in sleep, they are pained by any physical endurance, the activity of their mental powers will naturally associate the most horrible ideas with such suffering, and produce incubus, and all its frightful accompaniments.

Nightmare is sometimes attended with danger, when it becomes habitual. It may then give rise to apoplexy, and destroy life; or, in very nervous subjects, may occasion epileptic and hysterical affections, which prove extremely harassing. According to Cœlius Aurelianus, many people die of this complaint. Probably some of those who are found dead in bed have lost their lives in a fit of incubus, the circumstance being imputed to some other cause. Nightmare is thus, in some cases dangerous: and in all, when it becomes habitual, is such a source of misery, that sleep, instead of being courted as a period of blissful repose, is looked upon with horror, as the appointed season of inexpressible suffering and dread. It becomes, on this account, a matter of importance to contrive some method for preventing the attacks of so distressful a malady. The cause, whatever it may be, must, if practicable, be removed, and the symptoms thence arising will naturally disappear. If the disorder proceed from heavy suppers, or indigestible food, these things ought to be given up, and the person should either go supperless to bed, or with such a light meal as will not hurt his digestion. Salted provisions of all kinds must be abandoned, nor should he taste any thing which will lie heavily upon the stomach, or run into fermentation. For this reason, nuts, cucumbers, cheese, ham, and fruits are all prejudicial. If he be subject to heart-burn, flatulence, and other dyspeptic symptoms, he should make use of occasional doses of magnesia, or carbonate of potash or soda. I have known a tea-spoonful of either of the two latter, or three times that quantity of the former, taken before stepping into bed, prevent an attack, where, from the previous state of the stomach, I am convinced it would have taken place, had those medicines not been used. Great attention must be paid to the state of the bowels. For this purpose, the colocynth, the compound rhubarb, or the common aloetic pill, should be made use of, in doses of one, two, or three, according to circumstances, till the digestive organs are brought into proper play. The common blue pill, used with proper caution, is also an excellent medicine. In all cases, the patient should take abundant exercise, shun late hours, or too much study, and keep his mind in as cheerful a state as possible. The bed he lies on ought to be hard, and the pillow not very high. When the attacks are frequent, and extremely severe, Dr Darwin recommends that an alarm clock might be hung up in the room, so that the repose may be interrupted at short intervals. It is a good plan to have another person to sleep in the same bed, who might arouse him from the paroxysm; and he should be directed to lie as little as possible upon the back.

These points comprehend the principal treatment, and when persevered in, will rarely fail to mitigate or remove the disease. Sometimes, however, owing to certain peculiarities of constitution, it may be necessary to adopt a different plan, or combine other means along with the above: thus, Whyatt, who was subject to nightmare, could only insure himself against an attack, by taking a small glassful of brandy, just before going to bed; and some individuals find that a light supper prevents the fit, while it is sure to occur if no supper at all be taken. But these are rare exceptions to the general rule, and, when they do occur, must be treated in that manner which experience proves most effectual, without being bound too nicely by the ordinary modes of cure. Blood-letting, which some writers recommend, is useless or hurtful, except in cases where there is reason to suppose that the affection is brought on by plethora. With regard to the other causes of nightmare, such as asthma, hydrothorax, &c., these must be treated on general principles, and it, as one of their symptoms, will depart so soon as they are removed.

P

Some persons recommend opium for the cure of nightmare, but this medicine I should think more likely to aggrave than relieve the complaint. The late Dr Polydori, author of 'The Vampyre,' and of an 'Essay on Positive Pleasure,' was much subject to incubus, and in the habit of using opium for its removal. One morning he was found dead, and on the table beside him stood a glass, which had evidently contained laudanum and water. From this, it was supposed he had killed himself by his own treatment; but whether the quantity of laudanum taken by him would have destroyed life in ordinary circumstances, has never been ascertained.

CHAPTER VI.

DAYMARE.

I have strong doubts as to the propriety of considering this affection in any way different from the incubus, or nightmare. It seems merely a modification of the latter, only accompanied by no aberration of the judgment. The person endures precisely many of the same feelings, such as difficult respiration, torpor of the voluntary muscles, deep sighing, extreme terror, and inability to speak. The only difference which seem to exist between the two states is, that in daymare, the reason is *always* unclouded—whereas in incubus it is *generally* more or less disturbed.

Dr Mason Good, in his 'Study of Medicine,' takes notice of a case, recorded by Forestus, 'that returned periodically every third day, like an intermittent fever. The patient was a girl, nine years of age, and at these times was suddenly attacked with great terror, a constriction of both the lower and upper belly, with urgent difficulty of breathing. Her eyes continued open, and were permanently continued to one spot; with her hands she forcibly grasped hold of things, that she might breathe the more easily. When spoken to, she returned no answer. In the meantime, the mind seemed to be collected; she was without sleep; sighed repeatedly; the abdomen was elevated, the thorax still violently contracted, and oppressed with laborious respiration and heavy panting: she was incapable of utterance.'

During the intensely hot summer of 1825, I experienced an attack of daymare. Immediately after dining, I threw myself on my back upon a sofa, and, before I was aware, was seized with difficult respiration, extreme dread, and utter incapability of motion or speech. I could neither move nor cry, while the breath came from my chest in broken and suffocating paroxysms. During all this time, I was perfectly awake: I saw the light glaring in at the windows in broad sultry streams; I felt the intense heat of the day pervading my frame; and heard distinctly the different noises in the street, and even the ticking of my own watch, which I had placed on the cushion beside me. I had, at the same time, the consciousness of flies buzzing around, and settling with annoying pertinacity upon my face. During the whole fit, judgment was never for a moment suspended. I felt assured that I laboured under a species of incubus. I even endeavoured to reason myself out of the feeling of dread which filled my mind, and longed with insufferable ardour for some one to open the door, and dissolve the spell which bound me in its fetters. The fit did not continue above five minutes: by degrees I recovered the use of speech and motion: and as soon as they were so far restored as to enable me to call out and move my limbs, it wore insensibly away.

Upon the whole, I consider daymare and nightmare identical. They proceed from the same causes, and must be treated in a similar manner.

CHAPTER VII.

SLEEP-WALKING.

In simple dreaming, as I have already stated, some of the cerebral organs are awake, while others continue in the quiescence of sleep. Such, also, is the case in somnambulism, but with this addition, that the dream is of so forcible a nature as to stimulate into action the muscular system as well as, in most cases, one or more of the organs of the senses. If we dream that we are walking, and the vision possesses such a degree of vividness and exciting energy as to arouse the muscles of locomotion, we naturally get up and walk. Should we dream that we hear or see, and the impression be so vivid as to stimulate the eyes and ears, or, more properly speaking, those parts of the brain which take cognizance of sights and sounds, then we both see any objects, or hear any sounds, which may occur, just as if we were awake. In some cases, the muscles only are excited, and then we simply walk, without either seeing or hearing. In others, both the muscles and organs of sight are stimulated, and we not only walk, but have the use of our eyes. In a third variety, the activity of hearing is added, and we both walk, and see, and near. Should the senses of smell, taste, and touch be stimulated into activity, and relieved from the torpor into which they were thrown by sleep, we have them also brought into operation. If, to all this, we add an active state of the organs of speech, inducing us to talk, we are then brought as nearly as the slumbering state admits, into the condition of perfect wakefulness. The following passage from Dr Mason Good will illustrate some of the foregoing points more fully.

'If,' observes he, 'the external organ of sense thus stimulated be that of sight, the dreamer may perceive objects around him, and be able to distinguish them; and if the tenor of the dreaming ideas should as powerfully operate upon the muscles of locomotion, these also may be thrown into their accustomed state of action, and he may rise from his bed, and make his way to whatever place the drift of his dream may direct him, with perfect ease, and free from danger. He will see more or less distinctly, in proportion as the organ of sight is more or less awake: yet, from the increased exhaustion, and, of course, increased torpor of the other organs, in consequence of an increased demand of sensorial power from the common stock, to supply the action of the sense and muscles immediately engaged, every other sense will probably be thrown into a deeper sleep or torpor than if the whole had been quiescent. Hence, the ears may not be roused even by a sound that might otherwise awake the sleeper. He may be insensible not only to a slight touch, but a severe shaking of the limbs; and may even cough violently, without being recalled from his dream. Having accomplished the object of his visionary pursuit, he may safely return, even over the most dangerous precipices —for he sees them distinctly—to his bed: and the organ of sight being now quite exhausted, or there being no longer any occasion for its use, it may once more associate in the general inactivity, and the dream take a new turn, and consist of a new combination of images.'*

I suspect that sleep-walking is sometimes hereditary, at least I have known instances which gave countenance to such a supposition. Its victims are generally pale, nervous, irritable persons; and it is remarked that they are subject, without any apparent cause, to frequent attacks of cold perspiration. Somnambulism, I have had occasion to remark, is very common among children; and I believe that it more frequently affects childhood than any other age. In females, it sometimes arises from amenorrhœa; and any source of bodily or mental irritation may produce it. It is a curious, and not easily explained fact, that the aged, though they dream more than the middle-aged, are less addicted to somnambulism and sleep-talking. Indeed, these phenomena are seldom noticed in old people.

* Good's Study of Medicine, vol. iv. p. 175, 3d edit.

It has been matter of surprise to many, that somnambulists often get into the most dangerous situations without experiencing terror. But the explanation of this ought not to be attended with any real difficulty; for we must reflect, that alarm cannot be felt unless we apprehend danger, and that the latter, however great it may be, cannot excite emotion of any kind, so long as we are ignorant of its existence. This is the situation in which sleep-walkers, in a great majority of cases, stand. The reasoning faculties, which point out the existence of danger, are generally in a state of complete slumber, and unable to produce corresponding emotions in the mind. And even if danger should be perceived by a sleep-walker and avoided, as is sometimes the case, his want of terror is to be imputed to a quiescent state of the organ of *cautiousness;* the sense of fear originating in high excitement of this particular part of the brain. That the reasoning faculties, however, are sometimes only very partially suspended we have abundant evidence, in the fact of the individual not only now and then studiously avoiding danger, but performing offices which require no small degree of judgment. In the higher ranks of somnambulism, so many of the organs of the brain are in activity, and there is such perfect wakefulness of the external senses and locomotive powers, that the person may almost be said to be awake.

Somnambulism bears a closer analogy than a common dream to madness. 'Like madness, it is accompanied with muscular action, with coherent and incoherent conduct, and with that complete oblivion (in most cases) of both, which takes place in the worst grade of madness.'*

Somnambulists generally walk with their eyes open, but these organs are, nevertheless frequently asleep, and do not exercise their functions. This fact was well known to Shakspeare, as is apparent in the fearful instance of Lady Macbeth:

'*Doctor*. You see her eyes are open.'
Gentleman. Ay, but their sense is shut.'

The following is a remarkable instance in point, and shows that though the power of vision was suspended, that of hearing continued in full operation.

A female servant in the town of Chelmsford, surprised the family, at four o'clock one morning, by walking down a flight of stairs in her sleep, and rapping at the bed-room door of her master, who inquired what she wanted? when, in her usual tone of voice, she requested some cotton, saying that she had torn her gown, but hoped that her mistress would forgive her: at the same time bursting into tears. Her fellow-servant, with whom she had been conversing for some time, observed her get out of bed, and quickly followed her, but not before she had related the pitiful story. She then returned to her room, and a light having been procured, she was found groping to find her cotton-box. Another person went to her, when, perceiving a difference in the voice, she called out, 'That is a different voice, that is my mistress,' which was not the case—thus clearly showing, that she *did not see* the object before her, although her eyes were *wide open*. Upon inquiry as to what was the matter, she only said that she wanted some cotton, but that her fellow-servant had been to her master and mistress, making a fuss about it. It

* Rush's Medical Inquiries.

was now thought prudent that she should be allowed to remain quiet for some short time, and she was persuaded to lie down with her fellow-servant, until the usual hour of rising, thinking that she might then awake in her accustomed manner. This failing in effect, her mistress went up to her room, and rather angrily desired her to get up, and go to her work, as it was now six o'clock; this she refused, telling her mistress that if she did not please her, she might look out for another servant, at the same time saying, that she would not rise up at two o'clock, (pointing to the window,) to injure her health for any one. For the sake of a joke, she was told to pack up her things, and start off immediately, but to this she made no reply. She rebuked her fellow-servant for not remaining longer in bed, and shortly after this became quiet. She was afterwards shaken violently, and awoke. She then rose, and seeing the cotton-box disturbed, demanded to know why it had been meddled with, not knowing that she alone was the cause of it. In the course of the day, several questions were put to her in order to try her recollection, but the real fact of her walking, was not made known to her; and she is still quite unconscious of what has transpired.

The next case is of a different description, and exhibits a dormant state of the sense of hearing, while sight appears, throughout, to have been in active operation.

A young man named Johns, who works at Cardrew, near Redruth, being asleep in the sump-house of that mine, was observed by two boys to rise and walk to the door, against which he leaned; shortly after, quitting that position, he walked to the engine-shaft, and safely descended to the depth of twenty fathoms, where he was found by his comrades soon after. with his back resting on the ladder. They called to him, to apprize him of the perilous situation in which he was, but he did not hear them, and they were obliged to shake him roughly till he awoke, when he appeared totally at a loss to account for his being so situated.

In Lodge's 'Historical Portraits,' there is a likeness, by Sir Peter Lely, of Lord Culpepper's brother, so famous as a dreamer. In 1686, he was indicted at the Old Bailey, for shooting one of the Guards, and his horse to boot. He pleaded somnambulism, and was acquitted on producing nearly fifty witnesses, to prove the extraordinary things he did in his sleep.

A very curious circumstance is related of Dr Franklin, in the memoirs of that eminent philosopher, published by his grandson. 'I went out,' said the Doctor, 'to bathe in Martin's salt water hot bath, in Southampton, and, floating on my back, fell asleep, and slept nearly an hour, by my watch, without sinking or turning --a thing I never did before, and should hardly have thought possible.'

A case still more extraordinary occurred some time ago in one of the towns on the coast of Ireland. About two o'clock in the morning, the watchmen on the Revenue quay, were much surprised at descrying a man disporting himself in the water, about a hundred yards from the shore. Intimation having been given to the Revenue boat's crew, they pushed off and succeeded in picking him up, but strange to say, he had no idea whatever of his perilous situation: and it was with the utmost difficulty they could persuade him he was not still in bed. But the most singular part of this novel adventure, and which was afterwards ascertained, was that the man had left his house at twelve o'clock that night, and walked through a difficult, and, to him, dangerous road, a distance of nearly two miles, and had actually swum one mile and a half when he was fortunately discovered and picked up.

Not very long ago a boy was seen fishing off Brest, up to the middle in water. On coming up to him, he was found to be fast asleep.

I know a gentleman who, in consequence of dreaming that the house was broken into by thieves, got out of bed, dropped from the window (fortunately a low one) into the street; and was a considerable distance on his way to warn the police, when he was discovered by one of them, who awoke him, and conducted him home.

A case is related of an English clergyman who used to get up in the night, light his candle, write sermons, correct them with interlineations, and retire to bed again; being all the time asleep. The Archbishop of Bourdeaux mentions a similar case of a student, who got up to compose a sermon while asleep, wrote it correctly, read it over from one end to the other, or at least appeared to read it, made corrections on it, scratched out lines, and substituted others, put in its place a word which had been omitted, composed music, wrote it accurately down, and performed other things equally surprising. Dr Gall takes notice of a miller who was in the habit of getting up every night and attending to his usual avocations at the mill, then returning to bed; on awaking in the morning, he recollected nothing of what passed during night. Martinet speaks of a saddler who was accustomed to rise in his sleep and work at his trade; and Dr Pritchard of a farmer who got out of bed, dressed himself, saddled his horse, and rode to the market, being all the while asleep. Dr Blacklock, on one occasion, rose from bed, to which he had retired at an early hour, came into the room where his family were assembled, conversed with them, and afterwards entertained them with a pleasant song, without any of them suspecting he was asleep, and without his retaining after he awoke, the least recollection of what he had done. It is a singular, yet well authenticated fact, that in the disastrous retreat of Sir John Moore, many of the soldiers fell asleep, yet continued to march along with their comrades.

The stories related of sleep-walkers are, indeed, of so extraordinary a kind, that they would almost seem fictitious, were they not supported by the most incontrovertible evidence. To walk on the house-top, to scale precipices, and descend to the bottom of frightful ravines, are common exploits with the somnambulist; and he performs them with a facility far beyond the power of any man who is completely awake. A story is told of a boy, who dreamed that he got out of bed, and ascended to the summit of an enormous rock, where he found an eagle's nest, which he brought away with him, and placed beneath his bed. Now, the whole of these events actually took place; and what he conceived on awaking to be a mere vision, was proved to have had an actual existence, by the nest being found in the precise spot where he imagined he had put it, and by the evidence of the spectators who beheld his perilous adventure. The precipice which he ascended, was of a nature that must have baffled the most expert mountaineer, and such as, at other times, he never could have scaled. In this instance, the individual was as nearly as possible, without actually being so, awake. All his bodily, and almost the whole of his mental powers, appear to have been in full activity. So far as the latter are concerned, we can only conceive a partial defect of the judgment to have existed, for that it was altogether abolished is pretty evident from the fact of his proceeding to work precisely as he would have done, had he, in his waking hours, seriously resolved to make such an attempt; the defect lay in making the attempt at all; and still more in getting out of bed to do so in the middle of the night.

Somnambulism, as well as lunacy, sometimes bestows supernatural strength upon the individual. Mr Dubrie, a musician in Bath, affords an instance of this kind. One Sunday, while awake, he attempted in vain to force open the window of his bed-room, which chanced to be nailed down; but having got up in his sleep, he repeated the attempt successfully, and threw himself out, by which he unfortunately broke his leg.

Sleep-walking is sometimes periodical. Martinet describes the case of a watchmaker's apprentice who had an attack of it every fortnight. In this state, though insensible to all external impressions, he would perform his work with his usual accuracy, and was always astonished, on awaking, at the progress he had made. The paroxysm began with a sense of heat in the epigastrium extending to the head, followed by confusion of ideas and complete insensibility, the eyes remaining open with a fixed and vacant stare. This case, which undoubtedly originated in some diseased state of the brain, terminated in epilepsy. Dr Gall relates that he saw at Berlin a young man, sixteen years of age, who had, from time to time, very extraordinary fits. He moved about unconsciously in bed, and had no perception of any thing that was done to him; at last he would jump out of bed, and walk with rapid steps about the room, his eyes being fixed and open. Several obstacles which were placed by Dr Gall in his way, he either removed or cautiously avoided. He then threw himself suddenly again upon bed, moved about for some time, and finished by jumping up awake, not a little surprised at the number of curious people about him.

The facility with which somnambulists are awakened from the paroxysm, differs extremely in different cases. One man is aroused by being gently touched or called upon, by a flash of light, by stumbling in his peregrinations, or by setting his foot in water. Another remains so heavily asleep, that it is necessary to shout loudly, to shake him with violence, and make use of other excitations equally powerful. In this condition, when the sense of vision chances to be dormant, it is curious to look at his eyes. Sometimes they are shut; at other times wide open; and when the latter is the case, they are observed to be fixed and inexpressive, 'without speculation,' or energy, while the pupil, is contracted, as in the case of perfect sleep.

It is not always safe to arouse a sleep walker; and many cases of the fatal effects thence arising have been detailed by authors. Nor is it at all unlikely that a person, even of strong nerves, might be violently agitated by awaking in a situation so different from that in which he lay down. Among other examples, that of a young lady, who was addicted to this affection, may be mentioned. Knowing her failing, her friends, made a point of locking the door, and securing the window of her chamber in such a manner that she could not possibly get out. One night, these precautions were, unfortunately overlooked; and in a paroxysm of somnambulism, she walked into the garden behind the house. While there, she was recognised by some of the family, who were warned by the noise she made on opening the door, and they followed and awoke her; but such was the effect produced upon her nervous system, that she almost instantly expired.

The remote causes of sleep walking are so obscure, that it is seldom we are able to ascertain them. General irritability of frame, a nervous temperament, and bad digestion, will dispose to the affection. Being a modification of dreaming, those who are much troubled with the latter will, consequently be most prone to its attacks. The causes, however, are, in a great majority of cases, so completely unknown, that any attempt to investigate them would be fruitless; and we are compelled to refer the complaint to some idiosyncracy of constitution beyond the reach of human knowledge.

According to the report made by a Committee of the Royal Academy of Sciences in Paris, animal magnetism appears to have the power of inducing a peculiar species of somnambulism. The circumstances seem so curious, that, even authenticated as they are by men of undoubted integrity and talent, it is extremely difficult to place reliance upon them. The person who is thrown into the magnetic sleep is said to a acquire a new consciousness, and entirely to forget all the events of his ordinary life. When this sleep is dissolved, he gets into his usual state of feeling and recollection, but forgets every thing that happened during the sleep; being again magnetized, however, the remembrance of all that occurred in the previous sleep is brought back to his mind. In one of the cases above related, the patient, a lady of sixty-four years, had an ulcerated cancer in the right breast. She had been magnetized for the purpose of dissolving the tumor, but no other effect was produced than that of throwing her into a species of somnambulic sleep, in which sensibility was annihilated, while her ideas retained all their clearness. In this state her surgeon, M. Chapelain, disposed her to submit to an operation, the idea of which she rejected with horror *when awake.* Having formally given her consent she undressed herself, sat down upon a chair, and the diseased glands were carefully and deliberately dissected out, the patient conversing all the time and being perfectly insensible of pain. On awaking, she had no consciousnes whatever of having been operated upon; but being informed of the circumstance, and seeing her children around her, she experienced the most lively emotion, which the magnetizer instantly checked by again setting her asleep. These facts appear startling and incredible. I can give no opinion upon the subject from any thing I have seen myself; but the testimony of such men as Cloquet, Georget, and Itard, is not to be received lightly on any physiological point; and they all concur in bearing witness to such facts as the above. In the present state of knowledge and opinion, with regard to animal magnetism, and the sleep occasioned by it, I shall not say more at present, but refer the reader to the ample details contained in the Parisian Report; an able translation of which into English has been made by by Mr Colquhoun.

When a person is addicted to somnambulism, great care should be taken to have the door and windows of his sleeping apartment, secured, so as to prevent the possibility of egress, as he sometimes forces his way through the panes of glass: this should be put out of his power, by having the shutters closed, and bolted, in such a way that they cannot be opened without the aid of a key or screw, or some such instrument, which should never be left in the room where he sleeps, but carried away, while the door is secured on the outside. Some have recommended that a tub of water should be put by the bedside, that, on getting out, he might step into it, and be awaked by the cold; but this, from the suddenness of its operation, might be attended with bad consequences in very nervous and delicate subjects. It is a good plan to fix a cord to the bedpost, and tie the other end of it securely round the person's wrist. This will effectually prevent mischief if he attempt to get up. Whenever it can be managed, it will be prudent for another person to sleep along with him. In all cases, care should be taken to arouse him suddenly. This must be done as gently as possible, and when he can be conducted to bed without being awakened at all, it is still better. Should he be perceived in any dangerous situation as on the house-top, or the brink of a precipice, the utmost caution is requisite; for, if we call loudly upon him, his dread, on recovering, at finding himself in such a predicament, may actually occasion him to fall, where, if he had been left to himself, he would have escaped without injury.

To prevent a recurrence of somnambulism, we should remove, if possible, the cause which gave rise to it. Thus, if it proceed from a disordered state or the stomach, or biliary system, we must employ the various medicines used in such cases. Plenty of exercise should be taken, and late hours and much study avoided. If it arises from plethora, he must be blooded, and live low; should hysteria produce it, antispasmodics, such as valerian, ammonia, assafœtida, and opium may be necessary.

But, unfortunately, we can often refer sleep-walking to no complaint whatever. In this case, all that can be done is to carry the individual as safely as possible through the paroxysm, and prevent him from injury by the means we have mentioned. In many instances, the affection will wear spontaneously away: in others, it will continue in spite of every remedy.

CHAPTER VIII.

SLEEP-TALKING.

This closely resembles somnambulism, and proceeds from similar causes. In somnambulism, those parts of the brain which are awake call the muscles of the limbs into activity; while, in sleep-talking, it is the muscles necessary for the production of speech which are animated by the waking cerebral organs. During sleep, the organ of *language* may be active, either singly or in combination with other parts of the brain; and of this activity sleep-talking is the result.* If, while we dream that we are conversing with some one, the organ of *language* is in such a high state of activity as to rouse the muscles of speech, we are sure to talk. It often happens, however, that the cerebral parts, though sufficiently active to make us dream that we are speaking, are not excited so much as to make us actually speak. We only suppose we are carrying on a conversation, while, in reality, we are completely silent. To produce sleep-talking, therefore, the brain, in some of its functions, must be so much awake as to put into action the voluntary muscles by which speech is produced.

The conversation in this state, is of such subjects as our thoughts are most immediately occupied with; and its consistency or incongruity depends upon that of the prevailing ideas—being sometimes perfectly rational and coherent; at other times, full of absurdity. The voice is seldom the same as in the waking state. This I would impute to the organs of hearing being mostly dormant, and consequently unable to guide the modulations of sound. The same fact is observable in very deaf persons, whose speech is usually harsh, unvaried, and monotonous. Sometimes the faculties are so far awake, that we can manage to converse with the individual, and extract from him the most hidden secrets of his soul: circumstances have thus been ascertained which would otherwise have remained in perpetual obscurity. By a little address in this way, a gentleman lately detected the infidelity of his wife from some expressions which escaped her while asleep, and succeeded in finding out that she had a meeting arranged with her paramour for the following day. Lord Byron describes a similar scene in his 'Parisina:'

'And Hugo is gone to his lonely bed,
To covet there another's bride;
But she must lay her conscious head
A husband's trusting heart beside.
But fever'd in her sleep she seems,
And red her cheek with troubled dreams,
And *mutters she in her unrest*
A name she dare not breathe by day,
And clasps her lord unto her breast
Which pants for one away.'

From what has been said of somnambulism, the reader will be prepared for phenomena equally curious as regards sleep-talking. Persons have been known, for instance, who delivered sermons and prayers during sleep; among others, Dr Haycock, Professor of Medicine in Oxford. He would give out a text in his sleep, and deliver a good sermon upon it; nor could all the pinching and pulling of his friends prevent him. 'One of the most remarkable cases of speaking during sleep,' observes a writer in Frazer's Magazine, 'is that of an American lady, now (we believe) alive, who preached during her sleep, performing regularly every part of the Presbyterian service, from the psalm to the blessing. This lady was the daughter of respectable and even wealthy parents; she fell into bad health, and, under its influence, she disturbed and annoyed her family by her nocturnal eloquence. Her unhappy parents, though at first surprised, and perhaps flattered by the exhibition in their family of so extraordinary a gift, were at last convinced that it was the result of disease; and, in the expectation that their daughter might derive benefit from change of scene, as well as from medical skill, they made a tour with her of some length, and visited New York and some of the other great cities of the Union. We know individuals who have heard her preach during the night in steamboats; and it was customary, at tea parties in New York, (at the houses of medical practitioners,) to put the lady to bed in a room adjacent to the drawing-room, in order that the dilletanti might witness so extraordinary a phenomenon. We have been told by ear-witnesses, that her sermons, though they had the appearance of connected discourses, consisted chiefly of texts of scripture strung together. It is strongly impressed upon our memory, that some of her sermons were published in America.'

In the Edinburgh Journal of science, a lady who was subject to spectral illusions, is described as being subject to talk in her sleep with great fluency, to repeat great portions of poetry, especially when unwell, and even to *cap* verses for half an hour at a time, never failing to quote lines beginning with the final letter of the preceding till her memory was exhausted.

Dr Dyce, in the Edinburgh Philosophical Transactions, relates the case of Maria C——, who, during one paroxysm of somnambulism, recollected what took place in a preceding one, without having any such recollection during the interval of wakefulness. One of the occasions in which this young woman manifested the power in question, was of a very melancholy nature. Her fellow-servant, a female of abandoned character, having found out that, on awaking, she entirely forgot every thing which occurred during the fit, introduced by stealth into the house, a young man of her acquaintance, and obtained for him an opportunity of treating Maria in the most brutal and treacherous manner. The wretches succeeded in their object by stopping her mouth with the bed-clothes, by which and other means, they overcame the vigorous resistance she was enabled to make to their villany, even in her somnolent state. On awaking she had no consciousness whatever of the outrage; but some days afterwards, having fallen into the same state, it recurred to her memory, and she related to her mother all the revolting particulars. The state of mind in this case was perfectly analagous to that which is said to occur in the magnetic sleep; but the particular state of the brain which induces such conditions will, I believe, ever remain a mystery.*

* Among the insane, the organ just mentioned is occasionally excited to such a degree that even, in the waking state, the patient, however *desirous*, is literally *unable* to refrain from speaking. Mr. W. A. F. Browne has reported two cases of this nature in the 37th No. of the Phrenological Journal. The first is that of a woman in the hospital of 'La Salpetrière' in Paris. Whenever she encounters the physician or other of the attendants, she bursts forth into an address which is delivered with incredible rapidity and vehemence, and is generally an abusive or ironical declamation against the tyranny, cruelty, and injustice to which she is exposed. In the midst of her harangues, however, she introduces frequent and earnest parenthetical declarations 'that she does not mean what she says; that though she vows vengeance and showers imprecations on her medical attendant, she loves him, and feels grateful for his kindness and forbearance; and that, though anxious to evince her gratitude and obedience by silence, she is constrained by an invisible agency to speak.' In the other case, the individual speaks constantly; 'sleep itself does not yield an intermission; and there is strong reason to believe that a part, at least of his waking orations is delivered either without the cognizance of the other powers, or without consciousness on the part of the speaker.'

* A case, in some respects similar, was published in the Medical Repository, by Dr Mitchell, who received the particulars of it from Major Ellicot, Professor of Mathematics in the United States Military Academy at West Point. The subject was a

The following singular case of sleep-talking, combined with somnambulism, will prove interesting to the reader:—

'A very ingenious and elegant young lady, with light eyes and hair, about the age of seventeen, in other respects well, was suddenly seized with this very wonderful malady. The disease began with violent convulsions of almost every muscle of her body, with great, but vain efforts to vomit, and the most violent hiccoughs that can be conceived: these were succeeded in about an hour with a fixed spasm; in which, one hand was applied to her head, and the other to support it: in about half an hour these ceased, and the reverie began suddenly, and was at first manifest by the look of her eyes and countenance, which seemed to express attention. Then she conversed aloud with imaginary persons, with her eyes open, and could not, for about an hour, be brought to attend to the stimulus of external objects by any kind of violence which it was possible to use: these symptoms returned in this order every day for five or six weeks.

'These conversations were quite consistent, and we could understand what she supposed her imaginary companions to answer, by the continuation of her part of the discourse. Sometimes she was angry, at other times showed much wit and vivacity, but was most frequently inclined to melancholy. In these reveries, she sometimes sung over some music with accuracy, and repeated whole passages from tbe English poets. In repeating some lines from Mr Pope's works, she had forgot one word, and began again, endeavouring to recollect it; when she came to the forgotten word, it was shouted aloud in her ears, and this repeatedly, to no purpose; but by many trials she at length regained it herself.

'Those paroxysms were terminated with the appearance of inexpressible surprise and great fear, from which she was some minutes in recovering herself, calling on her sister with great agitation, and very frequently underwent a repetition of convulsions, apparently from the pain of fear.

'After having thus returned for about an hour a-day, for two or three weeks, the reveries seemed to become less complete, and some of the circumstances varied, so that she could walk about the room in them, without running against any of the furniture; though these motions were at first very unsteady and tottering. And afterwards, she once, drank a dish of tea, and the whole apparatus of the tea-table was set before her, and expressed some suspicion that a medicine was put into it; and once seemed to smell at a tuberose, which was in flower in her chamber, and deliberated aloud about breaking it for the stem, saying, 'It would make her sister so charmingly angry.' At another time, in her melancholy moments, she heard the bell, and then taking off one of her shoes as she sat upon the bed, 'I love the color black,' says she; 'a little wider and a little longer, and even this might make me a coffin!' Yet it is evident she was not sensible at this time, any more than formerly, of seeing or hearing any person about her; indeed, when great light was thrown upon her by opening the shutters of the window; she seemed less melancholy: and when I have forcibly held her hands, or covered her eyes, she appeared to grow impatient, and would say, she could not tell what to do, for she could neither see nor move. In all these circumstances, her pulse continued unaffected, as in health. And when the paroxysm was over, she could never recollect a single idea of what had passed.'*

Equally extraordinary is the following instance of combined sleep-talking and somnambulism:

'A remarkable instance of this affection occurred to a lad named George David, sixteen years and a half old, in the service of Mr Hewson, butcher, of Bridge-Road, Lambeth. At about twenty minutes after nine o'clock, the lad bent forward in his chair, and rested, his forehead on his hands, and in ten minutes started up, went for his whip, put on his one spur, and went thence to the stable; not finding his own saddle in the proper place, he returned to the house and asked for it. Being asked what he wanted with it, he replied, to go his rounds. He returned to the stable, got on the horse without the saddle, and was proceeding to leave the stable: it was with much difficulty and force that Mr Hewson, junior, assisted by the other lad, could remove him from the horse; his strength was great, and it was with difficulty he was brought in doors. Mr Hewson, senior, coming home at this time, sent for Mr Benjamin Ridge, an eminent practitioner, in Bridge-Road, who stood by him for a quarter of an hour, during which time the lad considered himself as stopped at the turnpike-gate, and took sixpence out of his pocket to be changed; and holding out his hand for the change, the sixpence was returned to him. He immediately observed, 'None of your nonsense—that is the sixpence again; give me my change;' when two pence halfpenny was given to him, he counted it over, and said, 'None of your gammon; that is not right; I want a penny more;' making the three pence halfpenny, which was his proper change. He then said, 'Give me my castor, (meaning his hat,) which slang term he had been in the habit of using, and then began to whip and spur to get his horse on. His pulse at this time was 136, full and hard; no change of countenance could be observed, nor any spasmodic affection of the muscles, the eyes remaining close the whole of the time. His coat was takan off his arm, shirt sleeves tucked up, and Mr Ridge bled him to 32 ounces; no alteration had taken place in him during the first part of the time the blood was flowing; at about 24 ounces, the pulse began to decrease; and when the full quantity named above had been taken, it was at 80—a slight perspiration on the forehead. During the time of bleeding, Mr Hewson related a circumstance of a Mr Harris, optician, in Holborn, whose son, some years since, walked out on the parapet of the house in his sleep. The boy joined the conversation, and observed, 'He lived at the corner of Brownlow-Street.' After the arm was tied up, he unlaced one boot, and said he would go to bed: in three minutes from this time, he awoke, got up, and asked what was the matter, (having then been one hour in the trance,) not having the slightest recollection of any thing that had passed, and wondered at his arm being tied up, and at the blood, &c. A strong aperient

young lady, of a good constitution, excellent capacity, and well educated. 'Her memory was capacious and well stored with a copious stock of ideas. Unexpectedly, and without any forewarning, she fell into a profound sleep, which continued several hours beyond the ordinary term. On waking, she was discovered to have lost every trait of acquired knowledge. Her memory was *tabula rasa*—all vestiges, both of words and things were obliterated and gone. It was found necessary for her to learn every thing again. She even acquired, by new efforts, the art of spelling, reading, writing, and calculating, and gradually became acquainted with the persons and objects around, like a being for the first time brought into the world. In these exercises she made considerable proficiency. But after a few months another fit of somnolency invaded her. On rousing from it, she found herself restored to the state she was in before the first paroxysm; but was wholly ignorant of every event and occurrence that had befallen her afterwards. The former condition of her existence she now calls the Old State, and the latter the New State; and she is as unconscious of her double character as two distinct persons are of their respective natures. For example, in her old state, she possesses all the original knowledge; in her new state, only what she acquired since. If a lady or gentleman be introduced to her in the old state, and *vice versa*, (and so of all other matters) to know them satisfactorily, she must learn them in both states. In the old state, she possesses fine powers of penmanship, while in the new, she writes a poor, awkward hand, having not had time or means to become expert. During four years and upwards, she has had periodical transitions from one of these states to the other. The alterations are always consequent upon a long and sound sleep. Both the lady and her family are now capable of conducting the affair without embarrassment By simply knowing whether she is in the old or new state, they regulate the intercourse and govern themselves accordingly.'

* Darwin's 'Zoonomia.'

medicine was then administered: he went to bed, slept well, and the next day appeared perfectly well, excepting debility from the bleeding, and operation of the medicine, and has no recollection whatever of what had taken place. None of his family or himself were ever affected in this way before.'*

Sleep-talking is generally such a trivial affection as not to require any treatment whatever. In every case the digestive organs must be attended to, and, if disordered, put to rights by suitable medicines. And should the affection proceed, or be supposed to proceed from hypochondria, hysteria, or the prevalence of any strong mental emotion, these states must be treated according to general principles. When it arises from idiosyncrasy, and becomes habitual, I believe that no means which can be adopted will be of much avail. As, in the case of somnambulism, it very frequently happens that the affection, after continuing for a long time, and baffling every species of treatment, disappears spontaneously.

CHAPTER IX.

SLEEPLESSNESS.

Sleep takes place as soon as the sensorial power that keeps the brain awake is expended, which, under common circumstances, occurs at our ordinary hour of going to rest, or even sooner, if any sophorific cause sufficiently strong should chance to operate. But the above power may be increased by various means, as in cases of physical suffering, or excited imagination, and, consequently, is not expended at the usual time. In this case, the person remains awake, and continues so till the period of its expenditure, which may not happen for several hours after he lies down, or even not at all, during the whole of that night. Now, whatever increases the sensorial power, whether it be balls, concerts, grief, joy, or bodily pain, is prejudicial to repose. By them the mind is exalted to a pitch of unnatural action, from which it is necessary it should descend before it can roll into the calm channel of sleep.

Whatever stimulates the external senses, however slightly, may prevent sleep. Thus, the ticking of a clock has this effect with very sensitive people; and a candle burning in the chamber is attended with the same result. Even when the eyes are shut this may take place, for the eye-lids are sufficiently transparent to transmit a sense of light to the retina. For the same reason, the light of day peering in at the window may awake us from or prevent slumber. It is said that Napoleon could never sleep if exposed to the influence of light, although, in other circumstances, slumber appeared at his bidding with surprising readiness.

A constitutional restlessness is sometimes brought on by habitually neglecting to solicit sleep when we lie down, by which means the brain is brought into such a state of irritability, that we can hardly sleep at all. Chronic wakefulness, originating from any mental or bodily affection, sometimes degenerates into a habit, in which the sufferer will remain for weeks, months, or even years, if authors are to be believed, awake. In the disease called delirium tremens, wakefulness is a constant symptom, and frequently continues for many successive days and nights. It is also an attendant upon all disorders accompanied by acute suffering, especially when the brain is affected, as in phrenitis, or fever. Maniacs, from the excited state of their sensorium, are remarkably subject to want of sleep; and this symptom is often so obstinate as to resist the most powerful remedies we can venture to prescribe.

Certain stimulating agents, such as tea or coffee, taken shortly before going to bed, have often the effect of preventing sleep. I would impute this to their irritative properties, which, by supplying the brain with fresh sensorial power, enable it to carry on uninterruptedly all its functions longer than it would otherwise do, and consequently prevent it from relapsing into slumber at the usual period.

* 'Lancet,' vol i.

Any uneasy bodily feeling has the same effect—both preventing the accession of sleep, and arousing us from it when it has fairly taken place. Thus, while moderate fatigue provoke slumber, excessive fatigue, owing to the pain and irritation it necessarily occasions, drives it away. Sickness, cold, heat, pregnancy, the ordinary calls of nature, a disagreeable bed, the want of an accustomed supper, too heavy a supper, or uneasiness of any kind, have the same result. Cold is most apt to induce sleeplessness, when partial, especially if it be confined to the feet; for when general and sufficiently intense, it has the opposite effect, and give rise to drowsiness. Certain diseases, such as hemicrania, tic doloureux, &c., have actually kept the person awake for three successive months; and all painful affections prevent sleep more or less. But the most violent tortures cannot altogether banish, however much they may retard it. Sooner or later the fatigue, which a want of it occasions, prevails, and slumber ultimately ensues.

Sleeplessness is sometimes produced by a sense of burning heat in the soles of the feet and palms of the hands, to which certain individuals are subject some time after lying down. This seems to proceed from a want of perspiration in these parts; owing generally to impaired digestion.

Mental emotions, of every description, are unfavorable to repose. If a man, as soon as he lays his head upon a pillow, can banish thinking, he is morally certain to fall asleep. There are many individuals so constituted, that they can do this without effort, and the consequence is, they are excellent sleepers. It is very different with those whose minds are oppressed by care, or over stimulated by excessive study. The sorrowful man, above all others, has the most need of sleep; but, far from shedding its benignant influence over him, it flies away, and leaves him to the communionship of his own sad thoughts:

> '*His* slumbers—if *he* slumber—are not sleep,
> But a continuance of enduring thought.'

It is the same with the man of vivid imagination. His fancy, instead of being subdued by the spell of sleep, becomes more active than ever. Thoughts in a thousand fantastic forms—myriads of waking dreams—pass through his mind, whose excessive activity spurns at repose, and mocks all his endeavors to reduce it to quiescence. Great joy will often scare away sleep for many nights; but, in this respect, it is far inferior to grief, a fixed attack of which has been known to keep the sufferer awake for several months. Those who meditate much, seldom sleep well in the early part of the night: they lie awake, for perhaps two or three hours, after going to bed, and do not fall into slumber till towards morning. Persons of this description often lie long, and are reputed lazy by early risers, although, it is probable, they actually sleep less than these early risers themselves. Long continued study is highly prejudicial to repose. Boerhaave mentions that, on one occasion, owing to this circumstance, he did not close his eyes for six weeks.

Nothing is so hurtful both to the mind and body as want of sleep. Deprived of the necessary portion, the person gets wan, emaciated and listless, and very soon falls into bad health; the spirit becomes entirely broken, and the fire of even the most ardent dispositions is quenched. Nor is this law peculiar to the human race, for it operates with similar power upon the lower animals, and deprives them of much of their natural ferocity. An illustration of this fact is afforded in the taming of wild elephants. These animals, when first caught, are studiously prevented from sleeping; in consequence of which, they become, in a few days, comparatively mild and harmless. Restlessness, when long protracted, may terminate in delirium, or confirmed insanity; and in many diseases, it is the most obstinate symptom we have to struggle against. By it alone, all the existing bad symptoms are aggravated; and as soon as we can succeed in overcoming it, every thing disagreeable and dangerous frequently wears away, and the person is restored to health.

In restlessness, both the perspiration and urinary secretions are usually much increased; there is also an accession of heat in the system, and a general feverish tendency, unless the want of sleep should proceed from cold.

With regard to the treatment of sleeplessness, a very few words will suffice: in fact, upon this head little more can be said, than a recommendation to obviate the causes from whence it proceeds, and it will naturally disappear. I may mention, however, that when there is no specific disease, either of body or mind, to which the want of sleep can be imputed, the person should keep himself in as cheerful a mood as possible—should rise early, if his strength permits it, and take such exercise as to fatigue himself moderately; and if all these means fail, that he ought to make use of opium. In all cases of restlessness, indeed, this medicine must be had recourse to, if the affection resists every other remedy, and continues so long as to endanger health. Those preparations of opium, the acetate and muriate of morphia, have latterly been a good deal used, and with excellent effect, for the same purpose. When neither opium nor its preparations agrees with the constitution, it becomes necessary to employ other narcotics, especially hyosciamus or hop. A pillow of hops sometimes succeeds in inducing sleep when other means fail. Such was the case with his late majesty, George III., who, by this contrivance, was relieved from the protracted wakefulness under which he laboured for so long a time. In giving medicines to produce sleep, great attention must be paid to the disease which occasions the restlessness; for, in phrenitis, high fever, and some other disorders, it would be most injurious to administer anodynes of any kind. In such cases, as the restlessness is merely a symptom of the general disease, its removal will depend upon that of the latter. When, however, the acute symptoms have been overcome, and nothing but chronic wakefulness, the result of debility, remains behind, it then becomes necessary to have recourse to opium, or such other remedies as may be considered applicable to the particular case. Studious men ought to avoid late reading; and, on going to bed, endeavour to abstract their minds from all intrusive ideas. They should try to circumscribe their thoughts within the narrowest possible circle, and prevent them from becoming rambling or excursive. I have often coaxed myself asleep by internally repeating half a dozen of times, any well known rhyme. While doing so, the ideas must be strictly directed to this particular theme, and prevented from wandering; for sometimes, during the process of repetition, the mind takes a strange turn, and performs two offices at the same time, being directed to the rhyme on the one hand, and to something else on the other; and it will be found that the hold it has of the former, is oftentimes much weaker than of the latter. The great secret is, by a strong effort of the will to compel the mind to depart from the favourite train of thought into which it has run, and address itself solely to the internal repetition of what is substituted in its place. If this is persevered in, it will generally be found to succeed; and I would recommend all those who are prevented from sleeping, in consequence of too active a flow of ideas, to try the experiment. As has been already remarked, the more the mind is made to turn upon a single impression, the more closely it is made to approach to the state of sleep, which is the total absence of all impressions. People should never go to bed immediately after studying hard, as the brain is precisely in that state of excitement which must prevent sleep. The mind ought previously to be relaxed by light conversation, music, or any thing which requires little thought.

In some cases of restlessness, sleep may be procured by the person getting up, and walking for a few minutes about the room. It is not easy to explain on what principle this acts, but it is certain, that by such means sleep sometimes follows, where previously it had been solicited in vain. It is customary with some people to read themselves into slumber, but dangerous accidents have arisen from this habit, in consequence of the lighted candle setting fire to the bed curtains. A safer and more effectual way is to get another person to read; in which case, sleep will very generally take place, especially if the subject in question is not one of much interest, or read in a dry monotonous manner. When sleeplessness proceeds from the heat of the weather, the person should lie very lightly covered, and let the air circulate freely through his room. A cold bath taken shortly before going to bed, or sponging the body with cold water, will often ensure a comfortable night's rest in the hot season of the year. When it arises from heat in the soles or palms, these parts should be bathed with cold vinegar and water, before lying down, and, if necessary, occasionally afterwards till the heat abates, which usually occurs in two or three hours. Attention must also be paid to the stomach and bowels.

An easy mind, a good digestion, and plenty of exercise in the open air, are the grand conducives to sound sleep;—and, accordingly, every man whose repose is indifferent, should endeavour to make them his own as soon as possible. When sleeplessness becomes habitual, the utmost care ought to be taken to overcome the habit, by the removal of every thing that has a tendency to cherish it.

CHAPTER X.

DROWSINESS.

Drowsiness is symptomatic of apoplexy and some other diseases, but sometimes it exists as an idiopathic affection. There are persons who have a disposition to sleep on every occasion. They do so at all times, and in all places. They sleep after dinner; they sleep in the theatre; they sleep in church. It is the same to them in what situation they may be placed: sleep is the great end of their existence—their occupation—their sole employment. Morpheus is the deity at whose shrine they worship—the only god whose influence over them is omnipotent. Let them be placed in almost any circumstances, and their constitutional failing prevails. It falls upon them in the midst of mirth; it assails them when travelling. Let them sail, or ride, or sit, or lie, or walk, sleep overtakes them—binds their faculties in torpor; and makes them dead to all that is passing around. Such are our dull, heavy-headed, drowsy mortals, those sons and daughters of phlegm—with passions as inert as a Dutch fog, and intellects as sluggish as the movements of the hippopotamus or the leviathan. No class of society is so insufferable as this. There is a torpor and obtuseness about their faculties, which render them dead to every impression. They have eyes and ears, yet they neither see nor hear; and the most exhilarating scenes may be passing before them without once attracting their notice. It is not uncommon for persons of this stamp to fall asleep in the midst of a party to which they have been invited; Mr Mackenzie, in one of his papers, speaks of an honest farmer having done so alongside of a young lady, who was playing on the harp for his amusement. The cause of this constitutional disposition to doze upon every occasion, seems to be a certain want of activity in the brain, the result of which is, that the individual is singularly void of fire, energy, and passion. He is of a phlegmatic temperament, generally a great eater, and very destitute of imagination. Such are the general characteristics of those who are predisposed to drowsiness: the cases where such a state coexists with intellectual energy are few in number.

Boerhaave speaks of an eccentric physician who took it into his head that sleep was the natural state of man, and accordingly slept eighteen hours out of the twenty-four—till he died of apoplexy, a disease which is always apt to be produced by excessive sleep.

Cases of constitutional drowsiness are in a great measure without remedy, for the soporific tendency springs from some natural defect, which no medicinal means can overcome.

Equally impossible of cure is the affection when it arises, as it very often does, from old age. Even long before this period of life, as at the age of fifty or sixty, people very often get into somnolent habits, and are pretty sure to fall asleep if they attempt to read, or even if they place themselves in an easy chair before the fire. I know of no cure for this indolent propensity, unless indeed the habits arise, as it sometimes does, from corpulency, in which case it is more manageable, in so far as its cause is occasionally capable of being removed.

Drowsiness sometimes proceeds from a fulness of blood in the head, or a disordered state of the digestive organs. When it originates from the former cause, it becomes necessary to have recourse to general or local blood-letting. The person, likewise, should use, from time to time, mild laxatives, live temperately, and take abundance of exercise. Medicines of a similar kind are necessary when the affection arises from the state of the stomach and bowels: so soon as these organs are restored to health, the symptomatic drowsiness will naturally disappear.

Persons who feel the disposition to drowsiness gaining upon them, should struggle vigorously against it; for when once the habit is fairly established, its eradication is very difficult. Exercise of body and mind, early rising and the cold bath, are among the best means for this purpose.

CHAPTER XI.

PROTRACTED SLEEP.

I have already mentioned a few instances of individuals remaining for days or weeks in a state of profound sleep. The nature of this extraordinary affection is in a great measure, unknown; it arises, in most cases, without any obvious cause, generally resists every method that can be adopted for removing it, and disappears of its own accord.

The case of Mary Lyall, related in the 8th volume of the 'Transactions of the Royal Society of Edinburgh,' is one of the most remarkable instances of excessive somnolency on record. This woman fell asleep on the morning of the 27th of June, and continued in that state till the evening of the 30th of the same month, when she awoke, and remained in her usual way till the 1st of July, when she again fell asleep, and continued so till the the 8th of August. She was bled, blistered, immersed in the hot and cold bath, and stimulated in almost every possible way, without having any consciousness of what was going on. For the first seven days she continued motionless, and exhibited no inclination to eat. At the end of this time she began to move her left hand; and, by pointing to her mouth, signified a wish for food. She took readily what was given to her; still she discovered no symptoms of hearing, and made no other kind of bodily movement than of her left hand. Her right hand and arm, particularly, appeared completely dead, and bereft of feeling; and even when pricked with a pin, so as to draw blood, never shrunk in the least degree. At the same time, she instantly drew back her left arm whenever it was touched by the point of the pin. She continued to take food whenever it was offered to her. For the first two weeks, her pulse generally stood at 50, during the third and fourth week, about 60; and on the day before her recovery, at 70 or 72. Her breathing was soft and almost imperceptible, but during the night-time she occasionally drew it more strongly, like a person who has first fallen asleep. She evinced no symptom of hearing, till about four days before her recovery. On being interrogated, after this event, upon her extraordinary state, she mentioned that she had no knowledge of any thing that had happened—that she had never been conscious of either having needed or received food, or of having been blistered; and expressed much surprise on finding her head shaved. She had merely the idea of having passed a long night in sleep.

The case of Elizabeth Perkins is also remarkable. In the year 1788, she fell into a profound slumber, from which nothing could arouse her, and remained in this state for between eleven and twelve days, when she awoke of her own accord, to the great joy of her relatives, and wonder of the neighbourhood. On recovering, she went about her usual business; but this was only for a short period, for in a week after she relapsed again into a sleep which lasted some days. She continued, with occasional intervals of wakefulness, in a dozing state for several months, when she expired.

There was lately at Kirkheaton a remarkable instance of excessive sleep. A poor paralytic, twenty years of age, was seldom, for the period of twelve months, awake more than three hours in the twenty-four. On one occasion, he slept for three weeks; he took not a particle of either food or drink; nothing could rouse him, even for a moment; yet his sleep appeared to be calm and natural.

The case of Elizabeth Armitage of Woodhouse, near Leeds, may also be mentioned. The age of this person was sixty-nine years. She had been for several months in a decline, during which she had taken very little sustenance, when she fell into a state of lethargic stupor, on the morning of the 1st of July, 1827, in which condition she remained, without uttering one word, receiving any food, or showing any signs of life, except breathing, which was at times almost imperceptible. In this state she continued for eight days, when she expired without a groan.

Excessively protracted sleep may ensue from the injudicious use of narcotics. A very striking instance of this kind occurred on 17th February, 1816, near Lymington. In consequence of a complaint with which a child had been painfully afflicted for some time previous, its mother gave it an anodyne, (probably laudanum,) for the purpose of procuring it rest. The consequence was, that it fell into a profound sleep, which continued for three weeks. In this case, in addition to an excessive dose, the child must have possessed some constitutional idiosyncrasy, which favoured the operation of the medicine in a very powerful manner.

One of the most extraordinary instances of excessive sleep, is that of the lady of Nismes, published in 1777, in the 'Memoirs of the Royal Academy of Sciences at Berlin.' Her attacks of sleep took place periodically, at sunrise and about noon. The first continued till within a short time of the accession of the second, and the second till between seven and eight in the evening—when she awoke, and continued so till the next sunrise. The most extraordinary fact connected with this case is, that the first attack commenced always at daybreak, whatever might be the season of the year, and the other always immediately after twelve o'clock. During the brief interval of wakefulness which ensued shortly before noon, she took a little broth, which she had only time to do, when the second attack returned upon her, and kept her asleep till the evening. Her sleep was remarkably profound, and had all the characters of complete insensibility, with the exception of a feeble respiration, and a weak but regular movement of the pulse. The most singular fact connected with her remains to be mentioned. When the disorder had lasted six months, and then ceased, she had an interval of perfect health for the same length of time. When it lasted one year, the subsequent interval was of equal duration. The affection at last wore gradually away; and she lived, entirely free of it, for many years after. She died in the eighty-first year of her age, of dropsy, a complaint which had no connexion with her preceding disorder.

There are a good many varieties in the phenomena of protracted sleep. In some cases, the individual remains for many days without eating or drinking; in others, the necessity for these natural wants arouses him for a short time from his slumber, which time he employs in satisfying hunger and thirst, and then instantly gets into his usual state of lethargy. The latter kind of somnolency is sometimes feigned by impostors for the purpose of extorting charity; on this account, when an instance of the kind occurs, it should be narrowly looked into, to see that there is no deception.

The power possessed by the body of subsisting for such a length of time in protracted sleep, is most remarkable, and bears some analogy to the abstinence of the polar bear in the winter season. It is to be observed, however, that during slumber, life can be supported by a much smaller portion of food than when we are awake, in consequence of the diminished expenditure of the vital energy which takes place in the former state.

All that can be done for the cure of protracted somnolency, is to attempt to rouse the person by the use of stimuli, such as blistering, pinching, the warm or cold bath, the application of sternutatories to the nose, &c. Blooding should be had recourse to, if we suspect any apopletic tendency to exist. Every means must be employed to get nourishment introduced into the stomach; for this purpose, if the sleeper cannot swallow, nutritious fluids should be forced, from time to time, into this organ by means of Jukes' pump, which answers the purpose of filling as well as evacuating it.

CHAPTER XII.

SLEEP FROM COLD.

This kind of sleep is so peculiar, that it requires to be considered separately. The power of cold in occasioning slumber, is not confined to man, but pervades a very extensive class of animals. The hybernation, or winter torpitude of the brown and Polar bear, results from this cause. Those animals continue asleep for months; and do not awake from their apathy till revived by the genial temperature of spring. The same is the case with the hedgehog, the badger, the squirrel, and several species of the mouse and rat tribes, such as the dormouse and marmot: as also with the land tortoise, the frog, and almost all the individuals of the lizard, insect, and serpent tribes. Fishes are often found imbedded in the ice, and though in a state of apparent death, become at once lively and animated on being exposed to heat. "The fish froze," says Captain Franklin, 'as fast as they were taken out of the nets, and in a short time became a solid mass of ice, and by a blow or two of the hatchet were easily split open, when the intestines might be removed in one lump. If, in this completely frozen state, they were thawed before the fire, they recovered their animation.' Sheep sometimes remain for several weeks in a state of torpitude, buried beneath wreaths of snow. Swallows are occasionally in the same state, being found torpid and insensible in the hollows of trees, and among the ruins of old houses during the winter season; but with birds this more rarely happens, owing, probably, to the temperature of their blood being higher than that of other animals, and thereby better enabling them to resist the cold. Almost all insects sleep in winter. This is particularly the case with the crysalis, and such grubs as cannot, at that season, procure their food. In hybernating animals, it is impossible to trace any peculiarity of structure which disposes them to hybernate, and enables life to be sustained during that period. So far the subject is involved in deep obscurity. According to Dr Edwards, the temperature of such animal sinks considerably during sleep, even in summer.

Want of moisture produces torpor in some animals. This is the case with the garden snail, which revives if a little water is thrown on it. Snails, indeed, have revived after being dried for fifteen years. Mr Baucer has restored the *vibris tritici* (a species of worm) after perfect torpitude and apparent death for five years and eight months by merely soaking it in water. The *furcularia anostobea*, a small microscopic animal, may be killed and revived a dozen times by drying it and then applying moisture. According to Spallanzani, animalculi have been recovered by moisture after a torpor of twenty-seven years. Larger animals are thrown into the same state from want of moisture. Such according to Humboldt, is the case with the alligator and boa constrictor during the dry season in the plains of Venezuela, and with the *centenes solosous*, a species of hedge hog found in Madagascar; so that dryness as well as cold, produces hybernation, if, in such a case, we may use that term.

The power of intense cold in producing sleep, is very great in the human subject, and nothing in the winter season is more common than to find people lying dead in fields and on the high highways from such a cause. An overpowering drowsiness steals upon them, and if they yield to its influence death is almost unevitable. This is the particularly the case in snowstorms, in which it is often impossible to get a place of shelter.

This state of torpor, with the exception perhaps of catalepsy, is the most perfect sleep that can be imagined: it approaches almost to death in its apparent annihilation of the animal functions. Digestion is at an end, and the secretions and excretions suspended: nothing seems to go on but circulation, respiration and absorption. The two former are extremely languid,* but the latter tolerably vigorous, if we may judge from the quantity of fat which the animal loses during its torpid state. The bear, for example, on going to its wintry rest, is remarkably corpulent; on awaking from it, quite emaciated; in which state, inspired by the pangs of hunger, it sallies forth with redoubled fury upon its prey. Life is sustained by the absorption of this fat, which for months serves the animal as provision. Such emaciation, however, is not common to all hybernating animals, some of whom lose little or nothing by their winter torpitude.

Hybernation may be prevented. Thus the polar bear in the menagerie at Paris never hybernated; and

* The extremely languid, or almost suspended state of these two functions, is demonstrated by the fact, that an animal in a state of hybernation may be placed for an hour in a jar of hydrogen without suffering death.

in the marmot and hedgehog hybernation is prevented if the animals be kept in a higher temperature. It is also a curious fact, that an animal, if exposed to a more intense cold, while hybernating, is awaked from its lethargy. Exposing a hybernating animal to light has also, in many cases the same effect.

Some writers, and Buffon among the rest, deny that such a state of torpor as we have here described, can be looked upon as sleep. This is a question into which it is not necessary at present to enter. All I contend for is, that the state of the mind is precisely the same here as in the ordinary sleep—that, in both cases, the organs of the senses and of volition are equally inert; and that though the condition of the secretive and circulating systems are different, so many circumstances are nevertheless identical, that we become justified in considering the one in a work which professes to treat of the other.

In Captain Cook's first voyage, a memorable instance is given of the power of intense cold in producing sleep. It occurred in the island of Terra del Fuego. Dr Solander, Mr Banks, and several other gentlemen had ascended the mountains of that cold region, for the purpose of botanizing and exploring the country. 'Dr Solander, who had more than once crossed the mountains which divide Sweden from Norway, well knew that extreme cold, especially when joined with fatigue, produces a torpor and sleepinesss that are almost irresistible. He, therefore, conjured the company to keep moving whatever pain it might cost them, and whatever relief they might be promised by an inclination to rest. 'Whoever sits down,' said he, 'will sleep; and whoever sleeps, will wake no more,' Thus at once admonished and alarmed, they set forward; but while they were still upon the naked rock, and before they had got among the bushes, the cold became suddenly so intense as to produce the effects that had been most dreaded. Dr Solander himself was the first who felt the inclination, against which he had warned others, irresistible; and insisted upon being suffered to lie down. Mr Banks entreated and remonstrated in vain; down he lay upon the ground, although it was covered with snow, and it was with great difficulty that his friend kept him from sleeping. Richmond, also, one of the black servants, began to linger, having suffered from the cold in the same manner as the Doctor. Mr Banks, therefore, sent five of the company, among whom was Buchan, forward, to get a fire ready at the first convenient place they could find; and himself, with four others remained with the Doctor and Richmond, whom, partly by persuasion and entreaty, and partly by force, they brought on; but when they had got through the greatest part of the birch and swamp, they both declared they could go no farther. Mr Banks again had recourse to entreaty and expostulation, but they produced no effect. When Richmond was told that, if he did not go on, he would in a short time be frozen to death, he answered, that he desired nothing but to lie down and die. The Doctor did not so explicitly renounce his life; he said he was willing to go on, but that he must first take some sleep, though he had before told the company, to sleep was to perish. Mr Banks and the rest found it impossible to carry them; and there being no remedy, they were both suffered to sit down, being partly supported by the bushes; and in a few minutes they fell into a profound sleep. Soon after, some of the people who had been sent forward, returned, with the welcome news that a fire was kindled about a quarter of a mile farther on the way. Mr Banks then endeavored to awake Dr Solander, and happily succeeded. But though he had not slept five minutes, he had almost lost the use of his limbs, and the muscles were so shrunk, that the shoes fell from his feet: he consented to go forward with such assistance as could be given him, but no attempts to relieve poor Richmond were successful.

It is hardly necessary to say any thing about the treatment of such cases. If a person is found in a state of torpor from cold, common sense points out the necessity of bringing him within the influence of warmth. When, however, the limbs, &c., are frost-bitten, heat must be very cautiously applied, lest reaction, ensuing in such debilitated parts, might induce gangrene. Brisk friction with a cold towel, or even with snow, as is the custom in Russia, should, in the first instance, be had recourse to. When by this means the circulation is restored, and motion and feeling communicated to the parts, the heat may be gradually increased, and the person wrapped in blankets, and allowed some stimulus internally, such as a little negus, or spirits and water. This practice should be adopted from the very first, when the parts are not frost-bitten; but when such is the case, the stimulating system requires to be used with great caution, and we must proceed carefully, proportioning the stimulus to the particular circumstance of the case.

If a person is unfortunate enough to be overtaken in a snow storm, and has no immediate prospect of extrication, he should, if the cold is very great, and the snow deep, sink his body as much as possible in the latter, leaving only room for respiration. By this plan, the heat of the body is much better preserved than when exposed to the influence of the atmosphere, and life has a greater chance of being saved; for the temperature of the snow is not lower than that of the surrounding air, while its power of absorbing caloric is much less. It is on this principle that sheep live for such a length of time enveloped in snow wreaths, while, had they been openly exposed, for a much less period, to a similar degree of cold, death would inevitably have ensued.

One of the best methods to prevent the limbs from being frost-bitten in intensely cold weather, is to keep them continually in motion. Such was the method recommended by Xenophon to the Greek troops, in the memorable 'retreat of the ten thousand,' conducted by that distinguished soldier and historian

CHAPTER XIII

TRANCE.

There is some analogy between suspended animation and sleep. It is not so striking, however, as to require any thing like a lengthened discussion of the former, which I shall only consider in so far as the resemblance holds good between it and sleep. I have already spoken of that suspension of the mind, and of some of the vital functions, which occurs in consequence of intense cold; but there are other varieties, not less singular in their nature. The principal of these are, fainting, apoplexy, hanging, suffocation, drowning and especially, trance. When complete fainting takes place, it has many of the characters of death—the countenance being pail, moist, and clammy; the body cold; the respiration extremely feeble; the pulsation of the heart apparently at an end; while the mind is in a state of utter abeyance. It is in the latter respect only that the resemblance exists between syncope and sleep; in every other they are widely different. The same rule holds with regard to apoplexy, in which a total insensibility, even to the strongest stimuli, takes place, accompanied also with mental torpor. In recoverable cases of drowning, hanging, and suffocation, a similar analogy prevails, only in a much feebler degree; the faculties of the mind being for the time suspended, and the actual existence of the vital spark only proved by the subsequent restoration of the individual to consciousness and feeling.

The most singular species, however, of suspended

animation is that denominated catalepsy, or trance. No affection, to which the animal frame is subject, is more remarkable than this. During its continuance, the whole body is cold, rigid, and inflexible; the countenance without color; the eyes fixed and motionless; while breathing and the pulsation of the heart are, to all appearance, at an end. The mental powers, also, are generally suspended, and participate in the universal torpor which pervades the frame. In this extraordinary condition, the person may remain for several days, having all, or nearly all, the characteristics of death impressed upon him. Such was the case with the celebrated Lady Russel, who only escaped premature interment by the affectionate prudence of her husband; and other well authenticated instances of similar preservation from burying alive, have been recorded.

The nature of this peculiar species of suspended animation, seems to be totally unknown; for there is such an apparent extinction of every faculty essential to life, that it is inconceivable how existence should go on during the continuance of the fit. There can be no doubt, however, that the suspension of the heart and lungs is more apparent than real. It is quite certain that the functions of these organs must continue, so as to sustain life although in so feeble a manner as not to come under the cognizance of our senses. The respiration, in particular, is exceedingly slight; for a mirror, held to the mouth of the individual, receives no tarnish whatever from his breath. One fact seems certain, that the functions of the nervous system are wholly suspended, with the exception of such a faint portion of energy, as to keep up the circulatory and respiratory phenomena: consciousness, in a great majority of cases, is abolished; and there is nothing wanting to indicate the unquestionable presence of death, but that decomposition of the body which invariably follows this state, and which never attends the presence of vitality.

The remote causes of trance are hidden in much obscurity; and, generally, we are unable to trace the affection to any external circumstance. It has been known to follow a fit of terror. Sometimes it ensues after hysteria, epilepsy, or other spasmodic diseases, and is occasionally an accompaniment of menorrhagia and intestinal worms. Nervous and hypochondriac patients are the most subject to its attacks; but sometimes it occurs when there is no disposition of the kind, and when the person is in a state of the most seeming good health.

'A girl named Shorigny, about twenty-five years old, residing at Paris, had been for two years past subject to hysteria. On the twenty-eighth day after she was first attacked, the physician who came to visit her was informed that she had died during the night, which much surprised him, as when he had left her the night before, she was better than usual. He went to see her, in order to convince himself of the fact; and, on raising the cloth with which she was covered, he perceived that though her face was very pale, and her lips discoloured, her features were not otherwise in the least altered. Her mouth was open, her eyes shut, and the pupils very much dilated; the light of the candle made no impression on them. There was no sensible heat in her body; but it was not cold and flabby like corpses in general. The physician returned the next day, determined on seeing her again before she was buried; and, finding that she had not become cold, he gave orders that the coffin should not be soldered down until putrefaction had commenced. He continued to observe her during five days, and at the end of that period, a slight movement was observed in the cloth which covered her. In two hours, it was found that the arm had contracted itself; she began to move; and it was clear that it had only been an apparent death. The eyes soon after were seen opened, the senses returned, and the girl began gradually to recover. This is an extraordinary, but incontestible fact: the girl is still alive, and a great many persons who saw her while she was in the state of apathy described, are ready to satisfy the doubts of any one who will take the trouble to inquire.'*

The case which follows is from the *Canton Gazette*, and is not less curious:—

'On the western suburbs of Canton, a person named Le, bought as a slave-woman a girl named Leaning. At the age of twenty-one, he sold her to be a concubine to a man named Wong. She had lived with him three years. About six months ago she became ill, in consequence of a large imposthume on her side, and on the 25th of the present moon died. She was placed in a coffin, the lid of which remained unfastened, to wait for her parents to come and see the corpse, that they might be satisfied she died a natural death. On the 28th, while carrying the remains to be interred in the north side of Canton, a noise or voice was heard proceeding from the coffin; and, on removing the covering, it was found the woman had come to life again. She had been supposed dead for three days.'

The case of Colonel Townsend, however, is much more extraordinary than either of the above mentioned. This gentleman possessed the remarkable faculty of throwing himself into a trance at pleasure. The heart ceased, apparently, to throb at his bidding, respiration seemed at an end, his whole frame assumed the icy chill and rigidity of death; while his face became colourless and shrunk, and his eye fixed, glazed, and ghastly: even his mind ceased to manifest itself; for during the trance it was utterly devoid of consciousness as his body of animation. In this state he would remain for hours, when these singular phenomena wore away, and he returned to his usual condition. Medical annals furnish no parallel to this extraordinary case. Considered whether in a physiological or metaphysical point of view, it is equally astonishing and inexplicable.

A variety of stories are related of people having had circumstances revealed to them in a trance, of which they were ignorant when awake: most of these tales have their origin in fiction, although there is no reason why they may not be occasionally true; as the mind, instead of being in torpor, as is very generally the case, may exist in a state analogous to that of dreaming, and may thus, as in a common dream, have long forgotten events impressed upon it.

The following case exhibits a very singular instance, in which the usual characteristic—a suspension of the mental faculties—was wanting. It seems to have been a most complete instance of suspended volition, wherein the mind was active, while the body refused to obey its impulses, and continued in a state of apparent death.

'A young lady, an attendant on the Princess ——, after having been confined to her bed, for a great length of time, with a violent nervous disorder, was at last, to all appearance, deprived of life. Her lips were quite pale, her face resembled the countenance of a dead person, and the body grew cold.

'She was removed from the room in which she died, was laid in a coffin, and the day of her funeral fixed on. The day arrived, and, according to the custom of the country, funeral songs and hymns were sung before the door. Just as the people were about to nail on the lid of the coffin, a kind of perspiration was observed to appear on the surface of her body. It grew greater every moment; and at last a kind of convulsive motion was observed in the hands and feet of the corpse. A few minutes after, during which time fresh signs of returning life appeared, she at once opened her eyes and uttered a most pitiable shriek. Physicians were quickly procured, and in the course of a few days she was considerably restored, and is probably alive at this day.

'The description which she gave of her situation is extremely remarkable, and forms a curious and authentic addition to psychology.

* Mentor.

'She said it seemed to her, as if in a dream, that she was really dead; yet she was perfectly conscious of all that happened around her in this dreadful state. She distinctly heard her friends speaking and lamenting her death, at the side of her coffin. She felt them pull on the dead-clothes, and lay her in it. This feeling produced a mental anxiety, which is indescribable. She tried to cry, but her soul was without power, and could not act on her body. She had the contradictory feeling as if she were in her body, and yet not in it, at one and the same time. It was equally impossible for her to stretch out her arm, or to open her eyes, or to cry, although she continually endeavored to do so. The internal anguish of her mind was, however, at its utmost height when the funeral hymns began to be sung, and when the lid of the coffin was about to be nailed on. The thought that she was to be buried alive, was the one that gave activity to her soul, and caused it to operate on her corporeal frame.'*

The following is different from either of the foregoing; I have given it on account of its singularity, although it does not altogether come under the denomination of trance.

'George Grokatzhi, a Polish soldier, deserted from his regiment in the harvest of the year 1677. He was discovered, a few days after, drinking and making merry in a common ale-house. The moment he was apprehended, he was so much terrified, that he gave a loud shriek, and was immediately deprived of the power of speech. When brought to a court martial, it was impossible to make him articulate a word; nay, he then became as immovable as a statue, and appeared not to be conscious of any thing that was going forward. In the prison, to which he was conducted, he neither ate nor drank. The officers and priests at first threatened him, and afterwards endeavored to soothe and calm him, but all their efforts were in vain. He remained senseless and immovable. His irons were struck off, and he was taken out of the prison, but he did not move. Twenty days and nights were passed in this way, during which he took no kind of nourishment: he then gradually sunk and died.'†

It would be out of place to enter here into a detail of the medical management of the first mentioned varieties of suspended animation, such as drowning, strangulation, &c., &c.; and with regard to the treatment of trance, properly so called, a very few words will suffice.

If we have reason to suppose that we know the cause of the affection, that, of course, must be removed whenever practicable. We must then employ stimuli to arouse the person from his torpor, such as friction, the application of sternutatories and volatile agents to the nostrils, and electricity. The latter remedy is likely to prove a very powerful one, and should always be had recourse to when other means fail. I should think the warm bath might be advantageously employed. When even these remedies do not succeed, we must trust to time. So long as the body does not run into decay, after a case of suspended animation arising without any very obvious cause, internment should not take place; for it is possible that life may exist, although, for the time being, there is every appearance of its utter extinction. By neglecting this rule, a person may be interred alive; nor can there be a doubt that such dreadful mistakes have occasionally been committed, especially in France, where it is customary to inter the body twenty-four hours after death. Decomposition is the only infallible mark that existence is at an end, and that the grave has triumphed.

CHAPTER XIV.

VOLUNTARY WAKING DREAMS.

The young and the imaginative are those who indulge most frequently in waking dreams. The scenes which life presents do not come up to the desires of the heart; and the pencil of fancy is accordingly employed in depicting others more in harmony with its own designs. Away into the gloomy back-ground goes reality with its stern and forbidding hues, and forward, in colours more dazzling than those of the rainbow, start the bright and airy phantoms of imagination. 'How often,' observes Dr Good,* 'waking to the roar of the midnight tempest, while dull and gluttonous indolence snores in happy forgetfulness, does the imagination of those who are thus divinely gifted mount the dizzy chariot of the whirlwind, and picture evils that have no real existence; now figuring to herself some neat and thrifty cottage where virtue delights to reside, she sees it swept away in a moment by the torrent, and despoiled of the little harvest just gathered in; now following the lone traveller in some narrow and venturous pathway, over the edge of the Alpine precipices, where a single slip is instant destruction, she tracks him alone by fitful flashes of lightning; and at length, struck by the flash, she beholds him tumbling headlong from rock to rock, to the bottom of the dread abyss, the victim of a double death. Or possibly she takes her stand on the jutting foreland of some bold terrific coast, and eyes the foundering vessel straight below; she mixes with the spent and despairing crew; she dives into the cabin, and singles out, perhaps from the rest, some lovely maid, who, in all the bloom of recovered beauty, is voyaging back to her native land from the healing airs of a foreign climate, in thought just bounding over the scenes of her youth, or panting in the warm embraces of a father's arms.' Such are waking dreams; and there are few who, at some happy moment or other, have not yielded to their influence. Often under the burning clime of India, or upon the lonely banks of the Mississippi, has the stranger let loose the reins of his imagination, calling up before him the mountains of his own beloved country, his native streams, and rocks, and valleys, so vividly, that he was transported back into the midst of them, and lived over again the days of his youth. Or the waking dream may assume a more selfish character. If the individual pines after wealth, his mind may be filled with visions of future opulence. If he is young and unmarried, he may conjure up the form of a lovely female, may place her in a beautiful cottage by the banks of some romantic stream, may love her with unfathomable affection, and become the fondest and most happy of husbands. The more completely a person is left to solitude, the more likely is his imagination to indulge in such fancies. We seldom build castles in the air in the midst of bustle, or when we have any thing else to think of. Waking dreams are the luxuries of an otherwise unemployed mind—the aristocratic indulgences of the intellect. As people get older and more coversant with life in all its diversified features, they are little inclined to indulge in such visions. They survey events with the eye of severe truth, amuse themselves with no impracticable notions of fancied happiness, and are inclined to take a gloomy, rather than a flattering, view of the future. With youthful and poetical minds, however, the case is widely different. Much of that portion of their existence, not devoted to occupation, is a constant dream. They lull themselves into temporary happiness with scenes which they know only to exist in their own imagination; but which are nevertheless so beautiful, and so much in harmony with every thing their souls desire, that they fondly clasp at the illusion, and submit themselves unhesitatingly to its spell.

These curious states of mind may occur at any time; but the most common periods of their accession are shortly after lying down, and shortly before getting up. Men, especially young men, of vivid, sanguine, imaginative temperaments, have dreams of this kind almost

* 'Psychological Magazine,' vol. v. part iii. page 15.

† Bonetus, '*Medic Septentrion.*' lib. i. sec. xvi. cap. 6.

* Book of Nature, vol. iii. p. 422.

every morning and night. Instead of submitting to the sceptre of sleep, they amuse themselves with creating a thousand visionary scenes. Though broad awake, their judgment does not exercise the slightest sway, and fancy is allowed to become lord of the ascendant. Poets are notorious castle-builders, and poems are, in fact, merely waking dreams—at least their authors were under the hallucination of such dreams while composing. Milton's mind, during the composition of Paradise Lost, must have existed chiefly in the state of a sublime waking dream; so must Raphael's, while painting the Sistine Chapel; and, Thorwaldson's, while designing the triumphs of Alexander. In waking dreams, whatever emotion prevails has a character of exaggeration, at least in reference to the existing condition of the individual. He sees every thing through the serene atmosphere of imagination, and imbues the most trite circumstances with poetical colouring. The aspect, in short, which things assume, bears a strong resemblance to that impressed upon them by ordinary dreams, and differs chiefly in this, that, though verging continually on the limits of extravagance, they seldom transcend possibility.

CHAPTER XV.

SPECTRAL ILLUSIONS.

Of the various faculties with which man is endowed, those which bring him into communication with the material world, constitute an important class. The organs of these faculties—termed perceptive—are situated in the middle and lower parts of the forehead. Their function is to perceive and remember the existence, phenomena, qnalities, and relations of external objects. *Individuality* takes cognizance of the existence of material bodies; *Eventuality*, of their motions or actions; *Form*, of their shape; *Size*, of their magnitude and proportions; *Weight*, of the resistance which they offer to a moving or restraining power; *Colouring*, of their colours; and *Locality*, of their relative position. *Time* and *Number* perceive and remember duration and numbers; *Language* takes cognizance of artificial signs of feeling and thought; and *Order* delights in regularity and arrangement. In ordinary circumstances, the mode of action of these organs is this. If any object—a horse for example—be placed before us, the rays of light reflected from its surface to our eye, form a picture of the animal upon the retina or back part of that organ. This picture gives rise to what, for want of more precise language, is called an impression, which is conveyed by the optic nerve to the cerebral organs already mentioned; and by them, in reality, the horse is perceived. The eye and optic nerve, it will be observed, do no more than transmit the impression from without, so as to produce that state of the internal organs which is accompanied by what is termed perception or *sensation*. When the horse is withdrawn, the impression still remains, to a certain extent, in the brain; and though the animal is not actually perceived, we still remember its appearance, and can almost imagine that it is before us. This faint semi-perception is called an *idea*, and differs from sensation only in being less vivid. The brain is more highly excited when it perceives a sensation, than when an idea only is present; because, in the former case, there is applied, through the medium of the senses, a stimulus from without, which, in the latter case, is not present. If, however, the brain be brought by *internal* causes to a degree of excitement, which, in general, is the result only of external impressions, ideas not less vivid than sensations ensue; and the individual has the same consciousness as if an impression were transmitted from an actual object through the senses. In other words, the brain, in a certain state, perceives external bodies; and any cause which induces that state, gives rise to a like perception, independently of the usual cause—the presence of external bodies themselves. The chief of these internal causes is inflammation of the brain: and when the organs of the perceptive faculties are so excited—put into a state similar to that which follows actual impressions from without—the result is a series of false images or sounds, which are often so vivid as to be mistaken for realities. During sleep, the perceptive organs seem to be peculiarly susceptible of such excitement. In dreaming, for instance, the external world, is inwardly represented to our minds with all the force of reality: we speak and hear as if we were in communication with actual existences. Spectral illusions are phenomena strictly analogous; indeed, they are literally nothing else than involuntary waking dreams.

In addition to the occasional cause of excitement of the perceptive organs above alluded to, there is another, the existence of which is proved by numerous facts, though its mode of action is somewhat obscure. I allude to a large development of the organ of *Wonder*. Individuals with such a development are both strongly inclined to believe in the supernaturality of ghosts, and peculiarly liable to be visited by them. This organ is large in the head of Earl Grey, and he is said to be haunted by the apparition of a bloody head. Dr Gall mentions, that in the head of Dr Jung Stilling, who saw visions, the organ was very largely developed. A gentleman who moves in the best society in Paris, once asked Gall to examine his head. The doctor's first remark was, 'You sometimes see visions, and believe in apparitions.' The gentleman started from this in astonishment, and said that he *had* frequent visions: but never till that moment had he spoken on the subject to any human being, through fear of being set down as absurdly credulous. How a large development of *Wonder* produces the necessary excitement of the perceptive organs is unknown, but the fact seems indisputable.

In former times, individuals who beheld visions, instead of ascribing them to a disordered state of the brain, referred them to outward impressions, and had a false conviction of the presence of supernatural beings. Hence the universal belief in ghosts which in these periods prevailed, even among the learned, and from which the illiterate are not yet entirely exempt.

We read in history of people being attended by familiar spirits; such was the case with Socrates in ancient, and with the poet Tasso, in modern times: their familiar spirits were mere spectral illusions. 'At Bisaccio, near Naples,' says Mr Hoole, in his account of the illustrious author of the Jerusalem Delivered, 'Manso had an opportuuity of examining the singnlar effects of Tasso's melancholy, and often disputed him concerning a *familiar spirit* which he pretended conversed with him: Manso endeavoured in vain to persuade his friend that the whole was the illusion of a disturbed imagination; but the latter was strenuous in maintaining the reality of what he asserted, and to convince Manso, desired him to be present at one of the mysterious conversations. Manso had the complaisance to meet him the next day, and while they were engaged in discourse, on a sudden he observed that Tasso kept his eyes fixed on a window, and remained in a manner immovable; he called him by his name, but received no answer; at last Tasso cried out, 'There is the friendly spirit that is come to converse with me; look! and you will be convinced of all I have said.'

Manso heard him with surprise; he looked, but saw nothing except the sunbeams darting through the window; he cast his eyes all over the room, but could perceive nothing; and was just going to ask where the pretended spirit was, when he heard Tasso speak with great earnestness, sometimes putting questions to the spirit, sometimes giving answers · delivering the whole in such a pleasing manner, and in such elevated expressions, that he listened with admiration, and had not the least inclination to interrupt him. At last the uncommon conversation ended with the departure of the spirit, as appeared by Tasso's own words, who, turning to Manso, asked him if his doubts were removed. Manso was more amazed than ever ; he scarce knew what to think of his friend's situation, and waived any farther conversation on the subject.'

The visions of angels, and the communications from above, with which religious enthusiasts are often impressed, arise from the operation of spectral illusions. They see forms and hear sounds which have no existence ; and, believing in the reality of such impressions, consider themselves highly favored by the almighty. These feelings prevailed very much during the persecutions in Scotland. Nothing was more common than for the Covenanter by the lonely hill side to have what he supposed a special message from God, and even to see the angel who brought it, standing before him, and encouraging him to steadfastness in his religious principles. Much of the crazy fanaticism exhibited by the disciples of Campbell and Irving, undoubtedly arises from a similar cause ; and it is probable that both of these individuals see visions and hear supernatural voices, as well as many of their infatuated followers.

Various causes may so excite the brain as to produce these phantasmata, such as great mental distress, sleeplessness, nervous irritation, religious excitement, fever, epilepsy, opium, delirium tremens, excessive study, and dyspepsia. I have known them to arise without the apparent concurrence of any mental or bodily distemper. I say *apparent*, for it is very evident there must be some functional derangement, however much it may be hidden from observation. An ingenious friend has related to me a case of this kind which occurred in his own person. One morning, while lying in bed broad awake, and, as he supposed, in perfect health, the wall opposite to him appeared to open at its junction with the ceiling, and out of the aperture came a little uncouth, outlandish figure, which descended from the roof, squatted upon his breast, grinned at him maliciously, and seemed as if pinching and pummelling his sides. This illusion continued for some time, and with a timorous subject might have been attended with bad consequences ; but he referred it at once to some disordered state of the stomach under which he imagined he must have labored at the time, although he had no direct consciousness of any such derangement of this organ. The same gentleman has related to me the case of one of his friends which attracted much notice at the time it happened, from the melancholy circumstance that attended it. It is an equally marked instance of hallucination arising without the individual being conscious of any physical cause by which it might be occasioned. It is as follows :—

Mr H. was one day walking along the street, apparently in perfect health, when he saw, or supposed he saw his acquaintance, Mr C., walking before him. He called aloud to the latter, who, however, did not seem to hear him, but continued moving on. Mr H. then quickened his pace for the purpose of overtaking him ; the other increased his also, as if to keep ahead of his pursuer, and proceeded at such a rate that Mr H. found it impossible to make up to him. This continued for some time, till, on Mr C. coming to a gate he opened it, passed in, and slammed it violently in Mr H.'s face. Confounded at such treatment, the latter instantly opened the gate, looked down the long lane into which it led, and, to his astonishment, no one was visible. Determined to unravel the mystery, he went to Mr C.'s house ; and what was his surprise when he learned that he was confined to his bed, and had been so for several days. A week or two afterwards, these gentlemen chanced to meet in the house of a common friend, when Mr H. mentioned the circumstance, and told Mr C. jocularly that he had seen his *wraith*, and that, as a natural consequence, he would soon be a dead man. The person addressed laughed heartily, as did the rest of the company, but the result turned out to be no laughing matter ; for, in a very few days, Mr C. was attacked with putrid sore throat, and died ; and within a very short period of his death Mr H. was also in the grave.

Some of the most vivid instances of spectral illusion are those induced by opium. Several of the 'English Opium-Eater's' visions were doubtless of this nature. Dr Abercrombie relates a striking instance of the kind which occurred to the late Dr Gregory. 'He had gone to the north country by sea to visit a lady, a near relation, in whom he felt deeply interested, and who was in an advanced state of consumption. In returning from the visit, he had taken a moderate dose of laudanum, with the view of preventing sea-sickness, and was lying on a couch in the cabin, when the figure of the lady appeared before him in so distinct a manner that her actual presence could not have been more vivid. He was quite awake, and fully sensible that it was a phantasm produced by the opiate, along with his intense mental feeling ; but he was unable by any effort to banish the vision.'* Indeed, any thing on which the mind dwells excessively, may by exciting the perceptive organs, give rise to spectral illusions. It is to this circumstance that the bereaved husband sees the image of a departed wife, to whom he was fondly attached—that the murderer is haunted by the apparition of his victim—and that the living with whom we are familiar, seem to be presented before our eyes, although at a distance from us. Dr Conolly relates the case of a gentleman, who, when in danger of being wrecked near the Eddystone lighthouse, saw the images of his whole family.

These illusive appearance sometimes occur during convalescence from diseases. In the summer of 1832, a gentleman in Glasgow, of dissipated habits, was seized with cholera, from which he recovered. His recovery was unattended with any thing particular, except the presence of a phantasmata—consisting of human figures about three feet high, neatly dressed in pea-green jackets, and knee-breeches of the same color. Being a person of a superior mind, and knowing the cause of the illusions, they gave him no alarm, although he was very often haunted by them. As he advanced in strength the phantoms appeared less frequently, and diminished in size, till at last they were not taller than his finger. One night, while seated alone, a multitude of these Lilliputian gentlemen made their appearance on his table, and favored him with a dance ; but being at the time otherwise engaged, and in no mood to enjoy such an amusement, he lost temper at the unwelcome intrusion of his pigmy visiters, and striking his fist violently upon the table, he exclaimed in a violent passion, 'Get about your business you little impertinent rascals ! What the devil are you doing here?' when the whole assembly instantly vanished, and he was never troubled with them more.

It generally happens that the figures are no less visible when the eyes are closed than when they are open. An individual in the west of Scotland, whose case is related in the Phrenological Journal,† whenever he shut his eyes or was in darkness, saw a procession move before his mind as distinctly as it had previously done before his eyes. Some years ago, a farmer from the neighbourhood of Hamilton, informed me, with feelings of great horror, that he had frequently the vision of a hearse drawn by four black horses, which were driven by a black driver. Not knowing the source of this illusion he was rendered extremely miserable by it ; and, to aggravate his unhappiness, was regarded by the ignorant country people, to whom he told his story, as

* Inquiries concerning the Intellectual Powers, p. 357.
† Vol. ii. p. 111.

having been guilty of some grievous crime. This vision was apparent to him chiefly by night, and the effect was the same whether his eyes were open or shut. Indeed, so little are these illusions dependant on sight, that the blind are frequently subject to them. A respected elderly gentleman, a patient of my own, who was afflicted with loss of sight, accompanied by violent headaches, and severe dispeptic symptoms, used to have the image of a black cat presented before him, as distinctly as he could have seen it before he became blind. He was troubled with various other spectral appearances, besides being subject to illusions of sound equally remarkable; for he had often the consciousness of hearing music so strongly impressed upon him, that it was with difficulty his friends could convince him it was purely ideal.

Considering the age in which Bayle lived, his notions of the true nature of spectral illusions were wonderfully acute and philosophical. Indeed, he has so well described the theory of apparitions, that the modern phrenological doctrine on this point seems little more than an expanded version of his own. 'A man,' says he, 'would not only be very rash, but also very extravagant, who should pretend to prove that there never was any person that imagined he saw a spectre; and I do not think that the most obstinate and extravagant unbelievers have maintained this. All they say, comes to this: that the persons who have thought themselves eye-witnesses of the apparition of spirits had a disturbed imagination. They confess that there are *certain places in our brain* that, being affected in a certain manner, *excite the image of an object which has no real existence out of ourselves*, and make the man, whose brain is thus modified, believe he sees, at two paces distant, a frightful spectre, a hobgoblin, a threatening phantom. The like happens in the heads of the most incredulous, either in their sleep, or in the paroxysms of a violent fever. Will they maintain after this, that it is impossible for a man awake, and not in a delirium, to receive, *in certain places of his brain, an impression* almost like that which, by the law of nature, is connected with the appearance of a phantom.' In one of Shenstone's Essays, entitled 'An Opinion of Ghosts,' the same theory is clearly enunciated.

It is worthy of remark, that the phenomena of apparitions are inconsistent with the prevalent theory that the brain is a single organ, with every part of which each faculty is connected. Were this theory sound, the same cause that vivifies the perceptive faculties must also vivify, or excite to increased action, the propensities, sentiments, and reflecting powers. This, however, is by no means the case.

The case of Nicolai, the Prussian bookseller, which occurred in the beginning of 1791, is one of the most remarkable instances of spectral illusion on record. 'I saw,' says he, 'in a state of mind completely sound, and—after the first terror was over—with perfect calmness, for nearly two months, almost constantly and involuntarily, a vast number of human and other forms, and even heard their voices, though all this was merely the consequence of a diseased state of the nerves, and an irregular circulation of the blood.' 'When I shut my eyes, these phantoms would sometimes vanish entirely, though there were instances when I beheld them with my eyes closed; yet when they disappeared on such occasions, they generally returned when I opened my eyes. I conversed sometimes with my physician and my wife of the phantasms which at the moment surrounded me; they appeared more frequently walking than at rest; nor were they constantly present. They frequently did not come for some time, but always reappeared for a longer or shorter period either singly or in company, the latter, however, being most frequently the case. I generally saw human forms of both sexes; but they usually seemed not to take the smallest notice of each other, moving as in a market-place, where all are eager to press through the crowd; at times, however, they seemed to be transacting business with each other. I also saw, several times, people on horseback, dogs, and birds. All these phantasms appeared to me in their natural size, and as distinct as if alive, exhibiting different shades of carnation in the uncovered parts, as well as in different colours and fashions in their dresses, though the colours seemed somewhat paler than in real nature; none of the figures appeared particularly comical, terrible, or disgusting, most of them being of an indifferent shape, and some presenting a pleasing aspect.'

Perhaps the most remarkable visionary, of whom we have any detailed account, was Blake the painter. This extraordinary man not only believed in his visions, but could often call up at pleasure whatever phantasms he wished to see; and so far from their being objects of annoyance, he rather solicited than wished to avoid their presence. He was in the habit of conversing with angels, demons, and heroes, and taking their likenesses; for they proved most obedient sitters, and never showed any aversion to allow him to transfer them to paper. 'His mind;' says Mr Cunningham, 'could convert the most ordinary occurrences into something mystical and supernatural.' ''Did you ever see a fairy's funeral, madam?' he once said to a lady who happened to sit by him in company, 'never, sir!' was the answer. 'I have,' said Blake, 'but not before last night. I was walking alone in my garden, there was great stillness among the branches and flowers, and more than common sweetness in the air; I heard a low and pleasant sound, and knew not whence it came. At last I saw the broad leaf of a flower move, and underneath I saw a procession of creatures of the size and color of the green and grey grasshoppers, bearing a body laid out on a rose leaf, which they buried with songs, and then disappeared. It was a fairy funeral.'' On being asked to draw the likeness of Sir William Wallace, that hero immediately stood before him, and he commenced taking his portrait. 'Having drawn for some time with the same care of hand and steadiness of eye, as if a living sitter had been before him, Blake stoped suddenly and said, 'I cannot finish him—Edward the first has stepped in between him and me.' 'That's lucky,' said his friend, 'for I want the portrait of Edward too.' Blake took another sheet of paper and sketched the features of Plantagenet; upon which his majesty politely vanished, and the artist finished the head of Wallace.'* The greater part of his life was passed in beholding visions and in drawing them. On one occasion he saw the ghost of a flea and took a sketch of it. No conception was too strange or incongruous for his wild imagination, which totally overmastered his judgment, and made him mistake the chimeras of an excited brain for realities.

What is called the *Second sight* originated, in most cases, from spectral illusions; and the seers of whom we so often read, were merely individuals visited by these phantoms. The Highland mountains, and the wild lawless habits of those who inhabited them, were peculiarly adapted to foster the growth of such impressions in imaginative minds; and, accordingly, nothing was more common than to meet with persons who not only fancied they saw visions, but, on the strength of this belief, laid claim to the gift of prophesy. The more completely the mind is abstracted from the bustle of life; the more solitary the district in which the individual resides; and the more romantic and awe-inspring the scenes that pass before his eyes, the greater is his tendency to see visions, and to place faith in what he sees. A man, for instance, with the peculiar temperament which predisposes to see, and believe in, spectral illusions, is informed that his chieftain and clan have set out on a dangerous expedition. Full of the subject, he forces their images before him—sees them engaged

* Cunningham's Lives of the British Painters, Sculptors, and Architects, vol. ii., Life of Blake.

in fight—beholds his chieftian cut down by the claymore of an enemy—the clansmen routed and dispersed, their houses destroyed, their cattle carried off. This vision he relates to certain individuals. If, as is not unlikely, it is borne out by the event, his prophecy is spread far and wide, and looked upon as an instance of the second sight; while, should nothing happen, the story is no more thought of by those to whom it was communicated. In some instances, it is probable that the accidental fulfilment of an ordinary dream was regarded as second sight.

The belief in fairies, no doubt, had also its origin in spectral illusions. In the days of ignorance and superstition nothing was more easy than for an excited brain to conjure up those tiny forms, and see them perform their gambols upon the greensward beneath the light of the moon.

The dimensions of the figures which are exhibited in spectral illusions vary exceedingly. Sometimes they appear as miniatures, sometimes of the size of life, at other times of colossal proportions. The same differences apply to their colour. In one case they are pale, misty, transparent; in another black, red, blue, or green. Sometimes we have them fantastically clothed in the costume of a former age, sometimes in that of our own. Now they are represented grinning, now weeping, now in smiles. 'White or grey Ghosts,' says Mr Simpson 'result from excited *Form*, with quiescent *Colouring*, the transparent cobweb effect being colourless. Pale spectres, and shadowy yet coloured forms, are the effect of partially excited *Colouring*. Tall ghosts and dwarf goblins, are the illusions of over-excited *Size*.' The jabbering of apparitions arises from an excited state of that part of the brain which gives us cognizance of sounds. This explanation seems highly probable, or rather quite satisfactory. There are points, however, which it is likely no one will ever be able to explain. Why, for instance should the disordered brain conjure up *persons* and *faces* rather than *trees* and *houses?* why should a ghost be dressed in *red* rather than *blue*, and why should it *smile* rather than *grin?* These are minutiæ beyond the reach of investigation at least in the present state of our knowledge.

Mr Simpson, in the second volume of the Phrenological Journal, has published a case of spectral illusion, which, for singularity and interest, equals any thing of the same kind which has hitherto been recorded. The subject of it was a young lady under twenty years of age, of good family, well educated, free from any superstitious fears, in perfect bodily health and of sound mind. She was early subject to occasional attacks of such illusions, and the first she remembered was that of a carpet which descended in the air before her, then vanished away. After an interval of some years, she began to see human figures in her room as she lay wide awake in bed. These figures were *whitish* or rather *grey*, and *transparent* like *cobweb*, and generally above the size of life. At this time she had acute headaches, very singularly confined to one small spot of the head. On being asked to indicate the spot, she touched, with her fore-finger and thumb, each side of the root of the nose, the commencement of the eyebrows, and the spot immediately over the top of the nose, the ascertained seats of *Form*, *Size*, and *Lower Individuality*. On being asked if the pain was confined to these spots, she answered that some time afterwards it extended to the right and left, along the eyebrows, and a little above them, and completely round the eyes, which felt as if they would burst from their sockets. On this taking place the visions varied. The organs of *Weight*, *Colouring*, *Order*, *Number*, and *Locality*, were affected, and the phantasmata assumed a change corresponding to the irritated condition of these parts. 'The whitish or cobweb spectres assumed the natural *colour* of the objects, but they continued often to present themselves, though not always, above the *size* of life.' '*Colouring* being over-excited, began to occassion its specifie and fantastical illusions. Bright spots, like stars on a back ground, filled the room in the dark, and even in day-light; and sudden, and sometimes gradual, illumination of the room during the night took place, so that the furnitnre in it became visible. Innumerable balls of fire seemed one day to pour like a torrent out of one of the rooms of the house down the staircase. On one occasion, the pain between the eyes, and along the lower ridge of the brow, struck her suddenly with great violence—when, *instantly*, the room filled with stars and bright spots. On attempting, on that occasion, to go to bed, she said she was conscious of an *inability to balance herself, as if she had been tipsy*, and she fell, having made repeated efforts to seize the bed-post; which, in the most unaccountable manner eluded her grasp *by shifting its place*, and also by presenting her with *a number of bed-posts instead of one*. If the organ of *Weight* situated between *Size* and *Colouring*, be the organ of the instinct to preserve, and power of preserving equilibrium, it must be the necessary consequence of the derangement of that organ to overset the balance of the person. Over-excited *Number* we should expect to produce multiplication of objects, and the first experience she had of this illusion, was the multiplication of the bed-posts, and subsequently of any inanimate object she looked at.'

'For nearly two years, Miss S. L. was free from her frontal headaches, and—mark the coincidence—untroubled by visions or any other illusive perceptions. Some months ago, however, all her distressing symptoms returned in great aggravation, when she was conscious of a want of health. The pain was more acute than before along the frontal bone, and round and in the eyeballs; and all the organs there situated recommenced their game of illusion. Single figures of absent and deceased friends were terribly real to her, both in the day and in the night, sometimes *cobweb*, but generally coloured. She sometimes saw friends on the street, who proved phantoms when she approached to speak to them; and instances occurred, where, from not having thus satisfied herself of the illusion, she affirmed to such friends that she had seen them in certain places, at certain times, when they proved to her the clearest *alibi*. The *confusion* of her spectral forms now distressed her.—(*Order* affected.) The oppression and perplexity were intolerable, when figures presented themselves before her in inextricable disorder, and still more when they changed—as with Nicolai—from whole figures to parts of figures—faces and half faces, and limbs—sometimes of inordinate size and dreadful deformity. One instance of illusive *Disorder*, which she mentioned, is curious; and has the farther effect of exhibiting (what cannot be put in terms except those of) the derangement of the just perception of gravitation or equilibrium. (*Weight.*) One night as she sat in her bed-room, and was about to go to bed, a *stream* of spectres, persons' faces, limbs, in the most shocking confusion, seemed to her to pour into her room from the window, in the manner of a cascade! Although the cascade continued, apparently, in rapid descending motion; there was no accumulation of figures in the room, the supply unaccountably vanishing, after having formed the cascade. *Colossal* figures are her frequent visiters. (*Size.*)'

In the fifth volume of the Phrenolagical Journal, page 319, a case is mentioned where the patient was tortured with horrid faces glaring at her, and approaching close to her in every possible aggravation of horror. 'She was making a tedious recovery in child-bed when these symptoms troubled her. Besides the forms, which were of natural colour, though often bloody, she was perplexed by their variation in size, from colossal to minute. She saw also entire human figures, but they were always as minute as pins, or even pin-heads, and were in great confusion and numbers.' 'She described the pain which *accompanied* her illusions, viz. acute pain in the upper part or root of the nose, the seat of the organ of *Form*, and all along the eyebrows, which takes in *Individuality*, *Form*, *Size*, *Weight*, *Order* and *Number*.' In the same volume, page 430, Mr Levison relates, that on asking an individual who saw apparitions, whether or not he felt pain at any part of his head, he answered, 'that every time before he experienced this peculiar power of seeing figures, he invariably felt pain in and between his eyes, and, in short, all over the eyebrows.' It does not appear, however, that pain is universally felt in such cases in the lower part of the forehead. Dr Andrew Combe informs me that, so far as he has observed, the pain, when it does exist, is more frequently in the exciting organ, generally *Wonder*.

Spectral illusions constitute the great pathognomonic sign of delirium tremens. In this disease they are usually of a horrible, a disgusting, or a frightful nature; the person being irresistibly impressed with the notion that reptiles, insects, and all manner of vermin are crawling upon him, which he is constantly endeavoring to pick off—that he is haunted by hideous apparitions —that people are in the room preparing to murder and rob him, and so forth. In the following case, with which I have been favored by Dr Combe, the illusive appearances were of a more pleasing kind than generally happen. 'In a case,' says he, 'of delirium tremens in an inn-keeper, about whom I was consulted, the spectral illusions continued several days, and had a distinct reference to a large and active cerebullum, (the organ of *Amativeness*) conjoined with *Wonder*. The man refused to allow me to look at a blister which had been placed between his shoulders, 'because he could not take off his coat *before the ladies who were in the room!*' When I assured him that there was nobody in the room, he smiled at the joke, as he conceived it to be, and, in answer to my questions, described them as several in number, well dressed, and good-looking. At my request he rose up to shake hands with them, and was astonished at finding them elude his grasp, and his hand strike the wall. This, however, convinced him that it was an illusion, and he forthwith took off his coat, but was unwilling to converse longer on the subject. In a few days the ladies vanished from his sight.'

Spectral illusions are more frequently induced by fever than by any other cause. Indeed, the premonitory stages of most fevers are accompanied by illusive appearances of one kind or another, such as luminous bodies, especially when the eyes are shut, hideous faces, streaks of fire, &c.; and in the advanced stages, they are not uncommon. A medical friend has informed me, that when ill of fever in Portugal, he was terribly harrassed by the vision of a soldier, whose picture was hanging in the room. Removing the picture failed to dissipate the illusion, which did not disappear till he was conveyed to another apartment. Dr Bostock, while under a febrile attack, was visited by spectral illusions of an unusual kind. The following are the particulars of his case, as described by himself:—

'I was laboring,' says he, 'under a fever, attended with symptoms of general debility, especially of the nervous system, and with a severe pain of the head, which was confined to a small spot situated above the right temple. After having passed a sleepless night, and being reduced to a state of considerable exhaustion, I first perceived figures presenting themselves before me, which I immediately recognised as similar to those described by Nicolai, and upon which, as I was free from delirium, and as they were visible about three days and nights with little intermission, I was able to make my observations. There were two circumstance which appeared to me very remarkable; first, that the spectral appearances always followed the motion of the eyes; and, secondly, that the objects which were the best defined and remained the longest visible, were such as I had no recollection of ever having previously seen. For about twenty-four hours I had constantly before me a human figure, the features and dress of which were as distinctly visible as that of any real existence, and of which, after an interval of many years, I still retain the most lively impression; yet, neither at the time nor since have I been able to discover any person whom I had previously seen who resembled it.

'During one part of this disease, after the disappearance of this stationary phantom, I had a very singular and amusing imagery presented to me. It appeared as if a number of objects, principally human faces or figures on a small scale, were placed before me, and gradually removed like a succession of medallions. They were all of the same size, and appeared to be all situated at the same distance from the face. After one had been seen for a few minutes, it became fainter, and then another, which was more vivid, seemed to be laid upon it or substituted in its place, which, in its turn, was superseded by a new appearance. During all this succession of scenery, I do not recollect that, in a single instance, I saw any object with which I had been previously acquainted, nor, as far as I am aware, were the representations of any of those objects, with which my mind was the most occupied at other times, presented to me; they appeared to be invariably new creations, or, at least, new combinations of which I could not trace the original materials.'*

The following very curious instance, is not less interesting: the subject of it was a member of the English bar.

'In December, 1823, A. was confined to his bed by inflammation of the chest, and was supposed by his medical attendant to be in considerable danger. One night, while unable to sleep from pain and fever, he saw sitting on a chair, on the left side of his bed, a female figure which he immediately recognised to be that of a young lady who died about two years before. His first feeling was surprise, and perhaps a little alarm; his second, that he was suffering from delirium. With this impression, he put his head under the bed-clothes, and, after trying in vain to sleep, as a test of the soundness of his mind, he went through a long and complicated process of metaphysical reasoning. He then peeped out and saw the figure in the same situation and position. He had a fire, but would not allow a candle or nurse in the room. A stick was kept by his side to knock for the nurse when he required her attendance. Being too weak to move his body, he endeavored to touch the figure with the stick, but, on a real object being put on the chair, the imaginary one disappeared, and was not visible again that night.

The next day he thought of little but the vision, and expected its return without alarm, and with some pleasure. He was not disappointed. It took the same place as before, and he employed himself in observations. When he shut his eyes or turned his head, he ceased to see the figure; by interposing his hand he could hide part of it; and it was shown, like any mere material substance, by the rays of the fire which fell upon and were reflected from it. As the fire declined it became less perceptible, and as it went out, invisible. A similar appearance took place on several other nights; but it became less perceptible, and its visits less frequent, as the patient recovered from his fever.

'He says the impressions on his mind were always pleasing, as the spectre looked at him with calmness and regard. He never supposed it real; but was unable to account for it on any philosophical principles within his knowledge.

In the autumn of 1825. A.'s health was perfectly

* Bostock's Physiology, vol. iii. p. 204.

restored, and he had been free from any waking vision for nearly eighteen months. Some circumstances occurred which produced in him great mental excitement. One morning he dreamed of the figure, which stood by his side in an angry posture, and asked for a locket which he usually wore. He awoke and saw it at the toilet, with the locket in its hand. He rushed out of bed and it instantly disappeared. During the next six weeks its visits were incessant, and the sensations which they produced were invariably horrible. Some years before, he had attended the dissection of a woman in a state of rapid decomposition. Though much disgusted at the time, *the subject* had been long forgotten; but was recalled by the union of its putrescent body with the spectre's features. The visits were not confined to the night, but frequently occurred while several persons were in the same room. They were repeated at intervals during the winter; but he was able to get rid of them by moving or sitting *in an erect position*. Though well, his pulse was hard, and generally from 90 to 100.'*

In March, 1829, during an attack of fever, accompanied with violent action in the brain, I experienced illusions of a very peculiar kind. They did not appear except when the eyes were shut or the room perfectly dark; and this was one of the most distressing things connected with my illness; for it obliged me either to keep my eyes open or to admit more light into the chamber than they could well tolerate. I had the consciousness of shining and hideous faces grinning at me in the midst of profound darkness, from which they glared forth in horrid and diabolical relief. They were never stationary, but kept moving in the gloomy background: sometimes they approached within an inch or two of my face: at other times, they receded several feet or yards from it. They would frequently break into fragments, which after floating about would unite —portions of one face coalescing with those of another, and thus forming still more uncouth and abominable images. The only way I could get rid of those phantoms was by admitting more light into the chamber and opening my eyes, when they instantly vanished; but only to reappear when the room was darkened or the eyes closed. One night, when the fever was at its height, I had a splendid vision of a theatre, in the arena of which Ducrow, the celebrated equestrian, was performing. On this occasion, I had no consciousness of a dark back ground like to that on which the monstrous images floated; but every thing was gay, bright, and beautiful. I was broad awake, my eyes were closed, and yet I saw with perfect distinctness the whole scene going on in the theatre, Ducrow performing his wonders of horsemanship—and the assembled multitude, among whom I recognized several intimate friends; in short, the whole process of the entertainment as clearly as if I were present at it. When I opened my eyes the whole scene vanished like the enchanted palace of the necromancer; when I closed them, it as instantly returned. But though I could thus dissipate the spectacle, I found it impossible to get rid of the accompanying music. This was the grand march in the Opera of Aladdin, and was performed by the orchestra with more superb and imposing effect, and with greater loudness, than I ever heard it before: it was executed, indeed, with tremendous energy. This air I tried every effort to dissipate, by forcibly endeavouring to call other tunes to mind, but it was in vain. However completely the vision might be dispelled, the music remained in spite of every effort to banish it. During the whole of this singular state, I was perfectly aware of the illusiveness of my feelings, and, though labouring under violent headache, could not help speculating upon them and endeavoring to trace them to their proper cause. This theatrical vision continued for about five hours; the previous delusions for a couple of days. The whole evidently proceeded from such an excited state of some parts of the brain, as I have already alluded to. *Ideality*, *Wonder*, *Form*, *Colour*, and *Size*, were all in intensely active operation, while the state of the reflecting organs was unchanged. Had the latter participated in the general excitement, to such an extent as to be unable to rectify the false impressions of the other organs, the case would have been one of pure delirium.

* Phrenological Journal, vol. v. p. 210.

Spectral illusions can only be cured by removing the causes which give rise to them. If they proceed from the state of the stomach, this must be rectified by means of purgatives and alterative medicines. Should plethora induce them, local or general blood-letting and other antiphlogistic means are requisite. If they accompany fever or delirium tremens, their removal will, of course, depend upon that of these diseases. Arising from sleeplessness, they will sometimes be cured by anodynes; and from nervous irritation, by the shower-bath and tonics. Where they seem to arise without any apparent cause, our attention should be directed to the state of the bowels, and blood-letting had recourse to

---

CHAPTER XVI.

REVERIE.

A state of mind somewhat analogous to that which prevails in dreaming, also takes place during reverie. There is the same want of balance in the faculties, which are almost equally ill regulated, and disposed to indulge in similar extravagancies. Reverie proceeds from an unusual quiescence of the brain, and inability of the mind to direct itself strongly to any one point: it is often the prelude of sleep. There is a defect in the *attention*, which, instead of being fixed on one subject, wanders over a thousand, and even on these is feebly and ineffectively directed. We sometimes see this while reading, or, rather, while attempting to read. We get over page after page, but the ideas take no hold whatever upon us; we are in truth ignorant of what we peruse, and the mind is either an absolute blank, or vaguely addressed to something else. This feeling every person must have occasionally noticed in taking out his watch, looking at it, and replacing it without knowing what the hour was, In like manner he may hear what is said to him without attaching any meaning to the words, which strike his ear, yet communicate no definite idea to the sensorium. Persons in this mood may, from some ludicrous ideas flashing across them, burst into a loud fit of laughter during sermon or at a funeral, and thus get the reputation of being either grossly irreverent or deranged. That kind of reverie in which the mind is nearly divested of all ideas, and approximates closely to the state of sleep, I have sometimes experienced while gazing long and intently upon a river. The thoughts seem to glide away, one by one, upon the surface of the stream, till the mind is emptied of them altogether. In this state we see the glassy volume of the water moving past us, and hear its murmur, but lose all power of fixing our attention definitively upon any subject: and either fall asleep, or are aroused by some spontaneous reaction of the mind, or by some appeal to the senses sufficiently strong to startle us from our reverie. Grave, monotonous, slowly repeated sounds—as of a mill, a waterfall, an Eolian harp, or the voice of a dull orator, have the effect of lulling the brain into repose, and giving rise to a pleasing melancholy, and to calmness and inanity of mind. Uniform gentle motions have a tendency to produce a similar state of reverie, which is also very apt to ensue in the midst of perfect silence; hence, in walking alone in the country, where there is no sound to distract our meditations, we frequently get into this state. It is also apt to take place when we are seated without books, companions, or amusement of any kind, by the hearth on a winter evening, especially when the fire is beginning to burn out, when the candles are becoming faint for want of topping, and a dim religious light, like that filling a hermit's cell from his solitary lamp, is diffused over the apartment. This is the situation most favourable for reveries, waking dreams, and all kinds of brown study, abstraction, ennui, and hypochondria.

Reverie has been known to arise from the mind sustaining temporary weakness, in consequence of long and excessive application to one subject. It is also, I believe, frequently induced by forcing young people to learn what they dislike. In this case, the mind, finding it impossible to direct itself to the hated task, goes wandering off in another direction, and thus acquires a habit of inattention, which, in extreme cases, may terminate in imbecility. Sometimes reveries arise from peculiarity of temperament, either natural or induced by mental or bodily weakness. The best regulated minds and strongest bodies, may, however, and, in fact, often have, occasional attacks: but when the feeling grows into a habit, and is too much indulged in, it is apt to injure the usefulness of the individual, and impair the whole fabric of his understanding. 'It is,' says Dr Good, 'upon the faculty of attention that every other faculty is dependent for its vigour and expansion: without it, the perception exercises itself in vain; the memory can lay up no store of ideas; the judgment draw forth no comparisons; the imagination must become blighted and barren; and where there is no attention whatever, the case must necessarily verge upon fatuity.' I conceive that persons in whom the organ of *Concentrativencss* is very small, arc peculiarly apt to fall into reverie.

The following is a remarkable instance of reverie arising from excessive application:—The subject of it was Mr Spalding, a gentleman well known as an eminent literary character in Germany, and much respected by those who knew him. The case was drawn up by himself, and published in the *Psychological Magazine.*

'I was this morning engaged with a great number of people who followed each other quickly, and to each of whom I was obliged to give my attention. I was also under the necessity of writing much; but the subjects, which were various and of a trivial and uninteresting nature, had no connexion the one with the other; my attention, therefore, was constantly kept on the stretch, and was continually shifting from one subject to another. At last it became necessary that I should write a receipt for some money I had received on account of the poor. I seated myself and wrote the two first words, but in a moment found that I was incapable of proceeding, for I could not recollect the words which belonged to the ideas that were present in my mind. I strained my attention as much as possible, and tried to write one letter slowly after the other, always having an eye to the preceding one, in order to observe whether they had the usual relationship to each other; but I remarked, and said to myself at the time, that the characters I was writing were not those which I wished to write, and yet I could not discover where the fault lay. I therefore desisted, and partly by broken words and syllables, and partly by gesture, I made the person who waited for the receipt understand he should leave me. For about half an hour there reigned a kind of tumultuary disorder in my senses, in which I was incapable of remarking any thing very particular, except that one series of ideas forced themselves involuntarily on my mind. The trifling nature of these thoughts I was perfectly aware of, and was also conscious that I made several efforts to get rid of them, and supply their place with better ones, which lay at the bottom of my soul. I endeavoured as much as lay in my power, considering the great crowd of confused images which presented themselves to my mind, to recall my principles of religion, of conscience, and of future expectation, these I found equally correct, and fixed as before. There was no deception in my external senses, for I saw and knew every thing around me; but I could not free myself from the strange ideas which existed in my head. I endeavoured to speak in order to discover whether I was capable of saying any thing that was connected; but although I made the greatest efforts of attention, and proceeded, with the utmost caution, I perceived that I uniformly spoke other words than those I intended. My soul was at present as little master of the organs of speech, as it had been before of my hand in writing. Thank God, this state did not continue very long, for, in about half an hour, my head began to grow clearer, the strange and tiresome ideas became less vivid and turbulent, and I could command my own thoughts with less interruption.

'I now wished to ring for my servant, and desire him to inform my wife to come to me; but I found it still necessary to wait a little longer to exercise myself in the right pronunciation of the few words I had to say: and the first half hour's conversation I had with her was, on my part, preserved with a slow and anxious circumspection, until at last I gradually found myself as clear and serene as in the beginning of the day, all that now remained was a slight headache. I recollected the receipt I had begun to write, and in which I knew I had blundered; and upon examining it, I observed to my great astonishment, that instead of the words *fifty dollars, being one half year's rate*, which I ought to have written, the words were *fifty dollars through the salvation of Bra—*, with a break after it, for the word *Bra* was at the end of a line. I cannot recollect any perception, or business which I had to transact, that could, by means of an obscure influence, have produced this phenomenon.'

Reverie, when proceeding, as in this case, from excessive application, will seldom be difficult of cure; the removal of the exciting cause will of itself naturally constitute the remedy. When it arises from such a defect in education as that already mentioned, the cure will be more difficult, although even then it is not always impracticable. In such a case, the person should be strongly directed to those subjects in which he feels most interest, and never be made to study what he has not a positive liking for. Active employment and gay and pleasant society, may effect much in restoring the intellectual balance. In all cases, whatever, he should never be left long alone; as nothing has such a tendency to foster this state of mind as solitude.

CHAPTER XVII.

ABSTRACTION.

Abstraction, or absence of mind, has been confounded with reverie, but it is, in reality, a different intellectual operation; for as in the latter a difficulty is experienced in making the mind bear strongly on any one point, in the former its whole energies are concentrated towards a single focus, and every other circumstance is, for the time, utterly forgotten. Such was the case with Sir Isaac Newton when, in a fit of absence, he made a tobacco stopper of the lady's finger, and with Archimedes, who remained unconscious and unmoved during the noise and slaughter of captured Syracuse. Though, in general, abstraction is easily broken by outward impressions, there have been instances where it has been so powerful as to render the individuals labouring under it insensible to pain. Pinel in his *Nosographie Philosophique* speaks of a priest who in a fit of mental absence was unconscious of the pain of burning; and Cardan brought himself into such a state as to be insensible to all external impression

Some men are naturally very absent; others acquire this habit from particular pursuits, such as mathematics, and other studies demanding much calculation. Indeed, all studies which require deep thinking, are apt to induce mental absence, in consequence of the sensorial power being drained from the general circumference of the mind, and directed strongly to a certain point. This draining, while it invigorates the organ of the particular faculty towards which the sensorial energy is concentrated, leaves the others in an inanimate state, and incapacitates them from performing their proper functions; hence persons subject to abstraction are apt to commit a thousand ludicrous errors; they are perpetually blundering—committing a multitude of petty, yet harmless offences against established rules, and for ever getting into scrapes and absurd situations. Nothing is more common than for an absent man to take the hat of another person instead of his own, to give away a guinea for a shilling, to mistake his lodgings, forget invitations, and so forth. When the fit of abstraction is very strong, he neither hears what is said to him, nor sees what is passing around. 'While you fancy,' says Budgell, in the 77th No. of the Spectator, 'he is admiring a beautiful woman, it is an even wager that he is solving a proposition in Euclid; and while you imagine he is reading the Paris Gazette, it is far from being impossible that he is pulling down and rebuilding his country house.' In some cases the individual requires to be shaken before he can be brought to take notice of any occurrence; and it is often difficult to make him comprehend even the simplest proposition. Abstraction, therefore, bears an analogy to dreaming, inasmuch as, in each of these states, some faculties are active, while others are at rest. In dreaming, however, the organs of the quiescent faculties are in a much deeper slumber, and less easily roused into activity than in abstraction; hence in the great majority of cases, abstraction is broken with greater facility than sleep.

It appears from the observations of the Edinburgh phrenologists, that individuals who have a large development of the organ of *Concentrativeness* are peculiarly liable to fall into a state of abstraction. The effect of such a development is fixity of ideas—the power and tendency to think consecutively and steadily upon one subject. 'In conversing with some individuals,' says Mr Combe,* 'we find them fall naturally into a connected train of thinking; either dwelling on a subject which interests them, till they have placed it clearly before the mind, or passing naturally and gracefully to a connected topic. Such persons uniformly have this organ large. We meet with others, who in similar circumstances, never pursue one idea for two consecutive seconds, who shift from topic to topic, without regard to natural connexion, and leave no distinct impression on the mind of the listener; and this happens even with individuals in whom reflection is not deficient; but this organ (*Concentrativeness*) is, in such persons, uniformly small.' A good endowment of the power in question adds very much to the efficiency of the intellect, by enabling its possessor to apply his mind continuously to a particular investigation, unannoyed by the intrusion of foreign and irrelevant ideas. It seems to have been very strong in Sir Isaac Newton, whose liability to abstraction has already been alluded to. 'During the two years,' says Biot, 'which he spent in preparing and developing his immortal work, *Philosophæ Naturalis Principia Mathematica*, he lived only to calculate and to think. Oftentimes lost in the contemplation of these grand objects, he acted unconsciously; his thoughts appearing to preserve no connexion with the ordinary affairs of life. It is said, that frequently, on rising in the morning, he would sit down on his bedside, arrested by some new conception, and would remain for hours together engaged in tracing it out, without dressing himself.' 'To one who asked him, on some occasion, by what means he had arrived at his discoveries, he replied, 'By always thinking unto them.' And at another time, he thus expressed his method of proceeding, —'I keep the subject constantly before me, and wait till the first dawning opens slowly, by little and little, into a full and clear light.' Again, in a letter to Dr Bentley, he says, 'If I have done the public any service this way, it is due to nothing but industry and patient thought.' Biot mentions farther, that, 'in general, the intensity of thinking was with him so great that it entirely abstracted his attention from other matters, and confined him exclusively to one object. Thus, we see that he never was occupied at the same time with two different scientific investigations.'

* System of Phrenology, p. 135.

The instances of abstraction upon record are so numerous that a volume might easily be filled with them. Hogarth, the illustrious painter, affords a good specimen. Having got a new carriage, he went in it to the Mansion-House, for the purpose of paying a visit to the Lord Mayor. On leaving the house he went out by a different door from that by which he entered, and found that it rained hard. Notwithstanding this, he walked homewards, and reached his own dwelling drenched to the skin. His wife seeing him in this state, asked him how it happened, and what had become of his carriage since he had not returned home in it. The truth was, that he had actually forgotten he had a carriage, or had gone in one at all.

The following case, from the pleasant style in which it is told, will amuse the reader.

'It is a case of one of the most profound and clear-headed philosophical thinkers, and one of the most amiable of men, becoming so completely absorbed in his own reflections, as to loose the perception of external things, and almost that of his own identity and existence. There are few that have paid any attention to the finance of this country, but must have heard of Dr Robert Hamilton's 'essay on the National debt,' which fell on the houses of parliament like a bombshell, or, rather, which rose and illuminated their darkness like an orient sun. There are other writings of his in which one knows not which most to admire—the profound and accurate, science, the beautiful arrangement, or the clear expression. Yet, in public, the man was a shaddow; pulled off his hat to his own wife in the streets, and apologized for not having the pleasure of her acquaintance; went to his classes in the college on the dark mornings, with one of her white stockings on the one leg, and one of his own black ones on the other, often spent the whole time of the meeting in moving from the table the hats of the students, which they as constantly returned; sometimes invited them to call on him, and then fined them for coming to insult him. He would run against a cow in the road, turn round, beg her pardon, 'madam,' and hope she was not hurt. at other times he would run against posts, and chide them for not getting out of his way; and yet his conversation at the same time, if any body happened to be with him, was perfect logic and perfect music. Were it not that there may be a little poetic license in Aberdeen story-telling, a volume might be filled with anecdotes of this amiable and excellent man, all tending, to prove how wide the distinction is between first rate thought and that merely animal use of the organs of sense which prevents ungifted mortals from walking into wells. The fish-market at Aberdeen, if still where it used to be, is near the Dee, and has a stream passing through it that falls into that river. The fish women expose their wares in large baskets. The doctor one day marched into that place, where his attention was attracted by a curiously figured stone in a stack of chimneys. He advanced towards it, till he was interrupted by one of the benches, from which, however, he tumbled one of the baskets into the stream, which was bearing the fish to their native element. The visage of the lady was instantly in lightning, and her voice in thunder; but the object of her wrath was deaf to the loudest sounds, and blind to the most alarming colors. She stamped, gesticulated, scolded, brought a crowd that filled the place; but the philosopher turned not from his eager gaze and his inward meditations on the stone. While the woman's breath held good, she did not seem to heed, but when that began to fail, and the violence of the act moved not one muscle of the object, her rage felt no bounds: she seized him by the breast, and yelling, in an effort of despair, 'spagh ta ma, or I'll burst,' sank down among the remnant of her fish in a state of complete exhaustion; and before she had recovered, the doctor's reverie was over, and he had taken his departure.'*

Many curious anecdotes of a similar kind are related of the Rev Dr George Harvest, one of the ministers of Thames Ditton. So confused on some occasion, were the ideas of this singular man, that he has been known to write a letter to one person, address it to a second, and send it to a third. He was once on the eve of being married to the bishop's daughter, when having gone a gudgeon-fishing, he forgot the circumstance, and overstaid the canonical hour, which so offended the lady, that she indignantly broke off the match. If a beggar happened to take off his hat to him on the streets, in hopes of receiving alms, he would make him a bow, tell him he was his most humble servant, and walk on. He has been known on Sunday to forget the days on which he was to officiate, and would walk into church with his gun under his arm, to ascertain what the people wanted there. Once, when he was playing at backgammon, he poured out a glass of wine, and it being his turn to throw, having the box in one hand and the glass in the other, and being extremely dry, and unwilling to lose any time, he swallowed down both the dice, and discharged the wine upon the dice-board. 'Another time,' says the amusing narrative which has been published of his peculiarities, in one of his absent fits, he mistoook his friend's house, and went into another, the door of which happened to stand open; and no servant being in the way, he rambled all over the house, till, coming into a middle room, where there was an old lady ill in bed of the quincy, he stumbled over the night stool, threw a close-horse down, and might not have ended there, had not the affrighted patient made a noise at his intrusion, which brought up the servants, who, on finding Dr Harvest in the room, instead of the apothecary that was momentarily expected, quieted the lady's fears, who by this time was taken with such an immoderate fit of laughter at his confusion, that it broke the quincy in her throat, and she lived many years afterwards to thank Dr Harvest for his unlucky mistake. 'His notorious heedlessness was so apparent, that no one would lend him a horse, as he frequently lost his beast from under him, or, at least from out of his hands, it being his frequent practice to dismount and lead the horse, putting the bridle under his arm, which the horse sometimes shook off, or the intervention of a post occasioned it to fall; sometimes it was taken off by the boys, when the parson was seen drawing his bridle after him; and if any one asked him after the animal, he could not give the least account of it, or how he had lost it.' In short the blunders which he committed were endless, and would be considered incredible, were they not authenticated by incontestible evidence. Yet, notwithstanding all this, Harvest was a man of uncommon abilities, and an excellent scholar.

Bacon, the celebrated sculptor, exhibited on one occasion, a laughable instance of absence of mind. 'Bacon was remarkably neat in his dress, and, according to the costume of the old school, wore, in fine weather, a powdered wig, ruffles, silver buckles, with silk stockings, &c., and walked with his gold-headed cane. Thus attired, he one day called at St. Paul's, shortly after having erected the statue of the benevolent Howard, and before the boarding which enclosed the statue had been removed. One of his sons was employed, at this time, in finishing the statue. After remaining a short time, he complained of feeling somewhat cold, on which the son proposed, as no one could overlook them, that he should put on, as a kind of temporary spencer, an old torn, green shag waistcoat, with a red stuff back, which had been left there by one of the workmen. He said it was a 'good thought,' and accordingly buttoned the waistcoat over his handsome new coat. Shortly afterwards, he was missing, but returned in about an hour, stating that he had been to call on a gentleman in Doctor's Commons, and had sat chatting with his wife and daughters, whom he had never seen before; that he found them to be exceedingly pleasant women, though perhaps a little disposed to laugh and titter about he knew not what. 'Sir,' said the son, 'I am afraid I can explain their mysterious behavior; surely you have not kept on that waistcoat all the time?' 'But, as sure as I am a living man, I have,' said he, laughing heartily, 'and I can now account not only for the strange behavior of the ladies, but for all the jokes that have been cracked about me as I walked along the street—some crying let him alone, he does it for a wager, &c. &c.; all which, from being quite unconscious of my appearance, I thought was levelled at some other quiz that might be following near me; and I now recollect that, whenever I looked round for the object of their pleasantry, the people laughed, and the more so, as, by the merry force of sympathy, I laughed also, although I could not comprehend what it all meant.'

I shall conclude by mentioning an anecdote of Mr Warton, the accomplished Professor of Poetry in the University of Oxford. 'This good divine having dined with some jolly company at a gentleman's house in that city, passing through the streets to the church, it being summer-time, his ears were loudly saluted with the cry of 'Live mackerel!' This so much dwelt upon the Doctor's mind, that after a nap while the psalm was performing, as soon as the organ ceased playing, he got up in the pulpit, and with eyes half open, cried out 'All alive, alive oh!' thus inadvertently keeping up the reputation of a Latin proverb, which is translated in the following lines:—

> 'Great wits to madness nearly are allied,
> And thin partitions do their bounds divide.'

'The Professor of Poetry perhaps supposed himself yet with his companions at the convivial table.'

Mental absence is generally incurable. In stout subjects, depletion, purging, and low diet, will sometimes be of use. Where the affection seems to arise from torpor of the nervous system, blistering the head and internal stimuli afford the most probable means of relief. The person should associate as much as possible with noisy, bustling people, and shun solitude and all such studies as have a tendency to produce abstraction.

CHAPTER XVIII.

SLEEP OF PLANTS.

During night, plants seem to exist in a state analogous to sleep. At this period they get relaxed, while their leaves droop and become folded together. Such is peculiarly the case with the tamarind tree, and the leguminous plants with pinnated leaves; but with almost all plants it takes place in a greater or lesser degree, although in some the change is much more striking than in others. The trefoil, the Oxalis, and other herbs with ternate leaves, sleep with their leaflets fold

* 'New Monthly Magazine,' vol. xxxviii. p. 510.

ed together in the erect posture. The cause of the different states in which plants exist during the day and night has never been correctly ascertained—some attributing it to the influence of light, some to the vicissitudes of temperature, and others to atmospherical humidity. Probably the whole of these influences are concerned. It is very evident that the presence of certain stimuli during the day puts the leaves in a state of activity, and excites their development; while the want of such stimuli in the night time throws them into repose, relaxes them, and occasions them to be weighed down, as if the sustaining principle which kept them in energy was suspended in the torpor of sleep. The principal of these stimuli is unquestionably light; indeed, Linnæus, from the observation of stove plants, seems to have demonstrated that it is the withdrawing of light, and not of heat, which produces the relaxation, or *Sleep of Plants*, as it is commonly denominated. The effect of light upon the leaves of the *Acacia* is peculiarly striking. At sunrise they spread themselves out horizontally; as the heat increases they become elevated, and at noon shoot vertically upwards: but as soon as the sun declines they get languid and droop, and during night are quite pendant and relaxed. During day, the leaves of some plants are spread out, and displayed, and at the same time inclined towards the sun. Those of the *Helianthus annuus*, the *Helianthemum annuum*, and *Croton tinctorium* follow the course of the sun in their position; and most buds and flowers have a tendency to turn their heads in the direction of the great luminary of day. As an instance of this let us look at the sun flower, which confronts the source of light with its broad yellow expansion of aspect, and hangs its gorgeons head droopingly so soon as the object of its worship declines. The leaves of a great number of vegetables present changes in their position corresponding to the different hours of the day. 'Who does not know,' says Wildenow, 'that the species of *Lupinus*, especially *Lupinus luteus* turn, in the open air, their leaves and stalks towards the sun, and follow its course in so steady a manner, as to enable us to specify the hour of the day from their direction.' Such phenomena were not unknown to Pliny and Theophrastus.

The analogy between animal and vegetable life is still farther demonstrated by the well known fact, that while some creatures, such as the cat and owl, sleep during the day, and continue awake at night, certain plants do the same thing. Such is the case with the *Tragopogon luteum*, which becomes closed, or in other words, goes to sleep at nine in the morning, and opens at night. Every hour of the day, indeed, has some particular plant which then shuts itself up: hence the idea of the Flower Dial by means of which the hour of the day can be told with tolerable accuracy. Some plants, which shut themselves up in the day time, flower at night. The night-flowering *Cereus*, a species of Cactus, is a beautiful instance of the kind; and there are other plants which exhibit the same interesting phenomenon. Nothing, indeed, can be more beautiful than the nocturnal flowering of certain members of the vegetable world. Linnæus used to go out at night with a lantern into his garden to have an opportunity of witnessing this remarkable peculiarity in the plants by which it is exhibited.

The analogy between the two kingdoms is rendered yet more striking, when it is recollected that (with such exceptions as the above,) plants increase much more rapidly during night, which is their time of sleep, than in the day-time, which may be considered the period of their active or waking existence.

The state in which plants exists in the winter season resembles the hybernation of animals: there is the same torpor and apparent extinction of vitality. Heat and light have the power of both reviving plants and putting an end to hybernation. Between plants and animals, however, there is this difference: that while *most* plants become torpid in winter, only a *small number* of animals get into that state; but even in such dissimilitude we can trace an analogy; for as there are animals upon which winter has no torpifying influence, so are there likewise plants. The *Helloborus hymalis* or christmas rose, flowers at the end of December, and the *Galanthus nivilis*, or snow-drop, in the month of February.

CHAPTER XIX.

GENERAL MANAGEMENT OF SLEEP.

In the foregoing pages, I have detailed at length all the principal phenomena of sleep; and it now only remains to state such circumstances as affect the comfort and healthfulness of the individual while in that condition. The first I shall mention is the nature of the chamber in which we sleep; this should be always large and airy. In modern houses, these requisites are too much overlooked; and, while the public rooms are of great dimensions, those appropriated for sleeping are little better than closets. This error is exceedingly detrimental to health. The apartments wherein so great a portion of life is passed, should always be roomy, and, if possible, not placed upon the ground-floor, because such a situation is more apt to be damp and ill ventilated than higher up.

The next consideration applies to the bed itself, which ought to be large, and not placed close to the wall, but at some distance from it, both to avoid any dampness which may exist in the wall, and admit a freer circulation of air. The curtains should never be drawn closely together, even in the coldest weather; and when the season is not severe, it is a good plan to remove them altogether. The bed or mattress ought to be rather hard. Nothing is more injurious to health than soft beds; they effeminate the individual, render his flesh soft and flabby, and incapacitate him from undergoing any privation. The texture of which the couch is made, is not of much consequence, provided it is not too soft: hence, feather-beds, or mattresses of hair or straw are almost equally good, if suitable in this particular. I may mention, however, that the hair mattress, from being cooler, and less apt to imbibe moisture, is preferable during the summer season, to a bed of feathers. Those soft yielding feather-beds, in which the body sinks deeply, are highly improper, from the unnatural heat and perspiration which they are sure to induce. Air-beds have been lately recommended, but I can assert, from personal experience, that they are the worst that can possibly be employed. They become very soon heated to such an unpleasant degree as to render it impossible to repose upon them with any comfort. For bed-ridden persons, whose skin has become irritated by long lying, the hydrostatic bed, lately brought into use in some of the public hospitals, is the best.

The pillow as well as the bed, should be pretty hard. When very soft, the head soon sinks in it, and becomes unpleasantly heated. The objection made to air-beds applies with equal force to air-pillows, which I several times attempted to use, but was compelled to abandon, owing to the disagreeable heat that was generated in a few minutes.

With regard to the covering, there can be no doubt that it is more wholesome to lie between sheets than blankets. For the same reason, people should avoid sleeping in flannel nightshirts. Such a degree of warmth as is communicated by those means is only justifiable in infancy and childhood, or when there is actual disease or weakness of constitution. Parents often commit a great error in bringing up their young people under so effeminate a system.

A common custom prevails of warming the bed before going to sleep. This enervating practice should be abandoned except with delicate people, or when the cold is very intense. It is far better to let the bed be chafed by the natural heat of the body, which, even in severe weather, will be sufficient for the purpose, provided the clothing is abundant.

We ought never to sleep overloaded with clothes, but have merely what is sufficient to maintain a comfortable warmth.

When a person is in health, the atmosphere of his apartment should be cool; on this account, fires are exceedingly hurtful, and should never be had recourse to, except when the individual is delicate, or the weather intolerably severe. When they become requisite, smoke must be carefully guarded against, as fatal accidents have arisen from this cause.

The window-shutters ought never to be entirely closed, neither ought they to be kept altogether open. In the first case, we are apt to oversleep ourselves, owing to the prevailing darkness with which we are surrounded; and in the second, the light which fills the apartment, especially if it be in the summer season, may disturb our repose, and waken us at an earlier hour than there is any occasion for. Under both circumstances, the eyes are liable to suffer; the darkness in the one instance, disposes them to be painfully affected, on exposure to the brilliant light of day, besides directly debilitating them—for, in remaining too much in the gloom, whether we be asleep or awake, these organs are sure to be more or less weakened. In the other case, the fierce glare of the morning sun acting upon them, perhaps for several hours before we get up, does equal injury, making them tender and easily affected by the light. The extremes of too much and too little light must, therefore, be avoided, and such a moderate portion admitted into the chamber as not to hurt the eyes, or act as too strong a stimulus in breaking our slumbers.

During the summer heats, the covering requires to be diminished, so as to suit the atmospheric temperature; and a small portion of the window drawn down from the top, to promote a circulation of air; but this must be done cautiously, and the current prevented from coming directly upon the sleeper, as it might give rise to colds, and other bad consequences. The late Dr Gregory was in the habit of sleeping with the window drawn slightly down during the whole year: and there can be no doubt that a gentle current pervading our sleeping apartments, is in the highest degree essential to health.

Nothing is so injurious as damp beds. It becomes every person, whether at home or abroad, to look to this matter, and see that the bedding on which he lies is thoroughly dry, and free from even the slightest moisture. By neglecting such a precaution, rheumatism, colds, inflammations, and death itself may ensue. Indeed these calamities are very frequently traced to sleeping incautiously upon damp beds. For the same reason, the walls and floor should be dry, and wet clothes never hung up in the room.

We should avoid sleeping in a bed that has been occupied by the sick, till the bedding has been cleansed and thoroughly aired. When a person has died of any infectious disease, not only the clothes in which he lay, but the couch itself ought to be burned. Even the bed-stead should be carefully washed and fumigated.

Delicate persons who have been accustomed to sleep upon feather-beds, must be cautious not to exchange them rashly for any other.

On going to sleep, all sorts of restraints must be removed from the body; the collar of the night-shirt should be unbuttoned and the neckcloth taken off. With regard to the head, the more lightly it is coverd the better: on this account, we should wear a thin cotton or silk night-cap; and this is still better if made of net-work. Some persons wear worsted, or flannel caps, but these are never proper, except in old or rheumatic subjects. The grand rule of health is to keep the head cool, and the feet warm; hence, the night-cap cannot be too thin. In fact, the chief use of this piece of clothing is to preserve the hair, and preserve it from being disordered and matted together.

Sleeping in stockings is a bad and uncleanly habit. By accustoming ourselves to do without any covering upon the feet, we shall seldom experience cold in these parts, if we have clothing enough to keep the rest of the system comfortable; and should they still remain cold, this can easily be obviated by wrapping a warm flannel cloth around them, or by applying to them, for a few minutes, a heated iron, or a bottle of warm water.

The posture of the body must be attended to. The head should be tolerably elevated, especially in plethoric subjects; and the position, from the neck downwards, as nearly as possible horizontal. The half-sitting posture, with the shoulders considerably raised, is injurious, as the thoracric and abdominal viscrea are thereby compressed, aud respiration, digestion, and circulation, materially impeded. Lying upon the back is also improper, in consequence of its tendency to produce nightmare. Most people pass the greater part of the night upon the side, which is certainly the most comfortable position that can be assumed in sleep. According to Dr A. Hunter, women who love their husbands generally lie upon the right side. This interesting point I have no means of ascertaining, although, doubtless, the ladies are qualified to speak decidedly upon the subject. I have known individuals who could not sleep except upon the back; but these are rare cases.

I have mentioned the necessity of a free circulation of air. On this account, it is more wholesome to sleep single, than double, for there is then less destruction of oxygen; and the atmosphere is much purer and cooler. For the same reason, the practice, so common in public schools, of having several beds in one room, and two or three individuals in each bed, must be deleterious. When more than one sleep in a single bed, they should take care to place themselves in such a position as not to breath in each other's faces. Some persons have a dangerous custom of covering their heads with the bedclothes. The absurdity of this practice needs no comment.

Before going to bed, the body should be brought into that state which gives us the surest chance of dropping speedily asleep. If too hot, its temperature ought to be reduced by cooling drinks, exposure to the open air, sponging, or even the cold bath; if too cold, it must be brought into a comfortable state by warmth; for both cold and heat act as stimuli, and their removal is necessary before slumber can ensue. A full stomach, also, though it sometimes promotes, generally prevents sleep; consequently, supper ought to be dispensed with, except by those who, having been long used to this meal, cannot sleep without it. As a general rule, the person who eats nothing for two or three hours before going to rest, will sleep better than he who does. His sleep will also be more refreshing, and his sensations upon waking much more gratifying. The Chinese recommended brushing the teeth previous to lying down: this is a good custom.

Sleeping after dinner is pernicious. On awaking from such indulgence, there is generally some degree of febrile excitement, in consequence of the latter stages of digestion being hurried on: it is only useful in old people, and in some cases of disease.

The weak, and those recovering from protracted illnesses, must be indulged with more sleep than such as are vigorous. Sleep, in them, supplies, in some measure, the place of nourishment, and thus becomes a most powerful auxiliary for restoring them to health. Much repose is likewise necessary to enable the system to recover from the effects of dissipation.

Too little and too much sleep are equally injurious. Excessive wakefulness, according to Hippocrates, prevents the aliment from being digested, and generates crude humours. Too much sleep produces lassitude and corpulency, and utterly debases and stupifies the mind. Corpulent people being apt to indulge in excessive sleep, they should break this habit at once, as, in their case, it is peculiarly unwholesome. They ought to sleep little, and that little upon hard beds.

The practice of sleeping in the open air, cannot be too strongly reprobated. It is at all times dangerous, especially when carried into effect under a burning sun, or amid the damps of night. In tropical climates, where this custom is indulged in during the day, it is not unusual for the person to be struck with a *coup-de-soleil*, or some violent fever; and in our own country, nothing is more common than inflammations, rheumatisms, and dangerous colds, originating from sleeping upon the ground, either during the heat of the day, or when the evening has set in with its attendant dews and vapours.

As respects the repose of children it may be remarked that the custom of rocking them asleep in the cradle, is not to be recommended, sanctioned though it be by the voice of ages. This method of procuring slumber, not only heats the infant unnecessarily, but, in some cases, disorders the digestive organs, and, in most, produces a sort of artificial sleep, far less conducive to health, than that brought on by more natural means. According to some writers, it has also a tendency to induce water in the head, a circumstance which I think possible, although I never knew a case of that disease which could be traced to such a source. the cradle, then, should be abandoned, so far as the rocking is concerned, and the child simply lulled to repose in the nurse's arms, and then deposited quietly in bed. Sleep will often be induced by gently scratching or rubbing the top of the child's head. This fact is well known to some nurses, by whom the practice is had recourse to for the purpose of provoking slumber in restless children. For the first month of their existence, children sleep almost continually, and they should be permitted to do so, for at this early age they cannot slumber too much: calm and long-continued sleep is a favourable symptom, and ought to be cherished rather than prevented, during the whole period of infancy. When, however, a child attains the age of three or four months, we should endeavour to manage so that its periods of wakefulness may occur in the daytime, instead of at night. By proper care, a child may be made to sleep at almost any hour; and, as this is always an object of importance, it should be sedulously attended to in the rearing of children. Until about the third year, they require a little sleep in the middle of the day, and pass half their time in sleep. Every succeeding year, till they attain the age of seven, the period allotted to repose should be shortened one hour, so that a child of that age may pass nine hours or thereabouts, out of the twenty-four, in a state of sleep. Children should never be awakened suddenly, or with a noise, in consequence of the terror and starting which such a method of arousing them produces: neither should they be brought all at once from a dark room into a strong glare of light, lest their eyes be weakened, and permanent injury inflicted upon these organs.

The position in which children sleep requires to be carefully attended to. Sir Charles Bell mentions that the *eneuresis infantum*, with which they are so often affected, frequently arises from lying upon the back, and that it will be removed or prevented by accustoming them to lie on the side. It is also of the greatest importance, that they be kept sufficiently warm. I believe that many infantile diseases arise from the neglect of this precaution. Children have little power of evolving heat; on this account, when delicate they should never be permitted to sleep alone, but made to lie with the nurse, that they may receive warmth from her body.

At whatever period we go to sleep, one fact is certain, that we can never with impunity convert day into night. Even in the most scorching seasons of the year, it is better to travel under the burning sunshine, than in the cool of the evening, when the dews are falling and the air is damp. A case in support of this statement, is given by Valangin in his work on Diet. Two colonels in the French army had a dispute whether it was not most safe to march in the heat of the day, or in the evening. To ascertain this point, they got permission from the commanding officer to put their respective plans into execution. Accordingly, the one with his division marched during the day, although it was in the heat of summer, and rested all night—the other slept in the day-time, and marched during the evening and part of the night. The result was that the first performed a journey of six hundred miles, without losing a single man or horse, while the latter lost most of his horses, and several of his men.

It now becomes a question at what hour we should retire to rest, how long our rest ought to continue, and when it should be broken in the morning. These points I shall briefly discuss, in the order in which they stand.

It is not very easy to ascertain the most appropriate hour for going to bed, as this depends very much upon the habits and occupation of the individual. Laborers and all hard wrought people, who are obliged to get up betimes, require to go to rest early; and in their case, nine o'clock may be the best hour. Those who are not obliged to rise early, may delay the period of retiring to rest for an hour or two longer; and may thus go to bed at ten or eleven. These are the usual periods allotted among the middle ranks of life for this purpose; and it may be laid down as a rule, that to make a custom of remaining up for a later period than eleven must be prejudicial. Those, therefore, who habitually delay going to bed till twelve, or one, or two, are acting in direct opposition to the laws of health, in so far as they are compelled to pass in sleep a portion of the ensuing day, which ought to be appropriated to wakefulness and exertion. Late hours are in every respect hurtful, whether they be employed in study or amusement. A fresh supply of stimulus is thrown upon the mind, which prevents it from sinking into slumber at the proper period, and restlessness, dreaming, and disturbed repose inevitably ensue. Among other things, the eyes are injured, those organs suffering much more from the candle-light, to which they are necessarily exposed, than from the natural light of day.

With regard to the necessary quantity of sleep, so much depends upon age, constitution, and employment, that it is impossible to lay down any fixed rule which will apply to all cases. Jeremy Taylor states that three hours only in the twenty-four should be devoted to sleep. Baxter extends the period to four hours, Wesley to six, Lord Coke and Sir William Jones to seven, and Sir John Sinclair to eight. With the latter I am disposed to coincide. Taking the average of mankind, we shall come as nearly as possible to the truth when we say that nearly one-third part of life ought to be spent in sleep: in some cases, even more may be necessary, and in few, can a much smaller portion be safely dispensed with. When a person in young, strong, and healthy, an hour or two less may be sufficient; but childhood and extreme old age require a still greater portion. No person who passes only eight hours in bed, can be said to waste his time in sleep. If, however, he exceeds this, and is, at the same time, in possession of vigor and youth, he lays himself open to the charge of slumbering away those hours which should be devoted to some other purpose. According to Georget, women should sleep a couple of hours longer than men. For the former he allows six or seven hours, for the latter eight or nine. I doubt, however, if the female constitution, generally speaking, requires more sleep than the male; at least it is certain that women endure protracted wakefulness better than men, but whether this may result from custom is a question worthy of being considered.

Barry, in his work on Digestion, has made an ingenious, but somewhat whimsical, calculation on the tendency of sleep to prolong life. He asserts, that the duration of human life may be ascertained by the number of pulsations which the individual is able to perform. Thus, if a man's life extends to 70 years, and his heart throbs 60 times each minute, the whole number of its pulsations will amount to 2,207,520,000; but if, by intemperance, or any other cause, he raises the pulse to 75 in the minute, the same number of pulsations would be completed in 56 years, and the duration of life abbreviated 14 years. Arguing from these data, he alleges, that sleep has a tendency to prolong life, as, during its continuance, the pulsations are less numerous than in the waking state. There is a sort of theoretical truth in this statement, but it is liable to be modified by so many circumstances, that its application can never become general. If this were not the case, it would be natural to infer that the length of a man's life would correspond with that of his slumbers; whereas it is well known, that too much sleep debilitates the frame, and lays the foundation of various diseases, which tend to shorten rather than extend the duration of life.

Those who indulge most in sleep, generally require the least of it. Such are the wealthy and luxurious, who pass nearly the half of their existence in slumber, while the hard-working peasant and mechanic, who would seem, at first sight, to require more than any other class of society, are contented with seven or eight hours of repose—a period brief in proportion to that expended by them in toil, yet sufficiently long for the wants of nature, as is proved by the strength and health which they almost uniformly enjoy.

For reasons already stated, more sleep is requisite in winter than in summer. Were there even no constitutional causes for this difference, we should be disposed to sleep longer in the one than in the other, as some of the circumstances which induce us to sit up late and rise early in summer, are wanting during winter; and we consequently feel disposed to lie longer in bed during the latter season of the year.

The hour of getting up in the morning is not of less importance than that at which we ought to lie down at night. There can be no doubt that one of the most admirable conducives to health is early rising. 'Let us,' says Solomon, 'go forth into the fields; let us lodge in the villages; let us *get up early* to the vineyards; let us see if the vine flourish—if the tender grape appear—if the pomegranates bud forth.'

Almost all men who have distinguished themselves in science, literature, and the arts, have been early risers. The industrions, the active-minded, the enthusiast in the pursuit of knowledge or gain, are up betimes at their respective occupations; while the sluggard wastes the most beautiful period of life in pernicious slumber. Homer, Virgil, and Horace are all represented as carly risers: the same was the case with Paley, Franklin, Priestly, Parkhurst, and Buffon, the latter of whom ordered his *valet de chambre* to awaken him every morning, and compel him to get up by force if he evinced any reluctance: for this service the valet was rewarded with a crown each day, which recompense he forfeited if he did not oblige his master to get out of bed before the clock struck six. Bishops Jewel and Burnet rose regularly every morning at four o'clock. Sir Thomas More did the same thing; and so convinced was he of the beneficial effects of getting up betimes, that, in his 'Utopia,' he represented the inhabitants attending lectures before sunrise. Napoleon was an early riser; so was Frederick the Great and, Charles XII; so is the Duke of Wellington; and so in truth, is almost every one distinguished for energy and indefatigability of mind.

Every circumstance contributes to render early rising advisable to those who are in the enjoyment of health. There is no time equal in beauty and freshness to the morning, when nature has just parted with the gloomy mantle which night had flung over her, and stands before us like a young bride, from whose aspect the veil which covered her loveliness, has been withdrawn. The whole material world has a vivifying appearance. The husbandman is up at his labour, the forest leaves sparkle with drops of crystal dew, the flowers raise their rejoicing heads towards the sun, the birds pour forth their anthems of gladness; and the wide face of creation itself seems as if awakened and refreshed from a mighty slumber. All these things, however, are hid from the eyes of the sluggard; nature, in her most glorious aspect, is, to him, a sealed book; and while every scene around him is full of beauty, interest, and animation, he alone is passionless and uninspired. Behold him stretched upon his couch of rest! In vain does the clock proclaim that the reign of day has commenced! In vain does the morning light stream fiercely in by the chinks of his window, as if to startle him from his repose! He hears not—he, sees not, for blindness and deafness rule over him with despotic sway, and lay a deadening spell upon his faculties. And when he does at length awake—far on in the day—from the torpor of this benumbing sleep, he is not refreshed. He does not start at once into new life—an altered man, with joy in his mind, and vigour in his frame. On the contrary, he is dull, languid, and stupid, as if half recovered from a paroxysm of drunkenness. He yawns, stretches himself, and stalks into the breakfast parlour, to partake in solitude, and without appetite, of his unrefreshing meal—while his eyes are red and gummy, his beard unshorn, his face unwashed, and his clothes disorderly, and ill put on. Uncleanliness and sluggishness generally go hand in hand; for the obtuseness of mind which disposes a man to waste the most precious hours of existence in debasng sleep, will naturally make him neglect his person.

The character of the early riser is the very reverse of the sloven's. His countenance is ruddy, his eye joyous and serene, and his frame full of vigour and activity. His mind, also, is clear and unclouded, and free from that oppressive languor which weighs like a nightmare upon the spirit of the sluggard. The man who rises betimes, is in the fair way of laying in both health and wealth; while he who dozes away his existence in unnecessary sleep, will acquire neither. On the contrary, he runs every chance of losing whatever portion of them he may yet be in possession of, and of sinking fast in the grade of society—a bankrupt both in person and in purse.*

The most striking instances of the good effects of early rising, are to be found in our peasantry and farmers, whose hale complexions, good appetites, and vigourous persons, are evidences of the benefit derived from this custom, conjoined with labour; while the wan, unhealthy countenances and enfeebled frames of those who keep late hours, lie long in bed, and pass the night in dissipation, study, or pleasure, are equally con-

* In the will of the late Mr James Sergeant of the borough of Leicester, is the following clause relative to early rising:—'As my nephews are fond of indulging in bed of a morning, and as I wish them to improve the time while they are young, I direct that they shall prove to the satisfaction of my executors, that have got out of bed in the morning, and either employed themselves in business, or taken exercise in the open air, from five o'clock every morning, from the 5th of April, to the 10th of October, being three hours each day, and from seven o'clock in the morning from the 10th of October to the 5th of April, being two hours every morning for two whole years; this to be done for some two years during the first seven years, to the satisfaction of my executors, who may excuse them in case of illness, but the task must be made up when they are well, and if they will not do this, they shall not receive any share of my property.'

clusive proofs of the pernicious consequences resulting from an opposite practice.

Early rising, therefore, is highly beneficial; but care should be taken not to carry it to excess. It can never be healthful to rise till the sun has been for some time above the horizon; for until this is the case, there is a dampness in the air which must prove injurious to the constitution, especially when it is not naturally very strong. Owing to this, early rising is injurious to most delicate people; and, in all cases, the heat of the sun should be allowed to have acquired some strength before we think of getting out of doors. No healthy man in the summer, should lie longer in bed than six o'clock. If he does so, he loses the most valuable part of the day, and injures his own constitution. Persons subject to gout, should always go to sleep early, and rise early. The former mitigates the violence of the evening paroxysm, which is always increased by wakefulness; and the latter lessens the tendency to plethora, which is favoured by long protracted sleep.

It is common in some of the foreign universities to go to bed at eight, and rise at three or four in the morning; and this plan is recommended by Willich in his 'Lectures on Diet and Regimen.' Sir John Sinclair, in allusion to it, judiciously observes, 'I have no doubt of the superior healthiness, in the winter time, of rising by day-light, and using candle-light at the close of the day, than rising by candle-light, and using it some hours before day-light approaches. It remains to be ascertained by which system the eyes are least likely to be affected.

Dr Franklin in one of his ingenious Essays, has some fine observations on early rising; and makes an amusing calculation of the saving that might be made in the city of Paris alone, by using the sunshine instead of candles. This saving he estimates at 96,000,000 of livres, or £4,000,000 sterling. This is mentioned in a satirical vein, but probably there is a great deal of truth in the statement. Indeed, if people were to go sooner to bed, and get up earlier, it is inconceivable what sums might be saved; but according to the absurd custom of polished society, day is, in a great measure, converted into night, and the order of things reversed in a manner at once capricious and hurtful.

To conclude. The same law which regulates our desire for food, also governs sleep. As we indulge in sleep to moderation or excess, it becomes a blessing or a curse—in the one case recruiting the energies of nature, and diffusing vigour alike over the mind and frame: in the other, debasing the character of man, stupifying his intellect, enfeebling his body, and rendering him useless alike to others and himself. The glutton, the drunkard, and the sloven bear the strictest affinity to each other, both in the violation of nature's laws, and in the consequences thence entailed upon themselves. What in moderation is harmless or beneficial, in excess is a curse; and sleep carried to the latter extreme, may be pronounced an act of intemperance almost as much as excessive eating or drinking.

THE END.

CONTENTS OF THE PHILOSOPHY OF SLEEP.

INDEX

TO THE PHILOSOPHY OF SLEEP.

THE

ANATOMY

OF

DRUNKENNESS.

BY

ROBERT MACNISH,

AUTHOR OF "THE PHILOSOPHY OF SLEEP," AND MEMBER OF THE FACULTY OF PHYSICIANS AND SURGEONS OF GLASGOW.

FROM THE FIFTH GLASGOW EDITION.

HARTFORD:
PUBLISHED BY SILAS ANDRUS & SON.
1850.

ANATOMY OF DRUNKENNESS.

ADVERTISEMENT.

In preparing the present edition of the Anatomy of Drunkenness for the press, I have spared no pains to render the work as complete as possible. Some parts have been re-written, some new facts added, and several inaccuracies, which had crept into the former edition, rectified. Altogether, I am in hopes that this impression will be considered an improvement upon its predecessors, and that no fact of any importance has been overlooked or treated more slightly than it deserves.

R. M.

September 20th, 1834.

CHAPTER I.

PRELIMINARY OBSERVATIONS.

Drunkenness is not, like some other vices, peculiar to modern times. It is handed down to us from 'hoar antiquity;' and, if the records of the antediluvian era were more complete, we should probably find that it was not unknown to the remotest ages of the world. The cases of Noah and Lot, recorded in the sacred writings, are the earliest of which tradition or history has left any record; and both occurred in the infancy of society. Indeed, wherever the grape flourished, inebriation prevailed. The formation of wine from this fruit, was among the earliest discoveries of man, and the bad consequences thence resulting, seem to have been almost coeval with the discovery. Those regions whose ungenial latitudes indisposed them to yield the vine, gave birth to other products which served as substititutes; and the inhabitants rivalled or surpassed those of the south in all kinds of Bacchanalian indulgence—the pleasures of drinking constituting one of the most fertile themes of their poetry, in the same manner as, in other climates, they gave inspiration to the souls of Anacreon and Hafiz.

Drunkenness has varied greatly at different times and among different nations. There can be no doubt that it prevails more in a rude than in a civilized society. This is so much the case, that as men get more refined, the vice will gradually be found to soften down, and assume a less revolting character. Nor can there be a doubt that it prevails to a much greater extent in northern than in southern latitudes.* The nature of the climate renders this inevitable, and gives to the human frame its capabilities of withstanding liquor: hence a quantity which scarcely ruffles the frozen current of a Norwegian's blood, would scatter madness and fever into the brain of the Hindoo. Even in Europe, the inhabitants of the south are far less adapted to sustain intoxicating agents than those of the north. Much of this depends upon the coldness of the climate, and much also upon the peculiar physical and moral frame to which that coldness gives rise. The natives, of the south are a lively, versatile people; sanguine in their temperaments, and susceptible, to an extraordinary degree, of every impression. Their minds seem to inherit the brilliancy of their climate, and are rich with sparkling thoughts and beautiful imagery. The northern nations are the reverse of all this. With more intensity of purpose, with greater depth of reasoning powers, and superior solidity of judgment, they are in a great measure destitute of that sportive and creative brilliancy which hangs like a rainbow over the spirits of the south, and clothes them in a perpetual sunshine of delight. The one is chiefly led by the heart, the other by the head. The one possesses the beauty of a flower-garden, the other the sternness of the rock, mixed with its severe and naked hardihood. Upon constitutions so differently organized, it cannot be expected that a given portion of stimulus will operate with equal power. The airy inflamable nature of the first, is easily roused to excitation, and manifests feelings which the second does not experience till he has partaken much more largely of the stimulating cause. On this account, the one may be inebriated, and the other remain comparatively sober upon a similar quantity. In speaking of this subject, it is always to be remembered that a person is not to be considered a drunkard because he consumes a certain portion of liquor; but because what he does consumes produces certain effects upon his system. The Russian, therefore, may take six glasses a-day, and be as temperate as the Italian who takes four, or the Indian who takes two. But even when this is acceded to, the balance of sobriety will be found in favour of the south: the inhabitants there not only drink less, but are, *bona fide*, more seldom intoxicated than the others. Those who have contrasted London and Paris, may easily verify this fact; and those who have done the same to the cities of Moscow and Rome, can bear still stronger testimony. Who ever heard of an Englishman sipping *eau sucree*, and treating his

* In making this observation, I have only in view the countries north of the equator; for as we proceed to the south of that line, the vice increases precisely in the same manner as in the opposite direction. To use the words of Montesquieu, 'Go from the equator to our pole, and you will find drunkenness increasing together with the degree of latitude. Go from the same equator to the opposite pole, and you will find drunkenness travelling south, as on this side it travels towards the north.'

friends to a glass of lemonade? Yet such things are common in France; and, of all the practices of that country, they are those most thoroughly visited by the contemptuous malisons of John Bull.

It is a common belief that wine was the only inebriating liquor known to antiquity; but this is a mistake. Tacitus mentions the use of ale or beer as common among the Germans of his time. By the Egyptians, likewise, whose country was ill adapted to the cultivation of the grape, it was employed as a substitute for wine. Ale was common in the middle ages; and Mr Park states that very good beer is made, by the usual process of brewing and malting, in the interior of Africa. The favourite drink of our Saxon ancestors was ale or mead. Those worshippers of Odin were so notoriously addicted to drunkenness, that it was regarded as honourable rather than otherwise; and the man who could withstand the greatest quantity was looked upon with admiration and respect: whence the drunken songs of the Scandinavian scalds; whence the glories of Valhalla, the fancied happiness of whose inhabitants consisted in quaffing draughts from the skulls of their enemies slain in battle. Even ardent spirit, which is generally supposed to be a modern discovery, existed from a very early period. It is said to have been first made by the Arabians in the middle ages, and in all likelihood may lay claim to a still remoter origin. Alcohol was known to the alchymists as early as the middle of the twelfth century, although the process of preparing it was by them, at that time, kept a profound secret. The spirituous liquor called arrack, has been manufactured in the island of Java, as well as in the continent of Hindostan, from time immemorial. Brandy appears to have been known to Galen, who recommends it for the cure of voracious appetite;* and its distillation was common in Sicily at the commencement of the fourteenth century. As to wine, it was so common in ancient times as to have a tutelar god appropriated to it: Bacchus and his companion Silenus are as household words in the mouths of all, and constituted most important features of the heathen mythology. We have all heard of the Falernian and Campanian wines, and of the wines of Cyprus and Shiraz. Indeed, there is reason to believe that the ancients were in no respect inferior to the moderns in the excellence of their vinous liquors, whatever they may have been in the variety. Wine was so common in the eastern nations, that Mahomet, foreseeing the baleful effects of its propagation, forbade it to his followers, who, to compensate themselves, had recourse to opium. The Gothic or dark ages seem to have been those in which it was least common: in proof of this it may be mentioned, that in 1298 it was vended as a cordial by the English apothecaries. At the present day it is little drunk, except by the upper classes, in those countries which do not natnrally furnish the grape. In those that do, it is so cheap as to come within the reach of even the lowest.†

In speaking of drunkenness, it is impossible not to be struck with the physical and moral degradation which it has spread over the world. Wherever intoxicating liquors become general, morality has been found on the decline. They seem to act like the simoom of the desert, and scatter destruction and misery around their path. The ruin of Rome was owing to luxury, of which indulgence in wine was the principal ingredient. Hannibal's army fell less by the arms of Scipio than by the wines of Capua; and the inebriated hero of Macedon after slaying his friend Clytus, and burning the palace of Persepolis, expired at last of a fit of intoxication, in his thirty-third year. A volume might be written in illustration of the evil effects of dissipation; but this is unnecessary to those who look carefully around them, and more especially to those who are conversant with the history of mankind. At the same time, when we speak of drunkenness as occurring in antiquity, it is proper to remark, that there were certain countries in which it was viewed in a much more dishonourable light than by any modern nation. The Nervii refused to drink wine, alleging that it made them cowardly and effeminate: these simple people had no idea of what by our seamen is called *Dutch courage;* they did not feel the necessity of elevating their native valour by an artificial excitement. The ancient Spartans held ebriety in such abhorrence, that, with a view to inspire the rising generation with a due contempt of the vice, it was customary to intoxicate the slaves and exhibit them publicly in this degraded condition. By the Indians, drunkenness is looked upon as a species of insanity; and, in their language, the word *ramgam,* signifying a drunkard, signifies also a madman. Both the ancients and moderns could jest as well as moralize upon this subject. 'There hangs a bottle of wine,' was the derisive exclamation of the Roman soldiery, as they pointed to the body of the drunken Bonosus, who, in a fit of despair, suspended himself upon a tree. 'If you wish to have a shoe of durable materials,' exclaims the facetious Matthew Langsberg, 'you should make the upper leather of the mouth of a hard drinker—for that never lets in water.'

If we turn from antiquity to our own times, we shall find little cause to congratulate ourselves upon any improvement. The vice has certainly diminished among the higher orders of society, but there is every reason to fear that, of late, it has made fearful strides among the lower. Thirty or forty years ago, a landlord did not conceive he had done justice to his guests unless he sent them from his table in a state of intoxication. This practice still prevails pretty generally in Ireland and in the highlands of Scotland, but in other parts of the kingdom it is fast giving way: and it is to be hoped that the day is not far distant when greater temperance will extend to these jovial districts, and render their hospitality a little more consonant with prudence and moderation. The increase of drunkenness among the lower classes may be imputed to various causes, and chiefly to the late abandonment of part of the duty on rum and whiskey. This was done with a double motive of benefiting agriculture and commerce, and of driving the 'giant smuggler' from the field. The latter object it has in a great measure failed of effecting. The smuggler still plies his trade to a considerable extent, and brings his commodity to the market with nearly the same certainty of acquiring profit as ever. It would be well if the liquor vended to the poor possessed the qualities of that furnished by the contraband dealer; but, instead of that, it is usually a vile compound of every thing spurious and pestilent, and seems expressly contrived for preying upon the vitals of the unfortunate victims who partake of it. The extent to which adulteration has been carried in all kinds of liquor, is indeed such as to interest every class of society. Wine, for instance, is often impregnated with alum and sugar of lead, the latter dangerous ingredient being resorted to by innkeepers and others, to take away the sour taste so common in bad wines. Even the colour of these liquids is frequently artificial; and the deep rich complexion so greatly admired by persons not in the secrets of the trade, is often caused, or at least heightened, by factitious additions, such as elder-berries, bilberries, red-woods, &c. Alum and sugar of lead are also common in spirituous liquors;

* Good's Study of Medicine, vol. i. p. 113, 2d edit.

† The quantity of wine raised in France alone is almost incredible. The vineyards in that country are said to occupy five millions of acres, or a twenty-sixth part of the whole territory. Paris alone consumes more than three times the quantity of wine consumed in the British Isles. It is true that much of the wine drank in the French capital is of a weak quality, being used as a substitute for small beer. But after every allowance is made, enough remains to show clearly, if other proofs were wanting, how much use of wine here is restricted by our exorbitant duties. It would be well for the morals of this country if the people abandoned the use of ardent spirits, and were enabled to resort to such wines as the French are in the habit of drinking.

and, in any cases, oil of vitriol, turpentine, and other materials equally abominable, are to be found in combination with them. That detestable liquor called British gin, is literally compounded of these ingredients: nor are malt liquors, with their multifarious narcotic additions, less thoroughly sophisticated or less detrimental to the health. From these circumstances, two conclusions must naturally be drawn; *viz.* that inebriating agents often contain elements of disease foreign to themselves; and that all persons purchasing them should endeavour to ascertain the state of their purity, and employ no dealer whose honour and honesty are not known to be unimpeachable. Liquors, even in their purest state, are too often injurious to the constitution without the admixture of poisons.*

The varieties of wine are so numerous as almost to defy calculation. Mr Brande, in his table, gives a list of no less than forty-four different kinds, and there are others which he has not enumerated. Ardent spirits are fewer in number, and may be mostly comprised under the names of rum, gin, brandy, and whiskey. The first is the prevailing drink over the West Indies, North America, and such cities of Great Britain as are intimately connected with these regions by commerce. The second is extensively used in Holland and Switzerland, the countries which principally furnish it, and has found its way pretty generally over the whole of Europe. The third is chiefly produced in Charente and Languedoc, and is the spirit most commonly found in the south. The fourth is confined in a great measure to Ireland and Scotland, in which latter country the best has always been made. Of malt liquors we have many varieties. Britain, especially England, is the country which furnishes them in greatest perfection They are the natural drinks of Englishmen—the *vinum Anglicorum*, as foreigners have often remarked. Every town of any consequence in the empire has its brewery; and in almost every one is there some difference in the quality of the liquor. Brown stout, London and Scotch porters, Burton, Dorchester, Edinburgh and Alloa ales, are only a few of the endless varieties of these widely-circulated fluids.

Besides wines, ardent spirits, and malt liquors, there are many other agents possessing inebriating properties. Among others, the *Peganum Harmala* or Syrian rue, so often used by the sultan Solyman; the *Hibiscus Saldarissa*, which furnishes the Indian bangue, and from which the *Nepenthes* of the ancients is supposed to have been made; the *Balsac*, or Turkish bangue, found on the shores of the Levant; the *Penang*, or Indian betle; the *Hyoscyamus Niger;* and the *Atropa Belladonna.* In addition to these, and many more, there are opium, tobacco, *Cocculus Indicus*, and the innumerable tribes of liqueurs and ethers, together with other agents of a less potent nature, such as clary, darnel, and saffron. The variety of agents capable of exciting drunkenness is indeed surprising, and in proportion to their number seems the prevalence of that fatal vice to which an improper use of them gives rise.

CHAPTER II.

CAUSES OF DRUNKENNESS.

The causes of drunkenness are so obvious, that few authors have thought it necessary to point them out: we shall merely say a few words upon the subject. There are some persons who will never be drunkards, and others who will be so in spite of all that can be done to prevent them. Some are drunkards by choice, and others by necessity. The former have an innate and constitutional fondness for liquor, and drink *con amore.* Such men are usually of a sanguineous temperament, of coarse unintellectual minds, and of low and animal propensities. They have, in general, a certain rigidity of fibre, and a flow of animal spirits which other people are without. They delight in the roar and riot of drinking clubs; and with them, in particular, all the miseries of life may be referred to the bottle.

The drunkard by necessity was never meant by nature to be dissipated. He is perhaps a person of amiable disposition, whom misfortune has overtaken, and who, instead of bearing up manfully against it, endeavours to drown his sorrows in liquor. It is an excess of sensibility, a partial mental weakness, an absolute misery of the heart, which drives him on. Drunkenness, with him, is a consequence of misfortune; it is a solitary dissipation preying upon him in silence. Such a man frequently dies broken-hearted, even before his excesses have had time to destroy him by their own unassisted agency.

Some become drunkards from excess of indulgence in youth. There are parents who have a common custom of treating their childern to wine, punch, and other intoxicating liquors. This, in reality, is regularly bringing them up in an apprenticeship to drunkenness. Others are taught the vice by frequenting drinking clubs and masonic lodges. These are the genuine academies of tippling. Two-thirds of the drunkards we meet with, have been there initiated in that love of intemperance and boisterous irregularity which distinguish their future lives. Men who are good singers are very apt to become drunkards and, in truth, most of them are so, more or less, especially if they have naturally much joviality or warmth of temperament. A fine voice to such men is a fatal accomplishment.

Ebriety prevails to an alarming degree among the lower orders of society. It exists more in towns than in the country, and more among mechanics than husbandmen. Most of the misery to be observed among the working classes spring from this source. No persons are more addicted to the habit, and all its attendant vices than the pampered servants of the great. Innkeepers, musicians, actors, and men who lead a rambling and eccentric life, are exposed to a similar hazard. Husbands sometimes teach their wives to be drunkards by indulging them in toddy and such fluids, every time they themselves sit down to their libations.

Women frequently acquire the vice by drinking porter and ale while nursing. These stimulants are usually recommended to them from well-meant but mistaken motives, by their female attendants. Many fine young women are ruined by this pernicious practice. Their persons become gross, their milk unhealthy, and a foundation is too often laid for future indulgence in liquor.

The frequent use of cordials, such as noyeau, shrub, kirsch-wasser, curacoa, and anissette, sometimes leads to the practice. The active principle of these liqueurs is neither more nor less than ardent spirits.*

Among other causes, may be mentioned the excessive use of spiritous tinctures for the cure of hypochondria and indigestion. Persons who use strong tea, especially green, run the same risk. The latter species is singularly hurtful to the constitution, producing hysteria, heartburn, and general debility of the chylopoetic viscera. Some of these bad effects are relieved for a time by the use of spirits; and what was at first employed as a medicine, soon becomes an essential requisite.

Certain occupations have a tendency to induce drunkenness. Innkeepers, recruiting-sergeants, pugilists, &c., are all exposed in a great degree to temptation in this respect; and intemperance is a vice which may be very often justly charged against them Commercial travellers, also, taken as a body, are open to the accusation of indulging too freely in the bottle, al-

* See Accum's Treatise on the Adulteration of Food; Child on Brewing Porter; and Shannon on Brewing and Distillation.

* Liqueurs often contain narcotic principles; therefore their use is doubly improper.

though I am not aware that they carry it to such excess as to entitle many of them to be ranked as drunkards. 'Well fed, riding from town to town, and walking to the houses of the several tradesmen, they have an employment not only more agreeable, but more conducive to health than almost any other dependant on traffic. But they destroy their constitutions by intemperance; not generally by drunkenness, but by taking more liquor than nature requires. Dining at the traveller's table, each drinks his pint or bottle of wine; he then takes negus or spirit with several of his customers; and at night he must have a glass or two of brandy and water. Few commercial travellers bear the employ for thirty years—the majority not twenty.'*

Some waiters allege that unmarried women, especially if somewhat advanced in life, are more given to liquor than those who are married. This point I am unable from my own observation to decide. Women who indulge in this way, are *solitary* dram-drinkers, and so would men be, had not the arbitrary opinions of the world invested the practice in them with much less moral turpitude than in the opposite sex. Of the two sexes, there can he no doubt that men are much the more addicted to all sorts of intemperance.

Drunkenness appears to be in some measure hereditary. We frequently see it descending from parents to their children. This may undoubtedly often arise from bad example and imitation, but there can be little question that, in many instances at least, it exists as a family predisposition.

Men of genius are often unfortunately addicted to drinking. Nature, as she has gifted them with greater powers than their fellows, seem also to have mingled with their cup of life more bitterness. There is a melancholy which is apt to come like a cloud over the imaginations of such characters. Their minds possess a susceptibility and delicacy of structure which unfit them for the gross atmosphere of human nature; wherefore, high talent has ever been distinguished for sadness and gloom. Genius lives in a world of its own: it is the essence of a superior nature—the loftier imaginings of the mind, clothed with a more spiritual and refined verdure. Few men endowed with such faculties enjoy the ordinary happiness of humanity. The stream of their lives runs harsh and broken. Melancholy thoughts sweep perpetually across their soul; and if these be heightened by misfortune, they are plunged into the deepest misery.

To relieve these feelings, many plans have been adopted. Dr Johnson fled for years to wine under his habitual gloom. He found that the pangs were removed while its immediate influence lasted, but he also found that they returned with double force when that influence passed away. He saw the dangerous precipice on which he stood, and, by an unusual effort of volition, gave it over. In its stead he substituted tea; and to this milder stimulus had recourse in his melancholy. Voltaire and Fontenelle, for the same purpose, used coffee. The excitements of Newton and Hobbes were the fumes of tobacco, while Demosthenes and Haller were sufficiently stimulated by drinking freely of cold water. Such are the differences of constitution.

'As good be melancholy still, as drunken beasts and beggars.' So says old Burton, in his Anatomy of Melancholy, and there are few who will not subscribe to his creed. The same author quaintly, but justly remarks, 'If a drunken man gets a child, it will never, likely, have a good brain.' Dr Darwin, a great authority on all subjects connected with life, says, that he never knew a glutton affected with the gout, who was not at the same time addicted to liquor. He also observes, 'it is remarkable that all the diseases from drinking spirituous or fermented liquors are liable to become hereditary, even to the third generation, gradually increasing, if the cause be continued, till the family becomes extinct.'*

* Thackrah on the Effects of the Principal Arts, Trades an Professions, p. 83.

We need not endeavour to trace farther the remote causes of drunkenness. A drunkard is rarely able to recall the particular circumstances which made him so. The vice creeps upon him insensibly, and he is involved in its fetters before he is aware. It is enough that we know the proximate cause, and also the certain consequences. One thing is certain, that a man who addicts himself to intemperance, can never be said to be sound in mind or body. The former is a state of partial insanity, while the effects of the liquor remain; and the latter is always more or less diseased in its actions.

CHAPTER III.

PHENOMENA OF DRUNKENNESS.

The consequences of drunkenness are dreadful, but the pleasures of getting drunk are certainly ecstatic. While the illusion lasts, happiness is complete; care and melancholy are thrown to the wind: and Elysium, with all its glories, descends upon the dazzled imagination of the drinker.

Some authors have spoken of the pleasure of being completely drunk; this, however, is not the most exquisite period. The time is when a person is neither 'drunken nor sober, but neighbor to both,' as Bishop Andrews says in his ''Ex—ale—tation of Ale.' The moment is when the ethereal emanations begin to float around the brain—when the soul is commencing to expand its wings and rise from earth—when the tongue feels itself somewhat loosened in the mouth, and breaks the previous taciturnity, if any such existed.

What are the sensations of incipient drunkenness? First, an unusual serenity prevails over the mind, and the soul of the votary is filled with a placid satisfaction: By degrees he is sensible of a soft and not unmusical humming in his ears, at every pause of the conversation. He seems, to himself, to wear his head lighter than usual upon his shoulders. Then a species of obscurity, thinner than the finest mist, passes before his eyes, and makes him see objects rather indistinctly. The lights begin to dance and appear double. A gayety and warmth are felt at the same time about the heart. The imagination is expanded, and filled with a thousand delightful images. He becomes loquacious, and pours forth, in enthusiastic language, the thoughts which are born, as it were, within him.

Now comes a spirit of universal contentment with himself and all the world. He thinks no more of misery; it is dissolved in the bliss of the moment. This is the acme of the fit—the ecstacy is now perfect. As yet the sensorium is in tolerable order; it is only shaken, but the capability of thinking with accuracy still remains. About this time, the drunkard pours out all the secrets of his soul. His qualities, good or bad, come forth without reserve; and now, if at any time, the human heart may be seen into. In a short period, he is seized with a most inordinate propensity to talk nonsense, though he is perfectly conscious of doing so. He also commits many foolish things, knowing them to be foolish. The power of volition, that faculty which keeps the will subordinate to the judgment, seems totally weakened. The most delightful time seems to be that immediately before becoming very talkative. When this takes place, a man turns ridiculous, and his mirth, though more boisterous, is not so exquisite. At first the intoxication partakes of sentiment, but latterly, it becomes mere animal.

After this the scene thickens. The drunkard's imagination gets disordered with the most grotesque con

* Botanic Garden.

ceptions. Instead of moderating his drink, he pours it down more rapidly than ever; glass follows glass with reckless energy. His head becomes perfectly giddy. The candles burn blue, or green, or yellow; and where there are perhaps only three on the table, he sees a dozen. According to his temperament, he is amorous, or musical, or quarrelsome. Many possess a most extraordinary wit; and a great flow of spirits is a general attendant. In the latter stages, the speech is thick, and the use of the tongue in a great measure lost. His mouth is half open, and idiotic in the expression; while his eyes are glazed, wavering, and watery. He is apt to fancy that he has offended some one of the company, and is ridiculously profuse with his apologies. Frequently he mistakes one person for another, and imagines that some of those before him are individuals who are, in reality, absent or even dead. The muscular powers are, all along, much affected: this indeed happens before any great change takes place in the mind, and goes on progressively increasing. He can no longer walk with steadiness, but totters from side to side. The limbs become powerless, and inadequate to sustain his weight. He is, however, not always sensible of any deficiency in this respect: and while exciting mirth by his eccentric motions, imagines that he walks with the most perfect steadiness. In attempting to run, he conceives that he passes over the ground with astonishing rapidity. To his distorted eyes, all men, and even inanimate nature itself, seem to be drunken, while he alone is sober. Houses reel from side to side as if they had lost their balance; trees and steeples nod like tipsy Bacchanals; and the very earth seems to slip from under his feet, and leave him walking and floundering upon the air. The last stage of drunkenness is total insensibility. The man tumbles perhaps beneath the table, and is carried away in a state of stupor to his couch. In this condition he is said to be *dead drunk*.

When the drunkard is put to bed, let us suppose that his faculties are not totally absorbed in apoplectic stupor; let us suppose that he still possesses consciousness and feeling, though these are both disordered; then begins 'the tug of war;' then comes the misery which is doomed to succeed his previous raptures. No sooner is his head laid upon the pillow, than it is seized with the strongest throbbing. His heart beats quick and hard against the ribs. A noise like the distant fall of a cascade, or rushing of a river, is heard in his ears: sough—sough—sough, goes the sound. His senses now become more drowned and stupified. A dim recollection of his carousals, like a shadowy and indistinct dream, passes before the mind. He still hears, as in echo, the cries and laughter of his companions. Wild fantastic fancies accumulate thickly around the brain. His giddiness is greater than ever; and he feels as if in a ship tossed upon a heaving sea. At last he drops insensibly into a profound slumber.

In the morning he awakes in a high fever. The whole body is parched; the palms of the hands in particular, are like leather. His head is often violently painful. He feels excessive thirst; while his tongue is white, dry, and stiff. The whole inside of the mouth is likewise hot and constricted, and the throat often sore. Then look at his eyes—how sickly, dull, and languid! The fire, which first lighted them up the evening before, is all gone. A stupor like that of the last stage of drunkenness still clings about them, and they are disagreeably affected by the light. The complexion sustains as great a change: it is no longer flushed with the gayety and excitation, but pale and wayworn, indicating a profound mental and bodily exhaustion, There is probably sickness, and the appetite is totally gone. Even yet the delirium of intoxication has not left him, for his head still rings, his heart still throbs violently; and if he attempt getting up, he stumbles with giddiness. The mind also is sadly depressed, and the proceedings of the previous night are painfully remembered. He is sorry for his conduct, promises solemnly never again so to commit himself, and calls impatiently for something to quench his thirst. Such are the usual phenomena of a fit of drunkenness.

In the beginning of intoxication we are inclined to sleep, especially if we indulge alone. In companies, the noise and opportunity of conversing prevent this; and when a certain quantity has been drunk, the drowsy tendency wears away. A person who wishes to stand out well, should never talk much. This increases the effects of the liquor, and hurries on intoxication. Hence, every experienced drunkard holds it to be a piece of prudence to keep his tongue under restraint.

The giddiness of intoxication is always greater in darkness than in the light. I know of no rational way by which this can be explained; but, certain it is, the drunkard never so well knows his true condition as when alone and in darkness. Possibly the noise and light distracted the mind, and made the bodily sensations be, for the time, in some measure unfelt.

There are some persons who get sick from drinking even a small quantity; and this sickness is, upon the whole, a favourable circumstance, as it proves an effectual curb upon them, however much they may be disposed to intemperance. In such cases, it will generally be found that the sickness takes place as soon as vertigo makes its appearance: it seems, in reality, to be produced by this sensation. This, however, is a rare circumstance, for though vertigo from ordinary causes has a strong tendency to produce sickness, that arising from drunkenness has seldom this effect. The nausea and sickness sometimes occurring in intoxication, proceed almost always from the surcharged and disordered state of the stomach, and very seldom from the accompanying giddiness.

Intoxication, before it proceeds too far, has a powerful tendency to increase the appetite. Perhaps it would be more correct to say, that inebriating liquors, by stimulating the stomach, have this power. We often see gluttony and drunkenness combined together at the same time. This continues till the last stage, when, from overloading and excess of irritation, the stomach expels its contents by vomiting.

All along, the action of the kidneys is much increased, especially at the commencement of intoxication. When a large quantity of intoxicating fluid has been suddenly taken into the stomach, the usual preliminary symptoms of drunkenness do not appear. An instantaneous stupefaction ensues; and the person is at once knocked down. This cannot be imputed to distention of the cerebral vessels, but to a sudden operation on the nervous branches of the stomach. The brain is thrown into a state of collapse, and many of its functions suspended. In such cases the face is not at first tumid and ruddy, but pale and contracted. The pulse is likewise feeble, and the body cold and powerless. When re-action takes place, these symptoms wear off, and those of sanguineous apoplexy succeed; such as turgid countenance, full but slow pulse, and strong stertorous breathing. The vessels of the brain have now become filled, and there is a strong determination to that organ.

Persons of tender or compassionate minds are particularly subject, during intoxication, to be affected to tears at the sight of any distressing object, or even on hearing an affecting tale. Drunkenness in such characters, may be said to melt the heart, and open up the fountains of sorrow. Their sympathy is often ridiculous, and aroused by the most trifling causes. Those who have a living imagination, combined with this tenderness of heart, sometimes conceives fictitious causes of distress, and weep bitterly at the woe of their own creating.

There are some persons in whom drunkenness calls forth a spirit of piety, or rather of religious hypocrisy, which is both ludicrous and disgusting. They become sentimental over their cups; and, while in a state of debasement most offensive to God and man, they will weep at the wickedness of the human heart, entreat you to eschew swearing and profane company, and have a greater regard for the welfare of your immortal soul. These sanctimonious drunkards seem to consider ebriety as the most venial of offences.

During a paroxysm of drunkenness, the body is much less sensible to external stimuli than at other times: it is particularly capable of resisting cold. Seamen, when absent on shore, are prone to get intoxicated; and they will frequently lie for hours on the highway, even in the depth of winter, without any bad consequences. A drunk man seldom shivers from cold. His frame seems steeled against it, and he holds out with an apathy which is astonishing. The body is, in like manner, insensible to injuries, such as cuts, bruises, &c. He frequently receives, in fighting, the most severe blows, without seemingly feeling them, and without, in fact, being aware of the matter, till sobered. Persons in intoxication have been known to chop off their fingers, and otherwise disfigure themselves, laughing all the while at the action. But when the paroxysm is off, and the frame weakened, things are changed. External agents are then withstood with little vigour, with even less than in the natural state of the body. The person shivers on the slightest chill, and is more than usually subject to fevers and all sorts of contagion.

External stimuli frequently break the fit. Men have been instantly sobered by having a bucket of cold water thrown upon them, or by falling into a stream. Strong emotions of the mind produce the same effect, such as the sense of danger, or a piece of good or bad news, suddenly communicated.

There are particular situations and circumstances in which a man can stand liquor better than in others. In the close atmosphere of a large town, he is soon overpowered; and it is here that the genuine drunkard is to be met with in the greatest perfection. In the country, especially in a mountainous district, or on the seashore, where the air is cold and piercing, a great quantity may be taken with impunity. The highlanders drink largely of ardent spirits, and they are often intoxicated, yet, among them, there are comparatively few who can be called habitual drunkards. A keen air seems to deaden its effects, and it soon evaporates from their constitutions. Sailors and soldiers who are hard wrought, also consume enormous quantities without injury; porters and all sorts of labourers do the same. With these men exercise is a corrective; but in towns, where no counteracting agency is employed, it acts with irresistible power upon the frame, and soon proves destructive.

A great quantity of liquors may also be taken without inebriating, in certain diseases, such as spasm tetanus, gangrene, and retrocedent gout.

Certain circumstances of constitution make one person naturally more apt to get intoxicated than another. Mr Pitt,' says a modern writer, 'would retire in the midst of a warm debate, and enliven his faculties with a couple of bottles of Port. Pitt's constitution enabled him to do this with impunity. He was afflicted with what is called a coldness of stomach; and the quantity of wine that would have closed the oratory of so professed a Bacchanalian as Sheridan, scarcely excited the son of Chatham.'*

All kinds of intoxicating agents act much more rapidly and powerfully upon an empty than a full stomach. In like manner, when the stomach is disordered, and subject to weakness, heartburn, or disease of any kind, ebriety is more rapidly produced than when this organ is sound and healthy.

The stomach may get accustomed to a strong stimulus, and resist it powerfully, while it yields to one much weaker. I have known people who could drink eight or ten glasses of raw spirits at a sitting without feeling them much, become perfectly intoxicated by half the quantity made into toddy. In like manner, he who is in the constant habit of using one spirit,—rum, for instance,—cannot, for the most part, indulge to an equal extent in another, without experiencing more severe effects than if he had partaken of his usual beverage. This happens even when the strength of the two liquors is the same.

The mind exercises a considerable effect upon drunkenness, and may often control it powerfully. When in the company of a superior whom we respect, or of a female in whose presence it would be indelicate to get intoxicated, a much greater portion of liquor may be withstood than in societies where no such restraints operate.

Drunkenness has sometimes a curious effect upon the memory. Actions committed during intoxication may be forgotten on a recovery from this state, and remembered distinctly when the person becomes again intoxicated. Drunkenness has thus an analogy to dreaming, in which state circumstances are occasionally brought to mind which had entirely been forgotten. The same thing may also occur in fevers, wherein even languages with which we were familiar in childhood or youth, but had forgotten, are renewed upon the memory and pass away from it again when the disease which recalled them is removed.

With most people intoxication is a gradual process, and increases progressively as they pour down the liquor; but there are some individuals in whom it takes place suddenly, and without any previous indication of its approach. It is not uncommon to see such persons sit for hours at the bottle without experiencing any thing beyond a moderate elevation of spirits, yet assume all at once the outrage and boisterous irregularity of the most decided drunkenness.

Some drunkards retain their senses after the physical powers are quite exhausted. Others, even when the mind is wrought to a pitch leading to the most absurd actions, preserve a degree of cunning and observation which enables them to elude the tricks which their companions are preparing to play upon them. In such cases, they display great address, and take the first opportunity of retaliating; or, if such does not occur, of slipping out of the room unobserved and getting away. Some, while the whole mind seems locked up in the stupor of forgetfulness, hear all that is going on. No one should ever presume on the intoxicated state of another to talk of him detractingly in his presence. While apparently deprived of all sensation, he may be an attentive listener; and whatever is said, though unheeded at the moment, is not forgotten afterwards, but treasured carefully up in the memory. Much discord and ill-will frequently arise from such imprudence.

There are persons who are exceedingly profuse, and fond of giving away their money, watches, rings, &c., to the company. This peculiarity will never, I believe be found in a miser: avarice is a passion strong under every circumstance. Drinking does not loosen the grasp of the covetous man, or open his heart: he is for ever the same.

The generality of people are apt to talk of their private affairs when intoxicated. They then reveal the most deeply-hidden secrets to their companions. Others have their minds so happily constituted that nothing escapes them. They are, even in their most unguarded moments, secret and close as the grave.

The natural disposition may be better discovered in drunkenness than at any other time. In modern society, life is all a disguise. Almost every man walks in masquerade, and his most intimate friend very often does not know his real character. Many wear smiles constantly upon their cheeks, whose hearts are unprin-

* Rede's Memoir of the right Hon. George Canning.

cipled and treacherous. Many with violent tempers have all the external calm and softness of charity itself. Some speak always with sympathy, who, at soul, are full of gall and bitterness. Intoxication tears off the veil, and sets each in his true light, whatever they may be. The combative man will quarrel, the amorous will love, the detractor will abuse his neighbour. I have known exceptions, but they are few in number. At one time they seemed more numerous, but closer observation convinced me that most of those whom I thought drunkenness had libelled, inherited at bottom the genuine dispositions which it brought forth. The exceptions, however, which now and then occur, are sufficiently striking, and point out the injustice of always judging of a man's real disposition from his drunken moments. To use the words of Addison, 'Not only does this vice betray the hidden faults of a man, and show them in the most odious colours, but often occasions faults to which he is not naturally subject. Wine throws a man out of himself, and infuses qualities into the mind which she is a stranger to in his sober moments.' The well known maxim '*in vino veritas*,' therefore, though very generally true, is to be received with some restrictions, although, these I am satisfied, are by no means so numerous, as many authors would have us to belive.

CHAPTER IV

DRUNKENNESS MODIFIED BY TEMPERAMENT.

Under the last head I have described the usual phenomena of intoxication ; but it is necessary to remark that these are apt to be modified by the physical and moral frame of the drinker. Great diversity of opinion exists with regard to the doctrine of the temperaments ; some authors affirming, and others denying their existence. Into this controversy it is needless to enter. All I contend for is, that the bodily and mental constitution of every man is not alike, and that on these peculiarities depend certain differences during a paroxysm of drunkenness.

1. *Sanguineous Drunkard.*—The sanguine temperament seems to feel most intensely the excitement of the bottle. Persons of this stamp have usually a ruddy complexion, thick neck, small head, and strong muscular fibre. Their intellect is in general *mediocre*, for great bodily strength and corresponding mental powers are rarely united together. In such people, the animal propensities prevail over the moral and intellectual ones. They are prone to combativeness and sensuality, and are either very good-natured or extremely quarrelsome. All their passions are keen : like the Irish women, they will fight for their friends or with them as occasion requires. They are talkative from the beginning, and, during confirmed intoxication, perfectly obstreporous. It is men of this class who are the heroes of all drunken companies, the patron of masonic lodges, the presidents and getters-up of jovial meetings. With them, eating and drinking are the grand ends of human life. Look at their eyes, how they sparkle at the sight of wine, and how their lips smack and their teeth water in the neighbourhood of a good dinner : they would scent out a banquet in Siberia. When intoxicated, their passions are highly excited : the energies of a hundred minds then seem concentrated into one focus. Their mirth, their anger, their love, their folly, are all equally intense and unquenchable. Such men cannot conceal their feelings. In drunkenness, the veil is removed from them, and their characters stand revealed, as in a glass to the eye of the beholder. The Roderick Random of Smollett had much of this temperament, blended, however, with more intellect than usually belongs to it.

II. *Melancholy Drunkard.*—Melancholy, in drunkards, sometimes arises from temperament, but more frequently from habitual intoxication or misfortune, Some men are melancholy by nature, but become highly mirthful when they have drunk a considerable quantity. Men of this tone of mind seem to enjoy the bottle more exquisitely than even the sanguineous class. The joyousness which it excites breaks in upon their gloom like sunshine upon darkness. Above all, the sensations, of the moment when mirth begins with its magic to charm away care, are inexpressible. Pleasure falls in showers of fragrance upon their souls ; they are at peace with themselves and all mankind, and enjoy, as it were, a foretaste of paradise. Robert Burns was an example of this variety. His melancholy was constitutional, but heightened by misfortune. The bottle commonly dispelled it, and gave rise to the most delightful images ; sometimes, however, it only aggravated the gloom.

III. *Surly Drunkard.*—Some men are not excited to mirth by intoxication : on the contrary, it renders them gloomy and discontented. Even those who in the sober state are sufficiently gay, become, occasionally thus altered. A great propensity to take offence is a characteristic among persons of this temperament. They are suspicious, and very often mischievous. If at some former period they have had a difference with any of the company, they are sure to revive it, although, probably, it has been long ago cemented on both sides, and even forgotten by the other party. People of this description are very unpleasant companions. They are in general so foul-tongued, quarrelsome, and indecent in conversation, that established clubs of drinkers have made it a practice to exclude them from their society.

IV. *Phlegmatic Drunkard.*—Persons of this temperament are heavy-rolling machines, and, like the above, are not roused to mirth by liquor. Their vital actions are dull and spiritless—the blood in their veins as sluggish as the river Jordan, and their energies stagnant as the Dead Sea. They are altogether a negative sort of beings, with passions too inert to lead them to any thing very good or very bad. They are a species of animated clods, but not thoroughly animated—for the vital fire of feeling has got cooled in penetrating their frozen frames. A new prometheus would require to breathe into their nostrils, to give them the ordinary glow and warmth of humanity. Look at a phlegmatic man—how dead, passionless and uninspired is the expression of his clammy lips and vacant eye ! Speak to him—how cold, slow, and tame is his conversation ! the words come forth as if they were drawn from his mouth with a pair of pincers : and the ideas are as frozen as if concocted in the bowels of Lapland. Liquor produces no effect upon his mental powers ; or, if it does, it is a smothering one. The whole energies of the drink fall on his almost impassive frame. From the first, his drunkenness is stupifying ; he is seized with a kind of lethargy, the white of his eyes turns up, he breathes loud and harshly, and sinks into an apoplectic stupor. Yet all this is perfectly harmless, and wears away without leaving any mark behind it.

Such persons are very apt to be played upon by their companions. There are few men who, in their younger days who have not assisted in shaving the heads and painting the faces of these lethargic drunkards.

V. *Nervous Drunkard.*—This is a very harmless and very tiresome personage. Generally of a weak mind and irritable constitution, he does not become boisterous with mirth, and rarely shows the least glimmering of wit or mental energy. He is talkative and fond of long winded stories, which he tells in a drivelling, silly manner. Never warmed into enthusiasm by liquor he keeps chatting at some ridiculous tale, very much in the way of a garrulous old man in his dotage.*

* The old gentleman who is represented as speaking, in Bun

VI. *Choleric Drunkard.*—There are a variety of drunkards whom I can only class under the above title. They seem to possess few of the qualities of the other races, and are chiefly distinguished by an uncommon testiness of disposition. They are quick, irritable, and impatient, but withal good at heart, and, when in humour, very pleasant and generous. They are easily put out of temper, but it returns almost immediately. This disposition is very prevalent among Welshmen and Highland lairds. Mountaineers are usually quick tempered: but such men are not the worst or most unpleasant. Sterne is undoubtedly right when he says that more virtue is to be found in warm than cold dispositions. Commodore Trunnion is a marked example of this temperament; and Captain Fluellen, who compelled the *heroic* Pistol to eat the leek, is another.

VII. *Periodical Drunkard.*—There are persons whose temperaments are so peculiarly constituted, that they indulge to excess *periodically*, and are, in the intervals of these indulgences, remarkably sober. This is not a very common case, but I have known more than one instance of it; and a gentleman, distinguished by the power of his eloquence in the senate and at the bar, is said to furnish another. In the cases which I have known, the drunken mania, for it can get no other name, came on three or four time a-year. The persons from a state of complete sobriety, felt the most intense desire for drink; and no power, short of absolute force or confinement, could restrain them from the indulgence. In every case they seemed to be quite aware of the uncontrollable nature of their passion, and proceeded systematically by confining themselves to their room, and procuring a large quantity of ardent spirits. As soon as this was done, they commenced and drank to excess till vomiting ensued, and the stomach absolutely refused to receive another drop of liquor. This state may last a few days or a few weeks according to constitutional strength, or the rapidity with which the libations are poured down. During the continuance of the attack, the individual exhibits such a state of mind as may be looked for from his peculiar temperament; he may be sanguineous, or melancholy, or surly, or phlegmatic, or nervous, or choleric. So soon as the stomach rejects enery thing that is swallowed, and severe sickness comes on, the fit ceases. From that moment recovery takes place, and the former fondness for liquor is succeeded by aversion or disgust. This gains such ascendency over him, that he abstains religiously from it for weeks, or months, or even for a year, as the case may be. During this interval he leads a life of the most exemplary temperance, drinking nothing but cold water, and probably shunning every society where he is likely to be exposed to indulgence. So soon as this period of sobriety has expired, the fit again comes on; and he continues playing the same game for perhaps the better part of a long life. This class of persons I would call periodical drunkards.

These different varieties are sometimes found strongly marked; at other times so blended together that it is not easy to say which predominates. The most agreeable drunkard is he whose temperament lies between the sanguineous and the melancholic. The genuine sanguineous is a sad noisy dog, and so common that every person must have met with him. The naval service furnishes a great many gentlemen of this description. The phlegmatic, I think, is rarer, but both the nervous and the surly are not unusual.

CHAPTER V.

DRUNKENNESS MODIFIED BY THE INEBRIATING AGENT.

Intoxication is not only influenced by temperament, but by the nature of the agent which produces it. Thus, ebriety from ardent spirits differs in some particulars from that brought on by opium or malt liquors, such as porter and ale.

I. *Modified by Ardent Spirits.*—Alcohol is the principle of intoxication in all liquors. It is this which gives to wine,* ale, and spirits, their characteristic properties. In the natural state, however, it is so pungent, that it could not be received into the stomach, even in a moderate quantity, without producing death. It can, therefore, only be used in dilution; and in this state we have it, from the strongest ardent spirits, to simple small beer. The first (ardent spirits) being the most concentrated of its combinations, act most rapidly upon the constitution. They are more inflammatory, and intoxicate sooner than any of the others. Swallowed in an overdose, they act almost instantaneously—extinguishing the senses and overcoming the whole body with a sudden stupor. When spirits are swallowed raw, as in the form of a dram, they excite a glow of heat in the throat and stomach, succeeded, in those who are not much accustomed to their use, by a flushing of the countenance, and a copious discharge of tears. They are strongly diuretic.

Persons who indulge too much in spirits rarely get corpulent, unless their indulgence be coupled with good living. Their bodies become emaciated; they get spindle-shanked; their eyes are glazed and hollow; their cheeks fall in; and a premature old age overtakes them. They do not eat so well as their brother drunkards. An insatiable desire for a morning dram makes them early risers, and their breakfast amounts to almost nothing.

The principal varieties of spirits, as already mentioned, are rum, brandy, whiskey, and gin. It is needless to enter into any detail of the history of these fluids. Brandy kills soonest; it takes most rapidly to the head, and, more readily than the others, tinges the face to a crimson or livid hue. Rum is probably the next in point of fatality; and, after that, whiskey and gin. The superior diuretic qualities of the two latter, and the less luscious sources from whence they are procured, may possibly account for such differences. I am at the same time aware that some persons entertain a different idea of the relative danger of these liquors: some, for instance, conceive that gin is more rapidly fatal than any of them; but it is to be remembered, that it, more than any other ardent spirit, is liable to adulteration. That, from this circumstance, more lives may be lost by its use, I do not deny. In speaking of gin, however, and comparing its effects with those of the rest of the class to which it belongs, I must be understood to speak of it in its pure condition, and not in that detestable state of sophistication in which such vast quantities of it are drunk in London and elsewhere. When pure, I have no hesitation in affirming that it is decidedly more wholesome than either brandy or rum; and that the popular belief of its greater tendency to produce dropsy, is quite unfounded.

An experiment has lately been made for the purpose of ascertaining the comparative powers of gin, brandy, and rum upon the human body, which is not less remarkable for the inconsequent conclusions deduced from it, than for the ignorance it displays in confounding dead animal matter with the living fibre. It was made as follows:—

A piece of raw liver was put into a glass of gin, another into a glass of rum, and a third into a glass of brandy. That in the gin was, in a given time, partially decomposed; that in the rum, in the same time, not diminished; and that in the brandy quite dissolved. It was concluded from these results, that rum was the most wholesome spirit of the three, and brandy the

bury's admirable caricature of the 'Long Story,' furnishes one of the best illustrations I have ever seen of this variety. It is worth consulting, both on account of the story-teller, and the effect his tedious garrulity produced upon the company.

* Alcohol appears to exist in wines, in a very peculiar state of combination. In the Appendix, I have availed myself of Dr Paris's valuable remarks on this subject.

least. The inferences deduced from these premises are not only erroneous, but glaringly absurd; the premises would even afford grounds for drawing results of the very opposite nature: it might be said, for instance, that though brandy be capable of dissolving dead animal matter, there is no evidence that it can do the same to the living stomach, and that it would in reality prove less hurtful than the others, in so far as it would, more effectually than they, dissolve the food contained in that organ. These experiments, in fact, prove nothing; and could only have been suggested by one completely ignorant of the functions of the animal economy. There is a power inherent in the vital principle which resists the laws that operate upon dead matter. This is known to every practitioner, and is the reason why the most plausible and recondite speculations of chemistry have come to naught in their trials upon the living frame. The only way to judge of the respective effects of ardent spirits, is by experience and physiological reasoning, both of which inform us that the spirit most powerfully diuretic must rank highest in the scale of safety. Now and then persons are met with on whose frames both gin and whiskey have a much more heating effect than the two other varieties of spirits. This, however, is not common, and when it does occur, can only be referred to some accountable idiosyncrasy of constitution.

II. *Modified by Wines.*—Drunkenness from wines closely resembles that from ardent spirits. It is equally airy and volatile, more especially if the light wines, such as Champagne, Claret, Chambertin, or Volnay, be drunk. On the former, a person may get tipsy several times of a night. The fixed air evolved from it produces a feeling analogous to ebriety, independent of the spirit it contains. Port, Sherry, and Madeira are heavier wines, and have a stronger tendency to excite headache and fever.

The wine-bidder has usually an ominous rotundity of face, and, not unfrequently, of corporation. His nose is well studded over with carbuncles of the claret complexion; and the red of his cheeks resembles very closely the hue of that wine. The drunkard from ardent spirits is apt to be poor, miserable, emaciated figure, broken in mind and in fortune; but the votary of the juice of the grape may usually boast the 'paunch well lined with capon,' and calls to recollection the bluff figure of Sir John Falstaff over his potations of sack.*

III. *Modified by Malt Liquors.*—Malt liquors under which title we include all kinds of porter and ales, produce the worst species of drunkenness; as, in addition to the intoxicating principle, some noxious ingredients are usually added, for the purpose of preserving them and giving them their bitter. The hop of these fluids is highly narcotic, and brewers often add other substances, to heighten its effect, such as hyoscyamus, opium, belladonna, cocculus Indicus, lauro cerasus, &c. Malt liquors, therefore, act in two ways upon the body, partly by the alcohol they contain, and partly by the narcotic principle. In addition to this, the fermentation which they undergo is much less perfect than that of spirits or wine. After being swallowed, this process is carried on in the stomach, by which fixed air is copiously liberated, and the digestion of delicate stomachs materially impaired. Cider, spruce, ginger, and table beers, in consequence of their imperfect fermentation, often produce the same bad effects, long after their first briskness has vanished.

Persons addicted to malt liquors increase enormously in bulk. They become loaded with fat; their chin gets double or triple, the eye prominent, and the whole face bloated and stupid. Their circulation is clogged, while the pulse feels like a cord, and is full and laboring, but not quick. During sleep, the breathing is stertorous. Every thing indicates an excess of blood; and when a pound or two is taken away, immense relief is obtained. The blood, in such cases, is more dark and sizy than in the others. In seven cases out of ten, malt liquor drunkards die of apoplexy or palsy. If they escape this hazard, swelled liver or dropsy carries them off. The abdomen seldom loses its prominency, but the lower extremities get ultimately emaciated. Profuse bleedings frequently ensue from the nose, and save life, by emptying the blood-vessels of the brain.

The drunkenness in question is peculiarly of British growth. The most noted examples of it are to be found in innkeepers and their wives, recruiting sergeants, guards of stage-coaches, &c. The quantity of malt liquors which such persons will consume in a day is prodigious. Seven English pints is quite a common allowance, and not unfrequently twice that quantity is taken without any perceptible effect. Many of the coal-heavers on the Thames think nothing of drinking daily two gallons of porter, especially in the summer season, when they labor under profuse perspiration. A friend has informed me that he knew an instance of one of them having consumed eighteen pints in one day, and he states that there are many such instances.*

The effects of malt liquors on the body, if not so immediately rapid as those of ardent spirits, are more stupifying, more lasting, and less easily removed. The last are particularly prone to produce levity and mirth, but the first have a stunning influence on the brain, and, in a short time, render dull and sluggish the gayest disposition. They also produce sickness and vomiting more readily than either spirits or wine.

Both wine and malt liquors have a greater tendency to swell the body than ardent spirits. They form blood with greater rapidity, and are altogether more nourishing. The most dreadful effects, upon the whole, are brought on by spirits, but drunkenness from malt liquors is the most speedily fatal. The former break down the body by degrees, the latter operate by some instantaneous apoplexy or rapid inflammation.

No one has ever given the respective characters of the malt liquor and ardent spirit drunkard with greater truth than Hogarth, in his Beer Alley and Gin Lane. The first is represented as plump, rubicund, and bloated; the second as pale, tottering, and emaciated, and dashed over with the aspect of blank despair.

IV. *Modified by Opium.*—The drunkenness produced by opium has also some characteristics which it is necessary to mention. The drug is principally employed by the Mahometans. By their religion, these people are forbidden the use of wine,† and use opium as a substitute. And a delightful substitute it is while the first excitation continues; for images it occasions in the mind are more exquisite than any produced even by wine.

There is reason to believe that the use of this medicine has, of late years, gained ground in Great Britain. We are told by the 'English Opium-Eater,' whose powerful and interesting 'Confessions' have excited so deep an interest, that the practice exists among the work people at Manchester. Many of our fashionable ladies have recourse to it when troubled with vapours, or low spirits; some of them even carry it about with them for the purpose. This practice is most perni-

* There is reason to believe that the Sack of Shakspeare was Sherry.—'Falstaff. You rogue! here's *lime* in this Sack too. There is nothing but roguery to be found in villanous man. Yet a coward is worse than a cup of Sack with lime in it.'—Lime, it is well known, is added to the grapes in the manufacture of Sherry. This not only gives the wine what is called its dry quality, but probably acts by neutralizing a portion of the malic or tartaric acid.

* 'It is recorded of a Welsh squire, William Lewis, who died in 1793, that he drank *eight gallons* of ale *per diem*, and weighed forty stones.'—*Wadd's Comments on Corpulency.*

† 'The law of Mahomet which prohibits the drinking of wine, is a law fitted to the climate of Arabia; and, indeed, before Mahomet's time, water was the common drink of the Arabs. The law which forbade the Carthaginians to drink wine, was also a law of the climate.'—*Montesquieu, Book*, xiv. *Chap.* x.

cious, and no way different from that of drunkards, who swallow wine and other liquors to drive away care. While the first effects continue, the intended purpose is sufficiently gained, but the melancholy which follows is infinitely greater than can be compensated by the previous exhilaration.

Opium acts differently on different constitutions. While it disposes some to calm, it arouses others to fury. Whatever passion predominates at the time, it increases; whether it be love, or hatred, or revenge, or benevolence. Lord Kames, in his Sketches of Man, speaks of the fanatical Faquirs, who, when excited by this drug, have been known, with poisoned daggers, to assail and butcher every European whom they could overcome. In the century before last, one of this nation attacked a body of Dutch sailors, and murdered seventeen of them in one minute. The Malays are strongly addicted to opium. When violently aroused by it, they sometimes perform what is called *Running-a-Muck*, which consists in rushing out in a state of phrensied excitement, heightened by fanaticism, and murdering every one who comes in their way. The Turkish commanders are well aware of the powers of this drug in inspiring an artificial courage; and frequently give it to their men when they put them on any enterprise of great danger.

Some minds are rendered melancholy by opium. Its usual effect, however, is to give rise to lively and happy sensations. The late Duchess of Gordon is said to have used it freely, previous to appearing in great parties, where she wished to shine by the gayety of her conversation and brilliancy of her wit. A celebrated pleader at the Scotch bar is reported to do the same thing, and always with a happy effect.

In this country opium is much used, but seldom with the view of producing intoxication. Some, indeed, deny that it can do so, strictly speaking. If by intoxication is meant a state precisely similar to that from over-indulgence in vinous or spiritous liquors, they are undoubtedly right; but drunkenness merits a wider latitude of signification. The ecstacies of opium are much more entrancing than those of wine. There is more poetry in its visions—more mental aggrandizement—more range of imagination. Wine, in common with it, invigorates the animal powers and propensities, but opium, in a more peculiar manner, strengthens those proper to man, and gives, for a period amounting to hours, a higher tone to the intellectual faculties. It inspires the mind with a thousand delightful images, lifts the soul from earth, and casts a halo of poetic thought and feeling over the spirits of the most unimaginative. Under its influence, the mind wears no longer that blank passionless aspect which, even in gifted natures, it is apt to assume. On the contrary, it is clothed with beauty 'as with a garment,' and colours every thought that passes through it with the hues of wonder and romance. Such are the feelings which the luxurious and opulent mussulman seeks to enjoy. To stir up the languid current of his mind, satiated with excess of pleasure and rendered sluggish by indolence, he has recourse to that remedy which his own genial climate produces in greatest perfection. Seated perhaps amid the luxuries of Oriental splendour—with fountains bubbling around, and the citron shading him with its canopy, and scattering perfume on all sides—he lets loose the reins of an imagination conversant from infancy with every thing gorgeous and magnificent. The veil which shades the world of fancy is withdrawn, and the wonders lying behind it exposed to view; he sees palaces and temples in the clouds; or the Paradise of Mahomet, with its houris and bowers of amaranth, may stand revealed to his excited senses. Every thing is steeped in poetic exaggeration. The zephyrs seem converted into aerial music, the trees bear golden fruit, the rose blushes with unaccustomed beauty and perfume. Earth, in a word, is brought nearer to the sky, and becomes one vast Eden of pleasure. Such are the first effects of opium; but in proportion as they are great, so is the depression which succeeds them. Languor and exhaustion invariably come after; to remove which, the drug is again had recourse to, and becomes almost an essential of existence.

Opium retains at all times its power of exciting the imagination, provided sufficient doses are taken. But, when it has been continued so long as to bring disease upon the constitution, the pleasurable feelings wear away, and are succeeded by others of a very different kind. Instead of disposing the mind to be happy, it now acts upon it like the spell of a demon, and calls up phantoms of horror and disgust. The fancy is still as powerful as ever, but it is turned in another direction. Formerly it clothed all objects with the light of heaven; now it invests them with the attributes of hell. Goblins, spectres, and every kind of distempered vision haunt the mind, peopling it with dreary and revolting imagery. The sleep is no longer cheered with its former sights of happiness. Frightful dreams usurp their place, till, at last, the person becomes the victim of an almost perpetual misery.* Nor is this confined to the mind alone, for the body suffers in an equal degree. Emaciation, loss of appetite, sickness, vomiting, and a total disorganization of the digestive functions, as well as of the mental powers, are sure to ensue, and never fail to terminate in death, if the evil habit which brings them on is continued.

Opium resembles the other agents of intoxication in this, that the fondness for it increases with use, and that at last, it becomes nearly essential for bodily comfort and peace of mind. The quantity which may be taken varies exceedingly, and depends wholly upon age, constitution, and habit. A single drop of laudanum has been known to kill a new-born child; and four grains of solid opium have destroyed an adult. Certain diseases such as fevers, phrensies, &c., facilitate the action of opium upon the system; others, such as diarrhœa, cramp, &c., resist it; and a quantity which would destroy life in the former, would have little perceptible effect in the latter. By habit, enormous quantities of the drug may be taken with comparative impunity. There are many persons in this country who make a practice of swallowing half an ounce of laudanum night and morning, and some will even take from one to two drachms daily of solid opium. The Teriakis, or opium-eaters of Constantinople, will sometimes swallow a hundred grains at a single dose. Nay, it is confidently affirmed that some of them will take at once three drachms in the morning, and repeat the same dose at night, with no other effect than a pleasing exhilaration of spirits. The 'English Opium-Eater' himself, furnishes one of the most extraordinary instances on record of the power of habit in bringing the body to withstand this drug. He took daily *eight thousand drops* of laudanum, containing *three hundred and twenty grains* of opium. This enormous quantity

* The following description, by a modern traveller, of a scene witnessed by him in the East, gives a lively picture of the effects of this drug:—

'There is a decoction of the head and seeds of the poppy, which they call Coquenar, for the sale of which there are taverns in every quarter of the town, similar to our coffee-houses. It is extremely amusing to visit these houses, and to observe carefully those who resort there for the purpose of drinking it, both before they have taken the dose, before it begins to operate, and while it is operating. On entering the tavern, they are dejected and languishing: soon after they have taken two or three cups of this beverage, they are peevish, and as it were enraged; every thing displeases them. They find fault with every thing, and quarrel with one another, but in the course of its operation they make it up again;—and, each one giving himself up to his predominant passion, the lover speaks sweet things to his idol—another, half asleep, laughs in his sleeps—a third talks big and blusters—a fourth tells ridiculous stories. In a word, a person would believe himself to be really in a mad-house. A kind of lethergy and stupidity succeed to this disorder y gayety; but the Persians, far from treating it as it deserves, call it an ecstacy, and maintain that there is something exquisite and heavenly in this state.'—*Chardin.*

he reduced suddenly, and without any considerable effort, to *one thousand drops*, or *forty grains*. 'Instantaneously,' says he, 'and as if by magic, the cloud of profoundest melancholy which rested upon my brain, like some black vapours which I have seen roll away from the summits of the mountains, drew of in one day—passed off with its murky banners, as simultaneously as a ship that has been stranded, and is floated off by the spring-tide.'

The circumstance of the body being brought by degrees to withstand a great quantity of opium is not solitary, but exists as a general rule with regard to all stimulants and narcotics. A person who is in the habit of drinking ale, wine, or spirits, will take much more with impunity than one who is not; and the faculty of withstanding these agents goes on strengthening till it acquires a certain point, after which it becomes weakened. When this takes place, their is either organic disease or general debility. A confirmed drunkard, whose constitution has suffered from indulgence, can not take so much liquor, without feeling it, as one who is in the habit of taking his glass, but whose strength is yet unimpaired. It is, I suspect, the same, though probably in a less degree, with regard to opium.

Mithridates, king of Pontus, affords an instance of the effects of habit in enabling the body to withstand poisons: and on the same principle, we find that physicians and nurses who are much exposed to infection, are less liable than those persons whose frames are not similarly fortified.

Opium resembles wine, spirit, and ales, in effecting the brain and disposing to apoplexy. Taken in an over-dose, it is fatal in from six to twenty-four hours, according to the quantity swallowed, and the constitution, habits, &c., of the persons submitted to its operation. The following are the principal symptoms of poisoning from opium. Giddiness succeeded by stupor; insensibility to light, while the eyes are closed, and the pupil immoveable, and sometimes dilated. The pulse is generally small and feeble, but, occasionally, slow and full, as in common apoplexy. The breathing at first is scarcely perceptible, but is apt to become stertorous. Foam sometimes issues from the mouth: in other cases there is vomiting. The countenance is cadaverous and pale or livid. A narcotic odour is often perceptible in the breath. The skin is cold, and the body exceedingly relaxed; now and then it is convulsed. By being struck shaken, or excited any way, the person sometimes recovers for a short period from his stupor, and stares wildly around him, but only to relapse into lethargy. At last death ensues, but shortly before this event, a deceitful show of animation occasionally makes its appearance, and may impose upon superficial observers.

I extract the following interesting case of opium-eating from a London paper:—

'An inquest was held at Walpole lately, on the body of Rebecca Eason, aged five years, who had been diseased from her birth, was unable to walk or articulate, and from her size, did not appear to be more than *five weeks* old. The mother had for many years been in the habit of taking opium in large quantities, (nearly a quarter of an ounce a day;*) and, it is supposed, had entailed a disease on her child which caused its death; it was reduced to a mere skeleton, and had been in that state from birth. Verdict; 'Died by the visitation of God; but from the great quantity of opium taken by the mother during her pregnancy of the said child, and of sucking it, she had greatly injured its health.' It appeared that the mother of the deceased had had five children; that she began to take opium after the birth and weaning of her first child, which was and is remarkably healthy; and that the other children have all lingered and died in the same emaciated state as the child who was the subject of this investigation. The mother is under thirty: she was severely censured by the coroner for indulging in so pernicious a practice.'

* Equal to nearly three thousand drops of laudanum.

V. *Modified by Tobacco.*—A variety of drunkenness is excited by tobacco. This luxury was introduced into Enrope from the new world, in 1559, by a Spanish gentleman, named Hernandez de Toledo, who brought a small quantity into Spain and Portugal. From thence, by the agency of the French ambassador at Lisbon, it found its way to Paris, where it was used in the form of powder by Catherine de Medicis, the abandoned instigator of the massacre of the Protestants on St. Bartholomew's day. This woman, therefore, may be considered the inventor of snuff, as well as the contriver of that most atrocious transaction. It then came under the patronage of the Cardinal Santa Crocé, the Pope's nuncio, who, returning from his embassy at the Spanish and Portuguese courts, carried the plant to his own country, and thus acquired a fame little inferior to that which, at another period, he had won by piously bringing a portion of the *real* cross from the Holy Land. It was received with general enthusiasm in the Papal States, and hardly less favorably in England, into which it was introduced by Sir Walter Raleigh, in 1585. It was not, however, without opposition that it gained a footing either in this country or in the rest of Europe. Its principal opponents were the priests, the physicians, and the sovereign princes; by the former, its use was declared sinful; and in 1624, Pope Urban VIII. published a bull, excommunicating all persons found guilty of taking snuff when in church. This bull was renewed in 1690 by Pope Innocent; and about twenty-nine years afterwards, the Sultan Amurath IV. made smoking a capital offence, on the ground of its producing infertility. For a long time smoking was forbidden in Russia, under the pain of having the nose cut off: and in some parts of Switzerland, it was likewise made a subject of public prosecution—the public regulations of the Canton of Berne, in 1661, placing the prohibition of smoking in the list of the ten commandments, immediately under that against adultery. Nay, that British Solomon James I. did not think it beneath the royal dignity to take up his pen upon the subject. He accordingly, in 1603, published his famous 'Counterblaste to Tobacco,' in which the following remarkable passage occurs:—'It is a custom loathsome to the eye, hateful to the nose, harmful to the brain, dangerous to the lungs, and, in the black stinking fume thereof, nearest resembling the horrible Stygian smoke of the pit that is bottomless.'* But notwithstanding this regal and sacerdotal wrath, the plant extended itself far and wide, and is at this moment the most universal luxury in existence.

The effects of tobacco are considerably different from those of any other inebriating agent. Instead of quickening, it lowers the pulse, and, when used to excess, produces languor, depression of the system, giddiness, confusion of ideas, violent pain in the stomach, vomiting, convulsions, and even death. Its essential oil is so intensely powerful, that two or three drops inserted into a raw wound, would prove almost instantly fatal.* Mr Barrow, in his travels, speaks of the use

* 'Tobacco,' King James farther observes, 'is the lively image and pattern of hell, for it hath, by allusion, in it all the parts and vices of the world, whereby hell may be gained; to wit, first, it is a smoke; so are all the vanities of this world. Secondly, it delightest them that take it; so do all the pleasures of the world delight the men of the world. Thirdly, it maketh men *drunken* and light in the head; so do all the vanities of the world, men are drunken therewith. Fourthly, he that taketh tobacco cannot leave it; it doth bewitch him; even so the pleasures of the world make men loath to leave them; they are, for the most part, enchanted with them. And, farther, besides all this, it is like hell in the very substance of it, for it is a stinking loathsome thing, and so is hell.' And, moreover, his majesty declares, that 'were he to invite the devil to a dinner, he should have three dishes; first, a pig; second, a poll of ling and mustard; and, third, a pipe of tobacco for digestion.'

† It appears from Mr. Brodie's experiments, that the essential

made by the Hottentots of this plant, for the purpose of destroying snakes. 'A Hottentot,' says he, 'applied some of it from the short end of his wooden tobacco pipe to the mouth of a snake while darting out his tongue. The effect was as instantaneous as an electric shock; with a convulsive motion that was momentary, the snake half untwisted itself, and never stirred more; and the muscles were so contracted, that the whole animal felt hard and rigid, as if dried in the sun.' When used in moderation, tobacco has a soothing effect upon the mind, disposing to placid enjoyment, and mellowing every passion into repose. Its effects, therefore, are inebriating; and those who habitually indulge in it may with propriety be denominated drunkards. In whatever form it is used, it produces sickness, stupor, bewilderment, and staggering, in those unaccustomed to its use. There is no form in which it can be taken that is not decidedly injurious and disgusting. The whole, from snuffing to plugging, are at once so utterly uncleanly and unnatural, that it is incredible in what manner they ever insinuated themselves into civilized society. A vast quantity of valuable time is wasted by the votaries of tobacco, especially by the smokers; and that the devotees of snuff are not greatly behind in this respect, will be shown by the following singular calculation of Lord Stanhope:—

'Every professed, inveterate, incurable snuff-taker,' says his Lordship, 'at a moderate computation, takes one pinch in ten minutes. Every pinch, with the agreeable ceremony of blowing and wiping the nose, and other incidental circumstances, consumes a minute and a half. One minute and a half out of every ten, allowing sixteen hours to a snuff-taking day, amounts to two hours and twenty-four minutes out of every natural day, or one day out of ten. One day out of every ten amounts to thirty-six days and a half in a year. Hence, if we suppose the practice to be persisted in forty years, two entire years of the snuff-taker's life will be dedicated to tickling his nose and two more to blowing it. The expense of snuff, snuff-boxes, and handkerchiefs, will be the subject of a second essay, in which it will appear that this luxury encroaches as much on the income of the snuff-taker as it does on his time; and that by proper application of the time and money thus lost to the public, a fund might be constituted for the discharge of the national debt.'

But this is not the worst of snuffing, for though a moderate quantity taken now and then, may do no harm, yet, in the extent to which habitual snuffers carry it, it is positively pernicious. The membrane which lines the nose gets thickened, the olfactory nerves blunted, and the sense of smell consequently impaired. Nor is this all, for, by the strong inspirations which are made when the powder is drawn up, some of the latter is pretty sure to escape into the stomach. This organ is thence directly subjected to a powerful medicine, which not only acts as a narcotic, but produces heartburn and every other symptom of indigestion. It is generally believed that Napoleon owed his death to the morbid state of his stomach produced by excessive snuffing. Snuffing has also a strong tendency to give a determination to the head, and on this account plethoric subjects should be the very last ever to enter upon the habit. If it were attended with nó other inconvenience, the black loathsome discharge from the nose, and swelling and rubicundity of this organ, with other circumstances equally disagreeable, ought to deter every man from becoming a snuffer.

The smoker, while engaged at *his* occupation, is even a happier man than the snuffer. An air of peculiar satisfaction beams upon his countenance; and as he puffs forth volumes of fragrance, he seems to dwell in an atmosphere of contented happiness. His illusions have not the elevated and magnificent character of those brought on by opium or wine. There is nothing of Raphael or Michael Angelo in their composition—nothing of the Roman or Venitian schools—nothing of Milton's sublimity, or Ariosto's dazzling romance; but there is something equally delightful, and in its way, equally perfect. His visions stand in the same relation to those of opium or wine, as the Dutch pictures of Ostade to the Italian ones of Paul Veronese—as Washington Irving to Lord Byron—or as Izaak Walton to Froissart. There is an air of delightful homeliness about them. He does not let his imagination run riot in the clouds, but restrains it to the lower sphere of earth, and meditates delightfully in this less elevated region. If his fancy be unusually brilliant, or somewhat heated by previous drinking, he may see thousands of strange forms floating in the tobacco smoke. He may people it, according to his temperament, with agreeable or revolting images—with flowers and gems springing up, as in dreams before him—or with reptiles, serpents, and the whole host of *diablerie*, skimming, like motes in the sunshine, amid its curling wreaths.

This all that can be said in favour of smoking, and quite enough to render the habit too common to leave any hope of its suppression, either by the weapons of ridicule, or the more summary plan of the Sultan Amurath. In no sense, except as affording a temporary gratification, can it be justified or defended. It pollutes the breath, blackens the teeth, wastes the saliva which is required for digestion, and injures the complexion. In addition to this, it is apt to produce dyspepsia, and other disorders of the stomach; and in corpulent subjects, it disposes to apoplexy. At the present moment, smoking is fashionable, and crowds of young men are to be seen at all hours walking the streets with cigars in their mouths, annoying the passengers. They seem to consider it manly to be able to smoke a certain number, without reflecting that there is scarcely an old woman in the country who would not beat them to naught with their own weapons, and that they would gain no sort of honour were they able to outsmoke all the burgomasters of Amsterdam. As the practice, however, seems more resorted to by these young gentlemen for the sake of effect, and of exhibiting a little of the *haut ton*, than for any thing else, it is likely soon to die a natural death among them; particularly as jockeys and porters have lately taken the field in the same way, being determined that no class of the community shall enjoy the exclusive monopoly of street smoking.

The observatians made upon the effects of snuffing and smoking, apply in a still stronger degree to chewing. This is the worst way for the health in which tobacco can be used. The waste of saliva is greater than even in smoking, and the derangements of the digestive organs proportionably severe. All confirmed chewers are more than usually subject to dyspepsia and hypochondriasis: and many of them are afflicted with liver complaint, brought on by their imprudent habit.

The most innocent, and at the same time most disgusting way of using tobacco, is plugging, which consists in inserting a short roll of the plant in the nostril, and allowing it to remain there so long as the person feels disposed. Fortunately this habit is as rare as it is abominable; and it is to be hoped that it will never become common in Great Britain.

I have observed, that persons who are much addicted to liquor have an inordinate liking to tobacco in all its different forms: and it is remarkable that in the early stages of ebriety almost every man is desirous of having a pinch of snuff. This last fact it is not easy to explain, but the former may be accounted for by that incessant

oil of tobacco operates very differently from the infusion. The former acts instantly on the heart, suspending its action, even while the animal continues to inspire, and destroying life by producing syncope. The latter appears to operate solely on the brain, leaving the circulation unaffected.

craving after excitement which cling to the system of the confirmed drunkard.

From several of the foregoing circumstances, we are justified in considering tobacco closely allied to intoxicating liquor, and its confirmed votaries as a species of drunkards. At least, it is certain that when used to excess, it gives birth to many of the corporeal and mental manifestations of ebriety.

VI. *Modified by Nitrous Oxide.*—The drunkenness, if it merit that name, from inhaling nitrous oxide, is likewise of a character widely differing from intoxication in general. This gas was discovered by Dr Priestley, but its peculiar effects upon the human body were first perceived in 1799, by Sir Humphrey Davy, who, in the following year, published a very elaborate account of its nature and properties, interspersed with details by some of the most eminent literary and scientific characters of the sensations they experienced on receiving it into their lungs.

According to these statements, on breathing the gas the pulse is accelerated, and a feeling of heat and expansion pervades the chest. The most vivid and highly pleasurable ideas pass, at the same time, through the mind; and the imagination is exalted to a pitch of entrancing ectascy. The hearing is rendered more acute, the face is flushed, and the body seems so light that the person conceives himself capable of rising up and mounting into the air. Some assume theatrical attitudes; others laugh immoderately, and stamp upon the ground. There is an universal increase of muscular power, attended with the most exquisite delight. In a few cases there are melancholy, giddiness, and indistinct vision but generally the feelings are those of perfect pleasure. After these strange effects have ceased, no debility ensues, like that which commonly follows high excitement. On the contrary, the mind is strong and collected, and the body unusually vigorous for some hours after the operation.

At the time of the discovery of the effects of nitrous oxide strong hopes were excited that it might prove useful in various diseases. These, unfortunately have not been realized. Even the alleged properties of the gas have now fallen into some discredit. That it has produced remarkable effects cannot be denied, but there is much reason for thinking that, in many cases, these were in a great measure brought about by the influence of imagination. Philosophers seem to be divided on this point and their conflicting testimonies it is not easy to reconcile. Having tried the experiment of inhaling the gas myself, and having seen it tried upon others, I have no doubt that there is much truth in the reports generally published of its properties, although in many cases, imagination has made these appear greater than they really are. The intoxication which it produces is entirely one *sui generis*, and differs so much from that produced by other agents, that it can hardly be looked upon as the same thing.

The effects of nitrous oxide upon myself, though considerable, were not so striking as I have seen upon others. The principal feelings produced, were giddiness and violent beating in the head, such as occur in the acme of drunkenness. There was also a strong propensity to laugh: it occurs to me, however, that in my own case, and probably in some others, the risible tendency might be controlled by a strong effort of volition, in the same way as in most cases of drunkenness, were the effort imperatively requisite. Altogether I experienced nearly the sensations of highly excited ebriety. There was the same seeming lightness and expansion of the head, the same mirthfulness of spirit, and the same inordinate propensity to do foolish things, knowing them to be foolish, as occur in drunkenness in general. I was perfectly aware what I was about, and could, I am persuaded, with some effort, have subjected the whimsies of fancy to the sober dictates of judgment. In a word, the gas produced precisely a temporary paroxysm of drunkenness, and such a determination of blood upwards as rendered the complexion livid, and left behind some degree of headache. Such are the effects upon myself, but with most people, there is a total unconsciousness of the part they are acting. They perform the most extravagant pranks, and on recovering their self-possession are totally ignorant of the circumstance. Sometimes the gas has an opposite effect, and the person instantly drops down insensible, as if struck by lightning: he recovers, however, immediately. Those who wish to know more of this curious subject, should read Sir H. Davy's work, but, above all, they should try the gas upon themselves. In the mean time I shall lay before the reader the details, in their own words, of the sensations experienced by Messrs Edgeworth and Coleridge, and by Dr Kinglake.

Mr Edgeworth's Case.—'My first sensation was an universal and considerable tremor. I then perceived some giddiness in my head, and a violent dizziness in my sight; these sensations by degrees subsided, and I felt a great propensity to bite through the wooden mouth-piece, or the tube of the bag through which I inspired the air. After I had breathed all the air that was in the bag, I eagerly wished for more. I then felt a strong propensity to laugh, and did burst into a violent fit of laughter, and capered about the room without having the power of restraining myself. By degrees, these feelings subsided, except the tremor, which lasted for an hour after I had breathed the air, and I felt a weakness in my knees. The principal feeling through the whole of the time, or what I should call the characteristical part of the effect, was a total difficulty of restraining my feelings, both corporeal and mental, or, in other words, not having any command of myself.'

Mr Coleridge's Case.—'The first time I inspired the nitrous oxide, I felt an highly pleasurable sensation of warmth over my whole frame, resembling that which I once remember to have experienced after returning from a walk in the snow into a warm room. The only motion which I felt inclined to make, was that of laughing at those who were looking at me. My eyes felt distended, and, towards the last, my heart beat as if it were leaping up and down. On removing the mouth-piece, the whole sensation went off almost instantly.

'The second time, I felt the same pleasurable sensation of warmth, but not, I think, in quite so great a degree. I wished to know what effect it would have on my impressions: I fixed my eye on some trees in the distance, but I did not find any other effect, except that they became dimmer and dimmer, and looked at last as if I had seen them through tears. My heart beat more violently than the first time. This was after a hearty dinner.

'The third time, I was more violently acted on than in the two former. Towards the last, I could not avoid, nor indeed felt any wish to avoid, beating the ground with my feet; and, after the mouth-piece was removed, I remained for a few seconds motionless, in great ecstacy.

'The fourth time was immediately after breakfast. The first few inspirations affected me so little, that I thought Mr Davy had given me atmospheric air; but soon felt the warmth beginning about my chest, and spreading upward and downward, so that I could feel its progress over my whole frame. My heart did not beat so violently; my sensations were highly pleasurable, not so intense or apparently local, but of more unmingled pleasure than I had ever before experienced.'

Dr Kinglake's Case.—'My first inspiration of it was limited to four quarts, diluted with an equal quantity of atmospheric air. After a few inspirations, a sense of additional freedom and power (call it energy, if you please) agreeably pervaded the region of the lungs; this was quickly succeeded by an almost delirious but highly pleasurable sensation in the brain, which was soon diffused over the whole frame, imparting to the muscular power at once an increased disposition and tone for action; but the mental effect of the excitement was such as to absorb in a sort of intoxicating placidity and delight, volition, or rather the power of voluntary motion. These effects were in a greater or less degree protracted during about five minutes, when the former state returned, with the difference however of feeling more cheerful and alert, for several hours after.

'It seemed also to have had the farther effect of reviving rheumatic irritations in the shoulder and knee-joints, which had not been previously felt for many months. No perceptible change was induced in the pulse, either at or subsequent to the time of inhaling the gas.

'The effects produced by a second trial of its powers, were more extensive, and concentrated on the brain. In this instance, nearly six quarts undiluted, were accurately and fully inhaled. As on the former occasion, it immediately proved agreeably respirable, but before the whole quantity was quite exhausted, its agency was exerted so strongly on the brain, as progressively to suspend the senses of seeing, hearing, feeling, and ultimately the power of volition itself. At this period, the pulse was much augmented both in force and frequency; slight convulsive twitches of muscles of the arms were also induced; no painful sensation, nausea, or languor, however, either preceded, accompanied or followed this state, nor did a minute elapse before the brain rallied, and resumed its wonted faculties, when a sense of glowing warmth extended over the system, was speedily succeeded by a re-instatement of the equilibrium of health.

'The more permanent effects were (as in the first experiment) an invigorated feel of vital power, improved spirits, transient irritations in different parts, but not so characteristically rheumatic as in the former instance.

'Among the circumstances most worthy of regard in considering the properties and administration of this powerfnl aerial agent, may be ranked, the fact of its being contrary to the prevailing opinion, both respirable, and salutary; that it impresses the brain and system at large with a more or less strong and durable degree of pleasurable sensation; that unlike the effect of other violently exciting agents, no sensible exhaustion or diminution of vital power accrues from the exertions of its stmulant property; that its most excessive operation even, is neither permanently nor transiently debilitating; and finally, that it fairly promises, under judicious application, to prove an extremely efficient remedy, as well in the vast tribe of diseases originating from deficient irritability and sensibility, as in those proceeding from morbid associations, and modifications of those vital principles.'*

CHAPTER VI.

ENUMERATION OF THE LESS COMMON INTOXICATING AGENTS.

In this chapter, I shall content myself with the enumeration of a few of the less common intoxicating agents. To detail all the productions of nature which have the power of inebriating, would be an endless and uninteresting topic.

Hemlock.—A powerful narcotic, producing giddiness, elevation of spirits, and other symptoms of ebriety. It was by an effusion of the leaf of this plant that Socrates was poisoned.

Leopard's-bane.—(*Arnica montana.*)—Properties analogous to those of hemlock and other narcotics.

Bangue.—This is the leaf of a species of wild hemp, growing on the shores of Turkey, and of the Grecian Archipelago. It possesses many of the properties of opium, and is used by the poorer classes of Mussulmen as a substitute for this drug. Before being used, it is dried, and the excissated leaves are either chewed entire, or reduced into a fine powder, and made into pills. Its effects are to elevate the spirits, dispel melancholy, and give increased energy to the corporeal faculties—followed by languor both of body and mind.

Hop.—Similar in its effects to opium, only inferior in degree. Used in porter brewing.

Wolf's-bane.—(*Aconitum napellus.*)—A most deadly narcotic, producing, in small doses, the usual symptoms of ebriety, such as giddiness, elevation of spirits, &c. When taken to excess it is inevitably fatal.

Cocculus Indicus.—The intoxicating powers of this berry are considerable. It is used by the brewers to increase the strength of porter and ales; and is sometimes thrown into ponds for the purpose of intoxicating the fishes, but they may thereby be more easily caught.

Foxglove.—(*Digitalis.*)—Likewise a powerful narcotic, and capable of producing many of the symptoms of drunkenness. It has the peculiar effect of lowering, instead of raising the pulse.

Nightshade.—(*Belladonna.*)—This is one of the most virulent narcotics we possess. Like opium, hop, and cocculus Indicus, it is used by brewers to augment the intoxicating properties of malt liquors. 'The Scots,' says Buchanan, 'mixed a quantity of the juice of the belladonna with the bread and drink with which, by their truce, they were bound to supply the Danes, which so intoxicated them, that the Scots killed the greater part of Sweno's army.'

'Some children ate, in a garden, the fruit of the belladonna, (*deadly nightshade.*) Shortly after, they had burning fever, with convulsions, and very strong palpitations of the heart; they lost their senses, and became completely delirious: one of them, four years of age, died the next day: the stomach contained some berries of the belladonna crushed, and some seeds; it exhibited three ulcers; the heart was livid, and the pericardium without serosity.'*

'One child ate four ripe berries of the belladonna, another ate six. Both one and the other were guilty of extravagancies which astonished the mother; their pupils were dilated; their countenances no longer remained the same; they had a cheerful delirium, accompanied with fever. The physician being called in, found them in a state of great agitation, talking at random, running, jumping, laughing sardonically; their countenances purple, and pulse hurried. He administered to each of them half a grain of emetic tartar and a drachm of glauber salt, in four or five ounces of water: they had copious evacuations during seven or eight hours, and the symptoms disappeared.'†

Henbane.—(*Hyoscyamus.*)—Similar in its properties to nightshade and opium. The intoxicating properties of hyoscyamus appear to have been known from a very early period. It was with this plant that the Assassin Prince, commonly called the 'Old Man of the Mountain,' inebriated his followers preparatory to installing them into his service. The following eloquent passage from a modern writer will prove interesting:—

'There was at Alamoot, and also at Masiat, in Syria, a delicious garden, encompassed with lofty walls, adorned with trees and flowers of every kind—with murmuring brooks and translucent lakes—with bowers of roses and trellises of the vine—airy halls and splendid kiosks, furnished with carpets of Persia and silks of Byzantium. Beautiful maidens and blooming boys were the inhabitants of this delicious spot, which resounded with the melody of birds, the murmur of

* The doses in these experiments, were from five to seven quarts

* Journal Générale de Médecine, lix. xxiv. p. 224.

† Gazette de Santé. 11 Thermidor, an xv. p. 508

streams, and the tones and voices of instruments—all respired contentment and pleasure. When the chief had noticed any youth to be distinguished for strength and resolution, he invited him to a banquet, where he placed him beside himself, conversed with him on the happiness reserved for the faithful, and contrived to administer to him an intoxicating draught, prepared from the *hyoscyamus*. While insensible, he was conveyed to the garden of delight, and there awakened by the application of vinegar. On opening his eyes, all Paradise met his view; the black-eyed and blue-robed houris surrounded him, obedient to his wishes; sweet music filled his ears; the richest viands were served up in the most costly vessels, and the choicest wines sparkled in golden cups. The fortunate youth believed himself really in the Paradise of the Prophet, and the language of his attendants confirmed the delusion. When he had had his filled enjoyment, and nature was yielding to exhaustion, the opiate was again administered, and the sleeper transported back io the side of the chief, to whom he communicated what had passed, and who assured him of the truth and reality of all he had experienced, telling him such was the bliss reserved for the obedient servants of the Imaum, and enjoining, at the same time, the strictest secrecy. Ever after, the rapturous vision possessed the imagination of the deluded enthusiast, and he panted for the hour when death, received in obeying the commands of his superior, should dismiss him to the bowers of Paradise.'*

Palm Wine.—This is prepared from the juice which exudes from the palm tree. Its properties are very inebriating; and it is an amusing fact to witness the stupor and giddiness into which the lizards frequenting these trees are thrown, by partaking of the juice which yields it. They exhibit all the usual phenomena of intoxication.

Camphor.—The intoxicating properties of camphor are considerable. It elevates the spirits, increases voluntary motion, and gives rise to vertigo; and these effects, as in the case of all narcotics, are succeeded by drowsiness, lassitude, and general depression. In large doses, syncope, convulsions, delirium, and even death, take place. It is sometimes used as a substitute for opium in cases of delirium, where, from particular circumstances, the latter either cannot be taken, or does not produce its usual effects. The common belief, however, of camphor being an antidote to this medicine, is quite unfounded. It neither decomposes opium, nor prevents it from acting poisonously upon the system: but, in consequence of its stimulating properties, it may be advantageously given in small doses to remove the stupor and coma produced by opium.

Saffron.—This aromatic possesses moderate intoxicating properties. Taken in sufficient doses, it accelerates the pulse, produces giddiness, raises the spirits, and gives rise to paroxysms of laughter. In a word, it exhibits many of the phenomena occasioned by over-indulgence in liquors, only in a very inferior degree.

Darnel.—Possesses slight intoxicating properties.

Clary.—Possesses slight intoxicating properties.

Carbonic Acid.—Carbonic acid partially inebriates, as is seen in drinking ginger beer, cider, Champagne, or even soda water, in which no alcoholic principle exists.

Ethers.—Ethers, when taken in quantity, give rise to a species of intoxication, which resembles that from ardent spirits in all respects, except in being more fugacious.

Intense Cold.—Intense cold produces giddiness, thickness of speech, confusion of ideas, and other symptoms of drunkenness. Captain Parry speaks of the effects so produced upon two young gentlemen who were exposed to an extremely low temperature. 'They looked wild,' says he, 'spoke thick and indistinctly, and it was impossible to draw from them a rational answer to any of our questions. After being on board for a short time, the mental faculties appeared gradually to return, and it was not till then that a looker-on could easily persuade himself that they had not been drinking too freely.'

* Von Hammer's Hist. of the Assassins.

CHAPTER VII.

DIFFERENCES IN THE ACTION OF OPIUM AND ALCOHOL.

The *modus operandi* of opium upon the body is considerably different from that of alcohol. The latter intoxicates chiefly by acting *directly* upon the nerves, the former by acting *secondarily* upon them, through the medium of absorption. This is easily proved by injecting a quantity of each into the cellular tissue of any animal, and comparing the effects with those produced when either is received into the stomach. M. Orfila* details some interesting experiments which he made upon dogs. In applying the watery extract of opium to them in the first manner, (by injection into the cellular tissue,) immediate stupor, convulsions, and debility ensue, and proved fatal in an hour or two. When, on the contrary, even a larger quantity was introduced into the stomach of the animal, it survived ten, twelve, or eighteen hours, although the œsophagus was purposely tied to prevent vomiting. The operation of alcohol was the reverse of this; for, when injected into the cellular substance, the effects were slight; but when carried into the stomach, they were powerful and almost instantaneous. This proves that opium acts chiefly by being taken up by the absorbents, as this is done much more rapidly by the drug being directly applied to a raw surface than in the stomach, where the various secretions and processes of digestion retard its absorption. Besides, alcohol taken in quantity produces instant stupefaction. It is no sooner swallowed than the person drops down insensible. Here is no time for absorption; the whole energies of the spirit are exerted against the nervous system. The same rapid privation of power never occurs after swallowing opium. There is always an interval, and generally one of some extent, between the swallowing and the stupor which succeeds. Another proof that opium acts in this manner, is the circumstance of its being much more speedily fatal than alcohol, when injected into the blood-vessels. Three or four grains in solution, forced into the carotid artery of a dog, will kill him in a few minutes. Alcohol, used in the same manner, would not bring on death for several hours.

In addition it may be stated, that a species of drunkenness is produced by inhaling the gas of intoxicating liquors. Those employed in bottling spirits from the cask, feel it frequently with great severity. This proves that there is a close sympathy between the nerves of the nose and lungs, and those of the stomach. From all these circumstances, it is pretty evident that intoxication from spirits is produced more by the direct action of the fluid upon the nerves of the latter organ, than by absorption.

Mr Brodie supposes that there is no absorption whatever of alcohol, and supports his views with a number of striking facts.* This, however, is a length to

* Toxiologi Générale.

† The following are the grounds on which he supports his doctrine:—'1. In experiments where animals have been killed by the injection of spirits into the stomach, I have found this organ to bear the marks of great inflammation, but never any preter natural appearances whatever in the brain. 2. The effects of spirits taken into the stomach, in the last experiment, were so instantaneous, that it appears impossible that absorption should have taken place before they were produced. 3. A person who is intoxicated frequently becomes suddenly sober after vomiting. 4. In the experiments which I have just related, I mixed tincture of rhubarb with the spirits, knowing, from the experiments of Mr Home and Mr William Brande, that this (*rhubarb*) when absorbed into the circulation, was readily separated from the blood by the kidneys, and that very small quantities might be

which I cannot go. I am inclined to think that though such absorption is not necessary to produce drunkenness, it generally takes place to a greater or lesser degree; nor can I conceive any reason why alcohol may not be taken into the circulation as well as any other fluid. My reasons for supposing that it is absorbed are the following:—1. The blood, breath, and perspiration of a confirmed drunkard differ from those of a sober man; the former being darker, and the two latter strongly impregnated with a spiritous odour. 2. The perspiration of the wine-drinker is often of the hue of his favourite liquor; after a debauch on Port, Burgundy, or Claret, it is not uncommon to see the shirt or sheets in which he lies, tinted to a rosy colour by the moisture which exudes from his body. 2. Madder, mercury, and sulphur, are received into the circulation unchanged; the former dyeing the bones, and the others exhaling through the pores of the skin, so as to communicate their peculiar odours to the person, and even discolour coins and other metallic substances in his pockets. The first of these reasons is a direct proof of absorption: the second shows, that as wine is received into the circulation, and passes throught it, alcohol may do the same; and the third furnishes collateral evidence of other agents exhibiting this phenomenon as well as spiritous liquors. The doctrine of absorption is supported by Dr Trotter,* who conceives that alcohol deoxygenizes the blood, and causes it to give out an unusual portion of hydrogen gas. The quantity of this gas in the bodies of drunkards is so great, that many have attempted to explain from it the circumstances of *Spontaneous Combustion*, by which it is alleged, the human frame has been sometimes destroyed, by being burned to ashes.

CHAPTER VIII.

PHYSIOLOGY OF DRUNKENNESS.

In administering medicines, the practitioner has a natural desire to learn the means by which they produce their effects upon the body. Thus, he is not contented with knowing that squill acts as a diuretic, and that mercury increases the secretion of the bile. He inquires by what process they do so; and understands that the first excites into increased action the secretory arteries of the kidneys, and the last the secretory veins of the liver. In like manner, he does not rest satisfied with the trite knowledge that wines, and spirits, and ales, produce intoxication: he extends his researches beyond this point, and is naturally anxious to ascertain by what peculiar action of the system these agents give rise to so extraordinary an effect.

All the agents of which we have spoken, with the exception of tobacco, whose action from the first is decidedly sedative, operate partly by stimulating the frame. They cause the heart to throb more vigorously, and the blood to circulate freer, while, at the same time, they exert a peculiar action upon the nervous system. The nature of this action, it is probable, will never be satisfactorily explained. If mere stimulation were all that was wanted, drunkenness ought to be present in many cases where it is never met with. It, or more properly speaking, its symptoms, ought to exist in inflammatory fever, and after violent exercise, such as running or hard walking. Inebriating agents, therefore, with few exceptions, have a twofold action. They both act by increasing the circulation, and by influencing the nerves; and the latter operation, there can be no doubt, is the more important of the two. Having stated this general fact, it will be better to consider the cause of each individual symptom in detail.

detected in the urine by the addition of potash; but though I never failed to find urine in the bladder, I never detected rhubarb in it.'—*Phil. Trans. of the Roy. Soc. of Lond.* 1811. part I. p. 178.

* Essay on Drunkenness.

I. *Vertigo.*—This is partly produced by the occular delusions under which the drunkard labours, but it is principally owing to other causes; as it is actually greater when the eyes are shut than when they are open—these causes, by the exclusion of light, being unaccountably increased. Vertigo, from intoxication, is far less liable to produce sickness and vomiting than from any other cause; and when it does produce them, it is to a very inconsiderable degree. These symptoms, in ninety-nine cases out of a hundred, arise from the disordered state of the stomach, and not, as we have elsewhere mentioned, from the accompanying giddiness. There are, indeed, a certain class of subjects who vomit and become pale, as soon as vertigo comes over them, but such are few in number compared with those whose stomachs are unaffected by this sensation. In swinging, smoking, sailing at sea, on turning rapidly round, sickness and vomiting are apt to occur; and there seems no doubt that they proceed in a great measure from the vertigo brought on by these actions. The giddiness of drunkenness, therefore, as it very rarely sickens, must be presumed to have some characters peculiar to itself. In this, as well as in some other affections, it seems to be the consequence of a close sympathy between the brain and nerves of the stomach; and whatever affects the latter organ, or any other viscus sympathizing with it, may bring it on equally with inebriating agents: calculi in the ureters or biliary ducts are illustrations of this fact. In intoxication, the giddiness is more strongly marked, because the powers both of body and mind are temporarily impaired, and the sensorium so disordered as to be unable to regulate the conduct.

A degree of vertigo may be produced by loading the stomach too rapidly and copiously after a long fast. Common food, in this instance, amounts to a strong stimulus in consequence of the state of the stomach, in which there was an unnatural want of excitement. This organ was in a state of torpor; and a stimulus which, in ordinary circumstances, would hardly have been felt, proves, in reality, highly exciting. For the same reason, objects have an unnatural luminousness when a person is suddenly brought from intense darkness to a brilliant light.

II. *Double Vision.*—The double vision which occurs in drunkenness may be readily accounted for by the influence of increased circulation in the brain upon the nerves of sight. In frenzy, and various fevers, the same phenomenon occurs. Every nerve is supplied with vessels; and it is conceivable that any unusual impulse of blood into the optics may so far affect that pair as to derange their actions. Whence, they convey false impressions to the brain, which is itself too much thrown off its just equilibrium to remedy, even if that under any circumstances were possible, the distorted images of the retina. The refraction of light in the tears, which are secreted more copiously than usual during intoxication, may also assist in multiplying objects to the eye.

III. *Staggering and Stammering.*—These symptoms are, in like manner, to be explained from the disordered state of the brain and nervous system. When the organ of sensation is affected, it is impossible that parts whose actions depend upon it can perform their functions well. The nervous fluid is probably carried to the muscles in a broken and irregular current, and the filaments which are scattered over the body are themselves directly stunned and paralyzed; hence, the insensibility to pain, and other external impressions. This insensibility extends everywhere, even to the organs of diglutition and speech. The utterance is thick and indistinct, indicating a loss of power in the lingual nerves which give action to the tongue; and the same want of energy seems to prevail in the gustatory branches which give it tase.

IV. *Heat and Flushing.*—These result from the strong determination of blood to the surface of the body. This reddens and tumefies the face and eyes, and excites an universal glow of heat. . Blood is the cause of animal heat, and the more it is determined to any part, the greater is the quantity of caloric evolved therefrom.

V. *Ringing in the Ears.*—This is accounted for by the generally increased action within the head, and more particularly by the throbbing of the internal carotid arteries which run in the immediate neighbourhood of the ears.

VI. *Elevation of Spirits.*—The mental pleasure of intoxication is not easily explained on physiological principles. We feel a delight in being rocked gently, in swinging on a chair, or in being tickled. These undoubtedly act upon the nerves, but in what manner, it would be idle to attempt investigating. Intoxicating agents no doubt do the same thing. The mental manifestations produced by their influence depend almost entirely upon the nerves, and are, unlike the corporeal ones, in a great measure independent of vascular excitement. The power of exciting the feelings inherent in these principles, can only be accounted for by supposing a most intimate relation to subsist between the body and the mind. The brain, through the medium of its nervous branches, is the source of all this excitement. These branches receive the impressions and convey them to their fountain-head, whence they are showered like sparkling rain-drops over the mind, in a thousand fantastic varieties. No bodily affection ever influences the mind but through the remote or proximate agency of this organ. It sits enthroned in the citadel of thought, and, though material itself, acts with wizard power both upon matter and spirit. No other texture has the same pervading principle. If the lungs be diseased, we have expectoration and cough; if the liver, jaundice or dropsy; if the stomach, indigestion; but when the brain is affected, we have not merely many bodily symptoms, but severe affections of the mind; nor are such affections ever produced by any organ but through the agency of the brain. It therefore acts in a double capacity upon the frame, being both the source of the corporeal feelings, and of the mental manifestations. Admitting this truth, there can be little difficulty in apprehending why intoxication produces so powerful a mental influence. This must proceed from a resistless impulse being given to the brain, by virtue of the peculiar action of inebriating agents upon the nerves. That organ of the mind is suddenly endowed with increased energy. Not only does the blood circulate through it more rapidly, but an action, *sui generis*, is given to its whole substance. Mere increase of circulation, as we have already stated, is not sufficient: there must be some other principle at work upon its texture; and it is this principle, whatever it may be, which is the main cause of drunkenness. At first, ebriety has a soothing effect, and falls over the spirit like the hum of bees, or the distant murmur of a cascade. Then to these soft dreams of Elysium succeed a state of maddening energy and excitement in the brain. The thoughts which emanate from its prolific tabernacle, are more fervid and original than ever—they rush out with augmented copiousness, and sparkle over the understanding like the aurora borealis, or the eccentric scintillations of light upon a summer cloud. In a word, the organ is excited to a high, but not a diseased action, for this is coupled with pain, and, instead of pleasurable, produces afflicting ideas. But its energies, like those of any other part, are apt to be over-excited. When this takes place, the balance is broken; the mind gets tumultuous and disordered, and the ideas inconsistent, wavering, and absurd. Then come the torpor and exhaustion subsequent on such excessive stimulus. The person falls into drowsiness or stupor, and his mind, as well as his body, is followed by languor corresponding to the previous excitation.

Such is a slight and unsatisfactory attempt to elucidate some of the more prominent phenomena of drunkenness. Some are omitted as being too obvious to require explanation, and others have been elsewhere cursorily accounted for in differents parts of the word.

CHAPTER IX

METHOD OF CURING THE FIT OF DRUNKENNESS.

1. *From Liquors.*—Generally speaking, there is no remedy for drunkenness equal to vomiting. The sooner the stomach is emptied of its contents the better, and this may, in most cases, be accomplished by drinking freely of tepid water, and tickling the fauces. On more obstinate occasions, powerful emetics will be necessary. The best for the purpose, are ten grains of sulphate of copper, half a drachm of sulphate of zinc, or five grains of tartar emetic. Either of these should be dissolved in a small quantity of tepid water, and instantly swallowed. Should this treatment fail in effecting vomiting, and dangerous symptoms supervene, the stomach pump should be employed. Cold applications to the head are likewise useful. In all cases, the head ought to be well elevated, and the neckcloth removed, that there may be no impediment to the circulation. Where there is total insensibility, where the pulse is slow and full, the pupils dilated, the face flushed, and the breathing stertorous, it becomes a question whether blooding might be useful. Darwin* and Trotter speak discouragingly of the practice. As a general rule I think it is bad; and that many persons who would have recovered, if left to themselves, have lost their lives by being prematurely bled. In all cases it should be done cautiously, and not for a considerable time. Vomiting and other means should invariably be first had recourse to, and if they fail, and nature is unable of her own power to overcome the stupor, blooding may be tried. In this respect, liquors differ from opium the insensibility from which is benefitted by abstraction of blood.

There is one variety of drunkenness in which both blooding and cold are inadmissible. This is when a person is struck down, as it were, by drinking suddenly a great quantity of ardent spirits. Here he is overcome by an instantaneous stupor: his countenance is ghastly and pale, his pulse feeble, and his body cold, While these symptoms continue, there is no remedy but vomiting. When, however, they wear off, and are succeeded, as they usually are by flushing, heat, and general excitement, the case is changed, and must be treated as any other where such symptoms exist.

The acetate of ammonia is said to possess singular properties in restoring from intoxication. This fact was ascertained by M. Masurer, a French chemist. According to him, from twenty to thirty drops in a glass of water, will, in most cases, relieve the patient from the sense of giddiness and oppression of the brain; or, if that quantity should be insufficient, half the same may be again given in eight or ten minutes after. In some csses the remedy will occasion nausea or vomiting, which, however, will be salutary to the patient, as the state of the brain is much aggravated by the load on the stomach and subsequent indigestion. It is also farther stated that the value of this medicine is greatly enhanced from its not occasioning that heat of the stomach and subsequent inflammation which are apt to be produced by pure ammonia. Whether it possesses all the virtues attributed to it, I cannot say from personal observation, having never had occasion to use it in any case which came under my management; but I think it at least promises to be useful, and is, at all events,

* Zoonomia.

worthy of a trial. I must mention, however, that the acetate of ammonia is seldom to be procured in the highly concentrated state in which it is used by M. Masurer. Owing to the great difficulty of crystallizing it, it is rarely seen except in the fluid state, in which condition it is recommended by the French chemist. The form in which it is almost always used in this country is that of the Aq. Acet. Ammon. or Spirit of Mindererus, in doses of half an ounce or an ounce, but whether in this shape it would be equally effectual in obviating the effects of drunkenness, remains to be seen.

Mr Broomley of Deptford recommends a draught composed of two drachms of Aq. Ammon. Aromat. in two ounces of water, is an effectual remedy in drunkenness.

The carbonate of ammonia might be used with a good effect. M. Dupuy, director to the veterinary school at Toulonse, tried a curious experiment with this medicine upon a horse. Having previously intoxicated the animal by injecting a demiletre of alcohol into the jugular vein, he injected five grains of the carbonate of ammonia, dissolved in an ounce of water, into the same vein, when the effects of the alcohol immediately ceased.

We have already mentioned that the excitement of drunkenness is succeeded by universal languor. In the first stage, the drunkard is full of energy, and capable of withstanding vigorously all external influences. In the second, there is general torpor and exhaustion, and he is more than usually subject to every impression, whether of cold or contagion. Persons are often picked up half dead in the second stage. The stimulus of intoxication had enabled them to endure the chill of the atmosphere, but the succeeding weakness left them more susceptible than before of its severity. In this state the body will not sustain any farther abstraction of stimuli; and blooding and cold would be highly injurious. Vomiting is here equally necessary, as in all other instances; but the person must be kept in a warm temperature, and cherished with light and nourishing food—with soups, if such can be procured, and even with negus, if the protrastration of strength is very great.

A paroxysm of *periodical* drunkenness may be sometimes shortened by putting such small quantities of tartar emetic into the liquor which the person indulges in, as to bring on nausea. This, however, must be done with secrecy and caution.

It may here be mentioned, though not with a view of recommending the practice, that the vegetable acids have a strong effect both in counteracting and removing drunkenness. To illustrate this fact, the following circumstance may be mentioned :—About twenty years ago, an English regiment was stationed in Glasgow, the men of which, as is common in all regiments, became enamoured of whskey. This liquor, to which they gave the whimsical denomination of *white ale*, was new to them—being nearly unknown in England : and they soon indulged in it to such an extent, as to attract the censure of their officers. Being obliged to be at quarters by a certain hour, they found out the plan of sobering themselves by drinking large quantities of vinegar, perhaps a gill or two at a draught. This, except in very bad cases, had the desired effect, and enabled them to enter the barrack-court, or appear on parade, in a state of tolerable sobriety. The power of the vegetable acids in resisting intoxication, is well shown in the case of cold punch—a larger portion of which can be withstood than of either grog or toddy, even when the quantity of spirit is precisely the same.

There is nothing which has so strong a tendency to dispel the effects of a debauch as hard exercise especially if the air be cold. Aperients and diaphoretics are also extremely useful for the same purpose.

For some days after drinking too much, the food should be light and unirritating, consisting principally of vegetables. Animal food is apt to heat the body and dispose it to inflammatory complaints.*

II. *From Opium.*—When a dangerous quantity of opium has been taken, the treatment, in the first instance is the same as with regard to spirits, or any other intoxicating fluid. Immediate vomiting, by the administration of similar emetics, is to be attempted, and when it has taken place, it should be encouraged by warm drinks till there is reason to believe that the stomach has been freed of the poison. These drinks, however, should not be given before vomiting is produced, for, in the event of their failing to excite it, they remain upon the stomach, and thus dissolve the opium and promote its absorption. But when vomiting occurs from the action of the emetics, it will in all probability be encouraged by warm drinks, and the stomach thus more effectually cleared of the poison. Large quantities of a strong infusion of coffee ought then to be given, or the vegetable acids, such as vinegar or lemon-juice, mixed with water. These serve to mitigate the bad consequences which often follow, even after the opium has been brought completely up. If the person show signs of apoplexy, more especially if he be of a plethoric habit, the jugular vein, or temporal artery should be opened, and a considerable quantity of blood taken away. Indeed, it may be laid down as a general rule, that as soon as the poison is rejected, the patient ought to be bled, and the operation should be repeated according to circumstances. Every means must be used to arouse him from stupor. He must be moved about, if possible, from room to room, hartshorn applied to his nostrils, and all plans adopted to prevent him from sinking into lethargy. For this purpose, camphor, assafœtida, or musk, might be administered with advantage. It is also a good practice to sponge the body well with cold water; and the effusion of cold water on the head and over the body, is still more effectual. In cases where vomiting cannot be brought about by the ordinary means, M. Orfila suggests that one or two grains of tartar emetic, dissolved in an ounce or two of water, might be injected into the veins. In desperate cases, the stomach pump must be had recourse to. Purgatives are latterly necessary.

Many practitioners consider vinegar and the other vegetable acids antidotes to opium. This opinion M. Orfila has most satisfactorily shown to be erroneous. In a series of well-conducted and conclusive experiments made by him, it appears that the vegetable acids aggravate the symptoms of poisoning by opium, whenever they are not vomited. They hurry them on more rapidly, render them more violent, produce death at an earlier period, and give rise to an inflammation of the stomach—an event which hardly ever occurs when they are not employed. These effects, it would appear, are partly produced by their power of dissolving opium, which they do better than the mere unassisted fluids of the stomach; consequently the absorption is more energetic. The only time when acids can be of any use, is after the person has brought up the poison by vomiting. They then mitigate the subsequent symptoms, and promote recovery; but if they be swallowed before vomiting takes place, and if this act cannot by any means be brought about, they aggravate the disorder,

* In speaking of the treatment, it is necessary to guard against confounding other affections with drunkenness :—'There is a species of delirium that often attends the accession of *typhus fever*, from contagion, that I have known to be mistaken for ebriety. Among seamen and soldiers, whose habits of intoxication are common, it will sometimes require nice discernment to decide; for the vacant stare in the countenance, the look of idiotism, incoherent speech, faltering voice, and tottering walk, are so alike in both cases, that the naval and military surgeon ought at all times to be very cautious how he gives up a man to punishment, under these suspicious circumstances. Nay, the appearances of his having come from a tavern, with even the effluvium of liquor about him, are signs not always to be trusted; for these haunts of seamen and soldiers are often the sources of infection. —*Trotter*.

and death ensues more rapidly than if they had not been taken.

Coffee has likewise a good effect when taken after the opium is got off the stomach; but it differs from the acids in this, that it does not, under any circumstances, increase the danger. While the opium is still unremoved, the coffee may be considered merely inert; and it is, therefore, a matter of indifference whether at this time it be taken or not. Afterwards, however, it produces the same beneficial effects as lemonade, tartaric acid, or vinegar. According to Orfila, the infusion is more powerful as an antidote than the decoction. Drunkenness or poisoning from the other narcotics, such as hemlock, belladonna, aconite, hyoscyamus, &c., is treated precisely in the same manner as that from opium.

III. *From Tobacco.*—If a person feel giddy or languid from the use of this luxury, he should lay himself down on his back, exposed to a current of cool air. Should this fail of reviving him, let him either swallow twenty or thirty drops of hartshorn, mixed with a glass of cold water, or an ounce of vinegar moderately diluted. When tobacco has been received into the stomach, so as to produce dangerous symptoms, a powerful emetic must immediately be given, and vomiting encouraged by copious drinks, till the poison is brought up. After this, vinegar ought to be freely exhibited, and lethargy prevented by the external and internal use of stimuli. If apoplectic symptoms appear, blooding must be had recourse to. The same rule applies here, with regard to acids, as in the case of opium. They should never be given till the stomach is thoroughly liberated of its contents by previous vomiting.

Accidents happen oftener with tobacco than is commonly supposed. Severe languor, retching, and convulsive attacks sometimes ensue from the application of ointment made with this plant, for the cure of the ring-worm; and Santeuil, the celebrated French poet, lost his life in consequence of having unknowingly drunk a glass of wine, into which had been put some Spanish snuff.

IV. *From Nitrous Oxide.* Though the inhalation of this gas is seldom attended with any risk, yet, in very plethoric habits, there might be a determination of blood to the head, sufficient to produce apoplexy. If a person therefore becomes after the experiment, convulsed, stupified, and livid in the countenance, and if these symptons do not soon wear away, some means must be adopted for their removal. In general, a free exposure to fresh air, and dashing cold water over the face, will be quite sufficient; but if the affection is so obstinate as to resist this plan, it will then be necessary to draw some blood from the arm, or, what is still better, from the jugular vein. When, in delicate subjects, hysteria and other nervous symptoms are produced, blooding is not necessary; all that is requisite to be done being the application of cold water to the brow or temples, and of hartshorn to the nostrils. In obstinate cases, twenty or thirty drops of the latter in a glass of water, may be administered with advantage.

CHAPTER X.

PATHOLOGY OF DRUNKENNESS.

The evil consequences of drinking, both in a physical and moral point of view, seem to have been known from the most remote antiquity. They are expressly mentioned in Scripture; nor can there be a doubt that the Homeric fiction of the companions of Ulysses being turned into swine by the enchanted cup of Circe, plainly implied the bestial degradation into which men bring themselves by coming under the dominion of so detestable habit. Having mentioned these circumstances in favour of the accuracy of ancient knowledge, we shall simply proceed to detail the effects of drunkenness so far as the medical practitioner is professionally interested in knowing them. The moral consequences belong more properly to the legislator and divine, and do not require to be here particularly considered.

I. *State of the Liver.*—One of the most common consequences of drunkenness is acute inflammation. This may affect any organ, but its attacks are principally confined to the brain, the stomach, and the liver. It is unnecessary to enter into any detail of its nature and treatment. These are precisely the same as when it proceeds from any other cause. The inflammation of drunkenness is, in a great majority of cases, chronic; and the viscus which, in nine cases out of ten, suffers, is the liver.

Liquors, from the earliest ages, have been known to affect this organ. Probably the story of Prometheus stealing fire from heaven and animating clay, alluded to the effects of wine upon the human body; and the punishment of having his liver devoured by a vulture may be supposed to refer to the consequences which men draw upon themselves, by over-indulgence—this organ becoming thereby highly diseased. Man is not the only animal so affected. Swine who are fed on the refuse of breweries, have their livers enlarged in the same manner. Their other viscera become also indurated, and their flesh so tough, that unless killed early, they are unfit to be eaten. Some fowl-dealers in London are said to mix gin with the food of the birds, by which means they are fattened, and their livers swelled to a great size. The French manage to enlarge this organ in geese, by piercing it shortly after the creatures are fledged.*

Neither malt liquors nor wine have so rapid and decided an effect upon the liver as ardent spirits. Indeed, it is alleged, although I cannot go this length, that the wine that is *perfectly pure* does not affect the liver; and the fact of our continental neighbours being much less troubled with hepatic complaints than the wine-drinkers among ourselves, gives some countenance to the allegation; for it is well known that to suit the British market, the vinous liquors used in this country are sophisticated with brandy. In wine that is perfectly pure the alcohol exists in such a state of chemical combination, as greatly to modify its effects upon the system. In the wine generally to be met with, much of it exists mechanically or uncombined, and all this portion of spirit acts precisely in the same manner as if separately used.†

The liver is a viscus which, in confirmed topers, never escapes; and it withstands disease better than any other vital part, except, perhaps, the spleen. Sometimes, by a slow chronic action, it is enlarged to double its usual size, and totally disorganized, and yet the person suffers comparatively little. The disease frequently arises in tropical climates, from warmth and other natural causes, but an excess in spirituous liquors is more frequently the cause than is generally imagined.

The consequences which follow chronic inflammation of the liver, are very extensive. The bile, in general, is not secreted in due quantity or quality, consequently digestion is defective, the bowels, from want of their usual stimulus, become torpid. The person gets jaundiced, his skin becoming yellow, dry, and rough, and the white of his eyes discoloured. As the enlargement goes on, the free passage of blood in the veins is impeded, and their extremities throw out lymph: this accumulating, forms dropsy, a disease with which a great proportion of drunkards are ultimately more or less affected.

The jaundice of drunkenness is not an original dis

* 'They have a custom of fostering a liver complaint in their geese, which encourages its growth to the enormous weight of some pounds; and this diseased viscus is considered a great delicacy.'—*Matthew's Diary of an invalid.*

† Vide Appendix No. 1.

ease, but merely a symptom of the one under consideration. A very slight cause will often bring it on; it is, consequently, not always dangerous. Dropsy is, for the most part, also symptomatic of diseased liver, but sometimes, more especially in dram-drinkers, it arises from general debility of the system. In the former case, effusion always takes place in the cavity of the abdomen. In the latter, there is general anasarca throughout the body, usually coupled with more or less topical affection. In every instance, dropsy, whether general or local, is a very dangerous disease.

II. *State of the Stomach, &c.*—Like the liver, the stomach is more subject to chronic than acute inflammation. It is also apt to get indurated, from long-continued, slow action going on within its substance. This disease is extremely insidious, frequently proceeding great lengths before it is discovered. The organ is often thickened to half an inch, or even an inch; and its different tunics so matted together that they cannot be separated. The pyloric orifice becomes, in many cases, contracted. The cardiac may suffer the same disorganization, and so may the œsophagus; but these are less common, and, it must be admitted, more rapidly fatal. When the stomach is much thickened, it may sometimes be felt like a hard ball below the left ribs. At this point there is also a dull uneasy pain, which is augmented upon pressure.

Indigestion or spasm may arise from a mere imperfect action of this organ, without any disease of its structure; but when organic derangement takes place, they are constant attendants. In the latter case it is extremely difficult for any food to remain on the stomach; it is speedily vomited. What little is retained undergoes a painful fermentation, which produces sickness and heartburn. There is, at the same time, much obstinacy in the bowels, and the body becomes emaciated.

This disease, though generally produced by dissipation, originates sometimes from other causes, and affects the soberest people. Whenever the stomach is neglected, when acidity is allowed to become habitual, or indigestible food too much made use of, the foundation may be laid for slow inflammation, terminating in schirrus and all its bad consequences.

Vomiting of bilious matter in the mornings, is a very common circumstance among all classes of drunkards. But there is another kind of vomiting, much more dangerous, to which they are subject; and that is when inflammation of the villous coat of the stomach takes place. In such a state there is not much acute pain, but rather a dull feeling of uneasiness over the abdomen, attended with the throwing up of a dark, crude matter, resembling coffee grounds. I have seen two cases in which the vomiting stopped suddenly, in consequence of metastasis to the head. In these, the affection soon proved fatal, the persons being seized with indistinctness of vision, low delirium, and general want of muscular power: the action of the kidneys was also totally suspended for three days before death. On examination, *post mortem*, there was effusion in the ventricles of the brain, besides extensive inflammation along the inner surface of the upper portion of the alimentary canal.

Bilious complaints, which were formerly in a great measure unknown to the common people, are now exceedingly common among them, and proceed in a great measure from the indulgence in ardent spirits to which that class of society is so much addicted.

There is nothing more indicative of health, than a good appetite for breakfast; but confirmed topers, from the depraved state of their stomachs, lose all relish for this meal.

Persons of this description are generally of a costive habit of body, but a debauch, with those who are constitutionally sober is, for the most part, followed by more or less diarrhœa.

In the latter stages of a drunkard's life, though he has still the relish for liquor as strongly as ever, he no longer enjoys his former power of withstanding it. This proceeds from general weakness of the system, and more particularly of the stomach. This organ gets debilitated, and soon gives way, while the person is intoxicated much easier, and often vomits what he has swallowed. His appetite likewise fails; and, to restore it, he has recourse to various bitters, which only aggravate the matter, especially as they are in most cases taken under the medium of ardent spirits. Bitters are often dangerons remedies. When used moderately, and in cases of weak digestion from natural causes, they frequently produce the best effects; but a long continuance of them is invariably injurious. There is a narcotic principle residing in most bitters, which physicians have too much overlooked. It destroys the sensibility of the stomach, determines to the head, and predisposes to apoplexy and palsy. This was the effects of the famous Portland powder,* so celebrated many years ago for the cure of gout; and similar consequences will, in the long run, follow bitters as they are commonly administered. Persons addicted to intemperance, have an inordinate liking for these substances; let them be ever so nauseous, they are swallowed greedily, especially if dissolved in spirits. Their fondness for purl, herb-ale, and other pernicious morning drinks, is equally striking.

There is nothing more characteristic of a tippler than an indifference to tea, and beverages of a like nature. When a woman exhibits this quality, we may reasonably suspect her of indulging in liquor. If drunkards partake of tea, they usually saturate it largely with ardent spirits. The unadulterated fluid is too weak a stimulous for unnatural appetites.

III. *State of the Brain.*—Inflammation of this organ is often a consequence of intemperance. It may follow immediately after a debauch, or it may arise secondarily from an excess of irritation being applied to the body during the stage of debility. Even an abstraction of stimulus, as by applying too much cold to the head, may bring it on in this latter state.

Dr Armstrong, in his lectures, speaks of a chronic inflammation of the brain and its membranes, proceeding, among other causes, from the free use of strong wines and liquors. According to him, it is much more common after, than before, forty years of age, although he has seen several instances occurring in young persons. The brain gets diseased, the diameter of the vessels being diminished, while their coats are thickened and less transparent than usual. In some places they swell out and assume a varicose appearance. The organ itself has no longer the same delicate and elastic texture, becoming either unnaturally hard, or of a morbid softness. Slight effusions in the various cavities are apt to take place. Under these cirunmstances, there is a strong risk of apoplexy. To this structure is to be ascribed the mental debasement, the loss of memory, and gradual extinction of the intellectual powers. I believe that the brains of all confirmed drunkards exhibit more or less of the above appearances.

IV. *State of the Kidneys.*—During intoxication the action of the kidneys is always much increased; and this is a favourable circumstance, as, more than any thing else, it carries off the bad effects of drinking. The kidney, however, in confirmed drunkards, is apt to become permanently diseased, and secrets its accustomed fluid with unusual activity, not only in the moments of drunkenness, when such an increase is useful, but at all periods, even when the persons abstains from every sort of indulgence. The disease called diabetes

* The Portland Powder consisted of equal parts of the roots of round birthwort and gentian, of the leaves of germander and ground pine, and of the tops of the lesser centaury, all dried. Drs Cullen, Darwin, and Murray of Gottingen, with many other eminent physicians, bear testimony to the pernicious effects of this compound.

is thus produced, which consists in a morbid increase of the secretion, accompanied with a diseased state of the texture of the kidneys. This affection is mostly fatal.

V. *State of the Bladder.*—Drunkenness affects this organ in common with almost every other; hence it is subject to paralysis, spasm, induration, &c., and to all bad consequences thence resulting—such as pain, incontinence, and retention of urine.

VI. *State of the Blood and Breath.*—The blood of a professed drunkard, as already stated, differs from that of a sober man. It is more dark, and approaches to the character of venous. The ruddy tint of those carbuncles which are apt to form upon the face, is no proof to the contrary, as the blood which supplies them crimsoned by exposure to the air, on the same principle as that by which the blood in the pulmonary arteries receives purificatien by the process of breathing. The blood of a malt-liquor drinker is not merely darker, but also more thick and sizy than in other cases, owing, no doubt, to the very nutritious nature of his habitual beverage.

The breath of a drunkard is disgustingly bad, and has always a spiritous odour. This is partly owing to the stomach, which communicates the flavour of its customary contents to respiration; and partly, also, there can be little doubt, to the absorption of the liquor by the blood, through the medium of the lacteals.

VII. *State of the Perspiration.*—The perspiration of a confirmed drunkard is as offensive as his breath, and has often a strong spiritous odour. I have met with two instances, the one in a Claret, the other in a Port drinker, in which the moisture which exuded from their bodies had a ruddy complexion, similar to that of the wine on which they had committed their debauch.

VIII. *State of the Eyes, &c.*—The eyes may be affected with acute or chronic inflammation. Almost all drunkards have the latter more or less. Their eyes are red and watery, and have an expression so peculiar, that the cause can never be mistaken. This, and a certain want of firmness about the lips, which are loose, gross, and sensual, betray at once the topor. Drunkenness impairs vision. The delicacy of the retina is probably affected; and it is evident, that, from long-continued inflammation, the tunica adnata which covers the cornea must lose its original clearness and transparency.

Most drunkards have a constant tenderness and redness of the nostrils. This, I conceive, arises from the state of the stomach and œsophagus. The same membrane which lines them is prolonged upwards to the nose and mouth, and carries thus far its irritability.

There is no organ which so rapidly betrays the Bacchanalian propensities of its owner as the nose. It not only becomes red and fiery, like that of Bardolph,* but acquires a general increase of size—displaying upon its surface various small pimples, either wholly of a deep crimson hue, or tipped with yellow, in consequence of an accumulation of viscid matter within them. The rest of the face often presents the same carbuncled appearance.

I have remarked that drunkards who have a foul, livid, and pimpled face, are less subject to liver complaint than those who are free from snch eruptions. In this casc the determination of blood to the surface of the body seems to prevent that fluid from being directed so forcibly to the viscera as it otherwise would be. The same fact is sometimes observed in sober persons who are troubled with hepatic affection. While there is a copious rush upon the face or body, they are comparatively well, but no sooner does it go in than they are annoyed by the liver getting into disorder.

IX. *State of the Skin.*—The skin of a drunkard, especially if he be advanced in life, has seldom the appearance of health. It is apt to become either livid or jaundiced in its complexion, and feels rough and scaly. There is a disease spoken of by Dr Darwin, under the title of *Psora Ebriorum*, which is peculiar to people of this description. 'Elderly people,' says he, 'who have been much addicted to spiritous drinks, as beer, wine, or alcohol, are liable to an eruption all over their bodies; which is attended with very afflicting itching, and which they probably propagate from one part of their bodies to another with their own nails by scratching themselves.' I have met with several cases of this disease, which is only one of the many forms of morbid action, which the skin is apt to assume in drunkards.

X. *State of the Hair.*—The hair of drunkards is generally dry, slow of growth, and liable to come out; they are consequently more subject to baldness than other people. At the same time, it would be exceedingly unjust to suspect any one, whose hair was of this description, of indulgence in liquors, for we frequently find in the soberest persons that the hairs are arid, few in number, and prone to decay. Baldness with such persons is merely a local affection, but in drunkards it is constitutional, and proceeds from that general defect of vital energy which pervades their whole system.

XI. *Inflammations.*—Drunkards are exceedingly subject to all kinds of inflammation, both from the direct excitement of the liquor, and from their often remaining out in a state of intoxication, exposed to cold and damp. Hence inflammatory affections of the lungs, intestine, bladder, kidneys, brain, &c., arising from these sources. Rheumatism is often traced to the neglect and exposure of a fit of drunkenness.

XII. *Gout.*—Gout is the offspring of gluttony, drunkenness, or sensuality, or of them all put together. It occurs most frequently with the wine-bibber. A very slight cause may bring it on when hereditary predisposition exists; but in other circumstances considerable excess will be required before it makes its appearance. It is one of the most afflicting consequences of intemperance, and seems to have been known as such from an early age—mention being made of it by Hippocrates, Aretæus, and Galen. Among the Roman ladies gout was very prevalent during the latter times of the empire; and, at the present day, there are few noblemen who have it not to hand down to their offspring as a portion of their heritage.

XIII. *Tremors.*—A general tremor is an attendant upon almost all drunkards. This proceeds from nervous irritability. Even those who are habitually temperate, have a quivering in their hands next morning, if they indulge over night in a debauch. While it lasts, a person cannot hold any thing without shaking, neither can he write steadily. Among those who have long devoted themselves to the mysteries of Silenus, this amounts to a species of palsy, affecting the whole body, and even the lips, with a sort of paralytic trembling. On awaking from sleep, they frequently feel it so strongly, as to seem in the cold fit of an ague, being neither able to walk steadily, nor articulate distinctly. It is singular that the very cause of this distemper should be employed for its cure. When the confirmed drunkard awakes with tremor, he immediately swallows a dram: the most violent shaking is quieted by this means. The opium-eater has recourse to the same

* 'Falstaff. Thou art our admiral: thou bearest the lanthorn in the poop; but 'tis in the *nose* of thee: thou art the knight of the burning lamp.

'Bardolph. Why, Sir John, my face does you no harm.

'Falstaff. No, I'll be sworn! I make as good use of it as many a man doth of a death's head or a memento mori. I never see thy face but I think of hell-fire.'—'When thou rann'st up Gads-hill in the night to catch my horse, if I did not think thou hadst been an *ignis fatuus*, or a ball of wildfire, there's no purchase in money. O! thou art a perpetual triumph—an everlasting bonfire light: thou hast saved me a thousand marks in links and torches, walking with me in the night betwixt tavern and tavern; but the Sack thou hast drunk me would have bought me lights as good cheap, at the dearest chandler's in Europe. I have maintained that salamander of yours with fire any time this two and thirty years—heaven reward me for it!'

method: to remove the agitation produced by one dose of opium, he takes another. This, in both cases, is only adding fuel to the fire—the tremors coming on at shorter intervals, and larger doses being required for their removal.

Drunkards are more subject than any other class of people to apoplexy and palsy.

XIV. *Palpitation of the Heart.*—This is a very distressing consequence of drunkenness, producing difficult breathing, and such a determination to the head as often brings on giddiness. Drunkards are apt to feel it as they step out of bed, and the vertigo is frequently so great as to make them stumble. There are some sober persons who are much annoyed by this affection. In them it may arise from spasmodic action of the fibres of the heart, nervous irritability, or organic disease, such as aneurism, or angina pectoris.

XV. *Hysteria.*—Female drunkards are very subject to hysterical affections. There is a delicacy of fibre in women, and a susceptibility of mind, which makes them feel more acutely than the other sex all external influences. Hence their whole system is often violently affected with hysterics and other varieties of nervous weakness. These affections are not always traced to their true cause, which is often neither more nor less than dram-drinking. When a woman's nose becomes crimsoned at the point, her eyes somewhat red, and more watery than before, and her lips full and less firm and intellectual in their expression, we may suspect that something wrong is going on.

XVI. *Epilepsy.*—Drunkenness may bring on epilepsy, or falling sickness, and may excite it into action in those who have the disease from other causes. Many persons cannot get slightly intoxicated without having an epileptic or other convulsive attack. These fits generally arise in the early stages before drunkenness has got to a height. If they do not occur early the individual will probably escape them altogether for the time.

XVII. *Sterility.*—This is a state to which confirmed drunkards are very subject. The children of such persons are, in general, neither numerous nor healthy. From the general defect of vital power in the parental system they are apt to be puny and emaciated, and more than ordinarily liable to inherit all the diseases of those from whom they are sprung. On this account, the chances of long life are much diminished among the children of such parents. In proof of this, it is only necessary to remark, that according to the London bills of mortality one-half of the children born in the metropolis die before attaining their third year; while of the children of the Society of Friends, a class remarkable for sobriety and regularity of all kinds one-half actually attain the age of forty-seven years. Much of this difference, doubtless, originates in the superior degree of comfort, and correct general habits of the Quakers, which incline them to bestow every care in the rearing of their offspring, and put it in their power to obtain the means of combating disease; but the mainspring of this superior comfort and regularity is doubtless temperance—a virtue which this class of people possess in an eminent degree.

XVIII. *Emaciation.*—Emaciation is peculiarly characteristic of the spirit drinker. He wears away, before his time, into the 'lean and slippered pantaloon' spoken of by Shakspeare in his 'Stages of Human life.' All drunkards, however, if they live long enough, become emaciated. The eyes get hollow, the cheeks fall in, and wrinkles soon furrow the countenance with the marks of age. The fat is absorbed from every part, and the rounded plumpness which formerly characterized the body soon wears away. The whole form gets lank and debilitated. There is a want of due warmth, and the hand is usually covered with a chill clammy perspiration.

The occurrence of emaciation is not to be wondered at in persons who are much addicted to ardent spirits, for alcohol, besides being possessed of no nutritive properties, prevents the due chymification of the food, and consequently deteriorates the quality, besides diminishing the quantity of the chyle. The principle of nutrition being thus affected, the person becomes emaciated as a natural consequence.

XIX. *Corpulency.*—Malt liquor and wine drinkers are, for the most part, corpulent, a state of body which rarely attends the spirit drinker, unless he be, at the same time, a *bon vivant.* Both wines and malt liquors are more nourishing than spirits. Under their use, the blood becomes, as it were, enriched, and an universal deposition of fat takes place throughout the system. The omentum and muscles of the belly are, in a particular manner, loaded with this secretion; whence the abdominal protuberance so remarkable in persons who indulge themselves in wines and ales. As the abdomen is the part which becomes most enlarged, so is it that which longest retains its enlargement. It seldom parts with it, indeed, even in the last stages, when the rest of the body is in the state of emaciation. There can be no doubt that the parts which first lose their corpulency are the lower extemities. Nothing is more common than to see a pair of spindle-shanks tottering under the weight of an enormous corporation, to which they seem attached more like artificial appendages, than natural members. The next parts which give way are the shoulders. They fall flat, and lose their former firmness and rotundity of organization. After this, the whole body becomes loose, flabby, and enelastic; and five years do as much to the constitution as fifteen would have done under a system of strict temperance and sobriety. The worst system that can befall a corpulent man, is the decline of his lower extremities.* So long as they continue firm, and correspondent with the rest of the body, it is a proof that there is still vigor remaining; but when they gradually get attenuated, while other parts retain their original fullness, there can be no sign more sure that his constitution is breaking down, and that he will never again enjoy his wonted strength.

XX. *Premature Old Age.*—Drunkenness has a dreadful effect in anticipating the effects of age. It causes time to pace on with giant strides—chases youth from the constitution of its victims—and clothes them prematurely with the gray garniture of years. How often do we see the sunken eye, the shrivelled cheek, the feeble, tottering step, and hoary head, in men who have scarcely entered into the autumn of their existence. To witness this distressing picture, we have only to walk out early in the mornings, and see those gaunt, melancholy shadows of mortality, betaking themselves to the gin-shops, as to the altar of some dreadful demon, and quaffing the poisoned cup to his honor, as the Carthaginians propitiated the deity of their worship, by flinging their children into the fire which burned within his brazen image. Most of these unhappy persons are young, or middle-aged men; and though some drunkards attain a green old age, they are few in number compared with those who sink untimely into the grave ere the days of their youth have well passed by.†

* This circumstance has not escaped the observation of Shakspeare;—'Chief Justice. Do you set down your name in the scroll of youth that are written down old, with all the characters of age! Have you not a moist eye, a dry hand, and a yellow cheek, a white beard, a *decreasing* leg, an increasing belly? Is not your voice broken, your wind short, your chin double, your wit single, and every part of you blasted with antiquity; and will you yet call yourself young? Fie, fie, fie, Sir John!'

† 'Let nobody tell me that there are numbers who, though they live most irregularly, attain, in health, and spirits, those remote periods of life attained by the most sober; for this argument being grounded on a case full of uncertainty and hazard, and which, besides, so seldom occurs as to look more like a mi-

Nothing is more common than to see a man of fifty as hoary, emaciated, and wrinkled, as if he stood on the borders of fourscore.

The effect of intemperance in shortening life is strikingly exemplified in the contrast afforded by other classes of society to the Quakers, a set of people of whom I must again speak favorably. It appears from accurate calculation, that in London only one person in forty attains the age of four-score, while among Quakers, whose sobriety is proverbial, and who have long set themselves against the use of ardent spirits, not less than one in ten reaches that age—a most striking difference, and one which carries its own inference along with it.

It is remarked by an eminent practitioner, that of more than a hundred men in a glass manufactory, three drank nothing but water, and these three appeared to be of their proper age, while the rest who indulged in strong drinks seemed ten or twelve years olders than they proved to be. This is conclusive.*

XXI. *Ulcers.*—Ulcers often break out on the bodies of drunkards. Sometimes they are fiery and irritable, but in general they possess an indolent character. Of whatever kind they may be, they are always aggravated in such constitutions. A slight cause gives rise to them; and a cut or bruise which, in health, would have healed in a few days, frequently degenerates into a foul sloughy sore. When drunkards are affected with scrofula, scurvy, or any cutaneous disease whatever, they always, *cæteris paribus*, suffer more than other people.

XXII. *Melancholy.*—Though drunkards over their cups are the happiest of mankind, yet, in their solitary hours, they are the most wretched. Gnawing care, heightened perhaps by remorse, preys upon their conscience. While sober, they are distressed both in body and mind, and fly to the bowl to drown their misery in oblivion. Those, especially, whom hard fate drove to this desperate remedy, feel the pangs of low spirits with seven-fold force. The weapon they employ to drive away care is turned upon themselves. Every time it is used, it becomes less capable of scaring the fiend of melancholy, and more effectual in wounding him that uses it.

All drunkards are apt to become peevish and discontented with the world. They turn enemies to the established order of things, and, instead of looking to themselves, absurdly blame the government as the origin of their misfortunes.

XXIII. *Madness.*—This terrible infliction often proceeds from drunkenness. When there is hereditary predisposition, indulgence in liquor is more apt to call it into action than when there is none. The mind and body act reciprocally upon one another; and when the one is injured the other must suffer more or less. In intemperance, the structure of the brain is no longer the same as in health; and the mind, that immortal part of man, whose manifestions depend upon this organ, suffers a corresponding injury.

Intoxication may effect the mind in two ways. A person, after excessive indulgence in liquor, may be seized with delirium, and run into a state of violent outrage and madness. In this case the disease comes suddenly on: the man is fierce and intractable, and requires a strait jacket to keep him in order. Some never get drunk without being insanely outrageous: they attack, without distinction, all who come in their way, foam at the mouth, and lose all sense of danger. This fit either goes off in a few hours, or degenerates into a confirmed attack of lunacy. More generally, however, the madness of intoxication is of another character, partaking of the nature of idiotism, into which state the mind resolves itself, in consequence of a long-continued falling off in the intellectual powers.

Drunkenness, according to the reports of Bethlehem Hospital, and other similar institutions for the insane, is one of the most common causes of lunacy. In support of this fact, it may be mentioned that of two hundred and eighty-six lunatics now in the Richmond Asylum, Dublin, one half owe their madness to drinking; and there are few but must have witnessed the wreck of the most powerful minds by this destructive habit. It has a more deplorable effect upon posterity than any other practice, for it entails, not only bodily disease upon the innocent offspring, but also the more afflicting diseases of the mind. Madness of late years has been greatly on the increase among the lower classes, and can only be referred to the alarming progress of drunkenness, which prevails now to a much greater extent among the poor than ever it did at any former period.*

XXIV. *Delirium Tremens.*—Both the symptoms and treatment of this affection require to be mentioned, because, unlike the diseases already enumerated, it invariably originates in the abuse of stimuli, and is cured in a manner peculiar to itself.

Those who indulge in spirits, especially raw, are most subject to delirium tremens, although wine, malt liquor, opium, and even ether, may give rise to it, if used in immoderate quantities. The sudden cessation of drinking in a confirmed toper, or a course of violent or long protracted intemperance may equally occasion the disease. A man, for instance, of the former description, breaks his leg, or is seized with some complaint, which compels him to abandon his potations. This man in consequence of such abstinence is attacked with delirium tremens. In another man, it is induced by a long course of tippling, or by a hard drinking-bout of several days' continuance.

The disease generally comes on with lassitude, loss of appetite, and frequent exacerbations of cold. The pulse is weak and quick, and the body covered with a chilly moisture. The countenance is pale, there are usually tremors of the limbs, anxiety, and a total disrelish for the common amusements of life. Then succeed retching, vomiting, and much oppression at the pit of the stomach, with sometimes slimy stools. When the person sleeps, which is but seldom, he frequently starts in the utmost terror, having his imagination haunted by frightful dreams. To the first coldness, glows of heat succeed, and the slightest renewed agitation of body or mind, sends out a profuse perspiration. The tongue is dry and furred. Every object appears unnatural and hideous. There is a constant dread of being haunted by spectres. Black or luminous bodies seem to float before the person: he conceives that vermin and all sorts of impure things are crawling upon him, and is constantly endeavouring to pick them off. His ideas are wholly confined to himself and his own affairs, of which he entertains the most disordered notions. He imagines that he is away from home, forgets those who are around him, frequently abuses his attendants, and is irritated beyond measure by the slightest contradiction. Calculations, buildings, and other fantastic schemes often occupy his mind; and a belief that

racle than the work of nature, men should not suffer themselves to be thereby persuaded to live irregularly, nature having been too liberal to those who did so without suffering by it; a favour which very few have any right to expect.'—*Carnaro on Health.*

* 'The workmen in provision stores have large allowances of whiskey bound to them in their engagements. These are served out to them daily by their employers, for the purpose of urging them, by excitement, to extraordinaty exertion. And what is the effect of this murderous system? The men are ruined, scarcely one of them being capable of work beyond fifty years of age, though none but the most able-bodied men can enter such employment.'—[Beecher's Sermons on Intemperance, with an introductory Essay by John Edgar. This is an excellent little work, which I cordially recommend to the perusal of the reader.

* It has been considered unnecessary to enter into any detail of the nature and treatment of the foregoing diseases, because they may originate from many other causes besides drunkenness; and when they do arise from this source, they acquire no peculiarity of character. Their treatment is also precisely the same as in ordinary cases—it being always understood, that the bad habit which brought them on must be abandoned before any good can result from medicine. The disease, however, which follows is different, and requires particular consideration.

every person is confederated to ruin him, is commonly entertained. Towards morning there is often much sickness and sometimes vomiting. This state generally lasts from four to ten days, and goes off after a refreshing sleep; but sometimes, either from the original violence of the disease, or from improper treatment, it proves fatal.

Such, in nine cases out of ten, is the character of delirium tremens. Sometimes, however, the symptoms vary, and instead of a weak there is a full pulse; instead of the face being pallid, it is flushed, and the eyes fiery; instead of a cold clammy skin, the surface is hot and dry. This state only occurs in vigorous plethoric subjects. A habitually sober man who has thoughtlessly rushed into a debauch, is more likely to be attacked in this manner than a professed drunkard. Indeed, I never met with an instance of the latter having this modification of the disease.

When the patient perishes from delirium tremens, he is generally carried off in convulsions. There is another termination which the disease sometimes assumes: it may run into madness or confirmed idiotism. Indeed, when it continues much beyond the time mentioned, there is danger of the mind becoming permanently alienated.

Subsultus, low delirium, very cold skin, short disturbed sleep, contracted pupil, strabismus, rapid intermittent pulse, and frequent vomiting, are indications of great danger. When the patient is affected with subsultus from which he recovers in terror, the danger is extreme.

In treating delirium tremens, particular attention must be paid to the nature of the disease, and constitution of the patient. In the first mentioned, and by far the most frequent variety, blooding, which some physicians foolishly recommend, is most pernicious. I have known more than one instance where life was destroyed by this practice. As there is generally much gastric irritation, as is indicated by the foul tongue, black and viscid evacuations and irritable state of the stomach, I commence the treatment by administering a smart dose of calomel. As soon as this has operated, I direct tepid water strongly impregnated with salt, to be dashed over the body, and the patient immediately thereafter to be well dried and put to bed. I then administer laudanum in doses of from forty to sixty drops, according to circumstances, combining with each dose from six to twelve grains of the carbonate of ammonia: this I repeat every now and then till sleep is procured. It may sometimes be necessary to give such doses every two hours, or even every hour, for twelve or twenty successive hours, before the effect is produced. The black drop in doses proportioned to its strength, which is more than three times that of laudanum, may be used as a substitute for the latter; the acetate or muriate of morphia in doses of a quarter or half a grain, is also a good medicine, having less tendency to produce stupor or headache than laudanum, and therefore preferable in cases where the patient is of a plethoric habit of body. It must be admitted, however, that their effects are less to be depended upon than those of laudanum, which, in all common cases will, I believe, be found the best remedy. The great object of the treatment is to soothe the apprehensions of the patient, and procure him rest. So soon as a sound sleep takes place there is generally a crisis, and the disease begins to give way; but till this occurs it is impossible to arrest its progress and effect a cure. A moderate quantity of wine will be necessary, especially if he has been a confirmed drinker, and labours under much weakness. Perhaps the best way of administering wine is along with the laudanum, the latter being dropped into the wine. Where wine cannot be had, porter may be advantageously given in combination with laudanum. The principal means, indeed, after the first purging, are opium, wine, ammonia, and tepid effusions: the latter may be tried two, three, or four times in the twenty-four hours, as occasion requires, The mind is, at the same time, to be soothed in the gentlest manner, the whimsical ideas of the patient to be humoured, and his fancies indulged as far as possible. All kinds of restraint or contradiction are most hurtful. Some recommend blisters to the head, but these are, in every case, injurious. So soon as all the symptoms of the disease have disappeared some purgative should be administered, but during its progress we must rely almost wholly upon stimulants. To cure, by means of stimuli, a complaint which arose from an over-indulgence in such agents, is apparently paradoxical; but experience confirms the propriety of the practice where, *a priori*, we might expect the contrary.

In the second variety of the disease, the same objections do not apply to blood-letting as in the first, but even there, great caution is necessary, especially if the disease has gone on for any length of time, if the pulse is quick and feeble or the tongue foul. At first, general blooding will often have an excellent effect, but should we not be called till after this stage it will prove a hazardous experiment. Local blooding will then sometimes be serviceable where general blooding could not be safely attempted. The patient should be purged well with calomel, have his head shaved, and kept cool with wet cloths, and sinapisms applied to his feet. When the bowels are well evacuated, and no symptoms of coma exist, opiates must be given as in the first variety, but in smaller and less frequently repeated doses.

Much yet remains to be known with reguard to the pathology of delirium tremens. I believe that physicians have committed a dangerous error, in considering these two varieties as modifications of the same disease. In my opinion they are distinct affections and ought to be known under different names. This cannot be better shown than in the conflicting opinions with regard to the real nature of the disease. Dr Clutterbuck, having apparently the second variety in his eye, conceives that delirium tremens arises from congestion or inflammation of the brain; while Dr Ryan, referring to the first, considers it a nervous affection, originating in that species of excitement often accompanying debility. It is very evident, that such different conditions require different curative means. The genuine delirium tremens is that described under the first variety, and I agree with Dr Ryan in the view he takes of the character of this singular disease.

General remarks.—Such are the principal diseases brought on by drunkenness. There are still several others which have not been enumerated—nor is there any affection incident to either the body or mind which the voice does not aggravate into double activity, The number of persons who die in consequence of complaints so produecd, is much greater than unprofessional people imagine. This fact is well known to medical men, who are aware that many of the cases they are called upon to attend, originate in liquor, although very often the circumstance is totally unknown either to the patient or his friends. This is particularly the case with regard to affections of the liver, stomach, and other viscera concerned in digestion. Dr Willan, in his reports of the diseases of London, states his conviction that considerably more than one-eight of all the deaths which take place in persons above twenty years old, happen prematurely through excess in drinking spirits. Nor are the moral consequences less striking: Mr Poynter, for three years Under-Sheriff of London and Westminster, made the following declaration before a committee of the House of Commons:—'I have long been in the habit of hearing criminals refer all their misery to drinking, so that I now almost cease to ask them the cause of their ruin. This evil lies at the root of all other evils of this city and elsewhere. Nearly all the convicts for murder with whom I have conversed, have admitted themselves to have been under the influence of liquor at the time of the act.' 'By due observation for nearly twenty years,' says the great Judge Hales, 'I have found that if the murders and manslaughters, the burglaries and robberies, and riots and tumults, and adulteries, fornications, rapes, and other great enormities, they have happened in that time, were divided into five parts, four of them have been the issues and product of excessive drinking—of tavern and ale-house meetings.' According to the *Caledonian Mercury* of October 26, 1829, no fewer than ninety males, and one hundred and thirty *females*, in a state of intoxication, were brought to the different police watch-houses of Edinburgh, in the course of the week—being the greatest number for many years. Nor is Glasgow, in this respect, a whit better than Edinburgh. On March 1, 1830, of forty-five cases brought before the police magistrate in Glasgow, forty were for drunkenness; and it is correctly ascertained that more than nine thousand cases of drunkenness are annually brought before the police, from this city and suburbs—a frightful picture of vice. In the ingenuous Introductory Essay attached to the Rev Dr Beecher's sermons on Intemperance, the following passage occurs, and I think, instead of exaggerating it rather underrates the number of drunkards in the quarter alluded to. 'Supposing that one-half of the eighteen hundred licensed houses for the sale of spirits which are in that city, send forth each a drunken man every day, there are, in Glasgow, nine hundred drunken men, day after day, spreading around them beggary, and wretchedness, and crime!' Had the author given to each licensed house, one drunkard, on an average, I do not think he would have overstepped the bounds of truth. As it is, what a picture of demoralization and wretchedness does it not exhibit!

CHAPTER XI.

SLEEP OF DRUNKARDS.

To enter at large upon the subject of sleep would require a volume. At present I shall only consider it so far as it is modified by drunkenness.

The drunkard seldom knows the delicious and refreshing slumbers of the temperate man. He is restless, and tosses in bed for an hour or two before falling asleep. Even then, his rest is not comfortable. He awakes frequently during night, and each time his mouth is dry, his skin parched, and his head, for the most part, painful and throbbing. These symptoms from the irritable state of his constitution, occur even when he goes soberly to bed; but if he lie down heated with liquor, he feels them with double force. Most persons who fall asleep in a state of intoxication, have much headach, exhaustion and general fever, on awaking. Some constitutions are lulled to rest by liquors, and others rendered excessively restless; but the first are no gainers by the difference, as they suffer abundantly afterwards. Phlegmatic drunkards drop into slumber more readily than the others: their sleep is, in reality a sort of apoplctic stupor.

I. *Dreams.*—Dreams may be readily supposed to be common, from the deranged manifestations of the stomach and brain which occur in intoxication. They are usually of a painful nature, and leave a gloomy impression upon the mind. In general, they are less palpable to the understanding than those which occur in soberness. They come like painful grotesque conceptions across the imagination; and though this faculty can embody nothing into shape, meaning, or consistence, it is yet haunted with melancholy ideas. These visions depend much on the mental constiution of the person, and are modified by his habitual tone of thinking. It is, however, to be remarked, that while the waking thoughts of the drunkard are full of sprightly images, those of his sleep are usually tinged with a shade of perplexing melancholy.

II. *Nightmare.*—Drunkards are more afflicted than other people with this disorder, in so far as they are equally subject to all the ordinary causes, and liable to others from which sober people are exempted. Intoxication is fertile in producing reveries and dreams, those playthings of the fancy; and it may also give rise to such a distortion of idea, as to call up incubus, and all its frightful accompaniments.

III. *Sleep-walking.* — Somnambulism is another affection to which drunkards are more liable than their neighbours. I apprehend that the slumber is never profound when this takes place, and that, in drunkenness in particular, it may occur in a state of very imperfect sleep. Drunkards, even when consciousness is not quite abolished, frequently leave their beds and walk about the room. They know perfectly well what they are about, and recollect it afterwards. but if questioned, either at the moment or at any future period, they are totally unable to give any reason for their con duct. Sometimes after getting up, they stand a little time and endeavour to account for rising, then go again deliberately to bed. There is often, in the behaviour of these individuals, a strange mixture of folly and rationality. Persons half tipsy have been known to arise and go out of doors in their night-dress, being all the while sensible of what they were doing, and aware of its absurdity. The drunken somnambulism has not always this character. Sometimes the reflecting faculties are so absorbed in slumber, that the person has no consciousness of what he does. From drinking, the affection is always more dangerous than from any other cause, as the muscles have no longer their former strength and are unable to support the person in his hazardous expeditions. If he gets upon a house-top, he does not balance himself properly, from giddiness; he is consequently liable to falls and accidents of every kind. It is considered, with justice, dangerous to awaken a sleep-walker In a drunken fit, there is less risk than under other circumstances, the mind being so far confused by intoxication, as to be, in some measure, insensible to the shock.

IV. *Sleep-talking.*—For the same reason that drunkards are peculiarly prone to somnambulism are they subject to sleep-talking, which is merely a modification of the other. The imagination, being vehemently excited by the drunken dream, embodies itself often in speech, which however is, in almost every case, extremely incoherent, and wants the rationality sometimes possessed by the conversation of sleep-talkers under other circumstances.

CHAPTER XII.

SPONTANEOUS COMBUSTION OF DRUNKARDS.

Whether such a quantity of hydrogen may accumu late in the bodies of drunkards as to sustain combustion, is not easy to determine. This subject is, indeed, one which has never been satisfactorily investigated; and, notwithstanding the cases brought forward in support of the doctrine, the general opinion seems to be, that the whole is fable, or at least so much involved in obscurity as to afford no just grounds for belief. The principal information on this point is in the *Journal de Physique*, in an article by Pierre Aime Lair, a copy of which was published in the sixth volume of the *Philosophical Transactions*, by Mr. Alexander Tilloch. A number of cases are there given: and it is not a little singular that the whole of them are those of women in advanced life. When we consider that writers like Vicq d'Azyr, Le Cat, Maffei, Jacobæus, Rolli, Bianchini, and Mason Good, have given their testimony in support of such facts, it requires some effort to believe them unfounded in truth. At the same time, in perusing the case themselves, it is difficult to divest the mind of an idea that some misstatement or other exists, either as to their alleged cause or their actual nature—and that their relaters have been led into an unintentional misrepresentation. The most curious fact connected with this subject is, that the combustion appears seldom to be sufficiently strong to inflame combustible substances with which it comes in contact, such as woollen or cotton, while it destroys the body, which in other circumstances is hardly combustible at all.* Sometimes the body is consumed by an open flame flickering over it—at other times there is merely a smothered heat or fire, without any visible flame. It is farther alleged that water, instead of allaying, aggravates the combustion. This species of burning, indeed, is perfectly *sui generis*, and bears no resemblance to any species of combustion with which we are acquainted. In most cases it breaks out spontaneously, although it may be occasioned by a candle, a fire, or a stroke of lightning; but in every case it is wholly peculiar to itself. M. Fodere remarks, that hydrogen gas is developed in certain cases of disease, even in the living body; and he seems inclined to join with M. Mere in attributing what is called spontaneous combustion, to the united action of hydrogen and electricity in the first instance, favoured by the accumulation of animal oil, and the impregnation of spiritous liquors. In the present state of our knowledge, it is needless to hazard any conjectures upon this mysterious subject. The best way is to give a case or two, and let the reader judge for himself.

Case of Mary Clues.—'This woman, aged fifty, was much addicted to intoxication. Her propensity to this vice had increased after the death of her husband, which happened a year and a half before: for about a year, scarcely a day had passed in the course of which she did not drink at least half a pint of rum or aniseed water. Her health gradually declined, and about the beginning of February she was attacked by the jaundice and confined to her bed. Though she was incapable of much action, and not in a condition to work, she still continued her old habit of drinking every day, and smoking a pipe of tobacco. The bed in which she lay stood parallel to the chimney of the apartment, at the distance from it of about three feet. On Saturday morning, the 1st of March, she fell on the floor, and her extreme weakness having prevented her from getting up, she remained in that state till some one entered and put her to bed. The following night she wished to be left alone: a woman quitted her at half past eleven, and, according to custom, shut the door and locked it. She had put on the fire two large pieces of coal, and placed a light in a candlestick on a chair at the head of the bed. At half past five in the morning, smoke was seen issuing through the window, and the door being speedily broken open, some flames which were in the room were soon extinguished. Between the bed and the chimney were found the remains of the unfortunate Clues; one leg and a thigh were still entire, but there remained nothing of the skin, the muscles, and the viscera. The bones of the cranium, the breast, the spine, and the upper extremities, were entirely calcined, and covered with a whitish efflorescence. The people were much surprised that the furniture had sustained so little injury. The side of the bed which was next the chimney had suffered most; the wood of it was slightly burned, but the feather-bed, the clothes, and covering were safe. I entered the apartment about two hours after it had been opened, and observed that the walls and every thing in it were blackened; that it was filled with a very disagreeable vapour; but that nothing except the body exhibited any very strong traces of fire.'

This case first appeared in the *Annual Register* for 1773, and is a fair specimen of the cases collected in the *Journal de Physique*. There is no evidence that the combustion was spontaneous, as it may have been occasioned either by lightning, or by contact with the fire. The only circumstance which militates against the latter supposition, is the very trifling degree of burning that was found in the apartment.

Case of Grace Pitt.—'Grace Pitt, the wife of a fishmonger in the Parish of St. Clement, Ipswich, aged about sixty, had contracted a habit, which she continued for several years, of coming down every night from her bed-room, half-dressed, to smoke a pipe. On the night of the 9th of April, 1744, she got up from her bed as usual. Her daughter, who slept with her, did not perceive she was absent till next morning when she awoke, soon after which she put on her clothes, and going down into the kitchen, found her mother stretched out on the right side, with her head near the grate; the body extended on the hearth, with the legs on the floor, which was of deal, having the appearance of a log of wood, consumed by a fire without apparent flame. On beholding this spectacle, the girl ran in great haste and poured over her mother's body some water contained in two large vessels in order to extinguish the fire; while the fœtid odour and smoke which exhaled from the body, almost suffocated some of the neighbours who had hastened to the girl's assistance. The trunk was in some measure incinerated, and resembled a heap of coals covered with white ashes. The head, the arms, the legs, and the thighs, had also participated in the burning. This woman, it is said, had drunk a large quantity of spiritous liquors in consequence of being overjoyed to hear that one of her daughters had returned from Gibraltar. There was no fire in the grate, and the candle had burned entirely out in the socket of the candlestick, which was close to her. Besides, there were found near the consumed body, the clothes of a child and a paper screen, which had sustained no injury by the fire. The dress of this woman consisted of a cotton gown.'

This case is to be found in the *Transactions of the Royal Society of London*, and is one of the most decided, and least equivocal instances of this species of combustion to be met with. It was mentioned at the time in all the journals, and was the subject of much speculation and remark. The reality of its occurrence was attested by many witnesses, and three several accounts of it, by different hands, all nearly coincide.

Case of Don Gio Maria Bertholi.—'Having spent the day in travelling about the country, he arrived in the evening at the house of his brother-in-law. He immediately requested to be shown to his destined apartment, where he had a handkerchief placed between his shirt and shoulders; and, being left alone, betook himself to his devotions. A few minutes had scarcely elapsed when an extraordinary noise was heard in the chamber, and the cries of the unfortunate man were particularly distinguished: the people of the house, hastily entering the room, found him extended on the floor, and surrounded by a light flame, which receded (*a mesure*) as they approached, and finally vanished. On the following morning, the patient was examined by Mr Battlaglia, who found the integuments of the right arm almost entirely detached, and pendant from

* 'At a period when criminals were condemned to expiate their crimes in the flames, it is well known what a large quantity of combustible materials was required for burning their bodies. A baker's boy named Renaud being several years ago condemned to be burned at Caen, two large cart loads of fagots were required to consume the body; and at the end of more than ten hours some remains were still visible. In this country, the extreme incombustibility of the human body was exemplified in the case of Mrs King, who, having been murdered by a foreigner, was afterwards burned by him; but in the execution of this plan he was engaged for several weeks, and, after all, did not succeed in its completion.'—*Paris and Fonblanque's Medical Jurisprudence.*

the flesh; from the shoulders to the thighs, the integuments were equally injured; and on the right hand, the part most injured, mortification had already commenced, which, notwithstanding immediate scarification, rapidly extended itself. The patient complained of burning thirst, was horribly convulsed, and was exhausted by continual vomiting, accompanied by fever and delirium. On the fourth day, after two hours of comatose insensibility, he expired. During the whole period of his sufferings, it was impossible to trace any symptomatic affection. A short time previous to his death, M. Battaglia observed with astonishment that putrefaction had made so much progress; the body already exhaled an insufferable odour; worms crawled from it on the bed, and the nails had become detached from the left hand.

'The account given by the unhappy patient was, that he felt a stroke like the blow of a cudgel on the right hand, and at the same time he saw a lambent flame attach itself to his shirt, which was immediately reduced to ashes, his wristbands, at the same time, being utterly untouched. The handkerchief which, as before mentioned, was placed between his shoulders and his shirt, was entire, and free from any traces of burning; his breeches were equally uninjured, but though not a hair of his head was burned, his coif was totally consumed. The weather, on the night of the accident, was calm, and the air very pure; no empyreumatic or bituminous odour was perceived in the room, which was also free from smoke; there was no vestige of fire, except that the lamp which had been full of oil, was found dry, and the wick reduced to a cinder.'

This case is from the work of Foderé, and is given as abridged by Paris and Fonblanque, in their excellent treatise on Medical Jurisprudence. It occurred in 1776, and is one of the best authenticated to be met with. I am not aware that the subject of it was a drunkard: if he were not, and if the facts be really true, we must conclude that spontaneous combustion may occur in sober persons as well as in the dissipated.

Case of Madame Millet.—'Having,' says Le Cat, 'spent several months at Rheims, in the years 1724 and 1725, I lodged at the house of Sieur Millet, whose wife got intoxicated every day. The domestic economy of the family was managed by a pretty young girl, which I must not omit to remark, in order that all the circumstances which accompanied the fact I am about to relate, may be better understood. This woman was found consumed on the 20th of February, 1725, at the distance of a foot and a half from the hearth in her kitchen. A part of the head only, with a portion of the lower extremities, and a few of the vertebræ, had escaped combustion. A foot and a half of the flooring under the body had been consumed, but a kneading trough and a powdering tub, which were very near the body, sustained no injury. M. Chriteen, a surgeon, examined the remains of the body, with every judicial formality. Jean Millet, the husband, being interrogated by the judges who instituted the inquiry into the affair, declared, that about eight in the evening, on the 19th of February, he had retired to rest with his wife who not being able to sleep, went into the kitchen, where he thought she was warming herself; that, having fallen asleep, he was awakened about two o'clock by an infectious odour, and that, having run to the kitchen, he found the remains of his wife in the state described in the report of the physicians and surgeons. The judges, having no suspicion of the real cause of this event prosecuted the affair with the utmost dilligence. It was very unfortunate for Millet that he had a handsome servant-maid, for neither his probity nor innocence were able to save him from the suspicion of having got rid of his wife by a concerted plot, and of having arranged the rest of the circumstances in such a manner as to give it the appearance of an accident. He experienced, therefore, the whole severity of the law; and though, by an appeal to a superior and very enlightened court, which discovered the cause of the combustion, he came off victorious, he suffering so much from uneasiness of mind, that he was obliged to pass the remainder of his days in an hospital.'

The above case has a peculiar importance attached to it, for it shows that, in consequence of combustion, possibly spontaneous, persons have been accused of murder. Forderé, in his work, alludes to several cases of this kind.

Some chemists have attempted to account for this kind of combustion, by the formation of phosphuretted hydrogen in the body. This gas, as is well known, inflames on exposure to the air; nor can there be a doubt that if a sufficient quantity were generated, the body might be easily enough consumed. If such an accumulation can be proved ever to take place, there is an end to conjecture; and we have before us a cause sufficiently potent to account for the burning. Altogether I am inclined to think, that although most of the related cases rest on vague report, and are unsupported by such proofs as would warrant us in placing much reliance upon them, yet sufficient evidence nevertheless exists, to show that such a phenomenon as spontaneous combustion has actually taken place, although doubtless the number of cases has been much exaggerated. Dr Mason Good, justly observes, 'There may be some difficulty in giving credit to so marvellous a diathesis: yet, examples of its existence, and of its leading to a migratory and fatal combustion are so numerous, and so well authenticated, and press upon us from so many different countries and eras, that it would be absurd to withhold our assent.' 'It can no longer be doubted,' says Dr Gordon Smith, 'that persons have retired to their chambers in the usual manner, and in place of the individual, a few cinders, and perhaps part of his bones, were found.' Inflammable eructations are said to occur occasionally in northern latitudes, when the body has been exposed to intense cold after excessive indulgence in spiritous liquors; and the case of a Bohemian peasant is narrated, who lost his life in consequence of a column of ignited inflammable air issuing from his mouth, and baffling extinction. This case, as well as others of the same kind, is alleged to have arisen from phosphuretted hydrogen, generated by some chemical combination of alcohol and animal substances in the stomach. What truth there may be in these relations I do not pretend to say. They wear unquestionably the aspect of a fiction; and are, notwithstanding, repeated from so many quarters, that it is nearly as difficult to doubt them altogether as to give them our entire belief. There is one thing, however, which may be safely denied; and that is the fact of drunkards having been blown up in consequence of their breath or eructations catching fire from the application of a lighted candle. These tales are principally of American extraction; and seem elaborated by that propensity for the marvellous for which our transatlantic brethren have, of late years, been distinguished.

Upon the whole, this subject is extremely obscure, and has never been satisfactorily treated by any writer. Sufficient evidence appears to me to exist in support of the occurrence, but any information as to the remote or proximate cause of this singular malady, is as yet exceedingly defective and unsatisfactory.

In a memoir lately read before the Académie des Sciences, the following are stated to be the chief circumstances connected with spontaneous combustion:

'1. The greater part of the persons who have fallen victims to it, have made an immoderate use of alcoholic liquors. 2. The combustion is almost always general, but sometimes is only partial. 3. It is much rarer among men than among women, and they are principally old women. There is but one case of the combustion of a girl seventeen years of age, and that was only partial. 4. The body and the viscera are invariably burnt, while the feet, the hands, and the top of the skull almost always escape combustion. 5. Although it requires several fagots to burn a common corpse, incineration takes place in these spontaneous combustions without any effect on the most combustible matters in the neighborhood. In an extraordinary instance of a double combustion operating upon two persons in one room, neither the apartment nor the furniture was burnt. 6. It has not been at all proved that the presence of an inflamed body is necessary to develope spontaneous human combustions. 7. Water, so far from extinguishing the flame, seems to give it more activity; and when the flame has disappeared, secret combustion goes on. 8. Spontaneous combustions are more frequent in winter than in summer. 9. General combustions are not susceptible of cure, only partial. 10. Those who undergo spontaneous combustions are the prey of a very strong internal heat. 11. The combustion bursts out all at once, and consumes the body in a few hours. 12. The parts of the body not attacked are struck with mortification. 13. In persons who have been attacked with spontaneous combustion, a putrid degeneracy takes place which soon leads to gangrene.'

In this singular malady medicine is of no avail. The combustion is kept up by causes apparently beyond the reach of remedy, and in almost every case, life is extinct before the phenomenon is perceived.

CHAPTER XIII.

DRUNKENNESS JUDICIALLY CONSIDERED.

Not only does the drunkard draw down upon himself many diseases, both of body and mind, but if, in his intoxication, he commit any crime or misdemeanor, he becomes, like other subjects, amenable to the pains of law. In this respect, indeed, he is worse off than sober persons, for drunkenness, far from palliating, is held to aggravate every offence: the law does not regard it as any extenuation of crime. 'A drunkard,' says Sir Edward Coke, 'who is *voluntarius demon*, hath no privilege thereby; but what hurt or ill soever he doeth, his drunkenness doth aggravate it.' In the case of the King *versus* Maclauchlin, March, 1737, the plea of drunkenness, set up in mitigation of punishment, was not allowed by the court. Sir George Mackenzie says he never found it sustained, and that in a case of murder it was repelled—Spott *versus* Douglass, 1667. Sir Matthew Hales, c. 4. is clear against the validity of the defence, and all agree that '*levis et modica ebrietas non excusat nec minuit delictum.*' It is a maxim in legal practice, that 'those who presume to commit crimes when drunk, must submit to punishment when sober.' This state of the law is not peculiar to modern times. In ancient Greece it was decreed by Pittacus, that 'he who committed a crime when intoxicated, should receive a double punishment,' *viz.* one for the crime itself, and the other for the ebriety which prompted him to commit it. The Athenians not only punished offences done in drunkenness with increased severity, but, by an enactment of Solon, inebriation in a magistrate was made capital. The Roman law was in some measure, an exception, and admitted ebriety as a plea for any misdeeds committed under its influence: *per vinum delapsis capitalis pœna remittitur.* Notwithstanding this tenderness to offences by drunkards, the Romans, at one period, were inconsistent enough to punish the vice itself with death, if found occurring in a woman. By two acts passed in the reign of James I., drunkenness was punishable with a fine, and, failing payment, with sitting publicly for six hours in the stocks; 4 Jac. I. c. 5, and 21 Jac. I. c. 7. By the first of these acts, Justices of the Peace may proceed against drunkards at the Sessions, by way of indictment: and this act remained in operation till the 10th of October, 1828, at which time, by the act of the 9 Geo. IV. c. 61, § 35, the law for the suppression of drunkenness was repealed, without providing any punishment for offenders in this respect. Previous to this period, the ecclesiastical courts could take cognizance of the offence, and punish it accordingly. As the law stands at present, therefore drunkenness, *per se*, is not punishable, but acts of violence committed under its influence are held to be aggravated rather than otherwise; nor can the person bring it forward as an extenuation of any folly or misdemeanor which he may chance to commit. In proof of this, it may be stated, that a bond signed in a fit of intoxication, holds in law, and is perfectly binding, unless it can be shown that the person who signed it was inebriated by the collusion or contrivance of those to whom the bond was given. A judge or magistrate found drunk *upon the bench*, is liable to removal from his office; and decisions pronounced by him in that state are held to be null and void. Such persons cannot, while acting *ex officio*, claim the benefit of the repeal in the ancient law—their offence being in itself an outrage on justice, and, therefore, a misdemeanor. Even in blasphemy, uttered in a state of ebriety, the defence goes for nothing, as is manifest from the following case, given in Maclaurin's Arguments and Decisions, p. 731.

'Nov. 22, 1694. Patrick Kinninmouth, of that Ilk, was brought to trial for blasphemy and adultery. The indictment alleged, he had affirmed Christ was a bastard. And that he had said, 'If any woman had God on one side, and Christ on the other, he would stow [cut] the lugs [ears] out of her head in spite of them both.' He pleaded chiefly that he was drunk or mad when he uttered these expressions, if he did utter them. The court found the libel relevant to infer the pains libelled, *i. e.* death; and found the defence, that the pannel was furious or distracted in his wits relevant: but repelled the alledgance of fury or distraction arising *from drunkenness.*'

It thus appears that the laws both of Scotland and England agree in considering drunkenness no palliation of crime, but rather the reverse; and it is well that it is so, seeing that ebriety could be easily counterfeited, and made a cloak for the commission of atrocious offences. By the laws, drunkenness is looked upon as criminal, and this being the case, they could not consistently allow one crime to mitigate the penalties due to another.

There is only one case where drunkenness can ever be alleged in mitigation of punishment—that is, where it has induced 'a state of mind perfectly akin to insanity.' It is, in fact, one of the common causes of that disease. The partition line between intoxication and insanity, may hence become a subject of discussion.

'William M'Donough was indicted and tried for the murder of his wife, before the supreme court of the State of Massachusetts, in November, 1817. It appeared in testimony, that several years previous he had received a severe injury of the head; that although relieved of this, yet its effects were such as occasionally to render him insane. At these periods he complained greatly of his head. The use of spiritous liquors immediately induced a return of the paroxysms, and in one of them, thus induced he murdered his wife. He was with great propriety found guilty. The *voluntary use* of a stimulus which, he was fully aware, would disorder his mind, fully placed him under the power of the law,'*

'In the state of New-York, we have a statue which places the property of habitual drunkards under the care of the chancellor, in the same manner as that of lunatics. The overseer of the poor in each town may, when they discover a person to be an habitual drunkard, apply to the chancellor for the exercise of his power

* Beck on Medical Jurisprudence.

and jurisdiction. And in certain cases, when the person considers himself aggrieved, it may be investigated by six freeholders, whether he is actually what he is described to be, and their declaration is, *prima facie*, evidence of the fact.'* [This act was passed March 16, 1821.]

'In Rydgway *v.* Darwin, Lord Eldon cites a case where a commission of lunacy was supported against a person, who, when sober, was a very sensible man, but being in a constant state of intoxication, he was incapable of managing his property.'†

CHAPTER XIV.

METHOD OF CURING THE HABIT OF DRUNKENNESS.

To remove the habit of drunkenness from any one in whom it has been long established, is a task of peculiar difficulty. We have not only to contend against the cravings of the body, but against those of the mind; and in struggling with both, we are, in reality, carrying on a combat with nature herself. The system no longer performs its functions in the usual manner; and to restore these functions to their previous tone of action, is more difficult than it would be to give them an action altogether the reverse of nature and of health.

The first step to be adopted, is the discontinuance of all liquors or substances which have the power of intoxicating. The only question is—should they be dropped at once, or by degrees? Dr Trotter, in his Essay on Drunkenness, has entered into a long train of argument, to prove that, in all cases, they ought to be given up *instanter*. He contends, that, being in themselves injurious, their sudden discontinuance cannot possibly be attended with harm. But his reasonings on this point, though ingenious, are not conclusive. A dark unwholesome dungeon is a bad thing, but it has been remarked, that those who have been long confined to such a place, have become sick if suddenly exposed to the light and pure air, on recovering their liberty: had this been done by degrees, no evil effects would have ensued. A removal from an unhealthy climate (to which years had habituated a man) to a healthy one, has sometimes been attended with similar consequences. Even old ulcers cannot always be quickly healed up with safety. Inebriation becomes, as it were, a second nature, and is not to be rapidly changed with impunity, more than other natures. Spurzheim* advances the same opinion. 'Drunkards,' says he, 'cannot leave off their bad habits suddenly, without injuring their health.' Dr Darwin speaks in like terms of the injurious effects of too sudden a change; and for these, and other reasons about to be detailed, I am disposed, upon the whole, to coincide with them.

If we consider attentively the system of man, we will be satisfied that it accommodates itself to various states of action. It will perform a healthy action, of which there is only one state, or a diseased action, of which there are a hundred. The former is uniform, and homogeneous. It may be raised or lowered, according to the state of the circulation, but its nature is ever the same: when that changes—when it assumes new characters—it is no longer the action of health, but of disease. The latter may be multiplied to infinity, and varies with a thousand circumstances; such as the organ which is affected, and the substance which is taken. Now, drunkenness in the long run, is one of those diseased actions. The system no longer acts with its original purity: it is operated upon by a fictitious excitement, and, in the course of time, assumes a state quite foreign to its original constitution—an action which, however unhealthy, becomes, ultimately, in some measure, natural. When we use opium for a long time, we cannot immediately get rid of it, because it has given rise to a false action in the system—which would suffer a sudden disorder if deprived of its accustomed stimulus. To illustrate this, it may be mentioned, that when Abbas the Great published an edict to prohibit the use of coquenar, (the juice of boiled poppies,) on account of its dismal effects on the constitution, a great mortality followed, which was only stopped at last by restoring the use of the prohibited beverage. Disease, under such circumstances, triumphs over health, and has established so strong a hold upon the body, that it is dislodged with difficulty by its lawful possessor. When we wish to get rid of opium, or any other narcotic to which we are accustomed, we must do so by degrees, and let the healthy action gradually expel the diseased one. Place spirits or wine in the situation of opium, and the results will be the same. For these reasons, I am inclined to think, that, in many cases at least, it would be improper and dangerous to remove intoxicating liquors all at once from the drunkard. Such a proceeding seems at variance with the established actions of the human body, and as injudicious as unphilosophical.

I do not, however, mean to say, that there are no cases in which it would be necessary to drop liquors all at once. When much bodily vigour remains—when the morning cravings for the bottle are not irresistible, nor the appetite altogether broken, the person should give over his bad habits instantly. This is a state of incipient drunkenness. He has not yet acquired the constitution of a confirmed sot, and the sooner he ceases the better. The immediate abandonment of drinking may also, in general, take place when there is any organic disease, such as enlarged liver, dropsy, or schirrus stomach. Under these circumstances, the sacrifice is much less than at a previous period, as the frame has, in a great measure, lost its power of withstanding liquors, and the relish for them is also considerably lessened. But even then, the sudden deprivation of the accustomed stimulus has been known to produce dangerous exhaustion; and it has been found necessary to give it again, though in more moderate quantities. Those drunkards who have no particular disease, unless a tremor and loss of appetite be so denominated, require to be deprived of the bottle by degrees. Their system would be apt to fall into a state of torpor if it were suddenly taken away, and various mental diseases, such as melancholy, madness, and de-

* Beck on Medical Jurisprudence.

† Collinson on Lunacy.

'The laws against intoxication are enforced with great rigour in Sweden. Whoever is seen drunk, is fined, for the first offence, three dollars; for the second, six, for the third and fourth, a still larger sum, and is also deprived of the right of voting at elections, and of being appointed a representative. He is, besides, publicly exposed in the parish church on the following Sunday. If the same individual is found committing the same offence a fifth time, he is shut up in a house of correction, and condemned to six months' hard labour; and if he is again guilty, of a twelvemonths' punishment of a similar description. If the offence has been committed in public, such as at a fair, an auction, &c., the fine is doubled; and if the offender has made his appearance in a church, the punishment is still more severe. Whoever is convicted of having induced another to intoxicate himself, is fined three dollars, which sum is doubled if the person is a minor. An ecclesiastic who falls into this offence loses his benefice: if it is a layman who occupies any considerable post, his functions are suspended, and perhaps he is dismissed. Drunkenness is never admitted as an excuse for any crime; and whoever dies when drunk is buried ignominiously, and deprived of the prayers of the church. It is forbidden to give and more explicitly to sell, any spirituous liquors to students, workmen, servants, apprentices, and private soldiers. Whoever is observed drunk in the streets, or making a noise in a tavern, is sure to be taken to prison and detained till sober, without, however, being on that account exempted from the fines. Half of these fines goes to the informers, (who are generally police officers,) the other half to the poor. If the delinquent has no money, he is kept in prison until some one pays for him, or until he has worked out his enlargement. Twice a-year these ordinances are read aloud from the pulpit by the clergy; and every tavern-keeper is bound under the penalty of a heavy fine, to have a copy of them hung up in the principal rooms of his house.'—*Schubert's Travels in Sweden.*

* View of the Elementary Principles of Education.

lirium tremens, might even be the result. With such persons, however, it must be acknowledged that there is very great difficulty in getting their potations diminished. Few have fortitude to submit to any reduction. There is, as the period of the accustomed indulgence arrives, an oppression and faintness at the *præcordia*, which human nature can scarcely endure, together with a gnawing desire, infinitely more insatiable than the longings of a pregnant woman.

To prove the intensity of the desire for the bottle, and the difficulty, often insurmountable, of overcoming it, I extract the following interesting and highly characteristic anecdote from a recent publication:—'A gentleman of very amiable dispositions, and justly popular, contracted habits of intemperance: his friends argued, implored, remonstrated; at last he put an end to all importunity in this manner:—To a friend who was addressing him in the following strain—'Dear Sir George, your family are in the utmost distress on account of this unfortunate habit; they perceive that business is neglected; your moral influence is gone; your health is ruined; and, depend upon it, the coats of your stomach will soon give way, and then a change will come too late.' The poor victim, deeply convinced of the hopelessness of his case, replied thus:—'My good friend, your remarks are just; they are, indeed, too true; but I can no longer resist temptation: if a bottle of brandy stood at one hand, and the pit of hell yawned at the other, and if I were convinced I would be pushed in as sure as I took one glass, I could not refrain. You are very kind. I ought to be grateful for so many kind good friends, but you may spare yourselves the trouble of trying to reform me: the thing is impossible.''

The observation of almost every man must have furnished him with cases not less striking than the above. I could relate many such which have occurred in my own practice, but shall at present content myself with one. I was lately consulted by a young gentleman of fortune from the north of England. He was aged twenty-six, and was one of the most lamentable instances of the resistless tyranny of this wretched habit that can possibly be imagined. Every morning, before breakfast, he drank a bottle of brandy: another he consumed between breakfast and dinner; and a third shortly before going to bed. Independently of this, he indulged in wine and whatever liquor came within his reach. Even during the hours usually appropriated to sleep, the same system was pursued—brandy being placed at the bed side for his use in the night-time. To this destructive vice he had been addicted since his sixteenth year and it had gone on increasing from day to day, till it had acquired its then alarming and almost incredible magnitude. In vain did he try to resist the insidious poison. With the perfect consciousness that he was rapidly destroying himself, and with every desire to struggle against the insatiable cravings of his diseased appetite, he found it utterly impossible to offer the slightest opposition to them. Intolerable sickness, faintings, and tremors, followed every attempt to abandon his potations; and had they been taken suddenly away from him, it cannot be doubted that delirium tremens and death would have been the result.

There are many persons that cannot be called drunkards, who, nevertheless, indulge pretty freely in the bottle, though after reasonable intervals. Such persons usually possess abundance of health, and resist intoxication powerfully. Here the stomach and system in general lose their irritability, in the same way as in confirmed topors, but this is more from torpor than from weakness. The springs of life become less delicate; the pivots on which they move get, as it were, clogged, and, though existence goes on with vigour, it is not the bounding and elastic vigour of perfect health. This proceeds, not from debility but from torpor; the muscular fibre becoming, like the hands of a labouring man hardened and blunted in its sensibilities. Such are the effects brought on by a *frequent* use of inebriating agents, but an *excessive* use in every case gives rise to weakness. This the system can only escape by a proper interval being allowed to elapse between our indulgences. But if dose be heaped on dose, before it has time to rally from former exhaustion, it becomes more and more debilitated; the blood ceases to circulate with its wonted force; the secretions get defective, and the tone of the living fibre daily enfeebled. A debauch fevers the system, and no man can stand a perpetual succession of fevers without injuring himself, and at last destroying life.

Drunkenness, in the long run changes its character. The sensations of the confirmed tippler, when intoxicated, are nothing, in point of pleasure, to those of the habitually temperate man, in the same condition. We drink at first for the serenity which is diffused over the mind, and not from any positive love we bear to the liquor. But, in the course of time, the influence of the latter, in producing gay images, is deadened. It is then chiefly a mere animal fondness for drink which actuates us. We like the taste of it, as a child likes sweetmeats; and the stomach, for a series of years, has been so accumstomed to an unnatural stimulus, that it cannot perform its functions properly without it. In such a case, it may readily be believed that liquor could not be suddenly removed with safety.

The habit will sometimes be checked by operating skilfully upon the mind. If the person has a feeling heart, much may be done by representing to him the state of misery into which he will plunge himself, his family, and his friends. Some men by a strong effort, have given up liquors at once, in consequence of such representations.

Some drunkards have attempted to cure themselves by the assumption of voluntary oaths. They go before a magistrate, and swear that, for a certain period, they shall not taste liquors of any kind; and it is but just to state, that these oaths are sometimes strictly enough kept They are, however, mnch oftener broken—the physical cravings for the bottle prevailing over whatever religious obligation may have been entered into. Such a proceeding is as absurd as it is immoral, and never answer the purpose of effecting any thing like a radical cure; for, although the person abides by his solemn engagement, it is only to resume his old habits more inveterately than ever, the moment it expires.

Many men become drunkards from family broils. They find no comfort at home, and gladly seek for it out of doors. In such cases, it will be almost impossible to break the habit. The domestic sympathies and affections, which oppose a barrier to dissipation, and wean away the mind from the bottle, have here no room to act. When the mother of a family becomes addicted to liquor, the case is very afflicting. Home instead of being the seat of comfort and order, becomes a species of Pandemonium: the social circle is broken up, and all its happiness destroyed. In this case there is no remedy but the removal of the drunkard. A feeling of perversity has been known to effect a cure among the fair sex. A man of Philadelphia, who was afflicted with a drunken wife, put a cask of rum in her way, in the charitable hope that she would drink herself to death. She suspected the scheme, and, from, a mere principle of contradiction, abstained in all time coming, from any sort of indulgence in the bottle. I may mention another American anecdote of a person reclaimed from drunkenness, by means not less singular. A man in Maryland, notoriously addicted to this vice, hearing an uproar in his kitchen one evening, felt the curiosity to step without noise to the door, to know what was the matter, when he beheld his servants indulging in the most unbounded roar of laughter at a couple of his negro boys, who were mimicking himself in his drunken fits, showing how he reeled and staggered—how he looked and nodded, and hiccupped and tumbled. The picture which these children of nature drew of him, and which had filled the rest with so much merriment, struck him so forcibly, that he became a perfectly sober man, to the unspeakable joy of his wife and children.

Man is very much the creature of habit. By drinking regularly at certain times, he feels the longing for liquor at the stated return of those periods—as after dinner, or immediately before going to bed, or whatever the period may be. He even feels it in certain companies, or in a particular tavern at which he is in the habit of taking his libations. We have all heard the story of the man who could never pass an inn on the roadside without entering it and taking a glass, and who, when, after a violent effort, he succeeded in getting beyond the spot, straightway returned to reward himself with a bumper for his resolution. It is a good rule for drunkards to break all such habits. Let the frequenter of drinking clubs, masonic lodges, and other Bacchanalian assemblages, leave off attending these places; and if he must drink, let him do so at home, where there is every likelihood his potations will be less liberal. Let him also forswear the society of boon companions, either in his own habitation or in theirs. Let him, if he can manage it, remove from the place of his usual residence, and go somewhere else. Let him also take abundance of exercise, court the society of intellectual and sober persons, and turn his attention to reading, or gardening, or sailing, or whatever other amusement he has a fancy for. By following this advice rigidly, he will get rid of that baleful habit which haunts him like his shadow, and intrudes itself by day and by night into the sanctuary of his thoughts. And if he refuses to lay aside the Circean cup, let him reflect that Disease waits upon his steps—that Dropsy, Palsy, Emaciation, Poverty, and Idiotism, followed by the pale phantom, Death, pursue him like attendant spirits, and claim him as their prey.

Sometimes an attack of disease has the effect of sobering drunkards for the rest of their lives. I knew a gentleman who had apoplexy in consequence of dissipation. He fortunately recovered, but the danger which he had escaped made such an impression upon his mind, that he never, till his dying day, tasted any liquor stronger than simple water. Many persons, after such changes, become remarkably lean; but this is not an unhealthy emaciation. Their mental powers also suffer a very material improvement—the intellect becoming more powerful, and the moral feelings more soft and refined.

In a small treatise on Naval Discipline, lately published, the following whimsical and ingenious mode of punishing drunken seamen is recommended:—'Separate for one month every man who was found drunk, from the rest of the crew: mark his clothes 'drunkard;' give him six-water grog, or, if beer, mixed one-half water; let them dine when the crew had finished; employ them in every dirty and disgraceful work, &c. This had such a salutary effect, that in less than six months not a drunken man was to be found in the ship. The same system was introduced by the writer into every ship on board which he subsequently served. When first lieutenant of the Victory and Diomede, the beneficial consequences were acknowledged—the culprits were heard to say that they would rather receive six dozen lashes at the gangway, and be done with it, than be put into the 'drunken mess' (for so it was named) for a month.'

Those persons who have been for many years in the habit of indulging largely in drink, and to whom it has become an *elixir vitæ* indispensable to their happiness, cannot be suddenly deprived of it. This should be done by slow degrees, and must be the result of conviction. If the quantity be forcibly diminished against the person's will, no good can be done; he will only seize the first opportunity to remunerate himself for what he has been deprived of, and proceed to greater excesses than before. If his mind can be brought, by calm reflection, to submit to the decrease, much may be accomplished in the way of reformation. Many difficulties undoubtedly attend this gradual process, and no ordinary strength of mind is required for its completion. It is, however, less dangerous than the method recommended by Dr Trotter, and ultimately much more effectual. Even although his plan were free of hazard, its effects are not likely to be lasting. The unnatural action, to which long intemperance had given rise, clings to the system with pertinacious adherence. The remembrance of liquor, like a delightful vision, still attaches itself to the drunkard's mind; and he longs with insufferable ardour, to feel once more the ecstacies to which it gave birth. This is the consequence of a too rapid separation. Had the sympathies of nature been gradually operated upon, there would have been less violence, and the longings had a better chance of wearing insensibly away.

Among the great authorities for acting in this manner, may be mentioned the celebrated Dr Pitcairn. In attempting to break the habit in a Highland chieftain, one of his patients, he exacted a promise that the latter would every day drop as much sealing-wax into his glass as would receive the impression of his seal. He did so, and as the wax accumulated, the capacity of the glass diminished, and, consequently, the quantity of whiskey it was capable of containing. By this plan he was cured of his bad habit altogether. In mentioning such a whimsical proceeding, I do not mean particularly to recommend it for adoption; although I am satisfied that the principle on which its eccentric contriver proceeded was substantially correct.

A strong argument against too sudden a change is afforded in the case of food. I have remarked that persons who are in the daily habit of eating animal food feel a sense of weakness about the stomach if they suddenly discontinue it, and live for a few days entirely upon vegetables. This I have experienced personally, in various trials made for the purpose; and every person in health, and accustomed to good living, will, I am persuaded, feel the same thing. The stomach, from want of stimulus, loses its tone; the craving for animal food is strong and incessant; and, if it be resisted, heart-burn, water-brash, and other forms of indigestion, are sure to ensue. In such a case vegetables are loathed as intolerably insipid, and even bread is looked upon with disrelish and aversion. It is precisely the same with liquors. Their sudden discontinuance, where they have been long made use of, is almost sure to produce the same, and even worse consequences to the individual.

I cannot give any directions with regard to the regimen of a reformed drunkard. This will depend upon different circumstances, such as age, constitution, diseases, and manner of living. It may be laid down as a general rule, that it ought to be as little heating as possible. A milk or vegetable diet will commonly be preferable to every other. But there are cases in which food of a richer quality is requisite, as when there is much emaciation and debility. Here it may even be necessary to give a moderate quantity of wine. In gout, likewise, too great a change of living is not always salutary, more especially in advanced years, where there is weakness of the digestive organs, brought on by the disease. In old age, wine is often useful to sustain the system, more especially when sinking by the process of natural decay. The older a person is, the greater the inconvenience of abstaining all at once from liquors, and the more slowly ought they to be taken away. I cannot bring myself to believe that a man who for half a century has drunk freely, can suddenly discontinue this ancient habit without a certain degree of risk; the idea is opposed to all that we know of the bodily and mental functions.

In attempting to cure the habit of drunkenness, opium may sometimes be used with advantage. By giving it in moderate quantities, the liquor which the person is in the habit of taking, may be diminished to a considerable extent and he may thus be enabled to leave them off altogether. There is only one risk, and it is this—that he may become as confirmed a votary of opium as he was before of strong liquors. Of two evils, however, we should always choose the least: and it is certain that however perniciously opium may act upon the system, its moral effects and its power of injuring reputation are decidedly less formidable than those of the ordinary intoxicating agents.

The following anecdote has been communicated to me by the late Mr Alexander Balfour, (author of "Contemplation,' 'Weeds and Wildflowers,' and other ingenious works,) and exhibts a mode of curing dram-drinking equally novel and effective:

About the middle of last century, in a provincial town on the east coast of Scotland, where smuggling was common, it was the practice for two respectable merchants to gratify themselves with a social glass of good Hollands, for which purpose they regularly adjourned at a certain hour, to a neighboring gin-shop. It happened one morning that something prevented one of them from calling on his neighbor at the usual time. Many a wistful and longing look was cast for the friend so unaccountably absent, but he came not. His disappointed companion would not go to the dram-shop alone; but he afterwards acknowledged that the want of his accustomed cordial rendered him uneasy the whole day. However, this feeling induced him to reflect on the bad habit he was acquiring, and the consequences which were likely to follow. He therefore resolved to discontinue dram-drinking entirely, but found it difficult to put his resolution into practice, until, after some deliberation, he hit upon the following expedient:—Filling a bottle with excellent Hollands, he lodged it in his back-shop, and the first morning taking his dram, he replaced it with simple water. Next morning he took a second dram, replacing it with water; and in this manner he went on, replacing the fluid subtracted from the bottle with water, till at last the mixture became insipid and ultimately nauseous, which had such an effect upon his palate, that he was completely cured of his bad habit, and continued to live in exemplary soberness till his death, which happened in extreme old age.

Dr Kain, an American physician, recommends tartar emetic for the cure of habitual drunkenness. 'Possessing,' he observes, 'no positive taste itself, it communicates a disgusting quality to those fluids in which it is dissolved. I have often seen persons who, from taking a medicine in the form of antimonial wine, could never afterwards drink wine. Nothing, therefore, seems better calculated to form our indication of breaking up the association, in the patient's feelings, between his disease and the relief to be obtained from stimulating liquors. These liquors, with the addition of a very small quantity of emetic tartar, instead of relieving, increase the sensation of loathing of food, and quickly produce in the patient an indomitable repugnance to the vehicle of its administration.' 'My method of prescribing it, has varied accordingly to the habits, age, and constitution of the patient. I give it only in alterative slightly nauseating doses. A convenient preparation of the medicine is eight grains dissolved in four ounces of boiling water—half an ounce of the solution to be put into half-pint, pint, or quart of the patient's favorite liquor, and to be taken daily in divided portions. If severe vomiting and purging ensue, I should direct laudanum to allay the irritation, and diminish the dose. In every patient it should be varied according to its effects. In one instance, in a patient who lived ten miles from me, severe vomiting was produced, more, I think, from excessive drinking, than the use of the remedy. He recovered from it, however, without any bad effects. In some cases, the change suddenly produced in the patient's habits, has brought on considerable lassitude and debility, which were of but short duration. In a majority of cases, no other effect has been perceptible than slight nausea, some diarrhœa, and a gradual, but very uniform, distaste to the menstruum.'*

Having tried tartar emetic in several instances, I can bear testimony to its good effects in habitual drunkenness. The active ingredient in Chambers's celebrated nostrum for the cure of ebriety, was this medicine. Tartar emetic, however, must always be used with caution, and never except under the eye of a medical man, as the worst consequences might ensue from the indiscreet employment of so active an agent.

It seems probable that, in plethoric subjects the habit of drunkenness might be attacked with some success by the application of leeches, cold applications and blisters to the head, accompanied by purgatives and nauseating doses of tartar emetic. Dr Caldwell of Lexington, conceives drunkenness to be entirely a disease of the brain, especially of the animal compartments of this viscus, and more especially of that portion called by phenologists the organ of *alimentiveness*, on which the appetite for food and drink is supposed mainly to depend. Should his views be correct, the above treatment seems eligible, at least in drunkards of a full habit of body, and in such cases it is certainly worthy of a full trial. I refer the reader to Dr Caldwell's Essay, in which both the above doctrine and the practice founded upon it are very ably discussed. It is, indeed, one of the ablest papers which has hitherto appeared upon the subject of drunkenness.†

It very often happens, after a long course of dissipation, and that the stomach loses its tone, and rejects almost every thing that is swallowed. The remedy, in this case, is opium, which should be given in the solid form in preference to any other. Small quantities of negus are also beneficial; and the carbonate of ammonia, combined with some aromatic, is frequently attended with the best effects. When there is much prostration of strength, wine should always be given. In such a case, the entire removal of the long-accustomed stimulus would be attended with the worst effects. This must be done gradually.

Enervated drunkards will reap much benefit by removing to the country, if their usual residence is in town. The free air and exercise renovate their enfeebled frames; new scenes are presented to occupy their attention; and, the mind being withdrawn from former scenes, the chain of past associations is broken in two.

Warm and cold bathing will occasionally be useful, according to circumstances. Bitters are not to be recommended, especially if employed under the medium of spirits. When there is much debility, chalybeates will prove serviceable. A visit to places where there are mineral springs is of use, not only from the waters, but from the agreeable society to be met with at such quarters. The great art of breaking the habit consists in managing the drunkard with kindness and address. This managment must, of course, be modified by the events which present themselves, and which will vary in different cases.

Persons residing in tropical climates ought, more than others, to avoid intoxicating liquors. It is too much the practice in the West Indies to allay thirst by copious draughts of rum punch. In the East Indies, the natives, with great propriety, principally use rice-

* American Journal of the Medical Sciences, No. IV.

† See Transylvania Journal of Medicine and the Associate Sciences, for July, August, and September, 1832.

water, (congee;) while the Europeans residing there, are in the habit of indulging in Champagne, Madeira, and other rich wines, which may in a great measure account for the mortality prevailing among them in that region. A fearful demoralization, as well as loss of life, is occasioned among the British troops in the East and West Indies, from the cheapness of spiritous liquors, which enables them to indulge in them to excess. 'Since the institution of the recorder's and supreme courts at Madras,' says Sir Thomas Hislop, 'no less than thirty-four British soldiers have forfeited their lives for murder, and most of them were committed in their intoxicated moments.' Dr Rollo relates, that the 45th regiment, while stationed in Grenada, lost within a very few weeks, twenty-six men out of ninety-six; at a time, too, when the island was remarkably healthy. On inquiry, it was found that the common breakfast of the men was raw spirits and pork. It is remarked by Desgennetts, in his medical history of the French army in Egypt, that, 'daily experience demonstrates that almost all the soldiers who indulge in intemperate habits, and are attacked with fevers, never recover.' In countries where the solar influence is felt with such force, we cannot be too temperate. The food should be chiefly vegetable, and the drink as unirritating as possible. It may be laid down as an axiom, that in these regions, wine and ardent spirits are invariably hurtful; not only in immediately heating the body, but in exposing it to the influence of other diseases.* A great portion of the deaths which occur among Europeans in the tropics, are brought on by excess. Instead of suiting their regimen to the climate, they persist in the habits of their own country, without reflecting that what is comparatively harmless in one region, is most destructive in another. There cannot be a stronger proof of this than the French troops in the West Indies having almost always suffered less in proportion to their numbers than the British, who are unquestionably more addicted to intemperance. 'I aver, from my own knowledge and custom,' observes Dr Mosely, 'as from the custom and observation of others, that those who drink *nothing but water*, are but little affected by the climate, and can undergo the greatest fatigue without inconvenience.'†

It is a common practice in the west of Scotland to send persons who are excessively addicted to drunkenness, to rusticate and learn sobriety on the islands of Loch Lomond. There are, I believe, two islands appropriated for the purpose, where the convicts meet with due attention, and whatever indulgences their friends choose to extend towards them. Whether such a proceeding is consistent with law, or well adapted to answer the end in view, may be reasonably doubted; but of its severity, as a punishment, there can be no question. It is indeed impossible to inflict any penalty upon drunkards so great as that of absolutely debarring them from indulging in liquor.

In the next chapter, I shall consider the method of curing and preventing drunkenness by means of temperance societies.

CHAPTER XV.

TEMPERANCE SOCIETIES.

Much has been said and written of late concerning temperance societies. They have been represented by their friends as powerful engines for effecting a total reformation from drunkenness, and improving the whole face of society, by introducing a purer morality, and banishing the hundred-headed monster, intemperance, and all its accompanying vices, from the world. By their opponents, they have been ridiculed as visionary and impracticable—as, at best, but temporary in their influence—as erroneous in many of their leading views—as tyrannical, unsocial, and hypocritical. Their members are represented as enthusiasts and fanatics; and the more active portion of them,—those who lecture on the subject, and go about founding societies,—traduced as fools or impostors. Such are the various views entertained by different minds of temperance societies; but, leaving it to others to argue the point, for or against, according to their inclinations, I shall simply state what I think myself of these institutions—how far they do good or harm—and under what circumstances they ought to be thought favourable of, or the reverse. Truth generally lies *in mediis rebus*, and I suspect they will not form an exception to the rule.

Temperance societies proceed upon the belief that ardent spirits are, *under all circumstances*, injurious to people in health, and that, therefore, they ought to be altogether abandoned. I am anxious to think favourably of any plan which has for its object the eradication of drunkenness; and shall therefore simply express my belief that those societies have done good, and ought therefore to be regarded with a favourable eye. That they have succeeded, or ever will succeed, in reclaiming any considerable number of drunkards, I have great doubts; but that they may have the effect of preventing many individuals from becoming drunkards, is exceedingly probable. If this can be proved,—which I think it may without much difficulty,—it follows that they are beneficial in their nature, and, consequently, deserving of encouragement. That they are wrong in supposing ardent spirits *invariably* hurtful in health, and they are also in error in advocating the instant abandonment, *in all cases*, of intoxicating liquors, I have little doubt; but that they are correct in their great leading views of the pernicious effects of spirits to mankind in general, and that their principles, if carried into effect, will produce good, is self-evident. Spirits when used in moderation, cannot be looked upon as pernicious; nay, in certain cases, even in health, they are beneficial and necessary. In countries subject to intermittents, it is very well known that those who indulge moderately in spirits are much less subject to these diseases than the strictly abstinent. 'At Walcheren it was remarked that those officers and soldiers who took schnaps, *alias* drams, in the morning, and smoked, escaped the fever which was so destructive to the British troops; and the natives generally insisted upon doing so before going out in the morning.'* The following anecdote is equally in point. 'It took place on the Niagara frontier of Upper Canada, in the year 1813. A British regiment, from some accident, was prevented from receiving the usual supply of spirits, and in a very short time, more than two-thirds of the men were on the sick list from ague or dysentery; while, the very next year, on the same ground, and in almost every respect under the same circumstances, except that the men had their usual allowance of spirits, the sickness was extremely trifling. Every person acquainted with the circumstances believed that the diminution of the sick, during the latter period, was attributable to the men having received the quantity of spirits to which they had been habituated.'† Indeed, I am persuaded that while, in the tropics, stimulating liquors are highly prejudicial, and often occasion, while they never prevent, disease, they are frequently of great service in accomplishing the latter object in damp foggy countries, especially when fatigue, poor diet, agues, dysenteries, and other diseases of debility are to be contended against. It

* In warm countries, the acqueous part of the blood loses itself greatly by perspiration; it must therefore be supplied by a like liquid. Water is there of admirable use; strong liquors would coagulate the globules of blood that remain after the transuding of the acqueous humour.—*Montesquieu, Book* xiv. *Chap.* x.

† Tropical Diseases.

* Glasgow Medical Journal, No. XV.

† Ibid.

has been stated, and, I believe with much truth, that the dystentery which has prevailed so much of late among the poorer classes in this country, has been in many cases occasioned, and in others aggravated, in consequence of the want of spirits, which, from the depressed state of trade, the working classes are unable to procure; and should this assertion turn out to be correct, it follows, that temperance societies, by the rigid abstinence urged upon their members, have contributed to increase the evil. The system is fortified against this disorder, as well as various others, by a proper use of stimuli; while excess in the indulgence of these agents exposes it to the attack of every disease, and invariably aggravates the danger. Water is unquestionably the natural drink of man, but in the existing condition of things, we are no longer in a state of nature, and cases consequently often occur wherein we must depart from her original principles. There are many persons who find a moderate use of spirits necessary to the enjoyment of health. In these cases it would be idle to abandon them. They ought only to be given up when their use is not required by the system. That such is the case in a great majority of instances, must be fully admitted; and it is to these that the principles of temperance societies can be applied with advantage. Considering the matter in this light, the conclusion we must come to is simply that ardent spirits sometimes do good, but much oftener mischief. By abandoning them altogether, we escape the mischief and lose the good. Such is the inevitable effect, supposing temperance societies to come into general operation. It remains, therefore, with people themselves to determine whether they are capable of using spirits only when they are beneficial, and then with a due regard to moderation. If they have so little self-command, the sooner they connect themselves with temperance societies the better. I believe that by a moderate indulgence in spirits no man can be injured, and that many will often be benefited. It is their abuse which renders them a curse rather than a blessing to mankind; and it is with this abuse alone I find fault, in the same way as I would object to excess in eating, or any other excess. People, therefore, would do well to draw a distinction between the proper use and the abuse of these stimulants, and regulate themselves accordingly.

Temperance societies, however, though erroneous in some of their principles, and injurious as applied to particular cases, may be of great use towards society in general. Proceeding upon the well-known fact that ardent spirits are peculiarly apt to be abused, and habitual drunkenness to ensue, they place these agents under the ban of total interdiction, and thus arrest the march of that baneful evil occasioned by their excessive use. So far, therefore, as the individual members of these institutions are concerned, a great good is effected at the sacrifice of comparatively little. On such grounds, I fully admit their beneficial effects, and wish them all success. At the same time, many sober persons would not wish to connect themselves with them, for the plain reason—that having never felt any bad effects from the small quantity of ardent spirits they are in the habit of taking, but, on the contrary, sometimes been the better for it—they would feel averse to come under any obligation to abstain from these liquors altogether. Such, I confess, are my own feelings on this subject; and in stating them I am fully aware that the advocates of the societies will answer—that a man's private inclinations should be sacrificed to public good, and that, for the sake of a general example, he should abandon that which, though harmless to him, in the limited extent to which he indulges in it, is pernicious to the mass of mankind. This argument is not without point, and upon many will tell with good effect, though, I believe, people in general will either not acknowledge its force, or, at least, refuse to act up to it.

T

Temperance societies have had one effect: they have lessened the consumption of spiritous liquors to a vast extent, and have left that of wines and malt liquors undiminished, or rather increased it; for although the more strict members avoid even them, their use is not interdicted by the rules of the societies. By thus diminishing the consumption of spirits, they have been the means of shutting up many small public houses; of keeping numerous tradesmen and laborers from the tavern; of encouraging such persons to sober habits, by recommending coffee instead of strong liquor; and, generally speaking, of promoting industry and temperance.

If a person were disposed to be very censorious, he might object to some other things connected with them, such as the inconsistency of allowing their members to drink wine and malt liquors, while they debar them from ardent spirits. They do this on the ground that on the two first a man is much less likely to become a drunkard than upon spirits—a fact which may be fairly admitted, but which, I believe, arises, in some measure, from its requiring more money to get drunk upon malt liquors and wine than upon spirits. In abandoning the latter, however, and having recourse to the others, it is proper to state, that the person often practices a delusion upon himself; for in drinking wine, such at least as it is procured in this country, he in reality consumes a large proportion of pure spirits; and malt liquors contain not only the alcoholic principle of intoxication, but are often sophisticated, as we have already seen, with narcotics. I believe that, though not in the majority of cases, yet in some, spirits in moderation are better for the system than malt liquors; this is especially the case in plethoric and dyspeptic subjects. Independently of this, it is much more difficult to get rid of the effects of the latter. Much exercise is required for this purpose; and if such is neglected, and the person is of full habit of body, it would have been better if he had stuck by his toddy than run the risk of getting overloaded with fat, and dropping down in a fit of apoplexy.

I know several members of the temperance society who are practising upon themselves the delusion in question. They shun spirits, but indulge largely in porter—to the extent perhaps of a bottle a-day. Nobody can deny that by this practice they will suffer a great deal more than if they took a tumbler or so of toddy daily; and the consequences are the more pernicious, because, while indulging in these libations, they imagine themselves to be all the while paragons of sobriety. Rather than have permitted such a license to their members, temperance societies should have proscribed malt liquors as they have done spirits. As it is, a person may be a member, and follow the rules of the societies, while he is all the time habituating himself to drunkenness. These facts, with all my respect for temperance societies, and firm belief in their utility, I am compelled to mention; and I do so the more readily, as there is a large balance of good in their favour, to overweigh whatever bad may be brought against them.

But notwithstanding this, the fact that a habit of drunkenness is far more likely to be caused by indulging habitually in spirits than in any thing else, is undeniable; and temperance societies, in lessening the consumption of spirits, have accomplished a certain good, in so far as they have thus been the means of diminishing, to a considerable extent, the vice of drunkenness, of reclaiming a few topers, and preventing many from becoming so who would certainly have fallen into the snare, had they not been timely checked by their influence and example.

In conclusion, I have to repeat that I do not agree with the societies in considering ardent spirits always hurtful in health, or in recommending the instant disuse of liquor in all cases of drunkenness. The reasons for entertaining my own opinions on these points are given in the work, and they are satisfactory to myself, whatever they may be to others. At the same time, I fully admit that these institutions may often prove eminently useful, and that the cases wherein they may be injurious to those connected with them, are not many, compared to the mass of good which they are capable of effecting. The man, therefore, who feels the appetite for liquor stealing upon him, cannot adopt a wiser plan than to connect himself with a body, the members of which will keep him in countenance in sobriety, and, by their example, perhaps wean him away from the bottle, and thus arrest him on the road to ruin.*

* The following account of temperance societies is by Professor Edgar, one of their most enthusiastic advocates:—

'Temperance societies direct their chief exertions against the use of distilled spirits, conceiving them to be the great bane of the community; but they do not exclude these to introduce other intoxicating liquors in their room. Their object is to disabuse the public mind respecting the erroneous opinions and evil practices which produce and perpetuate intemperance; and though they do not hold it to be sinful to drink wine, yet they are cheerfully willing to accord with the sentiment of inspiration,—'It is good neither to drink wine nor any thing whereby thy brother stumbleth, or is offended, or is made weak.' Were the wine spoken of in Scripture alone used in these countries, they do not believe that there would be a necessity for temperance societies; yet even from such wine, so different from that commonly in use, the Scriptures gave them the fullest liberty to refrain. Avoiding, however, all appearance of rigorous abstinence, they leave to every man's judgment and conscience, how far he shall feel himself warranted in the use of fermented liquors, and only insist, as their fundamental principle, on an abstinence from distilled spirits, and a discountenancing of the causes and practices of intemperance. Their regulations respect persons in health alone; with the prescriptions of physicians they do not interfere. Even the moderate use of distilled spirits they consider to be injurious; and they call upon their brethren for their own sake, to renounce it. The great mass of excellences attributed to intoxicating liquors, they believe to be fictitious; and though all the virtues attributed to them were real, they are cheerfully willing to sacrifice them, while they have the remotest hope of thus cutting off even one of the sources of drunkenness, or arresting one friend or neighbor on the road to ruin. They do not look on the use of intoxicating liquors as necessary either to their health or happiness; they do not love them, and therefore, they do not wish to represent an abstinence from them as, on their part, a great sacrifice; and they trust that they only require to be convinced that the good of their brother demands it, to induce them to do much more than they have yet done. They know that the only prospect of reformation for the intemperate is immediate and complete abstinence, and they joyfully contribute their influence and example to save him. They know that the present customs and practices of the temperate, are now preparing a generation for occupying the room of those who shall soon sleep in drunkards' graves, and it is their earnest wish to exercise such a redeeming influence on the public mind, that should the present race of drunkards refuse to be saved, there may be none to fill their place when they are no more. The abstinence of the temperate, they are convinced, will accomplish this, and that abstinence it is their business to promote by those means with which the God of truth has furnished them. They believe that such abstinence, instead of being productive of any injury to the community, will greatly benefit it; and already there are the fairest prospects of the great objects of such voluntary abstinence being effected, by associations sustaining one another in new habits, to make them reputable and common. They require no oaths, no vows; their bond of obligation is a sense of duty, and subscription to their fundamental principle, is merely an expression of present conviction and determination. The law of temperance societies, like the Gospel is the law of liberty—the law which binds to do that which is considered a delight and a privilege. They look forward to the time as not far distant, when the temperate, having withdrawn their support from the trade in ardent spirits, it shall be deserted by all respectable men, and shall gradually die away, as premature death thins the ranks of drunkards; they trust that the falsehoods by which temperate men have been cheated into the ordinary use of ardent spirits, will soon be completely exposed; and that full information and proper feeling being extended, respecting the nature and effects of intoxicating liquors they will occupy their proper place, and the unnumbered blessings of temperance on individuals and families, and the whole community, will universally prevail. Not only will temperance societies cut off the resources of drunkenness, but to the reformed drunkard, they will open a refuge from the tyranny of evil customs, and they will support and encourage him in his new habits. To promote these invaluable objects, they call for the united efforts of all temperate men; they earnestly solicit the assistance of physicians, of clergymen, of the conductors of public journals, of all men possessing authority and influence; and by every thing sacred and good, they beseech drunkards to turn from the wickedness of their ways and live.'

CHAPTER XVI.

ADVICE TO INVETERATE DRUNKARDS.

If a man is resolved to continue a drunkard, it may here be proper to mention in what manner he can do so with least risk to himself. One of the principal rules to be observed, not only by him, but by habitually sober people, is never to take any inebriating liquor, especially spirits, upon an empty stomach. There is no habit more common or more destructive than this: it not only intoxicates readier than when food has been previously taken, but it has a much greater tendency to impair the functions of the digestive organs. In addition, drunkards should shun raw spirits, which more rapidly bring on disease of the stomach, than when used in a diluted state. These fluids are safe in proportion to the state of their dilution; but to this general rule there is one exception, *viz.* punch. This, though the most diluted form in which they are used, is, I suspect, nearly the very worst—not from the weakness of the mixture, but from the acid which is combined with it. This acid, although for the time being, it braces the stomach, and enables it to withstand a greater portion of liquor than it would otherwise do, has ultimately the most pernicious effect upon this organ—giving rise to thickening of its coats, heartburn, and all the usual distressing phenomena of indigestion. Other organs, such as the kidneys, also suffer, and gravelly complaints are apt to be induced. A common belief prevails that punch is more salubrious than any other spirituous compound, but this is grounded on erroneous premises. When people sit down to drink punch they are not so apt—owing to the great length of time which elapses ere such a weak fluid produces intoxication—to be betrayed into excess as when indulging in toddy. In this point of view it may be said to be less injurious; but let the same quantity of spirits be taken in the form of punch, as in that of grog or toddy, and there can be no doubt that in the long run the consequences will be far more fatal to the constitution. If we commit a debauch on punch, the bad consequences cling much longer to the system than those proceeding from a similar debauch upon any other combination of ardent spirits. In my opinion, the safest way of using those liquids is in the shape of grog.* Cold toddy, or a mixture of spirits, cold water and sugar, ranks next in the scale of safety; then warm toddy; then cold punch—and raw spirit is the most pernicious of all.

The malt-liquor drunkard should, as a generla rule, prefer porter to strong ale. Herb ale and purl are very pernicious, but the lighter varities, such as small beer and home-brewed, are not only harmless but even useful. The person who indulges in malt liquor should take much exercise. If he neglects this, and yields to the indolence apt to be induced by these fluids, he becomes fat and stupid, and has a stong tendency to apoplexy, and other diseases of plethora.

As to the wine-bibber, no directions can be given which will prove very satisfactory. The varities of wines are so numerous, that any complete estimate of their respective powers is here impossible. It may, however, be laid down as a general rule, that those which are most diuretic, and excite least headach and fever are the safest for the constitution. The light dry wines, such as Hock, Claret, Burgundy, Bucellas, Rhenish, and Hermitage, are, generally speaking, more salubrious than the stronger varieties, such as Port, Sherry, or Madeira. Claret, in particular, is the

* The origin of the term 'grog' is curious. Before the time of Admiral Vernon, rum was given in its raw state to the seamen; but he ordered it to be diluted, previous to delivery, with a certain quantity of water. So incensed were the tars at this watering of their favourite liquor, that they nicknamed the Admiral *Old grog*, in allusion to a grogram coat which he was in habit of wearing: hence the name.

most wholesome wine that is known. Tokay,* Frontignac, Malmsey, Vino Tinto, Montifiascone, Canary, and other sweet wines, are apt, in consequence of their imperfect fermentation, to produce acid upon weak stomachs; but in other cases they are delightful drinks ; and when there is no tendency to acidity in the system, they may be taken with comparative safety to a considerable extent. Whenever there is disease, attention must be paid to the wines best adapted to its particular nature. For instance, in gout, the acescent wines, such as Hock and Claret, must be avoided, and Sherry, or Madeira substituted in their room ; and should even this run into the acetous fermentation, it must be laid aside, and replaced by weak brandy and water. Champagne, except in cases of weak digestion, is one of the safest wines that can be drunk. Its intoxicating effects are rapid, but exceedingly transient, and depend partly upon the carbonic acid which is evolved from it, and partly upon the alcohol which is suspended in this gas, being applied rapidly and extensively to a large surface of the stomach.

Drunkards will do well to follow the maxim of the facetious Morgan Odoherty, and never mix their wines. Whatever wine they commence with, to that let them adhere throughout the evening. If there be any case where this rule may be transgressed with safety, it is perhaps in favour of Claret, a moderate quantity of which is both pleasant and refreshing after a course of Port or Madeira. Nor is the advice of the same eccentric authority with regard to malt liquors, less just or less worthy of observance —the toper being recommended to abstain scrupulously from such fluids when he means beforehand to 'make an evening of it,' and sit long at the bottle. The mixture, unquestionably, not only disorders the stomach, but effectually weakens the ability of the person to withstand the forthcoming debauch.

CHAPTER XVII.

EFFECTS OF INTOXICATING AGENTS ON NURSES AND CHILDREN.

Women, especially in a low station, who act as nurses, are strongly addicted to the practice of drinking porter and ales, for the purpose of augmenttng their milk. This very common custom cannot be sufficiently deprecated. It is often pernicious to both parties, and may lay the foundation of a multitude of diseases in the infant. The milk, which ought to be bland and unirritating, acquires certain heating qualities, and becomes deteriorated to a degree of which those unaccustomed to investigate such matters have little conception. The child nursed by a drunkard is hardly ever healthy. It is, in a particular manner, subject to derangements of the digestive organs, or convulsive affections. With regard to the latter, Dr North† remarks, that he has seen them almost instantly removed by the child being transferred to a temperate woman. I have observed the same thing, not only in convulsive cases, but many others. Nor are liquors the only agents whose properties are communicable to the nursling. It is the same with regard to opium, tobacco, and other narcotics. Purgatives transmit their powers in a similar manner, so much so, that nothing is more common than for the child suckled by a woman who has taken physic, to be affected with bowel complaint. No woman is qualified to be a nurse, unless strictly sober; and though stout children are reared by persons who indulge to a considerable extent in liquor, there can be no doubt that they are thereby exposed to risk, and that they would have had a much better chance of doing well, if the same quantity of milk had been furnished by natural means. If a woman cannot afford the necessary supply without these indulgences, she should give over the infant to some one who can, and drop nursing altogether. The only cases in which a moderate portion of malt liquor is justifiable, are when the milk is deficient, and the nurse averse or unable to put another in her place. Here, of two evils, we choose the least, and rather give the infant milk of an inferior quality, than endanger its health, by weaning it prematurely, or stinting it of its accustomed nourishment.

Connected with this subject is the practice of administering stimulating liquors to children. This habit is so common in some parts of Scotland, that infants of a few days old are often forced to swallow raw whiskey. In like manner, great injury is often inflicted upon children by the frequent administration of laudanum, paregoric, Godfrey's cordial, and other preparations of opium. The child in a short time becomes pallid, emaciated, and fretful, and is subject to convulsive attacks, and every variety of disorder in the stomach and bowels. Vomiting, diarrhœa, and other affections of the digestive system ensue, and atrophy, followed by death, is too often the consequence.

An experiment made by Dr Hunter upon two of his children, illustrates in a striking manner the pernicious effects of even a small portion of intoxicating liquors, in persons of that tender age. To one of the children he gave, every day after dinner, a full glass of Sherry : the child was five years of age, and unaccustomed to the use of wine. To the other child, of nearly the same age, and equally unused to wine, he gave an orange. In the course of a week, a very marked difference was perceptible in the pulse, urine, and evacuations from the bowels of the two children. The pulse of the first child was raised, the urine high coloured, and the evacuations destitute of their usual quantity of bile. In the other child, no change whatever was produced. He then reversed the experiment, giving to the first the orange, and to the second the wine, and the results corresponded : the child who had the orange continued well, and the system of the other got straightway into disorder, as in the first experiment. Parents should therefore be careful not to allow their youthful offspring stimulating liquors of any kind, except in cases of disease, and then only under the guidance of a medical attendant. The earlier persons are initiated in the use of liquor, the more completely does it gain dominion over them, and the more difficult is the passion for it to be eradicated. Children naturally dislike liquors—a pretty convincing proof that in early life they are totally uncalled for, and that they only become agreeable by habit. It is, in general, long before the palate is reconciled to malt liquors ; and most young persons prefer the sweet home-made wines of their own country, to the richer varieties imported from abroad. This shows that the love of such stimulants is in a great measure acquired, and also points out the necessity of guarding youth as much as possible from the acquisition of so unnatural a taste.

CHAPTER XVIII.

LIQUORS NOT ALWAYS HURTFUL.

Though drunkenness is always injurious, it does not follow that a moderate and proper use of those agents which produce it is so. These facts have been so fully illustratated that it is unnecessary to dwell longer upon them ; and I only allude to them at present for the purpose of showing more fully a few circumstances in which all kinds of liquors may be indulged in, not only

* Catherine I. of Russia was intemperately addicted to the use of Tokay. She died of dropsy, which complaint was probably brought on by such indulgence.

† Practical Observations on the Convulsions of Infants.

without injury, but with absolute benefit. It is impossible to deny that in particular situations, as in those of hard-wrought sailors and soldiers, a moderate allowance is proper. The body, in such cases, would often sink under the accumulation of fatigue and cold, if not recruited by some artificial excitement. In both the naval and mercantile service the men are allowed a certain quantity of grog, experience having shown the necessity of this stimulus in such situations. When Captain Bligh and his unfortunate companions were exposed to those dreadful privations consequent to their being set adrift, in an open boat, by the mutineers of the Bounty, the few drops of rum which were occasionally doled out to each individual, proved of such incalculable service, that, without this providential aid, every one must have perished of absolute cold and exhaustion.* The utility of spirits in enabling the frame to resist severe cold, I can still farther illustrate by a circumstance personal to myself; and there can be no doubt that the experience of every one must have furnished him with similar examples. I was travelling on the top of the Caledonian coach, during an intensely cold day, towards the end of November, 1821. We left Inverness at five in the morning, when it was nearly pitch dark, and when the thermometer probably stood at 18° of Fahr. I was disappointed of an inside seat, and was obliged to take one on the top, where there were nine outside passengers besides myself, mostly sportsmen returning from their campaigns in the moors. From being obliged to get up so early, and without having taken any refreshment, the cold was truly dreadful, and set fear-noughts, fur-caps, and hosiery, alike at defiance. So situated, and whirling along at the rate of nearly nine miles an hour, with a keen east wind blowing upon us from the snow-covered hills, I do not exaggerate when I say, that some of us at least owed our lives to ardent spirits. The cold was so insufferable, that, on arriving at the first stage, we were nearly frozen to death. Our feet were perfectly benumbed, and our hands, fortified as they were with warm gloves, little better. Under such circumstances, we all instinctively called for spirits, and took a glass each of raw whiskey, and a little bread. The effect was perfectly magical: heat diffused itself over the system, and we continued comparatively warm and comfortable till our arrival at Aviemore Inn, where we breakfasted. This practice was repeated several times during the journey, and always with the same good effect. When at any time the cold became excessive, we had recourse to our dram, which insured us warmth and comfort for the next twelve or fourteen miles, without, on any occasion, producing the slightest feeling of intoxication. Nor had the spirits which we took any bad effects either upon the other passengers or myself. On the contrary, we were all, so far as I could learn, much the better of it; nor can there be a doubt, that without spirits, or some other stimulating liquor, the consequences of such severe weather would have been highly prejudicial to most of us. Some persons deny that spirits possess the property of enabling the body to resist cold, but, in the face of such evidence, I can never agree with them. That, under these circumstances, they steel the system, at least for a considerable time, against the effects of a low temperature, I am perfectly satisfied. Analogy is in favour of this assertion, and the experience of every man must prove its accuracy. At the same time, I do not mean to deny that wine or ale might have done the same thing equally well, and perhaps with less risk of ulterior consequences. We had no opportunity of trying their efficacy in these respects, and were compelled, in self-defence, to have recourse to what, in common cases ought to be shunned, *viz.* raw spirits. The case was an extreme one, and required an extreme remedy; such, however, as I would advise no one to have recourse to without a similar plea of strong necessity to go upon.

It follows, then, that if spirits are often perverted to the worst purposes, and capable of producing the greatest calamities, they are also, on particular occasions, of unquestionable benefit. In many affections, both they and wine are of more use than any medicine the physician can administer. Wine is indicated in various diseases of debility. Whenever there is a deficiency of the vital powers, as in the low stages of typhus fever, in gangrene, putrid sore throat, and generally speaking, whenever weakness, unaccompanied by acute inflammation, prevails, it is capable of rendering the most important services. Used in moderation, it enables the system to resist the attack of malignant and intermittent fevers. It is a promoter of digestion, but sometimes produces acidity, in which case, spirits are preferable. To assist the digestive process in weak stomachs, I sometimes prescribe a tumbler of negus or toddy to be taken after dinner, especially if the person be of a studious habit, or otherwise employed in a sedantary occupation. Such individuals are often benefited by the stimulus communicated to the frame by these cordials. In diarrhœa, dysentery, cholera, cramps, tremors, and many other diseases, both spirits and wine often tell with admirable effect, while they are contra-indicated in all inflammatory affections. Malt liquors also, when used in moderation, are often beneficial. Though the drunkenness produced by their excessive use is of the most stupifying and disgusting kind, yet, when under temperate management, and accompanied by sufficient exercise, they are more wholesome than either spirits or wine. They abound in nourishment, and are well adapted to the laboring man, whose food is usually not of a very nutritive character. The only regret is, that they are much adulterated by narcotics. This renders them peculiarly improper for persons of a plethoric habit, and also prevents them from being employed in other cases where they might be useful. Persons of a spare habit of body, are those likely to derive most benefit from malt liquors. I often recommend them to delicate youths and young girls who are just shooting into maturity, and often with the best effect. Lusty, full-bodied, plethoric people, should abstain from them, at least from porter and strong ale, which are much too fattening and nutritious for persons of this description. They are also, generally speaking, injurious to indigestion and bowel complaints, owing to their tendency to produce flatulence. In such cases, they yield the palm to wine and spirits. It is to be regretted that the system of making home-brewed ale, common among the English, has made so little progress in Scotland. This excellent beverage is free from those dangerous combinations employed by the brewers, and to the laboring classes in particular, is a most nourishing and salubrious drink. I fully agree with Sir John Sinclair in thinking, that in no respect is the alteration in diet more injurious than in substituting ardent spirits for ale—the ancient drink of the common people. Though an occasional and moderate allowance of spirits will often benefit a working man, still the tendency of people to drink these fluids to excess renders even their moderate indulgence often hazardous; and hence, in one respect, the superiority possessed over them by malt liquors.

In higher circles, where there is good living and

* 'At day-break,' says Captain Bligh, 'I served to every person a tea-spoonful of rum, our limbs being so much cramped that we could scarcely move them.'

'Being unusually wet and cold, I served to the people a tea-spoonful of rum each, to enable them to bear with their distressing situation.'

'Our situation was miserable: always wet, and suffering extreme cold in the night, without the least shelter from the weather. The little rum we had was of the *greatest service*—when our nights were particularly distressing, I generally served a tea-spoonful or two to each person, and it was always joyful tidings when they heard of my intention.'—*Family Library*, vol. xxv. *Mutiny of the Bounty.*

little work, liquors of any kind are far less necessary; and, till a man gets into the decline of life, they are, except under such circumstances as have been detailed, absolutely useless. When he attains that age, he will be the better of a moderate allowance to recruit the vigor which approaching years steal from the frame. For young and middle-aged men, in good circumstances and vigorous health, water is the best drink; the food they eat being sufficiently nutritious and stimulating without any assistance from liquor. For young people, in particular, liquors of all kinds are, under common circumstances, not only unnecessary in health, but exceedingly pernicious, even in what the world denominate *moderate* quantities. This is especially the case when the habit is daily indulged in. One of the first physicians in Ireland has published his conviction on the result of twenty years' observation—'That were ten young men on their twenty-first birth day, to begin to drink one glass (equal to two ounces) of ardent spirits, or a pint of Port wine or Sherry, and were they to drink this *supposed moderate quantity* of strong liquor daily, the lives of eight out of the ten would be abridged by twelve or fifteen years.' 'An American clergyman,' says Professor Edgar, 'lately told me that one of his parishoners was in the habit of sending to his son at school a daily allowance of brandy and water, before the boy was twelve years of age. The consequence was, that his son, before the age of seventeen, was a confirmed drunkard, and he is now confined in a public hospital.' The force of this anecdote must come home to every one. Nothing is more common, even in the best society, than the practice of administering wine, punch, &c., even to children—thus not only injuring their health, and predisposing them to disease, but laying the foundation for intemperance in their maturer years.

Having stated thus much, it is not to be inferred that I advocate the banishment of liquors of any kind from society. Though I believe mankind would be benefited upon the whole, were stimulants to be utterly proscribed, yet, in the present state of things, and knowing the fruitlessness of any such recommendation, I do not go the length of urging their total disuse. I only would wish to inculcate moderation, and that in its proper meaning, and not in the sense too often applied to it; for, in the practice of many, moderation, (so called) is intemperance, and perhaps of the most dangerous species, in so far as it becomes a daily practice, and insinuates itself under a false character, into the habits of life. Men thus indulge habitually, day by day, not perhaps to the extent of producing any evident effect either upon the body or mind at the time, and fancy themselves all the while strictly temperate, while they are, in reality, undermining their constitution by slow degrees—killing themselves by inches, and shortening their existence several years. The quantity such persons take at a time, is perhaps moderate and beneficial, if only occasionally indulged in, but, being habitually taken, it injures the health, and thus amounts to actual intemperance. 'It is,' says Dr Beecher, and I fully concur with him, 'a matter of unwonted certainty, that habitual tippling is worse than periodical drunkenness. The poor Indian who once a-month drinks himself *dead*, all but simple breathing, will outlive for years the man who drinks little and often, and is not perhaps suspected of intemperance. The use of ardent spirits *daily* as ministering to cheerfulness or bodily vigour, ought to be regarded as intemperance. No person probably ever did or ever will receive ardents spirits into his system once a-day and fortify his constitution against its deleterious effects, or exercise such discretion and self-government, as that the quantity will not be increased, and bodily infirmities and mental imbecility be the result; and, in more than half the instances, inebriation. Nature may hold out long against this sapping and mining of the constitution which daily tippling is carrying on, but, first, or last, this foe of life will bring to the assault enemies of its own formation, before whose power the feeble and the mighty will be alike unable to stand.

Let those, therefore, who will not abandon liquors, use them in moderation, and not *habitually* or *day by day*, unless the health should require it, for cases of this kind we sometimes do meet with, though by no means so often as many would believe. Abstractly considered, liquors are not injurious. It is their abuse that makes them so, in the same manner as the most wholesome food becomes pernicious when taken to an improper excess.

APPENDIX.

Excerpt from Paris' Pharmacologia.

'The characteristic ingredient of all wines is *alcohol*, and the quantity of this, and the condition or state of combination in which it exists, are the circumstances that include all the interesting and disputed points of medical inquiry. Daily experience convinces us that the same quantity of alcohol, applied to the stomach under the form of natural wine, and in a state of mixture with water, will produce very different effects upon the body, and to an extent which it is difficult to comprehend: it has for instance, been demonstrated that Port, Madeira, and Sherry, contain from one-fourth to one-fifth of their bulk of alcohol, so that a person who takes a bottle of either of them, will thus take nearly half a pint of alcohol, or almost a pint of pure brandy! and moreover, that different wines, although of the same specific gravity, and consequently containing the same absolute proportion of spirit, will be found to vary very considerably in their intoxicating powers; no wonder, then, that such results should stagger the philosopher, who is naturally unwilling to accept any tests of difference from the nervous system, which elude the ordinary resources of analytical chemistry; the conclusion was therefore drawn, that alcohol must necessarily exist in wine, in a far different condition from that in which we know it in a separate state, or, in other words, that its elements only could exist in the vinous liquor, and that their union was determined, and, consequently, alcohol produced by the action of distillation. That it was the *product* and not the *educt* of distillation, was an opinion which originated with Rouelle, who asserted that alcohol was not completely formed until the temperature was raised to the point of distillation: more lately, the same doctrine was revived and promulgated by Fabbronni, in the memoirs of the Florentine Academy. Gay-Lussac has, however, silenced the clamorous partisans of this theory, by separating the alcohol by distillation at the temperature of 66o Fah., and by the aid of a vacuum, it has since been effected at 56o; besides, it has been shown that by precipitating the colouring matter, and some of the other elements of the wine, by *sub-acetate* of *lead*, and then saturating the clear liquor with *sub-carbonate* of *potass*, the alcohol may be completely separated without any elevation of temperature; and this ingenious expedient, Mr Brande has been enabled to construct a table, exhibiting the proportions of combined alcohol which exist in the sev-ral kinds of wine: no doubt, therefore, can remain upon this subject, and the fact of the difference of effect, produced by the same bulk of alcohol, when presented to the stomach in different states of combination, adds another striking and instructive illustration to those already enumerated in the course of this work, of the extraordinary powers of chemical combination in modifying the activity of substances upon the living system. In the present instance, the alcohol is so combined with the extractive matter of the wine, that it is probably incapable of exerting its full specific effects upon the stomach, before it becomes altered in its properties, or, in other words, *digested;* and this view of the subject may be fairly urged in explanation of the reason why the intoxicating effects of the same wine are so liable to vary, in degree, in the same individual, from the peculiar state of his digestive organs at the time of his potation. Hitherto we have only spoken of pure wine, but it is essential to state, that the stronger wines of Spain, Portugal, and Sicily, are rendered remarkable in this country by the addition of brandy, and must consequently contain *uncombined* alcohol, the proportion of which, however, will not necessarily bear a ratio to the quantity added, because, at the period of its admixture, a renewed fermentation is produced by the scientific vintner, which will assimilate and combine a certain portion of the foreign spirit with the wine: this manipulation, in technical language, is called *fretting-in.* The free alcohol may, according to the experiments of Fabbroni, be immediately separated by saturating the vinous fluid with *sub-carbonate* of *potass*, while the combined portion will remain undisturbed: in ascertaining the fabrication and salubrity of a wine, this circumstance ought always to constitute a leading feature in the inquiry; and the tables of Mr Brande would have been greatly enhanced in practical value, had the relative proportions of *uncombined* spirit been appreciated in his experiments, since it is to this, and not to the *combined* alcohol, that the injurious effects of wine are to be attributed. 'It is well known,' observes Dr Macculloch, 'that diseases of the liver are the most common, and the most formidable of those produced by the use of *ardent* spirits; it is equally certain that no such disorders follow the intemperate use of *pure* wine, however long indulged in: to the concealed and unwitting consumption of spirit, therefore, as contained in the wines commonly drunk in this country, is to be attributed the excessive prevalence of those hepatic affections, which are comparatively little known to our continental neighbors.' Thus much is certain, that their ordinary wines contain no alcohol but what is disarmed of its virulence by the prophylactic energies of combination.'

THE END.

CONTENTS OF THE ANATOMY OF DRUNKENNESS.

THE

INFLUENCE OF LITERATURE

UPON

SOCIETY.

TRANSLATED FROM THE FRENCH

OF

MADAME DE STAEL-HOLSTEIN

TO WHICH IS PREFIXED,

A MEMOIR OF THE LIFE AND WRITINGS OF THE AUTHOR

HARTFORD:
PUBLISHED BY SILAS ANDRUS & SON
1850.

CONTENTS OF THE INFLUENCE OF LITERATURE

A CONCISE ACCOUNT

OF

THE PRIVATE AND LITERARY LIFE

OF THE

BARONESS DE STAEL-HOLSTEIN.

To become the depositary of those literary productions which the conscience of tyrants might be anxious to destroy, is one of the many eminent prerogatives of a free people living in the midst of nations that are enslaved; and of all the works which England has snatched from the unjust condemnation of the atrocious factions and oppressive violence under which France has groaned these twenty years, there are few more worthy of being preserved than the Essay of the Baroness de Stael-Holstein on *Literature, considered in its relations to social institutions.* Having witnessed the fatal consequences of a revolution, the storms of which were experienced alike by social institutions and literature, Madame de Stael was led to examine the mutual influence of religion, morals, and laws upon literature, and of literature upon religion, morals, and laws; and while she traced the progressive advances of nations towards literary eminence, she established the degree of perfection which this twofold influence has allowed them to attain.

The most enlightened philosophers have acknowledged perfectibility to be the lot of man in general; but none before Madame de Stael had ever applied it to literature in particular. This prudent restriction proved, however, inefficient to guard her against the unjust attacks of the feeble or wicked minds of those by whom the tenet is reprobated, because their foolish vanity or their criminal ambition represent the principles by which they are influenced, and the measures which they order, as absolutely perfect. They stigmatize as presumptuous those who believe in the possibility of doing better than has been done hitherto; while they themselves have the arrogance to fancy they are patterns of perfection. Dazzled by their vain errors they do not perceive that those who adopt the system of perfectibility, found it upon the principle that perfection is not within the reach of man, but that it is the object, to which religion and morality teach him to aspire. It is this object, which is never attained, that distinguishes mankind from the brute creation, and constitutes individuality. He who is nearest to perfection may still be excelled by those who follow: but of all the competitors that press forward in the same career, none ever stop precisely at the same point. Were it not for perfectibility all men would be alike.

The account which I am attempting to give of the private and literary life of Madame de Stael, will no doubt appear unsatisfactory to those who are desirous of being acquainted with the most minute biographical details of a lady whose writings have justly conferred on their author a great degree of celebrity. But, independently of the regard due to every living author, I have been prevented, by the present restrained communication with the continent, from obtaining that degree of information which might throw some interest upon this memoir.

Wilhelmina Necker is the daughter of James Necker and Susan Curchod. She was born in 1768, at Paris, where she was educated under the immediate superintendance of her parents. She had not reached her tenth year, when her father, who had acquired a considerable fortune as a partner in the house of a banker named Thellusson, and who, by some political pamphlets, particularly an eulogy of Colbert, which was crowned by the French Academy, had acquired an incipient celebrity, was appointed to the directorship of the finances of France under Lewis XVI. Her mother, whose virtues and talents had attracted the admiration of Gibbon during his residence in Switzerland, was the daughter of a Protestant clergyman. As he had endowed her with learning superior to her sex, she had, before her marriage, been a governess in the family of Madame de Vermenoux. Unacquainted with the Parisian manners, Madame Necker possessed none of the attractions of French women: but modesty, candor, and good-nature gave her charms of greater value. A virtuous education and solitary studies, says Marmontel, adorned her mind with all that instruction can add to an excellent natural understanding. She had no fault but a too passionate attachment to literature and an unbounded desire of obtaining a great celebrity for herself and for her husband. A kind mother, a faithful friend, a most affectionate wife, she united all the true characteristics of virtue, a firm religious belief, and a great elevation of soul. Her thoughts were pure: meditation, however, did not tend to enlighten her ideas; in amplifying them she thought to improve them, but in extending them she lost herself in hyperboles and metaphysical abstractions. She seemed to behold certain objects through a mist which magnified them to her eyes; her expressions, on such occasions, became so bombastic, that their meaning would have appeared ridiculous, had it not been known to be ingenuous. It might be truly said of her, that religion and justice formed the ground-work of all her duties. Her conduct proved at all times irreproachable and exemplary.

No sooner was Mr Necker appointed to the management of the finances, than Madame Necker made his power serve to enlarge the exercise of her active benevolence. She contributed to the improvement of the internal regulations of the infirmaries of the metropolis, and undertook the special superintendence of an hospital which she founded at her own expense, near Paris, and which became the model of foundations of that kind. All her literary productions attest her care for suffering humanity. *Her Essay on too precipitate Burials*, her *Observations on the founding of Hospitals*, and her *Thoughts on Divorce*, breathe an ardent zeal for the happiness of her fellow-creatures; and her sentiments were always in unison with her writings.

To make her husband known, to gain him the favour of literary men, the dispensers of fame, and to cause him to be handsomely spoken of in the highest circles, Madame Necker had formed a literary society, which used to meet once a week at her house. Along with *Thomas*, *Buffon*, *Diderot*, *Marmontel*, *Saint Lambert*, and other celebrated writers, who attended these meetings, they were honoured by the most distinguished residents of foreign courts, especially the *Marquis de Caraccioli*, ambassador of Naples, *Lord Stormont*, the ambassador of Great Britain, and *Count de Creutz*, the Swedish ambassador, whose mild philosophy, modest virtue, and eminent talents, received every where an equal share of esteem and admiration.

But, of all the academicians with whom Madame Necker had associated, in order to strengthen her mind by the aid of their genius, she placed none upon a level with *Thomas* and *Buffon*. The former she used to call the *man of the age*, and the latter *the man of all ages*. The veneration and attachment which she felt for these two persons, bordered on adoration; she considered their authority as part of her creed. It was particularly in the school of *Thomas*, a school so fertile in tinsel wit and confused metaphysics, that she became a slave to that affected style which, as it is continnally aiming at elevation and grandeur, conceals her amiable mind, and fatigues, without interesting the reader.

Under the guidance of such a mother, Miss Necker acquired with ease that immense variety of knowledge which astonishes in her writings, and that brilliant superiority of style which renders their study so delightful, notwithstanding a degree of affectation which they occasionally betray, though much less frequently than the works of Madame Necker. Charmed with their early display, her parents neglected nothing to cultivate her talonts. They were soon enabled to devote all their time to this object in a rural retreat.

Miss Necker was scarcely thirteen years old, when her father, impelled by an eager desire of praise, which tormented him during the whole course of his life, published the *Account rendered to the king of his administration*, and availing himself of the unexampled success with which it was received throughout France, demanded to be admitted into the privy council. It was in vain that his religion was urged as an obstacle. He flattered himself that the fear of losing him would overcome this religious scruple: he persisted, and threatened to resign; but he became the victim of his presumption. His resignation was accepted on the 25th of May, 1781. He retired to Switzerland, where he bought the baronial manor of Copet, and he there published his work *on the administration of the finances*.

At the end of a few years, Mr Necker re-appeared occasionally at Paris those of his friends who were truly his, and not the friends of his situation, visited his house as they had done while he was in office. Count de Creutz introduced to him the Baron de Stael Holstein, who had just been sent to him from Sweden, as one of the Swedish embassy, and the latter was immediately admitted into Mr Necker's society. Young, and of a handsome figure, he had the good fortune to please Miss Necker. As the king of Sweden shortly after recalled Count de Creutz, in order to place him at the head of the department of foreign affairs, in his own country, he was succeeded by the Baron de Stael Holstein. Invested with the dignity of a Swedish ambassador at the court of France, and professing the Protestant religion, Baron de Stael soon became the envied husband of a rich heiress who had been courted in vain by many French noblemen. His happiness however was not much to be envied; not that Madame de Stael was without attractions. Her appearance, though not handsome, was agreeable; her deportment noble. She was of the middle size, graceful in her expressions and in her manners. She had much vivacity in her eyes, and much acuteness in her countenance, which seemed to heighten the pointed wit of her remarks. Her faults consisted in too great a carelessness in her dress and an extreme desire of shining in conversation. She spoke little, but in aphorisms, and with the evident intention to produce effect. The unhappy anxiety to become renowned, which she derived from her father, and the pedantic tone which she could not help contracting in the society of her mother and Mr Thomas, must no doubt have been disagreeable to a man, simple and unaffected in his words and actions. But it was chiefly the great superiority of her talents over those of the Baron, that soon destroyed that happy harmony which reigns among couples more equally allied in this respect. The distance was indeed immense. The Baron had even few of those light graces by means of which French vivacity frequently conceals a want of intellectual resources.

It was, however, in consequence of this marriage, that Mr Necker settled again in France, at a time when the prodigality of his successor in the financial department must necessarily have increased his reputation. But as *Mr de Calonne* had attacked the veracity of his *Account* presented to the king, in the speech he pronounced at the opening of the meeting of the Notables in 1787, Mr Necker sent a justification of this account to Louis XVI; and although the monarch expressly desired that it might not become known, his love of importance and glory could not keep him from publishing it. As soon as the king was informed that his answer to the speech of *Mr de Calonne* was printed, he banished him to the distance of forty leagues from Paris. The Baroness de Stael, who in the month of August of the same year had given birth to a daughter, accompanied her father in his exile. It lasted only four months. On the 25th of August, 1788, the king recalled Mr Necker into administration immediately after he had published his work *On the Importance of Religious Opinions*.

The period of this second ministerial reign, which on the 11th of July, 1789, ended in a second exile, is the time when Madame de Stael entered the thorny path of literature. She began with some *Letters on the Writings and Character of J. J. Rousseau*, which met with deserved applause. The third edition is enriched with a letter of Madame de Vassy, and an answer to it by Madame de Stael. But prior to this time, and ere she had reached the age of twenty, she had tried her talents in writing three short novels, which she printed at Lausanne in 1795, with an Essay on Fictions and a poetic Epistle to Misfortune, composed during the tyranny of Robespierre and his infamous coadjutors; the whole under the title of a *Collection of detached Pieces*, the second edition of which was published, with corrections and additions, at Leipzic in

1796. In one of these short novels, called *Mirza*, Madame de Stael appears to have anticipated the plan which the African society of London is now endeavouring to realize. She makes a traveller in Senegal relate that 'the governor had induced a negro family to settle at the distance of a few leagues, in order to establish a plantation similar to those of St Domingo; hoping, no doubt, that such an example would excite the Africans to raise sugar, and that a free trade with this commodity in their own country would leave no inducement to Europeans to snatch them from their native soil, in order to submit them to the dreadful yoke of slavery.'

In her Essay on Fictions, Madame de Stael has endeavored to prove that novels, which should give a sagacious, eloquent, profound, and moral picture of real life, would be the most useful of all kinds of fictions. The imitation of truth constantly produces greater effects than are produced by supernatural means. Those protracted allegories, wherein, as in *Spenser's Fairy Queen*, each canto relates the battle of a knight representing a virtue against a vice his adversary, can never be interesting, whatever be the talent by which they are embellished. The reader arrives at the end, so fatigued with the romantic part of the allegory, that he has no strength left to understand its philosophical meaning. As for these allegories which aim at mingling jocular wit with moral ideas, Madame de Stael thinks that they attain their philosophical object but very imperfectly. When the allegory is really entertaining, most men remember its fable better than its result. *Gulliver* has afforded more amusement as a tale, than instruction as a moral composition.

Madame de Stael disapproves of novels founded upon historical facts. She pleads for natural fictions, and wishes to see the gift of exciting emotions applied to the passions of all ages, to the duties of all situations. Among the works of this kind, *Tom Jones* is that of which the moral is the most general. Love, in this novel, is introduced merely to heighten the philosophical result. To demonstrate the uncertainty of judgments built upon appearances, to show the superiority of natural and, as it were, involuntary qualities over reputations grounded on the mere respect of outward decorum, is the true object of *Tom Jones*. *Goodwin's Caleb Williams*, with all its tedious details and negligences, appears likewise to answer Madame de Stael's ideas of the inexhaustible kind of novels to which she alludes. Love has no share in the groundwork of his fiction. The unbridled passion of the hero of the novel for a distinguished reputation, and the insatiable curiosity of Caleb that leads him to ascertain whether Falkland deserves the esteem which he enjoys, are the only supports of the interest of the narrative.

These correct views show how intimately Madame de Stael was acquainted with English Literature even in her younger years. But she was not long permitted to enjoy her first literary successes in peace. The crisis of the revolution, which embittered her life, was fast approaching.

On the 11th of July, 1789, her father was going to sit down to table with several guests, when the Secretary of state for the naval department came to him, took him aside, and delivered to him a letter from the king, which commanded him to resign and to quit the French territory in silence. Madame Necker, whose health was rather precarious, did not take with her any domestic, nor any change of apparel, that their departure might not be suspected. They made use of the carriage in which they generally took a ride in the evening and hastened onwards night and day to Brussels. When the Baroness de Stael joined them three days afterwards with her husband, they were still wearing the same dress in which they were habited, when, after the grand dinner, during which no one had suspected their agitation, they had silently quitted France, their home, and their friends. Mr Necker set off from Brussels accompanied only by the Baron de Stael, to go to Basle through Germany. Madame Necker and the Baroness de Stael followed with a little less precipitation. They were overtaken at Frankfort by the bearer of letters from the king and the national assembly, which recalled Mr Necker for a third time into administration. As soon as Madame de Stael and her mother had joined him at Basle, he resolved to return to France. This journey from Basle, to Paris was the most interesting moment of Madame de Stael's life. Her father was as it were borne in triumph, and she anticipated for the future none but happy days.

But these deceitful hopes were very soon banished. During the fifteen months of his being in office for the last time, Mr Necker was constantly involved in a fruitless struggle in behalf of the executive power, and as he saw no prospect of being useful, he retired to his estate at Copet towards the end of 1790. Madame de Stael shortly after followed him thither. She returned to Paris in the first months of 1791, and took perhaps a more lively concern in the political events of the day than became the wife of a foreign ambassador. It has even been asserted, that, moved by the misfortunes with which Louis XVI. was threatened, she formed the project of saving him by affording him a secret retreat at an estate of the Duke of Orleans in Normandy, which was then to be disposed of: but the king preferred to entrust himself to Count de Fersen, and took the road to Montmidi. She has also been reproached for her intimacy with M. de Talleyrand Perigord, at that time bishop of Autun, Viscount Noailles, the Lameths, Barnave, Count Louis de Narbonne, Vergniaud, and other distinguished members of the constituent and first legislative assemblies; and it has been said that she accompanied Count Narbonne on his circuit to inspect the fortresses of the frontiers, immediately after his having been called to the head of the war department towards the end of 1791. Be this as it may, it is certain that she continued at Paris with her husband until the reign of terror. It was only in 1793 that she fled with him to Copet, and thence went over to England, where she resided several months. They did not return to France till the year 1795, after the Duke of Sudermannia, regent of the kingdom of Sweden, during the minority of the unfortunate Gustavus Adolphus IV., had appointed Baron de Stael his ambassador with the French republic. It was also nearly about this time that Madame de Stael published her *Thoughts on Peace, addressed to Mr Pitt and the French People*, which the illustrious Fox quoted in the House of Commons in support of his arguments for peace, and to which Sir Francis d'Ivernois replied by his *Thoughts on War*.

It is possible that, born with a lively disposition, and anxiously wishing for the return of order and tranquillity, Madame de Stael frequently armed herself with all her eloquence to animate her friends, in those disastrous times, to put an end to troubles that were continually renewed. In 1795, Legendre, that Parisian butcher, who was the friend of Marat, Danton, and Robespierre, declaimed more than once against her as being at the head of the intrigues that had a tendency to moderation. She says somewhere in her work on literature: 'If, to heighten her misfortune, it were in the midst of political dissentions that a female should acquire a remarkable celebrity, her influence would be supposed unbounded, though null in reality; she would be accused of the deeds of her friends; she would be hated for whatever is dear to her, and the defenceless objects would be attacked in preference to those who might yet be feared:' and it is her own experience which suggested these expressions. Madame de Stael has felt what she complains of; during the internal dissentions of France she has been crushed by all parties, astonished to find her an interested bystander during the conflict of their passions. Her having said, along with the Abbe Sieyes, that the constitution of 1795 'was not yet the good one,' has been imputed to her as a crime.

While calumny was embittering her days, her feeling heart was doomed to a more severe misfortune. Mr Necker having informed her that there was no hope of his wife's recovery from a long illness, which actually terminated her life shortly after, Madame de Stael eagerly hastened to her dying mother. She fond her extremely weak. Madame Necker was fond of hearing music during her illness: every evening she sent for some musicians, in order that the impression she received from harmonious sounds might keep her soul alive to those sublime thoughts from which alone death derives a character of melancholy and tranquillity. Once, during the last days of her sufferings, the musicians having neglected coming, Mr Necker requested his daughter to perform on the piano. After having played a few sonatas, she began to sing a song of Sacchini's composition, in his Œdipus at Colonna, the words of which recall the cares of Antigone.* Her father, on hearing this, shed a flood of tears, and threw himself at the feet of his dying consort. His profound emotion caused Madame de Stael to give over singing. On the very last day of Madame Necker's life, wind-instruments were still heard in a room close to her bed-chamber when she had already ceased to live. 'To describe,' says Madame de Stael, 'the melancholy contrast between the varied expressions of the musical sounds, and the uniform feeling of sadness with which death filled the heart, is impossible.' Thomas, who has celebrated Madame Necker in his verses addressed to Susanna, has left an indirect eulogy of her in his Essay on Women. 'Truly estimable,' says this academician, 'is the female who, though she has imbibed in the great world the charms of society, such as good taste, grace and wit, knows how to preserve her heart and her understanding from that unfeeling vanity and that false sensibility, the offspring of the higher circles; who, reluctantly obliged to submit to social forms and usages, never loses sight of nature, and by whom nature is yet regretted; who, forced by her rank to expense and luxury, prefers at least useful expenses, and enables industrious poverty to share in her wealth; who, while she cultivates literature and philosophy, loves these pursuits for their own sake and not for a vain reputation; she in fine who, in the midst of levity, does not lose her natural character; who, in the bustle of the world, retains a firm mind; who owns her friend in the midst of those by whom he is slandered; who boldly undertakes his defence, though he is never to know it; and who at home and abroad reserves her esteem for virtue, her contempt for vice, and her heart for friendship.' In order to assuage her grief for the loss of a parent, in every respect entitled to the most poignant regret, and to repel the malicious attacks to which she was exposed for opinions which were not hers, Madame de Stael composed at Lausanne the first part of a philosophical Essay *on the influence of the passions upon the happiness of individuals and nations*, which she published at Paris in 1796, and of which she printed the second part in 1797. The merit of this work has been acknowledged alike in France, in England and in Germany. It abounds in interesting remarks, and views many objects in a novel and striking manner. Its style is elegant throughout, and but very rarely obscure. It was translated into English in 1798.

Madame de Stael was with her father at Copet when the French troops entered Switzerland. By one of the decrees passed during the reign of terror, Mr Necker, although an alien, had been placed on the list of emigrants, and any one, whose name was on that fatal list, was to be condemned to death if found on a territory occupied by the French armies. But the French generals showed him the most respectful regard, and the Directory afterwards erased his name from the list.

This moderation induced Madame de Stael to repair once more to her husband in France. But at the end of a few months she grew tired of the various persecutions to which she was unceasingly exposed, and hastened back to her father, upbraiding herself for being unable to live like him in solitude, and to exist without that competition of thoughts and glory which doubles our existence and our powers.

In 1798, the declining health of Baron de Stael again called Madame de Stael to Paris, where he expired in her arms. About this time she published a work *On the influence of Revolutions upon Literature*, of which I have not been able to procure a copy; nor have I seen a dramatic piece of her composition called *The Secret Sentiment*. Madame de Stael, after the death of her husband, spent the greatest part of her time with her father at Copet and at Lausanne.

In 1800, when Buonaparte passed through Geneva he had the curiosity to visit Mr Necker at Copet where Madame de Stael happened to be with her father. The interview was not long, but it has been reported that Madame de Stael requested a private audience, during which she spoke to the First Consul of the powerful means which his situation afforded him to provide for the happiness of France, and made an eloquent display of some plans of her own, which she thought particularly calculated to accomplish this object. Buonaparte appeared to give her an attentive hearing: but when she ceased to speak, he coldly asked, 'Who educates your children, madame?'

It was chiefly in Switzerland that Madame de Stael wrote the novel called *Delphine*, the first edition of which was printed at Geneva in 1802. The moral object of this novel has been equally mistaken in France, England, and Germany, and yet it has been read every where with the same eagerness. It has had four or five editions in France, and has been translated in English and German, while the *Anti-Delphine* of a very sensible English young lady, which has drawn sweet tears from the eyes of tender females, has met with few readers in England, where Madame de Stael's novel has been loudly condemned.

The severity of the criticisms which from every corner of Europe were directed against a work written with a captivating energy of style, drew from the author an ingenious defence:—'In most novels, which have a moral object,' says Madame de Stael, 'personages that are perfect are contrasted with others who are completely odious. Such writings, I think, leave no impression on the only class of readers that are capable of amendment, namely, those who are both weak and honest. Utility consists in inspiring the dread of faults committed by beings that are naturally virtuous, delicate, and feeling; to these alone good advice may be serviceable; they alone may be deterred by a fatal example.—The vicious are, by their nature, so different from us, that whatever we may write effects no conviction in their minds: their language, sentiments, hopes and fears are so different; and nothing can have any effect upon them except the events of their own life. I need not observe, I hope, that a dramatic writer does not approve of the characters he delineates, and that, whether he paints a train of error and their fatal consequences, or a series of good actions and their rewards, he is still a severe moralist. I am almost ashamed to be obliged to repeat notions which are every where so fully acknowledged that they are deemed superfluous.'

One day Mr Necker, in a conversation with his daughter, respecting the novel of Delphine, which had been so much criticised, maintained, that domestic affections alone were capable of affording scenes as tragical as the passion of love; and to prove his

* Elle m'a prodigué sa tendresse et ses soins,
Son zèle dans mes maux m'a fait trouver des charmes

assertion, he composed a tale, entitled *The Fatal Consequences of a Single Error*, which Madame de Stael has inserted in the manuscripts of her father published at Geneva in 1804.

In the mean time, Madame de Stael could not habituate herself to live in a country which is not her native one, and where sciences are much more cultivated than literature. Her father perceived her struggles between her predilection for the brilliant societies at Paris and the sorrow she felt at the idea of leaving him. Though, in his character of a wise parent, he ought to have condemned, in a widow, the mother of three children, this fatal propensity for seeking happiness only in the crowded assemblies of the great world, whose votaries alike extol the sallies of false wit and the effusions of genius, to be applauded in their turn, Mr Necker, who himself was not yet cured of the same disease, encouraged her partiality for France. Fond of the remembrance which he had left behind in that country, he endeavored with all his might to preserve its affection for his family. As Madame de Stael was perhaps actuated by the secret desire of shining at the court of the First Consul, or at least of collecting in the metropolis of the French republic the flattering meed of praise due to her last literary successes, she easily yielded to the persuasions of her father, and he appeared at Paris in 1803. But her residence in that city was not of long duration. Whether the watchful activity of her superior genius, was still feared, or that she had ventured too sarcastic observations upon the events of the day, or whether the First Consul had so little generosity as to be revenged on the daughter for a work published against the consular government by the father, Buonaparte soon pronouuced against her a sentence of banishment to the distance of forty leagues from Paris; and it has been reported that Madame de Stael had the noble firmness to say to him: 'You are giving me a cruel celebrity; I shall occupy a line in your history.'

Madame de Stael at first retired to Auxerre; but not meeting with suitable society, she thought she might settle at Rouen; and as this city is only thirty-two leagues from Paris, she even fancied she might draw a little nearer to the metropolis, and took a house in the valley of Montmorency. But the French government ordered her to withdraw within the limits assigned in the sentence of her exile; she then set out for Frankfort, attended by her eldest daughter, and accompanied by the ex-tribune Benjamin Constant, her faithful protector. From Frankfort Madame de Stael repaired, in the midst of a severe winter, to the dominions of the king of Prussia, where she formed plans destined to make the French acquainted with German literature. In the spring of the year 1804 she felt herself happy at Berlin, the society of which city pleased her much; when, on the morning of the 18th of April, a friend brought her letters which informed her of her father's illness. She immediately set off, and until she reached Weimar, the idea that she might be deceived, that her father might be no more, had never entered her mind. Mr Necker had however died at Geneva on the 9th of April, 1804, after a short but painful illness. During his fever he expressed frequent apprehensions that his last work might prove fatal to his daughter, and in his delirium he often blessed her and her three children.

This unexpected blow changed the destiny of Madame de Stael. After her tears had flown in abundance upon the grave of a father whom she had affectionately loved, she sought for some alleviation to her grief in selecting the most interesting fragments among Mr Necker's papers; and published them at Geneva in 1804, together with a short account of the character and private life of her father, under the title of *Manuscripts of Mr Necker, published by his daughter*. She took care to insert in them a compliment paid to the character of Buonaparte in these words: 'The first consul is eminently distinguished by his firm and decisive character; it is a splendid will which seizes every thing, regulates every thing, fixes every thing, and which always moves and stops at the proper time. This faculty, which I describe after a great model, is the first quality for the chief ruler of a great empire. In the end, it is considered as a law of nature, and all opposition vanishes.' This mean flattery on the part of a man who had ruined France, to introduce republican forms, produced no alteration in the disposition of the First Consul towards Madame de Stael. The sentence of her banishment was not revoked, and the novel of *Corinna*, which appeared soon after Buonaparte had been raised to the imperial throne, has probably rendered it irrevocable.

To dispel her sadness and gloom, Madame de Stael determined to travel over the fine countries of Italy. The constant serenity of the sky, the variety of landscapes, a delightful music, and the contemplation of the ruins of that superb Rome, formerly mistress of the world, insensibly revived her talents and her enthusiasm, and even gave renewed elasticity to her genius. It is to this journey that learned Europe is indebted for *Corinna or Italy*, that splendid monument of the fine taste, the profound erudition, the lively sensibility and the ardent imagination of its author. The mind finds some difficulty in conceiving the combination of talents which that work possesses. It is written with an eloquence bordering on the sublime; it breathes throughout the purest attachment to the true principles of civil liberty; and England and Italy are contrasted in a manner little calculated to please those who would wish to destroy every free country. The exclamation of Corinna at the sight of the Roman forum: 'Honour then, everlasting honour to all courageous and free nations, since they thus captivate the attention of posterity!' resounds disagreeably in the ears of despots.

After this effort of genius, Madame de Stael, by way of relaxation, amused herself first with performing in tragedy at Geneva, and afterwards assuming the modest office of an editor. Some time after the appearance of Corinna, she published two volumes of *Letters and Reflections of Prince de Ligne*, and enriched them with a short preface worthy of her talents. I have given an English translation of this work, to which I attach some little value, because it has afforded me an opportunity of associating my name with that of such an editor; it is only in this character that I may be allowed to aspire to that honour. The literary world is anxiously expecting the work which Madame de Stael had commenced in 1804 upon Germany.

Far be it from me to imitate the numerous slanderers who have taken particular delight in publishing the errors of Madame de Stael, and falsely adding to their number. It belongs only to the pen of history which will immortalize her merit, to reveal the weaknesses by which that merit may be obscured. It is possible that Madame de Stael, as has been observed by her father, may be 'very susceptible of being misled:' she may sometimes have been guilty of 'an amiable thoughtlessness,' as Marmontel calls it: but she never can be dispossessd of the first rank among female authors who, in our times, have shed a lustre on French literature.

D. Boileau.

Brompton Road, Nov. 1st. 1811.

INTRODUCTION.

The object of the present work is to examine what influence Religion, Manner s,and Laws, have upon Literature; and reciprocally, how far Literature may effect Laws, Manners, and Religion. On the art of composition and the principles of taste there are extant, in the French tongue, treatises* the most accurate and complete : but it appears to me, that sufficient pains have not been taken to analyze the moral and political causes which modify and mark the character of Literature. Neither do I think that any attempt has hitherto been made to consider philosophically the gradual development of the human faculties, as it displays itself in the distinguished works that have afforded delight or instruction to mankind, from the age of Homer down to the present time.

The works of celebrity which have appeared in every age, afford unequivocal proofs of the successive progress and improvement of the human understanding. I have endeavored to explain the slow but, unceasing advance of the mental powers, in the field of Philosophy, and their rapid but desultory strides in the career of the Arts. From a curious observation of the characteristic traits which distinguish the contemporary writings of the Italians and the English, of the Germans and the French, I hold it to be demonstrable, that political and religious institutions had a principal share in the production of these continual diversities. Finally, from contemplating the gloom of despair and the dawn of hope which the French Revolution has, if I may be allowed the expression, confounded together ; I deemed it of some importance to ascertain what degree of influence that revolution has exerted upon the state of knowledge, and what are the probable consequences that may hereafter result from it, should liberty and order, republican, morality and independence, be wisely and politically combined.

But before I proceed farther to unfold the plan of the present work, it may be proper to touch a little upon the importance and advantages of literature, considered in its widest acceptation; that is, as it embraces the dogmas of philosophy and the effusions of imagination ;—every thing, in fine, connected with the operations of thought, with the exclusion only of physical and experimental science.

My first object, then, will be to take a general survey of literature as it is connected with virtue, with glory, with liberty, and with happiness: and if it be acknowledged without the possibility of contradiction, that it has a powerful influence upon these sublime sentiments, these master-springs of the human soul; how much more lively must be the interest with which, I flatter myself, the reader will accompany me in retracing the progress and observing the predominant character of the writers who have honoured every country and graced every age! Oh! that I could win over every enlightened mind to the pursuit and enjoyment of philosophical meditations ! But it frequently happens, that the contemporaries and eye-witnesses of a revolution cease to take any interest in the investigation of truth. The issue of so many events decided by force; the atrocity of so many crimes wiped off by success; the lustre of so many virtues tarnished by calumny; the sacredness of so many misfortunes profaned by the insolence of power; the dignity of so many generous sentiments sunk into objects of ridicule and scorn; the meanness of low calculations raised into subjects of philosophical discussion :—all these things tend to discourage and deaden hope, even in the breasts of men the most zealously devoted to the homage of reason. It should, however, re-animate their desponding spirits, to observe, that there is not to be found in the history of the human mind an useful discovery or a profound truth that does not carry the mark of its own age, and claim its peculiar admirers. Yet, doubtless, it is a melancholy reflection, that we must have to wade through futurity, to transfer our interest, and repose our hopes on posterity, on foreigners, or strangers, who can come in no point of contact with us; in a word, on the whole mass of mankind, the recollection or image of whom can never come home to our hearts or understandings. But, alas ! with the exception of a few select unalterable friends, the majority of those whom we recall to mind, after ten years of a Revolution, only sadden the soul, stifle its emotions, and over-awe the talents one may possess, not by any superiority on their part, but by the influence of that malevolence which gives pain only to delicate minds, and grieves those only who deserve to be strangers to sorrow.

Let us, then, raise ourselves above the pressures of life: let us not furnish our unmerited enemies, nor our ungrateful friends, with any opportunity to boast of having dejected our intellectual powers. Their malicious attempts will only compel those who would have remained satisfied with cultivating the milder affections, to aspire to the pursuit of glory. Since, then, it must be so; let us grasp at the bright attainment. These efforts of ambition will, indeed, be of little avail to assuage the sorrows of the soul; but they will shed a gleam of honour on the career of life. To devote our days wholly to the ever-deceitful hopes of happiness, would only tend to make them more miserable. Bet-

* The works of Voltaire, Marmontel, and Laharpe.

ter is it to concentrate the whole of our endeavors, that we may travel with some dignity, and with some reputation, down that road which leads from the morning of youth to the night of the grave.

OF THE IMPORTANCE OF LITERATURE, AS IT CONCERNS AND IS CONNECTED WITH VIRTUE.

Perfect virtue is the ideal *beautiful* of the moral world: and there is some similitude and affinity between the impression which virtue makes upon us, and that sentiment which is inspired by whatever is sublime, either amidst the productions of the finer arts or in the aspect of the physical world. The regular and graceful proportions of antique statues, the calm and pure expression of certain paintings, the harmony of music, the amenity of a beautiful prospect over a fruitful country, transport us with an enthusiasm by no means uncongenial to that admiration to which we are raised by the contemplation of generous and heroic actions. Fantastic appearances, whether the result of nature or of art, may strike the imagination with a momentary surprise; but the operations of thought can dwell only upon order and regularity.

In endeavoring to convey some idea of a future life, it has been said that the soul of man returned into the bosom of his creator. This was describing in some measure the emotion we feel, when, after being long bewildered in the labyrinth of the passions, we suddenly hear the august and awful voice of virtue, of pride, or of pity, and when our whole soul becomes alive to the call.

Literature can only derive its permanent beauties from the most delicate and refined morality. Men may devote their actions to vice; but vice can never control their judgment. Never was it in the power of any poet, however ardent his fancy or vivid his imagination, to draw forth a tragic effect from an incident which admitted the smallest tendency to an immoral principle. Opinion, which fluctuates so much respecting the events of real life, assumes a character of constancy and decision, when it has to pronounce on the productions of the imagination. Literary criticism is not unfrequently, indeed, a sort of treatise on morality. By yielding merely to the impulse and guidance of their talents, eminent writers might discover every thing that is heroic in self-devotion, and all that is affecting in the sacrifices we make of our interests or passions. By studying the art of moving the affections, we explore the recesses and discover the secrets of virtue.

The master-pieces of literature, independent of the fine models which they furnish, produce a kind of moral and physical emotion, an agitating transport of admiration, which excites us to the performance of generous deeds. The legislators of Greece attached no mean importance to the effect that might be produced by music of a martial or a voluptuous strain. Our organs are also acted upon by eloquence, poetry, the incidents of the dramatic scene, and the gloom of melancholy thoughts, though these are properly the objects of reason and reflection: it is then that virtue becomes a voluntary impulse, a movement that communicates itself to the blood, and hurries us irresistibly along like the most violent and imperious passions. It is much to be regretted, that the works which appear in our days, do not more frequently kindle that noble enthusiasm: our taste is, doubtless, formed by the study of the already received and acknowledged master-pieces of literature: but we become accustomed to them from our infancy: each of us is struck with their beauties at different periods of life, and separately receives the impressions they should produce. Were we to assist together in crowds at the first representation of a tragedy worthy of Racine,—were we to read together the enchanting pages of Rousseau, or have our ears saluted, for the first time, with the modulated periods of Cicero,—the interest excited by surprise and curiosity would rivet our attention upon truths that are now unheeded; and genius, assuming its empire over every mind, would repay to morality something of what it has received from morality: it would re-establish that homage to which it owes its inspiration.

The connexion that exists between all the faculties of man is such, that, even by improving his literary taste, you contribute to raise and dignify his character. We experience, within ourselves, a certain impression from the language which we use: the images it calls up in our minds, contribute to the better modification of our dispositions. Thus, when hesitating between different expressions, the writer or the orator gives a decided preference to that which suggests the most pure and delicate idea; his taste chooses between these expressions, in the same manner as his mind ought to determine respecting the actions of life; and the former habit often may conduce to the latter.

The sentiment of the intellectual *beautiful*, while it is employed upon literary objects, must inspire a repugnance for every thing mean or ferocious: and this involuntary aversion is as sure a guide as the most fixed and deeply meditated principles.

It would be humiliating to attempt the justification of wit; its advantages are so evident at the very first glance. Though some persons, by a sort of abuse of wit, have amused themselves by attempting to discover its disadvantages: but this is a paradox to which nothing but puns or equivocal expressions could have lent the appearance of reason. True genuine wit is no other than the faculty of seeing rightly: common sense approaches much nearer to it than false ideas. The more a man is endued with common sense, the more wit he possesses. And genius, what is it, but good sense intent upon new ideas? Genius augments the treasure of good sense; it adds its conquests to the dominions of reason. What it explores and discovers to-day, will soon be generally known; because important truths, when once discovered, strike every mind with equal force. Sophisms, conceits that are called *ingenious*, though they be devoid of justness, in a word, every thing that diverges from the proper point, should invariably be regarded as a defect. But when wit and genius concur, in all their relations, with the dictates of reason, they are equally incapable of producing any evil. When wit and genius, therefore, are encouraged by a nation; when those only who are gifted with those faculties are promoted to public stations, the surest means are employed to make the cause of morality prosper.

Not unfrequently do we hear imputed to wit the very faults that proceed from the absence of it. Your half-hints, the mere shadows of ideas, darken the mind instead of enlightening it. Virtue is both an affection of the soul, and a demonstrable truth: it must be either felt or understood. If you derive from reasoning only what misleads instinct, without attaining to that which can supply its place; then it is not the qualities you possess that become destructive, but rather those in which you are deficient. Of all human calamities the remedy should be looked for from above. If we raise our eyes towards heaven, our thoughts swell into a nobler nature: it is by soaring aloft that we breathe a purer air, and are cheered by a brighter light. Man should, in fine, be prompted to aspire to every kind of perfection and superiority: nothing can more contribute to improve and refine his morals. Superior talents excite an admiration, and win an affection, which disposes the mind of those who possess them to gentleness and lenity. Observe men of cruel dispositions; you will generally find they are deficient in intellectual endowments of the higher order: nature even seems to have given them a cast of countenance that disgusts and repels; and they would fain avenge themselves upon the social order for what nature has refused them. I would without the smallest fear or suspicion confide in those whom I find satisfied with their lot, and who, by some talent or other, can claim and do really merit the suffrage of mankind. But for the man who is incapable of obtaining from his fellow-men any pledge of voluntary approbation, what interest can he feel in the conservation of the human race? To him whom the world admires, the happiness of the world must be dear.

It has frequently been remarked, that historians, dramatic writers, all those, in short, who study men with a view to a description of their character, become themselves indifferent to virtue or to vice. An ordinary knowledge of mankind may, indeed, produce such an effect: but a deeper and more discerning knowledge leads to the very opposite result. He who draws mankind like Saint Simon or Duclos, only contributes to the levity of their opinions and of their morals: but the writer who can observe and appreciate mankind like Tacitus, must, of necessity, be useful to the age he lives in. The art of distinguishing characters, of unfolding their motives, and of drawing forth their discriminative colors, is armed with such a power and ascendant over opinion, that, in every country where the liberty of the press prevails, no public man, no man of consequence enough to be known, could withstand contempt, if it was inflicted on him by the hand of genius. With what fine bursts of indignation has the aspect of crime filled the mouth of eloquence! How powerfully and triumphantly does eloquence assert and avenge the cause of every generous sentiment! Nothing can equal the impression that is made by an animating strain of eloquence, or the portrait of a character boldly drawn. Pictures of vice leave an indelible impression, when they are the product of a writer of penetration: he analyzes the most secret sentiments and seizes the almost imperceptible shades and details of character; and frequently some energetic expression attaches to a bad man through life, and the man and the expression are but one and the same in the judgment of the public. Here, then, is another moral utility resulting from literary talent, which, by the very art of depicting* bad actions, brands them with an indelible stigma.

I have now to touch upon the objections that have been urged against those works, in which genius is employed in portraying reprehensible morals. It must indeed be confessed, that such writings are of a tendency to injure morality, if they could leave any deep impression: but the merely superficial marks they make are easily effaced by the influence of genuine and generous sentiments. Susceptibility is, with regard to love, what esteem is with respect to virtue: and as immorality can never gain esteem, so the tear of tenderness will never be shed but at the call of delicacy. Sprightly and amorous writings, in general, serve only as a transient relaxation of the mind, which rarely retains any recollection of them. Human nature is of a serious cast; and, in the silence of meditation, we attach ourselves solely to those works which are calculated to exercise our reason or our own sensibility. It is in in this kind of writing only that literary glory has been acquired, and in it alone can the real influence of literature be displayed.

Will it be said, that the pursuit of literary fame may divert a man from the performance of domestic duties, or of political services which he might render to his country? There no longer exist any models of those republics, which allotted to each citizen his share of influence over the destiny of his country; much farther are we removed from that patriarchal mode of life, in which every family entertained in their own bosom such sentiments as they most approved. But in the present state of Europe, the progress of literature must tend to unfold every species of generous notions. Were this advancement of literature to be checked, it would not be the cultivation of public virtues or of private affections that would be substituted in its room, but the greedy calculations of selfishness or of vanity.

The generality of mankind, dismayed by the frightful vicissitudes to which political events have given rise amongst us, seem to have lost all regard for the improvement of their minds, and are too deeply intimidated by the hazardous state of things, to allow the intellectual faculties to possess any ascendancy. If the French, however, were to exert themselves to obtain fresh successes in the career of literature and philosophy, it would be a first step made towards the improvement of their morals: the very pleasure that is produced by the success of self-love, would be the means of forming some bands of unity betwixt men. We should gradually emerge from that most degraded state of public spirit, where the selfishness of the state of nature is combined with the active multiplicity of the interests of society; where corruption is without politeness, and coarseness without candor; where civilization is unaccompanied by knowledge, and ignorance unprompted by enthusiasm: in a word, we should emerge from that kind of apathy, the distemper of a few superior men, with which little minds imagine themselves to be attacked; while wholly taken up with their own interest, they betray a total indifference for the suffering of the others.

OF LITERATURE, AS IT CONCERNS AND IS CONNECTED WITH GLORY.

If it be true, that literature can essentially contribute to the improvement of morals, it must, by that circumstance alone, have a powerful influence upon glory: for there can be no durable glory enjoyed by a country, in which due regard is not paid to the public morals. If a nation did not adopt certain invariable principles as the basis of its opinion, and if each individual were not strengthened and confirmed in his judgment by a conviction that that judgment was consentaneous to the universal assent, distinguished reputations would be nothing more than so many contingencies that succeeded each other by chance. The splendor of certain actions might dazzle and strike; but there must be a progression in the sentiments we feel, before we arrive at the sublimest of all,—admiration. All our judgments are formed upon comparison. Esteem, approbation and respect, are so many ingredients that are necessary to the composition of enthusiasm. Morality lays the foundations upon which glory may raise its superstructure; and literature, independently of its alliance and connexion with morals, contributes moreover, and in a manner still more direct, to the production and existence of that glory which is the noblest motive and highest incentive to all public virtues.

The love of one's country is an affection purely social. Man, whom nature has adapted for domestic intercourse, would not carry his ambition farther, if not urged by the irresistible attraction of general esteem: and upon that esteem, which grows out of the public opinion, literary talents exert the most powerful influence. At Athens, at Rome, in all the mistress cities of the civilized world, the powers of eloquence

* Most undoubtedly, the advantages that might be hoped for from the publicity of truth, may be counterbalanced by the repulsive libels with which France has been dishonored. But I merely intended speaking of the services that might be expected from genius; for genius dreads to disgrace itself by falsehood; it equally dreads confounding characters, as it would then forfeit the rank which it holds among mankind. In all the affairs of men, superiority alone encourages and secures; and what is most to be apprehended are the vices and defects that are inseparable from littleness of mind and poverty of spirit.

displayed in public harangues turned at will the inclinations of the people, and decided the general lot. In modern days, reading paves the way for great events, and by this men's minds are enlightened. What would become of populous nations, if the individuals who compose them did not communicate with each other by means of the press? Were silence to prevail in large assemblies of men, there never could be established any point of contact from which to elicit light, and the multitude could never enrich ther minds with the thoughts of superior intellects.

As the human species is constantly recruiting itself, an individual can create a void only in opinion; and in order to give existence to that opinion, there must be some means of understanding each other at a distance, and of uniting themselves in one universal sentiment, from a knowledge of the ideas and sentiments that are generally approved. Poets and moralists previously characterize the nature of glorions deeds. The study of literature enables a nation to reward its great men, by teaching it to appreciate their respective deserts. Military glory has existed among the most barbarous tribes; but no comparison should ever be instituted between ignorance and degradation. Should a people that have once been civilized by the love of letters, relapse into a state of indifference to genius and philosophy, and become dull and cold to every lively and generous sentiment; they then can only be distinguished by a spirit that endeavors to debase and vilify, and which prompts them under every circumstance to shut their minds against admiration. They are afraid of being deceived, should they attempt to bestow praise, and, like young fops who assume the air and tone of fashion, they imagine they distinguish themselves more by an unjust censure, than by too great a facility, to commend. Such a people, under such circumstances, generally sink into apathy and indifference; the frost of age seems to have benumbed their rational faculties: they have a sufficient knowledge of things to guard them against surprise, but not enough to qualify them for discriminating what deserves esteem. They may have destroyed a number of illusions, but have not established a single truth; through old age, they have relapsed into infancy: and through reasoning, into uncertainty: they have become strangers to the glow of mutual interest, and have sunk into that state which DANTE calls the *hell of the luke-warm.* Whoever aims at distinction, is sure immediately to raise an unfavorable prejudice against himself; the public is wearied, and sickens at the first appearance of a man who attempts to win any mark of its favor.

When a nation is daily acquiring new lights, it looks with fondness on great men as its precursors in the career which it has to run; but when a nation is conscious that it retrogades, the small number of superior minds that escape from the general degeneracy, appear, as it were, enriched with its spoils. It no longer takes a common interest in their successes; and the only emotions it feels are those that are prompted by envy.

The dissemination of knowledge, and the illumination that has been produced in Europe by the destruction of slavery and the discovery of printing, must lead to an unlimited melioration of things, or to a complete degradation of society. If the analyzing search of the philosopher ascended to the true principle of social institutions, it would add a new degree of strength to the truths it may have preserved; but that superficial analysis which decomposes only the first obvious ideas, without penetrating into the examination of the whole object, must infallibly tend to weaken and relax the spring of all bold opinions. Amidst a nation whose appetites are palled, whose energies are unstrung, the sentiment of an high admiration cannot possibly be found: even the eclat of military triumphs must fail to acquire an immortal reputation, if the culture of literary and philosophical ideas does not befit the mind for feeling, and for justly appreciating the glory of heroism.

It is by no means true that a great man rises to greater eminence by being the only celebrated person, than when he is surrounded by a number of distinguished names that yield to the first of all,—his own. It has been a maxim in politics, that the kingly power cannot support itself without a peerage and a nobility. Opinion, indeed, will not suffice: there must be added certain gradations of rank in order to secure supremacy. But what was a conqueror, who during the night of ignorance, led barbarians against barbarians? Is Cæsar so celebrated in history for no other reason than that he decided the fate of Rome, while Rome had her Ciceros, her Sallusts, her Catos, and because that bright host of talents and of virtues bent beneath the sword of a single man? Behind Alexander you still discover the shade of Greece. It is necessary, then, for thc glory of illustrious warriors, that they subjugate countries that are enriched with all the endowments of the human mind. I do not pretend to say, that the mental powers may one day free the world from the scourge of war; but till then, it is mind, it is eloquence, imagination, and even philosophy, which alone can give grace and relief to the achievement of martial exploits. After every thing else has faded away, and sunk into degradation, force may still bear sway over the world; but it will be surrounded by no real or genuine splendor: mankind would be a thousand times more degraded by the extinction of all emulation, than by all tha rageful jealousies of which glory was still the object.

OF LITERATURE AS IT RELATES TO LIBERTY.

Liberty, virtue, glory, knowledge, those kindred and closely allied ideas which form the proud retinue that attends on the natural dignity of man, cannot possibly be insulated in a separate state of existence; the perfection of each of them results from the union of them all.

Those minds which indulge in the idea, that the destiny of man is connected with the divine intelligence, behold in this comprehension of beings, in this intimate relation between every thing that is good, a strong additional proof of that moral unity, of that unity of conception which informs and directs the universe.

The advancement of literature, that is to say, the ulterior perfection of the art of thinking and of expressing one's thoughts, is necessary to the establishment and to the conservation of liberty. It is manifest, that the light of knowledge is the more indispensably necessary in a country, as all the citizens who inhabit it have a more immediate influence on the character and conduct of the government: and equally true is it, that political equality, a principle essentially inherent in every philosophical institution, cannot possibly exist, unless you class the differences of education with as minute an attention as was exerted, in feudal times, to maintain arbitrary distinctions. Purity of language, dignity of expression, that bespeak and picture out the nobleness of the soul, are more eminently necessary in a state that is bottomed on a democratical basis. Elsewhere, certain factitious barriers prevent the total confusion of different educations: but when power is only to be supported and upheld by the supposition of personal merit, what care should be taken to surround that merit with all the splendor of its external characteristics!

In a democratic state, it is continually to be feared that the love of popularity may beget an imitation of vulgar manners: soon then would a persuasion be entertained that it was useless, nay, perhaps prejudicial, to hold out a too strongly marked superiority over the multitude, whose favor a man may be prompted to wish to conciliate for the purpose of gratifying his ambition. The people would thence become accustomed to make choice of ignorant and illiberal magistrates : such magistrates would soon put out every light of knowledge ; and, by an inevitable consequence, the extinction of knowledge would bring back the degradation and slavery of the people.

It is impossible that, in a free state, the public authority can stand without the genuine, unbiassed assent of the citizens whom it governs. Reasoning and eloquence are the natural bonds that hold together a republican association. What power can you wield over the free will of men, if you be destitute of that vigour, that truth of expression, which penetrates into every soul, and inspires the very sentiments it expresses? If persons who are called to the helm of the commonwealth, do not possess the secret of persuading men's minds, the nation ceases to acquire lights, and individuals adhere to the opinion upon public affairs which chance has implanted in their understanding. Were eloquence to die away, one of the principal motives for regretting its extinction would be, that its loss would tend to insulate mankind from each other, by resigning them wholly and solely to their individual impressions. Those who cannot convince, must oppress ; and in all the different relations between the governing and the governed, the fewer qualities the former possess the more will be their encroachments on the latter.

The establishment of new institutions must create a new spirit in countries that aspire to be free. But what hold can be laid upon opinion without the aid and concurrence of able writers? In order to call forth such a spirit, it is not obedience that you are to enforce, but the desire of new institutions that you must suggest : and when a government is wisely inclined to promote the establishment of these institutions ; so tender should be the regard shown to public opinion, that government should only seem to anticipate the public wish. There is nothing but the sound writings of accomplished wits that, for any length of time, can direct and modify the bent of certain national habitudes. Man, in the secret recesses of his soul, secures an asylum for liberty, inaccessible to the attacks of force ; conquerors have often adopted the manners of the conquered ; but conviction alone has been able to change ancient customs. The cultivation and improvement of literature are the best means by which you can effectually combat the obstinacy of inveterate prejudices. In countries newly become free, in order to extirpate old deep-rooted errors, governments must employ ridicule, to give youth a disrelish to them ; and conviction, to obliterate them from maturer minds. In order to favor the foundation of new establishments, governments must stimulate hope, excite curiosity, kindle enthusiasm ; call forth, in a word, those sentiments of creative energy that have given birth to every thing that exists and stability to every thing that endures ; and by what powers can these sentiments be inspired, but by the art of eloquence and of fine composition? The love of activity so necessary in all free states, breaks out in a spirit of faction, unless the acquirement and diffusion of knowledge be an object of universal interest, and be formed into an occupation that opens impartially to every talent a field in which the general ambition may be exercised and displayed. It will also be necessary to encourage a close and constant study of history and philosophy, which alone can qualify the mind to penetrate into and disseminate the knowledge of the respective rights and duties of nations, and of the magistrates who rule them. In despotic empires, reason can only be of avail to induce the resignation of individuals ; but in free countries, it must watch over the general tranquillity and protect the general freedom

Among the various studies which tend to develop the human mind, it is philosophical literature, it is eloquence and reasoning, which I look upon as the chief stay and most permanent pledge of liberty. The sciences and the arts constitute a very important portion of our intellectual labours ; but the discoveries to which they lead, and the success with which they are crowned, exert no immediate influence upon that public opinion on which hangs the destiny of nations. Geometricians, natural philosophers, painters, and poets, may meet with protection and encouragement under the reign of the most potent monarchs : but before the eyes of such masters, political and religious philosophy would rise up in the shape of the most formidable insurrection.

Those who devote themselves to the study of the abstract sciences; as they have not to encounter, in their progress, the passions of mankind : so they gradually get accustomed to take that only into account, which is susceptible of mathematical demonstration : they almost invariably arrange in the class of delusions whatever they are unable to submit to the logic of calculation. The strength of government, no matter what its form may be, is the first thing they attend to and appreciate : and as they have scarcely any other desire than that of prosecuting unmolested the plan of their learned labours, they easily yield obedience to the ruling authority. The profound meditation so requisite in the combinations of the abstract sciences, weans the attention of the learned from the ordinary events of life ; and nothing so wonderfully suits the views and temper of absolute monarchs, as a description of men who are so wholly engrossed with contemplating the physical laws of the world, that they readily abandon the care of its moral order to any one who will take the trouble of directing it. It may indeed be true, that discoveries made in sciences will, in process of time, give a new spring and energy to that higher species of philosophy that sits in judgment on nations and on kings ; but a futurity so remote can have nothing in it to restrain and intimidate the audacity of tyrants. We have seen many tyrants who were ostentatious in their protection of the sciences and the arts : but all of them have dreaded the natural enemies of protection itself,—men who think and philosophize.

Poetry, of all the arts, is that which borders most closely on the province of reasoning. Poetry, however, admits neither analysis nor discussion ; which are both so conducive to the discovery and dissemination of philosophical ideas. The mind that is anxious to utter any bold and novel truth, would preferably express itself in a style of language that conveys its thoughts with exactness and precision : it would labour more after the ascendency of conviction than the colorings of the imagination. Poetry has more frequently been employed in flattering, than in censuring power ; and, in general, the fine arts may sometimes contribute, through the very enjoyments they procure, to fashion men to that mould in which tyrants would wish them to be cast. By the endless variety of pleasures which they daily hold out to enjoyment, the arts have a power to divert the mind from cherishing any predominant idea : they enlist men on the side of their sensations : they breathe into the soul a kind of voluptuous philosophy, a deliberate unconcernedness, a passion for the present, an indifference for the future ; than which nothing can be more favorable to tyranny. By a singular contrast, the arts, while they give a taste and relish for life, render us rather dull and indifferent to death. The passions alone make us cling forcibly to existence, by the ardent wish they inspire for the accomplishment of their object : but a life devoted to mere amusements, diverts without captivating ; and disposes to intoxication, to sleep, and to death During those periods which sanguinary proscriptions have consigned to infamy, the Romans and the French indulged themselves with extraordinary eagerness in all kinds of public amusements: but in well-constituted republics, grave occupations, domestic affections, the love and pursuit of glory, not unfrequently alienate the mind even from the enjoyments furnished by the fine arts. Indeed, the only literary engine that can be wielded with effect, so as to make all injurious powers tremble, even in the most elevated sphere, is manly eloquence, independent philosophy; which, and which alone, can arraign before the tribunal of reason all the opinions and institutions of mankind.

From an undue influence of a military spirit there also results very imminent danger to free states: nor can this danger be averted, but by diffusing the light of knowledge and the spirit of philosophy. If military men pretend to look down with disdain on men of letters, it is because the latter do not always unite with talents a sufficient decision and vigor of character. But the art of composition might also become a weapon, and eloquence might quicken into action, if it displayed the living energies of the soul;—if the sentiments of the writer soared to the elevation of his thoughts;—and if tyranny beheld itself exposed to the attacks of the most formidable of its foes, stern reason and generous indignation. Consideration would then no longer be exclusively attached to military talents, nor would liberty run the risk to which it must otherwise be necessarily exposed.

From among the troops that compose an army, every thing like opinion is banished by the severity of its discipline. So far this *esprit de corps* bears some resemblance to that which prevails among the priesthood: it in like manner excludes all reasoning and discussion, and admits no other guide or rule but the will of superiors. The constant, uninterrupted exercise of the omnipotence of arms must, in the end, inspire nothing but contempt for the slow and silent progress of persuasion.

The enthusiastic admiration which waits on the glory of triumphant generals, is wholly unconnected with the justice of the cause they espouse. The imagination is struck only with the decision of fortune in their favor, and the splendor of success which crowns their intrepidity. The enemies of liberty, it is true, may be overpowered in battle: but, in order to make the principles of that liberty take root and flourish in a country, the military spirit must be done away; thought and reasoning must be called in, and these seconded by the warrior's qualities of courage, ardour, and decision, in order to excite in the souls of its inhabitants something spontaneous, something voluntary, which dies away within them when they have been long inured to the triumphant prevalence of mere force.

In all ages and in all countries, a military spirit produces the same effects: it stamps no nation with any peculiar character; it weds no people to any particular institution: it is, indeed, calculated equally to defend and protect them all. Eloquence and philosophy can alone give the charms and endearments of *country* to any extent of territory, by framing the nation that inhabits it to a similarity of propensities and habits, of customs and sentiments. Force dispenses with the aid of time, and tramples down will; but by this very means it is rendered unfit for giving permanency to any thing among men. During the course of the French revolution, we have often heard it said, 'that a certain degree of despotism was necessary to the establishment of liberty.' This incongruous jumble of words passed into a kind of sentence: but that sentence can make no change in the real nature of things. Institutions established by force may, indeed, wear all the features and appearances of liberty, except its natural motion: they may exhibit all its forms, and shock you by the resemblance;—like those models that retain every thing that constitutes a likeness, but life.

OF LITERATURE, AS IT IS CONNECTED WITH HAPPINESS.

Every idea of happiness has been almost lost sight of amidst the very efforts that seemed at first to have been made for its attainment; and a sordid selfishness, by depriving each individual of the support and co-operation of others, has considerably diminished that portion of public happiness which the constitution of the social order had so fairly promised. In vain might hearts of sensibility endeavor to diffuse around them their expansive benevolence; insurmountable obstacles would obstruct and frustrate their generous intentions; they would be censured even by public opinion, which is ready enough to condemn those who would fain deviate from that sphere of self-love, which every one seems anxious to secure as an inviolable asylum. A man must, therefore, exist for himself alone, since a reciprocity of affection is no where to be found, and since it is even forbidden to assuage sorrow or alleviate distress. He must exist for himself alone, in order to preserve in his imagination the model of every thing that is sublime or beautiful; or to keep alive the sacred fire of genuine enthusiasm, and retain the image of virtue, such as in the freedom of meditation she always appears, and such as she has been portrayed by those exalted minds that have been the ornaments of every age.

What form of character would mankind assume, if they were never to hear the language of honest and generous sentiments;—if hearts of sensibility were condemned to live among frigid egotists;—if unbiassed reason was to be waging an ineffectual struggle against the sophistries of vice; and if the tender solicitudes of pity were incessantly exposed to the scorns and mockeries of unfeeling frivolity? In the end, perhaps, we should arrive at the total extinction even of self-esteem. Man finds himself necessitated to rely on the opinion of his fellow-man: he dreads lest his self-love should be taken for his conscience: he accuses himself of folly, if he sees nothing around him that bears any resemblance to himself: and such is the imbecility of human nature, such its dependence upon society, that man would, in some measure, repent of his good qualities, as of involuntary defects, if general opinion concurred in censuring them: but, in these moments of disquietude, he has recourse to his books; and they hold up to him the undisfigured monuments of those refined and noble sentiments that have exalted every age. If liberty be dear to him; if the name of republic, so powerful over the feelings of proud unbending minds, associates in his reflections with the image of all the virtues;—some of Plutarch's Lives; a letter from Brutus to Cicero; a few sentences of Cato, in the language of Addison; some of those reflections with which the hatred of tyranny inspired Tacitus; or, those sentiments, real or supposed, which historians and poets put into the mouths of their heroes; are sufficient to raise anew the soul after it has shrunk and sickened at the aspect of contemporary events. An exalted character is restored to self-approbation, if he finds his soul in union with these noble sentiments, and with those lofty virtues which imagination selects and embodies when she aspires to delineate a model for the imitation of every age. How abundant are the consolations which we derive from writings of a certain cast! If the great men of early antiquity were exposed, during their lives, to the shafts of calumny; their only retreat and asylum lay within their own breasts: but, in our days, we may have recourse to the Phædon of Socrates, to the animating master-pieces of eloquence that support the mind under the pressure of adversity. The philosophers of every country exhort and encourage us; and the persuasive language of morality drawn from an intimate knowledge of the human heart, seems to be addressed individually to all those whom it consoles.

How useful, how congenial is it to human nature, to

attach an high importance to the influence of reason and of literature! The type and form of what is virtuous and just, can no longer be destroyed. The man whom nature destines for virtue, can no longer want a guide: and, finally, (what is of infinite consequence,) grief may be sure always to meet a healing sympathy and condolence. From that arid sadness which we feel when abandoned and forlorn, from that icy hand with which misfortunes presses on us when we imagine ourselves to be deserted by pity and compassion, we are rescued in some measure by those writings that still bear the breathing impression of noble thoughts and virtuous affections. Such writings draw forth tears in every situation of life: they raise the mind to general meditations, which divert our attention from personal sufferings: they create a society for us, and a communion both with dead and living authors, and with all those who concur in admiring the works which we approve. In the desolation of exile, amidst the gloom of dungeons, at the approach of danger and of death, a particular passage of an affecting author may have often re-animated a prostrate soul: even I, who read, who now touch that page, methinks I discover on it the track of tears; and by indulging in similar emotions, I enter into a kind of intercourse and fellowship with those whose cruel destiny I so deeply deplore. Amidst the calm of ease, the sunshine of happiness, life is an easy labour: but in the gloominess of misfortune, it is difficult to conceive how strongly certain reflections and sentiments, that have sunk deeply into the heart, mark their era in the history of our solitary impressions. Grief can only be assuaged by the power of weeping over our destiny, and of taking that interest in what concerns ourselves, so as to divide us in some sort into two separate beings, the one of whom commisserates the other. But this resource, in misfortune, can only be enjoyed by a virtuous man. When adversity assails the vicious and the profligate, they have no retreat left them in their own reflections: as long as their criminal habits consign their soul to ferociousness and aridity, and until a sincere repentance re-establishes them in a moral disposition, their sufferings must be poignant and excruciating: the dark recesses of such minds can never admit even a gleam of consolation. The unfortunate man, who, by the malignant misrepresentations and aspersions of artful calumny, finds himself suddenly robbed of his reputation, and exposed to general censure and contempt, would likewise sink into the situation of the really guilty, were he not able to derive some comfort and encouragement from those writings, which might enable him to behold himself in his true colours; to confide in those who resemble him, and harbour the conviction, that in some corners of the world there exist persons who would sympathize with him in his downfal, and affectionately weep with him, could he but submit his case to their consideration and compassion.

How precious, therefore, are these ever-living lines, which supply to us the place of friends, of public esteem, of country! In an age like the present, when such accumulated calamities have visited the human race, how desirable is it that there should exist a writer, who, with a taste turned to such pursuits, would select and treasure up all those care-soothing reflections, all those efforts exerted by reason, that have contributed to solace the unfortunate in their miserable career! Such a work at least would open an abundant source of tears.

The voyager, whom a storm has cast on an unpeopled shore, engraves upon the surrounding rocks the names of the aliments he has discovered, and points out to those who may be involved in a similar fate, the resources which he employed against danger and death. We, whom the chances of this mortal life have reserved for a period of revolution, should also make it our business to transmit to future generations an intimate knowledge of those secrets of the soul, of those unexpected consolations which parent nature has employed to smooth our way through the rugged paths of life.

PLAN OF THE WORK.

After having collected some general ideas which ascertain the power exerted by literature over the destiny of man; I shall now proceed to develop them by a successive survey of those more enlightened periods that shine so conspicuously in the history of letters.

The first part of this work will contain a moral and philosophical analysis of Grecian and Latin literature: some reflections on the effects produced upon the human mind by the invasions of the northern nations, by the revival of letters, and by the establishment of the Christian religion; a rapid delineation of the discriminative traits of modern literature, with some more detailed observations on the master-pieces in Italian, English, German, and French languages, considered agreeably to the general scope of the work, that is to say, with a view to the relations that subsist between the political state of a country and the predominant spirit of its literature. I will endeavor to show the particular character which eloquence assumes under this or that form of government; the moral ideas which this or that religious creed is calculated to beget in the human mind; the effects of imagination that are produced by the credulity of the people; the poetical beauties that depend upon the influence of climate the degree of civilization that best promotes the strength and perfection of literature; the various changes that have been introduced into the art of composition, as well as into manners, by the different modes of existence of women before and after the establishment of the Christian religion; and, finally, the universal progress of knowledge resulting for the mere succession of ages. These considerations will form the subject-matter of the first part.

In the second, I will examine into the state of knowledge and of literature in France since the revolution; and I will hazard a few conjectures respecting what ought to be, and what certainly will be, their future state, if we are one day to enjoy the possession of republican freedom and morality. In order to attain to some knowledge respecting the unknown events which time has not yet developed, I shall avail myself of an analogical deduction from past events: and then, by restating the observations I shall have made in the first part of this work, respecting the influence of a particular religion, a form of government, or particular manners and customs, I shall be enabled to draw some inferences relative to my supposed future state of things. In this second part will be exhibited, at one view, both our present degradation and our future attainable perfection. This subject must sometimes lead me to observations on the political situation of France during the last ten years: but I shall touch on it only as far as it is connected with literature and philosophy, without diverging into any digression foreign to my general purpose.

As I survey the revolutions of the globe, and the succession of ages, one great idea is ever uppermost in my mind, from which I never allow my attention to be diverted; I mean that of the perfectibility of the human race. I cannot bring myself to think, that this grand work of moral nature has ever been abandoned; in the ages of light, as well as in those of darkness, the gradual advancement of the human intellect has never been interrupted.

This system of the perfectibility of human nature has, it is true, become odious in the eyes of some persons, on account of the atrocious consequences derived from it at certain disastrous periods of the revolution: nothing, however, has less connection with these consequences than that exalted system. As nature sometimes makes partial evils tend to the general good, a set of besotted barbarians imagined themselves transformed into supreme legislators, while they drew down upon the human race a train of calamities, the effects of which they vainly expected to direct; but which were in the end productive of nothing but misery and ruin. Philosophy may occasionally look back upon past calamities, and contemplate them as salutary lessons, and as instruments and means of reparation in the hand of time; but this observation can never sanction, under any circumstances whatever, the slightest departure from the positive laws of justice. As the human mind can never arrive at a certain knowledge of futurity, virtue alone should prompt its divinations. The consequences, whatever they may be, of human actions, can never contribute to render them either innocent or criminal: man is to be guided, not by fanciful and arbitrary rules, but by fixed unalterable duties; and experience itself has proved, that we fail in attaining the moral end we have in view, when guilty means are employed for its attainment. Because men of sanguinary minds have polluted and profaned the language of generous and noble feelings; does it follow that we are to be forbidden to let our breasts expand at the recollection of sublime sentiments and thoughts? The ruffian might thus tear from the man of virtue the dearest objects of his esteem: for it is ever under the name of some virtue that political crimes are perpetrated.

No, never can man's reason be detached from those ideas that hold out the promise of so many fortunate results. And, indeed, into what dejection must the human mind fall, were it no longer to be cheered with the hope that every day must add to the mass of knowledge,—that every day must more fully unfold the truths of philosophy! Persecutions, calumnies, sufferings of every hue, would become the lamentable lot of those who boldly think and soundly moralize. The votaries of ambition and avarice at one time endeavor to deride as fallacious the warnings of conscience; at another, they would insinuate that unworthy motives are the spring of generous actions. To such men it is intolerable, that any thing like morality should exist; and they persecute it with revengeful zeal, even to the very heart in which it attempts to take refuge. Envy is still attracted by that luminous ray which beams around the head of the moral man. This lustre, which the foul breath of their calumnies sometimes succeeds in eclipsing and concealing from the eyes of the world, never ceases to dazzle and dim their own. What then must be the fate of the worthy man whom so many enemies worry and persecute, if his misery were accomplished by their success in depriving him of the most consolatory and religious hope, which earthly existence can enjoy—that of the future improvement and perfection of his fellow-creatures?

To this philosophical creed do I cling with all the faculties of my mind: I perceive among its chief advantages, that it inspires an high sense of self-esteem, an elevation of soul; and I appeal to every mind of a certain cast, whether there be in this nether world a purer enjoyment than that conferred by this enlargement of mind? To it we are indebted, that there still are moments in which all these mean groveling beings, with all their sordid calculations of self-interestedness fade away and sink before their eyes. Our faculties are inspired with fresh vigor by contemplating the future state of knowledge, of virtue, and of glory: certain vague impressions crowd in upon us, certain sentiments that we cannot well define, which alleviate the load of life; while the whole moral man swells with the pride of virtue, and swims in the overflowings of happiness. If all our efforts were to be exerted in vain; if our intellectual labors were to be employed to no purpose, but irrevocably swallowed up in the oblivious gulf of time; where is the object which a virtuous man could propose to himself in his solitary meditations? For my own part, I have, throughout this work, incessantly adverted to every circumstance that tends to evince the perfectibility of the human species. Nor is this to be confounded with visionary theories; it is the result of observation, and stands on the evidence of facts. It is wise, indeed, to guard against that species of metaphysics which derives no support from experience: but at the same time, it should not be forgotten that, in times of degeneracy and corruption, the name of METAPHYSICS is given to every thing that is not circumscribed within the narrow limits of self-love, or that does not coincide with the calculations of self-interest.

THE

INFLUENCE OF LITERATURE

UPON

SOCIETY

PART FIRST.

OF THE STATE OF LITERATURE AMONG THE ANCIENTS AND THE MODERNS.

CHAPTER I.

THE FIRST ERA OF GRECIAN LITERATURE.

The astonishing success which crowned the literary labours of the Greeks, more especially in poetry, might be urged as an objection against the progressive perfectibility of the human mind. It may be said, that the first writers with whom we are acquainted, and particularly the first poet, have not been surpassed during a period of nearly three thousand years; and even that the successors and imitators of the Greeks have frequently fallen very far short of the perfection of their models.

Under the denomination of literature, I have comprehended poetry, eloquence, history, and philosophy, or the study of man as a moral agent. In tracing these different branches of literature, it may be proper to distinguish what appertains to the imagination from that which is the result of thought. It will likewise be necessary to investigate to what degree both these faculties are susceptible of perfection: we shall thence be able to ascertain the principal cause of the superiority of the Greeks in the cultivation of the fine arts; and we shall farther be helped to discern, whether their philosophical acquirements exceeded what the age they lived in, what their form of government, and what their state of civilization, might have led us to expect. It is very obvious, that some certain limit may be fixed to the progress of the arts; though the discoveries of a thinking mind are without a bound. Now, in moral nature, as soon as some end appears in view, the road that leads to it is speedily travelled over: but where a career is boundless, our progress must always appear slow. This observation, I think, may apply to a variety of other objects besides those that more particularly relate to the cultivation of literature. The fine arts are not susceptible of infinite perfection: thus we observe, that the imagination which gave them birth, is far more brilliant in its first impressions than in its fairest and most feltcitous recollections.

Modern poetry consists in images and sentiments. When viewed as consisting of imageries, it ranks among the imitations of nature: when looked upon as composed of sentiments, it then results from the eloquence of the passions. In poetry, considered in this first view, or in an animated description of external objects, the Greeks excelled, at the earliest period of their literature. In our endeavors to express what we feel, a poetical style is easily adopted, or recourse is had to imagery, in order to give greater strength to our impressions: but poetry, properly so called, is the art of painting by words, every thing that attracts and strikes our eyes, and the connection between sentiments and sensations is the first step towards philosophy. Here, however, we shall consider poetry as far only as it is an imitation of physical nature; and in that view, poetry is not susceptible of an indefinite perfection.

The same means may give rise to new effects, if they are adapted to different languages. But a portrait cannot do more than resemble, and our sensations are still limited by our senses. The description of spring, of a storm, of night, of beauty, of a battle, may be susceptible of infinite variety in the details: but the strongest impressions must have been produced by the first poet who succeeded in painting them. The elements may be combined, but cannot be multiplied. Perfection can only be displayed by the shades and gradations of light: but he who first of all made himself master of the primitive colours, will preserve the merit of invention, and give a brilliancy to his descriptions, which his successors will attempt in vain to emulate.

When the contrasts exhibited by nature, and the remarkable effects which strike alike every beholder, are first introduced into poetry; they present to the imagination the most energetic pictures, and the most marked and simple oppositions. The thoughts that are infused into poetry, produce an happy development of its beauties; but then it is not mere poetry. Aristotle, who first defined the term *poetry*, calls it 'an imitative art.' The powers of reason are daily unfolded, and continually extend themselves to new objects. In this respect, ages become the inheritors of ages: generations start from the point at which preceding generations had stopped; and thinking philosophers form, through the lapse of centuries, a chain of ideas which the hand of death does not interrupt. Not so with poetry. Poetry, at the first outset, may attain to certain beauties that cannot be afterwards surpassed: and whilst, in the progressive sciences, the last step is the most finished of all; so the power of the imagination is the more prominent, as the exercise of it is the more early and fresh.

The ancients were animated and hurried along by an enthusiastic imagination, the impressions of which they were not in the habit of analyzing by patient meditation. They took possession of a land hitherto unexplored, of a country not yet described. Delighted and surprised with every enjoyment and every production which nature held out to them, they placed a god over them, to enhance their value, and to secure their duration: their composition was shaped upon no other model than the objects themselves which they were occupied in delineating; they were guided by no antecedent system of literature. As long as poetical enthusiasm remains ignorant of its own emotions it derives from that circumstance alone a strength and a simplicity which no effort of study can attain; it is the charm of a first love. But as soon as the paths of literature have become trodden by the feet of other writers; then their successors in the same track cannot be but conscious that they are portraying sentiments which others had expressed before: they cease to be astonished at what arises in their own minds: they know themselves to be in a phrensy: they judge themselves to be enthusiasts: and consequently, they can no longer indulge the idea of a supernatural inspiration.

With respect to literature, the Greeks may indeed be considered as the *first* people that ever existed. The Egyptians, who preceded them had undoubtedly attained much proficiency in knowledge; but the uniformity of the rules to which they adhered, kept them as it were stationary in the field of imagination. The Egyptians certainly did not furnish the Greeks with a model for their poetry; the poetry of Greece, is incontestably, the first;* nor is it at all surprising, that the earliest poetry should, perhaps, be that which best deserves our praise and approbation: for to that circumstance alone does it chiefly owe the superiority it has attained. But this opinion seems to require a farther elucidation.

An attentive examination of the three different eras of Grecian literature, will enable us very distinctly to discover in them the natural progress of the human mind. As far as we are acquainted with the remote periods of Grecian history, we find that the Greeks derived their first celebrity from their poets. Homer stamped the character of his genius on the first epocha of Grecian literature: the age of Pericles was distinguished by a rapid progress in the drama, in eloquence, in morality, and by the first dawnings of philosophy. In the time of Alexander, a more profound study of the philosophical sciences became the principal occupation of those who possessed literary talents. It must indeed be acknowledged, that the powers of the human mind require to be unfolded to a certain degree, before it can reach the elevations of poetry; but it must likewise be confessed, that the range of a poetical fancy must be somewhat checked, when the progress of civilization and of philosophy has rectified all the errors of the imagination.

It has been frequently asserted, that the fine arts and poetry have most flourished in corrupt ages. This is merely saying, that the greater part of free nations have only been employed in the conservation of their morals and of their liberty; while kings and despotic chiefs were the voluntary promoters and encouragers of relaxations and amusements. But the origin of poetry,—the poem the most remarkable for the display of imagination, that of Homer, is the production of an age renowned for the simplicity of its manners. The progress of poetry is neither accelerated nor retarded by national virtue or depravity; but it is principally indebted to the recent state of nature, and to the infancy of civilization. The tender years of the poet cannot entirely compensate for the juvenile state of the human species: those whose ears can be enraptured by poetic strains, must be great admirers of the scenes of unadorned nature: they must feel flexible to her impressions, and astonishsd at her prodigies. A more philosophical disposition in an audience, might render them more fastidious and nice; but it could never contribute to enhance the beauties and charms of verse: it is among men who are easily moved, that inspiration arms the true poet with the most impressive powers.

The origin of societies, the formation of languages, (the first steps towards the progress of the human mind,) are wholly unknown to us; and, in general, nothing is more wearisome and disgusting than the metaphysical substitution of facts for the sake of supporting a theory, without ever attempting to lay down any positive observation as a fundamental basis. But here a reflection occurs to me, which, as it is necessarily connected with the subject I am treating, I will not omit to state: namely, that moral nature quickly acquires whatever is necessary to the development of itself; in the same manner as physical nature first discovers whatever is requisite to its own conservation. The creative power has been prodigal of whatever is needful. The productions that nourish our bodies, and the elementary ideas that first form the mind have in a manner, been holden out spontaneously to man He speedily came to the knowledge and attainment of those things which he felt the absolute necessity: but the advancement that followed the discoveries suggested by this necessity, have, in proportion, been infinitely more slow. It would seem as if man, in the researches necessary to his existence, had been conducted by a divine hand; which delivered him over to his own guidance, when he entered upon pursuits of a less immediate necessity. The theory of a language, for example the Greek, supposes an infinite variety of combinations far beyond the extent of the metaphysical acquirements of those writers, who, nevertheless, spoke the language with so much purity and perfection:—but language is an instrument indispensably requisite to the attainment of every other additional light; and that instrument by a kind of prodigy, is to be found at a period when it was not in the power of any man to attain, on any other subject whatsoever, to that degree of mental abstraction which the composition of a grammar necessarily requires. The Greek writers are not to be looked upon as gifted with that depth of thought which the metaphysical niceties of their language might lead us to suppose: they can be considered only as poets; and, as poets, every thing conspired in their favor.

The events, the characters, the superstitions, and the customs, which marked the complexion of the heroic ages, were peculiarly adapted to the display of poetic imaginary. Homer, great and sublime, as he must undoubtedly be acknowledged, is not a man superior to all other men: nor does he stand alone in the age he lived in; nor does he rise so far above those who figured many centuries before him. The comprehension of the most exalted genius bears always some proportion to the degree of literary light enjoyed by his contemporaries; and it may not perhaps be difficult to calculate, how far the intellectual powers of one man may exceed the extent of knowledge, to which the age he lived in had attained. Homer carefully collected all the traditions that were afloat in his days; and the history of the principal events of those days was, in itself, highly poetical. The fewer and more abstracted the commu-

* It is supposed, that the poetry of the Hebrews preceded that of Homer: but it appears that the Greeks were totally unacquainted with it.

nications between different countries were at that time, the more the narrative of facts was emblazoned by the imagination. The ruffian robbers and ferocious animal that then infested the earth, gave a higher and more dazzling value to the exploits of heroes, which were found necessary to the individual security of their fellow-citizens. As the tendency of public events had a direct influence upon the destiny and happiness of each person in particular, gratitude and fear conspired to kindle enthusiasm. Heroes aud gods were confounded, because they were each looked up to for the same protection; and the splendid achievements of war appeared nothing less than supernatural, to the afrighted senses. Thus the *marvellous* was mixed with the physical as well as with the moral nature. Philosophy, that is to say, the knowledge of causes and their effects, strikes the reflecting mind with admiration, and naturally leads the ideas to the great work of creation; but each part, considered singly, requires a particular description and explanation. When man acquires the faculty of foreseeing, he loses in a great measure, his astonishment; enthusiasm, like fear, is generally the effect of surprise.

Bodily strength was by the ancients holden in the highest veneration; they considered their safety as entirely depending on it. War had not yet become a science; and courage with them was much less a moral than a physical virtue: the feelings of mankind with regard to honor, and respect for the aged and defenceless, were the more exalted ideas of the subsequent ages. The Grecian heroes publicly accused themselves of cowardice: and a beautiful virgin was sacrificed by the son of Achilles in the eyes of all Greece; which, by its applause, declared its approbation of the horrid deed. Poets paint external objects in the most striking point of view; but they cannot draw characters where the moral beauty has been kept up without blemish to the conclusion of the poem or tragedy: the reason is plain; Such characters have no existence in nature. However sublime Homer may be esteemed in the beautiful and regular disposition of events, and the grandeur of his *dramatis personæ;* it has often happened that his commentators have been transported with admiration at some of the most common expressions in the language: as if the poet had been the first to discover the sense which was attached to them.

Homer and the other Grecian poets have been holden in high estimation for the variety and splendor of their imagery, but not for the depth of their reflections. The conceptions of a poet should be transmitted in the most lively manner to the imagination of his readers, who, it may be said, must see with his eyes, and commence poets also; they are to journey on with him through immense tracts of space; a rapid succession of events and imagery, more or less agreeable, is ever passing before their eyes; they believe, they admire, they are astonished, and the curiosity of puerile years is united to the turbulent passions of riper years. Homer describes every thing with the greatest minuteness, because every thing at that period interested his contemporaries: he tells you, that '*an island is a piece of land surrounded with water;' that corn is the chief support of man;'* and that *at mid-day the sun is vertical.*' It may be said, that Homer is sometimes given to repetitions; but he is never tiresome, because he is continually presenting new ideas: and he never fatigues his readers by abstract reasonings.

Metaphysics (the art of generalizing ideas) has greatly aided the progress of the human mind: but, in so doing, the knowledge acquired has lost much of its brilliancy. All objects presented themselves in succession to the eyes of Homer; who however did not make his choice with rigid accuracy, though he never failed to display them to the greatest advantage.

The Grecian poets, in general, gave themselves little trouble in connecting their ideas, and formed few combinations in their writings: they were fond of reciting the praise and adulation they were continually receiving. Such language by repitition created a degree of enthusiasm, which, heightened by the heat of their climate, produced, if the term may be admitted, a poetical delirium, that inspired their natural genius with words. The Italians derive their divine music from the soul-subduing sounds they draw from their own mellifluous organization; thus it is that the harmony of the Grecian language assimilates its poetry to the tones of the lyre; by this means uniting music and poetry as necessary and inseparable companions.

It has been remarked, that those who are really devoted to the science of music, in their admiration of it, seldom, if ever, pay any attention to the words of a fine air; they are more captivated with the undeterminate ideas which superior harmony alone inspires. It is the same with philosophy and poetry; the profound attention exacted by the former, prevents, in a great measure, that which the latter requires: though it certainly does not follow that a poet, in order to indulge his imagination in a favorite pursuit, should renounce forever the more abstruse philosophical ideas he may have acquired: there is little reason to doubt that a mind, sufficiently enlightened to receive perceptions of such a nature, would be continually brought back to a retrospect which could not fail to afford satisfaction: by the force af such reasoning, it would be as impossible for a modern writer to forget what he had acquired, as it would be for him to see and represent objects in the light in which they were seen and represented by the ancients.

Our great writers have united in their poetry all the richness of the language of the present age; but we are indebted to ancient literature for the forms that constitute the art of poetry; because it is impossible, as has been before observed, to pass a certain limit in the arts,—not even in poetry, esteemed one of the first amongst them.

It has been remarked, and with truth, that the greatest purity (except in a few instances that will be explained hereafter in speaking of theatrical productions) reigned throughout the first era of literature: but how could it have been otherwise? It was hardly possible their taste could have been vitiated whilst they were surrounded by new and pleasing objects; it is the want of variety that renders the mind whimsical and fastidious: but the Greeks, with the most beautiful imagery immediately within their view, and endowed with very lively perceptions, gave themselves up to the descriptions of what pleased them most; and their fine taste is owing to their pure and uncorrupted enjoyments of simple nature. Our refined theory, therefore, does nothing more than analyze their impressions.

The Greeks are indebted for their progress in the fine arts chiefly to their pagan religion: their pretended deities, always near to men, yet at the same time always exalted far above them, rendered the beauty and elegance of their paintings a matter of sacred observance: religion also was called to their aid in their master-pieces of literature. The priests and legislators turned the credulity of the people so entirely to poetical fiction, that the oracles, and all the mysteries of the Grecian mythology, appeared to be but the creation of a free and unbiassed imagination. The poets and painters also availed themselves of the general belief, in order to place in the skies the resources and secrets of their art. The habits and customs of the Greeks too gave an elevation to their ideas, and a dignity to their manners: the most ordinary employments of their lives were ennobled by the religious ceremonies which were mixed with them; their repasts were preceded by libations of wine offered on the steps of their doors to render the gods propitious; and they prostrated themselves before Jupiter Hospitalis. The occupations too of agriculture and hunting were much in fashion with the heroes of antiquity: and these pursuits tended greatly to the advantage of poetry, by combining matters of the highest political importance with the simple images of nature.

Slavery, that abominable scourge of the human species, by increasing the power of social distinctions, placed in a still more conspicuous view the grandeur of heroic characters: but the Greeks enjoyed more poetical advantages than any other nation; yet they were deficient in that which a philosophy more moral and a sensibility more profound would have added even to their poetry itself, namely, in the union of ideas and new impressions. It is a very easy task to follow the progress made by the Greeks in philosophy. Æschylus, Sophocles, and Euripides, successively introduced and advanced the moral of dramatic poetry; and the sole occupation of Socrates, and of Plato, was to inculcate virtue and morality. Aristotle made rapid strides in the science of analysis; Pindar composed his odes after the time of Homer and Hesiod, in that period of the age which was most remarkable for superior compositions in poetry; and even then their ideas of moral virtue were very undecided; they authorized anger, revenge, and all the impetuous passions of the soul. Herodotus, who existed about that period, speaks of virtue and vice with the presaging tongue of an oracle: a crime, he declares, appears to him like a bad omen; out he never appeals to conscience to prove that it is actually so. The word *virtue* had no positive signification with the Greek writers of that period: Pindar gave the appellation of *virtuous* to those who excelled and triumphed in the Olympic games, and also to those who were most skilful in the art of chariot-racing. Thus were their successes, their pleasures, the will of their gods, and the duties of man, all confounded by their inordinate imaginations; and their sensitive existence seemed alone capable of making any deep and lasting impression on them. But the incertitude of their morals is no proof of the depravity of that age; it simply proves how little their ideas were turned towards philosophy; every thing combined to divert them from meditation, and nothing induced them to return to it. Solid reflections are very seldom to be met with in the Greek poetry, and much less do we find a genuine spirit of sensibility.

Every man, without doubt, at some period of his life, has experienced the painful sensations of a troubled mind, and will feel and acknowledge the energetic descriptions of Homer: but the power of love seems to have kept pace with the other progresses of the human intellect. Certain prostitutes, lost to every sense of shame; slaves, rendered contemptible by their abject state; and women, secluded from the rest of the world, confined within their own houses, entire strangers to the interests of their husbands, and educated in such a manner as to render them unfit for comprehending any idea, any sentiment; these were the only ties of affection with which the Greeks were acquainted. Little or no respect was paid to mothers by their sons. Telemachus commands Penelope to keep silence; and Penelope retires, penetrated with admiration at the depth of her son's wisdom.

The Greeks never expressed, nor were they indeed acquainted with, the first and most noble of the sentiments of the human mind,—friendship in love! Nor, till women were called up to share the destiny of their husbands, were they supposed by them to be possessed of souls capable of as great and heroic deeds as their own. Love, as depicted by the ancients, was a distemper, a spell thrown over them by the gods; it was a kind of delirium, which sought for no moral perfection in the object beloved. What they understood by friendship, existed only between men; but the Greeks did not know, and the manners of the age they lived in did not permit them even to imagine, that women were beings capable of equaling them in sense and understanding: nor did they belive that, under the influence of sincere affection, they could become faithful companions for life; nor, that it would constitute their own supreme felicity to devote their time and talents towards rendering the object of thetr attachment happy. The total want of this sentiment is discovered, not only in the description of love, but in every circumstance which regards the delicacy of the heart.

Telemachus, when he takes his departure to go in search of Ulysses, says, '*that if he should be apprised of the death of his father, his first care on his return would be to erect a monument to his memory, and persuade his mother to take a second husband.* The Greeks paid all due honor to their dead; the dogmas of their religion expressly ordered them to watch over the funeral pomp; but a melancholy and lasting regret was not in their nature; it is in the hearts of women that sorrow takes up its abode. I shall often have occasion to remark the changes that have been made in literature since the period when women were admitted to partake of the moral life of men.

After having attempted to show whence arose the original beauties of the Greek poetry, and the defects which were incident to it at that remote period of civilization; it will remain to examine the extent of influence the government and the national spirit of Athens had in the rapid progress of all degrees of literature. It cannot be denied, that the legislation of a country is all-powerful in its influence over the habits, taste, and talents of its inhabitants; since Lacedæmon existed by the side of Athens, in the same century, under the same climate, with nearly the same religion; and yet nothing, it must with truth be observed, could be more different than their manners and customs. All the institutions of Athens were calculated to excite emulation. The Athenians had not always been free: but the spirit of encouragement never ceased to thrive among them in full vigor: no nation ever paid more homage to distinguished talents; and it was the desire of admiration, that gave birth to the superior productions which merited it.

The Greeks, even in their infant state, were the only civilized country, in the midst of a world of savages; they were few in number, but were looked up to with respect by the surrounding nations: they united the double advantages of having but a small territory to guard, and the great theatre of the world for action. That emulation which owes its birth to a certainty of being known in our own country, excites the ambition of immortal honor. Their population was very circumscribed, and the bonds of slavery, by which nearly one half were kept in subjection, diminished the class of citizens, and in a still greater degree, restricted the light of knowledge to a small number of competitors, who were continually stimulating each other, and making comparisons among themselves.

The democratical form of government, which called all the men of distinguished talents to situations of eminence, naturally occupied their minds with public affairs: nevertheless, the Athenians did not devote themselves entirely to the political interest of their country; they loved and cultivated the fine arts. They were jealous of preserving their rank as the first among the enlightened nations; and the hatred and contempt in which they held those whom they esteemed the barbarians, strengthened and confirmed them in their taste for the fine arts and *belles lettres*. It would not certainly be much better for mankind at large, if the light of knowledge was more generally spread throughout the world: but the emulation of the favored few who possess it, is heightened by its partial distribution: the life of a celebrated man was more *glorious* in ancient times; but that of an obscure individual is more *happy* in this modern period.

The predominant passion of the Athenians was amusement: and so much did they addict themselves to this, that they decreed a sentence of death against any person who should propose to employ, even towards the military service of their country, any part of the money appropriated for the public festivals. They were not, like the Romans, inspired with an ardent desire of conquest. They repelled the barbarians indeed; but this they did merely with a view of preserving their own superior taste and manners uncontaminated: and the highest value they set on liberty was, that it procured them a free and uninterrupted enjoyment of all kinds of pleasures. Neither were they possessed of that abhorrence of tyranny which a certain elevation of soul, and dignity of manners, gave to the Romans. They took no care to secure a permanency in their legislation; they simply wished to lighten it of every fatigue, and lay their chiefs under the necessity of pleasing, and keeping possession of the affections of the people.

All kinds of talents were applauded with rapture by the Athenians: and the homage paid to their great men, amounted almost to adoration. Nothing serves as a greater proof of the distrust with which their insatiable love of admiration and propensity to enthusiasm inspired them, than their Ostracism, or law of exile. Nothing was left undone that could create a thirst for glory, or add brilliancy to fame. The tragic authors, before they commenced their career, offered sacrifices on the tomb of Æschylus. Pindar and Sophocles, with their lyres in their hands, appeared at the public spectacles crowned with laurel, and covered with the designation of the oracle.

The art of printing, so favorable to the progress and diffusion of knowledge, is prejudicial to poetry; which may be studied, analyzed, and corrected, till much of its native beauty is destroyed by refinement:—whereas the Greeks sung their simple harmony, and received its original impressions accompanied with music, when the heart was exhilarated and expanded by conviviality, which inspired that festivity which men of kindred mind and manners never fail of communicating to each other. Some of the characters of the Grecian poetry may be attributed to the manner of its success; their compositions were even read in due form to the public: melancholy and reflection, those solitary occupants of the mind, are little suited to a crowd and the bustle of life.

When men are assembled together, their spirits are exhilarated, and the imagination naturally becomes more susceptible of receiving lively and agreeable impressions; of this truth the poets were sensible, and turned such knowledge to their own advantage. The monotony of the Pindaric hymns, which is so irksome to us, was esteemed quite the reverse at the Grecian festivals. Some airs, which have produced the greatest effect imaginable on the minds of those inhabiting dreary and mountainous countries, were artless, and composed of very few notes. It was, perhaps, the same with the ideas contained in the lyric poetry of the Greeks; for similar imagery, sentiments, and harmony, were certain of drawing the desired applause from the multitude.

The approbation of the Greeks was expressed in much more lively terms than the deliberate commendation of the moderns. A great deal of rivalry must necessarily exist in a country where such great encouragement was given to distinguished talents; but this competition, in itself, contributed to the advancement of the sciences. The most glorious triumph the Greeks could obtain, excited much less hatred than the limited applause resulting from the niggard hand of modern criticism.

Amongst the ancients, genius was allowed a certain degree of self-approbation; and those who fancied they had any claim to renown, were induced without fear to announce themselves as candidates for fame; the nation was even pleased to witness what they esteemed laudable ambition: but at the present period, superior talents are obliged to assume the disguise of mediocrity, to glide imperceptibly into celebrity, and to steal from men their admiration:—it is important, not only to calm their apprehensions by assuming the greatest humility, but a total indifference to applause must also be affected, if they wish to obtain it. The comprehensive mind is wounded by such restraint; elevated genius requires more latitude properly to expand itself, and is therefore disgusted by being thus cramped; and talents, which might have proved of the utmost consequence to mankind, are often crushed before they are sufficiently understood. It is true, that, among the Greeks, envy sometimes existed between rival candidates for fame: but in these days it has passed from them to the spectators, and, by one of the most unaccountable caprices that ever affected the mind of man, the bulk of mankind are jealous of the efforts made with an intention of adding to their pleasures, and to secure their approbation.

CHAPTER II.

OF THE GRECIAN TRAGEDIES.

It is from theatrical productions in particular, that we are enabled to form an accurate idea of the manners, customs, and laws of the country, in which they were composed and represented with success. A dramatic author, to acquire the reward of his merit, must, independently of his literary abilities, be thoroughly acquainted with men, their manners and their prejudices; and possess, in a certain degree, a knowledge of the politics of his country.

The fundamental bases of tragedy are affliction, and death, which are always softened and divested of their usual terrors by religion. We will now proceed to examine, how far the tragedies of the Greeks were influenced by their notion of religion, and what degree of power it possessed over the minds of men.

The religion of the Greeks was in itself highly theatrical: we are told, that the 'Eumenides,' a tragedy of Æschylus, produced one time so wondrous an impression, that pregnant woman could not endure the spectacle: but it was the terrific view of the infernal regions, and the power of superstition, more than the splendor of the drama, that caused these violent emotions.

The poet, in exciting the different passions of the human mind, disposed of its faith in religious matters at the same time. If this tragedy, which made so deep an impression on the minds of the Greeks, had been represented in another country, and in the presence of an audience of a different persuasion, the effects would have been totally changed. We shall have occasion to observe, in examining the state of literature in the northern countries, what kind of emotions were produced by a religion of a different description: and I shall endeavor to explain, in treating of modern literature, that the Christian religion is in itself too awful and mysterious to be introduced with propriety upon the stage. Our dramatic writers can only hope to excite an interest, and move the passions, by an energetic representation of them. But I shall at present confine myself to a farther description of the Greeks, endeavoring to elucidate what impressions the sight of sufferings and death made upon their minds, and in what manner they considered the illicit wanderings of the passions.

The religion of the Greeks attributed to their pretended gods a supreme power of inflicting remorse on the guilty: and their theatres represented the torments of criminals in so horrid a manner, as to fill the minds of the spectators with an insuperable terror: by means also of this sensation, the legislators were enabled to exercise a greater degree of power, and the principles of morality were more firmly binding among men.

The image of death presented a much less gloomy aspect to the ancients than to the moderns: their belief in paganism calmed their fears, by representing a future state in the most brilliant and pleasing colors. The ancients materialized it by their recitals, their descriptions, and their paintings; and the abyss which nature has placed between our existence and immortality, was as it were filled up by their mythology.

The Greeks were much less susceptible of calamity than any other nation of antiquity; their political institutions, and national spirit, disposed their minds more to pleasure and contentment; and examples of suicide were much less frequent with them than with the Romans; but the fortitude which enabled them to support misfortune, is chiefly to be attributed to their superstition. Their oracles, their dreams, their presentiments, and every circumstance which throws into the scale of human events the *extraordinary* and the *unforeseen*, did not suffer them to credit that any irrevocable calamity could happen. Thus was despair kept at a distance by hope, which, even in the most perilous situations, suggested, that some miracle might still be exerted in their favor. The calculation of moral probabilities might frequently have destroyed the delusion: but when the mind once imbibes supernatural ideas, the *impossible* appears to have no existence. The Greeks never felt, and could not therefore have explained, that dejection and depression of spirits so mournfully expressed in the writings of Shakspeare.

The great men of antiquity were exposed to severe trials; but they were never forgotten or overlooked by their country: great misfortunes astonished them, and they imputed their origin to supernatural causes, and the immediate displeasure of their gods. The religion of the Greeks is, to us, nothing more than poetry; for 't is impossible that their tragedies can ever inspire us with the same emotions they themselves experienced in hearing them recited. The Greek authors grounded their success on a number of tragical events which coincided with the dark credulity of the age in which they were written; and thus supplied by religious terrors their want of more natural emotions.

Almost every circumstance with the Greeks had novelty to recommend it; even the passion of grief, if the term may be admitted, was in its infancy. The expression of hope and ardent expectation was always certain of exciting a tender compassion; and the assurance that the audience would take the most lively interest in every species of distress, gave a confidence to the poet: he did not apprehend (what ought and would be feared in these more enlightened days, even in fiction,) that he should fatigue his hearers by his plaintive tale; as if misfortune, represented on the tablets of the imagination, were still in the presence of egotism.

The *distress* of the Greeks wore an august appearance; it furnished the painter with noble attitudes, and the poets with images which commanded respect; it also gave to religion a new and more solemn appearance: yet with all these advantages, the sentiments inspired by the modern tragedies are more profound and lasting. The representations of later times do not simply offer a picture of majestic *distress*, but distress, solitary, and without support,—distress such as nature and society have made it.

The Greeks did not, like us, require a continual change of situation and contrast of characters; the effect of their tragedies was not brightened by the opposition of shades; their dramatic art resembled their paintings, where the most vivid colors and the most various objects were placed upon the same plan, without any observance of perspective. The greater part of the Grecian tragedies being founded on the action and will of the gods, an exact appearance of truth, the gradation of natural events, was dispensed with, and the greatest effect was produced without any progressive gradation. The mind was prepared by their religion for the *horrific*, and by their faith for the *wonderful*. The Greeks had not to encounter the difficulties of the dramatic art; they did not attempt to draw characters with that philosophical truth attempted by the moderns; the contrast of virtue and vice, the struggles of conscience, the mixture and opposition of sentiments, which in these days must be delineated in order to interest the human heart, was by them hardly understood; the words of an oracle were at all times sufficient for the Greeks.

Orestes murdered his mother, and Electra encouraged him without a moment's hesitation or regret; the remorse of Orestes, after the death of Clytemnestra, did not arise from the struggles he had experienced before the act was committed: the oracle of Apollo had commanded the sacrifice! but when it was accomplished, the Furies unrelentingly seized the criminal. The sentiments of the man are with difficulty distinguished through his actions: the reflections, the doubts, the deliberations, and the fears, are all left for the chorus to develop: the heroes act only by order of the gods.

Racine, in some of his compositions written in imitation of the Greeks, explains the crimes that were commended by the gods, by reasons drawn from the passions of the human mind, and places a moral development by the side of fatalism: this explanation was certainly necessary in a country whose inhabitants had no belief in paganism; but with the Greeks, the tragic effects were still more terrible, as they were founded upon supernatural causes; and the confidence annexed to them by the Greeks rendered the mind effeminate, and deprived it of its independence. Every sentiment was decided by a religious dogma, in which they had such faith, that every tree, and every fountain, was personified as a divinity. Nobody could refrain from showing pity to one who might appear before him, bearing an olive-branch adorned with little fillets, or who could approach near enough to touch the sacred altar: this was the sole subject of the tragedy of the 'Suppliants.' The belief of the Greeks in the fabulous, gave a poetical elegance to every action of their lives; but it banished habitually every thing that had in it any irregularity, every thing unforeseen and irresistible, from the heart.*

Love, with the Greeks, was like all other violent passions,—it was nothing more than a fatality. In their tragedies, as well as in their poems, we are continually struck with observing how little they understood of the real affections of the heart, before women were called upon to feel and to judge. Alcestes gave his life for Admetus; but during his indecision, was he not urged in the strongest manner by Euripides to engage the father of Admetus to devote himself in her place? The Greeks could paint a generous action, but they were ignorant of the pleasure derived from braving death for a beloved object; neither did they conceive what jealousy may be attached to the being without a rival in this personal sacrifice.

It has been said with truth, that the greater part of the dramatic writings of the Greeks would be ill adapted to the modern theatres in France, were they to be literally translated: notwithstanding, so many original beauties would not fail to excite admiration; but the total want of delicacy in the exceptionable passages could not be endured at this enlightened period. We may be easily convinced of this truth by the comparison of the two Phædras. Racine once attempted to introduce love upon the French stage, in imitation of the Greeks; a love that was to be attributed to the vengeance of the gods: nevertheless, on the same subject, how much difference may be observed in the manners

* It happens sometimes, that the mythological dogmas, in the writings of the ancients, add to the effect of moving situations; but it happens more frequently, that the power of these dogmas dispenses with the examination of the springs whence arise the emotions of the heart; and the passions are consequently neither developed nor duly considered

and customs of the age? Euripides might have said to Phædra,

> 'Ce n'est plus une ardeur dans mes veines cachée,
> 'C'est Vénus toute entière à sa prose attachée.'

The following lines would never have been thought of by a Greek:

> 'Ils ne se verront plus;—
> '————ils s' aimeront toujours.'

The Greek tragedies were at that era much inferior to our modern compositions of the same description; because the dramatic talent of this time consists not only of the art of poetry, but a profound knowledge of the passions; which clearly discovers that the improvement in tragedy arises from the increased progress of the human intellect.

The Greeks are not less admirable in this kind of ambition than other nations: this truth is farther confirmed, when we compare their success with the period in which they flourished. They transferred to their theatres every thing that was beautiful in the imagination of the poets, with the characters of antiquity and the worship of their gods. And philosophy was much farther advanced in the time of Pericles, than in that of Homer: their dramatic writers began also to acquire some depth.

There is a very visible improvement in the three great tragedians, Æschylus, Sophocles, and Euripides; though there is too much distance between Æschylus and the two latter, to be able to account for his superiority by the natural progress of the human mind in so short a space of time: but Æschylus had witnessed only the prosperity of Athens: Sophocles and Euripides beheld the reverse; their dramatic genius was brought forward and ripened: calamity too has its fecundity.

No moral conclusion can be drawn from the works of Æschylus; he scarcely ever unites the sufferings of the body with those of the mind by any reflections. A shriek, a groan, a lamentation without any explanation, expresses the impression of the moment, and presents us with a portrait of what the mind was, before reflection had placed within us a witness of our interior emotions.

Sophocles often mixes philosophical axioms with the language of the heart. Euripides is lavish of his maxims in the discourses of his personages, without their always according with their particular situations and character.

In perusing the works of these three great tragic writers, we are made acquainted with their personal talents, and the development and progress of those of the age they lived in; but not one of them equaled the perfection of the English writers, in displaying melancholy sensations, and the extent of human wo. The modern writers excel in pathetic representation; they are aware of the tender sources that render men's hearts accessible to pity; and it requires a knowledge of calamity to create an interest sufficiently strong to present it with success to the view of the mind.

The numerous rewards bestowed by the Greeks on those who were possessed of a dramatic genius, encouraged, in a great measure, the progress of the art; but the exultation arising from the homage that was paid to them, proved, in a great measure, destructive to theatrical talents. The poet, rendered vain by extravagant applause, was himself in too tranquil a disposition of mind to give dignity to distress, and adequate strength to melancholy expression. In the modern tragedies, we are led to perceive by the character of the style, that the author has himself experienced some of the calamities which he represents.

The Grecian tragedies were remarkable for their purity of language. As they preceded all other writers, they could not have been imitators; their style at first might be considered as being too simple, rather than too studied.

Modern literature aimed at greater excellence, or at least, to differ from the ancients: it is certain that the Greeks, as they had nature alone for their model, might sometimes be accused of inelegance and coarseness of expression; but they could not be charged with affectation. The Greeks pursued the straight path of literary fame, and their efforts never failed of success

It may be said, that the productions which they introduced upon the stage were extended to an unreasonable length: but they were perfectly adapted to the age in which they were written: the spectators had not as yet learned to become weary at these representations; their attention being kept alive, they were far from wishing a rapid transition in the scenes presented to them; they were pleased with the details, and would have been dissatisfied had they been abridged.

The Greeks, according to the system of the present times, committed many errors with respect to women: in their tragedies, men appeared in female characters; and they were incapable of understanding the force and delicacy, annexed to charms, which the moderns attach to the persons of the softer sex. It must however be confessed, with the exceptions of a few criticisms, that the Greek tragedies possess, with much beauty, a perfect regularity. People so impetuous in their political discussions, had in all their arts, comedy excepted, a dignified moderation: it is to their religion that we must attribute their stability in whatever was noble or sublime.

The inhabitants of Athens did not pursue the present practice of the English theatrical writers; they objected to the grotesque and vulgar scenes of common life being mixed with grand and heroic characters. The Greeks represented their tragedies in those festivals which were consecrated to their gods; they were generally founded upon religion, and a pious veneration suggested the propriety of separating from their compositions, as they did from their sacred temples, every impure and ignoble idea. The heroes, as described by their dramatic writers, had not that steady elevation of character which was given them by Racine, but this difference cannot be attributed to a popular condescension; all the poets portrayed their characters in this manner, before monarchy and chivalry had given another turn to their ideas.

The greater part of the dramatic character of the Greeks was taken from the Iliad, or from the Heroic history of that period. The impressive idea which Homer gave of his heroes, was of singular utility to the dramatic writers of that age: the names alone of Ajax, Achilles, and Agamemnon, produced an emotion with which the remembrance of those heroes always inspired the Greeks. The greatest interest was next excited by their situations; their fate seemed the fate of each individual, and their cause was the cause of the nation: the dramatic poets, in representing them, had only to display the idea already received: they were not under the necessity of creating both character and situation; the greatest respect and interest were previously excited for the personages they wished to introduce.

Our modern writers have been indebted to the august celebrity of the tragic personages of antiquity; their finest and most natural passions are copied from the Greeks: it is not because they are superior to the moderns, but the Greeks certainly first pointed out the predominant affections and passions, the leading features of which must ever remain the same.

Our tragic representations of maternal tenderness have all in some degree a resemblance to that of Clytemnestra, and every filial sacrifice must bring to our remembrance that of Antigone.

In short, there exists in moral nature, as in the light of the sun, a certain number of rays which will produce either distinct or opposite colors, which you may vary by mixing them; but a single new one cannot be created. The three tragic authors of Greece wrote all upon the same subject, without giving themselves the trouble of inventing any thing new; it was neither expected nor desired by the spectators, nor thought of by the poet: and had they even attempted it, they might not have succeeded. The happy conception of extraordinary events is much more the production of tradition than of the poets: a connection of ideas may conduct us to philosophical discoveries; but our first devices and inventions, with regard to poetry, are almost always the effects of chance.

History, customs and manners, and even the popular tales, assist the imagination of the writers. Sophocles would never have invented the subject of Tancred from his own conceptions, nor Voltaire that of Œdipus. Nothing novel in the marvelous can be discovered, when the credulity of the multitude withdraws its aid.

The importance given to the chorusses, which stood forward as the representatives of the people, is almost the only trace of republican spirit which can be remarked in the Grecian tragedies; their comedies indeed frequently recall the recollection of the politics of the nation; but their tragedies were always filled with the misfortunes and distresses of kings,* which interested the spectators in their fate. A parade of regal pomp was still observed at Athens, although they loved and preferred a republican government. But it does not appear that the Greeks were possessed of that enthusiasm for liberty by which the Romans were distinguished; this arose probably from their having had less difficulties to struggle with in the obtaining it. They had not, like the Romans, to expel a race of cruel kings, the very remembrance of whom was capable of inspiring them with the greatest horror. The love of liberty was with the Greeks a habit, a manner of existence, but not a predominant passion.

The Athenians were partial to their own institutions and to their country; though it was not with them as with the Romans, an exclusive sentiment: they received new pleasures in whatever was represented before them. Their tragedies were a true characteristic of their democracy; their principal subjects were filled with reflections upon the rapid reverse of fate, and the uncertainty of fortune. The sudden and frequent revolutions of a popular government often lead the mind to observations of this nature.

Racine did not imitate the Greeks in this respect. Under the reign of a monarch so arbitrary as Louis XIV, his own decisions usurped the place of fate, and consequently no one dared to suppose him guilty of caprice; but in a country where the people predominate, that which most impresses the mind, is the fate of individuals; their sudden transitions being equally rapid and terrible, as they frequently fall from the pinnacle of grandeur into the abyss of adversity.

The Greek tragic authors always endeavor to revive those impressions which have been considered as the most affecting spectacles to the people who are to listen to them; the heart is often sensibly touched by retrospect, at least such a measure is always a step towards it. It is not necessary in sentiment as in the works of lighter fancy, to arrest the attention by novelty. No; when an audience is to be melted into tears, it is the *past* which must be recalled.

CHAPTER III.

OF THE GREEK COMEDIES.

Comedy requires a much deeper and more extensive knowledge of the human heart, than tragedy: it is less difficult to portray what so frequently strikes the imagination as the picture of distress: it may also be admitted, that tragic characters bear a certain resemblance toward each other, which excludes critical observation; and the models of heroic history have clearly pointed out the method which they must pursue.

But it was the labour of ages to bring the understanding to that requisite degree of taste and superior philosophy, which justly distinguished the dramatic works of Moliere; and even had as great a genius as this author possessed existed among the Athenians they would not have discovered the beauty of his productions, or even have understood his superior merit.

We look back with astonishment while reading the plays of Aristophanes, and find it difficult to conceive it possible that productions of such a nature could gain so great a degree of applause in the age of Pericles; and likewise that the Greeks, who possessed a superior taste in the fine arts, could be entertained with vulgarity of so disgusting a nature. We must thence conclude that their taste was only good when it was annexed to the imagination; but defective in what arose from morality and sentiment. The Greeks were fond of every species of the beautiful, yet they erred through want of delicacy, and even of the decency due to society.

The Athenians were ever inspired with more enthusiasm than respect for great and sublime characters; religion, power, misfortune genius, and whatever struck the imagination, excited in them a degree of fanaticism; but these impressions were of short duration, and gave place with equal facility to any other of as lively description.

Whatever requires to be performed by slow and cautious degrees, does not accord with democracy. As it was by the spectators that the actors were to be heard and applauded, authors were obliged, in a great measure, to conform to their taste, and amuse them by low incidents and sallies of wit; which, however, too frequently have a similar effect on those in higher stations.

Tragedy was less affected by this desire to please the multitude: it formed, as has been before observed, a part of their religious festivals. Besides, it is not necessary to consult either the taste or knowledge of the people in order to touch their feeling; the soft emotion of pity finds the same way to the heart in all ranks and conditions. It is to mankind at large that tragedy is addressed; but comedy relates only to the precise period in which it is written:—the people, the manners, and the customs must be understood and consulted, in order to obtain popular success. Mirth is derived from habit: but tears are drawn from nature.

The principles of morality commonly serve to regulate the taste of the lower orders of society, and often to enlighten them even in literature. The people of Athens did not possess that scrupulous morality which can supply the place of the finest principles: they resigned themselves entirely to religious superstitions, which afforded them a very imperfect idea of the reality of virtue; they transgressed all bounds of principle and decency in the eager pursuit of their amusements.

The exclusion of women from the Greek theatres was one of the chief causes of its imperfections. The authors have no motive for concealment, there was no restriction of language necessary to be observed; and nothing being left to the imagination, they were consequently deficient in that grace, elegance, and modesty, which is so striking to the modern reader. It is also a fact, that the masks, speaking-trumpets, and all the absurd fantastical customs of the ancient theatres, disposed the mind, like caricatures in drawing

* Barthelemy in his celebrated travels of the young Anacharsis, says, that the Athenians represented the misfortunes of kings upon their theatres, in order to fortify the republican spirit of the people; but I cannot think, that to be continually representing the misery and distress of kings, was the most proper or likely method to destroy the love of regal power: great disasters are in themselves highly dramatic, they affect and take deep root in the imagination; this then cannot be the means of conquering such prejudices, or indeed those of any other kind.

to study the grotesque and unnatural; but were totally contrary to the simplicity of nature.

Aristophanes sometimes availed himself of the gross jests and buffoonery of the populace: he likewise presented the reverse of what was vulgar and inelegant; but it was never a clear representation of situations, or an accurate description of characters that he explained; nor did he point out the irregularities of mankind to the ridicule of society.

The greater part of the dramatic works of Aristophanes were relatively connected with the events of the times in which they were written: they had not, at that early period, acquired the art of exciting popular curiosity, by a representation of romantic intrigue. The comic art, in its state of Grecian simplicity, certainly could not have existed without having recourse to allusions; they were not in possession of a sufficient knowledge of the secret passions of the human heart, to create any interest in the recital of them; but it was always an easy matter to please the people, by turning their chiefs into ridicule: thus were compositions founded on the circumstances of the moment, and they were certain of being received with applause; but they were not calculated to obtain a lasting reputation.

The portraits of living characters, and the epigrams upon contemporary events, like a family jest, were merely the whim and success of the day, which could not fail to fatigue and disgust the subsequent ages. Nothing could he more likely than that representations of this nature should annually decrease in the merit ascribed to them; because memory fails in retracing the subjects therein alluded to, and the judgment by this means is inadequate to unravel the beauty and gaiety of such writtngs: whenever it requires reflection in order to comprehend the point and sense of a jest, the effect of it must be entirely lost.

But in tragedy the case is very different; the spectators consider nothing farther than the illusion; they are sufficiently interested in the hero of the piece, to understand foreign manners and customs, and to transport themselves ideally into countries and places entirely new: the emotion of which they are susceptible, inclines them to conceive and adopt every thing presented to their view. In comedy the imagination of the audience is quiet and tranquil, and therefore does not afford the least assistance to the author: the impression of mirth is so light and spontaneous, that the most feeble efforts, or the slightest absence of mind, is enough to prevent the effect.

Aristophanes grounded his plays on the circumstances of the day: because the Greeks were destitute of that philosophical reflection, which admits the ready comprehension of characters, and which would have enabled them to understand a composition that would have proved interesting to men of all ages and nations.

The comedies of Menander and the characters of Theophrastus made a great progress; the one in theatrical decency, and the other in the observations of the human heart: but both these writers had the advantage of being in repute a century later than Aristophanes. In a country where democracy is established, authors in general are seduced to introduce upon the stage illusions to public affairs, by the irresistible hope and charm of popular applause; which will always prove inimical to the theatrical productions of a free people. I am ignorant whether such representations are a sign of liberty; but I am certain they are the destruction of the dramatic art.

The Athenians, as I have before observed, were extremely inclined to enthusiasm; but they were not the less partial to that species of satire which insulted men of superior station and abilities; the comedies of Athens, like the journals of France, were favorable to the display of a democratic levelling spirit; but with this difference, that the plays at that period were filled with personalities against existing characters; which was an attack so gross in its nature, that no man of honor in our times could reconcile it to his feelings.

In these days, we count too little upon admiration, not to be apprehensive of slander; and are too readily forsaken by our friends, not to guard against the machinations of our enemies. In Athens, persons accused could make themselves known, and justify themselves before the nation at large: but in our numerous associations, we could only oppose the tardy light of literature to the animated ridicule of the theatre; and against such an unequal contest, no character, no authority, could maintain its ground.

The republic of Athens itself owed its subjection entirely to the abuse of the comic powers; and the excessive love of the Athenians for that species of amusement which increased their inordinate desire of procuring constant diversion and frivolous occupations. The comedy of 'Nubes' prepared the minds of the populace for the accusation of Socrates. Demosthenes, in the following century, could not draw the attention of the people from their lighter pursuits to engage them against Philip. What was most seriously feared for the republic, was the too great ascendancy which might be acquired by one of its great men: but that which tended to its overthrow was its total indifference for them all.

After having sacrificed their glory to their amusements, the Athenians saw even their independence ravished from them, and with it those very enjoyments which they had preferred to the defence of their liberties.

CHAPTER IV.

OF THE PHILOSOPHY AND ELOQUENCE OF THE GREEKS.

Philosophy and eloquence were often united among the Athenians; the systems, metaphysics, and politics of Plato, contributed much less to his reputation than the beauty and grandeur of his style. The Greek philosophers were, generally speaking, extremely eloquent upon the subject of abstract ideas.

I must, however, first examine their system of philosophy, apart from their eloquence: and my design is, to investigate the progress of the human understanding: a knowledge of philosophy can alone point this out with any degree of certainty.

Whether in the poetical department, or in the interesting political discussions of a free nation, eloquence had attained that degree of perfection with the Greeks, which has served for a model to the subsequent ages, even down to the present time: but their philosophy appears to me much inferior to that of their imitators, the Romans. The modern philosophy has still greater superiority over that of the Greeks; and this is no more than might be expected, when we consider the advantages that must be derived from the lapse of two thousand years.

The Greeks improved themselves in a most remarkable manner during the course of three centuries: in the last, which was that of Alexander, Menander, Theophrastus, Euclid, and Aristotle, they were evidently distinguished by their progress, in every species of refinement: but one of the principal and final causes of the great events which are known to us, appears to be the civilization of the world. I shall explain this assertion more at large elsewhere: at present, what is immediately necessary to be observed is, simply, how far the Greeks were accessary to the diffusion of knowledge, and the means they pursued in order to excite that persevering spirit necessary to its attainment.

The Greek philosophers instituted sects;—an expedient which proved as useful to them, as it would be prejudicial to us; their searches after truth included every thing that could strike the imagination. The walks, beneath the expanse of a serene sky, where the young pupils would gather round their preceptor, and listen to the sublime sentiments he uttered;—the harmonious language which elevated the soul, even before it was fully impressed with the sense of what was spoken;—the mystery used at Eleusis in the discovery and communication of certain principles of morality;—all these things combined to give the greatest effect to their lessons of philosophy. The world, in its infancy, was taught truth by the assistance of the marvelous in mythology. Thus was a taste for study produced and preserved by a thousand different ways; and the encomiums bestowed on the disciples of philosophy, greatly augmented their number.

Nothing contributes more to give us an enlarged idea of the reputation of the ancients, than the astonishing effect produced by their works; but this is by no means an accurate rule by which they should be judged. The limited number of enlightened men which Greece held out to the admiration of the rest of the world, the great difficulties attending nautical discoveries, the ignorance in which the chief part of the community remained with regard to the reality of facts collected by the authors, the rarity of their manuscripts, all contributed to inspire the most lively curiosity for works of celebrity. The multiplied testimonies of the general interest excited the philosophers to overcome the greatest difficulties that were annexed to their studies, before they were abridged by method and generalizations. Modern fame would not have been considered an adequate compensation, for such extraordinary efforts of the mind: nothing less than the brilliant honors conferred on genius by the ancients, could have encouraged them to persevere in a task so laborious. It is granted, that the ancient philosophers acquired a more shining reputation than the moderns; but it is also true, that the moderns, in metaphysics, in morals, and in most of the sciences, are infinitely superior to the ancients.

The philosophers of antiquity may be said to have refuted some of the errors prevalent at that era; but they were not themselves entirely exempt from many of them. While we must admit, that the most absurd opinions were generally established, even the writers who appeal to the light of reason, cannot entirely divest themselves of the prejudicee by which they are encompassed. Sometimes they substitute one error in the place of another, which they had successfully combated; at other times, in making their attack upon generally received opinions, they are but too apt to retain a degree of superstition peculiar to themselves. Casual words appeared very formidable to Pythagoras, Socrates, and Plato, who had faith in the existence of familiar spirits; and Cicero was alarmed at the presages conveyed in dreams. But when calamity or distress of any description bears heavily on the human mind, it is difficult, if not impossible, entirely to eradicate the degree of superstition it is naturally inclined to admit: the interior sensation that should abolish such weakness, is not sufficiently strong; and the mind never feels itself secure, unless depending for support upon something independent of itself. Those who minutely study their own hearts, will find that, in every calamity of life, they are more inclined to rely on the opinion of others than on their own ideas and reflections; and to seek elsewhere for the motive of their hopes and fears, rather than apply to a more certain guide,—that of their own reason. A man, however superior his faculties may be, feels it a difficult task, by his own efforts, to free himself from a portion of the supernatural, which is inherent in his nature: the nation at large must unite with philosophy against absurd terrors and superstitions, or it would be impossible even for philosophy itself to be successful.

The minds of the Greeks were foolishly engrossed by researches into the different systems of the world. The smaller the progress they had made in science, the less they were acquainted with the extent of the human understanding. The philosophers delighted themselves particularly in the *unknown*, and the *incxplicable.* Pythagoras declared that '*there was nothing real, but what was spiritual; and that the material had no existence.*'—Plato, that writer whose imagination was so brilliant, is continually reverting to whimsical metaphysics relative to the world, to men, and to love; where the physical laws of the universe, and the verification of sentiments, are never observed. There is nothing more wearisome than the study of that species of metaphysics, which has neither facts for its foundation, nor method for its guide: and it is surely impossible not to be convinced of this truth, in reading the philosophical writings of the Greeks, notwithstanding we may fully admit the charms of their language.

The ancients were better skilled in morals than in philosophy: an accurate study of the sciences is necessary to rectify metaphysics: but nature has placed in the heart of man a guide to conduct him to virtue: nevertheless, nothing could be more unsettled and unconnected than the moral code of the ancients. Pythagoras seems to attach the same importance to proverbs, to counsels of prudence and of dexterity, as he did to the precepts of virtue. Rank and morals were confounded by many of the Greek philosophers: the love of study, and the performance of the first duties, were classed together. In their enthusiasm for the faculties of the mind, they allowed them a place of esteem beyond every thing else: they excited men to the acquirement of admiration; but they never looked with an eye of penetration into the heart.

I am doubtful whether the term *happincss* occurs once in any of the Greek writings, according to the modern acceptation of the word: nor did they annex any great importance to private virtues; the *political* was, with them, a branch of the *moral:* their meditations on men were made in society; and they seldom or ever judged them, but with relation to their fellow-citizens: and as the free states were but thinly peopled, and the women not considered as forming any part of it,* the actual existence of the men consisted in their social relations: it was to complete this political existence, that the studies of the philosopher were exclusively applied. Plato, in his Republic, proposes, as a means of promoting the happiness of the human race, the extirpation of conjugal and paternal affection, by a community of women and children. A monarchical government, and the extent of modern powers, have disunited the greater part of the inhabitants from the interest of public affairs: they have retired into the bosom of their families, and have not diminished their happiness by the exchange: but every circumstance excited the ancients to continue in the path of politics, and the very first object of their moral was an encouragement to pursue it. What is truly beautiful in their doctrine does not contradict the assertion. If it is requisite, in all situations, for men to exercise a great power over themselves; it is, above all, to those in public stations that this power is necessary. How admirably is this moral, which consists in the tranquillity and vigor of mind and the enthusiasm of wisdom, set forth in the apology of Socrates and in the Phædon. If it were possible to instill into the mind that accurate order of ideas, it seems as if it would be invincibly armed against mankind.

The ancients, it is true, often founded part of their support in error; but after all, they followed what they thought and acknowledged to be right: but what is wanting at the present era, is an insurrection against egotism; for the moral virtue of each individual is found to centre in his own personal interest.

The Greek philosophers were very limited in their

* There is not to be found, in the characters of Theophrastus, a single description of a female.

number; and being unable to obtain any assistance from the light of former ages, they were compelled to make their studies universal: it was therefore impossible for them to proceed to a great length in any particular pursuit; and they wanted that method which can only be acquired by an accurate knowledge of the sciences.

Plato could not have arranged in his memory that which the aid of method enables the young men of modern times to do with the greatest facility. Socrates himself, in the dialogues of Plato, in order to confute the Sophists, borrows some of their own defaults; but more especially that insufferable procrastination of a development, which could not be supported in those days. We must have recourse to the ancients, for their beautiful and simple taste in the fine arts; we must admire their energy and enthusiasm for every thing that was good and sublime; but we must consider all their philosophical ratiocinations as the scaffolding of an edifice which the human mind has to raise.

Aristotle, however, who lived in the third century of the Greeks, a century consequently superior in the efforts of the imagination to the two preceding: Aristotle, I say, substituted the force of observation in the place of the energy of theory: and this distinction alone would have been sufficient to have established his fame; but he did not stop there; he wrote upon literature, physic, metaphysics, and these subjects formed the analysis of ideas in his own times. Being the historian of the progress of the sciences at that period, he digested and placed them methodically in the very order in which they were conceived by himself This man was truly great, considering the age in which he lived; but it is difficult, if not altogether impossible, for the human mind to be continually employed in searching into antiquity for the truths of philosophy: this would be to carry the spirit of discovery to a retrospect of the past, when things present lay claim to their chief attention.

The ancients, but more particularly Aristotle, displayed a skill and judgment, in some of their political institutions, equal to those of the moderns, but this exception to the invariable rule of progression is entirely owing to the republican liberty which was enjoyed by the Greeks, but which is unknown to the moderns. Aristotle remained in the most profound ignorance respecting all general questions that had not been explained by preceding events in the history of his time: he does not admit of the existence of a natural right to slaves; and though an antagonist of Plato in many other respects, he does not appear to imagine it was possible that slavery could admit of modification. Plato speaks of the causes of revolutions, and the principles of government, with a superior penetration and judgment; but the greater part of his ideas were furnished by the examples of the Greek republic. If a republican government had existed since the time of Plato, the moderns would have been as much his superiors in the social arts, as they have been in every other intellectual study. The ideas must ever be informed by events: thus in examining the labors of the mind, we constantly observe that either time or circumstance is the clue by which genius is guided: reflection knows how to draw consequences from a single idea; but the first step in every thing is discovered by chance, and not by reflection.

The style of the Greek historians was remarkable for creating an interest, while it kept up without diminishing that beautiful simplicity so justly admired: their descriptions were full of vivacity, but they never investigated deeply into characters, nor judged by institutions: they caught at facts so eagerly, that they never carried their thoughts towards existing causes. In keeping pace with the events of their time, the Greek authors followed a certain impulse without considering whence it arose: it seems indeed, as if their inexperience of life rendered them ignorant, whether the then state of existence could ever be altered; and they transmitted to posterity moral truths as well as physical facts, fine discourses as well as bad actions, and their mildest laws as well as the commands of tyrants, without analyzing either the characters or the principles: it might almost be said, that they portrayed the conduct of men like the vegetation of plants, without bestowing upon them the judgment of reflection.* These observations are applicable to the historians of the first ages of the Greeks. Plutarch, and his contemporary Tacitus, lived in a different epoch of the advancement of the human understanding.

The eloquence of the Greek philosophers nearly equaled that of the Greek orators. Socrates and Plato preferred speaking to writing; because they felt, without exactly rendering to themselves an account of their talents, that their ideas belonged more to imitation than to analysis. They loved to have recourse to that impulse and elevation of thought which is produced by the animated language of conversation; and they searched with as much diligence for something to inflame the imagination, as the metaphysicians and moralists of our days would employ, to secure their works from the smallest appearance of the poetic.

The philosophical eloquence of the Greeks has a still greater effect upon us, by the grandeur and purity of the language: their mild yet energetic doctrines gave to their writings a character which time has not impaired. Ancient diction is very congenial to the simple beauties of composition, nevertheless we should find an insupportable monotony in the discourses of the Greek philosophers upon the affection, had they been written in these days: they have no power to create emotion, but are uniformly remarkable for melancholy and sensibility.

Morality and sensibility were not united in the opinions of the Stoics. Northern literature did not then exist, to instil a love of gloomy reflections: the human race if, the expression may be allowed, had not then reached the age of melancholy: men, when struggling with mental affliction, had recourse to violence, instead of that due resignation which d oes not endeavor to suppress pain, nor cause a blush at feeling regret: it is that submission alone, which can turn affliction tc our advantage, and make it subservient even to the sub limity of our talents,

The eloquence of the Tribune, in the republic of Athens, was as perfect as was necessary to bring over the opinion of the auditors: and in a country where so great a political result was produced by rhetoric, this talent must necessarily develop itself. Eloquence was converted by the Athenians, while they remained a free people, into a kind of gymnastic, in which the orators seemed wrestling with the populace, and forcing their arguments upon them as if they were determined to overcome them. The subject most frequently treated upon by Demosthenes was the indignation with which he was inspired by the Athenians: this wrath against the people, natural enough in a republic, was mixed in all his orations,—when he speaks of himself, it is with rapidity and indifference.

In the following chapter, I shall examine some of the reasons which caused the political distinction that existed between Cicero and Demosthenes. It is generally remarked of the Greek orators, that they make use of but a very small number of original ideas: whether it was owing to their being able to strike the minds of the people with only a few arguments forcibly expressed and fully explained, or whether the ha-

* Thucydides was certainly the most distinguished historian of the Greeks; all his descriptions are full of imagination, and his harangues, like those of Titus Livy, were composed in a style of the finest eloquence.

rangues of the ancients displayed the same uniformity as their writings, it is certain that, generally speaking, they had not a great variety of ideas: their writings resembled the music of the Scots, who composed their airs of a few fine but simple notes, the perfect harmony of which, while it defied criticism could not create a very deep interest in the hearers.

We feel little cause of regret in taking leave of the Greeks, though truly an astonishing people: and the obvious reason for this indifference is, that they were the people who merely began the civilization of the world. They had, it is true, all the qualities requisite to excite the development of the human understanding: but we do not feel a similar sensation of pain at their disappearance from history, as is caused by the loss of the Romans. The customs and habits, the philosophical knowledge, and the military successes of the Greeks, could be but transitory; they resembled seed driven by the wind to every corner of the world, till none remained in the place whence it originally came.

The love of fame was the motive that guided every action of the Greeks: they studied the sciences, in order to be admired; they supported pain, to create interest; they adopted opinions, to gain disciples; and they defended their country, for the sake of ruling it:* but they had not that internal sentiment, that national spirit, that devotion to their country, all which so eminently distinguished the Romans The Greeks gave the first impulse to literature and the fine arts; but the Romans gave to the world invaluable testimonies of their genuis.

CHAPTER V.

OF THE LATIN LITERATURE WHILE THE ROMAN REPUBLIC STILL EXISTED.

We must make a distinction in all the different stages of literature; dividing what is national from that which belongs to imitation. The Roman empire having succeeded to the dominion of Athens, the Latin literature followed the track which had been marked out by the Greeks: at first, because they might have considered it superior in many respects; and therefore to have swerved from it, would have been to have renounced truth and taste; and another probable reason why they conformed to it was, that they found a model which accorded with their own ideas and habits:—whenever this is the case, the mind is more inclined to adopt than create; necessity alone can produce invention, and mankind apply themselves in preference to improving, when they are saved the trouble of inventing.

The paganism of the Romans was very similar to that of the Greeks. The precepts of the fine arts and of literature, a great number of laws, and the greater part of their philosophical opinions, were transported successively from Greece into Italy. I shall not therefore attempt to analyze effects, which so nearly resemble each other, and which must have arisen from a similar cause: all that regards the Greek literature, the pagan religion, slavery, the customs and manners of the east, and the general spirit of antiquity before the invasion of the north, and the establishment of the Christian religion, will be found, with some few restrictions, among the Latins.

What are most worthy of observation and remark, appear to be the different characteristics of the Greek and Latin literature, and the progrèss of the human mind in the three successive periods of the literary history of the Romans; that which precedes the reign of Augustus; that which bears the name of that emperor; and likewise the term that may be reckoned after his death till the reign of the Antonines. The two first are in some measure confounded by their dates, but are extremely different in every other respect. Although Cicero died in the reign of the triumvirate of Octavius, his genius is limited entirely to the republic: and notwithstanding Ovid, Virgil, and Horace, were born during the time of the republic, their writings bear the character of monarchical influence: and in the reign of Augustus, some authors, particularly Titus Livy, discovered very often in their historical writings, that they were republicans at heart. But to analyze with accuracy the distinctions of these three different periods, we must examine their general colorings, and not dwell upon particular exceptions.

The Roman character was never fully displayed but in the time of the republic. A nation indeed has no character, unless it is free. The aristocracy of Rome possessed some of the advantages of an aristocracy made up of enlightened characters: and though they may be justly reproached, with regard to the nomination of their senators, it being entirely hereditary; nevertheless the government of Rome, within its own walls, was free and paternal. But their conquests gave an almost unlimited power to the chiefs of the state; and the principal Romans, being freely elected by their city, which they looked upon as the queen of the universe, considered themselves as possessing the government of the world. From this aristocratical sentiment in the nobles, and the exclusive superiority in the inhabitants of the city, arose the distinguished character of the Roman writings, their language, their moral habits and their dignity.

The Romans never displayed, under any circumstances, the tokens of violent emotion: when they most desired to affect and persuade by their eloquence, they then thought it of the greatest importance to preserve that equanimity of temper and that calm dignity of manners, which are the symbols of a strong mind; that they might not bring into question those sentiments of respect, which served as the basis of their political institutions as well as of their social relations. There was in their language an authority of expression, a gravity of tone, a regularity of periods, which is seldom, if ever, acquired by the broken accents of an agitated mind, or the lively and rapid sallies of wit and gaiety. Their bravery rendered them victorious in battle; but their *moral* strength consisted in that profound and solemn impression which was produced by the very name of *Romans*. They never permitted themselves to be seduced by any consideration; not even a present triumph could induce them to commit an action which would in any degree be detrimental to their subordination, their respect, or their prudence.

The Romans were a people whose power consisted more in their discretion than in the impetuosity of their passions; they were easily persuaded by the voice of reason, and restrained by esteem; they were also more religious and less fanatical than the Greeks; they paid a greater attention to political authority, and not possessing an equal share of enthusiasm, they were less jealous of the reputation of individuals, and were never deprived of the exercise of their reason by any event incident to human nature.

The Romans, in the early period of their history, despised the fine arts, and literature more particularly; but when philosophers, orators, and historians rendered the talent of writing useful to the affairs and morals of the people, th Romans then were the first to engage in the pursuit f literature: their works, moreover, had that advantage over those of the Greeks, which must always arise from a practical knowledge and administration: but they were necessarily obliged to use the utmost circumspection in the composition of them. It

* Alcibiades and Themistocles attempted to revenge themselves of their country by stiring up foreign enemies against it. But a Roman would never have been guilty of such a crime; Coriolanus is the only example;—he formed the plot, but could not acquire sufficient resolution to put it into practice.

was with the greatest timidity that Cicero first attacked the generally received ideas of the Romans: the opinions of the nation might not be set at defiance by those who wished to obtain their votes for the first places in the republic; and therefore the greatest ambition of the generality of writers was to defend and preserve the reputation of the statesmen.

In such a democracy as that which existed at Athens, the attention to political concerns, and the study of philosophy, were as rarely found united, as the man of reflection and the courtier are in a monarchy. The means by which the people acquired popularity, occupied nearly the whole of their time, and seemed to have little or no connection with the labor necessary for the increase of knowledge: the chiefs of the people had not, so to speak, the smallest idea of posterity; the storms of the then present times were so terrible, and had such an unlimited power over the posterity and adversity of every individual, that all their passions were absorbed in contemperaneous events. An aristocratical government proceeding in a slower and more measured career, excites in its subjects a more lively interest for the future: the light of philosophy is necessary to the reflection of a select society of men, while the resources of the imagination are sufficient to move an assembled multitude of the people.

With the exception of Xenophon, who himself took an active part in the military history which he related, (but who was never possessed of any power in the interior of the republic,) not one statesman of Athens was celebrated at the same period for his literary talents, or even imagined, like Cicero and Cæsar, that he could add by his writings to his political consequence. Scipio and Sallust were suspected, the one of being the concealed author of the Comedies of Terence, and the other to have been covertly engaged in the conspiracy of which he was the historian: but there is no instance, amongst the Athenians, of any individual having united the study of literature with affairs of state. The result of this nearly absolute distinction between the study of philosophy and the occupation of the statesman, was, that the Greek writers gave more latitude to their imagination; and the Latin authors regulated their ideas by the actual state of human affairs.

The Latin literature was the only one which commenced with philosophy; in every other, especially in that of the Greeks, they were entirely indebted to the imagination for the first efforts of the mind. The comedies of Plautus and of Terence are entirely the result of the ideas of the Greeks. The poets that preceded Cicero, are not worthy of being recorded, for, like Lucretius, they turned philosophy into poetry.* The *useful* was the first principle of the Latin literature; and want of amusement, that of the Greeks. The patricians, in condescension to the people, instituted shows, music, and festivals; but the power was wholly concentrated in the senate.

The Romans were allowed to be a celebrated nation, powerfully constituted, and wisely governed, long before the existence of any author in the Latin language. The talent of writing was not developed till a considerable time after action had had its full play; which induces a conclusion, that the Roman literature was of a quite different nature from that of a nation whose imagination was the first principle that was roused to action.

* This opinion having been called in question, I think it necessary to point out a few facts which will prove it. I have said, that the poets who preceded Cicero and Lucretius were not worthy of being recorded; an objection has been made to Ennius, Accius, and Pacuvius: Ennius, who in some respects had the advantage of the three, was incorrect, obscene, and possessed but a small share of political imagination; this opinion is grounded upon the fragments of his works, which are still extant; and it is confirmed by Virgil, whose judgment of Ennius was even proverbial. Horace, in some of his epistles, makes a jest of those who admired the ancient Roman poets, Ennius and his contemporaries. Ovid forbids the female sex to read the Annals of Ennius in verse; and, moreover, the greater number of the Latin commentators considered Ennius as a very moderate, not to say an indifferent author. I have advanced, that the Romans had philosophical writers amongst them, before they had poets; for the proof of this assertion I have the following dates: it was in the year 514 that the first comedies in verse, written by Titus Andronicus, were represented; and it was in the following year that Ennius was known; but it was five centuries before that epoch, that Numa wrote upon philosophy; and it was 150 years after Numa, that Pythagoras was received as a citizen of Rome; the philosophical sects of higher Greece had a continual connection with Rome; the Latin language borrowed many of the grammatical rules of Æolic Greece, which the colonies had transported into higher Greece. Ennius, before he attempted to compose in verse, embraced the sect of Pyth- [illegible]rism; and what still remains of his poems, treat more of phil- [illegible]ophical ideas than marvelous facts. The legislation which ought to be considered as a branch of philosophy, was carried to the greatest perfection at Rome, before they understood the meaning of a poet; public schools were instituted to study the laws, where they were analytically explained by the commentators. Sextus Porphyrius, Sextus Cœlius, Granius Flaccus, &c., wrote upon this subject, in the third, fourth, and fifth centuries of the republic: to methodize the twelve tablets, some of their people were sent by the Romans to consult with the most enlightened men of Greece; and it was the decree of the twelve tablets, which treated of religion and of the rights of men, both in public and in private; and they are quoted by Cicero, as superior to any the Philosophers had ever written on the subject. Paulus Emilius confided the education of his son to the philosopher Metrodon, who had accompanied him from Athens; and Cato the Elder, who disapproved of the Roman taste for Greek literature, and who expressed in the most pointed manner his contempt for Ennius, on account of his poetical talents, had himself been instructed by Nearchus, the Pythagorean, and distinguished himself both as a writer and as an orator; he entered the lists as an opponent to Carnades, a Greek philosopher of the Academical sect; and Diogenes the Stoic, who was sent to Rome at the same time with Carnades, was so kindly received by the Romans, that Scipio, Lælius, and many other senators, embraced his doctrines; it even appears that they were known and practised at Rome for a length of time before that embassy. If reference is to be obtained by the philosophy of the sophist it may with truth be said, that during the existence of the republic, the Romans constantly repulsed those false principles of the Greeks; but if we allow to philosophy the same honorable reception it met with from the ancients, we shall perceive that the Romans could not have been good statesmen, profound legislators, or great orators without philosophy. There were among the Romans many writers in prose before the time of Ennius; Posthumus Albinus wrote a history of Rome in Greek; Fabius Pictor wrote one also in Latin before Ennius was known. There were, among the Romans, many celebrated authors of whom Cicero speaks with admiration; the Gracchi and the Appii, some of whose discourses were extant in writing in the time of Cicero; in short, the republic were in possession of all the great men, before they were advanced in the cultivation of poetry. Is it possible to compare the progress of the human understanding in Rome to that which it followed in Greece? Homer, the most sublime of all poets, existed four centuries before the first composition written in prose that we are acquainted with; and Pherycides of Scyros existed 300 years before Solon, and one century before Lycurgus; when poetry, the first essay of the imagination in Greece, had attained to the highest degree of perfection, before their ideas were sufficiently enlightened upon other subjects, to establish a code of laws or form a political society. In short, to promote our desire of becoming acquainted with literature, we must attentively examine its general character. It has been said, that the Italian literature began with poetry; but in the time of Petrarch there existed several bad prosaic writers, whose names might have been objected to as well, in opposition to those of Ennins, Accius, and Pacuvius, to the great philosophers and political orators who perpetuate the glory of the first centuries of the Roman republic. If we were to recollect the great orator Cicero, only from his having attempted a poem on Moschus, in his juvenile days, it would not be understood who was meant by this appellation: it is the same with that shapeless, cold, and obscene poetry, which they desire to honor with the origin of the Latin literature. Instruction is sometimes better than erudition, because, in the right of antiquity, the imagination may easily get bewildered in the detail which will impede the progress of those who search after the truth of the whole.

The writers who were really celebrated before the century of Augustus, were Sallust, Cicero, and Lucretius; to whom may be added Plautus and Terence, who translated the Greek comedies; but it is difficult to determine the original poets in the Latin language that were deserving of any degree of fame before the time of Cicero; and likewise who is the poet that could boast of having an influence over the Latin literature before the century of Augustus, which can be in the least compared to that which Homer had over that of the Greek. Cicero was considered as being at the head of the Latin literature; as Homer was acknowledged to be of the Grecian; but with this difference, that a number of enlightened ages must have taken place before there could have existed a philosopher resembling Cicero; while it is entirely to the marvelous of the heroic age, and the imagination of the poet, that we are indebted for Homer. Should these observations be found too multiplied, I only beg it may be remembered, that they are written in answer to a charge which required to be refuted.

A greater refinement in taste, and a more accurate judgment than that possessed by the Greeks, was the natural consequence that arose from the distinction of classes at Rome. Those who were highest, ambitious to raise themselves higher, were not long in discovering that a good education and a noble deportment distinguished the different ranks in a much greater degree than the legal gradations could obtain. The Romans would never have endured on their theatres the coarse jests of Aristophanes; they would never have suffered their contemporaneous events, and their public characters, to have been thus given as a spectacle of ridicule to the public: they permitted, however, certain theatrical jests and manners to be exhibited in their presence, but without the smallest allusion to their domestic virtues. Pantomimes or farces, the subjects of which were taken from Greece, and the principal parts performed by Greek slaves, were allowed, but nothing that bore the slightest relation to the manners of the Romans. The ideas and sentiments expressed in these comedies were, in the opinion of the Roman spectators, as a fiction more than a work of imagination. Terence, however, preserved, in the use of those foreign subjects, that style of decency and restraint which are necessary to the dignity of mankind, even when there were no women amongst the auditors.

The condition of the female sex was of much more importance amongst the Romans than amongst the Greeks; but it was in their own families they obtained that ascendency, which they had not at that time acquired in society. The taste and urbanity of the Romans was of that masculine order, which borrows nothing from the delicacy of women, but was solely maintained by their austerity of manners.

Neither the thundering eloquence of the Greeks, nor the ingenious flattery of the French, were calculated for an aristocratical government; It is neither the individual person of the king, nor the people at large, whose esteem it is the most essential to cultivate; but that of a small body of men who unite in common their separate interest. In this order of things, it behoved the patricians mutually to respect each other, in order to command the esteem of the nation at large: they must also apply themselves to obtain a solid and lasting reputation: their qualifications must be solemn and grave, but at the same time such as might reflect honor on each individual of their number, and tend to the support of each separate existence equally with their own. Whatever is singular, or excites too large a share of applause or envy, is not suitable to the dignity of an august body of men. The Romans were not ambitious to distinguish themselves, like the Greeks, by extraordinary systems and useless sophisms, or by a manner of living fantastically philosophical.* What was most calculated to obtain the esteem of the patricians, was the object of general emulation; they might hate them, but they nevertheless wished to imitate them. Although the Romans attended less to literary pursuits than the Greeks, they were considered superior to them in their wisdom, and the extent of their moral and philosophical observations: besides, the Romans had the advantage of some centuries over the Greeks in the progress of the human understanding.

A democracy inspires a lively and almost universal emulation; but an aristocracy excites to the perfection of what it has begun. The writer who composes, ought ever to have the judges of his performance present to his imagination; that his works will then combine the genius of the author, and the knowledge of the public, which he was selected for his tribunal.

The Greeks had infinitely more practice than the Romans in smart and prompt repartees, which could not fail to insure popularity in the midst of a sprightly and witty nation: but the Romans had evidently the advantage of possessing real judgment: there was, consequently, a closer connection in their ideas, which laid them to examine with greater minuteness every species of reflection: and their advancement in philosophy is very apparent, from the era of Cicero to that of Tacitus. The literature of the imagination proceeded with a rapid but an unequal step; while the knowledge of the human heart, and the morals annexed to it, came by degrees to perfection. The principal foundation of the Roman philosophy was borrowed from the Greeks: but as the Romans adopted in their conduct in life, the principles of morality which the Greeks had only developed in their writings, the exercise of virtue rendered them greatly their superior. Every thing which relates to the code of moral duties, is explained by Cicero with more energy, more clearness, and greater force, than by any other who preceded him it was impossible to advance farther in the establishment of a beneficient religion, or in the abolishment of slavery, both political and civil.

The ancients did not investigate so deeply into the extent of the human passions, as some of the modern moralists have done: their ideas of virtue were in opposition to this examination. Virtue, with the ancients, consisted chiefly in the command they acquired over themselves, and the love of fame; which being more external than internal, did not permit an inquiry into the secrets of the heart, and therefore moral philosophy lost much in many respects.

The *opinion* of the Stoics was the *point of honor* with the ancients. A predominant virtue sustains every political association independent of their principles of government; that is to say, amongst all the different qualifications one must be preferred: unless this were the case, the others would lose their effect; but this one alone can supply the absence of all the rest; this quality is the tie, the distinguished character which unites citizens of the same country.

The predominant trait in the character of the Lacedemonians, was the contempt in which they held bodily pain; that of the Athenians was the distinction of talents; that of the Romans was the conquest of the mind over itself; and that of the French was the splendid display of their valor: and so great was the importance which a Roman attached to the exercise of an absolute command over himself, that, when alone, he would scarcely allow even to himself that he possessed those affections which he was expected to suppress. If the least apprehension of weakness at any time rendered him likely to betray it, he repulsed it with so much energy, that he did not indulge his inclination with sufficient latitude to investigate the private emotions of his own heart. It was much the same with the Roman philosophers; the tumultuous sensations of grief, anger, envy, or regret, and every involuntary feeling of the soul, were considered as effeminate; and they would have blushed even to have been suspected of approving of them; they had no desire to study them, either in their own case or that of others. Extremely ambitious of fame, they gave no latitude to their natural character; that which appeared, was altogether artificial: nevertheless, the Romans were not hypocrites by nature, but they acquired that appearance from ostentation.

Cicero is the only philosopher whose real character was evidently portrayed throughout his writings; and yet he brought his systems to oppose what his self-love had suffered to escape from him; and his philosophy was entirely composed of precepts without observations. Cicero, in his 'Offices,' speaks of *decorum*, that is, of exterior forms of virtue, as if it was a part of virtue itself; they taught as a moral duty, the several different methods of imposing respect, by purity of language, by elegance of pronunciation: in short, every

* What would the Romans have said to the singularities of Diogenes? Why, nothing at all; for he never would have committed them in a country where they would not have been successful in procuring him a reputation.

circumstance that could add to the dignity of man, was esteemed a virtue with the Romans. It was philosophical enjoyments and not the consolatory ideas of a sublime and elevated religion, which the Romans proposed as a recompense for their sacrifices. It was not to the consolations of the heart that they appealed to sustain the man; but to his pride. The more their nature resembled the *majestic*, the greater care was taken to banish from the mind even the smallest emotion of sensibility, had it even been the sole support of their severest morals.

It does not appear, that in the first epoch of their literature there was any work which discovered a profound knowledge of the human heart, the secret springs which actuate characters, or the numberless diversities of the moral nature. To have investigated the cause of those involuntary sensations of the heart, would have been probably an encouragement to them, whilst the Romans wished to remain ignorant even of the possibility of their existence. Their eloquence, singly considered, did not possess that irresistible emotion; it was the light and strength of reason, which never interrupted the tranquillity of the mind. The Romans were, nevertheless, possessed of more real sensibility than the Greeks; that austerity of manners which they imposed upon themselves, was a better preservative to the affections, than that licentiousness to which the Greeks abandoned themselves.

Plutarch relates that Brutus, when about to quit Italy, and just ready to embark, walked by the sea-side with Portia, whom he was going to leave; they entered into one of the temples, and addressed their prayers to the gods of protection; when a painting, which represented the parting scene of Hector and Andromache, caught their attention. Cato's daughter, who, till that moment, had supported herself with the greatest heroism, could no longer suppress the violence of her grief. Brutus, moved to pity by her tears, led her to some friends who had accompanied them, saying, 'I trust to your care this woman, who unites to every virtue peculiar to her own sex, the intrepidity of ours.' And with these expressive words he went his way.

I know not whether our civil commotions, in which the tender farewells of so many friends have proved their last, have added to the impression I felt in reading this recital; but it appears to me, that there are few more affecting: it is also true, that the austerity of the Roman character gives a more brilliant coloring to the feelings it excites. The stoic Brutus, whose rigid virtue never condescended to pity, showed, in his last days, and even in those moments which preceded his latest efforts, a sentiment so tender, that it surprises the heart with an unexpected emotion: the dreadful action and fatal destiny of this last of the Romans, encompass his image with ideas so melancholy which excite a sympathetic concern for the fate of Portia.*

Compare this affecting scene with that of Pericles, pleading before the Areopagus for the accused Aspasia: the splendor of power, the lustre of beauty, and even love itself, such as could be excited by seduction, were all found united in this pleader: and yet they do not penetrate to the heart. The sources of tenderness are also to be found in the secrets of consicience: neither the prejudices of society, nor the opinions of philosophers, can dispose of the affections of the heart: but virtue, such as it was given by heaven, and whether it is in love or in the sacrifice of the affections, is ever deltcate and equally consistent.

Although the Romans, from the purity of their morals and the progress of their understanding, were better qualified for deep and lasting affections than the Greeks; yet it was not till the reign of Augustus that we could perceive any traces, either in ideas or expressions, of that sensibility which those affections ought to have created. The habit of never suffering any personal impressions to appear, and their attention being chiefly engrossed by philosophy, gave an energy to their style; but it was sometimes productive of an unpleasant dryness and irregularity. 'As to the sentiment vulgarly termed love,' says Cicero, 'it is almost superfluous to attempt to demonstrate how much it is beneath the character of man.' He likewise declares, that the tears shed over the tombs of departed friends, and all testimonies of grief, are 'supportable only in women:' and he also adds, that 'they are a bad omen.' Thus was the man who wished to subdue human nature, himself the victim of superstition.

Without endeavoring to discuss the advantages which might result to a nation of such moral strength, and exalted by the united efforts of institutions and manners; I am certain that literature must have less variety when the genius of each man has its path marked out by the national spirit, and the exertions of each individual tend to one single point of perfection, instead of being directed to that for which his natural talents are best adapted.

The battles of the gladiators had for their object, strongly to impress the minds of the people with the representations of war, and the spectacle of death; but the Romans also required, that those unfortunate beings, whom fate had placed in their hands, the slaves of their barbarous amusement, should learn, in the practice of those sanguinary games, to triumph over pain: and they never omitted an occasion to put them to the proof. This continual subjection of their finer feelings was not favorable to the effect of tragedy, neither does the Latin literature contain any thing celebrated in that style.*

The Roman character possessed in a high degree the grandeur of tragedy; but it was too general to be theatrical: even the lowest classes of the people were distinguished by a certaiu dignity and gravity of manners. But in that derangement occasioned by misfortune, that cruel picture of physical nature torn and wrecked by the sufferings of the mind, and from which idea Shakspeare drew such heart-rending scenes, the Romans would have discovered nothing but the degradation of the human species. There is no instance, in their history, of any man or woman whose intellects were deranged by disappointment in any shape: nevertheless, suicide was very frequent amongst them, although the exterior signs of grief were rarely to be met with. The contempt which the language of complaint was sure to excite, imposed it as a law to conquer such weakness or to die. There is nothing in such a disposition that can furnish any great development of tragedy, neither would it have been possible to have transported into Rome that interest which the Greeks felt in their theatrical compositions on national subjects.† The Romans would not have permitted, on their stage, any representations which had the smallest allusion to their history, their affections, or their country: a religious sentiment, was what the Romans esteemed above all things. The Athenians believed in the same religious dogmas as the Romans, and like them defended their country, and like them were fond of liberty; but that respect which acts upon the thoughts, and drives from the imagination even the probability of committing a prohibited action, was known only to the Romans. At Athens, philosophy was cultivated as one of the fine arts by their people, enamored of every species of celebrity: but at

* Elle vint sur ce seuil accompagner ses pas,
Et ses infortunés ne se revirent pas.
[Les Gracques, par M. de Guibert.

* Horace complains, that often, in the midst of a representation, the Romans interrupted the performance by vociferations for the gladiators.

† There still exists one tragedy composed upon a Roman subject, entitled the Death of Octavius; but it was written, as the nature of the events will prove, some length of time after the destruction of the republic; and although it is inserted in the works of Seneca, we are ignorant of the author of it, nor is it clearly ascertained if it was ever represented.

Rome it was adopted as the support of virtue; the statesmen studied it as a means of enabling them to form a better code of laws; for the aggrandizement of the Roman republic was the sole object to which their labors and their ambition tended, and reflected more glory upon their warriors, their magistrates, and their writers, than all the honors which could have been individually conferred upon them. The same spirit and the same character, arising from the same cause, shone through the literature of the Roman republic; it is by the perfection and not by the variety, the dignity, and not by the ardor, and by the wisdom more than the invention, that the writings of those days were remarkable. There reigned throughout an authority of expression, a majesty of character, that commands respect, and assures the full acceptation of every word; but so far is it from suppressing or retrenching any part of the signification, that each term, on the contrary, seems to suppose more than it expresses. The Romans gave a great scope to the development of their ideas; but what belongs to their sentiments, is always expressed in a concise manner.

The first epoch of the Latin literature approaches so near to the close of the Greeks, that it is subject to the same imperfections, arising from a similar cause, namely, the infancy of civilization; many of their works were pregnant with errors, which evinced their profound ignorance of the subject they attempted to delineate; while others were extended to an insupportable length. The Romans were nevertheless superior to the Greeks in the connection of their ideas; but in this respect how much inferior are they to the moderns.

What most excites our admiration in perusing the smaller number of writings which remain of the epoch of the Roman literature, is the idea which such compositions afford us of their character and government. The history of Sallust, the letters of Brutus,* and the works of Cicero, are recalled most powerfully to the remembrance: we feel the strength of mind through the beauty of the style; we discover the man in the author, the nation in the man, and the universe at the feet of the nation. Neither Sallust nor Cicero were the greatest characters of the age in which they lived; but writers that possessed such extraordinary talents, must necessarily imbibe the spirit and beauties of so fine a century, and Rome lives in their writings. When Cicero pleads before the people, or the senate, or the priests, or before Cæsar, his eloquence changes its character; in his harangues may be observed, not only that style which was suitable to the Roman nation in general; but all his discourses were addressed and modified to the different tastes and habits of each.

The parallel which may be drawn between Cicero and Demosthenes, is most apparent in the comparison which may be made between the spirit and customs of the Greeks, and those of the Romans: in comparing the ingenious humor of Demosthenes with the prevailing eloquence of Cicero, and the means employed by Demosthenes to move the passions which he stands in need of, with the arguments which Cicero uses to repel those he wishes to oppose; his long developments, and the rapid impulse of the Greek orator, are all closely connected with the government and national character of the two people.

A private writer is absorbed in his own talents; but an orator who wishes to influence political deliberations, conforms with care to the national spirit, as an able general previously surveys the ground on which he is to give battle.

* Brutus, in his letters, does not confine himself to the art of writing; his aim was to be useful to the political interests of his country; and yet the letter which he addressed to Cicero, to reproach him for flattering the young Octavius, was perhaps one of the finest prose compositions ever written in the Latin language.

CHAPTER VI.

OF THE LATIN LITERATURE DURING THE REIGN OF AUGUSTUS.

Cicero and Virgil are generally considered as belonging to that century called the golden age of the Latin literature; but those writers whose genius and talents aimed at perfection in the midst of such furious struggles for liberty, should be distinguished by another character from those whose abilities were ripened in the last years of the peaceable despotism of Augustus: but those periods approached so near to each other, that their dates might be confounded, were it not that the general spirit of their literature, before and after the loss of their liberty, presents to the eye of observation a most striking difference.

Many of the republican customs were continued from habit for some years after the reign of Augustus, the proofs of which are visible in many of their historical writers; but were all recalled by the influence of the court, the greater part of which desiring to please Augustus, and being situated near him, gave to their writings that turn of character that must be assumed under the reign of a monarch who wishes to conciliate the good opinion of the people without diminishing in any degree the power he is possessed of. This is the only point of analogy which establishes the least relation between the Latin literature and that of the French in the reign of Louis XIV.; in other respects, these different periods bear not the least resemblance to each other.

Philosophy, in Rome, preceded poetry: this was inverting the common order of things, and was possibly the principal cause of the perfection of the Latin poets. Emulation was not carried to poetry till the reign of Augustus. The enjoyment of power and of political interest was generally preferred to any success that might arise purely from literature; and when, by the form of government, men of superior talents were called upon to the exercise of public occupations, it was towards eloquence, history, and philosophy, and to that species of literature which leads more immediately to the knowledge of men and events, that their labors were directed. But under the dominion of an empire it is quite the reverse; and the only means left, by which men of distinguished talents can acquire fame, is in the exercise of the fine arts: and if their tyranny should be tempered with lenity, the poets are, in general, too much inclined to illustrate the reign by their masterly pieces of adulation. Nevertheless, Virgil, Horace, and Ovid, though they were all prodigal of their flattery to Augustus; yet their writing discovered more philosophy and reflection than any other of the Latin poets: they were indebted for this advantage in part to the sound sense and solid judgment of the writers who preceded them. Every era of literature has its epoch of poetry; the beauties of imagery and of harmony have been succesively transplanted into many different and reformed languages; but when the poetical talent of a nation unfolds itself as it did at Rome, in the middle of an enlightened century, it is enriched by its knowledge and experience.

The poets, in the reign of Augustus, adopted in most of their compositions the Epicurean system; which is favorable to poetry, and appears to give a degree of consequence to indolence, a luxury to philosophy, and in a manner to dignify even slavery. This system, is immoral, but it is not servile: it gives up liberty like every other good that requires any effort to keep possession of; but it does not make despotism a principle, nor obedience to resemble fanaticism, as the flatterers of Louis XIV. were desirous of doing.

The idea of death, which Horace constantly intermixed with the most smiling images, established a kind philosophical equality by the side of flattery; but it was not from a virtuous sensibility that the poets portrayed the brevity of existence and the certain destiny of man: if they had been really capable of profound reflection, they would rather have opposed the tyranny than have celebrated the usurper. But life thus passed, is but a representation of the smooth gliding streams that refreshed their burning climate, and we are almost inclined to forgive their omission of morals and of liberty, when we see them inattentive to time and existence.

But notwithstanding the great effeminacy of character so remarkably prevalent in most of the poets during the reign of Augustus, there are found in them a number of reflected beauties: they borrowed from the Greeks great part of their poetical inventions, which the moderns have imitated in their turn: and it seems as if they would ever remain the standard of the art. But whatever is tender or philosophical in the Latin poets, may be ascribed entirely to themselves.

The love of a pastoral life, which inspired so many beautiful ideas, assumes a different character with the Romans, to that which was understood by the Greeks: these nations were both equally pleased with the same imagery, which was suitable to a similar climate. They each invoked the freshness bestowed by nature, and welcomed with delight the shade that screened them from a vertical sun: but the Romans required, to heighten the charms of rural life, a shelter that could defend them from tyranny; they retired from the bustle of inhabited cities, to repose their minds after the painful emotions they had been subjected to, and to lose sight, if possible, of the yoke which goaded and degraded them. Such a measure was favorable to moral reflections: they were interspersed with their descriptive poetry; and we imagine we perceive a tender regret, and a melancholy remembrance in all the compositions of that period. This circumstance, without doubt, is the cause why we feel a greater degree of interest for the Romans than for the Greeks. The Greeks lived as it were with futurity in view; but the Romans, like us, loved to carry their reflections to the past. As long as the republic existed, the Romans discovered a delicacy in their affection for the female sex: they had not, it is true, that independent spirit which is rendered permanent by the modern laws: but secluded, with their household gods, they breathed, like domestic divinities, certain religious sentiments. Those writers who existed in the period of the republic, never allowed themselves to express the affections which they felt: it was in that short interval betwixt the most rigid austerity of manners and the greatest degree of depravity, that the Latin poets showed a more tender sentiment than any we meet with in the Greek writings. In the reign of Augustus, they recollected the republican severity; and their portraits of love were indebted for a few charms to a virtuous retrospect.*

The verses of Tibullus to Delia, the fourth book of the Æneid, Ceyx and Alcyone, Baucis and Philemon, give a true description of the sentiments of the heart in the Latin language: their sublime and soft character inspires a great degree of respect; such an impression is created from this language which that of reason only would not be capable of producing with all its strength when employed in the expression of tenderness. True and genuine sensibility is, however, rarely to be met with during the reign of Augustus; the Epicurean system, the doctrine of fatality, and the manners and customs of antiquity before the establishment of the Christian religion and almost entirely in opposition to nature and the effusions of the heart.

Ovid, in many of his compositions, introduced a portion of affectation and antithesis in his language of love, which destroyed even the shadow of truth: such was also the vitiated taste of the age of Louis XIV. This mode of writing with cool deliberation on the passions and affections of the heart, must at all times and in all climates have nearly the same effect upon the readers: but Ovid's affectation was the error of his imagination, and in no degree connected with the general character of antiquity.

The comparison has been so often drawn between the age of Louis XIV. and that of Augustus, that it is needless, as it is impossible, for me to enter upon it here: I shall therefore confine myself to the development of one single observation, which is of the greatest importance to the system of perfectibility, which it is my desire to support. Descartes, Boyle, Pascal, Moliere, Labruyere, Bossuet, and the English philosophers, who were contemporaries at one period of his history of letters, do not admit of any comparison between the century of Louis XIV. in the advance of the progress of the human understanding. Nevertheless, we are tempted to inquire why amongst the ancients, and more especially amongst the Romans, there were found historians so correct, as never to have been equaled by the moderns; and particularly, why the French cannot furnish a single work of this description which is complete.

In the chapter which treats of the age of Louis XIV., I shall analyze the cause whence arises the mediocrity of the French historians: but I ought previously to make some reflections on the superiority of the ancients in history; and I am persuaded those reflections will prove, that their superiority was not unfavorable to the successive progress of their understanding. There exist some histories, which may justly be entitled philosophical: and there are others whose sole merit consists in the variety and animated style of their representations, and the energy and beauty of their language: it was in the latter period that the Greek and Latin historians were illustrious.

* I cite at hazard two examples, to substantiate what I have advanced concerning the sensibility of the Latin poets. When the travelling gods, in Ovid's Metamorphoses, demanded of Philemon, what Baucis and himself would most desire from the favor of heaven? Philemon answered:—

> Poscimus; et quoniam concordes egimus annos,
> Auferat hora duos eadem, nec conjugis unquam
> Busta meæ videam, neu sim tumulandus ab illâ

'As we have lived together many years in perfect harmony, we only ask that the same hour should terminate our existence; that I may not behold the tomb of my spouse, nor she be left to sorrow after me.'

I have selected from Virgil, the poet in whose verses is found the utmost sensibility, especially those in which paternal tenderness is so forcibly described, to cause that deep affection in the mind, without making use of the language of love, requires a much greater fund of sensibility. Evander on taking leave of his son Pallas, when he was preparing for battle, addressed heaven in these words:

> At vos, O superi, et divum tu maxime rector
> Jupiter, Arcadii quæso miserescite regis,
> Et patrias audite preces. Si numina vestra
> Incolumen Pallanta mihi, si fata reservant;
> Si visurus eum vivo, et venturus in unum;
> Vitam oro; patiar quemvis durare laborem.
> Sin aliquem infandum casum, Fortuna, minaris,
> Nunc o, nunc liceat crudelem abrumpere vitam
> Dum curæ ambiguæ, dum spes incerta futuri
> Dum te care puer, mea sera et sola voluptas,
> Complexu teneo: gravior ne nuncius aures
> Vulneret.——

> 'Ye gods! and mighty Jove, in pity bring
> Relief, and hear a father and a king.
> If fate and you reserve these eyes to see
> My son return with peace and victory;
> If the lov'd boy shall bless his father's sight;
> If we shall meet again with more delight,
> Then draw my life in length, let me sustain,
> In hopes of his embrace, the worst of pain.
> But if your hard decrees, which, O! I dread,
> Have doom'd to death this undeserving head;
> This, O! this very moment, let me die,
> While hopes and fears in equal balance lie;
> While yet possess'd of all his youthful charms,
> I strain him close within these aged arms;
> Before that fatal news my soul shall wound.'

A much more profound knowledge of mankind is necessary in order to become a great moralist, than what is required to be a good historian. Tacitus is the only writer of antiquity who united those qualities; the apprehension and sufferings which are always attached to servitude, ripened his reflection, and his experience was the result of extended observation. Titus Livy, Sallust, and the historians of an inferior order, Florus, Cornelius Nepos, &c., delight us by the grandeur and elegance of their recitals, by the beauty and eloquence of the harangues which they give to their characters, and by the dramatic interests which they knew how to afford to their representations. But those historians portrayed, as it may be said, nothing more than the mere externals of life; describing man such as he appears, in the light he wishes to display himself. Their coloring was strong, and finely contrasted with virtue and vice: but we do not find in the ancient history either a philosophical analysis of moral impressions, or a profound observation of characters. Montaigne, in his intellectual review, penetrates much farther into that subject, than any other ancient author. But this kind of superiority is not desirable in an historian: mankind must be represented at large; their grandeur of character must be left to the heroes, that they may appear great to the subsequent ages. The moralist may discover the foibles which are the hidden resemblances of one man to another; but the historian must be positive in pronouncing the difference.

The ancients delighted in what excited admiration, and were possessed of a quality which was as necessary to the interest of truth as to that of fiction; namely, they were as unbiassed in their contempt, as they were in their enthusiasm; they neither endeavored to diminish the odiousness of vice, nor to exalt the merit of virtue: and we often find characters much better supported in their history than in their works of imagination. Besides, is it possible to forget the astonishing advantage the ancient historians possessed over the moderns, even from the facts which they recited? A republican government produces a dignity of character in men as well as in events: while a despotic monarchical government, or the history of federal laws, can never inspire so much interests as the annals of a free people.

Suetonis, who was the historian of the reign of the emperors, Ammianus, Marcellinus, and Velleius Paterculus, could not have been compared, in the latter part of his writings, to any of those who wrote in the centuries of the republic; and if Tacitus surpassed his contemporaries, it was because he still cherished the republican resentment; and not considering the government of the emperors as legal, nor requiring the permission of any one to publish his works, his spirit was not subdued by prejudices, either natural or insisted on, which has enslaved our modern historians down to the present century.

Numerous are the considerations to which we are to attribute the superiority of the ancients in historical writings. One chief advantage arose from their peculiar art of describing and relating what they conceived to be the emotions, the interest, and the effects of the imagination, but not from any secret knowledge of the human heart, or the philosophical course of events. It was not likely that the ancients should have possessed this knowledge in an equal degree with those whom the lapse of centuries and multiplied generations have instructed by new examples, and who are inclined to contemplate, in a review of past history, so many crimes, misfortunes, and sufferings.

CHAPTER VII.

OF THE LATIN LITERATURE, FROM THE DEATH OF AUGUSTUS DOWN TO THE REIGN OF THE ANTONINES.

After the age of Louis XIV., and during that of Louis XV., an advanced progress was visible in philosophy, without either poetry or literature having acquired any greater degree of perfection. Nearly the same advancement in the arts may be observed from the period of Augustus to that of Antonines; but with this difference, that the emperors who reigned during that interval were such atrocious monsters, that the empire, unable to support itself against despotic tyranny, sunk under its influence; and the general spirit of the nation being thus broken, there was but a very small number of men who retained sufficient strength of mind to devote themselves to study.

The minds of men, enervated by that inglorious ease in which they indulged themselves in the reign of Augustus, lost even the remembrance of those heroic virtues to which Rome was indebted for her grandeur. Horace blushed not to avow in his verses, that he fled on the day of battle; and Cicero and Ovid both testified the greatest impatience at their exile, although there is the most striking difference in their manner of expressing it. The *De Tristibus* of Ovid are filled with the repinings of despondency, and the most servile flattery of his prosecutor; while Cicero, even in his familiar correspondence with Atticus, contrived to ennoble, by a thousand different methods, the grief he felt at his unjust banishment. The variation in their sensations and in their expression is not to be attributed entirely to the dissimilarity of their character, but to the different periods in which they lived. General opinion may be considered as the centre by which men are united: and if it does not change the character, it in some degree modifies the forms in which men chose to appear before the multitude.

After the flourishing reign of Augustus, there arose a more barbarous and oppressive tyranny, of which antiquity does not furnish a second example. Excess of misfortune had in a great measure broken the spirit of the nation; and the slothful indolence into which they had degenerated since the overthrow of the republic, enervated alike superior minds with those of the vulgar; while the horrid cruelties which were continually practised upon them, rendered the lower classes of the people still more servile and contemptible:—but in the midst of these dreadful calamities, a small number of enlightened men arose above the general despondency, and experienced more strongly the necessity of a social philosophy.

Seneca (of whom I shall only here form a judgment by his works,) Tacitus, Epictetus, and Marcus Aurelius, although in different situations, and with characters which bore not the least resemblance to each other, were all inspired with the same abhorrence of guilt and indignation against vice: their writings in both the Greek and Latin language are composed of a character totally different from the literature of the period of Augustus; they even possessed more force and energy than was to be found in the republican philosophers themselves. The morals of Cicero are principally directed to the effect they ought to produce on others; and those of Seneca express the self-command we should endeavor to acquire: the one seeks an honorable power; the other, an asylum to shelter him from affliction: the one wishes to support and animate virtue; the other, to inspire a contempt of vice. Cicero considers men only as they are connected with his country; while Seneca, who had no country, was engrossed entirely with what related to private individuals. There is a certain vein of melancholy which prevails throughout the works of Seneca; while those of Cicero are filled with energy and emulation.

When despotic tyrants menaced destruction, and philosophers were condemned like the most atrocious criminals, to suffer an ignominious death; men, not daring to act openly, retired within themselves, and devoted their time to a more minute investigation of the mind. Yet the writers of the third epoch of the

Latin literature had not arrived at that perfect knowledge and philosophical observation of general characters which we find in Montaigne and Labruyere; but they acquired a more intimate acquaintance with themselves; and their genius was confined by oppression to repose in their own bosoms.

Tyranny, like other public calamities, may assist the development of philosophy; but it is very destructive to literature, by suppressing emulation and corrupting the taste.

It has been maintained, that the decline of the arts, of letters, and of empires, must necessarily happen after they have arrived at a certain degree of splendor: but this idea is not just; for though I firmly believe that the arts have their limits, above which they are incapable of rising; it is however very possible they may remain at the same height without any retrogression:—and in every species of progressive knowledge, the moral nature ever tends to perfect itself. Precedent melioration is a cause of future melioration: the link of connection may be broken by accidental occurrences, which may impede future progress, but which can by no means be considered as any consequence of prior advancement.

Notwithstanding the dreadful nature of the circumstances the writers had to contend with in the period of the Emperors, they were much superior in philosophy to the writers of the age of Augustus: but the style of the Latin authors, in the third epoch of their literature, possessed much less elegance and purity: it was impossible that, under such rude and ferocious tyrants, they could preserve a delicacy of taste and expression. The multitude were rendered contemptible by a servile imitation of the manners of the reigning tyrant; while the smaller number of distinguished men found so much difficulty in communicating their ideas to each other, that it was impracticable for them to establish that critical, that literary legislation, which draws a positive line between that which is studied and that which is genuine, and marks likewise the difference between energy and exaggeration.

Under the tyranny of the Emperors it was not permitted, nor would it have been possible, to have moved the people by eloquence; neither philosophical nor literary labors tended in the least degree to influence public events: nor can we discover, in any of the writings of that period, such a character as is marked by the desire of being useful, or any measure for determining particular actions, or for inspiring by words an actual and positive result. Amusement must be afforded to the mind, in order to induce men who are separated from each other to literary pursuits, whose ambition is dormant, and who expect nothing from reflection. It is very probable, in such a situation, for the writers to be guilty of affectation; because it is of the utmost importance to them, to render the form of their style attractive and pleasing. Seneca, and particularly Pliny the Younger, are not entirely free from that foible. It is also pretty certain that, like Juvenal, they might have vitiated their taste by their different modes of trial to inspire the horror of vice in a people who were hardened by the repetition of crimes; and the sentiments of authors were so depraved by the predominant manners of the times, that they could not retain that purity of expression which requires greater force when employed in pointing out the most disgusting images. But those errors which cannot be denied, ought not to preclude us from acknowledging that the third epoch of the Roman literature was more celebrated for men of profound genius, judgment, and solid understanding, than any other which preceded it. The ideas of Quintilian, in his treatise upon the art of rhetoric, are certainly more novel and refined than any which are to be found in the writings of Cicero on the same subject. Quintilian united his sentiments with those of Cicero, and took his departure from the point Cicero relinquished. The philosophy of Seneca penetrates deeply into the human heart. Pliny the Elder is, of all the writers of antiquity, the one who approaches the nearest to truth in the sciences. Tacitus, in every respect, has an unlimited preference over the greatest Latin historians.

The first authors who wrote and comprehended superior language, were enraptured by the harmony of phrases; and neither Cicero himself, nor his auditors, felt at that time the want of a style more energetic than that which was furnished by their own ideas. But as they advanced in literature, their taste for the simple pleasures of imagination lessened by degrees, and the mind became more diligent in the search of abstract ideas. The intercourse between mankind increased with the progress of ages; their conceptions were better regulated, and a variety of circumstances produced new discoveries and combinations: thus, reflection may be pronounced the successor of time. It is this progressive style which is visible in the last epoch of the Latin literature, notwithstanding the local difficulties which at that time impeded the advancement of the human understanding.

During the tragical reign of the Emperors, it must be said, to the honor of the Romans, that most of the efforts of imagination sunk into oblivion. Lucan wrote but to revive the remembrance of the republic; and his death sufficiently attests the peril which attended the arduous task. It was in vain that the ferocious Emperors of Rome testified the greatest partiality for public amusements; not one theatrical production, worthy of any continued success, appeared during their reign; not one poetical essay remains, to remind us of the disgraceful leisure of servitude: the men of letters did not at that period so far degrade their talents, as to employ them in the decoration of tyranny; their sole occupation was the study of philosophy and eloquence,—weapons calculated to overthrow even oppression itself.

Flattery has tarnished the writings of some philosophers of that period, and their rhetorical figures were disgraceful: nevertheless, the art of printing being then unknown was a circumstance, in some respects, favorable to the freedom of the pen; despotism was less watchful over composition, when the means of publishing were so extremely limited. Polemical writings, as well as those which influence temporary opinions and contemporaneous events, could be of no service; neither could they have any power before the use of the press was discovered; as they could never be sufficiently diffused to produce any popular effect: the tribune alone could accomplish this point; but composition then confined itself to works upon general ideas, or anterior facts instructive to succeeding generations. Tyrants at that period were much less solicitous as to the liberty of the pen, than they are at the present era; posterity not being under their jurisdiction, they willingly left it to the philosophers.

We are ready to inquire, how it happened that, at this period, none of the Romans devoted themselves to the study of the sciences? It has frequently occurred that, under the yoke of tyranny, men of superior acquirements were unwilling to render themselves contemptible; but as they did not wish to revolt, they were employed in independent researches. But it may be apprehended, that the dangers which at the time threatened men of great talents, were too imminent to leave them sufficient leisure for the exercise and labors of genius. It is also possible that the Romans retained such a portion of republican indignation, as to withdraw entirely their attention from the destiny of their country. Philosophy calls forth the energies of the soul: while the sciences transport the ideas into quite a different channel. In short, at that period they had not discovered the best method of pursuit in the study of natural philosophy; neither were they excited by emutation to proceed with vigor, where no great success had as yet been obtained.

One of the principal causes of the destruction of the empires of antiquity, was their ignorance of several important discoveries in the sciences : which event established more equality between men and nations. The decline of empires is no more in the natural order of events, than that of letters and of knowledge. But before the civilization of Europe, before the political and military systems and the use of gunpowder, had placed nations nearer on an equality, and, in short, previous to the establishment of the art of printing, national spirit and national knowledge must of course have been victims to the barbarians, who were certainly more skilful as warriors, than other men. However, had the press existed, the acquirements and opinions of the people would daily have increased in strength, and the Roman character would have been preserved, and with it, the republic would have continued its superiority : we should not then have witnessed the banishment of a people who were fond of liberty without subordination, and glory divested of jealousy ; a people who, instead of requiring that men should degrade themselves to obtain their favor, had raised their ideas to the true appreciation of virtues and talents, in order to honor them with their esteem ; a people, whose admiration was directed by their judgment, but in whom judgment was never biassed by their admiration.

The genius of mankind, and above all, patriotism, would be entirely discouraged, if it could be proved that there was a moral necessity for the greatest nations to be eclipsed after having enlightened the world for a certain length of time. But this succession of dethroned people is not an inevitable fatality. If we study the sublime reflections of Montesquieu on the causes of the decline of the Romans, we shall clearly perceive that the greatest part of those causes do not exist in the present days. The part of Europe which was not included in the civilization, was likely to invade the one less enlightened ; for nature always inclines towards equality : and it was therefore absolutely necessary that the advantages of society should be universal ; that the diffusion of knowledge, the charms of a domestic life, and also commercial relations, by establishing more purity in their enjoyments, should appease by degrees the rivalry of nations.

The crimes scarcely to be credited, of which the Roman empire was the theatre, was one of the principal causes of their fall ; the disorderly lives they led, and the discrepancy of public opinions, could alone have permitted such horrible excesses.* If we except the reign of terror in France, atrocity is neither inherent in the nature or the manners of Europeans in the present era. The state of slavery, which exempted one class of men from the performance of any moral duty ; the small supply of means which could promote general instruction ; the diversity of philosophical sects, which threw the minds of men into incertitude with respect to what was just or unjust ; the indifference relative to suffering and death, an indifference which owed its birth to courage, but which terminated by exhausting the natural sources of sympathy ;—these were the several sources of that savage cruelty which existed among the Romans.

A disgusting depravity, which alike infringed upon nature and morality, completed the degradation of a people once so great ; and their debasement prepared an easy triumph for the Northern people. The civilization of Europe, the establishment of the Christian religion, the discovery of the sciences, and the diffusion of knowledge, were as so many bulwarks against depravation, and destroyed the ancient causes of barbarity : therefore the fall of nations, and in consequence that of letters, is now much less to be apprehended ;—a truth which I hope the following chapter will more clearly demonstrate.

* When Caligula went to make war in Britany, he sent Protogenes to the Senate : Scribonius, a senator, approached him with the intention of addressing him in some phrase of salutation upon his arrival ; when Protogenes, raising his voice, said, 'Is it possible that an enemy of the Emperors can allow himself to pay a compliment to me ?' The senators, who heard these words, immediately seized Scribonius, and as they were unarmed, they massacred him with their penknives. This trait certainly surpasses any instance of base intrepidity related in modern history.

CHAPTER VIII.

THE INVASION OF THE PEOPLE OF THE NORTH ; THE ESTABLISHMENT OF THE CHRISTIAN RELIGION ; AND THE REVIVAL OF LETTERS.

We may reckon in history a lapse of more than ten centuries, during which it is generally that the human understanding has been on the decline. It certainly would be a great objection to the system of progressive knowledge, that such a long course of years, so considerable a portion of the times with which we are acquainted, should have rolled along, and yet the important work of *perfectability* should have recoiled from the grasp of each ardent pursuers : but this objection, which I should regard as irrefragable, if it had any foundation in truth, I can confute in a very simple and satisfactory manner. I do not conceive that the human species have retrograded during this epoch ; on the contrary, it is admitted that, in the course of the above ten centuries, great efforts have been made in the propagation of knowledge, as well as in the development of the intellectual faculties.

We are convinced, by the study of history, that all principal events tend towards the same end, namely, the civilization of the world. In each century, we perceive new classes of people admitted to the benefits of social order ; and even war, notwithstanding its cruel disasters, has been known to extend the empire of knowledge.

The Romans civilized the people whom they conquered ; but they were indebted to Greece for the first ray of light, which appeared as a small brilliant speck in the midst of a region of darkness. Some centuries after, a warlike people united under the same laws a part of the world, in order to civilize it, which they had first won by conquest. The people of the north, although they banished for a time the arts and literature which flourished in the east, nevertheless acquired a share of the knowledge possessed by the vanquished ; and the inhabitants of more than one half of Europe, who till that period had remained ignorant of the nature of civilized society, participated in the advantages. Time has, therefore, discovered to us a regular design in a series of events, which appeared at first but the effects of chance. Thus we perceive thought always predominant in the minutiæ of actions and of ages.

The invasion of the barbarians was, without doubt, a calamity to the nations that were contemporaries of the revolution ; but the reality of the event was necessary to the propagation of knowledge. The enervated inhabitants of the east, in associating with the people of the north, were indebted to them for a degree of energy : whereas the people of the north acquired a mildness and docility that must have been of great service in completing their intellectual faculties. Whenever war is declared between two enlightened nations simply upon political interest, it may be considered as the most fatal scourge that ever resulted from the human passions : but the brilliant events recorded in the course of a war may occasionally enforce the adoption of certain ideas by the rapid authority of power

It has been asserted by many writers, that the

Christian religion was the cause of the degradation of letters and of philosophy : but I am fully convinced, that the Christian religion, at the period of its establishment, was indispensably necessary to civilization, and to the uniting of the spirit of the north with the manners of the east ; and I am farther of opinion, that the religious contemplations produced by Christianity to whatever object they might be applied developed the faculties of the mind, and prepared it for the reception of metaphysics, morality, and science.

There are certain periods in history, in which the love of glory and every other energetic passion appear to have been extinct. When calamity becomes general in a country, egotism is universal: a certain portion of happiness is absolutely necessary to the strength of a nation ; adversity cannot inspire with courage individuals whose spirits have been broken by it, except in the midst of a nation who have been so fortunate as to preserve the sensations of admiration or of pity ; but when all are equally overcome by affliction, public opinion loses its influence, and refuses its accustomed support to individuals : days and years may remain, but life has no aim, no end in view ; emulation has lost its vigor, and voluptuous pleasures become the sole interest of an inglorious existence, without honor and without morals. Such is described to be the state of the people of the east, under the chiefs of the lower empire.

Another nation, but who are equally as far from the true principles of virtue, made their appearance, and easily achieved a conquest over a people rendered pusillanimous by indolence and inactivity. The ferocity of despotism excited by war, in which ignorance was also predominant, had such an effect on the alarmed senses of men as to produce crimes, opposite indeed to the vile degradation of the people they had conquered, but more terrible in their effects. To civilize such conquerors, and to elevate such a race as had been conquered, was a task which nothing but enthusiasm could have effected ;—that forcible power of the mind which, it is true, sometimes leads it astray, but which alone subdues that habitual instinct of self-love and increasing personality, that causes happiness to consist in an individual sacrifice.

I would have it understood, that I do not mean to weaken the indignation which is inspired by the crimes and follies of superstition ; but to consider each great epoch of the philosophical history of thought, relative to the state the human mind was in at that time ; and the Christian religion, when it was firmly established, was, as it appears to me, necessary to the progress of reason.

The people of the north esteemed life as of little value : this disposition, though it inspired them with a degree of personal courage, could not but be productive of cruelty towards others They were possessed of genius, melancholy, and an inclination to the mysterious ; but at the same time they entertained a profound contempt for knowledge of every description, as incompatible with the spirit of a warrior. The women, possessing more leisure, were much better instructed than the men ; they were beloved, and the men were faithful to them : their affection naturally produced a degree of sensibility : but power and the loyal fidelity of a warrior, and truth as an attribute of power, were the only ideas they ever ascribed to virtue : the gratification of their vengeance was by them dignified with a place in the heavens. By exhibiting the scars in the foreparts of their bodies, by reciting the numbers of their enemies whose blood they had spilt, they thought to captivate the affections of the softer asx. They offered human victims to their mistresses, se to their gods. Their gloomy atmosphere presented nothing to their imagination but storms and darkness : they marked the revolution of days by the calculation of nights, and the progress of years by the winters. The giants of frosts presided over their exploits. According to their traditions, the deluge of the earth was a deluge of blood ; and they believed that Odin looked down from heaven to animate their carnage. Their rewards and punishments were all proportioned to their actions in war. Man, with them, seemed born but for the destruction of his fellow-man. They paid no respect to advanced age : they regarded every species of study with contempt ; and were utter strangers to humanity. The faculties of their mind were engrossed by one pursuit : —war was their sole occupation, and their only aim was conquest.

Such were the principles from which were to be extracted gentleness, morality, and a taste for letters ; nor was the task to be executed upon the people of the east less difficult ; the Roman character, so celebrated for national pride and political institutions, was totally extinct : the inhabitants of Italy were disgusted with the very idea of glory ; they were entirely devoted to voluptuousness and sensuality ; they acknowledged plurality of gods, and ordained festivals to their honor ; and they acknowledged their sovereigns at the hands of a few soldiers, who elevated or disgraced them agreeably to their caprice or pleasure : constantly subject to an arbitrary proscription, they were regardless of death, not from the ideas inspired by courage, but from the intoxication of vice : death interrupted no brilliant projects, no progression of useful suggestions ; it severed no tender ties, it only interfered with the pleasures and amusements with which possibly they had been previously wearied and disgusted. Universal corruption had destroyed even the remembrance of virtue ; and had any one showed merely an inclination to have recalled it, he would only have excited astonishment united with censure. The moral virtues of the people of the east were swallowed up by sensual enjoyments ; while those of the people of the north were lost sight of amidst martial exercises. If there still existed among this degenerate people a vestige of that innate taste for the arts, letters, and philosophy, it was directed towards metaphysical subtilties ; while the sophistical spirit left them in doubt as to the truth of argument, and indifference respecting the affections of the heart.

It was in the midst of this deplorable depression into which the people of the east had fallen, that the Christian religion offered its powerful aid ; and taught them to embrace the rules of duty, a voluntary devotion, and gave them good assurances for the establishment of a holy faith. But it may be asked, would it not have been more desirable that they should have been recalled to virtue by philosophy? In answer to which I observe, that it would have been impossible at that period to have acquired an influence over the human mind by any other means than the co-operation of the passions, which it may be said, are always in opposition to reason : religion alone is acquainted with the surest means to apply the passions most effectually to answer her own wise ends and purposes.

The nations of the earth were all influenced by enthusiasm : Mahomet, by fostering this propensity, gave birth to fanaticism, which advanced with the most astonishing facility. Mahomet was considered as a man certainly great in himself ; hut his prodigious success was owing to the moral disposition of the times : his religion, however, was only calculated for the people of the east, as its chief tendency was to revive the military spirit, by offering pleasures as the recompense of their exploits :—it created warriors, but did not in the least assist the intellectual improvement. This *general-prophet* employed himself entirely in the discipline of soldiers, and instilling obedience and enforcing it : but the dogma of fatality, which rendered them invincible in war, left them brutal and stupid during the time of peace. The Christian religion, having a egislator, whose grand aim was the perfection of morals, and to unite under the same banner nations of different manners and of a contrary belief, could not fail of being more favorable to the increase of virtue and the expansion of the faculties of the mind. Many combinations were necessary, in order to secure the confidence of two nations so opposite in their manners as the people of the north and those of the east. The Christian religion was chosen by the people of the north; it was favorable to their melancholy disposition and inclination for gloomy images, and also to their continual and profound contemplation relative to the destination of the dead. There was nothing in the principles of paganism which could have rendered it acceptable to the people of this character; the dogmas of the Christian religion, and the exalted spirit of the first secretaries, encouraged and directed the habitual depression inspired by their cloudy atmosphere. Some of their virtues, as truth, chastity, and a strict observance of their promises, were consecrated by the divine laws; thus religion, without altering the nature of their courage, contrived to divert it to another object; their customs required them to support every hardship with magnanimity, in order to be esteemed illustrious in war: religion enjoined them to brave all sufferings, and even death itself, in the defence of their faith and the fulfilment of their several duties: destructive intrepidity was changed into an unshaken resolution; and resistance, which had no other aim but to conquer force, was directed by principles of morality. The errors of fanaticism have often perverted the judgment and ruined the principles; but in this instance it caused a nation, till then invincible, to understand and acknowledge a power superior to their own; to substitute duties for laws, and the terror produced by religion proved a restraint on their actions. The man of inferior abilities menaced his superior, and the dawn of equality may be said to have first received its existence.

The people of the east, susceptible of enthusiasm, readily devoted themselves to a life of contemplation, which was analogous to their climate and inclinations. They were the first to receive with ardor the monarchical institutions. Austerities and mortifications were quickly adopted by a nation given up to a voluptuous satiety which naturally led to an exaggeration of religious observances. A people so ardent, credulous, and fanatic, were an easy prey to superstition, and to crimes at which nature and humanity shudder; religion was less beneficial to them than to the people of the north, on account of their more extended depravity and corruption of morals. The task is easier to civilize an ignorant race, than to elevate a corrupted people from their state of depravation.

The Christian religion gave new vigor to the principles of moral life in a set of men who were without connection, without any direct pursuit in view, or any tie that could endear their existence. It is true, it was incapable of restoring to them their country; but it elevated their thoughts, polluted with the vices of mankind, to a future state; and they found consolation in the hope of participating in a happy immortality. Thus many characters were awakened to energy by religion; and in consequence of the follies of martyrdom, resulted a renunciation of self-interest, and an abstraction of thought, which proved very favorable to the human intellect.

The Christian religion became a bond of union between the people of the north and those of the east; it blended manners and opinions that were before diametrically opposite; and, by reconciling the most inveterate enemies, formed nations, among whom energy has strengthed talents, and talents have awakened energy. This reciprocal benefit was, nevertheless, produced by slow degrees: eternal providence employs centuries in the accomplishment of its designs; while our finite existence feels irritated and amazed at the delay. But eventually the victors and the vanquished have formed but one united people in the different countries of Europe:—to this end the Christian religion has most powerfully contributed.

But before I proceed in analyzing some other advantages of the Christian religion, I must request permission to stop here, to make a few remarks upon what strikes me to be a resemblance between this epoch and the French revolution.

The nobility, or those who ranked in the first class of society, generally united all the advantages of a distinguished education; but they were enervated by prosperity, and by degrees lost those virtues which might have rendered their social pre-eminence excusable; while it may be observed, that the lower orders of the people had not advanced far in civilization; and their manners, which were restrained by laws, were likely to revert to their natural ferocity on the first dawn of liberty:—it may almost be said, that they made an invasion upon the superior classes of society; and that all we have suffered, and all we condemn in the revolution, arises from that fatal necessity of confiding the direction of affairs to those conquerors of the civil order, whose aim was certainly directed by philosophy, but whose education was many centuries behind those whom they conquered. Those who have been conquerors in the field, and victorious at home, bear a great resemblance in character to the men of the north; and in the vanquished we acknowledge the analogy to the acquirements, the prejudices, the vices, and the social description of the people of the east. But due latitude must be given for the education of conquerors, and the knowledge which was formerly confined to a few individuals, must be expanded before the leading rulers in France will be entirely divested of barbarity and vulgarity.

We are however led to hope, that the civilization of our northern nations will not require ten or twelve centuries; we make more rapid advances than our ancestors did, and the reason is obvious. Amongst a people deriving no advantage from education, men are frequently discovered who possesses a remarkably clear understanding and quick perception, added to the benefits resulting from the present enlightened century, the use of the press, and a knowledge of the surrounding nations; which must each of them necessarily contribute to aid the progress of a class of people newly admitted to the direction of political affairs. But it is difficult at present to anticipate what will be the final result of the war between the ancient possessors and the new conquerors. It will be a happy termination, if we shall discover, as at the epoch of the invasion of the northern nations, a philosphical system, a virtuous enthusiasm, and a solid and equitable legislation, that might prove to us the light the Christian religion appeared in to the ancients; sentiments in which the conqueror and the conquered may be said to have united. This reconciliation between the north and the east, which was so benificial to the world, was not the only advantage which resulted from the Christian religion; for it is generally believed, that the abolition of slavery was the consequence of its benign precepts: to this decree of justice we may add other benefits which it conferred upon mankind, namely domestic happiness and the sympathy of pity.

Every circumstance with the ancients, even their domestic concerns, bore the marks of that odious institution of slavery; the disposal of life and death was vested in parental authority: the repeated instances of that barbarous custom of publicly exposing their children;—the power of husbands, similar in many respects to that of fathers;—in short, all their civil laws bore some analogy to that detestible code which delivered man into the power of man; and created two classes, the one of which conceived themselves obliged by no relative duties towards the other: and this idea once adopted, it was only by slow gradations that they could arrive at liberty. The women during the term of their lives, and the children in a state of infancy, were subjected in a certain degree to the conditions of slavery.

In the degenerate ages of the Roman empire, the women were torn from their servitude by the most unbridled licentiousness, and plunged into the abyss of degradation; but the introduction of Christianity restored them, in respect to moral and religious duties at least, to a state of equality with the men. Christianity, by rendering marriage a sacred institution, secured the affection which arose from conjugal attachment; the dogmas of purgatory exacted the same punishments from both sexes, and promised the same recompense to each. The Evangelists, who recommended private virtues, an obscure destiny, and a pious humility, offered to both sexes the means of obtaining a religious palm. The mind is disposed towards religion by sensibility; on which account women surpassed men in that Christian emulation which Europe possessed during the first centuries of modern history.

The roving people of the north were, by the influence of religion, brought to a settled state of life and the enjoyments of domestic happiness they settled themselves in one country, and dwelt in society; and the legislation of civil life was reformed by an adherence to religious principles. It was at this period that women were admitted to their proper station in life; and from this time the sweets of domestic happiness begun to be experienced. A too great share of power is injurions to native goodness, and destroys all delicacy; with one part of the creation, neither virtues nor sentiments could resist the exercise of authority; and with the other, they would vanish by the means of habitual apprehension. The felicity of man arises from the independence of the object of his desires: he may conceive that he is beloved, when chosen by a free being who makes it their study to conform to his wishes, to obey him; and to relinquish her taste, her habits, and her time, to render his existence complete. How much the perfections of his mind, and the sentiments of his heart are increased by the ideas and the impressions of a union of this description, is obvious: the parties having languished a length of time in a solitary and joyless state, now enter, as it were into a new world of their own creating, by contributing to the moral existence of each other.

Few works of real superiority have been written by women: nevertheless, they have been eminently useful in the progress of literature, from the number of ideas with which men have been inspired by their constant intercourse with female delicacy and sensibility. Productions of every kind have been multiplied, since objects have been considered in a new point of view: the confidence inspired by a near and dear connection, has conveyed more instruction to the moral nature than all the treatises and systems which have been written by men,—such as they appear to each other, and not what they are in reality.

Commiseration for sufferings must, in every age, have naturally existed in the human heart; nevertheless, how different are the morals of antiquity from those of Christianity! The one is founded upon violence, and the other upon sympathy. The warlike spirit must have presided at the origin of societies, is discernible even in the philosophy of the Stoics: self-command was exercised, so to speak, with a warlike energy: the happiness of others was not the object of ancient morality, the principal aim of the philosophers being to render men independent of each other.

The Christian religion also requires self denial: this virtue has, by monkish fanaticism, been extended far beyond the austerity of ancient philosophy: but the principles of this sacrifice, so strongly enjoined by Christianity, are, perfect submission to the divine will, and meek humility towards our fellow-creatures;—not like the Stoics, to sacrifice every thing to the pride and dignity of our own character. By an attention to the literal sense of the gospel, unsullied by the false interpretations which have been given of it, we clearly perceive that a benevolent spirit of compassion towards the unhappy pervades its every page: and we there find it is considered as a duty incumbent upon man to feel deeply for the distresses incident to humanity.

In order to acquire a knowledge of the human heart, it was expedient to adopt a system of morality altogether sympathetic: and although religion in general enjoins a subjection of the passions, that of Christianity came much nearer than that of the stoics to the knowledge of their power. Its peculiar benignity and indulgence gave a greater latitude to the character of men to develop themselves; and philosophy, whose purpose is to study the movements of the human heart, certainly acquired much knowledge by it.

Literature was also considerably benefited by the effects produced by melancholy. It is true, that the religion of the people of the north inspired them at all times with a similar disposition; but it is to Christianity that the French orators were indebted for those powerful and gloomy ideas which added grandeur to their eloquence.

The Christian religion has been accused of producing a degree of relaxation in the human mind: but the intention of the gospel was to counteract a ferocious and cruel disposition: how then is it possible to inspire at the same time a great portion of humanity toward our fellow-creatures and a perfect indifference for ourselves? Murder must be represented in sanguinary colors; a sensation of horror must be excited for bloodshed and death; and nature itself will not suffer sympathy to remain entirely exterior.

It is admitted, that fanaticism has at different times obscured the sentiments of humanity which are annexed to the Christian religion: but it is its general spirit that I wish to examine; and in our own times, and in the countries where the reformation has been established, we may remark what salutary effects the gospel has had on the morals.

The toleration of paganism was regretted by the philosophers, when they compared it with the fanaticism inspired by the Christian religion. Strong passions frequently precipitate men into the commission of crimes which cooler reason would never have permitted: but there are events in history where the exertion of such passions invigorate society; reason, assisted by time, profits by the effects of great commotions; and many ideas have been discovered by the help of the passions, which would have remained in darkness without them.

The human mind requires a violent concussion, in order to annex its ideas to novel objects: even earthquakes and subterraneous fires have presented to mankind sources of wealth which time alone would not have been sufficient to have discovered. I think I discern another proof in favor of this opinion, in the great influence acquired by the study of theology beyond that of metaphysics; this pursuit has often been condemned as a very idle and useless method of employing talents; and it has also been alleged as one of the principal causes of the barbarity of the first centuries of our era. Nevertheless, it is a style of intellectual effort which has developed, in a singular manner, the faculties of the mind. If we judge the result of this labor only as connected with the arts suggested by imagination, nothing certainly can give a more unfavorable opinion of it. The noble elegance and graceful forms of antiquity are entirely obscured beneath the pedantic errors of theological writers; but that degree of understanding which is adapted to the study of the sciences, is acquired by disputing upon different opinions, notwithstanding their object is equally puerile and absurd. Attention and abstraction are naturally inherent in a mind of deep reflection; and those faculties are alone sufficient to aid the progress of the human understanding.

The talents and the imagination which are by this means derived, give new vigor to the memory: but it is entirely owing to metaphysical method that we are indebted for fresh ideas. The abilities of men are exercised by spiritual dogmas in the conception of abstract sentiments; and the extended contention of the mind, actuated by the subtle chain of theological consequences, prepares the faculties for the study of the more abstruse sciences. But it may be asked, how can a deep examination into the nature of error be serviceable towards bringing to light the knowledge of truth? It is that art of reasoning, and that strict meditation, by which we are enabled to pursue metaphysical references, and to create order and method, which is always an useful exercise for the faculties of thought, from whatever degree they are taken, and whatever end they wish to arrive at.

Without doubt, if the faculties which were thus developed had not since been directed to other objects, much mischief would have been produced to the human species; but in the discovery of the revival of letters we perceive ideas so quickly arise, and the sciences to advance in so rapid and extraordinary a manner, that we are led to believe, that even in pursuing a false bias, the mind acquired the strength and knowledge which accelerated its progress towards reason and philosophy.

Some men are disposed from inclination to study the abstract; but the greater number are tempted by party-interest. Political knowledge made rapid advances during the first years of the French revolution; because it served the ambition of some, and created general agitation. Theological questions, in their time, were objects creative of a lively interest and a profound analysis: the disputes to which they gave rise, were animated by the authority of power and the fear of persecution. If the spirit of faction had not introduced itself into metaphysics, and if ambition had not been interested in abstract discussions, men would not have felt a sufficient motive to have induced them to overcome those difficulties which are necessary to the discoveries and progress of the subsequent ages.

Thus instruction makes its way among all ranks of people. When the professed opinions upon any order of ideas whatever, become the cause and the weapons of parties; hatred, and rage, and jealousy, united to each report, engage on every side the objects in discussion, and agitate with violence every question depending: but when the passions have subsided, reason carefully looks round the field of contest for some fragments to assist in the researches after truth.

Every institution, merely beneficial in the moment of danger, may be considered in itself an insupportable abuse, after having corrected abuses still more atrocious. Chivalry was necessary to soften military ferocity; and tended to the cultivation of female society, and of religion: but chivalry, as an order, as a sect, as the cause of separating mankind instead of uniting them, ought to have been considered as a fatal evil the moment that it ceased to be of any essential utility.

The Roman jurisprudence, which they were happy to have received by a people whose extent of knowledge consisted in the right of conquest, became a cunning and pedantic study; it occupied the greater part of the learned men, who had relinquished for it the pursuit of theology. The knowledge of the ancient languages, which revived the true literary taste, inspired for some time an absurd mania for erudition; the present and the future were almost annihilated in the puerile examination of the most trifling circumstances which retrospect afforded; commentaries upon the works of the ancients preceded philosophical observations:—it appeared as if it were ordained that literary productions should interfere with mankind and nature. The great estimation in which erudition was holden, entirely engrossed the spirit of invention; and every event that concerned the ancients, acquired an equal degree of interest.

Nevertheless, these different foibles had their separate advantages; and we may perceive, on the revival of letters, that those nations which were esteemed barbarous were beneficial as well as others; first, they added to the number of civilized people; and secondly, they were of use in bringing the understanding to perfection.

If we consider the revival of letters only in its relation to the works of imagination and taste, we shall find, without doubt, that there have been nearly sixteen hundred years lost; and that, since the time of Virgil to the period of the Catholic mysteries represented on the Paris theatres, the human understanding, in the acquirement of arts, has been retrograding towards the most absurd barbarism. But this was not the case with philosophical works. Bacon, Machiavel, Montaigne, and Galileo, all nearly contemporaries, in three different countries, emerged all at once out of general obscurity; and shew themselves, for many centuries forward, the last writers of ancient literature, and, above all, the last philosophers of antiquity.

If the human understanding had not made some progress even in those centuries in which we can scarcely discover any traces of it; should we have seen, at the period of the revival of letters, men who, in morals, politics, and the sciences, surpassed the greatest geniuses of antiquity? If there exists an infinite distance between the late celebrated men of antiquity and those who are illustrious in letters and sciences; and if Bacon, Machiavel, and Montaigne, possessed ideas and knowledge superior to those of Pliny, Marcus Aurelius, &c.; is it not evident, that the human reason did not lie dormant during the centuries which separated the lives of those celebrated men? We must not lose sight of the principle which I enforced at the commencement of this work, namely, that the most distinguished genius never rises but a very few degrees above the knowledge of his own century. The history of the human understanding during the interval which elapsed between the time of Pliny and Bacon, Epictetus and Montaigne, Plutarch and Machiavel, is very little understood by us; because men and nations, generally speaking, were confounded together in the single event of war; but military exploits created a very feeble interest after the period of their power was past. There has never, since the commencement of the world, been any other standard for enlightened men to abide by, but the advancement of knowledge and of reason; nevertheless, let us observe, with the learned man, the secret manner in which nature combines her developments. The moralist perceives the combination of causes which, during the space of fourteen hundred years, have been bringing about the actual state of the sciences and of philosophy.

What strength of mind suddenly shone forth in the middle of the fifteenth century! What important discoveries were made! New methods were adopted in a few years! Such a rapid progress, such an astonishing success! must they not have some connection with something anterior? And even in the arts, was not all false taste quickly expelled? The progress of thought in a very short time discovered the principles of the really beautiful; and literature was rapidly brought to perfection, from the great exercise the mind had experienced on its return to the path of reason, during which it made speedy advances toward perfection.

One principal cause of the eager emulation which was excited by the revival of letters, was the great splendor it annexed to the name of a good writer. We are in some degree astonished at the homage obtained by Petrarch, and are equally surprised at the importance, that was attached to the publication of his sonnets. Wearied with the absurd military prejudice, the aim of which was to degrade and abolish literature, the people descended into the opposite extreme : it is also possible that the parade of recompensing opinions was necessary to excite men to the difficult labor required, three centuries since, to render modern languages perfect, to effect the regeneration of philosophical spirit, and the creation of a new method for metaphysics and the more difficult sciences.

But let us stop at that period which commences the new era ; whence we may reckon, without interruption, the most astonishing conquests of the genius of mankind ; and in comparing our literary treasures with those of antiquity, so far from suffering ourselves to be discouraged by a sterile admiration of the past, let us encourage ourselves with the fertile enthusiasm of hope ; let us unite our efforts; let us spread our sails, and catch every breeze that can waft us to futurity.

CHAPTER IX.

OF THE GENERAL SPIRIT OF MODERN LITERATURE.

It may be thought, and not to imagination, that we are indebted for the new acquisitions made to literature in the middle ages. Imitation, the principle of the fine arts, as I have before remarked, does not admit of unlimited perfection: the moderns, in this respect, can never proceed farther than by following the path traced out by the ancients. But if the images of poetry and description always remain nearly the same ; more eloquence is added to the passions by a new development of sensibility and a profound knowledge of character, which gives a charm to our superior specimens of literature, which cannot be attributed solely to poetical imagination.

The ancients esteemed men as their friends, while they considered women in no other light than as slaves designed by nature for that unhappy state ; and indeed the greater part of them were deserving of that appellation ; their minds were not furnished with a single idea that could distinguish them from the brute creation, nor were they enlightened by one generous sentiment: this circumstance, without doubt, was the cause why the ancients represented in their tender scenes merely sensations.

The preference of the ancients towards the softer sex was solely influenced by their beauty : but the moderns acknowledge, that superior talents and ties can alone insure their happiness or misery, in that predilection to which they owe the destiny of their lives.

Novels, those varied productions of modern genius, were almost entirely unknown to the ancients : it is true, they composed a few pastorals in that style, at a period when the Greeks endeavored to discover some employment as a relaxation during servitude. But before women had created an interest in domestic life, there was nothing sufficiently desirable to excite the curiosity of men, whose time was almost entirely occupied by political pursuits.

A greater number of shades were perceptible in the characters of women, which their wish to obtain power, and their fear of subjection, presented to general view ; but they were singularly useful in furnishing new secrets of emotion for the exercise of dramatic talents; their fear of death, their desire of life, the devotion of themselves, their resentments, and in short, every sentiment which they were suffered to deliver, embellished literature with new expressions. The women, it may be said, not being strictly answerable for their conduct, did not scruple to relate what their different sentiments naturally suggested. A solid understanding, with a scrutinizing discernment, may clearly perceive these developments of the human heart when it appears in a state of nature : it is for this reason that the modern moralists have, in general, so much the advantage over the ancients in regard to their subtility in the knowledge of mankind.

With the ancients, those who could not acquire fame, had no motive for development : but after the period when connections were formed in domestic life, the communications of the mind and the exercise of morals always existed, at least in a limited circle ; the children became dearer to the parents from reciprocal tenderness, which more closely united the conjugal tie ; and the different affections assumed the appearance of that divine alliance of friendship in love, of attraction and esteem, of a merited confidence and an involuntary seduction.

Advanced age that was crowned with glory and virtue, although it ceased to hope, might continue to be animated by the emotions of the heart, and was consoled with a pensive melancholy which allowed individuals to remember, to regret, and still to regard what had formerly claimed their affection. When moral reflections have been united to the violent passions of youth, they may be extended by an exalted remembrance to the termination of existence, and present the same pleasing picture through the awful variations of time.

A profound and melancholy sensibility is one of the greatest beauties perceptible in some of our modern writings : this, without doubt, is owing to the fair sex, who, being ignorant of most other things in life, except the art of pleasing, transmitted the softness of their impressions to the style of certain authors. In perusing those works which were composed since the renewal of letters, we may in every separate page remark those ideas which were wanting before they accorded to women a kind of civil equality.

Generosity, courage, and humanity, have in some respects a different meaning. The ancients founded the chief of their virtues on the love of their country : the qualities of women were exercised in a different and an independent manner :—a sympathy for misfortune, a pity for weakness, an elevation of soul, without any other aim than the enjoyment of that elevation, is much more in their nature than political virtues. The moderns, influenced by women, easily gave way to philanthropy, and the mind acquired a more philosophical liberty when thev were less under the empire of exclusive associations.

The only advantage which the writers of the last centuries have over the ancients in their works of imagination, is the talent of expressing a more delicate sensibility ; and that of giving greater variety to situations and characters, from a more intimate knowledge of the human heart. But how much superior are the philosophers of the present era in the sciences, in method, in analysis, in the arrangement of ideas, and the chain of events.

Mathematical arguments resemble the two great ideas of metaphysics, space and eternity ; millions of leagues may be added, and centuries multiplied ; each calculation is true, yet the term remains indefinite. The wisest step ever taken by the human understanding was, to renounce all doubtful systems, and adopt methods capable of demonstration.

Although modern eloquence may be deficient in the emulation of a free people; nevertheless it acquires from philosophy and a melancholy imagination a new character, which has a very powerful effect. I do not think, that among the ancients, there was one composition, or a single orator, that could equal Bossuet, Rousseau, or the English, in some of their poetry, or the German in some of their phrases, in the sublime art of affecting the heart. It is to the spirituality of the Christian ideas, and to the sombre truths of philosophy, that we must attribute the art of introducing, even into private discussions, general and affecting reflections which touched the heart, awakened recollection, and induced man to consider the interest of his fellow-creatures.

The ancients knew how to add vigor to the arguments necessary to be used on every occasion; but, at the present period, the mind, through a succession of ages, has become so indifferent to the interest of individuals and also to that of nations, that the eloquent writer finds it necessary to adopt a more pathetic style, in order to awaken the feelings which are common to all men. Without doubt, it is requisite to strike the imagination with a lively and forcible impression of the object intended to create an interest; but the appeal to pity is never irresistible, except when melancholy represents what the imagination has portrayed.

The moderns possess a readiness of expression, the sole aim of which is to engage the eloquence of thought: antiquity presents no model of this kind but Tacitus. Montesquieu, Pascal, and Machiavel, are eloquent by a single expression, by a striking epithet, or in a rapidity of imagery, the purpose of which is the elucidation of an idea, and the endeavor to enlarge and embellish what is intended to be explained. The impression given by this peculiar style, may be compared to the effect produced by the disclosure of an important secret: it seems likewise as if a number of thoughts had preceded that which had just been expressed, and each separate idea appears connected with the most profound meditations; and that suddenly, and by a single word, we are permitted to extend our ideas to those immense regions which have been accurately traced by the efforts of genius.

The ancient philosophers exercised, so to speak, a magistracy of instruction among men: having always in view the general benefit, they enforced certain rules, and left nothing undone that was likely to enlighten mankind. The knowledge of morals must have advanced with the progress of human reason; but philosophical demonstrations are considered more applicable to that moral which is of the intellectual order. We must not compare modern virtues with those of the ancients, as citizens: it is only in a free country where there can exist that constant duty and that generous relation between the citizens and their country. It is true that, in a despotic government, custom or prejudice may still inspire some brilliant acts of military courage; but the continued and painful attention given to civil employments and legislative virtues, added to the disinterested sacrifice of the greater part of their lives to the public, can only exist where there is a real passion for liberty: it is therefore in private qualities, sentiments of philanthropy, and in a few writings of a superior order, that we are to examine the progress of morals.

The principles of modern philosophy are much more conducive to happiness than those of the ancients: the duties imposed by our moralists are courtesy, docility, pity and affection. Filial reverence was holden in the highest estimation by the ancients, and parental attachment is viewed in the same light by the moderns; but without doubt, in the connection between father and son, it is more advantageous that the benefactor should be the individual whose tenderness is the strongest.

The ancients could not be exceeded in their love of justice, but they did not consider benevolence as a duty, justice may be enforced by the laws, notwithstanding general opinion is the criterion of beneficence, and is sufficient to exclude from esteem the being who is insensible to the miseries of his fellow-creatures.

The ancients only required of others to refrain from injuring them; and simply desired them not to *stand in their sunshine*, but that they might be left to nature and themselves. But the moderns, endowed with softer sentiments, solicit assistance, support, and that interest which their situation inspires. They have constituted into a virtue every thing that can be useful to mutual happiness; domestic ties are cemented by a rational liberty; and no one has an arbitrary power over his fellow-creature.

With the ancient people of the north, lessons of prudence, dexterity, and maxims which commanded a supernatural empire over their own afflictions, were placed among the first precepts of virtue: but the importance of duties is much better classed by the moderns; the reciprocal obligation from man to man holds the first rank; what regards ourselves, ought to be considered relatively to the influence which we may possess over the destiny of others. What each individual is to procure, to promote his own happiness, is a counsel and not an order: the strictest moral does not impute to man as a crime that grief which is natural, and which his feelings will not allow him to conceal, but that grief which he occasions to others.

In a word, that which both the gospel and philosophy alike inculcate, is the doctrine of humanity. We are taught to respect the gift of life; and the existence of man is now considered as sacred to man, and is not viewed with that political indifference which some of the ancients believed compatible with the true principles of virtue. We now feel a sensation of horror at the sight of blood; and the warrior who is entirely indifferent to his own personal danger, acquires a degree of honor when he shudders at being the necessary cause of destruction to another. If any circumstance at this period gives reason to apprehend, that a condemnation has been unjust, that an innocent person has fallen a victim to a supposed justice, nations will listen with terror to the lamentations which arise from an irreparable misfortune; the sensation caused by an unmerited death is recorded from one generation to another; and even children will listen with horror to the recital of so great a grievance. When the eloquent Lally, twenty years after the death of his father, demanded in France the re-establishment of his manes; those young men who could not have seen or known the victim whom he wished to reclaim, felt themselves violently agitated, and shed tears in abundance, as if that fatal day, when innocence was sacrificed, could never be effaced from their remembrance.

Thus ages rolled on towards the conquest of liberty for virtue is always its herald. Alas! by what means shall we banish the painful contrast which so forcibly strikes the imagination? One crime was recollected during a long succession of years; but we have since witnessed cruelties without number committed and forgotten at the same moment! And it was under the shadow of the republic, the noblest, the most glorious, and the proudest institution of the human mind, that those execrable crimes have been committed! Ah! how difficult do we find it to repel those melancholy ideas, every time we reflect upon the destiny of man: the horrid phantom of the revolution appears before us: in vain we wish to look back on times that are past; in vain we desire to recognise in late events the constant connection of abstract combinations: if in the regions of metaphysics one word awakens recollection, the emotions of the heart resume all their empire, and no longer supported by reflection, we are suddenly plunged into the abyss of despair.

Nevertheless, let us not yield to this despondency, but return to general observations and literary ideas; to any thing and every thing, in short, that can divert our attention from personal sentiments; they are of too painful a nature to be developed: talents may be animated by a certain degree of emotion: but long and heavy affliction stifles the genius of expression; and when sorrow is become habitual to the mind, the imagination loses even the wish to express what it feels.

CHAPTER X.

OF THE SPANISH AND ITALIAN LITERATURE.

The greatest part of the ancient manuscripts, the monuments of art, and in short, all the remains of Roman splendor and knowledge, existed in Italy : and considerable expenses and the authority of public power were necessary in order to make the researches requisite to bring them to light. It was consequently in this country, where the sources of all scientific pursuits were to be found, that literature first made its reappearance, and commenced its career under the auspices of princes : for the different means which are indispensably necessary to the first progress, are immediately dependent upon the power and will of government.

The protection of the Italian princes greatly contributed to the revival of letters : but it must have been an obstacle to the light of philosophy : and those obstacles would have existed even if religious superstition had not, in many instances, been detrimental to the investigation of truth.

I must once more explain the meaning which I have constantly attached to the word *philosophy* in the course of this work ; what I mean by the use of that term, is a more minute inquiry into the principles of political and religious institutions ; the analysis of characters, and the events of history : in a word, the study of the human heart, and the natural rights of man. Such a philosophy imagines a state of liberty, or must necessarily lead towards it.

The men of letters in Italy were farther from that independence requisite to this philosophy, than any other nation ; as they required pecuniary means and the approbation of princes, in order to discover those manuscripts of antiquity that were to serve them as guides.

There were in all the great cities of Italy numberless academies and universities : these associations were particularly proper for the learned researches that were to rescue from oblivion so many superior compositions of antiquity. But these public establishments, even from the nature of their institutions, were entirely under the subjection of government ; and the corporations, like all other orders, classes, and sects, were extremely useful to one particular aim, but much less favorable than the efforts of individual genius to the advancement of philosophy. We must add to these general reflections, that the long and patient researches requisite for the examination of the ancient manuscripts, was peculiarly adapted to a monastic life : and the monks, in fact, were the most active in the study of literature. Thus the same cause which produced the revival of letters, opposed the development of natural reason. The Italians took the first steps, and pointed out the way in which the human understanding has since made such immense progress ; but they were destined never to make any advance in the path which they themselves had laid open.

In Italy, the imagination was intoxicated by the inimitable charms of poetry and the fine arts : but the writers in prose were, in general, neither moralists nor philosophers, and their efforts to appear eloquent produced nothing but bombast. Nevertheless, as it is in the nature of the human understanding always to improve ; the Italians, to whom philosophy was interdicted, and who could not, in poetry, exceed the limit prescribed to all arts,—that of perfection the Italians, I say, rendered themselves illustrious by the astonishing progress which, by their perseverence, they affected in the sciences. After the century of Leo X, after Ariosto and Tasso, their poetry visibly assumed a retrograde course : but, in Galileo, Cassini, and in others still more recently, they acquired a number of useful discoveries in nature which associated them for the intellectual perfection of the human species.

Superstition made many attempts to persecute Galileo ; but a number of the Italian princes came to his relief. Religious fanaticism is very inimical to the arts and sciences, as well as to philosophy ; but absolute regal power, or federal aristocracy, have often protected them, and are only averse to a philosophical independence.

In a country where priesthood is predominant, every evil and every prejudice have been often found united : but the diversity of governments in Italy lightened the yoke of priesthood, by creating a rivalry between those states or princes, who secured the very limited independence necessary to the arts and sciences.

After having affirmed, that it was in the sciences only that the Italians advanced progressively, and furnished their tribute towards the general knowledge of the human species ; let us proceed to examine into each branch of intellectual learning, into philosophy, eloquence, and poetry, with the causes of the successes and failures of the Italian literature.

The subdivision of states in the same country is, in general, very favorable to philosophy : this is what I have occasion to show in speaking of the German literature. But in Italy, this subdivision did not produce its natural effect ; the despotism of the priests destroyed, in a great measure, the happy results which might have arisen from a federal government ; it would perhaps have been better, if the whole nation had been united under one government ; their recollection would have been more active, and the sentiments it inspired would have produced a retrospect favorable to virtue.

Principalities, whether under a federal or a theocratical government, have each of them been a prey to civil wars, parties, and factions ; altogether unfavorable to liberty. The minds of men were depraved by mutual hatred, instead of being enlarged by the love of their country. Even while they submitted to tyranny, they were familiar with assassination : incredulity was occasionally found the companion of fanaticism, but sound reason was never to be met with.

The Italians, notwithstanding their general incredulity and their universal professions, were much more addicted to pleasantry than reasoning : which led them to make a jest of their own existence. When they wished to lay aside their natural talent, the comic, and attempted eloquent orations, they were always mixed with the most absurd affectation. Their recollection of past grandeur, without one idea of present greatness, must necessarily produce the *stupendous*. The Italians might possess dignity, if there were any mixture of the gloomy or melancholy in their characters ; but when the successors of the Romans, deprived of all national splendor, and all political liberty, are yet the gayest people on earth, it shows that there is a natural want of elevation of soul.

It was perhaps from antipathy to the Italian bombast, that Machiavel used such extreme simplicity when he analyzed tyranny. It is very probable that he wished, that the horror of crimes should arise from the development of their principles ; and carrying his contempt rather too far even for the appearance of declamation, he left every thing to the imagination of his readers. The reflections of of Machiavel upon Titus Livy are far superior to his *Prince*. These reflections may be considered as one of the works in which the human understanding has showed itself to the greatest advantage : such a production belongs entirely to the genius of the author, and has no connection with the general character of the Italian literature.

The troubles of Florence, without doubt, contributed to give to the ideas of Machiavel a greater energy :

but it appears to me, that in studying his work, we can feel they are the productions of a man who fancied himself as standing alone in creation : he writes as if for himself solely, without concerning himself about the effects which his writings might produce on others.

Machiavel may be accused of not having foreseen the bad consequences that might have arisen from his books : but it is not to be credited, that a man of such extensive genius would have adopted the theory of vice ; which theory is too brief, and has too little of the prospective even in its most profound combinations.

Among the number of Italian historians there are none, not even Guichardin and F. Paolo, whom they esteem the most, who will in any degree bear a comparison with those of antiquity, or with the English historians amongst the moderns ; they certainly have erudition ; but they neither examine men nor ideas. But perhaps it was really dangerous under the Italian government to judge philosophically of institutions and characters : possibly this people, once so great, and now so degraded, were, like Rinaldo in the palace of Armida, importuned by every thought that could interrupt their pleasures and their repose.

It would have been natural to suppose, that the eloquence of the pulpit would have been superior in Italy to that of any other nation ; because they were under the dominion of a positive religion. Nevertheless, this country offers nothing celebrated in that style of eloquence ; while France can boast of the greatest talents of that description. The Italians, if we except a certain number of enlightened men, were alike in religion, in love, and in liberty ; fond of the bombast in every thing ; and felt no real sentiment in any thing. They were vindictive, yet servile ; they were slaves to the female sex, yet total strangers to the deep and lasting sentiments of the heart : they were the victims of superstition, strictly adhering to all Catholic ceremonies ; but they did not believe in an indissoluble alliance between religion and morals. Such is the effect that might naturally have been expected from fanatical prejudices ; from divers governments which never united in the love and defence of their country ; and from the heat of their climate, which excited every sensation, and rendered them prone to indulge every degree of voluptuousness, if its effects are not opposed, as with the Romans, by the energetic pursuit of politics. In shortl all countries where public authority sets the limits of superstition against researches into philosophical truths ; when emulation has exhausted itself on the fine arts ; enlightened men, having neither path to follow, nor aim or expectation in view, are naturally discouraged, and a total listlessness takes possession of their faculties, and scarcely leaves to the mind strength sufficient to find amusement for itself.

After having expressed, perhaps with some degree of severity, what was wanting in the Italian literature, we must return to the fascinating charms of their brilliant imagination.

That period of literature is worthy of being remarked, in which was discovered the secret of exciting the curiosity by the invention and recital of private adventures. The *romantic* was introduced into tho north and east by two distinct causes. In the north, the spirit of chivalry often gave rise to extraordinary events ; and in order to make their recitals interesting to the warriors, they were obliged to relate exploits similar to their own : to render literature subservient to the recital or the invention of the splendid achievements of chivalry was the only means to overcome the repugnance in which learning was holden by men who were even then but in a state of barbarity.

It may also be farther remarked, that Oriental despotism turned the mind to words of imagination ; moral truths could not be risked but under the form of a fable, and talents were exercised to invent and detail fictions : it was natural for slaves to take refuge in a world of fancy ; and as their imagination was further animated by the heat of their climate, there was a greater variety in the Arabian tales than in the romances of chivalry. But in Italy they were both united ; the invasion of the people of the north transported into the east the tradition of the exploits of chivalry ; and their connection with Spain enriched their poetry with a number of events taken from the Arabian tales. It is to this happy mixture that we are indebted for Ariosto and Tasso.

The art of exciting pity and terror by developing the passions of the heart, is a talent in which philosophy claims a great part : but the effects of the *marvelous* upon credulity is more powerful : as the explanation cannot be foreseen by any combination, and curiosity cannot be satisfied by the anticipation of any thing probable : all is therefore surprise and astonishment.

In the romances of chivalry, we may perceive a singular mixture of the Christian religion in which the writers believed, and the magic which they feared : and in the Oriental writings, a continual combat was visible between the new religion, and the ancient idolatry over which Mahomet triumphed. The Roman and Grecian mythology was a composition much more simple, and was more nearly connected with moral ideas ; being generally the emblem or the allegory. But the *wonderful* of the Arabians was more attractive to curiosity. The one appears like a dream of terror ; and the other a happy comparison of the moral and physical orders.

The literature of the Spaniards ought to have been more remarkable than that of the Italians ; it should have united the imagination of the north with that of the east, the Oriental grandeur with the splendor of chivalry, the martial spirit which repeated wars had exalted and the poetry which was inspired by the beauty of their climate : but regal power, which served as a prop for superstition, stifled in their birth those puerile dispositions to glory.

The subdivision of states, although it precluded Italy from becoming one nation, gave sufficient liberty for the study of the sciences : but the united despotism of Spain, in encouraging the active power of the Inquisition, left no pursuit for thought, no resource nor means of escaping the yoke. We may, however, judge what the Spanish literature might have been, by some essays which may yet be collected.

The romances of the Moors established in Spain. borrowed their respect for the fair-sex from chivalry, This respect was not to be found in the national manners of the east. The Arabs who remained in Africa, did not in this instance resemble the Arabs established in Spain : the Moors inspired the Spaniards with their spirit of magnificence ; and the Spaniards reciprocally taught their love and their chivalric honor to the Moors. No mixture could be more favorable to works of imagination, if literature had been encouraged in Spain. Amongst their romances, the 'Cid' gives us some idea of the grandeur which would have characterized the efforts of their genius. In the poem of Camoens, which is written in the same spirit as many of tho Spanish productions, we find a most beautiful fiction in the phantom which defends the entrance of the Indian seas. In the comedies of Calderoni, and of Lopez do Vega, an elevation of sentiment always shines through the cloud of faults by which their beauties are veiled. The love and jealousy of the Spaniards have quite a different character from the sentiments represented in the Italian pieces ; their expressions are neither very subtil, though not entirely insipid ; they never portray perfidy of character nor depravity of manners : it is true, they have too much pompousness of style ; but while we condemn their bombast, we are convinced of the truth of their sentiments. It is not the same in Italy : if the affectation of certain works were taken away, there would remain nothing at all : while, if we could remove that of the Spaniards, they would shortly attain to the perfection of dignity, courage, and the most affecting sensibility.

It was not possible that the elements of philosophy could be improved in Spain; the invasion of the north introduced nothing but the military spirit: and the Arabians were altogether enemies to philosophy: their absolute government, and the fatality of their religion, led them to detest the light of philosophy: this hatred caused them to burn the library of Alexandria. They however cultivated the sciences and poetry: but they studied the former like astrologers, and the latter like warriors. They cultivated their vocal talents, merely to sing their exploits; and they studied nature only with the hopes of attaining the magic art. They had no idea of strengthening their reason: and in reality, to what use could they have applied a faculty which would have overthrown what they most respected, despotism and superstition?

The Spaniards, strangers like the Italians to the labors of philosophy, were entirely diverted from all literary emulation by the gloomy and oppressive tyranny of the Inquisition. They drew no profit from the inexhaustible sources of poetic invention which the Arabians brought with them. Italy was in possession of the ancient monuments: was also immediately connected with the Greeks of Constantinople; and drew from Spain the Oriental style, which the Moors had introduced, but which the Spaniards neglected.

We may easily distinguish, in the Italian literature, what has arisen from the influence of the Greeks, and what belongs to the poetry and tradition of the Arabians. Pedantry and affectation were derived from the sophistry and theology of the Greeks, and the picture of poetic invention from the Oriental imagination. These two different characters may be distinctly perceived through the general character which the same language, the same climate, and similar manners, gave to the works of the same people.

Boiardo the first author who wrote in that style rendered so celebrated by Ariosto, displayed a great similarity in his poems to the Oriental tales; the same character of the inventive and the marvelous. Indeed, the spirit of chivalry, and the liberty granted to women in the north, constitute the only difference between Boiardo and the 'Thousand and One Nights.'

Although the Arabians were a warlike people, they fought for religion much more than for love or honor; while with the people of the north, whatever might be their respect for the belief they professed, personal glory was ever their first aim. Ariosto, as well as Boiardo, is an imitator of the Oriental style. Ariosto is certainly the greatest painter, and consequently, perhaps, the greatest poet amongst the moderns. One of the most striking originalities in his works is the art of extracting pleasantry from what is not only serious but bombastic. Nothing could be more agreeable to the Italians than this lively ridicule thrown upon all the serious and elevated notions of chivalry; it is natural to them to be fond of uniting, even in subjects of the highest importance, an exterior of gravity with levity of sentiments: and Ariosto is the most charming model of this national taste.

Tasso borrowed his most brilliant ideas from the Oriental imagination, but often joined with them a charm of sensibility peculiar to himself. Petrarch, the first poet of whom the Italians could boast, and one of those who was most admired, introduced that unfortunate style of antithesis and *concetti*, of which the Italian literature in many instances could never after be entirely corrected. All the poetical productions of the school of Petrarch and we must admit into the number the Aminta of Tasso, and the Pastor Fido of Guarini, drew their defects from the sophistry of the Greeks of the middle century. The spirit with which they animated their theology, was introduced by the Italians into their poems on the subject of love. There is some analogy between love and devotion; but there certainly can exist none between theology and the sentiments of the heart: nevertheless, at Constantinople they disputed in the same style upon the nature of the divinity, as in Italy upon the partiality or severity of their mistresses.*

All Europe, and France in particular, were in danger of losing the advantages of natural genius by imitating the writings of the Italians; the beauties which immortalized their poets, depended upon the imagination, the language, the climate, and a variety of circumstances which could not be transported elsewhere; but their defects were very contagious.

Affectation is, of all the faults incident to characters or writings, that which in the most irreparable manner checks the source of all good: even truth, when thus arrayed, sickens the mind, and we turn from it with disgust.

The language which has been employed in false ideas and cold exaggerations, becomes vapid if continued, and may at length lose the power of causing even the slightest emotion, if too often repeated upon the same subject; for this reason the Italian is, perhaps, of all the European languages, the least adapted for the passionate eloquence of love; as that of the French is now exhausted in declamations upon liberty.

At the same time that Petrarch introduced into his poetry a romantic exaggeration. Boccace adopted another extreme, and threw into his works the greatest indecency: and we may observe, that most of the Italian comedies are infinitely more obscene than any composed by the French authors. One of the destructive consequences of that affectation of sentiment is to inspire a taste for the opposite extreme, in order to rouse the mind from a languor and disgust which this sentimental tone never fails to occasion. The affectation of love leads the mind to licentiousness; as hypocrisy in religion generally ends in atheism: nevertheless, Petrarch and a few other celebrated poets who wrote in that style, are worthy of being read from the beauties of their harmonious language, which recalls to our minds in a degree the effects of that celestial music, with which it is so often accompanied: but it is not affirmed, that these sonorous words would be an advantage to all kinds of style, or to every description of poetry.

The brilliant consonance of the Italian language is not favorable to thought, either in the writer or the reader: there is not a sufficient conciseness in the ideas, nor enough of gloom to express the melancholy of sentiment; it is a language whose melody is so extraordinary, that even without giving attention to the sense of the words, it strikes and affects the mind like the chords of a musical instrument. Every one must be transported in reading this verse of Tasso:

> Chiama gli arbitator del ombre eterne
> Il rauco suon della Tartarea tromba,
> Treman le spaziose atre caverne,
> E l'aer cieco a quel ramor rimbomba.†

Yet when we examine the sense of it, we cannot find any thing sublime. Tasso like an able musician,

* Among a thousand instances of Italian affectation, I shall mention one.—Petrarch lost his mother when she was only thirty-eight years old; he then composed a sonnet in a manner assuredly most affecting and natural consisting exactly of thirty-eight verses, in honor of her memory, as well as to testify his own regret at having lost his mother at that comparatively early age.

† 'When the hoarse sound of the Tartarean trumpet called the inhabitants of the eternal shades, the vast and gloomy caverns trembled, while the tremendous roar was extended far and wide through the gloomy air.'

takes possession of the imagination. In this stanza he makes his hearers tremble by the harmony of numbers, and the grandeur of sounds; but one of the fine airs of Jiomelli would produce nearly a similar effect. This is the advantage of the Italian language, and we will now remark its inconvenience.

The death of Clorinda, murdered by Tancred, is perhaps the most affecting recital we are acquainted with in poetry: and the inexpressible beauties of the episode in Tasso, add still more to the effect; nevertheless the last verse of this composition,

Passa la bella donna, et par che dorma, *

is too soft and harmonious; it glides too smoothly upon the mind to accord with the profound expression such an event ought to produce.

The great number who have distinguished themselves by their facility in versification, has been cited as a proof of the poetical advantages of the Italian language; but it appears to me quite the reverse, and that this its extreme facility is one of its faults: great poets must find it an obstacle to the elevation and perfection of their style. The gradations of thought, and the shades of sentiment, require a profound meditation; while those agreeable words which offer themselves in such crowds to the fancy of the Italian poets, like a court of flatterers, dispense with the search, and by that means preclude the discovery of a real friend.

In Italy, every thing conspired to fill the life of man with the agreeable sensations which naturally arise from their fine arts and their unclouded sun; but since this country has lost the empire of the world, it seems as if its inhabitants disdained a political existence; and, according to the maxims of Cæsar, they aspired to the first rank in pleasure, rather than the second place in the annals of fame,

Dante having, as well as Machiavel, supported a character in the civil commotions of his country; in some of his poems we observe an energy in no degree analogous to the literature of his time: but the numberless faults with which we may reproach him, belonged without doubt to the century he lived in. It is only in the time of Leo X. that we remark a decided purity in the Italian literature: the ascendency of this prince was to the Italian government what unity might have been: the rays of knowledge were collected into one focus, in which taste also might have been concentrated, and literary judgments have proceeded from the same tribunal.

After the age of the Medici, the Italian literature made no progress of any kind, either because some central point was necessary to rally all the forces of the intellect, or, principally, because philosophy was not at all cultivated in Italy. When the literature of imagination has attained to the highest possible degree of perfection, the subsequent age belongs to philosophy, in order that the human understanding may not cease in its advancement towards perfection in some way or other. After Racine, we have seen Voltaire; because, in the eighteenth century, men were more profound thinkers than in the seventeenth. But what could have been added to the excellence of poetry after Racine?

The Italians have no romances like those of the French and English; because the love which inspired them, not being a passion of the mind capable of any long continuation, their customs and manners were too licentious to preserve any interest in this style. Their comedies were filled with that kind of buffoonery which arises from the absurdities and vices: but we do not find, if we except a few pieces of Goldoni, one striking and variegated picture of the vices of the human heart, such as are found in the French comedies. The Italians simply wished to create laughter; no serious aim can be discovered through the veil of flippancy, and their comedies are not the picture of human life, but its caricature.

The Italians, even in their theatres, have often turned their priests into ridicule, although in other respects they were entirely subjected to them: but it was not with a philosophical view that they attacked the abuses of religion: they had not, like some of our writers, a wish to reform the faults they complained of: it was easy to perceive that their real opinions were totally opposite to that kind of authority to which they were compelled to submit: but this spirit of opposition incited them to nothing more than a contempt for those who commanded esteem; it was like the cunning of children to their teachers; they were willing to obey them on condition they might be permitted to make sport of them.

It follows from this, that all the works of the Italians, except those which treat on physical sciences, have nothing useful in view; which is absolutely necessary in order to give a real strength and solidity to their reflections. The works of Beccaria, Filangieri, and a few others, make the only exception to what I have now advanced.

One question more remains to be decided before I close this chapter; which is, whether the Italians have carried the dramatic art to any length in tragedy?

For myself, in spite of the charms of Metastasio, and the energy of Alfieri, I do not think they have. The Italians have a lively invention in subjects, and a brilliancy in expression; but the personages which they represent, are not characterized in a manner to leave any lasting traces on the mind; and the affliction which they portray, excites but little sympathy. This may be occasioned by their moral and political situation, not allowing the mind its full display: their sensibility is not serious, their sadness is without melancholy, and their grandeur commands no respect. The Italian author was therefore obliged to have recourse entirely to himself; and, to compose a tragedy, he must not only forget all he sees, but renounce all his habitual ideas and impressions: and it is very difficult to find out the true basis of a tragedy which is so widely different from the general manners and customs of the time in which it was composed.

Vengeance is the passion which is the best described in the Italian tragedies: it is natural to their character to be suddenly roused by this sentiment in the midst of that habitual indolence in which they spent their lives; and their resentments were naturally expressed, because they really felt them.

The operas alone were followed, because at the opera was heard that enchanting music which was the glory and pleasure of Italy. The performers did not exert themselves in tragedy; fine acting would have been thrown away; they were not even heard; and it must ever be thus, when the art of touching the passions is not carried to a sufficient length to predominate over every other pleasure. The Italians did not require to be softened, and the authors for want of spectators, and the spectators for want of authors, did not give themselves up to the profound impressions of the dramatic art.

Metastasio, however, found out the secret of turning his operas almost into tragedies; and though compelled to struggle with all the difficulties imposed by the obligation of submitting to music, he still preserved many beauties of style and situation truly dramatic. It may be that there exist yet some other exceptions little known to strangers; but to draw the principal characters of any national literature, it is absolutely necessary to lay aside many details; there are no general ideas that are not contradicted by certain exemptions; but the mind would be incapable of ever forming any de-

* 'The beauteous nymph expired while seeming only to sleep.'

termination, if it were to stop at each particular instead of drawing a consequence from a collective whole.

Melancholy, that sentiment which is so fertile in works of genius, appears to have belonged almost exclusively to the people of the North. The Oriental style, which the Italians have often imitated, had a sort of melancholy of which we find some traces in the Arabian poetry, and likewise in the Hebrew psalms; but it has a character entirely distinct from that we shall find when we analyze the literature of the north.

The people of the east, whether Jews or Mahometans, were sustained and directed by their positive reliance on their religion. It was not that uncertain and undetermined apprehension which afforded the mind a more philosophical impression: the melancholy of the Orientals was that of men who were happy from every enjoyment of nature; they simply reflected with regret upon the brevity of human life, and the rapid decay of prosperity: while the melancholy of the people of the north was that which is inspired by the sufferings of the mind, the void which the absence of sensibility makes in the existence, and that continual musing upon the calamities of this life, and the uncertaintv of their destiny in a life to come.

CHAPTER XI.

OF THE LITERATURE OF THE NORTH.

There appear to be two distinct kinds of literature still extant, one derived from the east, the other from the north; the origin of the first may be traced to Homer, that of the last to Ossian. The Greeks, the Latins, the Italians, the Spanish, and the French of the century of Louis XIV., belong to that style of literature which I shall call eastern. The works of the English and Germans, with some of the Danish and Swedish writings, may be classed as the literature of the north. But before I attempt to characterize the English and German writers, I think it necessary, in a general manner, to consider the principal difference of the two hemispheres of their literature.

The English, as well as the Germans, have, without doubt, often imitated the ancients, and drawn very useful lessons from that fruitful study; but their original beauties carry a sort of resemblance, a certain poetic grandeur, of which Ossian is the most splendid example.

It may perhaps be remarked, that the English poets are celebrated for the spirit of philosophy which appears in all their works; and that the ideas of Ossian are not the ideas of reflection, but a series of events and impressions. I answer to this objection, that the most habitual images and ideas of Ossian are those which recall the shortness of life, the respect for the dead, the superstition connected with their memory, and the duty that remains towards those who are no more. If the poet has not united to those sentiments, morals, maxims, or philosophical reflections; it was because the human understanding, at that period, was not yet capable of the abstraction necessary to draw philosophical inferences; but the emotion caused by the songs of Ossian, disposed the mind to the most profound meditations.

Melancholy poetry is that which accords best with philosophy. Depression of spirits leads us to penetrate more deeply into the character and destiny of man, than any other disposition of the mind. The English poets who succeeded the Scots bards, added to their descriptions those very ideas and reflections which those descriptions ought to have given birth to: but they have preserved, from the fine imagination of the north, that gloom which is soothed with the roaring of the sea, and the hollow blast that rages on the barren heath, and, in short, every thing dark and dismal, which can force a mind dissatisfied with its existence here, to look forward to another state. The vivid imagination of the people of the north darting beyond the boundaries of a world whose confines they inhabited, penetrated through the black cloud that obscured their horizon, and seemed to represent the dark passage to eternity.

We cannot decide in a general manner between the two different styles of poetry, of which we may fairly say Homer and Ossian were the first models: my general impressions, and the force of my ideas, induce me to give a preference to the literature of the north; but my business at present is, to examine the decided difference of their characters.

The climate is certainly one of the principal causes of difference which existed between the images that pleased in the north and those which were admired in the east. The reveries of poets may produce extraordinary objects; but the impressions of habits are necessary in their compostions of every kind. To banish the remembrance of those impressions, would be to lose the greatest advantage, namely, that of portraying what they had themselves experienced.

The poets of the east intermingled with all their sentiments of life the ideas of tufted woods, limpid streams, and cooling zephyrs: they could not even describe the enjoyments of the heart, without introducing the idea of the sequestered bowers which preserved them from the scorching rays of their meridian sun. The bounty of nature by which they were surrounded, excited more emotion than thought.

He who said that the passions were more violent in the east than in the north, was, I think, wrong: it is true, we may see a greater variety of interests, but we perceive less ardor in the same sentiments.

The people of the north were less engaged in pleasure than in its opposite sensation; and this rendered their imagination more fertile: the prospects of nature had almost unbounded influence over them; but it affected them as it appeared in their climate, always dark and gloomy. Without doubt, many circumstances in life might sometimes vary this disposition to melancholy; but that alone stamps the character of the national spirit. We must look, in a nation, as well as in an individual, for the leading characteristic; all others may be the effects of chance, and depend on a thousand different circumstances; but this one alone characterizes the man.

The northern poetry was much more suitable than the eastern to the minds of a free people. The Athenians, who were the first inventors of eastern literature, were more jealous of their independence than any nation in the world: nevertheless, they were much more easily subdued to slavery than the people of the north; their love of the arts, the beauty of their climate, and the numberless enjoyments bestowed on the Athenians might, in a great measure, recompense for their want of liberty. But independence was the sole happiness of the northern nations: a certain haughtiness of soul, and indifference to life, which was inspired by their gloomy atmosphere and the rarity of their sun, would have rendered servitude insupportable: and long before the theory of constitutions, and the advantages of a representative government were known in England, the warlike spirit which shone with so much enthusiasm in the Erse and Scandinavian poetry, inspired man with a prodigious idea of his own strength and the power of his will. Independence existed for each one separately, before liberty was generally constituted.

At the revival of letters, philosophy first commenced with the northern nations; in whose religious habits reason found much less superstition to oppose than in those of the southern people. The ancient poetry of the north is infected with much less superstition than the Grecian mythology: there are a few absurd fables in the Edda; but almost all the religious ideas of the north owe their birth to exalted reason: the ghosts pending from the clouds, were but animated remembrances presented by sensibility.

The emotions which are produced by the poems of Ossian, may be re-produced in all countries and in all nations; because the means of awakening them are all taken from nature: but it must be talents of the highest order that could without affectation introduce the Grecian mythology into French poetry. There is nothing, generally speaking, that can appear more cold or insipid, than the dogmas of any religion, when transported into a country where there are only received as ingenious metaphors.

The poetry of the north was rarely allegorical; not one of its effects stood in need of local superstition to strike the imagination. A reflected enthusiasm, and a pure exaltation of mind, might equally be found in every nation: it is the true poetic inspiration, a sentiment which is in every heart, but the expression of which is the gift of genius alone. It creates a kind of celestial musing, which excites a love of solitude and the country, and often fills the mind with truly religious ideas.

Whatever is great and sublime, we owe to the painful sentiments of the imperfection of our nature: moderate understandings are in general satisfied with the common occurrences of life; they in a manner bring their existence to a period, and supply what is wanting by the illusions of vanity. But sublime sentiments and actions spring from the desire which great souls have of breaking those bounds which circumscribe the imagination. The heroism of morals, the enthusiasm of eloquence, and the ambition of fame, are supernatural enjoyments, necessary only to those minds which, at once exalted and melancholy, are wearied and disgusted with every thing transitory, and to which the idea of bounds is insupportable, though placed at ever so great a distance. This disposition of the mind, which is the source of every generous passion and every philosophical discovery, is excited in the most lively manner by the poetry of the north.

I am very far from wishing to compare the genius of Homer with that of Ossian. What we know of Ossian's, cannot properly be considered as a work; it is merely a collection of popular songs, which were sung in the mountains of Scotland. Before Homer composed his poems, without doubt, some ancient traditions existed in Greece. The poetry of Ossian is no farther advanced in the poetic art, than were the songs of the Greeks before the time of Homer. No comparison can, then, with justice be made between the Iliad and the poem of Fingal. But we may always judge whether the images of nature, such as they were represented in the latter, excited as noble and pure emotions as those of the north, or whether the imagery of the east, more brilliant in many respects, gave birth to so many ideas, which are immediately connected with the sentiment of the heart. Philosophical ideas naturally unite themselves to gloomy reflections, and the poetry of the east, far from according, like that of the north, with meditation, and inspiring what reflection ought to feel, excludes almost every idea of a noble and elevated nature.

Ossian is reproached with his monotony: this fault exists much less in the different English and German poems which have imitated his style. Cultivation, industry, and commerce, have varied the face of the country in many ways; nevertheless, the northern imagination always preserving nearly the same character, we can still find a sort of uniformity in Young, Thomson, Klopstock, and others.

There cannot be an endless variety in melancholy poetry: that deep emotion which thrills the blood, is a sensation that never varies. When this emotion is excited by poetry, it has a great analogy to the effects produced by the *harmonica*. When the mind, gently agitated, is willing to prolong the pleasing sensation while it is possible to support it; when we are enervated, the fault is not to be attributed to the poetry, but to the susceptibility and weakness of our organs; what we experience at that time, is not a disgust at the monotony, but the fatigue of a pleasure too long continued.

The grand effects of the English dramatics, and after them that of the German, were not borrowed from Grecian subjects, nor from mythological dogmas. The English and Germans excite terror by other superstitions more suitable to the credulity of the last centuries; above all, they have found the art of exciting it by the pictures of distress which was so forcibly felt by energetic minds. The effect which the ideas of death generally produce in the sentiments of men, depend, in a great measure, as I have observed before, upon their religious opinions. The Scottish bards have, at all times, had a more spiritual and gloomy devotion than those of the east: but the Christian religion, which, when divested of priestcraft, is nearly a-kin to pure Deism, banished that train of terrors with which imagination had surrounded men in the hour of death. The ancients peopled all nature with protecting beings: the forests and rivers were filled with inhabitants, which presided over the night as well as the day; nature had retired into solitude, and men's fears were increased. The Christian religion, the most philosophical of all others, is that which leaves man the most at his own disposal.

The tragic writers of the north, not always contented with the effects which sprung naturally from the representation of the affections of the heart, called to their aid ghosts and spectres; a superstition suited to their gloomy imagination; but however great the terror which may be produced by such means, it is always rather a fault than a beauty.

The talent of the dramatic poet augments by existing in a nation not too much given to credulity; because it is then a matter of necessity to search into the human heart for the source of that emotion which is felt from an elegant expression, a sentiment from the heart: solitary remorse, or any of those frightful phantoms which strike the imagination, the marvelous may surprise and astonish: but in whatever fashion it may appear, it can never equal the impression of a natural event, when that event collects all that can move the affections of the soul: for example, the furies pursuing Orestes is less horrific to the mind than the sleep of Lady Macbeth.

If we are to judge by the traditions in our possession, the southern nations had in all times a respect for women, which was entirely unknown to the people of the east: they seem to have enjoyed independence in the north, while in other parts of the world they were condemned to slavery:—this most probably is one of the principal causes of that sensibility which characterizes northern literature.

The history of love, in all countries, may be considered in a philosophical point of view. It seems as if the representation of this passion ought to depend entirely on the feelings of the writer who expresses it; but such is the ascendency which the reigning manners and customs have over the writers, that they submit to them even the language of their inmost sentiments. It is possible that Petrarch might have felt this passion more strongly than the author of 'Werter,' or many English poets, for instance, Pope, Thomson, Otway, &c. Nevertheless, in reading the writings of the north, we might be led to think men were of a different nature, and that they lived in another world. The perfection of some of this poetry proves beyond a doubt the genius of its author: but it is not less certain, that had those authors lived in Italy, their writings would not have been the same, even if they had felt similar passions; so true, it is, that in all literary works where aim is success, we find much less of the real character of the writer than the general spirit of his nation, and that of the century in which he lived.

It was the Protestant religion which inspired the modern people of the north with a more general spirit of philosophy than was possessed by those of the east. The reformation was certainly the epoch of history which essentially promoted the perfectibility of the human species. The Protestant religion contains no active seeds of superstition; while it gives to virtue every support which can be drawn from wisdom. In those countries where the Protestant religion is predominant, it maintains purity of manners, and does not in the least retard the progress of philosophy.

A greater development of this question would be foreign to my subject; but I leave it to the discussion of every enlightened thinker, whether, if there could exist a means of uniting morality with the ideas of a god, without this means becoming an instrument of power in the hands of men; and whether a religion thus founded, would not be the greatest happiness that could be insured to human nature!—to that nature which is so much to be pitied, and which every day breaks some tie formed by affection, delicacy, or goodness

CHAPTER XII.

OF THE PRINCIPAL FAULTS WHICH THE FRENCH COMPLAIN OF IN THE LITERATURE OF THE NORTH.

The French censure the literature of the north as deficient in taste. Northern writers reply, that this taste is an arbitrary legislation, which often deprives sentiments and ideas of their original beauties. But it appears to me, that there may exist a medium between these opinions: the rules of taste are not arbitrary, and we must not confound the principles and basis upon which universal truth is founded, with the modifications caused by local circumstances. The duties of virtue, that code of principles which is supported by the unanimous consent of the world, experience some small change from the manners and customs of different nations; and although the first principles remain the same, the estimation of many virtues varies according to the habits and forms of government.

If it may be permitted to compare taste with what is greatest among men, we might say it was also fixed in the general principles.

It has often been asked, Must genius be sacrificed to taste? Undoubtedly it must not: but taste does not require the sacrifice of genius. We often find, in the literature of the north, something ridiculous annexed to something of great beauty: what belongs to taste in such writings, is their beauties; and what ought to have been suppressed, was what taste condemned. There exists no necessary connection between defects and beauties but what arises from the weakness of human nature; which does not permit us to remain always at the same pitch of perfection.

Faults are not the natural consequence of beauties: and although they may be overlooked; so far from adding any brilliancy to talents, they often weaken the impression they ought to produce.

If it was a question, which was most to be preferred, a work in which there were great beauties and great faults, or a work of the middling kind perfecty correct; I would answer without the least hesitation, that we ought to prefer a work where there existed even one spark of genius. It is a weakness in any nation to attach itself only to the ridiculous; which is so easy to seize or to avoid; instead of searching into the characters of men, which would open the understanding and elevate the mind. A negative merit can afford no enjoyment: but there are many people who require nothing more in life than to be exempt from pain: or in writings, but to be exempt from faults; and, in short, an exemption in every thing: but strong minds wish for an active existence; to attain which, in matters of literature, they must meet with new ideas or passionate sentiments.

There are some works in the French language, in which we may find beauties of the first order, without the intermixture of bad taste; and those are the only models in which every literary quality is united.

Amongst the learned men of the north there existed a sort of caprice, that might be said to belong more to their party-spirit than to their judgment: they were attached to the faults of their writers almost as much as their beauties: while they might have observed, as a woman of sense once did in speaking of the weakness of some hero, '*It is not the cause of his greatness, but he is great in spite of it.*'

In works of imagination, men mostly seek for agreeable impressions: taste then is nothing more than the art of knowing and forseeing what may awaken those impressions. If you recall disgusting images, you excite unpleasant sensations, the reality of which every one would shun: and when, by the representation of scenes horrible in themselves, you change moral terror into physical fear; you lose all the charm of imitation, and excite nothing but a nervous commotion: and you may lose the power of causing even this painful sensation, if you try to carry it too far. For it is with the theatre as it is in life: when the exaggeration is perceived, we disregard even the reality. If you lengthen the development, or if you put an obscurity in the discourse, and an improbability in the event; you suspend or destroy the interest by fatiguing the attention. If you represent heroic personages in a base and ignoble point of view, it is to be feared you will find it difficult to resume the theatrical illusion: it is of a nature so extremely delicate, that the lightest circumstance may awaken the spectators from their enchantment. In simplicity, ideas gain rest and strength: but what is base and low, may prevent even the possibility of again feeling interested in what is noble and elevated.

The beauties of Shakspeare may triumph in England over his faults: but they are a great drawback to his fame with other nations. Surprise is certainly a great means of adding to theatrical effect: but it would be ridiculous to conclude from that, that every tragic scene should be preceded by a comic scene, in order to heighten the astonishment by the contrast. Surprise should spring from grandeur itself, and not from its opposition to meanness. *Shades*, but not *blemishes*, are necessary, in every style of painting, to raise the brilliancy of coloring; and the same principles should be followed in literature: Nature offers us the model and a good taste should be but a reflection from our observation of it.

These developments might be carried much farther; but I think they are sufficient to prove that taste in literature never exacts the sacrifice of any enjoyment, but, on the contrary, it indicates the means of augmenting them: and so far from the principles of taste being incompatible with genius, it is in studying it that they were first discovered.

I will not reproach Shakspeare with having set aside all rules of the art; they are infinitely less important than those of taste; because the one prescribes what must be done, while the other only forbids what must be avoided. It is impossible to prescribe limits to the different combinations of a man of genius; he may perhaps strike into some path entirely new, without missing the aim he set out upon. The rules of art are a calculation of probabilities upon the means of success: and if this success is obtained, it is of little importance to have submitted to them. But it is not the same with the rules of taste; to despise them, is to relinquish all beauties, even the beauties of nature; and they can never be surpassed.

Let us not then say that Shakspeare knew how to excel without taste, and to show himself superior to the regulations prescribed by his country; but let us acknowledge, on the contrary, that he displayed his taste in his sublimities, and was most deficient in it when he was least sublime.

CHAPTER XIII.

OF THE TRAGEDIES OF SHAKSPEARE.

The English entertain as profound veneration and enthusiasm for Shakspeare, as any nation perhaps has ever felt for any writer. A free people have a natural love for every thing that can do honor to their country; and this sentiment ought to exclude every species of criticism.

There are beauties of the first order to be found in Shakspeare, relating to every country and every period of time. His faults are those which belonged to the times in which he lived; and the singularities then so prevalent among the English, are still represented with the greatest success upon their theatres. These beauties and eccentricities I shall proceed to examine, as connected with the national spirit of England, and the genius of the literature of the north.

Shakspeare did not imitate the ancients; nor, like Racine did he feed his genius upon the Grecian tragedies. He composed one piece upon a Greek subject, *Troilus and Cressida;* in which the manners in the time of Homer are not at all observed. He excelled infinitely more in those tragedies which were taken from Roman subjects. But history, and the lives of Plutarch, which Shakspeare appears to have read with the utmost attention, are not purely a literary study; we may therein trace the man almost to a state of existence. When an author is solely penetrated with the models of the dramatic art of antiquity, and when he imitates imitations, he must of course have less originality: he cannot have that genius which draws from nature; that immediate genius, if I may so express myself, which so particularly characterizes Shakspeare. From the times of the Greeks down to this time, we see every species of literature derived one from another, and all arising from the same source. Shakspeare opened a new field of literature: it was borrowed, without doubt, from the general spirit and color of the north: but it was Shakspeare who gave to the English literature its impulse, and to their dramatic art its character.

A nation which has carved out its liberty through the horrors of civil war, and whose passions have been strongly agitated, is much more susceptible of the emotion excited by Shakspeare, than that which is caused by Racine. When misfortune lies heavy and for a long time upon a nation, it creates a character, which even succeeding prosperity can never entirely efface. Shakspeare, although he has since been equalled by both English and German authors, was the first who painted moral affliction in the highest degree: the bitterness of those sufferings of which he gives us the idea, might pass for the phantoms of imagination, if nature did not recognize her own picture in them.

The ancients believed in a fatality, which came upon them with the rapidity of lightning, and destroyed them like a thunderbolt. The moderns, and more especially Shakspeare, found a much deeper source of emotion in a philosophical distress, which was often composed of irreparable misfortunes of ineffectual exertions, and blighted hopes. But the ancients inhabited a world yet in its infancy; were in possession of but very few histories; and withal were so sanguine in respect to the future, that the scenes of distress painted by them, could never be so heart-rending as those in the English tragedies.

The terror of death was a sentiment, the effects of which, whether for religion or from stoicism, was seldom displayed by the ancients. Shakspeare has represented it in every point of view: he makes us feel that dreadful emotion which chills the blood of him, who, in the full enjoyment of life and health, learns that death awaits him. In the tragedies of Shakspeare, the criminal and the virtuous, infancy and old-age are alike condemned to die, and express every emotion natural to such a situation. What tenderness do we feel, when we hear the complaints of Arthur, a child condemned to death by the order of King John; or when the assassin Tirrel comes to relate to Richard III. the peaceful slumber of the children of Edward? When a hero is painted just going to be deprived of his existence, the grandeur of his character, and the recollection of his achievements, excite the greatest interest: but when men of weak minds, and doomed to an inglorious destiny, are represented as condemned to perish; such as Henry VI., Richard II., and King Lear; the great debates of nature between existence and non-existence absorb the whole attention of the spectators. Shakspeare knew how to point with genius that mixture of physical emotions and moral reflections which are inspired by the approach of death, when no intoxicating passion deprives man of his intellectual faculties.

Another sentiment which Shakspeare alone knew how to render theatrical, was pity unmixed with admiration for those who suffer;* pity for an insignificant being,† and sometimes for a contemptible one.‡ There must be infinity of talent to be able to convey this sentiment from real life to the stage and to preserve it in all its force: but when once it is accomplished, the effect which it produces is more nearly allied to reality than any other. It is for the man alone that we are interested, and not by sentiments which are often but a theatrical romance: it is by a sentiment so nearly approaching the impressions of life, that the illusion is still the greater.

Even when Shakspeare represents personages whose career has been illustrious, he draws the interest of the spectators towards them by sentiments purely natural. The circumstances are grand, but the men differ less from other men than those in the French tragedies. Shakspeare makes you penetrate entirely into the glory which he paints; in listening to him, you pass through all the different shades and gradations which lead to heroism; and you arrive at the height without perceiving any thing unnatural.

The national pride of the English, that sentiment displayed in their jealous love of liberty, disposed them much less to enthusiasm for their chiefs than that spirit of chivalry which existed in the French monarchy. In England, they wish to recompense the services of a good citizen; but they have no turn for that unbounded ardor which existed in the habits, the institutions, and the character of the French. That haughty repugnance to unlimited obedience, which at all times characterized the English nation, was probably what inspired their national poet with the idea of assailing the passions of his audience by pity rather than by admiration. The tears which were given by the French to the sublime characters of their tragedies, the English author drew forth for private sufferings; for those who were forsaken; and for such a long list of the unfortunate, that we cannot entirely sympathize with Shakspeare's sufferers without acquiring also some of the bitter experience of real life.

But if he excelled in exciting pity; what energy appeared in this terror? It was from the crime itself

* The death of Catherine of Arragon, in 'Henry VIII.'
† The Duke of Clarence, in 'Richard III.'
‡ Cardinal Wolsey, in 'Henry VIII.'

that he drew dismay and fear. It may be said of crimes painted by Shakspeare, as the bible says of death, that he is the KING OF TERRORS. How skilfully combined are the remorse and the superstition which increases with that remorse in Macbeth.

Witchcraft is in itself much more terrible in its theatrical effect than the most absurd dogmas of religion. That which is unknown, or created by supernatural intelligence, awakens fear and terror to the highest degree. In every religious system, terror is carried only to a certain length, and is always at least founded upon some motive. But the chaos of the magic bewilders the mind. Shakspeare, in 'Macbeth,' admits of fatality, which was necessary in order to procure a pardon for the criminal; but he does not on account of this fatality dispense with the philosophical gradations of the sentiments of the mind. This piece would be still more admirable, if its grand effects were produced without the aid of the marvelous, although this marvelous consists, as one may say, only of phantoms of the imagination, which are made to appear before the eyes of the spectators. They are not mythological personages bringing their fictitious laws or their uninteresting nature amongst the interest of men: they are the marvelous effects of dreams, when the passions are strongly agitated. There is always something philosophical in the supernatural employed by Shakspeare. When the witches announce to Macbeth, that he is to wear the crown; and when they return to repeat their prediction, at the very moment when he is hesitating to follow the bloody counsel of his wife; who cannot see that it is the interior struggle of ambition and virtue which the author meant to represent under those hideous forms?

But he had not recourse to these means in 'Richard III;' and yet he has painted him more criminal still than Macbeth: but his intention was to portray a character without any of those involuntary emotions, without struggles, without remorse, cruel and ferocious as the savage beasts which range the forests; and not as a man who, though at present guilty, had once been virtuous. The deep recesses of crimes were opened to the eyes of Shakspeare, and he descended into the gloomy abyss to observe their torments.

In England, the troubles and civil commotions which preceded their liberty, and which were always occasioned by their spirit of independence, gave rise much oftener than in France to great crimes and great virtues. There are in the English history many more tragical situations than in that of the French; and nothing opposes their exercising their talents upon national subjects.

Almost all the literature of Europe began with affectation. The revival of letters having commenced in Italy, the countries where they were afterwards introduced, naturally imitated the Italian style. The people of the north were much sooner enfranchised than the French in this studied mode of writing; the traces of which may be perceived in some of the ancient poets, as Waller, Cowley, and others. Civil wars and a spirit of philosophy have corrected this false taste, for misfortune, the impressions of which contain but too much variety, excludes all sentiments of affectation, and reason banishes all expressions that are deficient in justness.

Nevertheless, we find in Shakspeare a few of those studied turns connected even with the most energetic pictures of the passions. There are some imitations of the faults of Italian literature in 'Romeo and Juliet:' but how nobly the English poet rises from this miserable style!—how well does he know now to describe love, even in the true spirit of the north!

In 'Othello,' love assumes a very different character from that which it bears in 'Romeo and Juliet.' But how grand, how energetic it appears! how beautifully Shakspeare has represented what forms the tie of the different sexes, *courage* and *weakness!* When Othello protests before the Senate of Venice, that the only art which he had employed to win the affections of Desdemona were the perils to which he had been exposed;* how every word he utters is felt by the female sex; their hearts acknowledge it all to be true. They know that it is not flattery, in which consists the powerful art of men to make themselves beloved, but the kind protection which they may afford the timid object of their choice; the glory which they may reflect upon their feeble life, is their most irresistible charm.

The manners and customs of the English relating to the existence of women, were not yet settled in the time of Shakspeare; political troubles had been a great hindrance to social habits. The rank which women held in tragedy, was then absolutely at the will of the author: therefore, Shakspeare, in speaking of them, sometimes uses the most noble language, that can be inspired by love, and at other times the lowest taste that was popular. This genius, given by passion, was inspired by it, as the priests were by their gods: they gave out oracles when they were agitated; but were no more than men, when calm.

Those pieces taken from the English history, such as the two upon Henry IV., that upon Henry V., and the three upon Henry VI., have an unlimited success in England: nevertheless I believe them to be much inferior in general to his tragedies of invention, 'King Lear,' 'Macbeth,' 'Hamlet,' Romeo and Juliet,' &c. The irregularities of time and place are much more remarkable. In short Shakspeare gives up to the popular taste in these, more than in any other of his works. The discovery of the press necessarily diminished the condescension of authors to the national taste: they paid more respect to the general opinion of Europe; and though it was of the greatest importance that those pieces which were to be played should meet with success at the representation, since a means was found out of extending their fame to other nations; the writers took more pains to shun those illusions and pleasantries which could please only the people of their own nation. The English, however, were very backward in submitting to the general good taste; their liberty being founded more upon national pride than philosophical ideas, they rejected every thing that came from strangers, both in literature and politics.

Before it would be possible to judge of the effects of an English tragedy, which might be proper for the French stage; an examination remains to be made, which is, to distinguish in the pieces of Shakspeare, that which was written to please the people; the real faults which he committed; and those spirited beauties which the severe rules of the French tragedies exclude from their stage.

The crowd of spectators in England require that comic scenes should succeed tragic effects. The contrast of what is noble with that which is not, as I have observed before, always produces a disagreeable impression upon men of taste. A noble style must have shades; but a too glaring opposition is nothing more than fantasticalness. That play upon words, those licentious equivocations, popular tales, and that string of proverbs, which are handed down from generation to generation, and are, as one may say, the patrimonial ideas of the common people; all these are applauded by the multitude, and censured by reason. These have no connection with the sublime effects which Shakspeare drew from simple words and common circumstances artfully arranged, which the French most absurdly would fear to bring upon their stage.

* What charming verses are those which terminate the justification of Othello, and which La harpe has so ably translated into truth!

'She lov'd me for the dangers I had pass'd;
And I lov'd her, that she did pity them.'—
Shakspeare.

'Elle aima mes malheurs, et j'aimai sa pitie.'
La Harpe

Shakspeare, when he wrote the parts of vulgar minds in his tragedies, sheltered himself from the judgment of taste by rendering himself the object of popular admiration: he then conducted himself like an able chief, but not like a good writer.

The people of the north existed during many centuries, in a state that was at once both social and barbarous; which left for a long time the vestiges of the *rude* and *ferocious*. Traces of this recollection are to be found in many of Shakspeare's characters, which are painted in the style that was most admired in those ages, in which they only lived for combats, physical power, and military courage.

We may also perceive in Shakspeare some of the ignorance of his century with regard to the principles of literature; his powers are superior to the Greek tragedies for the philosophy of the passions, and the knowledge of mankind:* but he was inferior to many with regard to the perfection of the art. Shakspeare may be reproached with incoherent images, prolixity, and useless repetitions: but the attention of the spectators in those days was too easily captivated, that the author should be very strict with himself. A dramatic poet, to attain all the perfection his talents will permit, must neither be judged by impaired age, nor by youth, who find the source of emotion within themselves.

The French have often condemned the scenes of horror represented by Shakspeare; not because they excited an emotion too strong, but because they sometimes destroyed the theatrical illusion. They certainly appear to me susceptible of criticism. In the first place, there are certain situations which are only frightful; and the bad imitators of Shakspeare wishing to represent them, produced nothing more than a disagreeable invention, without any of the pleasures which the tragedy ought to produce: and again, there are many situations really affecting in themselves, which nevertheless require stage effect to amuse the attention, and of course the interest.

When the governor of the tower, in which the young Arthur is confined, orders a red-hot iron to be brought, to put out his eyes; without speaking of the atrociousness of such a scene, there must pass upon the stage an action, the imitation of which is impossible, and the attention of the audience is so much taken up with the execution of it, that the moral effect is quite forgotten.

The character of Caliban, in the 'Tempest,' is singularly original: but the almost animal figure, which his dress must give him, turns the attention from all that is philosophical in the conception of this part.

In reading 'Richard III.,' one of the beauties is what he himself says of his natural deformity. One can feel that the horror which he causes, ought to act reciprocally upon his own mind, and render it yet more atrocious. Nevertheless, can there be any thing difficult in an elevated style, or more nearly allied to ridicule, than the imitation of an ill-shaped man upon the stage? Every thing in nature may interest the mind; but upon the stage, the illusion of sight must be treated with the most scrupulous caution, or every serious effect will be irreparably destroyed.

Shakspeare also represented physical sufferings much too often. Philoctetes is the only example of any theatrical effect being produced by it; and in this instance, it was the heroic cause of his wounds that fixed the attention of the spectators. Physical sufferings may be related, but cannot be represented. It is not the author, but the actor, who cannot express himself with grandeur; it is not the ideas, but the senses, which refuse to lend their aid to this style of imitation.

In short, one of the greatest faults which Shakspeare can be accused of, is his want of simplicity in the intervals of his sublime passages. When he is not exalted, he is affected; he wanted the art of sustaining himself, that is to say, of being as natural in his scenes of transition, as he was in the grand movements of the soul.

Otway, Rowe, and some other English poets, Addison excepted, all wrote their tragedies in the style of Shakspeare: and Otway's 'Venice Preserved,' almost equalled his model. But the two most truly tragical situations ever conceived by men, were first portrayed by Shakspeare:—madness caused by misfortune, and misfortune abandoned to solitude and itself.

Ajax is furious; Orestes is pursued by the anger o the gods; Phædra is consumed by the fever of love. but Hamlet, Ophelia, and King Lear, with different situations and different characters, have all, nevertheless, the same marks of derangement: it is distress alone that speaks in them; every idea of common life disappears before this predominant one: they are alive to nothing but affection; and this affecting delirium of a suffering object seems to set it free from that timidity which forbids us to expose ourselves without reserve to the eyes of pity. The spectators would perhaps refuse their sympathy to voluntary complaints; but they readily yield to the emotion which arises from a grief that cannot answer for itself. Insanity, as portrayed by Shakspeare, is the finest picture of the shipwreck of moral nature, when the storm of life surpasses its strength.

It may be a question, whether the theatre of republican France, like the English theatre, will now admit of their heroes being painted with all their foibles, the virtues with their inconclusiveness, and common circumstances connected with elevated situations? In short, will the tragic characters be taken from recollection, from human life, or from the *beautiful ideal?*—This is a question which I propose to discuss after having spoken of the tragedies of Racine and Voltaire. I shall also examine, in the second part of this work, the influence which the French revolution is likely to have upon literature.

CHAPTER XIV.

OF ENGLISH PLEASANTRY.

We may distinguish many kinds of pleasantry in the literature of every country; and nothing is better adapted to give an insight into the manners of a nation, than the character of gayety generally adopted by its writers. People are serious when alone: and they are gay for others, especially in their writings; but they can excite laughter only by such ideas as are so familiar to those who listen to them, that they strike at the first instant, without the least effort of attention.

Although pleasantry cannot so easily pass in the esteem of a nation as a philosophical work; it is necessarily submitted, like every thing else appertaining to the mind, to the judgment of universal good taste. It requires no little ingenuity to account for the causes of comic effect; but it is by no means less true, that the general assent must be obtained for *chefs-d'œuvre* in this kind, as well as in all others.

The gayety which owes its birth to the inspiration of taste and genius, and that which is produced by the combination of understanding, and that species of it

* Among the great number of philosophical traits which are remarked even in the least celebrated works of Shakspeare, there is one with which I was singularly struck. In that piece entitled Measure for Measure, Lucien, the friend of Claudius, and brother to Isabella, presses her to go and sue for his pardon to the Governor Angelo, who had condemned this brother to die. Isabella, young and timid, answers, that she fears it would be useless; that Angelo was too much irritated, and would be inflexible, &c. Lucien insists, and says to her,

> ——Our doubts are traitors,
> And make us lose the good we might win
> By fearing to attempt.

Who can have lived in a revolution and not be sensible of the truth of these words?

which the English call *humor*, have scarcely any connection the one with the other; nor have I included constitutional gayety in any of those already mentioned; because a great number of examples have proved, that it is no way connected with the talent of lively writing. Sprightliness may be easily assumed by every man who is endowed with wit; but it must be the genius of one man, and the good taste of many, to inspire genuine comedy.

I shall, in the subsequent chapter, endeavor to discover why the French only could attain that perfection of taste, grace, and quick penetration into the human heart, which produced the best works of Moliere: but at present let us search into the reason why the manners of the English are so opposite to the true genius of gayety.

Most part of the inhabitants of England, entirely engrossed by business, seek pleasure merely as a relaxation: and as hunger that is excited by fatigue, renders the appetite less difficult to please: so the English relish any thing that is presented to them: continual labor, whether mental or corporeal, disposes the mind to be contented with every kind of diversion. The severity of their religious ideas, their serious occupations, their domestic life, and their heavy atmosphere, render the English very liable to the malady of *ennui*: and it is for this reason, that the delicate amusements of the mind are not sufficient for them; they require some animated diversions to rouse them from their dejection:—and their authors either partake of the taste of the spectators, or conform themselves to it.

It requires an accurate observation of characters, to compose a good comedy. In order to develop the comic genius, it is necessary to live a great deal in society; to attach a great importance to the success they may meet with, in society: they must also know how to connect that multitude of interests which have their source in vanity, and which give vigor to every shaft of ridicule, as well as to every combination of self-love. The English are generally retired in their own families, or collected in public assemblies for the discussion of national affairs. The intermediate state called *society*, hardly exists among them: nevertheless, it is in this frivolous space of life that the refinements of taste are formed.

The English have not among themselves one comic author that can be compared to Moliere: and even if they did possess one, they would not be able fully to appreciate his merit. In such pieces as 'L'Avare,' 'Le Tartuffe,' 'Le Misanthrope,' which represent human nature as it is in all countries, there are many instances of delicate pleasantness and shades of self-love, which the English would not even perceive: they would not recognize themselves in such a piece, however natural it might be: they do not even imagine that they might be thus minutely described; their strong passions and important occupations make them consider life more generally.

There is to be found in Congreve a great deal of pleasantry and penetrating wit: but we never meet with one natural sentiment. By a most singular contradiction, the more simplicity and purity there are in the private manners of the English; the more they exaggerate the picture of vice in their comedies. The obscenity of Congreve's plays could never have been tolerated on the French theatre: we find in the dialogue many ingenious ideas; but the manners which they represent, were taken from some of the worst kind of French novels, which never in the smallest degree painted the manners of the French. Nothing can resemble the English less than their comedies. One would think that, intending to be gay, they had thought it necessary to depart as much as possible from their natural character; or that such was their profound respect for those sentiments which constituted the happiness of domestic life, that they held them too sacred to admit of their being lavished upon the stage.

Congreve, and many of his imitators, heaped up immoralities without number, as well as without resemblance: their pictures are of no consequence with a nation such as the English, who amuse themselves with them as they would with tales or fantastical images of a world that was not their own. But the French comedies, in painting the real manners and customs of the times, might have an influence over them; for which reason, it becomes of the utmost consequence to impose severe rules on authors.

We rarely find, in the English comedies, characters which truly resemble the English; perhaps the dignity of a free people opposes with the English, as it did with the Romans, the representation of their manners upon the theatre: but the French willingly amuse themselves with their own foibles. Shakspeare, and some others, represented in their pieces some popular characters, such as Falstaff, Pistol, &c.; but they were so overcharged as almost entirely to exclude every resemblance. The common people of all nations are amused with vulgar pleasantries; but it is only in France where the most satirical gayety is at the same time the most delicate.

Mr Sheridan is the author of some comedies, in which the most brilliant and original wit appears in almost every scene. But, besides that *one* exception changes nothing in the general consideration, we must still make a distinction between a lively turn of mind and that species of gayety of which Moliere is the model. An author of my country who is capable of conceiving a great number of ideas, is sure of acquiring the art of opposing them in an agreeable manner to each other: but as the antitheses are not composed solely of eloquence, the contrasts are not the only secrets of gayety; and there is in the gayety of some of the French authors something at once the most natural, and the most inexplicable: the *thought* may be analyzed, but it is not produced by thought alone; it is a sort of electricity, communicated by the general spirit of the nation.

Gayety and eloquence are only connected so far as an involuntary inspiration carries the writer or the speaker to any degree of perfection in the one or the other. The spirit of the nation in which we live, develops the power of persuasion or of pleasantry much better than study and reflection can do. Sensations are produced from without; and every talent that depends immediately upon the sensations, requires an impulse from others. Gayety and eloquence are not the simple results of combination: to obtain success in talents of this sort, we must be agitated, we must be modified by the emotion from which either the one or the other might arise. But the disposition of the English in general, does not excite their writers to any species of gayety.

Swift, in his 'Gulliver,' and his 'Tale of a Tub,' like Voltaire in his works of philosophy, drew some of his most happy pleasantries from the opposition existing betwixt received errors and proscribed truths, betwixt institutions and the nature of things. The illusions, the allegories, the fictions of the mind, and all the disguises which it assumes, are so many combinations from which gayety may be produced; and, in every kind of style, the efforts of thought go a great way, though they can never amount to the facility of habit, or the unexpected happiness of spontaneous impressions.

Nevertheless, there is in some of the English writings a sort of gayety which has every character of originality and nature. To express this same gayety, which arises from the constitution nearly as much as from the mind, the English language has created a word, and called it *humor:* it is entirely dependent upon the climate, and the national manners; and would be altogether inimitble, where the same causes tended to develop it. Certain pieces of Fielding and Swift, 'Peregrine Pickle,' 'Roderick Random,' but more especially Sterne's works, give a complete idea of the style called *humor*.

There is a moroseness, I could almost say a gloominess, in this sort of gayety: the person who makes you smile, does not himself feel the smallest degree of the pleasure he communicates to others: you may easily perceive that he was melancholy when he wrote, and that he would be almost angry with you for being amused. But as praise is sometimes the more agreeable for being given under a rough form; so the gayety of pleasantry may receive an addition from the gravity of its author. The English very seldom admit upon their stage that style of *humor:* it would not have a theatrical effect.

There is a degree of misanthropy in the pleasantry of the English; and a sociability in that of the French: the one should be read when alone; the other strikes most amidst a number of auditors. What the English have of gayety, conducts almost always to a philosophical or moral result; that of the French has often no aim but pleasure: the English shine most in portraying whimsical characters: because there are a great many amongst themselves. Society does away singularities, but a retired life preserves them all.

There is seldom any quickness of perception in minds that are constantly employed on some material object. What is really useful, is easy to comprehend. A country where equality prevails, is also less sensible to the faults of uniformity: the nation being at unity with itself, its writers naturally accustom themselves to address their works to the judgment and sentiments of all classes; in short, every free country is and ought to be serious.

When the government is founded upon force, it has no occasion to fear a national turn for pleasantry, but when the authority depends upon the general confidence, and when the public is the principal spring; the talent and gayety which discover the ridicule, and delight in criticism, become exceedingly dangerous to liberty and political equality. We have spoken of the misfortunes of the Athenians which resulted from their immoderate love of pleasantry; and France would have furnished another example to the support of the first, if the great events of the revolution had left the national character to its natural development,

CHAPTER XV.

OF THE IMAGINATION OF THE ENGLISH IN THEIR POETRY AND NOVELS.

The invention of incidents, and the faculty of feeling and painting nature, are talents which are absolutely distinct: the one belongs more particularly to the literature of the east, and the other to that of the north. I have, I think, developed the different causes: what remains to be examined, is the particular character of the poetic imagination of the English.

The English have not invented any new subjects of poetry, like Tasso and Ariosto; neither are there romances founded upon marvelous incidents and supernatural events, like the Arabian and Persian tales; they still preserve a few images indeed of the religion of the north, but not a brilliant and various mythology like that of the Greeks: their poets however, have an inexhaustible fund of those sentiments and ideas which arise from the spectacle of nature. Supernatural events are limited; and are at most but circumscribed combinations, not susceptible of the progression which belongs to moral truths of every description. When the poets attach themselves to dress their philosophical ideas with the colors of the imagination, they in some measure enter that path in which enlightened men are continually advancing, unless a stop is put to their career by ignorance and tyranny.

The English, separated from the continent, have had but little connection at any period with the history and manners of their neighbors: they have a character peculiar to themselves in every style; their poetry does not resemble that of the French, nor even that of the Germans; but they have not attained the inventive excellence, both in fable and poetical incident, which was the principal glory of the Greek and Italian literature.

The English are accurate observers of nature, and know how to paint it; but they have not a creative genius: their superiority consists in the talent of expressing in a lively manner what they see and what they feel; they have the art of uniting philosophical reflections with the feelings excited by the beauties of the country. The aspect of the earth and sky, at all hours of the day or night, awakens in onr minds numberless different sensations; and those who give themselves up to ideas inspired by nature, will experience a series of the most pure and elevated impressions, always analogous to those deep reflections on morality and religion by which man is connected with futurity.

At the revival of letters, and at the commencement of English literature, many of the English poets swerved from the national character, to imitate the Italians. Waller and Cowley may be included amongst these: we may also add Donne, Chaucer, &c. The English, however, have been less successful in this style than any other people; they are very deficient in that graceful ease so essential to light writing; they also want that quickness and facility which are to be acquired by being habitually in the society of men whose only aim is pleasure.

Pope's works are peculiarly calculated for models of grace and eloquence; nevertheless there are a great many faults to be found in them, especially in the 'Rape of the Lock.' There is nothing in the world can be more tedious than Spenser's 'Fairy Queen.' The poem of 'Hudibras,' although spirited and witty, is filled with pleasantries which are lengthened out even to satiety. Gay's 'Fables' are witty but not natural Nor can any of the fugitive pieces of the English be compared with the writings of Voltaire, Ariosto, or La Fontaine. But it is not enough to know the affecting language of the passions; it is surely unnecessary to set a great value upon the rest.

How sublime are the *meditations* of the English! how fruitful in those sentiments which are developed by solitude! What profound philosophy is found in the 'Essay on Man!' It is possible that the mind or the imagination can be raised to a higher degree of elevation than in the 'Paradice Lost?' It is not the poetic invention which is the merit of this piece; the subject is almost entirely taken from the book of Genesis. But the allegory which the author was introduced in many places, is censured by taste; and we may often perceive that the poet is restrained and directed by his submission to orthodoxy. But what rendered Milton one of the greatest poets in the world, was the imposing grandeur of his character—the poetry we so much admire, was inspired by the wish of rendering the images equal to the conception of the understanding. It was to make his intellectual ideas understood, that the poet had recourse to the most terrible pictures that can strike the imagination. Before he gave form to Satan, he conceived him immaterial: he represented to himself his moral nature; he then accorded it with that gigantic figure, and the horrors of the place he inhabited. With what an infinity of talent he transports you from this hell into paradise! with what art he conducts you through the delightful paths of youth, nature and innocence! It is not the happiness of animated enjoyments; it is tranquillity which he contrasts wit crime, and the opposition appears still the greater The piety of Adam and Eve, the primitive difference of their characters and their destinies, are painted as philosophy and imgination ought to to have characterized them.*

Gray's 'Elegy in a country church-yard,' the 'Epistle upon Eaton College,' and Goldsmith's 'Deserted Village,' are filled with that noble melancholy which is the majesty of sensible philosophy. Where can we find more poetical enthusiasm than in Dryden's 'Ode to Music ?' What passion in the letters of Eloise ! Can there be a more charming picture of love in marriage, than that which terminates the first ode of Thomson upon Spring ?

What deep awful meditations in Young's 'Night Thoughts ;' where man is described as reflecting upon the progress and termination of his existence ; deprived of that happy illusion which leads us to feel an interest in the day before us, as well as in a century to come ; in the events of the present time, as well as in a speculation upon eternity ! Young judges of human life as if he did not belong to it ; his thoughts seem to have risen above himself, to search for an imperceptible spot in the immensity of the creation, where he might observe, himself unseen.

——————What is the world ?—a grave :
Where is the dust which has not been alive ?

And again,

——————What is life ?—a war,
Eternal war with woe,

This gloomy imagination, though more apparent in Young, is nevertheless the general color of the English poetry. If we find a monotony in Ossian on account of his images, which have little variety of themselves, not being interspersed with reflections that can interest the mind ; we cannot make the same complaint of the English poets ; they never fatigue, by giving way to their philosophical sadness ; it perfectly accords with the nature of our being, and even with its destiny. There is nothing can cause a more agreeable sensation, than to be able to read ourselves into the habitual course of our reflections : and if we were to recall the particular passages of any writings in any language, we shall find that they have almost all the same character of elevation and melancholy.

It may be asked, why the English, who are so happy in their government, and in their customs and manners, should have so much more melancholy in their disposition than the French ? The reason is, that liberty and virtue, the greatest result of the human reason require meditation ; and that meditation naturally conducts the mind to serious objects.

In France, persons distinguished either by their sense or their rank had, in general, a great deal of gayety : but the gayety of the first classes in society is not a sign of the happiness of the nation. In order that the political and philosophical state of a nation should answer the intentions of nature, the lot of the middling class should be the happiest ; those men who are superior in style, should be entirely devoted, and sacrifice every selfish interest, to the general good of the human species.

Happy is the country where the authors are melancholy, the merchants satisfied, the rich gloomy, and where the middling class of people are contented !

The English language, although not so harmonious or pleasing to the ear as the language of the east, has nevertheless, by the energy of its sound, a very great advantage in poetry : every word that is strongly accented, has an effect upon the mind, because it seems to come from a lively impression. The French language excludes from poetry a number of words as being too simple, which are really noble in English, from the manner in which they are articulated. I shall offer one example, When Macbeth, at the moment he is going to seat himself at the festive table, sees the place that was destined for him filled by the shade of Banquo, whom he had just assassinated, he exclaims with terror, '*The table is full !*' and all the spectators tremble. If these same words were to be repeated in French, '*La table est remplie* ;' the greatest actor in the world could not make the audience forget their common acceptation :—the French pronunciation does not admit of that accent which enobles every word by giving it animation.

The English poets, however, often take an undue advantage of the facility of their language and the genius of their nation : they exaggerate their images, they refine their ideas, they exhaust what they express, and taste does not warn them when to stop. But *much will be forgiven them* on account of the sincerity of their emotions. We judge of the faults of their writings as those of nature, and not as those of art.

The English have a great pre-eminence in a style of writing which they call *novels* ; these are entirely works of the imagination, without historical allusions, and without allegory ; founded, in general, upon the characters and events of private life. Love has till now been the subject of this sort of writing ; and the rank which women hold in England, is the principal cause of the inexhaustible fertility of these writings.

In no country whatever have the women enjoyed so much of that happiness which arises from domestic affection, as in England. We often find a great purity of manners in countries that are poor, and especially among the middling class of the people : but it belongs to the first class to set the example ; it is they alone who can choose their way of life, the others are forced to resign themselves to the one which is imposed on them by destiny : and when the mind is brought to the exercise of virtue by unpleasant circumstances, or personal privations, it is never accompanied with all the idea and sentiment which spring from that virtue which is the effect of choice. It is then, in general, the manners of the first class of society which influence the literature ; and when they are good, they are a preservation to love, and love is the inspirer of novels. Without stopping here to examine philosophically the destiny of women in the social order ; it is certain that, in general, their domestic virtues alone obtain from the men all the tenderness of which their parts are capable.

But although the women in England may be beloved, they are very far from enjoying those pleasures of society which France formerly afforded to the fair sex. But it is not from a picture of the enjoyments of self-love that an interesting novel can be composed ; although the history of life too often proves that many can be contented with such. The English manners furnish a great number of delicate shades and affecting situations for novels. One would be apt to imagine at first, that immorality, knowing no bounds, would give a wider scope for romantic invention ; but, on the contrary, we perceive that unfortunate facility to be barren and unfruitful. Passions without opposition sacrifices without regret, and connections without delicacy, take from novels their every charm : the small number of this kind possessed by the French, had scarcely any success, even in the societies which had served them for models.

The English novels, like all their other writings, are spun out to a great length ; but they are calculated for those who have adopted that style of life which

* ——————though both
Not equal, as their sexes not equal :
For contemplation he, and valor form'd ;
For softness she, and sweet attractive grace :
He for God only, she for God in him.

they represent; for those who lived retired in the country in the bosom of their families, for the leisure which they can spare from their regular occupations and domestic duties. If it were possible the French could support all that useless minuteness which is accumulated in those writings, it could only be from that curiosity which is inspired by the manners and customs of foreigners; they never tolerate any thing of that kind in their own works; in fact, those great lengths sometimes destroy the interest. But the English have a method of exciting interest by a series of just and moral observations upon the natural affections of life: attention is every thing with them, whether to describe what they see, or to discover what they seek.

'Tom Jones,' cannot be considered simply a novel; the abundance of philosophical ideas, the hypocrisy of society, and the contrast of natural qualities, are brought into action with an infinity of art; and love, as I have observed before,* it is only a vehicle to introduce all these.

But Richardson stands first in rank; and after his writings are an infinity of novels, the most part of which are the productions of female pens: these give a perfect idea of this sort of writing which is so inexpressibly interesting.

The old French novels are filled with the adventures of chivalry, which do not in the least recall the events of life. Rousseau's 'Eloise' is an elegant and eloquent composition: but it only characterizes the genius of one man, and not the manners of a nation: all the other French novels that we admire, we owe to the imitation of the English; the subjects are not the same; but the manner of treating them, and their general character, belong exclusively to the English writers. They first ventured to imagine that the pictures of private affections were sufficient to interest the mind and the heart of man; that neither elevation of character, nor the importance of rank, nor the marvelous in events, were necessary to captivate the imagination: they thought that the power of love was sufficient to renovate incessantly both the picture and the situation without occasioning satiety. In short, it was the English who first composed works of morality under the form of novels, where an obscure though virtuous destiny might find motives of exaltation, and create for itself a sort of heroism.

There reigns throughout these writings a calm and proud sensibility, at once energetic and affecting: we can no where better feel the charm of that protecting love, which exempts the feeble being from watching over her own destiny, and concentrates all her esteem and affection in the tenderness of her defender!

CHAPTER XVI.

OF THE PHILOSOPHY AND ELOQUENCE OF THE ENGLISH.

The political situation of the English is distinguished by three particular epochs: namely, that preceding the revolution, the revolution itself, and the constitution which they have possessed since the year 1688: the character of their literature must necessarily have varied with circumstances. Prior to the revolution, we meet with but one philosopher, the great Chancellor Bacon: Theology entirely absorbed the years during which the revolution actually lasted: and poetry almost exclusively occupied the men of genius under the despotic and voluptuous reign of Charles II. It is only from the year 1688, since which time a steady constitution has given repose and liberty to England, that we can observe with any certitude the order of events.

* Essay on Fictions

The writings of Bacon characterize his own genius, but not that of his country. He rushed alone into the field of sciences, sometimes obscure, sometimes scholastic: he nevertheless brought to light new ideas upon every subject, but never completed any thing. The man of genius may take a few steps in unknown paths, but it requires the united efforts of centuries, and of nations, to open the greatroad of science. The religious quarrels of the seventeenth century would have kept England in that state from which all Europe had been just emancipated, had not the knowledge which already existed in many countries, and even in England itself, risen in opposition to those vain disputes. Harrington, Sidney, and others, indifferent to theological questions, strenuously exerted themselves to re-unite men's minds to the principles of liberty; and their efforts were not entirely lost upon reason.

In short, at the end of the seventeenth century, the English philosophy assumed its real character; which it has sustained for a hundred years with increasing success.

The English philosophy is scientific; that is to say, the writers apply to moral ideas that kind of abstraction, those calculations and developments, which the learned make use of to arrive at discoveries, and to explain them.

The French philosophy belongs more to the *imagination* and to *sentiment*, but without being less profound; for these two faculties, when directed by reason, enlighten and assist the understanding to penetrate deeper into the knowledge of the human heart.

The Christian religion, such as it is professed in England, and the constitutional principles, such as they are established, give a great latitude to the researches of thought, either in morals or in politics: nevertheless, the English philosophers in general do not allow themselves to examine every thing; the *useful*, which is the main-spring of all their efforts, interdicts to a certain degree their independence. They have, it is true, developed in a superior manner the metaphysical theory of the faculties of man; but they have less knowledge of the character and the passions. Bruyere, the Cardinal De Retz, and Montaigne, have no equal among the English.

The English have treated politics as a science wholly intellectual. Hobbes, Fergusson, Locke, and others, searched, through different systems, to find out what was the primitive state of society, in order to arrive at the knowledge of what laws should be instituted for men. Smith, Hume, and Shaftesbury, studied sentiments and characters in a point of view almost entirely metaphysical; they wrote for instruction and meditation, but did not seem to think it necessary to captivate the interest, even while they solicited the attention. Montesquieu seems to give life to ideas, and, amidst the abstractions of the mind, recalls in each line the moral nature of man. The French writers, having always the tribunal of society present to their imagination, study to obtain the approbation of readers who are soon fatigued, by uniting the charms of sentiment to the analysis of ideas, and thus exhibit at one view a greater number of truths.

The English have made the same progress in the philosophical sciences, as they have in their commercial industry, by the aid of time and patience. The inclination of their philosophers for things in the abstract, might have drawn them into systems contrary to reason, had not the spirit of calculation regulated their application to abstract combinations; morality, the most experimental of all human ideas, commercial interest, and the love of liberty, always brought back the English philosophers to a practical result. How many works have they undertaken for the service of mankind, for the education of children, the relief of the unfortunate, the criminal legislation, the political economy, for the sciences, for morals, for metaphysics! what philosophy in every conception! and what respect for experience in the choice of the means!

And all this emulation and wisdom was owing to the enjoyment of liberty. But in France, the writers could so seldom flatter themselves with influencing the institutions of their country by their writings, that even in the most serious discussions, they only thought of showing a superiority of understanding. In consequence of which, systems that would have been right in some respects, were carried even to paradoxes; and reason not being able to produce any useful effect, they wished at least that their paradox should be brilliant. Besides, under an absolute monarchy, they might have spoken in praise of *pure* democracy, like Rousseau in his Social Contract; but no one would have dared to have sported ideas nearer the reality. All was wit and conceit in France, *except* the decrees of the king's council; while, in England, every one might say as he thought proper with regard to the resolutions of their representatives; and by this habit of comparing thoughts with actions, they accustom themselves to the love of public good, and to the hopes of being able to contribute towards it.

This principle of usefulness, if I may so express myself, which gave so much energy to the English literature, was nevertheless an hindrance to their arriving at that conciseness of style justly esteemed one of the greatest perfections of the art which the French have attained. Most of the English works are confused through prolixity. The patriotism which reigns in England, inspires a kind of family-interest for all questions of *general utility*. An Englishman feels himself as much interested in them, as in his own private affairs, and will be as long entertained in discussing them; but the authors, confiding in this disposition, often abuse the liberty which it gives. The English analyze all their ideas with as much minuteness as a tutor makes use of when addressing his pupils. This may possibly be the better means of disseminating knowledge among the people in general: but the philosophical method cannot in this way attain the summit of its perfection.

The French would compose a better work than the English; they would present the same ideas with more order and precision; and as they suppress much of the intermediate matter, their works require more attention in order to be understood; but the classification of ideas gains as much, whether from the rapidity with which they are expressed, or from the direct way through which the mind is led on. In England, fame is at first almost always acquired from the suffrages of the multitude: which afterwards they obtain from the superior classes. In France it always began with the superior classes; and from them descended to the multitude. I shall not examine which is preferable for the happiness of a nation; but I am certain that the art of writing, and the method of composing, cannot arrive to that perfection in England that it ought to have done in France, when authors looked almost exclusively to the first ranks of their country for approbation.

In England, authors either devote themselves to abstract systems, or researches which have some positive and practical utility in view; but this intermediate style, which unites reflection and eloquence, instruction and interest, fanciful expressions and just ideas, is scarcely known by the English: their productions have only a single aim, to be either useful or agreeable.

The English are great writers in verse, and carry eloquence of mind to the highest degree; but their works in prose scarcely partake of that life and energy which are found in their poetry. Blank-verse presenting very little difficulty, the English reserve for their poetry all that belongs to the imagination; they consider prose but as the language of logic: the only object of their style is to make their arguments understood, and not to create an interest by their expressions. The English language has not yet acquired that degree of perfection of which it is susceptible. As it has more often been employed in commercial affairs than in literature, it has never been displayed in all its shades of variety: and in any language much more correctness and refinement are required to write well in prose, than to write good verse.

Some English authors, however, such as Bolingbroke, Shaftesbury, and Addison, are reputed as good writers in prose: nevertheless, their images are deficient in energy, and their style in originality. The character of the writer is not imprinted in his style, nor his internal emotions felt by his readers. It seems as if the English feared to give too much scope to their fancy, except in their poetic inspiration: when they write in prose, a sort of *modesty* or *bashfulness* seems to keep their sentiments in capivity.

The English transport themselves into the ideal world of poetry; but we seldom or ever find any animation in their writing upon existing subjects. The French authors are justly reproached with their egotism, their vanity, and the importance which each one attaches to his own person, in a country where the *public* interest holds no place. But it is nevertheless certain that an author, in order to acquire eloquence, must express his own sentiments: it is not his interest but his emotion, it is not his self-love but his character, that must animate his writings.

In England, the spirit of business is applied to the principles of literature, and all appeal to the feelings and every thing that can in the least influence the judgment is interdicted in those works of reason. Mr Burke, the most violent enemy of France, has, in his work against that country, some resemblance to the eloquence of the French; and although he had many admirers in England, there are some who are tempted to accuse his *style* of bombast, as much as his *opinions*, and to find his manner of writing incompatible with justice.

The Letters of Junius are the most eloquent productions in the English prose: perhaps too, the principal cause of the great pleasure attached to this work, is the admiration which is felt for the liberty of a country, where the ministry, and even the king himself, might be thus attacked without disturbing in the least the public tranquillity or the organization of society, or yielding to the depositaries of public power the right to withdraw themselves under the most vehement expressions of individual censure.

The parliamentary debates are more animated than the style of any English author in prose: the necessity of the extempore, the subject of the debates, the opposition, the retort, and, in short, every thing appertaining to them excites an interest and causes an agitation that may hurry away the orators: nevertheless, argument is always the principal character of parliamentary discourse. But the popular eloquence of the ancients, and that of the first French orators, would produce in the House of Commons more astonishment than conviction. We will now take a cursory view of the causes of these differences.

The English revolution, which was occasioned by theological disputes, must have set every popular passion into motion. Eloquence, therefore, at this period, instead of receiving any great impulse, naturally took the form of argumentation agreeably to the nature of the subjects it treated on. The commercial and financial intererests were the first objects of all the English Parliaments; and every time that they were called upon to discourse with men upon the calculation of their interest, it was by argument alone that they obtained their confidence. The diplomatical situation of Europe was another subject of parliamentary debate, which required the greatest circumspection from its importance. The two parties which divided the parliament, did not contest, like the plebeians and patricians, with all the passions of men; there was generally some rivalry of individuals couched under the ambition that excited them. They were debates in which the opposition, wishing to give to the king a minister of its own party, always, even in their warmest disputes, kept up the respect that was necessary to obtain the aim which they had in view. The point of honor also prescribed bouuds to the violence of personal attacks. In short, the moderns have in general a respect for the laws, which must also in some measure change the character of their eloquence. Although there were laws enacted in the time of the ancients, popular authority had often both the will and the power to destroy and create them anew at their pleasure: while the moderns were generally constrained to comment upon the laws actually existing. Without pretending to deny the advantage of this constraint, it nevertheless follows that the spirit of discussion and analysis are of less weight in our present assemblies, than the talent of persuasion.

The logic of the orator, in the room of wrestling with men, like Demosthenes, should attack them with more suitable arms, the effect of which would be more indirect. A representative government necessarily draws into a narrow compass the objects which are discussed, and the number of those who are addressed; the eloquence of Demosthenes would bear no proportion with the auditory and the topic under discussion. The witnesses *known* and *counted*, by which the English orators* are surrounded; the table upon which they uniformly mark the repetition of the same arguments; every thing, in short, must remind them of a council of state rather than a popular assembly; and they must feel themselves engaged to make use of no other weapons than those of cool firmness, *argument*, or irony.

Many of the causes which I have mentioned, may be equally applied to the representative government of France; but the first epochs of the revolution offered subjects of antiquity for the discussion of its orators. Mirabeau, and some others after him, used a style of eloquence more attractive than that of the English: the habits of business are there less perceptible, and the successes of the mind much more so. Long developments will ever be less tolerated in France than in England.

The English orators, like Cicero, often repeat the same ideas, and frequently recur to the same eloquence which has been before employed with success: but the French are so jealous of the admiration they express, that if the orator wished to obtain applause twice upon the same sentiment, or the same happiness of expression, the auditors would reproach him with a consequential confidence, and would not only refuse a second acknowledgment of his talent, but would almost believe that they had not given it him at first.

This disposition in the French must elevate real talents to the highest degree; but it draws mediocrity into the most ridiculous and gigantic efforts: it also but too often favors, in a lamentable degree, the success of the most absurd assertions. If an argument is prolonged, its errors will be more easily discovered: if it could be refuted by those forms under which elementary truths are developed, the most common capacity would at least understand the object of the question. The English dialect is much less proper than that of the French for the success of sophisms; the declamatory style, which is so favorable to erroneous ideas, is seldom admitted by the English, the language of prose having arrived at a much higher degree of perfection in France than in England; the French orators who are truly eloquent, have a greater command over the human passions, and have the art of uniting a greater variety of talents in the same discourse. The English consider the art of speaking in the same point of view as they consider every other talent, *that of usefulness;* and this is what must occur in every nation after a certain time of repose founded upon liberty.

But the repose founded upon despotism produces a contrary effect; it leaves in existence the active principles of individual self-love, and renders the mind indifferent to nothing but the national interest: while the political importance of each citizen in a free country is such, that he holds in greater estimation his share of the public happiness than any personal advantages that would not serve to the benefit of the whole.

* The orator of the opposition party, not being engaged in the direction of affairs, is generally more eloquent than the minister; but at this present time, in England, it would be hard to decide between two men of such prodigious talents; nevertheless the inclination more naturally inclines towards the one who **is out of power.**

CHAPTER XVII.

OF GERMAN LITERATURE.

The present century, 1800, gave birth to German literature: prior to that period, the Germans had directed their attention very successfully to the sciences and to metaphysics; but their writings, which were more frequently in the Latin than in their native language, exhibited universally a want of originality of character. The same causes that have already conspired to retard the progress of German literature, still oppose themselves in some instances to its perfection.* And it is, moreover, an evident disadvantage to the literature of any nation to be formed at a later period than that of the surrounding countries; as, in such a case, imitative talents too often usurp the place of national genius. Before we proceed further, it may not be improper to consider what are the principal causes that have modified the spirit of literature in Germany, what the peculiar character borne by the works of intrinsic merit it has produced, and to suggest those inconveniences against which its authors ought to be guarded.

The division of the country into petty states, to the exclusion, as it were, of a single capital, in which the resources of the whole nation might concentrate; where all possessed of distinguished talents might be attracted to assemble;—must undoubtedly render it more difficult to acquire and form a discriminating taste in Germany than in France. In a number of small spheres, emulation multiplies its endeavors; but neither judgment nor criticism are exacted with severity, when every town can boast of possessing men of talents. It must also be difficult to find a standard for the language, when there are divers universities, and divers academies, equally authorized to decide in literary controversies: for in this case, many writers believe themselves privileged incessantly to coin new words; and confusion must necessarily ensue from such an abundance.

It is, I believe, generally acknowledged that federation is a political system very favorable to happiness and liberty; but it is almost always prejudicial to the greatest possible display of arts and talents; to promote which, taste must have attained perfection. The ha-

* I must here call to remembrance the purport of this work; by no means do I pretend to write an analysis of all the celebrated productions comprehended in the term Literature; I have only endeavored to characterize the general principle of its respective stages, in their relation to, and influence over laws, manners, and religion. It will be naturally supposed, that I could not treat on such a subject without quoting many writers, and many publications; but this I have done merely in support of my own arguments, without any intention of judging and discussing the merits of each author; a task that could not be performed without the aid of an universal library. This observation applies more especially to the present chapter than to any other. Germany abounds with excellent productions which I have passed over in silence, those already mentioned being alone sufficient to demonstrate the truth of the assertions I have advanced respecting the general character of German literature

bitual association of learned men, their union in one common centre, establishes a kind of literary legislature, well calculated to direct others to the most advantageous course of study.

The federal government to which Germany is subjected, deprives that country of the full enjoyment of all the political advantages attached to the federate system: nevertheless the German literature bears that distinguished character which stamps it as the literature of a free people; and the reason of this is evident. The learned there maintain a republic amongst themselves; and in proportion to the abuses introduced by the despotism of rank, they detach themselves from society and from public affairs. They consider all ideas in their natural relations; the institutions existing amongst them are too much in opposition to the simple notions of philosophy, to induce a compliance with them at the expense of their reason.

The English are less independent than the Germans in their general manner of considering whatever relates to religious or political opinions; they find repose and liberty in the order of things adopted by them, and consent to the modification of some philosophical principles. They respect their own happiness, and dispense with certain prejudices, as a man married to a woman whom he loves, would strenuously maintain the indissolubility of marriage. The philosophers of Germany, encompassed with faulty and imperfect institutions, devoid equally of reason and advantages, devote themselves entirely to a strict search into natural truths. A divided government, without giving political liberty, almost necessarily establishes the liberty of the press.

There can be no prevailing religion, nor prevailing opinion, in a country thus disunited; established powers are supported by the protection of higher powers; but the empire of each respective state over its subjects is extremely limited by opinion: every thing may become a subject of debate, although the possibility of taking active measures may be precluded.

Society also possessing fewer attractions in Germany than in England, its philosophers generally live in solitude; and the interest so warmly excited amongst the English respecting public affairs, is little, if at all, felt by the Germans. Their princes certainly treat men of letters with distinction, and frequently grant them tokens of honor: nevertheless the governments, in general, appoint only their ancient nobles to political departments; and it is moreover a fact, that none but representative governments can possibly inspire all classes of people with a direct interest in public affairs. The minds, therefore, of literary men ought to be directed to the contemplation of nature, and to a knowledge of themselves.

The Germans excel in delineating the tender passions of the mind, and in portraying the sombre scenes of melancholy. In this respect they bear a closer resemblance to the style of Ossian than any other northern writers; but their meditative habits of life inspire them with an enthusiasm for the sublime, and an indignation against the abuses of social order, which protects them from that *ennui* so sensibly felt by the English amongst all the vicissitudes of their career. Enlightened men, in Germany, live only to study; and their minds are self-supported by a kind of internal activity more uniform and more lively than that of the English.

The Germans delight most in the indulgence of their ideas. There is nothing sufficiently great and free in their governments to induce the philosophers to prefer the enjoyments of power to those of reflection; and the ardor of their mind is not damped by a too constant intercourse with mankind.

The German productions are less practically useful than those of the English: they indulge themselves more in systematic combinations; because, having no influence whatever over the institutions of their country by their writings, they abandon themselves, without any object in view, to the sport of their imaginations: and they adopt successively each sect of mystical religion, and beguile, in numberless ways, that time and life which they can only dedicate to meditation. But there is no country whose authors have more successfully dived into the sentiments of impassioned man, the sorrows of the heart, and the philosophical resources which are best calculated to support them. The general character of literature is the same in all the northern countries; but the distinguishing characteristics of that of the Germans spring from the political and religious situation of the country.

One of the most excellent works of the German writers, and which they may justly hold up in opposition to the master-pieces of other languages, is 'Werter.' As it is called a romance, many are ignorant that it is a work of higher consideration: and indeed, I am not acquainted with any production that displays a more striking and natural picture of the wanderings of enthusiasm; a deeper insight into misfortune; in a word, a search into that abyss of nature, where truth displays itself at once to the eye that is capable of discerning it.

The character of 'Werter' cannot be a common one: it discovers, in all their force, the injuries that may accrue to an energetic mind from a bad social order; instances of which are more frequent in Germany than in any other part of the world.

Some have blamed the author of 'Werter' for involving his hero in any other distress than that arising from love; for suffering the world to see that he felt his humiliation; and that he harbored a deep resentment against that pride of rank which caused it. This is however, in my opinion, one of the first traits in the work. Goethe wished to depict a being, suffering through all the various affections of a mind exquisitely sensible and proud: he wished to describe that complicated agony which alone can conduct the human mind to the deepest gulf of despair. Natural evils may still leave us some resource; society must contribute to infuse its poison into the wound, before our reason can be totally subverted, and death become the object of our wishes.

What a sublime union do we find, in 'Werter,' of thought and of sentiment, of the blind impetuosity of passion, and the sober reasonings of philosophy! Rousseau and Goethe alone knew how to paint reflecting passion; passion which judges yet knows that it cannot subdue itself. This search into his own feelings, made even while he is their victim, would have weakened the interest of the work, if described by any but a man of genius. As it is; nothing can be more affecting than this combination of agony and meditation, reasoning and insanity, which portray a miserable man contemplating and reflecting upon his situation, yet sinking under affliction; directing his imagination towards himself, courageously viewing his own sufferings, yet incapable of affording himself consolation or relief.

It has been said, that 'Werter' is a dangerous work; that it exalts the sentiments, instead of directing them, and that some instances of fanaticism which it has excited, are proofs of this assertion. The enthusiasm which it has awakened, particularly in Germany, proceeds from its being written entirely in the national taste. It is not Goethe who has created it, he has only painted it from the life.

Enthusiasm is universally prevalent in Germany; and 'Werter' is favorable to dispositions of that cast. The example of suicide never can become contagious; moreover, it is not the mere incident invented in a romance, but the sentiments conveyed through such a medium, that leave a deep impression: and that malady of the soul which derives its source from too exalted a mind, and eventually renders life hateful; that malady of the soul, I repeat, is perfectly described in 'Werter'

Every man possessed of sensibility and generosity, has at some period or other felt himself infected by it;

and frequently, perhaps, some excellent beings may have questioned themselves, whether life, under its present circumstances, could be supported by the virtuous, if the entire organization of society had not its weight with candid and affectionate dispositions, and did not render existence totally impossible.

The perusal of 'Werter' teaches that the most exalted sentiments, even of honor itself, may lead to insanity; it shows us at what degree sensibility becomes too highly wrought to allow the mind to support even the most natural occurrences. We are warned from our wrong propensities by every reflection, every circumstance, and every moral treatise: but when we know our disposition inclined to candor and sensibility, we trust ourselves implicitly to its guidance, and may be led to the lowest depth of misery without feeling or perceiving the succession of errors that have insensibly conducted us thither.

To characters of this description, the example of 'Werter's' fate is useful; it is a work that makes virtue itself acknowledge the necessity of reason.

Goethe has written many other works of high respect in Germany. Wilhelm Meister's Hermann and Dorothea, &c., the Odes of Klopstock, the Tragedies of Schiller, the writings of Wieland, the dramatic productions of Kotzebue, &c., would require many chapters, if we wished to examine their literary merit; but this task, as I have before observed, cannot enter into the general plan of my work.

The 'Messiah' of Klopstock, notwithstanding innumerable defects, prolixities, mysteries, and inexplicable obscurities, displays beauties of the first magnitude. The character of Abaddon, undergoing the fate of the guilty, while persevering in the love of virtue, uniting the faculties of an angel with the sufferings inflicted in the infernal regions, is an idea altogether new. Such conspicuous truth in the expressions of love, and the pictures of nature, amongst the most whimsical inventions of every kind, produces a very singular effect.

The consternation that would be occasioned by the idea of death, when thought of for the first time, is described with an affecting energy in one of the cantos of the 'Messiah.' An inhabitant of a planet where life is interminable, interrogates an angel who brings him intelligence from our globe on the nature of death. 'What!' he exclaims, 'can it be true that you are acquainted with a country where the son may be for ever separated from her who has lavished upon him the most tender marks of affection during the early years of his life?—where the mother may see herself deprived of the child on whom she had rested all her hopes of future happiness?—a country too where love is known; where two beings devoted to each other, live perhaps long together, then learn to exist alone? Can it be in that country possible to wish for life, where it serves only to form connections which death must dissolve; only to love what must be lost; only to cherish in the heart an image, whose object may disappear from the world where it leaves its wretched survivor?' When we first begin to read the 'Messiah,' we appear to enter into a gloom in which we are frequently bewildered; where sometimes, indeed, beautiful objects are distinguishable, but a uniform melancholy reigns throughout the whole; which however is not entirely devoid of sweetness.

The German tragedies, and particularly those of Schiller, contain beauties which always indicate a great mind. In France, a delicacy of mind, a feeling for the reigning customs, and a fear of ridicule, weaken, in some respects, the vivacity of impressions. Accustomed to watch over ourselves, we necessarily lose, in the midst of society, those impetuous emotions which develop to every eye the predominant affections of the soul. But in reading those German tragedies which have acquired celebrity, words, expressions, and ideas, may be often found, that awaken in ourselves some sentiments which the regular institutions and ties of society have stifled or restrained. These expressions re-animate and transport us; persuade us in a moment that we are about to be lifted above all factitious considerations, above all compulsatory forms; and that after a long restraint, the first friend we shall find is our own original character,—is, in fact, ourselves.

The Germans are highly distinguished as painters of nature. Gessner, Zacharias, many poets in the pastoral line, excite a love of country, and appear to be inspired with its sweet impressions. They describe it in such a manner, as must strike the attentive observer, when the toils of agriculture and the labors of the field, which claim the presence of man and the enjoyments of tranquil life, are in unison with the disposition of the soul.

We must indeed be in this peaceful temper, in order to relish such descriptions. When we are agitated by the passions, the exterior calm of nature adds to our sufferings. Prospects that are wild and gloomy, and every melancholy external object that surrounds us, aid us in the enduring of internal anguish.

The tragedy of Goetz de Berlichingen, as well as some other popular romances, are filled with those mementos of chivalry, which leave so strong an impression on the imagination, and which the Germans are so competent to introduce under varied and interesting forms.

After this cursory survey of the principal beauties of the German literature, I feel it incumbent upon me to direct the reader's attention towards the defects of its writers, as well as to the consequences that might result from those errors, if they were suffered to remain without correction.

The lofty style is, of all others, that in which we may be the most easily deceived. Great talents are necessary, to avoid departing from truth when we endeavor to paint a character raised above habitual prejudices; and in depicting enthusiasm, inferiority is insupportable. 'Werter' has given rise to a greater number of bad imitations than any other literary *chef-d'œuvre:* the aiming at an elevated style in a work of this kind, is the most ridiculous thing in the world. Wieland has shown with great success, in his 'Peregrinus Proteus,' the absurdities of that factitious enthusiasm so widely different from the genuine inspiration of genius. The Germans are much more indulgent in this respect than ourselves; they permit also, and often even applaud, an abundance of trivial notions in philosophy, concerning riches, beneficence, birth, merit, &c.; common-place subjects, which in France would at once repress and damp every kind of interest. The Germans also hear with pleasure the repetition of the most hackneyed thoughts, although their genius daily leads to the discovery of those which are genuine.

The language of the Germans is not yet determined; each author has his own peculiar style; and thousands in that country look upon themselves as authors. How can literature be established in a country where nearly three thousand volumes are published annually? It is a very easy matter to write the German language sufficiently well to be printed; too many obscurities are permitted, too much latitude allowed, common-place ideas are too frequently received, and too great a number of words united together or newly coined; whereas a difficulty of style must naturally discourage men of modern abilities. Genuine talent is at a loss to discover itself amidst such a numberless multitude of books; and though at length it may certainly be distinguishable, yet the general taste is more and more corrupted by insipidities, and literary pursuits must in course terminate in losing their respectability.

The Germans are sometimes deficient in taste, in writings which are the productions of their natural imagination: they fail of it still more frequently in works of imitation. Amongst their writers, those who are not possessed of an original genius, borrow sometimes the defects of English literature, and occasionally those of the French.

I have endeavored already to make it appear by analyzing Shakspeare, that his beauties can only be equalled by a genius similar to his own; and that his defects ought to be carefully avoided.

The Germans resemble the English in some respects: for this reason, they lose themselves less frequently in studying the English authors than the French: nevertheless they have also adopted the system of contrasting the vulgar with the heroic character: by which means they diminish the beauty of numbers of their best productions.

To this defect, which they possess in common with the English, is superadded a taste for metaphysical sentiments; which frequentlv serves to weaken the effect of the most affecting situations. As they are by nature given to thought and meditation, they insert the abstract ideas, the explanations and definitions, with which their heads are filled, in the most impassioned scenes; and their heroes, their women, the ancients, and the moderns, are all made to speak in the language of a German philosopher. This is a glaring defect, against which their writers ought to be guarded. Their genius frequently inspires them with the most simple expressions for the noblest passions; but when they lose themselves in obscurity, we are no longer interested, and our reason forbids our approbation.

The German writers have been frequently reproached for their want of grace and sprightliness. Some of them, apprehensive of a censure upon which the English pride themselves endeavor to imitate the French style; by which means they fall into worse errors: because, having once stepped out of their native character, they no longer possess those energetic and strikiug beauties which occasion their defects to be be glossed over and forgotten. Those charms of grace and sprightliness which characterized some of the French writers before the revolution, could have birth only from the circumstances peculiar to ancient France; and, even in that nation, could be produced only at Paris. There are numbers also amongst us, who have failed in their literary attempts, although surrounded by the best models. The Germans are by no means to be depended upon for making the best choice of authors for their imitation.

In Germany, perhaps, it may be thought that Crebillon and Dorat are writers remarkable for grace: they therefore overcharge the copy of a style already so inflated as to be almost insupportable to the French.

The German writers, who within their own minds might find all that could interest men of every country, by blending the mythology of the Greeks and the gallantry of the French, produce a medley from which they seem anxions to banish both nature and truth.

In France, the power of ridicule always terminates by leading us back to the paths of simplicity: but in a country like Germany, where the tribunal of society has so little influence, and is so little in unison in itself, nothing ought to be risked in a style which requires the most constant practice and the finest feeling of all the powers of the mind. They ought to confine themselves 'to the universal principles of the higher walks of literature, and write on those subjects in which nature and reason are competent guides.

The Germans have sometimes the fault of introducing into their philosophical works a sort of pleasantry, which is by no means adapted to serious writings. They think by this measure to accommodate themselves to their readers.* But we ought never to imagine that the capacities of our readers are inferior to our own; it is always better to express our thoughts just as we conceived them. We ought to put ourselves upon a level with the majority' but to aim at the highest possible point of perfection: the judgment of the public is always, in the end, that of the most distinguished men of the nation.

It is sometimes also through a mistaken wish to please the fair sex, that the Germans endeavor to blend the serious and the frivolous. The English never study the taste of females in their writings: the French, by the rank they have granted to them in society, have rendered them excellent judges of genius and taste. The Germans ought to entertain an affection for them, as their ancestors did formerly; who attributed to them some qualities attached to divinity. They ought to pay them the tribute of respect without descending too much in their correspondences with them.

In a word, in order to render philosophical truths admissible in a country where they are not yet publicly adopted, it has been thought necessary to dress them in the garb of tales, dialogues or fables: and Wieland especially has acquired great reputation in this style of writing. On some occasions, indeed, some artifice or disguise may perhaps be necessary in order to introduce truth. What they wished to communicate to the moderns, they might perhaps be obliged to put into the mouth of the ancients; and thus recalling the past, make it serve as an allegory for the use of the present times. We cannot judge how far the contrivances used by Wieland are politically requisite: but here* it may be repeated, that, with relation to literary merit, it is an error to believe that philosophical truths become more interesting by a medley of personages and incidents which serve merely as a pretext for want of arguments.

The analysis loses its solidity, and the romance its interest, by their being blended. To render fictitious incidents at all captivating, they ought to succeed each other with dramatic rapidity: to render arguments convincing, they must be duly connected, and conclusive. When the interest is abridged by discussion, and discussion by the interest, far from giving a respite to discriminating minds, their attention becomes wearied less execution is required to follow the thread of an idea as far as reflection can carry it, than incessantly to resume and to quit arguments of which the chain is broken, and impressions that are weakened by interruption.

The success of Voltaire has inspired some with a wish to follow his example in writing philosophical tales: but that animating gayety, that varied grace, which characterizes Voltaire in this kind of composition, defies imitation. There is, without doubt a philosophical inference to be found at the conclusion of his tales; but the pleasantry and the turn that he gives to his compositions is such, that his aim is not to be perceived till the catastrophe: like an excellent comedy, the moral of which we feel upon reflection, but at its first representation on the stage we are only struck with its interest and action.

Serious reason and eloquent sensibility are the allowed province of the German literature; its attempts in any other line have always been less successful. There is no nation more peculiarly adapted to philosophical studies. Their historians, amongst whom we must first rank Schiller and Muller, are as distinguished as it is possible to be in writing modern history. A feudal government is extremely prejudicial to the interest excited by incident and character. In that warlike age, our imagination is apt to fancy all great men clad in the same armor, and that their characters bear

* A German mythologist, descanting in one of his tracts upon a stone which he had not been able to discover, expresses himself thus upon the subject: 'This fugitive nymph escapes our search;' and exaggerating afterwards the properties of another stone, he exclaims, 'Ah, syren!'

* See the Essay on Fictions.

as close a resemblance to each other, as their helmets and their shields.

How much honor do the Germans reflect upon their nation by their persevering labors, by their researches into metaphysics, and into every other science! They have not a political country; but they have rendered it a literary and a philosophical country, and are animated with the most noble enthusiasm for its glory.

Nevertheless, a voluntary subjection prevents the Germans from being, in some respects, so enlightened a people as they might otherwise become: this subjection is the spirit of sect, which in a life of indolence, supplies the place of a spirit of party, and partakes of some of its inconveniences. Undoubtedly, before the number of followers of any sect is increased, individuals apply all their attention to judge of it, and decide in its favor, or otherwise, by the uncontrolled exercise of their reason. The first choice is free, but not so its consequences. As soon as a person is satisfied with its basis, he adopts, in order to maintain the sect, all the conclusions which the master may deduce from his own principles. A sect, however philosophical it may be in its aim, is never so in its means to attain that end. A blind confidence must always be inspired, to compensate for individual decision: for numbers, whilst their reason is uncontrolled, never give an assent to all the opinions of one man alone.

There is yet another important observation that may be made against the new systems of which it is attempted to compose a sect; the progress of the human mind is too gradual to admit of any succession of just ideas. A century discovers two or three additional ideas; and that century is therefore esteemed illustrious. How then can an individual conceive a chain of thoughts entirely new? Moreover, all truths are susceptible of evidence, and evidence makes no sect. Caprice, and mystery above all, are required to excite in men that which gives rise to spirits of sect, an ardent wish to distinguish themselves. This wish becomes really useful to the progress of the understanding, when it excites emulation in every species of talents; but not when it subjects many minds to dependence upon one only.

In order to conquer empires, disciplined armies must acknowledge the authority of a commander-in-chief: but in order to make a progress in the career of truth, each man must proceed by himself, guided by the light of the age he lives in, and not by the documents of any party.*

The enlightened amongst the Germans have generally a love of virtue and of the *beautiful* in all things; a circumstance which gives great character to their writings. The distinguishing feature of their philosophy is, that they have substitued the austerity of morality in lieu of religious superstition. In France, they have been contented to overthrow the empire of opinion. But of what utility would knowledge be to the happiness of nations, if that knowledge was only the harbinger of destruction;—if it never opened to the mind any principle of life;—if it did not inspire the soul with new sentiments and new virtues, for the support of former duties?

The Germans are eminently calculated to be free, since already, in their philosophical revolution, they have substituted in the place of the worn-out barriers of antiquity, the immutable bounds of natural reason.

If, by any invincible misfortune, France should ever be destined to lose all hope of liberty, Germany would become the central seat of learning: and in its bosom would be established, at some future epoch, the principles of political philosophy. Our wars with the English must have rendered them inimical to every thing that recalls France to their memory: but a more equitable impartiality would guide the opinions of the Germans.

They are more perfect than we are in the art of softening the lot of mankind; they enlighten the understanding, and lead the way to conviction; while we by force attempt every thing, undertake every thing, and in every thing have failed. We lay a foundation only for animosities; and the friends of liberty appear in the midst of the nation, with down-cast looks, blushing for the crimes of some, and calumniated by the prejudices of others.

Ye enlightened people! ye inhabitants of Germany! who perhaps will one day be, like us, enthusiasts in every republican idea; be invariably faithful to one determined principle, which is of itself a sufficient protection from all irreparable errors. Never indulge yourselves in an action which morality can disapprove; attend not to the pitiful arguments that may be holden out to you upon the difference that ought to be established between the morality of public and of private characters. This distinction proceeds from a perverted understanding, and a narrow mind; and if we should perish, it will be because we have adopted it.

Behold the effect of crimes in the interior of a nation:—the persecuting always agitated, the persecuted always implacable;—no opinion can appear innocent, and no argument can be heard;—a multitude of facts, calumnies, and falsehoods so accumulated on the heads of all, that amidst the whole body of people, there scarcely remains one upright consideration, one man to whom another man will vouchsafe the slightest mark of condescension, nor any one party faithful to the same principles: some individuals we see united by the tie of general consternation, a tie easily broken by the hope of self-preservation: in fine, so terrible a confusion between liberal opinions and culpable actions, between servile opinions and liberal sentiments, that esteem becomes unsettled, and knows not whereon to fix, and conscience hardly dares to confide in itself for its own security.

One single day, in the course of which we may, in thought or word, have countenanced and supported measures that have led to cruelty and suffering,—that one day may of itself suffice to embitter life, and fundamentally to destroy that internal calm, that universal benevolence of heart, which gave birth to hope of our finding friends wherever we found men. Oh! let nations still virtuous, let men gifted with political abilities, who are yet irreproachable, assidiously preserve such blessings! and if a revolution should commence amongst them, let them fear amidst themselves only those perfidious friends who advise them to persecute the vanquished.

Liberty supplies strength for its own defence; the concurrence of interest opens all the needful resources; the impulse of ages overthrows all that would struggle for the past against the future: but inhumanity sows discord, perpetuates war, divides a whole nation into inimical bands; and that offspring of the serpent of Cadmus, to whom an avenging god granted life only to condemn them to wage war till death,—that offspring of the serpent is the people amongst whom injustice has long reigned.

CHAPTER XVIII.

WHY ARE THE FRENCH POSSESSED OF MORE GRACE, TASTE, AND GAYETY, THAN ANY OTHER EUROPEAN NATION?

French gayety and French taste, have been proverbial in all the countries of Europe, and that taste and gayety have generally been attributed to the national char-

* All Kant's ingenuity of mind and elevation of principle are not, I think, sufficient objections against what I have just advanced respecting the spirit of sect.

acter: but what is a national character, if not the result of institutions and circumstances which influence the happiness, interests, and customs of a people? Since those circumstances and those institutions have been changed, and even in the most tranquil periods of the revolution, the most striking contrasts have not been the subject of one single epigram, or of one spirited pleasantry. Many of those men who have obtained great ascendency over the destiny of France, were destitute of every grace of expression and brilliancy of understanding; perhaps even they were indebted for some part of their influence to the gloom, silence, and chilling ferocity, that pervaded both their manners and their sentiments.

Religion and laws determine almost entirely the resemblance, or the difference of the genius of nations. The climate too may occasion some changes; but the general education of the higher ranks of society is always the result of the prevailing political institutions. The seat of government being the centre of the chief interests of the people, their customs and opinions follow the lead of their interests. Let us examine what advantages arose from the ambition prevalent in France, to be distinguished by the attractions of grace and gayety; that we may learn why this country offered such perfect models of both.

To please or displease, was the real source of those punishments and rewards which were not inflicted by the laws. Other countries had monarchical governments, kings absolute in authority, and magnificent courts; but no where could be found united the same circumstances which influenced the genius and the manners of the French.

Under limited monarchies, as in England and in Sweden, the love of liberty, the exercise of political rights, and the almost continual civil commotions, are a lesson to their kings, that it behooved them to choose such favorites as were possessed of certain defensive qualities; and also teach the courtiers, that, in order to obtain preferments with their respective kings, they must be able to support their authority by means that are independent and personal.

In Germany, long wars and the federation of its states prolonged the feudal spirit, and presented no common centre where all enlightened talents and general interests could unite.

The despots of the east and of the north were too much under the necessity of inspiring fear, to awaken in any degree the genius of their subjects; and the desire of pleasing their rulers was productive of a kind of familiarity with them, which merely tended to aggravate their tyranny.

In republics, however constituted they may be, it is so necessary for men to defend themselves, or to become subservient to each other, that neither harmony nor pleasure can be found amongst them.

The gallantry of the Moors, and the consequence which it gave to their women, would in some respects have raised the genius of the Spaniards nearly to a par with that of the French; but the superstitions to which they are devoted, have totally impeded their progress in any thing amiable or solid; and the indolence of the east has relinquished every exertion of talent to the diligence of the priesthood.

France, then, was the only country where the authority of the king being consolidated by the tacit consent of the nobility, the monarch possessed an absolute power; the right of which, notwithstanding, was in fact undetermined: this situation compelled him to study even his courtiers, as constituting a part of that body of victors which granted and secured to him France, their conquest.

The delicacy of the point of honor, one of the delusions of the privileged order, compelled the nobility to decorate the most abject submission with the forms of liberty. It was necessary that they should preserve, in their connection with their master, a spirit of chivalry; that they should engrave upon their shield, 'For my Mistress and King,' that they might be thought voluntarily to choose the yoke which they wore; and thus blending honor with slavery, they endeavored to bow without debasement. Grace was, if I may be allowed the expression, in their situation, a necessary policy, as that only could give the appearance of choice to obedience.

The king, on his part, duly considering himself, in some instances, as the dispenser of glory, and the representative of public opinion, could recompense only by applause, and punish only by degradation. He was obliged to support his power by a kind of public assent, which was doubtless principally directed by his will, but which frequently manifested itself independent of that will. Ties of the most delicate nature, and prejudices artfully conducted, formed the connection of the first subjects with their governor: these connections required great art and quickness of mind: grace was requisite in the monarch, or at least in the dispensers of his power; taste and delicacy were necessary in the choice of favors and of favorites, in order that neither the commencement nor the limits of the royal authority might be discerned. Some of its rights must be exercised without being acknowledged, some acknowledged without being exercised; and moral considerations were embraced by opinion with such subtlety, that one bad stroke of politics was universally felt, and might be the ruin of a minister, notwithstanding any support that government should be inclined to give him.

The king, of course, must call himself the first gentleman of his kingdom, that he might the more readily exercise a boundless authority over gentlemen; and to strengthen that authority over the nobility, a certain portion of flattery was necessarily directed to them. Arbitrary power not even then allowing a freedom of opinion, both parties perceived the necessity of pleasing each other, and the means of succeeding therein were multiplied. Grace and elegance of manners gradually passed from the customs of the court into the writings of literary men. The most elevated station, the source of all favor, is the object of general attention: and as in all free countries, the government gives the impulse to public virtue; so in monarchies, the court influences the mental genius of the nation, because an universal wish is excited to imitate that which distinguishes the most elevated rank.

When the government is so moderate, that no cruelty is apprehended from it, and so arbitrary, that all the enjoyments of power and fortune depend only upon its favor; all those who aspire to that favor, ought to possess a sufficient degree of mental tranquillity to render themselves amiable, and sufficient dexterity to make that frivolous accomplishment conducive to material success. Men of the first class of society in France often aspired to power; but they ran no dangerous hazards in that career; they gamed without risking the loss of a large stake, uncertainty turned only upon the extent of their advantage; hope alone then animated their exertions. Great perils give additional energy to the soul and to the reflecting powers; but security gives to the mind all the charms of ease and readiness.

The animation of gayety, still more than the polish of grace, banished the remembrance of all distinctions of rank without destroying any: by means of this, grandees dreamed of equality with kings, and poets with nobles; and inspired even the higher ranks with a more refined idea of their advantages, which, after a short forgetfulness, were called again to memory with renewed pleasure; and the highest perfection of taste and gayety was the result of this universal desire to please.

The affectation in ideas and sentiments, imported from Italy to spoil the taste of all the European nations was at first prejudicial to the grace of the French; but the understanding being more enlightened, reverted consequently to simplicity. Chaulieu, La Fontaine, and Madame de Sevigne, were the most unaffected writers, and plainly proved themselves to be possessed of inimitable grace. The Italians and the Spaniards were actuated by a desire to please the softer sex ; but nevertheless they were far from equalling the French in the delicate art of adulation. The flattery which serves ambitious purposes, requires much more understanding and skill than that which is addressed only to the fair sex ; all the passions of mankind, and all their different vanities, must be artfully studied, when the combination of the government and the manners is such that the success of men in their dealings with each other depends on their mutual talents of pleasing, and those talents are the only means to obtain eminent situations in power.

In France, grace and taste were not only conducive to the highest interests, but both the one and the other were preservatives against the misfortune they most dreaded, namely, ridicule. Ridicule is, in many respects, an aristocratical power ; the more ranks there are in society, the more connections exist between those ranks, and the greater is the necessity to know and to respect them. Among the higher classes are established certain customs, certain laws of politeness and elegance, which serve, so to speak, as a signal for rallying, and to be ignorant of which would betray a habit of different manners and different society. Those men who constitute these first classes, having at their disposal all the favors of the state, must necessarily have great sway over the public opinion ; for with the exception of a very few instances, power consists of good taste, interest has a certain portion of grace, and the happy are beloved.

That class which, in France, prevailed over the whole nation, was privileged to take up the slightest absurdities ; and as the *ridiculous* had the most striking effects upon the minds of the people, they were universally solicitous to shun the lash of ridicule. The apprehension of it was often an obstacle to originality of genius ; it might also in the political career, be detrimental to the energy of action ; but it developed in the minds of the French a kind of perspicacity singularly worthy of observation. Their writers had a greater insight into characters, and more ability to depict them, than any other nation : being obliged incessantly to study what might give offence or pleasure in society, this interest rendered them very observing.

Moliere, and, even since his time, some other comic writers, are superior in that walk to all the authors of any other nation. The French do not, like the English and the Germans, search deeply into the sentiments occasioned by misery ; they accustom themselves so much to shun it, that they cannot be well acquainted with its results : but those characters that give rise to comic effects, as, for instance, men seduced by vanity, deceived by self-love, or deceiving others through pride, that multitude of beings subservient and devoted to the opinion of others ; no nation on earth has ever arrived at the skill of painting these so well as the French.

Gayety leads us back to natural ideas ; and although the *bon ton* of French society was entirely formed upon fictitious grounds, it is to the gayety of that society that we must absolutely attribute all that remains of truth in ideas, and in the manner of expressing them.

There certainly was not much philosophy in the conduct of the greater part of enlightened characters ; they were themselves often subject to the very failings which they condemned in their own works : nevertheless, the effect of their writings and conversations was heightened by a sort of homage paid to philosophy ; the object of which was to show, that they could reason as well as the mind was capable of reasoning; and that, if necessary, they could laugh at their own ambition, their pride, and even their rank, although they were positively determined not to renounce an atom of any one of them.

The court wished to please the nation, and the nation the court ; the court pretended to philosophy, and the city to *bon ton.* The courtiers, when they associated with the inhabitants of the capital, wished to display a personal merit, a character, and a genius peculiar to themselves ; and the inhabitants of the capital exhibited an irresistible attraction to the polished manners of the courtiers. This reciprocal emulation did not accelerate the progress of solid and exalted truth ; but there was not one ingenious idea, not one delicate shade, that self-interest suffered to remain undiscovered to the mind.

A very animated work by Agrippa d'Aubigne, more than two centuries back, distinguished the real and the apparent, *l'etre et le paroitre,* in his delineation of the character of a Frenchman, the Duke d'Epernon. In the ancient system of things, all the French were more or less attentively engaged by the *apparent,* because the theatre of society inclines particularly to that side. The external appearance, indeed, ought to be attended to, when there is no opportunity to judge of any thing but the manners ; and in France, it was perfectly excusable to wish to succeed in society, since there existed no other field for the display of talents, and for gaining the notice of those in power. And, moreover, what numerous subjects for comedy must be found in a nation where the manners, not the actions, are the test of reputation ! All the studied graces and ridiculous pretensions, were inexhaustible sources of humour and comic scenery.

The influence of women is necessarily very great, when all events take place in the drawing-room and when all characters are judged by their conversation ; in such a case, women become a supreme power, and whatever pleases them is assiduously cultivated. The leisure which monarchy left to the generality of distinguished men in every department, conduced very much to bring the pleasures of the understanding and of conversation to perfection.

Power was attained in France neither by labor nor by study ; a *bon mot,* some peculiar gracefulness, was frequently the occasion of the most rapid promotions : and the frequent examples of this inspired a sort of careless philosophy, a confidence in fortune, and a contempt for studious exertions, which led every mind to be agreeable and accommodating. When diversion is not only permitted, but often useful, a nation ought to attain the utmost point of perfection to which it can be carried.

Nothing similar to this will ever be witnessed in France whilst under a government of a different nature, however it may be constituted ; which will be a convincing proof, that what was called French genius and French grace, were only the result of monarchical institutions and manners, such as they have for many past ages existed in France.

CHAPTER XIX.

OF LITERATURE IN THE AGE OF LOUIS XIV.*

The reign of literature has been revived in Europe by the study of the ancients ; but not till a considerable time after its revival, was an imitation of the ancients the guide of literary taste. The French culti-

* I shall not analyze all the particulars relating to French literature ; all that can be interesting, has been already said on this subject. I confine myself simply to trace the path pursued by genius from the age of Louis XIV. to the revolution in 1789.

vated the Spanish style of writing at the commencement of the seventeenth century; and this style had a degree of grandeur peculiar to itself, which preserved the French authors from some faults of Italian taste, then diffused all over Europe. Corneille, who first introduced the era of French genius, was greatly indebted to his study of the Spanish character.

The age of Louis XIV., the most remarkable of all in the annals of literature, is very inferior, in respect of philosophy, to the succeeding age. The monarchy, and above all a monarch who esteemed admiration an act of obedience; religious intolerance; and the superstitions at that time still prevalent; put a boundary to the extent of thought: an entire and consistent whole could not be conceived, nor could any analysis be permitted in a certain order of opinions, neither could an idea be followed up through all its connections and windings. Literature, in the age of Louis XIV., was the highest attainment of the imagination; but even this was not a philosophical power, since it was encouraged by an absolute king, and showed no signs of disapprobation at his despotism.

Literature like this, which had no aim but to indulge the sportive imaginations of the mind, could not possess such energy as that which has even gone so far as to make the very throne totter. Sometimes indeed, authors have been seen, who, like Achilles, have taken up weapons of war in the midst of frivolous ornaments; but in general, books at that time did not treat upon subjects of real importance; literary men retired to a distance from the active interests of life. An analysis of the principles of government, an examination into religious opinions, a just appreciation of men in power, every thing, in short, that could lead to any applicable result, was strictly forbidden them.

To publish such a work as Telemachus, was then a bold step: yet Telemachus contains only truths modified by a monarchical spirit. Massillon and Flechier hazarded some independent principles under the mask of religious errors; Pascal lived entirely in the intellectual world of science and religious metaphysics; La Rochefoucault and Labruyere described men in the circle of private life with prodigious skill and penetration: but as they touched upon nothing national, those great traits upon political characters, which are seen only in free institutions, could not be included in their designs.

The tragedies of Corneille, who drew nearer to the stormy period of the league, are often tinctured with republicanism: but what author in the age of Louis XIV. can boast of a philosophical independence worthy of being compared with that which is so conspicuous in the writings of Voltaire, Rousseau, Montesquieu, Raynall, &c.?

Purity of style cannot be carried to greater perfection than it is in the first rate works of the age of Louis XIV.: and in this respect they ought always to be considered as the models of French literature. They do not indeed possess, Bossuet excepted, all the beauties of eloquence; but they are exempt from all those faults which destroy the effect of the most striking beauties.

An aristocratic society is particularly favorable to the delicacy and polish of style. The habits of life constitute as essential a part of good writing, as even reflection itself: for although ideas may arise in solitude; the garb in which those ideas must be dressed, and the imagery necessary to illustrate them, depend in a great measure upon the impressions which education has left on the mind, and upon the society in which life has been passed.

In every country, but especially in France, words have, as it were, each its particular history: one may have been ennobled by some remarkable occurrence, whilst another may have been degraded by a similar circumstance. An author may throw a perpetual ridicule upon an expression which he has improperly applied: a custom, an opinion, or a mode of religious worship may, by a combination of ideas, dignify or debase the most natural image.

It is in the narrow circle of a few men superior in education or merit to the rest of the world, that the rules and elegance of style can be preserved. Surrounded by an unpolished society, how can we create in ourselves that delicacy of instinct which repels every thing that can be offensive to taste, without even having analyzed whence that repugnance proceeded?

The style in writing represents to the reader, if I may be allowed the observation, the deportment, the accent, the gesture of the person who addresses him: and in no case can vulgarity of manners add to the force either of ideas or of expressions. It is the same with style; there must alway be dignity in serious subjects. No thought, no sentiment, by this means loses its energy; elevation of language simply preserves that manly dignity in the presence of men, which he who lays himself open to their judgments ought never to lose sight of. For that assemblage of unknown persons whom an author, while writing, admits to a knowledge of himself, await not his familiarity; and the majesty of the public would be astonished, not without reason, at the assurance of the author.

Republican independence should therefore endeavor to imitate the correctness of those who wrote in the age of Louis XIV., in order that useful thoughts may be diffused, and that works of philosophy may at the same time rank as classical works in literature.

Many disputes have arisen, whether the imitation of nature, or the beautiful in idea, ought to be preferred in tragedies. I refer my readers to the second part of this work, to some reflections upon that system of tragedy most suitable to a republican state: this discussion belongs not to the present chapter.

The author who has attained the highest degree of perfection in style, in poetry, and in the art of painting,—the beautiful in idea, is Racine; a writer who, of all others, gives the most competent idea of the influence which laws and manners possessed over dramatic works in the reign of Louis XIV. The spirit of chivalry had introduced among the principles of honor a sort of delicacy, which necessarily gave rise to a sort of compact: that is to say, there existed a certain degree of heroism, indispensable as it were to the noblesse, and of which it was not allowable to suppose that a nobleman could be destitute: this point of honor, so susceptible that it could not tolerate even amongst the nearest relations the slightest expression capable of wounding the most exalted pride; this point of honor gave laws also to theatrical imitations, and to the sports of the imagination; and the diversity of characters that might be portrayed, were also obliged to be within the prescribed limits. Authors indeed were not allowed to carry that diversity to the full extent of nature; and a certain respect for the higher classes withheld them from representing any thing that might tend to degrade them in the public esteem.

Adulation towards the monarch raised to still greater perfection the *beautiful* in idea. A nation is annihilated when it is composed only of the worshippers of an individual. The factitious greatness which it was necessary to attribute to Louis XIV., inclined the poets always to represent some characters as perfect as that which flattery had invented. The imagination of the writer was at least to keep pace with his eulogiums; and the same model was frequently repeated in the scenes of the drama. The character of Achilles, in 'Iphigenia,' had some traits of French gallantry; and in 'Titus' again were found allusions to Louis XIV. The greatest genius in the world, Racine, did not allow himself to express such bold conceptions as his mind perhaps might have suggested to him; because those who would be the judges of them, were incessantly in his thoughts.

The formidable, but unknown, *public* of a tumultuous audience inspires less timidity than the *Areopagus* of a court, of which the author would wish personally to captivate each individual judge. Before such a tribunal, taste appears still more essential than energy. We feel a wish to attain great effects by many gradual shades; and in such a case those methods of which Shakspeare availed himself in order to attract the multitude who were adorers of his productions, would be improper and unavailing. The description of love, in the reign of Louis XIV., was also subjected to some acknowledged rules. Gallantry towards the women, introduced by the laws of chivalry, the polish of the court, the elegant language which the pride of rank reserved to itself as an additioal distinction, all served to render the undertaking more arduous. These difficulties enhanced the reputation of him who had skill sufficient to overcome them; but at the same time, a far-fetched or affected expresssion frequently chilled his emotion. A taste for madrigals displayed a perfect *sang-froid* even whilst attempting to describe the impetuosity of passion; and this of course gave birth to a language which was neither that of reason, nor of love.

Even Racine himself was somewhat deficient in the knowledge of the human heart, under those relations which philosophy alone can render evident. But if deep reflection was requisite to discern what might even yet have improved such master-pieces as his were; the limits of philosophy, in the age of Louis XIV., are discerned much more evidently in those literary works which belong not to the drama. These limits are one of the principal causes of the want of excellence in the historians.

The religious wars had given birth to a spirit of party, which converts many histories into theological briefs; the spirit of society, although different from the spirit of party, is equally far from the trnth, and alters facts with as unsparing a hand. In fine; the feudal code founding all institutions and all power upon pristine rights rendered sacred by time, it was not allowable to speak truth in what related to past events, however remote they might be; present authority depended upon them: errors of every kind impeded historians on all subjects, or, what was still more to be lamented, they themselves adopted those very errors as truths.

Man, surrounded by so many long-respected institutions, so many famous decisions, so many received conformities, could not appeal from them to the independence of his own reflections; his reason could not examine into every thing, and his mind was never freed from the yoke of general opinion; even solitude could not bring it back to natural ideas; the ascendency of the monarch, and the prevalence of monarchical reverence, had penetrated into the conviction of all. This was not a despotism which enslaved either the mind or the soul; but it was a despotism that appeared universally to be so blended with the nature of things, that the people conformed to it as they would to that invariable order which must necessarily exist.

One asylum yet remained,—religion: sheltered by this, one individual, Bossuet, asserted some bold truths. All the interests of life were subjected to the monarch; but, in the name of death, even to him equality might be mentioned. These dogmas, these ceremonies, this religious pomp, were then oniy barriers against power: this power was cited before eternity; for if men abandoned to an individual the disposal of their existence, they could appeal from him to a God who makes even kings to tremble.

In our days, if the absolute power of one individual were established in France, we could no longer have recourse to those majestic ideas which, levelling all human distinctions, offer the only consolation for casual misfortunes: for philosophical reasoning would oppose fewer obstacles to tyranny, than the unshaken belief and the intrepid devotion of religious enthusiasm.

CHAPTER XX.

FROM THE EIGHTEENTH CENTURY TO THE YEAR 1789.

In this epoch, literature has given impulse to philosophy. After the death of Louis XIV., the same abuses being no longer defended by the same power, reflection turned upon religious and political subjects, and a mental revolution commenced.

The English philosophers known in France, have been one of the primary causes of that spirit of analysis which has led the French writers to such unusual lengths; but independent of this particular cause, the age immediately succeeding an age of literature, is in all countries, as I have endeavored to prove, that of reflection. Happy if the French be so favored by destiny, that the thread of metaphysical progress, of scientific discoveries, and philosophical ideas, be not yet broken in their hands!

Liberty of opinion commenced in France by attacks upon the Catholic religion; at first, because such attacks were the only daring steps that produced no ill consequences to their author; and secondly, because Voltaire, the first man who made philosophy popular in France, found in this subject an inexhaustible fund of pleasantries, all in the French taste, and all in the taste of those about the court.

The courtiers, not aware of the intimate connection which must exist between all prejudices, hoped at once both to maintain their posts in stations founded upon error, and to deck themselves with a spirit of philosophy: they wished apparently to disdain some of their advantages, but nevertheless in reality to preserve them: they thought that only those who profited by abuses, could clear them up; and that the vulgar at large would continue in their credulity, whilst a small number of individuals enjoying, as formerly, their exalted rank, would add a superiority of understanding to that of their situation in life; they flattered themselves that they might yet for a long time look upon their inferiors as their dupes; and that those inferiors would never be tired of such a situation. No man was better able than Voltaire to profit by this disposition of the nobles of France; indeed it is not impossible that he himself partook of it.

Voltaire loved grandeur and royalty; he wished rather to enlighten society than to change it. The animated grace, the exquisite taste conspicuous in all his works, rendered it almost essential to him to be judged by the spirit of aristocracy. He wished learning to become fashionable, and philosophy to become general; but he did not call forth the strongest emotions of nature; he did not summon from the depth of the forests, like Rousseau, the tempest of primitive passions to shake the government upon its ancient foundations. By pleasantry, and the shafts of ridicule, Voltaire gradually weakened the importance of some errors; he destroyed the roots of that which the subsequent storm so easily overturned; but he neither foresaw nor wished for that revolution to which he prepared the way.

A republic founded upon a system of philosophical equality not even entering into his ideas, could not of course be his secret aim. There is no distant plan, no concealed design perceptible in his writings: that perspicuity and ease which distinguish his works, display every thing to the view, and leave nothing for the imagination to divine.

Rousseau, whose mind was suffering and wounded by the injustice, the ingratitude, and the blind contempt of careless and frivolous men, worn out moreover by the social order then existing, might indeed have recourse to ideas purely natural: whereas the fate of Voltaire was singularly happy in society, in the fine arts, and in monarchical civilization; he must even have feared to subvert the object of his attacks. The merit and the interest felt in most of his sallies of wit, depend upon the very existence of those prejudices which he ridicules.

Those works, the merit of which depends in any degree upon temporary circumstances, cannot preserve a lasting reputation. They may be considered as describing the manners of the day, but not as immortal productions. A writer who searches only into the immutable nature of man, into those thoughts and sentiments which must enlighten the mind in every age, is independent of events; they can never change the order of those truths which such a writer unfolds. But some of the prose works of Voltaire are already in the same case with the Provincial Letters; the turn of them is admired, but the subject is cast off and forsaken. How is it possible that, in the present day, we should relish pleasantries upon the Jews, or upon the Catholic religion? Their day is past: whereas the philippics of Demosthenes are always suitable to present times, because he addresses himself to men; and men are the same now as they were then.

In the age of Louis XIV. to bring the art of writing itself to perfection was the object of authors in general; but in the eighteenth century literature has assumed a very different character. It is no longer an art merely; it is a power; it is become a weapon to the human mind, which hitherto it had only instructed and amused.

Pleasantry was, in the time of Voltaire, like the fables in the east, an allegorical manner of making truth to be heard, even whilst subjected to the dominion of error. Montesquieu attempted this sort of raillery in his Persian Letters; but he had not the natural gayety of Voltaire, the want of which, however, was compensated by his brilliant understanding. Works of still greater merit leave proofs of this truth: his reflections have given birth to thousands of new reflections. He has analyzed political questions without enthusiasm, and without any positive system. He has displayed them all to view; others have made their choice: but should the social art ever attain in France the certainty of science in its principles and in its application, it is from Montesquieu that the commencement of its progress ought to be dated.

To him succeeded Rousseau: he has discovered nothing, but he has set all in a blaze: and the sentiment of equality, which is productive of many more disturbances than the love of liberty, and which gives birth to inquiries of a totally different order, and events of a far more terrible nature:—the sentiment of equality, both in its majesty and in its meanness, is portrayed in every line of the writings of Rousseau, and gains entire possession of mankind as well by means of the virtues as the vices of his nature.

Voltaire has entirely engrossed to himself that epoch of philosophy when men, like children, must be taught to sport with what they fear: then comes the moment, boldly to examine these formidable objects; and then finally to conquer and become masters of them. Voltaire, Montesquieu, and Rousseau have traced these various periods in the progress of reflection, and, like the gods of Olympus, they have gone over the ground in three steps.

The literature of the eighteenth century is enriched by the philosophical spirit which characterizes it. Purity of style and elegance of expression are incapable of farther progres after Racine and Fenelon: but the fashion of analyzing, by giving more independence to the mind, has attracted reflection to a multitude of new objects. Philosophical ideas have found admittance in tragedies, in tales, and eve in writings of mere amusement: and Voltaire, uniting the grace of the preceeding century to the philosophy of that in which he lived, embellished the charm of wit by all those truths, the application of which had till then been considered as impossible.

Voltaire has been the occasion of great improvement in the dramatic art although he has not equalled the poetry of Racine. But without imitating the incoherences of the English tragedies, and not even allowing himself to bring forward all their beauties upon the French stage, he has portrayed grief with more energy than any of the authors who preceeded him. In his productions, the incidents are more striking, passion is described more naturally, and theatrical style is bought nearer to truth.

When philosophy is progressive, every thing improves in proportion, and sentiments are displayed as well as ideas. A certain servility or subjection of mind prevents mankind from making observations upon their own feelings,—from confessing those sentiments to themselves or expressing them to others: philosophical independence, on the contrary, makes them better acquainted with themselves, and with human nature in general. The tragedies of Voltaire, therefore, are most felt; those of Racine are most admired. The sentiments, the incidents, the characters, presented to us by Voltaire, make a deeper impression on my memory. To promote the perfection of morality itself the theatre ought always to present models above us; but a much greater degree of sympathy is excited when the author brings our own feelings and sentiments to our consideration.

What character can be more affecting on the stage, than that of Tancred? Phedra inspires astonishment and creates enthusiasm; but her character is not that of a woman of sensibility and delicacy. We remember Tancred as a hero whom we had known, as a friend whom we had regretted. Bravery, melancholy, love, all that can at once make us value, yet sacrifice life,—all the luxurious enjoyments of the mind, are united in this admirable subject.

To defend the country from which he is banished; to save the woman he loves, even while he believes her guilty; to load her with acts of generosity; to be revenged of her only by devoting himself to death; how sublime, and yet how much in unison with every mind of sensibility! This heroism, explained by love, does not astonish until reflected upon. The interest which the piece inspires, so transports the audience, that every individual present believes himself capable of the same exalted conduct.

The great admiration of Amenaide for Tancred, and the respectful esteem of Tancred in return, greatly add to the poignancy of affliction. To Phedra, who is not beloved, of what importance can be the loss of life? But when we see happiness annihilated by fate; mutual confidence, that first of blessings, destroyed by calumny; the impression we feel, is so strong, that it could not be tolerated on the stage, if Tancred were to die without an assurance from Amenaide that she had never ceased to love him.

The heart-breaking scene in which we learn the catastrophe, is a kind of consolation. Tancred expires just at the moment he most wished to live; nevertheless he dies with more consoling reflections.

And indeed who is there that would not wish to descend into the grave with affections that render life an object of regret, rather than feel a solitariness of heart that was a death-blow to us even while we lived? In that uncertain future, of which we have only a confused idea beyond the term of our existence in this world, we hope perhaps those friends who loved us here may follow us: but if we have ceased to esteem their virtues, and to confide in their affection, where then could be the solace of such a hope? What emotion would then remain to direct the mind to heaven? In what heart would be left any traces of the transitory creature who solicits eternity? What petitions would then be offered to the supreme being to entreat him not to break the chain of recollection which blends, as it were, two separate existences together?

Those reflections which recall in any shape to the minds of men what is common to them all, must ever occasion great emotion; and it is in this point of view that the philosophical reflections introduced by Voltaire in his tragedies, when those reflections are not used too freely, occasion an universal interest to be felt throughout the various circumstances he brings forward on the stage. I will examine, in the second part of this work, whether some new beauties may not be adapted to the French theatre, that bear a still closer resemblance to nature; but it cannot be denied, that in this respect Voltaire has gained a step in the dramatic art, and the power of theatrical effect has arisen from it.

The literary lustre of the eighteenth century is principally due to its prose-writers. Bossuet and Fenelon ought undoubtedly to be quoted as the first who set the example of uniting in the same language all prosaic correctness and poetical imagination. But how much has the art of writing been enriched in France by Montesquieu's energetic expression of thought, and Rousseau's eloquent descriptions of passion! The regularity of versification inspires a sort of pleasure, to which prose can never attain; it is a physical sensation which excites emotion or enthusiasm; it is a difficulty surmounted, of the merit of which connoisseurs can judge, but it inspires even the ignorant with a pleasure they cannot analyze.

But we feel it incumbent upon us also to acknowledge all the charms of the poetical images and specimens of eloquence witnessed, when prose brought to perfection offers us such fine examples.

Racine himself sometimes sacrifices style to the rhyme, to the hemistich, and to the metre: and if it be true that just expression, that which gives even the most delicate shade, even the most fugitive trace of the connection of our ideas; if it also be true that this expression is unique in the language, that even to the choice of grammatical transitions of articles between the words, all may serve to illustrate an idea, to awaken a remembrance, to discard a useless affinity, to transmit an emotion just as it is felt, in a word, to bring to perfection that sublime talent which makes life communicate with life, and reveals to an isolated being the secrets of another heart, and the deeply felt impressions of another mind; if it be true that superior delicacy of style would not allow in eloquent periods even the slightest alteration without offending the ear; if there be but one method of composition that can be deemed perfect, is it possible, that whilst adhering to the prescribed rules of poetry, that one method can always be found?

Harmony of style has made a great progress in prose-writing; but this harmony ought not to imitate the musical effect of fine versification. If it were attempted, prose would become monotonous, the choice of expressions would no longer be free, and all the advantages thence arising would never repay the trouble of the attempt. The harmony of prose is that which nature herself points out to our organs. Under the influence of any emotion, the tone of the voice is softened when imploring compassion; its accents become more firm when expressing any generous determination; it is raised and dropped when we wish to bring over to our own opinions a wavering audience around us: genius, or talent, is the power of calling to our aid at pleasure, all the resources, all the effects of natural emotions; it is that susceptibility of soul which makes us feel, merely from the impressions of the imagination, those emotions which others experience only in consequence of events that have occurred in their own life. The finest specimens of prose at present known, are those in which the passions themselves, invoked by genius, become eloquent. A man destitute of literary talents would express himself in the very style we so much admire, if writing under the pressure of deeply felt calamity.

On the plains of Philippi, Brutus exclaimed, 'Oh Virtue, art thou but a name?' A tribune of the Roman soldiers leading them to inevitable death in order to force an important post, thus addressed his followers: 'There is a necessity to *go*, but there is no necessity to *return*.' *Ire illuc necesse est, unde redire non necesse.* Arria said to Pætus, when she presented him with the dagger, '*Pæte non dolet.*' Bossuet pronouncing an eulogium on Charles I. in the funeral oration upon the death of the Queen, suddenly stops, and pointing to her coffin, says, 'That heart which existed but for him, awakes, dust as it is, and beats again, even under the pall, at the name of a husband so beloved.' Emilius, at the point of avenging himself of his mistress, exclaims, '*Malheureux! fais lui donc un mal que tu ne sentes pas.*' In these expressions, how are we to distinguish what ought to be attributed to invention, and what to history; what to imagination, and what to reality? Heroism, eloquence, love, all that can exalt the soul and raise it above selfish considerations, all that aggrandizes and ennobles it, is the result of violent emotions.

From the moment when literature concerned itself with matters of serious import; from the moment when authors saw a ray of hope that they might influence the fate of their fellow-citizens by the display of some particular principles, and by rendering some truths peculiarly interesting; prose-writing gradually rose to perfection.

M. de Buffon took delight in the art of writing, and carried it to a great length; but although he lived in the eighteenth century, he has not stept into the circle of literary fame: he only aims in good language to write a good work; he asks nothing of mankind but their approbation; he does not seek to influence them, nor to inspire them with strong emotions; words are his aim, as well as the means to attain that aim; he therefore has never reached the perfection of eloquence. In countries where talents may change the fate of empires, those talents increase in proportion to the magnitude of the object to which they aspire: an aim so exalted incites to eloquent writing, by acting on those feeling which also render us capable of magnanimous actions. All the rewards, all the distinctions which monarchy can offer, will never inspire that energy which arises from the hope of being useful. Philosophy itself is but a frivolous employment in a country where the understanding cannot penetrate into the institutions. When reflection cannot amend or soften the lot of mankind, it becomes unmanly or pedantic. He who writes without having influenced, or without a wish to influence the destiny of others, has neither character, force, nor volition in his style.

Towards the eighteenth century, some French authors conceived for the first time a hope of usefully propagating their speculative ideas: their style has consequently assumed a bolder tone, their eloquence a warmth more genuine. A man of letters, living in a country where the patriotism of the citizen is only a barren sentiment, is, if I may be allowed so to express myself, obliged to fancy himself under the influence of passions, in order to describe them; to create fictitious emotions, to be enabled perfectly to comprehend their effects; to qualify himself to write, and in short, if possible, abstract himself, as it were, from his own existence, in order to examine what literary measures may be adopted from his opinions and sentiments.

Already we may perceive the outline of the great change which political liberty must produce in literature, by comparing the writers of the age of Louis XIV., with those of the eighteenth century: but to what strength would not talents attain in a government where they are a really existing power? The author, or the orator, feels himself ennobled by the moral or political importance of the subject on which he treats: if he pleads for the victim before the assassin, for liberty in presence of the oppressor; if the unfortunate wretches in whose defence he speaks, hear, tremblingly the sound of his voice, turn pale if he hesitates, and lose all hope if an expression of triumph escapes from the conviction of his mind; if the fate of the country itself is confided to him; he ought to endeavor to withdraw the selfish from their own interests and from their terrors, to excite in his auditors that emotion, that frenzy of virtue, which a certain lofty eloquence may inspire for a moment, even in the bosoms of the guilty. How is it possible under such circumstances, and with such a design, that he should not even surpass himself? He will find ideas and expressions which the ambition of doing good can alone inspire; he will feel all the powers of his genius raised; and when at some future time he shall read over what he has written, or what he recited at such a particular period, he may exclaim with Voltaire, when he heard some of his own verses repeated, 'No, it could not be I who wrote that.' And in fact it is not man independently, it is not man aided only by his own individual faculties, who attains by his own exertions to those strokes of eloquence whose irresistible authority disposes of our moral existence entirely at his own pleasure; but man when he feels himself called upon to defend and protect suffering innocence; man, when enabled to overthrow despotism; man, in a word, when he devotes himself to the happiness of the whole human race, who then believes and really feels a kind of supernatural inspiration.

And does the revolution inspire France with such emulation and such glory? This shall be inquired into in the second part of this work.

I here end my reflections upon the past, and shal now proceed to examine the general state of things, and offer some conjectures relative to the future. More lively interests and passions still in existence will judge of this new kind of search; but I feel, nevertheless, that I cannot analyze the present so impartially, as if time had already swallowed up the years of which we treat.

Of all the abstractions arising from solitary meditation, the most natural apparently is to make general observations upon the scenes passing before our eyes, as we should do upon the history of preceding centuries. A habit of reflection, more than any other employment in life, detaches us from all personal interests. The chain of ideas and the gradual progression of philosophical truths, fix the mind's attention much more than the passing incoherent and partial relations which may exist between our own private history and the events of the time in which we live.

ANCIENT AND MODERN LITERATURE.

PART SECOND.

OF THE PRESENT STATE OF MENTAL IMPROVEMENT IN FRANCE, AND OF ITS FUTURE PROGRESS.

CHAPTER I.

GENERAL PLAN OF THE SECOND PART.

I have traced the history of the human mind from the time of Homer to the year 1789. National pride led me to consider the French revolution as a new era in the intellectual world. Perhaps it is only a calamitous event!—perhaps the influence of long habits will not for a certain period of time suffer this event to be productive of one profitable institution, or one philosophical result: but whatever may be the case, as this second part will contain some general ideas respecting the progress of the human mind, it may not be useless to develop those ideas, even should the application of them be left to another nation or another century.

I think it always interesting to examine what would be the prevailing character of the literature of a great and enlightened people, in whose country should be established liberty, political equality, and manners in unison with its institutions: there is but one nation in the world to whom some of these reflections may be applied in the present day;—America. The American literature, indeed, is not yet formed; but when their magistrates are called upon to address themselves on any subject to the public opinion, they are eminently gifted with the power of touching all the affections of the heart, by expressing simple truth and pure sentiments; and to do this, is already to be acquainted with the most useful secret of elegant style. Let it be admitted then, that the following reflections, although intended for France in particular, are nevertheless sus ceptible, under various relations, of a more general application.

Whenever I speak of the modifications and amendment which may be hoped for in the French literature, I always suppose the existence and the duration of liberty and the political equality. Must it then be concluded, that I believe in the possibility of this liberty, and this equality? I do not undertake to solve such a problem, still less would I resolve to renounce such a hope: my aim is to endeavor to discover what influence over mental improvement and over literature would arise from the institutions necessary to such principles, and the manners which such institutions would introduce.

It is impossible to separate these observations, when they have France for their object, from the effects already produced by the revolution itself; those effects, it must be allowed, are detrimental to manners, to literature, and philosophy. In the course of this work I have shown how the confused mixture of the northern and eastern people had occasioned barbarism for a time, although the eventual result was a very considerable progress both in mental improvement and in civilization. The introduction of a new class into the French government may probably introduce a similar effect. This revolution may, in the course of time, enlighten a larger portion of mankind; but for many years vulgarity of manners and opinions must in many respects cause both taste and reason to become retrograde.

No one can deny that literature has suffered greatly in France, since the terrific system has swept away men, characters, sentiments, and ideas. But without analyzing the result of that dreadful period, which must be considered as totally out of the common course of things,—as a prodigious phenomenon which no stated or regular custom can either explain or produce, it is the nature of a revolution to check, for some years, the progress of mental improvement, and to give it afterwards a new impulsion. We must then first examine the two principal obstacles which oppose the development of the mind,—the loss of polished manners, and that of emulation, which the rewards of public opinion might excite. When I shall have laid before my readers the different ideas arising from this subject, I shall consider of what degree of perfectibility literature and philosophy are susceptible, if we correct ourselves of revolutionary errors, withont abjuring with them those truths which interest all Europe in its reflections upon the foundation of a republic virtuous and free.

My conjectures upon the future shall be the result of my observations upon the past. I have endeavored to prove that the democracy of Greece, the aristocracy of Rome, and the paganism of the two nations, gave a different character to philosophy and the fine arts; that the ferocity of the north being blended with the degenerate manners of the east, and both being softened by the Christian religion, have been the principal cause of the state of the mind in the middle century. I have endeavored to explain the singular inconsistencies in Italian literature by the remembrance of past liberty and habits of present superstition; a monarchy the most aristocratic in its manners, and a royal government the most republican in its customs, have appeared to me the first source of the striking difference between French and English literature. There yet remains to be examined, after the influence which laws, religion, and manners have at all times exercised over literature, what are the changes which the new institutions, in France, may occasion in its writings. If such and such political institutions have had certain results; we may foresee by analogy, how similar or different causes would act upon their respective effects. The new progress in literature and philosophy which I propose to point out, will be a continuation of the development of perfectibility, the grand advancement of which I have traced from the time of the Greeks. It is easy to show how much our progress in this line would be accelerated, if all those prejudices which now stand in the way of truth were removed, and if nothing remained to philosophy, but to proceed directly from demonstration to demonstration.

Such is the method adopted by the sciences, which every day advance to some new discovery, and never lose what they have gained. Yes, even if that future, on which my imagination delights to dwell, be still far distant; it may nevertheless be useful to inquire into what it may be. We must overcome the despondency which some terrible epochas have given rise to in the public mind: at such periods, the judgment is obscured by fears or calculations entirely foreign to the immutability of philosophical ideas. It is to obtain reputation or power, that we study the bias of temporary opinions; but if we aspire to think or to write, we ought to consult only the solitary conviction of contemplative reason.

We must banish from our minds the ideas which float around us, and which are indeed only the metaphorical representations of some personal interests; we must alternately take the lead of, or follow the popular opinion: this perhaps precedes, rejoins, or abandons us; but immutable truth abides with us.

Mental conviction cannot, however, be so strong a support as conscious feeling. The dictates of morality, as to action, are never doubtful; but we often hesitate, and frequently repent of our opinions when ill-disposed men take advantage of them, and make them serve as an excuse for their crimes, and the glimmering light of reason does not yet afford a sufficient solace in the calamities of life. Nevertheless, either the understanding is a useless faculty, or mankind must be continually making some new discoveries which may advance beyond the epocha in which they live. It is impossible to condemn reflection to retrace its steps with diminished hopes and increased regrets; the human mind, hopeless of futurity, would sink into the most abject state of degradation. Let us then seek that *future* in literary productions and philosophical ideas; one day, perhaps, those ideas in greater maturity may be applied to institutions; but in the meantime the faculties of the mind may, at least, be usefully directed; they still may be productive of national glory.

Those who, surrounded by human passions and frailties, are possessed of superior talents, will soon be persuaded that those very talents are misfortunes; but they will be found so many benefits, if their possessors can believe in the eventual perfectibility of mind; if they can find new relations between ideas and sentiments; if they can penetrate more deeply into the knowledge of mankind; if they can add one degree of new force to morality; if, in a word, they can flatter themselves with the possibility of uniting, by means of eloquence, the various opinions of all those who are the friends of liberal truths.

CHAPTER II.

OF TASTE AND URBANITY OF MANNERS; AND OF THEIR INFLUENCE IN LITERATURE AND POLITICS.

It has for some time been a prevailing opinion in France, that a revolution in literature was necessary, and that the laws of taste in every department ought to be indulged with the greatest possible latitude. Nothing could be more inimical to the progress of literature,—that progress which so effectually promotes the diffusion of philosophical light, and consequently the support of liberty; nothing can be more fatal to refinement of manners, one of the first aims that republican institutions ought to have in view The fastidious nicety of some societies of the ancient system have, undoubtedly, no connection with the true principles of taste, which are always in conformity with reason; but some prescribed laws might be abolished without subverting those barriers which point out the path of genius, and preserve both consistency and dignity in oratory as well as composition. The only motive alleged for an entire change in the style and forms which preserve respect and promote reflection, is the despotism which the aristocratic classes of a monarchy exercise over taste and customs. It is therefore useful to mark the defects which may be found in some of the pretensions, pleasantries, and exigencies of the societies of the ancient system, in order to show afterwards with more effect what disgusting consequences, both in literature and politics, have arisen from the boundless audacity, the awkward gayety, and the degrading vulgarity which it has been attempted to introduce in some periods of the revolution. From the opposition of these two extremes, from the factitious ideas of monarchy, and the gross systems of some individuals during the revolution, some just reflections must necessarily accrue respecting the noble simplicity which ought to characterize the oratory, the compositions, and the customs of a republican government.

The French nation was, in some respects, too much civilized; its institutions and social habits had usurped the place of natural affections. In the ancient republics, and above all at Lacedemon, the laws moulded the individual character of each citizen, formed them all upon the same model, and political sentiments absorbed all other sentiments. What Lycurgus effected by his laws in favor of the republican spirit, the French monarchy had done by its powerful prejudices in favor of the vanities of rank.

This vanity engaged almost exclusively the minds of each class; the life of man seemed dedicated to the desire of making a conspicuous figure, to obtain an acknowledged superiority over his immediate rival, and to excite that envy in others, to which he himself in his turn became a prey. From individual to individual, from class to class, suffering vanity could be happy only on the throne; in every other station, from the most elevated to the most abject, men wasted their lives in comparing themselves with their equals or their superiors; and far from rating themselves at their own intrinsic worth, they sought from the opinions of others to know in what estimation they stood with respect to their importance amongst their equals. This spirit of contention upon subjects totally frivolous, except in their influence over happiness; this ardent desire to succeed; this dread of offending; altered and often exaggerated the true principles of natural taste; there was a fashion of the day, a fashion of some particular class, in a word, that which must arise from the general opinion created by similar relations. Societies then existed, which could by allusions to their customs their interests, or even their caprices, ennoble the most hacknied phrases, or proscribe the most simple beauties. If we showed ourselves strangers to these manners in society, we publicly acknowledged ourselves to be of an inferior rank; and inferiority of rank is of itself an unsavory mouthful in a country where a distinction of rank exists. Individuals ridicule individuals, where the people are strangers to an education of liberty; and in France, even with the most exalted mind, it would have been only an absurdity in him who should endeavor to emancipate himself from that prevailing style which was established by the ascendency of the highest class.

This despotism of opinion being carried too far, must eventually be prejudicial to real talents; the laws of taste and politeness became daily more refined; the manners were continually growing more dissimilar from the impressions of nature. Ease of address existed without freedom of sentiments; politeness divided the people into classes instead of cementing a general union amongst them; and all that natural simplicity requisite to be perfectly graceful, did not prevent men from growing old either in a constant habit of attention, or a pretended inattention to the observance of the least marks of social distinction.

Nevertheless they wished to establish a sort of equality which placed all characters and all talents apparently upon the same level; an equality most undesirable to men of distinguished abilities, but at the same time most consoling to jealous mediocrity. It was necessary to speak and to be silent exactly like other people to know the reigning customs that no innovation might be hazarded; and it was only an assiduous imitation of received habits, that it was possible to acquire a reputation peculiar to ourselves. The art of avoiding the dangers of too brilliant an understanding was, in fact, the only use to which the understanding was applied: and real genius was consequently often smoothered by all these fashionable restrictions. This sort of taste, which ought rather to be deemed effeminate than refined, which is shocked at any new effort, at any daring sedition, or even at an energetic expression-checked all the flights of fancy; genius cannot pay a complaisant attention to all these artificial considerations; fame is impetuous, and its tumultous retinue must break through such slight oppositions.

But society, that is to say, relations without any aim, trifling concerns without subordination, a theatre, where merit was appreciated by marks the most foreign from its intrinsic value; society, I repeat, in France had endued ridicule with such power, that even, men of the most elevated minds could not brave it. Of all the weapons that can destroy the emulation of exalted characters, the most effectual is the aim of ridicule. A quick and subtile penetration into the failings of an exalted character, the weaknesses of brilliant talents, checks that confidence in its own powers, which is often so essential to genius; and the slightest lasting of cold and unfeeling raillery may, in a generous heart, prove a mortal wound to that lively hope which animated it to enthusiasm in glory and virtue.

Nature has supplied remedies for the great evils to which man is subject; has balanced genius with adversity, ambition with perils, and virtue with calumny; but ridicule can insinuate itself into life, can attach itself even to estimable qualities, and secretly and imperceptibly undermine them.

Disdainful indifference has also great power over enthusiasm of the most pure kind; grief even loses that eloquence with which nature has endued it, when it meets with a spirit of irony; energy of expression, an unstudied accent, action itself, freedom of action, is inspired by a sort of confidence in the sentiments of those around us; one cold pleasantry annihilates it.

A spirit of ridicule attaches itself to one who may hold an object in the world in high estimation: it laughs at all those who, advanced to a serious period of life, still confide in unfeigned sentiments and weighty interests. In this respect it may not be devoid of a philosophical tendency; but this same discouraging spirit checks the emotions of a soul worked up to enthusiasm; nay, so utterly does it disconcert, as frequently to excite the warmest indignation; it blights every youthful hope; in short, unblushing vice alone is out of the reach of its shafts; that indeed, ridicule seldom attempts to attack, but even shows an inclination to respect the character over which it has no power.

This tyranny of ridicule, which particularly characterized the latter years of the ancient government, after having given a polish to taste, terminated in violent measures, and literature must necessarily have felt the effects of them. In order, therefore, to give more elevation of style to composition, and more energy to character, we find it requisite that taste should not be subordinate to the elegant and studied habits of aristocratical societies, however remarkable they may be for the perfection of grace ; their despotism would produce the most serious ill-consequences to liberty, political equality, and even to the higher walks of literature : but how greatly would bad taste, carried even to grossness, be prejudicial to literary fame, to morality, to liberty, to all, in fact, of good and great that can exist in the relations and connections between man and man ?

Since the revolution, a disgusting vulgarity of manners has often been found united to the exercise of the highest authorities. Now the defects of power are contagious ; in France, above all, power not only influences the actions and conversations, but even the secret thoughts of the numerous flatterers who hover about men in power. Courtiers in all governments imitate those whom they extol ; they are penetrated with esteem for those who can be serviceable to them ; they forget, that even their own interest requires only exterior demonstrations, and that it is not necessary to violate their judgment also, in order to show themselves what they wish to appear.

Bad taste, such as we have seen it to prevail during some years of the revolution, is not only prejudicial to the relations of society and literature, but undermines morality : men indulge themselves in pleasantries upon their own baseness, their own vices, and shamelessly glory in them in order to ridicule those timid minds which still shrink from this degrading mirth. Those free-thinkers of a new description make a boast of their shame, and applaud themselves in proportion to the astonishment they have excited around them.

The gross or cruel expressions which some men in power have frequently allowed themselves in conversation, must in the course of time occasion depravity in their own minds, while they shock the morality of those who hear them.

An excellent law in England interdicts men, whose profession obliges them to shed the blood of animals, from the power of exercising judiciary functions. Indeed, independent of the morality which is founded upon reason, there is also that of natural instinct,—that whose impressions are unforeseen and irresistible. When we accustom ourselves to see animals suffer, we in time overcome the natural repugnancy of the sense of anguish, we become less accessible to pity even for our fellow creatures, at least we no longer involuntarily feel its impressions. Vulgar and ferocious expressions produce in some respects the same effect as the sight of blood, when we accustom ourselves to pronounce them the ideas which they excite become more familiar. Men in battle animate each other to those sentiments of revenge which ought to inspire them, by an incessant use of the grossest language. The justice and impartiality necessary for civil administration make it their duty to employ such forms and expressions as may calm both him who speaks and those who hear.

Good taste, in the language and in the manners of those who govern, by inspiring more respect, renders more terrific measures less necessary. A magistrate whose manners create disgust, can hardly avoid having recourse to persecution in order to obtain obedience.

Kings are wrapt in a certain cloud of illusions and recollections ; but deputies commanding in the name of their personal superiority, have need of all the exterior marks of that superiority : and what more evident mark can be found, than that good taste which, discovering itself in every word, gesture, accent, and even in every action, announces a peaceable and stately mind, which comprehends immediately whatever is brought before it, and which never loses sight of its own respectability nor of the respect due to others It is thus that good taste exercises a real influence in political affairs.

It is a truth generally received, that a spirit of republicanism requires a revolution in the character of literature. I believe this idea true, but in a different acceptation from that generally allowed. A republican spirit requires more correctness in good taste, which is inseparable from sound morality : it also, undoubtedly, permits more energetic beauties in literature, a more philosophical and more affecting picture of the important events of life. Montesquieu, Rousseau, and Condillac, belonged by anticipation to the republican systems ; and they have commenced the so desirable revolution in the character of French writings :— this revolution must be completed. The republic necessarily drawing forth stronger passions, the art of portraying must improve, while the subject becomes more exalted ; but, by a whimsical contrast, it is in the licentious and frivolous style that authors have most profited by the liberty which literature is supposed to have acquired.

The graceful models which the French possess in their language, may serve as a guide to them, but only as they will also serve foreign nations : the same spirit cannot be renewed in France without the style and habits of what was called good company. In a free country, society will be more engaged by political affairs than by attention to ceremony, or even the charms of pleasantry. In a nation where political equality shall subsist, all kinds of merit may gain admission : and there will no longer exist an exclusive society, dedicated only to bring itself to perfection, and uniting in itself all the ascendency of fortune and power. Now, unless such a tribunal constantly exists, the youthful mind cannot be formed to that delicacy of feeling, to those fine and correct shades which alone can give to the lighter kinds of writing that grace of conformity, and that finished taste so much admired in some French authors, and particularly in the fugitive pieces of Voltaire.

Literature will disgrace itself completely in France, if we multiply those affected attempts at grace and taste which only serve to render us ridiculous : some genuine humor may, nevertheless, still be found in good comedy ; but as to that playful gayety with which we have been inundated even amidst all our calamities, if we except some individuals who can still remember the times that are past, all new attempts in this style corrupt the taste for literature in France, and place the French below the level of all the serious nations in Europe.

Before the revolution it had been frequently remarked, that a Frenchman, unaccustomed to the society of the first class, made known his inferiority of rank the instant he attempted pleasantry : whilst the Englishman, whose manners are always serious and simple, scarcely ever betrayed by his conversation to what rank in society he belonged. In spite of the distinctions which will long exist between the two nations, French writers must shortly perceive that they no longer have the same means of succeeding in the art of pleasantry ; and far from believing that the revolution has given them greater latitude in this respect, they ought more than ever to pay an assiduous attention to good taste ; since the confusions in society produced by a revolution, no longer offer any good models, and do not inspire those daily habits which render grace and taste natural to us without the aid of reflection to recal them.

The laws of taste, as applied to republican literature, are in their nature more simple, but not less strict than those which were adopted by the authors of the age of Louis XIV. Under a monarchical government, a multitude of customs sometimes substituted conformity for reason, and the respect paid to society for the sentiments of the heart : but in a republic, taste ought to consist only in the perfect knowledge of all true and durable relations : to fail therefore in the principles of taste, would be nothing less than ignorance of the true nature of things.

In the time of the monarchy, it was frequently necessary to disguise a bold censure, to veil a new opinion under the form of received prejudices; and the taste which it was necessary to introduce in these different turns, required a singularly delicate ingenuity of mind: but the garb of truth, in a free country, accords with truth itself:—expression and sentiment ought to spring from the same source.

We are not obliged, where liberty reigns, to confine ourselves within the circle of the same opinions, neither is a variety of forms necessary to conceal a sameness of ideas. The interest of progression always exists, since prejudices do not limit the career of thought: the mind, therefore, having no longer to struggle against lassitude, acquires more simplicity, and does not hazard, in order to awaken attention, those studied graces which are repugnant to natural taste.

A bold and very difficult stratagem, allowed under the ancient government, was the art of offending against the manners without wounding taste, and to make a mockery of morality by proportioning delicacy of expressions to indecency of principles. Happily, however, this talent is as ill adapted to the virtue as to the genius of a republic: as soon as one barrier was overthrown, the rest would be disregarded, the relations of society would no longer have the power to curb those whom sacred ties could not restrain.

Moreover, extraordinary quickness of genius is requisite in order to succeed in this dangerous style, which unites grace of expression to depravity of sentiments; and by the strong exercise of our faculties, to which we are called in a republic, we lose that ingenuity. The most delicate touches are necessary to give to immorality that grace, without which even the most abandoned of mankind would repel with disgust the pictures and principles of vice.

In another chapter I shall make mention of the gayety of comedy—that which is so connected with the knowledge of the human heart: but it appears to me probable, that Frenchmen will no longer be cited as examples of that turn of mind at once amiable, elegant, and gay, which constituted the charm of the court. Time will sweep away those few who yet remain as models of this kind, and their remembrance will gradually be lost; for books alone will not suffice to retain such characters in our view. That which is of a more delicate nature than thought itself, can only be acquired by habit: if the society which inspired that kind of instinct, that rapid perception, is annihilated, the same instinct and perception must also perish with it. That which can be taught only by specified habits of life, and not by general combinations, can no longer be learned when these habits of life are ended.

It has been observed by an eminent man, that 'happiness is a serious state:' the same may be said of liberty. The dignity of a citizen is more important than that of a subject; for, in a republic, every man of talents is an additional obstacle to political usurpation. Exaltation of character can alone give some weight to this honorable mission with which we are vested by our own conscience.

We have formerly seen men unite dignity of manners with almost constant habits of pleasantry: but this union pre-supposes perfection of taste and delicacy, a conscious feeling of superiority, power, and rank, which cannot be excited by an education of equality. This grace, at once imposing and playful, cannot accord with republican manners; it characterizes too distinctly the habits of rank and fortune. Reflection is more democratic; it increases at the will of chance amongst all men who are sufficiently independent to possess any leisure. Reflection therefore ought to be encouraged by giving our attention less to those subjects in literature which belong exclusively to the grace of expression.

When we have experienced calamity, we are obliged to reflect; and if national misfortunes exalt the characters of men, it is by correcting them of frivolity, and concentrating in one point, by the terrible power of affliction, their scattered faculties.

Literary taste ought to be directed to a graceful expression of ideas: this will not diminish its utility; for it has been proved, that the most profound reflections, and most noble sentiments, produce no effect, if any striking defects in taste divert the attention, break the chain of thought, or interrupt the succession of emotions which lead the mind to important results and the soul to durable impressions.

We may perhaps censure the weakness of the human mind in attaching itself to some misplaced expression, rather than being uniformly engrossed by what is really essential: but in the most desperate situation in life, nay, even in the hour of death, we frequently see that ridiculous incidents can withdraw the mind from a sense of its own sufferings. How are we to hope, then, that any reflections, or any work can excite so deep an interest as that the defects of style may not divert the attention of the reader? Wonderful talents are requisite to withdraw readers from their self-love; but if the defects in style are such as to offer to judges, of whatsoever kind they may be, an opportunity of displaying their own wit, they seize it immediately, and no longer regard either the sentiments or ideas of the author.

The taste necessary for republican literature, in serious works as well as those of imagination, consists not merely in one talent, but in the perfection of all; and so far from being inimical to depth of sentiment or energy of expression, the simplicity it exacts, and the ease it inspires, are the only suitable ornaments to strength of mind.

Urbanity of manners, as well as good taste, (the former of which indeed constitutes a part of the latter,) are both very important in the literary and political world. Although literature may free itself, in a republic much more easily than in a monarchy, from the empire of any fashion generally received in society, yet it is not possible that the models of the greater number of works of imagination should be taken from other examples than from those which we see daily before our eyes. Now, what would become of those writings which necessarily bear the stamp of the manners of their time, if vulgarity, and that style of behavior which displays the defects and disadvantages of every character, should continue to prevail?

The literary men of France would still retain some ancient works, which might yet have power to affect them; but their imagination would not be inspired by the surrounding objects; it would gain food by reading, but never by any impressions which they themselves might feel. They would hardly ever unite, in their compositions, unaffected observation with nobleness of sentiment. Instead of availing themselves of their recollections, they must strive to banish them; nor, scarcely could even a collected mind ever inspire any truly beautiful ideas.

It will be said, perhaps, that politeness is so trifling an advantage, that even the privation of it would not in the least tarnish those great and valuable qualities which constitute strength and elevation of mind. If the ceremonies of gallantry in the age of Louis XIV. are called politeness, most certainly the first-rate men of antiquity had not the slightest idea of it; yet are they not the less to be esteemed, on this account, as the most striking models that history and imagination could offer to the admiration of succeeding ages: but if politeness is in reality that just propriety of conduct which ought to be maintained by man to man; if it indicates what we think ourselves to be, and what we really are; if it teaches others what they are, or what they ought to be; a vast number of sentiments and reflections are allied to politeness.

Its forms vary, of course, according to characters, and the same good-will may be expressed with gentleness or with bluntness; but in order to discuss philosophically the importance of politeness, we must consider the general sense of the word in its most extensive acceptation, without dwelling upon every diversity that may arise from each character.

Politeness is that tie which society has established between men who are strangers to each other. Virtue attaches us to our families, to our friends, and to the unfortunate; but in all those relative connections which have not assumed the character of duty, urbanity of manners softens the affections, opens the way to conviction, and preserves to every man the rank which his merit ought to obtain from him in society.

It points out the degree of consideration to which each individual has raised himself; and viewed in that light, politeness becomes the dispenser of those rewards which it has been the object of a whole life to gain. And now let us examine under how many different forms the fatal effects of vulgarity of manners present themselves, and what ought to be the peculiar character of the politeness adapted to a republican spirit.

Women and great men, love and glory, are the only subjects of reflection that can excite any very lively interest in the mind: but how are we to find pure and exalted models of the female character, in a country where the connections of society are not guarded with the most unsullied delicacy? Whence can we take the symbol of virtue, when even women themselves, those independent judges of the conflicts of life, have suffered the noble instinct of elevated sentiments to fade away in themselves? A woman loses part of her attractions, not only by allowing herself the use of indelicate expressions, but even by hearing them, or permitting them in her presence. In the bosom of her family, modesty and simplicity suffice to maintain the respect which is due to females: but in public life still more is requisite; elegance of language, and polish of manners, constitute a part of her dignity, and these alone never fail of inspiring deference.

During the monarchy, a spirit of chivalry, the pomp of rank, the splendor of wealth, every thing indeed that struck the imagination, supplied, in some respects, the place of real merit: but in a republic, women lose much of their dignity, if they cannot inspire awe by those qualities which characterize their natural elevation of mind. The instant we banish an allusion, we must substitute a reality; as soon as we eradicate an ancient prejudice, we stand in need of a new virtue. A republic, far from giving more liberty to the habitual relations of society, (as all its distinctions are founded solely upon personal qualiites,) requires in us a more scrupulous attention to preserve ourselves from fault. In this form of government, if our reputation is in the slightest degree tarnished, we cannot, as in a monarchy, renew our consequence by rank, by birth, nor by any advantage not arising from our own intrinsic worth.

What I have said of women is equally applicable to men engaged in stations of eminence. It will be necessary for them to keep up their own consequence with much more assiduity, than in a period when aristocratic dignities efficaciously secured to their possessors the esteem and respect of the multitude. Those existing opinions, which in a republic will be daily attacked or defended, must give a great importance to all that can influence the minds or the imaginations of mankind.

If from the partiality of opinion we pass to the support of legal power; we shall see, that authority is in itself an insupportable weight upon those over whom it extends itself. Those minds which are not created to be slaves, early experience a prejudice, against power. If a want of feeling in him who commands, aggravates this prejudice, it becomes perfect hatred. Every man of taste and possessing an elevated mind, ought to feel almost the necessity of apologizing for the power he possesses. Political authority is an inconvenience that must be submitted to for the sake of prosperity, order and security: but the depository of this authority ought always to justify himself in some measure by his comportment and his actions.

In the course of the last ten years, we have frequently seen the enlightened governed by the ignorant; whose arrogance of tone, and vulgarity of manners, inspired more disgust than even the shallowness of their intellects. Many of these people confounded republican opinions with unfeeling speeches and gross pleasantries; and spontaneous affecton was naturally banished from the republic.

Manners have a greater power of attracting or repelling, than opinions; I will almost venture to assert, even than sentiments. Possessed of a certain liberality of mind, we may live agreeably in the midst of a society professedly devoted to a different party from that to which we ourselves belong; we may even forget serious injuries, or fears, perhaps, justly inspired by the immorality of a man, if the nobleness of his language lulls us into an illusion as to the purity of his mind. But it is impossible to endure that vulgarity of education which betrays itself in every expression, every gesture, in the tone of the voice, the attitude, in short, in all the involuntary marks of the general habits of life.

I do not here speak of the esteem which arises from reflection, but of that involuntary impression which is every moment renewed. In great events, sympathetic minds discover each other by the sentiments of the heart; but in the minutiæ of society, we are known to each other by our manners; and vulgarity, carried to a certain length, makes the unfortunate object or witness of it experience a feeling of embarrassment, and even of shame which is altogether insupportable.

Happily, we are seldom compelled to endure vulgarity of manners from a respect to elevation of sentiment: strict integrity inspires a confidence so noble and a tranquillity so pure, that in whatever situation of life we find it, it is easy to discover what a good education would have produced under the same circumstances. That depraved vulgarity of which the French have so often been the victims, was almost alway a composition of depraved sentiments; of audacity, cruelty and insolence, which showed themselves under the most odious forms. Conformity is the image of morality; its representative in all circumstances which give no opportunity for proof; it preserves man in the habit of respecting the opinions of man. If the chiefs of a state neglect or condemn this virtue, they will no longer inspire that consequence of which themselves are the first to dispense the rudiments.

Another kind of rudeness may characterize men in power: it is not grossness; it is, if I may express myself so, a kind of political fatuity; the importance which a man attaches to his place; the effect which that place produces on himself, and with which he wishes to inspire others. Many of these instances must have been observed since the revolution. In the ancient government, places of the first importance were filled only by those individuals who had been accustomed from their infancy to the privileges and advantages of high rank; power effected no change in their usual habits; but since the revolution, eminent magistracies have been occupied by men of mean condition in life, and whose character was not naturally elevated: humble then as to their personal merit, but vain of their power, they have thought themselves obliged to adopt new manners, because they have obtained new employments. Of all the effects of vanity, this is the most contrary to that affection and respect which republican magistrates should inspire; affection and respect are attached to the individual character; and the man who believes himself to be another creature when appointed to any dignity, clearly indicates to you by his own manners, that if he loses it, your esteem and respect are to be transferred to his successor.

How can one man possibly recommend himself to another, better than by that dignity of manners and simplicity of expressions, which, brought forward on the stage, or related in history, inspire almost as much enthusiasm as magnanimous actions? I will, moreover, observe, that a succession of chances may lead a man to make himself conspicuous by some illustrious actions, who is, nevertheless, not gifted with a superior genius or an heroic character: but our words, accents, and comportment to those around us, are alone capable of constituting that true greatness of mind which defies imitation.

Some have thought, that reserve and dignity ought to be substituted for the once gracious manners of the French. Undoubtedly, the first citizens of a free state ought to display more seriousness in their behavior, than the flatterers of a monarch; but too much coldness would check the spring of all generous emotions. A man who is reserved in his manners, necessarily draws some importance to himself by showing he attaches none to you: but the painful sensation which he inspires, produces nothing useful in any shape: it is not familiar insolence, it is true goodness, it is elevation of mind, it is real superiority, which is humbled by this chilling reserve. Thus we see, manners can never be truly perfect but where they encourage the virtues that each individual may possess, and discountenance his vices.

We must not deceive ourselves as to the exterior marks of respect: to smother noble sentiments, or to dry the source of thought, is to produce only the ill effects of fear; but to elevate the minds of others to the standard of our own, to give to the understanding its full play, to encourage that confidence which all generous minds feel in each other; such is the art of inspiring durable respect.

It is of importance to create in France some ties which may connect parties now at variance; and urbanity of manners is an efficacious means to attain this desirable end. It would unite all enlightened men; and this class so firmly connected, might form a tribunal of opinion, which could distribute praise or censure with some justice.

This tribunal might also exercise its influence over literature: authors would know where to find taste and national spirit, and would strenuously endeavor to describe and to aggrandize it. But of all confusion, the most fatal is that which blends all modes of education without distinction, and separates nothing but the spirit of party. Of what consequence is it to agree in our political opinions, if we differ in mind and sentiments? How lamentable is the effect of civil commotions to attach more importance to a similarity of our views in public affairs, than to all those which constitute the only system of fraternity, whose impressions are indelible!

Urbanity of manners can alone soften the asperities of party spirit; it suffers us to see others long before we begin to esteem them, and to converse with them long before any acquaintance commences; and by degrees, that violent aversion which we might feel towards a man whom we had never accosted, grows weaker by the influence of respect and of esteem: hence a sympathy is created, and, in the event, we find our own sentiments inherent in the person whom we had been accustomed to consider as an enemy.

HAPTER III.

OF EMULATION.

Amongst the various methods of bringing the productions of the human mind to perfection, we must lay great stress upon the aim and end that are kept in view by those who devote themselves to intellectual studies. Either an indolent or an active life is more suited to the inclination of man, than meditation; and if we would have all the powers of his mind consecrated to the research of philosophical truth, his emulation must be encouraged by the hope of serving his country and influencing the destiny of his fellow-citizens.

Some minds will feed upon the mere pleasure of discovering new ideas; and in sciences requiring accuracy; above all, there are many men for whom this pleasure suffices: but when the experience of reflection tends to moral and political consequences, its object must necessarily be an influence over the destiny of mankind. The aim of those works which appertain to the higher departments of literature is, to effect useful changes; to accelerate some essential progress; to modify, in a word, both institutions and laws. But in a country where philosophy cannot be applied to any real purpose; when eloquence can obtain only literary fame; both one and the other would eventually appear mere occupations for leisure hours, and the incitement to pursue them would daily grow weaker.

I certainly cannot deny, that the situation of France for some years past has been more adverse to the development of talents and understanding, than most of the epochs of history: but I believe, that while we examine what is peculiarly necessary to philosophical emulation, we shall discover why a revolutionary spirit, during the time of its influence, is totally discouraging to reflection; how the ancient government humbled those whom it protected; and by what means the republic might carry to the greatest possible height the noble ambition of mankind to make progressive advances towards reason.

On a first view, we are inclined to think that civil commotions, by annihilating ancient rank, must give to the natural faculties the full use and development of all their powers: and in the beginning, this is undoubtedly the case; but at the expiration of a very short time, the factious party feel towards the enlightened a hatred at least equal to that felt by the ancient usurpers. Violent spirits make enlightened men subservient to their purposes, when they wish to triumph over the established power: but when they only aim to maintain their own ground, they endeavor to testify the most sovereign contempt for reason, and stupidly declare, that mental faculties and philosophical ideas can belong only to effeminate minds: and the feudal code appears again, only under new names.

Every despotic character, in whatsoever situation, detests reflection; and if blind fanaticism be the arm of authority, its most formidable enemy is, undoubtedly, the man who preserves the faculty of judging. Violent men can only be allied to narrow minds; they alone can submit or rebel at the will of their chief.

If revolutionary commotions be prolonged beyond the attainment of the object they ostensibly aim at, authority always descends another step amongst the ignorant classes of society. The greater the mediocrity of men, the more assiduous they seem to suit themselves: they repulse enlightened reason with disdain, as something heterogeneous to their nature, and which must be fatal to their empire.

If any party wish that injustice should triumph: it will, of course, avoid giving any encouragment to mental improvement; a man may disgrace his abilities by devoting them to the defence of injustice; but if the influence of reason is diffused in any nation, it must necessarily tend to bring general morality to perfection.

A revolutionary spirit traces out its own path, and forms its own language; and if any one should wish to vary, merely for the sake of eloquence, those established phrases introduced by party-interest, he would alarm his chiefs · they would tremble to see new sentiments and new thoughts advanced, which might serve their cause indeed to-day, but which to-morrow might prove undisciplinable, and take a new direction. There are, if I may be allowed the expression, certain received formulas of cruelty, from which men, even in whom the greatest confidence is placed, are never permitted to deviate.

Suspicions, jealousies, the calculations of ambition, all unite to withdraw superior minds from revolutionary struggles; violent and obscure men range themselves in their proper place only when order is established; in the overthrow of all ideas and sentiments, they think themselves authorized to perpetuate the confusion which exists; and having, amidst their Saturnalia (to borrow the term from antiquity,) become masters of talent and of virtue, captive reflection is compelled to bear all the weight of their ignorance and vanity.

In the crisis of popular factions, independence of judgment must be banished first of all. Speech serves only to perpetuate anger, and to fix its first emotions as decrees. The infuriated gave the name of aristocracy to the most republican sentiments in the world, —the love of reason and of virtue. The spirit of cruelty struggles against philosophy, defies education, and shows itself more indulgent to the vices of the heart than to the talents of the mind.

If this state of things continue, we shall no longer possess any distinguished characters except in the career of arms: nothing can damp the ardor for military fame: this always attains the end it desires, and demands from the general voice whatever applause it has a right to expect. But in this free interchange, whence results the glory of authors and philosophers, ideas arise, if I may so say, from that very approbation which men are disposed to grant them.

Bravery may struggle against the ascendency of a reigning faction; but the inspiration of talent is smothered by it. The tyranny of an individual would not with equal certainty produce such an effect; but the tyranny of a party, often assuming the form of public opinion, inflicts a much deeper wound upon emulation.

If we were to compare the lot of enlightened men under Louis XIV. with that in which they have been involved by revolutionary violence, every thing would appear in favor of the monarchy; but what connection could exist between the patronage of a king and republican emulation, when at length it should assume its real character?

Strength of mind does not wholly display itself, except in attacks upon power; it is by opposition that the English acquire the talents requisite in a prime minister. When, on the contrary, the favors of opinion depend also upon the favor of one man, reflection cannot feel itself free in any of its conceptions: far from devoting itself to the discovery of truth, its powers are in every way limited: the mind must incessantly recoil upon itself. Scarcely is it possible, amidst works of imagination, amidst the domain of invention which legal power infringes not; scarcely, I say, is it possible to forget, that the amusement of the sovereign and his courtiers is the grand point of success that is aimed at.

In all languages, literature may flourish for a certain time without having recourse to philosophy; but when the beauty of expressions images, and political turns, is no longer new; when all the beauties of antiquity are adapted to modern genius; we feel the necessity of that progressive reason, which each day attains some useful end, and which offers an unlimited field to improve: nevertheless, how was it possible to write philosophically, in a country where the rewards bestowed by one individual, the king, were the representative shadows of glory.

The dependent state of existence of men of literature under the French monarchy, gave them no authority whatever in those important questions which relate to the destiny of mankind. How could they acquire any dignity in a social order of this nature, unless by showing themselves adverse to it? And what a miserable medley of flattery and truth do we find in the writings of those philosophers, at once incredulous submissive and protected!

Rousseau has freed himself, in this century, from the greater part of prejudices and monarchical considerations. Montesquieu, although with more caution, knew well enough how, when occasion served, to display the boldness of an independent spirit. But Voltaire, who often wished to unite the favors of a court with philosophical independence, shows us the contrast, and evidences the difficulty of such a design in the most forcible manner.

What we call *encouraging* literary men, is to place them below the power from which they receive their recompense; it is to consider literary genius apart from the social world, and from political interests; to treat it in the same manner as we should a talent for music or painting; or, in a word, for any art in which reflection, in which the whole mind indeed must be absorbed.

But to encourage literature itself in its highest walks, and of this I am exclusively speaking in the present chapter; to do this, is indeed true glory; the glory of Cicero, the glory of Cæsar also, and of Brutus. The first saved his country by his oratorical eloquence and his consular talents; the second, in his commentaries, wrote the history of his exploits; and the third, by the eloquence of his style, the philosophical elevation by which his letters are characterized made himself beloved as a man exemplary for the assassination he committed.

It is only in free states that the genius of action can be united to that of reflection. In the ancient government, literary talents almost always pre-supposed the absence of political ones. A turn for public business cannot be discovered by any given signs, until it is displayed in important posts; men of mediocrity are interested in persuading others that they alone are possessed of this talent; and in order to gain credit for it, they pique themselves upon those qualities of which they are destitue, upon that energy which they have not, those ideas which they are incapable of comprehending, and upon the success which they disdain: these are the guarantees of their political capacity.

It seems a general wish in absolute monarchies, that a sort of mystery should be observed as to the qualities which are adapted to government, in order that a self-importance and cold mediocrity may distance a superior understanding, and declare it incapable of contemplations much more simple than those in which it has been constantly occupied.

In the language adopted by a coalition of certain men, a knowledge of the human heart consists in never being guided, either in our aversions or our preferences, by indignation against vice, or enthusiasm in the cause of virtue; to be versed in the science of business, is to be never influenced in one decision by any generous or philosophical motive. The republic, discussing at large many of its interests, and submitting every thing to the general voice, must enfranchise us from that blind faith which was formerly exacted as to the secrets of the art of government.

Undoubtedly, great talents are necessary for a good administration; but it was in order to banish talents, that people endeavored to inspire a belief that those reflections, which serve to form the profound philosopher, the eminent author, and the eloquent orator, have no connection with the principles by which the chiefs of a nation ought to be guided. The great Chancellor Bacon, Sir William Temple, L'Hopital, &c., were philosophers and men of literature, and have shown themselves to be the first of statesmen.*

* The Chancellor Bacon was guilty of the most atrocious in-

Frederic II., Marcus Aurelius, and indeed the generality of the kings or heroes whose fame has been the boast of their nation, possessed at the same time minds enlightened by philosophy; their learning, and their talents in civil matters, rendered them dear to posterity, and gained them, during life, the obedience of admiration,—that obedience which gives to absolute power the most delightful attribute of free government; the voluntary assent of public opinion.

Certainly there is no career so limited, so confined, as that of literature, if we view it in the light in which it is frequently considered,—as detached from all philosophy, having no aim but to amuse the leisure hours of life and fill up the void of the mind: such an occupation renders us incapable of the least employment that can require positive knowledge, or that obliges us to render our ideas applicable. A boundless vanity is generally the attendant of literature thus humbled and confined; its possessor belies his reason by the value which he attaches to words without ideas, and to ideas without consequences; he is, of all men, the most occupied with himself, and the most ignorant of what interests others. Literature must often assume such a character, when it is cultivated by men removed from all affairs of importance.

The most degrading circumstance to literature was its inutility; that which rendered the maxims of government illiberal, was such an entire disunion of politics and philosophy, that those who had devoted their talents to instruct and enlighten mankind, were immediately judged incapable of governing them. Traces still remain of this absurd prejudice; but they must daily become more faint. Philosophy disqualifies us only for that arbitrary and despotic method of governing, which is degrading to the human species. While we bring the ancient spirit of the court into the new republic, let us not pretend that, in administration, any thing can be more essential than reflection, more certain than reason, or more impressive than virtue.

The object of celebrated writers under a free government is not, as in a monarchy, to give vigor to a state of existence without any fixed aim; but for the important purpose of giving to truth all its persuasive expression, when any material resolution may depend upon some acknowledged axiom. We devote ourselves to the study of philosophy, not as a consolation for the prejudices respecting birth, which, under the ancient government, might debar us from all future prospects, but in order to render ourselves qualified for the magistracies of a country where authority is vested only in the hands of reason.

If military power alone prevailed in any state, and disdained literature and philosophy, mental improvement would take a retrograde course, however great the influence to which it might previously have attained: such a power would unite itself with some dispicable talents calculated to throw a veil over authority, with men who would boast of their pretended powers of reflection in order to abuse them: but reason would be transformed into sophistry, and the mind become cunning and subtle in proportion to the degradation of the character.

The tumult inseparable from a republican government frequently endangers liberty; and if the chiefs do not offer to view the double security of courage and understanding, ignorant power, or perfidious cunning, will sooner or later plunge the government into despotism. To promote the happiness of the human race, it is essential that the great men to whom its destiny is confided should possess, almost in an equal degree, a certain number of apposite qualities; as a superiority in one respect only, is not sufficient to captivate the esteem of so many different opinions: neither, if I may thus express myself, does it sufficiently personify the idea which we love to entertain of a celebrated man.

gratitude; and his delicacy in pecuniary matters has been strongly suspected: but here, his talents only are called in question, and not his morality; a distinction which we have but too well learned to make within the last ten years.

If words have not eloquently instructed us as to the motive of actions, and if actions have not proved the truth of words; memory can retain only an isolated recollection of either words or actions. The soldier without an enlightened mind, or the orator without bravery, cannot captivate the imagination: certain sentiments with us still remain uninfluenced, and our own ideas are still left to decide for ourselves. The ancients felt a passionate admiration for their illustrious chiefs, whose native greatness stamped their characters with divers talents and glory of various kinds. A variety of superior qualities not only elevates him who possesses them; but establishes a greater connection between this extraordinary man and his fellow-creatures. Any one faculty out of proportion to the rest, appears a caprice of nature; whilst a union of many tranquilizes the mind and attracts affection. The moral character of a great man ought to present to our view that organization, that balance, that perfect justice, which alone, either in a character or a government, can give the idea of repose and stability.

But perhaps it will be observed, that in a republic this enthusiasm respecting an individual ought of all things to be feared the most; and far from desiring that perfection of character which I have just said is almost essential, those instruments of success ought rather to be sought, who compile discourses, make decrees, or gain conquests, in the same manner as men exercise an exclusive profession, without having one idea beyoud it.

Nothing can be less philosophical, that is to say, nothing can tend less to happiness, than that jealous system which would deprive nations of their rank in history, by levelling the reputation of individuals. General instructions ought to be most assiduously promoted; but in the same level with the interest of the advancement of mental improvement, we must also leave the aim of individual glory. A republic ought to give greater encouragement, than any other government, to the multiplied endeavors which it inspires; a small number only reach the goal, but all join in the race; and although fame rewards nothing but success, every attempt is doubtless of some remote utility.

The love of glory must not be extinguished in great minds, nor the sentiment of admiration in the people: to this sentiment every degree of affection between the governors and the governed owes its existence. Of what benefit is an appreciating and cool judgment in our numerous modern associations? Can millions of men decide upon any thing, each according to his respective understanding? Is it not necessary that a more animated impulse should communicate itself to that multitude whom it is so difficult to unite in one common opinion? If a nation is cold with respect to worth and merit, its contempt will not be regarded; and if some libellous detractors confound in their writings the virtuous man with the guilty, the citizens will no longer feel that emotion of pure affection toward their benefactor, which leads them to repel calumny as a sacrilege.

You cannot attach the people even to the idea of virtue, unless you explain it by the generous actions and the moral character of some particular individuals. Some think more effectually to secure the independence of a people by endeavoring to interest it only by abstract principles; but the multitude comprehend ideas only by events; it displays its justice in hatreds and affections; it will not cease to respect, until it is utterly depraved; and by esteeming its magistrates, it learns to love the government.

The glory of great men is the patrimony of a free country; after their death, it becomes the inheritance of the people at large. The love of our country is constituted by recollections. How is it possible not to admire, in the eloquence of the ancients, the respectful sentiments which they felt for their illustrious dead; the homage paid to their memory; and the examples offered in their names to their successors? Nature has given animation to all existence; and would man change that animation for mere abstraction?

The principle of a republic where political equality is holden as sacred, ought to be the establishment of the most marked distinctions amongst men, according to their talents and their virtues. Free nations ought to have in their tribunals judges inexorably determined to do justice to all, without being laid away either by indignation or enthusiasm; but when such nations have endured their magistrates with the relentless execution of the laws, they may abandon themselves to the freedom of approbation and censure: they may offer to their great men that reward to which alone they aspire,—the opinion of the present time and that of posterity; opinion, the sole recompense, the sole illusion, from which even virtue has never the power to detach itself.

And Cæsar, and Cromwell, some one perhaps will ask; think you that the enthusiasm which they inspired, did not in the end prove fatal to the liberty of their country?

The enthusiasm inspired by military glory, is the only kind that can become dangerous to liberty; but even this is unattended by any fatal consequences, except in those countries where divers causes have destroyed the admiration merited by moral qualities or civil state talents. Thus we have seen a republic overthrown at Rome, and in England; each nation being wearied of granting its esteem by a long continuance of crimes and misfortunes.

Yet let us consider what that power was which struggled singly against Cæsar? It was neither the political institutions of the Romans, nor their senate, nor their armies; it was the greatness of one man; it was the respect which was still universally felt for Cato; this respect balanced the destiny of Cæsar and Cato, nor could Cæsar feel himself secure in the authority, unless his rival should cease to exist.

Cato exemplified the power of virtue on earth; and Rome testified for him that admiration which is an honor to the nation that feels it, and which presents to tyranny a far more considerable obstacle than all the confusion of names, actions, and characters. They might endeavor to give to this confusion the name of a philosophical republic; but, in fact, it would only be combats without victory, disorders without any object in view, and calamities without end.

The reputation and the homage constantly attendant upon men who have gone through an honorable career in public affairs, are amongst the first means of preserving liberty: but what most effectually contributes to the progress of mental improvement is, as was the custom amongst the ancients, to blend together military, legislative, and philosophical pursuits: nothing animates and methodizes intellectual meditations so much as the hope of being immediately useful to the human race. When thought may be the forerunner of action; when a happy reflection may be instantaneously transformed into a beneficent institution; how deep an interest must every man feel in communicating the result of his contemplations: he no longer fears that the light of his reason will be extinguished without having in the least contribted to enlighten the path of active life; he no longer experiences that kind of shame which genius, condemned to pursuits merely speculative, must feel in the presence of the most inferior person, provided that person is vested with a power that may enable him to wipe away a tear, to render a material service, or even to be useful to any individual in existence.

When reflection can efficaciously contribute to the happiness of man, its mission is ennobled and its aim is more exalted: it is then no longer a melancholy reverie, dwelling upon the calamities incident to human life, without the ability to relieve them; it is a powerful weapon bestowed by nature, the liberty of using which must give assurance of its triumph.

Conquerors fear even the soldiers who assisted them to gain their empire; priests fear the very fanaticism on which their power depends; ambition is suspicious of its own instruments: but enlightened men, who have obtained places of the highest importance in the state, can never cease to value and diffuse knowledge. Reason has nothing to fear from reason, and philosophical minds establish their own power upon their equals.

After having examined the various principles of emulation amongst men, it may be useful to consider what influence women may have over mental improvement. This shall be the subject of the following chapter.

CHAPTER IV

OF FEMALE LITERATURE.

Misfortune resembles the black mountain of Bember, situated at the extremity of the burning kingdom of Lahor: while we ascend it, we see before us only barren rocks; but no sooner do we reach the summit, than we perceive the heavens over our head, and the kingdom of Cachemire at our feet.

The Indian Cottage: by Bernardine de St. Pierre.

The rank which women hold in society is still, in many respects, indeterminate; a desire to please draws forth their natural understanding, while reason advises them to remain unknown, and their success is as abso lute as their failure.

I cannot but think, that a period will arrive, when philosophical legislators will bestow a serious attention upon the education of women, upon the civil laws by which they are protected, the duties incumbent upon them, and the happiness which may be secured to them: but, in the present state of things, they are placed neither in the order of nature, nor in the order of society; what some succeed in, proves the destruction of others; their good qualities are sometimes prejudicial to them, while their faults befriend them: one moment they are every thing, the next perhaps they are nothing. Their destiny is, in some respects, similar to that of freed-men in a monarchy; if they attempt to acquire any ascendency,—a power which the laws have not given them, it is imputed to them as a crime; if they remain slaves, they are persecuted and oppressed.

Generally speaking, it would certainly be far better if women would devote themselves wholly to domestic virtues: but a strange caprice in the judgment of men with respect to women is, that they esteem a total inattention to essential duties more pardonable in a female, than the crime of attracting attention by distinguished talents; even an abasement of the heart is tolerated in favor of an inferior understanding, whilst the most unsullied integrity can scarcely obtain forgiveness for real superiority.

Let us lay open to view the divers causes of this eccentricity. I shall begin by considering what is the fate of literary women in a monarchy, and also what awaits them in a republic. My first object must be to characterize the principal differences which may arise from these two political situations in the destiny of such females as may aspire to literary fame; and afterwards to consider at large, what degree of happiness those women who pretend to celebrity may reasonably expect from it.

In a monarchy they have ridicule to fear, and in a republic, hatred.

It is to be expected from the nature of things, that in a monarchy where a strict conformity to fashion and prejudice prevails, every extraordinary action, every attempt to move out of the sphere in which you are placed, must at first appear ridiculous. What is required of you by your situation in life, or by any peculiar circumstauces in which you may be placed, meets with general approbation; but inventions that are not necessary, or to which you are not compelled, are even anticipated by the severest censure. The jealousy natural to all men is not to be appeased, unless you apologize, if I may so speak, for your success, by representing it as the result of necessity; but if you will not veil the reputation you have acquired under the pretence of amending your situation in life and promoting your welfare; if, in fact, you are suspected of only wishing to distinguish yourself, you will inevitably become an annoyance to those whose ambition is directed to similar views.

Indeed, men may always disguise their self-love, and their desire of applause, under the mask or the reality of the most energetic and noble passions: but when women take up the pen; as their first motive is generally supposed to be a wish to display their abilities, the public is not easily persuaded to grant them its approbation, and, knowing this approbation to be essential to them, feels still more inclined to withhold it. In every situation of life it may be observed, that no sooner does a man perceive himself to be eminently necessary to you, than his conduct is changed into a cold reserve. Thus it is when a woman publishes any work; she puts herself so entirely in the power of opinion, that the dispensers of that opinion fail not to make her painfully sensible of her dependence.

To these general causes, which are common to all countries, may be added various circumstances peculiar to the French monarchy. A spirit of knight-errantry which still existed, was in some instances an obstacle to the too assiduous cultivation of literature amongst men. This same spirit must also inspire increased disgust towards those women who suffered themselves to be so exclusively engaged by literary pursuits, as to divert their attention from their first interest, the sentiments of the heart. An honorable delicacy may occasion even men to feel some repugnance to submit to all those criticisms which public notice must draw upon them: how much greater reason, therefore, have they to be displeased at seeing those beings whom it is their duty to protect, their wives, their sisters, or their daughters, expose themselves to the public judgment, and boldly render themselves the general topic of conversation?

Great talents, undoubtedly, would triumph over all these objections; but, nevertheless, a woman must find it extremely difficult to carry off with credit to herself the reputation of an authoress; to unite it with the independence of elevated rank, and to lose nothing, in consequence of such reputation, of that dignity, that grace, that ease, and those unaffected manners, which ought to characterize her habitual manner and conduct.

Women are readily allowed to sacrifice their domestic pursuits to fashion and dissipation, but every serious study is treated in them as pedantry; and if they do not from the first rise superior to the pleasantries levelled at them from all sides, those very pleasantries will in the end discourage genius, and check the course of well-grounded confidence and elevation of mind.

Some of these disadvantages will not be met with in any republic, and particularly in that where the general aim is to promote the progress of mental improvement. Perhaps it may be natural to expect that, in such a state, literature, properly so called, may fall entirely to the lot of women; while men devote themselves solely to the higher branches of philosophy.

The education of women has, in all free countries, been adapted to the peculiar constitution established in each: at Sparta they were accustomed to the exercise of war; at Rome, austere and patriotic virtues were required of them. If, therefore, it is wished that the principal object of the French republic should be emulation in mental improvement and philosophy, it would surely be a rational plan to promote the cultivation of the female mind, in order that men may find companions with whom they may converse on subjects the most interesting to themselves.

Nevertheless, since the revolution, men have thought it politically and morally desirable to reduce the female mind to the most absurd mediocrity: the conversation they have addressed to women, has been in a language as devoid of delicacy as of sense; and consequently the latter have had no inducement to excite the powers of their understanding. We do not, however, find that all this has tended to the improvement of manners. It is not by contracting the sphere of ideas, that the simplicity of the primitive ages can be restored; and the only result of such a system is, that less understanding has produced less delicacy, less respect for public opinion, and fewer means of supporting solitude. What is applicable to every thing that regards the understanding, has in this instance come to pass. It has always been thought, that to enlighten the mind has been productive of evil consequences; to repair which, reason has been made to make a retrograde course: whereas the evil arising from mental improvement can be corrected only by a still farther progress in that very improvement. Either morality is a fable, or the more enlightened we are, the more attached to it we become.

If, indeed, the French could inspire their women with all the virtues of the English women, with their modest manners, and their taste for solitude; they would do well to prefer such qualities to all the shining gifts of shining abilities: but probably all they could obtain from their countrywomen would be, to read nothing and to know nothing; in conversation, to be totally incapable of an interesting idea, a happy expression, or an elegant diction; and, far from being more domesticated by this charming scene of ignorance, their children would become less dear to them in proportion as themselves were less able to superintend their education.

The world would become at once more necessary and more dangerous to them, as love would be the only subject of conversation that could be addressed to them; and this subject could no longer be treated with that sort of delicacy which has hitherto been a substitute for morality.

Many advantages highly important to the morality and happiness of a country would be at once lost, if women should ever be rendered totally insipid or frivolous: they would possess fewer means to soften the irritable passions of men; they would no longer, as formerly, maintain a useful ascendency over matters of opinion, which they have ever animated in every thing that respects humanity, generosity, and delicacy. Women, only apart from the interests of politics, and the pursuits of ambition, cast an odium upon all base actions, contemn ingratitude, and honor misfortunes when noble sentiments have brought them on. If in France there no longer existed women sufficiently enlightened to have their judgment attended to, and sufficienlly dignified in their manners to inspire real respect, the opinion of society would no longer have any influence over the actions of men.

I believe firmly, that in the ancient government, where opinion held so salutary an authority, that authority was the work of women distinguished by their sense and good character; women who were quoted as examples of eloquence, when inspired by some generous resolution, when pleading in the cause of misfortune, or when boldly expressing some sentiment which required the courage to offend against power.

During the course of the revolution, those same women have given the most numerous and convincing proofs of energy and intrepidity. Frenchmen can never become such absolute republicans, as wholly to anni hilate the independence and pride natural to the female character. Women had undoubtedly, under the ancient government, too much ascendency in public affairs; but will they become less dangerous, when destitute of all mental improvement, and consequently of reason? From their influence would then arise an immoderate rage for wealth; preferences without discernment, and affection without delicacy; and instead of ennobling, they would degrade the objects of their attachment. Will the state be a gainer by this? The rarely-experienced danger of finding a woman whose superiority is out of proportion to the lot of her sex in general; ought it to deprive the republic of that celebrity which France enjoyed by the art of pleasing and of living in society? Now, without women, society can be neither agreeable nor interesting; but if they be devoid of sense, or destitute of that grace in conversation which pre-supposes a distinguished and elegant education, such women are a nuisance instead of an ornament to society; they introduce a sort of foolery, a party-spirit of slander, a tiresome insipid gayety, which must eventually banish all sensible men from their meetings; and thus the once brilliant assemblies of Paris would be reduced to young men who have nothing to do, and young women who have nothing to say.

It is true, that inconveniences will arise in all human affairs: some undoubtedly may be found in the superiority of women, and even in that of men, in the self-love of people of understanding, in the ambition of heroes, the imprudence of superior minds, the irritability of independent character, the impetuosity of courage and in many other cases. And must we for these reasons resist with all our power the natural bent of the mind, and direct all our institutions to discourage genius and talents? Indeed it is hardly certain, that such discouragement would be favorable either to domestic or public authority. Those women who are destitute of conversible powers, and unversed in literature, have generally the most art in fleeing from their duty; and unenlightened nations know not how to be free, and therefore perpetually change their governors.

To enlighten, to instruct, to perfect the education of women as well as that of men, of nations as well as that of individuals; such is still the best secret to attain all reasonable ends, all social and political relations which we wish to be founded on a durable basis.

The mental improvement of women can surely become an object of fear only through a delicate concern for their happiness. It is possible, that to enlighten their reason may be to give them an insight into the calamities which so frequently fall to their lot: but the same argument would be equally applicable to the general effect of mental improvement upon the happiness of the human race; and for my part, I entertain not a doubt upon the subject.

If the condition of the female world in the civil order of things is very defective; surely to alleviate their situation and not to degrade their mind, is the object most desirable. Assiduously to call forth female sense and reason, is useful both to mental improvement and the happiness of society; only one serious misfortune can accrue from the cultivated education which they may have received; and this would be, if by chance any should acquire such distinguished talents, an eager desire of fame: but even this chance would not be prejudicial to society at large, as it could affect only that small number of women whom nature might devote to the worst of torments,—an importunate thirst for superiority.

Let us suppose some female existing, who seduced by the celebrity of talents, would ardently endeavor to obtain it: how easy would it be to dissuade her, if she had not already advanced too far, to recede? Let her only see how formidable is the destiny she was preparing for herself. Look but into social order, some one might say; and you will soon perceive it is armed at all points against a woman who dares aspire to raise herself to a reputation on a level with that of men.

No sooner is a woman pointed out as a distinguished person, than the public is in general prejudiced against her. The vulgar can never judge but after certain rules which may be adhered to without danger. Every thing which is out of the common course of events, is at first displeasing to those who consider the beaten track of life as the protection for mediocrity; even a man of superior talents somewhat startles them: but a woman of shining abilities being a still greater phenomenon, astonishes, and consequently incommodes them much more. Nevertheless, a distinguished man being almost always destined to pursue some important career, his talents may become useful to those very persons who annex but a trifling value to the charms of reflection. A man of genius may become a man of power; and from this consideration the envious and the weak pay court to him; but a woman of talents can only offer them what they feel no interest about,—new ideas or elevated sentiments; the sound of her praise, therefore, only fatigues them.

Fame itself may be even a reproach to a woman; because fame is the reverse of what nature intended for her. Severe virtue condemns celebrity even in what is really praise-worthy in itself, as being in some measure inimical to perfect modesty.

Men of sense, astonished to find rivals amongst the fair sex, can neither judge them with the generosity of an adversary, nor with the indulgence of a protector; and in this new conflict they adhere neither to the laws of honor nor to those of good nature.

If, as the greatest misfortune that could befall her, a woman chanced to acquire remarkable celebrity in a time of political dissension, her influence would be thought boundless, even when she attempted not to exert any; the actions of her friends would be all attributed to her; she would be hated for whatever she loved; and this poor defenceles object would be atacked before those who are really formidable were even thought of.

Nothing gives greater scope to vague conjectures, than the uncertain existence of a woman whose name is celebrated, and whose life has been obscure. If the vanity of one man excites derision; if the abhorred character of another makes him sink under the burden of public contempt; if a man of inferior talents fails of some desired success; all are ready to attribute these events to the invisible agency of female power. The ancients persuaded themselves, that fate had thwarted their designs, when they could not accomplish them; in our days, self-love, in like manner, wishes to attribute its failures to some secret cause, and not to itself; and the supposed influence of celebrated women might in cases of necessity, be a substitute for fatality.

Women have no means of manifesting the truth, nor of explaining the particulars of their life: if any calumny is spread concerning them, the public hears it but their intimate friends alone can judge of the truth. What authentic means can a woman have to prove the falsity of scandalous reports? A calumniated man replies by his actions to an accusing world, and may justly say,

'Let the tenor of my life speak for me.'

But of what service is such a testimony to a woman? Some private virtues; some good deeds, scarcely known; some sentiments confined to the narrow circle in which she was destined to move; some writings which may render her name celebrated in countries of which she is not an inhabitant and at a time when, perhaps, she has ceased to exist.

A man may, even in his works, refute the calumnies of which he is become the object: but as to women, to defend themselves is an additional disadvantage, to justify themselves a new alarm. They are conscious of a purity and a delicacy in their nature, which the notice even of the public will tarnish; sense, talents, an impassioned mind, may induce them to emerge from the cloud in which they ought always to be enveloped; but they never cease to recur to it with regret as their safest asylum.

Women, however distinguished they may be, tremble at the aspect of malevolence; and although courageous in adversity, enmity intimidates them: they are exalted by reflection, but weakness and sensibility must ever be the leading features of their character. The generality of those whose superior talents have inspired them with a desire of fame, resemble Herminius clothed in a coat of mail; the warriors perceive the helmet, the lance, and the dazzling plume; they expect to meet with equal force; they begin the onset with violence, and the first wound cuts to the heart.

Injustice may not only destroy female happiness and peace, but it may detach the heart from the first object of its affections; who knows whether the effects produced by slander may not sometimes obliterate truth from the memory? Who can tell whether the authors of this calumny, having already embittered life, may not even after death deprive an amiable woman of those regrets which are universally due to her memory?

In this description I have hitherto portrayed only the injustice of men towards any distinguished female:—is not that of her own sex equally to be feared? Do they not secretly endeavor to awaken the ill-will of men against her? Will they ever unite, in order to aid, to defend, and support her in her path of difficulty?

Nor is this all: opinion seems to exempt men from all those attentions usually paid to the sex in all that concerns an individual whose superior abilities are generally allowed; towards such, men may be ungrateful, deceitful, and ill designing, without being called to account by the public. 'Is she not an extraordinary woman?' Every thing is comprised in these words: she is left to the strength of her own mind, to struggle as she can with her afflictions. The interest usually inspired by females, the power which is the safeguard of men, all fail her at once: she drags on her isolated existence like the Parias of India, amongst all those distinct classes into none of which she can ever be admitted, and who consider her as fit only to live by herself, as an object of curiosity, perhaps of envy, although, in fact, deserving of the utmost commiseration.

CHAPTER V.

OF WORKS OF IMAGINATION.

It is easy to point out the defects which are prohibited by the laws of good taste in any literary production; but it is not equally so to trace out the path which imagination ought in future to follow in order to produce new effects. There are certain methods to attain literary success, the very foundations of which have been destroyed by the revolution. Let us begin by examining what these methods are; and we shall be naturally led to some information as to the new resources which may yet be discovered.

Works of imagination operate upon the mind in two different ways; by depicting such scenes as excite mirth, or such as awaken the emotion of the soul. These emotions spring from those concatenations which are inherent in human nature: gayety is frequently only the result of the various, and sometime whimsical relations established in society. The emotions of the soul have then a permanent cause, which experiences but few changes from political events; whilst gayety is in many respects dependent upon circumstances.

The more we simplify institutions, the more we efface those contrasts from which a philosophical mind can produce striking effects. Voltaire has shown, better than any other author, how many resources pleasantry would be deprived of by a reasonable scheme of politics. Voltaire incessantly contrasts what *ought to be* with what really *was;* exterior pedantry with internal frivolity, the austerity of religious dogmas with the libertine manners of those who instituted them. In a word, almost all his writings display institutions the reverse of every thing that is rational; and institutions, moreover, so powerful that the pleasantry which dares attack them has, at least, the merit of being fearless. If such a religion was not sanctioned in such a country, there would be no more wit in ridiculing it, than there would be on an European stage to make a jest of the ceremonies of the Bramins.

The same may be said of the prejudice of rank, and of the disgusting abuses which they may occasion: the inhabitants of a country in which these abuses had no existence, would scarely think any jests on such a subject worth a smile.

The Americans scarcely perceived the merit of such comic descriptions as alluded only to institutions foreign to their government: they listened, perhaps, to what might be said of them, on account of their connections with Europe; but their own writers would assuredly not exercise their genius on such subjects; every pleasantry levelled at irrationality, in civil and political institutions, loses its effect the instant it attains its end, the reformation of social order.

The Greeks made a jest of their magistrates, but not of their institutions. Their poetical religion had an entire hold of their imagination: they were always governed either by an authority of their own choice, or by a tyrant who had reduced them to the most abject slavery. They never were, like the French, in that sort of intermediate situation, which is of all others the most fruitful in animated contrasts.

The French made choice of their national hardships as the objects of their pleasantries: ridiculed by their wit what they idolized by their ceremonies; affected to appear indifferent to their most important interests; and consented to tolerate even despotism, provided they might make a jest of themselves for having endured it.

The Greek philosophers did not, like the philosophers of monarchial governments, set themselves up in opposition to the institutions of their country; they had no idea of those hereditary rights which have, generally speaking, been the foundation of power amongst the modern nations since their invasion from the north. The authority of the magistrates, in Greece, owed its strength to the consent of the nation itself; consequently, nothing could have appeared more inconsistent than the endeavor to throw ridicule upon a political order which was entirely dependent upon the public will. Moreover, a free people attaches too much importance to the institutions by which they are governed to abandon them to the chance of thoughtless ridicule.

If the constitution of France be free and its institutions philosophical; pleasantries upon the government being no longer of any ability, will cease to create any interest; even those which are levelled against the human race, as we see them in the 'Candid' of Voltaire, are not applicable, in many respects, under a republican government.

When despotism exists, the poor slaves must be consoled by a belief that the general lot of all mankind is unhappy; but that elevation of mind essential to republican liberty, ought to inspire a disgust towards every thing that tends to degrade human nature. A disrelish to life does not animate fortitude ; the thing most important is, to place the enjoyments of virtue above those of life, and to dignify all the sentiments of the heart in order still more to ennoble that first of sentiments, a love of goodness and of our fellow-creatures.

The great secret of pleasantry is, in general, to check all enthusiasm ; fearlessly to attack every thing, and to weaken passion by indifference. This secret is of material use in opposing pride and prejudice ; but liberty and patriotic virtue must be maintained by an active interest in the happiness and glory of the nation ; and the vivacity of this sentiment is destroyed, if distinguished men are led so to contemn all human things, that they are alike indifferent to good and evil.

When society advances progressively in the path of reason, nothing can be so wrong as to dishearten ; and pleasantries which, after having been useful in weakening the power of prejudice, could no longer act, unless to diminish the influence of truth ;—such pleasantries, I repeat, would undermine the principles of moral existence which ought to be the support of individuals and of mankind at large. Thus 'Candid' and all other writings of the same kind, which indulge their satirical philosophy even to make a jest of the importance attached to the most noble interests of life, are hurtful in a repubiic, where it is necessary to esteem our equals, to confide in the good we may be able to do, and to animate our minds to make daily sacrifices by the religion of hope.

In works of invention there may certainly be another kind of gayety than that which depends almost entirely on pleasantries upon social order, or upon the lot of humanity: this is a penetrating and delicate observation of the passions and characters. The genius of Moliere presents the most sublime model of this superior talent. Voltaire was unable to produce any theatrical effect from pleasantry of this description, notwithstanding the habitual address and ingenuity of his mind.

It yet remains for us to examine what subjects of comedy may be most successful under a free government.

There are two distinct kinds of ridicule amongst mankind: that which is borrowed from nature ; and that which is diversified according to the different modifications of society. This latter kind of ridicule must be almost without support in a country where political equality is established, where the relations of society are more nearly allied to those of nature, and a conformity to them may exist without offence to reason. A man might be possessed of very great merit under the ancient government, and yet have rendered himself very ridiculous by an absolute ignorance of established customs; whereas, in a free state, the habits of society can be shocked only by real defects in the head or the heart.

During the monarchy, it was frequently necessary to conciliate the jarring claims of dignity and interest, of external courage and imperceptible flattery, an air of indifference and a constant attention to self-advancement, the reality of slavery and an affectation of independence. So many difficulties to surmount, might readily attach ridicule to him who knew not how to steer clear of them. Greater simplicity, with respect to manners and situations in life, would furnish authors under a republic, with fewer subjects for comedy.

Amongst the productions of Moliere, there are some which are founded entirely upon established prejudices ; such as 'Le Bourgeois Gentilhomme,' 'George Dandin,' &c. : but there are also some, such as 'l'Avare,' 'le Tartuffe,' &c., which describe man as he is in all countries and at all periods. Such pieces as these would suit a free government, if not in every point of their character, yet at least when the whole is taken together.

The ridicule that attacks the vices of the human heart, is more striking and more bitter than that which describes mere absurdities or whimsical institutions. We feel something like melancholy even in the most comic scenes of 'the Tartuffe :' because they bring natural depravity to view. But when pleasantry merely sets before us the contradictions arising from certain prejudices, or perhaps the prejudices themselves ; the hope we always entertain of correcting them, diffuses a more lively gayety over the impression caused by ridicule. We can neither have a talent, nor indeed any occasion, for that sort of light gayety, in a government founded upon reason, where the mind ought rather to be turned towards the highest department of comedy,—the most philosophical of all the works of imagination, and that which pre-supposes the most profound and extensive knowledge of the human heart. The republic may excite a new emulation in this career.

In a monarchy, we take pleasure in ridiculing such manners as do not accord with received customs ; in a republic, the proper objects of ridicule are those vices of the heart which may be detrimental to the public good. It may not be amiss to quote a remarkable example of the new subjects which comedy may treat of, and of the new aim which it may have in view:

In the 'Misanthrope' of Moliere, Philinte appears the reasonable man, and we laugh at the absurdities of Alceste. A modern author, developing these two characters in their progress in life, has shown Alceste to be generous and enthusiastic in friendship, and Philinte to be secretly avaricious and selfish, even to tyranny. This author has, I think, in his productions, taken the exact point of view in which comedy should henceforth be presented : those vices which arise from the absence of virtuous qualities, negative vices, if I may so call them, are what the stage ought now to attack : it ought to expose those mere exteriors, under the shelter of which so many men set their consciences at ease, and indulge themselves in wickedness under the semblance of decency.

A spirit of republicanism requires positive and acknowledged virtues. Many vicious men have no other ambition than to escape ridicule : they ought to know, and indeed it is necessary to possess sufficient talents to prove to them, that successful vice affords a wider field for ridicule, than uncouth virtue.

For some time past it has been the fashion to give the name of *firmness of mind* to that perseverance which will pursue its interest in defiance to all its duties ; and to call him a *man of sense*, who breaks successively, but with art, every tie, however solemn, that he has formed. Virtue, in short, is represented as a hypocrite ; and vice passes for the noble assurance of superior talents. It ought, therefore, to be the aim of comedy, to make men feel that immorality is a proof of narrowness of mind ; to wound the self-love of the depraved amongst mankind ; and to give a new direction to the shafts of ridicule. Formerly it was the foible of men to take pleasure in representing certain defects as even graceful, and every estimable quality as insipid ; whereas, in the present day, it is desirable to devote our talents to re-establish every thing according to the true meaning of nature ; to exhibit stupidity and vice ; and to show the near relationship between genius and virtue.

But, it may be asked, what is become of our contrasts ; and how shall we produce effects ? Assuredly, some very unexpected ones will arise from this proposed alteration : for example, the immoral conduct of men towards the softer sex has been unceasingly represented on the stage with a view to cast a ridicule upon deluded women. The confidence which women too generally feel in the sentiments they inspire, may reasonably afford a subject for raillery ; but the subject would be more worthily treated, and would also afford a greater scope for talents, if the deceiver himself were rendered the object of that satire, which would be better directed against the aggressor than the injured. It is easy to censure gravely what is culpable in itself; but the difficulty is, dexterously to place the fool's cap and bells upon the head of the guilty ; and even this is very possible.

Those men who would impose their crimes and vices upon you as additional graces, and whose desire to be thought clever is such, that they would boast even to yourself of having dexterously betrayed you, if they did not think that it would sooner or later come to your knowledge ; men who would conceal their incapacity by their villainy, flattering themselves that a spirit so daring against universal morality will not be suspected of imbecility in its political conceptions ;—these minds, so careless of the opinion of the good, and so anxious to obtain the favor of the powerful ; these retailers of vice, who carp at elevated principles, and trifle with sensibility, ought themselves to become the victims of that ridicule which they prepare for others ; the mask should be torn off, and they should be made the laughing stock of children. To direct against such characters, the energetic power of indignation is, in fact, to do nothing ; they must be deprived of that reputation for address and insolence, upon which they pride themselves, as a compensation for the loss of esteem.

In countries where the political institutions are rational, ridicule ought to assume the province of contempt. Vice, however elegant, circumspect, or dexterous, ought nevertheless to be abandoned to the sarcasms of ridicule,—the sole avenger that dares attack successful vice ; the sole weapon that has yet the power to wound, where shame and remorse are ineffectual.

The morality of the French is perverted by the ardent desire they feel to distinguish themselves in any way; but most by the brilliancy of their wit. When the qualities they already possess are insufficient for this purpose, they have recourse to vice in order to render themselves conspicuous : this gives them that confident address, that assurance and firmness, at least against the misfortunes of others, which may occasion some illusion. Comedy ought to oppose this detestable disposition of mind, by disappointing it of its object. Indignation attacks vice as a formidable power ; comedy ought to represent it as a contemptible weakness arising from a wretched degradation of the mind.

The literature of free countries, as I have already observed, has very rarely turned upon good comedy : the facility of obtaining success by allusions to the existing circumstances of the day, and the serious concerns of important political interests, have by turns been equally prejudicial, in various nations, to the art of comedy. But in France, the power of self-love is still in such full vigor, that it will furnish for a long time to come many pleasant subjects for comedy. Horace has described the just man standing firm and erect upon the ruins of the world : it is the same with the opinion which a Frenchman entertains of himself: this survives, unmolested, all the faults that he commits, and becomes superior to all the revolutions of fortune with which it is encompassed. While this feature of the French character remains uneffaced among them, their comic authors will always have some interesting subject to treat upon, and ridicule will have as much influence in the progress of philosophy, as reason and sentiment.

Those affections which never very, properly come under the department of tragedy ; whose descriptons being chiefly of the pathetic kind, the source of its effects are inxhaustible. Nevertheless, like all other productions of the human mind, it is modified by social institutions and the customs dependent on them.

The subjects of the ancients and their imitators, produce less effect in a republic than in a monarchy : the distinctions of rank rendered the pains of misfortune still more acute : they placed between it and the throne an immense interval which imagination could not clear without trembling. Social order, which amongst the ancients created slaves, rendered still deeper the abyss of misery, gave greater elevation to fortune, and rendered the various lots of human destiny truly theatrical. It certainly is possible to feel an interest in situations which have no parallel in our own country ; but, nevertheless, the philosophical spirit which ought at length to result from free institutions and political equality diminishes every day the power of social illusions.

Royality had been often banished, often annihilated in the governments of the ancients : but in our days it has been analyzed : and this at once destroys the effects of imagination. The splendor of power, the respect which it inspires, the pity which we feel for those who lose it, when we believe they are entitled to possess it ; all these sentiments act upon the mind, independent of the talents of the author ; and their effect would be very much weakened in the political order which I am now supposing. Already man has suffered too much as *man* only, to feel much additional emotion for the misfortunes, and other circumstances which are peculiar to the destiny of those individuals who are possessed of dignity and power.

Nevertheless, tragedy must not be converted into a drama : and in order effectually to avoid a fault of this nature, we ought carefully to study the difference of these two styles of writing. This difference, perhaps, does not consist merely in the rank of the personage represented, but in the grandeur of the characters, and the energy of the passions when properly decribed.

Many attempts have been made to introduce on the French stage the beauties of the English genius, and the effects of the German theatre ; but with the exception of a very small number,* these attempts have obtained success only for the moment, and no lasting reputation ; and for this evident reason, that the emotion produced by tragedy, like the laughter excited by comedy is only a passing impression. If the cause of this impression has not awakened in you one new idea ; if the tragedy at which you have shed tears, has left in your mind neither the remembrance of one moral observation, nor of any novelty of situation, drawn from the impulses of the passions ; the emotion which it has excited in you is a pleasure more innocent certainly than that excited by the combats of gladiators, but equally unimproving to reflection and sentiment.

I have met with an observation in some German work, which appears to me perfectly just : it is, that tragedy, when really good, ought to strengthen the mind after having weakened it. And indeed, true greatness of character, however heavy the calamities under which it is represented, generaly inspires the spectators with an enthusiastic admiration, which renders them more capable of enduring misfortune.

A principle of utility is found in this style, as well as in all others. What is truly great, improves the man ; and withont studying the rules of taste, if we feel that any theatrical production acts upon the character in any manner that can make it better, we may rest assured that it contains some marks of true genius.

It is not any maxim of morality, it is the development of characters, and the combination of natural events, which produce this effect upon the stage : and by taking this rule as a guide, we may judge what foreign productions we may add to our own store.

* Ducis, in some scenes of all his productions ; Chénier, in his fourth act of 'Charles IX. ;' Arnault, in the fifth act of the 'Vénitiens ;' have introduced upon the French stage a new and remarkable sort of effect, which belongs more to the genius of the northern poets than to that of the French.

It is not enough to affect the heart; we must enlighten the mind: and all that stage-scenery which strikes the eyes only, such as tombs, executions, spectres, combats, &c., ought merely to be permitted as directly conducive to the portraying of some exalted character, or some profound sentiment; all the affections of a reflecting mind have a rational object in view. An author merits real fame only when he makes the power of emotion subservient to some great moral truths.

The circumstances of private life suffice for the effect of the drama; whilst in general, it is necessary that the interest of nations should be included in the events that can be worthy to become the subjects of tragedy. Nevertheless, it is in lofty ideas and profound sentiments, rather than in historical remembrances and illusions, that we must seek for the dignity of tragedy.

Vauvenargue has observed, that 'sublime thoughts proceed from the heart.' Tragedy is an exemplification of this exalted truth. Fenelon has composed a piece founded upon a fact which is entirely within the province of the drama. The very name of M. de Malesherbes, his noble, but dreadful destiny, would, with a serious nation, be a subject for the most affecting tragedy in the world. Exalted virtue and extensive genius are the new dignities which ought to characterize tragedy, and, above all, the sentiments arising from misfortune; such as, in our days, we have learned to experience.

I am entirely of opinion, that the moral nature is more energetic in its expressions, than our French tragedies, in all other respects admirable, have described it. The splendor derived from exalted rank, introduces into tragical subjects a sort of respect which prevents the characters from meeting on equal terms: this respect must sometimes occasion a cold manner of characterizing the emotions of the soul. Expressions veiled, sentiments restrained, and proceedings always cautious, require great talents in this peculiar style; but the passions cannot, through all these difficulties, be represented with that heart-rending energy, that deep penetration, which complete independence must inspire.

Under a republican government, the reflection must be most deeply affected by virtue; while the imagination will be powerfully influenced by misfortune. I know not whether even glory, the only pomp of life which can be holden in any estimation by the philosophical mind, would effect a republican spectator so deeply, as the representation of those emotions which correspond with our inmost feelings, by their analogy to human nature.

That spirit of philosophy which generalizes our ideas, together with the system of political equality, must give a new character to our tragedies. This indeed is no reason why historical subjects should be rejected; but great men ought to be portrayed with such sentiments as may awaken in their favor the sympathy of every heart, and set off obscure facts by dignity of character:—our nature ought to be ennobled instead of aiming at perfection in ideas of mere conformity. It is not the irregularity and the inconclusiveness of the English and German productions that ought to be the object of our imitation; but it would be a new kind of beauty in the French theatres, as well as in those of many other nations, could they learn the art of giving dignity to common circumstances, and to paint with simplicity events of the greatest importance.

The stage is real life, exalted perhaps, but still it ought to be real life: and if the most common circumstance can serve as a contrast to great effects, we must know how to introduce it with propriety, in order to enlarge the boundaries of the art without giving offence to taste. In the style of the ideal *beautiful*, the first-rate tragedians of the French can never be equaled: an attempt therefore must be made, under the guidance of reason and talents, to introduce more frequently those dramatic arts which awaken and recall individual recollections: for nothing can excite such deep emotions as these.*

Conformity on the stage is inseparable from aristocracy in the government; one cannot be supported without the other. The dramatic art, deprived of all these factitious resources, cannot improve by any means but those of philosophy and sensibility; but, with these aids, it becomes unlimited; for grief is one of the most powerful methods of developing the human mind.

Life glides away, as it were, unperceived by the happy; but in affliction, reflection enlarges itself to search for some hope, or to discover a motive for regret; it examines the past, and tries to drive into the future; and this faculty of observation, which, when the mind is at ease, turns entirely upon exterior objects, in misfortune is exercised only upon the impressions we feel. The ceaseless operation of uneasiness upon the mind causes in the heart a fluctuation of ideas and sentiments, which agitate our internal feelings, as if every moment were teeming with some new event. What an inexhaustible source of reflection does this afford to genius.

The rules of the tragic art are not of themselves such impediments to the subjects we may choose, as are the difficulties attached to the exigencies of poetry. What would be very sensible and true in common language, may be even ridiculous in verse: the metre, the harmony, and the rhyme, interdict expressions which, in such a given situation, might produce a fine effect. The conformities of the theatre are required by the dignity of the moral nature; poetical conformity depends upon the mere act of versification; and although it may often heighten the impression made by some peculiar style of beauty, it limits the bold career which genius, with a knowledge of the human heart, might otherwise fearlessly engage in.

And in fact, we should not think much of the grief of any one who could express in verse his regret for the loss of some friend whom he had sincerely loved. A certain degree of grief inspires a turn for poetry; one degree more destroys it. There is, therefore, undoubtedly, a severity of distress, a style of truth, the effect of which would be weakened by being expressed in poetry: there are also common circumstances in life that may be rendered terrible by the power of affliction; but these cannot be versified and clothed in all the imagery which versification requires, without introducing ideas altogether foreign to the natural chain of sentiments. Nevertheless, it cannot be denied that a tragedy in prose, however eloquent its language, would in France excite much less admiration than the capital pieces in verse. The merit of a difficulty overcome, and the charm of an harmonious rhyme, served at once to display the double merit of the poet and the dramatic author. The union of these two talents has been one of the principal causes of the great difference existing between the French and English tragedy.

* A French audience is not generally willing to encourage any innovation in the theatrical line: justly admiring the master-pieces already in its possession, any deviation from the path which Racine has pointed out, appears to be prejudicial to the art. I do not however believe, that it is impossible to succeed in a new track, if some effects not yet hazarded upon the stage were introduced with great caution and superior talents; but if we would wish this enterprise to succeed, it must be conducted by the most rigid and critical taste. A general knowledge of the precepts of literature will be sufficient for us, if we submit to received rules; but if we wish to triumph over the repugnance which a French audience naturally feel towards the English or German style, as they call it, we ought scrupulously to watch over even the lightest shades which the most delicate taste could reprove. We should be bold in our conceptions, but prudent in the execution of them; and in this respect follow, in literature, a principle which equally holds good in politics; the more hazardous the project altogether, the more cautious, and even timid we ought to be in the execution of each separate part.

The inferior characters of Shakspeare speak in prose; his scenes of transition are in prose; and even when he does make use of verse, that verse being generally without rhyme, does not require, as in the French language, an almost continual poetic splendor. I do not, however, recommend these prose tragedies to the imitation of France, where the ear could hardly be reconciled to them; but the art of simple and natural versification ought to be brought to such perfection, that it may not, even by poetical beauties, divert the audience from those sentiments of emotion which ought to absorb every other idea. In a word, if we would open a new source of theatrical effects, we must find some intermediate style between the strict conformity of the French poets, and the defective taste of the northern writers.

Philosophy extends itself over all the arts of imagination, as well as over all the works of reason; and man, in this enlightened age, has no longer any curiosity but that which respects the passions of human nature. Every thing external is known and considered: the moral being, in his interior sentiments, remains the sole object of wonder, and can alone excite any deep emotion. The style of tragedy most affecting to the human heart, is neither that which retraces the customary ideas of common life, nor that which portrays characters and events as much out of nature as the marvelous in a fairy tale; it is that style alone which awakens in the mind of man the purest sentiment he has ever experienced, and recalls the feelings of an audience to the noblest emotions of their past life.

Poetry of the imagination will make no farther progress in France; verse will be filled with philosophical ideas, or passionate sentiments; but the human mind is so enlightened in this century, that it can no longer admit the illusions, nor the enthusiasm, which create such pictures and tales as are calculated to strike the imagination. France, indeed, has never excelled in this style of composition; and in the present times, the effect of poetry cannot be heightened but by expressing, in the eloquent language of the French, the new observations with which time may have enriched them.

To make use of the mythology of the ancients in these days, would be indeed to become childish through old age; the poet may indulge himself in all the creations arising from a temporary delirium; but still we must confide in the sincerity of his feelings. Now mythology is to a modern neither an invention nor a sentiment: he must search his memory for what the ancients found in their habitual impressions. These poetical forms borrowed from paganism, are, to us, only the imitation of an imitation: to use them is, indeed, to portray nature through the medium of the effect which it has produced upon other men.

When the ancients personified love and beauty; far from weakening the idea which might be conceived of them, they gave strength to that idea, and adapted it to the capacities of men who had but a confused idea of their own sensations. But the moderns have traced every emotion of the mind with such accuracy, that they need only know how to describe them, to be at once eloquent and energetic; and if they adopted fictions anterior to this profound knowledge of nature and of man, their representations would become devoid at once of energy, gradation, and truth.

In the works even of the ancients how much do we prefer their observations upon the human heart to all the brilliancy of their most splendid fictions! The image of love, borrowing the features of Ascanius to awaken the passions of Dido, is surely less descriptive of the origin of an impassioned sentiment, than those fine verses expressive of the affections and emotions which nature has implanted in the hearts of all.

The ancients being incessantly reminded by every surrounding object, of the gods of paganism, the remembrance and the image of them were blended in all their impressions: but when the moderns imitate the ancients in this particular, we cannot be ignorant that they have sought in books for resources to embellish those subjects to which sentiment alone would have given sufficient animation. It is always easy to distinguish a labored style, however dexterously an author may seek to conceal it; and we are no longer seduced by that involuntary talent, if I may so express myself, which feels an emotion instead of seeking it, and abandons itself to its impressions instead of selecting the best method of producing effects. The true objects of the poetical style ought to be, to excite, by images at once novel and just, an interest in mankind to gain a knowledge of those ideas and sentiments which they unconsciously experience: poetry ought to proceed, like every thing else which is the result of reflection, in the philosophical steps of its day.

The models of antiquity ought to be studied with a view to create and animate our taste and love of simplicity; but not in order to fill modern productions with the ideas and fictions of the ancients: we may attempt to mingle invention with mythological imagery, but they will never coincide. To whatever perfection we may carry our study of the works of the ancients, we can only imitate them, but are unable to create new fictions in their style. If we wish to equal them, we must not exactly follow their steps: they have gathered in the harvest from their fields,—we had better reap our own.

The few mythological ideas we find in the northern poets, are more analogous to French poetry; because they are more compatible, as I have endeavored to prove, with philosophical notions. Imagination, in the present century, cannot be assisted by illusion; it may indeed give exaltation to sentiments founded on fact; but it is necessary that reason should always approve and comprehend what enthusiasm renders charming.*

A new style of poetical composition exists in the prose works of Rousseau and Bernardine de St. Pierre: this arises from the observation of nature, in its relations to the sentiments with which it inspires man. The ancients, in personifying flowers, rivers, and trees, had lost sight of simple and natural sensations, and adopted in their stead brilliant chimeras: but Providence has so closely connected physical objects with the moral existence of man, that nothing can be added to the study of the one, which does not at the same time lead to a farther knowledge of the other.

We cannot but call to mind the roaring of the billows, the gloom of the atmosphere, and the terrified inhabitants of the air, in the recital of the deep emotions which filled the souls of Julia and St. Preux, when upon the lake which they were crossing together, '*their hearts beat in unison for the last time.*'

The fertility of the Isle of France, that quick and multiplied vegetation prevailing within the tropics, those tremendous tempests which suddenly succeed to days of cloudless calm, are all connected in our imagination with the return of Paul and Virginia; who, full of youth, of hope, and love, guided by their faithful negro, confidently look forward to a life of happiness in each other's company, while the unseen tempest is gathering over their heads, which shortly after is to overwhelm them.

As soon as we banish the marvelous, we find a connection throughout all nature; and our writings ought to imitate its consistency and general appearance. Philosophy, by still more generalizing the ideas, adds grandeur to poetical imagery. A knowledge of logic gives to passion a greater facility of speech. A constant progression of ideas, an aim at utility, ought to be perceived in all works of imagination. We allow no relative merit, nor can we even feel an interest in difficulties overcome, when the mind acquires nothing from

* De Lille, St. Lambert, and Fontanes, the best French poets in the descriptive style, have already approached very near to the character of the English poets.

them. Human nature must either be analyzed or improved. Romances, poetry, dramatic productions, and all those writings which appear to have no other object than to amuse, cannot attain even to that without some philosophical tendency. Romances, containing nothing but wonderful events, would be soon thrown aside.* Poetry also which had nothing to boast but fiction, verse whose harmony was its only merit, must soon become wearisome to the mind, which is most desirous of such discoveries as may lay open to view the sentiments and characters of mankind.

The uncontrollable passions excited by civil commotions, annihilate all curiosity, except that which is awakened by those writings which penetrate into the thoughts and sentiments of man, or which serve to acquaint us with the power and the bent of the multitude. We are curious respecting those works only, which portray characters, and put them in action, in some shape or other; and we admire only such writings as may show the influence of exalted sentiment over the heart.

The celebrated German metaphysician, Kant, in his search into the cause of the pleasure arising from eloquence, from the fine arts, and all the finest works of imagination, says, that this pleasure arises from the desire we feel to place at a greater distance the limits of human destiny: those limits which painfully contract the heart, are forgotten for a while in a vague emotion, or an elevated sentiment; the soul delights in the indescribable sensation it feels from whatever is exalted and sublime, and the narrow bounds of earth disappear, when the glorious career of genius and virtue is opened to our view. Indeed, a man of superior mind and feelings submits with difficulty to the shackles of life, and is glad to solace his melancholy imagination by momentary visions of eternity.

A disgust to life, when it does not lead to despair, but simply produces an indifference to the things of this world; such a disgust, together with a love of glory, may inspire great beauty of sentiment; every thing is viewed, as it were, from an eminence, and every object appears in a new strength of coloring. The ancients were better poets in proportion as their imagination was more captivated: amongst the moderns, the imagination ought to be as free from the illusions of hope, as reason itself; for it is thus only that a philosophical imagination can produce striking effects.

Even when surrounded by pictures of prosperity, some appeal to the sentiments of the heart should awaken us to the pensive turn of the poet. At the period in which we live, melancholy is the genuine inspiration of true genius: whoever is not conscious of this affection of the mind, must not aspire to any great celebrity as an author; for this is the price at which such celebrity must be purchased.

Indeed, even in the most corrupt age of the world, considering morality only in its relation to literature, it may be with truth asserted, that works of imagination will not produce any great effect, unless they tend to the honor and exaltation of virtue.

We have attained to a period in which the character of the people resembles, in some respects, that which prevailed at the time of the fall of the Roman empire, and the invasion from the north. At that momentous epoch, the human race seemed to stand in need of enthusiasm and austerity. The more depraved the manners of France are in the present day, the nearer the French approach to a disgust at vice, and the more their feelings are irritated against the endless calamities arising from immortality: the restlessness which at present torments them, will terminate in an animated and desided sentiment of which able writers ought to avail themselves beforehand. The period of a return to virtue is not far distant; and the heart already pants after uprightness, although reason may not at present have insured its triumph.

If we would succeed in works of imagination, we must offer a mild morality in the midst of rigid manners: but when the manners are corrupt, we must constantly hold up to view an austere morality. This general maxim may be more particularly applied to the age in which we live.

So long as the imagination of a people is inclined to fiction, every distant idea is confounded and lost in the whimsical flights of a creative reverie, but when all the power which is left to imagination, consists in the art of giving animation to moral and philosophical truths by sentiments and descriptions; what can be drawn from such truths, that can be adapted to high-flown poetry? One boundless thought, one enthusiastic sentiment which will stand the test of reason, the love of virtue, that inexhaustible source of all good, can at once bring to perfection every art, and every production of the mind; can unite in the same subject, and in the same work, the pleasures of imagination, and the approbation of reason.

* The romances which have of late been given to the public, in which the aim is to excite terror by descriptions of impenetrable darkness, ancient castles, long corridors, and blasts of wind, are amongst the most useless of all productions, and consequently are in the end more fatiguing to the mind than any others. They are a species of fairy-tales; more monotonous indeed than the genuine ones, because they admit of fewer combinations. But those romances which are descriptive of manners and characters, are frequently the means of conveying more knowledge respecting the human heart, than history itself. In works of this kind, under the mask of invention, we are told many things which we should never learn from history. Female writers in the present day, both in France and in England have excelled in the style of romance; because women study with care, and characterize with skill the emotions of the heart. Moreover, romances have hitherto been dedicated solely to portraying the passion of love, with the delicate shades of which women alone are acquainted. Amongst the modern French romances written by female authors, we ought to distinguish with particular nottice, Caliste, Claire d'Albe, Adele de Senanges, and especially he works of Madame de Genlis, whose skill in descriptive scenery and observation in sentiment render her deserving of a high rank amongst good authors.

CHAPTER VI.

OF PHILOSOPHY.

We must not be weary of repeating, that philosophy ought to be considered only as a search into truth by the guidance of reason; and viewed in this light, which is the true one conveyed by the primitive sense of the word, philosophy can be opposed only by those who admit of contradictions in ideas, or supernatural causes in events. It may be justly observed, that there are but two methods of supporting our arguments upon external objects—philosophy, or miracles. Now, in our days, as we do not flatter ourselves that we shall be enlightend by miracles; what is there we can substitute for philosophy? Reason, perhaps, will be the answer. But philosophy itself is nothing but reason generalized. We are clever enough to raise a dispute about two similar propositions; and we believe that we have two distinct ideas, becanse, by making use of equivocal terms, objects appear double.

Religious ideas are not at variance with philosophy, because they record with reason; neither can it be contrary to philosophy to maintain those principles which are the basis of social order; since those very principles are at unity with reason: but the partisans of prejudice, that is to say, of unjust claims, superstitious doctrines, and oppressive privileges, endeavor to excite an apparent opposition between reason and philosophy, in order that they may be enabled to support their assertion, that arguments may exist, which proscribe the investigation of reason; truths which must be credited unsearched; principles which we are compelled to admit, but must not analyze; in a word, a sort of exercise of the reflection which can serve only to convince us of its own inutility. For my own part, I confess, I shall never be able to comprehend by what operation of the mind we can attain the art of giving one half of our faculties the right of prohibiting the use of the other half. If moral organization could be aptly portrayed by sensible objects, I should think it would be by representing a man exerting his best endeavors under the guidance of all the powers of his mind and judgment, rather than by the image of a being who should be laboring with one hand to fetter the other. Providence surely has not given us any moral perception, of which we are forbidden the use; the more the mind is enlightened, the farther it will penetrate into the essence of things; at least, if we suffer our mental powers to be directed by a method which can connect and guide them. This method is in itself no more than the result of the most extensive human knowledge and reflection; it is to the study of physical science that we owe that justness of discussion and analysis which gives us a certainty of attaining truth when we sincerely deserve it: it is, therefore, by applying as much as possible the philosophy of positive sciences to the philosophy of intellectual ideas, that we may be enabled to make a useful progress in that moral and political career, where passion incessantly obstructs the path.

In the sciences, and particularly in mathematics, France can boast of the greatest men in Europe. The civil commotions amongst the French, far from discouraging emulation in this line, have inspired a wish to take refuge in the study of it. Inestimable advantage of the present period! Although every moral idea be absorbed in the disorders of intestine tumult, there yet remain some truths, whose nature is immutable, and whose paths are known. Men of reflection, disgusted on all sides by the follies of party-spirit, attach themselves to these studies: and as the power of reason is always the same, to whatever object it may be applied; the human mind, which would undoubtedly degenerate, had it no other food than the altercation of factions, exercises itself upon the accurate sciences, until it regains an opportunity of exerting the powers of reflection upon those subjects which are connected with the glory and happiness of society.

Errors of every kind, whether in politics or morals, must shortly be dissipated by that prodigious assemblage of knowledge and discoveries which has enlightened every subject within the limits of physical order: all superstitions, prejudices, false conclusions, and inapplicable principles, will sink into annihilation in the presence of that calm yet decisive reason, which does not concern itself, it is true, in the interests of the moral world, but which teaches all mankind the most efficacious method of proceeding in their researches into truth.

An examination into the actual state of mental improvement, will easily prove to us that the sciences are the only true riches. I have endeavored to show how much the general taste, with respect to literature, must have been changed in France: it is the same with politics; the course of *ideas* having been rapidly surpassed by that of *events*, those ideas must become proportionally retrograde. This is a natural effect of those precipitated institutions which are not the result of good instruction, and consequently not according to the general wish.

If the imagination, impressed with a just horror at the crimes which the French have been witnesses of, should attribute them to any abstract causes; it will become inveterate against principles as well as individuals; and this inveteracy, of which a principle perhaps is the object, will extend itself to every current which flows from it, how distant soever from the source. Did we thus estimate the present state of mental acquirements, we should think the human mind had gone back more than a century within the last ten years: but the nature of those arguments which we allege in favor even of our prejudices, is an incontestable proof of the progress which reason has made amongst us.

In order to justify the various kinds of subserviency towards which divers sentiments may lead, we have recourse, at least, to general ideas; to motives drawn from the happiness of nations, and arguments founded upon the wishes of the people. When the mind has once taken this bent; whether it momentarily advances or retreats, its future improving progress is secure; it can analyze, and therefore cannot long defend what is really erroneous. At the present period, the French have not acquired a perfect acquaintance with political and moral truths; but almost all parties, however opposite to each other, acknowledge *reason* as the basis of their discussions, and *public utility* as the only right and sole aim of social institutions.

When this generation which has suffered so many cruelties, shall give place to a generation that will not seek to be revenged on mankind for their ideas, it is impossible but that the human understanding should commence a philosophical career. Let us consider this career in its proper point of view, that is, as the only hope and support of the mind, ready to be precipitated into the gulf of despair, by a painful contemplation of the past.

The philosophy of the ancients had in it more imagination, but was less methodical than that of the moderns; it was also much less susceptible of a certain and positive progress; and while it made a more lively impression upon the mind, it was more apt to lead it astray by the spirit of system.

A chain of principles had not yet been established by means of analysis, from the origin of metaphysical ideas to their indefinite term. Locke and Condillac had much less imagination than Plato; but they followed the tract of geometrical demonstration; and that method alone can present a regular and unbounded progress.

In speaking of *style*, I shall examine whether it be not possible, if not even necessary, that an union should subsist betwixt what strikes the imagination and what acts upon the judgment: but at present I shall only consider the possible applications and advantages that may result from philosophy as a science.

Descartes discovered a method of solving the problems of geometry by algebra. But if, in the calculation of probabilities, we might one day discover a method suitable to objects wholly moral, what an immense step it would be in the career of reason!

A mathematical method has already been applied with success to the metaphysics of the human understanding: and it is a great triumph for philosophy, that the forms of demonstration have been employed to explain the theory of intellectual faculties. For example, what repose and happiness would it not procure to the human species, if political questions could arrive to that degree of evidence and clearness, that the majority of men might give their assent as to a calculated truth?

Without doubt, it would be very difficult to subject moral combinations to the rules of calculation; all the foundations of the exact sciences are invariable: but in moral ideas every thing depends upon circumstances; nothing can be decided but by a multitude of different considerations, many of which are so fugitive, that they escape from the mind before they can reach the lip: how much sooner, then, would they escape from calculations? Nevertheless, M. de Condorcet has clearly demonstrated, in his Essay on Probabilities, that i would be possible to know before-hand, almost to a certainty, what would be the opinions of an assembly upon any subject whatever. The calculation of probabilities, when applied to a great number of chances, presents a result morally infallible: it serves as a guide to all gamesters, although their object appears to be given up to every caprice of hazard: and why may it not have the same application to the multitude of facts of which the science of politics is composed?

The catalogue of births and deaths will present a certain and invariable result, as long as there subsits a regular order of habitual circumstances: and the number of divorces, of thefts, and murders, that will be committed in a country where the population and the religious and political situation remain the same, may be calculated with the greatest precision: and thus we see those events, which depend upon the daily concurrence of all the human passions, arrive as exactly at their stated periods, as those that are subjected only to the laws of nature.

In calculating the proportion of ten years, it may be known exactly how many divorces have yearly taken place at Berne, and how many assassinations have been committed at Rome: if these then can be calculated to a certainty, is it not possible to prove that combinations of the moral order are as regular as combinations of the physical order, and to form a positive calculation from those combinations?

But these calculations must be founded upon a constant uniformity of the mass and not on the diversity of particular examples; all things are different in the moral order, if taken separately; but if a hundred thousand chances are admitted, and the calculation is made from a hundred thousand different men taken promiscuously, you will know by a just approximation what number of enlightened men, what number of villains, what number of weak-minded, and what number distinguished by a superior understanding, are contained in the whole. This calculation would be still more exact, if the interest of each class was taken into the combination; and in joining a calculation of the knowledge derived from any institution whatever, political power might be founded upon a basis nearly amounting to certainty. The resistance they were to meet with, might be measured and balanced betwixt themselves from the real action, and obstacles might be influenced from the very actions themselves. Why should we not be enabled one day to draw up a list that would be a solution of every political question, from the positive facts which may be collected from each country? We might then be enabled to say, the administration of such a people requires such a sacrifice of individual liberty: such laws, or such a government, are suitable to such an empire: such a degree of strength will be necessary, in the executive power, for such an extent of country: such a state of authority is proper for such a country, and tyranny for another: such an equilibrium is necessary betwixt different powers for their mutual defence: such constitutions cannot maintain their power, and others are despotic from necessity. These examples might be prolonged; but as the real difficulty of this idea is not in the abstract conception, but to apply it with precision, the indication of it will suffice.

I think they were wrong who blamed the French *publicists*, when they had it in view to apply calculations to politics: it was also wrong to have condemned them for having attempted to generalize causes: but there has often been reason to accuse them of a want of observation of those very facts which alone could have conducted to a discovery of causes.

The science of politics must be created: we can only as yet perceive at an obscure distance those principles and combinations of experience which are to lead to a result so certain, that the concatenation of most sciences may be, as we may say, submitted to the evidence of mathematical conclusions. The elements of sciences are not fixed; what we call general ideas, are no more than special facts, which present only one side of a question, without permitting us to see the whole. Thus each new fact gives us a new but confused impulsion.

One year, all the declamation will be against the executive power: and another year, against the legislative assembly: one year, it will be against the liberty of the press; and the next, against its subjection.

As long as this disorder of favorable circumstances shall exist, a happy hazard may establish, in some countries, institutions conformable to reason: but the general principles of politics will not be fixed, nor will the application of those principles to the modifications of social order be upon a sure foundation.

It is thus in America, that a great number of political problems appear to be solved, because the citizens are happy and independent: but this favorable hazard depends entirely upon particular circumstances, from which we cannot determine before-hand, what those principles are, nor what application they are susceptible of in other countries.

Neither can the long duration, and almost indestructible stability of some governments in Europe, be given as a proof of the progress of the human understanding in politics, because supported by their power; and while maintaining a claim amongst themselves, they have secured to men some advantages of association. Despotism dispenses with political science, as force dispenses with knowledge, and as authority renders persuasion superfluous: but those means cannot be admitted when the interests of nations are discussed. Force is a hazardous combination, and destructive to every thing that belongs to thought and argument, both of which require the free exercise of liberty.

Despotism cannot, then, be an object for the calculations of the human mind: let us therefore examine the natural resources possessed by the understanding, to avoid going astray in its progressive march; and not those means of violence and brutality, which can only preserve from error by stopping every progress.

The analyzing and uniting of ideas in mathematical order has this inestimable advantage, that it takes from the mind even the idea of opposition. Every subject that becomes susceptible of evidence, is out of the dominion of the passions, which then lose the hope of gaining the ascendency: in the moral, as well as in the physical order, there are already many truths beyond the reach of their influence.

Since the time of Newton, there has been no new system upon the origin of colors, nor upon the motion of the earth. Since Locke, no one talks of innate ideas: it is now universally agreed, that all ideas are derived from the senses. But to acknowledge the evidence of political questions, is infinitely more difficult; the passions have their interest to render it so: there are, however, some even of those questions already solved, and thus leave no farther hopes of debate to the spirit of party.

The state of slavery, the feudal system, and even religious disputes themselves, will never again excite to war: the light of knowledge is so generally unfolded upon these objects, that the most vehement spirits cannot now entertain the least hope of ever being able again to represent them under different aspects, and to form two parties, founded upon two different manners of judging and viewing the same ideas.

The philosophers ought then, in politics, to submit to positive combination those facts that are known to them, in order to draw a certain result from the number and nature of chances.

Algebraists will not tell you that you are going to throw such a number; but they will calculate in how many turns of the dice this number ought to return; and will not find themselves deceived. It will be the same with politicians: they will be certain of a return of the same events in a given time, provided the institutions remain the same.

It is however true, that no calculations require a greater multiplicity of different combinations. If the effects of a physical experience can be destroyed, only because a trifling degree, more or less, of heat or cold, had been overlooked in the process ; what a profound study of the human heart is necessary to determine what influence should be given to government, that it should be able to enforce obedience without using the means of becoming unjnst, and the action necessary to be employed by administration, in order to unite the nation in the same spirit, without shackling the genius of individuals ? How much experience is requisite to mark the exact point at which the executive power would cease to be an advantage, as that in which its absence would become an evil ? There is no problem composed of a greater number of terms, or in which an error would be productive of more dangerous consequences.

An abstract opinion that becomes an object of fanaticism, produces in the minds of men the most remarkable effects : ideas diametrically opposite to each other admitted, and exist simultaneously : the mind admits, one by one, every proposition, without even attempting to judge them ; it then creates factitious reports, the seeming abstraction of which pleases and exalts it ; for the imagination is as easily prepossessed by the abstract as by the most animated pictures of truth : the soaring of boundless ideas is singularly adapted to the exaltation of the mind.

When once the dogmas on metaphysical systems are adopted, people are then apt to stand up in defence of every thing, even of those ideas which they know to be false ; and by a singular effect of controversy, that which they have supported from argument, or from obstinacy, becomes at last that which they believe : and by always seeking for arguments to support one side of the question, they entirely lose sight of those by which they can be confuted their vanity is awakened and their passions exalted by the irritation which their self-love receives from contradiction ; and after a series of actions, at first inspired by opinion, their interest becomes united with the success of that opinion, and they find themselves irresistibly pushed forward by that interest : there pass in the interim many combats which they refuse to acknowledge even to themselves, and which they at last contrive to stifle altogether.

The devotees carry their scruples even to their most secret thoughts, and finish by making a crime of those transient doubts which sometimes shoot across their imagination ; it is the same with all kinds of fanaticism ; imagination is as fearful of the return of reason, as of an enemy that would trouble the good understanding that existed between their chimeras and their weaknesses.

Fanaticism in politics, as in religion, is agitated by those rays of truth which appear at intervals even to the firmest belief ; and men persecute in others those doubts, the very first idea of which arose in their own minds ; and the faculty of belief, fantastical in its vehemence, is irritated by its own suspicion, in place of making use of it to arrive at the truth.

In this disposition of mind there are found arguments for every thing ; the most absurd opinions, and the most detestable maxims are received, when they once have acquired the form of general ideas. The contradictions are reconciled by a sort of geometrical logic, which, if not analyzed with the strictest scrutiny, is apt to appear like the severity of reason.

'This law, (said Couthon, when he proposed that of the twenty-second Praireal,) *assigns patriotic judges for the defence of the innocent ; but it assigns none for conspirators.*' Is not every part of the doctrine in this maxim perfectly correct ? And yet is it possible to unite more atrocious absurdities in so small a compass of words.

This flowery style which often seduces the most upright minds, and which the strongest reason is hardly able to shake it, is one of the greatest scourges of imperfect metaphysics ; for argument then becomes the weapon of folly and criminality, the abuse of abstract forms is united with the fury of persecution ; and man, by a monstrous mixture, combines the frenzy of superstition with all that is arid in philosophy

It is impossible not to feel the want of a new doctrine to throw a light on this frightful mass of shapeless pretences, which serves as a screen to men of false principles, the villain and the little-minded ; as if transforming error into principle, and sophistry into consequence, could change the radical fallacy of a first assertion, and palliate the detestable effect of this abominable logic !

This new doctrine may now repose itself on a double basis, morality and calculation : but this principle is invariable, that whenever the calculations do not agree with morality, however incontestable their exactitude may appear at first sight, their result must be erroneous.

It has been said, that in the French revolution, barbarous speculators, founding their bloody laws on mathematical calculations, had coldly sacrificed millions of individuals to promote the supposed happiness of the greater number.

These monsters of human nature might have imagined, that they could have rendered their calculations more simple, by striking out sentiment, sufferings, and recollection ; but they could not have had the most distant idea of general truths, those truths which are composed of every individual existence, and every particular fact. The calculation is neither good nor useful, till it embraces every exception and regulates every variety : if you suffer one single circumstance to escape, your result must be false ; as the smallest error in arithemetic will render the solution of a problem impracticable.

The proof of the combinations of the mind is in the sentiment and in the experience : argument, under whatever form it may be presented, can never change nor modify the nature of things ; it can only analyze what already exists.

It has been advanced as a mathematical truth, that the smaller number ought to be sacrificed to the good of the greater : but nothing can be more erroneous, even with regard to political combinations : for the effects of injustice are such, that they must necessarily disorganize a state. If you sacrifice innocence to what may be deemed the good of the nation ; it is the nation itself which you devote to destruction. From action to re-action, from vengeance to vengeance, the victims that are immolated at the pretended altar of general good, will rise again from their ashes, and emerge from their exile ; and such as would have remained in obscurity, if justice had been exercised towards them, will receive a name and a consequence from the very persecutions of their enemies. It is the same with all political problems in which virtue is interested ; it is always possible to prove, by simple argument, that the solutions of those problems are false, if the calculation recedes in the smallest degree from the laws of morality.

Morality is to be placed above calculation ; for morality is the *nature* of the intellectual order : and as in the physical order, all calculations take their procedure from the *nature of things*, upon which they can produce no change ; so, in the intellectual order, it should proceed from the same point, that is to say, morality.

The cause of those absurd and atrocious errors which have discredited the use of abstract ideas in politics, is fully exemplified by the reflection, that in lieu of making morality the fundamental basis and supreme legislator, it was considered, at best, but as one of the elements of calculation, and not as its constant rule ; and sometimes only as an auxiliary, that might be modified or sacrificed at pleasure.

Let us then, in the first place, establish morality as

a fixed point; let us then subject politics to calculations that take their procedure from this point; and we shall then see, those *inconveniences* which have attended the application of metaphysics to social institutions and the interest of the human species, and with which they are so justly reproached to this day, would totally disappear.

Politics can be submitted to calculation, because, being always applied to a community, it is founded upon general combinations which are abstract, of course; but morality, the aim and end of which is the particular conversation of the rights and happiness of each man, is absolutely necessary in order to force politics to respect, in their general combinations, the happiness of individuals. Morality should direct our calculations, and our calculations should direct our politics.

This place assigned to morality above calculation, is equally suitable both to public and private morals: it is to the omission of it, in the first case, that we are to ascribe those innumerable evils, the fatal effects of which we have so cruelly experienced. The rendering public morality subordinate to that which it ought itself to hold in subjection, has often been the ruin of thousands of individuals, under pretence of promoting the general good. There are likewise certain philosophical systems, which threaten private morals with the like degradation. The completion of every thing must ultimately be submitted to virtue: and although virtue is susceptible of a demonstration founded on the calculation of usefulness; yet this calculation is not sufficient to serve it for a basis. As virtue has to encounter numerous obstacles, she has received from nature a variety of supports.

The sciences of morality are only susceptible of the calculation of probabilities: and this calculation can only be founded on a very great number of facts, of which the approximate result has previously been examined. As the science of politics is only applicable to men when united in a community, the probabilities in that science may almost amount to certainties, through the multitude of chances from which they are taken: and the institutions established on this foundation, applying likewise of themselves to the happiness of the multitude, cannot miss their aim. But morality includes each man individually, each fact, and each circumstance: and although a great majority of circumstances prove that a virtuous conduct is the best regard to the interests of this life; yet it cannot be affirmed, that there are no exceptions to this general rule.

If, then, you wish to submit those exceptions to the same laws; if you wish to inspire each man individually with morality, in whatever situation he may be; you will find for each individual an animating and constant supply, which is renovated every day, yea every moment.

The moral alone, of all the human thoughts, is that which stands in need of any other regulator than reason: all the ideas that inflame the destiny of divers men at the same time, are founded on their personal interests: yet if we were to give to each man his own personal interest for the guide of his conduct; even if this guide did not lead him astray, it would always result, that the effects of this principle would be to dry up the source of every great and generous action.

Doubtless, it must appear that morality is always conformable to the interests of mankind: but to give it this sort of motive for a point of support, is to deprive the mind of the energy necessary for the sacrifices required by virtue.

There is no reasoning, however subtile, that can represent a generous act of self-devotion as a regular egotism: to do this, the grammatical acceptation of the word must be adopted in preference to the sentiment which it revives in the hearts of those who listen to it. Every thing brings us back to our own interest, because every thing centres in ourselves: and yet no one would say, *Glory is my interest; heroism is my interest; the sacrifice of my life is my interest:* it would be degrading to virtue to tell a man it was merely his interest; for if you acknowledge that his first motive should be honesty, you cannot surely refuse him some liberty in the judgment of his own concerns: and there are various circumstances in which it is impossible not to believe that morality and interest are at variance with each other. How then is it possible to convince a man, that an event entirely new and unexpected had been foreseen by those who had presented him with the general rules of conduct? The rules of prudence, (and virtue which is founded solely on interest, amounts to no more,)—even those of its rules that are most known, are subject to a multitude of exceptions: why should virtue, when considered as a calculation of personal interest, be exempted? There remains, then, no method of proving that virtue is always in unison with our interest, except that of returning to the idea of placing the happiness of man in the peaceful security of his own conscience; which simply signifies, that the interior enjoyments of virtue are preferable to all the advantages of egotism.

It is not true, however, that personal interest is the most powerful spring of the actions of mankind: for pride, vanity, anger, self-love, and a variety of other circumstances, will easily make them sacrifice this interest; and in virtuous minds, there exists a principle of action totally different from any single calculation whatever.

I have attempted in this chapter to develop how important it is to submit all the ideas of the human mind to mathematical demonstration: but although this kind of proof may be applied to morality, it is to the principles of life that it is more peculiarly attached: its impulsion precedes every kind of argument. The same creative power which sends back the blood towards the heart, inspires *courage* and *sensibility*, two sensations and two enjoyments wholly moral; the empire of which you totally destroy, if you analyze them by personal interest, as you would destroy the charms of beauty by describing it as an anatomist.

The elements of our being, pity, courage, and humanity, act within us before we are capable of any calculation. In studying the various parts of nature, we must necessarily suppose some endowments anterior to the search of man. The impulse of virtue must ever take place of reasoning. Our organization, and the developments which the habits of infancy give to that organization, are the true causes of whatever is great in human actions, of the delights which the mind experiences in doing good. The religious ideas which pure minds are so fond of indulging, animate and consecrate this spontaneous elevation, and are the noblest and surest guarantees of morality. 'In the breast of a virtuous man (says Seneca) there resides a god; but I am ignorant what god.' If this sentiment were translated into the language of the most enlightened egotism, what effect would it produce?

It might be said, that this mode of expression belongs entirely to the imagination, and that the real sense of this idea, as of every other, is submitted to argument. Doubtless, reason is the faculty that judges all the other faculties: but it is not reason that constitutes the identity of the moral being. If we study ourselves, we shall find that the love of virtue precedes the faculty of reflection; that this sentiment is intimately connected with our physical nature; and that its impressions are often involuntary. Morality must be considered in man, as an inclination, as an affection, the principle of which is inherent in himself, and which is guided by his judgment. This principle may be strengthened by whatever enlarges the mind and expands the intellect.

There certainly exists a method of improving even the theory of morality itself, by calculation and reflection: but that method, though useful when considered only as an auxiliary, becomes insufficient and fatal, if we attempt to substitute it in the place of sentiment, as it would contract the limits of morality, instead of extending them.

Philosophy, among its observations, recognizes primitive causes, pre-existing energies: and in the number of these, virtue must certainly be counted. Virtue is the offspring of creation, and not of analysis: it appeared almost at the same time with that instinct which prompts us to self-preservation: and compassion for others developes itself almost as soon as the dread of any ill that might happen to ourselves. I shall certainly not disavow what the wisdom of philosophy may add to the morality of sentiments: but as we should do an injury to national love in believing it to be only the result of reason, we must select in every virtue what is purely natural, and reserve to ourselves afterwards to throw a new light upon the best manner of directing its spontaneous movements.

Philosophy may discover the cause of the sentiments which we experience; but it should only follow the course which those sentiments mark out for it. Instinct and reason teach us the same moral: thus Providence has twice repeated certain important truths to man, that they may not be lost to him when they especially concern his welfare, nor elude his diligent researches.

The man who loses himself in physical sciences, is re-conducted into the path of truth, by the applications he is to make of his combinations with material facts: but the man who devotes himself to the abstract ideas of which the moral sciences are composed, how can he be assured that his conceptions will be either good or just in the execution? How can he dispense with the knowledge of experience, and carry his views towards futurity with any degree of certainty? It can only be done in subjecting reason to morality; without which nothing can subsist, nothing can prosper in opposition to its injunctions. The consolotary idea of an eternal Providence can fill the space of every other reflection; but we must be on our guard, and distrust even morality itself, when it refuses to acknowledge a God for its author.

CHAPTER VII.

OF THE STYLE OF AUTHORS, AND THAT OF MAGISTRATES.

Before the career of philosophical ideas had excited the emulation of enlightened men in France, those works in which questions of literature and morality were discussed, when they were written with elegance, sublimity, and correctness, were holden in the highest estimation. Before the revolution, there existed a number of writers who had acquired a prodigious reputation, without ever considering objects in a general point of view, in carrying the ideas, both moral and political, entirely to literature, instead of subjecting literature to the ideas of morality and politics.

It is impossible, at this time, to feel any great degree of interest for writings which are only ingenious, and do not embrace the whole of the subjects on which they treat, never exhibiting them but on one side, and by such particulars as are no way connected with the first ideas, nor the profound impressions of which the nature of man is composed.

The style must necessarily have undergone some changes from the revolution which has taken place in the minds of men, as well as in institutions; for style, not consisting in the grammatical turning of a period, cannot be looked upon as a single form, but as closely connected with the ideas and nature of the mind. Style in writing, is like the character of a man; and this character cannot be a stranger either to his opinions or his sentiments, but modifies his whole being. Let us, then, examine what style is most proper for philosophical minds under a free government.

The images, the sentiments, and the ideas, represent the same truths to man under three different forms: and yet there subsist the same connections and the same consequences in these three provinces of the understanding. When you discover a new idea, you will find in nature some image that will serve to depict it, and in the heart, a sentiment that corresponds, by a resemblance which reflection causes you to discover. No writer can carry conviction and enthusiasm to any high degree, till he has acquired the knowledge of touching those three chords at the same time, the unison of which is no other than the harmony of the creation.

It is from the more or less perfect combination o. the means of influencing the sentiments, the imagination, or the judgment, that we may appreciate the merit of different authors. There is no style worthy of praise, if it do not contain two out of those three qualities, which, when united, form the perfection of the art of writing.

Fine conceptions, subtile ideas which do not connect themselves with the great chain of general truths, and ingenious relations which exercise the genius to detach itself from the mind instead of applying to it for its principal support, can never place an author in the first rank.

If you particularize your ideas over-much, they slide into mere images and sentiments which conglomerate instead of separating. Neither are abstract combinations which sentiment repels, and which exhaust the imagination, more congenial to this universal nature, the sublimity of which is to be represented by the beauties of style. Images that throw no light on any idea, are no more than whimsical phantoms, or simply pictures of amusement: sentiments that awake no moral idea, no general reflection, are most certainly affected, and can answer to nothing real in any style.

Marivaux, for example, presented always the studied side of the discoveries of the mind: his writings possessed neither philosophical ideas, nor lively descriptions. It is impossible that sentiments which do not proceed from just ideas, can be susceptible of natural images. Those thoughts that may be offered under the double aspect of sentiment and imagination, are the first of the moral order: but when the ideas are too much refined, they have no terms of comparison in animated nature.

In the positive sciences, you only need abstract forms; but when you treat upon other philosophical subjects, you must remain where you can make use at once of reason, imagination, and sentiment; faculties that all combine, by different means, to the development of the same truths.

Fenelon joins soft and pure sentiments to the images that properly belong to them: Bossuet unites philosophical ideas with those pictures that command respect. Rousseau combines the passions of the heart with the natural effects which produce them: Montesquieu, in his dialogue of Eucrate and Sylla, comes very near to uniting all the qualities of style, connection of ideas, the profundity of sentiment, and the force of imagery. There are found in those dialogues all the grandeur and elevation of fine ideas, with as much of the figurative as is necessary to the complete development of philosophic conception. We do not feel, while perusing the beautiful pages of Montesquieu, that tenderness which an impassioned eloquence ought to give birth to, but the sensation caused by what is truly admirable in every style: it is that kind of emotion felt by strangers on entering St Peter's, at Rome; where every instant they discover some new beauty that absorbs, as we may say, the striking effect of the whole.

Malbranche endeavored to combine ideas with images, in his Essay on Metaphysics: but as his ideas were not founded on truth, we can but very imperfectly discover the union he wished to establish between them and his brilliant images. Garat, in his Lessons to the Normal Schools, is a model of perfection in that style: and Rivarol, in spite of some studied expressions, makes you perfectly conceive the possibility of this perfect harmony, between the images drawn from nature, and the ideas which serve to form the chain of principles and their deductions in the moral order. Who can tell to what length this power of analysis may be carried, which, when united to imagination, so far from being destructive to any thing, adds new life to every thing, and, imitating nature, concentrates the divers elements of life in the same focus?

A work upon the principles of taste, upon music, or painting, may become a work of philosophy, if it be addressed to man altogether; if it excite in his breast those sentiments and thoughts which aggrandize every question; while a discourse upon the most important interests of human society, may fatigue the mind, if it contain nothing but mere circumstances, or if it present important subjects crowded into a narrow compass, and does not carry the mind to general considerations by which it is interested.

The charm of style dispenses with the efforts required by the conception of abstract ideas; figurative expressions rouse every spark of life within; and an animated picture encourages you to pursue a long chain of ideas and arguments. There is no longer any occasion to struggle with absence of mind, when the imagination is captivated; it commands of itself the power of attention.

If works purely literal do not contain that sort of analysis which aggrandizes every object it comprehends; if it does not characterize the particulars without losing sight of the whole; and if they do not prove at the same time their knowledge of men, and their study of life; they must appear but as works of puerility. In a free country, when a man renders himself remarkable by his writing, it is required that he should indicate, in those writings, the important qualities that the nation may one day claim from some one of her citizens, of whatever class or denomination: but a work that is not philosophically written, may class its author among artists, but can never elevate him to the rank of thinkers.

Since the revolution, the French have launched into a fault that is particularly destructive to the beauties of style: they wished, by employing new verbs, to abridge all their phrases, and render all their expressions abstruse:* but nothing can be more contrary to the talent of a great writer. Concision does not consist in the art of diminishing the number of words: much less does it consist in the privation of images. The concision which we should be ambitious of attaining, is such a one as that of Tacitus, which is at once both eloquent and energetic:—energy, so far from being prejudicial to that brevity of style we so justly admire, that figurative expressions are those by which the greater number of ideas are retraced in the smallest compass. Neither can the invention of new words contribute towards perfection of style. Masters of the art may secure the reception of a few when they are involuntarily created by a sudden impulse of thought; but in general, the invention of words is a sure symptom of a sterility of ideas. When an author permits himself to make use of a new word: the reader, who is not accustomed to it, stops to judge it; and this breaking in upon the attention hurts the general and continued effect of the style.

All that has been said of bad taste, may be equally applied to the faults of the language which has been employed by many writers, for these ten years past. Nevertheless, there are some of those faults which more particularly belong to the influence of political events; which I propose to discuss in speaking of eloquence.

* Utiliser, activer, préciser, &c.

When philosophy makes a new progress, style must necessarily proceed on to perfection. The literary principles that may be applied to the art of writing, have been almost all developed; but the knowledge and study of the human heart ought each day to add to the sure and rapid means which have effect upon the mind. Every time that an impartial public are not moved and persuaded by a discourse, or a work, the fault *must* lie in the author: but it is almost always to what he is deficient in as a moralist, that his fault as a writer must be attributed.

It often happens in society, when listening to those who have the desire of persuading their auditors of their sensibility, or their virtue; that we cannot help remarking how little they have observed that nature, whose characteristic signs they wish to imitate: and authors are for ever falling in the same error, when they wish to develop moral truths or profound sentiments. Doubtless, there are some subjects in which art cannot supply what is really experienced by nature; but there are others which might be handled with success, if profound reflections were first made upon the impressions that are experienced by the greater part of mankind, and the means of giving birth to them.

It is the gradation of terms, the agreement and choice of suitable words, the rapidity of certain forms, the development of certain motives, or lastly, the style itself perhaps, which actuate the opinions, and insinuate themselves into the persuasion of men. An expression which at the bottom changes nothing of the idea, but which has not a natural application, must become an object of speculation to most readers. Too strong an epithet may entirely destroy the effect of an argument founded on truth; and the slightest shade may entirely turn aside the imagination that was proposed to follow you. An obscurity in the arrangement, which reflection might easily have penetrated, takes away, all at once, the interest you have inspired. In short, style requires some of those qualities that are necessary to govern mankind: we must know their faults, sometimes spare, and sometimes subdue them; but the utmost care must be taken to guard against that pride which, inciting men to accuse a nation rather than themselves, refuse to admit the general opinion, as the supreme judge of their talents.

Ideas in themselves are independent of the effects which they produce: but the aim of style being precisely to engage mankind to adopt the ideas which it expresses; if the author does not obtain his aim, it is because his penetration has not yet discovered the road which leads to the secrets of the heart, and the principles of judgment; which he must first become master of himself, in order to influence the opinion of others.

It is in this style, above all, that we may remark that grandeur of soul which distinguishes the character of the *man* in the *writer*. The purity and grandeur of the language add greatly to the consideration of those who govern, particularly in a country where a political equality is established. Real dignity of language is the best method of pronouncing all moral distinctions: it also inspires a respect that improves those who experience it. In short, it is possible that the art of writing may one day become one of the principal powers of a free state.

When the first legislators of a country are possessed of this power, it forms of itself an union betwixt those who govern and those who are governed. Doubtless, actions are the best guarantees for the morality of mankind: nevertheless, I believe there exists an accent in words, and, of course, a character in the forms of style, which attests the qualities of the mind with more certitude than even actions themselves. This sort of style is not an art that may be acquired by the understanding; it is the real exhibition of the heart.

Men of imagination, by transporting themselves into the character of another, may discover what that other might have said: but when they speak in their own character, it is their own sentiments which appear, even in defiance of their efforts to conceal them. There never existed an author who, in speaking of himself, knew how to give an idea superior to the truth. A word, a false transition, an exaggerated expression, reveals what they most wish to conceal.

If a man of great talents as an orator, was accused, and had to plead his own cause before a tribunal; it would be easy to judge, by his manner of defence, whether he was innocent or guilty, every time that words are called in testimony. It is not possible to take from language that character of truth implanted by nature: it is no longer a deceptive art; what they feel, escapes in a thousand different ways from what they relate.

The virtuous man has a proof of his innocence which the wicked cannot deprive him of; it is a mark set upon him by his Creator, which his fellow-men cannot misconstrue. The calm and dignified expression of an elevated sentiment, the clear and simple manner of announcing a fact, that style of reason which belongs only to virtue, cannot be counterfeited: this language is not only the result of virtuous sentiments, but they are also forcibly inspired by it.

The noble and simple beauties of certain expressions command respect even from those who pronounce them; and among other woes attached to self-contempt, we must also add the loss of this language, which causes the most exalted and pure emotions to those who are worthy of using it.

This style of the mind, if I may thus express myself, is one of the greatest supports of a free government; it arises from such a train of sentiments as must be in concordance with those of every honest man, and from such a confidence and respect for the public opinion, that it is a certain proof of much present happiness, and a sure guarantee of much happiness to come.

When an American, in announcing the death of General Washington, said, '*Divine Providence hath been pleased to withdraw from the midst of us this man, the first in war, the first in peace, and the first in the affections of his country!*' what sentiments, what ideas are recalled to the mind by those expressions! Does not this acknowledgment of divine Providence indicate, that, in this enlightened country, no ridicule is thrown upon religious ideas, nor on those regrets expressed in the tenderness of the heart? This simple encomium on a great man, and the gradation which gives for the last term of his glory, '*the affections of his country*,' conveys to the heart a deep and tender emotion.

How many virtues, in fact, are comprehended in the love of a free nation for their first legislator! for a man who, after twenty years of unblemished reputation in a public character, became, by his own choice, a private individual! It appears as if he had only traversed the fields of power, in the journey of life, as a road that led to retirement; a retirement honored by the most noble, elevating, and pleasing recollections!

Never, in any crisis of the French revolution, was there to be found a man who could have spoken the language of which I have recited the above few remarkable words; but in every report that hath reached us of the connection that subsisted between the American legislators and the citizens, there are to be found this purity and grandeur of style, which can only be inspired by the conscience of an honest man.

Every pure government is called, by the form of institutions, to develop and comment upon the motives of its resolves. When, in the moment of peril, the French legislators addressed the people in those eloquent phrases which they were accustomed to use among themselves, they produced no effect on the mind of a public weakened by every ineffectual effort that was attempted to rouse in them the wished for enthusiasm; but enthusiasm was farther from reviving than ever, though often having been solicited in vain.

I think I may venture to affirm, that my father was the first, and hitherto one of the most perfect models of the art of writing, for a man in a public capacity: he possessed in full the talent of appealing to the opinions of mankind, and making them serviceable to the support of government, and of re-animating the principles of morality in the breasts of mankind; a power, of which the magistrates ought to look upon themselves as the representatives; a power, which alone can give them the right of demanding any sacrifice of the nation. In spite of our losses of every kind, since the time of M. Necker, there exists a visible progress in the language used by the chiefs of government: they have called reason to their discussions, and sometimes sentiments: but even then, they appear to me much inferior in precise eloquence, to M. Necker.

When once the power of words is admitted into political interests, they become of the highest importance in those states where despotic law strikes silently on the heads of individuals; the first consideration is then precisely, that silence which leaves the supposition of every thing to hope or fear. But when the government enters with the nation into the examination of its interests, the grandeur and the simplicity of the expressions which they employ, are the only means of gaining them the esteem and confidence of the multitude.

Certainly, all the great men we are acquainted with, have not distinguished themselves as writers; but there are very few who have not exercised the empire of words: all the grand discourses and celebrated expressions of the heroes of antiquity are models of style; they are expressions which were inspired by genius or by virtue, which talent has collected or imitated. The laconism of the Spartans, and the energetic expressions of Phocion, harmonized as well, and often better, than the most regularly sustained discourses, the necessary attributes of the power of language: this manner of expression acted on the imaginations of the people, characterized the motives of the actions of government, and set forth in a conspicuous manner the sentiments of the legislators.

Such are the principal aids that political authority can derive from the art of speaking to mankind; such are the advantages which may be secured to order, to morality, and to the public spirit, by the measured, solemn, and occasionally affecting style of those men who are called to the government of the states. But this is as yet only one point gained of the power of language; and the boundaries of the career we now run, will long recede before us: we shall see that power rise to a much higher degree, if we contemplate it when defending liberty, protecting innocence, or struggling with oppression; if, in one word, we examine it in the appearance of eloquence.

CHAPTER VIII.

OF ELOQUENCE.

In free countries, the political destiny of nations being decided by their own will, men seek and acquire in the highest degree, the means of influencing that will; and the first of all is *eloquence.* Efforts of all kinds acquire strength in proportion as they are recompensed; and when power and honor are holden out by government as a reward of genius; those who are worthy of obtaining the prize, are not tardy in presenting themselves to demand it. Emulation will develop talents, which would have remained unknown in a state where no remuneration could be offered worthy of the acceptance of a great mind.

Let us, neverthelesss, examine the reason, why, since the first years of the revolution, eloquence in France has been altered so much for the worse, instead of following its natural progress in the deliberating assemblies; let us examine how it may revive and come to perfection; and conclude by a general observation upon its utility towards the progress of the human understanding and the support of liberty.

Energy in discourse cannot be separated from measure. If every thing is permitted, nothing can produce any great effect. To treat moral confederations with caution, is to respect talents, services, and virtues; it is to honor, in each man, the rights which his life has given him to the public esteem. If you confound by a gross and scrupulous equality what distinguishes the inequality of nature; the social state would resemble the confusion of a battle, in which nothing is to be heard but the shouts of war or fury. What power then remains to eloquence, and what means can it employ to strike the mind by new ideas or happy expressions, by the contrast of vice with virtue, or by praise or blame distributed by the hand of justice? In that chaos of sentiment and ideas that existed for some time in France no orator could flatter by his esteem, or dishonor by his contempt: as no man at that time could be either honored or degraded.

In such a state of affairs, what could it avail to accuse or defend? Where was the tribunal that could absolve or condemn? What was there that was impossible? or what was there that was certain? If you were audacious, whom would you astonish? and if you were peaceable, who would notice it? Where is the dignity, if nothing is in its proper place? What difficulties are there to overcome, if there exists no obstacle! But, above all, what monument can be erected without a basis? Praise and abuse may be distributed in every direction, without creating either enthusiasm or hatred. It was no longer known what was to fix the esteem of man: calumny commanded by the spirit of party, and praises excited by terror, rendered every thing doubtful; and words, wandering from reason, struck upon the ear without aim or effect.

When Cicero defended Murena against the authority of Cato, he was eloquent, because he knew how to honor the virtues, while opposing the authority of a man like Cato. But in our assemblies, where every kind of invective was admitted; who would have noticed the delicate shades in the expressions of Cicero? or who would think of imposing an useless restraint upon himself, when no one would understand the motive, or receive the impression? The voice of a senator shouting from the tribunal, *Cato is a revolutionary, a stipendiary of our enemies; I require that the death of this culprit should satisfy the national justice;* would soon have made them forget the eloquence of Cicero.

In a country where the ascendency of moral ideas is annihilated, the mind can only be moved by the fear of dissolution: words, it is true, still retain the power of a destructive weapon; but all intellectual force is gone; they are dreaded as a danger, but not as an insult; they can no longer injure the reputation of any one. This multitude of calumnious writers blunt even the resentment which they inspire, and successively take their power from every expression they make use of. A delicate mind experiences a sort of disgust for a language, the expressions of which are found in the writings of such men. A contempt of confederation deprives eloquence of every effect that is connected with wisdom, sobriety and the knowledge of mankind; and reasoning can have no empire in a country where they disdain even the appearance of truth.

In many periods of the revolution, the discourses were filled with the most abominable sophisms: the party phrases which the orators repeated, with the desire of excelling each other, fatigued the ear, and dishonored the heart. There is no variety but in nature; and new ideas can only be inspired by just sentiments. What effect could be produced by that monotonous violence, that power of words, which left the mind so langoid? *It is time you should be acquainted with the real truth. The nation was buried in a slumber worse than that of death; but the representatives of the nation were there. The people are at last aroused from their lethargy, &c.* Or, in other words, *the time of abstractions is past; social order is re-seated on its basis, &c.*

I must stop here, or this imitation would become as tiresome as the reality itself: but there may be extracted from journals, from discourses, and addresses, numberless pages in which we may see words without thoughts, without sentiment, and without truth; it was a kind of litany as if they wished to exercise eloquence and reason, by a certain number of set phrases.

What talent could rise through expressions so absurd, insignificant, false, exaggerated, and vulgar? How was it possible that the mind should not be hardened against words by such a number of untruths? How was it possible to convince reason, fatigued by error, and rendered suspicious by sophisms? Individuals of the same party, united by the most important interest, were accustomed, in France, to look upon discourses only as the order of the day, that was to rally soldiers serving under the same banner. It would have been less burdensome to the mind, and eloquence would not have been entirely lost, if they had contented themselves by commanding in their deliberations, as in battle, by a simple sign of the will.

But in France, force, while having recourse to terror, wished, nevertheless, to patch up a species of argumentation; and vanity, uniting itself to vehemence, was eager to justify by discourse, the most absurd doctrines and unjustifiable actions. But to whom were those discourses addressed? Not to the victims; it would have been difficult to have convinced them of the usefulness of their misfortunes: it could not have been to the tyrants; for they were not to be brought to a decision even by the arguments which they themselves made use of: and it could not have been to posterity, whose inflexible judgment is formed on the nature and consequence of things. But their aim was to avail themselves of political fanaticism, and to blend, under certain heads, the truth of some principles with the most iniquitous and ferocious consequences that might be drawn from them by the passions; and thus to create a reasoning despotism, mortally fatal to the empire of knowledge.

The voice of truth, which conveys to the mind such exalted and pleasing sentiments, and those just and noble expressions of a heart at ease and of a character without reproach, were no where to be heard; it was not known to whom, or to what opinion they were to be addressed, or under what roof they would have been listened to: and that pride which was the natural inheritance of a Frenchman, induced them rather to be silent than to exhaust themselves in useless efforts.

The first of moral truths is that also which is most fruitful in eloquence: but when a licentious philosophy delights to debase, in order to confound every thing; what virtue can be honored by your voice? what brilliancy can you throw upon any object in this universal darkness of the mind? or how will you raise enthusiasm in men who have nothing to hope and nothing to fear from the voice of fame; and who did not recognize, even amongst themselves, the same principles as judges of the same actions?

Morality is inexhaustible in sentiments, and fruitful in ideas for the man of genius, who can penetrate into and avail himself of them. What was deemed a divine spirit by the ancients, was doubtless the consciousness of virtue in the mind of the just, the power of truth united to a talent of eloquence. But in our days, how many men shrink from morality, lest they should find in it the accuser of their own lives! how many others will admit no general ideas, till they have compared them with their own private actions and interest! and, again, how many, though inapprehensive on their own accounts, dare not speak with enthusiasm of justice and equity, through fear of galling the recollection of some of their auditors, and try to present morality sideways as it were, to give it the form of public utility, to throw a veil upon principle, and to make an agreement with pride and remorse at the same time, which mutually warn each other of their irritable interest.

Crimes may cloud the judgment, and turn reason aside by the force of vehemence; but virtue would not dare entirely to unveil herself: though it might wish to convince, it would fear to offend: and it is morally impossible for any one to be eloquent, while he is obliged to abstain from truth. Those barriers that are imposed by respectable convenience, as I have already observed, are useful even to the successes of eloquence: but when, by condescension for injustice or egotism, the movements of an elevated mind must be repressed; when not only facts and their application must be avoided, but even the general considerations that might offer to the imagination all ideas of truth, and all energy arising from sentiments of honesty; no man subjected to such restraints, can be eloquent; and the esteemed orator who is compelled to speak under such circumstances, naturally chooses those phrases that have been most used, upon which the experience of the passions has been already made, and which having been acknowledged inoffensive, pass through the rage of fury without exciting it.

Factions are also serviceable to the progress of eloquence, while they stand in need of the opinion of impartial men, and whilst they dispute betwixt themselves the voluntary assent of the nation: but when political movements have arrived at that term where force only can decide between the parties; what assistance they receive from words, of the resources of discussion, serve only to the degradation of the mind and the destruction of eloquence, instead of developing it: to speak in the midst of unjust power, is to impose on self the most complete servitude. Every absurdity must be supported that forms the long chain which conducts to criminal resolutions; and the character would, if possible, retain more integrity after having committed a blameable action inspired by passion, than after one of those discourses in which meanness and cruelty are distilled, drop by drop, with a sort of art which they in a manner forced themselves to render ingenious.

But how shameful, how degrading to human nature, to prostitute sense in support of rigor and oppression! How shameful to feel a self-love, when all pride is lost! and to think of personal success in sacrificing the life and happiness of others! to employ in the service of unjust power that sort of talent devoid of conscience, which, like the satellites of force, lend to men in power ideas and expressions, which they employ as forerunners of authority to clear the way before injustice!

No one will attempt to maintain, that eloquence has not entirely changed its nature for some years back: but many affirm, that it is impossible it should ever revive, and again acquire any perfection: while others pretend, that the talent of oratory is destructive to the repose, and even to the liberty of the nation. These two errors I shall attempt to refute.

It may be asked, What ground of hope have you, that eloquent men should make themselves heard? Eloquence cannot compose itself of moral ideas or virtuous sentiments: and what hearts would now be opened to sentiments of generosity? After ten years of revolution, who would be moved by virtue, delicacy, or bounty? If Cicero and Demosthenes, the greatest orators of antiquity, existed in these days, could they agitate the steady coolness of vice? could they raise a blush in the cheeks of those on whom the presence of an honest man has no effect? Tell those quiet possessors of the enjoyments of life, that their interest is at stake; and you will disquiet their impassibility: but what can they learn from eloquence? It would draw upon them the contempt of virtue. Alas! have they not known for a long time past, that each one of their days is covered with opprobrium? Would you address yourself to men eager in the pursuits of fortune, new as they are to the habits and the enjoyments which it permits? If you could for a moment inspire them with a noble design, they would be deficient in the courage necessary to put it into execution. Would you attempt to preach benevolence to hatred and ill-will? You would find yourself equally repulsed. If, indeed, you speak in the name of power; you will be heard with respect, whatever may be your language: but if you put in your claim for the weak; if your generosity has made you prefer the cause forsaken by favor and adopted by humanity; you will excite nothing but the resentment of the predominant faction. You live in an era in which misfortune excites nothing but indignation, and oppression nothing but contempt; where anger is inflamed by the aspect of the vanquished; where tenderness is moved, or men exult in power, as soon as it happens that they are to become sharers therein.

What would become of eloquence in the midst of such sentiments as these; eloquence, which, to be affecting and sublime, must have some peril to brave, some unfortunate to defend, and glory holden up as the reward of courage? Can it thus make its appeal to the nation? Alas! has not this unfortunate nation heard the names of every virtue prostituted in the defence of crimes? Is it possible it could yet recognize the voice of truth? The most respectable of our citizens repose in the tomb; and the multitude which remain, live neither for enthusiasm, for morality, nor for glory; they live for repose, which is almost equally disturbed by the fury of crimes, and the generous flights of virtue.

These objections might for some time damp the most sanguine hopes, and discourage expectation; nevertheless, it appears to me impossible but that what there is of good in us, should at last acquire an ascendency; and I shall ever believe that the orators or the writers are in fault, when a discourse pronounced in the midst of a great number of men, or a book that has the public for its judges, produces no effect.

Doubtless, if you address yourself to a few individuals who are united by one common interest, or one common fear; it is certain that no talents can influence them: in their hearts the natural sources have long been dried up, which the voice of a prophet could draw even from a stone. But when you are surrounded by a multitude that contains all the different elements; if you speak to human nature, it will answer you; if you possess the secret of giving that electrical commotion, the principles of which are likewise contained in the moral being, you need no more be afraid of the coolness of indifference; the mockery of injustice, the calculations of egotism, or the ridicule of the envious; all that multitude is your own: should they escape from the beauties of the tragic art, the divine sounds of celestial music, or the enthusiasm inspired by the songs of warriors, they may still be captivated by reason: should the mind feel the want of exaltation, seize the inclination, inflame the desire, and you will carry the opinion.

If we call to mind the cold and phlegmatic countenances that we meet in the world, I own that it seems next to an impossibility to move their hearts; but the attention of the greater part of those men who are known, is taken up by their past actions, their present interest, or in politics. But contemplate a crowd; how many features will you discover whose mild and friendly expression presages a heart not yet known, a heart that would understand your own, and coincide with your sentiments! This multitude is the true representative of the nation. You must forget what you know and what you fear, from such and such men, and give yourself entirely up to your own ideas and emotions; and in spite of every obstacle, you will draw after you every free affection, and every mind that has not received the impression of some yoke, or the price of servitude.

But by what means can we flatter ourselves that we shall be enabled to bring eloquence to perfection, if it be true that we yet hope for success? Eloquence, belonging more to sentiment than to ideas, appears less susceptible of an indefinite progress than philosophy: nevertheless, as new sentiments are developed by new ideas, the progress of philosophy ought to furnish eloquence with new means of bringing itself to perfection.

Intermediate ideas may be traced in a more rapid manner, when the concatenation of a great number of truths is generally understood: the mind may constantly be sustained in the regions of thought, and interested by moral reflections that are universally understood without having been rendered common. What is sublime in some of the ancient discourses, are words which can neither be foreseen nor forgotten, and which, like great actions, leave their traces through subsequent ages. But if the method and precision of argument, the style and necessary ideas, are susceptible of perfection; surely the modern discourses may acquire by their example great superiority over the models of antiquity; and what belongs to imagination, must necessarily produce more effect, if nothing weakens that effect, but on the contrary every thing serves to strengthen it.

That which characterizes eloquence, the movement which actuates the genius that develops it, requires the greatest independence of the mind, at least a momentary one, from every thing that surrounds us; we must rise above personal danger, above the opinions which we attack, and the men whom we oppose; and, in short, above every thing but conscience and posterity. Philosophical ideas will naturally lead to this elevation, when the expression of truth becomes so easy that the images and energies which serve to paint it, present themselves to the mind, animated with the purest and most exalted ardor.

This elevation takes nothing from that vivacity of sentiment so necessary to eloquence, or that ardor which alone can give the accent that irresistible energy and character of domination, that men acknowledge in themselves; which they often call in question, but against which they have no defence.

A man whom reflection had rendered totally insensible to the surrounding events, a character resembling that of Epictetus; should he write, his style would not be eloquent: but when the spirit of philosophy reigns in the enlightened classes of society, it unites itself to the most vehement passions; it is no longer the result of the ascendency of each man over himself, but an opinion established from infancy; an opinion that, mixing with every sentiment of nature, aggrandizes the ideas, but without rendering the mind insensible. There were but very few of the ancients who adopted the maxims of the Stoics, which repress the movements of the heart: the philosophy of the moderns, although it acts more on the mind than on the character, is only a peculiar manner of considering every object. This manner of seeing, once adopted by enlightened men, though influencing the general tenor of their conduct, cannot triumph over the affections of the heart; it destroys neither love nor ambition, nor any of the important interests by which the minds of men are continually occupied, even where their reason is no longer deceived by them: but this meditative philosophy throws a melancholy into the picture of the passions, which adds another degree of profundity and eloquence to their language.

This character of melancholy, which will be more and more developed by the subsequent ages, may give a very great character to eloquence. The man who is ardent in his wishes; if he is endowed with a superior genius, constantly feels himself above the aim he is in pursuit of; and this idea, vague and gloomy, renders the expression at once affecting and imposing. But if moral truths should ever arrive to demonstration, and the language that is to express them, nearly to a mathematical precision; what will become of eloquence? All that belongs to virtue, would certainly be derived from another source, and be founded on another principle than that of reasoning; and yet with all this, eloquence will always reign in the empire which it ought to possess. It is true, it would not be exercised any more in political sciences where there are abstract ideas of any kind; but it would be still more respected, as it could not be represented as dangerous when concentrated in its natural focus, in the power of sentiment upon the mind.

There has been for some time past an absurd system established with regard to eloquence; struck with the abuse that has been made use of since the revolution, they now declare against eloquence; they even wish to take every precaution to guard against danger, which is as yet certainly not very imminent: and, as if the French nation were condemned to move forever in the circle of false ideas, and because men have once maintained injustice with violence, and even with vulgarity, they now refuse to suffer the power of sentiment to be called to the aid of justice.

It appears to me, on the contrary, that it might be maintained, that eloquence and truth are synonymous; that is to say, that in pleading an unjust cause, it is the reasoning that is false; but eloquence, properly speaking is always founded on truth, although it is very easy to deviate in the application or the consequence; in which case the error certainly lies in the argument. Eloquence requiring the impulsion of the mind, addresses itfelf to the sentiments: and the sentiments of the multitude are always on the side of virtue. It has often happened that an individual, when alone, has yielded to dishonest motives; but man, in the presence of man, will only submit to such sentiments as he may own without a blush.

Religion and political fanaticism have occasioned the most horrible excesses, by moving the multitude with inflammable expressions; but it was the falsity of their arguments, and not the interior movements of the heart, which rendered their words so fatal.

What is eloquent in religious fanaticism, is the sentiment which reconciles the sacrifice of ourselves to what may please the beneficent creator: but what is false, is the reasoning by which we are persuaded it is right to assassinate those of a different opinion; and that such sacrifices are pleasing, and even required by the supreme being.

What is real in political fanaticism, is the love of our country, of liberty, and justice: which every man has an equal right to, as to the providence of the eternal; but that which is false, is the reasoning which justifies every crime to arrive at the aim which a man believes to be useful.

Let us examine all the different subjects of discussion among men, and all the celebrated discourses that have been employed in those discussions; and we shall perceive that eloquence was always founded upon the truth of the question; and that its nature was only changed by reasoning: because sentiment cannot err in itself, and the only possible errors are the consequences drawn from it by argument: and those errors will never exist, while the language of logic is not fixed in a positive manner, and adapted to the understanding of the greater number.

I am well aware that there are many arguments which men may try to direct against eloquence; nevertheless, it is with this as with every other advantage permitted by our destiny, they have all their inconveniences, which are brought forward by the wind of faction. But in the strict examination of things, what gifts of nature are there which are wholly exempt from evil? The imperfection of human nature always leaves one side defenceless; the only use of reason is to decide for the majority of advantages against partial inconveniences.

Didactic arguments are not always sufficient for the defence of liberty: when there is danger to be braved, or a generous resolution to be taken, eloquence alone has power to give the necessary impulse. A very small number of characters really distinguished may be decided, in the calm of retirement, solely by the sentiment of virtue: but when courage is requisite to the accomplishment of a duty, the generality of men do not confide in their own strength till their minds are affected, nor forget their own interest till their blood is agitated. Eloquence affects the mind like martial music, and hardens it against danger. An assembled body of men will have the courage and virtue of the most distinguished among them. By eloquence, the virtue of one individual is conveyed to every one by whom he is surrounded. If eloquence be interdicted, an assembly of men will always be influenced by the most vulgar sentiments: for in the habitual state those sentiments are predominant; and it is to the talent of speech that we are indebted for every noble and intrepid resolution which has ever been adopted.

To interdict eloquence, would be the total destruction of glory: a free scope must be given to the expressions of enthusiasm, to inspire it in others: there must be freedom in every thing, in order to give to applause that character which commands respect from reason and prosperity.

In fine, if the belief be persisted in, that eloquence is dangerous; let reflection pause for an instant upon what would be requisite to stifle it; and it will plainly be perceived, that it is with that as with liberty, and every other grand development of the human understanding. It may be, that some evils are attached to those advantages; but in order to guard against those evils, every thing that is useful, great, and generous, in the exercise of moral faculties, must be annihilated. This is the last idea which I propose to develop, before I conclude this work.

CHAPTER IX.

CONCLUSION.

The perfectibility of the human species has become an object of derision to those who look upon intellectual occupations as a kind of imbecility of the mind, and only hold in estimation those faculties which are immediately connected with the interests of life. This system of perfectibility is also opposed by some men of reflection; but above all, at this moment it meets with the greatest opposition in France, from those sentiments, void of reflection, and those affections composed of nothing more than passion, which, by confounding the greatest oppositions, becomes entirely subservient to men whose designs are criminal, by giving them the appearance of honorable motives.

When philosophy is accused of the crimes of the revolution, it is wrongfully attaching base and unworthy actions to the most noble and exalted ideas; the elucidation of which belongs to the subsequent ages. Would it not be better to render the abyss which separates virtue from vice still greater, by uniting the love of knowledge to that of morality, and winning over to her side every thing that is grand or elevated among men, in order to deliver up guilt to every species of shame, ignorance, and ignominy? But whatever may be the received opinion of those conquests of time over the indefinite empire of reason, it appears to me that there exists an argument which may be equally applicable to all.

It is said that the development of knowledge, and every advantage thence derived, as eloquence, political liberty, and the independence of religious opinions, are destructive to the repose and happiness of the human species. But let us contemplate for a moment the means that must be employed to avert the natural desire of knowledge inherent in mankind: how is a stop to be put to this evil, if it be really one, without having recourse to means horrible in themselves, and which after all would prove ineffectual?

I have attempted to show with what force philosophical reason, in spite of every obstacle, and after every misfortune, has always known how to open itself a way, and has successively developed itself in every country, as soon as a toleration, however limited, gave to men the liberty of thinking. How then is it possible to force the human reason to retrograde? And even if this melancholy success could be obtained, how is it possible to foresee and prevent all those circumstances that may give a new impulse to moral faculties? It is the first desire even of kings, that a progress should be made in literature and the fine arts: this progress is necessarily connected with all those ideas which must carry reflection much farther than the subjects which they have given birth to. When the aim of a literary work is to influence the mind, it must necessarily partake of philosophical ideas: and philosophical ideas will ever lead to the discovery of truth.

If they could imitate the Inquisition of Spain, and the despotism of Russia, they still could not be certain that no other institutions could be established in other countries of Europe: for even the simple concerns of commerce, when every other was interdicted, would terminate by becoming the means of communicating the knowledge of one country to another.

The aim of physical sciences being of immediate utility, no country would choose, even if it had the power, to interdict them; this being the case, would not the study of nature destroy the belief of certain dogmas? And would not a religious independence lead to the free examination of every authority? It may perhaps be said, that without shackling knowledge it might be possible to restrain its excesses: but by whom are those excesses to be repressed? By government! Surely that can never be considered as an impartial power: and would the bounds prescribed by them to the researches after truth, be precisely those which ardent spirits would wish to overleap?

If the spirit of a nation be entirely directed to amusement and sensuality; and if ever courageous quality be enervated in order to destroy thought; who is to defend it from the attacks of hostile neighbors? And if it escape from being conquered by a hostile power; yet every vice would find an easy admittance, because there would exist among men nothing but the interest of pleasure, and, of course, that of money; and among all the springs of human actions, there is none more base or contemptible.

If all were to be inspired with the love of war; perhaps the contempt of thought might be revived, but the nation would be subjected to all the evils of feudality; and after all, their hopes would be deceived: for when a strong impulse is given to the mind, it is very difficut to put a stop to its progress. Heroic valor, that quality which produces a new enthusiasm, and combines all that can strike the imagination or intoxicate the mind;—that spirit of war, which you call to the assistance of despotism, will inspire the love of glory; and the love of glory will soon become the most formidable enemy to despotism.

The most remarkable words, and the most brilliant discourses, have been pronounced on the eve of battle, in the midst of dangers, under those perilous circumstances which, by elevating the courageous man, develop at once all his powers. This eloquence of the field would soon be imitated in civil contests: and when generous sentiments, of whatever nature they may be, are expressed without control; eloquence, this talent which appears so easy to stifle, because it is so rarely attained, revives, develops itself, and at length seizes on every subject of importance.

Wherever there has existed any wise institution, whether for the amendment of administration, for the security of liberty, the toleration of religion, or to excite the courage and pride of the nation, the progress of knowledge has immediately become visible: it is only by slavery, and the most absolute debasement, that it can be totally subdued. The earthquakes of Calabria, the plagues of Turkey, and the continual snows of Russia and Kamischatka, and every scourge of nature, are the real allies of that system which militates against the development of the faculties of man: for every misfortune, and every vice, must be invoked before a final stop could be put to the progress of knowledge.

Every thing that is said for or against knowledge, resembles the advantages and conveniences that may be attributed to life; if it were possible for men to enjoy that sort of repose which nature has bestowed on the animal creation, it might perhaps be counted a blessing, as the faculty of suffering would be greatly diminished. But man must be incessantly tormented, before it would be possible to bring him to this state, from which he is by nature excited to escape: to put a final stop to that inclination, he must be precipitated by affliction into brutishness and stupidity. But there is a point on which the enemies as well as the partisans of knowledge ought equally to agree, if they are the friends of humanity; which is the impossibility of restraining the natural bent of the human mind, without plunging it into calamities a thousand times more fatal than those which might arise from the progress of knowledge.

But on the contrary, if the advancement of knowledge is conducted to wise ends and purposes, it is an endless source of enjoyment; if the greater part of mankind have felt the need of a resting-place beyond this world; a something to appeal to in the time of trouble; ought there not to be, even in this world, a decisive principle betwixt those opinions which have no connection with morality, and upon which it has no power? Philosophical truths may be said to acquire the same empire over enlightened minds, who admit them as virtues: upon that of an honest man those truths are a source of emulation independent of circumstances; a consolation in adversity, that does not submit happiness to circumstances. If the road to the perfection of human faculties were not imperiously traced out, we should incessantly observe the predominant opinions of each day consumed in calculations to discover the actual advantages of resolution: we should also observe them consumed with regret, if the effects of that resolution did not tend to immediate utility. In this situation, what ascendency could a man acquire over himself but what could be base and degrading to reason? What is man, when he submits to follow the passions of man; if he does not search after truth for its own sake; if he does not strive to attain the elevation of ideas and sentiments? There is a bright inducement in every career, which an ardent mind springs forward to attain: to warriors, it is glory: to men of thought, liberty; and to men of sensibility, it is a God.

These movements of enthusiasm must not be extinguished; no kind of exaltation should be diminished; the end and aim of legislation should be to unite what is great and good in one career, to what is equally so in another; it should moderate ambition by glory, and liberty by virtue: it should direct knowledge by reasoning, and submit reasoning to humanity: and assemble in the same focus all that is useful in nature, great and good in sentiments, and the most efficacious faculties, in order to combine all the powers of the mind instead of reducing it to the necessity of combating its own developments; to chain down a passion not by virtue, but by a contrary passion; to oppose evil to evil, when all might be united, all might be reduced to perfect harmony by the single sentiment of morality.

What an inestimable gift of heaven is morality! It is through this blessing that we are enabled to understand and appreciate the beauties of nature; it is that alone which adds stability to the gifts of life. What we admire in great men, is always virtue in the form of glory; it is true that many have been guilty of criminal actions; and mediocrity, which confounds every thing, is persuaded that the destiny of a man of genius is illustrated even by the crimes he commits: but if we were to examine into the cause of our admiration, we should always perceive that it was the moral from which it was derived. But from the imperfections to which human nature is condemned, great and generous qualities are too apt to make us forget any dreadful excesses, provided the character or grandeur still remains impressed upon the person guilty of those excesses; if the virtues are felt through the passions; and if, in short, we feel that we may confide in those extraordinary men who, often blamed and often feared, are nevertheless faithful to some noble ideas, and were never known to betray misfortune or retire from danger. Yes, I dare maintain, that all is morality in the sources of enthusiasm; military courage is the sacrifice of self; the love of glory is the exalted thirst after esteem; and the exercise of great faculties in the happiness of the human species; for it is only in doing good that thoughts find a sufficient space for action.

Let us call to mind all the illustrious names which have been transmitted to us through revolving centuries: and we shall find that there is not a single character, of which history does not record at least one virtue. Morality and knowledge are mutually useful to each other; the more our thoughts are elevated, the more shame we feel for having been made to believe that there could exist any wisdom in what was immoral, or a grandeur in those resolutions of which wisdom was not the object. When the circle of relations is enlarged, morality becomes a talent, and then a genius, and afterwards the sublimity of reason and character. Doubtless, no one can promise himself to walk in this noble career without stumbling: but what every man owes to himself, and to the human species, is to direct in the best manner the means in his power, and to invoke all those of others, in order to repeat to mankind, that the depth of reason and profundity of morality are two qualities that are inseparable; and that, so far from being obliged by destiny to make a choice betwixt genius and virtue, those talents which venture forth without his guide, are successively overturned in a thousand different ways. Neither is it true, that morality is more steady and lasting among men of little knowledge: probity, unaccompanied by superior talents, may suffice to direct men in the ordinary offices of life; but in places of eminence, real knowledge is the surest guarantee of morality. We are generally deceived with regard to the wisdom of great and political conceptions: can the art of deceiving be called wisdom? or the art of tormenting individuals and nations? Can it be called wisdom to regulate a fortune according to the interests of personal avidity? What can possibly arise from all those efforts, but often a reverse, and always an internal regret? But the wisdom which is really remarkable, and the intelligence which is truly enlightened, shine in the man who chooses virtue, and knows how to put it into practice; to whom truth is the power of government, and generosity his main strength. In this light the great men of antiquity are described: they ennobled, they elevated the nation, who were desirous of following their example, and their contemporaries trusted in virtue: these are the signs by which a transcendant wisdom is to be known, the formation of which demands the most important of all combinations, namely, that of knowledge and morality.

It has been my wish to comprise in this work every motive that can inspire a love for the progress of knowledge: to give convincing proofs of what is necessary to that progress; and, of course, to engage every virtuous mind to direct towards it that irresistible force, the source of which is to be found in moral nature, as the principles of motion are contained in physical nature. Nevertheless, I must own that in every page of this work, where there appears that love of philosophy and liberty, which neither their friends nor their enemies have been able to stifle in my bosom, I tremble through fear, lest an unjust and perfidious interpretation should represent me as indifferent to those crimes which I detest, and those misfortunes which I have alleviated with all the power that could belong to a mind void of cunning, and a heart without disguise. Some can brave malevolence, while others oppose calumny with indifference or disdain; but for myself, I cannot boast of such courage: I cannot say to those who accuse me unjustly, that they do not disturb the tranquillity of my life. No, I cannot say it; and whether I disarm or excite injustice by thus avowing its power over my happiness, I shall not affect a strength of mind which every day of my life would tend to contradict. I cannot comprehend what kind of characters those have received from heaven, who have no desire for the suffrage of mankind; whose hearts are not dilated by a look of benevolence; and who, when vexed by hatred and injustice, are not long before they can acquire sufficient strength of mind to treat it with contempt.

Nevertheless, this weakness of heart ought not to divert the judgment which is carried to general objects: we must brave the pain to which we expose ourselves in expressing them. Man can never usefully develop any principle of which they are not entirely persuaded themselves. The opinions which we would wish to sustain against our better judgment, cannot be examined by analysis, nor animated by expression: the more natural the reason, the more incapable it is of supporting itself when the prop of conviction is wanting. We should then, if it were possible, divest ourselves of those painful fears which destroy the independence of meditation, and confide our lives to morality, our happiness to those we love, and our thoughts to time—to time which is ever the faithful ally to conscience and truth.

What a melancholy appeal, nevertheless, for those minds who stand in need of obtaining each day the constant approbation of those who surround them! Ah! how happy were they ten years back, when entering into the world relying with full confidence on their own strength, on the friendship that was offered them, and on life itself, which had not as yet belied its promises;—they did not then meet with parties of injustice, envenomed hatred, nor rivals, nor jealousy; all then was delirium and hope! But in ten years after, the route of existence is already traced out; the opinions which have appeared, have jostled against interest, passions, and sentiments; and reason and thought, intimidated by the tumult, no longer dare to force themselves into the presence of those irritated judges. Is it possible that the imagination can resist the crowd of painful recollections which lay siege to it every moment? Reflection, it is true, may predominate; but I much fear it will be impossible to preserve that character of youth when the heart is ever open to friendship, and the amiable candor of a mind that has never known disappointment, which gives a gloss to style, however imperfect it may be, by the sensibility and confidence of the expressions.

I, however, present this book, such as it is, to the public: when one has ceased to be unknown, it is better to give a true idea of oneself, than to trust to the perfidious hazard of calumnious inventions. But it may be that one might wish, even at the expense of the remaining half of life, one had never entered the career of letters, and the publicity by which one is followed! How delightful are the first steps that are taken in the hopes of acquiring reputation; what satisfaction to hear our name recited, to obtain a rank in opinion, to be distinguished among the multitude! But alas! when we are arrived at this envied height; what terror takes possession of the mind, what a frightful solitude surrounds us! We then wish, but in vain, to re-enter our wonted associations: but the time is past. Nothing is so easy as to lose the small portion of fame we may have acquired; but it is not so easy a matter to obtain that benevolent reception which is accorded with pleasure to an obscure individual.

Of how much importance is the first impulse given to our destiny, as on that depends the happiness of our lives! It is to no purpose that tastes are modified, inclinations are changed as well as characters: we are then forced to remain the same, because it is believed that we are so. What then remains, but to obtain new successes, since we are still hated for those that are past? we are condemned to drag the chain of recollection of our first years, of the judgment which has been passed upon us, and, in fine, of our existence,—not such as it is in reality, but such as it is supposed to be.

Oh! life of misery! of tenfold misery! which perhaps drives from us beings whom we should have loved, and who might have attached themselves to us, had not those affections which are nourished by serenity and silence, been frightened away by vain reports. And yet we are compelled to follow this course of life, such as it is formed, since the first lines have been traced out by the imprudence of youth, and to try to find in those affections which still remain, and in the pleasures of thought, a balm to heal the wounds of the heart.

I am fully sensible how much I subject myself to blame for thus mixing the affections of the heart with the general ideas contained in this work: but it is impossible to separate the ideas from the sentiments: the affections incite us to reflection: the affections alone can give a rapid and profound penetration to the mind. Our opinions on every subject are modified by our affections. Such a work pleases, because it is analogous to some misfortunes we have ourselves experienced, or recalls to the mind some recollection that steals imperceptibly on our attention. But above all, some writings are admired, because they move every moral power. But cold and phlegmatic characters only wish to be presented with the discoveries of reason, without joining those movements of regret and those wanderings of reflection, which can never excite the smallest interest in them. I resign myself to their criticism: for how is it possible I can avoid it? By what means can a distinction be made betwixt the talents and the mind? How can we set aside what we feel, when we trace what we think? how impose silence on those sentiments which live in us, without losing any of the ideas which those sentiments have inspired? What kind of writings would result from these continual combats? Had we not better yield to all the faults which may arise from the irregularities of nature?

THE END

REFLECTIONS ON SUICIDE.

BY MADAME DE STAEL.

TO HIS HIGHNESS THE PRINCE ROYAL OF SWEDEN.

Stockholm, December, 1812.

My Lord,

I wrote these Reflections on Suicide, at a time when misfortune rendered the solace of meditation necessary to sustain me. Near you, my lord, my troubles have been alleviated ; my children and I, like the shepherds of Arabia, when they see a storm approaching, have sought shelter in the shade of the laurel. You, my lord, have ever considered death only in the light of devotion to your country ; your mind has never been touched by the mortification which sometimes afflicts those who believe themselves useless upon earth. But to your superior mind no philosophical subject is strange ; and your views are taken from so great an elevation that nothing can escape you. I have ever until now dedicated my works to the memory of my father but I have requested of you, my lord, the honor of doing you homage, because your public life is an exhibition to the world of sterling virtues which alone deserve the admiration of reflecting minds.

Intrepidity personally distinguishes you amidst the brave ; but this intrepidity is directed by a feeling not less sublime ; the blood of the warrior, the tears of the poor, even the cares of the unfortunate are objects of your watchful humanity. You dread the sufferings of your fellow creatures, and the exalted station in which you are placed will never be able to banish sympathy from your heart. A Frenchman said of you, my lord, that to 'the chivalry of republicanism you united the chivalry of royalty :' in truth generosity, in whatever manner it can be displayed, appears to be natural to you.

In your intercourse with the world, you never impose restraint, by factitious formality, upon the minds of those who surround you. You might, if I may be allowed the expression, gain the hearts of a whole nation, one by one, if each individual of which it is composed, had but the happiness of a few minutes' conversation with you ; combined with this affability, so full of grace, your manly energy attaches to you all heroic characters.

The Swedish nation, formerly so celebrated for its exploits, and which still preserves its early reputation, cherishes in you the presage of its glory. You respect the rights of this nation, both from inclination and duty ; and we have beheld you under many trying circumstances, as firm in supporting the constitutional barriers, as others are impatient of their restraint.

Duty never seems to you a restraint, but a support ; and it is thus that your habitual deference for the experienced wisdom of the king gives a new lustre to the power he confides to you.

Pursue, my lord, the career which offers to you so fine a futurity, and you will teach the world anew, what it seems to have forgotten, that the most enlightened wisdom sheds a glory on morality, and that the greatest heroes, far from despising, believe themselves superior to their fellow-men, only by the sacrifices which they make to them.

I am with respect, my lord,
Your royal highness'
most humble, and obedient servant,

Necker.
Baroness de Stael-Holstein.

REFLECTIONS

ON

SUICIDE.

I would impart consolation to the afflicted; the children of prosperity are instructed by their own experience only, and to them general reflections on most subjects appear useless: but it is not thus with the wretched: reflection is their best asylum, since separated by adversity from the distractions of the world, they fly to self-examination, and endeavor, like the invalid on the couch of pain, to find every alleviation of suffering.

Excess of misery gives birth to the idea of suicide, and this subject cannot be too thoroughly investigated: it involves the whole moral organization of man, I will endeavor to throw some new light upon the motives which lead to this action, as well as on those which prevent its perpetration I will examine the subject without prejudice or pride. We ought not to be offended with those who are so wretched as to be unable to support the burden of existence, nor should we applaud those who sink under its weight, since, to sustain it, would be a greater proof of their moral strength.*

The opponents of suicide, feeling themselves on the ground of duty and reason, too often employ, in support of their arguments, an intolerate manner, offensive to their adversaries; and also frequently mingle unjust invective against enthusiasm, generally, with their well-merited reprobation of an unjustifiable action. It appears to me, on the contrary, that we can easily demonstrate from the principles themselves of true enthusiasm, or, in other words, from the love of pure morality, how far resignation to destiny is superior to rebellion against it.

I propose to present the question of suicide in three different points of view: I shall first examine, 'what is the influence of suffering on the mind;' secondly, I shall show, 'what are the laws which the Christian religion imposes on us in relation to suicide;' and thirdly, I shall consider 'in what consists the greatest moral dignity of man in this world.'

SECTION I.

WHAT IS THE INFLUENCE OF SUFFERING ON THE MIND?

We cannot dissemble that there is in the effect of impressions, produced by grief as much difference between individuals, as can exist relatively with genius and character. Not only the circumstances, but the manner of feeling them, differ so essentially, that people otherwise estimable may misunderstand each other in this respect; and yet, of all the limits of the understanding, the most grevious is that which prevents us from comprehending one another.

It appears to me that happiness consists in a destiny harmonizing with our faculties. Our desires are the offspring of the moment, and often are of fatal consequence to us; but our faculties are permanent, and their necessities are unceasing: hence the conquest of the world may have been as necessary to Alexander, as the possession of a cottage to a shepherd. It does not follow, however, that the human race should have served but as nourishment to the gigantic faculties of Alexander; but it may be admitted that, according to the constitution of his nature, there were no other means of happiness for him.

A capacity to love, an activity of mind, a value attached to opinion, are the sources of happiness to some and altogether productive of infelicity to others. The inflexible law of duty is the same for all, but moral strength is purely individual; and in forming an opinion of the happiness or unhappiness of those who are constituted differently from ourselves, a profound knowledge of the human heart is essential to the philosophical and just conclusion.

It appears to me then that we should never dispute the feelings of others; counsel can only operate on conduct, the laws of religion and virtue providing alike for all situations; but the causes of misery, and its intensity, vary equally with circumstances and individuals. We might as well attempt to count the waves of the sea, as to analyze the combinations of destiny and character. Conscience alone exists within us as a pure and unchangeable being, from whom we can all obtain what we all most need, the repose of the soul. The greater part of men resemble each other, not so much in their actions as in their powers, and no one capable of reflection will deny, that, in committing sins against morality, we always feel we might have avoided them. If then we admit that it is part of our condition here to endure affliction, we cannot excuse ourselves, either by the weight of this affliction, or by the acuteness of the felling which it produces. We all have within us the means of performing our duty; and what is most wonderful in moral as well as in physical nature, is, how equally and universally what is necessary to us is disturbed, while what is superfluous is diversified in a thousand ways.

* In my work 'On the Influence of the Passions' I have applauded suicide, and I have ever since repented of that inconsiderate expression. I was then in all the pride and vivacity of early youth; bnt of what use is life, without the hope of improvement?

Physical and moral pain are one and the same thing in their effect upon the mind; for corporeal and mental affliction are both productive of pain; but the one destroys the body, while the other regenerates the soul.

It is not enough to believe with the stoics that 'pain is not an evil;' to submit to it with resignation, we must be convinced that it is a blessing. The least evil would be insupportable, if we considered it as purely accidental; individual irritability governing sensibility, there would be no more justice in blaming him who should destroy himself on account of the prick of a pin, than for an attack of the gout; for some slight difficulty, than for a real calamity. The smallest sensation of pain may excite rebellious dispositions in the mind, if it tend not towards its perfection; for there is more injustice in a light evil, if unnecessary, than in the heaviest affliction, if it have a noble end in view.

It is not necessary here to recur to the grand metaphysical question of the origin of evil, in the discussion of which philosophers have so vainly interested themselves. We can have no conception of free-will without admitting the possibility of evil; we can have no conception of virtue without free-will; nor of life eternal, without virtue;—this chain, the first link of which is, at the same time, incomprehensible and indispensable, ought to be considered as the condition of our being. If reflection and feeling lead us to believe that there is ever, in the ways of providence, a latent or apparent justice, we cannot consider suffering as either accidental or arbitrary. If we believe that the deity could endow us with unlimited faculties or powers, and that the infinite were thus transferable, we should have as much right to complain of some happiness withheld, as of some trouble imposed. Why should not man as well be incensed at not having always existed, as that he must cease to exist? In short, on what ground do his complaints rest? Is it against the system of the universe that he rebels, or against the part allotted to him in a system, subject to immutable laws? Affliction is one of the essential elements of the means of happiness; and it is impossible to form a conception of the one without the other. The vivacity of our desires is always in proportion to the difficulties with which they have to contend; the height of our enjoyments, to the fear of losing them; the strength of our affections, to the dangers which menace the objects of our regard. In a word, the Gordian knot of pleasure and of pain can only be severed by the stroke that terminates existence. Let us submit, say the unfortunate, to the balance of good and evil which belongs to the ordinary course of events; but when we are treated as enemies by destiny we have a right to endeavor to escape its malignity: and yet the regulator which determines the result of this balance is entirely within ourselves: the same sort of life, which reduces one to despair, would fill another with joy, who is placed in a sphere of less elevated hopes. This reflection is not incompatible with what I have said as to the respect we owe to the various modes of feeling: without doubt, the happiness of one may not accord with the character of another; but resignation belongs equally to all. If there are in physical nature two opposite powers, impulse and gravity, which are the causes of the motion of the earth, it may also be asserted that the desire of action, and the necessity of submission, volition, and resignation, are the two poles of moral being, and that the equilibrium of reason is only to be found between them.

The greater part of men can scarcely comprehend more than two powers in life, destiny, and their own will, which is of itself, they believe, sufficient to influence destiny; and hence the general transition from irritation to pride. When they are in a state of irritation, they inveigh against destiny, as children beat the table against which they hurt themselves; and when they are satisfied with the events of life, they attribute them entirely to themselves, deriving a degree of complacency from the means they have employed to direct them, and considering these means as the only source of their felicity. Both these modes of judging are erroneous.

The will of man acts commonly, it is true, in concurrence with destiny; but when this destiny is the result of necessity, that is to say, when it is unalterable, it becomes the manifestation of the designs of providence towards us. A man of genius has observed that 'necessity invigorates.' We must rise to a great elevation of thought to adopt this expression in its full extent; but it is certain that we should always have a sort of respect for destiny. It is a power which, sooner or later, unforeseen or anticipated, seizes on a certain epoch of life and determines the course of it; but far from destiny being blind, as we are pleased to imagine it, we have reason to believe that it comprehends us thoroughly, for it scarcely ever fails to assail our inmost weaknesses. It is the secret tribunal which pronounces judgment on us, and when it may appear unjust, perhaps we alone can tell what it would intend and what it would exact.

There is no doubt of our coming forth, sensibly improved, from the trials of adversity, when we submit to them with a becoming fortitude. The greatest faculties of the soul are developed only by suffering, and this purification of ourselves restores us, after a time, to happiness; for the circle closes up again, and carries us back to those days of innocence which preceded our faults. We then abandon virtue when we fly to suicide as a refuge from misfortune; we reject the enjoyments that virtue would bestow by enabling us to triumph over our distresses. The disciples of Plato said that 'the soul had need of a certain period of sojournment upon earth to become purified from guilty passions.' We should, in fact, believe that the end of life is properly to renounce it. Physical nature accomplishes this work by destruction, and moral nature by sacrifice. Human existence, rightly conceived, is but the abdication of personality to gain admission into universal order. Children only comprehend themselves, young people each other and the friends who are a part of themselves; but when the presages of decay appear, we must seek consolation in general reflections, or abandon ourselves to all the terrors which the latter part of life presents; for the unfortunate or fortunate circumstances of each individual are of little consequence in comparison with the inflexible laws of nature. Old age and death, much more than our peculiar distresses, should fill us with despair; but we readily submit to an universal condition, and yet rebel against our own portion, without reflecting that the universal condition is found in each lot, and that the distinction is more apparent than real.

In treating of the moral dignity of man, I shall strenuously insist upon the difference which exists between suicide and self-devotion, that is to say, between the sacrifice of ourselves to others, or which is the same thing, to virtue; and the renunciation of existence because it is a burden to us. The motives which lead to this act change entirely the nature of it; for when we abdicate life in order to do good to others, we immolate, if I may use the expression, our body to our soul, whilst, when we destroy ourselves from impatience under misfortune, we sacrifice almost always our conscience to our passions.

It is nevertheless wrong to contend that suicide is an act of cowardice: this strained assertion never convinced any one; but we ought here to distinguish between courage and fortitude. The act of suicide implies contempt of death, but to be unable to endure suffering shows a want of fortitude. A species of frenzy is necessary to subdue in us the instinct of self-preservation, when no religious feeling demands the sacrifice. The generality of those who have unsuccessfully endeavored to destroy themselves have not renewed the attempt. because there is in suicide, as in every extravagant act of the will, a certain degree of folly, which is appeased when it nearly accomplishes the end it had in view. Unhappiness is scarcely ever absolute; its associations with our recollections or our hopes, often constitutes the greater part of it; and when we experience a lively check, our affliction frequently presents itself to our imagination under a very different aspect.

Observe, after a period of ten years, a person who has sustained some great privation, of whatever nature it may be, and you will find that he suffers and enjoys from other causes than those from which ten years ago his misery was derived. It does not, therefore, follow that he is restored to happiness; but hope and fear have changed their course in him; and of the activity of these two passions moral life is composed.

There is one cause of suicide which interests the hearts of most women: it is love. The spell of this passion is no doubt the principal cause of the errors we commit in our judgment on the question of self-destruction. We are willing that love should subjugate the highest powers of the soul, and that nothing should be beyond his empire. All sorts of enthusiasm having encountered the attacks of mocking incredulity, romances have still maintained the delusion of sentiment in those countries of the world, to which good faith has retired: but of all the miseries of love there is but one, it appears to me, which should subdue the energy of the soul; it is the death of the object we love and by whom we are beloved.

An inward horror pervades our nature when the heart with which our existence was blended rests cold in the tomb. This affliction, the only one perhaps which surpasses the strength god has given us to resist suffering, has nevertheless been considered by several moralists as easier to be supported than those in which offended pride is in any respect mingled. In fact, in the misery which is produced by the infidelity of the object of our love, though the heart receives the wound, self-love instills its poisons. Without doubt also, a sentiment nobler than self-love rends our hearts when we are obliged to relinquish the esteem we had conceived for the first object of our affections; when there remains no more of an enthusiasm so profound, than the remembrance of the delusive appearances which gave birth to it. We must, however, in strictness urge, that, in an intimate and sincere union, such as ought to exist between true and pure beings, from the moment that either is unfaithful, or that either has deceived, he becomes unworthy of the sentiment he had inspired. I do not wish by this reasoning to imitate those pedants who reduce the troubles of life to syllogisms. We suffer in a thousand ways, we suffer from various, opposite and contending feelings; and no one has a right to contest the causes of our miseries: but in all the sufferings of the soul, in which self-love has its share, it is as unwise as reprehensible to seek our own destruction: for all that partakes of vanity is necessarily fleeting and we must not accord to that which is fleeting the right to precipitate us into eternity.

A misfortune entirely free from all emotion of pride is then the only one which should lead to suicide; but for the very reason that such a misfortune originates entirely in sensibility, religion can deprive it of its bitterness. Providence, which desires not that the wounds of the human soul should be without a cure, brings relief to him whom he has afflicted beyond his strength. Often, at such a time, the wings of the angel of peace overshadow our dejected heads, and who can say that this angel is not the very object of our regret? who can say that, touched by our tears, it has not obtained from heaven the power of watching over us?

The pains of sensibility, which self-love embitters, are necessarily moderated by time; and those of an affecting nature, without any mixture of the emotion of pride, inspire a religious disposition, which leads the soul to resignation. The most frequent causes of suicide in modern times are ruin and dishonor. A reverse of fortune, as society is constituted, produces a most acute unhappiness, which multiplies itself in a thousand different ways. The most cruel of all, however, is the loss of the rank we occupied in the world. Imagination has as much to do with the past, as with the future, and we form with our possessions an alliance, whose rupture is most grievous; but, after a time, a new situation presents a new perspective to almost all men. Happiness is so composed of relative sensations, that it is not things in themselves, but their connection with yesterday and to-morrow, which affects the imagination. If destiny or the menaces of a tyrant have led a man to apprehend a certain degree of unhappiness, and he learns that he is to be spared the half of what he dreaded, his impressions will be very different from those he would have experienced, if he had not suffered so great a terror. Destiny has almost always much to do in the composition of our miseries; we may say that he also sometimes repents as well as other sovereigns of causing too much evil.

Opinion exercises over most individuals a degree of influence whose power it is difficult to diminish: the words, 'I am dishonored,' affect the whole mind of a social being, and it is not possible to avoid pitying him who sinks under the weight of this misfortune; for, since he feels it so bitterly, it is, in all probability, unmerited: but yet we must range the causes of dishonor in two principal classes; those which are derived from faults with which our conscience reproaches us; and those which originate in involuntary error and are in no wise criminal.

Repentance is necessarily connected with our ideas of divine justice, for if we did not regulate our actions by this supreme standard of equity, we should experience in life nothing but discontent. We must consider existence in two points of view; either as a game, the gain or loss of which consists in the advantages of this world; or as a noviciate for immortality. If we regard it as a game, we shall be able to trace in our own conduct only the consequences of true or false reasoning; if we have the life to come in view, it is intention only to which our conscience clings. The man whose views are limited to the interests of this world may suffer discontent, but repentance belongs only to the religious man; and being such, he necessarily feels that expiation is the first duty, and that conscience commands us to endure the consequences of our transgressions, to the end that we may repair them, if possible, by doing good. Merited dishonor is then, to the religious man, a just punishment, from which he believes he has no right to fly; for, although, among human actions, there may be many more perverse than suicide, there is not one which seems so formally to deprive us of the protection of god.

Our passions lead us to many culpable actions which have happiness for their end; but, in suicide, there is a renunciation of all succor from above, that cannot be reconciled with any pious disposition.

He who is truly affected by repentance will exclaim, with the prodigal son: 'I will arise, and go to my father, and will say unto him, father, I have sinned against heaven, and before thee, and am no more worthy to be called thy son.' With this affecting resignation would a religious being express himself, for the more criminal he believes himself to be, the less would he arrogate to himself the right to quit life, since he has not used the gift as the bestower of it exacts. As for those guilty beings who do not believe in a future existence, and who have lost their consequence in this world, suicide, according to their manner of thinking, has no other inconvenience than to deprive them of the happy chances that might yet remain for them, and each individual can estimate these chances as he chooses, from his calculation of probabilities.

I believe we may affirm that unmerited dishonor is never of long duration. The influence of truth on the public is such, that patience only is requisite to restore us to our station. Time has something sacred in it, and seems to act independently of the events it embraces. It is a support for the weak and unfortunate, and, in fact, is one of those mysterious ways by which the deity manifests himself to us. The world, which is in most respects so different a thing from the individual, the world, which is a sensible being, although composed of so many stupid ones, the world, which is liberal, although follies without number are committed by those who make a part of it, the world always concludes by returning to justice, as soon as predominating and momentary circumstances have disappeared. 'In patience possess ye your souls,' says the gospel, and this counsel of piety is also that of reason. When we reflect on the holy writings, we find in them an admirable combination of the best precepts for conducting ourselves with success in this world, and often also the best means of obtaining it. Physical suffering, incurable infirmity, in short, all such miseries as are inseparable from corporeal existence, would seem to constitute one of the most plausible causes of suicide; and yet, scarcely ever, particularly among the moderns, does this species of misery occasion it. Miseries which are in the ordinary course of events may overcome us, but do not excite us to rebel against our condition. It is essential that irritation should be mingled with our feelings before we can be enraged against destiny, and wish to liberate ourselves from its evils, or revenge ourselves against it, as an oppressor. There is a singular kind of error in the manner in which most men consider their destiny. This error has so much influence on the impressions of the mind, that we cannot too often contemplate it under its various aspects. Indeed, a community of suffering is sufficient to make us resigned to the most distressing events, and we find injustice only in those afflictions which are peculiarly our own. And yet, are not these varieties, as well as these resemblances, for the most part counterbalanced? and are they not all, I repeat it, equally comprised in the laws of nature? I shall not dwell upon the common consolations that may be derived from the hope of a change in our circumstances; there are some afflictions which are not susceptible of this sort of comfort: but I believe we may boldly affirm, that all who have resorted to an active and steady employment have found an alleviation of their distress. There is an object in all occupations, and it is an object that man constantly requires. Our faculties devour us, like the vulture of Prometheus, when they have no external cause of action, and employment exercises and directs these faculties: in short, when we possess imagination, and most people in sorrow have a great deal, we can always find renovated pleasure in the master-pieces of the human mind, either as amateurs or artists. A celebrated woman has remarked that 'ennui is mingled in all our distresses,' and this reflection is full of profundity. True ennui, that of active minds, is the absence of all interest in what surrounds us, combined with faculties, which render this interest essential to us; it is thirst without the possibility of quenching it. Tantalus is a just image of the soul in this state. Occupation gives a zest to existence, and the fine arts contain, at the same time, the originality of particular objects, and the grandeur of universal ideas. They preserve our relation with nature; we might love her without the aid of these charming mediators, but they teach us the better to appreciate her.

We must not disdain, in whatever misery we may be plunged, the primitive gifts of our creator, life and nature. A social being places too much importance upon the tissue of circumstances of which his individual history is composed. Existence is in itself a marvelous thing; the happiness of the savage is derived from it alone; sick people often pray for nothing else; the prisoner considers liberty as the supreme good; the blind man would willingly give all he possessed for the blessing of sight; the climates of the south, which give life to colors, and develop perfumes, produce an undefinable impression; the consolations of philosophy have less empire over us than the enjoyments we derive from the spectacle of heaven and earth. Among our means of happiness then the power of reflection is most valuable. We are so contracted in ourselves, so many things agitate and wound us, that we have constantly need to plunge into this boundless sea of thoughts, where we must, as in the Styx, become invulnerable, or altogether resigned.

No one will venture to say that we can endure every calamity we are subjected to in this world, nor will any one dare to place such confidence in his own strength as to make this assertion. There are but few beings endowed with such superior faculties that despair has not reached them more than once; and life appears but as a protracted shipwreck, the fragments of which are friendship, love and glory. The borders of the stream of time are covered with them; but if we have preserved the internal harmony of the soul, we may yet hold communion with the works of the deity.

The mercy of heaven, the stillness of death, the beauty of the universe, which was not designed to show man his own insignificance, but as an earnest of better days; some noble thoughts, always the same; are like the harmony of creation, and restore us to tranquillity when we are accustomed to comprehend them. From these sources the hero and the poet draw their inspirations; why then would not some drops from the cup, which elevates them above humanity, be salutary for all?

We accuse destiny of malignity because its blows are always aimed at the tenderest part of us. This is not attributable to the malignity of destiny but to the impetuosity of our desires, which precipitates us against the obstacles we encounter, as we run deeper upon the sword of our adversary in the ardor of combat: and besides, the instruction we should receive from misfortune necessarily applies to that part of our character which stands most in need of reproof. We cannot admit the belief of a god without supposing that he directs destiny in its influence upon men: we cannot then consider this destiny as a blind power; it remains to be considered whether he who governs it has given to man the liberty of submitting to or flying from it. I shall examine this in the second part of these reflections.

SECTION II.

WHAT ARE THE LAWS WHICH THE CHRISTIAN RELIGION IMPOSES ON US, IN RELATION TO SUICIDE?

When the ancient man of sorrows, Job, was stricken with every evil, when he had lost his fortune and his children, and when frightful physical afflictions made him suffer a thousand deaths, his wife advised him to renounce life. 'Curse god,' said she, 'and die.'— 'What,' replied he, 'I have received good at the hand of god, and shall I not receive evil?' And in whatsoever depth of depair he was plunged, he was resigned to his fate, and his patience was rewarded. It is supposed that Job preceded Moses; he existed, at least, long before the coming of Jesus Christ, and at a time when the hope of the soul's immortality was not yet assured to mankind. What would he then have thought at the present time? We see in the bible, men, such as Samson and the Maccabees, who devoted themselves to death, to accomplish a design they believed to be noble and salutary; but in no part do we find examples of suicide, of which disgust to life or its troubles is the only cause; in no part has that species of suicide, which is only a desertion from destiny, been considered as possible. It has been frequently asserted, that there is no passage in the gospel which indicates a formal disapprobation of this act. Jesus Christ, in his discourses, rather ascends to the principles of action than enters into a particular application of the law; but is it not enough, that the general spirit of the gospel tends to hallow resignation?

'Blessed are they that mourn,' said Jesus Christ, 'for thay shall be comforted. If any man will come after me, let him deny himself, and take up his cross and follow me. Blessed are ye, when men shall revile you, and persecute you, for my sake.' Jesus Christ every where announces that his mission is, to teach man that the design of misfortune is the purification of the soul, and that celestial happiness is obtained by pious endurance of our miseries on earth. The interpretation of the doubtful meaning of affliction, is the special intention of the doctrine of Jesus Christ.

We find many good things respecting social morality in the Hebrew prophets and in the Pagan philosophers; but it was to teach charity, patience, and faith, that Jesus Christ descended upon earth; and these three virtues all alike tend to the relief of the unhappy. The first, charity, teaches us our duty towards them; the second, patience, teaches them to what consolations they ought to have recourse, and the third faith, announces to them their recompense. Most of the precepts of the gospel would want foundation if suicide were permitted; for, from misfortune we learn the necessity of appealing to heaven, and the insufficiency of the goods of this world is what, above all, renders another life necessary.

It is seldom that individuals, in the intoxication of prosperity, preserve a holy respect for sacred things. The allurements of this world are so brilliant as to darken all other joys, even the glory of a future existence. A German philosopher, disputing with his friends, once said, 'To obtain such a thing, I would give millions of years of my eternal felicity,' and he was singularly moderate in the sacrifice he offerred; for temporal enjoyments have generally much more activity than religious hopes; and spiritual life, or Christianity, which is the same thing, would not exist, if sorrow dwelt not in the heart of man. Premeditated suicide is incompatible with Christian faith, because this faith rests chiefly on the different duties of resignation. With respect to suicide resulting from a moment of delirium, from an excess of despair, it is not probable the divine legislator of men had occasion to notice it among the Jews, who rarely offered examples of this sort of offence. He unceasingly combated, in the Pharisees, the vices of hypocrisy, of unbelief, and of hardness of heart. Indeed, he appears to have considered the faults of the passions as the disease of the soul, and not as its habitual state, and always to have appealed rather to the general spirit of morality than to the precepts which grow out of circumstances.

Jesus Christ constantly directed man to occupy himself with life as it has relation to immortality only. 'Then, why take ye thought for raiment,' said he, 'consider the lillies of the field, they toil not, neither do they spin; yet Solomon, in all his glory, was not arrayed like one of these.' It is not slothfulness nor indifference that Jesus Christ inculcates by this passage, but a sort of calm which would be useful even as it regards the interests of this world. Warriors call this sentiment confidence in their good fortune; religious men, the hope of divine assistance; but both the one and the other find in this internal disposition of the soul a support, which, while it enables them to form a clearer judgment of the circumstances of this life, at the same time affords the means of escaping from them. We believe we can obtain our emancipation from the tyranny of human events by determining to destroy ourselves if we do not attain the end of our desires. Under this idea, we consider ourselves as entirely at our own disposal; and free to relinquish life when we are no longer content with the condition of it. If the gospel accorded with this manner of thinking, we should find in it some lessons of prudence; but all those which relate to virtue would have a very limited application, for virtue consists only in the preference we give to others, that is to say, to our duty over our personal interests: now, when we renounce life, merely because we are not happy, we prefer ourselves to all the world, and become, if I may be allowed the expression, egotists in suicide.

Of all the religious arguments which have been adduced against suicide, that which has been most frequently reiterated, is that it is formally comprised in the prohibition expressed by the commandment of god: 'Thou shalt not kill.' Without doubt, this argument might also be admitted; but as it is impossible to consider the suicide in the same light with the assassin, the true point of view of this question is, that happiness not being the end of human life, man ought to aim at perfection, and consider his duties as necessarily connected with his sufferings. Marcus Aurelius said that 'there was no more crime in leaving him than a room that smokes:' certainly, if it were so, instances of suicide would be still more frequent than they are; for it is difficult, when the illusion of youth is past, to reflect on the course of things, and still to preserve our attachment to existence. We might adhere to this existence, through fear of leaving it; but if this motive alone retained us upon earth, all those who have conquered fear, by the force of military habits, all those whose imaginations are more terrified by the phantom of life than by that of death, would spare themselves their latter days, which repeat in so melancholy a tone the brilliant airs of our youth.

J. J. Rousseau, in his letter in favor of suicide, says, 'Why, if we are allowed to cut off a leg, are we not also permitted to take away our lives?' Has not the will of god given us the one as well as the other?' A passage of the gospel seems to reply texturally to this sophism: 'If thy right hand offend thee,' says Jesus Christ 'cut it off. If thine eye offend thee, pluck it out, and cast it from thee.' What the gospel here says, applies to temptation, and not suicide; but nevertheless it is sufficient to refute the argument of J. J. Rousseau. Man is permitted to seek a cure for all his evils; but it is forbidden him to destroy his being, or in other words, the power he has received of choosing between good and evil. He exists by this power, he ought to be regenerated by it, and to this principle of action, to which the exercise of free will entirely belongs, every thing is subordinate.

Jesus Christ, in encouraging man to endure the pains of life, repeats unceasingly the efficacy of prayer. 'Knock,' says he, and it shall be opened unto you; ask and it shall be given unto you.' But the hopes he presents relate not to the events of this life; it is the disposition of the soul upon which prayer exerts the greatest influence. Peace of mind and the prosperities of the world are both alike denominated by the word happiness; and yet, no two things are so different as these sources of enjoyment. The philosophers of the eighteenth century have founded morality on the positive advantages it procures in this world, and have considered it as personal interest, well understood. Christians have fixed the centre of our greatest enjoyments in the bottom of the soul. Philosophers promise temporal benefits to those who are virtuous; they are right, in some respects; for, in the ordinary course of things, it is very probable that the blessings of this life will accompany a course of moral conduct; but if our confidence in this should be deceived, despair would then be lawful; for, considering virtue only as a speculation, when it is unsuccessful we may abandon existence. Christianity, on the contrary, places happiness above all, in the impressions we receive from conscience. Have we not experienced, independently of religious feelings, and our internal disposition has not always agreed with our circumstances, and that we have often felt more or less happy, than we ought to be, after an examination of our situation? If the mere force of the mobility of our nature is sufficient to produce such an effect, how much more power ought the holy and secret operation of piety to have upon the soul! How often have those virtuous beings whom affliction has visited, found an unexpected calm in the bottom of their hearts! An unknown celestial music is heard in the desert, and seems to announce that the fountain will soon spring, even from the bosom of the rock.

When we have beheld Louis XVI, the purest and most respectable victim that faction could immolate, led to the scaffold, we cannot but demand what relief the hand of god stretched forth to him in the abyss of misery? Of a sudden. the voice of an angel is heard, who under the form of a minister of the church, says to him, 'Son of Saint Louis, rise to heaven? His worldly grandeur, his heavenly hopes were all united in these simple words. They uplifted him, by recalling to him his illustrious race from the debasement into which man had wished to plunge him; they invoked the shades of his ancestors, who, without doubt, already stretched forth their crowns to welcome the coming of the august saint to heaven. Perhaps, at this moment, the eye of faith made him fancy he described them. He approached the limits of time, and our calculation of its hours concerned him no longer. Who knows with what blissful emotion a single moment of tender reflection at that time filled his soul!

While the blood-stained executioner bound those hands, which has wielded the sceptre of France, the same missionary of god said to his king, 'Sire, it was thus that our lord was led to death.' What aid did he not impart to the martyr, by presenting to his view his divine model! In fact, is not the most glorious example of the sacrifice of life the basis of the Christian's belief? And does not this example mark the difference which exists between the martyr and the suicide? The martyr serves the cause of virtue, by yielding up his blood for the instruction of the world: the suicide perverts all idea of courage, and scandalizes even death itself. The martyr teaches man the power of conscience, it subdues the most powerful physical instinct; the suicide also proves the power of will, over instinct, but it is that of an unsteady charioteer, who can no longer hold the reins, but precipitates himself into the abyss, instead of conducting in safety to the goal. Indeed, in committing this terrible act, the soul is wrought to a pitch of frenzy, which concentrates, in an instant, an eternity of pain.

The last scene of the life of Jesus Christ appears destined, above all, to confound those who believe they have the right to destroy themselves in order to escape misfortune. The dread of suffering seized upon him, who had voluntarily devoted himself to the death, as well as to the life of man. He prayed a long time to his father, on the mount of Olives, and his soul was exceedingly sorrowful, even unto death. 'My father,' cried he, 'if it be possible let this cup pass from me!' Three times he repeated this prayer, his countenance bathed in tears. All our pains had passed into his divine being. He feared, like us, the outrageous of man; like us, perhaps, he regretted those he had loved, his mother and his disciples; like us, and more than us, perhaps, he loved this fruitful earth, and the celestial pleasures of an active beneficence, for which he returned thanks to his father every day. But not being able to avert the cup to which he was destined, he cried, 'Nevertheless, not my will, but thine be done, O, my father,' and replaced himself in the hands of his enemies. What more would we seek in the gospel on resignation in affliction, and the duty of supporting it with courage and patience? The resignation we obtain from religious faith is a species of moral suicide, and it is in that it so much differs from suicide, properly so called, for the renunciation of self has for its end the sacrifice of ourselves to our fellow creatures; while suicide, caused by a disgust of life, is only the bloody mourning of personal happiness. Saint Paul says, 'She that liveth in pleasure, is dead while she liveth.' In every line of the holy writings we see this great misunderstanding between the beings of time and those of eternity; the first make life consist in what the last regard as death. It is then plain that the opinion of beings of time consecrates the suicide, while that of the beings of eternity exalts the martyr: for he who grounds morality on the happiness it may produce upon earth, hates life when it does not realize its promises; whilst he who makes true felicity consist in the internal emotion, which sentiments and thoughts in communication with the deity excite, can be happy in spite of men, and, if I may use the expression, in defiance of destiny. When the experience of existence has taught us the vanity of our own strength, and the almighty power of god, it often works in the soul a sort of regeneration, the delights of which are inexpressible.—Then it is that we become accustomed to judge ourselves, as we judge of others; to place our conscience as a third person between our personal interests and those of our adversaries; we are passive as to our destiny. certain that we cannot direct it; we are passive also as regards our self-love, certain that it is not ourselves but the world that casts our character: we are passive, in fine, as to that hardest of all human trials, the wrongs and injuries of friendship; whether it be by recollection of our own imperfections, or by confiding to the tomb of the being who has best loved us our most secret thoughts; or, finally, by raising towards heaven the sensibility it has bestowed upon us. How great is the difference between this religious denial of terrestrial strife, and the frenzy which leads to suicide as a refuge from suffering. The renunciation of ourselves is in every respect opposed to suicide.

Besides, how can we be assured that suicide will deliver us from the evils which pursue us? What certainty can atheists have of annihilation, or philosophers of the mode of existence nature has reserved for them? While Socrates taught to the Greeks the immortality of the soul, many of his disciples committed suicide, greedy to taste of this intellectual life, of which the confused images of paganism had not given them the idea. The emotion excited by so novel a doctrine led their ardent imaginations astray; but, can Christians, to whom the promises of a future life have been extended only in connection with menaces of punishment to the guilty, can they hope that suicide will be the means of extricating them from the troubles which overwhelm them? If the soul survive death, will not the sentiment which filled it entirely, whatever may be its nature, still make a part of it? Who among us knows what connection is established between the recollections of earth and celestial enjoyments? Is it for us to draw near, by our own resolution, to this unknown region, from which, at the same time a secret dread repulses us? How can we annihilate, by the caprice of our will, (and I denominate thus every act not founded upon duty) the work of god in us? How shall we determine our death, when we had no power over our birth? How answer for our eternal destiny, when the most trifling actions of this brief existence have often filled us with the most bitter regret? Who will dare believe himself wiser and stronger than destiny, and venture to say to it—this is too much?

Suicide draws us from nature as well as from its author. Natural death is almost always softened by the enfeebling of our strength, and the exaltation of virtue sustains us in the sacrifice of life to our duty: but the suicide seems to spring with hostile arms beyond the borders of the tomb, and defies alone the images of horror and of darkness.

Oh! what despair is required for such an act! May pity, the most profound pity, be granted to him who is guilty of it! but, at least, let him not mingle human pride with it. Let not the wretch believe himself the more a man, for being the less a Christian, and let a reflecting being know ever where to place the true moral dignity of man.

SECTION III.

OF THE MORAL DIGNITY OF MAN.

Almost every individual aims here below either at his physical well-being or at his consideration in the world, and the greater part of mankind at both united: but consideration, in the estimation of some, consists in the ascendency which power and fortune bestow, and in that of others, in the respect which talents and virtue inspire. Those who seek riches and power are also desirous to be thought possessed of moral qualities, and above all, of superior faculties; but this last is a secondary end, which must give place to the first; for a certain depraved knowledge of the human race, teaches us, that the solid advantages of life command the interests of men still more than their esteem.

We will set aside, as foreign from our subject, those whose ambition has only power and riches for its end; but we will examine with attention in what the moral dignity of man consists; and this examination will lead us necessarily to judge the action of self-destruction under two opposite points of view; the sacrifice inspired by virtue, and the disgust which results from mistaken passions. We have opposed, in respect to religion, the martyr to the suicide; we may also, in respect to moral dignity, present the contrast of devotion to duty, with rebellion against our condition.

Devotion generally leads us rather to submit to death, than to be instrumental in bringing it upon ourselves; yet, there were among the ancients suicides from devotion. Curtis, precipitating himself to the depth of the abyss, that he might cause it to close; Cato, stabbing himself to teach the world that there still existed a soul free under Cæsar's dominion, did not destroy themselves to escape from misery; the one wished to save his country, and the other gave the universe an example whose ascendency still continues. Cato passed the night preceding his death in reading the Phaedon of Socrates, and the Phaedon explicitly condemns suicide, but this great citizen knew that he did not die for himself but for the cause of liberty; and, according to circumstances, this cause may teach us to await death, like Socrates, or to be ourselves the instrument of it, like Cato.

The characteristic of the true moral dignity of man, is devotion to duty. What we do for ourselves may have a sort of grandeur which excites surprise; but admiration is only due to the sacrifice of selfish feeling, under whatever form it may appear. Elevation of soul constantly tends to free us from what is purely individual, for the purpose of uniting us to the great views of the creator of the universe. Love and reflection comfort and exalt us only by withdrawing us from all egotistical impressions. Devotion and enthusiasm infuse a purer air into our breasts. Self-love, irritation, impatience, are the enemies against which conscience obliges us to combat, and the tissue of our lives is almost entirely composed of the continual action and reaction of internal strength against external circumstances, and of external circumstances against internal strength. Conscience is the true standard of the greatness of man, but it has only a claim to our admiration in the generous being, who opposes duty himself, and can sacrifice himself when duty commands him to do so.

Genius and talent can produce great effects upon this earth; but when the object of their exercise is the personal ambition of him who possesses them, they no longer constitute the divine nature in man. They only serve for address, for prudence, for all those worldly qualities, the type of which is found in animals, although the perfection of them belongs to man. The paw of the fox, and the pen of him who barters his opinion for his interest, are one and the same thing in respect to moral dignity. The man of genius who serves himself at the expense of the happiness of his fellow-creatures, whatever eminent faculties he may be endowed with, acts always with regard to self; and in this respect the principle of his conduct is the same with that of animals. What distinguishes conscience from instinct is sentiment and the knowledge of duty, and duty always consists in the sacrifice of self to others, The whole problem of moral life is included in this principle; the whole dignity of the human being is in proportion to its strength, not only against death, but against the interests of existence. The other impulse, that is to say, that which overthrows the obstacles opposed to our desires, has success for its recompense, as well as its end; but it is not more wonderful to make use of our intelligence to subject others to our passions, than to employ our feet in walking, or our hands in taking, and, in the estimate of moral qualities, it is the motive of actions which alone determines their worth.

Hegesippus of Cyrene, a disciple of Aristippus, discoursed in favor of suicide as well as sensuality. He contended that man should have no object but pleasure in this world; but as it is very difficult to insure our own enjoyments, he advised death to those who could not obtain them. This doctrine is one of those by which we can best determine the motives of suicide, and it evinces the species of egotism which mingles, as I have before observed, in the very act by which we would annihilate ourselves.

A Swedish professor, named Robeck, wrote a long work upon suicide, and killed himself after having composed it: he says in his book, that we should encourage a contempt of life, even to suicide. Do not the most profligate also despise life? Every thing consists in the sentiment to which we make the sacrifice. Suicide, regarding only self, which we have carefully distinguished from the sacrifice of existence to virtue, proves but one thing in point of courage, which is, that the will of the soul overcomes physical instinct: thousands of soldiers afford constant evidence of this truth. Animals, it is said, never kill themselves. Actions, which are the result of reflection, are incompatible with their nature; they appear to be enchained by the present, ignorant of the future, and gathering only habits from the past: but as soon as their passions become roused, they brave pain, and this greatest pain which we term death; of which, without doubt, they have not the least idea. The courage of a great many men also partakes of this want of thought. Robeck was wrong in extolling the contempt of life so highly. There are two ways of sacrificing life, either because we give duty the preference, or because we give our passions this preference, in not wishing to live when we have lost the hope of happiness. This last sentiment cannot merit esteem: but to fortify ourselves by our own thoughts, in the midst of the reverses of life; to make ourselves a defence against ourselves, in opposing the calm of conscience to the irritation of temperament: this is true courage, in comparison with which, that which springs from instinct, is very little, and that which is the fruit of self-love, still less. Some people pretend, that there are circumstances in which, feeling ourselves a burden upon others, we may make a duty of ridding them of the incumbrance. One of the great means of introducing errors in morality is, to fancy situations, to which there would be nothing to reply, if it were not that they do not exist. Who is so unfortunate as to find no fellow-creature to whom he may impart consolation? Who is so unhappy, that by his patience and his resignation, he may not give an example to move the soul, and give birth to sentiments, that the best precepts have never been able to inspire. The half of life is its decline: what has then been the intention of the creator in presenting this melancholy perspective to man, to man whose imagination has need of hope, and who counts as nothing what he has, except as the means of obtaining yet more! It is clear that the creator has willed that mortal man should obtain a mastery over self, and that he should commence this great act of disinterestedness long before the degradation of his strength should render it more easy to him.

When you reach the age of maturity, you are already in every thing reminded of your death. Do you marry your children? You make an estimate yourself of the fortune they may have when you shall be no more. Paternal duty consists in a continual devotion; and as soon as children attain the age of reason, almost all the enjoyments they afford are grounded on the sacrifices we make to them. If then happiness were the only end of life, we should destroy ourselves as soon as we cease to be young, as soon as we descend the mountain, whose summit appeared environed with so many brilliant illusions.

A man of wit, who was complimented on the fortitude with which he had supported great reverses, replied, 'I have sufficient consolation in being only twenty-five years old.' In fact, there are very few griefs more bitter than the loss of youth. Man accustoms himself to it by degrees, it will be said. Without doubt, time is an ally of reason, and weakens the resistance it meets with in us; but where is the impetuous soul, which is not irritated at the approaches of old age? Do the passions always decay with the faculties? Do we not often see the spectacle of the punishment of Mezentius renewed by the union of a soul still alive and a ruined body, inseparable enemies? Of what use would this sad herald be, which nature causes to precede dissolution, if it were not ordained that we should exist without happiness, and abdicate each day, flower after flower, the crown of life.

Savages, having no idea of the religious or philosophical destiny of man, believe they perform a duty to their parents by depriving them of life when they become old; this act is founded on the same principle as suicide. It is certain that happiness, in the acceptation given it by the passions, that the enjoyments of self-love at least, exist but in a small degree for old age; but it is this, which, by the development of moral dignity, seems to announce the approach of another life, as in the long days of the north, the twilight of the evening is confounded with the dawn of the ensuing day. I have seen these venerable countenances absorbed entirely with the future; they seem to announce, as a prophet, the old man who no longer interests himself with the remainder of his life, but is regenerated, by the elevation of his soul, as if he had already passed the barriers of the tomb. It is thus we must arm ourselves against misfortune; it is thus that in the strength of life itself, destiny often gives the signal of this detachment from existence, that time sooner or later exacts from us. 'You have very humble thoughts,' some men will say, convinced that pride consists in what we exact from destiny, and from others; while, on the contrary, it consists in what we exact from ourselves. These very men contrast Christianity with the philosophy of the ancients, and pretend that their doctrine was much more favorable to energy of character, than that whose foundation is resignation: but certainly we must not confound resignation to the will of god with condescension to the power of man. Those heroic citizens of antiquity, who would have endured death rather than slavery, were capable of a pious submission to the power of heaven; while modern writers, who pretend that Christianity weakens the soul, could very well bend, notwithstanding their apparent strength, to tyranny, with more suppleness than a feeble but Christian-like old man.

Socrates, that saint of sages, refused to make his escape from prison after he was condemned to death. He believed he ought to set an example of obedience to the magistrates of his country, although they were unjust to him. Does not this sentiment belong to the true firmness of character? What greatness likewise was there not in that philosophical discourse on the immortality of the soul, continued so calmly, even to the very moment when the poison was brought to him! For two thousand years, men of profound thought, heroes, poets, and artists, have consecrated the death of Socrates by their praise; but the thousands of instances of suicide, caused by disgust and ennui, with which the annals of every corner of the world are filled, what traces have they left in the remembrance of posterity?

If the ancients were proud of Socrates, Christians, even without including the martyrs, can present a grea number of examples of this noble strength of mind, in comparison with which the irritation or the depression, which leads us to destroy ourselves, is deserving only of pity. Sir Thomas More, Chancellor of Henry VIII., during a whole year of close confinement in the tower of London, refused day after day, the offers that an all-powerful king made him, to return to his service, if he would suppress the scruples of conscience which withheld him. Thomas More knew how to confront death during a year: and to abandon life, still loving it, redoubles the greatness of the sacrifice. A celebrated writer, he loved those intellectual occupations which fill every hour with a still increasing interest. A beloved daughter capable of appreciating the genius of her father, diffused an habitual charm throughout his household; he was in a dungeon, through the grates of which only a glimmering light, broken by the dark bars, could penetrate. While near this horrible abode, a delicious estate on the verdant borders of the Thames offered to him the union of every pleasure that the affection of his family and philosophical studies could impart. Nevertheless, he was immoveable; the scaffold could not intimidate him: his health, cruelly impaired, weakened not his resolution; he found strength in that fire of the soul, which is inexhaustible because it is eternal. He met death because it was his choice, sacrificing happiness, with life, to conscience; immolating every enjoyment to this sentiment of duty, the greatest wonder of moral nature; that which fertilizes the heart, as, in physical order, the sun enlightens the world. England, the birth-place of this virtuous man, where so many other citizens have so unostentatiously sacrified their lives to virtue, England, I say, is nevertheless the country in which suicide is most frequently committed: and we are, with reason, astonished that a nation, in which religion exercises so noble an empire, should offer the example of such an aberration: but they, who represent the English as cold in character, suffer themselves to be entirely deceived by the reserve of their manner. The English character, in general, is very active, and even impetuous; their admirable constitution, which develops the moral faculties in the highest degree, is of itself able to sustain their need of action and reflection; monotony of existence does not suit them, although they often inflict it upon themselves; they then diversify, by the exercises of the body, the sort of life which to us appears uniform.

No nation loves enterprise so much as the English,

and from one end of the world to the other, from the falls of the Rhine, to the cataracts of the Nile, if any thing singular and daring is attempted, it is by an Englishman. Extraordinary wagers, sometimes even blameable excesses, are a proof of the vehemence of their character. Their respect for all laws, that is to say, for moral law, for political law, and the laws of decorum, represses the outward indications of their natural ardor; but it does not the less exist; and when circumstances do not give it nourishment, when ennui takes possession of their lively imaginations, it produces incalculable ravages.

It is also maintained, that the climate of England tends particularly to melancholy: I cannot judge of it, for the sky of liberty has always appeared to me purer than any other; but I cannot think that we ought to attribute the frequent examples of suicide altogether to this physical cause. The climate of the north is much less agreeable than that of England, and yet they are less subject to disgust of life, because the mind has there less need of impulse and variety. Another cause also which renders suicide more frequent in England is the extreme importance which is attached to public opinion: as soon as a man's reputation is impaired, life becomes insupportable to him. This great dread of censure is certainly a very salutary restraint for most men; but there is something still more sublime in having an asylum in ourselves, and there to find, as in a sanctuary, the voice of god inviting us to repent of our faults, or recompensing us for our secret good intentions.

Suicide is very rare among the people of the south. The air they breathe attaches them to life; the empire of public opinion is less absolute in a country where there is less need of society; the enjoyments of nature suffice for the rich as well as the poor; there is something in the spring of Italy which communicates happiness to every being.

Germany furnishes many examples of suicide, but the causes are various, and often whimsical, as is natural amongst a people, where a metaphysical enthusiasm prevails, which has yet no fixed object nor useful end. The defects of the Germans are much more the result of their situation, than of their character, and they will no doubt correct them, when there shall exist among them a political state of things, that will call into action men worthy of being citizens.

An event that happened recently at Berlin, may give an idea of the singular exaltation of which the Germans are susceptible.* The particular motives, which could lead any two individuals astray, are of little importance; but the enthusiasm with which an act has been spoken of, which ought rather to sue for indulgence, merits the most serious attention. If two persons, profoundly unhappy, had destroyed themselves after imploring the commiseration of sensible beings, and recommending themselves to the prayers of the pious, no one could have refused a tear to grief, that had driven them to distraction, whatever had been the species of folly to which it prompted. But can any one represent a mutual assassination as the sublime of reason, of religion, and of love! Can we give the name of virtue to the conduct of a woman, who voluntarily absolves herself from the duties of daughter, wife, and mother,—to that of a man who lends her his courage, thus to get rid of life!

What! this woman has sufficient confidence in the action she is committing, to write before she dies, 'that she will watch over her daughter from heaven:' and while the righteous often tremble on the bed of death, she feels assured of celestial happiness! Two beings, said to be estimable, introduce religion as a third, into the most bloody of actions! two Christians bring murder into comparison with the communion, by leaving open beside them the canticle, chanted by the faithful, when they meet together to offer up their vows of obedience to the divine model of patience and resignation! What delirium in the woman, and what an abuse of faculties in the man! for must he not have regarded himself as an assassin, although he had obtained the consent of the wretched being he destroyed? Did the ever-fluctuating will of a human being give to a fellow-creature the right of infringing the eternal principles of justice and humanity! He killed himself, it will be said, almost at the same moment with his friend; but can any one believe he has so ferocious a right over the life of another, at the same time also that he takes away his own!

And had this man, who wished to die, no country? Could he not have fought for it? Was there no noble or perilous enterprise in which he might have set a glorious example? What is that he has given? He did not expect, I imagine, that mankind would one day agree to renounce, in the sight of heaven, the gift of life; and yet, what other consequence could be drawn from the suicide of these two persons, who, as is supposed, knew no other misfortune than that of existence?

What then: there remained to these faithful friends a year perhaps, at least a day, to see and hear each other, and they voluntarily destroyed this happiness. One of them was capable of deforming those features in which he had read noble thoughts; the other no longer wished to hear the voice which had excited them in her soul; and every thing descriptive of hatred they called love! The most perfect innocence, we are assured, was mingled with it; is this enough to justify so barbarous a weakness? And what advantage do not such delusions give to those who consider enthusiasm as an evil? True enthusiasm should be the companion of reason, because it is the heat that develops it. Can there exist opposition between two qualities natural to the soul, and which are both rays of the same fire? When we say that reason is irreconcileable with enthusiasm, it is because we put calculation in the place of reason, and folly in the place of enthusiasm. There is reason in enthusiasm, and enthusiasm in reason, whenever they spring from nature and are without any mixture of affectation.

We are astonished at discovering affectation and vanity in a suicide; those sentiments, so contemptible even in this life, what do they not become in the presence of death? It appears that nothing is so profound, nor so powerful, as to prove a barrier against the most terrible of acts: but man has so much difficulty in picturing to himself the end of his existence, that he associates even with the tomb the most miserable interests of this world. In fact, we cannot avoid discerning sentimental affectation on the one side, and philosophical vanity on the other, in the manner in which the double suicide at Berlin was accomplished. The mother sends her daughter to an entertainment the night before she intended to kill herself, as if the death of a mother ought to be considered as a festival by her child, and as if it were already necessary to fill her young heart with the most false impressions of a bewildered imagination! This mother clothes herself in new attire as a holy victim; in her letter to her family she enters into a minute detail of household affairs, in order to show her indifference as to the act she is about to commit; indifference, great god, in disposing of herself without hy order! in passing from life to death without the aid of duty or nature to overleap the abyss!

The man, who, about to kill his friend, solemnizes a festival with her, and excites himself by songs and liquors, as if he feared the return of just and reasonable emotions: this man, I say, does he not resemble an

* M. de K—— and Madame de V——, two persons of very estimable character, left Berlin, the place of their abode, towards the end of the year 1811, to repair to an inn at Potsdam, where they passed some time in taking refreshment, and in singing together the canticles of the holy sacrament. Then, by mutual consent, the man blew the woman s brains out, and killed himself the minute after. Madame de V—— had a father, a husband, and a daughter. M. de K—— was a poet, and an officer of merit.

author destitute of genius, who has recourse to a real catastrophe to produce effect she could not attain in fiction? True superiority of every kind has nothing of caprice in it: it is a more energetic and profound intensity in the impressions which the mass of mankind experiences. Genius is, in many respects, popular; that is to say, it has points of contact with the manner in which most people feel. It is not thus, with a bombastic mind, or a disordered imagination: those who torment themselves to attract public attention, by withdrawing it from others, fancy they have made discoveries in the unexplored regions of the human heart. They go so far as to imagine that what is revolting to the feelings of the greater part of the world is of a more elevated character than that which touches and captivates them. What a gigantic vanity is that which places us, if I may so speak, out of our kind. The eloquence and the inspiration of genius revives what had often existed in the hearts of the most obscure individuals, and subdues their apathy or vulgar interests. Great minds, by their writings or their actions, sometimes scatter the ashes which covered the sacred fire: but to create, so to speak, a new world, in which it will be virtuous to abandon our duties; religious, to rebel against divine authority; affectionate, to immolate what is dear to us; is the melancholy result of sentiments without harmony, of faculties without force, and of a desire of that celebrity, to the attainment of which, the gifts of nature are not subsidiary.

I should not have taken the pains to dwell upon an act of madness, which may be excused by peculiar circumstances, of the details of which we are to a certain extent ignorant, if the event had not found apologists in Germany. The taste of German writers for the spirit of hypothesis is found in almost all the relations of life; they cannot be prevailed upon to devote all the powers of the soul to simple and acknowledged truths; it may be said they are as ambitious to make innovations in sentiment and conduct as in literature. Yet physical nature invents nothing better than the sun, the sea, forests, and rivers. Why then should not the affections of the heart also be always the same in their principle although varied in their effects? Is there not much more soul in what is understood by all, than in these human creations, invented, so to speak, like a fiction made at pleasure?

The Germans are endowed with most excellent qualities, and most extensive understandings; but it is from books the greater part of them are formed, and the result is a habit of analysis and sophistry, a certain research after ingenuity, which effects the manly decision of their conduct. The energy that knows not where to employ itself, inspires the most extravagant resolutions: but when they shall be able to consecrate their powers to the independence of their country, when they shall be regenerated as a nation, and thus reanimate the heart of Europe, paralyzed by slavery, we shall hear no more of sickly sentimentality; of literary suicides; of abstracted commentaries on subjects which shock the soul; they must then imitate those strong and hardy people of antiquity, whose character, constant, upright, and resolute, never suffered them to undertake any thing arduous without accomplishing it; who considered it as pusillanimous for a citizen to shrink from a patriotic resolution, as for a soldier to fly on the day of battle

The gift of existence is a constant miracle; the thoughts and feelings, which compose it, have something so sublime in them, that we cannot, without astonishment, contemplate our being by the aid of the faculties of this being. Shall we then squander, in a moment of impatience and ennui, the breath by which we have felt love, recognized genius, and adored the deity! Shakspeare says, in speaking of suicide,

> ——'And then, what's brave, what's noble,
> Let's do it after the high Roman fashion,
> And make death proud to take us.'

In short, if we are incapable of that Christian resignation, which makes us submit to the ordeal of life, at least we should return to the classical beauty of character of the ancients, and make glory our divinity, when we do not feel ourselves able to sacrifice this glory itself to the highest of all virtues.

We believe we have shown that suicide, whose end is, to rid ourselves of life, carries with it no character of devotion to duty, and cannot, of course, merit the name of enthusiasm.

Genius, and even courage, are only worthy of commendation when they tend to this devotion, which is able to produce greater miracles than genius. We have seen the greatest ability overcome, but the combination of religious and patriotic sentiment never is subdued. There is nothing truly great without the mixture of some virtue; every other rule of judgment necessarily leads to error. The events of this world, however important they may appear to us, are sometimes moved by the smallest springs, and chance has much to do with them. But there is neither littleness nor chance in a generous sentiment; whether it impel us to offer up life, or only exact the sacrifice of a day; whether it win a diadem, or be lost in oblivion; whether it inspire master-pieces of art, or prompt to obscure benefits, is of no consequence; it is still a generous sentiment, and it is by this standard alone that man ought to admire the words and actions of man.

There are examples of suicide in the French nation, but we cannot generally attribute them to the melancholy of their character, nor to the elevation of their ideas. Positive evils have led some Frenchmen to this act, and they have committed it with intrepidity, but also with the thoughtlessness which often characterize them. Nevertheless, the multitude of emigrants, which the revolution produced, have supported the most cruel privations with a sort of equanimity, of which no other nation would have been capable. Their genius disposes them more to action than to reflection, and this manner of life diverts them from the troubles of existence. What cost most to Frenchmen is separation from their country; and, indeed, what a country was theirs before faction had rent, before despotism had degraded it! What a country should we not see regenerated, if it were the voice of the nation that disposed of it? Imagination paints to us this beautiful France, which would welcome us under its azure heavens;—those friends who would melt with tenderness in beholding us again;—those recollections of youth, those traces of our relatives we should find at every step: and this return appears to us like a terrestrial resurrection; like another life granted to us here below:—but, if celestial goodness has not reserved for us this happiness, wherever we may be, we will offer up our prayers for this country, which will be so glorious, if it ever learns to appreciate liberty, or, in other words, the political guarantee of justice.

NOTICE OF LADY JANE GRAY.

Lady Jane Gray was grand-niece of Henry VIII, by her grandmother Mary, sister of that king, and widow of Louis XII; she married Lord Guildford, son of the duke of Northumberland, who caused Edward, son of Henry VIII, to call him to the throne by his will, in 1533, to the exclusion of Mary and Elizabeth. Catherine of Arragon, was the mother of the former; her intolerant catholicism made her dreaded by the English Protestants,—and the birth of the daughter of Anna Boleyn was liable to be contested.

The duke of Northumberland urged these motives

Edward VI. Lady Jane Gray, not being herself satisfied of the validity of her right to the crown, refused at first to accede to the will of Edward, but at length the entreaties of her husband, whom she tenderly loved, and over whom Northumberland exercised great authority, drew from her the fatal consent they desired. She reigned nine days, or rather her father-in-law, the Duke of Northumberland, availed himself of her name to govern during that time.

Mary, eldest daughter of Henry VIII, however overcame her in spite of the resistance of the partisans of the reformation: and her cruel and vindictive character signalized itself by the death of the Duke of Northumberland, his son Guildford, and the innocent lady Jane Gray. She was but eighteen years of age when she perished: yet her name was celebrated for her profound knowledge of ancient and modern languages, and her letters in Latin and Greek, still extant, evince very uncommon faculties for her years. She possessed the most perfect piety, and her whole existence was marked by sweetness and dignity. Her father and mother strongly urged her, notwithstanding her repugnance, to ascend the throne of England; her mother herself bore the train of her daughter on the day of her coronation; and her father, the duke of Suffolk, made an attempt to revive her party, while she was still a prisoner, and had been for some months condemned to death. It was this attempt which served as a pretext for executing her sentence, and the Duke of Suffolk perished a short time after his daughter.

The following letter might have been written in the month of February, 1554. It is certain that at this period, which is that of the death of lady Jane Gray, she cultivated in her prison, a constant correspondence with her family and friends, and that even to her latest moments her philosophical disposition and religious firmness never forsook her.

Lady Jane Gray to Doctor Alymer.

'It is to you, my worthy friend, I owe that religious instruction, that life of faith, which can alone endure for ever: my last thoughts are addressed to you in the solemn trial to which I am condemned. Three months have elapsed since the sentence of death, which the queen caused to be pronounced against my husband and myself, as a punishment for that unhappy reign of nine days, for that crown of thorns, which rested on my head only to mark it for destruction. I believed, I avow to you, that the intention of Mary was, to intimidate me by this sentence, but I did not imagine that she wished to shed my blood, which is also hers. It appeared to me my youth would have been sufficient to excuse me, when it should be proved that for a long time I resisted the melancholy honors with which I was menaced, and that my deference to the wishes of the Duke of Northumberland my father-in-law, was alone able to mislead me to the fault I have committed; but it is not to accuse my enemies, I write to you; they are the instruments of the will of god, like every other event of this world, and I ought to reflect but upon my own emotions. Enclosed in this tower, I live upon my thoughts, and my moral and religious conduct consists only in conflicts within myself.

Yesterday our friend Ascham came to see me, and the sight of him at first gave me a lively pleasure; it recalled to my mind the recollection of the delightful and profitable hours I have passed with him in the study of the ancients. I wished to converse with him only on those illustrious deaths, the descriptions of which have opened to me a train of reflections without end. Ascham, you know, is serious and calm; he leans upon old age as a support against the evils of existence; in fact, the old age of a reflecting being is not feeble; experience and faith fortify it, and when the space which remains is so short, a last effort is sufficent to bear us over it; the goal is yet nearer to me than to an old man, but the sufferings accumulated upon my last days will be bitter.

Ascham announced to me that the queen permitted me to breathe the air in the garden of my prison, and I cannot express the joy I felt at it; it was such that our poor friend had not at first the courage to disturb it. We descended together, and he permitted me to enjoy for some time that nature of which I had been for several months deprived; it was one of those days at the close of winter which announces spring. I know not if that beautiful season itself would so much have affected my imagination as this presentments of its return; the trees turned their still leafless branches towards the sun; the grass was already green; a few premature flowers seemed, by their perfume, to form a prelude to the melody of nature, when she shonld reappear in all her magnificence! The air was of an undefinable softness it seemed as if I heard the voice of god, in the invisible and all-powerful breath, which, at every moment restored me again to life—to life! What have I said! I have thought until this day that it was my right, and now I receive its last benefits as the adieus of a friend.

I advanced with Ascham towards the borders of the Thames, and we seated ourselves in the yet leafless wood, which was soon to be clothed with verdure; the waves seemed to sparkle with the reflection of the light of heaven; but although this spectacle was brilliant as a festival, there is always something melancholy in the course of the waves and no one can long contemplate them, without yielding to those reveries whose charm consists, above every thing, in a sort of detachment from ourselves. Ascham perceived the direction of my thoughts, and suddenly seizing my hands, and bathing it with tears, 'Oh thou,' said he, 'who art ever my sovereign, is it for me to acquaint you with the fate which menaces you? Your father has assembled your partisans to oppose Mary, and this queen, justly detested, charges you with all the love your name has excited.' His sobs interrupted him. 'Continue,' said I to him; 'Oh, my friend, remember those contemplative beings, who with a firm countenance, have looked upon the death even of those who were dear to them; they knew whence we came, and whether we go, that is enough. 'Well,' said he 'your sentence is to be executed, but, I bring that succor which has delivered so many illustrious men from the proscription of tyrants.' This old man, the friend of my youth, then tremblingly offered me the poison, with which he wonld have saved me, at the peril of his life. I remembered how often we had together admired certain voluntary deaths among the ancients, and I fell into profound reflection, as if the lights of Christianity were suddenly extinguished in me, and I was abandoned to that indescision, from which even man, in the most simple occurrence, finds so much diffiuclty in extricating himself. Ascham fell on his knees before me; his gray head was bowed down in my presence, and covering his eyes with one hand, with the other he presented me the fatal resource he had prepared. I gently repulsed his hand; and renovating myself through prayer, found power to answer him as follows—

'Ascham,' said I, 'you now with what delight I read with you the philosophers and poets of Greece and Rome; the masculine beauties of their language, the simple energy of their minds, will for ever remain incomparable. Society, such as is constituted in our days, has filled most minds with frivolity and vanity, and we are not ashamed to live without reflection, without endeavoring to understand the wonders of the world, which are created to instruct man by brilliant and durable symbols. The ancients have gone much beyond us in this respect, because they made themselves; but what revelation has planted in the soul of a Christian is greater than man. From the ideal of the arts, even to the rules of conduct, every thing should have relation to religious faith, since life has no other end than to teach mortality. If I fly from the signal misfortune to which I am destined, I should not fortify, by my example, the hope of those on whom my fate ought to have an influence. The ancients elevated their souls by the contemplation of their own powers—Christians have a witness before whom they must live and die; the ancients sought to glorify human nature; Christians consider themselves but as the manifestation of god upon earth; the ancients placed in the first rank of virtues, that death which freed them from the power of their oppressors, Christians prefer that devotion, which subjects us to the will of Providence. Activity and patience have their times by turns; we must make use of our will as long as we may thus serve others and perfect ourselves; but when destiny is, in a manner, face to face with us, our courage consists in awaiting it; and to look steadily on our fate is more noble than to turn from it. The soul thus concentrating itself in its own mysteries, every external action becomes more terrestrial than resignation.' 'I will not seek,' said Ascham, 'to dispute with you opinions whose unshaken firmness may be necessary to you; I am troubled only on account of the sufferings to which your fate condemns you; will you be able to support them? And this expectation of a mortal stroke, of a fixed hour, will it not be beyond your strength? If you should terminate your fate yourself, would it not be less cruel?' 'We must,' replied I, 'let the divine spirit take back what he has given. Immortality commences on this side the tomb, when by our own will we break off with life; in this situation, the internal impressions of the soul are more delightful than you can imagine. The source of enthusiasm becomes altogether independent of the objects which surrounds us, and god alone then constitutes all our destiny, in the most inward sanctuary of our souls.' 'But,' replied Ascham, 'why give to your enemies, to the cruel queen, to a worthless crowd, the unworthy spectacle——'

He could not proceed.

'If I should free myself,' said I, 'even by death, from the fury of the queen, I should irritate her pride, and should not serve as the instrument of her repentance. Who knows how far the example I shall give may do good to my fellow-creatures? How can I judge of the place my remembrance shall occupy in the chain of the events of history? By destroying myself, what shall I teach man but the just horror inspired by a violent outrage, and the sentiment of pride which leads us to avoid it? But, in supporting this terrible fate by the firmness which religion imparts to me, I inspire vessels, beaten, like myself, by the storm, with a greater confidence in the anchor of faith, which has sustained me.'

'The people,' said Ascham, 'believe all those guilty who perish as criminals.' 'Falsehood,' replied I, 'may deceive individuals for a while, but nations and time always make truth triumphant: there is an eternity for all that belongs to virtue, and what we have done for her will advance even to the sea, however small the rivulet we may have been during our life.

'No, I shall not blush to submit to the punishment of the guilty, for it is my innocence itself calls me to it, and I should impair this sentiment of innocence by perpetrating an act of violence; we cannot accomplish it ourselves, without disturbing the serenity the soul should feel on its approach towards heaven—' 'Oh! what is there more violent,' cried our friend, 'than this bloody death?' 'Is not the blood of martyrs,' replied I, 'a balm for the wounds of the unfortunate?' 'This death,' answered he, 'inflicted by man, by the murderous ax, that a ruffian shall dare to raise over your royal head!' 'My friend,' said I, 'if my last moments were encompassed with respect, they would not the less inspire me with dread; does death bear a diadem on his pale front? Is he not always armed with the same terrors? If it were to *nothing* he conducted us, would it be worth while to dispute with this shadow? If it is the call of god through this veil of darkness, then day is behind this night, and heaven is concealed from us only by vain phantoms.'

'What!' said our friend, with a still agitated voice, and whom, at all other times, I had seen so calm, 'are you aware that this punishment may be grievous, that it may be protracted, that an unskilful hand—' 'Stop,' said I, 'I know it, but this will not be.' 'Whence comes this confidence?' 'From my own weakness,' replied I. 'I have always dreaded physical suffering, and my efforts to acquire courage to brave it, have been vain. I believe, therefore, I shall be always spared it; for there is much secret protection extended towards Christians, even when they seem most miserable, and what we feel to be above our strength, scarcely ever happens to us. We generally know only the exterior of man's character; what passes within himself, may still afford new hints during thousands of ages. Irreligion has rendered the mind superficial; we are captivated by the external appearance of things, by circumstance, by fortune; the true treasures of thought, as well as of imagination, are the relations of the human heart with its creator; there are to be found presentiments, there prodigies, there oracles, and all that the ancients believed they saw in nature, was but the reflection of what they experienced within themselves, without their knowledge.'

Ascham and I were silent for some time; an uneasiness pervaded me, and I dared not express it, so much did it trouble me. 'Have you seen my husband?' said I. 'Yes,' replied Ascham. 'Did you consult him on the offer you were about to make me?' 'Yes,' answered he again. 'Finish, I pray you,' said I. 'If Guildford and my conscience do not agree, which of these two powers should be imperative on me?' 'Lord Guildford,' said he, 'did not express an opinion on the part you ought to take, but, as to him, his resolution to perish on the scaffold, is immovable.' 'Oh, my friend,' cried I, 'how I thank you for having left me the merit of a choice; if I had sooner known of the resolution of Guildford, I should not even have deliberated, and love would have been sufficient to animate me to what religion commands. Should I not share the fate of such a husband? Should I spare myself a single one of his sufferings? And does not every step of his towards death mark my path also?' Ascham then perceiving my resolution not to be shaken, departed from me, sad and pensive, promising to see me again.

Doctor Feckenham, chaplain to the queen, came a few hours after, to announce to me, that the day of my death was fixed for the next Friday, from which five days still separated me. I acknowledge to you, it seemed as if I were prepared for nothing, so much did the designation of a day appal me. I tried to conceal my emotion, but Feckenham undoubtedly perceived it, for he hastened to avail himself of my trouble, to offer me life, if I would change my religion. You see, my worthy friend, that God came to my assistance at that moment, for the necessity of repulsing an offer, so unworthy of me, restored to me the strength I had lost.

Doctor Feckenham wished to enter into controversy with me, which I prevented, by observing to him, 'that my understanding being necessarily obscured by the situation in which I was placed, I should not, dying as I was, discuss truths of which I had been convinced when my mind was in all its strength.' He endeavored to intimidate me, by saying that he should see me no more, neither in this world nor in heaven, from which my religious belief had excluded me. 'You would occasion me more alarm than my executioners,' replied I, 'if I could believe you; but the religion to which we sacrifice life, is always the true one for the heart. The light of reason is very vacillating in questions of such moment, and I cling to the principle of sacrifice; of that I can have no doubt.'

This conversation with doctor Feckenham revived my dejected soul; providence had just granted what Ascham desired for me, a voluntary death; I did not destroy myself, but I refused to live;—and the scaffold, accepted by my will, seemed no longer but as the altar chosen by the victim. To renounce life when we can purchase it but at the price of conscience, is the only kind of suicide which should be permitted to a virtuous being.

Convinced I had done my duty, I dared to count upon my courage; but soon again my attachment to existence, with which I had sometimes reproached myself, in the days of my felicity, revived in my feeble heart. Ascham came again the next day, and we visited once more the borders of the Thames, the pride of our delightful country. I endeavored to resume my habitual subjects of conversation. I recited some passages from the beautiful poetry of the Iliad and from Virgil, that we had studied together; but poetry serves above all, to penetrate us with a tender enthusiasm for existence; the seductive mixture of thoughts and images, of nature and the soul, of harmony, of language, and of the emotions it retraces, intoxicates us with the power of feeling and admiring; and these pleasures no longer exist for me! I then turned the conversation to the more severe writings of the philosophers. Ascham considers Plato as a soul predestined to Christianity; but even he, and the greater part of the ancients, are too proud of the intellectual strength of the human mind; they enjoy so much of the faculty of thought, that their desires do not lead them towards another life; they believe they can produce an evocation of it in themselves, by the energy of contemplation: I also once derived the purest delight from meditating upon heaven, genius, and nature. At the remembrance of this, a senseless regret of life took possession of me. I represented it to myself in colors compared with which, the world to come appeared no more than an abstraction destitute of charms. 'How,' said I to myself, 'will the eternal duration of sentiment be equal to this succession of hope and fear, which renews, in so lively a manner, the tenderest affections? Will the knowledge of the mysteries of the universe ever equal the inexpressible attraction of the veil which covers them? Will certainty have the flattering illusion of doubt? Will the brilliancy of truth ever afford as much enjoyment, as the research and the discovery of it? What will youth, hope, memory, affection be, if the course of time is arrested? In fine, can the supreme being, in all his glory, give to the creature a more enchanting present than love?'

I humbly confess to you, my worthy friend, that these fears were impious. Ascham, who, in our conversation the evening before, had appeared less religious than myself, at once availed himself of my rebellious grief. 'You ought not,' said he, 'to make use of benefits to cast a doubt upon the power of the benefactor, whose gift is this life that you regret? And if its imperfect enjoyments seem to you so valuable, why should you believe them irreparable? Certainly our imagination itself may conceive of something better than this earth; but, if it be unequal to this, is it for us to consider the deity merely as a poet, who is unable to produce a second work superior to the first?' This simple reflection restored me to myself, and I blushed at the obliquity into which the dread of death had betrayed me! Oh! my friend! what it costs me to fathom this thought! Abysses, still deeper and deeper, open under each other!

In four days I shall no longer exist; that bird which flies through the air will survive me; I have less time to live than he; the inanimate objects which surround me will preserve their form, and nothing of me will remain upon earth, but the remembrance of my friends Inconceivable mystery of the soul, which foresees its end here below, and yet cannot prevent it. The hand directs the coursers who conduct us: thought cannot obtain a moment's victory over death! Pardon my weakness, oh my father in religion, you, who have so tenderly cherished me: we shall be reunited in heaven; but shall I still hear that affecting voice which revealed to me a god of mercy? Shall these eyes contemplate your venerable features? Oh, Guildford! oh, my husband! you whose noble figure is unceasingly present to my heart, shall I behold you again, such as you are, among the angels whose image you are upon earth? But what do I say? My feeble soul desires nothing beyond the tomb but the actual return of life!—

THURSDAY.

My husband has requested to see me to-day for the last time. I have avoided that moment in which joy and despair would be too closely blended. I dreaded the loss of the resignation I now feel. You have seen that my heart has had but too much attachment to happiness; let me not relapse into it again. My father, do you approve of me? Has not this sacrifice expiated all? I no longer fear that existence will still be dear to me.

THE MORNING OF THE EXECUTION.

Oh! my father! I have seen him! he marched to his execution with as firm a step as if he had commanded those by whom he was conducted. Guildford raised his eyes towards my prison, then directed them still higher; I understood him: he continued on his way. At the turn of the road which leads to the place where death is prepared for both of us, he stopped to behold me once more; his last looks blessed her, who was his companion upon the throne and upon the scaffold!

AN HOUR AFTER.

They have carried the remains of Guildford under the windows of the tower; a sheet covered his mutilated corpse;—through his sheet a horrible image presented itself. If the same stroke was not reserved for me, could earth support the weight of my affliction? My father, how could I regret life so deeply? Oh holy death! gift of heaven as well as life! thou art now my tutelary angel! thou restorest me to serenity! my sovereign master has disposed of me, but since he will reunite me to my husband, he has demanded nothing of me surpassing my strength, and I replace my soul without fear in his hands?

TREATISE

ON

SELF-KNOWLEDGE;

SHOWING THE

NATURE AND BENEFIT

OF

THAT IMPORTANT SCIENCE,

AND THE WAY TO ATTAIN IT:

INTERMIXED WITH VARIOUS

REFLECTIONS AND OBSERVATIONS

ON

HUMAN NATURE.

BY JOHN MASON, A. M.

TO WHICH IS ADDED

A SKETCH OF THE LIFE OF THE AUTHOR.

'Man know thyself, all knowledge centers there.'
Dr. Young.

HARTFORD:
PUBLISHED BY SILAS ANDRUS & SON.
1850.

CONTENTS OF THE TREATISE ON SELF-KNOWLEDGE.

PART II.

Showing the great Excellencies and Advantage of this Kind of Science.

PART III.

Shewing how Self-Knowledge is to be attained.

SKETCH OF THE LIFE

OF THE

REV. JOHN MASON. A. M.

We find John Mason, author of the 'Treatise on Self-Knowledge,' was born at Dunmow, in Essex, about the year 1705: his father is said to have been a dissenting minister, and to have presided over a congregation, first at Daventry, in Northamptonshire, and after at Dunmow, in Essex; then at Spaldwick, in Lincolnshire, at which place he died, in the year 1723; and had a brother, William Mason, a clergyman, who held two livings in the established church. These two brothers were the children of the Rev. John Mason M. A., Rector of Water Stratford, Bucks, author of 'Select Remains,' published after his death, and strongly recommended by Dr Watts: he died, A. D. 1694, after twenty years residence, universally beloved as a faithful servant of his master, whose doctrine he cultivated with fervor of spirit seldom equalled, if ever surpassed.

It appears the author of 'Self-Knowledge' received his education under the Rev. John Jennings, master of the seminary at Kilworth, in Leicestershire, and in the 1720, removed to Hinkley, in the same county. Having finished his studies, he accepted the offer of private tutor and chaplain to — Freak, and resided at his seat, near Hatfield. He remained but a short time in this situation; and in the year 1730, became pastor of a congregation at Dorking, in Surry. He had resided ten years at Dorking before he published any of his works; and the first was a sermon, published at the desire of his friends; the subject was, 'Subjection to the Higher Powers:' and in 1743, was published, but without his name, 'A Plain and Modest Plea for Christianity; or, a Sober and Rational Appeal to Infidels.' This established the author's fame, and brought him many friends; among the number, Dr Walker, master of the academy at Mile End; who, unasked for, procured for the author the degre of M. A. from the college of Edinburgh. In the year 1745, his 'Treatise on Self-Knowledge' was published, which, his fame being already established, contributed to bring forth numerous friends. It is supposed to be one of the most valuable treatises on piety that was ever published in the English language, or in any foreign one; which has induced it to be translated, and published in several languages on the continent.

In the preface, our author thus describes his motive for publishing this work—

'The subject of the ensuing treatise is of great importance; and yet I do not remember to have seen it cultivated with exactness, perspicuity, and force, with which many other moral and theological themes have been managed. And indeed, it is but rarely that we find it particularly and fully recommended to us in a set and regular discourse either from the pulpit or the press. This consideration, together with a full persuasion of its great and extensive usefulness, hath led me to endeavor to make it more familiar to the minds of Christians.

'And the principal view that I had in putting these thoughts together, was the benefit of youth, and especially such of them as are students and candidates for the sacred ministry; for which they will find no science more immediately necessary, next to a good acquaintance with the word of god, than that which is recommended to them in the following treatise; to which every branch of human literature is subordinate, and ought to be subservient. For it is certain, that the great end of all philosophy, both natural and moral, is to know ourselves, and to know god. The highest learning is to be wise, and the greatest wisdom is to be good.

'It was a very just and sensible answer which Agesilaus, the Spartan king, returned to one who asked him, What that was in which youth ought principally to be instructed? He replied, That which they will have most need to practice when they are men. Were this single rule but carefully attended to in the method of education, it might probably be conducted in a manner much more to the advantage of our youth than it ordinarily is. And what is there in life which youth will have more frequent occasion to practice than this? What is there, of which they afterwards more regret the want? What is there, in which they want greater help and assistance, than the right government of their passions and prejudices? And what more proper season to receive those assistances, and to lay a foundation for this difficult, but very important science, than the early part of youth?

'It may be said, that it is properly the office and care of parents to watch over and correct the tempers of their children, in the first years of their infancy, when it may easiest be done. But if it be not done effectually then, as it very seldom is, there is the more necessity for it afterwards. But the truth is, it is the proper office and care of all who have the charge of youth, and ought to be looked upon as the most important and necessary part of education.

'It was the observation of a great divine and reformer, that he who acquires his learning at the expense of his morals, is the worse for his education. And we may add, that he who does not improve his temper, together with his understanding, is not much the better for it. For he ought to measure his progress in science by the improvement of his morals; and to remember, that he is no farther a learned man, than he is a wise and good man; and that he cannot be a finished philosopher till he is a Christian.'

From Dorking, Mr Mason removed to Cheshunt, in Hertfordshire. In his farewell address to his congregation at Dorking, which was published at their particular request, is this striking passage:—

'During the whole course of my preaching among you, I have avoided controversial subjects as much as possible: that is, as far as is consistent with ministerial fidelity. And those that I have handled were most such as were of the greatest importance to common Christianity; which I have always endeavored to treat in the plainest manner I could. But my chief aim hath been to affect your minds and my own with a deeper sense of those great, uncontroverted principles of Christianity, which enter into the very essence of religion, and without an habitual regard to which, our profession for it, and that of every party, is vain. For I have often thought, it is much more necessary to endeavor to mend the heart than stuff the head. And that Christians in general have more need to have their spirits improved, than their understandings informed; and want more zeal, rather than more light; better tempers, rather than better notions; and that a bad heart with right notions is much worse than a good heart with wrong notions; for if the heart be wrong, it matters little that the head is right.'

At Cheshunt, he was indefatigable, both as a preacher and an author. His work, 'The Lord's Day Evening Entertainment,' in four volumes, of fifty-two sermons, was published during his residence here; and a second edition of this work was published in the year 1754.

In the year 1758, he published, in one volume, 'Fifteen Discourses on the Behavior of God's People towards him, in the several periods of the Jewish and Christian churches.'

In the year 1761 was published, his 'Christian Morals,' in two volumes. I must give a short extract from this work. 'O,' says he, 'did deep humility, divine love, fervent faith, and heart-felt charity, but once shed their heavenly influence in our souls; how soon should we learn to despise that light chaff of mystic, or minute subtleties in divinity which some are so fond of, and to bend all our cares and efforts, in dependence on divine grace, to cultivate in ourselves those holy dispositions, which constitute all our happiness, both in this world and forever.

'To contribute somewhat to this great end, I have once more cast in my mite, as what I judged to be of the greatest service I am capable of doing the cause and gospel of Christ, whilst I live.'

And in the second volume is a sermon on the death of George II.

In the same year he published his popular work, 'The Student and Pastor, or Directions how to attain to Eminence and Usefulness in those respective Characters;' and is supposed to be next in merit to his 'Treatise on Self Knowledge,' the most eminent of his works.

Mr Mason published, in the year 1750, 'An Essay on Elocution,' &c., to which he did not think proper to add his name; and it was not till it had run through two or three editions that his name was affixed. His next work was, 'Essays on Poetical and Prosaic Numbers,' &c. In the year 1761, Mr Mason collected the several essays, and published them in one volume. There are several small tracts, as, 'A Letter to a Friend, upon his Entrance on the Ministerial Office;' and a number of others, such as a course of lectures read to his pupils, which were printed in the Protestant Magazine for 1794, 1795, and 1796.

Mr Mason's illness, which occasioned his death, was from taking cold in visiting one of his congregation, some distance from Cheshunt, on a very foggy evening; when he returned, he complained of illness, and from that evening never went out of his house. He left a widow, the daughter of the Rev. James Waters, of Uxbridge, but no children; and was buried in the church-yard of Cheshunt, with the following inscription to his memory:—

Here rests all that was mortal
of the late reverend, learned, and pious,
JOHN MASON, M. A.
who was minister to the
congregation of
Protestant Dissenters in this parish 17 years.
He ceased from his labors,
and was called to receive his reward,
Feb. 10, 1763, aged 58 years.
'Be followers of them, who, through faith and patience, inherit the promises.'

With a few observations taken from a sermon, preached by the Rev. John Hodge, on occasion of his death, we shall conclude this brief sketch:—

'His religion appears to me to have been thoroughly Catholic, and therein truly Christian. He himself called and he taught you accordingly, to call no man father, or master, on earth. While he honestly taught you the truth, as it is in Jesus, according as it appeared to him, from his diligent converse with the lively oracles: it was without any mixture of unkind rash censures, or exciting your angry passions against those who might be otherwise minded from him in some particular points of speculation. While he himself, from principle, adhered to the cause of Protestant non-conformity, amidst all its present discouragements, as apprehending it to have the nearest connection with the cause of truth and liberty, and serious godliness; still he kept himself at the greatest distance from every thing of a narrow party spirit, by confining Christianity to his own particular communion; on the contrary, he was free to converse with others as with Christian brethren, ready to discern and acknowledge real merit, and esteem true learning and piety wherever he met with it.

'His removing from us (so it pleased unerring wisdom to appoint) was after no long previous confinement, but of few days at most; during which, and under all the pains with which he had then to struggle, his mind appeared remarkably serene and composed: not a single murmuring, hardly a complaining word, was ever heard from him. As through the goodness of an indulging providence, he retained the use of his reasoning powers to the last, so he was found, to the last, calm and resigned: his end truly was peace.

'Providence hath taken him away in the midst of his days and usefulness; when considering only his age, and the apparent vigor of his constitution, his continued life, and further usefulness in the church of god, might have been with reason hoped for through many future years. But the supreme lord of life and death hath done his pleasure; and it is your duty, Christians, to submit, and adore.'

TREATISE

ON

SELF KNOWLEDGE.

PART THE FIRST

CHAPTER I.

THE NATURE AND IMPORTANCE OF THE SUBJECT.

A desire of knowledge is natural to the mind of man; and nothing discovers the true quality and disposition of the mind more than the particular kind of knowledge it is most fond of.

Thus we see that low and little minds are most delighted with the knowledge of trifles, as in children; an indolent mind, with that which serves only for amusement, or the entertainment of the fancy; a curious mind is best pleased with facts; a judicious penetrating mind, with demonstrations and mathematical science; a worldly mind esteems no knowledge like that of the world; but a wise and pious man, before all other kinds of knowledge, prefers that of god and his own soul.

But some kind of knowledge or other the mind is continually craving after: and by considering what that is, its prevailing turn and temper may easily be known.

This desire of knowledge, like other affections planted in our nature, will be very apt to lead us wrong, if it be not well regulated. When it is directed to improper objects, or pursued in a wrong manner, it degenerates into a vain and criminal curiosity. A fatal instance of this in our first parents we have upon sacred record; the unhappy effects of which are but too visible in all.

Self-knowledge is the subject of the ensuing treatise: a subject, which the more I think of, the more important and extensive it appears. So important, that every branch of it seems absolutely necessary to the right government of the life and temper; and so extensive, that the nearer view we take of its several branches, more are still opening to the view, as nearly connected with it as the other. Like what we find in microscopical observations on natural objects, the better the glasses, and the nearer the scrutiny, the more wonders we explore; and the more surprising discoveries we make of certain properties, parts, or affections, belonging to them, which were never before thought of. For, in order to a true self-knowledge, the human mind, with its various powers and operations, must be narrowly inspected; all its secret springs and motives ascertained; otherwise our self-acquaintance will be but partial and defective; and the heart after all will deceive us. So that, in treating this subject, there is no small danger, either of doing injury to it, by a slight and superficial examination on the one hand, or of running into a research too minute and philosophical for common use on the other. The two extremes I shall keep in my eye, and endeavor to steer a middle-course between them.

Know thyself, is one of the most useful and comprehensive precepts in the whole moral system: and it is well known in how great a veneration this maxim was held by the ancients, and in how high esteem the duty of self-examination, as necessary to it. Thales, the Milesian, the prince of the philosophers, who flourished about A. M. 3330; and was contemporary with Josiah, King of Judah, is said to be the first author of it; who used to say, that 'for a man to know himself is the hardest thing in the world.' (See Stanley's Life of Thales.) It was afterwards adopted by Chylon, the Lacedemonian; and is one of those three precepts which Pliny affirms to have been consecrated at Delphos in golden letters. It was afterwards greatly admired, and frequently adopted by others; till at length it acquired the authority of a divine oracle, and was supposed to have been given originally by Apollo himself. Of which general opinion Cicero gives us this reason:—'Because it hath such a weight of sense and wisdom in it, as appears too great to be attributed to any man.' And this opinion, of its coming originally from Apollo himself, perhaps was the reason that it was written in golden capitals over the door of his temple at Delphos.

And why this excellent precept should not be held in as high esteem in the Christian world as it was in the heathen, is hard to conceive. Human nature is the same now as it was then; the heart as deceitful; and the necessity of watching, knowing, and keeping it, the same. Nor are we less assured that this precept is divine. Nay, we have a much greater assurance of this than the heathens had; they supposed it came down from heaven—we know it did; what they conjectured, we are sure of. For this sacred oracle is dictated to us in a manifold light, and explained to us in various views by the holy spirit, in that revelation which god hath been pleased to give us as our guide to duty and happiness; by which, 'as in a glass,' we may survey ourselves, and know 'what manner of persons we are.' James i. 23.

This discovers ourselves to us, pierces into the inmost recesses of the mind; strips off every disguise; lays open the inward part; makes a strict scrutiny into the very soul and spirit; and critically judges of the thoughts and intents of the heart. It shows us with what exactness and care we are to search and try our spirits, examine ourselves, and watch our ways, and keep our hearts, in order to acquire this important self-science, which it often calls us to do. 'Examine yourselves; prove your ownselves; know you not yourselves.' 2 Cor. xiii. 5. 'Every Christian ought to try himself, and may know himself, if he be faithful in examining. The frequent exhortations of scripture hereunto imply both these; viz. that the knowledge of ourselves is attainable; and that we should endeavor after it. Why should the apostle put them upon examining and proving themselves, unless it was possible to know themselves upon such trying and proving.' Bennet's Christ. Oratory, p. 568. 'Let a man examine himself.' 1 Cor. xi. 28. Our Saviour upbraids his disciples with their self-ignorance, in not knowing what manner of spirit they were of.' Luke ix. 55. And, saith the apostle, 'If a man,' through self-ignorance, 'thinketh himself to be something, when he is nothing, he deceiveth himself. But let every man prove his work, and then shall he have rejoicing in himself, and not in another.' Gal. vi. 3. 4. Here we are commanded, instead of judging others, to judge ourselves; and to avoid the inexcusable rashness of condemning others for the very crimes we ourselves are guilty of, (Rom. ii. 1, 21, 22,) which a self-ignorant man is very apt to do; nay, to be more offended at a small blemish in another's character, than at a greater in his own; which folly, self-ignorance, and hypocrisy, our Saviour, with just severity, animadverts upon, Matt. vii. 3—5.

And what stress was laid upon this, under the old Testament dispensation, appears sufficiently from those expressions: 'Keep thy heart with all diligence. Prov. iv. 23. 'Commune with your own heart.' Psalm iv. 4. 'Search me, O god, and know my heart; try me, and know my thoughts.' Psalm cxxxix. 23. 'Examine me, O lord, and prove me: try my reins and my heart.' Psalm xxvi. 2. 'Let us search and try our ways.' Lam. iii. 4. 'Recollect, recollect yourselves, O nation! not desired.' Zeph. ii. 1. The verb properly signifies, to clean, or gather together, scattered sticks or straws; as appears from all the places where the word is used in the Old Testament. Exod. v. 7. 12. Numb. xv. 32. 1. Kings xvii 13. Hence, by an easy metaphor, it signifies, to recollect, or gather the scattered thoughts together; and ought to be so rendered, when used in the reflective form, as here it is. So saith R. Kimchi, Est proprie stipulas colligere. Id sit accurata scrutatione hanc dicitur de qualibet Inquisitione. Whence I think it is evident that the word should be rendered as above. And all this is necessary to that self-acquaintance which is the only proper basis of solid peace.

Were mankind but more generally convinced of the importance and necessity of this self-knowledge, and possessed with a due esteem for it; did they but know the true way to attain it; and under a proper sense of its excellence, and the fatal effects of self-ignorance, did they but make it their business and study every day to cultivate it; how soon should we find a happy alteration in the manners and tempers of men! But the misery of it is, men will not think; will not employ their thoughts in good earnest about the things which most of all deserve and demand them. By which unaccountable indolence, and aversion to self-reflection, they are led blindfold and insensibly into the most dangerons paths of infidelity and wickedness, as the Jews were heretofore; of whose amazing ingratitude and apostacy god himself assigns this signal cause: 'My people do not consider.' (Is. i. 3.) 'There is nothing men are more deficient in than knowing their own characters. I know not how this science comes to be so much neglected. We spend a great deal of time in learning useful things, but take no pains in the study of ourselves, and in opening the folds and doubles of the heart.' Reflections on Ridicule

Self-knowledge is that acquaintance with ourselves which shows us what we are, and do, and ought to be, in order to our living comfortably and usefully here, and happily herafter. The means of it is self-examination; the end of it is self-government and self-enjoyment. It principally consists in the knowledge of our souls; which is attained by a particular attention to their various powers, capacities, passions, inclinations, superstitions, state, happiness, and temper. For a man's soul is properly himself. Matt. xvi. 26, compared with Luke ix. 25. The body is but the house; the soul is the tenant that inhabits it: the body is the instrument: the soul the artist that directs it. 'When you talk of a man, I would not have you tack flesh and blood to the notion, nor those limbs neither which are made out of it; these are but tools for the soul to work with; and no more part of a man, than an axe or a plane is a piece of a carpenter. It is true, nature hath glued them together, and they grow as it were to the soul; and there is all the difference.'—Collier.

This science, which is to be the subject of the ensuing treatise, hath these three peculiar properties in it, which distinguish it from, and render it preferable to all other:—1. It is equally attainable by all. It requires no strength of memory, or force of genius, no depth of penetration, as many other sciences do, to come at a tolerable degree of acquaintance with them: which therefore renders them inaccessible by the greatest part of mankind. Nor is it placed out of their reach through a want of opportunity, and proper assistance and direction how to acquire it, as many other parts of learning are. Every one of a common capacity hath the opportunity and ability to attain it, if he will but recollect his rambling thoughts, turn them in upon himself, watch the emotions of his heart, and compare them with this rule. 2. It is of equal importance to all; and of the highest importance to every one

"'Tis virtue only makes our bliss below:
And all our knowledge is, 'ourselves to know!"
Pope.

Other sciences are suited to the various conditions of life; some more necessary to some; others to others. But this equally concerns every one that hath an immortal soul, whose final happiness he desires and seeks. 3. Other knowledge is very apt to make a man vain; this always keeps him humble. Nay, it is for want of this knowledge, that men are vain of what they have. 'Knowledge puffeth up.'—1. Cor viii. 1. A small degree of knowledge often hath this effect on weak minds; and the reason why greater attainments in it have not so generally the same effect is, because they open and enlarge the views of the mind so far, as to let into at the same time a good degree of self-knowledge. For the more true knowledge a man hath, the more sensible he is of the want of it; which keeps him humble.

And now, reader, whoever thou art, whatever be thy character, station, or distinction in life, if thou art afraid to look into thine heart, and hast no inclination to self-acquaintance, read no farther: lay aside this book; for thou wilt find nothing here that will flatter thy self-esteem; but perhaps something that may abate it. But if thou art desirous to cultivate this important kind of knowledge, and to live no longer a stranger to thyself, proceed; and keep thine eye open to thine own image, with whatever unexpected deformity it may present itself to thee; and patiently attend, whilst by divine assistance. I endeavor to lay open thine own heart to thee, and lead thee to the true knowledge of thyself in the following chapters.

CHAPTER II.

THE SEVERAL BRANCHES OF SELF-KNOWLEDGE. WE MUST KNOW WHAT SORT OF CREATURES WE ARE, AND WHAT WE SHALL BE.

That we may have a more distinct and orderly view of this subject, I shall here consider the several branches of self-knowledge; or some of the chief particulars wherein it consists; whereby perhaps it will appear to be a more copious and comprehensive science than we imagine—And,

1. To know ourselves, is to know and seriously consider what sort of creatures we are, and what we shall be.

1. What we are.

Man is a complex being, a tripartite person, or a

compound creature made up of three distinct parts, viz. the body, which is the earthly or mortal part of him ; the soul, which is the animal or sensitive part ; and the spirit of mind, which is the rational and immortal part.* Each of these three parts have their respective offices assigned them ; and a man then acts becoming himself, when he keeps them duly employed in their proper functions, and preserves their natural subordination. But it is not enough to know this merely as a point of speculation ; we must pursue and revolve the thought, and urge the consideration to all the purposes of a practical self-acquaintance.

We are not all body, but mere animal creatures. We find we have a more noble nature than the inanimate, or brutal part of the creation. We can not only move and act freely, but we observe in ourselves a capacity of reflection, study, and forecast ; and various mental operations, which irrational animals discover no symptoms of. Our souls, therefore, must be of a more excellent nature than theirs : and from the power of thought with which they are endowed, they are proved to be immaterial substances ; and consequently in their own nature capable of immortality ; and that they are actually immortal, or will never die, the sacred scriptures do abundantly testify. As nature delights in the most easy transitions from one class of beings to another, and as the nexus utriusque generis is observable in several creatures of ambiguous nature, which seem to connect the lifeless and vegetable, the vegetable and animal, the animal and rational worlds together, (see Nemesius de Nat. Hom. cap. 1. p. 6.) why may not the soul of brutes be considered as the nexus between material and immaterial substances, or matter and spirit, or something between both ? The great dissimilitude of nature in these two substances, I apprehend, can be no solid objection to this hypothesis, if we consider besides our own ignorance of the harm of spirits, but how nearly they approach in other instances, and how closely they are united in man. Let us then hereupon seriously recollect ourselves in the following soliloquy.

'O my soul, look back a few years, and thou wast nothing! And how didst thou spring out of that nothing? Thou couldst not make thyself. That is quite impossible. Most certain it is, that that almighty, self-existent, and eternal power, which made the world, made thee also out of nothing; called thee into being when thou wast not; gave thee these reasoning and reflecting faculties, which thou art now employing in searching out the end and happiness of thy nature. It was he, O my soul, that made thee intelligent and immortal. It was he that placed thee in this body, as in a prison ; where thy capacities are cramped, thy desires debased, and thy liberty lost. It was he that sent thee into this world, which by all circumstances appears to be a state of short discipline and trial. And wherefore did he place thee here, when he might have made thee a more free, unconfined, and happy spirit? But check that thought ;—it looks like a too presumptuous curiosity. A more needful and important inquiry is, what did he place thee here for? and what doth he expect from thee whilst thou art here ; what part hath he allotted thee to act on the stage of human life ; where he, angels, and men, are spectators of thy behavior? The part he hath given thee to act here is, doubtless, a very important one ; because it is for eternity.* And what is it but to live up to the dignity of my rational and intellectual nature, and as becomes a creature born for immortality?

'And tell me, O my soul, for as I am now about to cultivate a better acquaintance with thee, to whom I have been too long a stranger, I must try thee, and put many a close question to thee ; tell me, I say, whilst thou confinest thy desires to sensual gratifications, wherein dost thou differ from the beasts that perish? Captivated by bodily appetites, dost thou not act beneath thyself? Dost thou not put thyself upon a level with the lower class of beings, which were made to serve thee, offer an indignity to thyself, and despise the work of thy maker's hands? O remember thy heavenly extract ; remember thou art a spirit. Check then the solicitations of the flesh ; and dare to do nothing that may diminish thy native excellence, dishonor thy high original, or degrade thy noble nature.

'I am too noble, and of too high a birth,' saith that excellent moralist, 'to be a slave to my body ; which I look upon only as a chain thrown upon the liberty of my soul.'

But let me still urge it. 'Consider, I say, O my soul! that thou art an immortal spirit. Thy body dies; but thou, thou must live for ever ; and thine eternity will take its tincture from the manner of thy behavior, and the habits thou contractest, during this, thy short co-partnership with flesh and blood. O! do nothing now, but what thou mayest with pleasure look back upon a million of ages hence. For know, O my soul! that thy self-consciousness and reflecting faculties will not leave thee with thy body ; but will follow thee after death, and be the instrument of unspeakable pleasure or torment to thee in that separate state of existence.'†

2. In order to a full acquaintance with ourselves, we must endeavor to know not only what we are, but what we shall be.

And O! what different creatures shall we soon be, from what we are now! Let us look forwards then, and frequently glance our thoughts towards death, though they cannot penetrate the darkness of passage, or reach the state behind it. That lies veiled from the eyes of our mind ; and the great god has not thought fit to throw so much light upon it, as to satisfy the anxious and inquisitive desires the soul hath to know it. However, let us make the best use we can of that little light

* This doctrine, I think, is established beyond all dispute, not only by experience, but by authority. It was received by almost all the ancient philosophers. The Pythagoreans, as we learn from Jamblicus, vid. Protept. p. 34, 55. The Platonists, as appears from Nemesius, Sallust, and Lærtius, vid. Di. Lærtius, lib. iii. p. 219. The Stoics, as appears from Antoninus, who saith expressly, 'There are three things which belong to a man ; the body, the soul, and the mind. And as to the properties of the division, sensation belongs to the body, appetite to the soul, and reason to the mind. It appears also to have been the opinion of most of the fathers, vid. Irenæus, lib. 5. cap. 9 lib. 2. cap. 33. Ed. Par. Clem. Alex. Strom. 3. p. 542. Ed. Oxon. Origin. Philocal. p. 8. Ignat. Ep. ad Philadelph. ad calcem. See also Joseph. Antiq. lib. 1. cap. 2. p. 5. Constitut. Apostol. lib. 7. cap. 34. But above all these, is the authority of scripture, which, speaking of the original formation of man, mentions the three distinct parts of his nature ; Gen ii. 7. viz. 'the dust of the earth,' or the body ; 'the living soul,' or the animal and sensitive part; and 'the breath of life,' i. e. the spirit or rational mind. In like manner, the apostle Paul divides the whole man into the spirit, the soul, and the body. 1 Thess. v. 23. They who would see more of this, may consult Nemesius de Natura Hominis, cap. 1. and Whiston's Prim. Christ. vol. 4. p. 262.

All the observations I shall make hereupon is, that this consideration may serve to soften the prejudices of some against the account which scripture gives us of the mysterious manner of the existence of the divine nature ; of which every man (as 'created in the image of God') carries about him a kind of emblem, in the threefold distinction of his own ; which if he did not every minute find it by experience to be a fact, would doubtless appear to him altogether as mysterious and incomprehensible as the scripture doctrine of the trinity.

'Homo habet tres patres, spiritum, animam, et corpus ; itaque homo est imago S. S. Trinitatis.'—August. Tractat. de Symbolo.

* It is said when the prince of the Latin poets was asked by his friend, why he studied so much accuracy in the plan of his poem, the propriety of his characters, and the purity of his diction ; he replied, In æternum pingo. 'I am writing for eternity.' What more weighty consideration to justify and enforce the utmost vigilance and circumspection of life, than this—In æternum vivo, 'I am living for eternity.'

† As it is not the design of this treatise to enter into a nice and philosophical disquisition concerning the nature of the human soul, but to awaken men's attention to the inward operations and affections of it (which is by far the most necessary part of self-knowledge ;) so they who would be more particularly informed concerning its nature and original, and the various opinions of the ancients about it, may consult Nemes. de Nat. Hom. cap. 1 a treatise called, The Government of the Thoughts, chap. 1 and Chambers's Cyclopædia, under the word 'Soul.'

which scripture and reason have let in upon this dark and important subject.

'Compose thy thoughts, O my soul! and imagine how it will fare with thee, when thou goest a naked, unembodied spirit, into a world, an unknown world of spirits, with all thy self-consciousness about thee, where no material object shall strike thine eye; and where thy dear partner and companion, the body, cannot come nigh thee; but where without it thou will be sensible of the most noble satisfactions, or the most exquisite pains. Embarked in death, thy passage will be dark; and the shore, on which it will land thee, altogether strange and unknown. It doth not yet appear what we shall be.'*

The revelation which god hath been pleased to make of his will to mankind, was designed rather to fit us for the future happiness, and direct our way to it, than open to us the particular glories of it, or distinctly show us what it is. This it hath left still very much a mystery; to check our too curious inquiries into the nature of it, and to bend our thoughts more intently to that which more concerns us; viz. an habitual preparation for it. And what that is, we cannot be ignorant, if we believe either our bible or our reason; for both these assure us, that that which makes us like to god, is the only thing that can fit us for the enjoyment of him. Here then let us make a stand. Let our great concern be, to be 'holy as he is holy!' and then, and then only, are we sure to enjoy him, 'in whose light we shall see light.' And be the future state of existence what it will, we shall some way be happy there; and much more happy than we can now conceive; though in what particular manner we know not, because god hath not revealed it.

CHAPTER III

THE SEVERAL RELATIONS IN WHICH WE STAND TO GOD, TO CHRIST, AND TO OUR FELLOW CREATURES.

II. Self-knowledge requires us to be well acquainted with the various relations in which we stand to other beings, and the several duties that result from these relations. And,

1. Our first and principal concern is to consider the relation wherein we stand to him who gave us being.

We are the creatures of his hand, and the objects of his care. His power upholds the being his goodness gave us; his bounty accommodates us with the blessings of this life; and his grace provides for us the happiness of a better. Nor are we merely his creatures, but his rational and intelligent creatures. It is the dignity of our natures, that we are capable of knowing and enjoying him who made us. And as the rational creatures of god, there are two relations especially that we bear to him; the frequent consideration of which is absolutely necessary to a right self-knowledge. For as our creator, he is our king and father; and as his creatures, we are the subjects of his kingdom, and the children of his family.

We are the subjects of his kingdom. And as such we are bound.

1. To yield to a faithful obedience is of the laws of his kingdom. And the advantages by which these come recommended to us above all human laws, are many—they are calculated for the private interests of every one, as well as that of the public; and are designed to promote our present, as well as our future happiness—they are plainly and explicitly published; easily understood and in fair and legible character writ in every man's heart; and the wisdom, reason, and necessity of them are readily discerned—they are urged with the most weighty motives that can possibly affect the human heart: and if any of them are difficult, the most effectual grace if freely offered, to encourage and assist our obedience: advantages which no human laws have to enforce the observance of them. 2. As his subjects, we most readily pay him the homage due to his sovereignty. And this is no less than the homage of the heart; humbly acknowledging that we hold every thing of him and have every thing from him. Earthly princes are forced to be contented with verbal acknowledgements, or mere formal homage; for they can command nothing but what is external: but god, who knows and looks at the hearts of all his creatures, will accept of nothing but what comes from thence He demands the adoration of our souls, which is most justly due to him who formed them, and gave them the very capacities to know and adore him. 3. As faithful subjects, we must cheerfully pay him the tribute he requires of us. This is not like the tribute which earthly kings exact, who as much depend upon their subjects for the support of their power as their subjects do upon them for the protection of their property. But the tribute god requires of us, is a tribute of praise and honor, which he stands in no need of from us; for his power is independent, and his glory immutable; and he is infinitely able of himself to support the dignity of his universal government. But it is the most natural duty we owe him as creatures: for to praise him, is only to show forth his praise; to glorify him, to celebrate his glory; and to honor him, is to render him and his ways honorable in the eyes and esteem of others. And as this is the most natural duty that creatures owe to their creator, so it is a tribute he requires of every one of them in proportion to their respective talents and abilities to pay it. 4. As dutiful subjects, we must contentedly and quietly submit to the methods and administrations of his government, however dark, involved, or intricate. All governments have their arcana imperii, or secret of state; which common subjects cannot penetrate. And therefore they cannot competently judge of the wisdom or rectitude of certain public measures, because they are ignorant either of the springs of them, or the ends of them, or the expediency of the means arising from the particular situation of things in the present juncture. And how much truer is this with regard to god's government of the world; whose wisdom is far above our reach, and whose ways are not as ours! Whatever, then, may be the present aspect and appearance of things, as dutiful subjects, we are bound to acquiesce; to ascribe wisdom and 'righteousness to our maker,' in confidence that the king and 'judge of all the earth will do right.' Again. 5. As good subjects of god's kingdom we are bound to pay a due regard and reverence to his ministers; especially if they discover an uncorrupted fidelity to his cause, and a pure unaffected zeal for his honor; if they do not seek their own interest more than that of their divine master. The ministers of earthly princes too often do this; and it would be

* 'Thou must expire, my soul, ordain'd to range
Thro' unexperienc'd scenes, and myst'ries strange;
Dark the event, and dismal the exchange
But when compell'd to leave this house of clay,
And to an unknown somewhere wing thy way;
When time shall be eternity, and thou
Shalt be thou know'st not what, nor where, nor how,
Trembling and pale, what wilt thou see or do?
Amazing state! No wonder that we dread
The thoughts of death, or faces of the dead.
His black retinue strongly strikes our mind;
Sickness and pain before, and darkness all behind.
'Some courteous ghost, the secret then reveals;
Tells us what you have felt, and we must feel.
You warn us of approaching death, and why
Will you not teach us what it is to die?
But having shot the gulf. you love to view
Succeeding spirits plung'd along like you;
Nor lend a friendly hand to guide them through.
'When dire disease shall cut, or age untie
The knot of life, and suffer us to die;
When after some delay, some trembling strife,
The soul stands quiv'ring on the ridge of life;
With fear and hope she throbs, then curious tries
Some strange hereafter and some hidden skies.'

Norris.

happy if all the ministers and ambassadors of the heavenly king were entirely clear of the imputation. It is no uncommon thing for the honor of an earthly monarch to be wounded through the sides of his ministers. The defamation and slander that is directly thrown at them, is obliquely intended against him; and such it is taken. So, to attempt to make the ministers of the gospel, in general, the objects of decision, as some do, plainly shows a mind very dissolute and disaffected to god and religion itself; and is to act a part very unbecoming the dutiful subjects of his kingdom. Lastly. As good subjects, we are to do all we can to promote the interest of his kingdom; by defending the wisdom of his administrations, and endeavoring to reconcile others thereunto, under all the darkness and difficulties that may appear therein, in opposition to the profane censure of the prosperous wicked, and the doubts and dismays of the afflicted righteous. This is to act in character as loyal subjects of the king of heaven: and whoever forgets this part of his character, or acts contrary to it, shows a great degree of self-ignorance.

But, 2. As the creatures of god, we are not only the subjects of his kingdom, but the children of his family. And to this relation, and the obligations of it, must we carefully attend, if we would attain the true knowledge of ourselves. We are his children by creation; in which respect he is truly our father. Is. lxiv. 8. 'But now, O Lord, thou art our father: we are the clay, and thou our potter: and we all are the work of thine hands.' And, in a more special sense, we are his children, by adoption. Gal. iii. 26. 'For ye are all the children of god, by faith in Christ Jesus.' And therefore, 1. We are under the highest obligations to love him as our father. The love of children to parents is founded on gratitude for benefit received, which can never be requited; and ought in reason to be proportioned to those benefits, especially if they flow from a conscience of duty in the parent. And what duty more natural than to love our benefactors? What love and gratitude, then, is due to him, from whom we have received the greatest benefit, even that of our being, and every thing that contributes to the comfort of it? 2. As his children, we must honor him; that is, must speak honorably of him, and for him: and carefully avoid every thing that may tend to dishonor his holy name and ways. Mal. 1. 6. 'A son honoreth his father: if then I be a father, where is mine honor?' 3. As our father, we are to apply to him for what we want. Whither should children go, but to their father, for protection, help, and relief, in every danger, difficulty, and distress? And, 4. We must trust his power and wisdom, and paternal goodness, to provide for us, take care of us, and do for us that which is best; and what that is he knows best. To be anxiously fearful what will become of us, and discontented and perplexed under the apprehension of future evils, whilst we are in the hands, and under the care, of our father who is in heaven, is not to act like children. Earthly parents cannot avert from their children all the calamities they fear, because their wisdom and power are limited; but our all-wise and almighty father in heaven can. 'They may possibly want love and tenderness for their offspring, but our heavenly father cannot for his.' Is. xlix. 15, 5. As children, we must quietly acquiesce in his disposals, and not expect to see into the wisdom of all his will. It would be indecent and undutiful in a child, to dispute the authority, or question the wisdom, or neglect the orders of his parents, every time he could not discern the reason and design thereof. Much more unreasonable and unbecoming is such a behavior towards god, 'who giveth not account of any of his matters; whose judgments are unsearchable, and whose ways are past finding out.' Job xxiii. 13.—Rom. xi. 33. Lastly, As children, we must patiently submit to his discipline and correction. Earthly parents may sometimes punish their children through passion, or caprice; but our heavenly father always corrects his for their profit, and only if need be, (1 Pet. i. 6.) and never so much 'as their iniquities deserve.' Ezra ix. 13. Under his fatherly rebukes, let us be ever humble and submissive. Such now is the true filial disposition. Such a temper, and such a behavior, should we show towards god, if we would act in character as his children.

These, then, are the two special relations which, as creatures, we stand in to god. And not to act towards him in the manner before mentioned, is to show that we are ignorant of, or have not yet duly considered, our obligations to him, as his subjects, and his children; or that we are as yet ignorant both of god and ourselves. Thus, we see how directly the knowledge of ourselves leads us to the knowledge of god. So true is the observation of a late pious and very worthy divine, that, 'he that is a stranger to himself, is a stranger to god, and to every thing that may denominate him wise and happy.'

But, 2. In order to know ourselves, there is another important relation we should often think of, and that is, that in which we stand to Jesus Christ, our redeemer.

The former was common to us men; this is peculiar to us as Christians, and opens to us a new scene of duties and obligations, which a man can never forget, that does not grossly forget himself. For, as Christians, we are the disciples, the followers, and the servants of Christ, redeemed by him.

And, 1. As the disciples of Christ, we are to learn of him; to take our religious sentiments only from his gospel, in opposition to all the authoritative dictates of men, who are weak and fallible as ourselves. 'Call no man master on earth.' Whilst some affect to distinguish themselves by party-names, as the Corinthians formerly did; for which the apostle blames them. one saying, 'I am of Paul;' another, 'I am of Apollos;' another, 'I am of Cephas;' 1 Cor. i. 12. let us remember, that we are the disciples of Christ; and in this sense, make mention of his name only. It is really injurious to it, to seek to distinguish ourselves by any other. There is more mischief in such party-distinctions, denominations, and attachments, than many good persons are aware of; though not more than the apostle Paul who was unwillingly placed at the head of one himself, hath apprized them of, Cor. iii. 4. We are of Christ; our concern is to honor that superior denomination, by living up to it; and to adhere inflexibly to his gospel, as the only rule of our faith, the guide of our life, and the foundation of our hope, whatever contempt or abuse we may suffer, either from the profane or bigotted part of mankind, for so doing.

2. As Christians, we are followers of Christ; and therefore bound to imitate him, and copy after that most excellent pattern he hath set us: who hath left us an example, that we should follow his steps. 1 Pet. ii. 21. To see that the same holy temper be in us which was in him; and to exhibit in the same manner he did and upon like occasions. To this he calls us, Mat, xi. 29; and no man is any farther a Christian, than as he is a follower of Christ; aiming at a more perfect conformity to that most perfect example, which he hath set us, of universal goodness.

3. As Christians, we are the servants of Christ; and the various duties which servants owe to their masters, in any degree, those we owe to him, in the highest degree; who expects we should behave ourselves in his service with that fidelity and zeal, and steady regard to his honor and interest, at all times, which we are bound to, by virtue of this relation; and which his unmerited and unlimited goodness and love lay us under infinite obligations to.

Lastly, We are moreover his redeemed servants; and, as such, are under the strongest motives to love and trust him.

This deserves to be more particularly considered

because it opens to us another view of the human nature, in which we should often survey ourselves, if we desire to know ourselves; and that is, as depraved or degenerate beings. The inward contest we so sensibly feel, at some seasons especially, between a good and a bad principle, called in scripture language, the flesh and the spirit, of which some of the wisest heathens seemed not to be ignorant:—

> 'A fatal inbred strife does lurk within,
> The cause of all this misery and sin.'

This, I say, is demonstration, that some way or other, the human nature hath contracted an ill bias, and how came that about, the sacred scriptures have sufficiently informed us; and that it is not what it was when it came originally out of the hands of its maker; so that the words which St Paul spake, with reference to the Jews in particular, are justly applicable to the present state of mankind in general; 'There is none righteous; no, not one: they are all gone out of the way; they are together become unprofitable: there is none that doeth good; no, not one.' Rom. iii. 10, 12.

This is a very mortifying thought; but an undeniable truth, and one of the first principles of that science we are treating of, and very necessary to be attended to, if we would be sensible of the duty and obligations we owe to Christ, as the great redeemer; in which character he appears, for the relief and recovery of mankind, under this, their universal depravity.

Two miserable affects of the human apostacy are,

1. That perverse dispositions grow up in our mind from early infancy, that soon settle into vicious habits and render us weak and unwilling to obey the dictates of conscience and reason: this is commonly called the dominion of sin. And,

2. At the same time, we are subject to the displeasure of god, and the penalty of his law; which is commonly called, the condemnation of sin. Now, in both these respects, did Christ, 'the lamb of god, come to take away the sin of the world;' i. e. to take away the reigning power of it by the atonement of his blood; to sanctify us by his spirit, and justify us by his death: by the former, he reconciles us to god, and by the latter, he reconciles god to us,'* and is at once our righteousness and strength. He died to purchase for us the happiness we had forfeited, and sends his grace and spirit to fit us for that happiness he hath thus purchased. So complete is his redemption! so precisely adapted is the remedy he hath provided, to the malady we had contracted.

'O blessed redeemer of wretched ruined creatures, how unspeakable are the obligations I owe thee! But, ah! how insensible am I to those obligations! The saddest symptoms of degeneracy I find in my nature, is that base ingratitude of heart, which renders me so unaffected with thine astonishing compassions. Till I know thee, I cannot know myself! and when I survey myself, may I ever think of thee! May the daily consciousness of my weakness and guilt lead my thoughts to thee! and may every thought of thee kindle in my heart the most ardent glow of gratitude to thee, O thou divine, compassionate friend, lover, and redeemer of mankind!'

Whoever then he be that calls himself a Christian; that is, who professes to take the gospel of Christ for a divine revelation, and the only rule of his faith and practice; but at the same time, pays a greater regard to the dictates of men, than to the doctrines of Christ; who loses sight of that great example of Christ, which should animate his Christian walk, is unconcerned about his service, honor, and interest, and excludes the consideration of his merits and atonement, from his hope of happiness,—he forgets that he is a Christian;—he does not consider in what relation he stands to Christ, which is one great part of his character, and consequently discovers a great degree of self-ignorance.

* By this phrase, I do not mean, that god was implacable, or absolutely irreconcileable to us, till he was pacified by the vicarious sufferings of his son; for how then could he have appointed him to die, as our propitiatory sacrifice? But that the death of Christ is the clearest demonstration of god's willingness to be actually reconciled to us.

3. Self-knowledge, moreover, implies a due attention to the several relations in which we stand to our fellow creatures; and the obligations that result from thence.

If we know ourselves, we shall remember the condescension, benignity, and love, that is due to inferiors; affability, friendship, and kindness, we ought to show to equals; the regard, deference, and honor, which belongs to superiors; and the candor, integrity, and benevolence, we owe to all.

The particular duties requisite in these relations are too numerous to be here mentioned. Let it suffice to say, that if a man doth not well consider the several relations of life in which he stands to others, and does not take care to preserve the decorum and propriety of those relations, he may justly be charged with self-ignorance.

And this is so evident in itself, and so generally allowed, that nothing is more common than to say, when a person does not behave with due decency towards his superiors, such a one does not understand himself. But why may not this, with equal justice, be said of those who act in an ill manner towards their inferiors? The expression, I know, is not so often thus applied; but I see no reason why it should not, since one is as common, and as plain an instance of self-ignorance as the other. Nay, of the two, perhaps men are in general more apt to be defective in their duty and behavior towards those beneath them, than they are towards those that are above them. And the reason seems to be, because an apprehension of the displeasure of their superiors, and the detrimental consequences which may accrue from thence, may be a check upon them, and engage them to pay the just regards which they expect. But there being no check to restrain them from violating the duties they owe to inferiors, from whose displeasure they have little to fear, they are more ready, under certain temptations, to treat them in an unbecoming manner. And as wisdom and self-knowledge will direct a man to be particularly careful, lest he neglect the duties he is most apt to forget; so, as to the duties he owes to inferiors, in which he is most in danger of transgressing, he ought more strongly to urge upon himself the indispensable obligations of religion and conscience. And if he does not, but suffers himself, through the violence of ungoverned passion, to be transported into the excesses of rigor, tyranny, and oppression, towards those whom god and nature have put into his power, it is certain he does not know himself; is not acquainted with his own particular weakness; is ignorant of the duty of his relations; and, whatever he may think of himself, hath not the true spirit of government; because he wants the art of self-government. For he that is unable to govern himself, can never be fit to govern others.

Would we know ourselves, then, we must consider ourselves as creatures, as Christians, and as men; and remember the obligations which, as such, we are under to god, to Christ, and our fellow men, in the several relations we bear to them, in order to maintain the propriety, and fulfil the duties, of those relations.

CHAPTER IV.

WE MUST DULY CONSIDER THE RANK AND STATION OF LIFE, IN WHICH PROVIDENCE HATH PLACED US; AND WHAT IT IS THAT BECOMES AND ADORNS US.

III. A man that knows himself will deliberately con

sider and attend to the particular rank and station of life in which providence hath placed him ; and what is the duty and decorum of that station ; what part is given him to act ; what character to maintain ; and with what decency and propriety he acts that part, or maintains that character.

For a man to assume a character, or aim at a part, that does not belong to him, is affectation. And whence is it that affectation of any kind appears so ridiculous, and exposes men to universal and ust contempt, but because it is a certain indication of self-ignorance ! Whence is it that many seem so willing to be thought something, when they are nothing ; and seek to excel in those things in which they cannot, whilst they neglect those things in which they may excel ? Whence is it that they counteract the intention of nature and providence ; that when these intended them one thing, they fain would be another ? Whence, I say, but from an ignorance of themselves, the rank of life they are in, and of the part and character which properly belongs to them ?

It is a just observation, and an excellent document of a moral heathen. 'That human life is a drama, and mankind the actors ; who have their several parts assigned them by the master of the theatre, who stands behind the scenes, and observes in what manner every one acts. Some have a short part allotted them, and some a long one ; some a low, and some a high one. It is not he that acts the highest, or most shining part on the stage, that comes off with the greatest applause ; but he that acts his part best, whatever it be. To take care, then, to act our respective parts in life well, is ours ; but to choose what part in life we shall act, is not ours, but God's.'* But a man can never act his part well, if he does not attend to it—does not know what becomes it ; much less is he affected to act, another, which nature never assigned him. It is always self-ignorance that leads a man to act out of character.

Is it a mean and low station of life thou art in ? Know then, that providence calls thee to the exercise of industry, contentment, submission, patience, hope, and a humble dependence on him ; and a respectful deference to thy superiors. In this way, thou mayest shine through thine obscurity, and render thyself admirable in the sight of god and man ; and not only so, but find more satisfaction, safety, and self-enjoyment, than they who move in a higher sphere, from whence they are in danger of falling.

But hath providence called thee to act in a more public character, and for a more extensive benefit to the world ? Thy first care then ought to be, that thy example, as far as its influence reaches, may be an encouragement to the practice of universal virtue. And next, to shine in those virtues especially, which best adorn thy station ; as benevolence, charity, wisdom, moderation, firmness, and inviolable integrity ; with an undismayed fortitude to press through all opposition in accomplishing those ends, which thou hast a prospect and probability of attaining, for the apparent good of mankind.

And as self-acquaintance will teach us what part in life we ought to act, so the knowledge of that will ow us whom we ought to imitate, and wherein. We not to take example of conduct from those who e a very different part assigned them from ours, ss in those things that are universally ornamental exemplary. If we do, we shall but expose our affectation and weakness, and ourselves to contempt, for acting out of character ; for what is decent in one may be ridiculous in another. Nor must we blindly follow those who move in the same sphere, and sustain the same character with ourselves ; but only in those things that are befitting that character. For it is not the person, but the character we are to regard ; and to imitate him no farther than he keeps to that.

This caution particularly concerns youth, who are apt to imitate their superiors very implicitly, and especially such as shine in the profession they themselves are intended for ; but, for want of judgment to distinguish what is fit and decent, are apt to imitate their very foibles ; which a partiality for their persons make them deem as excellencies : and thereby they become doubly ridiculous, both by acting out of character themselves, and by a weak and servile imitation of others, in the very things in which they do so too. To maintain a character, then, with decency, we must keep our eye only upon that which is proper to it.

In fine, as no man can excel in every thing, we must consider what part is allotted us to act in the station in which providence hath placed us, and to keep to that, be it what it will, and seek to excel in that only.

CHAPTER V.

EVERY MAN SHOULD BE WELL ACQUAINTED WITH HIS OWN TALENTS AMD CAPACITIES ; AND IN WHAT MANNER THEY ARE TO BE EXERCISED AND IMPROVED TO THE GREATEST ADVANTAGE.

IV. A man cannot be said to know himself, till he is well acqnainted with his proper talents and capacities ; knows for what ends he received them ; and how they may be most fitly applied and improved for those ends.

A wise and self-understanding man, instead of aiming at talents he hath not, will set about cultivating those he hath ; as the way in which providence points out his proper usefulness.

As, in order to the edification of the church, the spirit of god at first conferred upon the ministers of it a great variety of spiritual gifts, (1 Cor. xii. 8—10) so, for the good of the community, God is pleased now to confer upon men a great variety of natural talents ; and 'every one hath his proper gift of god ; one after this manner, another after that.' 1 Cor. vii. 7. And every one is to take care, 'not to neglect, but to stir up the gift of god, which is in him,' (1 Tim. iv. 4. 2 Tim. i. 6) because it was given *him* to be improved : and not only the abuse, but the neglect of it, must hereafter be accounted for. Witness the doom of that unprofitable servant, who 'laid up his single pound in a napkin,' (Luke xix. 20, 24.) and of him who went 'and hid his talent in the earth.' Mat. xxv. 25, 30.

It is certainly a sign of great self-ignorance, for a man to venture out of his depth, or attempt any thing he wants opportunity or capacity to accomplish. And therefore a wise man will consider with himself, before he undertakes any thing of consequence, whether he hath abilities to carry him through it, and whether the issue of it is likely to be for his credit ; lest he sink under the weight he lays upon himself, and incur the just censure of rashness, presumption, and folly. See Luke xiv. 28—32.

He that takes up a burden that is too heavy for him, is in a fair way to break his back.

In every business, consider, first what it is you are about ; and then your own ability, whether it be sufficient to carry you through it.

'Examine well, ye writers weigh with care
What suits your genius, what your strength can bear ;

fe is a stage-play : it matters not how long we act, so we act It is not life, but living well, that is the blessing. Some- similar to this, is the epigram by Dr Doddridge, on 'dum us vivamus ;' which he assumed as his motto :

Live, while you live, the epicure would say,
And seize the pleasures of the present day :
Live, while you live, the sacred preacher cries,
And give to god each moment as it flies.
Lord ! in my views let both united be !
I live in pleasure, when I live in thee

For when a well proportion'd theme you choose,
Nor words, nor method, shall their aid refuse.
In this, or I mistake, consists the grace,
And force of method ; to assign a place
For what with present judgment we would say,
And for some happier time the rest delay.'
Francis's Horace.

It is no uncommon thing for some who excel in one thing, to imagine they may excel in every thing ; and not content with that share of merit which every one allows them, are still catching at that which doth not belong to them. Why should a good orator wish to be thought a poet ? Why must a celebrated divine set up for a politician ? or a statesman affect the philosopher ? or a mechanic the scholar ? or a wise man labour to be thought a wit ? This is a weakness that flows from self-ignorance, and is incident to the greatest men. Nature seldom forms an universal genius ; but deals out her favors in the present state with a parsimonious hand. Many a man, by this foible, hath weakened a well established reputation.*

CHAPTER VI.

WE MUST BE WELL ACQUAINTED WITH OUR INABILITIES, AND THOSE THINGS IN WHICH WE ARE NATURALLY DEFICIENT AS WELL AS THOSE IN WHICH WE EXCEL.

V. We must, in order to a thorough self-acquaintance, not only consider our talents, and proper abilities, but have an eye to our frailties, and deficiencies, that we may know where our weakness, as well as our strength lies. Otherwise, like Samson, we may run ourselves into infinite temptatiou and trouble.

Every man hath a weak side. Every wise man knows where it is, and will be sure to keep a double guard there.

There is some wisdom in concealing a weakness. This cannot be done till it be first known ; nor can it be known without a degree of self-acquaintance.

It is strange to observe what pains some men are at to expose themselves ; to signalize their own folly ; and to set out to the most public view, those things which they ought to be ashamed to think should ever enter into their character. But so it is ; some men seem to be ashamed of those things which would be their glory, whilst others 'glory in their shame.' Phil. iii. 19.

The greatest weakness in a man, is to publish his weaknesses, and to appear fond to have them known. But vanity will often prompt a man to this ; who, unacquainted with the measure of his capacity, attempts things out of his power, and beyond his reach ; whereby he makes the world acquainted with two things to his disadvantage, which they were ignorant of before ; viz. his deficiency, and his self-ignorance, in appearing so blind to it.

It is ill judged (though very common,) to be less ashamed of a want of temper than understanding. For it is no real dishonor, or fault, in a man, to have but a small ability of mind, provided he hath not the vanity to set up for a genius ; which would be as ridiculous, as for a man of small strength and stature of body, to set up for a champion ; because this is what he cannot help. But a man may in a good measure correct the fault of his natural temper, if he be well acquainted with it, and duly watchful over it. And therefore, to betray a prevailing weakness of temper, or an ungoverned passion, diminishes a man's reputation much more than to discover a weakness of judgment or understanding. But what is most dishonorable of all, is, for a man at once to discover a great genius and an ungoverned mind. Because that strength of reason and understanding he is master of, gives him a great advantage of the government of his passions. And therefore his suffering himself, notwithstanding, to be governed by them, shows that he hath too much neglected or mis-applied his natural talent, and willingly submitted to the tyranny of those lusts and passions, over which nature had furnished him with abilities to have secured an easy con quest.

A wise man hath his foibles, as well as a fool. But the difference between them is, that the foibles of the one are known to himself, and concealed from the world ; the foibles of the other are known to the world, and concealed from himself. The wise man sees those frailties in himself, which others cannot ; but the fool is blind to those blemishes in his character, which are conspicuous to every body else. Whence it appears, that self-knowledge is that which makes the main difference between a wise man and a fool, in the moral sense of that word.

* Cæcelius, a famous Rhetorician of Sicily, who lived in the time of Augustus, and wrote a treatise on the sublime, which is censured by Longinus, in the beginning of his, was a man of a hasty and enterprising spirit, and very apt to overshoot himself on all occasions ; and particularly ventured out of his depth in his comparison of Demosthenes and Cicero. Whereupon Plutarch makes this sage and candid remark : 'If,' saith he, 'it was a thing obvious and easy for every man to know himself, possible that saying had not passed for a divine oracle.' Plut. Liv. vol. vii. p 347.

CHAPTER VII.

CONCERNING THE KNOWLEDGE OF OUR CONSTITUTIONAL SINS.

VI. Self-acquaintance shows a man the particular sins he is most exposed and addicted to ; and discovers, not only what is ridiculous, but what is criminal, in his conduct and temper.

A man's untoward actions are generally the plainest index of his inward dispositions : and by the allowed sins of his life, you may know the reigning vices of his mind. Is he addicted to luxury and debauch ? Sensuality then appears to be his prevailing taste. Is he given to revenge and cruelty ? Choler and malice then reigns in his heart. Is he confident, bold, and enterprising ? Ambition appears to be the secret spring. Is he sly and designing, given to intrigue and artifice ? You may conclude there is a natural subtlety of temper that prompts him to this ; and this secret disposition is criminal, in proportion to the degree in which these outward actions, which spring from it, transgress the bounds of reason and virtue.

Every man hath something peculiar in the turn or cast of his mind, which distinguishes him as much as the particular constitution of his body. And both these, viz. his particular turn of mind and constitution of body, not only incline and dispose him to some kind of sins, more than to others ; but render the practice of certain virtues much more easy.*

* Men with regard to their bodies, and bodily appetites, are pretty much alike ; but with regard to their souls, and their mental tastes and dispositions, they are often as different as if they were quite of another species ; governed by different views, entertained with different pleasures, animated with different hopes, and affected by different motives, and distinguished by as different tempers and inclinations, as if they were not of the same kind. So that I am very ready to believe, that there is not a greater difference between an angel and some of the best and wisest of men, or between a devil and some of the worst and wickedest of men with regard to their tempers and dispositions, than there is between some sort of men and some others. And what inclines me to this sentiment is, considering the easy transition which nature always observes in passing from one order or kind of beings to another, which I have before taken notice of, together with the prodigious difference there appears to be between some and others of the human species, almost in every thing belonging to their souls. For some there are 'in whom,' as one expresses it, 'one would think nature had placed every thing the wrong way ;' depraved in their opinions unintelligible in their reasoning, irregular in their actions, and

Now these sins to which men are commonly most inclined, and the temptations which they have least power to resist, are, and not improperly, called their constitutional sins, their peculiar frailties; and in scripture, (Psalm xviii. 23.) their 'own iniquities,' and the sins which (Heb. xii. 1.) 'do most easily beset them.'

'As in the humors of the body, so in the vice of the mind, there is one predominant, which has an ascendant over us, and leads and governs us. It is in the body of sin, what the heart is in the body of our nature; it begins to live first, and dies last: and whilst it lives, it communicates life and spirit to the whole body of sin; and when it dies, the body of sin expires with it. It is the sin to which our constitution leads, our circumstances betray, and custom enslaves us; the sin to which not our virtues only, but vices too, lower their topsails, and submit; the sin which, when we could impose upon god and our consciences, we excuse and disguise with all imaginable artifice and sophistry; but, when we are sincere with both, we oppose first, and conquer last. It is, in a word, the sin which reigns and rules in the unregenerate, and too often alarms and disturbs (ah! that I could say more) the regenerate.'

Some are more inclined to the sins of the flesh; sensuality, intemperance, uncleanliness, sloth, self-indulgence, and excess in animal gratifications. Others, to the sins of the spirit, pride, malice, covetousness, ambition, wrath, revenge, envy, &c. And I am persuaded there are few, but, upon a thorough search into themselves, may find, that some one of these sins hath ordinarily a greater power over them than the rest.—Others often observe it in them, if they themselves do not. And for a man not to know his predominant iniquity, is great self-ignorance indeed; and a sign that he has all his life lived far from home; because he is not acquainted with that, relating to himself, which every one, who is but half an hour in his company perhaps may be able to inform him of. Hence proceeds that extreme weakness which some discover, in censuring others for the very same faults they are guilty of themselves, and perhaps in a much higher degree; on which the apostle Paul animadverts, Rom. ii. 1.

It must be owned, it is an irksome and a disagreeable business for a man to turn his own accuser; to search after his own faults, and keep his eyes upon that which gives him shame and pain to see. It is like tearing open an old wound. But it is better to do this, than to let it mortify. The wounds of the conscience, like those of the body, cannot be well cured, till they are searched to the bottom: and they cannot be searched without pain. A man who is engaged in the study of himself, must be content to know the worst of himself.

Do not therefore shut your eyes against your darling sin, or be averse to find it out. Why should you study to conceal or excuse it, and fondly cherish that viper in your bosom? 'Some men deal by their sins, as some ladies do by their persons. When their beauty is decayed, they seek to hide it from themselves by false glasses, and from others by paint. So, many seek to hide their sins from themselves by false glasses, and from others by excuses, or false colors;' but the greatest cheat they put upon themselves: 'They that cover their sins shall not prosper.'—Prov. xxviii. 13. It is dangerous self-flattery, to give soft and smoothing names to sin, in order to disguise their nature. Rather lay your hand upon your heart, and 'thrust it into your bosom, though it come out, as Moses' did, leprous as snow.'* Exod. iv. 6.

And to find out our most beloved sin, let us consider, what are those worldly objects or amusements which give us the highest delight; this, it is probable, will lead us directly to some one of our darling iniquities, if it be a sin of commission: and what are those duties which we read or hear of from the word of god, to which we find ourselves most disinclined. And this, in all likelihood, will help us to detect some of our peculiar sins of omission; which, without such previous examination, we may not be sensible of. And thus we may make a proficiency in one considerable branch of self-knowledge.

It is a good argument for a reformed mind, that it sees those vices in itself, which it was before ignorant of.

A man's predominant sin usually arises out of his predominant passion; which, therefore, he should diligently observe. The nature and force of which is beautifully described by Pope:

> 'On different senses, different objects strike;
> Hence different passions more or less inflame,
> As strong or weak the organs of the frame:
> And hence one master-passion in the breast,
> Like Aaron's serpent, swallows up the rest.
> Nature its mother, habit is its nurse;
> Wit, spirit, faculties, but make it worse;
> Reason itself but gives it edge and power,
> As heaven's blest beam turns vinegar more sour.
> Ah! if she lend not arms as well as rules,
> What can she more than tell us, we are fools?
> Teach us to mourn our nature, not to mend:
> A sharp accuser, but a helpless friend!'

CHAPTER VIII.

THE KNOWLEDGE OF OUR MOST DANGEROUS TEMPTATIONS NECESSARY TO SELF-KNOWLEDGE.

VII. A man that rightly knows himself, is acquainted with his peculiar temptations; and knows when, and in what circumstances, he is in the greatest danger of transgressing.

Reader, if ever you would know yourself, you must examine this point thoroughly. And if you have never done it, make a pause when you have read this chapter, and do it now. Consider in what company you are most apt to lose the possession and government of yourself; on what occasion you are apt to be most vain and unguarded, most warm and precipitant. Flee that company, avoid those occasions, if you would keep your conscience clear. What is it that robs you most of your time and temper? If you have a due regard to the improvement of the one, and the preservation of the other, you will regret such a loss: and shun the occasions of it, as carefully as you would a road beset with robbers.

But especially must you attend to the occasions which most usually betray you into your favorite vices; and consider the spring from whence they arise, and the circumstances which most favor them. They arise doubtless from your natural temper, which strongly disposes and inclines you to them. That temper, then, or particular turn of desire, must be carefully watched over, as a most dangerous quarter; and the opportunities and circumstances which favor those inclinations, must be resolutely avoided, as the strongest temptations. For the way to subdue a criminal inclination, is, first, to avoid the known occasions that excite it; and then to curb the first motions of it. And thus, having no opportunity of being indulged, it will of itself, in time, lose its force, and fail of its wonted victory.

The surest way to conquer, is sometimes to decline

vicious in every disposition. Whilst in some others, we see almost every thing amiable and excellent that can adorn and exalt the human mind, under the disadvantages of mortality.

* The knowledge of sin is the first step towards amendment: for he that does not know that he hath offended is not willing to be reproved. You must therefore find out yourself, before you can amend yourself. Some glory in their vices. And do you imagine they have any thought about reforming, who place their very vices in the room of their virtues? Therefore, reprove thyself: search thyself very narrowly. First turn accuser to thyself, then a judge, and then a suppliant; and dare for once to displease thyself.

a battle; to weary out the enemy, by keeping him at bay. Fabius Maximus did not use this stratagem more successfully against Hannibal, than a Christian may against his peculiar vice, if he be but watchful of his advantages. It is dangerous to provoke an unequal enemy to the fight, or to run into such a situation, where we cannot expect to escape, without a disadvantageous encounter.

It is of unspeakable importance, in order to self-knowledge and self-government, to be acquainted with all the accesses and avenues to sin, and to observe which way it is that we ourselves too often approach it; and to set reason and conscience to guard those passes, those usual inlets to vice, which if a man once enters, he will find a retreat extremely difficult.

'Watchfulness, which is always necessary, is chiefly so when the first assaults are made: for then the enemy is most easily repulsed; if we never suffer him to get within us; but upon the very first approach, draw up our forces, and fight him without the gate. And this will be more manifest, if we observe by what methods and degrees temptations grow upon us. The first thing that presents itself to the mind, is a plain single thought; this straight is improved into a strong imagination; that again enforced by a sensible delight; then follow evil notions; and when these are once stirred, there wants nothing but the assent of the will, and then the work is finished. Now the first steps to this are seldom thought worth our care; sometimes not taken notice of! so that the enemy is frequently got close up to us, and even within our trenches, before we observe him.'

As men have their particular sins, which do most easily beset them; so they have their particular temptations, which do most easily overcome them. That may be a very great temptation to one, which is none at all to another. And if a man does not know what are his greatest temptations, he must have been a great stranger indeed to the business of self-employment.

As the subtle enemy of mankind takes care to draw men gradually into sin, so he usually draws them by degrees into temptation. As he disguises the sin, so he conceals the temptation to it; well knowing, that were they but once sensible of the danger of their sin, they would be ready to be on their guard against it. Would we know ourselves thoroughly then, we must get acquainted, not only with our most usual temptations, that we be not unawares drawn into sin; but with the previous steps, and preparatory circumstances, which make way for those temptations, that we be not drawn unawares into the occasions of sin; for those things which lead us into tempations are to be considered as temptations, as well as those which immediately lead us into sin. And a man that knows himself will be aware of his remote temptations, as well as the more immediate ones; e. g. if he find the company of a passionate man is a temptation, (as Solomon tells us it is, Prov. xxii. 24, 25.,) he will not only avoid it, but those occasions that may lead him into it. And the petition in the lord's prayer makes it as much a man's duty to be upon his guard against temptation, as under it. Nor can a man pray from his heart that god would not lead him into temptation, if he take no care himself to avoid it.

CHAPTER IX.

SELF-KNOWLEDGE DISCOVERS THE SECRET PREJUDICES OF THE HEART.

VIII. Another important branch of self-knowledge is, for a man to be acquainted with his own prejudices, or those secret prepossessions, of his heart, which, though so deep and latent that he may not be sensible of them, are often so strong and prevalent, as to give a mighty, but imperceptible, bias to the mind.

There is no one particular, that I know of, wherein self-knowledge, more eminently consists, than it does in this. It being, therefore so essential a branch of my subject, and a point to which men seldom pay attention equal to its importance, I beg leave to treat it with a little more precision.

These prejudices of the human mind may be considered with regard to opinions, persons, and things.

1. With regard to opinions.

It is a common observation, but well expressed by a late celebrated writer, 'That we set out in life with such poor beginnings of knowledge, and grow up under such remains of superstition and ignorance, such influences of company and fashion, such insinuations of pleasure, &c., that it is no wonder if men get habits of thinking only in one way; that these habits in time grow rigid and confirmed: and so their minds come to be overcast with thick prejudices, scarce penetrable by any ray of truth, or light of reason.' See 'Religion of Nature Delineated, p. 129.

There is no man but is more attached to one particular set or scheme of opinions in philosophy, politics, and religion, than he is to another; mean, if he hath employed his thoughts at all about them. The question we should examine then is, how came we by those attachments? Whence are we so fond of these particular notions? Did we come fairly by them? or were they imposed upon us, and dictated to our easy belief, before we were able to judge of them? This is most likely. For the impressions we early receive generally grow up with us, and are those we least care to part with. However, which way soever we came by them, they must be re-examined, and brought to the touchstone of sound sense, solid reason and plain scripture. If they will not hear this, after hard drubbing, they must be dismissed, as no genuine principles of truth, but as counterfeits, imposed upon us, under guise und semblance of it.

And as reason and scripture must discover our prejudices to us, so they only can help us to get rid of them. By these we are to rectify, and to these are we to conform, all our opinions and sentiments in religion, as our only standard, exclusive of all other rules, light, or authority, whatsoever.

And care must farther be taken, that we do not make scripture and reason bend and buckle to our notions; which will rather confirm our prejudices than cure them. For whatever cannot evidently be proved, without the help of overstrained metaphors and the arts of sophistry, is much to be suspected; which used to make Archbishop Tillotson say, 'Non amo argutias in theologia; 'I do not love subleties in divinity.' But,

2. The human mind is very apt to be prejudiced either for or against certain persons, as well as certain sentiments. And as prejudice will lead a man to talk very unreasonably with regard to the latter, so will it lead him to act as unreasonably with regard to the former.

What is the reason, for instance, that we cannot help having a more hearty affection for some persons than others? Is it from a similarity of taste and temper? or something in their address, that flatters our vanity? or something in their humour, that hits our fancy? or something in their conversation, that improves our understanding? or a certain sweetness, of disposition, and agreeableness of manner, that is naturally engaging? or by benefits received or expected from them? or from some eminent and distinguished excellency in them? or from none of these but something else, we cannot tell what? Such sort of inquiries will show us whether our esteem and affections be lightly placed; or flow from mere instinct, blind prejudice, or something worse.

And so, on the other hand, with regard to our disaffection towards any one, or the disgust we have taken against him ; if we would know ourselves, we must examine into the bottom of this ; and see not only what is the pretended, but true cause of it : whether it be justifiable, and our resentments duly proportioned to it. Is his manner of thinking, talking, and acting, quite different from mine, and therefore, what I cannot approve ? Or have I received some real affront, or injury, from him ? Be it so, my continual resentment against him, on either of these accounts, may be owing, notwithstanding, more to some unreasonable prejudice in me, than to any real fault in him.

For, as to the former, his way of thinking, or talking, or acting, may possibly be juster than my own; which the mere force of custom and habit only makes me prefer to his. However, be it ever so wrong, he may not have had the same advantage of improving his understanding, address, and conduct, as I have had ; and therefore his defects herein are more excusable. And he may have many other kind of excellencies which I have not. 'But he is not only ignorant and unmannered, but insufferably vain, conceited, and overbearing, at the same time.' Why that, perhaps, he cannot help. It is the fault of his nature. He is the object of pity, rather than resentment. And had I such a disposition by nature, I should, perhaps, with all my self-improvement, find it a difficult thing to manage. And therefore, though I can never choose such an one for an agreeable companion, yet I ought not to harbor a dislike to him ; but love, and pity, and pray for him, as a person under a great misfortune ; and be thankful that I am not under the same. 'But he is quite blind to this fault of his temper, and does not appear to be in the least sensible of it. 'Why, that is a greater misfortune still ; and he ought to be the more pitied.'

And as to the other pretended ground of disgust.— 'He hath often offended and injured me ; let me consider, 1. Whether any offence was really intended ; whether I do not impute that to ill-nature which was only owing to ill-manners ; or that to design, which proceeded only from ignorance. Do I not take offence before it is given ? If so, the fault is mine, and not his ; and the resentment I have conceived against him, I ought to turn upon myself.'

'For every trifle, scorn to take offence ;
That always shows great pride, or little sense ;
Good nature and good sense must always join ;
To err is human, to forgive divine.'

Again, 2. Did I not provoke him to it, when I knew his temper ? The fault is still my own. I did, or might know, the pride, passion, and perverseness, of his nature ; why did I then exasperate him ? A man that would needlessly rouse a lion, must not expect always to come off so favorably as the hero of La Mancha. But 3. Suppose I were not the aggressor ; yet, how came I into his company ? who led me into the temptation ! He hath acted according to his nature, in what he hath done ; but I have not acted according to my reason, in laying myself so open to him. , I knew him ; why did I not shun him, as I would any other dangerous animal, that does mischief by instinct ; If I must needs put my finger into a wasp's nest, why should I blame them for stinging me ? Or, 4. If I could not avoid his company, why did I not arm myself ? why did I venture defenceless into such danger ? Or, 5. Suppose he hath done me a real and undeserved injury, without any fault or provocation ; yet does not my discontent aggravate it ? Does it not appear greater to me than it does to any body else ? or than it will to me, after the present ferment is over ? And, lastly, after all must I never forgive ? How shall I be able to repeat the lord's prayer, or read our saviour's comment upon it, (Matt. vi. 14, 15,) with an unforgiving temper ? Do I not hope to be forgiven 'ten thousand talents ?' and cannot I forgive my 'fellow servant thirty pence ?' when I know not but he hath repented, and god hath forgiven him whose forgiveness I want infinitely more than my greatest enemy does mine.*

Such considerations are of great use to soften our prejudices against persons ; and at once to discover the true spring, and prevent the bad effects of them. And happy would it be for a Christian, could he but call to mind and apply to his relief half the good things which that excellent heathen emperor and philosopher, Marcus Antoninus, could say upon this subject. Some of which I have, for the benefit of the English reader, extracted.

In the morning, remember to say to thyself,—This day, perhaps, I may meet with some impertinent, ungrateful, peevish, tricking, envious, churlish fellow. Now all these ill qualities in him proceeds from his ignorance of good and evil. And since I am so happy as to understand the natural beauty of a good action, and the deformity of an ill one; and since the person that disobliges me is of near kin to me; and though not just of the same blood and family, yet of the same divine extract, as to the mind ; and, finally, since I am convinced that no one can do me real injury, because he cannot force me to do a dishonest thing ;—for these reasons, I cannot find in my heart to hate him, or so much as to be angry with him. Marc. Anton. Medit. book 2. sect. 1.

You are just taking leave of the world : and have you not yet learned to be friends with every body ? and that to be an honest man is the only way to be a wise one ? B. 4. sect. 37.

To expect an impossibility is madness. Now it is impossible for ill men not to do ill things. Id. b. 5. sect. 17.

It is the privilege of human nature, above brutes, to love those that offend us. In order to this, consider, 1. that the offending party is of kin to you; 2. and acts thus because he knows no better. 3. He may have no design to offend you. 4. You will both of you quickly be in your graves. But, above all, 5. you have received no harm from him; for your mind, or reason, is the same as it was before. B. 7. sect. 22.

Think upon your last hour, and do not trouble yourself about other people's faults, but leave them there, where they must be answered for. Id. b. 7. sect. 29.

Do not return the temper of ill-natured people upon themselves, nor treat them as they do the rest of mankind. Id. b. 7. sect. 55.

Though the gods are immortal, yet they not only patiently bore with a wicked world through so many

* A man despises me ; what then ? Did he know me more, he would perhaps despise me more. But I know myself better than he can know me, and therefore despise myself more. And though his contempt in this instance may be groundless, yet in others it would be but too well founded. I will therefore not only bear with, but forgive it. Contemendus est ipse contemptus, saith Seneca. But such retorted scorn is more becoming the character of a stoic than a Christian.

It has been reckoned a wise and witty answer, which one of the philosophers returned to his friend, who advised him to revenge an injury that had been done to him ; 'What,' says he, 'if an ass kick me, must I needs kick him again ?' And perhaps there is more wit than wisdom in that reply. It seems, indeed, to carry in it something of a true greatness of mind ; but does it not, at the same time, discover a kind of haughty and contemptuous spirit ? The truth is, as a judicious writer observes upon it, 'it is at best but a lame and mishappen charity ; it has more of pride than of goodness. We should learn of the holy Jesus, who was not only meek, but lowly. We should contemn the injury, and pity the weakness ; but should not disdain or despise the persons of our enemies.—'Charity vaunteth not herself, is not puffed up, doth not behave itself unseemly.' See Scougal's 'Duty of Loving our Enemies.'

ages; but, what is still more, liberally provided for it: and are you, who are just going off the stage, weary with bearing, though you are one of those unhappy mortals yourself? Id. b. 7. sect. 70.

Never disturb yourself; for men will do the same untoward actions over again, though you burst with spleen. Id. b. 8. sect. 4.

Reform an injurious person, if you can; if not, remember your patience was given you to bear with him; that the gods patiently bear with such men, and sometimes bestow upon them health, and fame, and fortune. Id. b. 9. sect. 11.

When people treat you ill, and show their spite, and slander you, enter into their little souls; go to the bottom of them; search their understandings; and you will soon see, that nothing they may think or say of you need give you one troublesome thought. Id. b. 9. sect. 27.

That is the best thing for a man which god sends him; and that is the best time when he sends it. B. 10. sect. 2.

It is sometimes a hard matter to be certain whether you have received ill usage or not; for men's actions oftentimes look worse than they are; and one must be thoroughly informed of a great many things before he can rightly judge. Id. b. 11. sect. 18.

Consider how much more you often suffer from your anger and grief, than from those very things for which you are angry and grieved. Id. b. 11. sect. 18.

When you fancy that any one hath transgressed, say thus to yourself—'How do I know it is a fault? But admit it is, it may be his conscience hath corrected him; and then he hath received his punishment from himself.' B. 12.

To these I shall add two more quotations, out of the sacred writings, of incomparably greater weight and dignity than any of the aforementioned. 'The discretion of a man deferreth his anger: and it is his glory to pass over a transgression.' Prov. xix. 11. 'If thine enemy hunger, feed him; if he thirst, give him drink; for in so doing thou shalt heap coals of fire on his head. Be not overcome of evil, but overcome evil with good.' Rom. xii. 20, 21.

3. The mind is apt to be prejudiced against, or in favor of, certain things and actions, as well as certain sentiments and persons.

Do you not sometimes find dull disagreeable ideas annexed to certain places, seasons, or employments, which give you a secret aversion to them? These arise from the remembrance of some unpleasing incidents you have heretofore met with, and which you apprehend may again befall you on such occasions. But they are often nothing more than the mere misrepresentations of fancy; and ought to be repelled, because they will be apt to lead you to neglect the duties of your character.

If, therefore, you find in yourself a secret disinclination to any particular action or duty, and the mind begins to cast about for excuses and reasons to justify the neglect of it—consider the matter well; go to the bottom of that reluctance; and search out what it is that gives the mind this aversion to it. Whether it be the thing or action itself, or some discouraging circumstances that may attend it; or some disagreeable consequences that may possibly flow from it; or your supposed unfitness for it at present. Why, all these things may be only imaginary; and to neglect a plain and positive duty, upon such considerations, shows that you are governed by appearances more than realities, by fancy more than reason, and by inclination more than conscience.

But let fancy muster up all the discouraging circumstances, and set them in the most formidable light, to bar your way to a supposed duty. For instance, 'it is very difficult; I want capacity; at least, I am so indisposed to it at present, that I shall make nothing of it; and then it will be attended with danger to my person, reputation, or peace; and the opposition I am like to meet with is great,' &c. But, after all, is the call of providence clear? Is the thing a plain duty; such as reason, conscience, and scripture, your office, character, or personal engagements, call upon you to discharge? If so, all the aforesaid objections are vain and delusive; and you have nothing to do but to summon your courage, and, in dependence on divine help, to set about the business immediately, and in good earnest, and in the best and wisest manner you can; and you may depend upon it you will find the greatest difficulty to lie only in the first attempt; these frightful appearances to be all visionary—the mere figments of fancy, turning lambs into lions, and mole-hills into mountains; and that nothing but sloth, and folly, and self-indulgence, thus set your imagination on work, to deter you from a plain duty. Your heart would deceive you; but you have found out the cheat, and do not be imposed upon.*

Again, suppose the thing done; consider how it will look then. Take a view of it as past; and whatever pains it may cost you, think whether it will not be abundantly recompensed by the inward peace and pleasure which arise from a consciousness of having acted right. It certainly will. And the difficulties you now dread will enhance your future satisfaction. But think again, how you will bear the reflections of your own mind, if you wilfully neglect a plain and necessary duty; whether this will not occasion you much more trouble than all the pains you might be at in performing it. And a wise man will always determine himself by the end, or by such a retrospective view of things, considered as past.

Again, on the other hand, if you find a strong propension to any particular action, examine that with the like impartiality. Perhaps it is what neither your reason nor conscience can fully approve. And yet every motive to it is strongly urged, and every objection against it slighted. Sense and appetite grow importunate and clamorous, and want to lead, while reason remonstrates in vain. But turn not aside from that faithful and friendly monitor, whilst, with a low still voice, she addresses you in this soft, but earnest language:—'Hear me, I beseech you, but this one word more. The action is indeed out of character; what I shall never approve. The pleasure of it is a great deal over-rated; you will certainly be disappointed. It is a false appearance that now deceives you. And what will you think of yourself when it is past, and you come to reflect seriously on the matter? Believe it, you will then wish you had taken me for your counsellor, instead of those enemies of mine, your lusts and passions, which have so often misled you, though you know I never did.'

Such short reflections as these, and a little leisure to take a view of the nature and consequences of things, or actions, before we reject or approve them, will prevent much false judgment and bad conduct; and by degrees wear off the prejudices which fancy has affixed in the mind, either for or against any particular action; teach us to distinguish between things and their appearances; strip them of those false colors that so often deceive us; correct the sallies of the imagination, and leave the reigns in the hand of reason.

Before I dismiss this head, I must observe, that some of our strongest prejudices arise from an excessive self-esteem, or too great a complacency in our own good sense and understanding. Philautus, in every thing, shows himself well satisfied with his own wisdom: which makes him very impatient of contradiction, and gives him a distaste to all who shall presume to oppose their judgment to his, in any thing. He had rather

* 'The wise and prudent conquer difficulties by daring to attempt them. Sloth and folly shiver and shrink at sight of toil and danger, and make the impossibility they fear.'
Rowe.

persevere in a mistake than retract it, least his judgment should suffer; not considering that his ingenuity and good sense suffer much more by such obstinacy. The fulness of his self-sufficiency makes him blind to those imperfections which every one can see in him but himself. So that, however wise, sincere, and friendly, however gentle and seasonable your remonstrance may be, he takes it immediately to proceed from ill-nature or ignorance in you, but from no fault in him.

Seneca, I remember, tells us a remarkable story, which very well illustrates this matter. Writing to his friend Lucilius, 'My wife,' says he, 'keeps Harpastes in her house still; who, you know, is a sort of family fool, and no small incumbrance upon us. For my part, I am far from taking any pleasure in such prodigies. If I have a mind to divert myself with a fool, I have not far to go for one; I can laugh at myself. This silly girl, all on a sudden, lost her eye-sight; and (which perhaps may seem incredible, but is very true) she does not know she is blind, but is every now and then desiring her governess to lead her abroad, saying the house is dark. Now what we laugh at in this poor creature, we may observe happens to us all. No man knows that he is covetous, or insatiable. Yet with this difference: the blind seek somebody to lead them, but we are content to wander without a guide. But why do we thus deceive ourselves? The disease is not without us, but fixed deep within; and therefore is the cure so difficult, because we do not know that we are sick.'

CHAPTER X.

THE NECESSITY AND MEANS OF KNOWING OUR NATURAL TEMPERS.

IX. Another very important branch of self-knowledge is, the knowledge of those governing passions or dispositions of the mind, which generally form what we call a man's natural temper.

The difference of natural tempers seems to be chiefly owing to the different degrees of influence the several passions have upon the mind; e. g. if the passions are eager, and soon raised, we say the man is of a warm temper; if more sluggish, and slowly raised, he is of a cool temper; according as anger, malice, or ambition prevail, he is of a fierce, churlish, or haughty temper; the influence of the softer passions of love, pity, and benevolence, forms a sweet, sympathizing, and courteous temper; and where all the passions are duly poised, and the milder and pleasing ones prevail, they make what is commonly called, a quiet, good-natured man.

So that it is the prevalence or predominance of any particular passion, which gives the turn or tincture to a man's temper, by which he is distinguished, and for which he is loved and esteemed, or shunned and despised, by others.

Now what this is, those we converse with are soon sensible of. They presently see the fault of our temper, and order their behavior accordingly. If they are wise, and well mannered, they will avoid striking the string which they know will jar and raise a discord within us. If they are our enemies, they will do it on purpose to set us on tormenting ourselves. And our friends, we must suffer sometimes, with a gentle hand, to touch it, either by way of pleasant raillery, or faithful advice.

But a man must be greatly unacquainted with himself, if he is ignorant of his predominant passion, or distinguished temper, when every one else observes it. And yet, how common is this piece of self-ignorance! The two apostles, Peter and John, discovered it in that very action, wherein they meant to express nothing but a hearty zeal for their master's honor; which made him tell them, 'That they knew not what manner of spirit they were of,' (Luke ix. 5.) that is, instead of a principle of love and genuine zeal for him, they were at that time governed by a spirit of pride, revenge, and cruelty, and yet knew it not. And that the apostle John should be liable to this censure, whose temper seemed to be all love and sweetness, is a memorable instance how difficult a thing it is for a man at all times to know his own spirit; and that that passion which seems to have the least power over his mind, may, on some occasions, insensibly gain a criminal ascendant there.

The necessity of a perfect knowledge of our reigning passions appears farther, from hence: that they not only give a tincture to the temper, but to the understanding also; and throw a strong bias on the judgment. They have much the same effect upon the eye of the mind, as some distempers have upon that of the body. If they do not put it out, they weaken it; or throw false colors before it, and make it form a wrong judgment of things; and, in short, are the source of those forementioned prejudices, which so often abuse the human understanding.

Whatever the different passions themselves, that reign in the mind, may be owing to; whether to the different texture of the bodily organs, or the different quantity or motion of the animal spirits, or to the native turn and cast of the soul itself; yet, certain it is, that men's different ways of thinking are much according to the predominance of their different passions; and especially with regard to religion. Thus, e. g. we see melancholy people are apt to throw too much gloom upon their religion, and represent it in a very uninviting and unlovely view, as all austerity and mortification; whilst they who are governed by the more gay and cheerful passions, are apt to run into the other extreme, and too much to mingle the pleasures of sense with those of religion; and are as much too lax as the others are too severe; and thus, by the prejudice or bias of their respective passions, or the force of their natural temper, they are led into different mistakes.

'So that, would a man know himself, he must study his natural temper, his constitutional inclinations, and favorite passions; for, by these, a man's judgment is easily perverted, and a wrong bias hung upon his mind. These are the inlets of prejudice, the unguarded avenues of the mind; by which a thousand errors and secret faults find admission, without being observed or taken notice of.'

And that we may more easily come at the knowledge of our predominant affections, let us consider what outward events do most impress and move us, and in what manner? What is it that usually creates the greatest pain or pleasure in the mind? As for pain, a stoic indeed may tell us, 'that we must keep things at a distance: let nothing that is outward come within us; let externals be externals still.' But the human make will scarce bear the rigor of that philosophy. Outward things, after all, will impress and affect us; and there is no harm in this, provided they do not get the possession of us, overset our reason, or lead us to act unbecoming a man or a Christian. And one advantage we may reap from hence is, the manner or degree in which outward things impress us, may lead us into a better acquaintance with ourselves, discover to us our weak side, and the passions which most predominate in us.

Our pleasures will likewise discover our reigning passions, and the true temper and disposition of the soul. If it be captivated by the pleasures of sin, it is a sign its prevailing taste is very vicious and corrupt; if with the pleasures of sense, very low and sordid; if imaginary pleasures, and the painted scenes of fancy and romance, do most entertain it, the soul hath then a trifling turn; if the pleasures of science, or intellectual improvements, are those it is most fond of, it has then a noble and refined taste; but if its chief satisfactions derive from religion and divine contemplation, it has then its true and proper taste; its temper is as it should be, pure, divine, and heavenly; provided these satisfactions spring from a true religious principle, free from that superstition, bigotry, and enthusiasm, under which it is often disguised.

And thus, by carefully observing what it is that gives the mind the greatest pain and torment, or the greatest pleasure and entertainment, we come at the knowledge of its reigning passions, and prevailing temper and disposition.

'Include thyself, then, O my soul, within the compass of thine own heart; if it be not large, it is deep; and thou wilt there find exercise enough. Thou wilt never be able to sound it; it cannot be known, but by him who tries the thoughts and reins. But dive into this subject as deep as thou canst. Examine thyself; and this knowledge of that which passes within thee will be of more use to thee than the knowledge of all that passes in the world. Concern not thyself with the wars and quarrels of public or private persons; take cognizance of those contests which are between thy flesh and thy spirit; betwixt the law of thy members, and that of thy understanding. Appease those differences. Teach thy flesh to be in subjection; replace reason on its throne, and give it piety for its counsellor. Tame thy passions, and bring them under bondage. Put thy little state in good order; govern wisely and holily those numerous people which are contained in so little a kingdom; that is to say, that multitude of affections, thoughts, opinions, and passions, which are in thine heart.'

CHAPTER XI.

CONCERNING THE SECRET SPRINGS OF OUR ACTIONS.

X. Another considerable branch of self-acquaintance is, to know the true motives and secret springs of our actions.

This will sometimes cost us much pains to acquire. But for want of it, we shall be in danger of passing a false judgment upon our actions, and of entertaining a wrong opinion of our conduct.

It is not only very possible, but very common, for men to be ignorant of the chief inducements of their behavior; and to imagine they act from one motive, whilst they are apparently governed by another. If we examine our views, and look into our hearts narrowly, we shall find that they more frequently deceive us in this respect than we are aware of; by persuading us that we are governed by much better motives than we really are. The honor of god, and the interest of religion, may be the open and avowed motive; whilst secular interest, and secret vanity, may be the hidden and true one. While we think we are serving god, we may be only sacrificing to mammon. We may, like Jehu, boast our 'zeal for the lord,' (2 Kings x. 16.) when we are only animated by the heat of our natural passions; may cover a censorious spirit under a cloak of piety; and giving admonition to others, may be only giving vent to our spleen.

Many come to the place of public worship out of custom, or curiosity, who would be thought to come thither only out of conscience. And whilst their external and professed view is to serve god, and gain good to their souls, their secret and inward motive is only to show themselves to advantage, or to avoid singularity, and prevent others making observations on their absence. Munificence and almsgiving may often proceed from a principle of pride and party-spirit; and seeming acts of friendship from a mercenary motive.

By thus disguising our motives, we may impose upon men: but, at the same time, we impose upon ourselves; and whilst we are deceiving others, our own hearts deceive us; and, of all impostures, self-deception is the most dangerous, because least suspected.

Now, unless we examine this point narrowly, we shall never come to the bottom of it; and unless we come at the true spring and real motive of our actions, we shall never be able to form a right judgment of them; and they may appear very different in our own eye, and in the eye of the world, from what they do in the eye of god. 'For the lord seeth not as man seeth: for man looketh on the outward appearance, but the lord looketh on the heart,' (1 Sam. xvi. 7.) And hence it is, that that which is highly esteemed among men, is oftentimes 'abomination in the sight of god,' (Luke xiv. 15.) 'Every way of man is right in his own eyes: but the lord pondereth the heart.' Prov. xxi. 2.

CHAPTER XII.

EVERY ONE THAT KNOWS HIMSELF IS, IN A PARTICULAR MANNER, SENSIBLE HOW FAR HE IS GOVERNED BY A THIRST FOR APPLAUSE.

XI. Another thing necessary to unfold a man's heart to himself, is to consider what is his appetite for fame, and by what means he seeks to gratify it.

This passion in particular, having always so main a stroke, and oftentimes so unsuspected an influence on the most important parts of our conduct, a perfect acquaintance with it is a very material branch of self-knowledge, and therefore requires a distinct consideration.

Emulation, like the other passions of the human mind, shows itself much more plainly, and works much more strongly, in some, than it does in others. It is in itself innocent, and was planted in our natures for very wise ends; and, if kept under proper regulations is capable of serving very excellent purposes; otherwise it degenerates into a mean and criminal ambition.

When a man finds something within him that pushes him on to excel in worthy deeds, or in actions truly good and virtuous, and pursues that design with a steady and unaffected ardor, without reserve or falsehood, it is a true sign of a noble spirit; for that love of praise can never be criminal, that excites and enables a man to do a great deal more good than he could do without it. And perhaps there never was a fine genius, or a noble spirit, that rose above the common level, and distinguished itself by high attainments in what is truly excellent, but was secretly, and perhaps insensibly, prompted by the impulse of this passion.

But, on the contrary, if a man's views center only in the applause of others, whether it be deserved or not; if he pants after popularity and fame, not regarding how he comes by it; if his passion for praise urge him to stretch himself beyond the line of his capacity, and to attempt things to which he is unequal; to condescend to mean arts and low dissimulation, for the sake of a name; and, in a sinister, indirect way, sue hard for a little incense, not caring from whom he receives it; his ambition then becomes vanity. And if it excites a man to wicked attempts, and makes him willing to sacrifice the esteem of all wise and good men, to the acclamations of a mob; to overleap the bounds of decency and truth, and break through the obligations of honor and virtue, it is then not only vanity, but vice; a vice the most destructive to the peace and happiness of human society, and which, of all others, hath made the greatest havoc and devastation among men.

What an instance have we here of the wide difference between common opinion and truth! That a vice so big with mischief and misery, should be mistaken for a virtue! And that they who have been most in-

.amous for it, should be crowned with laurels, even by those who have been ruined by it; and have those laurels perpetuated by the common consent of men through after ages! Seneca's judgment of Alexander is cer-'ainly more agreeable to truth than the common opinion, who called him 'a public cut throat, rather than a hero; and who, in seeking only to be a terror to mankind, arose to no greater an excellence, than what belonged to the most hurtful and hateful animals on earth.'

How different from this, is the judgment of Plutarch, in this matter; who, in his 'Oration concerning the fortune and virtue of Alexander,' exalts him into a true hero; and justifies all the waste he made of mankind, under (the same color with which the Spaniards excused their inhuman barbarities towards the poor Indians, viz:) a pretence of civilizing them. And in attributing all his success to his virtue, he talks more like a soldier, serving under him in his wars, than an historian, who lived many years afterwards, whose business it was to transmit his character impartially to future ages. And in whatever other respects Mr Dryden may give the preference to Plutarch before Seneca, which he does, with much zeal, in his preface to Plutarch's Lives, yet it must be allowed, that, in this instance at least, the latter shows more in the philosopher. See Plu. Mor. vol. i. ad. fin.

Certain it is, that these false heroes, who seek their glory from the destruction of their own species, are, of all men, the most ignorant themselves: and by this wicked ambition, entail infamy and curses upon their name, instead of that immortal glory they pursued. According to the prophet's words, 'Woe to him that coveteth an evil covetousness to his house, that he may set up his nest on high; that he may be delivered from the power of evil. Thou hast consulted shame to thy house, by cutting off many people; and hast sinned against thy soul,' (Hab. ii. 9, 10,)—'that gaineth a wicked gain.'

Now no man can truly know himself, till he be acquainted with this, which is so often the secret and unperceived spring of his actions, and observes how far it governs him in his conversation and conduct; for virtue and real exellence will rise to view, though they be not mounted on the wings of ambition; which, by soaring too high, procures but a more fatal fall.

O sons of earth! Attempt ye still to rise,
By mountains pil'd on mountains, to the skies?
Heav'n still with laughter the vain toil surveys,
And buries madmen in the heaps they raise,
Who wickedly is wise, or madly brave,
Is but the more a fool, or more a knave.—POPE.

And to correct the irregularity and extravagance of this passion, let us but reflect how airy and unsubstantial a pleasure the highest gratifications of it afford; how many cruel mortifications it exposes us to, by awakening the envy of others; to what meanness it often makes us submit; how frequently it loseth its end, by pursuing it with too much ardor; and how much more solid pleasure the approbation of conscience will yield, than the acclamations of ignorant and mistaken men; who, judging by externals only, cannot know our true character; and whose commendations a wise man would rather despise than court. 'Examine but the size of people's sense, and the condition of their understanding, and you will never be fond of popularity, nor afraid of censure; nor solicitous what judgment they may form of you, who know not how to judge rightly of themselves.'

CHAPTER XIII.

WHAT KIND OF KNOWLEDGE WE ARE ALREADY FURNISHED WITH, AND WHAT DEGREE OF ESTEEM WE SET UPON IT.

XII. A man can never rightly know himself, unless he examines into his knowledge of other things.

We must consider, then, the knowledge we have, and whether we do not set too high a price upon it, and too great a value upon ourselves, on its account; of what real use it is of, and what effect it has upon us; whether it does not make us too stiff, unsociable, and assuming; testy and supercilious; and ready to despise others for their supposed ignorance. If so, our knowledge, be it what it will, does us more harm than good. We were better without it; ignorance itself would not render us so ridiculous. Such a temper, with all our knowledge, shows that we know not ourselves.

'A man is certainly proud of that knowledge he despises others for the want of.'

How common is it for some men to be fond of appearing to know more than they do, and of seeming to be thought men of knowledge! To which end they exhaust their fund almost in all companies, to outshine the rest; so that, in two or three conversations, they are drawn dry, and you see to the bottom of them much sooner than you could at first imagine. And even that torrent of learning, which they pour out upon you at first so unmercifully, rather confounds than satisfies you; their visible aim is not to inform your judgment, but display their own. You have many things to query and except against; but their loquacity gives you no room; and their good sense, set off to so much advantage, strikes a modest man dumb. If you insist upon your right to examine, they retreat, either in confusion or equivocation; and like the scuttle-fish, throw a large quantity of ink behind them, that you may not see where to pursue. Whence this foible flows is obvious enough. Self-knowledge would soon correct it.

But as some ignorantly affect to be more knowing, so others vainly affect to be more ignorant, than they are; who, to show they have greater insight and penetration than other men, insist upon the absolute uncertainty of science; will dispute even first principles; grant nothing as certain, and so run it into downright Pyrrhonism; the too common effect of abstracted debates excessively refined.

Every one is apt to set the greatest value upon that kind of knowledge in which he imagines he himself most excels; and to undervalue all other in comparison of it. There wants some certain rule, then, by which every man's knowledge is to be tried, and the value of it estimated. And let it be this:—'That is the best and most valuable kind of knowledge, that is most subservient to the best ends; i. e. which tends to make a man wiser and better, or more agreeable and useful, both to himself and others. For knowledge is but a mean that relates to some end. And as all means are to be judged of by the excellency of the end, and their expediency to produce it; so that must be the best knowledge that hath the directest tendency to promote the best ends; viz. a man's own true happiness, and that of others; in which the glory of god, the ultimate end, is ever necessarily comprised.

Now, if we are to judge of the several kinds of science by this rule, we should find, 1. Some of them to be very hurtful and pernicious; as tending to pervert the true end of knowledge; to ruin a man's own happiness, and make him more injurious to society. Such is the knowledge of vice, the various temptations to it, and the secret ways of practising it, especially the arts of dissimulation, fraud, and dishonesty. 2. Others will be found unprofitable and useless; as those parts of knowledge, which, though they may take up much time and pains to acquire, yet answer no valuable purpose; and serve only for amusement, and the entertainment of the imagination. For instance, an acquaintance with plays, novels, games, and modes in which a man may be very critical and expert, and yet not a whit the wiser or more useful man. 3. Other kinds of knowledge are good only relatively, or conditionally, and may be more useful to one than to another; viz. a skill in a man's particular occupation or calling, on which his credit, livelihood, or usefulness in the world depends. And as this kind of knowledge is valuable in proportion to its ends, so it ought to be cultivated with a diligence and esteem answerable to that. Lastly. Other kinds of knowledge are good absolutely and universally; viz. the knowledge of god and ourselves; the nature of our final happiness, and the way to it. This is equally necessary to all. And how thankful should we be, that we who live under the light of the gospel, and enjoy that light in its perfection and purity, have so many happy means and opportunities of attaining this most useful and necessary kind of knowledge.

A man can never understand himself, then, till he makes a right estimate of his knowledge; till he examines what kind of knowledge he values himself most upon, and most diligently cultivates; how high a value he sets upon it; what good it does him; what effect it hath upon him; what he is the better for it; what end it answers now; or what it is like to answer hereafter.

There is nothing in which a man's self-ignorance discovers itself more, than in the esteem he hath for his understanding, or for himself, on account of it. It is a trite and true observation, 'that empty things make the most sound.' Men of the least knowledge are most apt to make a show of it, and to value themselves upon it; which is very visible in forward confident youth; raw, conceited academics; and those who, uneducated in their childhood, betake themselves in latter life to reading, without taste or judgment, only as an accomplishment, and to make a show of scholarship, who have just learning enough to spoil company, and render themselves ridiculous; but not enough to make themselves, or others at all the wiser.

But beside the fore-mentioned kinds of knowledge, there is another, which is commonly called false knowledge; which though it often imposes upon men under the show and semblance of true knowledge is really worse than ignorance. Some men have learned a great many things, and have taken a great deal of pains to learn them, and stand very high in their own opinion on account of them, which yet they must unlearn, before they are truely wise. They have been at a vast expense of time, and pains, and patience, to heap together, and to confirm themselves in a set of wrong notions; which they lay up in their minds as a fund of valuable knowledge; which, if they try by the fore-mentioned rules; viz. 'The tendency they have to make them wiser and better, or more useful and beneficial to others,' will be found to be worth just nothing at all.

Beware of this false-knowledge: for as there is nothing of which men are more obstinately tenacious, so there is nothing that renders them more vain, or more averse to self-knowledge. Of all things, men are most fond of their wrong notions.

The apostle Paul often speaks of these men, and their self-sufficiency, in very poignant terms; 'who, though they seem wise, yet,' says he, 'must become fools, before they are wise.' (1 Cor. iii. 18.) Though they think they know a great deal, 'know nothing yet as they ought to know,' (1. Cor. viii. 2.) 'but deceive themselves, by thinking themselves something, when they are nothing,' (1 Gal. vi. 3.) And whilst they desire to be teachers of others, 'understand not what they say, nor whereof they affirm, (1 Tim. i. 7.) 'and want themselves to be taught what are the first rudiments and principles of wisdom.' 1 Heb. v. 12.

CHAPTER XIV.

CONCERNING THE KNOWLEDGE, GUARD AND GOVERNMENT OF OUR THOUGHTS.

XIII. Another part of self-knowledge consists in a due acquaintance with our own thoughts, and inward workings of the imagination.

The right government of the thoughts requires no small art, vigilance, and resolution. But it is a matter of such vast importance to the peace and improvement of the mind, that it is worth while to be at some pains about it. A man that hath so numerous and turbulent a family to govern as his own thoughts, which are too apt to be at the command of his passions and appetites ought not to be long from home. If he be, they will soon grow mutinous and disorderly, under the conduct of those two headstrong guides, and raise great clamors and disturbances. And sometimes on the slightest occasions And a more dreadful scene of misery can hardly be imagined, than that which is occasioned by such a tumult and uproar within, when a raging conscience, or inflamed passions, are let loose, without check or control. A city in flames, or the mutiny of a drunken crew aboard, who have murdered the captain, and are butchering one another, are but faint emblems of it. The torment of the mind, under such an insurrection and ravage of the passions, is not easy to be conceived. The most revengeful man cannot wish his enemy a greater.

Of what vast importance, then, is it for a man to watch over his thoughts, in order to a right of government of them! To consider what kind of thoughts find the easiest admission; in what manner they insinuate themselves, and upon what occasions.

It was an excellent rule which a wise heathen prescribed to himself, in his private meditations: 'Manage,' saith he, 'all your actions and thoughts in such a manner, as if you were just going out of the world.' Again, saith he, 'A man is seldom, if ever, unhappy for not knowing the thoughts of others; but he that does not attend to the motions of his own, is certainly miserable.'

Nothing can be more unhappy than that man who ranges every where, ransacks every thing, digs into the bowels of the earth, dives into other men's bosoms, but does not consider all the while that his own mind will afford him sufficient scope for inquiry and entertainment; and that the care and improvement of himself, will give him business enough.

Your disposition will be suitable to that which you most frequently think on; for the soul is, as it were, tinged with the color and complexion of its own thoughts,

It may be worth our while then to discuss this matter a little more precisely, and consider, first, what kind of thoughts are to be excluded or rejected; and, second, what ought to be indulged and entertained.

First. Some thoughts ought to be immediately banished, as soon as they have found entrance. And if we are often troubled with them, the safest way will be to keep a good guard on the avenues of the mind by which they enter, and avoid those occasions which commonly excite them. For sometimes it is much easier to prevent a bad thought entering the mind, than to get rid of it when it is entered. More particularly.

1. Watch against all fretful and distcontented thoughts, which do but chafe and wound the mind to no purpose. To harbor these, is to do yourself more injury than it is in the power of your greatest enemy to do you. It is equally a Christian's interest and duty to 'learn, in whatsoever state he is, therewith to be content.' Phil iv. 2.

2. Harbor not too anxious and apprehensive thoughts. By giving way to tormenting fears, suspicions of some approaching danger or troublesome event, we not only anticipate, but double the evil we fear; and undergo much more from the apprehension of it before it comes, than from the whole weight of it when present. This is a great, but common weakness, which a man should endeavor to arm himself against

by such kind of reflections as these. 'Are not all these events under the certain direction of a wise providence ? If they befall me, they are then that share of suffering which god hath appointed me ; and which he expects I should bear as a Christian. How often hath my too timorous heart magnified former trials, which I found to be less in reality, than they appeared upon their approach ! And perhaps the formidable aspect they put on, is only a stratagem of the great enemy of my best interest, designed on purpose to divert me from some point of duty, or to draw me into some sin, to avoid them. However, why should I torment myself to no purpose ? The pain and affliction the dreaded evil will give me, when it comes, is of god's sending : the pain I feel in the apprehension of it, before it comes, is of my own procuring. Whereby, I often make my sufferings more than double ; for this overplus of them, which I bring upon myself, is often greater than that measure of them which the hand of providence immediately brings upon me.'

3. Dismiss, as soon as may be, all angry and wrathful thoughts. These will but canker and corrode the mind, and dispose it to the worst temper in the world ; viz that of fixed malice and revenge. Anger may steal into the heart of the wise man ; but it 'rests only in the bosom of fools.' Make all the most candid allowances for the offender. Consider his natural temper Turn your anger into pity. Repeat 1 Cor. xxi. Think of the patience and meekness of Christ, and the petition in the lord's prayer ; and how much you stand in need of forgiveness yourself, both from god and man ; how fruitless, how foolish is indulged resentment ; how tormenting to yourself You have too much good nature willingly to give others so much torment ; and why should you give it yourself ? Your are commanded to love your neigbor as yourself ; but not forbidden to love yourself as much And why should you do yourself that injury, which your enemy would be glad to do you !

But, above all, be sure to set a guard on the tongue, whilst the fretful mood is upon you. The least spark may break out into a conflagration, when cherished by a resentful heart, and fanned by the wind of an angry breath. Aggravating expressions, at such a time, are like oil thrown upon flames, which always makes them rage the more.—Especially,

4. Banish all malignant and revengeful thoughts. A spirit of revenge is the very spirit of the devil ; than which nothing makes a man more like him ; and nothing can be more opposite to the temper which Christianity was designed to promote. If your revenge be not satisfied, it will give you torment now ; if it be, it will give you greater hereafter. None is a greater self tormentor, than a malicious and revengeful man, who turns the poison of his own temper in upon himself.

5. Drive from the mind all silly, trifling, and unreasonable thoughts ; which sometimes get into it, we know not how, and seize and possess it before we are aware, and hold it in empty idle amusements, that, yield it neither pleasure nor profit, and turn to no manner of account in the world, only consume time, and prevent a better employment of the mind. And indeed there is little difference whether we spend the time in sleep, or in these walking dreams. Nay if the thoughts which thus insensibly steal upon you be not altogether absurd and whimsical, yet if they be impertinent and unseasonable, they ought to be dismissed, because they keep out better company.

6. Cast out all wild and extravagant thoughts, all vain and fantastical imaginations. Suffer not your thoughts to roam upon things that never were, and perhaps never will be ; to give you a visionary pleasure, n the prospect of what you have not the least reason to hope, or a needless pain, in the apprehension of what you have not the least reason to fear. The truth is, next to a clear conscience and a sound judgment there is not a greater blessing than a regular and well governed imagination ; to be able to view things as they are, in their true light and proper colors, and to distinguish the false images that are painted on the fancy, from the representations of truth and reason ; for how common a thing is it for men, before they are aware, to confound reason and fancy, truth and imagination, together ! To take the flashes of the animal spirits for the light of evidence, and think they believe things to be true, or false, when they only fancy them to be so ; and fancy them to be so, because they would have them so ; not considering, that mere fancy is only the ignis fatuus of the mind, which often appears brightest when the mind is most covered with darkness, and will be sure to lead them astray who follow it as their guide. Near akin to these are,

7. Romantic and chimerical thoughts. By which I mean that kind of wild-fire, which the briskness of the animal spirits sometimes suddenly flashes on the mind, and excites images that are so extremely ridiculous and absurd, that one can scarce forbear wondering how they could get admittance. These random flights of the fancy are soon gone ; and herein differ from that castle-building of the imagination before mentioned, which is a more settled amusement. But these are too incoherent and senseless to be of long continuance ; and are the maddest sallies, and the most ramping reveries of the fancy that can be. I know not whether my reader understands now what I mean ; but if he attentively regards all that passes through his mind, perhaps he may hereafter by experience.

8. Repel all impure and lascivious thoughts, which taint and pollute the mind ; and, though hid from men, are known to god, in whose eye they are abominable. Our saviour warns us against these, as a kind of spiritual fornication, (Mat. v. 28.) and inconsistent with that purity of heart which his gospel requires.

9. Take care how you too much indulge gloomy and melancholy thoughts. Some are disposed to see every thing in the worst light. A black cloud hangs hovering over their minds, which, when it falls in showers through their eyes, is dispersed, and all within is serene again. This is often purely mechanical ; and owing either to some fault in the bodily constitution, or some accidental disorder in the animal frame. However, one that consults the peace of his own mind, will be upon his guard against this, which so often robs him of it.

10. On the other hand, let not the imagination be too sprightly and triumphant. Some are as unreasonably exalted as others are depressed ; and the same person, at different times, often runs into both extremes, according to the different temper and flow of the animal spirits ; and, therefore, the thoughts which so eagerly crowd into the mind at such times, ought to be suspected and well guarded, otherwise they will impose upon our judgment, and lead us to form such a notion of ourselves and of things, as we shall soon see fit to alter, when the mind is in a more settled and sedate frame.

Before we let our thoughts judge of things, we must set reason to judge our thoughts ; for they are not always in a proper condition to execute that office. We do not believe the character which a man gives us of another, unless we have a good opinion of his own ; so, neither should we believe the verdict which the mind pronounces, till we first examine whether it be impartial and unbiassed ; whether it be in a proper temper to judge, and have proper lights to judge by. The want of this previous act of self-judgment, is the cause of much self-deception and false judgment.

Lastly. With abhorrence reject immediately all profane and blasphemous thoughts ; which are sometimes suddenly injected into the mind, we know not how, though we may give a pretty good guess from whence. And all those thoughts which are apparently temptations and inducements to sin, our lord hath, by his example, taught us to treat in this manner, Matt. iv. 10.

These then are the thoughts we should carefully guard against. And as they will (especially some of them) be frequently insinuating themselves into the heart, remember to set reason at the door of it, to guard the passage, and bar their entrance, or drive them out forthwith when entered, not only as impertinent, but mischievous intruders.

But, second, there are other kinds of thoughts which we ought to indulge, and, with great care and diligence, retain and improve.

Whatever thoughts give the mind a rational or religious pleasure, and tend to improve the heart and understanding, are to be favored, often recalled, and carefully cultivated. Nor should we dismiss them, till they have made some impressions on the mind, which are like to abide there.

And to bring the mind into a habit of recovering, retaining, and improving such thoughts, two things are necessary.

1. To habituate ourselves to a close and rational way of thinking; and, 2. To moral reflections and religious contemplations.

(1.) To prepare and dispose the mind for the entertainment of good and useful thoughts, we must take care to accustom it to a close and rational way of thinking.

When you have started a good thought, pursue it; do not presently lose sight of it, or suffer any trifling suggestion that may intervene to divert you from it. Dismiss it not till you have sifted and exhausted it, and well considered the several consequences and inferences that result from it. However, retain not the subject any longer than you find your thoughts run freely upon it; for, to confine them to it when it is quite worn out, is to give them an unnatural bent, without sufficient employment; which will make them flag, or be more apt to run off to something else.

And to keep the mind intent on the subject you think of, you must be at some pains to recall and refix your desultory and rambling thoughts. Lay open the subject in as many lights and views as it is capable of being represented in. Clothe your best ideas in pertinent and well chosen words, deliberately pronounced; or commit them to writing.

Whatever be the subject, admit of no inferences from it, but what you see plain and natural. This is the way to furnish the mind with true and solid knowledge; as, on the contrary, false knowledge proceeds from not understanding the subject, or drawing inferences from it which are forced and unnatural, and allowing to those precarious inferences, or consequences drawn from them, the same degree of credibility as to the most rational and best established principles.

Beware of a superficial, slight, or confused view of things. Go to the bottom of them, and examine the foundation; and be satisfied with none but clear and distinct ideas (when they can be had) in every thing you read, hear, or think of: for resting in imperfect and obscure ideas is the source of much confusion and mistake.

Accustom yourself to speak naturally, pertinently, and rationally, on all subjects, and you will soon learn to think so on the best; especially if you often converse with those persons that speak, and those authors that write, in that manner

Such a regulation and right management of your thoughts and rational powers, will be of great and general advantage to you in the pursuit of youthful knowledge, and a good guard against the levities and frantic sallies of the imagination. Nor will you be sensible of any disadvantage attending it, excepting one; viz. its making you more sensible of the weakness and ignorance of others, who are often talking in a random, inconsequential manner; and whom it may oftentimes be more prudent to bear with, than contradict. But the vast benefit this method will be of, in tracing out truth, and detecting error; and, the satisfaction it will give you, in the cool and regular exercise of self-employment, and in the retaining, pursuing, and improving good and useful thoughts, will more than compensate that petty disadvantage.

(2.) If we would have the mind furnished and entertained with good thoughts, we must inure it to moral and religious subjects.

It is certain the mind cannot be more nobly and usefully employed, than in such kind of contemplations, because the knowledge it thereby acquires is, of all others, the most excellent knowledge; and that both in regard of its object and its end; the object of it being god, and the end of it eternal happiness.

The great end of religion is, to 'make us like god, and conduct us to the enjoyment of him.' And whatever hath not this plain tendency, (and especially if it have the contrary) men may call religion, if they please; but they cannot call it more out of its name. And whatever is called religious knowledge, if it does not direct us in the way to this end, is not religious knowledge, but something else, falsely so called. And some are unhappily accustomed to such an abuse of words and understanding, as not only to call, but to think, those things religion, which are quite reverse of it; and those notions religious knowledge, which lead them the farthest from it.

The sincerity of a true religious principle cannot be better known, than by the readiness with which the thoughts advert to god, and the pleasure with which they are employed in devout exercises. And though a person may not always be so well pleased with hearing religious things talked of by others, whose different taste, sentiments, or manner of expression, may have something disagreeable; yet, if he have no inclination to think of them himself, or to converse with himself about them, he hath great reason to suspect that his heart is not right with god. But if he frequently and delightfully exercise his mind in divine contemplations, it will not only be a good mark of his sincerity, but will habitually dispose it for the reception of the best and most useful thoughts, and fit it for the noblest entertainments.

Upon the whole, then, it is of as great importance for a man to take heed what thoughts he entertains, as what company he keeps; for they have the same effect upon the mind. Bad thoughts are as infectious as bad company; and good thoughts solace, instruct, and entertain the mind, like good company. And this is one great advantage of retirement, that a man may choose what company he pleases, from within himself.

As, in the world, we oftener light into bad company than good; so, in solitude, we are oftener troubled with impertinent and unprofitable thoughts, than entertained with agreeable and useful ones: and a man that hath so far lost the command of himself, as to lie at the mercy of every foolish or vexing thought, is in much the same situation as an host whose house is open to all comers; whom, though ever so noisy, rude, and troublesome, he cannot get rid of: but with this difference, that the latter hath some recompense for his trouble, the former none at all; but is robbed of his peace and quiet for nothing.

Of such vast importance to the peace, as well as the improvement of the mind, is the right regulation of the thoughts: which will be my apology for dwelling so long on this branch of the subject; which I shall conclude with this one observation more: that it is a very dangerous thing to think, as many are apt to do, that it is a matter of indifference what thoughts they entertain in their hearts; since the reason of things concurs with the testimony of the holy scriptures to assure us, 'that the allowed thought of foolishness is sin.'* (Prov. xxxiv. 9.)

CHAPTER XV.

CONCERNING THE MEMORY.

XIV. A man that knows himself will have a regard not only to the management of his thoughts, but the improvement of his memory.

The memory is that faculty of the soul which was designed for the store-house, or repository, of its most useful notions, where they may be laid up in safety, to be produced upon proper occasions.

Now, a thorough self-acquaintance cannot be had without a proper regard to this, in two respects. (1.) Its furniture. (2.) Its improvement.

(1.) A man that knows himself will have a regard to the furniture of his memory; not to load it with trash and lumber, a set of useless notions, or low conceits, which he will be ashamed to produce before persons of taste and judgment.

If the retention be bad, do not crowd it; it is of as ill consequence to overload a weak memory as a weak stomach: and that it may not be cumbered with trash, take heed what company you keep, what books you read, and what thoughts you favor; otherwise a great deal of useless rubbish may fix there before you are aware, and take up the room which ought to be possessed by better notions. But let not a valuable thought slip from you, though you pursue it with much time and pains before you overtake it; the regaining and refixing it may be of more avail to you than many hour's reading.

What pity it is that men should take such immense pains, as some do, to learn those things which, as soon as they become wise, they must take as much pains to unlearn. A thought that should make us very curious and cautious about the proper furniture of our minds.

(2.) Self-knowledge will acquaint a man with the extent and capacity of his memory, and the right way to improve it.

There is no small art in improving a weak memory, so as to turn it to as great an advantage as many do theirs which are much stronger. A few short rules to this purpose may be no unprofitable digression.

1. Beware of every sort of intemperance, in the indulgence of the appetites and passions. Excesses of all kinds do a great injury to the memory.

2. If it be weak, do not overload it. Charge it only with the most useful and solid notions. A small vessel should not be stuffed with lumber: but if its freight be precious, and judiciously stowed, it may be more valuable than a ship of twice its burden.

3. Recur to the help of a common-place-book, according to Mr. Locke's method;† and review it once a year. But take care that, by confiding to your minutes, or memorial aids, you do not excuse the labor of the memory; which is one disadvantage attending this method.

4. Take every opportunity of uttering your best thoughts in conversation, when the subject will admit it; that will deeply imprint them. Hence the tales which common story-tellers relate, they never forget though ever so silly.

5. Join to the idea you would remember, some other that is more familiar to you, which bears some similitude to it, either in its nature, or in the sound of the word by which it is expressed; or that hath some relation to it, either in time or place. And then, by recalling this, which is easily remembered, you will, by that concatenation, or connection of ideas, which Mr Locke takes notice of, draw in that which is thus linked or joined with it; which otherwise you might hunt after in vain. This rule is of excellent use to help you to remember names.

6. What you are determined to remember, think of before you go to sleep at night, and the first thing in the morning, when the faculties are fresh; and recollect at evening every thing worth remembering the day past.

7. Think it not enough to furnish this store-house of the mind with good thoughts, but lay them up there in order, digested or ranged under proper subjects or classes; that whatever subject you have occasion to think or talk upon, you may have recourse immediately to a good thought, which you heretofore laid up there, under that subject. So that the very mention of the subject may bring the thought to hand; by which means you will carry a regular common-place-book in your memory. And it may not be amiss sometimes to take an inventory of this mental furniture, and recollect how many good thoughts you have treasured up under such particular subjects, and whence you had them.

Lastly. Nothing helps the memory more than often thinking, writing, or talking, on those subjects you would remember. But enough of this.

* 'Guard well thy thoughts: our thoughts are heard in heaven.' [Young.

† See Appendix at the the end of the volume, in which Mr Locke's method of keeping a common-place-book is fully explained.

CHAPTER XVI.

CONCERNING THE MENTAL TASTE.

XV. A man that knows himself is sensible of, and attentive to, the particular tastes of his mind, especially in matters of religion.

As the late Mr Howe judiciously observes, in his 'Humble Request both to Conformists and Dissenters,' 'There is, beside bare understanding and judgment, and diverse from that heavenly gift, which in the scripture is called grace, such a thing as gust and relish belonging to the mind of man, and, I doubt not, with all men, if they observe themselves, and which are as unaccountable and as various as the relishes and disgusts of sense. This they only wonder at who understand not themselves, or will consider nobody but themselves. So that it cannot be said universally, that it is a better judgment, or more grace, that determines men the one way or the other; but somewhat in the temper of their minds, distinct from both, which I know not how better to express, than by mental taste. And this, hath no more of mystery in it, than that there is such a thing belonging to our natures as complacency and displacency, in reference to the objects of the mind. And this, in the kind of it, is as common to men as human nature; but as much diversified in individuals, as men's other inclinations are.'

Now this different taste in matters relating to religion, though it may be sometimes natural, or what is born with a man, generally arises from the difference of education and custom. And the true reason why some persons have an inveterate disrelish to certain circumstantials of religion, though ever so justifiable; and at the same time a fixed esteem for others, that are more exceptionable, may be no better than what I have heard some very honestly profess; viz. that the one they have been used to, and the other not. As a person, by long use and habit, acquires a greater relish for coarse and unwholesome food, than the most delicate diet; so, a person long habituated to a set of phrases, notions, and modes, may, by degrees, come to have such a veneration and esteem for them, as to despise and condemn others which they have not been accustomed to, though perhaps more edifying, and more agreeable to scripture and reason.

This particular taste in matters of religion differs very much, as Mr Howe well observes, both from judgment and grace.

However, it is often mistaken for both: when it is mistaken for the former, it leads to error; when mistaken for the latter, to censoriousness.

This different taste of mental objects is much the same with that, which, with regard to the objects of sense, we call fancy; for, as one man cannot be said to have a better judgment in food than another, purely because he likes some kind of meats better than he; so, neither can he be said to have a better judgment in matters of religion, purely because he hath a greater fondness for some particular doctrines and forms.

But though this mental taste be not the same as the judgment, yet it often draws the judgment to it; and sometimes very much perverts it.

This appears in nothing more evidently than in the judgment people pass upon the sermons they hear. Some are best pleased with those discourses that are pathetic and warming; others with what is more solid and rational; and others with the sublime and mystical; nothing can be too plain for the taste of some, or too refined for that of others. Some are for having the address only to their reason and understanding; others only to their affections and passions; and others to their experience and consciences. And every hearer or reader is apt to judge according to his particular taste, and to esteem him the best preacher or writer who pleases him most; without examining his own particular taste, by which he judgeth.

It is natural, indeed, for every one to desire to have his own taste pleased; but it is unreasonable in him to set it up as the best, and make it a test and standard to others; but much more unreasonable to expect, that he who speaks in public, should always speak to his taste; which might as reasonably be expected by another, of a different one. It is equally impossible, that what is delivered to a multitude of hearers, should alike suit all their tastes, as that a single dish, though prepared with ever so much art and exactness, should equally please a great variety of appetites; among which there may be some, perhaps, very nice and sickly.

It is the preacher's duty to adapt his subjects to the taste of his hearers, as far as fidelity and conscience will admit; because it is well known, from reason and experience, as well as from the advice and practice of the apostle Paul, (Rom. xv. 2—1 Cor. ix. 22.) that this is the best way to promote their edification. But if their taste be totally vitiated, and incline them to take in that which will do them more harm than good, and to relish poison more than food, the most charitable thing the preacher can do in that case is, to endeavor to correct so vicious an appetite, which loathes that which is most wholesome, and craves pernicious food; this, I say, it is his duty to attempt, in the most gentle and prudent manner he can, though he run the risk of having his judgment or orthodoxy called into question by them, as it very possibly may; for commonly they are the most arbitrary and unmerciful judges in this case, who are least of all qualified for that office.

There is not, perhaps, a more unaccountable weakness in human nature than this,—that, with regard to religious matters, our animosities are generally greatest where our differences are least; they who come pretty near to our standard, but stop short there, are more the objects of our disgust and censure, than they who continue at the greatest distance from it. And in some cases it requires much candor and self-command to get over this weakness. To whatever secret spring in the human mind it may be owing, I shall not stay to inquire; but the thing itself is too obvious not to be taken notice of.

Now we should all of us be careful to find out and examine our proper taste of religious things; that, if it be a false one, we may rectify it; if a bad one, mend it; if a right and good one, strengthen and improve it: for the mind is capable of a false gust, as well as the palate, and comes by it in the same way; viz. by being long used to unnatural relishes, which, by custom, become grateful. And having found out what it is, and examined it by the test of scripture, reason and conscience, if it be not very wrong, let us indulge it, and read those books that are most suited to it; which, for that reason, will be most edifying. But, at the same time, let us take care of two things: 1. That it do not bias our judgments, and draw us into error. 2. That it do not cramp our charity, and lead us to censoriousness.

CHAPTER XVII

OF OUR GREAT AND GOVERNING VIEWS IN LIFE.

XVI. Another part of self-knowledge is, to know what are the great ends for which we live?

We must consider what is the ultimate scope we drive at; the general maxims and principles we live by; or whether we have not yet determined our end, and are governed by no fixed principles; or by such as we are ashamed to own.

'The first and leading dictate of prudence is that a man propose to himself his true and best interest for his end; and the next is, that he make use of all those means and opportunities whereby that end is to be obtained. This is the most effectual way that I know of to secure to one's self the character of a wise man here, and the reward of one hereafter. And between these two there is such a close connection, that he does not do the latter, cannot be supposed to intend the former. He that is not careful of his action, shall never persuade me that he seriously proposes to himself his best interest as his end; for if he did, he would as seriously apply himself to the regulation of the other, as the means.'

There are few that live so much at random, as not to have some main end in eye; something that influences their conduct, and is the great object of their pursuit and hope. A man cannot live without some leading views: a wise man will always know what they are; whether it is fit he should be led by them or no; whether they be such as his understanding and reason approve, or only such as fancy and inclination suggest. He will be as much concerned to act with reason, as to talk with reason; as much ashamed of a solecism and contradiction in his character, as in his conversation.

Where do our views center? In this world we are in; or in that we are going to? If our hopes and joys center here, it is a mortifying thought, that we are every day departing from our happiness: but if they are fixed above, it is a joy to think that we are every day drawing nearer to the object of our highest wishes.

Is our main care to appear great in the eye of man, or good in the eye of god? If the former, we expose ourselves to the pain of a perpetual disappointment. For it is much if the envy of men do not rob us of a good deal of our just praise, or if our vanity will be content with that portion of it they allow us. But if the latter be our main care, if our chief view is to be approved of god, we are laying up a fund of the most lasting and solid satisfactions. Not to say, that this is the truest way to appear great in the eye of men, and to conciliate the esteem of all those whose praise is worth our wish.

'Be this, then, O my soul, thy wise and steady pursuit; let this circumscribe and direct thy views, be this a law to thee, from which account it a sin to depart, whatever disrespect or contempt it may expose thee to from others; be this the character thou resolvest to live up to, and at all times to maintain, both in public and private; viz. a friend and lover of god, in whose favor thou centerest all thy present and future hopes. Carry this view with thee through life, and dare not, in any instance, to act inconsistently with it.'

CHAPTER XVIII.

HOW TO KNOW THE TRUE STATE OF OUR SOULS; AND WHETHER WE ARE FIT TO DIE.

Lastly, the most important point of self-knowledge, after all, is, to know the true state of our souls towards god, and in what condition we are to die.

These two things are inseparably connected in their nature, and therefore I put them together. The knowledge of the former will determine the latter; and is the only thing that can determine it: for no man can tell whether he is fit for death, till he is acquainted with the true state of his own soul.

This, now, is a matter of such vast moment, that it is amazing any considerate man, or any who thinks what it is to die, can be satisfied, so long as it remains an uncertainty. Let us trace out this important point, then, with all possible plainnesss; and see if we can come to some satisfaction in it, upon the most solid principles.

In order to know, then, whether we are fit to die, we must first know what it is that fits us for death. And the answer to this is very natural and easy; viz. that only fits us for death, which fits us for happiness after death.

This is certain. But the question returns. What is it that fits us for happiness after death?

Now, in answer to this, there is a previous question necessary to be determined; viz. What that happiness is?

It is not a fool's paradise, or a Turkish dream of sensitive gratifications. It must be a happiness suited to the nature of the soul, and what it is capable of enjoying in a state of separation from the body. And what can that be, but the enjoyment of god, the best of beings, and the author of ours?

The question then comes to this, what is that which fits us for the enjoyment of god, in the future state of separate spirits?

And methinks we may bring this matter to a very sure and short issue, by saying, it is that which makes us like to him now. This only is our proper qualification for the enjoyment of him after death, and therefore our only proper preparation for death. For how can they, who are unlike to god here, expect to enjoy him hereafter? And if they have no just ground to hope that they shall enjoy god in the other world, how are they fit to die?

So, that the great question, Am I fit to die? resolves itself into this, Am I like to god? for it is this only that fits me for heaven; and that which fits me for heaven, is the only thing that fits me for death.

Let this point, then, be well searched into, and examined very deliberately and impartially.

Most certain it is, that god can take no real complacency in any but those that are like him; and it is as certain, that none but those that are like him, can take pleasure in him. But god is a most pure and holy being; a being of infinite love, mercy and patience; whose righteousness is invariable, whose veracity inviolable, and whose wisdom unerring. These are the moral attributes of the divine being, in which he requires us to imitate him; the express lineaments of the divine nature, in which all good men bear a resemblance to him; and for the sake of which only, they are the objects of his delight: for god can love none but those that bear this impress of his own image on their souls. Do we find, then, these visible traces of the divine image there? Can we make out our likeness to him in his holiness, goodness, mercy, righteousness, truth, and wisdom? If so, it is certain we are capable of enjoying him, and are the proper objects of his love. By this we know we are fit to die; because by this we know we are fit for happiness after death.

Thus, then, if we are faithful to our consciences, and impartial in the examination of our lives and tempers, we may soon come to a right determination of this important question, What is the true state of our soul towards god; and in what condition we are to die? which, as it is the most important, so, is the last instance of self-knowledge I shall mention; and with it close the first part of this subject.

Nor do I apprehend the knowledge of our state (call it assurance, if you please) so uncommon and extraordinary a thing, as some are apt to imagine. Understand, by assurance, a satisfactory evidence of the thing, such as excludes all reasonable doubts and disquieting fears of the contrary, though, it may be, not all transient suspicions and jealousies. And such an assurance and certainty multitudes have attained, and enjoy the comfort of; and indeed it is of so high importance, that it is a wonder any thoughtful Christian, that believes an eternity, can be easy one week or day without it.' Bennet's Christ. Orat.

A TREATISE

ON

SELF-KNOWLEDGE.

PART THE SECOND.

SHOWING THE GREAT EXCELLENCY AND ADVANTAGES OF THIS KIND OF SCIENCE.

Having, in the former part of the subject, laid open some of the main branches of self-knowledge, or pointed out the principal things which a man ought to be acquainted with, relating to himself; I am now, reader, to lay before you the excellency and usefulness of this kind of knowledge, as an inducement to labor after it, by a detail of the several great advantages attending it; which shall be recounted in the following chapters.

CHAPTER I.

SELF-KNOWLEDGE THE SPRING OF SELF-POSSESSION.

I. One great advantage of self-knowledge is, that it gives a man the truest and most constant self-possession.

A man that is endowed with this excellent knowledge, is calm and easy,—

1. Under affronts and defamation; for he thinks thus: 'I am sure I know myself better than any man can pretend to know me. This calumniator hath, indeed, at this time, missed his mark, and shot his arrows at random; and it is my comfort, that my conscience acquits me of his angry imputation. However, there are worse crimes, which he might more justly accuse me of; which, though hid from him, are known to myself. Let me set about reforming them; lest, if they come to his notice, he should attack me in a more defenceless part, find something to fasten his obloquy, and fix a lasting reproach upon my character

If you are told that another reviles you, do not go about to vindicate yourself, but reply thus: 'My other faults, I find are hid from him, else I should have heard of them too.'

There is a great deal of true and good sense in that common saying and doctrine of the stoics, though they might carry it too far, 'That it is not things, but thoughts, that disturb and hurt us.' 'It is not things, but men's opinion of things, that disturb them.' 'Remember, it is not he that reviles or assaults you, that injures you; but your thinking that they have injured you.' 'No man can hurt you, unless you please to let him; then only are you hurt, when you think yourself so.' Epict. Ench.

'Things do not touch the mind, but stand quietly without; the vexation comes from within, from our suspicions only.' Again, 'Things themselves cannot affect the mind; for they have no entrance into it, to turn and move it; it is the mind alone that turns and moves itself.' Marc. Anton. Med.

Now, as self-acquaintance teaches a man the right government of the thoughts, (as is shown above, part 1. chap. xiv.) it will help him to expel all anxious, tormenting, and fruitless thoughts, and retain the most quieting and useful ones; and so keep all easy within. Let a man but try the experiment, and he will find, that a little resolution will make the greatest part of the difficulty vanish.

2. Self-knowledge will be a good ballast to the mind, under any accidental hurry or disorder of the passions. It curbs their impetuosity; puts the reins into the hands of reason; quells the rising storm, ere it makes shipwreck of the conscience; and teaches a man, to 'leave off contention, before it be meddled with,' (Prov. xvii. 14.); it being much safer to keep the lion chained, than to encounter it in its full strength and fury. And thus will a wise man, for his own peace, deal with the passions of others as well as his own.

Self-knowledge, as it acquaints a man with his weaknesses and worst qualities, will be his guard against them, and a happy counterbalance to the faults and excesses of his natural temper.

3. It will keep the mind sedate and calm, under the surprise of bad news, or afflicting providences.

'For am I not a creature of god? And my life and comforts are they not wholly at his dispose, from whom I have received them; and by whose favor I have so long enjoyed them; and by whose mercy and goodness I have still so many left?

'A heathen can teach me, under such losses of friends or estate, or any comfort, to direct my eyes to the hand of god, by whom it was lent me, and is now recalled; that I ought not to say it is lost, but restored. And though I be injuriously deprived of it, still the hand of god is to be acknowledged; for what is it to me, by what means he, who gave me that blessing, takes it from me again?'

He that rightly knows himself, will live every day dependent on the divine author of his mercies, for the continuance and enjoyment of them; and will learn, from a higher authority than that of a heathen moralist, that he hath nothing he can call his own, or ought to depend upon as such; that he is but a steward employed to dispense the good things he possesses according to the direction of his lord, at whose pleasure he holds them; and to whom he should be ready, at any time, cheerfully to resign them. Luke xvi. 1.

4. Self-knowledge will help a man to preserve an equanimity and self-possession, under all the various scenes of adversity and prosperity.

Both have their temptations; to some the temptations of prosperity are the greatest; to others, those of adversity. Self-knowledge shows a man which of these are greatest to him; and, at the apprehension, of them, teaches him to arm himself accordingly; that nothing may deprive him of his constancy and self-possession, to lead him to act unbecoming the man, or the Christian.

We commonly say, no one knows what he can bear, till he is tried. And many persons verify the observation, by bearing evils much better than they feared. Nay, the apprehension of an approaching evil often gives a man a greater pain than the evil itself. This is owing to inexperience and self-ignorance.

A man that knows himself, his own strength and weakness, is not so subject as others to the melancholy presages of the imagination; and whenever they intrude, he makes no other use of them, than to take the warning, collect himself, and prepare for the coming evil; leaving the degree, duration, and the issue of it with him, who is the sovereign disposer of all events, in a quiet dependence on his power, wisdom and goodness.

Such self-possession is one great effect and advantage of self knowledge.

CHAPTER II.

SELF-KNOWLEDGE LEADS TO A WISE AND STEADY CONDUCT.

II. As self-knowledge will keep a man calm and equal in his temper, so it will make him wise and cautious in his couduct.

A precipitant and rash conduct is ever the effect of a confused and irregular hurry of thought; so, that when, by the influence of self-knoledge, the thoughts become cool, sedate, and rational, the conduct will be so too. It will give a man that even, steady, uniform behavior, in the management of his affairs, that is so necessary for the despatch of business; and prevent many disappointments and troubles, which arise from the unsuccessful execution of immature, or ill-judged projects.

In short most of the troubles which men meet with in the world, may be traced up to this source, and resolved into self-ignorance. We may complain of providence, and complain of men; but the fault, if we examine it, will commonly be found to be our own. Our imprudence, which arises from self-ignorance, either brings our troubles upon us, or increases them. Want of temper and conduct will make any affliction double.

What a long train of difficulties do sometimes proceed from one wrong step in our conduct, into which self-ignorance or inconsideration betrays us! And every evil that befalls us, in consequence of that, we are to charge upon ourselves.

CHAPTER III.

HUMILITY THE EFFECT OF SELF-KNOWLEDGE.

III. True self knowledge always produces humility.

Pride is ever the offspring of self-ignorance. The reason men are vain and self-sufficient is, because they do not know their own failings; and the reason they are not better acquainted with them is, because they hate self-inspection. Let a man but turn his eyes within scrutinize himself, and study his own heart, and he will soon see enough to make him humble. 'Behold, I am vile,' (Job xi. 4.) is the language only of self-knowledge.

Whence is it that young people are generally so vain, self-sufficient, and assured, but because they have taken no time or pains to cultivate a self-acquaintance? And why does pride and stiffness appear so often in advanced age but because men grow old in self-ignorance? A moderate degree of self-knowledge would cure an inordinate degree of self-complacency.

Humility is not more necessary to salvation, than self-knowledge to humanity.

It would effectually prevent that bad disposition which is too apt to steal upon and infect some of the best human minds, especially those who aim at singular and exalted degrees of piety ; viz. a religious vanity, or spiritual pride ; which, without a good deal of self-knowledge and self-attention, will gradually insinuate into the heart, taint the mind, and sophisticate our virtues, before we are aware : and, in proportion to its prevalence, make the Christian temper degenerate into the pharisaical.

'Might I be allowed to choose my own lot, I should think it much more eligible to want my spiritual comforts, than to abound in these, at the expense of my humility. No, let a penitent and a contrite spirit be always my portion ; and may I ever so be the favorite of heaven, as never to forget, that I am chief of sinners. Knowledge in the sublime and glorious mysteries of the Christian faith, and ravishing contemplations of god and a future state, are most desirable advantages ; but still I prefer charity, which edifieth, before the highest intellectual perfections of that knowledge which puffeth up. 1 Cor. viii. 1. Those spiritual advantages are certainly best for us, which increase our modesty and awaken our caution and dispose us to suspect and deny ourselves. The highest in god's esteem are meanest in their own : and their excellency consists in the meekness, and truth, not in the pomp and ostentation of piety, which affects to be seen and admired of men. Stanhope's Thom. a Kemp. b. 2. chap. xi.

Christ. 'My son, when thou feelest thy soul warmed with devotion and holy zeal for my service, it will be adviseable to decline all those methods of publishing it to the world, which vain men are so industrious to take ; and content thyself with its being known to god and thy own conscience. Rather endeavor to moderate and suppress those pompous expressions of it, in which some place the very perfection of zeal. Think meanly of thy own virtues. Some, of a bold ungoverned zeal, aspire at things beyond their strength, and express more vehemence than conduct in their actions. They are perfectly carried out of themselves with eagerness ; forget that they are still poor insects upon earth, and think of nothing less than building their nests in heaven. Now these are often left to themselves, and taught, by sad experience, that the faint flutterings of men are weak and ineffectual ; and that none soars to heaven, except I assist his flight, and mount him on my own wings. Virtue does not consist in abundance of illumination and knowledge ; but in lowliness of mind, in meekness, and chastity ; in a mind entirely resigned to god, and sincerely disposed to serve and please him ; in a just sense of every man's vileness ; and not only thinking very meanly of one's-self, but being well content to be so thought of by others.'—Id. book 3. chap. viii.

'It is a dangerous drunkenness, I confess, that of wine ; but there is another more dangerous. How many souls do I see in the world drunk with vanity, and a high opinion of themselves ? This drunkenness causes them to make a thousand false steps, and a thousand stumbles. Their ways are all oblique and crooked. Like men in drink, they have always a great opinion of their own wisdom, their power, and their prudence ; all which often fail them. Examine well thyself, my soul ; see if thou art not tainted with this evil. Alas ! if thou deniest it, thou provest it. It is great pride to think one has no pride ; for it is to think you are as good, indeed, as you esteem yourself. But there is no man in the world but esteems himself better than he truly is.

'Thou wilt say, it may be, thou hast a very ill opinion of thyself. But be assured, my soul, thou dost not despise thyself so much as thou art truly despicable. If thou dost despise thyself, indeed, thou makest a merit of that very thing ; so that pride is attached to this very contempt of thyself.'—Jurieu's Method of Devotion, page 8. chap x.

C c

CHAPTER IV.

CHARITY ANOTHER EFFECT OF SELF-KNOWLEDGE.

IV. Self-knowledge greatly promotes a spirit of meekness and charity.

The more a man is acquainted with his own failings, the more he is disposed to make allowances for those of others. The knowledge he hath of himself will incline him to be as severe in his animadversions on his conduct, as he is on that of others ; and as candid to their faults, as to his own.

There is an uncommon beauty, force, and propriety, in that caution which our saviour gives us : 'And why beholdest thou the mote that is in thy brother's eye, but considerest not the beam that is in thine own eye ? Or how wilt thou say to thy brother, let me pull out the mote out of thine eye, and behold a beam is in thine own eye? Thou hypocrite, first cast the beam out of thine own eye, and then shalt thou see clearly to cast out the mote out of thy brother's eye,' Mat. vii. 3—5. In which words these four things are plainly intimated. 1. That some are much more quick sighted to discern the faults and blemishes of others than their own : can spy a mote in another's eye sooner than a beam in their own. 2. That they are often the most forward to correct and cure the foibles of others, who are most unqualified for that office. The beam in their own eye makes them altogether unfit to pull out the mote from their brother's. A man half blind himself should never set up for an oculist. 3. They who are inclined to deal in censure, should always begin at home. 4 Great censoriousness is great hypocrisy. 'Thou hypocrite,' &c. all this is nothing but the effect of woful self-ignorance.

This common failing of the human nature, the heathens were very sensible of, and imagined it in the following manner : Every man, say they, carries a wallet, or two bags, with him ; the one hanging before him, and the other behind him ; into that before, he puts the faults of others ; into that behind, his own. By which means, he never sees his own failings, whilst he has those of others always before his eyes.

But self-knowledge now helps us to turn this wallet, and place that which hath our own faults, before our eyes, and that which hath in it those of others, behind our back. A very necessary regulation this, if we would behold our own faults in the same light in which they do. For we must not expect that others will be as blind to our foibles, as we ourselves are : they will carry them before their eyes, whether we do or no. And to imagine that the world takes no notice of them, because we do not, is just as wise as to fancy, that others do not see us, because we shut our eyes.

CHAPTER V.

MODERATION, THE EFFECT OF SELF-KNOWLEDGE.

V. Another genuine offspring of self-knowledge, is moderation.

This, indeed, can hardly be conceived to be separate from that meekness and charity before mentioned ; but I choose to give it a distinct mention, because I consider it under a different view and operation ; viz , as that which guards and influences our spirits, in all matters of debate and controversy.

Moderation is a great and important Christian virtue, very different from that bad quality of the mind under which it is often misrepresented and disguised ; viz. lukewarmness and indifference about the truth. The former is very consistent with a regular and well corrected zeal ; the latter consists in the total want of it : the former is sensible of, and endeavors, with peace and prudence, to maintain the dignity and importance of divine doctrines ; the latter hath no manner of concern about them : the one feels the secret influences of them ; the other is quite a stranger to their power and efficacy : the one laments in secret the sad decay of vital religion ; the other is an instance of it. In short the one proceeds from true knowledge ; the other from great ignorance : the one is a good mark of sincerity, and the other a certain sign of hypocrisy. And to confound two things together, which are so essentially different, can be the effect of nothing but great ignorance, or inconsideration, or an over-heated injudicious zeal.

A self-knowing man can easily distinguish between these two. And the knowledge which he has of human nature in general, from a thorough contemplation of his own in particular, shows him the necessity of preserving a medium (as in every thing else, so especially) between the two extremes, of a bigoted zeal, on the one hand, and indolent lukewarmness, on the other. As he will not look upon every thing to be worth contending for, so, he will look upon nothing worth losing his temper for in the contention. Because, though the truth be of ever so great importance, nothing can do a greater disservice to it, or make a man more incapable of defending it, than intemperate heat and passion ; whereby he injures and betrays the cause he is ever anxious to maintain. 'The wrath of man worketh not the righteousness of god.' James i. 20.

Self-knowledge heals our animosities, and greatly cools our debates about matters of dark and doubtful speculation. One who knows himself, sets too great a value upon his time and temper, to plunge rashly into those vain and fruitless controversies, in which one of them is sure to be lost, and the other is in great danger of being so ; especially when a man of bad temper and bad principles is the opponent : who aims rather to silence his adversary with overbearing confidence, dark unmeaning language, authoritative airs, and hard words, than convince him with solid argument ; and who plainly contends, not for truth, but victory. Little good can be done to the best cause, in such a circumstance ; and a wise and moderate man who knows human nature, and knows himself, will rather give his antagonist the pleasure of imaginary triumph, than engage in so unequal a combat.

An eagerness and zeal for dispute, on every subject, and with every one, shows great self-sufficiency ; that never failing sign of great self-ignorance : and true moderation, which creates an indifference to little things, and a wise and well proportioned zeal for things of importance, can proceed from nothing but true knowledge, which has its foundation in self-acquaintance.

CHAPTER VI.

SELF-KNOWLEDGE IMPROVES THE JUDGMENT.

VI. Another great advantage of being well acquainted with ourselves is, that it helps us to form a better judgment of other things.

Self-knowledge, indeed, does not enlarge or increase our natural capacities, but it guides and regulates them ; leads us to the right use and application of them : and removes a great many things which obstruct their due exercise ; as pride, prejudice, and passion, &c. which oftentimes so miserably pervert the rational powers.

He that hath taken a just measure of himself, is thereby better able to judge of other things.

1. He knows how to judge of men and human nature better ;—for human nature, setting aside the difference of natural genius, and the improvements of education and religion, is pretty much the same in all. There are the same passions and appetites, the same natural infirmities and inclinations, in all mankind ; though some are more predominant and distintinguishable in some, than they are in others. So that, if a man be but well acquainted with his own, this, together with a very little observation on human life, will soon discover to him those of other men ; and show him, very impartially, their particular failings and excellencies ; and help him to form a much truer sentiment of them, than if he were to judge only by their exterior—the appearance they make in the eye of the world, or the character given of them by others ; both which are often very fallacious.

2. Self-knowledge will teach us to judge rightly of facts, as well as men. It will exhibit things to the mind in a proper light, and true colors, without those false glosses and appearances which fancy throws upon them, or in which the imagination often paints them. It will teach us to judge, not with the imagination, but with the understanding ; and will set a guard upon the former, which so often represents things in wrong views, and gives the mind false impressions.—See Part 1. chap. iv.

3. It helps us to estimate the true value of all worldly good things. It rectifies our notions of them, and lessens that enormous esteem we are apt to have for them. For when a man knows himself, and his true interests, he will see how far, and in what degree, these things are suitable to him, and subservient to his good ; and how far they are unsuitable, ensnaring, and pernicious. This, and not the common opinion of the world, will be his rule of judgment concerning them. By this he will see quite through them ; see what they really are at bottom ; and how far a wise man ought to desire them. The reason why men value them so extravagantly, is because they take but a superficial view of them, and only look upon their outside, where they are most showy and inviting. Were they to look within them, consider their intrinsic worth, their ordinary effects, their tendency, and their end, they would not be so apt to over-value them. And a man that has learned to see through himself, can easily see through these. Riches, honors, power, and the like, which owe all their worth to our false opinion of them, are too apt to draw the heart from from virtue. We know not how to prize them ; they are not to be judged of by the common vogue, but by their nature. They have nothing to attract our esteem, but that we are used to admire them ; they are not cried up, because they are things that ought to be desired ; but they are desired, because they are generally cried up.

CHAPTER VII.

SELF-KNOWLEDGE DIRECTS TO THE PROPER EXERCISE OF SELF-DENIAL

VII. A man that knows himself best, knows how, and wherein, he ought to deny himself.

The great duty of self-denial, which our saviour so expressly requires of all his followers, plain and necessary as it is, has been much mistaken and abused ; and that not only by the church of Rome, in its doctrines of penance, fasts, and pilgrimages ; but by some Protestant Christians, in the instances of voluntary abstinence, and unnecessary austerities ; whence they are sometimes apt to be too censorious against those who indulge themselves in the use of those indifferent things, which they make it a point of conscience to abstain from. Whereas, would they confine their exercise of self-denial to the plain and important points of practice, devoutly performing the necessary duties they are most averse to, and resolutely avoiding the known sins they are most inclined to, under the direction of scripture; they would soon become more solid, judicious, and exemplary Christians; and did they know themselves, they would easily see, that herein there is occasion and scope enough for self-denial; and that to a degree of greater severity and difficulty, than there is in those little corporeal abstinences and mortifications they enjoin themselves.

1. Self-knowledge will direct us to the necessary exercises of self-denial, with regard to the duties our tempers are most averse to.

There is no one but, at some times, finds a great backwardness and indisposition to some duties, which he knows to be seasonable and necessary. This, then, is a proper occasion for self-discipline. For, to indulge this indisposition, is very dangerous, and leads to an habitual neglect of known duty; and to resist and oppose it, and to prepare for a diligent and faithful discharge of the duty, notwithstanding the many pleas and excuses that carnal disposition may urge for the neglect of it, this requires no small pains and self-denial; and yet it is very necessary to the peace of conscience.

And for our encouragement to this piece of self-denial, we need only remember, that the difficulty of the duty, and our unfitness for it, will, upon the trial, be found to be much less than we apprehended. And the pleasure of reflecting, that we have discharged our consciences, and given a fresh testimony of our uprightness, will more than compensate the pains and difficulty we found therein. And the oftener these criminal propensions, to the willful neglect of duty, are opposed and conquered, the seldomer they will return, or the weaker they will grow; till at last, by divine grace, they will be wholly overcome; and in the room of them will succeed an habitual 'readiness to every good work,' (Tit. iii. 1.) and a very sensible delight therein: a much happier effect than can be expected from the severest exercises of self-denial, in the instances before mentioned.

2. A man that knows himself will see an equal necessity for self-denial, in order to check and control his inclinations to sinful actions; to subdue the rebel within; to resist the solicitations of sense and appetite; to summon all his wisdom to avoid the occasions and temptations to sin, and all his strength to oppose it.

All this, especially if it be a favorite constitutional iniquity, will cost a man pains and mortification enough. For instance, the subduing a violent passion, or taming a sensual inclination, or forgiving an apparent injury and affront. It is evident, such a self-conquest can never be attained without much self-knowledge and self-denial.

And that self-denial that is exercised this way, as it will be a better evidence of our sincerity, so it will be more helpful and ornamental to the interests of religion, than the greatest zeal in those particular duties which are most suitable to our natural tempers, or than the greatest austerities in some particular instances of mortification, which are not so necessary, and perhaps not so difficult or disagreeable to us as this.

To what amazing heights of piety may some be thought to mount, raised on the wings of a flaming zeal, and distinguished by uncommon preciseness and severity about little things, who all the while, perhaps, cannot govern one passion, and appear yet ignorant of, and slaves to, their daring iniquity! Through an ignorance of themselves, they misapply their zeal, and misplace their self-denial; and by that means blemish their characters with a visible inconsistency.

CHAPTER VIII.

SELF-KNOWLEDGE PROMOTES OUR USEFULNESS IN THE WORLD.

VIII. The more we know of ourselves, the more useful we are like to be in those stations of life, in which providence has fixed us.

When we know our proper talents and capacities, we know in what manner we are capable of being useful; and the consideration of our characters and relations in life will direct us to the proper application of these talents; show us to what ends they were given us, and to what purposes they ought to be improved.

'Many of those who set up for wits, and pretend to a more than ordinary sagacity and delicacy of sense, do, notwithstanding, spend their time unaccountably; and live away whole days, weeks, and sometimes months together, to as little purpose, though it may be not so innocently, as if they had been asleep all the while. But if their parts be so good as they would have others believe, sure they are worth improving; if not, they have the more need of it. Greatness of parts is so far from being a discharge from industry, that I find men of the most exquisite sense, in all ages, were always most curious of their time. And, therefore, I very much suspect the excellency of those men's parts, who are dissolute and careless mis-spenders of it.

It is a sad thing to observe how miserably some men debase and prostitute their capacities. Those gifts and indulgences of nature, by which they outshine many others, and by which they are capable of doing real service to the cause of virtue and religion, and of being eminently useful to mankind, they either entirely neglect, or shamefully abuse, to the dishonor of god, and the prejudice of their fellow creatures, by encouraging and emboldening them in the ways of vice and vanity: for the false glare of a profane wit will sometimes make such strong impressions on a weak unsettled mind, as to overbear the principles of reason and wisdom, and give it too favorable sentiments of what it before abhorred: whereas, the same force and sprightliness of genius would have been very happily and usefully employed in putting sin out of countenance, and in rallying the follies, and exposing the inconsistencies, of a vicious and profligate character.

'The more talents and abilities men are blessed with, the more pains they ought to take.' This is Chrysostom's observation. And the reason is obvious; because they have more to answer for than other men: which I take to be a better reason than what is assigned by his father; viz. because they have more to lose.

When a man once knows where his strength lies, wherein he excels, or is capable of excelling, how far his influence extends, and in what station of life providence hath fixed him, and the duties of that station, he then knows what talents he ought to cultivate, in what manner, and to what objects they are to be particularly directed and applied, in order to shine in that station, and be useful in it. This will keep him even and steady in his pursuits and views, consistent with himself, uniform in his conduct, and useful to mankind; and will prevent his shooting at a wrong mark, or missing the right one he aims at; as thousands do, for want of this necessary branch of self-knowledge. See part 1. chap. v.

CHAPTER IX

SELF-KNOWLEDGE LEADS TO A DECORUM AND CONSISTENCY OF CHARACTER.

IX. A man that knows himself knows how to act

with discretion and dignity in every station and character.

Almost all the ridicule we see in the world takes its rise from self-ignorance : and to this, mankind, by common assent, ascribe it, when they say of a person that acts out of character, he does not know himself. Affectation is the spring of all ridicule, and self-ignorance the true source of affectation. A man that does not know his proper character, nor what becomes it, cannot act suitably to it. He will often affect a character that does not belong to him ; and will either act above or beneath himself ; which will make him equally contemptible in the eyes of them that know him.

A man of superior rank and character, that knows himself, knows that he is but a man ; subject to the same sickness, frailties, disappointments, pains, passions, and sorrows, as other men ; that true honor lies in those things in which it is possible for the meanest peasant to excel him ; and therefore he will not be vainly arrogant. He knows that they are only transitory and accidental things that set him above the rest of mankind ; that he will soon be upon a level with them ; and therefore learns to condescend : and there is a dignity in this condescension ; it does not sink, but exalts his reputation and character.

A man of inferior rank, that knows himself, knows how to be content, quiet, and thankful, in his lower sphere. As he has not an extravagant veneration and esteem for those external things which raise one man's circumstances so much above another's, so he does not look upon himself as the worse or less valuable man, purely because he has them not ; much less does he envy them that have them. As he has not their advantages, so neither has he their temptations ; he is in that state of life which the great arbiter and disposer of all things hath allotted him ; and he is satisfied : but as deference is owing to external superiority, he knows how to pay a proper respect to those that are above him, without that abject and servile cringing, which discovers an inordinate esteem for their condition. As he does not over-esteem them for those little accidental advantages in which they excel him, so neither does he over-value himself for those things in which he excels others.

Were hearers to know themselves, they would not take upon them to dictate to their preachers, or teach their ministers how to teach them, (which, as St Austin observes, is the same thing, as if a patient, when he sends for a physician, should prescribe to him what he would have him prescribe,) but if they happen to hear something not quite agreeable to their former sentiments, would betake themselves more diligently to the study of their bibles, to know 'whether those things were so.' Acts xvii. 11.

And were ministers to know themselves, they would know the nature and duty of their office, and the wants and infirmities of their hearers, better than to domineer over their faith, or shoot over their heads, and seek their own popularity, rather than their benefit. They would be more solicitous for their edification, than their approbation (the most palatable food is not always the most wholesome ;) and, like a faithful physician, would earnestly intend and endeavor their good, though it be in a way they may not like ; and rather risk their own characters with weak and captious men, than withhold any thing that is needful for them, or be unfaithful to god and their own consciences. Patients must not expect to be always pleased, nor physicians to be always applauded.

CHAPTER X.

PIETY THE EFFECT OF SELF-KNOWLEDGE.

X. Self-knowledge tends greatly to cultivate a spirit of true piety.

Ignorance is so far from being the mother of devotion, that nothing is more destructive of it ; and, of all ignorance, none is a greater bane to it than self-ignorance. This, indeed, is very consistent with superstition, bigotry, and enthusiasm ; those common counterfeits of piety, which, by weak and credulous minds, are often mistaken for it. But true piety and real devotion can only spring from a just knowledge of god and ourselves ; and the relation we stand in to him, and the dependence we have upon him. For when we consider ourselves as the creatures of god, whom he made for his honor, and as creatures incapable of any happiness, but what results from his favor ; and as entirely and continually dependent upon him for every thing we have and hope for ; and whilst we bear this thought in our minds, what can induce or prompt us more to love, and fear, and trust him, as our god, our father, and all-sufficient friend and helper ?

CHAPTER XI.

SELF-KNOWLEDGE TEACHES US RIGHTLY TO PERFORM THE DUTIES OF RELIGION.

XI. Self-knowledge will be a good help and direction to us in many of our devout and Christian exercises ; particularly,—

1. In the duty of prayer ; both as to the matter and mode. He that rightly knows himself, will be very sensible of his spiritual wants : and he that is well acquainted with his spiritual wants, will not be at a loss what to pray for.

'Our hearts would be the best prayer-books, if we were skillful in reading them. Why do men pray, and call for prayers when they come to die, but that they begin a little better to know themselves ? And were they now but to hear the voice of god and conscience, they would not remain speechless. But they that are born deaf are always dumb.' Baxter.

Again, self-knowledge will teach us to pray, not only with fluency, but fervency ; will help us also to keep the heart, as well as order our speech, before god ; and so promote the grace as well as gift of prayer. Did we but seriously consider what we are, and what we are about ; whom we pray to, and what we pray for ; it is impossible we should be so dead, spiritless, and formal, in this duty, as we too often are : the very thought would inspire us with life, and faith, and fervor.

2. Self-knowledge will be very helpful to us in the duty of thanksgiving, as it shows us both how suitable and how seasonable the mercies are which we receive. A Christian, that keeps up an intelligence with himself, considers what he hath, as well as what he wants ; and is no less sensible of the value of his mercies, than his unworthiness of them ; and this is what makes him thankful. For this reason it is, that one Christian's heart even melts with gratitude for those very mercies, which others disesteem and depreciate, and perhaps despise, because they have not what they think greater. But a man that knows himself, knows that he deserves nothing, and therefore is thankful for every thing ; for thankfulness as necessarily flows from humility, as humility does from self-acquaintance.

3. In the duties of reading and hearing the word of god, self-knowledge is of excellent use, to enable us to understand and apply that which we read or hear. Did we understand our hearts better, we should understand the word of god better ; for that speaks to the heart. A man that is acquainted with his own heart, presently sees how deeply the divine word penetrates and explores, searches and lays over, its most inward parts : he feels what he reads ; and finds that a quickening spirit, which, to a self-ignorant man, is but a dead letter.

Moreover, this self-acquaintance teaches a man to apply what he reads and hears of the word of god. He sees the pertinence congruity, and suitableness of it to his own case; and lays it up faithfully in the store-room of his mind; to be digested and approved by his after-thoughts. And it is by this art of applying scripture, and urging the most suitable instructions and admonitions of it home upon our consciences, that we receive the greatest benefit by it.

4. Nothing is of more eminent service in the great duty of meditation; especially in that part of it which consists in heart converse. A man who is unacquainted with himself, is as unfit to converse with his heart, as he is with a stranger he never saw, and whose taste and temper he is altogether unacquainted with. He knows not how to get his thoughts about him; and when he has, he knows not how to range and fix them; and hath no more the command of them, than a general has of a wild undisciplined army, that has never been exercised or accustomed to obedience and order. But one, who hath made it the study of his life to be acquainted with himself, is soon disposed to enter into a free and familiar converse with his own heart; and in such a self-conference improves more in true wisdom, and acquires more useful and substantial knowledge, than he could do from the most polite and refined conversation in the world. Of such excellent use is self-knowledge in all the duties of devotion and piety.

CHAPTER XII.

SELF-KNOWLEDGE THE BEST PREPARATION FOR DEATH.

XII. Self-knowledge will be an habitual preparation for death, and a constant guard against the surprise of it; because it fixes and settles our hopes of future happiness. That which makes the thoughts of death so terrifying to the soul, is its utter uncertainty what will become of it after death. Were this uncertainty to be removed, a thousand things would reconcile us to the thoughts of dying. It is this makes us averse to death,—that it translates us to objects we are unacquainted with; and we tremble at the thoughts of those things that are unknown to us. We are naturally afraid of being in the dark; and death is a leap in the dark.

'Distrust and darkness of a future state,
Is that which makes mankind to dread their fate:
Dying is nothing; but 'tis this we fear,
To be, we know not what,—we know not where.'

Now, self-knowledge, in a good degree, dissipates this gloom, and removes this dreadful doubt; for as the word of god hath revealed the certainty of a future state of happiness, which the good man shall enter upon after death, and plainly described the requisite qualifications for it; when, by a long and laborious self-acquaintance, he comes distinctly to discern those qualifications in himself, his hopes of heaven soon raise him above the fens of death: and though he may not be able to form any clear or distinct conception of the nature of that happiness, yet, in general, he is assured that it will be a most exquisite and extensive one, and will contain in it every thing necessary to make it complete; because it will come immediately from god himself. Whereas, they who know what they are, must necessarily be ignorant what they shall be. A man that is all darkness within, can have but a dark prospect forward.

Who expos'd to other's eyes,
Into his own heart never pries,
Death's to him a strange surprise.

O, what would we not give for solid hope in death! Reader! wouldst thou have it, know god and know thyself!

A TREATISE

ON

SELF-KNOWLEDGE.

PART THE THIRD.

SHOWING HOW SELF-KNOWLEDGE IS TO BE ATTAINED.

From what hath been said under the two former parts of the subject, self-knowledge appears to be in itself so excellent, and in its effect so extensively useful and conducive to the happiness of human kind, that nothing need farther be added, by way of motive or inducement, to excite us to make it the great object of our study and pursuit. If we regard our present peace, satisfaction, and usefulness, or our future and everlasting interests, we shall certainly value and prosecute this knowledge above all others; as what will be most ornamental to our characters, and beneficial to our interest, in every state of life, and abundantly recompense all our labor.

Were there need of any farther motives to excite us to this, I might lay open the many dreadful effects of self-ignorance, and show how plainly it appears to be the original spring of all the follies and incongruities we see in the characters of men, and of most of the mortifications and miseries they meet with here. This would soon appear, by only mentioning the reverse of those advantages before specified, which result from self-knowledge; for what is it, but a want of self-knowledge and self-government, that makes us so unsettled and volatile in our dispositions? so subject to transport and excess of passions, in the varying scenes of life? so rash and unguarded in our conduct? so vain and self-sufficient? so sensorious and malignant? so eager and confident? so little useful in the world, in comparison of what we might be? so inconsistent with ourselves? so mistaken in our notions of true religion? so generally indisposed to, or unengaged in the holy duties of it,? and, finally, so unfit for death, and so afraid of dying?—I say, to what is all this owing, but self-ignorance? the first and fruitful source of all this long train of evils: and, indeed, there is scarce any, but what may be traced up to it. In short, it brutifies man, to be ignorant of himself. 'Man that is in honor, and understandeth not,' himself especially 'is as the beasts that perish.' Ps. xlix 20.

'Come home, then, O my wandering, self-neglecting soul; lose not thyself in a wilderness or tumult of impertinent, vain, distracting things. Thy work is nearer thee; the country thou shouldst first survey and travel, is within thee; from which thou must pass to that above thee; when, by losing thyself in this without thee, thou wilt find thyself, before thou art aware, in that below thee. Let the eyes of fools be in the corners of the earth; leave it to men beside themselves, to live as without themselves; do thou, then, keep at home, and mind thine own business. Survey thyself, thine own make and nature, and thou wilt find full employ for all thy most active thoughts. But dost thou delight in the mysteries of nature? Consider well the mystery of thy own. The compendium of all thou studiest is near thee, even within thyself, being the epitome of the world. [Who can sufficiently admire the noble nature of that creature man, who hath in him the mortal and immortal, the rational and irrational, natures united, and so carries about with him the image of the whole creation; whence he is called microcosm, or the little world: for whose sake, so highly is he honored by god, all things are made, both present and future; nay, for whose sake god himself became man! So that it was not unjustly said by Gregory Nessene, that man was the microcosm, and the world without the microcosm.] If either necessity or duty, nature or grace, reason or faith, internal inducements, external impulses, or eternal motives, might determine the subject of thy study and contemplation, thou wouldst call home thy distracted thoughts, and employ them more on thyself and thy god.'—Baxter.

Now, then, let us resolve, that henceforth the study of ourselves shall be the business of our lives; that, by the blessing of god, we may arrive at such a degree of self-knowledge, as may secure to us the excellent benefits before-mentioned. To which end, we should do well to attend diligently to the rules laid down in the following chapters.

CHAPTER I.

SELF-EXAMINATION NECESSARY TO SELF-KNOWLEDGE.

I. The first thing necessary to self-knowledge, is self-inspection.

We must often look into our hearts, if we would know them. They are very deceitful; more than we can imagine, till we have searched, and tried, and watched them well. We may meet with frauds and faithless dealings from men; but, after all, our own hearts are the greatest cheats: and there are none who are in greater danger than ourselves. We must first suspect ourselves, then examine ourselves, then watch ourselves, if we expect ever to know ourselves. How is it possible there should be any self-acquaintance, without self-converse?

Were a man to accustom himself to such self-employment, he need not live 'till thirty, before he suspects himself a fool; or till forty, before he knows it.'

Men could never be so bad as they are, if they did but take a proper care and scope in this business of self-examination: if they did but look backwards to what they were, inwards to what they are, and forwards to what they shall be.

And, as this is the first and most necessary step to self-acquaintance, it may not be amiss to be a little more particular in it. Therefore,

1. This business of self-scrutiny must be performed with great care and diligence, otherwise our hearts will deceive us, even whilst we are examining them. 'When we set ourselves to think, some trifle or other presently interrupts, and draws us off from any profitable recollection. Nay, we ourselves fly out, and are glad to be diverted from a severe examination into our own state; which is sure, if diligently pursued, to present us with objects of shame and sorrow, which will wound our sight, and soon make us weary of this necessary work.'

Do not let us flatter ourselves, then, that this is a mighty easy business. Much pains and care are necessary sometimes to keep the mind intent; and more to keep it impartial; and the difficulty of it is the reason that so many are averse to it, and care not to descend into themselves.

Reader, try the experiment; retire now into thyself, and see if thou canst not strike out some light within, by closely urging such questions as these: 'What am I? for what was I made? and to what end have I been preserved so long, by the favor of my maker? Do I remember, or forget those ends? Have I answered or perverted them? What have I been doing since I came into the world? What is the world or myself the better for my living so many years in it? What is my allowed course of action? Am I sure it will bear the future test? Am I now in that state I shall wish to die in? And, O, my soul! think, and think again, what it is to die! Do not put that most awful event far from thee; nor pass it by with a superficial thought. Canst thou be too well fortified against the terrors of that day? And art thou sure that the props which support thee now will not fail thee then? What hopes hast thou for eternity? Hast thou, indeed, that godly temper, which alone can fit thee for the enjoyment of god? Which world art thou most concerned for? What things do most deeply affect thee? O, my soul! remember thy dignity: think how soon the scene will shift. Why should thou forget that thou art immortal?'

2. This self-excitation and scrutiny must be frequently made. They who have a great deal of important business on their hands should often look over their accounts, and frequently adjust them, lest they should be going backwards, and not know it; and custom will soon take off the difficulty of this duty, and make it delightful.

In our morning retreat, it will be proper to remember, that we cannot preserve throughout the day that calm and even temper we may then be in; that we shall very probably meet with some things to ruffle us; some attack on our weak side. Place a guard there now. Or, however, if no incidents happen to discompose us, our tempers will vary; our thoughts will flow pretty much with our blood; and the dispositions of the mind be a good deal governed by the motions of the animal spirits: our souls will be serene or cloudy, our tempers volatile or phlegmatic, and our inclinations sober or irregular, according to the briskness or sluggishness of the circulation of the animal fluids, whatever may be the natural and immediate cause of that: and therefore we must resolve to avoid all occasions that may raise any dangerous ferments there; which, when once raised, will excite in us very different thoughts and dispositions from those we now have; which, together with the force of a fair opportunity and urgent temptation, may overset our reason and resolution, and betray us into those sinful indulgences, which will wound the conscience, stain the soul, and create bitter remorse in our cooler reflections. Pious thoughts and purposes in the morning will set a guard upon the soul, and fortfy it, under all the temptations of the day.

But such self-inspection, however, should not fail to make part of our evening devotions, when we should review and examine the several actions of the day, the various tempers and dispositions we have been in, and the occasions that excited them. It is an advice worthy of a Christian, though it first dropped from a heathen pen: That before we betake ourselves to rest, we review and examine all the passages of the day, that we may have the comfort of what we have done aright, and may redress what we find to have been amiss, and make the shipwrecks of one day be as marks to direct our course on another. A practice that has been recommended by many of the heathen moralists of the greatest name; as Plutarch, Epictetus, Marcus Antoninus, and particularly Pythagorus, in the verses that go under his name, and are called his Golden Verses; wherein he advises his scholars every night to recollect the passages of the day, and ask themselves these questions:—'Wherein have I transgressed this day? What have I done? What duty have I omitted?' &c.

Seneca recommends the same practice. 'Sectius,' saith he, 'did this. At the close of the day, before he betook himself to rest, he addressed his soul in the following manner:—What evil of thine hast thou cured this day? What vice withstood? In what respect art hou better?' Passion will cease, or become more cool, when it knows every day it is to be thus called to account. What can be more advantageous than this constant custom of searching through the day?—And the same course,' saith Seneca, 'I take myself, and every day sit in judgment on myself: and at even, when all is hush and still, I make a scrutiny into the day; look over my words and actions, and hide nothing from myself; conceal none of my mistakes, through fear; for why should I, when I have it in my power to say thus,—This once I forgive thee; but see thou do so no more? In such a dispute, I was too keen. Do not, for the future, contend with ignorant men; they will not be convinced, because they are unwilling to show their ignorance. Such a one I reproved with too much freedom; whereby I have not reformed, but exasperated him. Remember hereafter to be more mild in your censures; and consider not only whether what you say be true, but whether the person you say it to can bear to hear the truth.' Thus far that excellent moralist.

Let us take a few other specimens of a more pious and Christian turn, from a judicious and devout writer.

'This morning, when I arose, instead of applying myself to god in prayer, (which I generally find it best to do, immediately after a few serious reflections) I gave way to idle musing, to the great disorder of my heart and frame. How often have I suffered, for want of more watchfulness on this occasion! When shall I be wise? I have this day shamefully trifled, almost through the whole of it; was in my bed, when I should have been upon my knees; prayed but coolly in the morning; was strangely off my guard in the business and conversation I was concerned with in the day, particularlarly at;—I indulged in very foolish, sinful, vile thoughts, &c.; I fell in with a strain of conversation too common amongst all sorts; viz. speaking evil of others; taking up a reproach against my neighbor. I have often resolved against this sin, and yet run into it again. How treacherous this wicked heart of mine! I have lost several hours this day, in mere sauntering and idleness. This day I had an instance of my own infirmity, that I was a little surprised at, and I am sure I ought to be humbled for: the behavior of——, from whom I can expect nothing but humor, indiscretion, and folly, strangely ruffled me; and that after I have had warning over and over again. What a poor, impotent, contemptible creature am I! This day I have been kept, in a great measure, from my too frequent failings. I had this day very comfortable assistances from god, upon an occasion not a little trying—what shall I render?'—

3. See that the mind be in the most composed and disengaged frame it can, when you enter upon this business of self-judgment. Choose a time when it is most free from passion, and most at leisure from the cares and affections of life. A judge is not like to bring a cause to a good issue, that is either intoxicated with liquor on the bench, or has his mind distracted with other cares, when he should be intent on the trial. Remember, you sit in judgment upon yourself, and have nothing to do at present, but to sift the evidence which conscience may bring in, either for or against you, in order to pronounce a just sentence; which is of much greater concernment to you at present, than any thing else can be: and therefore it should be transacted with the utmost care, composure, and attention.

4. Beware of partiality, and the influence of self-love, in this weighty business; which, if you do not guard against it, will soon lead you into self-delusion; the consequences of which may be fatal to you. Labor to see yourself as you are; and view things in a just light, and not in that in which you would have them appear. Remember, that the mind is always apt to believe those things which it would have to be true, and backward to credit what it wishes to be false; and this is an influence you will certainly lie under, in this affair of self-judgment.

You need not be much afraid of being too severe upon yourself: your great danger will generally be, of passing a too favorable judgement. A judge ought not, indeed, to be a party concerned; and should have no interest in the person he sits in judgment upon. But this cannot be the case here, as you yourself are both judge and criminal; which shows the danger of pronouncing a too favorable sentence. But remember, your business is only with the evidence and the rule of judgment; and that, however you come off now, there will be a re-hearing in another court, where judgment will be according to truth.

'However, look not uneqally, either at the good or evil that is in you; but view them as they are. If you observe only the good that is in you, and overlook the bad; or search only after your faults, and overlook your graces, neither of these will bring you to a true acquaintance with yourself.' Baxter.

And to induce you to this impartiality, remember, that this business (though it may be hid from the world) is not done in secret: god sees how you manage it, before whose tribunal you must expect a righteous judgment. 'We should order our thoughts so,' saith Seneca, 'as if we had a window in our breasts, through which any one might see what passes there: and indeed there is one that does. For what does it signify that our thoughts are hid from men? From god, nothing is hid.'

5. Beware of false rules of judgment. This is a sure and common way to self-deception: e. g. some judge of themselves by what they have been. But it does not follow, if men are not so bad as they have been, that therefore they are as good as they should be. It is wrong to make our past conduct implicitly the measure of our present; or our present the rule of our future; when our past, present, and future conduct, must be all brought to another rule. And they who thus 'measure themselves by themselves, and compare themselves with themselves, are not wise.' (2 Cor. x. 12.) Again, others are apt to judge of themselves by the opinions of men; which is the most uncertain rule that can be: for in that very opinion of theirs, you may be deceived. How do you know they have really formed so good an idea of you as they profess? But, if they have, may not others have formed as bad? And why should not the judgment of these be your rule, as well as the opinion of those? Appeal to self-flattery for an answer. However, neither one nor the other of them, perhaps, appear even to know themselves; and how should they know you? How is it possible they should have opportunities of knowing you better than you know yourself? A man can never gain a right knowledge of himself from the opinion of others, which is so various, and generally so ill-founded; for men commonly judge by outward appearances, or inward prejudice; and therefore, for the most part, think and speak of us very much at random.

Again, others are for judging themselves by the conduct of their superiors, who have opportunities and advantages of knowing, acting, and being better: and yet, without vanity be it spoken,' say they, 'we are not behind hand with them.' But what then? Neither they, nor you, perhaps, are what the obligations of your character indispensably require you to be, and what you must be, ere you can be happy. But consider how easily this argument may be retorted. You are better than some, you say, who have greater opportunities and advantages of being good than you have; and therefore your state is safe. But you yourself have greater opportunities and advantages of being good than some others have, who are, nevertheless, better than you; and therefore, by the same rule, your state cannot be safe. Again, others judge of themselves by the common maxims of the vulgar world, concerning honor and honesty, virtue and interest; which maxims, though generally very corrupt, and very contrary to those of reason, conscience, and scripture, men will follow as a rule, for the sake of the latitude it allows them: and fondly think, that if they stand right in the opinion of the lowest kind of men, they have no reason to be severe upon themselves. Others, whose sentiments are more delicate and refined, they imagine, may be mistaken, or may overstrain the matter. In which persuasion they are confirmed, by observing how seldom the consciences of the generality of men smite them for those things which these nice judges condemn as heinous crimes. I need not say how false and pernicious a rule this is. Again, others may judge of themselves and their state, by sudden impressions they have had, or strong impulses upon their spirits, which they attribute to the finger of god; and by which they have been so exceedingly affected, as to make no doubt but that it was the instant of their conversation. But whether it was or not, can never be known but by the conduct of their after lives. In like manner, others judge of their good state by their good frames; though very rare it may be, and very transient; soon passing off, like a morning cloud, or as the early dew. 'But we should not judge of ourselves by that which is unusual or extraordinary with us; but by the ordinary tenor and drift of our lives. A bad man may seem good, in some good mood; and a good man may seem bad, in some extraordinary falls. To judge of a bad man by his best hours, and a good man by his worst, is the way to be deceived in them both.' And the same way may you be deceived in yourself. Pharaoh, Ahab, Herod, and Felix, had all of them their softenings, their transitory fits of goodness; but yet they remain upon record under the blackest characters.

These, then, are all wrong rules of judgment; and to trust to them, or try ourselves by them, leads to fatal self-deception. Again,

6. In the business of self-examination, you must not only take care you do not judge by wrong rules, but that you do not judge wrong by right rules. You must endeavor, then, to be well acquainted with them. The office of judge is not only to collect the evidence and the circumstances of facts, but to be well skilled in the laws by which those facts are to be examined.

Now, the only right rules by which we are to examine, in order to know ourselves, are reason and scripture. Some are for setting aside these rules, as too severe for them; too stiff to bend to their perverseness; too straight to measure their crooked ways: are against reason, when reason is against them; decrying it as carnal reason: and against scripture, when scripture is against them; depreciating it as a dead letter. And thus, rather than be convinced they are wrong, they reject the only means that can set them right.

And, as some are for setting aside these rules, so, others are for setting them one against the other,—reason against scripture, and scripture against reason—when they are both given us by the god of our natures, not only as perfectly consistent, but as proper to explain and illustrate each other, and prevent our mistaking either; and to be, when taken together as they always should be, the most complete and only rule by which to judge both of ourselves, and every thing belonging to our salvation, as reasonable and fallen creatures.

1. Then one part of that rule which god hath given us to judge of ourselves by, is right reason; by which I do not mean the reasoning of any particular man, which may be very different from the reasoning of another particular man; and both, it may be, very different from right reason; because both may be influenced, not so much by the reason and nature of things, as by partial prepossessions, and the power of passions; but, by right reason, I mean those common principles, which are readily allowed by all who are capable of understanding them, and not notoriously perverted by the force of prejudice; and which are confirmed by the common consent of all the sober and thinking part of mankind; and may be easily learned by the light of nature. Therefore, if any doctrine or practice, though supposed to be founded in, or countenanced by, revelation, be nevertheless apparently repugnant to these dictates of right reason, or evidently contradict our natural notions of the divine attributes, or weaken our obligations to universal virtue, that, we may be sure, is no part of revelation; because then one part of our rule would clash with, and be opposite, to the other. And thus reason was designed to be our guard against a wild and extravagant construction of scripture.

2. The other part of our rule is the sacred scriptures, which we are to use as our guard against the licentious excursions of fancy, which is often imposing itself upon us for right reason. Let any religious scheme or notion, then, appear ever so pleasing or plausible, if it be not established on the plain principle of scripture it is forthwith to be discarded; and the sense of scripture, that is violently forced to bend towards it, is very much to be suspected.

It must be very surprising, to one who reads and studies the sacred scriptures with a free unbiased mind, to see what elaborate, fine-spun flimsy glosses men will invent and put upon some texts as the true and genuine sense of them, for no other reason, but because it is most agreeable to the opinion of their party; from which, as the standard of their orthodoxy, they durst never depart; who, if they were to write a critique in the same manner, on any Greek or Latin author, would make themselves extremely ridiculous in the eyes of the learned world. But, if we would not pervert our rule, we must learn to think as scripture speaks, and not compel that to speak as we think.

Would we know ourselves, then, we must often view ourselves in the glass of god's word. And when we have taken a full survey of ourselves from thence, let us not soon forget 'what manner of persons we are. Jam. i. 23, 24. If our own image do not please us, let us not quarrel with our mirror, but set about mending ourselves.

The eye of the mind, indeed, is not like that of the body, which can see every thing else but itself, for the eye of the mind can turn itself inward, and survey itself. However, it must be owned, it can see itself, much better when its own image is reflected upon it from this mirror: and it is by this only that we can come at the bottom of our hearts, and discover those secret prejudices, and carnal prepossessions, which self-love would hide from us.

This, then, is the first thing we must do, in order to self-knowledge. We must examine, scrutinize, and judge ourselves, diligently, leisurely, frequently, and impartially: and that not by the false maxims of the world, but by the rules which god hath given us,—reason and scripture; and take care to understand those rules, and not set them at variance.

CHAPTER II.

CONSTANT WATCHFULNESS NECESSARY TO SELF-KNOWLEDGE.

II. Would we know ourselves we must be very watchful over our hearts and lives.

1. We must keep a vigilant eye upon our hearts; i. e. our tempers, inclinations, and passions. A more necessary piece of advice, in order to self-acquaintance, there cannot be, than that which Solomon gives us. (Prov. iv. 23): 'Keep your heart with all diligence,' or as it is in the original 'above all keeping.' Q D. Whatever you neglect or overlook, be sure you mind your heart.' 'Look within; for within is the fountain

of good' Narrowly observe all its inclinations and aversions, all its motions and affections, together with the several objects and occasions which excite them. And this precept we find in scripture enforced with two very urgent reasons. The first is, because 'out of it are the issues of life;' i. e. as our heart is, so will the tenor of our life and conduct be. As is the fountain, so are the streams; as is the root, so is the fruit. (Matt. vii. 18.) And the other is, 'because it is deceitful above all things.' (Jer. xvii. 9.) And therefore without a constant guard upon it, we shall insensibly run into many hurtful self-deceptions. To which I may add, that, without this careful keeping of the heart, we shall never be able to acquire any considerable degree of self-acquaintance, or self-government.

2. To know ourselves, we must watch our life and conduct, as well as our hearts; and by this the heart will be better known, as the root is best known by the fruit. We must attend to the nature and consequences of every action we are disposed or solicited to, before we comply; and consider how it will appear in a future review. We are apt enough to observe and watch the conduct of others; a wise man will be as critical and as severe upon his own; for, indeed, we have a great deal more to do with our own conduct than that of other men: as we are to answer for our own, but not for theirs. By observing the conduct of other men, we know them; by carefully observing our own, we must know ourselves.

CHAPTER III.

WE SHOULD HAVE SOME REGARD TO THE OPINIONS OF OTHERS CONCERNING US, PARTICULARLY OF OUR ENEMIES.

III. Would we know ourselves, we should not altogether neglect the opinions which others may entertain concerning us.

Not that we need be very solicitous about the censure or applause of the world, which generally are very rash and wrong; and proceed from the particular humors and prepossessions of men: and he that knows himself, will soon know how to despise them both. 'The judgment which the world makes of us, is generally of no manner of use to us; it adds nothing to our souls or bodies, nor lessens any of our miseries. Let us constantly follow reason,' says Montaigne, 'and let the public approbation follow us the same way, if it pleases.'

But still, I say, a total indifference in this matter is unwise. We ought not to be entirely insensible of the reports of others; no, not to the railings of an enemy: for an enemy may say some things out of ill-will to us, which it may concern us to think of coolly, when we are by ourselves; to examine whether the accusation be just; and what there is in our conduct and temper which may make it appear so: and by this means, our enemy may do us more good than he intended; and discover to us something in our hearts which we did not before advert to. A man that hath no enemies, ought to have very faithful friends; and one who hath no such friends, ought to think it no calamity that he hath enemies to be his effectual monitors. 'Our friends, says Mr Addison, very often flatter us as much as our own hearts. They either do not see our faults, or conceal them from us; or soften them by their representations, after such a manner, that we think them too trivial to be taken notice of. An adversary, on the contrary, makes a stricter search into us, discovers every flaw and imperfection in our tempers; and though his malice may set them in too strong a light, it has generally some ground for what it advances A friend exaggerates a man's virtues; an enemy inflames his crimes. A wise man should give a just attention to both of them, so far as it may tend to the improvement of the one, and the diminution of the other. Plutarch has written an essay on the benefits which a man may receive from his enemies; and, among the good fruits of enmity, mentions this, in particular,—That by the reproaches it casts upon us, we see the worst side of ourselves, and open our eyes to several blemishes and defects in our lives and conversations, which we should not have observed, without the help of such ill-natured monitors.

'In order, likewise, to come at a true knowledge of ourselves, we should consider, on the other hand, how far we may deserve the praises and approbations which the world bestow upon us; whether the actions they celebrate proceed from laudable and worthy motives, and how far we are really possessed of the virtues which gain us applause amongst those with whom we converse. Such a reflection is absolutely necessary, if we consider how apt we are either to value or condemn ourselves by the opinions of others, and to sacrifice the report of our own hearts to the judgment of the world.'

In that treatise of Plutarch here referred to, there are a great many excellent things pertinent to this subject; and therefore I thought it not improper to throw a few extracts out of it into the margin.*

It is the character of a dissolute mind, to be entirely insensible to all that the world says of us; and shows such a confidence of self-knowledge, as is usually a sure sign of self-ignorance. The most knowing minds are ever least presumptuous: and true self-knowledge is a science of so much depth and difficulty, that a wise man would not choose to be ever confident that all his notions of himself are right, in opposition to the judgment of all mankind; some of whom, perhaps, have better opportunities and advantages of knowing him, at some seasons, especially, than he has of knowing himself; because herein they never look through the same false medium of self-flattery.

* The foolish and inconsiderate spoil the very friendship they are engaged in; but the wise and prudent make good use of the hatred and enmity of men against them.

Why should we not take an enemy for our tutor, who will instruct us gratis in those things we knew not before? For an enemy sees and understands more, in matters relating to us, than our friends do, because love is blind; but spite, malice, ill-will, wrath, and contempt, talk much, are very inquisitive, and quick-sighted.

Our enemy, to gratify his ill-will towards us, acquaints himself with the infirmities both of our bodies and minds; sticks to our faults, and makes his invidious remark upon them, and spreads them abroad by his uncharitable and ill-natured reports. Hence we are taught this useful lesson for the direction and management of our conversation in the world: viz. that we be circumspect and wary in every thing we speak or do, as if our enemy stood at our elbow, and overlooked our actions.

Those persons whom that wisdom hath brought to live soberly, which the fear and awe of enemies hath infused, are by degrees drawn into a habit of living so, and are composed and fixed in their obedience to virtue, by custom and use.

When one asked Diogenes, How he might be avenged of his enemies? he replied, 'To be yourself a good and honest man.'

Antisthenes spake incomparably well, 'That if a man would live a safe and unblamable life, it was necessary that he should have very ingenuous and faithful friends, or very bad enemies; because the first, by their kind admonitions, would keep him from sinning; the latter, by their invectives.'

If any man, with opprobrious language, objects to you crimes you know nothing of, you ought to inquire into the causes or reasons of such false accusations; whereby you may learn to take heed for the future, lest you should unwarily commit those offences which are unjustly imputed to you.

Whenever any thing is spoken against you that is not true, do not pass by, or despise it, because it is false; but forthwith examine yourself, and consider what you have said or done that may administer a just occasion of reproof.

Nothing can be a greater instance of wisdom and humanity, than for a man to bear silently and quietly the follies and revilings of an enemy; taking as much care not to provoke him, as he would to sail safely by a dangerous rock.

It is an eminent piece of humanity, and a manifest token of a nature truly generous, to put up with the affronts of an enemy, at a time when you have a fair opportunity to revenge them.

Let us carefully observe those good qualities, wherein our enemies excel us: and endeavor to excel them, by avoiding what is faulty, and imitating what is excellent, in them.

CHAPTER IV

FREQUENT CONVERSE WITH SUPERIORS A HELP TO SELF-KNOWLEDGE.

IV. Another proper means of self-knowledge is, to converse as much as you can with those who are your superiors in real excellence.

'He that walketh with wise men shall be wise.' (Prov. xiii. 20.) Their example will not only be your motive to laudable pursuits, but a mirror to your mind; by which you may probably discern some failings, deficiences, or neglects in yourself, which before escaped you. You will see the unreasonableness of your vanity and self-sufficiency, when you observe how much you are surpassed by others in knowledge and goodness. Their proficiency will make your defects the more obvious to you: and by the lustre of their virtues, you will better see the deformity of your vices: your negligence, by their diligence; your pride, by their humility; your passion, by their meekness; and your folly, by their wisdom.

Examples not only move, but teach and direct, much more effectually than precepts; and show us not only that such virtues may be practised, but how; and how lovely they appear when they are. And therefore, if we cannot have them always before our eyes, we should endeavor to have them always in our mind; and especially that of our great head and pattern, who hath set us a perfect example of the most innocent conduct, under the worst and most disadvantageous circumstances of human life.

CHAPTER V.

OF CULTIVATING SUCH A TEMPER AS WILL BE THE BEST DISPOSITION TO SELF-KNOWLEDGE.

V. If a man would know himself, he must, with great care, cultivate that temper which will best dispose him to receive this knowledge.

Now, as there are no greater hindrances to self-knowledge, than pride and obstinacy; so, there is nothing more helpful to it, than humility and an openness to conviction.

1. One who is in quest of self-knowledge, must, above all things, seek humility. And how near an affinity there is between these two, appears from hence; that they are both acquired the same way. The very means of attaining humility are the properest means for attaining self-acquaintance. By keeping an eye every day upon our faults and wants, we become more humble; and by the same means, we become more self-intelligent. By considering how far we fall short of our rule and our duty, and how vastly others exceed us, and especially by a daily and diligent study of the word of god, we come to have meaner thoughts of ourselves; and, by the very same means, we come to have a better acquaintance with ourselves.

A proud man cannot know himself. Pride is that beam in the eye of the mind, which renders him quite blind to any blemishes there. Hence, nothing is a surer sign of self-ignorance, than vanity and ostentation.

Indeed, true self-knowledge and humility are so necessarily connected, that they depend upon, and mutually beget each other. A man that knows himself, knows the worst of himself, and therefore cannot but be humble; and an humble mind is frequently contemplating its own faults and weakness, which greatly improves it in self-knowledge: so that self-acquaintance makes a man humble; and humility gives him still a better acquaintance with himself.

2. An openness to conviction is no less necessary to self-knowledge than humility.

As nothing is a greater bar to true knowledge than an obstinate stiffness in opinion, and a fear to depart from old notions, which, before we are capable of judging, perhaps, we had long taken up for the truth; so, nothing is a greater bar to self-knowledge, than a strong aversion to part with those sentiments of ourselves which we have been blindly accustomed to, and to think worse of ourselves than we are wont to do.

And such an unwillingness to retract our sentiments in both cases proceed from the same cause; viz. a reluctance to self-condemnation. For he that takes up a new way of thinking, contrary to that which he hath long received, therein condemns himself of having lived in an error; and he that begins to see faults in himself he never saw before, condems himself of having lived in ignorance and sin, and what self-flattery can by no means endure.

By such an inflexibility of judgment, and hatred of conviction, is a very unhappy and hurtful turn of mind; and a man that is resolved never to be in the wrong, is in a fair way never to be in the right.

As infallibility is no privilege of the human nature, it is no diminution to a man's good sense or judgment to be found in an error, provided he is willing to retract it. He acts with the same freedom and liberty as before; whoever be his monitor, it is his own good sense and judgment that still guides him; which shines to great advantage, in thus directing him against the bias of vanity and self-opinion; and in thus changing his sentiments, he only acknowledges that he is not, what no man ever was, incapable of being mistaken. In short, it is more merit, and an argument of a more excellent mind, for a man freely to retract when he is in the wrong, than to be overbearing and positive when he is in the right.

A man, then, must be willing to know himself, before he can know himself. He must open his eyes, if he desires to see; yield to evidence and conviction, though it be at the expense of his judgment, and to the mortification of his vanity.

CHAPTER VI.

TO BE SENSIBLE OF OUR OWN FALSE-KNOWLEDGE IS A GOOD STEP TO SELF-KNOWLEDGE.

VI. Would you know yourself, take heed and guard against self-knowledge.

See that the 'light that is within you be not darkness;' that your favorite and leading principles be right. Search your furniture, and consider what you have to unlearn: for oftentimes there is as much wisdom in casting off some knowledge which we have, as in acquiring that which we have not; which, perhaps, was what made Themistocles reply, when one offered to teach him the art of memory, 'That he had much rather he would teach him the art of forgetfulness.'

A scholar, that hath been all his life collecting books, will find in his library at last a great deal of rubbish; and, as his taste alters, and his judgment improves, he will throw out a great many as trash and lumber, which, it may be, he once valued and paid dear for; and replace them with such as are more solid and useful. Just so should we deal with our understandings; look over the furniture of the mind; separate the chaff from the wheat, which are generally received into it together; and take as much pains to forget what we ought not to have learned, as to retain what we ought not to forget. To read froth and trifles all our life, is the way always to retain a flashy and juvenile turn; and only to contemplate our first (which is generally our worst) knowledge, cramps the progress of the understanding, and makes our self-survey extremely deficient. In short, would we improve the understanding to the valuable purposes of self-knowledge, we must take as much care what books we read, as what company we keep.

'The pains we take in books or arts, which treat of things remote from the use of life, is a busy idleness. If I study, says Montaigne, it is for no other science, than what treats of the knowledge of myself, and instructs me how to live and die well.'

It is a comfortless speculation, and a plain proof of the imperfection of the human understanding, that, upon a narrow scrutiny into our furniture, we observe a great many things which we think we know, but do not; and many which we do know, but ought not: that a good deal of the knowledge we have been all our lives collecting, is no better than mere ignorance, and some of it worse; to be sensible of which is a very necessary step to self-acquaintance.

CHAPTER VII.

SELF-INSPECTION PECULIARLY NECESSARY UPON SOME PARTICULAR OCCASIONS.

VII. Would you know yourself, you must very carefully attend to the frame and emotions of your mind, under some extraordinary incidents.

Some sudden accidents which befall you when the mind is most off its guard, will better discover its secret turn and prevailing disposition, than much greater events you are prepared to meet; e. g.

1. Consider how you behave under any sudden affronts or provocations from men. 'A fool's wrath is presently known.' (Prov. xii. 16.) i. e. a fool is presently known by his wrath.

If your anger be soon kindled, it is a sign that secret pride lies lurking in the heart; which, like gunpowder, takes fire at every spark of provocation that lights upon it. For, whatever may be owing to a natural temper, it is certain, that pride is the chief cause of frequent and wrathful resentments. For pride and anger are as nearly allied, as humility and meekness. 'Only by pride cometh contention.' Prov. xiii. 10. And a man would not know what mud lay at the bottom of his heart, if provocation did not stir it up.

Athenodorus, the philosopher, by reason of his old age, begged leave to retire from the court of Augustus; which the emperor granted him: and in his compliments of leave, 'Remember,' said he, 'Cæsar, whenever you are angry, you say or do nothing, before you have distinctly repeated to yourself the four-and-twenty letters of the alphabet.' Whereupon Cæsar, catching him by the hand, 'I have need,' says he, 'of your presence still, and kept him a year longer. This is celebrated by the ancients as a rule of excellent wisdom. But a Christian may prescribe to himself, a much wiser: viz. 'When you are angry, answer not till you have repeated the fifth petition of the lord's prayer. 'Forgive us our trespasses, as we forgive them that trespass against us;' and our saviour's comment upon it, 'For if ye forgive men their trespasses, your heavenly father will also forgive you; but if you forgive not men their trespasses, neither will your father forgive your trespasses.' Mat. vi. 14. 15.

It is a just and seasonable thought, that of Marcus Antoninus, upon such occasions: 'A man misbehaves himself towards me,—what is that to me? The action is his; and the will that sets him upon it is his; and therefore let him look to it. The fault and injury belong to him, not to me. As for me, I am in the condition providence would have me, and am doing what becomes me.'

But after all, this amounts only to a philosophical contempt of injuries; and falls much beneath the dignity of a Christian forgiveness, to which self-knowledge will happily dispose us: and therefore, in order to judge of our improvements therein, we must always take care to examine and observe in what manner we are affected in such circumstances.

2. How do you behave under a severe and unexpected affliction from the hand of providence? which is another circumstauce, wherein we have a fair opportunity of coming to a right knowledge of ourselves.

If there be an habitual discontent or impatience lurking within us, this will draw it forth; especially if the affliction be attended with any of those aggravating circumstances which accumulated that of Job.

Afflictions are often sent with this intent, to teach us to know ourselves ;and therefore ought to be carefully improved to this purpose.

And much of the wisdom and goddness of our heavenly father is seen by a serious and attentive mind, not only in proportioning the degrees of his corrections to his children's strength, but in adapting the kinds of them to their tempers; afflicting one in one way, another in another, according as he knows they are most easily wrought upon, and as will be most for their advantage; by which means, a small affliction of one kind may as deeply affect us, and be of more advantage to us, than a much greater of another kind.

It is a trite but true observation, that a wise man receives more benefit from his enemies than from his friends; from his afflictions, than from his mercies: by which means his enemies become in effect his best friends, and his afflictions his greatest mercies. Certain it is, that a man never has an opportunity of taking a more fair and undisguised view of himself, than in these circumstances; and therefore, by diligently observing in what manner he is affected at such times, he may make an improvement in the true knowledge of himself, very much to his future advantage, though, perhaps, not a little to his present mortification: for a sudden provocation from man, or a severe affliction from god, may detect something which lay latent and undiscovered so long at the bottom of his heart, that he never once suspected it to have had any place there. Thus, the one excited wrath in the meekest man, (Psal. cvi. 33.) and the other passion in the most penitent, (Job iii. 3.)

By considering, then, in what manner we bear the particular afflictions god is pleased to allot us, and what benefit we receive from them, we may come to a very considerable acquaintance with ourselves.

3. What is our usual temper and disposition in a time of peace, prosperity, and pleasure, when the soul is generally most unguarded.

This is the warm season that nourishes and impregnates the seeds of vanity, self-confidence, and a supercilious contempt of others. If there be such a root of bitterness in the heart, it will be very apt to shoot forth in the sunshine of an uninterrupted prosperity; even after the frost of adversity had nipped it, and, as we thought, killed it.

Prosperity is a trial, as well as adversity; and is commonly attended with more dangerous temptations: and were the mind but as seriously disposed to self-reflection, it would have a greater advantage of attaining a true knowledge of itself under the former than under the latter; but the unhappiness of it is, the mind is seldom rightly turned for such an employment, under those circumstances. It has something else to do; has the concerns of the world to mind; and is too much engaged by the things without it, to advert to those within; and is more disposed to enjoy than examine itself. However, it is a very necessary season for self-examination, and a very proper time to acquire a good degree of self-acquaintance, if rightly improved.

Lastly. How do we behave in bad company? And that is to be reckoned bad company in which there is no probability of our doing or getting any good, but apparent danger of our doing or getting much harm; I mean, our giving offence to others by an indiscreet zeal, or incurring guilt to ourselves by a criminal compliance.

Are we carried down by the torrent of vanity and vice? Will a flash of wit or brilliant fancy make us excuse a profane expression? If so, we shall soon come to relish it, when thus seasoned, and use it ourselves.

This is a time when our zeal and wisdom, our fortitude and firmness, are generally put to the most delicate proof; and when we may too often take notice of the unsuspected escapes of folly, fickleness, and indiscretion.

At such seasons as these, then, we may often discern what lies at the bottom of our hearts, better than we can in the more even and customary scenes of life, when the passions are all calm and still. And therefore, would we know ourselves, we should be very attentive to our frame, temper, disposition, and conduct, upon such occasions.

CHAPTER VIII.

TO KNOW OURSELVES, WE MUST WHOLLY ABSTRACT FROM EXTERNAL APPEARANCES.

VIII. Would you know yourself, you must, as far as possible, get above the influence of exteriors, or mere outward show.

A man is what his heart is. The knowledge of himself is the knowledge of his heart, which is entirely an inward thing; to the knowledge of which, then, outward things such as a man's condition and state in the world can contribute nothing: but, on the other hand, is too often a great bar and hindrance to him in his pursuit of self-knowledge.

1. Are your circumstances in the world easy and prosperous? Take care you do not judge of yourself too favorably on that account.

These things are without you, and therefore can never be the measure of what is within: and however the world may respect you for them, they do not in the least make you either a wiser or more valuable man.

In forming a true judgment of yourself, then, you must entirely set aside the consideration of your estate and family, your wit, beauty, genius, health, &c., which are all but the appendages or trappings of a man; a smooth and shining varnish, which may lacker over the basest metal.

A man may be a good and happy man without these things, and a bad and wretched one with them; nay he may have all these, and be the worse for them. They are so far from being good and excellent in themselves, that we often see providence bestows them upon the vilest of men, and in kindness, denies them to some of the best. They are oftentimes the greatest temptations, and put a man's faith and wisdom to the most dangerous trial.

2. Is your condition in life mean and afflicted? Do not judge the worse of yourself for not having those external advantages which others have.

None will think the worse of you for the want of them, but those who think the better of themselves for having them: in both which they show a very depraved and perverted judgment. These are things entirely without us, and out of our power; for which a man is neither the better nor the worse, but according as he uses them; and therefore you ought to be as indifferent to them as they are to you. A good man shines amiably through all the obscurity of his low fortune; and a wicked man is a poor little wretch in the midst of all his grandeur.

> Pygmies are pygmies still, tho' plac'd on alps;
> And pyramids are pyramids in vales. Young.

Were we to follow the judgment of the world, we should indeed think otherwise of these things; and by that mistake be led into a wrong notion of ourselves. But we have a better rule to follow; to which, if we adhere, the consideration of our external condition in life, whatever it be, will have no undue influence on the mind, in its search after self knowledge.

CHAPTER IX.

THE PRACTICE OF SELF-KNOWLEDGE A GREAT MEANS TO PROMOTE IT.

IX. Let all your self-knowledge be reduced into practice.

The right improvement of that knowledge we have, is the best way to attain more.

The great end of self-knowledge is self-government: without which, it is but a useless speculation. And, as all knowledge is valuable in proportion to its end, so this is the most excellent, only because the practice of it is of the most extensive use.

'Above all other subjects,' says an ancient pious writer, 'study thine own self. For no knowledge that terminates in curiosity or speculation is comparable to that which is of use; and of all useful knowledge, that is most so which consists in the due care and just notions of ourselves. This study is a debt which every one owes himself. Let us not, then, be so lavish, so unjust, as not to pay this debt, by spending some part, at least, if we cannot all, or most, of our time and care upon that which has the most indefeasible claim to it. Govern your passions; manage your actions with prudence; and where false steps have been made, correct them for the future. Let nothing be allowed to grow headstrong and disorderly; but bring all under discipline. Set all your faults before your eyes; and pass sentence upon yourself with the same severity as you would do upon another, for whom no partiality hath biased your judgment.'

What will our most exact and diligent self-researches avail us, if, after all, we sink into indolence and sloth? Or what will it signify to be convinced that there is a great deal amiss in our deportments and dispositions, if we sit still contentedly under that conviction, without taking one step towards a reformation? It will, indeed, render us but the more guilty in the sight of god. And how sad a thing will it be to have our self-knowledge hereafter rise up in judgment against us!

'Examination is in order to correction and amendment: we abuse it and ourselves, if we rest in the duty without looking farther. We are to review our daily walk, that we may reform it; and consequently a daily review will point out to us the subject and matter of our future daily care. 'This day,' saith the Christian, upon his review of things at night, 'I lost so much time; particularly at ——. I took too great a liberty; particularly in ——. I omitted such an opportunity, that might have been improved to better purpose. I mismanaged such a duty. I find such a corruption often working; my old infirmity still cleaves to me; how easily doth this sin beset me! Oh! may I be more attentive for the time to come; more watchful over my heart; take more heed to my ways! May I do so the next day!' The knowledge of a distemper is a good step to a cure; at least, it directs to proper methods and applications in order to it. Self-acquaintance leads to self-reformation. He that at the close of each day calls over what is past, inspects himself, his behavior and manners, will not fall into that security, and those uncensured follies, that are so common and so dangerous.'

And it may not be improper, in order to make us

sensible of, and attentive to, some of the more secret faults and foibles of our tempers, to pen them down at night, according as they appeared during the transactions of the day. By which means, we shall not only have a more distinct view of that part of our character to which we are generally most blind, but shall be able to discover some defects and blemishes in it, which perhaps we never apprehended before: for the wiles and doublings of the heart are sometimes so hidden and intricate, that it requires the nicest care, and most steady attention, to detect and unfold them.

For instance; This day I read an author, whose sentiments were very different from mine, and who expressed himself with much warmth and confidence. It excited my spleen, I own, and I immediately passed a severe censure upon him; so that, had he been present, and talked in the same strain, my ruffled temper would have promoted me to use harsh and ungrateful language, which might have occasioned a very unchristian contention. But I now recollect, that though the author might be mistaken in those sentiments, as I still believe he was, yet, by his particular circumstances in life, and the method of his education, he has been strongly laid into that way of thinking; so that his prejudice is pardonable; but my uncharitableness is not; especially considering that in many respects he has the ascendant of me. This proceeded, then, from uncharitableness, which is one fault of my temper I have to watch against; and which I never was before so sensible of as I am now, upon this recollection. Learn more moderation, and make more allowances for the mistaken opinions of others, for the future. Be as charitable to others who differ from you, as you desire they should be to you, who differ as as much from them; for it may be, you cannot be more assured of being in the right than they are.

Again: This day I found myself strongly inclined to put in something, by way of abatement, to an excellent character given of an absent person, by one of his great admirers. It is true, I had the command of myself to hold my tongue; and it is well I had: for the ardor of his zeal would not have admitted the exception, though I still think that, in some degree, it was just; which might have raised a wrangling debate about his character, perhaps at the expense of my own; or, however, occasioned much animosity and contention. But I have since examined the secret spring of that impulse, and find it to be envy; which I was not then sensible of; but my antagonist had certainly imputed it to this; and had he taken the liberty to have told me so, I much question whether I should have had the temper of the philosopher, who, when he was really injured, being asked, whether he was angry or no? replied, 'No; but I am considering with myself whether I ought not to be so.' I doubt I should not have had so much composure; but should have immediately resented it as a false and malicious aspersion. But it was certainly envy, and nothing else; for the person who was the object of the encomium, was much my superior, in many respects; and the exception that arose to my mind was the only flaw in his character, which nothing but a quick-sighted envy could descry. Take heed, then, of that vice, for the future.

Again: This day I was much surprised to observe in myself the symptoms of a vice, which, of all others, I ever thought myself most clear of, and have always expressed the greatest detestation of in others; and that is covetousness; for what else could it be that prompted me to withhold my charity from my fellow-creature in distress, on pretence that he was not in every respect a proper object; or to dispense it so sparingly to another, who I knew was so, on pretence of having lately been at a considerable expense upon another occasion? This could proceed from nothing else but a latent principle of covetousness; which, though I never before observed in myself, yet it is likely others have. O how inscrutable are the depths and deceits of the human heart! Had my enemy brought against me a charge of indolence, self-indulgence, or pride, and impatient, or a too quick resentment of affronts and injuries, my own heart must have confirmed the accusation, and forced me to plead guilty. Had he charged me with bigotry, self-opinion, and censoriousness, I should have thought it proceeded from the same temper in himself, having rarely any thing like it in my own. But had he charged me with covetousness, I should have taken it for calumny, and despised the censure with indignation and triumph; and yet after all, I find it had been but too true a charge. O how hard a thing is it to know myself! This like all other knowledge, the more I have of it, the more sensible I am of my want of it.*

The difficulty of self-government and self-possession arises from the difficulty of a thorough self-acquaintance, which is necessary to it: I say, a thorough self-acquaintance, such as has been already set forth, in its several branches, Part 1. For as self-government is simply impossible, I mean, considered as a virtue, where self-ignorance prevails, so the difficulty of it will decrease in proportion to the degree in which self-acquaintance improves.

Many, perhaps, may be ready to think this a paradox, and imagine that they know their predominant passions and foibles very well, and still find it extremely difficult to correct them. But let them examine this point again, and perhaps they may find, that that difficulty arises either from their defect of self-dnowledge for it is in this as in other kinds of knowledge, wherein some are very ready to think themselves much greater proficients than they are, or else, from their neglect to put in practice that degree of self-knowledge they have. They know their particular failings, yet will not guard against the immediate temptations to them; and they are often betrayed into the immediate temptations which overcome them, because they are ignorant of, or do not guard against, the more remote temptations, which lead them into those that are more immediate and dangerous, which may not improperly be called the temptations to temptations; in observing and guarding against which consists a very necessary part of self-knowledge, and the great art of keeping clear of danger, which, in our present state of frailty, is the best means of keeping clear of sin.

To correct what is amiss, and to improve what is good in us, is supposed to be our hearty desire, and the great end of all our self-research. But if we do not endeavor after this, all our labor after self-knowledge will be in vain; nay, if we do not endeavor it, we cannot be said heartily to desire it; 'For there is most of the heart where there is most of the will; and there is most of the will where there is most endeavor; and where there is most endeavor there is generally most success: so that endeavor must prove the truth of our desire, and success will generally prove the sincerity of our endeavor.' This, I think, we may safely say, without attributing too much to the power of the human will, considering that we are rational and free agents, and considering what effectual assistance is offered to them who seek it, to render their en-

Cicero was, without doubt, the vainest man in life, or he never could have had the face to beseech Cocceius, in writing the Roman History, to set the administration of his consulship in the most distinguished point of glory, even at the expense of historical truth; and yet, when he is begging a favor of the like kind, even of Cato himself, he has these astonishing words: Si quisquam fuit unquam remotus et natura et magis etiam, ut mihi quidem sentire videor, ratione atque doctrina ab inani laude et ser monibus vulgi, ego profecto is sum. Lib. 15. Ep. 4. If ever any man was a stranger to vain glory, and the desire of popular applause, it is myself; and this disposition which I have by nature, is, methinks, grown yet stronger by reason and philosophy. Ah! how secretly doth self-ignorance not only insinuate itself into, but conceal itself within, the most improved and best cultivated minds!—Reader, beware

deavors successful, if they are sincere; which introduces the subject of the following chapter.

CHAPTER X.

FERVENT AND FREQUENT PRAYER THE MOST EFFECTUAL MEANS FOR ATTAINING TRUE SELF-KNOWLEDGE.

Lastly. The last means to self-knowledge which I shall mention, is frequent and devout application to the fountain of light, and the father of our spirits, to assist us in this important study, and give us the true knowledge of ourselves.

This I mention last, not as the least, but, on the contrary, as the greast and best means of all, to attain a right and thorough knowledge of ourselves, and the way to render all the rest effectual; and, therefore, though it be the last means mentioned, it is the first that should be used.

Would we know ourselves, we must often converse, not only with ourselves in meditation, but with god in prayer; in the lowest prostration of soul, beseeching the father of our spirits to discover them to us; 'in whose light we may see light,' where before there was nothing but darkness; to make known to us the depths and devices of our hearts; for, without the grace and influence of his divine illuminations and instructions, our hearts will, after all our care and pains to know them, most certainly deceive us; and self-love will so prejudice the understanding, as to keep us still in self-ignorance.

The first thing we are to do, in order to self-knowledge, is, to assure ourselves that our hearts 'are deceitful above all things;' and the next is, to remember, that, 'the lord searcheth the hearts, and trieth the reins;' Jer. xvii. 10. i. e. that he, the 'Searcher of all hearts,' Chron. xxviii. 9., hath a perfect knowledge of them, deceitful as they are: which consideration, as it suggesteth to us the strongest motive to induce us to labor after a true knowledge of them ourselves, so it directs us, at the same time, how we may attain this knowledge; viz. by an humble and importunate application to him, to whom alone they are known, to make them known to us. And this, by the free and near access which his holy spirit hath to our spirits, he can effectually do various ways; viz. by fixing our attentions; by quickening our apprehensions; removing our prejudices, which, like a false medium before the eye of the mind, prevents its seeing things in a just and proper light; by mortifying our pride; strengthening the intellective and reflecting faculties; and enforcing upon the mind a lively sense and knowledge of its greatest happiness and duty: and so awakening the soul from that carnal security and indifference about its best interests, into which a too serious attention to the world is apt to betray it.

Besides, prayer is a very proper expedient for attaining self-knowledge, as the actual engagement of the mind, in this devotional exercise, is, in itself, a great help to it; for the mind is in a better frame than when it is intently and devoutly engaged in this duty. It has then the best apprehensions of god, the truest notions of itself, and the justest sentiments of earthly things; the clearest conceptions of its own weakness; and the deepest sense of its own vileness; and, consequently, is in the best disposition than can be, to receive a true and right knowledge of itself.

And, oh! could we but always think of ourselves in such a manner, or could we but always be in a disposition to think of ourselves in such a manner, as we sometimes do in the fervor of our humiliations before the throne of grace, how great a progress should we soon make in this important science! Which evidently shows the necessity of such devout and humble engagements of the soul, and how happy a means they are to attain a just self-acquaintance.

And now, reader, whoever thou art, that hast taken the pains to peruse these sheets, whatever be thy circumstances or condition in the world, whatever thy capacity or understanding, whatever thy occupations and engagements, whatever thy favorite sentiments and principles, or whatever religious sect or party thou espousest, know for certain, that thou hast been deeply interested in what thou hast been reading, whether thou hast attended to it or no: for it is of no less concern to thee than the security of thy peace and usefulness in this world, and thy happiness in another; and relates to all thy interests, both as a man and a Christian. Perhaps thou hast seen something of thine own image in the glass that has now been held up to thee: and wilt thou go away, and soon 'forget what manner of person thou art?' Perhaps thou hast met with some things thou dost not well understand or approve. But shall that take off thine attention from those things thou dost understand and approve, and art convinced of the necessity of? If thou hast received no improvement, no benefit, from this plain practical treatise thou hast perused, read it over again. The same thought, you know, often impresses one more at one time than another: and we sometimes receive more knowledge and profit by the second perusal of a book than by the first. And I would fain hope that thou wilt find something in this that may set thy thoughts on work, and which, by the blessing of god, may make thee more observant of thy heart and conduct; and, in consequence of that, a more solid, serious, wise, and established Christian.

But will you, after all, deal by this book ye have now read, as you have dealt by many sermons you have heard,—pass your judgment upon it according to your received and establised set of notions; and condemn or applaud it, only as it is agreeable or disagreeable to them; and commend or censure it, only as it suits or does not suit your particular taste; without attending to the real weight, importance, and necessity of the subject, abstracted from those views? Or, will you barely content with the entertainment and satisfaction which some parts of it may possibly have given you, to assent to the importance of the subject, the justness of the sentiment, or the propriety of some of the observations you have been reading, and so dismiss all, without any farther concern about the matter? Believe it, O Christian reader! if this be all the advantage you gain by, it were scarce worth while to have confined yourself so long to the perusal of it. It has aimed, it has sincerely aimed, to do you a much greater benefit; to bring you to a better acquaintance with one you express a particular regard for, and who is capable of being the best friend, or the worst enemy, you have in the world; and that is—yourself. It was designed to convince you, that, would you live and act consistently, either as a man or a Christian, you must know yourself; and to persuade you, under the influencee of the foregoing motives, and by the help of the forementioned directions, to make self-knowledge the great study, and self-government the great business of your life. In which resolution may almighty god confirm you; and in which great business may his grace assist you against all future discouragements and distractions! With him I leave the success of the whole, to whom be glory and praise for ever!

APPENDIX,

REFERRED TO FROM PAGE 23.

The advantage of a common-place book, or register of things deemed worthy of retention in the course of a person's reading, must be so obvious to the mind of every reader, that any comment on it is deemed unnecessary.

The following plan, embracing an improvement on that recommended by Mr. Locke, is conceived sufficiently clear to be understood by the meanest capacity.

By the method here recommended, an alphabetical index is formed, each letter occupying a page; which is divided into six parts, affixing a vowel to each compartment. In this index is to be written at length in the page at the top of which its initial letter is found, and in the division occupied by its first vowel; or its second, if the initial letter be a vowel the word which forms the head of the subject referred to in the body of the book; with the number of the page allotted to that subject; which must be repeated when any fresh matter is inserted under the same head in a different part of the book.

When the initial letter is a vowel, and there is no other in the word, that vowel is to be considered as both the first and second. The word ART, therefore, should be inserted in the division A a;—EGG in the division E e.

In inserting any article in your Common-Place Book you must select some general term by which the subject may be understood, and, taking a left hand page, enter it in conspicuous characters at the top, on the outside corner; placing the subject you wish to insert within the ruled lines; observing that you do not occupy the following page by a new head; but leaving it for any subsequent matter that may occur on the same subject. However, should all the pages on the left hand be occupied, those on the right, that remain blank, might be taken, when it is not probable that the heads on the left will be continued.

It will be found convenient to reserve a blank in the margin of the Common-Place Book, for brief notes on the matter entered; as also at the foot of the page, for references from one head to another; as it often happens that an article placed under one head, may be illustrative of another;—for example, AIR and ATMOSPHERE.

Annexed is a page of the Index, with two pages of the Common-Place Book (printed as one,) which will serve as an elucidation of the preceding instructions.

A.

a	ANACARDIUM, (Cashew Nut, or Marking Nut,(9. ART .16.	*o*	ASTRONOMY. 24.
e	ANGEL, 22.	*u*	AUTUMN, 28, 32.
i	ADDISON, 10.	*y*	ARMY, 26.

ANACARDIUM.

	Cashew Nut, or Marking Nut. The liquor found between the rind and the thin outer shell of this nut forms a useful marking ink; as any thing written on linen or cotton with it is of a brown color, which gradually grows blacker, and is very durable. Nicholson's Chem. Dict. 8vo. 1808.	Marking Ink.
	See Ink, p. 28.	

ADDISON. 10

	One may justly apply to him what Plato, in his allegorical language, says of Aristophanes, that the Graces having searched all the world for a temple, wherein they might for ever dwell, settled at last in the breast of Mr Addison. Fitzosborne's Letters, xxiv. xxix.	

THE END.

www.ingramcontent.com/pod-product-compliance
Lightning Source LLC
LaVergne TN
LVHW021135110826
845150LV00005B/1035

* 9 7 8 1 4 2 5 5 4 9 8 7 9 *